SHIFTING THE CENTER
Understanding Contemporary Families

Third Edition

Susan J. Ferguson
Grinnell College

Higher Education

Boston   Burr Ridge, IL   Dubuque, IA   Madison, WI   New York
San Francisco   St. Louis   Bangkok   Bogotá   Caracas   Kuala Lumpur
Lisbon   London   Madrid   Mexico City   Milan   Montreal   New Delhi
Santiago   Seoul   Singapore   Sydney   Taipei   Toronto

The **McGraw·Hill** Companies

With love to my parents, Jim and Janet Ferguson

Mc
Graw **Higher Education**
Hill

This book is printed on acid-free paper.

3 4 5 6 7 8 9 0 DOC/DOC 0 9 8 7

ISBN-13: 978-0-07-282585-5
ISBN-10: 0-07-282585-5

Editor in Chief: *Emily Barrosse*
Publisher: *Philip Butcher*
Sponsoring Editor: *Sherith Pankratz*
Marketing Manager: *Dan Loch*
Project Manager: *Stacy Shearer*
Production Service: *Publishing Support Services*
Designer: *Cassandra Chu*
Photo Research: *Brian Pecko*
Production Supervisor: *Richard DeVitto*
Composition: 10/12 Book Antiqua by International Typesetting & Composition
Printing: *R.R. Donnelley & Sons*
Cover: *Phoenix Color*
Cover: Michael James. *Rehoboth Meander: Quilt #150.* 1993, cotton and silk, 134.6 × 133.4 cm. Copyright 1993 Michael F. James. Renwick Gallery, Smithsonian American Art Museum, Washington, DC, U.S.A. Photo © Smithsonian American Art Museum, Washington, DC/Art Resource, NY.

Library of Congress Cataloging-in-Publication Data

Shifting the center: understanding contemporary families/[compiled by] Susan J. Ferguson.—3rd ed.
    p. cm.
    Includes bibliographical references.
    ISBN: 978-0-07-282585-5 (software)
        1. Family—United States. 2. Marriage—United States. 3. Kinship—United States. I. Ferguson, Susan J.
    HQ536.S488 2007
    306.8'0973—dc22   2005049123

www.mhhe.com

Contents

FATHERHOOD

PART VII. AGING AND MULTIGENERATIONAL RELATIONSHIPS

PART VIII. DIVORCE, REMARRIAGE, AND BLENDED FAMILIES

PART IX. FAMILIES AND VIOLENCE

Preface

The family is changing, not disappearing.
We have to broaden our understanding of it,
look for the new metaphors.

— *Mary Catherine Bateson*

This anthology originated in the classroom. Over the years, students have challenged me to bring in readings on the family that integrate material on race-ethnicity, social class, gender, and sexual orientation. The lack of fully integrated family texts has been frustrating and puzzling to me; most anthologies on the family "lump" family diversity into one section, which often appears at the end of the book. This placement is problematic because it still marginalizes those families that differ from the idealized traditional family of the dominant culture. Instead, the analysis and discussion of diverse family forms should occur throughout the selected topics of a family course. To achieve an integrated framework, I often have compiled large packets of material to bring diverse family experiences and a multicultural perspective into my classroom. After years of teaching family courses this way, I realized that a new anthology could and *should* be created to integrate the voices and experiences of diverse families. This book represents a collection of articles that meets four pedagogical goals: (1) to deconstruct the notion of a universal family over time and across cultures; (2) to reflect cutting-edge scholarship by well-known family scholars; (3) to integrate race-ethnicity, social class, gender, and sexuality in the analysis; and (4) to promote critical reading and thinking.

The title of this anthology, *Shifting the Center: Understanding Contemporary Families,* was inspired by Margaret Andersen and Patricia Hill Collins' essay "Shifting the Center and Reconstructing Knowledge" in *Race, Class, and Gender: An Anthology* (1995). In their essay, Andersen and Hill Collins argue for the need to shift the center of analysis away from the dominant culture to the experiences of all racial-ethnic and social class groups. In her book *Feminist Theory: From Margin to Center* (1984), bell hooks, too, argues that "much of feminist theory emerges from privileged women who live at the center, whose perspectives on reality rarely include knowledge and awareness of the lives of women and men who live in the margin" (p. x). Thus, hooks argues that in order for us to have an improved understanding of all human lives, we must place the experiences and knowledge of women of color at the center of feminist theorizing and activism. The same argument can be made for any area of scholarship, including the study of families.

In this anthology on families, "shifting the center" means that the research on families of color, gay and lesbian families, and working-class families is moved from the margins of analysis to the center of the analytical framework. In many texts, these family forms are treated as "alternative" or "deviant." Shifting our focus of inquiry away from family structures based only on traditional marriage helps students to better understand that numerous family structures coexist. This anthology examines several family forms, including arranged marriages, cohabitation, heterosexual marriage, single-parent households, stepfamilies, and gay and lesbian families. "Shifting the center" encourages students to compare these diverse family forms to one another. This shift also enables instructors to deconstruct the idealized, white, middle-class family and enables students to see how present conceptualizations of family have been socially constructed over time and across cultures.

To understand that the family is a social creation, students need to study the family both historically and comparatively. Historical and cross-cultural readings can help shatter the idea that one universal family form is constant across cultures and time. Thus, some of the articles I have selected show how current patterns of family formation and dissolution in the United States differ from those in our past and in other countries. The articles on various racial-ethnic families in the United States, including the selections on immigrant families, also demonstrate how families within a particular cultural group change over time. As family historian Stephanie Coontz argues in her book *The Way We Never Were* (1992), the study of family history enables students to dispel many myths about families in the United States. As students study family history, they more easily separate nostalgic misconceptions about the family from the realities of contemporary families.

In addition, the articles in this anthology use social science research to show how the institution of the family is related to other social institutions in society and how those institutions affect the intimate center of family lives. Thus, the readings encourage students to discern the relationships between families and society and among individuals within a family. For example, to help students see that family relations are inherently gendered, I have included selections that show how gender is constructed and maintained within the institution of the family and how gender affects power dynamics, communication, and intimacy among family members. Moreover, by reading articles on families, work, and poverty, students gain a better understanding of how socioeconomic class positions can affect family structure and relations. Reading articles that illuminate either the macrolevel of family structure in society or the microlevel of social interaction within families helps students perceive the multiple linkages between society, families, and individuals. Furthermore, when articles address the intersection of race-ethnicity, gender, social class, and sexual orientation at these two levels of study, students get a fuller picture of contemporary family diversity, including an understanding of how diverse families affect individual identities.

The articles in this anthology should enhance students' abilities to compare social science research findings with the assumptions underlying public debates about the family. Students will be better able to utilize research evidence in evaluating images of family life offered in the popular culture, especially in film, on television, and in music lyrics. If students learn to evaluate empirical evidence, they will be able to make better-informed decisions about public policy issues concerning families and perhaps, in the future, to shape better social policies for *all* families.

Ultimately, it is my hope that this anthology will instill a sociological imagination in students. By encouraging students to think critically about what they are reading, this anthology helps students understand the difference between family concerns that are "public issues" and those that are "private troubles." This anthology contains the most current, innovative work by family scholars — work that highlights the concepts, theories, and research methodologies currently used to study the family. I have tried to choose articles that are accessible, timely, and substantive that will engage students and promote critical thinking. Thus, my assumption throughout has been not only that students are capable of understanding rigorous social science research on families, but that the research also can inspire students to think more critically about families and our social world.

Changes to the Third Edition

With this third edition, I maintain my commitment to having the articles meet the four pedagogical goals described earlier: (1) to deconstruct the notion of a universal family over time and across cultures; (2) to reflect cutting-edge scholarship by well-known family scholars; (3) to integrate race-ethnicity, social class, gender, and sexuality in the analysis; and (4) to promote critical reading and thinking. Since I revised the first edition in 2000, there has been an explosion of scholarship in the sociology of the family. Therefore, I have extensively revised the second edition to incorporate more of this cutting-edge scholarship. Specifically, I have added 30 new selections that either focus on timely social issues in contemporary family life (that is, lesbian and gay dating relationships, the deinstitutionalization of marriage, transnational marriage markets, cohabitation, commitment ceremonies, transnational motherhood, stepfathering, elder care, stepfamilies and public policy, elder abuse, the "mommy tax," and child care) or enhance the racial-ethnic diversity of family scholarship already contained in earlier volumes. In particular, I have added eight new articles that examine marriage and family in a multiracial society, the scholarship on black families, Latinas and dating, Vietnamese American and Vietnamese marriages, child rearing in black and white families, Navajo teen mothers, Filipina mothers, and low-income African American men who live away from their children. The four readings in the section on Families and Poverty are all new as well. Another new feature of the third edition is the expansion of several sections to better accommodate the diverse literature on family life. These expanded sections are (1) Marriage, Cohabitation, and Partnership; (2) Parents and Children;

(3) Divorce, Remarriage, and Blended Families; and (4) Families, Work, and Carework. This expansion should enable professors and students to examine aspects of family life in greater depth. Of course, for all of the readings, I have tried to choose selections that are interesting and accessible to students. To that end, I have edited several of the longer readings to make them more accessible. I also have written an accompanying test manual that contains many examination and discussion questions for each reading. As the editor of this anthology, I developed these items with the goal of helping instructors test students' understanding of key sociological concepts and themes. Please note that I always welcome feedback from professors and students on this edition of *Shifting the Center: Understanding Contemporary Families*.

Acknowledgments

Several people contributed to the research and development of this anthology on families. My original thinking on the sociology of the family was greatly influenced by my graduate school professors and fellow graduate students at the University of Massachusetts at Amherst. It was there that I worked as a teaching assistant in family courses, began my own research on the never married, and taught my first classes on the family. I especially want to acknowledge and thank professors Naomi Gerstel, Suzanne Model, and Alice Rossi for sharing with me their insights on the family.

At Grinnell College, I am grateful for the ongoing support of both my colleagues and the students in the Sociology Department. I particularly want to acknowledge the Grinnell students who have taken my family seminar over the past 12 years and have suggested new readings or ways of understanding contemporary family life. This anthology was written for them, and they continue to provide insight into how it can be better improved. I also appreciate the labor provided by my student research assistants on the third edition. I am especially indebted to Keli Campbell, Rachel Scheckter, and Madison Van Oort. Keli's hard work in locating new research on the family was invaluable, Rachel helped me draft questions for the test bank, and Madison did Internet searches on family scholars and typed reference lists for me. The Carnegie faculty secretaries, Karen Groves, Linda Price, and Stephanie Puls, helped photocopy articles and type portions of the manuscript.

My special thanks also go to the reviewers of the this edition: Kristin L. Anderson, Western Washington University; Gloria Boutte, University of North Carolina—Greensboro; Wilson B. Fleming, University of Delaware; Louella Fong, Western Kentucky University; Gina Carreño, Florida State University; Barbara E. Johnson, University of South Carolina—Aiken; Alfred T. Kisubi, University of Wisconsin—Oshkosh; Johnston Njoku, Western Kentucky University.

PART I

Introduction to the Study of Families

The sociological study of the family is a broad and ever-changing field. The family is one of the most private and pervasive social institutions in society: private in that many of the social problems related to families, such as child care, divorce, and family violence, are especially difficult to deal with; and pervasive in that it is the first institution with which we, as individuals, have contact, and it tends to remain at the center of social life. Thus, all of us have had contact with at least one family, and many of us will be involved in several different families during our lifetimes. The family also is undergoing numerous transformations. To help us better understand these changes, recent social science research and data on the family are presented in this anthology.

Because your experience of the family is very personal and individual, what you read may not fit with your personal experience. That is to be expected, not only because of the vast diversity in family relationships and interaction on a microlevel, but also because you will be studying the institution of the family on a macrolevel as well. A family researcher named R. D. Laing (1971) once said, "The first family to interest me was my own. I still know less about it than I do about other families." Laing's quote makes sense because we are often too close, too emotionally involved, to study our own families objectively. Moreover, the experience of family varies considerably not only between unrelated persons but also between related persons within the same family. The family you experience is very different from the one your siblings and parents experience. We each have a unique perception about our own families, and it is difficult to be unbiased about them.

To help us better understand the social institution of the family, this anthology has several themes: (1) we need to deconstruct idealized and stereotypical notions about the family, especially the idealized white, middle-class family, as the only family form; (2) we need to study the history of the family to understand contemporary families; (3) we need to examine diverse family forms, including diverse racial-ethnic, cultural, and gay and lesbian families; and (4) we need to understand that the family is shaped by other social institutions, including the economy, law, politics, and religion. Our analysis of the institution of the family will begin with a discussion about how to define family. All four articles in this section delineate different definitions of the family and address the themes listed above. In sum, all four selections argue that the institution of the family is socially constructed.

Social Construction of the Family

I often begin my first day of teaching the sociology of the family with a visualization exercise. I ask my students to close their eyes and think about the family. I ask them, "When you hear the word *family* what do you think of? What images do you see when you hear the word *family* ?" I repeat the word *family* several times before I have the students open their eyes. I ask them to share the images or thoughts they had about family, and I write them on the blackboard. My students say over and over again that they see a husband and a wife, some children, maybe a family pet, often in front of a house with a minivan or an SUV. Next, as a class, we analyze the patterns in their images of family. Ultimately, the images are overwhelmingly positive, typically of biological mothers and fathers playing with children or a family having Thanksgiving dinner or going on vacation. I then ask my students, "Where are the other images of family life, such as sibling rivalry, divorce, or other types of family conflict?" As we investigate the images further, it becomes clear that most students have an idealized and even romanticized image of the family. Why is this problematic? To understand the implicit meanings of these images, I ask my class to define what a family is based on the list on the blackboard. I ask, "Which people are included, and which people are excluded? What activities define a family? Why do societies need families?" What becomes immediately clear to the students is that their idealized images of families are often based on white, middle-class assumptions about what a family should be. They quickly identify all of the people missing from their images, including unmarried heterosexual couples, cohabitors, same-sex couples, single parents, teen mothers, adopted and foster children, couples who are voluntarily or involuntarily childless, and so on. We talk about how families might vary on the basis of social class or race-ethnicity. In brief, I ask them to deconstruct their stereotyped notions about family.

There are many different definitions of family. George Murdock, a prominent anthropologist, defines family as "a social group characterized by common residence, economic cooperation, and reproduction" (quoted in Morgan 1975:20). While this definition appears to suffice, it would not take long to think of many exceptions. For example, many families do not share common residences, especially commuter families, families separated by divorce, or different generations living in different households. In some societies, the husbands and wives belong to different domestic groups. They may ritually see each other a couple of times a year but live separately the rest of the time. We also can think of many families that are not based on economic cooperation (that is, families with child-support disputes, pre- and postnuptial agreements, etc.) or on the sexual reproduction of children. Many couples are voluntarily or involuntarily childless. If a couple does *not* have children, are they disqualified from being a family?

The sociological definition of family also varies. Early sociological definitions are similar to those from anthropology as is evidenced in the work of Ernest Burgess, an early family researcher. Burgess defines family as "persons sharing a residence and a household who are related by biological ties, marriage, social customs, or adoption" (quoted in Sussman 1986). Burgess also argues that the family is "a unity of interacting personalities existing chiefly for the development and gratification of its members . . . held together by internal cohesion rather than external pressure" (quoted in Sussman 1986). Similar to the blackboard exercise described earlier, Burgess is attempting to delineate who can be members of a family and what functions the institution of the family fulfills. Again, exceptions can be found utilizing his criteria. Thus, there is great difficulty in defining what a family is, and there are problems with most anthropological and sociological definitions.

Still, if we are going to study the family, we will need a working definition of the family that will be broad enough to include diverse members and functions, but detailed enough to apply to the study of families across cultures. The working definition of family I often use in class is that the family is a social institution which provides three things: (1) it gives support to its members (whether it be emotional nurturing, physical caretaking, economic support, or some combination of the three); (2) it binds the individual to a primary social group (it gives us our roots so to speak, a base to build from); and (3) it socializes the person for participating in society outside of the family. This definition of family is broad enough to include families of diverse domestic forms, whether married or unmarried, with or without children, and regardless of the sexual orientation of the members. The last two points of the working definition come from the work of sociologists Talcott Parsons and Robert Bales, who argued in 1955 that the only two remaining functions of the family are the stabilization of adults and the socialization of children. In Parsons' and Bales' eyes, over time the multiple functions of the historic institution of the family had been reduced to two. However, these remaining two functions are important because they provide all individuals with the critical experience of childhood socialization and adults with a defining membership in a primary group.

The first reading in this section, "The Family in Question: What Is the Family? Is It Universal?" by a British anthropologist, Diana Gittins, examines how the family has been defined in both the anthropological and sociological research literature. She concludes that many of the "classic" definitions of family are too restrictive and that no one "universal" family form exists. Instead, Gittins argues, the family is socially constructed—that is, "family" is defined distinctively in different cultures and historical time periods. Thus, the meaning of family and the social functions fulfilled by the institution of the family vary greatly. By defining the family as a social institution which performs certain functions in society, Gittins is arguing that the family is a *social construct*, shaped by the social forces of the society in which it exists. In other words, the structure, content, and purpose of family vary by culture, historical context, race-ethnicity, gender, social class, and sexuality. There is no fixed or universal definition of family. Instead, the family is a social construction that varies between cultures and over time. To say the family is socially constructed means that each society defines the institution depending on its social, cultural, and economic contexts. Moreover, individuals within a given society also may define their experience of family differently from one another.

The Institution of the Family Is Shaped by Race–Ethnicity, Gender, and Sexual Orientation

The second reading in this section, "Feminist Rethinking from Racial-Ethnic Families" by Maxine Baca Zinn, builds on Gittins' argument that there is no universal definition of family. Baca Zinn is a professor of sociology at Michigan State University, where she is also a senior faculty associate with the Julian Samora Research Institute. Baca Zinn specializes in race relations, gender, and the sociology of the family, and the article that follows is representative of Baca Zinn's abilities to effectively combine these three research areas. Similar to Gittins' argument, Baca Zinn argues that the family is socially constructed and linked to other social structures and institutions. In addition, Baca Zinn argues that social science scholarship on the family benefits from feminist and racial-ethnic perspectives. In particular, family scholars need to examine race, social class, and gender simultaneously in order to understand how these variables interact to shape both the structural and the relational dimensions of families.

One important theme in this volume is that the family is a gendered institution. That is, the family is based on gender roles and the control of sexuality and reproduction. Baca Zinn looks at how productive and reproductive labor in the family vary not only by gender but by race-ethnicity as well. Other family scholars, including Scott Coltrane, also argue that gender is a critical lens to look through in order to understand the family. Coltrane, in his book *Gender and Families* (1998), states that "gender relations and family life are so intertwined that it is impossible to understand one without paying attention to the other" (p. 1). In fact, according to Coltrane, we often take the gender dynamics in the family for granted or see them as natural, biologically determined roles that men and women fulfill; or people argue that current gender role arrangements are the way they have always been, a part of tradition that Mother always cooks the holiday dinners or Father always does the yard work. In fact, these gender roles and the sexual division of labor are socially constructed. They are not biologically innate or unchangeable. Thus, to argue that the family is gendered also means recognizing that power dynamics often influence family relationships. Many of the readings in this volume will address the relationship between gender and families, and whether these gender dynamics influence power differences within the family.

The third reading in this section, "Exiles from Kinship," is by Kath Weston, a sociocultural anthropologist currently working in women's studies at Harvard University. This selection is taken from Weston's book *Families We Choose: Lesbians, Gays, Kinship* (1991). Like Gittins and Baca Zinn (see

Readings 1 and 2), Weston challenges traditional definitions of family and demonstrates that the family is a social construction. Specifically, Weston argues that the conventional notion that family is based on biological or blood ties often assumed that gays and lesbians were anti-family and unable to establish families on their own. Weston explains how this monolithic and narrow definition of family has changed over time to become more inclusive of social relationships based on choice instead of on biology. Not only are many gays and lesbians accepted by their families of origin, but many also create their own families with friends, partners, and others in their communities. Moreover, gay and lesbian families are increasingly including children, via adoption, alternative insemination, and procreation.

Contemporary Debates about Families

The increasing numbers of gays and lesbians who are raising children is one of many contemporary debates about families in the United States. This debate usually revolves around the question, Is the institution of the family in decline, or is it changing? Some researchers see the institution of the family as dying and in moral decay because of the high rates of divorce, teen pregnancy, domestic violence, and, of course, the lesbian baby boom. Others argue that this debate about the family is a reflection of the larger culture wars going on in the United States (Hunter 1991), or that the debate about the family reflects the stress that exists in many other parts of society. Regardless, there can be no denying the ideological import of the family.

The last reading in this section, "Marriage and Family in a Multiracial Society," is an excerpt from a larger report on the family using data from the 2000 U.S. Census. The authors of this selection, Daniel T. Lichter and Zhenchao Qian, are family demographers and sociologists at Ohio State University who utilize population data to understand larger societal changes in marriage, fertility, and poverty. Similar to earlier readings in this section, Lichter and Qian address questions related to the definition of family and the current debates about family values. Lichter and Qian argue that these definitions and debates must be informed by an understanding of the increasing racial-ethnic diversity of America's population and their distinctive family forms. After defining the family using definitions from the U.S. Census Bureau, Lichter and Qian utilize demographic data to analyze contemporary changes and trends in American families. Specifically, they find that the institution of the family is being affected by larger changes in the macrostructure of society, such as immigration and economic change, and by demographic changes within the structure of the family itself. According to Lichter and Qian, the five major demographic trends that have reshaped American families and households in the past 25 years include delayed marriage, more individuals living alone, the decline in traditional families, the rise in single-parent families, and the surge in the number of cohabiting couples. Many readings in this anthology will discuss these trends in detail.

REFERENCES

Coltrane, Scott. 1998. *Gender and Families.* Thousand Oaks, CA: Pine Forge Press.

Hunter, James Davison. 1991. *Culture Wars: The Struggle to Define America.* New York: Basic Books.

Laing, R. D. 1971. *The Politics of the Family and Other Essays.* New York: Pantheon Books.

Morgan, D. H. J. 1975. *Social Theory and the Family.* London: Routledge & Kegan Paul.

Parsons, Talcott and Robert F. Bales. 1955. *Family, Socialization and Interaction Process.* Glencoe, IL: Free Press.

Sussman, Marvin B. 1986. *Handbook of Marriage and the Family.* New York: Plenum Press.

Weston, Kath. 1991. *Families We Choose: Lesbians, Gays, Kinship.* New York: Columbia University Press.

1

THE FAMILY IN QUESTION
What Is the Family? Is It Universal?

DIANA GITTINS

U ntil recently, most sociological studies of the family have been dominated by functionalist definitions of what the family is and what "needs" it fulfills in society. Functionalists' theories of the family are treated elsewhere at length (Gittins 1982; Morgan 1975), but it is worth examining some of their main assumptions briefly. Generally, functionalists have argued that the family is a universal institution which performs certain specific functions essential to society's survival. Murdock, for instance, defined the family as a "social group characterised by common residence, economic co-operation, and reproduction. It includes adults of both sexes, at least two of whom maintain a socially approved sexual relationship, and one or more children, own or adopted, of the sexually cohabiting adults."[1] The four basic functions of the family, therefore, are seen as common residence; economic co-operation, reproduction, sexuality. Let us examine each of these in more detail.

Household is the term normally used to refer to co-residence. Murdock's assumption is that it is also a defining characteristic of "the family," and vice versa. It is generally assumed that a married couple, or parent and child(ren), will form a household, and that family implies and presupposes "household." Yet this is by no means always so. Margaret Mead (1971) showed how Samoan children chose the household where they wanted to reside, and often changed their residence again later. Sibling households — or frérèches — were common in parts of Europe, and are a dominant form of household among the Ashanti (Bender 1979:494).

There are numerous examples in contemporary society of families who do not form households, or only form households for periods of time. Families where the husband is in the armed services, is a traveling salesman or travels frequently abroad may only have the husband/father resident for short periods of time. Families where partners have jobs some distance away from one another may maintain a second household where one of them lives during the week. Children who are sent to boarding school may spend little more than a third of the year residing with their parent(s).

Gutman (1976) found that it was common among black slave families in the USA for a husband and wife to live on different plantations and see one another for a few hours once or twice a week. Soliende de Gonzalez (1965) found this type of household very common in Black Carib society: "there are groupings which I have called 'dispersed families' in which the father, although absent for long periods of time, retains ultimate authority over a household for which he provides the only support, and where affective bonds continue to be important between him and his wife and children" (p. 1544). Obviously people can consider themselves "family" without actually co-residing, and can also co-reside without considering themselves to be "family."

On the other hand, households might be characterised by a shared set of activities such as sleeping, food preparation, eating, sexual relations, and caring for those who cannot care for themselves. Some have argued that a household can be defined to some extent in terms of a range of domestic activities. "Sharing the same pot" has traditionally been the boundary drawn by census enumerators for demarcating one household from another. Yet these activities need not necessarily, and often do not, occur within one household. Some members of a household may eat there all the time, while others only part of the time. Similarly, as mentioned before, some members may not always sleep in the household for a majority of the time. They may well consider themselves notwithstanding to be a family. Conversely, pris-oners eat and sleep under the same roof, but do not consider themselves to be a family.

There is no hard-and-fast rule, much less a definition in universal terms, that can be applied to a household in terms of domestic activities. Whether in modern industrial society or in Africa or Asia "there is no basis for assum-ing that such activities as sleeping, eating, child-rearing and sexual relations must form a complex and must always occur under one roof" (Smith 1978:33). Household is thus in some ways just as nebulous a term as family, although it lacks the ideological implications that "family" carries.

Murdock further posits "economic co-operation" as a defining charac-teristic of all families. This is a very broad term and can encompass a wide range of activities from cooking to spinning to resources in terms of people and skills. Economic co-operation is something which can, and does, occur throughout all levels of society and is not specific to the family. Economic co-operation frequently occurs *between* households as well as between individ-uals within households. Undoubtedly households do entail an economic relationship in various ways; in particular, they entail the distribution, pro-duction and allocation of resources. Resources include food, drink, material goods, but also service, care, skills, time and space. The notion of "co-operation," moreover, implies an equal distribution of resources, yet this is seldom so. Allocating food, space, time and tasks necessitates some kind of a division of labour; different tasks need doing every day and may vary by week and by season. The number of people living together will be finite but also changeable — not just in terms of numbers, but also in terms of age, sex, marital status, and physical capacity.

All resources are finite and some may be extremely scarce; some form of allocation therefore has to occur, and this presupposes power relationships. Food, work, and space are rarely distributed equally between co-residing individuals, just as they differ between households and social sectors. Most frequently, the allocation of resources and division of labour is based on differences according to sex and age. Rather than using Murdock's definition of "economic co-operation," it is thus more useful to understand families in terms of the ways in which gender and age define, and are defined by, the division of labour within, and beyond, households. These divisions also presuppose power relationships and inequality — in effect, patriarchy — rather than co-operation and equality.

Power relationships define and inform concepts of sexuality, Murdock's third defining category. His definition of sexuality is *hetero*sexuality, although[1] this is only one of various forms of sexuality. Presumably this is because the final — and perhaps most important — "function" of families as seen by such theorists is reproduction, which necessitates heterosexual relations, at least at times. Sexuality is not something specific to families; rather, the assumption is that heterosexuality *should* be a defining characteristic of families. It also, according to Murdock, presupposes a "socially approved relationship" between two adults.

Social recognition of mating and of parenthood is obviously intimately bound up with social definitions and customs of marriage. It is often assumed that, in spite of a variety of marriage customs and laws, marriage as a binding relationship between a man and a woman is universal. Yet it has been estimated that only 10 per cent of all marriages in the world are actually monogamous; polyandry and polygyny are common in many societies, just as serial monogamy is becoming increasingly common in our own. Marriage is not always a heterosexual relationship; among the Nuer, older women marry younger women. The Nuer also practise a custom known as "ghost marriages," whereby when an unmarried or childless man dies, a relation of his then marries a woman "to his name" and the resulting children of this union are regarded as the dead man's children and bear his name (see Edholm 1982:172).

Marriage customs are not only variable between cultures and over time, but also vary between social classes. Moreover, Jessie Bernard (1973) has shown that the meanings which men and women attribute to the same marriage differ quite markedly. Undoubtedly marriage involves some form of status passage and public avowal of recognizing other(s) as of particular importance in one way or another, yet it does not occur universally between two people, nor between two people of the opposite sex, nor is it always viewed as linked to reproduction. Marriage, in the way in which we think of it, is therefore not universal.

Similarly, definitions of sexuality with regard to incest have not been universal or unchanging. In medieval Europe it was considered incestuous to have sexual relations with anyone less than a seventh cousin, and marriage between cousins was proscribed. Now it is possible to marry first cousins.

In Egypt during the Pharaonic and Ptolemaic period, sibling marriages were permitted, and, in some cases, father–daughter marriages. This was seen as a way of preserving the purity of royalty and was not endorsed for the whole of society—although it was permitted for everyone after the Roman conquest of Egypt.

Incestuous marriages were also permitted among royal families in Hawaii and Peru. The Mormons of Utah allowed incest (and polygamy) as a means of ensuring marriage within their church; this was not banned until 1892 (Renvoize 1982:32). Obviously these examples are more related to marriage customs and inheritance or descent problems, but serve to illustrate that even an incest taboo cannot be taken as a universal defining characteristic of families: "who could Adam's sons marry except their sisters?" (ibid., p. 32). Nevertheless, the almost universal existence of some form of incest taboo is a useful illustration of the fact that all societies do, in a myriad of ways, have some form of social organisation of sexuality, mating and reproduction.

Murdock's definition does not take adequate account of the diversity of ways in which co-residence, economic relations, sexuality and reproduction can be organised. Various theorists have made amendments and refinements to Murdock's definition of the family, but all tend to make similar errors. In particular, they translate contemporary western (and usually middle-class) ideas and ideals of what a family should be into what they assume it is everywhere.

Far more precise attempts at definition and analysis have been made by anthropologists who prefer the term kinship to that of family. A feminist anthropologist recently defined kinship as "the ties which exist between individuals who are seen as related both through birth (descent) and through mating (marriage). It is thus primarily concerned with the ways in which mating is socially organised and regulated, the ways in which parentage is assigned, attributed and recognised, descent is traced, relatives are classified, rights are transferred across generations and groups are formed" (Edholm 1982:166). This definition of kinship is a vast improvement on functionalist definitions of family because, first, it stresses the fact that kinship is a social construction, and, second, it emphasises the variability of kinship depending on how it is defined. The social nature of kinship has been stressed by many others elsewhere,[2] and yet there remains a strong common-sense belief that kinship is in fact a quite straightforward biological relationship. It is not.

We assume that because we (think we) know who our parents are and how they made us that kinship is therefore a biological fact. Consider, however, stories we have all heard about children who were brought up by parent(s) for perhaps twenty years, who all along believed their parents were their biological parents, but then discovered that they had in fact been adopted. Such people often suffer severe "identity crises" because they no longer know "who they are" or who their parents are. Their suffering is caused by the way in which we define kinship in our society, namely, in strictly biological terms, differentiating clearly between a "biological" and a "social" parent. The biological parent is always seen by our society as the "real" parent with whom a child should have the strongest ties and bonds. Knowledge of parenthood through families is the central way in which individuals are "located" socially and economically in western society. This, however, is a culturally and historically specific way of defining parenthood and kinship. Other cultures and groups in modern society believe that the person who rears a child is by definition the real parent, regardless of who was involved in the actual reproduction process.

In many poor families in Western Europe and America well into this century it was not uncommon for children to be raised by a grandparent, other kin, or friend, and such children often thought of those who raised them as their parents, even though acknowledging that they also had biological parents who were different. R. T. Smith (1978) found such practises common in Guyana and Jamaica, and reports how "close and imperishable bonds are formed through the act of 'raising' children, irrespective of genetic ties. . . . What is erroneously termed 'fictive kinship' is a widespread phenomenon. . . . While a father may be defined minimally as the person whose genetic material mingled with that of the mother in the formation of the child during one act of sexual intercourse, the father 'role' varies a good deal in any but the most homogeneous societies" (p. 353).

Others have shown the ways in which kinship is a social construction, and how those who are not biologically related to one another come to define themselves as kin: "Liebow, Stack, Ladner and others describe fictive kinship, by which friends are turned into family. Since family is supposed to be more reliable than friendship, 'going for brothers,' 'for sisters,' 'for cousins,' increases the commitment of a relationship, and makes people ideally more responsible for one another. Fictive kinship is a serious relationship" (Rapp 1980:292). It is possible to argue that this is how all kinship began and becomes constructed. Kinship, whether we choose to label it as "biological," "social" or "fictive," is a way of identifying others as in some way special from the rest, people to whom the individual or collectivity feel responsible in certain ways. It is a method of demarcating obligations and responsibility between individuals and groups.

It is thus essential to get away from the idea that kinship is a synonym for "blood" relations — *even though it may often be expressed in those terms* — and to think of it as a social construction which is highly variable and flexible. Some anthropologists recently have argued that kinship is no more and no less than a system of meanings and symbols and that it is "absolutely distinct from a biological system or a system of biological reproduction. Animals reproduce, mate, and undoubtedly form attachments to each other, but they do not have kinship systems" (Smith 1978:351). Indeed, just as Marx argued that it is labour that distinguishes people from animals, it could equally be argued that it is kinship systems that do just that.

This is not to say that many kinship relations do not have some sort of biological base — many do — but the fact that not all of them do, and that the type of base is highly variable, means that it cannot be assumed that there is some universal biological base to kinship. There is not. As Edholm (1982) argues: "notions of blood ties, of biological connection, which to us seem relatively unequivocal, are highly variable. Some societies of which we have anthropological record recognize only the role of the father or of the mother in conception and procreation. . . . Only one parent is a 'relation,' the other is not. In the Trobriand Islands . . . it is believed that intercourse is not the cause of conception, semen is not seen as essential for conception . . . (but) from the entry of a spirit child into the womb . . . it is the repeated intercourse of the same partner which 'moulds' the child" (p. 168).

Because fatherhood is always potentially unknown, and always potentially contestable, it is therefore also always a social category. Motherhood, on the other hand, is always known. Yet apart from carrying and giving birth to a child, the biological base of motherhood stops there. The rest is socially constructed, although it may be—and often is—attributed to biology or "maternal instinct." Whether or not women breastfeed their children has been historically and culturally variable. Baby bottles are no modern invention, but were used in ancient Egypt and in other cultures since. Historians have noted the number of babies given to "wet nurses" in earlier times in Europe as a sign of lack of love and care for infants on the part of mothers. But we can never really know the emotions felt by people hundreds of years ago or their motivations for their practices. The most we can do is to note that their customs were different. To use our own ideology of motherhood and love and apply it universally to all cultures is a highly ethnocentric and narrow way of trying to understand other societies.

Notions of motherhood and "good mothering" are highly variable:

> In Tahiti young women often have one or two children before they are considered, or consider themselves to be, ready for an approved and stable relationship. It is considered perfectly acceptable for the children of this young woman to be given to her parents or other close kin for adoption. . . . The girl can decide what her relationship to the children will be, but there is no sense in which she is forced into "motherhood" because of having had a baby. (Edholm 1982:170)

Who cares for children and rears them is also variable, although in most cases it is women who do so rather than men. Often those women who rear children may well claim some kinship tie to the biological mother—for example, grandmother or aunt—but this tie may simply be created as a result of rearing another woman's child. Motherhood, therefore, if taken to mean both bearing and rearing children, is not universal and is not a biological "fact."

Nor can it be argued that there is such a thing as maternal "instinct," although it is commonly believed to exist. Women are capable of conceiving children today from the age of 13 or 14, and can continue to bear children approximately every two years until they are 45 or 50. This could mean producing around eighteen or nineteen children (although fecundity declines as women age), and this, of course, seldom occurs. Few women in western society marry before they are 18 or 19, and few women in contemporary society have more than two or three children. Contraceptives control conception, not instincts, and unless it were argued that women are forced to use contraceptives,[3] there is little scope to argue for such a thing as maternal instinct.

Consider further that women who conceive babies now when they are *not* married are not hailed as true followers of their natural instinct, but are considered as "immoral," "loose," "whores," and so on. As Antonis (1981) notes: "maternal instinct is ascribed to *married women* only" (p. 59). That women can conceive and bear children is a universal phenomenon; that they do so by instinct is a fallacy. So is the notion that they always raise them. From the moment of birth, motherhood is a social construction.

Sociological and historical studies of the family have tended to pay most attention to the vertical relationships between parents and children. Less attention is paid to the lateral relationships between siblings. Yet in other cultures, and in Western Europe in earlier times, the sibling tie has often formed the basis of households and may be seen as more important than that between parent and child. Among the poorer sectors of western society until quite recently it was common for the eldest daughter to take responsibility for supervising and caring for younger siblings from quite an early age, thereby freeing her mother to engage in waged or domestic work. This remains common in many contemporary societies. In Morocco, for instance, girls "from the age of about four onwards look after younger siblings, fetch and carry, clean and run errands. The tasks themselves are arranged in a hierarchy of importance and attributed to women and girls according to their authority within the household. . . . Boys tend to be freed from domestic tasks and spend their time in groups of peers who play marbles or trap birds" (Maher 1981:73–74).

The content and importance of sibling ties varies, and this is partly a result of different interpretations of reproduction. In societies where the role of the male is seen as peripheral or unimportant — or even non-existent — in reproduction, then his children by another woman are not seen as having any relation to those of the first mother, or vice versa if the mother's role is seen as unimportant. The salience of sibling ties also depends on the organisation of kinship generally. The relative neglect of studying sibling ties as an important aspect of — or even basis of — kinship betrays our own assumptions about the primacy of parenthood in families and, particularly, the assumption that reproduction is the "essence" of kinship, with the mother and child forming the universal core of kinship. As Yanagisako (1977) points out in writing about Goodenough: "while he is undoubtedly right that in every human society mothers and children can be found, to view their *relationship* as the universal nucleus of the family is to attribute to it a social and cultural significance that is lacking in some cases" (pp. 197–98).

Implicit in definitions of kinship is a way of perceiving the social organisation of reproduction and mating, at the centre of which therefore is an organisation of relations between the sexes. The organisation of, and differentiation between, male and female takes many different forms, but all societies do have a social construction of the sexes into gender. Gender is an inherent part of the manner in which all societies are organised and is also a crucial part of the different ways in which kinship has been constructed and defined. The social, economic and political organisation of societies has been initially at least based on kinship—and thus also on gender. Understanding society means understanding the ways in which a society organised kinship and gender, and how these influence one another. Gender and kinship are universally present—as are mothers and children—but the content of them, and the meanings ascribed to them, is highly variable.

The most basic divisions of labour within any society, as pointed out by Durkheim (1933) and others, are based on age and sex. While age as a category can eventually be achieved, sex is ascribed, permanent, and immutable. The biological differences between men and women are such that only women can conceive and lactate; only men can impregnate. In spite of these obvious differences, none of them is great enough to be adequate grounds for allocating one kind of work to women and another to men. Indeed, cross-culturally and historically there are very few jobs that can be claimed to be specifically and universally performed by either men or women. Women have ploughed and mined and still do; men have laundered, gathered fruit and minded children. Hunting and warfare have almost always been male activities, while care of the young and sick has usually been a female activity. But allocation of tasks is also strongly based on age, so it is important to remember that it may be *young* men who hunt and *old* men or women who care for children; old women may be responsible for cooking, while both young men and women may work in the fields or mines.

Age is an important factor to consider in trying to understand the organisation of kinship and households. Nobody remains the same age—contrary to contemporary images in the media of the "happy family" where the couple is permanently 30 and the children forever 8 and 6. As individuals age, so the composition and structure of the unit in which they live change. Consider the ways in which the household composition and resources of a couple change as, first, aged 20, they marry and both work; second, aged 25, they have had two children and the wife has left the labour market for a few years to rear the children until they attend school; third, at 30, one partner leaves or dies and one parent is left with total care of the children; fourth, at 35, one or both may remarry someone who perhaps has three children from an earlier marriage, or may take in an elderly parent to care for, and so on. The number of wage earners and dependants changes over a household's cycle, just as it changes for the individuals within the household.

Thinking in terms of "the" family leads to a static vision of how people actually live and age together and what effects this process has on others within the household in which they live. Moreover, the environment and conditions in which any household is situated are always changing, and these changes can and often do have important repercussions on individuals and households. As Tamara Hareven (1982) points out, it is important when analysing families to differentiate between individual time, family time, and historical time. Thus in considering the structure and meaning of "family" in any society it is important to understand how definitions of dependency and individual time vary and change, how patterns of interaction between individuals and households change, and how historical developments affect all of these.

The notion of there being such a thing as "the family" is thus highly controversial and full of ambiguities and contradictions. Childbearing, childrearing, the construction of gender, allocation of resources, mating and marriage, sexuality and ageing all loosely fit into our idea of family, and yet we have seen how all of them are variable over time, between cultures and between social sectors. The claim that "the family" is universal has been especially problematic because of the failure by most to differentiate between how small groups of people live and work together, and what the ideology of appropriate behaviour for men, women and children within families has been.

Imbued in western patriarchal ideology, as discussed previously, are a number of important and culturally specific beliefs about sexuality, reproduction, parenting and the power relationships between age groups and between the sexes. The sum total of these beliefs makes up a strong *symbol-system which is labelled as the family*. Now while it can be argued that all societies have beliefs and rules on mating, sexuality, gender and age relations, the content of rules is culturally and historically specific and variable, and in no way universal. Thus to claim that patriarchy is universal is as meaningless as claiming that the family is universal.

If defining families is so difficult, how do we try to understand how and why people live, work and form relationships together in our own society? First, we need to acknowledge that while what we may think of as families are not universal, there are still trends and patterns specific to our culture which, by careful analysis, we can understand more fully. Second, we can accept that while there can be no perfect definition, it is still possible to discover certain defining characteristics which can help us to understand changing patterns of behaviour and beliefs. Finally, and most important, we can "deconstruct" assumptions usually made about families by questioning what exactly they mean. Before doing this, however, it is useful to attempt some definition of what is meant by "family" in western society.

Problematic though it may be, it is necessary to retain the notion of co-residence, because most people have lived, and do live, with others for much of their lives. Thus "household" is useful as a defining characteristic, while bearing in mind that it does not necessarily imply sexual or intimate relationships, and that, moreover, relationships *between* households are a crucial aspect of social interaction. "Household" should not be interpreted as a homogeneous and undivided unit. Virtually all households will have their own division of labour, generally based on ideals and beliefs, as well as the structure, of age and sex. There will always tend to be power relationships within households, because they will almost invariably be composed of different age and sex groups and thus different individuals will have differential access to various resources.

Because the essence of any society is interaction, a society will always be composed of a myriad of relationships between people, from the most casual to the most intimate. Relationships are formed between people of the same sex, the opposite sex, the same age group, different age groups, the same and different classes, and so on. Some of these relationships will be sexual—and sexual relations can occur in any type of relationship. Some relationships will be affectionate and loving, others will be violent or hostile. They may be made up of very brief encounters or may extend over the best part of a person's life cycle. Thus while relationships are extremely varied in the ways in which they are formed, their nature and duration, *ideologically* western society has given highest status to long-term relationships between men and women, and between parents and children. Ideologically, such relationships are supposed to be loving and caring, though in reality many are not. They are presented as "natural," but as we have seen, they are not. These ideals have become reified and sanctified in the notion of "family," virtually to the exclusion of all other long-term or intimate relationships.

Ideals of family relationships have become enshrined in our legal, social, religious and economic systems which, in turn, reinforce the ideology and penalise or ostracise those who transgress it. Thus there are very real pressures on people to behave in certain ways, to lead their lives according to acceptable norms and patterns. Patriarchal ideology is embedded in our socioeconomic and political institutions, indeed, in the very language we use, and as such encourages, cajoles and pressures people to follow certain paths. Most of these are presented and defined in terms of "the family," and the family is in turn seen as the bulwark of our culture. The pressures of patriarchal ideology are acted out—and reacted against—in our interpersonal relationships, in marriage and non-marriage, in love and hate, having children and not having children. In short, much of our social behaviour occurs in, and is judged on the basis of, the ideology of "the family."

Relationships are universal, so is some form of co-residence, of intimacy, sexuality and emotional bonds. But the *forms* these can take are infinitely variable and can be changed and challenged as well as embraced. By analysing the ways in which culture has prescribed certain, and proscribed other, forms of behaviour, it should be possible to begin to see the historical and cultural specificity of what is really meant when reference is made to "the family."

ENDNOTES

1. Murdock quoted in Morgan (1975), p. 20.
2. Notably B. J. Harris, J. Goody, W. Goode.
3. For a full discussion of power relationships between men and women with regard to contraceptive practice see Gittins (1982).

REFERENCES

Antonis, B. 1981. "Motherhood and Mothering." In *Women and Society,* edited by Cambridge Women's Study Group. London: Virago.

Bender, D. R. 1979. "A Refinement of the Concept of Household: Families, Co-residence and Domestic Functions." *American Anthropologist* 69.

Bernard, Jessie. 1973. *The Future of Marriage.* London: Souvenir Press.

Durkheim, Émile. 1933. *The Division of Labour in Society.* London: Collier-Macmillan.

Edholm, F. 1982. "The Unnatural Family." In *The Changing Experience of Women,* edited by Whitelegg et al. Oxford: Martin Robertson.

Gittins, Diana. 1982. *Fair Sex: Family Size and Structure, 1990–1939.* London: Hutchinson.

Goode, William J. 1975. "Force and Violence in the Family." In *Violence in the Family,* edited by Steinmetz and Straus. New York: Harper & Row.

Goody, J. 1972. "The Evolution of the Family." In *Household and Family in Past Time,* edited by Laslett and Wall. Cambridge: Cambridge University Press.

———. 1976. "Inheritance, Property and Women: Some Comparative Considerations." In *Family and Inheritance: Rural Society in Western Europe, 1200–1800,* edited by J. Goody, J. Thirsk, and E. P. Thompson. Cambridge: Cambridge University Press.

Goody, J., J. Thirsk, and E. P. Thompson, eds. 1976. *Family and Inheritance: Rural Society in Western Europe, 1200–1800.* Cambridge: Cambridge University Press.

Gutman, Herbert. 1976. *The Black Family in Slavery and Freedom, 1750–1925.* Oxford: Basil Blackwell.

Hareven, Tamara. 1982. *Family Time and Industrial Time.* New York: Cambridge University Press.

Harris, Barbara J. 1976. "Recent Work on the History of the Family: A Review Article." *Feminist Studies* (Spring):159–72.

Ladner, Joyce A. 1971. Tomorrow's Tomorrow: The Black Woman. Garden City, NY: Doubleday.

Liebow, Elliott. 1967. *Tally's Corner: A Study of Negro Streetcorner Men.* Boston: Little, Brown.

Maher, V. 1981. "Work, Consumption and Authority within the Household: A Moroccan Case." In *Of Marriage and Market,* edited by Young et al. London: CSE Books.

Mead, Margaret. 1971. *Male and Female.* Harmondsworth: Penguin.

Morgan, D. H. J. 1975. *Social Theory and the Family.* London: Routledge & Kegan Paul.

Murdock, George. 1949. *Social Structure.* New York: Macmillan.

Rapp, Rayna. 1980. "Family and Class in Contemporary America: Notes Towards an Understanding of Ideology." *Science and Society* 42.

Renvoize, J. 1982. *Incest: A Family History.* London: Routledge & Kegan Paul.

Smith, R. T. 1978. "The Family and the Modern World System: Some Observations from the Caribbean." *Journal of Family History* 3.

Soliende de Gonzalez, N. 1965. "The Consanguineal Household and Matrifocality." *American Anthropologist* 67.

Stack, Carol. 1974. *All Our Kin: Strategies for Survival in a Black Community.* New York: Harper & Row.

Yanagisako, Sylvia J. 1977. "Family and Household: The Analysis of Domestic Groups." *Annual Review of Anthropology* 8.

2

FEMINIST RETHINKING FROM RACIAL–ETHNIC FAMILIES

MAXINE BACA ZINN

U nderstanding diversity remains a pressing challenge for family scholars. Innumerable shortcomings in dominant social science studies render much thinking ill-suited to the task. The growing diversity movement in women's studies, together with new thinking on racial-ethnic groups, holds the promise of a comprehensive understanding of family life.

The Family Transformation in Western Feminism

Two decades of feminist thinking on the family have demystified the idea of the natural and timeless nuclear family. "By taking gender as a basic category of analysis" (Thorne 1992:5), feminist theory has produced new descriptions of family experience, new conceptualizations of family dynamics, and identified new topics for investigation. The following themes show how conventional notions of the family have been transformed:

1. The family is socially constructed. This means that it is not merely a biological arrangement but is a product of specific historical, social, and material conditions. In other words, it is shaped by the social structure.
2. The family is closely connected with other structures and institutions in society. Rather than being a separate sphere, it cannot be understood in isolation from outside factors. As a result, "the family" can be experienced differently by people in different social classes and of different races, and by women and men.
3. Since structural arrangements are abstract and often invisible, family processes can be deceptive or hidden. Many structural conditions make family life problematic. Therefore, families, like other social institutions, require changes in order to meet the needs of women, men, and children.

These themes have made great strides in challenging the myth of the monolithic family, "which has elevated the nuclear family with a breadwinner husband and a full time wife and mother as the only legitimate family form" (Thorne 1992:4). Viewing family life within wider systems of economic and political structures has uncovered great complexity in family dynamics and important variation among families within particular racial and ethnic groups. Despite these advances, women of color theorists contend that Western feminists have not gone far enough in integrating racial differences into family studies.

Differing Feminist Perspectives on the Family

Issues that are rooted in racial (and class) differences have always produced debates within feminist scholarship. Racial differences have evoked deeply felt differences among feminists about the meaning of family life for women. Rayna Rapp's description of a typical feminist meeting about the family captured well the essence of the debate in the late 1960s and early 1970s:

> Many of us have been at an archetypical meeting in which someone stands up and asserts that the nuclear family ought to be abolished because it is degrading and constraining to women. Usually, someone else (often representing a third world position) follows on her heels, pointing out that the attack on the family represents a white middle-class position and that other women need their families for support and survival. (Rapp 1982:168)

Women of color feminists have disagreed with several feminist notions about the meaning of family life for women. As Patricia Zavella recounts the differences:

> In particular, we had problems with the separatist politics (automatically uncooperative with men) in some early women's organizations, and with the white middle-class focus of Americans' feminism, a focus implicitly and sometimes explicitly racist. . . . Both the lack of race and class consciousness in much 1970s feminist political and scholarly work came in for severe criticism. (Zavella 1991:316)

Western feminism became more contextual in the 1980s. As women of color continued to challenge the notion that gender produced a universal woman's family experience, feminism in general worked to broaden feminist studies beyond issues important to White, middle-class, heterosexual women (Ginsburg and Tsing 1990:3). Although gender remains the basic analytical category, scholars now acknowledge the relationships between families and other social divisions (Thorne 1992). The discovery that families are differentiated by race and class has had limited impact on family theorizing across groups. Feminist social scientists now routinely note the importance of race and class differences in family life. Yet we have been more successful in offering single studies of particular groups of families and women than in providing systematic comparisons of families in the same society. Although Western feminist thought takes great care to underscore race and class differences, it still marginalizes racial-ethnic families as special "cultural" cases. In other words, when it comes to thinking about family patterns, diversity is treated as if it were an intrinsic property of groups that are "different," rather than as being the product of forces that affect all families, but affect them in different ways. Feminism has taken on the challenge of diversity, yet it continues to treat race as epiphenomenal—in other words, to treat racial inequality and the social construction of race as secondary to gender (Zavella 1989:31). So far, mainstream feminism has failed to grapple with race as a power system that affects families throughout society and to apply that understanding to "the family" writ large. As Evelyn Nakano Glenn (1987) says, "Systematically incorporating hierarchies of race and class into the feminist reconstruction of the family remains a challenge, a necessary next step into the development of theories of family that are inclusive" (p. 368).

Inclusive Feminist Perspectives on Race and Family

Families and household groups have changed over time and varied with social conditions. Distinctive political and economic contexts have created similar family histories for people of color. Composite portraits of each group show them to have family arrangements and patterns that differ from those of White Americans. Although each group is distinguishable from the others, African Americans, Latinos, and Asians share some important commonalities (Glenn with Yap 1993). These include an extended kinship structure and informal support networks spread across multiple households. Racial-ethnic families are distinctive not only because of their ethnic heritage but also because they reside in a society where racial stratification shapes family resources and structures in important ways.

New thinking about racial stratification provides a perspective for examining family diversity as a structural aspect of society. Race is a socially constructed system that assigns different worth and unequal treatment to groups on the basis of its definition of race. While racial definitions and racial meanings are always being transformed (Omi and Winant 1986), racial hierarchies operate as fundamental axes for the social location of groups and individuals and for the unequal distribution of social opportunities. Racial and ethnic groups occupy particular social locations in which family life is constructed out of widely varying social resources. The uneven distribution of social advantages and social costs operates to strengthen some families while simultaneously weakening others.

By looking at family life in the United States across time and in different parts of the social order, we find that social and economic forces in society have produced alternative domestic arrangements. The key to understanding family diversity lies in the relationship between making a living and maintaining life on a daily basis. Feminist scholars call these activities productive and reproductive labor (Brenner and Laslett 1986:117).

Productive Labor

Historically, racial differences in how people made a living had crucial implications for domestic life. In short, they produced different family and household arrangements on the part of slaves, agricultural workers, and industrial workers. European ethnics were incorporated into low-wage industrial economies of the North, while Blacks, Latinos, Chinese, and Japanese filled labor needs in the colonial labor system of the economically backward regions of the West, Southwest and South. These colonial labor systems, while different, created similar hardships for family life. They required women to work outside of the home in order to maintain even minimal levels of family subsistence. Women's placement in the larger political economy profoundly influenced their family lives.

Several women of color theorists have advanced our understanding of the shaping power of racial stratification, not only for families of color but also for family life in general. For example, Bonnie Thornton Dill (1994) uncovers strong connections in the way racial meanings influence family life. In the antebellum United States, women of European descent received a certain level of protection within the confines of the patriarchal family. There is no doubt that they were constrained as individuals, but family life among European settlers was a highly valued aspect of societal development, and women—to the extent that they contributed to the development of families and to the economic growth of the nation—were provided institutional support for those activities. Unlike White migrants, who came voluntarily, racial-ethnics either were brought to this country or were conquered to meet the need for a cheap and exploitable labor force. Little attention was given to their family and community life. Labor, and not the existence or maintenance of families, was the critical aspect of their role in building the nation.

Women of color experienced the oppression of a patriarchal society (public patriarchy) but were denied the protections and buffering of a patriarchal family (private patriarchy). Thus, they did not have the social structural supports necessary to make their families a vital element in the social order. Family membership was not a key means of access to participation in the wider society. Families of women of color sustained cultural assaults as a direct result of the organization of the labor systems in which their groups participated. The lack of social, legal, and economic support for racial-ethnic families intensified and extended women's reproductive labor, created tensions and strains in family relationships, and set the stage for a variety of creative and adaptive forms of resistance.

Dill's study suggests a different conceptualization of the family, one that is not so bound by the notion of separate spheres of male and female labor or by the notion of the family as an emotional haven, separate and apart from the demands of the economic marketplace. People of color experienced no separation of work and family, no haven of private life, no protected sphere of domesticity. Women's work outside of the home was an extension of their family responsibilities, as family members—women, men, and children—pooled their resources to put food on the table (Du Bois and

Ruiz 1990:iii). What we see here are families and women who are buffeted by the demands of the labor force and provided no legal or social protection other than the maintenance of their ability to work. This research on women of color demonstrates that protecting one's family from the demands of the market is strongly related to the distribution of power and privilege in the society. The majority of White settlers had the power to shelter their members from the market (especially their women and children), and to do so with legal and social support. People of color were denied these protections, and their family members were exploited and oppressed in order to maintain the privileges of the powerful. As Leith Mullings (1986) has said, "It was the working class and enslaved men and women whose labor created the wealth that allowed the middle class and upper middle class domestic lifestyles to exist" (p. 50).

Despite the harsh conditions imposed on family life by racial labor systems, families did not break down. Instead, they adapted as best they could. Using cultural forms where possible, and creating new adaptations where necessary, racial-ethnics adapted their families to the conditions thrust upon them. These adaptations were not exceptions to a "standard" family form. They were produced by forces of inequality in the larger society. Although the White middle-class model of the family has long been defined as the rule, it was neither the norm nor the dominant family type. It was, however, the measure against which other families were judged.

Reproductive Labor

Racial divisions in making a living shape families in important ways. They also determine how people maintain life on a daily basis. Reproductive labor is strongly gendered. It includes activities such as purchasing household goods, preparing and serving food, laundering and repairing clothing, maintaining furnishings and appliances, socializing children, providing care and emotional support for adults, and maintaining kin and community ties (Glenn 1992:1). According to Evelyn Nakano Glenn, reproductive labor has divided along racial as well as gender lines. Specific characteristics of the division have varied regionally and changed over time—shifting parts of it from the household to the market:

> In the first half of the century racial-ethnic women were employed as servants to perform reproductive labor in white households, relieving white middle-class women of onerous aspects of that work; in the second half of the century, with the expansion of commodified services (services turned into commercial products or activities), racial-ethnic women are disproportionately employed as service workers in institutional settings to carry out lower-level "public" reproductive labor, while cleaner white collar supervisory and lower professional positions are filled by white women. (Glenn 1992:3)

The activities of racial-ethnic women in "public" reproductive labor suggest new interpretations of family formation. Knowing that reproductive labor has divided along racial lines offers an understanding of why the idealized family has often been a luxury of the privileged.

Family Patterns as Relational

The distinctive place assigned to racial-ethnic women in the organization of reproductive labor has far-reaching implications for thinking about racial patterns in family diversity. Furthermore, insights about racial divisions apply to White families as well as racial-ethnic families. The new research reveals an important *relational* dimension of family formation. "Relational means that race/gender categories are positioned and that they gain meaning in relation to each other" (Glenn 1992:34). As Bonnie Thornton Dill (1986) puts it, when we examine race, class, and gender simultaneously, we have a better understanding of a social order in which the privileges of some people are dependent on the oppression and exploitation of others (p. 16). This allows us to grasp the benefits that some women derive from their race and their class while also understanding the restrictions that result from gender. In other words, such women are subordinated by patriarchal family dynamics. Yet race and class intersect to create for them privileged opportunities, choices, and lifestyles. For example, Judith Rollins (1985) uses the relationships between Black domestics and their White employers to show how one class and race of women escapes some of the consequences of patriarchy by using the labor of other women. Her study, *Between Women*, highlights the complex linkages among race, class, and gender as they create both privilege and subordination. These are simultaneous processes that enable us to look at women's diversity from a different angle.

The relational themes of privilege and subordination appear frequently in studies of domestic service (Romero 1992). Victoria Byerly (1986) found that White women who worked in the Southern textile mills hired African Americans as domestic workers. The labor of these domestics enabled the White women to engage in formal work. Vicki Ruiz (1988) describes how Mexican American women factory workers in Texas have eased their housework burdens by hiring Mexican domestic workers (Ward 1990:10–11). These studies highlight some of the ways in which race relations penetrate households, intersecting with gender arrangements to produce varied family experiences.

Theorizing across Racial Categories

Historical and contemporary racial divisions of productive and reproductive labor challenge the assumption that family diversity is the outgrowth of different cultural patterns. Racial stratification creates distinctive patterns in the way families are located and embedded in different social environments. It structures social opportunities differently, and it constructs and positions groups in systematic ways. This offers important lessons for examining current economic and social changes that are influencing families, and influencing them differently. Still, the knowledge that family life differs significantly by race does not preclude us from theorizing across racial categories.

The information and service economy continues to reshape family life by altering patterns associated with marriage, divorce, childbearing, and household composition. A growing body of family research shows that although some families are more vulnerable than others to economic marginalization, none are immune from the deep structural changes undermining "traditional" families. Adaptation takes varying forms, such as increased divorce rates, female-headed households, and extended kinship units. Although new patterns of racial formation will affect some families more than others, looking at social contexts will enable us to better understand family life in general.

The study of Black families can generate important insights for White families (Billingsley 1988). Families may respond in a like manner when impacted by larger social forces. To the extent that White families and Black families experience similar pressures, they may respond in similar ways, including the adaptation of their family structures and other behaviours. With respect to single-parent families, teenage parents, working mothers, and a host of other behaviours, Black families serve as barometers of social change and as forerunners of adaptive patterns that will be progressively experienced by the more privileged sectors of U.S. society.

On the other hand, such insights must not eclipse the ways in which racial meanings shape social perceptions of family diversity. As social and economic changes produce new family arrangements, some alternatives become more tolerable. Race plays an important role in the degree to which alternatives are deemed acceptable. When alternatives are associated with subordinate social categories, they are judged against "the traditional family" and found to be deviant. Many alternative lifestyles that appear new to middle-class Americans are actually variant family patterns that have been traditional within Black and other ethnic communities for many generations. Presented as the "new lifestyles of the young mainstream elite, they are the same lifestyles that have in the past been defined as pathological, deviant, or unacceptable when observed in Black families" (Peters and McAdoo 1983:228). As Evelyn Brooks Higginbotham (1992) observes, race often subsumes other sets of social relations, making them "good" or "bad," "correct" or "incorrect" (p. 255). Yet, many of the minority family patterns deemed "incorrect" by journalists, scholars, and policymakers are logical life choices in a society of limited social opportunities.

Growing Racial Diversity and "the Family Crisis"

Despite the proliferation of studies showing that families are shaped by their social context, conservative rhetoric is fueling a "growing social and ideological cleavage between traditional family forms and the emerging alternatives"

(Gerson 1991:57). This is complicated further by the profound demographic transformation now occurring in the United States. The unprecedented growth of minority populations is placing a special spotlight on family diversity.

Racial minorities are increasing faster than the majority population. During the 1980s Asians more than doubled, from 3.5 million to 7.3 million, and Hispanics grew from 14.6 to 22.4 million. The Black increase was from 16.5 to 30.0 million. The result of these trends is that whereas Whites in 1980 were 80 percent of the population, they will be only 70 percent by 2000 (Population Reference Bureau 1989:10). Immigration now accounts for a large share of the nation's population growth. The largest ten-year wave of immigration in U.S. history occurred during the 1980s, with the arrival of almost 9 million people. More immigrants were admitted during the 1980s than any decade since 1900–1910. By 2020, immigrants will be more important to the U.S. population growth than natural increase (Waldrop 1990:23). New patterns of immigration are changing the racial composition of society. Among the expanded population of first-generation immigrants, "the Asian-born now outnumber the European-born. Those from Latin America — predominantly Mexican — outnumber both" (Barringer 1992:2). This contrasts sharply with what occurred as recently as the 1950s, when two-thirds of legal immigrants were from Europe and Canada.

Changes in the racial composition of society are creating new polarizations along residential, occupational, educational, and economic lines. Crucial to these divisions is an ongoing transformation of racial meaning and racial hierarchy. Family scholars must be alert to the effects of these changes because the racial repositioning will touch families throughout the racial order.

New immigration patterns will escalate the rhetoric of family crises as immigrant lifestyles and family forms are measured against a mythical family ideal. Inevitably, some interpretations of diversity will revert to cultural explanations that deflect attention from the social opportunities associated with race. Even though pleas for "culturally sensitive" approaches to non-White families are well-meaning, they can unwittingly keep "the family" ensnared in a White middle-class ideal. We need to find a way to transcend the conflict among the emerging array of "family groups" (Gerson 1991:57). The best way to do this is to abandon all notions that uphold one family form as normal and others as "cultural variations." Immigration will undoubtedly introduce alternative family forms; they will be best understood by treating race as a fundamental structure that situates families differently and thereby produces diversity.

REFERENCES

Barringer, Felicity. 1992. "As American as Apple Pie, Dim Sum or Burritos." *New York Times,* May, sec. 4, p. 2.

Billingsley, Andrew. 1988. "The Impact of Technology on Afro-American Families." *Family Relations* 7:420–25.

Brenner, Johanna and Barbara Laslett. 1986. "Social Reproduction and the Family." In *The Social Reproduction of Organization and Culture,* edited by Ulf Himmelstrand. Newbury Park, CA: Sage.

Byerly, Victoria. 1986. *Hard Times Cotton Mill Girls: Personal Histories of Womanhood and Poverty in the South.* Ithaca, NY: ILR Press.

Dill, Bonnie Thornton. 1986. *Our Mothers' Grief: Racial Ethnic Women and the Maintenance of Families.* Research Paper No. 4. Memphis, TN: Center for Research on Women, Memphis State University.

——. 1994. "Fictive Kin, Paper Sons, and Compadrazgo: Women of Color and the Struggle for Family Survival." In *Women of Color in U.S. Society,* edited by Maxine Baca Zinn and Bonnie Thornton Dill. Philadelphia: Temple University Press.

Du Bois, Ellen Carol and Vicki L. Ruiz, eds. 1990. "Introduction." In *Unequal Sisters: A Multicultural Reader in U.S. Women's History.* New York: Routledge.

Gerson, Kathleen. 1991. "Coping with Commitment: Dilemmas and Conflicts of Family Life." In *America at Century's End,* edited by Alan Wolfe. Berkeley: University of California Press.

Ginsburg, Faye and Anna Lowenhaupt Tsing. 1990. *Uncertain Terms: Negotiating Gender in American Culture.* Boston: Beacon Press.

Glenn, Evelyn Nakano. 1987. "Gender and the Family." In *Analyzing Gender,* edited by Beth B. Hess and Myra Marx Ferree. Newbury Park, CA: Sage.

——. 1992. "From Servitude to Service Work: Historical Continuities in the Racial Division of Paid Reproductive Labor." *Signs: Journal of Women in Culture and Society* 18 (1): 1–43.

Glenn, Evelyn Nakano, with Stacey H. Yap. 1993. "Chinese American Families." In *Minority Families in the United States: Comparative Perspectives,* edited by Ronald L. Taylor. Englewood Cliffs, NJ: Prentice-Hall.

Higginbotham, Evelyn Brooks. 1992. "African-American Women's History and the Metalanguage of Race." *Signs: Journal of Women in Culture and Society* 17 (2): 251–74.

Mullings, Leith. 1986. "Uneven Development: Class, Race, and Gender in the United States Before 1900." In *Women's Work,* edited by Eleanor Leacock and Helen I. Safa. New York: Bergin and Garvey.

Omi, Michael and Howard Winant. 1986. *Racial Formation in the United States.* London: Routledge & Kegan Paul.

Peters, Marie and Harriette P. McAdoo. 1983. "The Present and Future of Alternative Lifestyles in Ethnic American Cultures." In *Contemporary Families and Alternative Lifestyles,* edited by Eleanor D. Macklin and R. H. Rubin. Beverly Hills, CA: Sage.

Population Reference Bureau. 1989. *America in the 21st Century: Human Resource Development.* Washington, DC: Population Reference Bureau.

Rapp, Rayna. 1982. "Family and Class in Contemporary America: Notes toward an Understanding of Ideology." In *Rethinking the Family: Some Feminist Questions,* edited by Barrie Thorne and Marilyn Yalom. New York: Longman.

Rollins, Judith. 1985. *Between Women: Domestics and Their Employers.* Philadelphia: Temple University Press.

Romero, Mary. 1992. *Maid in the U.S.A.* New York: Routledge.

Ruiz, Vicki. 1988. "By the Day or the Week: Mexican Domestic Workers in El Paso." In *Women in the U.S.-Mexico Border,* edited by Vicki Ruiz and Susan Tiano. Boston: Allen & Unwin.

Thorne, Barrie. 1992. "Feminism and the Family: Two Decades of Thought." In *Rethinking the Family: Some Feminist Questions,* 2d ed., edited by Barrie Thorne and Marilyn Yalom. Boston: Northeastern University Press.

Waldrop, Judith. 1990. "You'll Know It's the 21st Century When . . ." *American Demographics* 13 (December): 22–27.

Ward, Kathryn. 1990. *Women Workers and Global Restructuring.* Ithaca, NY: Cornell University Press.

Zavella, Patricia. 1989. "The Problematic Relationship of Feminism and Chicana Studies." *Women's Studies* 17:25–36.

——. 1991. "Mujeres in Factories: Race and Class Perspectives on Women, Work, and Family." In Gender at the Crossroads of Knowledge, edited by Micaela di Leonardo. Berkeley: University of California Press.

3

EXILES FROM KINSHIP

KATH WESTON

Indeed, it is not so much identical conclusions that prove minds to be related as the contradictions that are common to them.

— Albert Camus

For years, and in an amazing variety of contexts, claiming a lesbian or gay identity has been portrayed as a rejection of "the family" and a departure from kinship. In media portrayals of AIDS, Simon Watney (1987) observes that "we are invited to imagine some absolute divide between the two domains of 'gay life' and 'the family,' as if gay men grew up, were educated, worked and lived our lives in total isolation from the rest of society" (p. 103). Two presuppositions lend a dubious credence to such imagery: the belief that gay men and lesbians do not have children or establish lasting relationships, and the belief that they invariably alienate adoptive and blood kin once their sexual identities become known. By presenting "the family" as a unitary object, these depictions also imply that everyone participates in identical sorts of kinship relations and subscribes to one universally agreed-upon definition of family.

Representations that exclude lesbians and gay men from "the family" invoke what Blanche Wiesen Cook (1977:48) has called "the assumption that gay people do not love and do not work," the reduction of lesbians and gay men to sexual identity, and sexual identity to sex alone. In the United States, sex apart from heterosexual marriage tends to introduce a wild card into social relations, signifying unbridled lust and the limits of individualism.

If heterosexual intercourse can bring people into enduring association via the creation of kinship ties, lesbian and gay sexuality in these depictions isolates individuals from one another rather than weaving them into a social fabric. To assert that straight people "naturally" have access to family, while gay people are destined to move toward a future of solitude and loneliness, is not only to tie kinship closely to procreation, but also to treat gay men and lesbians as members of a nonprocreative species set apart from the rest of humanity (cf. Foucault 1978).

It is but a short step from positioning lesbians and gay men somewhere beyond "the family" — unencumbered by relations of kinship, responsibility, or affection — to portraying them as a menace to family and society. A person or group must first be outside and other in order to invade, endanger, and threaten. My own impression from fieldwork corroborates Frances Fitz-Gerald's (1986) observation that many heterosexuals believe not only that gay people have gained considerable political power, but also that the absolute number of lesbians and gay men (rather than their visibility) has increased in recent years. Inflammatory rhetoric that plays on fears about the "spread" of gay identity and of AIDS finds a disturbing parallel in the imagery used by fascists to describe syphilis at mid-century, when "the healthy" confronted "the degenerate" while the fate of civilization hung in the balance (Hocquenghem 1978).

A long sociological tradition in the United States of studying "the family" under siege or in various states of dissolution lent credibility to charges that this institution required protection from "the homosexual threat." Proposition 6 (the Briggs initiative), which appeared on the ballot in California in 1978, was defeated only after a massive organizing campaign that mobilized lesbians and gay men in record numbers. The text of the initiative, which would have barred gay and lesbian teachers (along with heterosexual teachers who advocated homosexuality) from the public schools, was phrased as a defense of "the family" (in Hollibaugh 1979:55):

> One of the most fundamental interests of the State is the establishment and preservation of the family unit. Consistent with this interest is the State's duty to protect its impressionable youth from influences which are antithetical to this vital interest.

Other antigay legislative initiative campaigns adopted the slogans "save the family" and "save the children" as their rallying cries. In 1983 the *Moral Majority Report* referred obliquely to AIDS with the headline "Homosexual Diseases Threaten American Families" (Godwin 1983). When the *Boston Herald* opposed a gay rights bill introduced into the Massachusetts legislature, it was with an eye to "the preservation of family values" (Allen 1987).

Discourse that opposes gay identity to family membership is not confined to the political arena. A gay doctor was advised during his residency to discourage other gay people from becoming his patients, lest his waiting room become filled with homosexuals. "It'll scare away the families," warned his supervisor (Lazere 1986). Discussions of dual-career families and the implications of a family wage system usually render invisible the financial obligations of gay people who support dependents or who pool material resources with lovers and others they define as kin. Just as women have been accused of taking jobs away from "men with families to support," some lesbians and gay men in the [San Francisco] Bay Area recalled co-workers who had condemned them for competing against "people with families" for scarce employment. Or consider the choice of words by a guard at that "all-American" institution, Disneyland, commenting on a legal suit brought by two gay men who had been prohibited from dancing with one another at a dance floor on the grounds: "This is a family park. There is no room for alternative lifestyles here" (Mendenhall 1985).

Scholarly treatments are hardly exempt from this tendency to locate gay men and lesbians beyond the bounds of kinship. Even when researchers are sympathetic to gay concerns, they may equate kinship with genealogically calculated relations. Manuel Castells and Karen Murphy's (1982) study of the "spatial organization of San Francisco's gay community," for instance, frames its analysis using "gay territory" and "family land" as mutually exclusive categories.

From New Right polemics to the rhetoric of high school hallways, "recruitment" joins "reproduction" in allusions to homosexuality. Alleging that gay men and lesbians must seduce young people in order to perpetuate (or expand) the gay population because they cannot have children of their own, heterosexist critics have conjured up visions of an end to society, the inevitable fate of a society that fails to "reproduce."[1] Of course, the contradictory inferences that sexual identity is "caught" rather than claimed, and that parents pass their sexual identities on to their children, are unsubstantiated. The power of this chain of associations lies in a play on words that blurs the multiple senses of the term *reproduction*.

Reproduction's status as a mixed metaphor may detract from its analytic utility, but its very ambiguities make it ideally suited to argument and innuendo.[2] By shifting without signal between reproduction's meaning of physical procreation and its sense as the perpetuation of society as a whole, the characterization of lesbians and gay men as nonreproductive beings links their supposed attacks on "the family" to attacks on society in the broadest sense. Speaking of parents who had refused to accept her lesbian identity, a Jewish woman explained, "They feel like I'm finishing off Hitler's job." The plausibility of the contention that gay people pose a threat to "the family" (and, through the family, to ethnicity) depends upon a view of family grounded in heterosexual relations, combined with the conviction that gay men and lesbians are incapable of procreation, parenting, and establishing kinship ties.

Some lesbians and gay men in the Bay Area had embraced the popular equation of their sexual identities with the renunciation of access to kinship, particularly when first coming out. "My image of gay life was very lonely, very weird, no family," Rafael Ortiz recollected. "I assumed that my family was gone now — that's it." After Bob Korkowski began to call himself gay, he wrote a series of poems in which an orphan was the central character. Bob said the poetry expressed his fear of "having to give up my family because I was queer." When I spoke with Rona Bren after she had been home with the flu, she told me that whenever she was sick, she relived old fears. That day she had remembered her mother's grim prediction: "You'll be a lesbian and you'll be alone the rest of your life. Even a dog shouldn't be alone."

Looking backward and forward across the life cycle, people who equated their adoption of a lesbian or gay identity with a renunciation of family did so in the double-sided sense of fearing rejection by the families in which they had grown up, and not expecting to marry or have children as adults. Although few in numbers, there were still those who had considered "going straight" or getting married specifically in order to "have a family." Vic Kochifos thought he understood why:

> It's a whole lot easier being straight in the world than it is being gay. . . . You have built-in loved ones: wife, husband, kids, extended family. It just works easier. And when you want to do something that requires children, and you want to have a feeling of knowing that there's gonna be someone around who cares about you when you're 85 years old, there are thoughts that go through your head, sure. There must be. There's a way of doing it gay, but it's a whole lot harder, and it's less secure.

Bernie Margolis had been sexually involved with men since he was in his teens, but for years had been married to a woman with whom he had several children. At age 67 he regretted having grown to adulthood before the current discussion of gay families, with its focus on redefining kinship and constructing new sorts of parenting arrangements:

> I didn't want to give up the possibility of becoming a family person. Of having kids of my own to carry on whatever I built up. . . . My mother was always talking about she's looking forward to the day when she would bring her children under the canopy to get married. It never occurred to her that I wouldn't be married. It probably never occurred to me either.

The very categories "good family person" and "good family man" had seemed to Bernie intrinsically opposed to a gay identity. In his fifties at the time I interviewed him, Stephen Richter attributed never having become a father to "not having the relationship with the woman." Because he had envisioned parenting and procreation only in the context of a heterosexual relationship, regarding the two as completely bound up with one another, Stephen had never considered children an option.

Older gay men and lesbians were not the only ones whose adult lives had been shaped by ideologies that banish gay people from the domain of kinship. Explaining why he felt uncomfortable participating in "family occasions," a young man who had no particular interest in raising a child commented, "When families get together, what do they talk about? Who's getting married, who's having children. And who's not, okay? Well, look who's not." Very few of the lesbians and gay men I met believed that claiming a gay

identity automatically requires leaving kinship behind. In some cases, people described this equation as an outmoded view that contrasted sharply
with revised notions of what constitutes a family.

Well-meaning defenders of lesbian and gay identity sometimes assert
that gays are not inherently "antifamily," in ways that perpetuate the association of heterosexual identity with exclusive access to kinship. Charles
Silverstein (1977), for instance, contends that lesbians and gay men may
place more importance on maintaining family ties than heterosexuals do
because gay people do not marry and raise children. Here the affirmation
that gays and lesbians are capable of fostering enduring kinship ties ends up
reinforcing the implication that they cannot establish "families of their own,"
presumably because the author regards kinship as unshakably rooted in heterosexual alliance and procreation. In contrast, discourse on gay families cuts
across the politically loaded couplet of "profamily" and "antifamily" that
places gay men and lesbians in an inherently antagonistic relation to kinship
solely on the basis of their nonprocreative sexualities. "Homosexuality is not
what is breaking up the Black family," declared Barbara Smith (1987), a black
lesbian writer, activist, and speaker at the 1987 Gay and Lesbian March on
Washington. "Homophobia is. My Black gay brothers and my Black lesbian
sisters are members of Black families, both the ones we were born into and
the ones we create."

At the height of gay liberation, activists had attempted to develop alternatives to "the family," whereas by the 1980s many lesbians and gay men
were struggling to legitimate gay families as a form of kinship. When
Armistead Maupin spoke at a gathering on Castro Street to welcome home
two gay men who had been held hostage in the Middle East, partners who
had stood with arms around one another upon their release, he congratulated
them not only for their safe return, but also as representatives of a new
kind of family. Gay or chosen families might incorporate friends, lovers, or
children, in any combination. Organized through ideologies of love, choice,
and creation, gay families have been defined through a contrast with what
many gay men and lesbians in the Bay Area called "straight," "biological,"
or "blood" family. If families we choose were the families lesbians and gay
men created for themselves, straight family represented the families in
which most had grown to adulthood.

What does it mean to say that these two categories of family have been
defined through contrast? One thing it emphatically does *not* mean is that heterosexuals share a single coherent form of family (although some of the lesbians and gay men doing the defining believed this to be the case). I am not
arguing here for the existence of some central, unified kinship system vis-à-vis
which gay people have distinguished their own practice and understanding of
family. In the United States, race, class, gender, ethnicity, regional origin, and
context all inform differences in household organization, as well as differences
in notions of family and what it means to call someone kin.[3]

In any relational definition, the juxtaposition of two terms gives meaning to both.[4] Just as light would not be meaningful without some notion of

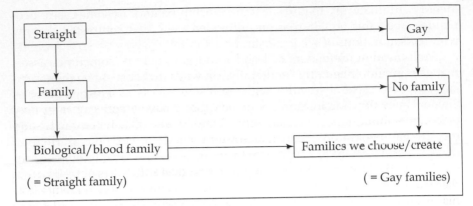

FIGURE 1.   Mapping Family Relationships

darkness, so gay or chosen families cannot be understood apart from the families lesbians and gay men call "biological," "blood," or "straight." Like others in their society, most gay people in the Bay Area considered biology a matter of "natural fact." When they applied the terms "blood" and "biology" to kinship, however, they tended to depict families more consistently organized by procreation, more rigidly grounded in genealogy, and more uniform in their conceptualization than anthropologists know most families to be. For many lesbians and gay men, blood family represented not some naturally given unit that provided a base for all forms of kinship, but rather a procreative principle that organized only one possible *type* of kinship. In their descriptions they situated gay families at the opposite end of a spectrum of determination, subject to no constraints beyond a logic of "free" choice that ordered membership. To the extent that gay men and lesbians mapped "biology" and "choice" onto identities already opposed to one another (straight and gay, respectively), they polarized these two types of family along an axis of sexual identity.[5]

The chart in Figure 1 recapitulates the ideological transformation generated as lesbians and gay men began to inscribe themselves within the domain of kinship. What this chart presents is not some static substitution set, but a historically motivated succession.[6] To move across or down the chart is to move through time. Following along from left to right, time appears as process, periodized with reference to the experience of coming out. In the first opposition, coming out defines the transition from a straight to a gay identity. For the person who maintains an exclusively biogenetic notion of kinship, coming out can mark the renunciation of kinship, the shift from "family" to "no family" portrayed in the second opposition. In the third line, individuals who accepted the possibility of gay families after coming out could experience themselves making a transition from the biological or blood families in which they had grown up to the establishment of their own chosen families.

Moving from top to bottom, the chart depicts the historical time that inaugurated contemporary discourse on gay kinship. "Straight" changes from a category with an exclusive claim on kinship to an identity allied with a specific kind of family symbolized by biology or blood. Lesbians and gay men, originally relegated to the status of people without family, later lay claim to a distinctive type of family characterized as families we choose or create. While dominant cultural representations have asserted that straight is to gay as family is to no family (lines 1 and 2), at a certain point in history gay people began to contend that straight is to gay as blood family is to chosen families (lines 1 and 3).

What provided the impetus for this ideological shift? Transformations in the relation of lesbians and gay men to kinship are inseparable from socio-historical developments: changes in the context for disclosing a lesbian or gay identity to others, attempts to build urban gay "community," cultural inferences about relationships between "same-gender" partners, and the lesbian baby boom associated with alternative (artificial) insemination. If Pierre Bourdieu (1977) is correct, and kinship is something people use to act as well as to think, then its transformations should have unfolded not only on the "big screen" of history, but also on the more modest stage of day-to-day life, where individuals have actively engaged novel ideological distinctions and contested representations that would exclude them from kinship. . . .

Kinship and Procreation

Since the time of Lewis Henry Morgan, most scholarly studies of familial relations have enthroned human procreation as kinship's ultimate referent. According to received anthropological wisdom, relations of blood (consanguinity) and marriage (affinity) could be plotted for any culture on a universal genealogical grid. Generations of fieldworkers set about the task of developing kinship charts for a multitude of "egos," connecting their subjects outward to a network of social others who represented the products (offspring) and agents (genitor/genetrix) of physical procreation. In general, researchers occupied themselves with investigations of differences in the ways cultures arranged and divided up the grid, treating blood ties as a material base underlying an array of cross-cultural variations in kinship organization.

More recently, however, anthropologists have begun to reconsider the status of kinship as an analytic concept and a topic for inquiry. What would happen if observers ceased privileging genealogy as a sacrosanct or objective construct, approaching biogenetic ties instead as a characteristically Western way of ordering and granting significance to social relations? After a lengthy exercise in this kind of bracketing, David Schneider (1972, 1984) concluded that significant doubt exists as to whether non-Western cultures recognize kinship as a unified construct or domain. Too often unreflective recourse to the biogenetic symbolism used to prioritize relationships in Anglo-European societies subordinates an understanding of how particular cultures construct social ties to the project of cross-cultural comparison. But suppose for a moment that blood is not intrinsically thicker than water. Denaturalizing the genealogical grid would require that procreation no longer be postulated as kinship's base, ground, or centerpiece.

Within Western societies, anthropologists are not the only ones who have implicitly or explicitly subjected the genealogical grid to new scrutiny. By reworking familiar symbolic materials in the context of nonprocreative relationships, lesbians and gay men in the United States have formulated a critique of kinship that contests assumptions about the bearing of biology, genetics, and heterosexual intercourse on the meaning of family in their own culture. Unlike Schneider, they have not set out to deconstruct kinship as a privileged domain, or taken issue with cultural representations that portray biology as a material "fact" exclusive of social significance. What gay kinship ideologies challenge is not the concept of procreation that informs kinship in the United States, but the belief that procreation *alone* constitutes kinship, and that "nonbiological" ties must be patterned after a biological model (like adoption) or forfeit any claim to kinship status.

In the United States, the notion of biology as an indelible, precultural substratum is so ingrained that people often find it difficult to take an anthropological step backward in order to examine biology as symbol rather than substance. For many in this society, biology is a defining feature of kinship: they believe that blood ties make certain people kin, regardless of whether those individuals display the love and enduring solidarity expected to characterize familial relations. Physical procreation, in turn, produces biological links. Collectively, biogenetic attributes are supposed to demarcate kinship as a cultural domain, offering a yardstick for determining who counts as a "real" relative. Like their heterosexual counterparts, lesbians and gay men tended to naturalize biology in this manner.

Not all cultures grant biology this significance for describing and evaluating relationships. To read biology as symbol is to approach it as a cultural construct and linguistic category, rather than a self-evident matter of "natural fact." At issue here is the cultural valuation given to ties traced through procreation, and the meaning that biological connection confers upon a relationship in a given cultural context. In this sense, biology is no less a symbol than choice or creation. Neither is inherently more "real" or valid than the other, culturally speaking.

In the United States, Schneider (1968) argues, "sexual intercourse" is the symbol that brings together relations of marriage and blood, supplying the distinctive features in terms of which kinship relations are defined and differentiated. A relationship mediated by procreation binds a mother to a daughter, a brother to a sister, and so on, in the categories of genitor or genetrix, offspring, or members of a sibling set. Immediately apparent to a gay man or lesbian is that what passes here for sex per se is actually the *heterosexual* union of two differently gendered persons. While all sexual activity among heterosexuals certainly does not lead to the birth of children, the isolation of heterosexual intercourse as a core symbol orients kinship studies toward a dominantly procreative reading of sexualities. For a society like the United States, Sylvia Yanagisako and Jane Collier's (1987) call to analyze gender and kinship as mutually implicated constructs must be extended to embrace sexual identity.

The very notion of gay families asserts that people who claim nonprocreative sexual identities and pursue nonprocreative relationships can lay claim to family ties of their own without necessary recourse to marriage, childbearing, or child rearing.[7] By defining these chosen families in opposition to the biological ties believed to constitute a straight family, lesbians and gay men began to renegotiate the meaning and practice of kinship from within the very societies that had nurtured the concept. Theirs has not been a proposal to number gay families among variations in "American kinship," but a more comprehensive attack on the privilege accorded to a biogenetically grounded mode of determining what relationships will *count* as kinship.

It is important to note that some gay men and lesbians in the Bay Area agreed with the view that blood ties represent the only authentic, legitimate form of kinship. Often those who disputed the validity of chosen families were people whose notions of kinship were bound up with their own sense of racial or ethnic identity. "You've got one family, one biological family," insisted Paul Jaramillo, a Mexican American man who did not consider his lover or friends to be kin.

> They're very good friends and I love them, but I would not call them family. Family to me is blood. . . . I feel that Western Caucasian culture, that it's much more broken down, and that they can deal with their good friends and neighbors as family. But it's not that way, at least in my background.

Because most individuals who expressed this view were well aware of the juxtaposition of blood family with families we choose, they tended to address gay kinship ideologies directly. As Lourdes Alcantara explained:

> I know a lot of lesbians think that you choose your own family. I don't think so. Because, as a Latin woman, the bonds that I got with my family are irreplaceable. They can't be replaced. They cannot. So my family is my family, my friends are my friends. My friends can be more important than my family, but that doesn't mean they are my family. . . . 'Cause no matter what, they are just friends — they don't have your blood. They don't have your same connection. They didn't go through what you did. For example, I starved with my family a lot of times. They know what it is like. If I talk to my friends, they will understand me, but they will never feel the same.

What Lourdes so movingly described was a sense of enduring solidarity arising from shared experience and symbolized by blood connection. Others followed a similar line of reasoning (minus the biological signifier) when they contended that a shared history testifies to enduring solidarity, which can provide the basis of creating familial relationships of a chosen, or nonbiological, sort.

In an essay on disclosing a lesbian or gay identity to relatives, Betty Berzon (1979) maintains that "from early on, being gay is associated with going against the family" (p. 89). Many people in the Bay Area viewed families as the principal mediator of race and ethnicity, drawing on folk theories of cultural transmission in which parents hand down "traditions" and identity (as well as genes) to their children.[8] If having a family was part of what it meant to be Chicana or Cherokee or Japanese American, then claiming a lesbian or gay identity could easily be interpreted as losing or betraying that cultural heritage, so long as individuals conceived kinship in biogenetic terms (cf. Clunis and Green 1988:105; Tremble et al. 1989). Kenny Nash had originally worried that coming out as a gay man would separate him from other African Americans.

> *Because I related to the black community a lot as far as politics, and . . . unfortunately, sexual politics in some parts of the black movement are not very good. Just as there is this continuing controversy about feminism and black women in the women's movement. It's a carry-over, I think, into [ideas] about gay people, gay men and lesbians. Because there are some people who think of [being gay] as the antithesis of building strong family institutions, and that's what we need: role models for people, bringing up children, and all that stuff.*

Condemnations of homosexuality might picture race or ethnicity and gay identity as antagonists in response to a history of racist attributions of "weak" family ties to certain groups (e.g., blacks), or in response to anything that appeared to menace the legacy of "strong" kinship bonds sometimes attributed to other categories of people (e.g., Latinos, Jews). In either case, depicting lesbian or gay identity as a threat to ethnic or racial identity depended upon the cultural positioning of gay people outside familial relations. The degree to which individuals construct racial identity *through* their notions of family remains a relatively unexplored aspect of why some heterosexuals of color reject gay or lesbian identity as a sign of assimilation, a "white thing."

Not all lesbians and gays of color or whites with a developed ethnic identity took issue with the concept of chosen families. Many African Americans, for instance, felt that black communities had never held to a strictly biogenetic interpretation of kinship. "Blacks have never said to a child, 'Unless you have a mother, father, sister, brother, you don't have a family'" (Height 1989:137).[9] Discourse and ideology are far from being uniformly determined by identities, experiences, or historical developments. Divergent perceptions of the relation between family ties and race or ethnicity are indicative of a situation of ideological flux, in which procreative and nonprocreative interpretations vie with one another for the privilege of defining kinship. As the United States entered the final decade of the twentieth century, lesbians and gay men from a broad spectrum of racial and ethnic identities had come to embrace the legitimacy of gay families.

From Biology to Choice

Upon first learning the categories that framed gay kinship ideologies, heterosexuals sometimes mentioned adoption as a kind of limiting case that appeared to occupy the borderland between biology and choice. In the United States, adopted children are chosen, in a sense, although biological offspring can be planned or selected as well, given the widespread availability of birth control. Yet adoption in this society "is only understandable as a way of creating the social fiction that an actual link of kinship exists. Without biological kinship as a model, adoption would be meaningless" (Schneider 1984:55). Adoption does not render the attribution of biological descent culturally irrelevant (witness the many adopted children who, later in life, decide to search for their "real" parents). But adoptive relations — unlike gay families — pose no fundamental challenge to either procreative interpretations of kinship or the culturally standardized image of a family assembled around a core of parent(s) plus children.

Mapping biological family and families we choose onto contrasting sexual identities (straight and gay, respectively) places these two types of family in a relation of opposition, but *within* that relation, determinism implicitly differentiates biology from choice and blood from creation. Informed by contrasting notions of free will and the fixedness often attributed to biology in this culture, the opposition between straight and gay families echoes old dichotomies such as nature versus nurture and real versus ideal. In families we choose, the agency conveyed by "we" emphasizes each person's part in constructing gay families, just as the absence of agency in the term "biological family" reinforces the sense of blood as an immutable fact over which individuals exert little control. Likewise, the collective subject of families we choose invokes a collective identity — who are "we" if not gay men and lesbians? In order to identify the "we" associated with the speaker's "I," a listener must first recognize the correspondence between the opposition of blood to choice and the relation of straight to gay.

Significantly, families we choose have not built directly upon beliefs that gay or lesbian identity can be chosen. Among lesbians and gay men themselves, opinions differ as to whether individuals select or inherit their sexual identities. In the aftermath of the gay movement, the trend has been to move away from the obsession of earlier decades with the etiological question of what "causes" homosexuality. After noting that no one subjects heterosexuality to similar scrutiny, many people dropped the question. Some lesbian-feminists presented lesbianism as a political choice that made a statement about sharing their best with other women and refusing to participate in patriarchal relations. In everyday conversations, however, the majority of both men and women portrayed their sexual identities as either inborn or a predisposition developed very early in life. Whether or not to act on feelings already present then became the only matter left to individual discretion. "The choice for me wasn't being with men or being a lesbian," Richie Kaplan explained. "The choice was being asexual or being with women."

In contrast, parents who disapproved of homosexuality could convey a critical attitude by treating gay identity as something elective, especially since people in the United States customarily hold individuals responsible for any negative consequences attendant upon a "free choice." One man described with dismay his father's reaction upon learning of his sexual identity: "I said, 'I'm gay.' And he said, 'Oh. Well, I guess you made your choice.'" According to another, "My father kept saying, 'Well, you're gonna have to live by your choices that you make. It's your responsibility.' What's there to be responsible [about]? I was who I *am*." When Andy Wentworth disclosed his gay identity to his sister:

> She asked me, how could I choose *to do this and to ignore the health risks . . . implying that this was a conscious, "Oh, I'd like to go to the movies today" type of choice. And I told her, I said, "Nobody in their right mind would go through this* hell *of being gay just to satisfy a whim." And I explained to her what it was like growing up. Knowing this other side of yourself that you can't tell anybody about, and if anybody in your family knows they will be upset and mortified.*

Another man insisted he would never forget the period after coming out when he realized that he felt good about himself, and that he was not on his way to becoming "the kind of person that they're portraying gay people to be." What kind of person is that? I asked. "Well, you know, wicked, evil people who *decide* that they're going to be evil."

Rather than claiming an elective gay identity as its antecedent, the category "families we choose" incorporates the meaningful *difference* that is the product of choice and biology as two relationally defined terms. If many gay men and lesbians interpreted blood ties as a type of social connectedness organized through procreation, they tended to associate choice and creativity with a total absence of guidelines for ordering relationships within gay families. Although heterosexuals in the Bay Area also had the sense of creating something when they established families of their own, that creativity was often firmly linked to childbearing and child rearing, the *pro* in procreation. In the absence of a pro-creative referent, individual discretion regulated who would be counted as kin. For those who had constructed them, gay families could evoke utopian visions of self-determination in the absence of social constraint. . . .

Certainly lesbians and gay men, with their range of backgrounds and experiences, did not always mean the same thing or advance identical cultural critiques when they spoke of blood and chosen families. Ideological contrasts utilized and recognized by all need not have the same significance for all.[10] Neither can an examination of ideology alone explain why choice should have been highlighted as an organizing principle of gay families. Only history, material conditions, and context can account for the specific content of gay kinship ideologies, their emergence at a particular point in time, and the variety of ways people have implemented those ideologies in their daily lives. In themselves, gay families comprise only a segment of the historical transformation sequence that mapped the contrast between straight and gay first onto "family/no family," and then onto "biological family/families we choose." Gone are the days when embracing a lesbian or gay identity seemed to require a renunciation of kinship. The symbolic groundwork for gay families, laid during a period when coming out to relatives witnessed a kind of institutionalization, has made it possible to claim a sexual identity that is not linked to procreation, face the possibility of rejection by blood or adoptive relations, yet still conceive of establishing a family of one's own.

ENDNOTES

1. See Godwin (1983) and Hollibaugh (1979).
2. For an analysis that carefully distinguishes among the various senses of reproduction and their equivocal usage in feminist and anthropological theory, see Yanagisako and Collier (1987).
3. On the distinction between family and household, see Rapp (1982) and Yanagisako (1979).
4. On relational definition and the arbitrariness of signs, see Saussure (1959).
5. For Lévi-Strauss (1963:88), most symbolic contrasts are structured by a mediating third term. Apparently conflicting elements incorporate a hidden axis of commonality that allows the two to be brought into relationship with one another. Here sexual identity is the hidden term that links "straight" to "gay," while kinship mediates the oppositions further down in the chart. This sort of triadic relation lends dynamism to opposition, facilitating ideological transformations while ensuring a regulated, or structured, relationship between the old and the new.

    My overall analysis departs from a Lévi-Straussian structuralism by historically situating these relations, discarding any presumption that they form a closed system, and avoiding the arbitrary isolation of categories for which structuralism has justly been criticized in the past (see Culler 1975; Fowler 1981; Jenkins 1979). The symbolic oppositions examined in this chapter incorporate indigenous categories in all their specificity (e.g., straight versus gay), rather than abstracting to universals of increasing generality and arguably decreasing utility (e.g., nature versus culture). Chronicled here is an ideological transformation faithful to history, process, and the perceptions of the lesbians and gay men who themselves identified each opposition included in the chart. For the deployment of these categories in everyday contexts, read on.
6. Notice how the contrasts in the chart map a relationship of difference (straight/gay) first onto a logical negation (family/no family, or A/NA), and then onto another relation of difference (biological [blood] family/families we choose [create], or A:B). On the generative potential of dichotomies that are constituted as A/B rather than A/NA, see N. Jay (1981:44).
7. See Foucault (1978) on the practice of grouping homosexuality together with other nonprocreative sex acts, a historical shift that supplanted the earlier classification of homosexuality with adultery and offenses against marriage. According to Foucault, previous to the late eighteenth century acts "contrary to nature" tended to be understood as an extreme form of acts "against the law," rather than something different in kind. Only later was "the unnatural" set apart in the emerging domain of sexuality, becoming autonomous from adultery or rape. See also Freedman (1982): "Although the ideological support for the separation of [erotic] sexuality and reproduction did not appear until the twentieth century, the process itself began much earlier" (p. 210).

8. See di Leonardo (1984), who criticizes the transmission model for its lack of attention to the wider socioeconomic context that informs the ways people interpret the relation of kinship to ethnicity.

9. See also Joseph and Lewis (1981:76), Kennedy (1980), McAdoo (1988), and Stack (1974). For a refutation and historical contextualization of allegations that African Americans have developed "dysfunctional" families, or even no families at all, see Gresham (1989).

10. Abercrombie et al. (1980) lay out many of the objections to treating culture as a shared body of values and knowledge determinative of social relations. For theoretical formulations critical of the assumption that ideology mechanically reflects a more fundamental set of material conditions, see Jameson (1981), Lichtman (1975), and R. Williams (1977). For different approaches to examining the influence of context, embodiment, and power relations on the formulation and interpretation of cultural categories, see Rosaldo (1989), Vološinov (1973), and Yanagisako (1978, 1985).

REFERENCES

Abercrombie, Nicholas, Stephen Hill, and Bryan S. Turner. 1980. *The Dominant Ideology Thesis.* Boston: Allen & Unwin.

Allen, Ronnie. 1987. "Times Have Changed at the *Herald.*" *Gay Community News,* June 28–July 4.

Berzon, Betty. 1978. "Sharing Your Lesbian Identity with Your Children." Pp. 69–74 in *Our Right to Love: A Lesbian Resource Book,* edited by Ginny Vida. Englewood Cliffs, NJ: Prentice-Hall.

——. 1979. "Telling the Family You're Gay." Pp. 88–100 in *Positively Gay,* edited by Betty Berzon and Robert Leighton. Los Angeles: Mediamix Associates.

Bourdieu, Pierre. 1977. *Outline of a Theory of Practice.* New York: Cambridge University Press.

Castells, Manuel and Karen Murphy. 1982. "Cultural Identity and Urban Structure: The Spatial Organization of San Francisco's Gay Community." Pp. 237–59 in *Urban Policy under Capitalism,* edited by Norman I. Fainstein and Susan S. Fainstein. Beverly Hills, CA: Sage.

Clunis, D. Merilee and G. Dorsey Green. 1988. *Lesbian Couples.* Seattle, WA: Seal Press.

Cook, Blanche Wiesen. 1977. "Female Support Networks and Political Activism: Lillian Wald, Crystal Eastman, Emma Goldman." *Chrysalis* 3:44–61.

Culler, Jonathan. 1975. *Structuralist Poetics: Structuralism, Linguistics and the Study of Literature.* Ithaca, NY: Cornell University Press.

di Leonardo, Micaela. 1984. *The Varieties of Ethnic Experience: Kinship, Class, and Gender among California Italian-Americans.* Ithaca, NY: Cornell University Press.

FitzGerald, Frances. 1986. *Cities on a Hill: A Journey through Contemporary American Cultures.* New York: Simon & Schuster.

Foucault, Michel. 1978. *The History of Sexuality.* Vol. 1. New York: Vintage Books.

Fowler, Roger. 1981. *Literature as Social Discourse: The Practice of Linguistic Criticism.* Bloomington: University of Indiana Press.

Freedman, Estelle B. 1982. "Sexuality in Nineteenth-Century America: Behaviour, Ideology, and Politics." *Reviews in American History* 10:196–215.

Godwin, Ronald S. 1983. "AIDS: A Moral and Political Time Bomb." *Moral Majority Report,* July.

Gresham, Jewell Handy. 1989. "The Politics of Family in America." *The Nation,* July 24–31, pp. 116–22.

Height, Dorothy. 1989. "Self-Help—A Black Tradition." *The Nation,* July 24–31, pp. 136–38.

Hocquenghem, Guy. 1978. *Homosexual Desire.* London: Alison & Busby.

Hollibaugh, Amber. 1979. "Sexuality and the State: The Defeat of the Briggs Initiative and Beyond." *Socialist Review* 9 (3): 55–72.

Jameson, Frederic. 1981. *The Political Unconscious: Narrative as a Socially Symbolic Act.* Ithaca, NY: Cornell University Press.

Jay, Nancy. 1981. "Gender and Dichotomy." *Feminist Studies* 7 (1): 38–56.

Jenkins, Alan. 1979. *The Social Theory of Claude Lévi-Strauss.* New York: St. Martin's Press.

Joseph, Gloria I. and Jill Lewis. 1981. *Common Differences: Conflicts in Black and White Feminist Perspectives.* Garden City, NY: Anchor/Doubleday.

Kennedy, Theodore R. 1980. *You Gotta Deal with It: Black Family Relations in a Southern Community.* New York: Oxford University Press.

Lazere, Arthur. 1986. "On the Job." *Coming Up!,* June.

Lévi-Strauss, Claude. 1963. *Totemism.* Boston: Beacon Press.

Lichtman, Richard. 1975. "Marx's Theory of Ideology." *Socialist Revolution* 5 (1): 45–76.

McAdoo, Harriette P. 1988. *Black Families.* 2d ed. Newbury Park, CA: Sage.

Mendenhall, George. 1985. "Mickey Mouse Lawsuit Remains Despite Disney Dancing Decree." *Bay Area Reporter,* August 22.

Rapp, Rayna. 1982. "Family and Class in Contemporary America: Notes toward an Understanding of Ideology." Pp. 168–87 in *Rethinking the Family,* edited by Barrie Thorne with Marilyn Yalom. New York: Longman.

Rosaldo, Renato. 1989. *Culture and Truth: The Remaking of Social Analysis.* Boston: Beacon Press.

Saussure, Ferdinand de. 1959. *Course in General Linguistics.* New York: McGraw-Hill.

Schneider, David M. 1968. *American Kinship: A Cultural Account.* Englewood Cliffs, NJ: Prentice-Hall.

——. 1972. "What Is Kinship All About? In *Kinship Studies in the Morgan Centennial Year,* edited by Priscilla Reining. Washington, DC: Anthropological Society of Washington.

——. 1984. *A Critique of the Study of Kinship.* Ann Arbor: University of Michigan Press.

Silverstein, Charles. 1977. *A Family Matter: A Parents' Guide to Homosexuality.* New York: McGraw-Hill.

Smith, Barbara. 1987. "From the Stage." *Gay Community News,* November 8–14.

Stack, Carol B. 1974. *All Our Kin: Strategies for Survival in a Black Community.* New York: Harper & Row.

Tremble, Bob, Margaret Schneider, and Carol Appathurai. 1989. "Growing Up Gay or Lesbian in a Multicultural Context." Pp. 253–64 in *Gay and Lesbian Youth,* edited by Gilbert Herdt. New York: Haworth Press.

Vološinov, V. N. 1973. *Marxism and the Philosophy of Language.* New York: Seminar Press.

Watney, Simon. 1987. *Policing Desire: Pornography, AIDS, and the Media.* Minneapolis: University of Minnesota Press.

Williams, Raymond. 1977. *Marxism and Literature.* New York: Oxford University Press.

Yanagisako, Sylvia J. 1978. "Variance in American Kinship: Implications for Cultural Analysis." *American Ethnologist* 5 (1): 1529.

——. 1979. "Family and Household: The Analysis of Domestic Groups." *Annual Review of Anthropology* 8:161–205.

——. 1985. *Transforming the Past: Tradition and Kinship among Japanese Americans.* Stanford, CA: Stanford University Press.

Yanagisako, Sylvia Junko and Jane Fishburne Collier. 1987. "Toward a Unified Analysis of Gender and Kinship." Pp. 14–50 in *Gender and Kinship: Essays toward a Unified Analysis,* edited by Jane Fishburne Collier and Sylvia Junko Yanagisako. Stanford, CA: Stanford University Press.

4

MARRIAGE AND FAMILY IN A MULTIRACIAL SOCIETY

DANIEL T. LICHTER • ZHENCHAO QIAN

Background

Today's American family is hard to define. The so-called "traditional family" — working husband, his stay-at-home wife, and their children — represents only a small fraction of all American households. In "Leave It to Beaver," the popular late-1950s television show, the Cleaver family — Ward and June and their children, Wally and Theodore ("the Beaver") — epitomized the American dream of economic success, a happy marriage, loving parents, respectful children, a nice house in the suburbs, and a big car in the garage. But the Cleaver family model represents only about 10 percent of all households today. The most popular television shows in recent years were about urban single people: "Seinfeld," "Friends," and "Sex and the City."

Television shows undoubtedly reflect America's changing family and demographic profile. Marriage rates have plummeted. Unmarried cohabitation has supplanted marriage as the first coresidential union for most young adults. Married couples have only one or two children, some couples have no children, and out-of-wedlock childbearing has become common. Many couples get divorced, yet many divorced people marry again and begin new families. Serial monogamy may have become the new norm. Many gays and lesbians seek legal changes that would allow same-sex marriages or civil unions that include the same rights and benefits enjoyed by heterosexual couples.

These general demographic trends are no longer news to most of us. In fact, we are often inured to them, mostly because we have experienced them firsthand. Preachers, politicians, and pundits worry that the decline in marriage and the breakdown of the traditional family are responsible for many societal ills: child poverty, racial inequality, delinquency, mental illness, and moral decay. Some people look back nostalgically to the old ways. Others are more sanguine, viewing today's family patterns as a natural response to relentless cultural or economic pressures in our fast-paced society that make marriage less central in people's lives or more difficult to maintain.

History tells us that family change is inevitable and often adaptive, and therefore should not be a source for alarmist rhetoric. Family change may also be the price of personal freedom and the rise of individualism over communalism. It also reflects growing gender equality both in the home and in the workplace, as well as changing economic exigencies of modern American life, such as geographic mobility and job dislocation, work–family imbalances, and work-related stress. Sociologist Andrew Cherlin has argued that most Western societies have moved to "individualized marriage," placing much greater emphasis on personal choice and self-development rather than companionship.[1] He suggests that marriage is being deinstitutionalized, which simply means that the family values and norms that proscribe appropriate behaviour regarding mate selection processes, gender relations, and marital interaction have weakened. The rules of courtship and marriage are less widely shared today.

Debates about cultural and family values require up-to-date information on America's changing marriage and family patterns, especially in light of rapid demographic and economic shifts over recent decades. More than ever before, these debates must also be informed by America's new racial and ethnic mix and its distinctive family forms. National statistics on marriage and living arrangements may misrepresent or even distort the family circumstances of many average Americans, especially racial minorities and recent immigrants from Latin America and Asia. Foreign nationals and other immigrants living in the United States often remain separated in fundamental ways by race and ethnicity, national origin, social class, and geography. Family forms and relationships often differ widely from one group to another; but, as history shows, these forms and relationships also can converge quickly over time as social mobility and economic assimilation take root. Growing racial diversity makes it difficult to project the future of the family in the United States. One type of family (U.S.-born whites) is becoming less dominant, and the future characteristics of the family will increasingly be influenced by what minority families look like and do.

America can no longer be viewed in simple black and white terms; the fastest-growing segments of the U.S. population must not be ignored in the family debate or in family policy. The 2000 Census revealed that Hispanics were replacing non-Hispanic blacks as the largest minority in America. By 2002, the foreign-born population numbered 33 million, or more than 11 percent of the total population.[2] Hispanics accounted for 52 percent of this total. When we add U.S.-born children of foreign-born parents, these numbers increase even more dramatically. For example, recent estimates suggest that these second-generation children of immigrants represented 15 percent of the U.S. population under age 18.[3] . . .

To fully understand today's families and tomorrow's future requires a fuller appreciation of the different cultural traditions rooted in the marriage patterns and family lives of America's racial and ethnic minorities. As in the past, America's next generation of adults promises to be very different from the current one, especially if intermarriage among groups accelerates. When today's children and youth grow into adulthood and start families of their own, their definitions of the ideal family are likely to differ from their grandparents' or even their parents'.

The 2000 Census provides an unusual opportunity to highlight family and household diversity in our increasingly multicultural and multiethnic society. Most surveys, even large ones, simply do not provide samples of sufficient size for some population groups (such as Koreans or Puerto Ricans) to give reliable family indicators for these groups. The usual, but often unsatisfactory, practice is to identify and analyze various panethnic groups, such as Asian Americans and Hispanics, that include smaller populations that may or may not share common cultural traits or economic circumstances. The Public Use Microdata Sample (PUMS) from the 1990 and 2000 U.S. censuses, because of its large sample sizes and national geographic coverage, provides an unprecedented opportunity to uncover major changes in the American family.

But, what is a family? The U.S. Census Bureau uses a very specific definition of households and families. A *household* contains all people living in a housing unit. Households are distinguished by whether they are family households (or families) or nonfamily households. A *family* includes household members who are related by blood, marriage, or adoption, and who share a common domicile. *Family households* include families in which a family member is the householder—the person who owns or rents the residence. These households can also include nonfamily members, such as a boarder or a friend. A *nonfamily household* includes the householders who live alone or who share a residence with individuals unrelated to the householder, such as two college friends sharing an apartment. Some nonfamily households sometimes substitute for traditional families and serve many of the same functions: Same-sex couples are one example. Close friends living together also sometimes regard themselves as a family, but this type of household does not satisfy the Census Bureau's strict definition.

Why Marriage and Family Matter

Attitude surveys indicate that the large majority of Americans expect to marry, and most will marry at some point in their lives.[4] Survey data indicate that, in 1997 and 1998, 72 percent of respondents reported that "having a good marriage and family life is 'extremely important.'"[5] At the same time, Americans are more tolerant today than in the past about alternative living arrangements. The stigma associated with single motherhood, unmarried cohabitation, and gay unions has lessened. Perhaps paradoxically, this increased tolerance has validated the significance of marriage as a freely chosen lifestyle decision rather than as a normative "requirement" or an expectation. Choosing to marry or not is a life-changing decision. Indeed, the symbolic significance and cultural meanings attached to marriage have perhaps never been more important to average Americans, or more hotly contested.

Disagreement about the significance of declines in marriage and traditional families is at the heart of the broader debate about the culture wars in America.[6] Many view the decline in marriage and the family as a cause of society's most pressing social problems. For example, delays in marriage, coupled with earlier and more frequent nonmarital sexual activity, have placed young women at much greater risk of out-of-wedlock childbearing than in the past. But, declines in marriage and marital fertility, not increases in nonmarital fertility, are most responsible for the post-1960s rise in the share of out-of-wedlock births.[7] Roughly one of every three births in the United States occurs outside of marriage, mostly to single women in their late teens and early 20s. Not so long ago, a pregnant teenage girl would have to leave her home and community, returning only after her baby was born and given up for adoption.

There also was a time when the woman married the man if she became pregnant with his child, but these marriages are no longer the cultural norm or viewed as necessary to legitimize the birth of the child. Demographer R. Kelly Raley has shown that, in the early 1990s, only about one of every 10 pregnant women ages 15 to 29 is married before the birth of their babies.[8] The corresponding figure in the early 1970s was four of every 10.

High divorce rates have reinforced the rise in female-headed families. Nearly one-half of all marriages end in divorce.[9] More than 1 million marriages end in divorce each year.[10] About one-half of all divorces involve children, who usually live with their mothers despite recent increases in joint custody arrangements. The economic implications of these trends are obvious and serious. In 2002, about 40 percent of children living with single mothers fell below the poverty line.[11] The rise in female-headed families with children is associated with higher rates of family and child poverty and welfare dependency. And the growth in female-headed families with children—growth that occurred disproportionately among historically disadvantaged racial and ethnic minorities—has slowed progress toward racial economic equality.[12] Understanding family change is arguably key to better understanding racial inequality, but researchers disagree on the direction of this association and whether it is causal. One theory is that racial economic inequality is the cause for existing racial differences in marriage and family structure.

Other deleterious effects of family change are largely indirect, but nonetheless important. Children and adolescents raised in married-couple families have, on balance, clear emotional and cognitive advantages over children from single-parent families.[13] Youths who grow up in single-parent families are at greater risk for delinquency, school dropout, and teenage pregnancy and childbearing. Children who live with stepparents fare no better than children living alone with single parents. For adults, marriage appears to confer physical and emotional health advantages and promotes longevity; marriage provides social support and buffers the deleterious health effects of stress. Marriage also appears to make men more productive in the workplace.[14] This large body of empirical evidence is now difficult to ignore. Yet, the health and productivity effects of marriage may also simply reflect the self-selection of healthy and productive people.

Not surprisingly, the widely acknowledged statistical association between marriage and positive social and economic outcomes has given impetus to the marriage movement. We see this in men's groups such as the Promise Keepers; in nonprofit organizations like Smart Marriages; in rallies like the Million Man March; in the proliferation of faith-based initiatives that aim to strengthen traditional marriage; and in new legislative efforts to legally define marriage as only between a man and a women.[15] Indeed, we see increasing government involvement in family life. The 1996 welfare reform law, the Personal Responsibility and Work Opportunity Reconciliation Act, included among its goals the promotion of marriage as a context for childbearing and childrearing. The new law encourages the formation and support of two-parent families and promotes job preparation, work, and marriage. Many Americans believed that the old welfare system (administered through Aid to Families with Dependent Children) trapped families in poverty and reinforced an antifamily subculture that encouraged out-of-wedlock childbearing, single parenting, and welfare dependency. To date, however, welfare reform has apparently had only a modest, if any, effect on promoting marriage and two-parent families.[16] Goals of the reauthorized welfare bill, as currently proposed by the U.S. Congress, place less emphasis on marriage *per se* but more on "healthy marriages" that are emotionally satisfying and financially secure, and are beneficial for children.

Other official efforts to promote marriage have sought to remove its existing economic disincentives. These efforts include eliminating the marriage penalty in the tax code and in the Earned Income Tax Credit for low-income workers with children, and upping the earnings disregards of husbands (income counted against the welfare grant) in determining women's eligibility for welfare under Temporary Assistance for Needy Families (TANF). Some states have sought to reduce divorce rates by providing marriage preparation and enrichment courses that emphasize relationship skills and conflict management. But critics argue that such proposals are unlikely to gain widespread public approval or be successful because they ignore structural conditions (such as a bad economy) that predispose couples to greater conflict. Covenant marriages, such as the recent marriage legislation initiated in Louisiana, give couples greater opportunity to strengthen their commitment to marriage and make it more difficult to dissolve because of longer waiting periods for divorce. To date, however, few couples have chosen covenant marriages, and these marriages have not been shown to lower divorce rates.[17]

The politics of family changes have also been disconcerting to many social and political observers. Policy debates are often contentious, and appropriate policy courses often lack clear and widely shared goals. But marriage is likely to continue to occupy a distinctive place in the lives of most Americans. Most Americans seem to understand the positive economic, social, and psychological benefits of marriage; they also understand that children benefit from being raised in economically stable and loving married-couple families. Even poor single mothers do not have to be convinced of the value of marriage.[18]

Opponents of government programs that promote marriage fear government intrusion into their private lives, and they fear that official efforts to promote marriage will unfairly privilege marriage at the expense of other viable personal and family relationships, such as single-parent families, cohabiting couples, or same-sex couples. These observers worry that abused women will face new obstacles to ending bad marriages or will be forced out of economic necessity to stay in relationships that neither benefit them nor their children. They are also concerned about the reemergence of patriarchy and traditional views of marriage that historically undermined women's equality in the home and workplace. But these scenarios are unlikely. The American public gives little indication that they want to return to the days when the rules of courtship and marriage, gender relations, and appropriate marital roles were clearly defined. Those days are now viewed as overly restrictive, old-fashioned, and sexist.

Families in America

The American family has experienced major changes over the past 25 years. But in *Continuity and Change in the American Family,* authors Lynne Casper and Suzanne Bianchi refer to a "quieting" of family change over the past several years.[19] Some trends, such as the rise in female-headed families, have slowed or even reversed for some groups. Some analysts claim that divergent trajectories of American family life are rooted in the unequal economic fortunes and access to opportunity of different segments of American society. Harvard professors David Ellwood and Christopher Jencks, for example, argue that income inequality has inevitably led to growing differences in marriage and family structure across population groups.[20] Ellwood and Jencks worry that current economic trends not only disadvantage those at the bottom of the income distribution but also reduce one's chances for marriage and for raising children with an economically and emotionally supportive spouse or partner.

More than ever before, merchants and marketers also have both the interest and the ability to target particular ethnic and economic segments of the American population, thus potentially crystallizing differences between groups rather than fostering cultural homogeneity or even assimilation. For example, the programs on Spanish-speaking television stations in most large cities reflect and reinforce distinct cultural values and appetites. The growing diversity and economic balkanization of American family life also is evident in less obvious ways. In 2000, labor force participation rates among mothers in white middle-class couples declined for the first time in decades.[21] Yet, the growth of low-wage jobs and the new work requirements of recent welfare reform legislation pushed employment rates among single mothers to an all-time high.[22]

Recent Trends

The typical or average American family is difficult to characterize accurately. In this report, we discuss five trends that have reshaped American families and households over the past 20 years: the decline in traditional families; delayed marriage; the rise in single-parent families; more individuals living alone; and the surge in the number of cohabiting couples.

Decline in Traditional Families   One marker of the changing American family is the decline in the share of families and households headed by married couples. In 1970, 71 percent of all American households were headed by married couples. By 2000, the percentage had dropped to 53. More significant, married couples today are more likely than in the past to be dual earners and to have no children. The percentage of married-couple families with children has declined over the last three decades. In 1970, 25 million married-couple families included children. In 2000, the number remained largely unchanged but represented a much smaller percentage of all married-couple families or all family households.

These patterns reflect increases in childlessness, but the patterns also are the result of more effective control of unwanted fertility — especially at older reproductive ages — through modern contraception, voluntary surgical sterilization, and legal abortion. Increases in life expectancy also mean that growing shares of married couples have, literally and figuratively, survived the childrearing stage. Their children have grown up and moved away. Married couples may have half a lifetime to spend together without dependent minor children.

Delays in Marriage   Without question, the decline in the traditional American family has been shaped by the retreat from marriage. The marriage rate (marriages per 1,000 unmarried women) declined from 76 in 1970 to 54 in 1990, according to the National Center for Health Statistics. This means that only about 5 percent of unmarried women marry in a given year. On the other hand, from 1960 to 1980, the divorce rate increased from 9 to 23 divorces per 1,000 married women, and this rate has remained relatively constant and high. For women who married in the late 1970s, 39 percent divorced within 10 years, a figure much higher than for women who married in the late 1940s (14 percent).

Between 1970 and 1990, the remarriage rate among divorced women dropped from 123 to 76 per 1,000 divorced or widowed women. Despite this drop, more than one-half of those who had previously divorced were remarried in 1996.[23] About nine in 10 remarriages followed a divorce rather than the death of a spouse. Most remarriages took place within three years of divorce. For a large percentage of Americans, getting a divorce does not deter them from trying marriage again: Divorce rates are no lower for second marriages than for first marriages.[24]

America's retreat from marriage is revealed most easily in the changing marital status composition of the adult population. The percentage of American women who are married declined only modestly from 56 percent in 1970 to 52 percent in 2000, while the percentage of divorced women grew from 6 percent to 13 percent. Data on marital status by age are more dramatic. Young adults are much less likely today to be married. Among women ages 20 to 24, for example, the percentage of never-marrieds grew from 36 percent in 1970 to a stunning 73 percent in 2000. Among women ages 30 to 34, an even larger gap exists between 1970 and 2000—from nearly 11 percent never married to 39 percent never married. Americans today clearly are less likely to get married at younger ages.

As a result, the entry into marriage is less useful today as a key marker of adult status. In the past, marriage typically coincided with leaving home for the first time and the end of formal schooling. Marriage also began one's regular sexual activity and childbearing with the only intimate partner young adults would have in their lifetimes. Today, most young adults have had sex before marriage, often with several different partners. Most young adults will leave home long before they marry, and a significant percentage will experience pregnancy and childbirth before marriage. The end of formal schooling no longer segues directly into marriage, but typically begins a period of single living and personal independence.[25] More formal education, strong career aspirations, and greater financial independence mean that marriage is no longer the only or main defining role of young women today. Women of all ages have choices that their mothers were denied.

More Single-Parent Families   The usual progression of love, marriage, and babies is being reordered in American society. For a majority of adolescents and young adults today, sexual intimacy often comes before love. Children increasingly come before marriage; in 2002, one-third of all births were to unmarried women.[26] Many Americans believe that premarital sexual activity and out-of-wedlock childbearing are responsible for the rise in single-parent families, poverty, and welfare dependency. In truth, most single-parent families are not poor or welfare-dependent, and single-parent families are more often a consequence of divorce than of out-of-wedlock-childbearing. At the same time, single-parent families are heterogeneous and difficult to stereotype. Nontraditional families, including single-parent families with children, increased by over 50 percent between 1970 and 2000, and grew from 11 percent to 16 percent of all families. Declines in marriage and increases in divorce have played obvious roles.

The fact that single parents are less likely now than in the past to live with other family members also has increased family and child poverty rates.[27] Such changes have been fueled by declines in the stigma associated with raising children alone and with changing cultural values regarding economic and residential independence from parents. With increasing education and higher occupational status among women over this period, many single mothers are no longer economically dependent. They can now choose to live on their own if they prefer and can afford it. Indeed, the poverty rate for single mothers with children in 2003 — 32.5 percent — was the lowest level on record.[28] Despite this bit of good news, this figure is a high rate of poverty using almost any standard in the developed world.

In the 1979 movie "Kramer vs. Kramer," actor Dustin Hoffman played a newly divorced father struggling in his unexpected role as primary caretaker of his young son and fighting a battle to maintain custody. The 1970s had been a period of rapidly increasing divorce rates in America, and this box-office hit movie resonated with many single fathers. The movie helped increase public sensitivity to the estrangement of many single fathers from their children and to the situation of divorced men faced with the legal challenges of gaining physical custody of their children. More than 20 years after that movie, however, only about 17 percent of all children who live with a single parent live with their unmarried fathers.[29]

Rise in People Living Alone   Over the past three decades, the number of households containing only one person rose sharply, from 17 percent in 1970 to more than 25 percent of all households by 2000. These are important changes that reflect delays in marriage: The years between leaving school and marriage have increased rapidly over this period, thus increasing the chances that young adults live alone. Data from the U.S. Census Bureau's Current Population Survey indicate that, between 1970 and 2000, the median age at first marriage increased from 20.8 years to 25.1 years for women, and from 23.2 years to 26.8 years for men. Increases in persons living alone are not just limited to young adults. Today, single people of all ages are more likely than in the past to live alone rather than to live with family or friends.[30] This trend undoubtedly reflects increasing individualism; the desire for personal privacy; greater financial independence; and less pressure for nonmarried adults, especially women, to live with family or others.

The rise in single-person households also results from the aging of the population and the growing mortality differential between older men and women. Simply put, traditional families are less significant numerically because many families end through the death of a partner, and there are simply not enough older men for widows to marry. In 2000, the sex ratio for the population age 65 or older was 70, meaning that there were only 70 elderly men for every 100 elderly women.[31] At ages 85 and older, the sex ratio drops to 41. The demographic implications are clearly apparent in older men's and women's living arrangements. Men over age 75 are more likely than men at other ages to live with a spouse (67 percent), while women over age 75 are most likely to live alone. Unlike previous generations, today's growing population of widows are better able financially to live on their own rather than to live with other relatives or in a group home.

The Recent Surge in Cohabitation   The recent decline in marriage has been offset completely by increases in cohabitation — unmarried couples living together. Age at first marriage has increased significantly over the past decade or two, but studies suggest that age at first union (marriage or cohabitation) has hardly changed over this period.[32] Couples have not stopped partnering in early adulthood: They simply are not marrying like they used to. The U.S. Census Bureau estimates that the number of opposite-sex cohabiting couples grew from 440,000 in 1960 to 3.8 million in 2000. Cohabitation now appears to be a normative step in the marriage process: Similar percentages of whites, blacks, and Hispanics experience cohabitation. Significantly, most cohabitors (about 75 percent) expect to marry their partners, but these partners do not necessarily discuss marriage plans before entering into a cohabiting union.[33]

Scholars have hotly debated the reasons for the upward climb in unmarried cohabitation. Some attribute this climb to America's changing sexual attitudes and behaviour. The wide availability of the birth control pill in the 1960s helped separate sex from reproduction. Nonmarital sexual activity, especially for women, also became much less stigmatized. Another view is that the rise in divorce has made young couples more cautious about entering marriage. After witnessing and experiencing the effects of their own parents' divorce, these observers say, many couples fear the possibility of their own divorce. Cohabitation may give some couples greater confidence that they can get along with their partners; it gives them some idea about what to expect in marriage. But regardless of motivation, cohabitation is a short-lived arrangement. Most cohabiting couples end their relationships in a year or two. For many heterosexual couples, cohabitation is one step in the progression to marriage. This step also may soon be true for same-sex couples. For other heterosexual couples, cohabitation is an alternative to marriage, one that provides a marriage-like living arrangement without the legal ramifications associated with dissolution. Cohabitation can also be an adaptation to economic hardship or uncertainty—a kind of "poor person's" marriage.

The implications of cohabitation for American society and its families are difficult to forecast. Cohabitation is associated with delays in marriage and childbearing for many young couples, and thus is partly responsible for the recent delays in first marriage. Perhaps surprisingly, divorce rates are unusually high for cohabiting couples who later marry—around 30 percent to 40 percent higher than for couples who do not cohabit. Cohabitation may simply attract individuals who are less committed to marriage as an institution, which means they may also be at greater risk of later dissolution if things go wrong. Cohabitation itself may undermine the stability of subsequent marriage. In fact, the experience of cohabitation may not be representative of the kinds of interactions couples actually experience in marriage.[34] In this sense, cohabitation may not be a good testing ground for marriage. Cohabitation may provide little preparation for making difficult decisions about spending priorities, work, or childbearing and childrearing. A seemingly idyllic or carefree cohabiting experience may thus set the stage for later disillusionment when tough decisions about children and money in marriage require a new level of negotiation and compromise to avoid conflict. Some cohabiting couples also may be poorly matched and therefore at greater risk of subsequent divorce. Many enter sexual and cohabiting relationships quickly and without much forethought about whether their partner is "Mr. or Ms. Right."[35] Intimate relationships, even quickly formed or unhealthy ones, often take on a momentum of their own as the relationship progresses inexorably toward marriage. This dynamic plays itself out later in higher divorce rates.

Explanations for Family Change

Many scholars ultimately attribute family changes to fundamental shifts in gender roles in American society. In his seminal 1991 book, *A Treatise on the Family*, Nobel Prize–winning economist Gary Becker identifies declining gender specialization in families as the cause of shifts away from marriage and rising divorce.[36] As the argument goes, men and women bring different comparative advantages to the marriage bargaining table. In the traditional breadwinner–homemaker marriage, men specialize in market work and women specialize in home production, including bearing and rearing children. Men and women "trade" their main assets in the marriage market; each is presumably better off by marrying than by remaining single. In the trade, men who make a good living presumably gain access through marriage to companionship, a sexual partner, someone to keep house, and children (who, in earlier periods of America history, were economic assets available to work on the farm or in the factory). As homemakers, women benefit from men's economic support and protection. This trade is especially the case when women face discrimination in the workplace and lack opportunities for economic self-sufficiency and upward mobility. The gains to marriage also increase if the trade is equitable—that is, when partners share similar characteristics such as physical attractiveness, socioeconomic background, race, and education.

Conversely, the blurring of traditional gender roles reduces the gains to marriage. Not surprisingly, observers often attribute recent declines in marriage to the rapid entry of women into the labor force and to the growth of women's earnings. The benefits of marriage presumably have declined with women's rapid entry into the labor force. Women have become less economically dependent on men, and these economic gains have removed a major incentive for women to marry. Working women are less likely to marry and more likely to divorce when faced with unhappy marriages.

The declining economic fortunes of young men—especially low-skilled minority men—and the rise in the welfare state have presumably reinforced declines in marriage. With greater economic independence, marriage-seeking women are more inclined to search longer for economically attractive male partners. Work subsidizes the marital search. For poorly educated men with low wages, their diminished ability to attract a wife is reflected in their rapidly declining marriage rates over the past several decades. The declines in real wages among low-educated workers as well as rising underemployment, especially in poor minority communities and neighborhoods, have presumably accelerated marriage declines among low-income and minority populations. Sociologist Valerie Oppenheimer has argued that men's changing circumstances—not women's work patterns—have steered America's marriage trends throughout history.[37]

At the same time, government-sponsored subsidies have arguably provided an alternative source of economic support and, therefore, a disincentive to—even a substitute for—marriage. According to critics of welfare, cash assistance has helped women leave their husbands, while also encouraging out-of-wedlock childbearing. The empirical evidence supporting this view, however, is weak.[38]

The benefits from marriage increase with the specialization along traditional gender roles. When mutually beneficial, marriage is the preferred state, and marriage rates are high. To many people, especially the romantically inclined, this coldly rational view of marriage undoubtedly seems anathema to their idealistic notions about the institution. They much prefer to believe that mate selection is largely beyond their control, governed by uncontrollable strong emotions.

Economic perspectives also provide a plausible explanation for racial differences in marriage and family structure. For example, black women's historically higher rates of labor force participation mean that they have always had greater economic independence than white women. Moreover, black men face higher rates of unemployment than do white men, and black men are also less likely to earn a family wage. The marriage imperative, therefore, is lower for black women and other disadvantaged minorities, and marriage rates are expected to be lower for these groups than for economically advantaged populations.

The empirical evidence on these questions, however, is much less compelling.[39] For one thing, delays in marriage have been broadly observed across almost all segments of the U.S. population. This trend has not simply been observed among high-earning (and economically independent) women, low-earning or economically unattractive men, or welfare-dependent women. Indeed, highly educated women—those with the *greatest* earnings potential—are more likely than poor women to marry today. And declines in marriage rates have been especially pronounced among the most highly educated men.[40] This decline is seemingly contrary to most economic models of marriage.

Robert Moffitt, a welfare expert at Johns Hopkins University, suggests that the decline in marriage for low-income women reflects the declining earnings of low-educated, low-skilled men who are available for those women to marry.[41] For highly educated women, on the other hand, declines in marriage presumably reflect increases in economic independence associated with their own higher earnings. The important lesson is straightforward: Changes in marriage and family forms may have different causes for different segments of the American population. There is no single cause for declines in marriage, and there is no silver bullet or single prescription that will return America to the days when virtually everyone expected to marry, to stay married, and to have children cared for by a stay-at-home mom.

Widespread declines in marriage among most population groups and the upsurge in alternative living arrangements suggest another explanation for recent changes to family forms in the United States. Pervasive changes in cultural values and attitudes regarding marriage may have played a key role in family change. What causes these cultural values and attitudes to change? Some observers believe that marriage attitudes and values ultimately respond to changes in the economy and to urbanization. Technological changes have also played a large role. The introduction of modern contraception in the early 1960s changed the risks associated with sexual intercourse outside of marriage, including the risk of unintended pregnancy. The media, and television in particular, have also undoubtedly exposed Americans to alternative living arrangements and greater acceptability of sexual activity outside of marriage, while reducing the stigma associated with single parenthood, divorce, and homosexuality. But these media messages may also simply reflect preexisting public attitudes and behaviour.

Race and the Family

Any discussion of racial variation in the family must begin with an acknowledgment of the long-standing debate about the strengths and weaknesses of the black family. Ever since the 1965 publication of Daniel Patrick Moynihan's *The Negro Family: The Case for National Action*, the discussion of racial and ethnic group variation in America's families has been culturally sensitive.[42] As Moynihan argued: "At the center of the tangle of pathology is the weakness of the family structure. Once or twice removed, it will be found to be the principal source of most of the aberrant, inadequate, or antisocial behaviour that did not establish but now serves to perpetuate the cycle of poverty and deprivation." Critics charged that Moynihan unfairly blamed the victims.

We have learned a good deal more about changing marriage and family patterns among African Americans and other ethnic groups since Moynihan's prescient comments. The family life of blacks remains distinctive in many ways, as we shall report in the next section, and black family trends may be harbingers of change for all Americans.[43]

Nearly 70 percent of African American children are born outside of marriage. Most black children today grow up in female-headed families, which are often poor. If rates of marriage are our measure, traditional marriage occupies a much less central place in the lives of most American blacks than for other Americans. A disproportionate share of young black mothers have a series of relationships with live-in partners and have children from multiple partners.[44] For black women who do marry, the large majority of their marriages do not last. The implications for intergenerational poverty, long-term welfare dependency, and children's developmental trajectories are real and profound.

These are the unvarnished facts. Their interpretation, however, has been the subject of much debate. Statistics on the black family beg the question about the root causes of these shifts. Are blacks themselves to blame for situations such as unwed childbearing, serial partners, and lack of education? Or are changes in the black family a product of racial oppression, economic inequality, and the lack of equal access to mainstream social and educational institutions? Is this trend a failure of our economic or political system? Or is the current state of the black family a cultural legacy of matrifocal family patterns extending back to slavery — when legal marriage was often denied to blacks, when the family unit centered on slave women and their children, and when black men were denied their traditional patriarchal roles as the family head and economic provider?

Census data alone cannot answer all these questions. The data can, however, provide a first glimpse of the changes in black marriage and family patterns from 1990 to 2000. A voluminous literature on African American family life also provides a social and political context for studying other minority and immigrant groups. Sociologist R. Salvador Oropesa, for example, has coined the term "paradox of Mexican American nuptiality," meaning that the currently high rates of marriage among both U.S.-born and immigrant Mexicans suggest a strong basis for cultural explanations of marriage.[45] Indeed, Mexican Americans, while often sharing the same impoverished circumstances as African Americans, exhibit much different patterns of marriage and family structure. Culture may trump economics. Whether foreign-born Mexicans will adopt the marriage and family patterns of the white majority as they blend into American society, or instead will maintain their cultural heritage of strong families, is far from certain. Mexican Americans are also much more likely than blacks to marry whites.

The typically stable families of most Asian Americans have been widely applauded as a source of great strength and upward social mobility. But in many ways, Asian Americans, as a panethnic group, are considerably more heterogeneous than Hispanics, who come from different Spanish-speaking countries but share certain cultural traits such as language and religion. Pan-Asian averages, on the other hand, may mask wide differences among different Asian-origin populations. Asians differ widely on language, religion, and economic resources. Chinese and Japanese have been in the United States in large numbers for more than 100 years, while other Asian minorities have only recently arrived in the United States. Many are refugees, such as Cambodians and Vietnamese, who lack the same economic resources that often characterize Asian and other immigrants who entered the country long ago. The experiences of recent Asian immigrant groups have been different in uncertain ways from those of other Asian immigrant groups with large third-generation populations. Fortunately, the 2000 Census provides an unprecedented opportunity to chart the family and demographic experiences of diverse pan-Asian ethnic groups, and also to compare these groups with diverse groups of African Americans, Hispanics, and non-Hispanics whites.

REFERENCES

1. Andrew J. Cherlin, "The Deinstitutionalization of American Marriage," *Journal of Marriage and the Family* 66, no. 4 (2004): 848–61.

2. Diane Schmidley, "The Foreign Born Population in the United States, March 2002," *Current Population Reports* P20-539 (2003): 1–2.

3. According to *Child Trends* in 2001, 15 percent of all children has at least one foreign-born parent.

4. Matthew D. Bramlett and Willam D. Mosher, "First Marriage Dissolution, Divorce, and Remarriage, United States," *Advanced Data from Vital and Health Statistics* 323 (Hyattsville, MD: National Center for Health Statistics, 2001); and Maureen R. Waller, "High Hopes: Unwed Parents' Expectations About Marriage," *Children and Youth Services Review* 23, nos. 6–7 (2001): 457–84.

5. Arland Thornton and Linda Young-DeMarco, "Four Decades of Trends in Attitudes toward Family Issues in the United States: The 1960s through the 1990s," *Journal of Marriage and the Family* 63, no. 4 (2001): 1009–37.

6. Scott Coltrane, "Marketing the Marriage 'Solution': Misplaced Simplicity in the Politics of Fatherhood," *Sociological Perspectives* 44, no. 4 (2001): 387–418; Daniel T. Lichter, *Marriage as Public Policy* (Washington, DC: Progressive Policy Institute, 2001); Theodora Ooms, *Toward More Perfect Unions: Putting Marriage on the Public Agenda* (Washington, DC: Family Impact Seminar, 1998); and Isabel Sawhill, "Is Lack of Marriage the Real Problem?" *The American Prospect*, Spring Supplement (2002): 8–9.

7. Herbert L. Smith, S. Philip Morgan, and Tanya Koropeckyj-Cox, "A Decomposition of Trends in the Nonmarital Fertility Ratios of Blacks and Whites in the United States, 1960–1992," *Demography* 33, no. 2 (1996): 141–52.

8. R. Kelly Raley, "Increasing Fertility in Cohabiting Unions: Evidence of the Second Demographic Transition in the United States?" *Demography* 38, no. 1 (2001): 59–66.

9. Bramlett and Mosher, "First Marriage Dissolution, Divorce, and Remarriage"; and Robert Schoen and Nicola Standish, "The Retrenchment of Marriage: Results from Marital Status Life Tables for the United States, 1995," *Population and Development Review* 27, no. 3 (2001): 553–63.

10. The crude divorce rate in 2002 was 4.0 divorces per 1,000 population. With a U.S. population of roughly 290 million in 2004, we estimate that about 1.2 million marriages result each year in divorce.

11. See http://ferret.bls.census.gov/macro/032003/pov/new02_100_01.htm, accessed on May 1, 2004.

12. David J. Eggebeen and Daniel T. Lichter, "Race, Family Structure, and Changing Poverty among American Children," *American Sociological Review* 56, no. 6 (1991): 801–17; and John Iceland, "Why Poverty Remains High: The Role of Income Growth, Economic Inequality, and Changes in Family Structure, 1949–1999," *Demography* 40, no. 3 (2003): 499–519.

13. Sara McLanahan and Gary Sandefur, *Growing Up with a Single Parent* (Cambridge, MA: Harvard University Press, 1994).

14. Jeffery S. Gray, "The Fall in Men's Return to Marriage: Declining Productivity Effects or Changing Selection," *Journal of Human Resources* 32, no. 3 (1997): 481–504.

15. In June 2000, the Coalition for Marriage, Family and Couples Education issued *The Marriage Movement: A Statement of Principles*. The document asked for a reconsideration of no-fault divorce laws; greater support of marriage over cohabitation and more communication to children about the value of abstinence and marriage;

the promotion of *covenant* marriages, which make divorce more difficult; greater government effort to promote marriage as a goal of family policy; more government effort to collect complete statistics on marriage and divorce; reform of court-connected divorce education to facilitate reconciliation; the use of welfare funds to finance promarriage programs; and encouragement of marriage counseling to support troubled marriages.

16. Marianne P. Bitler et al., "The Impact of Welfare Reform on Marriage and Divorce," *Demography* 41, no. 2 (2004): 213–36; and John M. Fitzgerald and David C. Ribar, "Welfare Reform and Female Headship," *Demography* 41, no. 2 (2004): 189–212.

17. Laura Sanchez, Stephen L. Nock, and James D. Wright, "Setting the Clock Forward or Back? Covenant Marriage and the 'Divorce Revolution,'" *Journal of Family Issues* 23, no. 1 (2002): 91–120; and Katherine B. Rosier and Scott L. Feld, "Covenant Marriage: A New Alternative for Traditional Families," *Journal of Comparative Family Studies* 31, no. 3 (2000): 385–94.

18. Daniel T. Lichter, Christie M. Batson, and J. Brian Brown, "Welfare Reform and Marriage Promotion: The Marital Expectations and Desires of Single and Cohabiting Mothers," *Social Service Review* 748, no. 1 (2004): 2–25.

19. Lynne M. Casper and Suzanne M. Bianchi, *Continuity and Change in the American Family* (Thousand Oaks, CA: Sage Publications, 2002).

20. David T. Ellwood and Christopher Jencks, "The Uneven Spread of Single-Parent Families: What Do We Know? Where Do We Look for Answers?" in *Social Inequality,* ed. Kathryn Neckerman (New York: Russell Sage Foundation, 2004).

21. David Cotter, Joan Hermsen, and Reeve Vanneman, *Gender Inequality at Work* (New York: Russell Sage Foundation, 2004).

22. Daniel T. Lichter and Rukamalie Jayakody, "Welfare Reform: How Do We Measure Success?" *Annual Review of Sociology* 28 (2002): 117–41.

23. Rose M. Kreider and Jason M. Fields, "Number, Timing, and Duration of Marriages and Divorces: 1996," *Current Population Reports* P70–80 (2002): 6.

24. Teresa Castro Martin and Larry L. Bumpass, "Recent Trends in Marital Disruption," *Demography* 26, no. 1 (1989): 37–51.

25. See www.cdc.gov/nchs/releases/95facts/fs_4312s.htm, accessed on May 2, 2004. Based on evidence from 1995, June was (and still is) the most popular month for marriage, with more than twice as many marriages (280,218) as January (117,310), the least popular month.

26. Joyce A. Martin et al., "Births: Final Data for 2002," *National Vital Statistics Reports* 52, no. 10 (2003): 8–9.

27. Maria Cancian and Deborah Reed, "Changes in Family Structure: Implications for Poverty and Related Policy," *Focus* 21, no. 2 (2000): 21–26.

28. Joseph Dalaker, "Poverty in the United States," *Current Population Reports* P60–214 (2001).

29. Jason Fields, "Children's Living Arrangements and Characteristics: March 2002," *Current Population Reports* P20–547 (2003): 4–5.

30. George Masnick and Mary Jo Bane, *The Nation's Families: 1960–1990* (Cambridge MA: The Joint Center for Urban Studies of MIT and Harvard University, 1980).

31. U.S. Census Bureau, "Age Groups and Sex: 2000," Census 2000 Summary File 1, accessed online at http://factfinder.census.gov/servlet/SAFFPeople?_sse=on, on Nov. 5, 2004.

32. Larry L. Bumpass, James A. Sweet, and Andrew Cherlin, "The Role of Cohabitation in Declining Rates of Marriage," *Journal of Marriage and the Family* 53, no. 4 (1991): 913–27; and Larry Bumpass and James A. Sweet, "National

Estimates of Cohabitation," *Demography* 26, no. 4 (1989): 615–25.

33. Susan L. Brown, "Moving From Cohabitation to Marriage: Effects on Relationship Quality," *Social Science Research* 33, no. 1 (2004): 1–19; and Sharon Sassler, "The Process of Entry in Cohabiting Unions," *Journal of Marriage and the Family* 66, no. 2 (2004): 491–505.

34. Steven L. Nock, "A Comparison of Marriages and Cohabiting Relationships," *Journal of Family Issues* 16, no. 1 (1995): 53–76. Nock shows that the quality of cohabiting relationships is typically lower on a number of dimensions than for married couples. This finding contributes to his view that cohabitation remains an incomplete institution.

35. Sassler, "The Process of Entry in Cohabiting Unions."

36. Gary Becker, *A Treatise on the Family* (Cambridge: MA: Harvard University Press, 1991).

37. Valerie Kincade Oppenheimer, "A Theory of Marriage Timing," *American Journal of Sociology* 94, no. 3 (1988): 563–91.

38. Robert Moffitt, "The Effect of Welfare on Marriage and Fertility: What Do We Know and What Do We Need to Know?" in *Welfare, the Family, and Reproductive Behaviour: Research Perspectives*, ed. Robert A. Moffitt (Washington, DC: National Academies Press, 1998): 50–97.

39. Ellwood and Jencks, "The Uneven Spread of Single-Parent Families."

40. Andrew J. Cherlin, "Toward a New Home Socioeconomics of Union Formation," in *Ties That Bind: Perspectives on Marriage and Cohabitation*, ed. Linda Waite et al. (New York: Aldine de Gruyter, 2000): 126–44.

41. Robert A. Moffitt, "Female Wages, Male Wages, and the Economic Model of Marriage: The Basic Evidence," in *Ties That Bind: Perspectives on Marriage and Cohabitation*, ed. Linda Waite et al. (New York: Aldine de Gruyter, 2000): 302–19.

42. Daniel Patrick Moynihan, *The Negro Family: The Case for National Action* (Washington, DC: U.S. Department of Labor, 1965).

43. The family situation of blacks in the 1960s is similar to the situation of whites today: Roughly one of every five children is born to an unmarried woman. Whites have followed similar family trajectories to blacks, but have lagged by a quarter-century.

44. Ronald B. Mincy, "Who Should Marry Whom? Multiple-Partner Fertility among New Parents," *Center for Research on Child Well-Being Working Paper* 02-03FF (Princeton, NJ: Princeton University Press, 2002).

45. R. S. Oropesa, Daniel T. Lichter, and Robert A. Anderson, "Marriage Markets and the Paradox of Mexican-American Nuptiality," *Journal of Marriage and the Family* 56, no. 4 (1994): 889–907.

PART II

Historical Changes and Family Variations

In this section, we examine the diverse history of American families and the variety of family forms and experiences that have occurred across cultural groups. The study of the history of the family is important in order to understand the contemporary family. Remember the argument from Part I that there is no one universal family form; instead, the family is socially constructed. The historical study of the family helps us to see how the family is socially constructed over time and across different cultures. Moreover, it enables us to deconstruct notions of the white, middle-class family as the dominant family form. By examining diverse family forms, including those of different racial-ethnic, cultural, and social class groups, we begin to understand the plurality of families that have historically coexisted and still coexist within the United States today. Thus, the study of family history shows that family forms and experiences vary distinctively between groups, and that many myths and assumptions we hold about families are historically inaccurate. Finally, studying the history of the family helps us to understand how the institution of the family is shaped by other institutions, including the economy, law, politics, and religion.

Tamara K. Hareven, a historian of the family, has argued that recent historical research on the family has challenged some myths and generalizations about family life and society. But the current work of historical research is much more complicated due to a recognition that families, themselves, are continually changing. She states:

> Contemporary historians of the family have sought to reintroduce human experience into historical research and to emphasize the complexity of historical change. The challenge for such scholars is the reconstruction of a multi-tiered reality—the lives of individual families and their interactions with major social, economic, and political forces. This enterprise is complicated by our increasing appreciation of the changing and diverse nature of "the family," rendered fluid by shifts in internal age and gender configurations across regions and over time. The formidable goal is to understand the family in various contexts of change, while allowing the levels of complexity to play themselves out at different points in historical time. In short, it represents an effort to understand the interrelationship between individual time, family time, and historical time. (Hareven 1994:13–14)

Thus, Hareven argues that contemporary historians must be aware of not only the microexperience of interactions within families, but also the macroexperience of how families are being shaped by other social, economic, and political forces. This research is challenging because the family is continually in flux based on changes both internal and external to the institution.

This challenge of studying the diversity of family history is addressed in the first reading in this section, "Historical Perspectives on Family Diversity," by Stephanie Coontz. Coontz is a social historian at Evergreen State College in Olympia, Washington, and she has written several books on the social history of the American family, including *The Way We Never Were: American Families and the Nostalgia Trap* (1992) and *The Way We Really Are: Coming to Terms with America's Changing Families* (1997). In both books, Coontz shatters many of the myths we have about families. The selection included here continues her use of history to challenge myths and misconceptions about family diversity in Europe and in the United States. Similar to Diana Gittins' arguments (see Reading 1), Coontz argues that there is no universal definition of family. Instead, there are many different historical definitions of family and the experience of family varies greatly in different societies and time periods. Thus, not only do the forms and definition of family vary over time and across cultures, but so do the emotional meanings attached to families. In this selection, Coontz focuses her analysis primarily on the diversity of American families, including Native American families, African American slave families, Mexican and Chicano families, and the families of European immigrants.

One important theme of Coontz's article is her linking of family history to the history of economic systems. That is, in any given time period, the economy shapes the institution of the family, and as the institution of the economy changes, the institution of the family also changes. Thus, as societies move from subsistence economies, to agrarian economies, to early industrialization, to global capitalism, the family is forced to adapt to and to accommodate changes in economic incentives and structures. Family scholars continually ask: How is the economy affecting the family? How does capitalism shape the family? Historical analysis helps us to understand this interrelationship between the economy and the family. For example, while historically the family was a site for both production and consumption, today both the productive and reproductive labor done within families has changed. The family not only is shaped by who is in the paid workforce, but it also serves as a site for consumerism. As the next reading shows, this historical relationship between the economy and the family is central to the diversity of forms and experiences of African American families.

African American Families

The second reading in this section, "Black Families: Beyond Revisionist Scholarship," by Shirley A. Hill, builds on many arguments made by Coontz in the first reading. Hill is a professor of sociology at the University of Kansas, where she teaches family sociology, medical sociology, and social inequality. In this selection, taken from her recent book *Black Intimacies: A Gender*

Perspective on Families and Relationships (2005), Hill echoes Diana Gittins' argument (Reading 1) about the incorrect assumption that there is a "universal" family. She agrees with Gittins that there is no one ideal family form that explains family variation across racial-ethnic and social class lines in the United States. Hill argues that in order to understand contemporary African American families, scholars must examine both the historical legacy of slavery and the revisionist scholarship on black families. Hill reviews this historical scholarship on black families and incorporates a gender lens into the study of African American families by focusing on the active, decision-making roles of black women in family formation. After reviewing both the legacy of slavery thesis and the revisionist perspectives, Hill proposes a postmodern perspective to understand black families.

Mexican American Families

The third reading in this section, *"La Familia: Family Cohesion among Mexican American Families in the Urban Southwest, 1848–1900,"* is by Richard Griswold del Castillo, a professor of Mexican American Studies at San Diego University. Griswold del Castillo wrote this essay on Mexican and Chicano families as one of a series of chapters for his book *La Familia: Chicano Families in the Urban Southwest: 1848 to the Present* (1984). For this essay, Griswold del Castillo used historical statistics to study extended-family formation as an expression of family solidarity. Trained as a humanist scholar at UCLA in the 1960s, he became fascinated with computer analyses of historical data, spending long hours at his terminal trying to figure out statistical methods. Griswold del Castillo became convinced that illustrating historical trends with quantitative data was useful only if the user was sophisticated about levels of significance and tests of association. Thus, this reading demonstrates some of the limitations of using census data to study family patterns. It also demonstrates the application of sociological theory about families, especially life-course analysis, to a historical era. By coincidence, Griswold del Castillo finds that his own personal life has followed virtually the same patterns he discerned for Mexican Americans in the nineteenth century: He now lives in a family that any census taker would consider to be extended, but that is, in fact, a stepfamily.

Chinese American Families

The fourth reading in this section extends our understanding of racial-ethnic diversity by examining Chinese American families. The reading, "Split Household, Small Producer, and Dual Wage Earner: An Analysis of Chinese-American Family Strategies," is by Evelyn Nakano Glenn. A professor of women's studies and ethnic studies at the University of California at Berkeley, Glenn has studied Asian American families for over 30 years. Building on

Hareven's arguments mentioned earlier, Glenn utilizes a macroperspective to challenge cultural analyses of Chinese American families. Glenn argues that, instead of utilizing a cultural approach, one needs to use an institutional approach to better understand the historical realities of Chinese American family life. In particular, Glenn states that "a fuller understanding of the Chinese American family must begin with an examination of the changing constellation of economic, legal, and political constraints that have shaped the Chinese experience in America." She argues that these constraints have shaped Chinese family life and have led Chinese Americans to create a number of strategies that have enabled them to survive as immigrants in the United States. Thus, this selection is similar to Shirley Hill's article (Reading 6) in challenging Eurocentric analyses of family. It also builds on Coontz's arguments (Reading 5) about how the economy and other social institutions shape the family.

REFERENCES

Coontz, Stephanie. 1992. *The Way We Never Were: American Families and the Nostalgia Trap.* New York: Basic Books.
———. 1997. *The Way We Really Are: Coming to Terms with America's Changing Families.* New York: Basic Books.
Griswold del Castillo, Richard. 1984. *La Familia: Chicano Families in the Urban Southwest: 1848 to the Present.* Notre Dame, IN: University of Notre Dame Press.
Hareven, Tamara K. 1994. "Recent Research on the History of the Family." Pp. 13–43 in *Time, Family, and Community: Perspectives on Family and Community History,* edited by Michael Drake. Cambridge, MA: Blackwell.
Hill, Shirley A. 2005. *Black Intimacies: A Gender Perspective on Families and Relationships.* Walnut Creek, CA: Altamira Press.

5

HISTORICAL PERSPECTIVES ON FAMILY DIVERSITY

STEPHANIE COONTZ

Variability in the European and American Historical Record

In the ancient Mediterranean world, households and kin groupings were so disparate that no single unit of measurement or definition could encompass them. By the late 14th century, however, the English word *family*, derived from the Latin word for a household including servants or slaves, had emerged to designate all those who lived under the authority of a household head. The family might include a joint patrilocal family, with several brothers and their wives residing together under the authority of the eldest, as was common in parts of Italy and France before 1550, as well as in many Eastern European communities into the 19th century. Or it might be a stem family, in which the eldest son brought his bride into his parents' home upon marriage, and they lived as an extended family until the parents' deaths. The son's family then became nuclear in form, until the eldest son reached the age of marriage. Owing to late marriages and early mortality, most such families would be nuclear at any particular census, but most of them would pass through an extended stage at some point in their life cycle (Berkner 1972; Coontz 1988; Hareven 1987).

Until the early 19th century, most middle-class Europeans and North Americans defined *family* on the basis of a common residence under the authority of a household head, rather than on blood relatedness. This definition thus frequently included boarders or servants. Samuel Pepys began his famous 17th-century English diary with the words: "I lived in Axe Yard, having my wife, and servant Jane, and no more in family than us three." In 1820 the publisher Everard Peck and his wife, of Rochester, New York, childless newlyweds, wrote home: "We collected our family together which consists of seven persons and we think ourselves pleasantly situated" (Coontz 1988; Hareven 1987).

Among the European nobility, an alternative definition of family referred not to the parent–child grouping, but to the larger descent group from which claims to privilege and property derived. Starting in the late

17th century, other writers used the word to refer exclusively to a man's offspring, as in the phrase *his family* and *wife*. Not until the 19th century did the word *family* commonly describe a married couple with their coresident children, distinguished from household residents or more distant kin. This definition spread widely during the 1800s. By the end of the 19th century, the restriction of the word to the immediate, coresidential family was so prevalent that the adjective *extended* had to be added when people wished to refer to kin beyond the household (Williams 1976).

Diversity in Emotional and Sexual Arrangements

. . . [Family diversity extends] not just to forms and definitions, but to the emotional meanings attached to families and the psychological dynamics within them. Whereas 17th-century Mediterranean families were organized around the principle of honor, which rested largely on the chastity of the family's women, other groups did not traditionally distinguish between "legitimate" and "illegitimate" children. When Jesuit missionaries told a Montagnais-Naskapi Indian that he should keep tighter control over his wife to ensure that the children she bore were "his," the man replied: "Thou hast no sense. You French people love only your own children; but we love all the children of our tribe" (Leacock 1980:31; see also Gutierrez 1991).

What is considered healthy parent–child bonding in our society may be seen as selfishness or pathological isolation by cultures that stress the exchange and fostering of children as ways of cementing social ties. The Zinacantecos of southern Mexico do not even have a word to distinguish the parent–child relationship from the house, suggesting that the emotional saliency of the cooperating household unit is stronger than that of blood ties per se. In Polynesia, eastern Oceania, the Caribbean, and the West Indies (and in 16th-century Europe), to offer your child to friends, neighbors, or other kin for adoption or prolonged coresidence was not considered abandonment but a mark of parental love and community reciprocity (Collier, Rosaldo, and Yanigasako 1982; Peterson 1993; Stack 1993).

Modern Americans stress the need for mother–daughter and father–son identification, but in matrilineal societies, where descent is reckoned in the female line, a man usually has much closer ties with his nephews than with his sons. Among the Trobriand Islanders, for instance, a child's biological father is considered merely a relation by marriage. The strongest legal and emotional bonds are between children and their maternal uncles. Conversely, among the patrilineal Cheyenne, mother–daughter relations were expected to be tense or even hostile, and girls tended to establish their closest relationships with their paternal aunts (Collier et al. 1982).

What counts as healthy family dynamics or relationships also varies *within* any given society. Research on contemporary families has demonstrated that parenting techniques or marital relationships that are appropriate to middle-class white families are less effective for families that must cope with economic deprivation and racial prejudice (Baumrind 1972; Boyd-Franklin and Garcia-Preto 1994; Knight, Virdin, and Roosa 1994).

Values about the proper roles and concerns of mothers and fathers differ as well. Today women tend to be in charge of family rituals, such as weddings and funerals. In colonial days, however, this was a father's responsibility, while economic activities were far more central to a colonial woman's identity (and occupied much more of her time) than was child rearing. Contemporary American thought posits an inherent conflict between mothering and paid work, but breadwinning is an integral part of the definition of mothering in many cultural traditions. One study found that "traditional" Mexicanas in the United States experience *less* conflict or guilt in integrating the worlds of home and paid employment than do their Chicana counterparts who have internalized the notions of good mothering portrayed in the American mass media (Calvert 1992; Gillis 1996).

Even something as seemingly "natural" as sexual behavior and identity shows amazing variation across time and cultures. Categories of gender and sexuality have not always been so rigidly dichotomous as they are in modern Euro-American culture. Among many Native American societies, for instance, the *berdache* has a spiritual, social, economic, and political role that is distinct from either men's or women's roles. Neither he nor the female counterparts found in other Native American groups can be accurately described by the sexual identity we know as homosexual. Similarly, in traditional African culture, a person's sexual identity was not separable from his or her membership and social role in a family group (Herdt 1994; Jeater 1993; Schnarch 1992; Williams 1986).

Ever since the spread of Freudian psychiatric ideas at the beginning of the 20th century, Europeans and North Americans have tended to see a person's sexual behavior as the wellspring or driving force of his or her identity. The ancient Greeks, in contrast, thought that dreams about sex were "really" about politics. Until comparatively recently in history, a person's sexual acts were assumed to be separate from his or her fundamental character or identity. Indeed, the term *homosexual* did not come into use until the end of the 19th century. A person could commit a sexual act with a person of the same sex without being labeled as having a particular sexual "orientation." This lack of interest in identifying people by their sexual practices extended to heterosexual behavior as well. In mid-17th century New England, Samuel Terry was several times convicted for sexual offenses, such as masturbating, in public, but this behavior did not prevent his fellow townspeople from electing him town constable (D'Emilio and Freedman 1988; Padgug 1989).

Since the early 20th century, most American experts on the family have insisted on the importance of heterosexual intimacy between husband and wife in modeling healthy development for children, yet in the 19th century, no one saw any harm in the fact that the closest bonds of middle-class women were with other women, rather than with their husbands. Men were often secondary in women's emotional lives, to judge from the silence or nonchalance about them in women's diaries and letters, which were saturated with expressions of passion that would immediately raise eyebrows by modern standards of sexual categorization. Although the acceptability of such passionate bonds may have provided cover for sexual relations between some women, these bonds were also considered compatible with marriage. Men, too, operated in a different sexual framework than today. They talked matter-of-factly about sleeping with their best friends, embracing them, or laying a head on a male friend's bosom—all without any self-consciousness that their wives or fiancées might misinterpret their "sexual orientation" (Duberman, Vicinus, and Chauncey 1989; Faderman 1981; Rotundo 1993; Smith-Rosenberg 1985). . . .

Families in the Cauldron of Colonization

At the time of European exploration of the New World, Native American families in North America orbited around a mode of social reproduction based on kinship ties and obligations. Kinship provided Native Americans with a system of assigning rights and duties on the basis of a commonly accepted criterion—a person's blood relationship (although this relationship might have been fictive) to a particular set of relatives. Kinship rules and marital alliances regulated an individual's place in the overall production and distribution of each group's dominant articles of subsistence and established set patterns in the individual's interactions with others.

Among groups that depended on hunting and gathering, such as those of the northern woods or Great Basin, marriage and residence rules were flexible and informal. In other Native American societies, typically those that had extensive horticulture, people were grouped into different sections, moieties or phratries, and clans, each of which was associated with different territories, resources, skills, duties, or simply personal characteristics. Exogamy, the requirement that an individual marry out of his or her natal group into a different clan or section, ensured the widest possible social cooperation by making each individual a member of intersecting kin groups, with special obligations to and rights in each category of relatives. Marriage and residence rules also organized the division of labor by age and gender (Coontz 1988; Leacock and Lurie 1971; Spicer 1962).

Unlike a state system, which makes sharp distinctions between family duties and civil duties, domestic functions and political ones, North American Native Americans had few institutions (prior to sustained contact with Europeans) that were set up on a basis other than kinship. Some groups, such as the Cherokee, might have had a special governing body for times of war, and the influence of such groups was invariably strengthened once Native Americans engaged in regular conflicts with settlers, but most of the time village elders made decisions. There was no opposition between domestic or "private" functions and political or public ones. North American Native Americans had no institutionalized courts, police, army, or other agencies to tax or coerce labor. Kin obligations organized production, distributed surplus products, and administered justice. Murder, for example, was an offense not against the state but against the kin group, and, therefore, it was the responsibility and right of kin to punish the perpetrator. To involve strangers in this punishment, as modern state judicial systems deem best, would have escalated the number of groups and individuals involved in the conflict (Anderson 1991; Coontz 1988).

The nuclear family was not a property-holding unit, since resources and land either were available to all or were held by the larger kin corporation, while subsistence tools and their products were made and owned by individuals, rather than families. Its lack of private property meant that the nuclear family had less economic autonomy vis-à-vis other families than did European households. The lack of a state, on the other hand, gave Native American families more political autonomy because people were not bound to follow a leader for any longer than they cared to do so. However, this political autonomy did not seem to create a sense of exclusive attachment to one's "own" nuclear family. The nuclear family was only one of many overlapping ties through which individuals were linked. It had almost no functions that were not shared by other social groupings (Leacock and Lurie 1971; Spicer 1962).

Native American kinship systems created their own characteristic forms of diversity. North American Indians spoke more than 200 languages and lived in some 600 different societies with a wide variety of residence, marital, and genealogical rules. Among nomadic foragers, residence rules were flexible and descent was seldom traced far back. Horizontal ties of marriage and friendship were more important in organizing daily life than were vertical ties of descent. More settled groups tended to have more extensive lineage systems, in which rights and obligations were traced through either the female or the male line of descent. Most of the Great Plains and prairie Indians were patrilineal; matrilineal descent was common among many East Coast groups; the Creeks, Choctaws, and Seminoles of the South; and the Hopi, Acoma, and Zuni groups of the Southwest (Axtell 1981, 1988; Catlin 1973; Coontz 1988; Gutierrez 1991; Leacock and Lurie 1971; Mindel, Habenstein, and Wright 1988; Peters 1995; Snipp 1989).

Native American family systems produced land-use and fertility patterns that helped maintain the abundance of game and forests that made the land so attractive to European settlers. But they also made the Native Americans vulnerable to diseases brought by the Europeans and their animals, as well as to the Europeans' more aggressive and coordinated methods of warfare or political expansion (Axtell 1985, 1988; Cronon 1983).

The impact of European colonization on Native American family systems was devastating. Massive epidemics, sometimes killing 60%–90% of a group's members, devastated kin networks and hence disrupted social continuity. Heightened warfare elevated the role of young male leaders at the expense of elders and women. In most cases, the influence of traders, colonial political officials, and Christian missionaries fostered the nuclear family's growing independence from the extended household, kinship, and community group in which it had traditionally been embedded. In other instances, as with Handsome Lake's revival movement among the Iroquois, Native

Americans attempted to adapt European family systems and religious values to their own needs. Either way, gender and age relations were often transformed, while many Native American groups were either exterminated or driven onto marginal land that did not support traditional methods of social organization and subsistence. Native American collective traditions, however, were surprisingly resilient, and Euro-Americans spent the entire 19th century trying to extinguish them (Adams 1995; Anderson 1991; Calloway 1997; Coontz 1988; Mindel et al. 1988; Peters 1995).

The European families that came to North America were products of an international mercantile system whose organizing principles of production, exchange, ownership, and land use were on a collision course with indigenous patterns of existence. Europeans also had the support of a centralized state apparatus whose claims to political authority and notion of national interests had no counterweight among Native Americans. Colonial families had far more extensive property and inheritance rights than did Native American families, but they were also subjected to far more stringent controls by state and church institutions. The redistribution duties of wealthy families, however, were much more limited than those of Native Americans, so there were substantial differences in wealth and resources among colonial families, with the partial exception of those in the New England colonies right from the beginning (Coontz 1988; Mintz and Kellogg 1988).

These features of colonial society led to a different kind of family diversity than that among Native Americans. In addition to differences connected to the national, class, and religious origins of the settlers, the sex ratio of different colonizing groups, and the type of agriculture or trade they were able to establish, the colonies were also characterized by larger disparities in the wealth and size of households. Poorer colonists tended to concentrate in propertied households as apprentices, servants, or temporary lodgers.

At the same time as European settlers were destroying the Native American kinship system, they were importing an African kinship system, which they also attempted to destroy. But because the colonists depended on African labor, they had to make some accommodations to African culture and to African American adaptations to the requirements of surviving under slavery. The slaves were at once more subject to supervision and manipulation of their families and more able than Native Americans to build new kinship networks and obligations. They adapted African cultural traditions to their new realities, using child-centered, rather than marriage-centered, family systems; fictive kin ties; ritual coparenting or godparenting; and complex naming patterns that were designed to authenticate extended kin connections, all in the service of building kin ties within the interstices of the slave trade and plantation system. But African American families also had their own characteristic forms of diversity, depending on whether they lived in settlements of free blacks, on large plantations with many fellow slaves, or on isolated small farms in the South (Franklin 1997; Gutman 1976; Stevenson 1996).

Slave families were not passive victims of the traffic in human beings nor organized in imitation of or deference to their masters' values. However, they could never be free of the constraints imposed by their white owners. They emerged out of a complex set of struggles and accommodations between both groups. But slaveowners' families were *also* derived from the dialectic of slavery. Anxieties about social control and racial-sexual hierarchies, fears of alliances between blacks and poor whites, and attempts to legitimate slavery in the face of Northern antislavery sentiment created a high tolerance for sexual hypocrisy; pervasive patterns of violence within white society, as well as against slaves; and elaborate rituals of patriarchy, both in family life and in the community at large (Edwards 1991; Isaacs 1982; McCurry 1995; Mullings 1997; Stevenson 1996).

Families in the Early Commercial and Industrializing Economy

From about the 1820s, a new constellation of family systems emerged in the United States, corresponding to the growth of wage labor, a national market economy, and the specialization of many occupations and professions. Merchants, manufacturers, and even many farmers consolidated production and hired employees to work for a set number of hours, rather than purchased supplies or raw materials from independent producers. Such producers, along with the apprentices and journeymen whom wage workers replaced, lost older routes to self-employment or accession to family farms. At the same time, married women's traditional household production was taken over by unmarried girls working in factories.

In an attempt to avoid becoming wage laborers and to find new professions or sources of self-employment for them and their children, a growing number of middle-class families developed a more private nuclear family orientation, keeping their children at home longer instead of sending them away for training or socialization elsewhere. Meanwhile, immigrants from Europe poured into the growing towns to work in factories or tenement workshops, while westward expansion drew new Mexican and Native American groups into the economy. Such trends in the early development of American capitalism reshaped ethnic traditions and class relations and led to the emergence of "whiteness" as a category that European immigrants could use to differentiate themselves from other groups near the bottom of the economic hierarchy (Johnson 1978; Jones 1997; Roediger 1988; Ryan 1981).

The gravitational force that was pulling families into new orbits in this period was the emergence of wage labor in the context of competing older values and an inadequately developed set of formal supporting institutions for capitalist production—schools, credit associations, unions, and even a developed consumer industry. Families who sought to escape wage labor by moving west, setting up small businesses, or trying to compete with factory-made goods through household production were just as surely affected by the progress of capitalism as were families who either owned or had to work in the larger workshops and factories that increasingly supplanted apprenticeship arrangements in separate households or farms. At the same time, few families could yet free themselves from some reliance on household production or community sponsorship and social ties.

The gradual separation of work and home—market production and household reproduction—created new tensions between family activities and "economic" ones. Households could no longer get by primarily on things they made, grew, or bartered. However, they could not yet rely on ready-made purchased goods. Even in middle-class homes, the labor required to make purchased goods usable by the families was immense (Strasser 1982).

These competing gravitational pulls produced a new division of labor among middle-class families and many workers. Men (and in working-class families, children as well) began to specialize in paid work outside the home. Wives took greater responsibility for child care and household labor. A new ideology of parenting placed mothers at the emotional center of family life and romanticized the innocence of children, stressing the need to protect them within the family circle. What allowed middle-class white families to keep children at home longer and to divert the bulk of maternal attention from the production of clothes and food to child rearing was the inability of many working-class families to adopt such domestic patterns. The extension of childhood and the redefinition of motherhood among the middle class required the foreshortening of childhood among the slaves or sharecropping families who provided cotton to the new textile mills, the working-class women and children whose long hours in the factory made store-bought clothes and food affordable, and the Irish or free African American mothers and daughters who left their homes to work in what their mistresses insisted in defining as a domestic sanctuary, rather than a workplace. In addition to its class limitations, domesticity (along with its corollary, female purity) was constructed in opposition to the way that women of color were defined (Baca Zinn and Eitzen 1990; Dill 1998; Glenn 1992).

Even as many wives gave up their traditional involvement in production for sale or barter, others followed their domestic tasks out of the household and into the factories or small workshops that made up "the sweated trades." Still, as wage labor increasingly conflicted with domestic responsibilities, most families responded by trying to keep one household member near home. Although most wives of slaves and freed blacks continued to participate in the labor force, wives in most other racial and ethnic groups were increasingly likely to quit paid work outside the home after marriage. After the Civil War, freed slaves also attempted to use new norms of sexually appropriate work to resist gang labor, in a struggle with their former masters and current landlords that helped produce the sharecropping system in the South (Franklin 1997; Hareven 1976; Jones 1985; Lerner 1969; Mullings 1997).

But these superficially similar family values and gender-role behaviors masked profound differences, since working-class families continued to depend on child labor and support networks of neighbors beyond the family and the work of women within the home or neighborhood varied immensely by class. For example, "unemployed" wives among the working class frequently took in boarders or lodgers, made and sold small articles or foodstuffs, and otherwise kept far too busy with household subsistence tasks to act like the leisured ladies of the upper classes or the hovering mothers of the middle classes (Boydston 1990; Hareven 1987).

Among the wealthy, fluid household membership and extended family ties remained important in mobilizing credit, pooling capital, and gaining political connections. In the working class, family forms diverged. Single-person and single-parent households multiplied among the growing number of transient workers. But the early factory system and its flip side, the sweated trades, reinforced the notion of the family as a productive unit, with all members working under the direction of the family head or turning their wages over to him.

After the Civil War, industrialization and urbanization accelerated. As U.S. families adapted to the demands and tensions of the industrializing society, different groups behaved in distinctive ways, but some trends could be observed. It was during this period that American families took on many of the characteristics associated with "the modern family." They became smaller, with lower fertility rates; they revolved more tightly around the nuclear core, putting greater distance between themselves and servants or boarders; parents became more emotionally involved in child rearing and for a longer period; couples oriented more toward companionate marriage; and the separation between home and work, both physically and conceptually, was sharpened (Coontz 1988; Mintz and Kellogg 1988).

Yet these trends obscure tremendous differences among and within the changing ethnic groups and classes of the industrializing United States. Between 1830 and 1882, more than 10 million immigrants arrived from Europe. After the Civil War, new professions opened up for middle-class and skilled workers, while job insecurity became more pronounced for laborers. Class distinctions in home furnishings, food, and household labor *widened* in the second half of the 19th century. There was also much more variation in family sequencing and form than was to emerge in the 20th century. Young people in the 19th century exhibited fewer uniformities in the age of leaving school and home, marrying, and setting up households than they do today. No close integration between marriage and entry into the workforce existed: Young people's status as children, rather than marriage partners, determined when and where they would start work. Family decisions were far more variable and less tightly coordinated throughout the society than they would become in the 20th century (American Social History Project 1992; Baca Zinn and Eitzen 1990; Graff 1987; Modell 1989).

In addition to this diversity in the life cycle, family forms and household arrangements diverged in new ways. The long-term trend toward nuclearity slowed between 1870 and 1890 when a number of groups experienced an increase in temporary coresidence with other kin, while others took in boarders or lodgers. American fertility fell by nearly 40% between 1855 and 1915, but this average obscures many differences connected to occupation, region, race, and ethnicity. The fertility of some unskilled and semiskilled workers actually *rose* during this period (Coontz 1988; Hareven 1987).

Another form of family and gender-role diversity in the late 19th century stemmed from mounting contradictions and conflicts over sexuality, which was increasingly divorced from fertility. In the middle class, birth control became a fact of life, despite agitated attempts of conservatives, such as Anthony Comstock, to outlaw information on contraceptives. In the working class, fertility diverged from sexuality, in another way—not only in the growth of prostitution in the cities, but with the emergence of a group of single working women who socialized with men outside a family setting. The opportunities for unsupervised sexual behavior in the cities also increased the possibilities for same-sex relationships, and even entire subcultures, to develop (D'Emilio and Freedman 1988).

The changes that helped produce more "modern" family forms, then, started in different classes, meant different things to families who occupied different positions in the industrial order, and did not proceed in a unilinear way. The "modernization" of the family was the result not of some general evolution of "the" family, as early family sociologists originally posited, but of *diverging* and *contradictory* responses that occurred in different areas and classes at various times, eventually interacting to produce the trends we now associate with industrialization. As Katz, Doucet, and Stern (1982) pointed out:

> The five great changes in family organization that have occurred are the separation of home and work place; the increased nuclearity of household structure; the decline in marital fertility; the prolonged residence of children in the home of their parents; and the lengthened period in which husbands and wives live together after their children have left home. The first two began among the working class and among the wage-earning segment of the business class (clerks and kindred workers). The third started among the business class, particularly among its least affluent, most specialized, and most mobile sectors. The fourth began at about the same time in both the working and business class, though the children of the former usually went to work and the latter to school. (P. 317)

The fifth trend did not occur until the 20th century and represented a reversal of 19th-century trends, as did the sixth major change that has cut across older differences among families: the reintegration of women into productive work, especially the entry of mothers into paid work outside the home and the immediate neighborhood.

The Family Consumer Economy

Around the beginning of the 20th century, a new constellation of family forms and arrangements took shape, as a consolidated national industrial system and mass communication network replaced the decentralized production of goods and culture that had prevailed until the 1890s. The standardization of economic production, spread of mass schooling into the teenage years, abolition of child labor, growth of a consumer economy, and gradual expansion of U.S. international entanglements created new similarities and differences in people's experience of family life.

In the 1920s, for the first time, a bare majority of children came to live in a male-breadwinner, female-homemaker family, in which the children were in school rather than at work. Numerous immigrant families, however, continued to pull their children out of school to go to work, often arousing intense generational conflicts. African American families kept their children in school longer than any immigrant group, but their wives were much more likely than other American women to work outside the home (Hernandez 1993).

A major reorientation of family life occurred in the middle classes and in the dominant ideological portrayals of family life at that time. For the 19th-century middle class, the emotional center of family life had become the mother–child link and the wife's networks of female kin and friends. Now it shifted to the husband–wife bond. Although the "companionate marriage" touted by 1920s sociologists brought new intimacy and sexual satisfaction to married life, it also introduced two trends that disturbed observers. One was increased dissatisfaction with what used to be considered adequate relationships. Great expectations, as the historian May (1980) pointed out, could also generate great disappointments. These disappointments took the form of a jump in divorce rates and a change in the acceptable grounds for divorce (Coontz 1996; May 1980; Mintz and Kellogg 1988; Smith-Rosenberg 1985).

The other was the emergence of an autonomous and increasingly sexualized youth culture, as youths from many different class backgrounds interacted in high schools. The middle-class cult of married bliss and the new romance film industry led young people increasingly to stress the importance of sexual attractiveness and romantic experimentation. At the same time, the model of independent courting activity provided by working-class youths and the newly visible African American urban culture helped spread the new institution of "dating" (Bailey 1989; D'Emilio and Freedman 1988).

Another 20th-century trend was the state's greater intervention into the economy in response to the growth of the union movement, industry's need to regulate competition, the expanding international role of the United States, and other related factors. Families became increasingly dependent on the state and decreasingly dependent on neighborhood institutions for regulating the conditions under which they worked and lived. This change created more zones of privacy for some families but more places for state intervention in others. Sometimes the new state institutions tried to impose nuclear family norms on low-income families, as when zoning and building laws were used to prohibit the coresidence of augmented or extended families or children were taken away from single parents. But in other cases, state agencies imposed a female-headed household on the poor, as when single-parent families were the only model that entitled people to receive governmental subsidies (Gordon 1988; Zaretsky 1982).

Diversity, however, continued to be a hallmark of American family life. Between 1882 and 1930, more than 22 million immigrants came to America, many of them from southern and Eastern Europe, rather than from the traditional Western European suppliers of labor to the United States. They brought a whole range of new customs, religions, and traditions that interacted with their point of entry into the U.S. economy and with the new ethnic prejudices they encountered. By 1910 close to a majority of all workers in heavy industry were foreign born (Baca Zinn and Eitzen 1990).

These immigrants enriched urban life and changed the nature of industrial struggle in the United States. They neither "assimilated" to America nor retained their old ways untouched; rather, they used their cultural resources selectively to adapt to shifting institutional constraints and opportunities. For many groups, migration to America set up patterns of life and interaction with the larger mainstream institutions that forged a new cultural identity that was quite different from their original heritage. But this identity, in turn, changed as the socioeconomic conditions under which they forged their family lives shifted (Baca Zinn and Eitzen 1990; Glenn 1983; Sanchez 1993).

Space does not permit me to develop the history of diversity in 20th-century families, but one of the backdrops to the current debate about family life is that for some years there was a seeming reduction in family diversity, especially after restrictions on immigration in the 1920s began to take effect. For the first two-thirds of the 20th century, there was a growing convergence in the age and order in which young people of all income groups and geographic regions left home, left school, found jobs, and got married. The Great Depression, World War II, and the 1950s contributed to the impression of many Americans, even those in "minority" groups, that family life would become more similar over the course of the 20th century. Most families were hurt by the Great Depression, although the impact differed greatly according to their previous economic status. Marriage and fertility rates fell during the 1930s for all segments of the population; desertion rates and domestic violence increased. World War II spurred a new patriotism that reached across class and racial lines. It also disrupted or reshuffled families from all social and ethnic groups, albeit in different ways, ranging from the removal of Japanese Americans to internment camps to the surge in divorce rates as GIs came home to wives and children they barely knew (American Social History Project 1992; Coontz 1992; Graff 1987; Mintz and Kellogg 1988).

At the end of the 1940s, for the first time in 60 years, the average age of marriage and parenthood fell, the proportion of marriages ending in divorce dropped, and the birth rate soared. The percentage of women remaining single reached a 100-year low. The percentage of children being raised by breadwinner fathers and homemaker mothers and staying in high school until graduation reached an all-time high. The impression that the United States was becoming more homogeneous was fostered by the intense patriotism and anti-communism of the period, by the decline in the percentage of foreign-born persons in the population, and by powerful new media portrayals of the "typical" American family (Coontz 1992; May 1988; Skolnick 1991).

We now know, of course, that the experience of many families was literally "whited out" in the 1950s. Problems, such as battering, alcoholism, and incest, were swept under the rug. So was the discrimination against African Americans and Hispanics, women, elders, gay men, lesbians, political dissidents, religious minorities, and the handicapped. Despite rising real wages, 30% of American children lived in poverty, a higher figure than today. African American married-couple families had a poverty rate of nearly 50%, and there was daily violence in the cities against African American migrants from the South who attempted to move into white neighborhoods or use public parks and swimming areas (Coontz 1992, 1997; May 1988).

Yet poverty rates fell during the 1950s as new jobs opened up for blue-collar workers and the government gave unprecedented subsidies for family formation, home ownership, and education of children. Forty percent of the young men who started families at the end of World War II were eligible for veterans' benefits. Combined with high rates of unionization, heavy corporate investment in manufacturing plants and equipment, and an explosion of housing construction and financing options, these subsidies gave young families a tremendous economic jump start, created predictable paths out of poverty, and led to unprecedented increases in real wages. Sociologists heralded the end of the class society, and the popular media proclaimed that almost everyone was now "middle class." Even dissidents could feel that social and racial differences were decreasing. The heroic struggle of African Americans against Jim Crow laws, for example, finally compelled the federal government to begin to enforce the Supreme Court ruling against "separate but equal" doctrines.

Despite these perceptions, diversity continued to prevail in American families, and it became more visible during the 1960s, when the civil rights and women's liberation movements exposed the complex varieties of family experiences that lay behind the Ozzie and Harriet images of the time. In the 1970s, a new set of divisions and differences began to surface. The prolonged expansion of real wages and social benefits came to an end in the 1970s. By 1973, real wages were falling for young families in particular, and by the late 1970s, tax revolts and service cuts had eroded the effectiveness of the government's antipoverty programs that had proliferated in the late 1960s and brought child poverty to an all-time low by 1970. A new wave of immigrants began to arrive, but this time the majority were from Asian, Latin American, and Caribbean countries, rather than from Europe. By the 1980s, racial and ethnic diversity was higher than it had been since the early days of colonization, while it was obvious to most Americans that the reports of the death of class difference had been greatly exaggerated (Coontz 1992, 1997; Skolnick 1991).

Race relations were also no longer as clear-cut as in earlier times, despite the persistence of racism. They had evolved "from a strictly enforced caste system," in which there was unequivocal subordination of all blacks to whites to a more complex "system of power relations incorporating elements of social status, economics, and race" (Allen and Farley 1986:285). Although long-term residential segregation and discrimination in employment ensured that the deterioration of the country's inner cities would hit African Americans especially hard, resulting in deepening and concentrated poverty, some professional African Americans made impressive economic progress in the decades after the 1960s, leading to a shift in the coding of racism and often to the rediscovery of white ethnicity by Americans who were seeking to roll back affirmative action (Coontz, Parson, and Raley 1998; Rubin 1994; Wilson 1978, 1996).

In one important way, family life has changed in the same direction among all groups. In 1950 only a quarter of all wives were in the paid labor force, and just 16% of all children had mothers who worked outside the home. By 1991 more than 58% of all married women in the United States, and nearly two-thirds of all married women with children, were in the labor force, and 59% of children, including a majority of preschoolers, had mothers who worked outside the home. Women of color no longer have dramatically higher rates of labor force participation than white women, nor do lower-income and middle-income groups differ substantially in the labor force participation of wives and mothers. Growing numbers of women from all social and racial-ethnic groups now combine motherhood with paid employment, and fewer of them quit work for a prolonged period while their children are young (Spain and Bianchi 1996).

But the convergence in women's participation in the workforce has opened up new areas of divergence in family life. Struggles over the redivision of household labor have created new family conflicts and contributed to rising divorce rates, although they have also led to an increase in egalitarian marriages in which both spouses report they are highly satisfied. Women's new economic independence has combined with other social and cultural trends to produce unprecedented numbers of divorced and unwed parents, cohabitating couples (whether heterosexual, gay, or lesbian), and blended families. Yet each of these family types has different dynamics and consequences, depending on such factors as class, race, and ethnicity (Coontz 1997; Cowan, Cowan, and Kerig 1993; Gottfried and Gottfried 1994; Morales 1990). . . .

Implications of Historical Diversity for Contemporary Families

The amount of diversity in U.S. families today is probably no larger than in most periods of the past. But the ability of so many different family types to demand social recognition and support for their existence is truly unprecedented. Most of the contemporary debate over family forms and values is not occasioned by the *existence* of diversity but by its increasing *legitimation*.

Historical studies of family life can contribute two important points to these debates. First, they make it clear that families have always differed and that no one family form or arrangement can be understood or evaluated outside its particular socioeconomic context and relations with other families. Many different family forms and values have worked (or not worked) for various groups at different times. There is no reason to assume that family forms and practices that differ from those of the dominant ideal are necessarily destructive.

Second, however, history shows that families have always been fragile, vulnerable to rapid economic change, and needful of economic and emotional support from beyond the nuclear family. *All* families experience internal contradictions and conflicts, as well as external pressures and stresses. Celebrating diversity is no improvement over ignoring it unless we analyze the changing social conditions that affect families and figure out how to help every family draw on its potential resources and minimize its characteristic vulnerabilities.

REFERENCES

Adams, D. 1995. *Education for Extinction: American Indians and the Boarding School Experience, 1877–1928.* Lawrence: University Press of Kansas.

Allen, W. and R. Farley. 1986. "The Shifting Social and Economic Tides of Black America, 1950–1980." *American Review of Sociology* 12:277–306.

American Social History Project. 1992. *Who Built America? Working People and the Nation's Economy, Politics, Culture, and Society.* Vols. 1 and 2. New York: Pantheon.

Anderson, K. 1991. *Chain Her by One Foot: The Subjugation of Women in Seventeenth-Century New France.* New York: Routledge.

Axtell, J. 1981. *The Indian Peoples of Eastern America: A Documentary History of the Sexes.* New York: Oxford University Press.

———. 1985. *The Invasion Within: The Contest of Cultures in Colonial America.* New York: Oxford University Press.

———. 1988. *After Columbus: Essays in the Ethnohistory of Colonial North America.* New York: Oxford University Press.

Baca Zinn, M. 1990. "Feminism, Family, and Race in America." *Gender & Society* 4:68–82.

———. 1994. "Feminist Thinking from Racial-Ethnic Families." In *Women of Color in U.S. Society,* edited by M. B. Zinn and B. T. Dill. Philadelphia: Temple University Press.

Baca Zinn, M. and S. Eitzen. 1990. *Diversity in American Families.* New York: Harper-Collins.

Bailey, B. 1989. *From Front Porch to Back Seat: Courtship in Twentieth-Century America.* Baltimore: Johns Hopkins University Press.

Baumrind, D. 1972. "An Exploratory Study of Socialization Effects on Black Children: Some Black-White Comparisons." *Child Development* 43:261–67.

Berkner, L. 1972. "The Stem Family and the Developmental Cycle of the Peasant Household." *American Historical Review* 77:398–418.

Boyd-Franklin, N. and N. Garcia-Preto. 1994. "Family Therapy: The Cases of African American and Hispanic Women." Pp. 239–64 in *Women of Color: Integrating Ethnic and Gender Identities in Psychotherapy,* edited by L. Lomas-Diaz and B. Greene. New York: Guilford Press.

Boydston, J. 1990. *Home and Work: Housework, Wages, and the Ideology of Love in the Early Republic.* New York: Oxford University Press.

Calloway, C. 1997. *New Worlds for All: Indians, Europeans, and the Remaking of Early America.* Baltimore: Johns Hopkins University Press.

Calvert, K. 1992. *Children in the House.* Boston: Northeastern University Press.

Catlin, G. 1973. *Letters and Notes on the Manners, Customs and Conditions of the North American Indians.* New York: Dover.

Collier, J., M. Rosaldo, and S. Yanigasako. 1982. "Is There a Family? New Anthropological Views." Pp. 25–39 in *Rethinking the Family,* edited by B. Thorne. White Plains, NY: Longman.

Coontz, S. 1988. *The Social Origins of Private Life: A History of American Families, 1600–1900.* London: Verso.

———. 1992. *The Way We Never Were: American Families and the Nostalgia Trap.* New York: Basic Books.

———. 1996. "Where Are the Good Old Days?" *Modern Maturity* 34:36–43.

———. 1997. *The Way We Really Are: Coming to Terms with America's Changing Families.* New York: Basic Books.

Coontz, S., M. Parson, and G. Raley, eds. 1998. *American Families: A Multicultural Reader*. New York: Routledge.

Cowan, P., C. Cowan, and P. Kerig, eds. 1993. *Family, Self, and Society: Toward a New Agenda for Family Research*. Hillsdale, NJ: Lawrence Erlbaum.

Cronon, W. 1983. *Changes in the Land: Indians, Colonists, and the Ecology of New England*. New York: Hill & Wang.

D'Emilio, J. and E. Freedman. 1988. *Intimate Matters: A History of Sexuality in America*. New York: Harper & Row.

Dill, B. T. 1998. "Fictive Kin, Paper Sons, and *Compadrazgo*: Women of Color and the Struggle for Family Survival." Pp. 2–19 in *American Families*, edited by S. Coontz, M. Parson, and G. Raley. New York: Routledge.

Duberman, M., M. Vicinus, and G. Chauncey. 1989. *Hidden from History: Reclaiming the Gay and Lesbian Past*. New York: New American Library.

Edwards, L. 1991. "Sexual Violence, Gender, Reconstruction, and the Extension of Patriarchy in Granville County, North Carolina." *North Carolina Historical Review* 68:237–60.

Faderman, L. 1981. *Surpassing the Love of Men: Romantic Friendship and Love between Women from the Renaissance to the Present*. New York: William Morrow.

Franklin, D. 1997. *Ensuring Inequality: The Structural Transformation of the African–American Family*. New York: Oxford University Press.

Gillis, J. 1996. *A World of Their Own Making: Myth, Ritual, and the Quest for Family Values*. New York: Basic Books.

Glenn, E. N. 1983. "Split Household, Small Producer, and Dual Wage-Earner." *Journal of Marriage and the Family* 45:35–46.

———. 1992. "From Servitude to Service Work: Historical Continuities in Racial Division of Paid Reproductive Labor." *Signs* 18:1–43.

Gordon, L. 1988. *Heroes of Their Own Lives: The Politics and History of Family Violence, Boston 1880–1960*. New York: Viking.

Gottfried, A. and A. Gottfried. 1994. Redefining Families: Implications for Children's Development. New York: Plenum.

Graff, H., ed. 1987. *Growing Up in America: Historical Experiences*. Detroit: Wayne State University Press.

Gutierrez, R. 1991. *When Jesus Came, the Corn Mothers Went Away: Marriage, Sexuality, and Power in New Mexico, 1500–1846*. Stanford, CA: Stanford University Press.

Gutman, H. 1976. *The Black Family in Slavery and Freedom, 1750–1925*. New York: Pantheon.

Hareven, T. 1976. "Women and Men: Changing Roles." Pp. 93–118 in *Women and Men: Changing Roles, Relationships and Perceptions Report of a Workshop*, edited by L. A. Cater, A. F. Scott, and W. Martyna. Palo Alto, CA: Aspen Institute for Humanistic Studies.

———. 1987. "Historical Analysis of the Family." In *Handbook of Marriage and the Family*, edited by M. B. Sussman and S. K. Steinmetz. New York: Plenum.

Herdt, G., ed. 1994. *Third Sex, Third Gender: Beyond Sexual Dimorphism in Culture and History*. New York: Zone.

Hernandez, D. 1993. *America's Children: Resources from Family, Government, and the Economy*. New York: Russell Sage Foundation.

Isaacs, R. 1982. *The Transformation of Virginia, 1740–1790*. Chapel Hill: University of North Carolina Press.

Jeater, D. 1993. *Marriage, Perversion, and Power: The Construction of Moral Discourse in Southern Rhodesia, 1894–1930*. New York: Oxford University Press.

Johnson, P. 1978. *A Shopkeeper's Millennium: Society and Revivals in Rochester, New York, 1815–1837*. New York: Hill & Wang.

Jones, J. 1985. *Labor of Love, Labor of Sorrow: Black Women, Work, and the Family from Slavery to the Present*. New York: Basic Books.

———. 1997. *American Work: Four Centuries of Black and White Labor*. New York: W. W. Norton.

Katz, M., M. Doucet, and M. Stern. 1982. *The Social Organization of Industrial Capitalism.* Cambridge, MA: Harvard University Press.

Knight, G. P., L. M. Virdin, and M. Roosa. 1994. "Socialization and Family Correlates of Mental Health Outcomes among Hispanic and Anglo-American Children." *Child Development* 65:212–24.

Leacock, E. 1980. "Montagnais Women and the Program for Jesuit Colonization." In *Women and Colonization: Anthropological Perspectives,* edited by M. Etienne and E. Leacock. New York: Praeger.

Leacock, E. and N. O. Lurie. 1971. *North American Indians in Historical Perspective.* New York: Random House.

Lerner, G. 1969. "The Lady and the Mill Girl: Changes in the Status of Women in the Age of Jackson, 1800–1840." *Midcontinent American Studies Journal* 10:5–14.

May, E. T. 1980. *Great Expectations: Marriage and Divorce in Post-Victorian America.* Chicago: University of Chicago Press.

——. 1988. *Homeward Bound: American Families in the Cold War Era.* New York: Basic Books.

McCurry, S. 1995. *Masters of Small Worlds: Yeoman Households, Gender Relations, and the Political Culture of the Antebellum South Carolina Low Country.* New York: Oxford University Press.

Mindel, C., R. Habenstein, and R. Wright, eds. 1988. *Ethnic Families in America: Patterns and Variations.* New York: Elsevier.

Mintz, S. and S. Kellogg. 1988. *Domestic Revolutions: A Social History of American Family Life.* New York: Free Press.

Modell, J. 1989. *Into One's Own: From Youth to Adulthood in the United States, 1920–1975.* Berkeley: University of California Press.

Morales, E. S. 1990. "Ethnic Minority Families and Minority Gays and Lesbians." Pp. 217–39 in *Homosexuality and Family Relations,* edited by F. W. Bozett and M. B. Sussman. New York: Harrington Park Press.

Mullings, L. 1997. *On Our Own Terms: Race, Class, and Gender in the Lives of African-American Women.* New York: Routledge.

Padgug, R. 1989. "Sexual Matters: Rethinking Sexuality in History." Pp. 54–64 in *Hidden from History: Reclaiming the Gay and Lesbian Past,* edited by M. B. Duberman, M. Vicinus, and G. Chauncey Jr. New York: New American Library.

Peters, V. 1995. *Women of the Earth Lodges: Tribal Life on the Plains.* North Haven, CT: Archon Books.

Peterson, J. 1993. "Generalized Extended Family Exchange: A Case from the Philippines." *Journal of Marriage and the Family* 55:570–84.

Roediger, D. 1988. *The Wages of Whiteness: Race and the Making of the American Working Class.* London: Verso.

Rotundo, A. 1993. *American Manhood.* New York: Basic Books.

Rubin, L. 1994. *Families on the Fault Line.* New York: Basic Books.

Ryan, M. 1981. *Cradle of the Middle Class: The Family in Oneida County, New York.* New York: Cambridge University Press.

Sanchez, G. 1993. *Becoming Mexican-American: Ethnicity, Culture, and Identity in Chicano Los Angeles, 1900–1945.* New York: Oxford University Press.

Schnarch, B. 1992. "Neither Man nor Woman: Berdache–A Case for Non-Dichotomous Gender Construction." *Anthropologica* 34:106–21.

Skolnick, A. 1991. *Embattled Paradise: The American Family in an Age of Uncertainty.* New York: Basic Books.

Smith-Rosenberg, C. 1985. *Disorderly Women: Visions of Gender in Victorian America.* New York: Oxford University Press.

Snipp, M. 1989. *American Indians: The First of This Land.* New York: Russell Sage Foundation.

Spain, D. and S. M. Bianchi. 1996. *Balancing Act: Motherhood, Marriage, and Employment among American Women.* New York: Russell Sage Foundation.

Spicer, E. H. 1962. *Cycles of Conquest: The Impact of Spain, Mexico, and the United States on the Indians of the Southwest, 1533–1960.* Tucson: University of Arizona Press.

Stack, C. 1993. "Cultural Perspectives on Child Welfare." Pp. 344–49 in *Family Matters: Readings on Family Lives and the Law,* edited by M. Minow. New York: New Press.

Stevenson, B. E. 1996. *Life in Black and White: Family and Community in the Slave South.* New York: Oxford University Press.

Strasser, S. 1982. *Never Done: A History of American Housework.* New York: Pantheon.

Wilson, W. J. 1978. *The Declining Significance of Race: Blacks and Changing American Institutions.* Chicago: University of Chicago.

———. 1996. *When Work Disappears: The World of the New Urban Poor.* New York: Alfred A. Knopf.

Williams, R. 1976. *Keywords: A Vocabulary of Culture and Society.* New York: Oxford University Press.

Williams, W. L. 1986. *The Spirit and the Flesh: Sexual Diversity in American Indian Culture.* Boston: Beacon Press.

Zaretsky, E. 1982. "The Place of the Family in the Origins of the Welfare State." Pp. 188–224 in *Rethinking the Family,* edited by B. Thorne. White Plains, NY: Longman.

6

BLACK FAMILIES
Beyond Revisionist Scholarship

SHIRLEY A. HILL

In form, African American families have been some of the most flexible, adaptable, and inclusive kinship institutions in America. In function, they have been among the most accepting and nurturing of children, and the most supportive of adults.

— NIARA SUDARKASA[1]

The latter half of the twentieth century witnessed a proliferation of revisionist scholarship on African American families, most of it aimed at challenging negative stereotypes and images and highlighting their strengths and diversity. Despite this work, the century began and ended with black people at the center of the country's most contentious family issue: the escalating number

Shirley A. Hill, "Black Families: Beyond Revisionist Scholarship" from *Black Intimicies: A Gender Perspective on Families and Relationships.* Reprinted with the permission of AltaMira Press.

of single-mother families formed outside marriage, living in poverty, and dependent on welfare.

By the close of the century, the significant minority of black families historically headed by single mothers clearly had turned into a sizable majority, a trend made even more alarming by the growing separation of marriage and parenthood, the economic decline of urban areas, the demise of extended family support, the growing number of black children placed in foster care, and an unprecedented expansion of the welfare rolls. By 2000, fewer than one-third of all African American women were married and living with a spouse, and a significant majority of black children—nearly 70 percent—were being born outside marriage.[2] Nonmarital childbearing was especially associated with welfare dependency for black women who, in the year prior to the elimination of the Aid to Families with Dependent Children (AFDC) program, comprised 40 percent of all welfare beneficiaries.[3] Never-married single mothers exemplified the concerns of political conservatives decrying a loss of "family values," and so wedded were race, poverty, and welfare in the minds of many Americans that the black family was often seen as consisting of a poor, single mother with several children, fathered by several different men. Claims by policymakers that a decline in family values and overly generous welfare benefits were fostering higher rates of single motherhood fueled support for ending the more than sixty-year-old AFDC program, which was originally designed to enable mothers to care for their own children, and for implementing new "workfare" (employment) and "wedfare" (marriage) policies.

The current focus on welfare and single-mother families represents the latest chapter in a long debate aimed at understanding why African Americans—or at least significant numbers of them—seem unable or unwilling to bring their sexual, marital, and family norms into compliance with mainstream cultural ideologies. While white slave owners had garnered immense economic profits for more than two centuries by insisting that enslaved black people disregard dominant family structures and ideologies, emancipation created the need to reorganize and stabilize the agricultural labor force, and it thus ushered in the first campaign to get African Americans married. The extent of their compliance to the marriage mandate became the focal point of scholarly work on black families, especially as the sociological study of families blossomed in the early 1900s. By then, most scholars had uncritically accepted the new ideology of marriage based on free choice and romantic love, and the family ideally as nuclear in structure with a breadwinner–homemaker division of labor. White, middle-class families were praised for their modernity and suitability for the new industrial economy, and the handful of researchers who turned their lens beyond that model of family saw only disorder, dysfunction, and pathology.

The early social scientists who unwittingly proffered a social deficit perspective on African American families were usually liberal scholars who failed to question the validity of dominant family structures. For them, the mission was to show that slavery and racism had crippled black families, leaving them with too few resources to form strong families and fostering the creation of matriarchal families. Indeed, marriage was unlikely to offer black women the option of full-time domesticity or economic security, as the southern sharecropping system demanded the labor of all family members.[4] Sharecropping and poverty diminished the resiliency of black families, but few championed decent jobs for black men as the solution to the dilemma, nor were there calls to exclude black women from their economic roles. Northward migration enhanced the number and visibility of single-mother families, and critics of "sexually promiscuous" black women who had children out of wedlock and ran their own families became more vocal. Not until the civil rights era was the "matriarchy" theme put to rest by revisionist scholars; however, much of their work has failed to stand the test of time.

In this [reading], I present a postmodern gender perspective on the cultural and structural forces that historically affected the marriage and family decision making of black women. I contend that, at least for a significant minority of black women, the cultural and economic resources they had garnered during slavery, their sense of autonomy and independence, and the viable female-centered families they had formed led them to resist efforts to force them to marry. During the post–civil rights era, the loss of these resources and traditions, due to factors such as public policies, racial integration, class polarization, and patriarchal leanings, fostered a proliferation of impoverished single-mother families that became the target of welfare reform initiatives.

Objectives

This [reading] has three major objectives. The first is to bring a gender analysis to the study of African American families by focusing on the active, decision-making roles of black women in family formation. I maintain that while the concept of gender is prominent and well developed in most feminist work on families, it has remained in its nascent stages in research on African American families. . . .

While the substantial focus on single-mother families introduced the issue of gender to black family studies and produced a rich literature on the experiences of African American women, one rarely finds even a single chapter in black family books devoted to a discussion of gender; in fact, the word *gender* does not even appear in most indices. For the most part, research on black families has either praised the strength or criticized the behavior of poor single mothers or highlighted the ability of more affluent black women to combine their work and family roles with social activism. In some cases, black feminists have met the contention of families as a source of oppression for women with the reprisal that they can also be sources of support and encouragement—although the families they speak of are rarely the nuclear, gender-ordered ones criticized by feminists. African American scholars have also noted that being a full-time homemaker can be a cherished role for black women, as economic necessity has often forced them to work outside the home.[5] Considerable energy has been spent debating whether black women are matriarchal, simply strong, or victims of multiple oppression—yet the focus on these issues has done little to promote an understanding of how gender, and the resources and power associated with it, has affected their family and marriage decision making.

The second objective of this chapter is to provide an analytical overview of the history of black families and bring a gender lens to the two dominant perspectives—the legacy of slavery thesis and the revisionist approach. In addition, I articulate a third "postmodern perspective" that draws on themes from more recent research on the history of black families. While both the legacy of slavery and revisionist perspectives imply at least a modicum of support for diverse family structures, their central thrust has been to accept the legitimacy of hegemonic family and gender structures and explain why blacks have failed to embrace them. . . .

I describe this analysis as postmodern as it rejects the idea of uniformity in the family ideologies and experiences of black people, unmasks the gender experiences of women, and focuses on that segment of the black population that actively resisted compliance with family and gender systems that were foreign to their traditions and inconsistent with their status and resources. It draws on recent strands of research that show what slaves had in common was forced labor and a legal status of property, beyond that, they varied greatly in the marriage patterns, work demands, and gender relationships. While studies of black families have alternately castigated their deficiencies and trumpeted their resiliency, the objective here is to understand black women as active agents in their own lives who made decisions to protect themselves, their children, and their cultural and material resources by resisting conformity to dominant family norms. Thus, despite formidable forces urging them to do so, black women were often unwilling to forsake the kinship systems that evolved over centuries of slavery in favor of male-dominated marriage, not simply because of economic and racial barriers, but also because doing so was inconsistent with their cultural values and resources. The survival of black families has hinged on their ability to create a variety of family structures, and, drawing on their cultural and economic resources, they did so.

Single-mother and extended families have a long tradition among African Americans; however, the post–civil rights era saw a remarkable decline in the strength and well-being of those families. The epidemics of joblessness, gang violence, drug abuse, nonmarital childbearing, and welfare dependency in black urban areas mocked the implication of revisionist thought that removing racial barriers and creating greater opportunity would strengthen black families and bring them into conformity with the dominant societal norm.

Thus, the third and final objective of this [reading] is to explore the decline in black families, especially those headed by single mothers, in an era where racial integration and equal employment policies have diluted racism and racial barriers to success. Structural theorists explained the problem in terms of a loss in the availability of industrial jobs for young African American men, while many embracing a cultural approach emphasized the changing and even pathological values of disadvantaged urban black people. I contend that a more complex array of factors have challenged the strength of single-mother families, including growing class diversity of black people and the decline in the traditional authority of black women.

The Legacy of Slavery Thesis

> *Whatever social organization may have prevailed in their native Africa, whatever family arrangements, forms, and usages found in the mores of the preexistent cultures, these were stripped from, or eventually lost, to the Negroes brought to America.*
>
> —S. A. QUEEN AND R. W. HABENSTEIN[6]

Family sociology emerged during the early 1900s, as concern over the disruptive impact of industrialization on family life gave way to ideologies of the modern, nuclear family as ideally suited to meet the needs of the new economy. Prior to the 1950s, however, many Americans lacked the economic resources to create such families, and racial and economic forces made such families even more elusive for black people. Nevertheless, racist ideologies attributing African Americans' inability to abide by these family traditions to their biological and moral inferiority were prevalent. In a series of studies initiated in the 1930s, E. Franklin Frazier worked tirelessly to redirect the focus of theories from racial inferiority to an analysis of the impact of slavery on black families. While Africans did not arrive on the shores of the Americas bereft of family traditions, slavery had taken a devastating toll on those traditions. Slavery had precluded the right of black people to marry legally, resulted in the sale of spouses and family members, undermined men as authority figures and providers in their families, and forced women to take on demeaning sexual and economic roles.

From the beginning of slave trade, ethnocentrism and the prospect of economic gain undoubtedly led the first white Europeans who encountered Africans to see them as savages and to misunderstand their family system, and these observations grew in significance as the slave trade flourished. Slavery destroyed the African heritage of blacks, claims Kenneth Stamps, and left them living in "cultural chaos" since the family patterns of whites were "meaningless and unintelligible" to them.[7] Moreover, the definition of slaves as property was one of many efforts to negate their humanity and deny the significance of their personal and family lives. Slaves' property status precluded them from entering a legal marriage contract, as the law recognized no form of marriage among slaves, "whether they 'take up' with each other by expression of their owners, or from mere impulse of nature, or in obedience to the command to 'multiply and replenish the earth.'"[8] With no standing before the law, slave marriages could be and were ended at any time at the discretion of slave owners.

Matriarchal Women and the Insignificant Black Male

Frazier acknowledges that slavery had given rise to both two-parent and single-mother families. While two-parent (male-headed) families appeared to function well, with some even achieving middle-class status, Frazier devotes most of his attention to single-mother or matriarchal families. Poor, female-headed families, Frazier argues, had their origins in the sale and separation of slaves, the definition of the black family as a mother and her children, and sexual relationships between female slaves and their owners. He understands that these maternal families had often functioned quite well in the rural South yet were being increasingly undermined by destabilizing forces such as northward migration. Implied in Frazier's analysis of the "black matriarchate," as well as the work of other legacy of slavery theorists, is the idea that slavery either abolished or severely curtailed dominant patriarchal traditions. One result, according to Frazier, was an unusual boldness and strength among black women, who often defied white authority in ways that black men would never have gotten away with. "Neither economic necessity nor tradition had instilled in her the spirit of subordination to masculine authority," writes Frazier, who describes these black women as playing a dominant role in families and seeking sexual satisfaction outside marriage.[9]

A similar theme is present in the work of Jessie Bernard, who argues that slavery had given black women an "unnatural superiority" over black men. Slavery was a more flagrant violation of masculinity than femininity, according to Bernard, as "enforced subordination and subservience was not so far out of line with the Western world's definition of a 'woman's place.'"[10] Highlighting the general sassiness of black women, for example, she notes that in matters of marriage, it "didn't pay, really, [for slave owners] to tangle with those spirited women. If they wanted a man, they seem usually to have got him; if they did not want him, it was . . . hard to force him on them."[11]

The flip side of the strong black women premise was the notion that slavery had deprived black men of their masculinity and rendered them irrelevant to family life. Slavery controlled the economic and reproductive labor of men and women; it denied men the right to provide for, protect, or be recognized as the heads of their families; and forced women to prioritize productive labor over their domestic roles. In doing so, it embodied numerous assaults of patriarchal families, including prohibiting slaves from entering legal marriage contracts, the sexual exploitation of black women by slave owners, the provision of separate housing for black spouses, the definition of black families as comprised of mothers and their children, and the sale of family members—all arrangements that allowed slave owners to maximize the exploitation of their slaves. Because black men could not protect their families from the abuses of slave masters, wrote one historian, some vowed either never to marry or to marry women from other plantations, as they did not want to "be forced to watch as she was beaten, insulted, raped, overworked, or starved without being able to protect her."[12]

Patriarchal traditions were also undermined by the frequent meddling of slave owners into the affairs of black families. To varying degrees, slave owners governed the marriage decisions and relationships, child-bearing and child-rearing practices, and the economic well-being of black families. They sometimes intervened heavily into the affairs of black families, whipping slaves for domestic discord and, ironically, for violating monogamous standards of sexuality.[13]

In Search of Freedom: Emancipation and Northward Migration

Innumerable tasks undoubtedly faced newly emancipated African Americans, not the least of which was survival in a society where racism was thoroughly entrenched and few were willing to hire, feed, or clothe black people. Emancipation diminished whatever stability slave families had achieved, as armies invaded and disrupted plantation life, setting thousands of black people adrift and leading many to abandon their spouses and children.[14] Although many African Americans had fought in the Civil War and had high aspirations for freedom, black men lost many of the skilled occupations they had held during slavery and, frequently charged with vagrancy, rape, and crime, faced an increased risk of being lynched, incarcerated, or forced into labor contracts with whites.[15] Most black people wound up on farms and plantations working under the sharecropping system, as the potential loss of their free labor was a major threat to the southern economy. For black men and women alike, the decision not to work after slavery was nearly impossible, as economic necessity and the power of whites forbade it.[16] To ensure an adequate supply of workers, some states created and enforced labor contracts between black workers and white landowners, justifying them on the premise that employment was essential to the transition from slavery to citizenship.[17]

The need for cheap labor also made it difficult for black parents to gain or retain custody of their children. Some states passed laws allowing former slave owners to "indenture" (or essentially reenslave) children under the age of twelve if their parents were either unmarried or unemployed.[18] Indeed, policymakers during the late nineteenth century often argued that children were generally better off living in orphan institutions than with poor, "immoral" parents, and, since black parents were often unemployed and unmarried, their parental rights were most likely to be under assault. Although these economic and family policies allowed some whites to profit from the absence of legal marriages among blacks, the abolition of slavery for the most part sparked a major campaign to get blacks married, as the long-standing patterns of non-marital sexuality and childbearing that had served slave owners well were now seen as threatening.

The hope of escaping the racial caste system of the South and securing job opportunities fueled a massive northward migration of African

Americans during the late 1800s and first half of the twentieth century. While the fortunes of a significant segment of the black population had risen after the abolition of slavery, these gains proved short-lived when Reconstruction ended, racial segregation became the law of the land, and southern blacks were disenfranchised and displaced from many jobs. By 1890, 90 percent of African Americans still lived in the rural South, and most of them worked in agriculture; less than a century later, 90 percent had migrated to urban areas, often in the North and West.[19]

As Carole Marks has explained, the active recruitment activities of northern industrialists played a major role in orchestrating this mass migration. Faced with a disruption in the flow of immigrants from Europe during World War I and growing labor unrest in factories, industrialists used black workers to perform low-wage, dirty work and to serve as strikebreakers. Black women were also actively recruited, sometimes signing domestic labor contracts in exchange for their transportation expenses and taking on jobs as cooks, laundresses, and maids that were crucial in supporting their families.

Black women often had an added incentive to migrate northward, as they were fleeing from the adversities of marriage and family life and sexual exploitation by black and white men.[20] While their maternal families and extended kin networks often functioned well in the South, the women who headed them were locked into low-wage agricultural and domestic jobs that were increasingly waning, and they were excluded from the benefits of social welfare programs. The northward migration of poor single mothers created a "moral panic" among black leaders in urban areas and state authorities, who often saw poor single black women as sexually and socially dangerous,[21] yet most survived by acquiring low-wage domestic or factory jobs and relying on the support of family networks. Migration brought higher wages, but northern families often insisted on live-in domestics,[22] making the work of black women more labor-intensive and keeping them away from their own families. As Jacqueline Jones has noted, in some cases their work in the homes of white families led to a re-creation of the mistress–slave roles that had existed under slavery. More often, black female domestic workers were exposed to the risk of being raped by employers, and they constantly instructed each other on "how to run, or always not be in the house with the white man or big sons."[23] "No white man had to fear prosecution for sexually attacking a black women," write Hines and Thompson, but "all black women, of whatever class or reputation, had to fear sexual assault, exploitation, and rape."[24]

Black women found their hopes for racial justice, economic advancement, and a more stable family life in the "promised land" of the North diminished by the racial oppression. Even the prospects for marriage were few due to black men's confinement in poor-paying jobs and their increasing criminalization for an array of petty offenses that dramatically increased their rates of incarceration during the early 1900s.[25] Abysmal housing, poor sanitation, malnutrition, and demanding, high-risk jobs increased rates of mortality and morbidity among African Americans, especially rates of infant and childhood mortality.[26]

Thus, as Frazier points out, northward migration further undermined the two-parent family. As blacks moved north, negative portrayals of single black women as sexually degenerate, the rise in single-mother families in urban areas, and greater access by black mothers to government welfare policies all conspired in creating the image of the pathological, matriarchal black family.

Migration and concentration in urban areas significantly increased the visibility of black people, while the dashed hopes for racial and economic equality gradually ignited their political consciousness. The racial unrest that began to foment in the early 1900s gradually turned into an organized protest movement, as blacks became more openly critical of racial inequality. Yet in 1965, an official government policy report on black families issued by Senator Moynihan revived Frazier's matriarchy thesis by implying that female-headed families were thwarting black progress. Moynihan focused on the growing number of single-mother families in urban areas and saw them as the result of a slavery system that was "profoundly different from," and "indescribably worse than, any recorded servitude, ancient or modern."[27] Though issued at the height of the civil rights movement, the now-infamous study suggested that policy should focus on strengthening black families rather than eliminating racism, segregation, and poverty.

Although he focused on single-mother families, Moynihan also repeatedly recognized growing class diversity among black families, emphatically dismissed genetic explanations of black poverty, and championed greater economic opportunity for black men. He argued that while there was nothing inherently wrong with matriarchal families, they caused problems because they were out of step with mainstream society. Whether for practical or ideological reasons, he equated strong families with male-headship and argued that black children were often being neglected by employed mothers.

The Revisionist Perspective

Black women shared the doubtful advantage of greater equality with black men — usually the equal privilege of working with hoes and axes in the tobacco, corn, and grain fields.

— L. WALSH[28]

If slavery bred strong women, it hardly emasculated black men.

— P. MORGAN[29]

The legacy of slavery and the black matriarch thesis deflected attention from the growing demand for racial justice by castigating black families as pathological and failing to abide by the family values of other Americans, thus sparking a genre of myth-dispelling research by revisionist scholars determined to provide a more accurate view of the black family. In his 1968 book *Black Families in White America*, Andrew Billingsley drew on functionalist theory to explain the adaptive nature of African American family structures, arguing that they should be evaluated based on their viability and survival rather than their stability and/or conformity to white cultural norms. Robert Hill delineated gender role flexibility, religiosity, a strong achievement orientation, and resilient kinship bonds as the particular strengths of black families. Similarly, Carol Stack provided a vivid ethnographic portrait of black, single mothers that made a lasting contribution to our understanding of the complex networks of exchange and reciprocity they used to survive. Other scholars criticized the seeming inordinate focus on poor, single-mother families as perpetuating a distorted, stereotypical image of the "typical" black family. Noting that most black families were neither poor nor headed by single women, researchers such as Charles Willie, Bart Landry, John Scanzoni, Walter Allen, and Harriette McAdoo extended the research lens to middle- and working-class black families, usually pointing out that they were quite similar to their white counterparts. Speaking of the diversity of black families, McAdoo contended that, "contrary to what many people seem to think, there is no such thing as 'the' African American family."[30]

While revisionist research constituted a thorough reassessment of black families, such as recasting single-mother families as strong and functional and highlighting the diversity of black families, its most enduring legacy has been to reject the notion that slavery had destroyed the black family. John Blassingame became the first of many scholars to document the strength and importance of slave families:

> The family, while it had no legal existence in slavery, was in actuality one of the most important survival mechanisms for the slave. In his family he found companionship, love, sexual gratification, sympathetic understanding of his sufferings; he learned how to avoid punishment, to cooperate with other blacks, and to maintain his self-esteem.[31] . . .

Thus, slaves were allowed to experience some of the gratifications of courtship, marriage, and family life, as such relationships fostered loyalties and boosted the morale and stability of the slave population. These factors became especially vital to the survival of slavery after 1807, when importing additional slaves into the United States was officially prohibited. While the family lives of slaves were scarcely allowed to interfere with their profitability, the few prerogatives they received were shaped by gender.

Rediscovering the Patriarchal Slave Family

> *An accurate portrait of the African women in bondage must debunk the myth of the matriarchate.*
>
> — ANGELA DAVIS[32]

Notable in the work of revisionist scholars was the rediscovery of patriarchy, with the linchpin being Herbert Gutman's argument that a majority of enslaved black families living on plantations were composed of two parents. Other research has contributed to constructing the patriarchal black family by emphasizing how male prerogatives shaped patterns of courtship, marriage, freedom of mobility, and occupational diversity. Historian P. Morgan, for example, finds evidence of patriarchy in the fact that, as customary in some African traditions, husbands were often seven to eleven years older than their wives, thus strengthening male-dominant marriages. Men usually initiated courtship and proposed marriage, and they were often described by slave owners as domineering husbands.[33] Families were organized along gender lines, with slave women doing most of the domestic chores and caring for children, and men often buttressing their status in the family by providing additional material resources. The greater geographic mobility of black men also hinted at male privilege: Compared to black women, men traveled more, either to run errands for their masters or to visit families on other plantations, and naming practices often favored men. Black masculinity was also expressed through social protest; for example, while there is ample evidence that women were also involved, men dominated when it came to organizing slave rebellions and conspiracies.[34]

Work assignments and other privileges granted slaves were also organized along the lines of gender, usually giving men greater privileges than women. Black men, for example, were given opportunities for more varied jobs, while women spent more time in monotonous drudgery. The greater occupational diversity and training available to black men is illustrated by data from South Carolina showing that by the late 1700s, nearly 25 percent of rural slave men worked outside the fields, compared to only 5 percent of rural slave women. Not only was the occupational structure for women narrow, but nearly all skilled and privileged positions were held by men.[35] Their occupational roles often enabled them to provide special gifts for their wives and children:

> Slave ironworkers in the Chesapeake purchased small luxuries and domestic items for their wives. During the 1730s, one skilled hand . . . used his overwork pay to purchase a bed, two blankets, and a rug for his wife and children. In 1797, a slave named Phil, who worked at John Blair's foundry in Virginia, bought shoe leather and seven and half yards of ribbon for his wife. Even ordinary field hands could provide for their womenfolk.[36]

Thus, enslaved black men made symbolic and important economic contributions to their families, as patriarchal traditions enabled them to claim the most prestigious occupations available to blacks and to be recognized as authorities in their families.

Free black families also took advantage of a gendered labor system that favored men, according to Thomas Bogger, who studied the family and occupational structures of free blacks in Norfolk, Virginia, during the mid-1800s. During this era, black men were listed as employed in nearly fifty different occupations, compared to only nine for black women. A slight majority of black families were male headed, despite a significant shortage of men, and only 25 percent of free black women worked outside the home—all of whom were married to men with low-paying jobs.

Drawing on the West African legacy of black families further strengthened the revisionist account of patriarchy, often by showing that male dominance could exist even when women had strong productive and family roles.

Most prominent among those scholars linking black families to their African ancestry are Afrocentric theorists such as Wade Nobles, who has argued that the structure and function of the black family is "ultimately traceable to its African value system and/or some modification thereof."[37] That value system described patriarchy, polygyny, extended families, respect for the elderly, the primacy of mother–child relationships, and women as economic providers as characteristic African family life, and it noted that all were practiced and even reinforced to some extent during slavery. Despite their economic roles, African women were subordinated to men in virtually every aspect of life, from denial of the best food to enforced sexual chastity to female circumcision.[38] Polygyny itself is usually indicative of male domination, although the short supply of black women, especially during the early decades of slavery, curtailed the practice and heightened the status and importance of black women. Some have argued black women were less likely to be slated for slavery because of the value of their work roles in West African society.[39] Overall, however, the dual family and economic roles of African American women were not seen as diminishing the significance of men in families.

Feminist Analysis of the Family

Despite its revival of black masculinity and implicit support for two-parent families, the work of revisionist scholars often dovetailed nicely with the feminist critique of families. Gender as socially constructed based on economic factors and patriarchy was the cornerstone of modern feminist thought, and the experiences of African American families offered ample evidence of this contention. Barrie Thorne summarized feminist family policies as endorsing a broader array of sexual and household arrangements as families, supporting women's right to abortion, and ending male authority, female dependency, and the relegation of nurturing to women in families.[40]

Claims by revisionist scholars that black families took a diversity of forms, that female-headed families could be strong and viable, that black women had effectively combined labor market and family work, and that black marriages were based on relative equality between men and women embodied much of the feminist vision for families. Black feminists expanded the revisionist focus on racial oppression as shaping African American families by placing it within the larger framework of intersectionality theory. Rose Brewer, for example, asserted that poor, single-mother families could not be understood unless historically grounded in the "social construction of a racist/sexist social order," noting that

> gender, race, ideology, culture, state, and economy operate simultaneously and interactively in the family formation and change process. Capitalist racial patriarchy profoundly shapes male and female relations generally but is also conflated with cultural and ideological realities. I mean by capitalist racial patriarchy a structure of White male-dominated social arrangements. These institutional arrangements severely disadvantage Black women, men, and children.[41]

Rethinking the Revisionist Paradigm

Born of the civil rights era struggle to control images of the black family and contest racist explanations for the proliferation of single-mother families among African Americans, revisionists highlighted the strengths and survival of black families, rejected the notion that most were headed by single mothers, and eventually challenged the dominant paradigm contending that slavery had destroyed black families. They essentially argued that African Americans had conformed to the dominant family model as best they could and sought to refute the theme of matriarchal families with evidence that slavery did not thwart the patriarchal inclinations of black men. Yet this claim itself, advanced to redeem black families from the accusation of deliberately ignoring dominant family conventions, offers significant implicit support for the superiority of two-parent families and introduces a "masculinist bias" into the study of black families. Moreover, attributing their family structures solely to racism denies any active decision making on the part of African Americans in assessing the value of white cultural family forms.

In many cases the revisionist perspective also inadvertently produced a more "humane" version of slavery, countering evidence of the harsh realities of slave life with the notion that it honored or at least sought to sustain the family ties of slaves. Genovese wrote that slaveholders "rarely if ever denied the moral content of the [marriage] relationship" between their slaves, and credited them with often showing "tender concern for black women who suffered abuse from their husbands."[42] He additionally claimed that slaves were fed well and that married life served effectively to keep the white sexual aggression to a minimum, contributing to a revisionist view of slavery recently described by Wilma A. Dunaway as more of a "Disney script than scholarly research."[43]

Perhaps more important, the notion that black people managed to maintain a reasonable semblance of the two-parent family during slavery produced a monolithic picture of the black family during slavery. Postrevisionist historians, criticizing earlier work as drawing too heavily on documents from large plantations, have produced a much more complex picture of the family lives of black people during slavery. Moving beyond debates over matriarchy and patriarchy, they have sought to show how an array of factors, such as region and size of plantation, affected black families. Dunaway, for example, criticizes the dominant revisionist paradigm as having neglected the study of family life on small plantations, although 88 percent of slaves resided in locations where there were fewer than fifty slaves.[44] In doing so, she argues that revisionists have overstated the prevalence of two-parent families and exaggerated the agency of slaves in resisting family breakup. On small plantations, enslaved black people experienced more family separations, greater brutality, and more sexual exploitation. The following postmodern perspective builds on emerging research by highlighting how structural forces gave rise to cultural traditions and resources that often empowered African American women and led to a great deal of activism and autonomy in their family decisions.

A Postmodern Gender Perspective

In *Cane River*, Lalita Tademy weaves a wealth of archival data into an elo-
quent, poignant story of her African American foremothers that dates back to
the 1800s. These four valiant black women—Elizabeth, Suzette, Philomene,
and Emily—endured the numerous indignities of slavery on plantations in
central Louisiana where they often worked side-by-side with their white slave
owners. Seldom able to marry or sustain marriages with freely chosen partners or to control their own sexuality, all had children fathered by white men
they were unable to marry, yet they mustered the courage to manipulate their
dire life situations and their relationships with white male partners to their
own advantage. Tademy writes that her research led her to challenge everything she thought she knew about slavery, race, class, and Louisiana, where
blacks in some areas were as likely as whites to own slaves. Slavery undoubtedly played itself out in a multitude of unique dramas, and Tademy's focus on
the family decision making of her female ancestors stands in sharp contrast to
male-centered revisionist accounts of black enslaved families doing their best
to mirror their white counterparts. It highlights the saliency of female bonds
and the agency of black women in forming families, and it resonates with
postrevisionist research showing that slavery produced a diversity of black
families, not simply because of the inclinations and whims of individual slave
owners but also because it evolved differently based on region and economic
factors.

The impact of slavery on the black family structure, argues Donna
Franklin in *Ensuring Inequality*, depended on the plantation's size, work organization, and economic solvency. African customs, restrictive sexual norms, and
stable slave marriages were more characteristic of large plantations, where
there were more potential marital partners, less likelihood of slaves being sold,
and greater segregation between whites and blacks. Slaves living on smaller
plantations had fewer marital partners, more interracial interaction with their
white owners, and were more likely to be sold to resolve economic crises. On
these plantations, early sexuality, teenage childbearing, master–slave sexual
relationships, and single-mother families were common. Moreover, while
revisionist writers have often drawn on the systematic records of large plantation owners,[45] the dominant image of slaves living on large, wealthy plantations is countered by the fact that by 1860, the 10 percent of whites still owning slaves had an average of seven to nine slaves each.[46] Tademy's story stands
as a case in point to the diversity of family experiences among slaves. Her
female ancestors lived on a small plantation where they worked alongside
their owners and faced the constant threat of family members being sold and
of coercive sexual encounters with white men.

In this postmodern gender perspective on African American families, I try
to illustrate some of the diversity in black women's responses to freedom
and the opportunity (and often demand) that they marry, based on their own
appraisal of their resources and their active decision making. Theorists agree
that blacks were neither allowed to enter legal marriages during slavery nor

guaranteed that the unions they formed would not be separated by sale, yet revisionists insist that emancipation produced heroic efforts by black people to legalize marriages, and they have marshaled evidence in support of that claim. Missing from their work, however, has been a critical analysis of the relevance of the marriage contract to the newly freed blacks, the coercive state policies and class politics that urged marriage, the fragility of black marital unions, the frequent failure by early census takers to determine if couples living together were married, and the resources of African American women that militated against their entry into patriarchal marriages. Marriage and patriarchy are essentially universal institutions and are "naturalized" as the bases for family life; so, it is certainly not surprising that scholars have found substantial ideological support for both among black people. Still, neither the African heritage of black people nor centuries of American slavery had prepared them for the marriage-centered family arrangements of mainstream society.

By forbidding legal and/or permanent marital ties among black people, slavery curtailed access to the rights and benefits of marriage but also sanctioned the separation of sex, marriage, and childbearing. It diminished patriarchal power among enslaved African men, yet revisionists have found that male prerogatives existed in that they initiated courtship and marriage, married younger women, enjoyed more freedom of movement, engaged in a broader array of occupations, contributed economically to their families, led rebellions, and expected their wives to perform the bulk of the domestic work. Less, however, has been said about how the resources garnered by black women during slavery may have thwarted their interest in marriage. Slavery not only reinforced West African traditions that valued women's economic and reproductive work, privileged the mother–child relationship, and focused on female-centered kinship ties and blood ties more than marriage; it also equipped black women with a sense of autonomy and authority that did not bode well for marriage. Thus, while the freedom to formalize marriages after slavery ended undoubtedly held appeal for many African Americans, I argue that black women had often garnered important gender, cultural, and economic resources that precluded a simple rush to get married.

Despite its romanticization and cultural sanctification, marriage is a quintessentially gendered institution, embodying expectations of male dominance and female subservience inherently at odds with the race and class position accorded many African Americans and their long-standing cultural traditions. These factors led to an abiding nonmarriage ethos among a significant number of black women and a tendency among women who did marry to define their marital roles differently. Resistance to families that relegated women to a dependent status and the nonmarriage cultural ethos that emerged among blacks reflect the tension between dominant families ideologies and the cultural norms and economic resources of African Americans. This resistance was strengthened by the fact that enslaved black women had often garnered significant tangible and intangible resources that afforded them some autonomy in their family decision making.

Most important of these were their important economic roles, as many had performed labor as arduous and valuable as that of men. Despite a gender division of labor, slavery had equally appropriated the productive work of black men and women, treating them as "almost equal, independent units of labor."[47] The importance of their labor is reflected in the fact that by the mid-1600s Virginia had declared the labor of black women as "tithable" (or taxable), making an important distinction between the labor of white female indentured servants and African women by defining the latter as having the productive capacity equivalent to that of men, and imposing a special tax on free black men who married them.[48]

In addition to their work roles, black women's sexuality, reproductive work, communal-oriented family systems, and closer association in the intimate, daily activities of white family life were important sources of power. Jacqueline Jones's seminal work on the historic labor roles of black women found that most black women worked in the fields, but those performing domestic work often had a higher status and gained more cultural capital through their contact with the plantation mistress, whose "privileged status . . . rested squarely on the backs of their female slaves."[49] Domestic service gave black women greater access to food and other resources than was available to those who worked in fields, which they used to help their own families and communities. House servants were often privy to vital information about most issues or events on the plantation and were intimately involved in caring for and nurturing white children. Most legendary was the image of the "mammy" — the black woman who held a vital position in the white family by performing domestic work, child care, and generally ruling the household with a "rod of iron." Deborah Gray White has described the stereotypical mammy "as a woman who could do anything, and do it better than anyone else. Because of her expertise in all domestic matters, she was the premier house servant and all others were her subordinates."[50] Few male roles provided black men similar entry into white society or comparable respect and authority.

The communal organization of family work among slaves also empowered black women by giving them the opportunity to socialize and build relationships with each other. Sex-segregated living situations in Africa were replicated in the United States, in that women worked together and often shared child rearing and domestic work. In many cases, spousal visits were confined to the weekends, so black men were only marginally involved in the daily work of family life. Older black women were especially relied on for child care and support, as well as for their practical and philosophical wisdom. Their special knowledge of the use of roots and herbs in healing earned them power and respect as conjurers, and they were often seen as usurping the position of white physicians by delivering babies.[51] For many African American women, family was more about sharing the work of feeding and rearing children with other women than marriage. Stevenson writes that matrifocality was widespread among Virginia slave families in the 1800s, with a malleable extended kin unit as the only discernible ideal.

Single-mother families were also common among free blacks: Steven Ruggles had found that in 1850, nearly half of all free black children lived with one or neither of their parents, and by the 1880s, parental absence was five times more likely among blacks than whites.

The power African American women gained through their work roles, reproductive activities, family work, and intimate relationships with white families often made them "ferocious and formidable" in dealing with slave owners, despite their marginal roles in organized social protest.[52] Many also had children fathered by white men, which gave them a source of power and privilege not available to black men. Children fathered by white men and free or slave black women were often referred to as "natural children" and left in the will of their fathers.[53] Black children stood to lose the advantages of their mixed racial heritage if their mothers married black men; moreover, since mothers passed their free status on to her children, children could sometimes fight for freedom based on their maternal descent.[54] Thus, black women had reason to distance themselves from black men, especially those who were enslaved. As Kathleen Brown has written:

> As free parents, black women often formed the first line of defense against encroachments upon the freedom of children, making possible free black family and community life. Many free women may have participated in relationships unrecognized by white courts and churches, either because marriage ceremonies were not conducted according to white law or because white or enslaved men could not legally become their husbands.[55]

Affluent black women whose wealth and status were tied to their relationships with white men whom they were unable to marry usually had nothing to gain by marrying a black man. Darlene Clark Hine and Kathleen Thompson have pointed out that French men in New Orleans, for example, customarily had black mistresses who inherited land and wealth, although laws forbade any formal recognition of these interracial unions. These relationships "gave a large group of free black women in New Orleans—and their children—a considerable degree of independence, wealth and power. . . . Property records of the second half of the eighteenth century list dozens of free black women who owned prime real estate in New Orleans in their own names, had houses built on the properties, and passed them on to their children."[56]

Among the less privileged, emancipation had a destabilizing effect on the black family and/or marriage relationships that had existed during slavery, as it led to starvation, separation, and the desertion of spouses and children. Yet the reorganization of slave labor into the sharecropping system yielded few protections from the abuse of black women. The dominant cultural mandate became the crusade to get African Americans married; however, the impact of the marriage campaign was mediated by the long-standing cultural and gender traditions of black women, the resources they had garnered during slavery, and their active agency in defining and protecting the well-being of their families. . . .

ENDNOTES

1. Sudarkasa, N. 1996. *The Strength of Our Mothers: African and African American Women and Families: Essay and Speeches.* Trenton, NJ: Africa World. P. 1.

2. Hemmons, W. M. 1996. *Black Women in the New World Order: Social Justice and the African American Female.* Westport, CT: Praeger.

3. See, for example, Moffitt, R. A. and P. T. Gottschalk. 2001. "Ethnic and Racial Differences in Welfare Receipt in the United States." Pp. 152–71 in *America Becoming: Racial Trends and Their Consequences,* edited by N. J. Smelser, W. J. Wilson, and F. Mitchell. Washington, DC: National Academy Press.

4. See Jones, J. 1985. *Labor of Love, Labor of Sorrow: Black Women, Work, and the Family from Slavery to the Present.* New York: Basic Books; and Dill, B. T. 1988. "Our Mothers' Grief: Racial Ethnic Women and the Maintenance of Families." *Journal of Family History* 13:415–31.

5. King, D. 1988. "Multiple Jeopardy, Multiple Consciousness: The Context of Black Feminist Ideology." Signs: *Journal of Women in Culture and Society* 14:42–72.

6. Queen, S. A., and R. W. Habenstein. 1967. *The Family in Various Cultures.* Philadelphia: Lippincott. P. 315.

7. Quoted in Gutman, H. G. 1976. *The Black Family in Slavery and Freedom, 1750–1925.* New York: Pantheon. Pp. 304–305.

8. Queen and Habenstein, 1967, note 6.

9. Frazier, E. F. [1939] 1966. *The Negro Family in the United States.* Chicago: University of Chicago Press.

10. Bernard, J. 1966. *Marriage and Family among Negroes.* Englewood Cliffs, NJ: Prentice Hall. P. 68.

11. Ibid.

12. Blassingame, J. W. 1972. *The Share Community: Plantation Life in the Antebellum South.* New York: Oxford University Press.

13. Brown, K. M. 1996. *Good Wives, Nasty Wenches, and Anxious Patriarchs: Gender, Race, and Power in Colonial Virginia.* Chapel Hill: University of North Carolina Press. P. 360.

14. Frazier [1939] 1966, note 9, p. 313.

15. Booker, C. B. 2000. *"I Will Wear No Chain!" A Social History of African American Males.* Westport, CT: Praeger.

16. Jones, J. 1985. *Labor of Love, Labor of Sorrow: Black Women, Work, and the Family from Slavery to the Present.* New York: Basic Books.

17. Franklin, D. L. 2000. *What's Love Got to Do with It? Understanding and Healing the Rift between Black Men and Women.* New York: Touchstone.

18. Scott, R. J. 1985. "The Battle Over the Child: Child Apprenticeship and the Freedmen's Bureau in North Carolina." Pp. 193–207 in *Growing Up in America: Children in Historical Perspective,* edited by N. R. Hiner and J. M. Hawes. Chicago: University of Chicago Press.

19. Billingsley, A. 1992. *Climbing Jacob's Ladder: The Enduring Legacy of African-American Families.* New York: Simon & Schuster.

20. Hine, D. C. 1995. "Rape and the Inner Lives of Black Women in the Middle West: Preliminary Thoughts on the Culture of Dissemblance." Pp. 380–87 in *Words of Fire: An Anthology of African-American Feminist Thought,* edited by B. Guy-Sheftall. New York: New Press.

21. Carby, H. V. 1995. "Policing the Black Woman's Body in an Urban Context." Pp. 115–32 in *Identities,* edited by K. A. Appiah and H. L. Gates. Chicago: University of Chicago Press.

22. Marks, C. 1989. *Farewell–We're Good and Gone: The Great Black Migration.* Bloomington: Indiana University Press.

23. Hine, D. C. and K. Thompson. 1998. *A Shining Thread of Hope.* New York: Broadway. P. 215.

24. Ibid.

25. Marks 1989, note 22.

26. Ibid.

27. Rainwater, L. and W. L. Yancey. 1967. *The Moynihan Report and the Politics of Controversy.* Cambridge, MA: MIT Press. P. 15.

28. Walsh, L. 1985. "The Experience and Status of Women in the Chesapeake." Pp. 1–18 in *The Web of Southern Social Relations: Women, Family and Education,* edited by W. Fraser, R. F. Saunders, and J. Wakelyn. Athens: University of Georgia Press. P. 13.

29. Morgan, P. D. 1998. *Slave Counterpoint: Black Culture in the Eighteenth-Century Chesapeake and Low Country.* Durham: University of North Carolina Press. P. 315.

30. McAdoo, H. P. 1990. "A Portrait of African American Families in the United States." Pp. 71–93 in *The American Woman,* 1990–1991, edited by S. E. Rix. New York: Norton. P. 74.

31. Blassingame, 1972, note 12, p. 261.

32. Davis, A. Y. 1995. "Reflections on the Black Woman's Role in the Community of Slaves." Pp. 200–218 in *Words of Fire: An Anthology of African-American Feminist Thought,* edited by B. Guy-Sheftall. New York: New Press. P. 201.

33. Bogger, T. L. 1997. *Free Blacks in Norfolk Virginia 1790–1860: The Darker Side of Freedom.* Charlottesville: University Press of Virginia.

34. See Sidbury, J. 1997. *Ploughshares into Swords: Race, Rebellion, and Identity in Gabriel's Virginia, 1730–1810.* Cambridge: Cambridge University Press; and Booker, C. B. 2000. *"I Will Wear No Chain!" A Social History of African American Males.* Westport, CT: Praeger.

35. Walsh, 1985, note 28; Bogger 1997, note 33.

36. Morgan, 1998, note 29.

37. Nobels, W. W. 1974. "Africanity: Its Role in Black Families." *Black Scholar* 5:10–17.

38. Hine and Thompson 1998, note 23.

39. Terborg-Penn, R. 1986. "Women and Slavery in the African Diaspora: A Cross-Cultural Approach to Historical Analysis." *Sage: A Scholarly Journal on Black Women* 3:11–15.

40. Thorne, B. 1982. "Feminist Rethinking of the Family: An Overview." Pp. 1–24 in *Rethinking the Family: Some Feminist Questions,* edited by B. Thorne and M. Yalom. New York: Longman. P. 7.

41. Brewer, R. 1995. "Gender, Poverty, Culture, and Economy: Theorizing Female-Led Families." Pp. 164–78 in *African American Single Mothers: Understanding Their Lives and Families,* edited by B. J. Dickerson. Thousand Oaks, CA: Sage. P. 166.

42. Genovese, E. D. 1974. *Roll, Jordon, Roll: The World the Slaves Made.* New York: Pantheon. Pp. 453, 484.

43. Dunaway, W. A. 2003. *The African-American Family in Slavery and Emancipation.* New York: Cambridge University Press. P. 270.

44. Ibid. p. 3.

45. Gutman 1976 (note 7), for example, draws heavily from the records kept for nearly one hundred years by the Good Hope Plantation in South Carolina, which still had 175 slaves when slavery ended.

46. Hurst, C. E. 2004. *Social Inequality: Forms, Causes, and Consequences.* Boston: Pearson Education.

47. Dill 1988, note 4.

48. Brown 1996, note 13, p. 118.

49. Jones 1985, note 16.

50. White, D. G. 1985. *Ar'nt I A Woman? Female Slaves in the Plantation South.* New York: Norton. P. 47.

51. Jones 1985, note 16.

52. Sidbury 1997, note 34.

53. Clinton, C. 1985. "Caught in the Web of the Big House: Women and Slavery." Pp. 19–34 in *The Web of Southern Social Relations: Women, Family and Education,* edited by W. Fraser, R. F. Saunders, and J. Wakelyn. Athens: University of Georgia Press.

54. Sidbury 1997, note 34.

55. Brown 1996, note 13, p. 229.

56. Hine and Thompson 1998, note 23, p. 44.

7

LA FAMILIA
Family Cohesion among Mexican American Families in the Urban Southwest, 1848–1900

RICHARD GRISWOLD DEL CASTILLO

You didn't have to ask for anyone's help. They would just come to you. Whenever my mother had a child, the house would be filled with other women who would take care of us children, cook for her, bathe her and the baby, help her in every possible way.

> —Reminiscence of a woman from South Texas in Foley, Mota, Post, and Lozano, *From Peones to Politicos: Ethnic Relations in a South Texas Town 1900–1977,* p. 59.

Contemporary sociologists studying the Mexican American family have found that *la familia* among the Spanish speaking is often a broad and encompassing term, not one limited to a household or even to biologically related kin. Close bonds of affection and assistance among members of the family household and a wide network of kinfolk have been found to be one

---

of the most important characteristics of Mexican American family life.[1] The network of *la familia* usually includes a number of *compadres,* or coparents, established through rituals of *compadrazgo* (god parenthood). This family, conceived in its broadest sense, is often an important source of emotional and economic support. Family members are expected to be warm and nurturing, and to be willing to provide security for one another throughout their lives. Individuals, as members of a family, whether in a nuclear household or as members of an extended network, are expected to place their personal welfare second only to the welfare of *la familia.*[2] While there is some debate over the exact structural form this extended *familia* has taken in present-day Mexican American society, most experts agree that it is a pervasive characteristic of familial life.[3]

This chapter is concerned with the interplay of economic and cultural forces as they have affected kinship networks and family solidarity. The approach taken here is . . . an attempt to compare the ideology of family solidarity with the empirical evidence of household structures. The Mexican American experience within the extended family is contrasted with that of Anglo Americans and offered as a way to evaluate significant differences and similarities between the two groups.

Without entering into an analysis of contemporary sociological literature regarding Mexican American family solidarity and kinship support, my concern here is rather to describe something of this phenomenon in times past. [My future research] will discuss contemporary aspects of Chicano family life in comparison to what we know about the nineteenth century.

The Origins and Development of Familism

Some have argued that familism, or the values, attitudes, beliefs, and behaviors associated with the Mexican American extended family, has it roots in the pre-Hispanic social world. The Mexica-Aztec family emphasized the individual's subordination to community-defined norms of behavior. Rigid sex roles were determined at birth, and women were regarded as subordinate to men and morally weak. The emphasis in rhetorical orations was on the family's role in promoting proper ritual behavior, maintaining honor, and fostering self-control.[4] The community *calpulli* system of clan organization and the Aztec-Nahua teachings regarding male and female family obligations influenced the Mestizo family, which emerged as a result of mixture with Europens.[5] Indeed, in many respects the Mexica-Aztec attitudes surrounding family life closely resembled the Iberian-Spanish. The social transitions under Spanish domination in the succeeding centuries reinforced the older pre-Columbian values, while accommodations resulted in a renewed sense of the importance of the Indian community.[6]

Iberian-Spanish family ideology also influenced Mexican and subsequently Mexican American values regarding familism. A 700-year-long conflict with the Moors, who invaded and occupied Spain in the eighth century, heightened the importance of family honor and pure lineage. Struggles between Spanish families over the privileges, titles, and lands that were gained during the reconquest reinforced the importance of family solidarity. A close and prolonged contact with the Moors and Jews in Spain loaded a family's claim to *limpieza de sangre,* or pure blood, with religious and political connotations. In the New World the Spanish attempted to preserve their concept of honor and pure descent by regulating racial mixture. By the laws embodied in the *Regim de Castas,* they ranked various degrees of race and ethnic mixture with the supposedly pure Spanish. Family status came to be associated with the degree to which its members had intermarried with "inferior" castes.[7]

The psychological and social meanings of kinship and family bonds differed according to a family's class position. For the landed aristocracy in Mexico and in Spain a continuity in the inheritance of real property, titles, and social status was of utmost importance. For the landless poor the extended *familia* served more as a form of social insurance against hard times. On Mexico's far northern frontier the paternalistic hacienda system was less well established, and the benevolent institutions of the church and state were not well funded or organized. For the poor in this agrarian and pastoral society family solidarity was a necessity, involving the widest possible links with members of the community. The extended family was essential to provide for protection in a hostile environment.[8]

One way that families enlarged their ties to others in the community was through *compadrazgo.* The custom of god parenthood made nonbiologically related individuals of a community members of the extended family. *Compadrazgo* evolved in Mediterranean folk custom as a formal ritual sanctioned by the Catholic Church. Godparents were required for the celebration of the major religious occasions in a person's life: baptism, confirmation, first communion, and marriage. At these times *padrinos,* or godfathers, and *madrinas,* or godmothers, entered into special religious, social, and economic relationships with the godchild, or *ahiado,* as well as with the parents of the child with whom they became *compadres* or *comadres.*[9] In the ideal, *padrinos* acted as coparents to their *ahiados,* providing discipline and emotional and financial support when needed. They could expect from their godchildren obedience, respect, and love in return. As *compadres* they were expected to become the closest friends of the parents and integral members of the extended family.

Historical evidence of *compadrazgo* is scattered throughout the letters and reminiscences of the Spanish-Mexican frontier aristocracy in the nineteenth century. In 1877, for example, Antonio Coronel in Los Angeles remembered that "the obligations of the godparents was that they should take the place of the parents should they (the parents) die."[10] In their private correspondence the aristocracy sometimes referred to their *padrinos* and *madrinos* as mother (*madre*) and father (*padre*). They expressed obligations to behave toward these kinfolk much in the same manner as they would toward their biological parents. Frequent visits, celebration of namesake saint days (*mañanitas*), anniversaries, and intimate communications with godparents were part of an *ahiado's* normal family life.[11]

Visiting between *comadres* was an important social activity among women, especially in the more isolated rural regions. They often took care of one another's children and had a good deal of authority over them. A teenage diarist in San Antonio during the 1880s told of numerous visits of her mother's *comadre*. Often the *comadre*, Adina de Zavala, stayed with the girl's family for many days.[12] These visits of relatives, *comadres*, and their families were, for this young girl, high points in what she thought was a drab and cloistered life. And so it must have been for many others in a frontier society where so many were so poor and where there were so few amusements for women outside the home environment. Visiting among the families of friends and relatives was perhaps the major form of recreation.

Extended family members including *compadres* and *comadres* also were important during times of crisis. When a woman gave birth or a family member took seriously ill, *comadres* and female relatives automatically came to each other's assistance. Sometimes they even moved their own families into the stricken household on a temporary basis.[13] James Tafolla, living in South Texas during the 1870s and 1880s, recalled that on more than one occasion relatives came to live with his family when he and his wife were sick.[14] And Juan Bandini sadly noted in his diary of having to send his two daughters to live with his sister during a period of personal financial hardship.[15] In these cases and in others it was expected and often true that extended family members would help when needed. Adina de Zavala, a San Antonio matron, expressed this feeling in her journal entry of 1882 when she wrote: "My life is only for my family. My whole life shall be worth while [sic] if I can render happy and comfortable the declining years of my parents and see my brothers safely launched on life's troubled seas."[16]

An important way that families strengthened their support networks outside the immediate kinship arena was through their participation in *mutualistas*, or mutual-aid societies. In both rural and urban areas Mexican Americans sought to insure themselves against the tragedies of death and economic disaster by forming societies where they could pool their meager resources. Most often these *mutualistas* became sources of emergency loans as well. Families often used *mutualistas* like community banks. The mutual-aid societies frequently became a focal point for the community's social life by organizing dances, fiestas, fund raisers, and the like. Occasionally, in conjunction with the Mexican consular offices, they played an important role in helping labor unions during strikes. They also provided help for recent Mexican immigrants by providing temporary housing, food, and job assistance.[17]

The *mutualista* movement among Mexican Americans appears to have been particularly strong in the cities and towns of the Southwest during the late nineteenth century. In Los Angeles, La Sociedad Hispano Americana de Beneficia Mutual was established in 1875 and La Sociedad Progresista Mexicana in 1883. In San Antonio, Mexicanos organized La Sociedad de la Unión in 1886 and La Sociedad de Protección Mutua de Trabajadores Unidos in 1890. These are only a few examples of the many mutual-aid associations which sprang up throughout the last part of the nineteenth century.

A detailed examination of the books of at least one mutual-aid society, that of La Sociedad de la Unión in San Antonio in 1886, reveals that members paid monthly dues of about one dollar and that the average accumulated savings ran between 80 and 90 dollars. Members of La Unión frequently borrowed small sums against their accumulated dues.[18] Thus, the society and others like it acted as community banks, extending credit to persons who normally would have found it difficult to get loans from banks.

Perhaps the largest and longest-lived *mutualista* was La Alianza Hispano Americana in Tucson.[19] Organized in 1894 by Carlos Ignacio Velasco, editor of *El Fronterizo*, and Mariano Samaniego, a wealthy freighter and rancher, La Alianza grew rapidly from a dozen or so subscribers to over 17,000 members in eight states. Like the other mutual-aid societies of that era, La Alianza was at first exclusively a men's organization, but families also participated in the social activities. By 1913 La Alianza began to admit women to equal membership in the organization.

Mutual-aid societies proved to be very popular among the Mexican immigrants who had regular wage-paying jobs. As fraternal societies they provided the kind of support that was often difficult for poor families to provide—a guarantee of a decent funeral was important for the Catholic immigrants. The societies also provided an important source of entertainment and social activities for members of the working class. They were often a common meeting ground for the immigrant and the native-born Mexican Americans. Not incidentally the *mutualistas* provided status and some economic security for those who were considered aliens by the majority society.

Familism and the Extended Household

Anglo Americans were frequently impressed by the warmth and closeness they found in Mexican American families. Frederick Law Olmstead in 1858 observed that "their manners toward one another is engaging and that of the children and the parents most affectionate." A Protestant missionary in South Texas wrote that the "Tejanos were kindly in home life, particularly to the aged, and clannish to a degree whole families of several generations occupying one hut."[20] A closeness of affection characterized Mexican American families in the nineteenth century. The roots of this family cohesion, as an emotional reality, lay in religious ideologies and folk customs, as well as in a common poverty.

Family cohesion among the poorer classes can best be studied by analyzing household structures in the nineteenth-century censuses. The surviving documents, letters, and diaries of the Spanish speaking are usually cryptic and incomplete. In any case they reflect the experience of only a handful of upper-class individuals. The degree to which families were willing and able to provide food and shelter for relatives can be viewed as a significant indicator of how families realized, in part, their commitment to a larger extended network. While almost everyone, except the recent immigrants from Mexico, had kin who lived in the same town, only a few were likely to have, at any given moment, a household which they shared with relatives. Extended family households were a temporary and impermanent creation of circumstance arising out of old age, sickness, death, or economic misfortune. Nevertheless, the incidence of extended-family household structures in the general population is one way to determine how families interacted with their *familia.*

Mexican American households may be defined in several ways. Not all households were composed of married couples with or without children (termed "nuclear families"). It was quite common in the nineteenth century for there to be a wide variety of "others" living in households. Boarders, adopted and visiting children, friends, *compadres*, and servants often shared dwellings with married couples. The "extended-family household" was an ideal type, where nuclear families lived with other individuals who were clearly related to the head of the household. These relatives were not always adults, but more often teenagers and children who had come to live with relatives for a variety of reasons. Extended-family households often had "others" such as relatives on the wife's side of the family, servants, boarders, and friends as well as multiple families. Nuclear families who lived in homes without clearly determined relatives but with these "others" may be called the "nuclear-plus-other" type of household. Those households where apparently none of the individuals were related I have termed "no-family" households.

Within these ideal types a good deal of variation in composition and relationship was possible. A couple could be married, sharing the same last name, or live in *unión libre.* Widows and widowers could live alone, with others, or with relatives (a stem family in the last case). Older brothers and sisters could live together with or without children from previous marriages. And a great variety of adults in varying numbers and related by *compadrazgo* or distant kinship could be present in all types of households.

An analysis of the proportions of extended households in comparison to "no-family" households is one way to assess the changing patterns of familism. No-family households were groups of individuals who were obviously living separate from their extended families. The members of these no-family households may have participated in an extended-family network located in the same town or a nearby village or farm. Some may have had nuclear families of their own living in Mexico or elsewhere in the Southwest. But their household status, as boarders, travelers, visitors, transients, or simply unattached individuals, meant that they had weaker ties to family than those individuals who reside with kin. Table 1 shows the relative proportions of extended-family households in comparison to no-family households in the urban Southwest.

Generally, the proportions of extended-family households declined throughout the period. A notable exception to this trend occurred in San Antonio in 1860, where extended households exceeded 27 percent, representing a huge jump from the previous decade. A possible explanation for this

TABLE 1   Proportions of Extended and No-Family Households, 1850–1880

	1850	1860	1870	1880
Los Angeles				
No-family	14.4	26.9	20.6	22.8
Extended	11.5	10.1	15.2	10.2
Tucson				
No-family	—	—	23.9	16.2
Extended	—	—	15.3	10.3
Santa Fe				
No-family	11.8	21.7	30.9	14.4
Extended	15.8	15.2	9.4	13.3
San Antonio				
No-family	17.0	17.8	11.1	18.7
Extended	14.0	27.7	13.2	3.7

unusual increase would be the decade of civil strife in South Texas and Mexico. A series of anti-Mexican riots, the Cart War of 1857, the Cortina rebellion in the Matamoros–Brownsville area in 1859, and the wars of the reform in Mexico (1857–1862) displaced hundreds of families from their ancestral homes in Mexico and the South Texas region.[21] Many Mexicans fleeing the violence in the surrounding countryside may have sought safety with relatives and friends in the comparative security of the large city of San Antonio.

Los Angeles also had a slight increase in extended family households in 1870. This was probably caused by the sudden collapse of the ranching industry in Southern California, which increased unemployment and put pressures on families to consolidate their resources.[22] Barbara Laslett in her study of Los Angeles has found that by 1870 those families that owned real and personal property were more likely to live in extended households than in any others. This had not been the case earlier, indicating that economic pressures were at work.[23]

It should be noted that in Los Angeles and Santa Fe the extended-family household remained about as prevalent in 1880 as it had been in 1850 despite the very different socioeconomic histories of the two towns. Only in San Antonio and Tucson was there a big decline in extended-family households. The expected effect of variations in regional economic development thus did not appear to have an influence on extended-family formation. Indeed, no single set of variables appears to account for these patterns; this underscores the truism that family solidarity was a complex of beliefs, attitudes, and customs that varied often irrespective of the economic cycle.

The pattern of no-family households presents a similar problem of explanation. Generally, at any given census year there were proportionally more unattached individuals than people living in extended families. San Antonio, Santa Fe, and Los Angeles had a net increase in no-family households over the forty-year period. There were progressively more unattached "family-less" individuals in the Mexican American population. This suggests a probable decline in the cohesiveness of the family unit, especially when seen in conjunction with the net decline in extended-family households.

The pattern could also have been caused by increased geographic mobility and by economic pressures. Young men and women left their families of origin to seek adventure and fortune or perhaps in the hope of helping their families to survive. The patterns of the two types of households, the no-family and the extended, seem to have been related. The number of no-family households rose when the proportion of extended households declined. No-family households declined in years when extended households were increasing. It appears that familism, as measured in terms of household organization, acted as a safety valve for temporary dislocations. In Laslett's theoretical view . . . the formation of extended families was a strategy for family survival.

The Formation of Extended–Family Households

The formation of extended-family households among Mexican Americans was influenced by a number of factors: socioeconomic class, nativity, age, sex, and marital status of the head of household. Over the forty-year period most extended families were headed by married, lower-working-class, native-born men under the age of twenty-five. As the decades progressed, Mexican-born immigrants established more and more extended families, and this indicated a progressive stabilization of immigrant family life. Little wonder that extended-family living was most prevalent among the poor and young: both were more likely to be dependent on relatives for support. The stem family, with young newly married couples living with older parents, existed hardly at all among the Mexican Americans. Early in the American era single parents with children did not tend to live in extended families. The majority of extended households were of heads of nuclear families with children. A noticeable trend later in the century was for more and more extended families to be headed by single, unmarried individuals without children. Obviously, the nature of family solidarity changed during the decades — away from the nuclear core families to other more complex family relationships.

One case history points out this process. In 1860 Francisco Solano lived in Tucson with his wife, Ramona. The census marshall in that year recorded that they had six children. Four years later the territorial census taker listed them as having thirteen children, all with the same last name as the father. Six years later, in 1870, the Solanos had only seven children, a housekeeper, and a married son with his common-law wife.[24] Without an exhausting and probably fruitless genealogical search we will probably never know how the Solano family mysteriously expanded and contracted during these years. In only ten years the Solanos had progressed from being a purely nuclear family to being one more complex.

In analyzing the question of why individuals entered into extended-family relationships, it is useful to compare the Anglo American population

TABLE 2 Distribution of Mexican American (MA) and Anglo American (AA) Households, 1850–1880 (expressed as a percentage)

	1850		1860		1870		1880	
	MA	*AA*	*MA*	*AA*	*MA*	*AA*	*MA*	*AA*
N in Sample	(385)	(106)	(687)	(218)	(756)	(376)	(986)	(299)
No-Family	14.5	34.0	24.9	28.0	21.4	30.3	19.8	27.1
Nuclear Family	50.2	42.4	40.9	43.5	45.6	44.7	48.4	45.8
Nuclear plus Other	22.3	17.9	20.8	20.2	19.2	17.0	18.4	20.1
Extended	13.0	5.7	13.4	8.3	13.8	8.0	9.9	7.0

with the Mexican American. Through this comparison we get a better idea of the role of culture in family solidarity.

Table 2 shows the decennial proportions of household types in the four towns for Mexican Americans and Anglo Americans. As might be expected, given the value of *la familia* in Mexican culture, Mexican Americans regularly had larger proportions of extended-family households and fewer no-family households than did the Anglo Americans. There was very little difference, however, with regard to other forms of household organization. Anglo American as well as Mexican immigrants, most of whom were recent arrivals to these southwestern towns, were unlikely to have many extended-family members and more likely to be single and unattached. The native-born Spanish speaking, however, had historic kinship ties in the region. For them extended-family households accounted for a significant proportion of all types of households until 1880. Over the decades, Mexican Americans and Anglo Americans became more similar in their family structures. This was largely due to the fact that more and more Anglo Americans formed extended families, while the proportions of Mexican Americans who lived in these kinds of households remained the same.

Notwithstanding the possibility that it was more difficult for Anglos to create large extended families on the frontier, their proportions of these types exceeded the national averages in the rest of the country except in 1880. Carl Degler, studying the families who migrated west in the late nineteenth century, found some evidence to show that many Anglo Americans either brought kinfolk with them or financed a serial migration of relatives from back east.[25] During the late nineteenth century the eastern seaboard cities underwent rapid urbanization and industrialization. The industrial Northeast had the highest percentages of extended families in the nation.

Rudy Ray Seward, who studied this unusual occurrence, believed that economic and residential pressures in these eastern cities sometimes forced families to lure wage-paying relatives to come and live with them.[26] The population east of the Mississippi also felt the demographic effects of the Civil War, which created many broken households and resulted in higher incidences of extended households. Moreover, in the industrial cities newly arriving European migrants tended to cluster along Old World family and town lines, often sharing the same tenements, apartments, or neighborhoods.

By 1880 the proportions of extended families east of the Mississippi reached high levels. These same high levels had existed among Mexican Americans in the urban Southwest for thirty years prior to that time. It is not at all clear that the prevalence of extended families among the Spanish speaking was due to the same factors that were operating in the East. Of all the forms of household organization the extended family in the southwestern cities was most related to ethnicity.[27]

Cultural Factors in Extended–Family Formation

In considering why it was that Mexican Americans tended to have more extended households than did Anglo Americans, inevitably the problem of cultural determinism arises. The question of causation is not easily dismissed by simply arguing that because of their cultural traditions Mexican Americans preferred to live with their kin rather than alone or in other types of arrangements. If this were indeed the case, we should have trouble explaining why it was that at no point in the late nineteenth century did the majority of the Spanish speaking live in extended-family households. Most lived separate from kin.

One would expect that the kinship organizations of both Americans and Mexican Americans would be disrupted by geographic mobility. Evidence from nineteenth-century western towns on this point suggests that both groups tended to be highly transient. In San Antonio only 32 percent of the total population continued to live in the town between 1880 and 1890.[28] Geographic mobility was most related to socioeconomic status. With the laboring classes being the period 1870–1900, I found only 7 percent of the skilled and unskilled workers continued to live in the city. The rates of persistence were much higher for the middle and upper classes.[29] In Los Angeles only about 11 percent of the Spanish-surnamed population remained in the town during the twenty-year period 1860–1880. Only twenty-two heads of households remained in the town between 1850 and 1880.[30]

There were systematic differences in the composition of Mexican American and Anglo American extended families. Mexican Americans differed most from Anglo Americans with regard to age and occupational status. After 1860 young Mexican Americans tended to be overrepresented in extended households. For Anglos age was not as important. The young were as likely as the aged to be the relatives residing in households. As can be seen in Table 3, the overwhelming majority of Mexican American extended-family members were under twenty-nine years of age in every census year. This was not the case for Anglo Americans.

That so many young people should have been relatives in these Spanish-speaking families seems unusual given our contemporary notions about the family as a collective source of economic support. Few of these young people

TABLE 3   Age Characteristics of Mexican American and Anglo American
Relatives Living in Extended Households, 1850–1880 (expressed as a percentage)

Age Categories	1850		1860		1870		1880	
	MA	*AA*	*MA*	*AA*	*MA*	*AA*	*MA*	*AA*
1–19	55.2	25.0	57.5	56.5	58.6	19.2	57.9	50.0
20–29	23.2	37.5	24.6	21.7	14.8	19.2	22.2	7.1
30–49	17.3	37.5	11.0	13.1	19.5	34.6	11.1	14.3
50–	4.3	0	6.0	8.7	7.1	27.0	8.8	28.6

could contribute much in the way of wages to the households. Some of the older teenagers and young adults worked outside the home to supplement their family's income. But in the census the majority of the young adults were classified as unemployed. Of course there were other ways a young person could help the family, even though not employed in a full-time occupation. He or she could take part-time care for younger children and perform housework, freeing others to enter the job market.

Some of these young relatives probably were newly married spouses who were just starting out and who needed a place to live. In the Spanish and Mexican eras it had been a custom for newlyweds to reside with the bride's parents for a period of time.[31] Other young members of extended households were probably relatives who may have been visitors or orphans.

Indeed, visiting was probably responsible for a significant number of these child relatives. The great distances which sometimes separated extended-family members led to protracted visits whenever they got together. In the early 1900s, for example, Dolores Aguirre sent her daughter to visit relatives in El Paso, Texas. Lupe stayed with her aunt Dolores P. de Bennet three weeks and then was sent to visit her cousins in Juárez for another month.[32] Many of the wealthier families had guest rooms that they used to put up friends and relatives during their stays. The Ochoa family in Tucson, for example, had three or four rooms set aside for this purpose. The house was reportedly always full of friends and relatives, who visited for long periods of time.[33] A general ethic of hospitality and sharing was traditional in Spanish-speaking society. This had the domestic result of reducing isolation and integrating family members with a great variety of others. Mutual respect and formality ensured a degree of privacy. By and large the family's home was available and open to almost everyone of good will. To be sure, the ability of a family to support visitors depended on its economic resources, although even the poorer classes were quick to share their meager food and humble abodes with visitors and relatives.

It may be stretching the point to call these households "extended" when many had this structure only because of the presence of young visitors, cousins, siblings, adopted children, stepchildren, and distant kinfolk. The presence of these youthful relatives also suggests that some nuclear families were unable to provide a supporting home environment for children.

Judge Benjamin Hayes recounted one example of how children came to be displaced from a nuclear family. In 1856 he told the story of a native California woman who came to him for legal advice. Months earlier she had applied for a divorce from her husband, who had been mistreating her. At this time the husband along with the children moved into his mother's home. Subsequently the couple had been reconciled, but the mother-in-law refused to forgive her son's wife, and she would not allow her to have her children back. "This mother (the mother-in-law) fired with wrath whenever the subject was mentioned, and warned the son that if he received his repentant wife she would give him her malediction, a mother's curse, a wish that he might go out upon the earth in rags, with neither bread to eat nor water to drink, a dire malediction dreaded by the son with a terror he cannot overcome, for it appears that Religion had no exorcismal value."[34]

The story of the wrathful mother-in-law indicates how much influence parents in Mexican American society had over their married children's lives. From the mother-in-law's perspective, her son's wife had violated a taboo against divorce and thus was not worthy of raising her own children. Stories like this illustrate the importance of tradition and ideology in family life. It also points out the occasional role that culture, and not incidentally emotion, played in breaking up nuclear families.

Comparisons with Other Extended Households

Economic factors seem to have been relatively more important in the formation and maintenance of Anglo American extended households. Most relatives in Mexican American extended households were unemployed or under the age of 19. But in every census year except 1880 proportionally more Anglo relatives tended to have wage-paying jobs. Thus Anglo American extended households tended to benefit economically from the incomes of their relatives. This was not true of the majority of Mexican American households. For Anglo relatives, joining a nuclear family appeared to be more a matter of individual choice and, perhaps, negotiation. Both the individual and the receiving family stood to benefit. The American extended families appeared less to be the result of crises than economic and perhaps residential convenience.

This point of view is strengthened by evidence from studies of extended families in industrial cities in both America and England during the late nineteenth century. Howard Chudacoff and Tamara Hareven studied Essex County, Massachusetts, between 1860 and 1889 and found that it became progressively more difficult for young people to find inexpensive housing. Newly married couples and young people who were anxious to leave home were pressured by the difficulty of finding suitable housing. For economic reasons they continued to live with their parents. During their prolonged stay they contributed to the family by having jobs. The "empty nest" syndrome was less common among Americans in these cities than later in the twentieth century.[35] . . .

The evidence surrounding family solidarity among Mexican Americans suggests that the kinship network functioned primarily as a support system during times of crisis. It seems to have served the same function among blacks. In Herbert Gutman's view, "extended and augmented families were important 'adaptive strategies' to deal with the poverty most Blacks knew." Indeed the proportions of extended and augmented families among blacks seem to have increased when more and more families moved to the cities. In 1880 approximately 36 percent of all black households in Mobile and Richmond were extended or augmented. By 1900 samples from the same urban areas showed rates of family extension as high as 59 percent.[36]

In the nineteenth century the extended-family household among Mexican Americans was an important institution, much more so than now. It functioned primarily as a place to take care of displaced children. Contrary to the contemporary ideal conceptualizations of the Chicano family, there were very few aged *abuelos* and *abuelitas* (grandfathers and grandmothers) who lived with nuclear families. In fact, the probability that the aged would find shelter with the families of their children was greater for Anglo Americans than it was for Mexican Americans.

Extended households among the Spanish speaking were more important as emotional support systems than was true for other Americans in the West. They were vital to ensure the proper rearing of children and were less important as a means of economic security for adults.

The Diversity of Household Organization

Neither the majority of Anglo Americans nor of Mexican Americans lived in extended or in nuclear households. In fact, a great diversity of living arrangements characterized both groups. Table 2 illustrated four different types of households found among Mexican Americans and Anglo Americans. Throughout the decades there were few differences between the two groups with respect to the proportions of households containing nuclear, nuclear-plus-other families, or "no-family" households. The most important differences, those that relate how the culture and the economy affected Mexican Americans, were the higher numbers of female-headed households and extended households among the Spanish speaking. The former seems to have resulted primarily from economic pressures, while the latter, the extended-family household, from cultural patterns.

Given the wide diversity of household types and a lack of geographic stability for both Anglo Americans and Mexican Americans, it seems likely that family solidarity was realized in a great variety of settings, not just in extended-household situations. Fluid and dynamic family structures changed to meet the needs of individuals. The kinds of support and degree of interaction between kin and the members of households varied according to a great variety of factors: the residential proximity of kinfolk, the social status and economic class of the family in relation to kinfolk, the type of relationship to the head of household (biological or fictive), generational differences, and the personality preferences of individuals.

In sum, it appears that the economic changes in the nineteenth-century urban Southwest did not clearly alter the role of *la familia* as a support network, particularly among the working classes. In fact, for the poorest members of Mexican American society, economic insecurities may have resulted in strengthened bonds of family unity. This was despite the fact that the economy also worked to disrupt traditional familistic behavior, mainly by creating broken homes. The existence of extended households which had little economic support from resident kin was evidence that cultural ideals of familism continued to provide strategies for survival during hard times.

ENDNOTES

1. Jaime Sena-Rivera, "Extended Kinship in the United States: Competing Models and the Case of La Familia Chicana," *Journal of Marriage and the Family* 41(1) (February 1979): 121–29; Oscar Ramírez and Carlos H. Arce, "The Contemporary Chicano Family: An Empirically Based Review," in *Explorations in Chicano Psychology,* ed. Augustine Barron, Jr. (New York: Praeger, 1981), pp. 3–28.

2. Nathan Murillo, "The Mexican American Family," in *Chicanos: Social and Psychological Perspectives,* ed. Nathaniel N. Wagner and Marsha Haug (St. Louis: Mosby, 1971), p. 102; Alfredo Mirandé, "The Chicano Family: A Reanalysis of Conflicting Views," *Journal of Marriage and the Family* 39(4) (November 1977): 751–52.

3. See, for example, Ramírez and Arce, "The Contemporary Chicano Family," pp. 9–11, for a review of the literature on the extended family and its importance.

4. For a full discussion of the Nahuatl attitudes and practices regarding family matters, see Colin M. MacLachlan and Jaime E. Rodríguez, *The Forging of the Cosmic Race: A Reinterpretation of Colonial Mexico* (Berkeley: University of California Press, 1980), pp. 45–50.

5. Ramírez and Arce, "The Contemporary Chicano Family," p. 10; Alfredo Mirandé and Evangelina Enríquez, *La Chicanas: The Mexican-American Woman* (Chicago and London: University of Chicago Press, 1979), pp. 17–23.

6. MacLachlan and Rodríguez, *The Forging of the Cosmic Race,* p. 206.

7. Ramón Gutiérrez, "Marriage, Sex and the Family: Social Change in Colonial New Mexico, 1680–1848" (Ph.D. dissertation, history, University of Wisconsin—Madison, 1980), pp. 93–95, 108.

8. The importance of family ties on the frontier is documented in the histories of Frances Leon Swadesh, *Los Primeros Pobladores: Hispanic Americans of the Ute Frontier* (Notre Dame and London: University of Notre Dame Press, 1974); David J. Weber, ed., *Foreigners in Their Native Land: Historical Roots of the Mexican Americans* (Albuquerque: University of New Mexico Press, 1973); and Father Angélico Chávez, *Origin of New Mexico Families in the Spanish Colonial Period* (Santa Fe: Gannon, 1975).

9. Margaret Clark, *Health in the Mexican American Culture: A Community Study* (Berkeley: University of California Press, 1959), pp. 157–58.

10. Antonio Coronel, "Cosas de California" (ms., Bancroft Library, Berkeley; CA), p. 231.

11. See, for example, Josefa del Valle to her father (ms., May 29, 1876, Coronel Callection, Los Angeles County Museum of Natural History).

12. "Diary of a Young Child" (ms., Adina de Zavala Collection, Benson Library, University of Texas, Austin, 1889).

13. Douglas Foley, Clarice Mota, Donald E. Post, and Ignacio Lozano, *From Peones to Politicos: Ethnic Relations in a South Texas Town, 1900–1977,* University of Texas Monograph No. 3 (Center for Mexican American Studies, 1979), pp. 52, 59.

14. James Tafolla, "Nearing the End of the Trail" (typescript), p. 65.

15. Juan Bandini, *Diary* (typescript, H. E. Huntington Library, San Marino, CA).

16. Adina de Zavala, *Journal,* January 15, 1882 (ms., Benson Library, University of Texas, Austin).

17. See David Maciel, *La Clase Obrera en la Historia de Mexico: Al Norte del Rio Bravo (pasado inmediato) (1930–1980),* Vol. 17 (Mexico DF: Siglo Veintiuno, 1982), for a detailed discussion of *mutualista* activity in relation to the labor movement. See also José Amaro Hernández, *Mutual Aid for Survival: The Case of the Mexican American* (Malabar, FL: Krieger, 1983).

18. Sociedad de la Unión, *Membership Books* (ms., Catholic Archives of San Antonio, Books 1–4 [1886–1935]).

19. Kay Lynn Briegal, "La Alianza Hispano Americana, 1894–1965: A Mexican American Fraternal Insurance Society" (Ph.D. dissertation, history, University of Southern California, 1974).

20. Arnoldo De Leon, *The Tejano Community, 1830–1900* (Albuquerque: University of New Mexico Press, 1982), pp. 127–30.

21. Frederick Law Olmstead, *A Journey through Texas: Or, A Saddle-Trip on the Southwestern Frontier* (1857; reprint edition, Austin: University of Texas Press, 1978), p. 164; Acúna, *Occupied America,* pp. 46–50; Weber, *Foreigners in Their Native Land,* pp. 152–53.

22. Richard Griswold del Castillo, *The Los Angeles Barrio* (Berkeley: University of California Press, 1980), pp. 41–50.

23. Barbara Laslett, "Social Change and the Family: Los Angeles, California, 1850–1870," *American Sociological Review* 42(2) (April 1977): 227.

24. Francisco Solano, "Historical Address" (ms., Arizona Historical Society).

25. Carl Degler, *At Odds: Women and the Family in America from the Revolution to the Present* (New York: Oxford University Press, 1980), p. 105.

26. Rudy Ray Seward, *The American Family: A Demographic History* (Beverly Hills, CA: Sage, 1978), pp. 130–31; this explanation of the increases in urban industrial extended families also has been advanced by Michael Anderson, who has studied the industrial towns of Lancashire, England. See Michael Anderson, "Family, Household and the Industrial Revolution," in *The American Family in Sociohistorical Perspective,* 2d ed., ed. Michael Gordon (New York: St. Martin's Press, 1978), pp. 67, 82.

27. The statistical association of ethnicity with extended-family households (Anglos = 1, Mexican Americans = 0) was a Lambda of $-.639$ with family-type dependent. For all household types the association was a Tau C score of .051 at a significance level of .0001 ($\chi^2 = 101.8$, sig. .0001).

28. Stephen Thernstrom, *The Other Bostonians: Poverty and Progress in an American Metropolis* (Cambridge, MA: Harvard University Press, 1973), pp. 222–23.

29. Alwyn Barr, "Occupational and Geographic Mobility in San Antonio, 1870–1900," *Social Science Quarterly* 5(2) (September 1970): 401.

30. Griswold del Castillo, *The Los Angeles Barrio,* pp. 36–38.

31. Ibid., p. 65.

32. Dolores P. de Bennet to Dolores Aguirre (ms., Samaniego Collection, Arizona Historical Society, Tucson, 1910).

33. Mrs. Juana Armizo, "Reminiscences of Juana Armizo" (typescript, Arizona Historical Society, Tucson).

34. Judge Benjamin Hayes, *Pioneer Notes from the Diaries of Judge Benjamin Hayes, 1849–1878* (Los Angeles: privately printed, 1929), p. 153.

35. Howard P. Chudacoff and Tamara K. Hareven, "Family Transitions into Old Age," in *Transitions: The Family and Life Course in Historical Perspective*, ed. Tamara K. Hareven (New York: San Francisco: Academic Press, 1976), pp. 217–43.

36. Herbert Gutman, *The Black Family in Slavery and Freedom, 1750–1925* (New York: Pantheon Books, 1976), pp. 448–49.

8

SPLIT HOUSEHOLD, SMALL PRODUCER, AND DUAL WAGE EARNER
An Analysis of Chinese American Family Strategies

EVELYN NAKANO GLENN

Most research on family patterns of black and other urban poor minorities points to the decisive impact of larger institutional structures. Particular attention has been paid to structures that lock certain classes of people into marginal employment and/or chronic unemployment (Drake and Cayton 1962; C. Valentine 1968). It has been argued that many characteristics of family organization—for example, reliance on female-based kinship networks—represent strategies for coping with the chronic poverty brought about by institutional racism (Stack 1974; Valentine 1978). Structural factors are considered sufficiently powerful to outweigh the influence of cultural tradition, especially in the case of blacks.

Chinese Americans, despite their historical status as an economically exploited minority, have been treated in almost exactly opposite terms. Studies of the Chinese American family have largely ignored social and economic conditions. They focus on purely cultural determinants, tracing characteristics of family life to Chinese values and traditions. The resulting

Evelyn Nakano Glenn, "Split Household, Small Producer, and Dual Wage Earner: An Analysis of Chinese American Family Strategies" from *Journal of Marriage and Family 45*, No. 1 (1983): 35–46. Copyright © 1983 by the National Council on Family Relations. Reprinted with permission.

portrayal of the Chinese American family has been highly favorable; the family is depicted as stable and problem-free—low in rate of divorce (Huang 1976), delinquency (Sollenberger 1968), and welfare dependency (Light 1972). These virtues are attributed to the family-centered values of Chinese society.

Given this positive assessment, the absence of challenges to the cultural approach is understandable. Still, the case of the Chinese cannot be disengaged from controversies involving other minority groups. The apparent fortitude of the Chinese has been cited as evidence supporting the view of black and Hispanic families as disorganized. Along with other "model" minorities, notably the Japanese and Cubans, the Chinese seem to have offered proof that some groups possess cultural resources that enable them to resist the demoralizing effects of poverty and discrimination. By implication, the difficulties experienced by blacks and Hispanics are due in some measure to the cultural weaknesses of these groups.

On the basis of an historical review and informant interviews,[1] this study argues that a purely cultural analysis does not adequately encompass the historical realities of Chinese American family life. It argues furthermore that a fuller understanding of the Chinese American family must begin with an examination of the changing constellation of economic, legal, and political constraints that have shaped the Chinese experience in America. When followed by an analysis of the strategies adopted to cope with these constraints, such an examination reveals the many institutionally created problems the Chinese have confronted in forming and maintaining family life, and the variety of strategies they have used to overcome limitations. By positing a more or less passive cultural determinism and a continuity of Chinese culture, the cultural approach used up to now by many writers tends to obscure not only the problems and struggles of Chinese American families but also their heterogeneity over time.

Cultural vs. Institutional Approaches to the Chinese American Family

The cultural approach grows out of the dominant assimilative perspective in the race- and ethnic-relations field (Gordon 1964; Park 1950). This perspective focuses on the initial cultural and social differences among groups and attempts to trace the process of assimilation over time; much literature on Chinese Americans is framed in these terms (Hirata 1976). The rather extreme emphasis on traditional *Chinese* culture, however, seems to require further explanation. The emphasis may be due in part to the prevailing conception of the Chinese as perpetual foreigners or "strangers" (Wolff 1950). The image of the Chinese as strange, exotic, and different seems to have preceded their actual arrival in the United States (Miller 1969). Since arriving, their marginal position in the larger society, combined with racist ideology, has served to perpetuate and popularize the image. First, laws excluding the Chinese from citizenship and preventing them from bringing over spouses and children ensured that for over 130 years a large proportion of the Chinese American population consisted of non-English-speaking alien residents. Second, discriminatory laws and practices forced the Chinese to congregate in ethnic ghettos and to concentrate in a narrow range of enterprises such as laundries, restaurants, and tourist-oriented businesses (Light and Wong 1975) that simultaneously reinforced and exploited their foreignness. Moreover, because of distinctive racial features, Americans of Chinese ancestry have been lumped together in the public mind with Chinese foreign nationals and recent immigrants, so that third-, fourth- or even fifth-generation Americans are assumed to be culturally as well as racially Asian. It is not surprising, therefore, to find that until recently studies of Chinese Americans interpreted social and community organizational patterns as products of Chinese culture rather than as responses to economic and social conditions in the United States (Lyman 1974 is an exception; see also Hirata 1976 and Kwong 1979 for related critiques).

Studies of family life follow in this same mold. Authors typically begin by examining traditional Chinese family patterns, then attempt to show how these patterns are expressed in a new setting and undergo gradual change through acculturation (e.g., Haynor and Reynolds 1937; Hsu 1971; Kung 1962; Sung 1971; Weiss 1974). The features identified as typical of Chinese American families and as evidence of cultural continuity are (a) stable family units as indicated by low rates of divorce and illegitimacy; (b) close ties between generations, as shown by the absence of adolescent rebellion and juvenile delinquency; (c) economic self-sufficiency, demonstrated by avoidance of welfare dependency; and (d) conservatism, expressed by retention of Chinese language and customs in the home.

Each of these characteristics is interpreted in terms of specific aspects of Chinese culture. For example, the primacy of the family unit over the individual in Chinese society is credited for the rarity of divorce. Similarly, the principles of Confucianism (filial piety, respect for elders, and reverence for tradition) are cited as the philosophical bases for close control over children by parents and retention of Chinese language and customs in the home; and the family-based production system in the Chinese agricultural village is seen as the precedent for immigrants' involvement in family enterprise and economic self-sufficiency.

An institutional approach starts at a different point, looking not at Chinese society but at conditions in the United States. More specifically, it focuses on the legal and political restrictions imposed on the Chinese, particularly with respect to immigration, citizenship, residential mobility, and economic activity. The Chinese were the first group excluded on racial grounds for legally immigrating, starting in 1882 and continuing until the mid-1950s. When they were allowed entry, it was under severe restrictions which made it difficult for them to form and maintain families in the United States. They also were denied the right to become naturalized citizens, a right withheld until 1943. This meant that for most of their 130-year history in the United States, the

Chinese were categorically excluded from political participation and entrance into occupations and professions requiring citizenship for licensing (see Konvitz 1946). In addition, during the latter part of the nineteenth century and through the early twentieth, California and other western states in which the Chinese were concentrated imposed head taxes and prohibited Chinese from carrying on certain types of businesses. The Chinese were routinely denied most civil rights, including the right to testify in court, so they had no legal recourse against injury or exploitation (Jacobs and Landau 1971; Wu 1972). Having initially worked in railroad building, agriculture, and mining, the Chinese were driven out of smaller towns, rural areas, and mining camps during the late nineteenth century and were forced to congregate in urban ghettos (Lyman 1977). The effect of these various restrictions was to keep the Chinese in the status of alien guests or commuters going back and forth between China and America. In addition, the restrictions led to a population made up disproportionately of male adults, concentrated in Chinatowns, and limited to a few occupations and industries.

These circumstances provide an alternative explanation for some of the features previously described as originating in Chinese culture: (a) low divorce rates result when spouses are forced to stay together by the lack of economic options outside of family enterprises; (b) low delinquency rates may reflect the demographic composition of the population which, up to the mid-1950s, contained few adolescents who, therefore, could be more effectively controlled by community sanctions; (c) avoidance of welfare is necessitated by the illegal status of many immigrants and the lack of access to sources outside the community; (d) retention of Chinese language and custom is a logical outcome of ghetto life and denial of permanent membership in American society.

Being able to generate plausible explanations does not itself constitute support for one approach over the other. However, in addition to offering alternative interpretations, the two approaches lead to quite different expectations regarding the degree of types of changes which the Chinese American family has undergone over time. By tracing family patterns to a specific cultural system, the *cultural approach* implies a continuity in family organization over time, with change occurring gradually and linearly via acculturation. By connecting family patterns to contemporaneous institutional structures, the *institutional approach* implies that family organization could and probably would undergo dramatic change with alteration in external constraints. A related point is that the cultural approach suggests that Chinese American family patterns are unique to this group, while the institutional approach suggests that other groups with differing cultural traditions might display similar patterns under parallel conditions.

The analysis that follows tests these expectations against the historical evidence by documenting the existence of qualitatively different family forms among Chinese Americans in different historical periods, with occasional reference to similar family forms among other groups in comparable circumstances. Three distinct family types are identified, corresponding to three periods demarcated by shifts in institutional constraints.

TABLE 1   Chinese Population in the United States, by Sex, Sex Ratio, Percentage Foreign Born, and Percentage Under Age 15, 1860–1970

Year	Total	Male	Female	Male/Female Ratio	% Foreign Born	% Aged 14 or Under
1860	34,933	33,149	1,784	18.58		
1870	63,199	58,633	4,566	12.84	99.8	
1880	105,465	100,686	4,779	21.06	99.0	
1890	107,475	103,607	3,868	26.79	99.3	
1900	89,863	85,341	4,522	18.87	90.7	3.4
1910	71,531	66,856	4,675	14.30	79.3	
1920	61,639	53,891	7,748	6.96	69.9	12.0
1930	74,954	59,802	15,152	3.95	58.8	20.4
1940	77,504	57,389	20,115	2.85	48.1	21.2
1950	117,140	76,725	40,415	1.90	47.0	23.3
1960	236,084	135,430	100,654	1.35	39.5	33.0
1970	431,583	226,733	204,850	1.11	46.9	26.6

Source: U.S. Censuses for the years 1872, 1883, 1895, 1902, 1913, 1922, 1933, 1943, 1953, 1963, and 1973. List of specific tables available upon request.

The Split–Household Family

For the first seventy years of Chinese presence in the United States, from 1850 to 1920, one can hardly speak of family life since there were so few women or children (Lyman 1968; Nee and Nee 1974). As Table 1 shows, from the late nineteenth to the early twentieth century, the ratio of males to females ranged from 13:1 to 20:1. In 1900 less than 4 percent of the Chinese population consisted of children fourteen years and under, compared to 37.4 percent of the population of whites of native parentage (U.S. Bureau of the Census 1902).

The first thirty-two years, from 1850 to 1882, was a period of open immigration when over 300,000 Chinese left Guangdong Province to work in California and the West (Lyman 1974). Most were able-bodied young men, recruited for labor on the railroads and in agriculture, mining, and manufacturing. Although some men of the merchant class came and brought wives or concubines, the vast majority of immigrants were laborers who came alone, not intending to stay; over half left wives behind in China (Coolidge 1909). Many were too impoverished to pay for passage and came on the credit ticket system, which obligated them to work for a fixed term, usually seven years, to pay for transport (Ling 1912). These "birds of passage" labored to send remittances to relatives and to accumulate capital to enable them to acquire land in China. Two-thirds apparently succeeded in returning, as there were never more than 110,000 Chinese in the United States at any one time.

It is possible that, like other Asian immigrants, Chinese laborers eventually would have sent for wives, had open immigration continued. The passage of the Chinese Exclusion Act of 1882 precluded this possibility. The Act barred laborers and their relatives but exempted officials, students, tourists, merchants, and relatives of merchants and citizens. Renewals of the Act in 1892 and 1902 placed further restrictions on entry and return. Finally, the Immigration Act of 1924 cut off all immigration from Asia (Wu 1972). These acts achieved their aim, which was to prevent the Chinese from settling in the United States. With almost no new immigration and the return of many sojourners to China, the Chinese population dwindled from a high of 107,000 in 1890 to 61,000 in 1920. Chinese men of the laboring class—faced with an unfavorable sex ratio, forbidden as non-citizens from bringing over wives, and prevented by laws in most western states from marrying whites—had three choices: (a) return permanently to China; (b) if single, stay in the United States as bachelors; or (c) if married, remain separated from families except for occasional visits.

Faced with these alternatives, the Chinese nevertheless managed to take advantage of openings in the law; if they had not, the Chinese population in the United States would have disappeared. One category for which entry was still allowed was relatives of citizens. Men born in the United States could return to China, marry, and father children, who were then eligible for entry. The 1906 earthquake and fire in San Francisco that destroyed most municipal records proved a boon for the large Chinese population of that area. Henceforth, residents could claim American birth without officials being able to disprove the contention (Sung 1971). It became common practice for American-born Chinese (actual or claimed) to visit China, report the birth of a son, and thereby create an entry slot. Years later the slot could be used by a relative, or the papers could be sold to someone wanting to immigrate. The purchaser, called a "paper son," simply assumed the name and identity of the alleged son.

Using these openings, many families adopted a strategy of long-term sojourning. Successive generations of men emigrated as paper sons. To ensure loyalty to kin, young men were married off before leaving. Once in America, they were expected to send money to support not only wives and children but also parents, brothers, and other relatives. In some villages, overseas remittances constituted the main source of income. It has been estimated that between 1937 and 1940 overseas Chinese remitted more than $2 billion, and that an average of $7 million per annum was sent from the United States in the years between 1938 and 1947 (Lyman 1968; Sung 1971). In one typical family history, recounted by a 21-year-old college student, great-grandfather arrived in the United States in the 1890s as a paper son and worked for about twenty years as a laborer. He then sent for the grandfather, who helped great-grandfather run a small business. Great-grandfather subsequently returned to China, leaving grandfather to carry on the business and forward remittances. In the 1940s grandfather sent for father. Up to this point, none of the wives had left China; finally, in the late 1950s, father returned to China and brought back his wife, so that after nearly seventy years, a child was finally born in the United States.

The sojourning strategy led to a distinctive family form, the *split-household family*. A common sociological definition of a family is: a group of people related by blood or marriage, cooperating to perform essential domestic tasks such as production, consumption, reproduction, and socialization. In the split-household family, production would be separated from other functions and carried out by a member living far away (who, of course, would be responsible for his own consumption needs). The other functions—reproduction, socialization, and the rest of consumption—would be carried out by the wife and other relatives in the home village. The family would remain an interdependent, cooperative unit, thereby fulfilling the definition of a family, despite geographic separation. The split-household form made possible the maximum exploitation of the worker. The labor of prime-age male workers could be bought relatively cheaply, since the cost of reproduction and family maintenance was borne partially by unpaid subsistence work of women and old people in the village. The sojourner's remittances, though small by U.S. standards, afforded a comfortable standard of living for family members in China.

The split household is not unique to the Chinese and, therefore, cannot be explained as a culturally preferred pattern. Sojourning occurs where there are (a) large differences in the level of economic development of receiving vs. sending regions, and (b) legal/administrative barriers to integration of the sending group. Three examples of the phenomenon are guest workers in Western Europe (Castles and Kosack 1973); gold-mine workers in South Africa (Boserup 1970); and Mexican braceros in the American Southwest (Power 1979). In all three cases, prime-age workers from disadvantaged regions are issued limited-duration permits to reside in regions needing low-wage labor but are prevented from bringing relatives or settling permanently. Thus, the host country benefits from the labor of sojourners without having to incorporate them into the society. Although the persistence of sojourning for several generations makes the Chinese somewhat unusual, there is evidence that legal restrictions were critical to maintaining the pattern. Other societies to which the Chinese immigrated did not prohibit intermarriage or limit economic competition—for example, Peru and the Philippines. In these societies, a high proportion of the Chinese intermarried with the native population (Hunt and Walker 1974; Wong 1978).

The life of the Chinese sojourner in the United States has been described in sociological and historical studies (see Lyman 1977; Nee and Nee 1974). Employed as laborers or engaged in small enterprises, the men lived in rented rooms alone or with other "bachelors." In place of kin ties, they relied on immigrant associations based on fictive clan relationships. As is common in predominantly male societies, many sojourners found outlets in gambling, prostitution, and drugs. Those successful enough or frugal enough to pay for passage returned periodically to China to visit and to father more children. Others, as a result of bad luck or personal disorganization, could never save enough to return. Even with movement back and forth, many sojourners gradually came to feel remote from village ties, and attached to life in the Chinese American colony. Thus, they ended up staying in the United States more or less by choice (Siu 1952).

The situation of wives and relatives in China has not been documented in the literature. According to informants, wives generally resided with in-laws; and remittances were sent to the husband's kin, usually a brother or son, to ensure that wives remained chaste and subject to the ultimate control of their husbands. Despite the lack of formal authority, most wives had informal influence and were consulted on major decisions. An American-born informant, the daughter of an herbalist and his concubine, was sent as a young girl to be raised by her father's first wife in China. This first wife never wanted to join her husband, as she lived quite comfortably in the village; with remittances from her husband, she maintained a large house with two servants and oversaw substantial landholdings and investments. The father's concubine led an arduous life in the United States, raising several children, running the household, and working long hours in the shop.

Parent–child relations were inevitably affected by separation. The mother–child tie was strengthened by the absence of the father. The mother's tie with her eldest son, normally an important source of leverage within an extended-kin household, became particularly close. In contrast, prolonged absence made the father's relationship with his children more formal and distant. The long periods between visits meant that the children were spaced far apart, and the father was often middle-aged or elderly by the time the youngest child was born. The age gap between fathers and later children added to the formality of the relationship.

The Small–Producer Family

Despite obstacles to family formation, the presence of families was evident in the major U.S. Chinatowns by the 1920s. As Table 1 shows, the male–female ratio fell, and the proportion of children nearly doubled between 1920 and 1930. These early families were started primarily by small entrepreneurs, former laborers who had accumulated enough capital to start a small business alone or in partnership. Due to occupational restrictions and limited capital, the enterprises were confined to laundries, restaurants, groceries, and other small shops. Once in business they could register as merchants, return to China, and bring over wives and children. There was an economic incentive to bring over families; besides providing companionship and affection, women and children were a source of free labor for the business.

The number of families grew steadily, then jumped dramatically during the 1950s due to changes in immigration regulations. The first small opening was created in 1943 with the repeal of the Chinese Exclusion Act. In recognition of China's position as an ally in World War II, a token quota of 105 entrants per year was granted, and permanent residents were declared eligible for citizenship. A larger opening was created by the "Brides Act" of 1946, which permitted entry to wives and children of citizens and permanent residents, and by the Immigration Act of 1953, which gave preference to relatives of citizens (Lee 1956; Li 1977b). For the first time in over sixty years, sizable legal immigration flowed from China; and for the first time in history, the majority of entrants were women. The women fell into two general categories: wives separated from their husbands for periods ranging up to thirty years or more, and brides of servicemen and other citizens who took advantage of the 1946 and 1953 laws to visit China and get married (Lee 1956). The marriages were usually arranged hastily; Chinese families were eager to have eligible daughters married to Americans, so the men had no problem finding prospects on short notice. At the same time, parents of American-born men often preferred Chinese-born brides (Lee 1956). An American-born woman explained why; she once had an engagement broken off because her fiancé's parents objected to the marriage:

> *They thought American girls will be bossy; she'll steal the son and go out freely. They said, "She will ruin your life. She'll be free spending with money." Also, she won't support the parents the rest of their life. They want a typical Chinese girl who will do what the father wants. [Interview with subject]*

At his parent's urging, the fiancé later visited China and brought back a wife.

During the period from about 1920 to the mid-1960s, the typical immigrant and first-generation family functioned as a productive unit in which all members, including children, worked without wages in a family business. The business was profitable only because it was labor-intensive and members put in extremely long hours. Often, for reasons of thrift, convenience, or lack of options, the family's living quarters were located above or behind the shop; thus, the workplace and home were physically joined.

Some flavor of the close integration of work and family life is seen in this description of the daily routine in a family laundry, provided by a woman who grew up in Boston's Chinatown during the 1930s and 1940s. The household consisted of the parents and four children. The work day started at 7:00 in the morning and did not end until midnight, six days a week. Except for school and a short nap in the afternoon, the children worked the same hours as the parents, doing their homework between midnight and 2:00 A.M. Each day's routine was the same. All items were marked or tagged as they were brought in by customers. A commercial cleaner picked up the laundry, washed it, and brought it back wet. The wet laundry was hung to dry in a back room heated by a coal burner. Next, items were taken down, sprinkled, starched, and rolled for ironing. Tasks were allocated by age and sex. Young children of six or seven performed simple tasks such as folding socks and wrapping parcels. At about age ten they started ironing handkerchiefs and underwear. Mother operated the collar and cuff press, while father hand-ironed shirts and uniforms. Only on Sunday did the family relax its hectic regimen to attend church in the morning and relax in the afternoon.

This family may have been unusually hard working, but this sort of work-centered family life was common among the generation that grew up between 1920 and 1960. In fact, the close-knit small-business family was portrayed in several popular autobiographies covering this period (Kingston 1976; Lowe 1943; Wong 1950). These accounts describe a life of strict discipline, constant toil, and frugality. Family members constantly interacted, but communication tended to revolve around concrete details of work. Parents directed and admonished the children in Chinese as they worked, so that the American-born Chinese became fluent in Chinese as well as in English, which they learned in school. Education was stressed, so that children's time was fully occupied by studying, working, and caring for younger siblings. Not so apparent in these accounts was the high incidence of disease, including tuberculosis, due to overcrowding and overwork (Lee, Lim, and Wong 1969).

The small-producer family had several distinct characteristics. First was the lack of any clear demarcation between work and family life. Child care, domestic maintenance, and income-producing activities occurred simultaneously in time and in the same location. Second was the self-contained nature of the family as a production and consumption unit. All members contributed to family income and domestic maintenance, including the children. Third was the division of labor by age and gender, with gradations of responsibility according to capacity and experience. Elder siblings were responsible for disciplining and taking care of younger siblings, who in turn were expected to defer to their older brothers and sisters. Finally, there was an emphasis on the collectivity over the individual. With so many individuals working in close quarters for extended periods of time, a high premium was placed on cooperation. Self-expression, which might engender conflict, had to be curbed.

While these features are in some way similar to those found in Chinese peasant families, they do not necessarily represent carryovers of Chinese patterns; they can be attributed equally to the particular material and social conditions arising from the family's involvement in small enterprise, an involvement dictated by limited economic options. There is evidence that these features are common to small-producer families in various societies and times (see, for example, Demos' 1970 account of the early Puritan families of the Massachusetts Bay Colony). Moreover, the Chinese American small-producer family had some features that differed from those of rural Chinese families due to circumstances of life in America. Of great significance was the family's location in a society whose dominant language and customs differed greatly. Children had the advantage in this regard. Once they started school, children quickly learned to speak and write English, while parents were rarely able to acquire more than rudimentary English. The parents came to depend on their children to act as mediators in relation to the outside society. As a result, children gained a great deal of status at an early age, in contrast to the subordinate position of children in China. American-born Chinese report that, starting at age eight or nine, they helped their parents in business and domestic matters by reading documents and contracts, accompanying them to the bank to fill out slips, negotiating with customers, and translating notices in stores.

A second circumstance was the age composition of immigrant communities, which were made up primarily of childbearing-aged men, and later, women. In the initial period of family formation, therefore, there were no grandparents; and households tended to be nuclear in form. In China the preferred pattern was for sons to live with parents, and wives were required to defer to mothers-in-law. The young immigrant mother, however, did not have to contend with in-laws. As a result of this, and the fact that she was an equal producer in the family economy, the wife had more autonomy. Many informants recall their mothers as the disciplinarians and central figures in the household.

The Dual Wage Earner Family

Following World War II, particularly after the Civil Rights Movement of the 1960s, discrimination against Asian Americans eased. College-educated Chinese Americans were able to enter white-collar occupations and industries formerly barred to them and to move into previously restricted neighborhoods. Among these socially mobile families, the parents still shop and visit friends in Chinatown, but their children tend not to have ties there. The lowering of barriers also speeded the integration of the so-called scholar-professional immigrants. Educated in Hong Kong, mainland China or Taiwan, many are Mandarin-speaking, in contrast to the Cantonese-speaking resident population. The older segment of this group arrived as students in the 1940s and 1950s and stayed, while the younger segment entered under the 1965 immigration act, which did away with national quotas and gave preference to relatives of citizens and permanent residents and to those in needed occupations. Employed as professionals, this group tends to live in white neighborhoods and to have little connection with Chinatown. Thus, for the socially mobile American-born and the scholar/professional immigrants, the trend has been toward assimilation into the mainstream of American society.

At the same time, however, there has been a countertrend that has re-Sinicized the Chinese American population. The same immigration law that brought in professionals and scholars has brought in an even larger influx of working-class Chinese. Under the liberalized law, over 20,000 Chinese have entered the United States each year since 1965, primarily via Hong Kong (U.S. Department of Justice 1977).[2] About half the immigrants can be classified as working class, having been employed as service workers, operatives, craftsmen, or laborers in Hong Kong (Nee and Nee 1974). After arrival, moreover, a significant proportion of professional, managerial, and white-collar immigrants experience a drop in occupational status into blue-collar and service jobs because of language and licensing difficulties (U.S. Department of Health, Education, and Welfare 1974).

Unlike the earlier immigrants who came over as individuals, most new immigrants come over in family groups—typically a husband, wife, and unmarried children (Li 1977a). The families have pulled up stakes in order to gain greater political security, economic opportunity, and educational advantages for their children. Since the law gives preference to relatives, most families use kinship ties with previous immigrants to gain entry. Frequently, the ties are used in a chainlike fashion (Li 1977b). For example, a couple might sponsor the wife's sister, her husband, and her children; the sister's husband in turn sponsors his parents, who later bring over one of their children, and so forth. In this way an extended-kin network is reunited in the United States.

Initially, the new immigrants usually settle in or near Chinatown so that they can trade in Chinese-speaking stores, use bilingual services, and find employment. They are repopulating and stimulating growth in Chinatowns at a time when these communities are experiencing declines due to the mobility of American-born Chinese (Hong 1976). The new immigrants have less dramatic adjustments to make than did earlier immigrants, having lived for some years in an urban society that exposed them to Western goods and lifestyles. In addition, although bilingual social services are frequently inadequate, municipal and county agencies now provide medical care, advice on immigration problems, family counseling, and the like. The immigrants rely on these public services rather than on the clan associations which, thus, have lost their old influence.

Despite the easier adjustment and greater opportunities for mobility, problems of language, and discrimination in small trade, construction and craft unions still affect immigrants who are not professionally trained. Having given up property, businesses or jobs, and having exhausted their resources to pay for transportation and settlement, they must quickly find a way to make a living and establish their families in a highly industrialized economy. The strategy most families have adopted is for husband and wife to find employment in the secondary labor market, the labor-intensive, low-capital service and small manufacturing sectors. The wage each earns is low, but by pooling income a husband and wife can earn enough to support a family. The typical constellation is a husband, who works as a waiter, cook, janitor, or store helper, and a wife who is employed in a small garment shop (Ikels and Shiang 1979; Nee and Nee 1974; "Tufts' lease . . ." 1981; cf. Lamphere, Silva, and Sousa 1980 for parallels with Azorean immigrants).

Although many women have been employed in Hong Kong, for most it is a new experience to juggle full-time work outside the home with child care and housework. In Hong Kong, mothers could do piecework at home, stitching or assembling plastic flowers during spare hours (Ikels and Shiang 1979). In the United States, employment means a long complicated day involving dropping off children at school, going to work in a shop for a few hours, picking up children from school, preparing food, and returning for a few more hours of work in the shop. Another change in many families is that the women's earnings comprise a greater share of family income in the United States. The pay differential between men and women, which is large in Hong Kong, becomes less or even reversed because of the downward shift in the husband's occupation (Hong 1980). Wives and husbands become more or less coequal breadwinners.

Perhaps the most striking feature of the dual-worker family is the complete segregation of work and family life. As a result, in contrast to the round-the-clock togetherness of the small-producer family, parents and children in the dual-worker family are separated for most of the day. While apart they inhabit totally different worlds. The parents' lives are regulated by the discipline of the job, while children lead relatively unstructured and unsupervised lives, often in the company of peers whose parents also work (Nee and Nee 1974). Furthermore, although mothers are usually at home by early evening, the father's hours may prevent him from seeing the children at all. The most common shift for restaurant workers runs from 2:00 in the afternoon until 11:00 at night. The sons and daughters of restaurant workers reported that they saw their fathers only on their days off.

The parents' fatigue, the long hours of separation, and the lack of common experiences combine to undermine communication. Children complain that their parents are not around much and, when they are, are too tired to talk. One young student notes, "We can discuss things, but we don't talk that much. We don't have that much to say." In addition, many parents suffered serious trauma during World War II and the Chinese Revolution, which they refuse to discuss. This refusal causes blocks to intimacy between parents and children since certain topics become taboo. For their part, parents complain that they have lost control over their children. They attribute the loss of influence to the fact that children adjust to American ways and learn English much more quickly than parents. Over a period of years, a language barrier frequently develops. Since parents are not around to direct and speak to children in Chinese, the children of wage-earning parents lost the ability (or willingness) to speak Chinese. When they reach adolescence, moreover, children can find part-time employment, which gives them financial independence as well as money to spend on outside recreation.

The absence of a close-knit family life among dual-worker families has been blamed for the eruption of youth rebellion, delinquency, and gang violence in Chinatowns during the 1960s and 1970s (Lyman 1974; Nee and Nee 1974). While the change in family patterns undoubtedly has been a factor, other demographic and social changes have contributed to the surfacing of youth problems (Light and Wong 1975). Adolescents make up a higher proportion of the new immigrants than they did in previous cohorts, and many immigrants arriving as adolescents encounter difficulties in school because of the language barrier. When they leave school they face unemployment or the prospect of low-wage service jobs. Similar obstacles were faced by the early immigrants, but they take on a new meaning in the present era when expectations are higher and when there is more awareness of institutional racism.

In a similar vein, dual-worker families are beset by the chronic difficulties that plagued Chinese American families in the past—rundown crowded housing, low incomes, immigration problems, and language difficulties; but their impact is different now that the family faces them in a less unified fashion.

Social workers employed in Chinatown report that the immigrant family is torn by a multiplicity of problems.[3] Ironically, the resilience of the Chinese American family until recently has retarded efforts at relief. It has taken the visible outbreak of the youth unrest mentioned above to dramatize the fact that the Chinese American family cannot endure any and all hardships without support. For the first time, social services, housing programs, and other forms of support are being offered to Chinese American families.

Summary and Conclusions

This sociohistorical examination of the Chinese American immigrant family has emphasized three main points: first, throughout their history in the United States, Chinese Americans have faced a variety of economic, social and political constraints that have had direct effects on family life. Second, Chinese American families have displayed considerable resourcefulness in devising strategies to overcome structural obstacles and to take advantage of the options open to them. Third, the strategies adopted have varied according to the conditions prevailing during given historical periods, resulting in three distinct family types. . . .

The split-household type, prevalent until 1920, adopted the strategy of sending married men abroad to specialize in income-producing activities. This created two separate households, one in the United States consisting of a primary individual—or, in some cases, a pair of related males such as a father and son—and another in China, consisting of the relatives of the sojourner—wife, children, parents, and brothers and their wives. Production was separated from the rest of family life, with the husband/father engaging in paid work abroad while the other relatives engaged in subsistence activities (e.g., small-scale farming) and carried out other domestic functions. Husband and wife, therefore, led completely separate existences, with the husband's relation to parents taking precedence over his relation to his wife, and the wife forming her primary attachment with children.

The small-producer type succeeded the split-household type around 1920 and became more common after the late 1940s when women were allowed to join their spouses in the United States. The economic strategy was to engage in small-scale enterprises that relied on the unpaid labor of husband, wife, and children. The nuclear household was the basic unit, with no separation between production and family life, and was focused around work. Close parent–child relations resulted from the enforced togetherness and the constant interaction required to carry on the business. The economic roles of husband and wife were basically parallel, and most daily activities were shared in common.

Finally, the dual-wage type, which has predominated among immigrants arriving after 1965, is based on a strategy of individual wage work, with husband and wife engaged in low-wage employment. The pooling of two wages provides sufficient income to support the family. The household is primarily nuclear, with production and family life separate, as is common in industrial society. The clearest division of labor is between parents and children, with parents specializing in income-producing activities while children are economically inactive. The roles of husband and wife are symmetrical; that is, they engage in similar proportions of paid and unpaid work but in separate settings (cf. Young and Wilmott 1973). Because parents' employment schedules often keep them away from home, there is little shared activity. The parent–child tie becomes attenuated, with children involved in a separate world of peers.

The existence of three distinctly different family types corresponding to different historical periods calls into question the adequacy of purely cultural explanations of Chinese American family patterns. If cultural patterns were the sole or primary determinants, we would expect to find greater continuity in family patterns over time; instead, we find discontinuities associated with shifts in institutional conditions. These discontinuities underline the importance of the larger political economic structures in which the family is embedded.

At the same time, the family is shown as actively striving to survive and maintain ties within the constraints imposed by these structures. The persistence of ties and the variety of strategies adopted by Chinese American families testify to their resilience and resourcefulness in overcoming obstacles. Further insights into the relationships among and between culture, larger institutional structures, and family strategies might be gained through comparative historical analysis of different racial and ethnic groups.

ENDNOTES

The author is grateful to Gloria Chun, Judy Ng, and Yee Mei-Wong for discussions that provided valuable insights; and to Ailee Chin, Gary Glenn, Larry Hong, Charlotte Ikels, Peter Langer, S. M. Miller, T. Scott Miyakawa, and Barbara Vinick for comments on earlier drafts. A previous version of this paper was presented at the meetings for the Study of Social Problems, Toronto, August, 1981.

1. The analysis is based on review of the English-language literature on Chinese Americans and informant interviews of twenty-nine individuals of varying ages, nativity, and family status, mainly residing in the Boston area. Informants were interviewed about family immigration histories, economic activities, household composition, residence, and relations among family members. Social and community workers provided broader information on typical tensions and problems for which help was sought.

2. Although the immigrants enter via Hong Kong, they mostly originate from the same region of southern China as the earlier immigrants. They or their parents fled Guangdong during the Sino-Japanese War or during the land reform following the Communist victory. Hence, they tend to have kinship ties with earlier immigrants.

3. According to community workers and government agencies, the most common problems are low, though not poverty-level, family income; substandard and dilapidated housing; language difficulties; legal problems with immigration; and unresolved past traumas, including separation between family members.

REFERENCES

Boserup, E. 1970. *Women's Role in Economic Development.* New York: St. Martin's Press.

Castles, S. and G. Kosack. 1973. *Immigrant Workers and Class Structure in Western Europe.* London: Oxford University Press.

Coolidge, Mary. 1909. *Chinese Immigration.* New York: Henry Holt.

Demos, John. 1970. *A Little Commonwealth.* London: Oxford University Press.

Drake, S. C. and H. R. Cayton. 1962. *Black Metropolis.* Rev. ed. New York: Harper and Row.

Gordon, M. M. 1964. *Assimilation in American Life: The Role of Race, Religion, and National Origin.* New York: Oxford University Press.

Haynor, N. S. and C. N. Reynolds. 1937. "Chinese Family Life in America." *American Sociological Review* 2:630–37.

Hirata, L. C. 1976. "The Chinese American in Sociology." Pp. 20–26 in *Counterpoint: Perspectives on Asian Americans,* edited by E. Gee. Los Angeles: Asian American Studies Center, University of California, Los Angeles.

Hong, L. K. 1976. "Recent Immigrants in the Chinese American Community: Issues of Adaptations and Impacts." *International Migration Review* 10 (Winter): 509–14.

———. 1980. Personal communication.

Hsu, F. L. K. 1971. *The Challenge of the American Dream: The Chinese in the United States.* Belmont, CA: Wadsworth.

Huang, L. J. 1976. "The Chinese American Family." Pp. 124–47 in *Ethnic Families in America,* edited by C. H. Mindel and R. W. Habenstein. New York: Elsevier.

Hunt, C. I. and L. Walker. 1974. "Marginal Trading Peoples: Chinese in the Philippines and Indians in Kenya." Chap. 4 in *Ethnic Dynamics: Patterns of Intergroup Relations in Various Societies.* Homewood, IL: Dorsey Press.

Ikels, P. and J. Shiang. 1979. "The Chinese in Greater Boston." Interim Report to the National Institute of Aging.

Jacobs, P. and S. Landau. 1971. *To Serve the Devil.* Vol. 2, *Colonials and Sojourners.* New York: Vintage Books.

Kingston, M. H. 1976. *The Woman Warrior.* New York: Knopf.

Konvitz, M. G. 1946. *The Alien and Asiatic in American Law.* Ithaca, NY: Cornell University Press.

Kung, S. W. 1962. *Chinese in American Life: Some Aspects of Their History, Status, Problems, and Contributions.* Seattle: University of Washington Press.

Kwong, P. 1979. *Chinatown, New York: Labor and Politics, 1930–1950.* New York: Monthly Review Press.

Lamphere, L., F. M. Silva, and J. P. Sousa. 1980. "Kin Networks and Family Strategies; Working Class Portuguese Families in New England." Pp. 219–45 in *The Versatility of Kinships,* edited by L. S. Cordell and S. Beckerman. New York: Academic Press.

Lee, L. P., A. Lim, and H. K. Wong. 1969. Report of the San Francisco Chinese Community Citizen's Survey and Fact Finding Committee (abridged ed.). San Francisco: Chinese Community Citizen's Survey and Fact Finding Committee.

Lee, R. H. 1956. "The Recent Immigrant Chinese Families of the San Francisco-Oakland Area." *Marriage and Family Living* 18 (February): 14–24.

Li, P. S. 1977a. "Occupational Achievement and Kinship Assistance among Chinese Immigrants in Chicago." *Sociological Quarterly* 18 (4): 478–89.

———. 1977b. "Fictive Kinship, Conjugal Tie and Kinship Claim among Chinese Immigrants in the United States." *Journal of Comparative Family Studies* 8 (1): 47–64.

Light, I. 1972. *Ethnic Enterprise in America.* Berkeley and Los Angeles: University of California Press.

Light, I. and C. C. Wong. 1975. "Protest or Work: Dilemmas of the Tourist Industry in American Chinatowns." *American Journal of Sociology* 80:1342–68.

Ling, P. 1912. "The Causes of Chinese Immigration." *Annals of the American Academy of Political and Social Sciences* 39 (January): 74–82.

Lowe, P. 1943. *Father and Glorious Descendant*. Boston: Little, Brown.

Lyman. S. M. 1968. "Marriage and the Family among Chinese Immigrants to America, 1850–1960." *Phylon* 29 (4): 321–30.

——. 1974. *Chinese Americans*. New York: Random House.

——. 1977. "Strangers in the City: The Chinese in the Urban Frontier." In *The Asians in North America*. Santa Barbara, CA: ABC Clio Press.

Miller, S. C. 1969. *The Unwelcome Immigrant: The American Image of the Chinese, 1785–1882*. Berkeley: University of California Press.

Nee, V. G. and B. Nee. 1974. *Longtime Californ'*. Boston: Houghton Mifflin.

Park, R. E. 1950. *Race and Culture*. Glencoe, IL: Free Press.

Power, J. 1979. *Migrant Workers in Western Europe and the United States*. Oxford: Pergamon Press.

Siu, P. C. T. 1952. "The Sojourners." *American Journal of Sociology* 8 (July): 32–44.

Sollenberger, R. T. 1968. "Chinese American Childbearing Practices and Juvenile Delinquency." *Journal of Social Psychology* 74 (February): 13–23.

Stack, C. B. 1974. *All Our Kin: Strategies for Survival in a Black Community*. New York: Harper and Row.

Sung, B. L. 1971. *The Story of the Chinese in America*. New York: Collier Books.

"Tufts' Lease on Two Kneeland Street Buildings Threatens Over 600 Jobs in Chinatown." 1981. *Sampan*, May.

U.S. Bureau of the Census. 1872. *Ninth Census. Vol. I: The Statistics of the Population of the United States*. Washington, DC: Government Printing Office.

——. 1883. *Tenth Census. Statistics of the Population of the United States*. Washington, DC: Government Printing Office.

——. 1895. *Eleventh Census. Report on Population of the United States, Part I*. Washington, DC: Government Printing Office.

——. 1902. *Twelfth Census of the United States Taken in the Year 1900. Census Reports, Vol. II: Population, Part II*. Washington, DC: United States Census Office.

——. 1913. *Thirteenth Census of the United States Taken in the Year 1910. Vol. I: Population, General Report and Analysis*. Washington, DC: Government Printing Office.

——. 1922. *Fourteenth Census Taken in the Year 1920. Vol. II: Population, General Report and Analytic Tables*. Washington, DC: Government Printing Office.

——. 1933. *Fifteenth Census of the United States: 1930. Population, Vol. II: General Report, Statistics by Subject*. Washington, DC: Government Printing Office.

——. 1943. *Sixteenth Census of the Population: 1940. Population Characteristics of the Non-White Population by Race*. Washington, DC: Government Printing Office.

——. 1953. *U.S. Census of the Population: 1950. Vol. IV: Special Reports, Part 3, Chapter B, Non-White Population by Race*. Washington, DC: Government Printing Office.

——. 1963. *U.S. Census of the Population: 1960. Subject Reports. Non-White Population by Race. Final Report PC(2)-1C*. Washington, DC: Government Printing Office.

——. 1973. *Census of Population: 1970. Subject Reports. Final Report PC(2)-1G, Japanese, Chinese and Filipinos in the United States*. Washington, DC: Government Printing Office.

U.S. Department of Health, Education, and Welfare. 1974. *A Study of Selected Socioeconomic Characteristics of Ethnic Minorities Based on the 1970 Census. Vol. II: Asian Americans*. HEW Publication No. (OS) 75–121. Washington, DC: U.S. Department of Health, Education, and Welfare.

U.S. Department of Justice. 1977. *Immigration and Naturalization Service Annual Report*. Washington, DC: U.S. Department of Justice.

Valentine, B. L. 1978. *Hustling and Other Hard Work*. New York: Free Press.

Valentine, C. 1968. *Culture and Poverty: Critique and Counter-Proposals*. Chicago: University of Chicago Press.

Weiss, M. S. 1974. *Valley City: A Chinese Community in America*. Cambridge, MA: Schenkman.

Wolff, K. 1950. *The Sociology of Georg Simmel*. Glencoe, IL: Free Press.

Wong, B. 1978. "A Comparative Study of the Assimilation of the Chinese in New York City, and Lima, Peru." *Comparative Studies in Society and History* 20 (July): 335–58.

Wong, J. S. 1950. *Fifth Chinese Daughter.* New York: Harper and Brothers.

Wu, C. 1972. *"Chink": A Documentary History of Anti-Chinese Prejudice in America.* New York: Meridian.

Young, M. and P. Wilmott. 1973. *The Symmetrical Family.* London: Routledge and Kegan Paul.

PART III

Courtship, Dating, and Power

How do we select a marriage or life partner? Traditionally, courtship and dating were the processes used to select a mate. But courtship and dating are about numerous other things in addition to screening for potential marriage partners and for finding romantic love. Courtship and dating are also about economic relationships, family control (or the lack thereof), power dynamics, competition, popularity, having sex, recreation, and consumption patterns. In this section we examine the history of courtship in Western societies to discover when it evolved into a modern pattern of dating. This history reveals that courtship, and, later, dating reflect changing norms about who controls mate selection. Over time, Western societies have moved from collective and community control over marriage selection to increased family and parental control to individual control. Moreover, this history of courtship and dating practices shows changing gender norms and power dynamics. In particular, it reveals the changing social status of women and the changing social norms concerning relationships and sexuality. Thus, we examine the history of courtship and its contemporary counterpart: dating. We also examine cultural variations in dating and courtship, the importance of dating among gay, lesbian, and bisexual youth, and whether U.S. society is a postdating culture.

History of Courtship

Historically, courtship and mating were *not* distinctive from marriage. Courtship, with or without premarital sex, had the sole purpose of finding a spouse. Love was not the basis of marriage; instead, relationships were based on economic and family considerations. Because marriage was a financial arrangement between two families, parents often exercised control over their children's choice of mates. Arranged marriages are an excellent example of this premise. Parents or village elders would select prospective spouses based on financial and status concerns. A bride price or dowry may be arranged as well to reaffirm the economic nature of this relationship. In some societies, if love developed after an arranged marriage occurred, that was considered to be a bonus. However, in other societies, romantic love was seen as problematic in a marriage relationship because it interfered with the work that needed to be done. Instead, romantic love occurred outside of marriage. In medieval Europe, for example, knights tried to seduce married ladies and sonnets were written to strangers about undying love. Thus, romantic love was *not* always central to courtship activities.

Today, the United States is often described as a culture with a "romantic love complex." That is, compared to many other societies, the dominant U.S.

culture places a high value on romance as a precondition for relationships. Some scholars argue that our expectations for romantic love are so extreme, relationships have a difficult time matching this ideal and thus we have high divorce rates. Moreover, most Americans expect love prior to marriage and look down on those who marry for reasons other than love. The recent *Who Wants to Marry a Millionaire* television program is an excellent example of cultural condemnation of individuals who would marry for money instead of love. In this program, 50 women compete with each other (somewhat like a beauty contest) to win the approval of a wealthy man, who asks the winner to marry him at the end of the "contest." Other examples of courtship and dating television shows include *The Bachelor* and *The Bachelorette* series, in which a man or a woman is supposed to be able to select a mate from a group of opposite-sex contestants after a series of dates. These television shows similarly reveal cultural values about dating, love, marriage, and compulsory heterosexuality.

Dating

Unlike courtship, dating is more romanticized and also ensures more individual choice in the selection of a partner. The first article in this section, "Choosing Mates — The American Way," by Martin King Whyte, focuses on this transition from courtship to dating that occurred around the turn of the twentieth century in the United States. Whyte, a professor of sociology at Harvard University, argues that, in the late 1800s, an intermediary practice termed "calling" often occurred in middle- and upper-class families. A male suitor would ask a woman to have the privilege of "calling" on her. If the woman said yes, he would visit her home and spend time socializing with her. Their interaction was often supervised and controlled by a parent, usually the mother. Thus, little premarital intimacy could occur. A popular young woman would have several male suitors calling on her, and she would have to select which one to marry. Thus, the purpose of calling was for the woman to select a marriage partner. Whyte's article then focuses on how individuals select the person they will marry in a modern dating context and why dating is *not* a good predictor of marital success.

Moreover, dating has other purposes than just finding a marriage partner (Laner 1995). In fact, many people will argue that dating is not about looking for a life partner. Instead, dating is supposed to be for fun and recreation. Young people are expected by society to fall in love at earlier ages, but they are also expected to marry later. Thus, dating is supposed to fill in the gap of time between one's teen years and the time one marries, if she or he does. Sociologist Willard Waller (1937) argues that dating is not for fun or recreation; rather, it serves as a status sorting device. Waller, who studied dating at Penn State in the 1930s, found that young people rank their peers as more or less desirable. This ranking system varies between youths and adults and between the sexes. In particular, Waller found that men and women rank potential dating partners in terms of their physical and personality characteristics. Only a few individuals are placed at the top of the ranking system, and they are the highest in demand for dates. Waller called this system the "campus rating complex," and it rates individuals on a scale of 1 to 10, with 10 being the most desirable. Variations of this rating and dating system are common in each high school or peer group. Thus, Waller argued that dating has much more to do with competition and popularity than with finding romantic love or a marriage partner.

Power in Dating Relationships

One important theme in the literature on courtship and dating is *power*. Power dynamics are found in all human relationships, but are especially evident in family relationships. For example, there is power in the person who controls whom you can date and whom you can marry. Historically, this power resided in the parents, especially in the patriarchal father, to determine who their children could court or date. Today, in most Western societies, individuals have more control over dating and marriage choices. Thus, dating reflects a movement from family control over mate selection to individual control. Instead of parents overseeing dating rituals, peers have more control over dating. As Whyte argues in his article (Reading 9), this movement from family to individual control over dating also has been paralleled by another change, the movement from women having more power in a calling or dating relationship to men having more power. Thus, many power shifts have occurred in courtship and dating relationships over time, including a generational shift from parents to children; a gender shift from women to men; and the most recent shift from family control to more peer influences over dating.

This changing balance of power in dating relationships is observed more acutely in many first- and second-generation families in the United States. Some families emigrating to the United States come from cultures that have distinctive values and traditions about courtship and dating that do not necessarily align with dominant culture values of dating in the United States. In particular, many immigrant families still exert a great deal of family or community control over the courtship and mate selection of their children. Reading 10, "'She's 16 Years Old and There's Boys Calling Over to the House': An Exploratory Study of Sexual Socialization in Latino Families," investigates the role that diverse cultural beliefs have on the adolescent romantic and sexual behavior in Latino families. Marcela Raffaelli, an associate professor of psychology and ethnic studies at the University of Nebraska, Lincoln, conducted this research with a human development graduate student, Lenna L. Ontai. Ontai is currently the child and family cooperative extension specialist in the Human and Community Department at the University of California at Davis. In this interview study, Raffaelli and Ontai explore parental concerns about dating, family rules and communication about dating and sexuality, and actual dating experiences of a sample of Latinas living in the Midwest. Their study reveals that not all Latino families in the United States conform to dominant culture beliefs about dating and courtship, and that many young people grow up exposed to two very different cultural systems about dating and sexuality: that of their family and that of the dominant culture. These cultural differences in dating and courtship also reveal significant differences in beliefs about gender roles, power dynamics in relationships, and authority within the family.

The third article in this section, "Dating and Romantic Relationships among Gay, Lesbian, and Bisexual Youths," also illustrates well the influence of the dominant culture in defining what is a "normal" relationship and the cultural ideals of finding romantic love. The author of this selection, Ritch C. Savin–Williams, is chair of the Department of Human Development at Cornell University. Savin–Williams also is a clinical and developmental psychologist who has spent numerous hours with gay youth talking about the difficulties of dating and having romantic relationships with same-sex partners in a homophobic society. This reading also builds nicely on Whyte's article (Reading 9), which discusses the changing functions of courtship and dating over time. Savin–Williams argues that if dating is the means by which romantic relationships are practiced and established, and if dating serves a number of important functions, such as entertainment, recreation, socialization, mate selection, and enhances peer status and self-confidence, what happens to gay youth, who face so many barriers to same-sex dating? What is it like to be gay and wanting to date when one attends a very homophobic high school? Savin–Williams examines how gay youth cope with these barriers to form relationships and the effects of heterosexism and homophobia on their relationships and on their sense of self.

Postdating Society

Is the United States a postdating society? Teenagers and college students say they do not go out on formal dates anymore, whereby one person asks another to go out. Instead, they hang out together in groups, or a couple may "go" with each other; that is, spend additional time together and "hook up" (Taylor 1996). However, going with someone does not imply commitment nor an intention to marry that person. In addition, going with someone does not necessarily mean you are going somewhere, as in a traditional date, whereby a couple would go out to dinner or to the movies or partake in some other activity. Many scholars attribute the change in dating relationships to changing gender roles, especially the increase in closer platonic relationships between males and females; to changing peer culture, where young people spend more time in group-oriented social activities; and to increased fears of relationship failures and the unknown. Given the high incidence of dating violence and sexually transmitted diseases, it makes sense that people are more cautious about dating today.

Simon Rodberg, a student at Yale University, comments on the lack of romantic love on college campuses today. Rodberg argues that college students feel nostalgia for the ideal of the pre-1960s dating scene where parties had "dance cards, big bands, and good wine rather than keg beer." Instead of the Friday-night dating scene, college life today is marked by random hook-ups.

> Hook-ups, Mr. Rodberg and his classmates suggest, are the easiest, most physically gratifying way to find refuge from the pressures of finding and maintaining the ever-elusive "relationship." That, he notes, is because those relationships are an enormous source of pressure, especially for students accustomed to analyzing, deconstructing, planning and achieving—particularly in the era of AIDS and high divorce rates. The fundamental problem, Mr. Rodberg writes, is that "history and popular culture promised us true love and great sex, but reality taught us how much we could get hurt." (*Academe Today* 1999)

Thus, according to Rodberg, not only do college students miss the idealized and romanticized dating of past decades, they also are more cautious and pessimistic about dating.

Economic changes, such as the rise of capitalism and consumerism, also have greatly influenced dating patterns. For example, researcher Beth Bailey argues in her book on dating, *From the Front Porch to the Back Seat* (1988), that the development of the automobile, drive-in movies and other technologies, such as contraceptives, greatly altered the content and meaning of dating in the 20th century. Currently, we could examine the role of other technologies, such as the Internet, video technology, and cell phones for their effects on contemporary dating. We also could examine the increased amount of disposable income that people have to spend on social activities, dating services, or single's cruises and vacations. Thus, many dating behaviors still reflect social status differences and access to wealth and technology.

Dating has changed in other ways as well. People have busier schedules now, and it is difficult for many single adults to meet each other, especially after the completion of high school or college. One interesting new dating trend is "speed dating," whereby single men and women attend a special bar or club that enables them to have multiple short dates in one evening through either video screening or five-minute interviews. Like a game of musical chairs, people rotate to their next date after spending five minutes trying to make a good impression on each potential date. Many people also look for dating partners via newspaper or Internet personal ads or dating services that attempt to match people based on their interests and values. Most newspapers now carry personal ads categorized by sexual preference in which individuals advertise what they are looking for in a relationship. The Right One, a national dating service, advertises services in 53 U.S. cities and 5 cities in Canada. Their promotion materials state:

> At The Right One, our professional Membership Consultants will spend time talking with you about your background, your relationship history,

your work, what you like to do in your free time and what you are looking for in a potential partner. This one-on-one personal approach helps
us introduce you to the type of people you are compatible with—which
makes dating more comfortable and enjoyable. *It's sensible, safer and it
works!* (The Right One 1999)

It is interesting to note that this dating service emphasizes how logical and
safe this route to dating is. Members are led to believe that the service is
screening out potentially dangerous or unbecoming alternatives. The Right
One costs a couple thousand dollars per person to join. For that amount, the
individual receives six introductions over a period of time. Each introduction
has been carefully matched based on the answers clients give to a survey of
questions on their values, hobbies, and relationship preferences. The success
rate of these programs in helping people find a long-term mate is debatable.
Moreover, similar to what many family scholars already have argued, maybe
the *real* goal of contemporary dating is not about finding a long-term mate.
Maybe dating is more about having fun, spending time with peers, and displaying one's social status.

REFERENCES

Academe Today. 1999. "Nostalgia for Collegiate Romance." From the Daily Report of
the *Chronicle for Higher Education,* May 5. Retrieved from <daily@chronicle.com>.
Bailey, Beth. 1988. *From the Front Porch to the Back Seat.* Baltimore: Johns Hopkins
University Press.
Laner, Mary Riege. 1995. *Dating: Delights, Discontents, and Dilemmas.* 2d ed. Salem,
WI: Sheffield Publishing Company.
Taylor, Matthew. 1996. "Hanging Out Together Replaces Going Out on Dates." *Des
Moines Register,* November 21, p. 3T.
The Right One. 1999. Promotional materials mailed to single adults. Retrieved from
<www.therightone.com>.
Waller, Willard. 1937. "Rating and Dating Complex." *American Sociological Review*
2:737–39.

9

CHOOSING MATES–THE AMERICAN WAY

MARTIN KING WHYTE

A s America's divorce rate has been soaring, popular anxieties about marriage have multiplied. Is it still possible to "live happily ever after," and if so, how can this be accomplished? How can you tell whether a partner who leaves you breathless with yearning will, as your spouse, drive you to distraction? Does "living together" prior to marriage provide a realistic assessment of how compatible you and your partner might be as husband and wife? Questions such as these suggest a need to examine our American way of mate choice. How do we go about selecting the person we marry, and is there something wrong with the entire process?

For most twentieth-century Americans, choosing a mate is the culmination of a process of dating. Examination of how we go about selecting mates thus requires us to consider the American dating culture. Dating is a curious institution. By definition it is an activity that is supposed to be separate from selecting a spouse. Yet, dating is expected to provide valuable experience that will help in making a "wise" choice of a marital partner. Does this combination work?

How well dating "works" may be considered in a number of senses of this term. Is it easy or difficult to find somebody to go out with? Do dates mostly lead to enjoyable or painful evenings? However, these are not the aspects of dating I wish to consider. The issue here is whether dating works in the sense of providing useful experience that helps pave the way for a successful marriage.

Dating is a relatively new institution. The term, and the various practices associated with it, first emerged around the turn of the century. By the 1920s dating had more or less completely displaced earlier patterns of relations among unmarried Americans. Contrary to popular assumptions, even in colonial times marriages were not arranged in America. Parents were expected to give their approval to their children's nuptial plans, a practice captured in our image of a suitor asking his beloved's father for her hand in marriage. Parental approval, especially among merchants and other prosperous classes, put some constraint on the marriages of the young. For example, through the eighteenth century, children in such families tended to marry in birth order and marriage to cousins was not uncommon. (Both practices had declined sharply by the nineteenth century.) However, parents rarely directly arranged the marriages of their children. America has always exhibited

Martin King Whyte, "Choosing Mates—The American Way" from *Society* 29, No. 3 (March/April 1992): 71–77. Copyright © 1992 by Transaction Publishers, Inc. Reprinted with permission.

"youth-driven" patterns of courtship. Eligible males and females took the initiative to get to know each other, and the decision to marry was made by them, even if that decision was to some degree contingent on parental approval. (Of course, substantial proportions of later immigrant groups from Southern and Eastern Europe, Asia, and elsewhere brought with them arranged marriage traditions, and contention for control over marriage decisions was often a great source of tension in such families.)

How did young people get to know one another well enough to decide to marry in the era before dating? A set of customs, dominant for the two centuries, preceded the rise of the dating culture. These activities came to be referred to as "calling" and "keeping company." Young people might meet in a variety of ways—through community and church socials, informally in shops or on the street, on boat and train trips, or through introductions from friends or relatives. (America never developed a system of chaperoning young women in public, and foreign observers often commented on the freedom unmarried women had to travel and mix socially on their own.) Usually young people would go to church fairs, local dances, and other such activities with family, siblings, or friends, rather than paired off with a partner. Most activities would involve a substantial degree of adult and community supervision. Nonetheless, these gatherings did encourage some pairing off and led to hand holding, moonlit walks home, and other romantic exploration.

As relationships developed beyond the platonic level, the suitor would pay visits to the home of the young woman. By the latter part of the nineteenth century, particularly among the middle and upper classes, this activity assumed a formal pattern referred to as "calling." Males would be invited to call on the female at her home, and they were expected to do so only if invited. (A bold male could, however, request an invitation to call.) Invitations might be extended by the mother of a very young woman, but eventually they would come from the young woman herself. Often a woman would designate certain days on which she would receive callers. She might have several suitors at one time, and thus a number of men might be paying such calls. A man might be told that the woman was not at home to receive him, and he would then be expected to leave his calling card. If this happened repeatedly, he was expected to get the message that his visits were no longer welcome.

Initiative and control in regard to calling were in the hands of women (the eligible female and her mother). Although some variety in suitors was possible, even in initial stages the role of calling in examining potential marriage partners was very clear to all involved. The relatively constrained and supervised nature of calling makes it certain that enjoyment cannot have been a primary goal of this activity. (During the initial visits the mother was expected to remain present; in later visits she often hovered in an adjacent room.) If dating is defined as recreational and romantic pairing off between a man and a woman, away from parental supervision and without immediate consideration of marriage, then calling was definitely not dating.

The supervised and controlled nature of calling should not, however, lead us to suppose that propriety and chastity were always maintained until marriage. If the relationship had deepened sufficiently, the couple might progress from calling to "keeping company," a precursor of the twentieth-century custom of "going steady." At this stage, the primary activity would still consist of visits by the suitor to the woman's home. However, now she would only welcome calls from one man, and he would visit her home on a regular basis. Visits late into the evening would increasingly replace afternoon calls. As the relationship became more serious, parents would often leave the couple alone. Nineteenth-century accounts mention parents going off to bed and leaving the young couple on the couch or by the fireplace, there to wrestle with, and not infrequently give in to, sexual temptation.

Even though some women who headed to the altar toward the end of the nineteenth century had lost their virginity prior to marriage, premarital intimacy was less common than during the dating era. (The double standard of the Victorian era made it possible for many more grooms to be non-virgins at marriage than brides. Perhaps 50 percent or more of men had lost their virginity prior to marriage, as opposed to 15 to 20 percent of women, with prostitutes and "fallen women" helping to explain the differential.) What is less often realized is that the formalization of the calling pattern toward the end of the nineteenth century contributed to a decline in premarital sexual intimacy compared to earlier times. America experienced not one but two sexual revolutions—one toward the end of the eighteenth century, at the time of the American Revolution, and the other in the latter part of the twentieth century.

The causes of the first sexual revolution are subject to some debate. An influx of settlers to America who did not share the evangelical puritanism of many early colonists, the expansion of the population into the unsettled (and "unchurched") frontier, the growth of towns, and the individualistic and freedom-loving spirit of the American Revolution may have contributed to a retreat from the fairly strict emphasis on premarital chastity of the early colonial period. Historians debate the extent to which the archetypal custom of this first sexual revolution, bundling (which allowed an unmarried couple to sleep together, although theoretically fully clothed and separated by a "bundling board"), was widespread or largely mythical. Whatever the case, other evidence is found in studies of communities, such as those by Daniel Scott Smith and Michael Hindus, which found that the percentage of married couples whose first births were conceived premaritally increased from about 11 percent before 1700 to over 33 percent in the last decades of the eighteenth century.

This first sexual revolution was reversed in the nineteenth century. The reasons for its demise are also not clear. The closing of the frontier, the rise of the middle class, the defensive reactions of that new middle class to new waves of immigrants, the growth of Christian revivalism and reform movements, and the spread of models of propriety from Victorian England (which were in turn influenced by fear of the chaos of the French Revolution)—all these have been suggested as having contributed to a new sexual Puritanism in the nineteenth century. According to Smith and Hindus, premarital conceptions decreased once again to about 15 percent of first births between 1841 and 1880.

It was in the latter time period that the customs of calling and keeping company reached their most formal elaboration—calling, in less ritualized forms, can be traced back to the earliest colonial period. Not long after reaching the formal patterns described, calling largely disappeared. In little more than a generation, dating replaced calling as the dominant custom.

Dating involved pairing off of couples in activities not supervised by parents, with pleasure rather than marriage as the primary goal. The rules governing dating were defined by peers rather than by adults. The initiative, and much of the control, shifted from the female to the male. The man asked the woman out, rather than waiting for her invitation to call. The finances and transportation for the date were also his responsibility. The woman was expected to provide, in turn, the pleasure of her company and perhaps some degree of romantic and physical intimacy. By giving or withholding her affection and access to her body, she exercised considerable control over the man and the date as an event. Nonetheless, the absence of parental oversight and pressure to respond to a man's initiatives placed a woman in a weaker position than she was in the era of calling.

The man might pick up the woman at her home, but parents who tried to dictate whom their daughters dated and what they did on dates generally found such efforts rejected and evaded. Parents of a son might not even know where junior was going or whom he was dating. Dates were conducted mostly in the public arena, and in some cases—such as at sporting events or school dances—adults might be present. But dates often involved activities and venues where no adults were present or where young people predominated—as at private parties or at local dance halls. Or in other cases the presence of adults would have little inhibiting effect, as in the darkened balconies of movie theaters. American youths also developed substantial ingenuity in finding secluded "lovers' lanes" where they could escape the supervision of even peers. (Localities varied in the places used for this purpose and how they were referred to. In locales near bodies of water, young people spoke of "watching submarine races"; in the rural area of upstate New York where I grew up, the phrase was "exploring tractor roads.") Community dances and gatherings for all generations and ages practically disappeared in the dating era.

Greater privacy and autonomy of youths promoted romantic and physical experimentation. Not only kissing but petting was increasingly accepted and widespread. Going beyond petting to sexual intercourse, however, involved substantial risks, especially for the female. This was not simply the risk of pregnancy in the pre-pill era. Dating perpetuated the sexual double standard. Men were expected to be the sexual aggressors and to try to achieve as much intimacy as their dates would allow. But women who "went too far" risked harming their reputations and their ability to keep desirable men interested in them for long. Women were expected to set the limits, and they had to walk a careful line between being too unfriendly (and not having males wanting to date them at all) and being too friendly (and being dated for the "wrong reasons").

During the initial decades of the dating era, premarital intimacy increased in comparison with the age of calling, but still a majority of women entered marriage as virgins. In a survey in the greater Detroit metropolitan area, I found that of the oldest women interviewed (those who dated and married prior to 1945), about one in four had lost her virginity prior to marriage. (By the 1980s, according to my survey, the figure was closer to 90 percent.) Escape from parental supervision provided by dating weakened, but did not immediately destroy, the restraints on premarital intimacy.

When Americans began dating, they were primarily concerned with enjoyment, rather than with choosing a spouse. Indeed, "playing the field" was the ideal pursued by many. Dates were not suitors or prospects. Seeing different people on successive nights in a hectic round of dating activity earned one popularity among peers. One of the early students and critics of the dating culture, Willard Waller, coined the term "rating and dating complex" to refer to this pattern. After observing dating among students at Pennsylvania State University in the 1930s, Waller charged that concern for impressing friends and gaining status on campus led to superficial thrill-seeking and competition for popularity, and eliminated genuine romance or sincere communication. However, Waller has been accused of both stereotyping and exaggerating the influence of this pattern. Dating was not always so exploitative and superficial as he charged.

Dating was never viewed as an endless stage or an alternative to courtship. Even if dates were initially seen as quite separate from mate selection, they were always viewed as only the first step in a progression that would lead to marriage. By the 1930s, the stage of "going steady" was clearly recognized, entailing a commitment by both partners to date each other exclusively, if only for the moment. A variety of ritual markers emerged to symbolize the increased commitment of this stage and of further steps toward engagement and marriage, such as wearing the partner's high school ring, being lavaliered, and getting pinned.

Going steady was a way-station between casual dating and engagement. Steadies pledged not to date others, and they were likely to become more deeply involved romantically and physically than casual daters. They were not expected explicitly to contemplate marriage, and the majority of women in our Detroit survey had several steady boyfriends before the relationships that led to their marriages. If a couple was of a "suitable age," though, and if the steady relationship lasted more than a few months, the likelihood increased of explicit talk about marriage. Couples would then symbolize their escalated commitment by getting engaged. Dating arose first among middle and upper middle class students in urban areas, and roughly simultaneously at the college and high school levels. The practice then spread to other groups — rural young people, working-class youths, to the upper class, and to employed young people. But what triggered the rapid demise of calling and the rise of dating?

Financial Reasons
— Middle Class

One important trend was prolonged school attendance, particularly in public, co-educational high schools and colleges. Schools provided an arena in which females and males could get to know one another informally over many years. Schools also organized athletic, social, and other activities in which adult supervision was minimal. College campuses generally allowed a more total escape from parental supervision than high schools.

Another important influence was growing affluence in America. More and more young people were freed from a need to contribute to the family economy and had more leisure time in which to date. Fewer young people worked under parental supervision, and more and more fathers worked far from home, leaving mothers as the primary monitors of their children's daily activities. These trends also coincided with a rise in part-time and after-school employment for students, employment that provided pocket money that did not have to be turned over to parents and could be spent on clothing, makeup, movie tickets, and other requirements of the dating culture. Rising affluence also fueled the growth of entire new industries designed to entertain and fill leisure time—movies, popular music recording, ice cream parlors, amusement parks, and so on. Increasingly, young people who wanted to escape from supervision of their parents found a range of venues, many of them catering primarily to youth and to dating activities.

Technology also played a role, and some analysts suggest that one particular invention, the automobile, deserves a lion's share of the credit. Automobiles were not only a means to escape the home and reach a wider range of recreation spots. They also provided a semiprivate space with abundant romantic and sexual possibilities. New institutions, such as the drive-in movie theater, arose to take advantage of those possibilities. As decades passed and affluence increased, the borrowed family car was more and more replaced by cars owned by young people, advancing youth autonomy still further.

All this was part of a larger trend: the transformation of America into a mass consumption society. As this happened, people shifted their attention partially from thinking about how to work and earn to pondering how to spend and consume. Marketplace thinking became more and more influential. The image of the individual as *homo economicus* and of modern life typified by the rational application of scientific knowledge to all decisions became pervasive. The new ideological framework undermined previous customs and moral standards and extended to the dating culture.

Dating had several goals. Most obviously and explicitly, dates were expected to lead to pleasure and possibly to romance. It was also important, as Waller and others have observed, in competition for popularity. But a central purpose of dating was to gain valuable learning experience that would be useful later in selecting a spouse. Through dating young people would learn how to relate to the opposite sex. Dating would increase awareness of one's own feelings and understanding of which type of partner was appealing and which not. Through crushes and disappointments, one would learn to judge the character of people. And by dating a variety of partners and by increasingly intimate involvement with some of them, one would learn what sort of person one would be happy with as a marital partner. When it came time to marry, one would be in a good position to select "Mr. Right" or "Miss Right." Calling, which limited the possibilities of romantic experimentation, often to only one partner, did not provide an adequate basis for such an informed choice.

What emerged was a "marketplace learning viewpoint." Selecting a spouse is not quite the same as buying a car or breakfast cereal, but the process was seen as analogous. The assumptions involved in shopping around and test driving various cars or buying and tasting Wheaties, Cheerios, and Fruit Loops were transferred to popular thinking about how to select a spouse.

According to this marketplace learning viewpoint, getting married very young and without having acquired much dating experience was risky, in terms of marital happiness. Similarly, marrying your first and only sweetheart was not a good idea. Neither was meeting someone, falling head over heels in love, and marrying, all within the course of a month. While Americans recognized that in some cases such beginnings could lead to good marriages, the rationale of our dating culture was that having had a variety of dating partners and then getting to know one or more serious prospects over a longer period of time and on fairly intimate terms were experiences more likely to lead to marital success.

Eventually, this marketplace psychology helped to undermine America's premarital puritanism, and with it the sexual double standard. The way was paved for acceptance of new customs, and particularly for premarital cohabitation. Parents and other moral guardians found it increasingly difficult to argue against the premise that, if sexual enjoyment and compatibility were central to marital happiness, it was important to test that compatibility before marrying. Similarly, if marriage involved not just hearts and flowers, but also dirty laundry and keeping a budget, did it not make sense for a couple to live together prior to marriage to see how they got along on a day-to-day basis? Such arguments on behalf of premarital sex and cohabitation have swept into popular consciousness in the United States, and it is obvious that they are logical corollaries of the marketplace learning viewpoint.

Our dating culture thus is based upon the premise that dating provides valuable experience that will help individuals select mates and achieve happy marriages. But is this premise correct? Does dating really work? What evidence shows that individuals with longer dating experience, dates with more partners, or longer and more intimate acquaintances with the individuals they intend to marry end up with happier marriages? Surprisingly, social scientists have never systematically addressed this question. Perhaps this is one of those cherished beliefs people would prefer not to examine too closely. When I could find little evidence on the connection between dating and other premarital experiences and marital success in previous studies, I decided to conduct my own inquiry.

My desire to know whether dating experiences affected marriages was the basis for my 1984 survey in the Detroit area. A representative sample of

459 women was interviewed in three counties in the Detroit metropolitan area (a diverse, multi-racial and multi-ethnic area of city and suburbs containing about 4 million people in 1980). The women ranged in ages from 18 to 75, and all had been married at least once. (I was unable to interview their husbands, so unfortunately marriages in this study are viewed only through the eyes of women.) The interviewees had first married over a sixty-year span of time, between 1925 and 1984. They were asked to recall a variety of things about their dating and premarital experiences. They were also asked a range of questions about their marital histories and (if currently married) about the positive and negative features of their relations with their husbands. The questionnaire enabled us to test whether premarital experiences of various types were related to marital success, a concept which in turn was measured in several different ways. (Measures of divorce and of both positive and negative qualities in intact marriages were used.)

The conclusions were a surprise. It appears that dating does not work and that the "marketplace learning viewpoint" is misguided. Marrying very young tended to produce unsuccessful marriages. Premarital pregnancy was associated with problems in marriage. However, once the age of marriage is taken into account, none of the other measures—dating variety, length of dating, length of courtship or engagement, or degree of premarital intimacy with the future husband or others—was clearly related to measures of marital success. A few weak tendencies in the results were contrary to predictions drawn from the marketplace learning viewpoint. Women who had dated more partners or who had engaged in premarital sex or cohabited were slightly less likely to have successful marriages. This might be seen as evidence of quite a different logic.

Perhaps there is a "grass is greener" effect. Women who have led less sheltered and conventional lives prior to marriage may not be as easily satisfied afterward. Several other researchers have found a similar pattern with regard to premarital cohabitation. Individuals who had been living together prior to marriage were significantly less likely to have successful marriages than those who did not.

In the Detroit survey, these "grass is greener" patterns were not consistent or statistically significant. It was not that women with more dating experience and greater premarital intimacy had less successful marriages; rather, the amount and type of dating experience did not make a clear difference one way or the other.

Women who had married their first sweethearts were just as likely to have enduring and satisfying marriages as women who had married only after considering many alternatives. Similarly, women who had married after only a brief acquaintance were no more (nor less) likely to have a successful marriage than those who knew their husbands-to-be for years. And there was no clear difference between the marriages of women who were virgins at marriage and those who had had a variety of sexual partners and who had lived together with their husbands before the wedding.

Dating obviously does not provide useful learning that promotes marital success. Although our dating culture is based upon an analogy with consumer purchases in the marketplace, it is clear that in real life selecting a spouse is quite different from buying a car or breakfast cereal. You cannot actively consider several prospects at the same time without getting your neck broken and being deserted by all of them. Even if you find Ms. Right or Mr. Right, you may be told to drop dead. By the time you are ready to marry, this special someone you were involved with earlier may no longer be available, and you may not see anyone on the horizon who comes close to being as desirable. In addition, someone who is well suited at marriage may grow apart from you or find someone else to be with later. Dating experience might facilitate marital success if deciding whom to marry was like deciding what to eat for breakfast (although even in the latter regard tastes change, and toast and black coffee may replace bacon and eggs). But these realms are quite different, and mate selection looks more like a crap-shoot than a rational choice.

Is there a better way? Traditionalists in some societies would argue that arranged marriages are preferable. However, in addition to the improbability that America's young people will leave this decision to their parents, there is the problem of evidence. The few studies of this topic, including one I have been collaborating on in China, indicate that women who had arranged marriages were less satisfied than women who made the choice themselves. So having Mom and Dad take charge is not the answer. Turning the matter over to computerized matchmaking also does not seem advisable. Despite the growing sophistication of computers, real intelligence seems preferable to artificial intelligence. As the Tin Woodman in *The Wizard of Oz* discovered, to have a brain but no heart is to be missing something important.

Perhaps dating is evolving into new patterns in which premarital experience will contribute to marital success. Critics from Waller onward have claimed that dating promotes artificiality, rather than realistic assessment of compatibility. Some observers suggest that the sort of superficial dating Waller and others wrote about has become less common of late. Dating certainly has changed significantly since the pre–Second World War era. Many of the rigid rules of dating have broken down. The male no longer always takes the initiative; neither does he always pay. The sexual double standard has also weakened substantially, so that increasingly Americans feel that whatever a man can do a woman should be able to do. Some writers even suggest that dating is going out of style, replaced by informal pairing off in larger groups, often without the prearrangement of "asking someone out." Certainly the terminology is changing, with "seeing" and "being with" increasingly preferred to "dating" and "going steady." To many young people the latter terms have the old-fashioned ring that "courting" and "suitor" had when I was young.

My daughter and other young adults argue that current styles are more natural and healthier than the dating experienced by my generation and the generation of my parents. Implicit in this argument is the view that, with formal rules and the "rating and dating" complex in decline, it should be possible to use dating (or whatever you call it) to realistically assess compatibility and romantic chemistry. These arguments may seem plausible, but I see no evidence that bears them out. The youngest women we interviewed in the Detroit survey should have experienced these more informal styles of romantic exploration. However, for them dating and premarital intimacy were, if anything, less closely related to marital success than was the case for the older women. The changes in premarital relations do not seem to make experience a better teacher.

While these conclusions are for the most part quite negative, my study leads to two more positive observations. First, marital success is not totally unpredictable. A wide range of features of how couples structure their day-to-day marital relations promote success—sharing in power and decision-making, pooling incomes, enjoying similar leisure-time activities, having similar values, having mutual friends and an active social life, and other related qualities. Couples are not "doomed" by their past histories, including their dating histories, and they can increase their mutual happiness through the way they structure their marriages.

Second, there is something else about premarital experience besides dating history that may promote marital success. We have in America not one, but two widely shared, but quite contradictory, theories about how individuals should select a spouse: one based on the marketplace learning viewpoint and another based on love. One viewpoint sees selecting a spouse as a rational process, perhaps even with lists of criteria by which various prospects can be judged. The other, as songwriters tell us, is based on the view that love conquers all and that "all you need is love." Love is a matter of the heart (perhaps with some help from the hormonal system) and not the head, and love may blossom unpredictably, on short notice or more gradually. Might it not be the case, then, that those couples who are most deeply in love at the time of their weddings will have the most successful marriages? We have centuries of poetry and novels, as well as love songs, that tell us that this is the case.

In the Detroit study, we did, in fact, ask women how much they had been in love when they first married. And we did find that those who recalled being "head over heels in love" then, had more successful marriages. However, there is a major problem with this finding. Since we were asking our interviewees to recall their feelings prior to their weddings—in many cases weddings took place years or even decades earlier—it is quite possible and even likely that these answers are biased. Perhaps whether or not their marriage worked out influenced these "love reports" from earlier times, rather than having the level of romantic love then explain marital success later. Without either a time machine or funds to interview couples prior to marriage and then follow them up years later, it is impossible to be sure that more intense feelings of love lead to more successful marriages. Still, the evidence available does not question the wisdom of poets and songwriters when it comes to love. Mate selection may not be a total crap-shoot after all, and even if dating does not work, love perhaps does.

REFERENCES

Bailey, Beth. 1988. *From Front Porch to Back Seat*. Baltimore: Johns Hopkins University Press.

Burgess, Ernest W. and Paul Wallin. 1953. *Engagement and Marriage*. Chicago: Lippincott.

Modell, John. 1983. "Dating Becomes the Way of American Youth." In *Essays on the Family and Historical Change*, edited by Leslie P. Moch and Gary Stark. College Station: Texas A&M University Press.

Rothman, Ellen K. 1984. *Hands and Hearts: A History of Courtship*. New York: Basic Books.

Smith, Daniel S. and Michael Hindus. 1975. "Premarital Pregnancy in America, 1640–1971: An Overview and Interpretation." *Journal of Interdisciplinary History* 4:537–70.

Waller, Willard. 1937. "Rating and Dating Complex." *American Sociological Review* 2:737–39.

Whyte, Martin King. 1990. *Dating, Mating, and Marriage*. New York: Aldine de Gruyter.

10

"SHE'S 16 YEARS OLD AND THERE'S BOYS CALLING OVER TO THE HOUSE"
An Exploratory Study of Sexual Socialization in Latino Families

MARCELA RAFFAELLI • LENNA L. ONTAI

Introduction

As primary agents of socialization, families play a major role in shaping developmental experiences during childhood and adolescence. Parents act as models, engage in direct and indirect teaching, attempt to mould their children's behaviour in specific ways and expose their children to, or protect them from, an array of experiences (Burgental and Goodnow 1998, Parke

Marcela Raffaelli and Lenna L. Ontai, " 'She's 16 Years Old and There's Boys Calling over to the House': An Exploratory Study of Sexual Socialization in Latino Families" from *Culture, Health & Sexuality 3(3):* 295–310. Copyright © 2001 by Taylor & Francis Ltd. Reprinted with permission.

and Buriel 1998). Although there is a rich literature showing the importance of parents in the socialization process, one aspect of socialization that has received less attention is sexual socialization.

There is widespread agreement that parents influence their children's sexual development in significant ways (see Katchadourian 1990; Udry and Campbell 1994). Family influences on sexuality operate through a complex web of factors, including direct communication (Casper 1990; Fox and Inazu 1980; Holtzman and Rubinson 1995; Jaccard and Dittus 1993), social control practises (Miller et al. 1986), and emotional qualities of the relationship (Jaccard, Dittus, and Gordon 1998).

The exact mechanisms of influence may be unknown but ultimately family socialization affects the formation of sexual scripts, or guidelines for sexual interaction (Simon and Gagnon 1986). According to scripting theory, sexual behaviour results from the interplay between cultural scenarios, interpersonal scripts and intrapsychic scripts (Simon and Gagnon 1986, 1987). Cultural scenarios provide the basic framework for sexual interactions, delineating the roles of individuals in a sexual encounter, whereas interpersonal and intrapsychic scripts are the outcome of individual "fine-tuning" through experience and practice.

Scripting theory gives a prominent place to culture, which has become a central concern of developmental scholars in recent years. Culture assumes a significant role in the socialization process by shaping the specific beliefs and values held by parents (McDade 1993). Parents of ethnically diverse children face a dual socialization challenge of not only transmitting their own beliefs and values, but also those of the larger population (Parke and Buriel 1998). Thus, to gain a full understanding of sexual socialization among different ethnic groups, parents' cultural beliefs must be taken into account. The current analysis draws on a retrospective study of sexual socialization in a sample of women of Latin American origin or descent living in the United States. This focus was initially prompted by the fact that U.S. Latinas are at high risk for negative sexual outcomes.

In contrast to the general decline in sexual activity among teenagers in the USA, the proportion of Latinas of this age reporting sexual activity increased between 1988 and 1995 (from 49% to 55%) whereas contraceptive use at most recent sexual intercourse decreased (from 69% to 53%) (*Child Trends* 2000). In 1995, 50% of White females reported sexual activity, and 71% used contraception at last intercourse; 60% of Black females were sexually active, with 70% reporting contraceptive use. Given these ethnic disparities, it is perhaps not surprising that in 1997 the teen birth rate among Latinas was almost twice the national average (National Campaign to Prevent Teen Pregnancy 1999). Hispanic women are moreover disproportionately represented among AIDS cases in the USA. Although Hispanic women aged 15 and older represent just 7% of the U.S. female population, they account for 20% of cumulative female AIDS cases (CDC 1999). In an effort to understand these health statistics, researchers have explored both demographic (e.g., poverty, discrimination, barriers to health care) and cultural factors.

Although some scholars critique depictions of traditional Latin cultures for being stereotypical and invalid (e.g., Amaro 1988; De La Cancela 1989, Singer et al. 1990), there is also agreement about a number of shared cultural values (Marin 1988, 1989, Taylor 1996) that are likely to be important influences on family socialization practises. These include *familismo*, an emphasis on the family as the primary source of social support and identity, and *respeto*, the need to maintain respectful hierarchical relationships.

Another set of cultural beliefs relevant to the socialization of daughters in particular pertains to the importance of virginity until marriage. Within Latino families much of the socialization of daughters is influenced by historical beliefs in religion and family codes of honour. Historical religious influences led to a high value for female chastity; violation of this value resulted in dishonour for both the individual woman and her family (Espin [1984] 1997). Because chastity of women within a family was one avenue through which honour was attained for the family as a whole, families vigorously safeguarded the virginity of unmarried women.

Other cultural beliefs relevant to sexual socialization include traditional gender role expectations and norms that promote female reticence and lack of knowledge about sexuality. These long-standing beliefs about female sexuality often conflict with conditions encountered by Latino families in the USA and are likely to be most salient as daughters enter adolescence. It has been suggested that the value of virginity may become a focal concern for some Latino parents who view US women as being promiscuous and link becoming "Americanized" with being sexually promiscuous (Espin [1984] 1997).

Prior research has identified specific cultural values and norms related to sexuality among Latino families, but the way that these beliefs influence the sexual socialization of children and adolescents remains largely unexplored (Barkley and Mosher 1995; Hurtado 1995). One study of 10–15-year-old Puerto Rican and Mexican girls and their mothers (Villaruel 1998) revealed that to maintain daughters' virginity, families often established rules regarding dating and contact with males and tried to keep daughters close to home. Similar patterns have been reported by clinicians who work with Latina adolescents (Espin [1984] 1997).

Other researchers have found that Latino parents are often reluctant to give their daughters information regarding sexuality (Baumeister, Flores, and Marin 1995; Darabi and Asencio 1987; Marin and Gomez 1997), communicating less about sexual topics than parents of other ethnic groups (CDC 1991). This lack of information and experience leads Latinas to be less knowledgeable about their own sexual anatomy and the basic physiological aspects of sexuality than non-Latino women (Barkley and Mosher 1995; Marin and Gomez 1997).

This body of research suggests that aspects of traditional culture influence sexual socialization in Latino families, but the small number of studies conducted to date limits conclusions that can be drawn. Moreover, prior research has not examined how specific parenting practises emerge from cultural beliefs, or how families negotiate a balance between old and new cultures. In an effort to add to the knowledge base about how Latino families socialize their daughters, the current analysis examined family experiences related to sexuality in a sample of adult Latinas who were interviewed about their experiences while growing up. We were particularly interested in examining how parental beliefs and values were enacted in everyday interactions around issues connected to sexuality and dating.

Methods

Procedures and Participants

The study drew on an opportunity sample of Latina/Hispanic women who responded to mailings to Latino faculty and staff at a large Midwestern University or to informational flyers posted in public locations. Several participants also referred friends who subsequently participated. Recruitment materials targeted 20 to 45 year old Latino/Hispanic women who had grown up in Spanish-speaking families but had lived in the USA for at least 8 years. After providing informed consent, women took part in individual in-depth interviews conducted in English by the first author. Participants received $20 for taking part in the study to cover their time, transportation, and childcare costs.

Twenty-two women had complete data and are included in the analyses. . . . The average age of the sample was 31.2 years (median 27 years; range 20–45). Two-fifths (41%) of the respondents had never been married, 41% were currently married, and 18% were separated or divorced. Two (9%) of the women reported no religious affiliation; 68% were Catholic and 23% reported other religious affiliations.

All of the respondents had graduated from high school; 32% had attended college but not graduated; 18% had graduated from college; and 18% had post-graduate education. In contrast, parental levels of education were lower; over half of the respondents' fathers (57%) and mothers (55%) had not graduated from high school, with the majority of these parents leaving school by the ninth grade. A number of parents had graduated from high school (14% of fathers, 23% of mothers) and the remainder had attended or graduated from college (29% of fathers, 23% of mothers).

All respondents self-identified as Latino/Hispanic; 16 (73%) were of Mexican origin or descent and the remainder were from other Latin American or Caribbean countries. In terms of generation of immigration, the majority ($n = 19$) had been born in the USA. Eleven (50%) of the women had at least one parent born outside the USA (in ten cases, Mexico) and the remaining 11 had two US-born parents. Only three of the respondents had two US-born grandparents; the rest had one or both grandparents born outside the USA. . . .

Measures

The interview guide consisted of open-ended and structured questions dealing with three main topic areas. The first area was sexual socialization within the family of origin, including gender role socialization (e.g., How did your parents teach you about how girls and boys "should" behave? Do you remember any specific examples? Did your parents ever get angry or upset when you didn't behave in a certain way?), sexual communication (e.g., Did your parents ever talk to you about sex? What did they tell you about sex?), and reactions to the daughter's emerging sexuality (e.g., Tell me about when you started developing physically. What did your parents say/do?). The second area was early romantic and sexual experiences, including parental rules and messages about dating (e.g., When were you allowed to date or go out with boys? What kinds of rules did your family have about dating? What did your parents tell you about boys? Did you ever get in trouble for breaking the rules?). The final area was sexuality-related beliefs, attitudes, and behaviour, including pregnancy history, contraceptive use, and lifetime partners. . . .

Results

The current analysis examines four domains related to adolescent sexual socialization: parental concerns regarding dating, family communication about sexual issues, family rules about dating, and actual dating experiences and early sexual behaviour. . . .

Parental Concerns

All the respondents described parental concerns regarding interactions with boys and men during adolescence. A major cause for concern stemmed from parental mistrust of males, as several women described:

> *I think [mother] was real concerned about whether or not we would be taken advantage of . . . . I always wondered was it that she didn't trust us or she didn't trust them and I think it was more she didn't trust them.* (Lupe, 41)

Mistrust of males was linked to fear of premarital pregnancy, which was described as a parental concern by a number of participants:

> *My friends attest he [father] would give us all lectures about how, you know, we can't let boys get in our way, because boys are bad and boys are, you know, just, they just want one thing and whatever I do don't get pregnant and that was just, I mean I would leave and "We don't want you coming home pregnant" . . . it was just whatever you do don't be pregnant or whatever you do don't get pregnant.* (Silvia, 21)

Several respondents also mentioned that their parents worried about how a daughter's behaviour might affect the family's image in the community. Sandra (aged 40) explained that she was not allowed to date because "we came from a pretty good family, and so it would be a disgrace if anything . . . you know." Another respondent described her father's reaction when she brought a boyfriend to church:

> *When I talked to my father after the mass, he was kind of upset, he was like, he didn't want me to bring any of my boyfriends there. He said, "Unless, until*

you're married I don't want you bringing your boyfriends around," because he didn't want the community to get the idea that I was promiscuous or dating around. (Victoria, 24) . . .

Thus, to many parents, daughters' dating behaviour was seen as a potential source of embarrassment because it might expose the family to shame in the community.

Another reason for parental concern about dating was that US-style dating violated traditional patterns of courtship and marriage. Teresa (45) described the situation she experienced growing up in a predominately Mexican-American neighbourhood:

. . . if the guys wanted to court you they would be outside. You would be outside the house and you just talked, there was no such thing as you went to the car and you took off, you know, you wanted to talk to somebody you would be outside the house and then your parents would tell you, you have to come in and that was it, but it was no kissing or holding hands or nothing, actually it was just talking, getting to know each other actually until you decided whether you wanted to get married and then . . . the guy would have to tell whoever the parent was then, ask for your hand in marriage. . . .

The tension between traditional courtship styles and the reality of life in the USA was expressed by one 26-year-old woman's description of conversations with her Mexican-born father, who moved to the USA before she was born:

I have asked him before, I've said, so, Dad, do you think that, that it is appropriate for us to go ahead and have boyfriends, to find out if this is the person that we want to marry, you know, how else are you going to find out if this is the person that you're going to marry, unless you meet this person, go out with this person, and so on the one hand it's like, you know, ah, intellectually he knows, okay, yeah, that makes sense, but it's almost as if though his social upbringing, you know, his, ah, it keeps him back from, you know, it's kind of like he's in between, you know, he's here in the United States, but yet he has all of this stuff that has told him that women are not allowed to go out with boyfriends. (Rosita, 26)

Silvia (21 years old) said her stepfather had begun pressuring her to be married because "according to him whenever I get married is when he can stop worrying. . . . It means I'll be in another household . . . and I'm no longer his worry, he doesn't, you know, I'll be taken care of."

Communication about Sexual Issues

Respondents were asked about family communication about different sexual topics, including menstruation, physical development, facts about sex, morality, appropriate behaviour, and boys/dating. The overall experience reported by study participants was for limited discussions about "biological" topics accompanied by extensive communication about the dangers of sexual activity. Only six (27%) of the respondents had discussed physical development with their parents, and eight (36%) had talked about the "facts of life" (i.e., intercourse and pregnancy). The most commonly discussed "biological" topic was menstruation, which fifteen (68%) of the women had discussed with a parent. In contrast, the majority of women had discussed appropriate behaviour ($n = 20$; 91%), boys and dating ($n = 18$; 82%) and moral aspects of sexuality ($n = 13$; 59%).

Parental expectations about sexuality often took the form of warnings or prohibitions. For example, when asked if there were any rules she had to follow when she went out, Gabriela (27) responded, "don't let a guy, don't let a boy touch me." Inez (23) reported:

> *I do remember, I'm not sure exactly when it was, but I imagine probably when I was still in grade school my mother telling us that both her and my father were virgins when they got married and that's how it should be.*

Other respondents described parental messages that were much more indirect:

> *I think it was comments, you know, that you would hear about, you know, I had an aunt who got pregnant and, and how that was so shameful. I mean it was just awful, you know, how could she do that. . . . [There was] always the recognition that there were good girls and bad girls and, you know, the talk about them and it wasn't just mother, it was the aunts, the tias, that would sit around and . . . you'd sit there and you . . . heard them talk . . . so the message was very clear, very indirect, but very clear that, that was not acceptable.* (Lupe, 41)

The bulk of family communication focused on avoidance of sexual involvement, with few families providing information about sexuality or physical development.

Family Rules about Dating

Parental concerns about their daughters' premature or inappropriate romantic and sexual involvement led to the implementation of a number of strategies to protect daughters. In some cases, parents attempted to shield their daughters from male attention by prohibiting the use of make up or revealing clothes. One woman described how her Mexican-born father reacted to her and her sisters' adolescence:

> *He didn't want us to wear make up or shave our legs, I can remember times when he would check my sisters' and my legs to see if we were shaving them . . . and he was just really, really cautious about us talking to guys and just growing up and becoming you know, puberty stage and just actually becoming women. Um, he's a good father though. He's, he's been supportive as far as our education. Sure there were times when he ah, he threatened not to let us go to school anymore if, you know, we kept doing, you know, saying things that he didn't want us to do.* (Yolanda, 27)

Some parents did not allow daughters to have social contact with males, as Silvia (21) succinctly described when asked what her parents' rules about social life were: "No boys." Similarly, when Victoria (24) was a teenager her father told her "he didn't want us to go out with, ah, to date, and he didn't want us to bring anyone, any boys to the house. That was a definite no." Another woman described her experience as follows:

> *I was absolutely to do nothing. I came home from school with my school work and that was it. I didn't dare ask to go to games, movies, 'cause I just had to be home. . . . I would try, I tried once or twice. And after that it was like "NO." . . . I think they didn't trust me. So I thought what have I done that you don't trust me. Obviously I couldn't have done anything, so it was like that. I stopped asking. If I had to stay at home, I had to stay at home.* (Sandra, 40)

Parents used a variety of tactics to monitor their daughters' romantic activity. One strategy was to set an age before which daughters were not allowed to date. When asked whether their parents had rules about the age at which dating was allowed, eight women (38%) said they were not supposed to date while living at home, nine (43%) were expected to wait until after age 15, and four (19%) said no explicit age limits were set. In a number of cases, group or chaperoned dates were permitted, but one-on-one dating was not.

Parents also restricted the locations where social interactions occurred. For example, some respondents were allowed to interact with boys or men in public or at social gatherings at which parents and relatives were present (e.g., weddings or community dances):

> *I was never allowed to have any boys in the house. . . . They didn't allow me to go to other people's houses. It had to be public, you know, a dance or a picnic or public thing.* (Carmen, 45)

Parental rules about dating reflected the expectations that parents held for their daughters. Overall, the 'script' for adolescent sexuality was characterized by delayed and circumscribed romantic involvement on the part of their daughters, with the ultimate goal being marriage. However, actual dating and sexual behaviour described by respondents often deviated from this ideal, resulting in familial and personal stress.

Dating and Sexual Behaviour

Respondents reported a wide variation in their adolescent dating experiences. Six (29%) began dating by age 14, ten (48%) by age 15 or 16, and five (24%) did not date until age 17 or older. The average age at which respondents began dating was 15.7 years, with early dating experiences often occurring without parental knowledge or permission.

Parental expectations that daughters would not date resulted in some respondents waiting until they left home to have boyfriends. Olivia (25), who was born in Mexico and moved to the USA as a young child, described her situation:

> *. . . because you're a girl you can't date until a certain age and there never really was a real idea of what age you were supposed to be, because the whole*

time I was in high school or even in college coming back home you couldn't date, because you were at home and that's not why you come home and so I always thought how are we supposed to get married if we can't even meet somebody?

In other cases, daughters engaged in covert dating to circumvent parental restrictions. About half of the respondents said they had dated without parental permission. For example, when asked about when she started dating, Lupe (41) replied, "the end of my sophomore year and it was sneak dating." Similarly, other women described their involvement in covert dating activities:

. . . in 8th grade, I snuck out, well, I didn't sneak out, I went with a girlfriend to the movies but my Mom didn't know we were meeting up with two guys and I got in trouble for that. (Antonia, 26)

. . . I can recall as a senior in high school, ah, sneaking out, 'cause by that time I had my car and, ah, a driver's license, so I'd wait until my parents went to bed and then I'd sneak out and sometimes I'd get in trouble for that. (Inez, 23)

Several other respondents said their mother helped them go out without their father's knowledge, as Olivia (25) described:

She would like lie for us to my Dad, so that we could do maybe like a high school social kind of thing also if we had dates or whatever if she knew the guy she would tell my dad that we were working and let us to go out for a little bit, or send one of us to chaperone. . . .

In other families, open dating was allowed but was surrounded with an atmosphere of tension and distrust. When Juanita (44) and her sisters came home after their curfew "[m]y Mom used to call us names . . . you know, bad names . . . she would just, using a Spanish word, she called us sluts and stuff like that." Other parents made their displeasure felt in less obvious ways:

Up to when I was a senior, I probably only had four dates and my Mom was not very nice to these poor boys when they came to my house, it was so embarrassing to me that I never did it until probably the middle of my senior year. (Gloria, 41)

Because of parental suspicion and displeasure, for many women dating was a source of tension and guilt. Of the 22 women interviewed, only a handful described their parents as supportive of their adolescent dating experiences.

Despite parental attempts to protect their daughters from premarital sexual involvement, 19 of the 22 respondents had engaged in premarital sexual intercourse. The mean age of sexual initiation was 18.2 years. Eleven of these 19 respondents did not use birth control the first time they had sex. A number of the women attributed their non-use of birth control to their ignorance about sex. Juanita (44), who became involved at 16 with a man in his 20s (and became pregnant the next year by another man), describes her early sexual encounters:

I told him we weren't going to have sex if we didn't use something and he said, "Oh, I'll take care of it" and he didn't. . . . I was so naïve or dumb or something that I thought, you know, he's doing something . . . he's taking care of it.

Similarly, Isadora became pregnant at 17 by her first sexual partner, a 21-year-old man who told her, "Oh, come on, nothing is going to happen the first time." Of the 19 women who had sexual experience, six (32%) became pregnant soon after they began having sex.

Although the direct links between early family environment and eventual dating and sexual experiences could not be examined systematically due to sample size limitations, a number of the respondents talked about having difficulties dealing with relationships as a result of their upbringing. Many of the women reported feeling guilty after their first sexual experience, because having sex was a "betrayal" of their family's values and expectations. Yolanda (27), who had sex with a 16-year-old boy when she was 12 years old, said that she "had broken every rule that my Mom and Dad were trying to raise me with" and felt so guilty that she did not date until years later, when she was in college. Lupe (41) said that "I really think that I lived most of my adolescent life in fear that either God would get me or my parents in terms of behaviour, specifically sexual." Rosita (26), who was not allowed to have boyfriends while living at home and was not sexually active at the time of the interview, reflected on the experiences of her older sisters, who both became pregnant soon after initiating sexual relations as young adults:

> . . . I do really think that had an effect on us when we were growing up because my sisters, the first time that they went out . . . pretty much I want to say on a serious relationship [became pregnant] so to me that's telling me, OK, part of that is it could be because they were not allowed to have boyfriends when they were younger therefore now when you finally get to this point where you can have a boyfriend this is very serious.

Discussion

The goal of the current study was to examine how sexual socialization practises in Latino families emerge from cultural values and to begin exploring how early experiences influences the later sexual behaviour of Latinas. To integrate the findings, we draw on the framework of scripting theory, which holds that sexual behaviour results from the interplay between cultural scenarios, interpersonal scripts, and intrapsychic scripts (Simon and Gagnon 1986, 1987).

Cultural scenarios provide the basic framework for sexual interactions, delineating the roles and possible actions of individuals in a sexual encounter. The cultural scenarios espoused by many of the respondents' parents depicted adolescent women as sexually vulnerable and in need of protection. All of the women in the study said their parents expressed concerns regarding interactions with boys and men. Reasons for parental concern included mistrust of males, fear of premarital pregnancy, concern about how a daughter's behaviour might be viewed by members of the community, and the fact that US-style dating conflicted with "traditional" patterns of courtship and marriage. Parental expectations regarding their daughters' involvement in romantic activity can be seen in the fact that nearly two-fifths (38%) of the respondents said they were not supposed to date while living at home and over two-fifths (43%) said they were expected to wait until after they turned 15. Interestingly, 15 is the age at which the traditional coming-of-age ceremony for Latina girls, the *quinceañera*, is held (Cantu 1999; Davalos 1996;). Also consistent with traditional Latin culture, female romantic involvement outside of marriage was described as dishonourable to the family, and many parents expressed a desire to maintain traditional courtship patterns even when they were aware that those behaviours were not typical of the larger society. Similar cultural norms have been reported in other research with Latino families (Espin [1984] 1997; Villaruel 1998). However, cultural norms reflect ideals that may or may not be reflected in actual behaviour. The current study extends prior research by identifying specific ways that parental concerns were manifested during their daughters' adolescence, which has implications for the development of interpersonal and intrapsychic scenarios.

According to scripting theory, interpersonal scenarios develop from an individual's actual experience in romantic and sexual situations. The women in the current study described family experiences that limited the degree to which they could engage in romantic or sexual behaviours as adolescents. Parents used a variety of tactics to curtail their daughters' sociosexual involvement, including restricting the age at which daughters were allowed to date, monitoring their clothes and use of make-up, and permitting heterosexual interactions only in specific locations or circumstances. Parental expectations that daughters would not date during early adolescence resulted in over half the respondents engaging in "sneak dating." Moreover, many respondents described the gap between parental expectations and actual dating practises as a source of conflict and tension. Also of relevance to the formation of interpersonal scenarios was the low level of family communication regarding sexuality. Less than one quarter of respondents had discussed the "sexual facts and physiology" with their parents, echoing what has been reported in prior research (Baumeister et al. 1995; Darabi and Asencio 1987; de Anda, Becerra, and Fielder 1990; Marin and Gomez 1997; Pavich 1986; Soto 1983). Parental messages were most often centered on the importance of not having sex, with little information being provided on how to avoid sexual involvement or prevent negative sexual outcomes. Based on these analyses, we speculate that family practises related to sexuality have important implications for the intrapsychic scripts formed by women. Women who conformed to parental restrictions on sexual experimentation reported later relationship difficulties due to their inexperience, whereas women who rebelled against parental restrictions described feelings of guilt. Similar tensions regarding sexual choices among Latinas have been described by Espin ([1984] 1997), who works primarily with clinical populations.

The current analysis provides some hints about why US Latinas may be at increased risk of negative sexual outcomes (e.g., elevated rates of teenage pregnancy and HIV/AIDS infection) compared to women from other ethnic groups. As Espin ([1984] 1997) has noted, immigrant and ethnic minority groups may preserve aspects of their traditional culture related to sexuality long after they have adopted other aspects of the host culture. Although parental adherence to traditional values and restriction of daughters' sexual opportunities have potential benefits in terms of protecting daughters from negative outcomes, there are also potential risks to this strategy. In industrialized societies, individuals are expected to set limits on their sexual behaviour without many of the external restraints that characterize "traditional" societies (e.g., arranged marriages, gender segregation) (Brooks-Gunn and Paikoff 1997). As a result, the teenage years represent a crucial time "to practice managing sex and gender" (Thompson 1994:219), as individuals are exposed to romantic and sexual situations in an age-graded fashion.

Our analysis suggests that many Latinas have limited romantic and sexual experience prior to leaving home. If traditional marriage arrangements were maintained, this limited experience would not be problematic. However, given the courtship patterns now prevalent in the USA, Latinas are faced with the task of negotiating sexual encounters when they eventually do leave home, and they may be ill equipped to do so. The women in the current study were highly educated . . . , yet over one half did not use birth control the first time they had sex and nearly one third had an unplanned pregnancy. The exploratory analysis described in this [reading] suggests that to understand the sexual behaviour of US Latinas, researchers must examine more closely sexual socialization within the family of origin and take parents' culturally-influenced beliefs and practises into account.

Authors' Note: This research was supported by grants to the first author form the University of Nebraska Research Council and the National Institutes of Mental Health. The authors thank Jennifer Crispo, Stephanie Hewitt, Lynn Marcus, Nicole Miller, Tammy Pfeifer, Katie Pickett, Julie Siepker, Kathryn Wilke and Byron Zamboanga for their contributions to the project.

REFERENCES

Amaro, H. 1988. "Women in the Mexican-American Community: Religion, Culture, and Reproductive Attitudes and Experiences." *Journal of Community Psychology* 16:6–20.

Barkley, B. H. and E. S. Mosher. 1995. "Sexuality and Hispanic Culture: Counseling with Children and Their Parents." *Journal of Sex Education and Therapy* 21:255–67.

Baumeister, L. M., E. Flores, and B. V. Marin. 1995. "Sex Information Given to Latina Adolescents by Parents." *Health Education Research* 10:233–39.

Brooks-Gunn, J. and R. Paikoff. 1997. "Sexuality and Development Transitions during Adolescence." Pp. 190–219 in *Health Risks and Developmental Transitions during Adolescence,* edited by J. Schulenberg, J. L. Maggs, and K. Hurrelmann. Cambridge: Cambridge University Press.

Burgental, D. B. and J. J. Goodnow. 1998. "Socialization Processes." Pp. 389–462 in *Social, Emotional, and Personality Development,* 5th ed, vol. 3, edited by N. Eisenberg. New York: Wiley.

Cantu, N. E. 1999. "La Quinceañera: Toward an Ethnogrpahic Analysis of a Life-Cycle Ritual." *Southern Folklore* 56:73–101.

Casper, L. M. 1990. "Does Family Interaction Prevent Adolescent Pregnancy?" *Family Planning Perspectives* 22:190–14.

Centers for Disease Control (CDC). 1991. "Characteristics of Parents Who Discuss AIDS with Their Children—United States 1989." *MMWR* 40:789–91.

Centers for Disease Control (CDC). 1999. *HIV/AIDS Surveillance Report* 11:1.

Child Trends Research Brief. 2000. "Trends in Sexual Activity and Contraceptive Use among Teens." Washington DC: Child Trends (http://www.childtrends.org).

Darabi, K. F. and M. Asencio. 1987. "Sexual Activity and Childbearing among Hispanics in the U.S." *SIECUS Report* 15:6–8.

Davalos, K. M. 1996. "La Quinceañera: Making Gender and Ethnic Identities." *Frontiers* 16:101–27.

de Anda, D., R. M. Becerra, and E. Fielder. 1990. "In Their Own Words: The Life Experiences of Mexican-American and White Pregnant Adolescents and Adolescent Mothers." *Child and Adolescent Social Work* 7:301–18.

De La Cancela, V. 1989. "Minority AIDS Prevention: Moving beyond Cultural Perspectives towards Sociopolitical Empowerment." *AIDS Education and Prevention* 1:141–53.

Espin, O. M. [1984] 1997. "Cultural and Historical Influences on Sexuality in Hispanic/Latin Women: Implications for Psychotherapy. Pp. 83–96 in *Latina Realities: Essays on Healing, Migration, and Sexuality,* edited by E. Espin. Boulder, CO: Westview Press.

Fox, G. L. and J. K. Inazu. 1980. "Patterns and Outcomes of Mother–Daughter Communication about Sexuality." *Journal of Social Issues* 36:7–29.

Holtzman, D. and R. Rubinson. 1995. "Parent and Peer Communication Effects on AIDS-Related Behavior among U.S. High School Students." *Family Planning Perspectives* 27:235–68.

Hurtado, A. 1995. "Variations, Combinations, and Evolutions: Latino Families in the United States." Pp. 40–61 in *Understanding Latino Families: Scholarship, Policy, and Practice,* edited by R. E. Zambrana. Thousand Oaks, CA: Sage.

Jaccard, J. and P. J. Dittus. 1993. "Parent–Adolescent Communication about Premarital Pregnancy." *Families in Society* 74:329–43.

Jaccard, J., P. J. Dittus, and V. V. Gordon. 1998. "Maternal Correlates of Adolescent Sexual and Contraceptive Behavior." *Family Planning Perspectives* 28:159–85.

Katchadourian, H. 1990. "Sexuality." Pp. 330–51 in *At the Threshold: The Developing Adolescent,* edited by S. S. Feldman and G. R. Elliott. Cambridge, MA: Harvard University Press.

Marin, B. 1988. *AIDS Prevention in Non–Puerto Rican Hispanics.* Rockville, MD: NIDA.

Marin, B. V. 1989. "Hispanic Culture: Implications for AIDS Prevention." Pp. 1–26 in *Sexuality and Disease: Metaphor, Perceptions, and Behavior in the AIDS Era,* edited by J. Boswell, R. Hexter, and J. Reinisch. New York: Oxford University Press.

Marin, B. V. and C. A. Gomez. 1997. "Latino Culture and Sex: Implications for HIV Prevention." Pp. 73–93 in *Psychological Interventions and Research with Latino Populations,* edited by J. Garcia and M. Zea. Boston: Allyn and Bacon.

Marin, G., F. Sabogal, B. V. Marin, R. Otero-Sabogal, and E. J. Perez-Stable. 1987. "Development of a Short Acculturation Scale for Hispanics." *Hispanic Journal of Behavioral Sciences* 9:183–205.

McDade, K. 1993. "How We Parent: Race and Ethnic Differences" Pp. 283–300 in *American Families: Issues in Race and Ethnicity,* vol. 30, edited by J. C. K. et. al. New York: Garland Publishing,

Miller, B. C., J. K. McCoy, T. D. Olson, and C. M. Wallace. 1986. "Parental Discipline and Control Attempts in Relation to Adolescent Sexual Attitudes and Behavior." *Journal of Marriage and the Family* 48:503–12.

National Campaign to Prevent Teen Pregnancy. 1999. "Fact Sheet: Teen Pregnancy and Childbearing among Latinos in the United States." National Campaign to Prevent Teen Pregnancy (http://www.teenpregnancy.org).

Parke, R. D. and R. Buriel. 1998. "Socialization in the Family: Ethnic and Ecological Perspectives." Pp. 463–552 in *Social, Emotional, and Personality Development,* 5th ed, vol. 3, edited by N. Eisenberg. New York: Wiley.

Pavich, E. G. 1986. "A Chicana Perspective on Mexican Culture and Sexuality." *Journal of Social Work and Human Sexuality* 4:47–65.

Raffaelli, M. and M. Suarez-Al-Adam. 1998. "Reconsidering the HIV/AIDS Prevention Needs of Latino Women in the United States." Pp. 7–41 in *Women and AIDS: Negotiating Safer Practices, Care, and Representation,* edited by N. L. Roth and L. K. Fuller. New York: Haworth.

Simon, W. and J. H. Gagnon. 1986. "Sexual Scripts: Permanence and Change." *Archives of Sexual Behavior* 15:97–120.

——. 1987. "A Sexual Scripts Approach." Pp. 363–83 in *Theories of Human Sexuality,* edited by J. H. Geer and W. T. O'Donohue. New York: Plenum Press.

Singer, M., C. Flores, L. Davison, G. Burke, Z. Castillo, K. Scanlon, and M. Rivera. 1990. "SIDA: The Economic, Social, and Cultural Context of AIDS among Latinos." *Medical Anthropology Quarterly* 4:72–114.

Soto, E. 1983. "Sex-Role Traditionalism and Assertiveness in Puerto Rican Women Living in the United States." *Journal of Community Psychology* 11:346–54.

Taylor, J. M. 1996. "Cultural Stories: Latina and Portuguese Daughters and Mothers." Pp. 117–31 in *Urban Girls: Resisting Stereotypes, Creating Identities,* edited by B. J. R. Leadbeater and N. Way. New York: New York University Press.

Thompson, S. 1994. "Changing Lives, Changing Genres: Teenage Girls' Narratives about Sex and Romance, 1978–1986." Pp. 209–32 in *Sexuality across the Life Course,* edited by A. S. Rossi. Chicago: University of Chicago Press.

Udry, J. R. and B. C. Campbell. 1994. "Getting Started on Sexual Behavior." Pp. 187–207 in *Sexuality across the Life Course,* edited by A. S. Rossi. Chicago: University of Chicago Press.

Villaruel, A. M. 1998. "Cultural Influences on the Sexual Attitudes, Beliefs, and Norms of Young Latina Adolescents." *Journal of the Society of Pediatric Nurses* 3:69–79.

11

DATING AND ROMANTIC RELATIONSHIPS AMONG GAY, LESBIAN, AND BISEXUAL YOUTHS

RITCH C. SAVIN–WILLIAMS

The Importance of Dating and Romance

According to Scarf (1987), the developmental significance of an intimate relationship is to help us "contact archaic, dimly perceived and yet powerfully meaningful aspects of our inner selves" (p. 79). We desire closeness within the context of a trusting, intimate relationship. Attachment theory posits that humans are prewired for loving and developing strongly felt emotional attachments (Bowlby 1973). When established, we experience safety, security, and nurturance. Early attachments, including those in infancy, are thought to circumscribe an internal blueprint that profoundly affects future relationships, such as the establishment of intimate friendships and romances in adolescence and adulthood (Hazan and Shaver 1987).

Developmentally, dating is a means by which romantic relationships are practiced, pursued, and established. It serves a number of important functions, such as entertainment, recreation, and socialization, that assist participants in developing appropriate means of interacting. It also enhances peer group status and facilitates the selection of a mate (Skipper and Nass 1966). Adolescents who are most confident in their dating abilities begin dating during early adolescence, date frequently, are satisfied with their dating, and are most likely to become involved in a "committed" dating relationship (Herold 1979).

The establishment of romantic relationships is important for youths regardless of sexual orientation. Isay (1989) noted that falling in love was a critical factor in helping his gay clients feel comfortable with their gay identity and that "the self-affirming value of a mutual relationship over time cannot be overemphasized" (p. 50). Browning (1987) regarded lesbian love relationships as an opportunity to enhance

> . . . the development of the individual's adult identity by validating her personhood, reinforcing that she deserves to receive and give love.

A relationship can also be a source of tremendous emotional support as the woman explores her goals, values, and relationship to the world. (P. 51)

Because dating experience increases the likelihood that an intimate romantic relationship will evolve, the absence of this opportunity may have long-term repercussions. Malyon (1981) noted some of the reverberations:

> Their most charged sexual desires are usually seen as perverted, and their deepest feelings of psychological attachment are regarded as unacceptable. This social disapproval interferes with the preintimacy involvement that fosters the evolution of maturity and self-respect in the domain of object relations. (P. 326)

Culture's Devaluation of Same-Sex Relationships

Relatively speaking, our culture is far more willing to turn a blind eye to sexual than to romantic relationships among same-sex adolescent partners. Same-sex activity may appear "temporary," an experiment, a phase, or a perverted source of fun. But falling in love with someone of the same gender and maintaining a sustained emotional involvement with that person implies an irreversible deviancy at worst and a bad decision at best. In our homes, schools, religious institutions, and media, we teach that intense relationships after early adolescence among members of the same sex "should" raise the concern of good parents, good friends, and good teachers. One result is that youths of all sexual orientations may become frightened of developing close friendships with same-sex peers. They fear that these friendships will be viewed as sexually intimate.

It is hardly surprising that a sexual-minority adolescent can easily become "the loneliest person . . . in the typical high school of today" (Norton 1976:376):

> For the homosexual-identified student, high school is often a lonely place where, from every vantage point, there are couples: couples holding hands as they enter school; couples dissolving into an endless wet kiss between school bells; couples exchanging rings with ephemeral vows of devotion and love. (Sears 1991:326–27)

The separation of a youth's homoerotic passion from the socially sanctioned act of heterosexual dating can generate self-doubt, anger, and resentment, and can ultimately retard or distort the development of interpersonal intimacy during the adolescent years. Thus, many youths never consider same-sex dating to be a reasonable option, except in their fantasies. Scientific and clinical writings that ignore same-sex romance and dating among youth contribute to this conspiracy of silence. Sexual-minority youth struggle with issues of identity and intimacy because important impediments rooted in our cultural values and attitudes deter them from dating those they love and instead mandate that they date those they cannot love.

Empirical Studies of Same–Sex Romantic Relationships among Youth

Until the last several years same-sex relationships among sexual-minority youths were seldom recognized in the empirical, scientific literature. With the recent visibility of gay, bisexual, and lesbian youths in the culture at large, social and behavioral scientists are beginning to conduct research focusing on various developmental processes of such youths, including their sexuality and intimacy.

Bisexual, lesbian, and gay youths, whether in Detroit, Minneapolis, Pennsylvania, New York, or the Netherlands, report that they desire to have long-lasting, committed same-sex romantic relationships in their future (D'Augelli 1991; Sanders 1980; Savin–Williams 1990). According to Silverstein (1981), establishing a romantic relationship with a same-sex partner helps one to feel "chosen," to resolve issues of sexual identity, and to feel more complete. Indeed, those who are in a long-term love relationship generally have high levels of self-esteem and self-acceptance.[1]

Although there are few published studies of teens that focus primarily on their same-sex dating or romantic relationships, there are suggestive data that debunk the myth in our culture that gays, lesbians, and bisexuals neither want nor maintain steady, loving same-sex relationships. In two studies of gay and bisexual male youths, same-sex relationships are regarded as highly desirable. Among 29 Minnesota youths, 10 had a steady male partner at the time of the interview, 11 had been in a same-sex relationship, and, most tellingly, all but 2 hoped for a steady male partner in their future (Remafedi 1987). For these youths, many of whom were living independently with friends or on the street, being in a long-term relationship was considered to be an ideal state. With a college-age sample of 61 males, D'Augelli (1991) reported similar results. One half of his sample was "partnered," and their most troubling mental health concern was termination of a close relationship, ranking just ahead of telling parents about their homosexuality.

The difficulty, however, is to maintain a visible same-sex romance in high school. Sears (1991) interviewed 36 Southern late adolescent and young adult lesbians, gays, and bisexuals. He discovered that although nearly everyone had heterosexually dated in high school, very few dated a member of the same sex during that time. Because of concerns about secrecy and the lack of social support, most same-sex romances involved little emotional commitment and were of short duration. None were overt.

Research with over 300 gay, bisexual, and lesbian youths between the ages of 14 and 23 years (Savin–Williams 1990) supports the finding that sexual-minority youths have romantic relationships during adolescence and young adulthood. Almost 90 percent of the females and two thirds of the males reported that they have had a romantic relationship. Of the total number of romances listed, 60 percent were with same-sex partners. The male youths were slightly more likely than lesbian and bisexual female youths to begin their romantic career with a same-sex, rather than an opposite-sex, partner.

In the same study, the lesbians and bisexual females who had a high proportion of same-sex romances were most likely to be "out" to others. However, their self-esteem level was essentially the same as those who had a high percentage of heterosexual relationships. If she began same-sex dating early, during adolescence, then a lesbian or bisexual female also tended to be in a current relationship and to experience long-lasting romances. Gay and bisexual male youths who had a large percentage of adolescent romantic relationships with boys had high self-esteem. They were more likely to be publicly "out" to friends and family if they had had a large number of romances. Boys who initiated same-sex romances at an early age were more likely to report that they have had long-term and multiple same-sex relationships.

The findings from these studies are admittedly sparse and do not provide the depth and insight that are needed to help us better understand the experience of being in a same-sex romantic relationship. They do illustrate that youths have same-sex romances while in high school. Where there is desire, some youths will find a way. Sexually active same-sex friendships may evolve into romantic relationships (Savin–Williams, 1995), and those most publicly out are most likely to have had adolescent same-sex romances. Certainly, most lesbian, gay, and bisexual youths value the importance of a same-sex, lifelong, committed relationship in their adult years.

Perhaps the primary issue is not the absence of same-sex romances during adolescence, but the hidden nature of the romances. They are seldom recognized and rarely supported or celebrated. The research data offer little information regarding the psychological impact of not being involved in a same-sex romantic relationship or of having to hide such a relationship when it exists. For this, one must turn to stories of the personal struggles of adolescents.

Personal Struggles

Youths who have same-sex romances during their adolescence face a severe struggle to have these relationships acknowledged and supported. Gibson (1989) noted the troubling contradictions:

> The first romantic involvements of lesbian and gay male youth are a source of great joy to them in affirming their sexual identity, providing them with support, and assuring them that they too can experience love. However, society places extreme hardships on these relationships that make them difficult to establish and maintain. (P. 130)

A significant number of youths, perhaps those feeling most insecure regarding their sexual identity, may fantasize about being sexually intimate with a same-sex partner but have little hope that it could in fact become a reality. One youth, Lawrence, reported this feeling in his coming-out story:

> *While growing up, love was something I watched other people experience and enjoy. . . . The countless men I secretly loved and fantasized about were only in private, empty dreams in which love was never returned. I seemed to be the only*

person in the world with no need for love and companionship. . . . Throughout high school and college I had no way to meet people of the same sex and sexual orientation. These were more years of isolation and secrecy. I saw what other guys my age did, listened to what they said and how they felt. I was expected to be part of a world with which I had nothing in common. (Curtis 1988:109–110)

A young lesbian, Diane, recalled that "love of women was never a possibility that I even realized could be. You loved your mother and your aunts, and you had girlfriends for a while. Someday, though, you would always meet a man" (Stanley and Wolfe 1980:47). Girls dated boys and not other girls. Because she did not want to date boys, she did not date.

Another youth knew he had homoerotic attractions, but he never fathomed that they could be expressed to the boy that he most admired, his high school soccer teammate. It took alcohol and the right situation:

I knew I was checking out the guys in the shower after soccer practice. I thought of myself as hetero who had the urge for males. I fought it, said it was a phase. And then it happened. Derek was my best friend. After soccer practice the fall of our junior year we celebrated both making the "A" team by getting really drunk. We were just fooling around and suddenly our pants were off. I was so scared I stayed out of school for three days but we kept being friends and nothing was said until a year later when I came out to everyone and he came up to me with these tears and asked if he made me homosexual. (Savin–Williams 1995)

It is never easy for youths to directly confront the mores of peers whose values and attitudes are routinely supported by the culture. Nearly all youths know implicitly the rules of socially appropriate behavior and the consequences of nonconformity. This single, most influential barrier to same-sex dating, the threat posed by peers, can have severe repercussions. The penalty for crossing the line of "normalcy" can result in emotional and physical pain.

Peer Harassment as a Barrier to Dating

Price (1982) concluded, "Adolescents can be very cruel to others who are different, who do not conform to the expectations of the peer group" (p. 472). Very little has changed in the last decade. For example, 17-year-old actor Ryan Phillippe worried about the consequences on his family and friends if he played a gay teen on ABC's soap opera *One Life to Live* (Gable 1992:3D). David Ruffin, 19, of Ferndale, Michigan, explained why he boycotted his high school senior prom: "The kids could tell I was different from them, and I think I was different because I was gay. And when you're dealing with young people, different means not cool" (Bruni 1992:10A).

Unlike heterosexual dating, little social advantage, such as peer popularity or acceptance, is gained by holding hands and kissing a same-sex peer in school hallways, shopping malls, or synagogues. Lies are spun to protect secrets and to avoid peer harassment. One lesbian youth, Kim, felt that she had to be an actress around her friends. She lied to friends by creating "Andrew" when she was dating "Andrea" over the weekend (Bruni 1992).

   To avoid harassment, sexual minority adolescents may monitor their interpersonal interactions. They may wonder, "Am I standing too close?" or "Do I appear too happy to see him(her)?" (Anderson 1987). Herrick and Martin (1987) found that youths are often apprehensive to show "friendship for a friend of the same sex for fear of being misunderstood or giving away their secretly held sexual orientation" (p. 31). If erotic desires become aroused and threaten expression, youths may seek to terminate same-sex friendships rather than risk revealing their secret. For many adolescents, especially bisexual youths, relationships with the other sex may be easier to develop. The appeal of such relationships is that the youths will be viewed by peers as heterosexual, thus peer acceptance will be enhanced and the threat of harassment and rejection will be reduced. The result is that some sexual-minority youths feel inherently "fake" and they therefore retreat from becoming intimate with others. Although they may meet the implicit and explicit demands of their culture, it is at a cost—their sense of authenticity.

Faking It: Heterosexual Sex and Dating

Retrospective data from gay, bisexual, and lesbian adults reveal the extent to which heterosexual dating and sex are commonplace during the adolescent and young adult years (Bell and Weinberg 1978; Schafer 1976; Troiden and Goode 1980). These might be one-night stands, brief romances, or long-term relationships. Across various studies, nearly two-thirds of gay men and three-quarters of lesbians report having had heterosexual sex in their past. Motivations include fun, curiosity, denial of homoerotic feelings, and pressure to conform to society's insistence on heterosexual norms and behaviors. Even though heterosexual sex often results in a low level of sexual gratification, it is deemed a necessary sacrifice to meet the expectations of peers and, by extension, receive their approval. Only later, as adults, when they have the opportunity to compare these heterosexual relationships with same-sex ones do they fully realize that which they had missed during their younger years.

   Several studies with lesbian, bisexual, and gay adolescents document the extent to which they are sexually involved with opposite-sex partners. Few gay and bisexual [male] youth had *extensive* sexual contact with females, even among those who began heterosexual sex at an early age. Sex with one or two girls was usually considered "quite enough." Not infrequently these girls were best friends who expressed a romantic or sexual interest in the gay boys. The male youths liked the girls, but they preferred friendships rather than sexual relations. One youth expressed this dilemma:

> She was a year older and we had been friends for a long time before beginning dating. It was a date with the full thing: dinner, theater, alcohol, making out, sex.

> *At her house and I think we both came during intercourse. I was disappointed because it was such hard work—not physically I mean but emotionally. Later on in my masturbation my fantasies were never of her. We did it once more in high school and then once more when we were in college. I labeled it love but not sexual love. I really wanted them to occur together. It all ended when I labeled myself gay.* (Savin–Williams 1995)

An even greater percentage of lesbian and bisexual female adolescents engaged in heterosexual sexual experiences—2 of every 3 (Herdt and Boxer 1993), 3 of every 4 (Sears 1991), and 8 of 10 (Savin–Williams 1990). Heterosexual activity began as early as second grade and as late as senior year in high school. Few of these girls, however, had extensive sex with boys—usually with two or three boys within the context of dating. Eighteen-year-old Kimba noted that she went through a heterosexual stage:

> . . .*trying to figure out what was so great about guys sexually. I still don't understand. I guess that, for straights, it is like it is for me when I am with a woman. . . . I experimented in whatever ways I thought would make a difference, but it was no go. My closest friends are guys; there is caring and closeness between us.* (Heron 1983:82)

Georgina also tried to follow a heterosexual script:

> *In sixth and seventh grades you start wearing makeup, you start getting your hair cut, you start liking boys—you start thinking about letting them "French kiss" you. I did all those major things. But, I still didn't feel very satisfied with myself. I remember I never really wanted to be intimate with any guy. I always wanted to be their best friend.* (Sears 1991:327)

One young lesbian, Lisa, found herself "having sex with boys to prove I wasn't gay. Maybe I was even trying to prove it to myself! I didn't enjoy having sex with boys" (Heron 1983:76). These three lesbian youths forfeited a sense of authenticity, intimacy, and love because they were taught that emotional intimacy can only be achieved with members of the other sex.

The reasons sexual-minority adolescents gave as to why they engaged in heterosexual sex were similar to those reported in retrospective studies by adults. The youths needed to test whether their heterosexual attractions were as strong as their homoerotic ones—thus attempting to disconfirm their homosexuality—and to mask their homosexuality so as to win peer- and self-acceptance and to avoid peer rejection. Many youths believed that they could not really know whether they were lesbian, gay, bisexual, or heterosexual without first experiencing heterosexual sex. For many, however, heterosexual activities consisted of sex without feelings that they tried to enjoy without much success (Herdt and Boxer 1993). Heterosexual sex felt unnatural because it lacked the desired emotional intensity. One young gay youth reported:

> *We'd been dating for three months. I was 15 and she, a year or so older. We had petted previously and so she planned this event. We attempted intercourse in*

her barn, but I was too nervous. I didn't feel good afterwards because it was not successful. We did it every week for a month or so. It was fun but it wasn't a big deal. But then I did not have a great lust or drive. This was just normal I guess. It gave me something to do to tell the other guys who were always bragging. (Savin–Williams 1995)

Similarly, Kimberly always had a steady heterosexual relationship: "It was like I was just going through the motions. It was expected of me, so I did it. I'd kiss him or embrace him but it was like I was just there. He was probably enjoying it, but I wasn't" (Sears 1991:327).

Jacob, an African American adolescent, dated the prettiest girls in his school in order to maintain his image: "It was more like President Reagan entertaining heads of state. It's expected of you when you're in a certain position" (Sears 1991:126–127). Another Southern male youth, Grant, used "group dates" to reinforce his heterosexual image. Rumors that he was gay were squelched because his jock friends came to his defense: "He's not a fag. He has a girlfriend" (Sears 1991:328).

These and other personal stories of youths vividly recount the use of heterosexual sex and dating as a cover for an emerging same-sex or bisexual identity. Dating provides opportunities to temporarily "pass" as straight until the meaning of homoerotic feelings are resolved or youths find a safe haven to be lesbian or gay. Heterosexual sex and dating may be less pleasurable than same-sex encounters, but many sexual-minority youths feel that the former are the only safe, acceptable options.

Impediments and Consequences

The difficulties inherent in dating same-sex partners during adolescence are monumental. First is the fundamental difficulty of finding a suitable partner. The vast majority of lesbian, bisexual, and gay youths are closeted, not out to themselves, let alone to others. A second barrier is the consequences of same-sex dating, such as verbal and physical harassment from peers. A third impediment is the lack of public recognition or "celebration" of those who are romantically involved with a member of the same gender. Thus, same-sex dating remains hidden and mysterious, something that is either ridiculed, condemned, or ignored.

The consequences of an exclusively heterosexually oriented atmosphere in the peer social world can be severe and enduring. An adolescent may feel isolated and socially excluded from the world of peers. Sex with others of the same gender may be associated exclusively with anonymous, guilt-ridden encounters, handicapping the ability to develop healthy intimate relationships in adulthood. Denied the opportunity for romantic involvement with someone of the same sex, a youth may suffer impaired self-esteem that reinforces the belief that one is unworthy of love, affection, and intimacy. One youth, Rick, even doubted his ability to love:

> *When I started my senior year, I was still unclear about my sexuality. I had dated women with increasing frequency, but never felt love for any of them. I discovered that I could perform sexually with a woman, but heterosexual experiences were not satisfying emotionally. I felt neither love nor emotional one-ness with women. Indeed, I had concluded that I was incapable of human love.* (Heron 1983:95–96)

If youths are to take advantage of opportunities to explore their erotic sexuality, it is sometimes, at least for males, confined to clandestine sexual encounters, void of romance, affection, and intimacy but replete with mis-givings, anonymity, and guilt.

> *Ted was 21 and me, 16. It was New Year's Eve and it was a swimming pool party at my rich friend's house. Not sure why Ted was there but he really came on to me, even putting his arm around me in front of everyone. I wasn't ready for that but I liked it. New Year's Day, every time Ted looked at me I looked away because I thought it was obvious that we had had sex. It did clarify things for me. It didn't feel like I was cheating on [my girlfriend] Beth because the sex felt so different, so right.* (Savin-Williams 1995)

A gay youth may have genital contact with another boy without ever kissing him because to do so would be too meaningful. Remafedi (1990) found this escape from intimacy to be very damaging: "Without appropriate opportunities for peer dating and socialization, gay youth frequently eschew intimacy altogether and resort to transient and anonymous sexual encounters with adults" (p. 1173). One consequence is the increased risk for contracting sexually transmitted diseases, including HIV. This is particularly risky for youths who turn to prostitution to meet their intimacy needs (Coleman 1989).

When youths eventually match their erotic and intimacy needs, they may be surprised with the results. This was Jacob's experience (Sears 1991) when he fell in love with Warren, an African American senior who also sang in the choir. Sex quickly evolved into "an emotional thing." Jacob explained: "He got to the point of telling me he loved me. That was the first time any-body ever said any thing like that. It was kind of hard to believe that even after sex there are really feelings" (p. 127).

Equally common, however, especially among closeted youths, is that les-bian, bisexual, and gay teens may experience a poverty of intimacy in their lives and considerable social and emotional isolation. One youth, Grant, enjoyed occasional sex with a star football player, but he was devastated by the subsequent exclusion the athlete meted out to him: "We would see each other and barely speak but after school we'd see each other a lot. He had his image that he had to keep up and, since it was rumored that I was gay, he didn't want to get a close identity with me" (Sears 1991:330).

Largely because of negative peer prohibitions and the lack of social support and recognition, same-sex romances that are initiated have difficulty flourishing. Irwin met Benji in the eighth grade and was immediately attracted to him (Sears 1991). They shared interests in music and academics and enjoyed long conversations, playing music, and riding in the countryside. Eventually, their attractions for each other were expressed and a romantic, sexual relationship began. Although Irwin was in love with Benji, their relationship soon ended because it was no match for the social pressures and personal goals that conflicted with Irwin being in a same-sex relationship.

Georgina's relationship with Kay began dramatically with intense feelings that were at times ambivalent for both of them. At one point she overheard Kay praying, "Dear Lord, forgive me for the way I am" (Sears 1991:333). Georgina's parents demanded that she end her "friendship" with Kay. Georgina told classmates they were just "good friends" and began dating boys as a cover. Despite her love for Kay, the relationship ended when Georgina's boyfriend told her that no one liked her because she hung around "that dyke, Kay." In retrospect, Georgina wished: "If everybody would have accepted everybody, I would have stayed with Kay" (p. 334).

Given this situation, lesbian, bisexual, and gay youths in same-sex relationships may place unreasonable and ultimately destructive demands on each other. For example, they may expect that the relationship will resolve all fears of loneliness and isolation and validate all aspects of their personal identity (Browning 1987).

A Success Story

A vivid account of how a same-sex romantic relationship can empower a youth is depicted in the seminal autobiography of Aaron Fricke (1981), *Reflections of a Rock Lobster*. He fell in love with a classmate, Paul:

> With Paul's help, I started to challenge all the prejudice I had encountered during 16 1/2 years of life. Sure, it was scary to think that half my classmates might hate me if they knew my secret, but from Paul's example I knew it was possible to one day be strong and face them without apprehension. (Fricke 1981:44)

Through Paul, Aaron became more resilient and self-confident:

> His strengths were my strengths. . . . I realized that my feelings for him were unlike anything I had felt before. The sense of camaraderie was familiar from other friendships; the deep spiritual love I felt for Paul was new. So was the openness, the sense of communication with another. (Fricke 1981:45)

Life-gained significance. He wrote poems. He planned a future. He learned to express both kindness and strength. Aaron was in love, with another boy. But no guidelines or models existed on how best to express these feelings:

> Heterosexuals learn early in life what behavior is expected of them. They get practice in their early teens having crushes, talking to their friends about their feelings, going on first dates and to chaperoned parties, and figuring out their feelings. Paul and I hadn't gotten all that practice; our relationship was formed without much of a model to base it on. It was the first time either of us had been

in love like this and we spent much of our time just figuring out what that meant for us. (Fricke 1981:46)

Eventually, after a court case that received national attention, Aaron won the right to take Paul to the senior prom as his date. This victory was relatively minor compared to the self respect, authenticity, and pride in being gay that their relationship won for each of them.

Final Reflections

As a clinical and developmental psychologist, I find it disheartening to observe our culture ignoring and condemning sexual-minority youth. One consequence is that myths and stereotypes are perpetuated that interfere with or prevent youths from developing intimate same-sex relationships with those to whom they are erotically and emotionally attracted. Separating passion from affection, engaging in sex with strangers in impersonal and sometimes unsafe places, and finding alienation rather than intimacy in those relationships are not conducive to psychological health. In one study the most common reason given for initial suicide attempts by lesbians and gay men was relationship problems (Bell and Weinberg 1978).

A youth's limited ability to meet other bisexual, lesbian, and gay adolescents compounds a sense of isolation and alienation. Crushes may develop on unknowing friends, teachers, and peers. These are often cases of unrequited love with the youth never revealing their true feelings (Gibson 1989:131).

Sexual-minority youths need the validation of those around them as they attempt to develop a personal integrity and to discover those similar to themselves. How long can gay, bisexual, and lesbian adolescents maintain their charades before they encounter difficulty separating the pretensions from the realities? Many "use" heterosexual dating to blind themselves and others. By so doing they attempt to disconfirm to themselves the growing encroachment of their homoerotic attractions while escaping derogatory name calling and gaining peer status and prestige. The incidence of heterosexual sex and relationships in the adolescence of gay men and lesbians attests to these desires.

Future generations of adolescents will no doubt find it easier to establish same-sex relationships. This is due in part to the dramatic increase in the visibility that adult same-sex relationships have received during the last few years. Domestic partnership ordinances in several cities and counties, victories for spousal equivalency rights in businesses, court cases addressing adoption by lesbian couples and challenges to marriage laws by several male couples, the dramatic story of the life partnership of Karen Thompson and Sharon Kowalski, and the "marriage" of former Mr. Universe Bob Paris to male Supermodel Rod Jackson raise public awareness of same-sex romantic relationships. Even Ann Landers (1992) is spreading the word. In a column, an 18-year-old gay teen from Santa Barbara requested that girls quit hitting on him because, as he explained, "I have a very special friend who is a student at the local university . . . and [we] are very happy with each other" (Landers 1992:2B).

A decade after Aaron Fricke fought for and won the right to take his boyfriend to the prom, a dozen lesbian, gay, and bisexual youths in the Detroit-Ann Arbor area arranged to have their own prom. Most felt excluded from the traditional high school prom, which they considered "a final, bitter postscript to painful years of feeling left out" (Bruni 1992: 10A). Seventeen-year-old Brenda said, "I want to feel rich for one moment. I want to feel all glamorous, just for one night" (Bruni 1992:10A). Going to the "Fantasy" prom was a celebration that created a sense of pride, a connection with other sexual-minority teens, and a chance to dance—"two girls together, unguarded and unashamed, in the middle of a room filled with teenagers just like them" (Bruni 1992:10A). One year later, I attended this prom with my life partner and the number of youths in attendance had increased sixfold.

We need to listen to youths such as Aaron, Diane, and Georgina, to hear their concerns, insights, and solutions. Most of all, we need to end the invisibility of same-sex romantic relationships. It is easily within our power to enhance the well-being of millions of youths, including "Billy Joe," a character in a famous Bobbie Gentry song. If Billy Joe had seen an option to a heterosexual life style, he might have considered an alternative to ending his life by jumping off the Tallahatchie Bridge.

ENDNOTE

The causal pathway, however, is unclear (Savin–Williams 1990). That is, being in a same-sex romance may build positive self-regard, but it may also be true that those with high self-esteem are more likely to form love relationships and to stay in them.

REFERENCES

Anderson, D. 1987. "Family and Peer Relations of Gay Adolescents." Pp. 162–78 in *Adolescent Psychiatry: Developmental and Clinical Studies: Vol. 14*, edited by S. C. Geinstein. Chicago: The University of Chicago Press.

Bell, A. P. and M. S. Weinberg. 1978. *Homosexualities: A Study of Diversity among Men and Women*. New York: Simon and Schuster.

Bowlby, J. 1973. *Attachment and Loss*. Vol. 2, *Separation*. New York: Basic Books.

Browning, C. 1987. "Therapeutic Issues and Intervention Strategies with Young Adult Lesbian Clients: A Developmental Approach." *Journal of Homosexuality* 14:45–52.

Bruni, F. 1992. "A Prom Night of Their Own to Dance, Laugh, Reminesce." *Detroit Free Press*, May 22, pp. 1A, 10A.

Coleman, E. 1989. "The Development of Male Prostitution Activity among Gay and Bisexual Adolescents." *Journal of Homosexuality* 17:131–49.

Curtis, W. ed. 1988. *Revelations: A Collection of Gay Male Coming Out Stories*. Boston: Alyson.

D'Augelli, A. R. 1991. "Gay Men in College: Identity Processes and Adaptations." *Journal of College Student Development* 32:140–46.

Fricke, A. 1981. *Reflections of a Rock Lobster: A Story about Growing Up Gay*. Boston: Alyson.

Gable, D. 1992. "'Life' Story Looks at Roots of Homophobia." *USA Today*, June 2, p. 30.

Gibson, P. 1989. "Gay Male and Lesbian Youth Suicide." In *Report of the Secretary's Task Force on Youth Suicide*, vol. 3, *Prevention and Interventions in Youth Suicide (3-110-3-142)*, edited by M. R. Feinleib. Rockville, MD: U.S. Department of Health and Human Services.

Hazan, C. and P. Shaver. 1987. "Romantic Love Conceptualized as an Attachment Process." *Journal of Personality and Social Psychology* 52:511–24.

Herdt, G. and A. Boxer. 1993. *Children of Horizons: How Gay and Lesbian Teens Are Leading a New Way Out of the Closet*. Boston: Beacon.

Herold, E. S. 1979. "Variables Influencing the Dating Adjustment of University Students." *Journal of Youth and Adolescence* 8: 73–79.

Heron, A., ed. 1983. *One Teenager in Ten*. Boston: Alyson.

Herrick, E. S. and A. D. Martin. 1987. "Developmental Issues and Their Resolution for Gay and Lesbian Adolescents." *Journal of Homosexuality* 14:25–44.

Isay, R. A. 1989. *Being Homosexual: Gay Men and Their Development*. New York: Avon.

Landers, A. 1992. "Gay Teen Tired of Advances from Sexually Aggressive Girls." *Detroit Free Press*, May 26, p. 2B.

Malyon, A. K. 1981. "The Homosexual Adolescent: Developmental Issues and Social Bias." *Child Welfare* 60:321–30.

Norton, J. L. 1976. "The Homosexual and Counseling." *Personnel and Guidance Journal* 54:374–77.

Price, J. H. 1982. "High School Students' Attitudes toward Homosexuality." *Journal of School Health* 52:469–74.

Remafedi, G. 1987. "Male Homosexuality: The Adolescent's Perspective." *Pediatrics* 79:326–30.

——. 1990. "Fundamental Issues in the Care of Homosexual Youth." *Adolescent Medicine* 74:1169–79.

Sanders, G. 1980. "Homosexualities in the Netherlands." *Alternative Lifestyles* 3:278–311.

Savin-Williams, R. C. 1990. *Gay and Lesbian Youth: Expressions of Identity*. New York: Hemisphere.

——. 1994. "Dating Those You Can't Love and Loving Those You Can't Date." Pp. 196–215 in *Personal Relationships during Adolescence*, vol. 6, *Advances in Adolescent Development*, edited by R. Montemayor, G. R. Adams, and T. P. Gullotta. Newbury Park, CA: Sage.

——. 1995. *Sex and Sexual Identity among Gay and Bisexual Males*. Manuscript in preparation, Cornell University, Ithaca, NY.

Scarf, M. 1987. *Intimate Partners: Patterns in Love and Marriage*. New York: Random House.

Schafer, S. 1976. "Sexual and Social Problems of Lesbians." *Journal of Sex Research* 12:50–69.

Sears, J. T. 1991. *Growing Up Gay in the South: Race, Gender, and Journeys of the Spirit*. New York: Harrington Park Press.

Silverstein, C. 1981. *Man to Man: Gay Couples in America*. New York: William Morrow.

Skipper, J. K., Jr., and G. Nass. 1966. "Dating Behavior: Framework for Analysis and an Illustration." *Journal of Marriage and the Family* 27:412–20.

Stanley, J. P. and S. J. Wolfe, eds. 1980. *The Coming Out Stories*. New York: Persephone.

Troiden, R. R. and E. Goode. 1980. "Variables Related to the Acquisition of a Gay Identity." *Journal of Homosexuality* 5:383–92.

PART IV

Marriage, Cohabitation, and Partnership

In this section, we examine various forms of family formation; namely, marriage, cohabitation, and partnership. These three family forms are examples of *coupling:* how couples come together to form a family relationship. It should be noted, however, that there are additional types of coupling and family formation, such as communes, where a group of people live together as a family; polygamy, whereby an individual marries more than one spouse; and polyamorous relationships, in which more than two people are involved in a love relationship. There are also a number of people who will never marry and, possibly, who will never cohabit but are in ongoing relationships. Thus, as students of the family, we need to recognize the diversity of family forms that exist in our society and other societies beyond traditional, heterosexual marriage. We also need to recognize that the personal experience of any one family form is also diverse depending on a person's race-ethnicity, social class, gender, and sexual orientation.

Given that diversity, what is known about marriage, cohabitation, and partnership?

Marriage

Even with the increasing numbers of individuals who choose to cohabit or to never marry, the majority of individuals in the United States eventually marry. Unlike cohabitation, however, there is abundant research on the institution of marriage (the macrolevel) and on the personal experience of marriage (the microlevel). At the macrolevel, marriage is a social institution that is influenced by other institutions, including legal, religious, economic, and political institutions. Norval D. Glenn, a well-known family scholar, has argued that marriage is an institution of social control because it regulates individual behavior. Glenn (1996) also has studied the paradox that, while marriage is important to most adult Americans, the proportion of Americans ever-married has declined and the proportion successfully married has declined even more. What is happening to the institution of marriage? The first reading in this section, "The Deinstitutionalization of American Marriage" by Andrew J. Cherlin, addresses this question. Cherlin, a professor of sociology at Johns Hopkins University, has studied families for 30 years. In this selection, Cherlin examines the weakening of social norms in the institution of heterosexual marriage. Instead of heterosexual marriage, more people are cohabiting, having children outside of marriage, or pursuing same-sex marriage or commitment ceremonies as the basis of their family formation.

The second article in this section, "Clashing Dreams: Highly Educated Overseas Brides and Low-Wage U.S. Husbands," by Hung Cam Thai, builds on Cherlin's arguments (Reading 12) about the deinstitutionalization of marriage in the United States. Cam Thai, an assistant professor of Asian American Studies at the University of California, Santa Barbara, examines how migration and economic globalization are changing the institution of marriage for Vietnamese and Vietnamese Americans. Cam Thai studied 69 Vietnamese transpacific marriages to see how men, women, and their families navigate the changing social and cultural norms of this transpacific marriage market between Vietnam and the United States. Cam Thai's findings are fascinating in what they reveal about cultural traditions, gender roles, and the changing social statuses that education and work give an individual in a transnational marriage market and the potential conflicts that can result. Cam Thai's research raises several interesting questions such as, What does marriage mean in Vietnam, to Vietnamese Americans in the United States, and to Vietnamese women of high social status who emigrate to the United States to marry Vietnamese American men of lower social status?

The third article in this section, "Peer Marriage" by Pepper Schwartz, is an excerpt from Schwartz's book *Peer Marriage: How Love Between Equals Really Works* (1995). Since her graduate school days at Yale, Schwartz, a professor of sociology at the University of Washington, has studied gender, relationships, and power dynamics. Schwartz chose to study peer marriage because everyone said it could not exist but she knew it could because she has been in a peer marriage for more than 15 years and knows other couples in peer marriages. She says she has always believed that equality and equity are important principles for respect and happiness. Regarding her research, Schwartz also says:

> It was and is important for me to show that men and women do not have to be in hierarchical relationship—and that women, in particular, do not have to settle for anything less than a fair deal in a loving partnership. (*Personal Interview 1997*)

Schwartz divides her respondents into three groups: traditional couples, Near Peer Couples, and Peer Couples. Each type of marital coupling has strengths and weaknesses, including the fact that a peer or egalitarian marriage requires a great deal of work on the couple's part. Peer Couples have to work every day on sustaining the communication and balance of power in their relationship.

Cohabitation

In the United States, even though cohabitation has existed for centuries, it is a fairly modern alternative to heterosexual marriage. The numbers of cohabiting couples in the United States did not begin to grow rapidly until after 1960. According to the U.S. Bureau of the Census, the number of cohabiting couples has risen from 439,000 in 1960 to 4,236,000 in 1998 (U.S. Bureau of the Census 1998).[1] Prior to 1960, cohabitation was considered to be socially deviant. Couples were thought to be "living in sin" or "shacking up" together. Social attitudes about cohabitation began to change during the 1960s and 1970s due to the influences of the sexual revolution and the feminist movement, which brought renewed attention to sexual freedom and to the traditional, and often oppressive, gender roles in marriage. During this time period, many "anti-marriage" groups began to form as part of the anti-establishment movement. Divorce rates also began to rise during this time period, and with the increasing public criticism of marriage, more young couples chose to live together either as an alternative to marriage or as a trial marriage. Today, cohabitors are usually one of three types: (1) couples planning to marry, but living together first; (2) couples cohabiting as a temporary alternative to marriage; and (3) couples cohabiting as a permanent alternative to marriage.

Unlike many other areas of study on the family, until recently there has not been much research on cohabitation. Most of the research on cohabitation focuses on how cohabitation affects marriage rates or marital stability. There is also some research on how cohabitation affects divorce rates and on the role cohabitation plays in relationships formed after a divorce. In fact, a growing number of cohabitors are individuals over age 45 who, after experiencing divorce, would rather cohabit than remarry. These individuals do not want to bear the legal and emotional complications of marrying again. Another area of study within the cohabitation literature is the influence cohabitation has on children. Manning and Lichter (1996) estimate that more than 2.2 million, or roughly 1 in 7, children live in the household of a cohabiting couple. Their research examines the emotional and financial well-being of children in cohabiting households versus that of children in married households.

The fourth article in this section, "Families Formed Outside of Marriage" by Judith A. Seltzer, reviews the current scholarship on cohabitation. Seltzer is a professor of sociology at the University of California at Los Angeles. As a family demographer and a social scientist, Seltzer is interested in studying the changes in family-formation patterns and household living arrangements caused by more people never marrying or choosing to cohabit after a divorce instead of remarrying. In this reading, Seltzer addresses several important questions: What are the social contexts and individual expectations of cohabitation in the United States and other societies? What are the current rates of cohabitation and group differences in those rates? Is cohabitation a stage in the courtship process or an end in itself? What is the stability of cohabiting unions, and how does cohabiting affect children?

---

[1]Note that these data reflect the numbers of heterosexual couples living together, not those cohabitors who are same-sex couples. The U.S. Bureau of the Census did not begin to collect data on same-sex couples sharing a household until the 1990 census. Moreover, in general, most of the research on cohabitation focuses on heterosexual couples, not on same-sex couples.

Partnership

Many individuals, regardless of sexual orientation, decide that marriage is not for them, and they decide, instead, to form commitments called "partnerships." The meaning and recognition of these partnerships vary because the government primarily recognizes legal, heterosexual marriages. Thus, some couples try to form domestic partnerships through employment or local governments to give their relationships recognition and rights similar to those of married couples. Other couples are less concerned about the legal recognition of their relationship but want to have a committed relationship outside of marriage. They may decide to create a private or public commitment ceremony to honor their relationship. In recent years, there has been increased research on the commitment ceremonies of gay and lesbian couples, including Suzanne Sherman's book *Lesbian and Gay Marriage: Private Commitments, Public Ceremonies* (1992) and Ellen Lewin's book *Recognizing Ourselves: Ceremonies of Lesbian and Gay Commitment* (1998).

The final article in this section, "From This Day Forward: Commitment, Marriage, and Family in Lesbian and Gay Relationships," is excerpted from Gretchen A. Stiers' 1999 book of the same title. Stiers conducted 90 interviews with gay and lesbian couples to examine the partnerships they formed in their efforts to create families. Stiers is particularly interested in how gay men and lesbians define commitment in their relationships and what their motivations are for having commitment ceremonies. Stiers also addresses the question of whether same-sex ceremonies are acts of accommodation or acts of resistance to the dominant culture. Stiers' research is especially timely given the current public debate on same-sex marriage. The debate is being waged in many states, including a number of states that have passed "Defense of Marriage" Acts that will make same-sex marriages contracted elsewhere illegal in their state. Many gay, lesbian, bisexual, and transgendered people see having the right to marry as being an important civil right. Other gay activists are critical of the oppressive nature of the institution of heterosexual marriage in terms of having sexist gender roles and the privileging of monogamous, long-term coupling as the only legitimate form of family relationship. Many people also are concerned that hundreds of economic and legal benefits conferred by the state to heterosexuals who marry are denied to heterosexuals and bisexuals who do not legally marry and to gay couples who cannot legally marry. Allowing gay couples to marry and gain access to these economic and legal benefits would not eliminate the marital-status discrimination faced by other groups of people who do not or cannot legally marry (such as cohabitors, single parents with children, and people who live alone). Thus, these scholars and activists advocate separating the legal, economic, and health care benefits from marriage and, instead, *granting all people,* regardless of their marital status, basic health care benefits and economic and legal rights.

REFERENCES

Bumpass, Larry L. and James A. Sweet. 1989. "National Estimates of Cohabitation." *Demography* 26 (4): 615–25.

Glenn, Norval D. 1996. "Values, Attitudes, and the State of American Marriage." Pp. 15–33 in *Promises to Keep: Decline and Renewal of Marriage in America,* edited by David Popenoe, Jean Bethke Elshtain, and David Blankenhorn. Lanham, MD: Rowman and Littlefield.

Lewin, Ellen. 1998. *Recognizing Ourselves: Ceremonies of Lesbian and Gay Commitment.* New York: Columbia University Press.

Manning, Wendy and Daniel Lichter. 1996. "Parental Cohabitation and Children's Economic Well-Being." *Journal of Marriage and the Family* 58:998–1010.

Schwartz, Pepper. 1995. *Peer Marriage: How Love Between Equals Really Works.* New York: The Free Press.

Sherman, Suzanne, Ed. 1992. *Lesbian and Gay Marriage: Private Commitments, Public Ceremonies.* Philadelphia: Temple University Press.

Stiers, Gretchen A. 1999. *From This Day Forward: Commitment, Marriage, and Family in Lesbian and Gay Relationships.* New York: St. Martin's Press.

U.S. Bureau of the Census. 1998. *Marital Status and Living Arrangements: March 1998. Current Population Reports,* Series P20-514. Washington, DC: U.S. Bureau of the Census.

12

THE DEINSTITUTIONALIZATION
OF AMERICAN MARRIAGE

ANDREW J. CHERLIN

A quarter century ago, in an article entitled "Remarriage as an Incomplete Institution" (Cherlin 1978), I argued that American society lacked norms about the way that members of stepfamilies should act toward each other. Parents and children in first marriages, in contrast, could rely on well-established norms, such as when it is appropriate to discipline a child. I predicted that, over time, as remarriage after divorce became common, norms would begin to emerge concerning proper behavior in stepfamilies—for example, what kind of relationship a stepfather should have with his stepchildren. In other words, I expected that remarriage would become institutionalized, that it would become more like first marriage. But just the opposite has happened. Remarriage has not become more like first marriage; rather, first marriage has become more like remarriage. Instead of the institutionalization of remarriage, what has occurred over the past few decades is the deinstitutionalization of marriage. Yes, remarriage is an incomplete institution, but now, so is first marriage—and for that matter, cohabitation.

By deinstitutionalization I mean the weakening of the social norms that define people's behavior in a social institution such as marriage. In times of social stability, the taken-for-granted nature of norms allows people to go about their lives without having to question their actions or the actions of others. But when social change produces situations outside the reach of established norms, individuals can no longer rely on shared understandings of how to act. Rather, they must negotiate new ways of acting, a process that is a potential source of conflict and opportunity. On the one hand, the development of new rules is likely to engender disagreement and tension among the relevant actors. On the other hand, the breakdown of the old rules of a gendered institution such as marriage could lead to the creation of a more egalitarian relationship between wives and husbands.

This perspective, I think, can help us understand the state of contemporary marriage. It may even assist in the risky business of predicting the future of marriage. To some extent, similar changes in marriage have occurred in the United States, Canada, and much of Europe, but the American situation may be distinctive. Consequently, although I include information about Canadian and European families, I focus mainly on the United States.

The Deinstitutionalization of Marriage

Even as I was writing my 1978 article, the changing division of labor in the home and the increase in childbearing outside marriage were undermining the institutionalized basis of marriage. The distinct roles of homemaker and breadwinner were fading as more married women entered the paid labor force. Looking into the future, I thought that perhaps an equitable division of household labor might become institutionalized. But what happened instead was the "stalled revolution," in Hochschild's (1989) well-known phrase. Men do somewhat more home work than they used to do, but there is wide variation, and each couple must work out their own arrangement without clear guidelines. In addition, when I wrote the article, 1 out of 6 births in the United States occurred outside marriage, already a much higher ratio than at midcentury (U.S. National Center for Health Statistics 1982). Today, the comparable figure is 1 out of 3 (U.S. National Center for Health Statistics 2003). The percentage is similar in Canada (Statistics Canada 2003) and in the United Kingdom and Ireland (Kiernan 2002). In the Nordic countries of Denmark, Iceland, Norway, and Sweden, the figure ranges from about 45% to about 65% (Kiernan). Marriage is no longer the nearly universal setting for child-bearing that it was a half century ago.

Both of these developments — the changing division of labor in the home and the increase in childbearing outside marriage — were well under way when I wrote my 1978 article, as was a steep rise in divorce. Here I discuss two more recent changes in family life, both of which have contributed to the deinstitutionalization of marriage after the 1970s: the growth of cohabitation, which began in the 1970s but was not fully appreciated until it accelerated in the 1980s and 1990s, and same-sex marriage, which emerged as an issue in the 1990s and has come to the fore in the current decade.

The Growth of Cohabitation

In the 1970s, neither I nor most other American researchers foresaw the greatly increased role of cohabitation in the adult life course. We thought that, except among the poor, cohabitation would remain a short-term arrangement among childless young adults who would quickly break up or marry. But it has become a more prevalent and more complex phenomenon. For example, cohabitation has created an additional layer of complexity in stepfamilies. When I wrote my article, nearly all stepfamilies were formed by the remarriage of one or both spouses. Now, about one fourth of all step-families in the United States, and one half of all stepfamilies in Canada, are formed by cohabitation rather than marriage (Bumpass, Raley, and Sweet 1995; Statistics Canada 2002). It is not uncommon, especially among the low-income population, for a woman to have a child outside marriage, end her relationship with that partner, and then begin cohabiting with a different partner. This new union is equivalent in structure to a stepfamily but does not involve marriage. Sometimes the couple later marries, and if neither has been married before, their union creates a first marriage with stepchildren. As a result, we now see an increasing number of stepfamilies that do not involve marriage, and an increasing number of first marriages that involve stepfamilies.

More generally, cohabitation is becoming accepted as an alternative to marriage. British demographer Kathleen Kiernan (2002) writes that the acceptance of cohabitation is occurring in stages in European nations, with some nations further along than others. In stage one, cohabitation is a fringe or avant garde phenomenon; in stage two, it is accepted as a testing ground for marriage; in stage three, it becomes acceptable as an alternative to marriage; and in stage four, it becomes indistinguishable from marriage. Sweden and Denmark, she argues, have made the transition to stage four; in contrast, Mediterranean countries such as Spain, Italy, and Greece remain in stage one. In the early 2000s, the United States appeared to be in transition from stage two to stage three (Smock and Gupta 2002). A number of indicators suggested that the connection between cohabitation and marriage was weakening. The proportion of cohabiting unions that end in marriage within 3 years dropped from 60% in the 1970s to about 33% in the 1990s (Smock and Gupta), suggesting that fewer cohabiting unions were trial marriages (or that fewer trial marriages were succeeding). In fact, Manning and Smock (2003) reported that among 115 cohabiting working-class and lower middle-class adults who were interviewed in depth, none said that he or she was deciding between marriage and cohabitation at the start of the union. Moreover, only 36% of adults in the 2002 United States General Social Survey disagreed with the statement, "It is alright for a couple to live together without intending to get married" (Davis, Smith, and Marsden 2003). And a growing share of births to unmarried women in the United States (about 40% in the 1990s) were to cohabiting couples (Bumpass and Lu 2000). The comparable share was about 60% in Britain (Ermisch 2001).

Canada appears to have entered stage three (Smock and Gupta 2002). Sixty-nine percent of births to unmarried women were to cohabiting couples in 1997 and 1998 (Juby, Marcil-Gratton, and Le Bourdais forthcoming). Moreover, the national figures for Canada mask substantial provincial variation. In particular, the rise in cohabitation has been far greater in Quebec than elsewhere in Canada. In 1997 and 1998, 84% of unmarried women who gave birth in Quebec were cohabiting (Juby, Marcil-Gratton, and Le Bourdais, forthcoming). And four out of five Quebeckers entering a first union did so by cohabiting rather than marrying (Le Bourdais and Juby, 2002). The greater acceptance of cohabitation in Quebec seems to have a cultural basis. Francophone Quebeckers have substantially higher likelihoods of cohabiting than do English-speaking Quebeckers or Canadians in the other English-speaking provinces (Statistics Canada 1997). Céline Le Bourdais and Nicole Marcil-Gratton (1996) argue that

Francophone Quebeckers draw upon a French, rather than Anglo-Saxon, model of family life. In fact, levels of cohabitation in Quebec are similar to levels in France, whereas levels in English-speaking Canada and in the United States are more similar to the lower levels in Great Britain (Kiernan 2002).

To be sure, cohabitation is becoming more institutionalized. In the United States, states and municipalities are moving toward granting cohabiting couples some of the rights and responsibilities that married couples have. Canada has gone further: Under the Modernization of Benefits and Obligations Act of 2000, legal distinctions between married and unmarried same-sex and opposite-sex couples were eliminated for couples who have lived together for at least a year. Still, the Supreme Court of Canada ruled in 2002 that when cohabiting partners dissolve their unions, they do not have to divide their assets equally, nor can one partner be compelled to pay maintenance payments to the other, even when children are involved (*Nova Scotia [Attorney General] v. Walsh* 2002). In France, unmarried couples may enter into Civil Solidarity Pacts, which give them most of the rights and responsibilities of married couples after the pact has existed for 3 years (Daley 2000). Several other countries have instituted registered partnerships (Lyall 2004).

The Emergence of Same-Sex Marriage

The most recent development in the deinstitutionalization of marriage is the movement to legalize same-sex marriage. It became a public issue in the United States in 1993, when the Hawaii Supreme Court ruled that a state law restricting marriage to opposite-sex couples violated the Hawaii state constitution (*Baehr* v. *Lewin* 1993). Subsequently, Hawaii voters passed a state constitutional amendment barring same-sex marriage. In 1996, the United States Congress passed the Defense of Marriage Act, which allowed states to refuse to recognize same-sex marriages licensed in other states. The act's constitutionality has not been tested as of this writing because until recently, no state allowed same-sex marriages. However, in 2003, the Massachusetts Supreme Court struck down a state law limiting marriage to opposite-sex couples, and same-sex marriage became legal in May 2004 (although opponents may eventually succeed in prohibiting it through a state constitutional amendment). The issue has developed further in Canada: In the early 2000s, courts in British Columbia, Ontario, and Quebec ruled that laws restricting marriage to opposite-sex couples were discriminatory, and it appears likely that the federal government will legalize gay marriage throughout the nation. Although social conservatives in the United States are seeking a federal constitutional amendment, I think it is reasonable to assume that same-sex marriage will be allowed in at least some North American jurisdictions in the future. In Europe, same-sex marriage has been legalized in Belgium and the Netherlands.

Lesbian and gay couples who choose to marry must actively construct a marital world with almost no institutional support. Lesbians and gay men already use the term "family" to describe their close relationships, but they usually mean something different from the standard marriage-based family.

Rather, they often refer to what sociologists have called a "family of choice": one that is formed largely through voluntary ties among individuals who are not biologically or legally related (Weeks, Heaphy, and Donovan 2001; Weston 1991). Now they face the task of integrating marriages into these larger networks of friends and kin. The partners will not even have the option of falling back on the gender-differentiated roles of heterosexual marriage. This is not to say that there will be no division of labor; one study of gay and lesbian couples found that in homes where one partner works longer hours and earns substantially more than the other partner, the one with the less demanding, lower paying job did more housework and more of the work of keeping in touch with family and friends. The author suggests that holding a demanding professional or managerial job may make it difficult for a person to invest fully in sharing the work at home, regardless of gender or sexual orientation (Carrington 1999).

We might expect same-sex couples who have children, or who wish to have children through adoption or donor insemination, to be likely to avail themselves of the option of marriage. (According to the United States Census Bureau [2003b], 33% of women in same-sex partnerships and 22% of men in same-sex partnerships had children living with them in 2000.) Basic issues, such as who would care for the children, would have to be resolved family by family. The obligations of the partners to each other following a marital dissolution have also yet to be worked out. In these and many other ways, gay and lesbian couples who marry in the near future would need to create a marriage-centered kin network through discussion, negotiation, and experiment.

Two Transitions in the Meaning of Marriage

In a larger sense, all of these developments—the changing division of labor, childbearing outside of marriage, cohabitation, and gay marriage—are the result of long-term cultural and material trends that altered the meaning of marriage during the 20th century. The cultural trends included, first, an emphasis on emotional satisfaction and romantic love that intensified early in the century. Then, during the last few decades of the century, an ethic of expressive individualism—which Bellah et al. (1985) describe as the belief that "each person has a unique core of feeling and intuition that should unfold or be expressed if individuality is to be realized" (p. 334)—became more important. On the material side, the trends include the decline of agricultural labor and the corresponding increase in wage labor; the decline in child and adult mortality; rising standards of living; and, in the last half of the 20th century, the movement of married women into the paid workforce.

These developments, along with historical events such as the Depression and World War II, produced two great changes in the meaning of marriage during the 20th century. Ernest Burgess famously labeled the first one as a transition "from an institution to a companionship" (Burgess and Locke 1945). In describing the rise of the companionate marriage, Burgess was referring to the single-earner, breadwinner—homemaker marriage that flourished in the 1950s. Although husbands and wives in the companionate marriage usually adhered to a sharp division of labor, they were supposed to be each other's companions — friends, lovers — to an extent not imagined by the spouses in the institutional marriages of the previous era. The increasing focus on bonds of sentiment within nuclear families constituted an important but limited step in the individualization of family life. Much more so than in the 19th century, the emotional satisfaction of the spouses became an important criterion for marital success. However, through the 1950s, wives and husbands tended to derive satisfaction from their participation in a marriage-based nuclear family (Roussel 1989). That is to say, they based their gratification on playing marital roles well: being good providers, good homemakers, and responsible parents.

During this first change in meaning, marriage remained the only socially acceptable way to have a sexual relationship and to raise children in the United States, Canada, and Europe, with the possible exception of the Nordic countries. In his history of British marriages, Gillis (1985) labeled the period from 1850 to 1960 the "era of mandatory marriage." In the United States, marriage and only marriage was one's ticket of admission to a full family life. Prior to marrying, almost no one cohabited with a partner except among the poor and the avant garde. As recently as the 1950s, premarital cohabitation in the United States was restricted to a small minority (perhaps 5%) of the less educated (Bumpass, Sweet, and Cherlin 1991). In the early 1950s, only about 4% of children were born outside marriage (U.S. National Center for Health Statistics 1982). In fact, during the late 1940s and the 1950s, major changes that increased the importance of marriage occurred in the life course of young adults. More people married — about 95% of young adults in the United States in the 1950s, compared with about 90% early in the century (Cherlin 1992) — and they married at younger ages. Between 1900 and 1960, the estimated median age at first marriage in the United States fell from 26 to 23 for men, and from 22 to 20 for women (U.S. Census Bureau 2003a). The birth rate, which had been falling for a century or more, increased sharply, creating the "baby boom." The post–World War II increase in marriage and childbearing also occurred in many European countries (Roussel 1989).

But beginning in the 1960s, marriage's dominance began to diminish, and the second great change in the meaning of marriage occurred. In the United States, the median age at marriage returned to and then exceeded the levels of the early 1900s. In 2000, the median age was 27 for men and 25 for women (U.S. Census Bureau 2003a). Many young adults stayed single into their mid to late 20s, some completing college educations and starting careers. Cohabitation prior to (and after) marriage became much more acceptable. Childbearing outside marriage became less stigmatized and more accepted. Birth rates resumed their long-term declines and sunk to all-time lows in most countries. Divorce rates rose to unprecedented levels. Same-sex unions found greater acceptance as well.

During this transition, the companionate marriage lost ground not only as the demographic standard but also as a cultural ideal. It was gradually overtaken by forms of marriage (and nonmarital families) that Burgess had not foreseen, particularly marriages in which both the husband and the wife worked outside the home. Although women continued to do most of the housework and child care, the roles of wives and husbands became more flexible and open to negotiation. And an even more individualistic perspective on the rewards of marriage took root. When people evaluated how satisfied they were with their marriages, they began to think more in terms of the development of their own sense of self and the expression of their feelings, as opposed to the satisfaction they gained through building a family and playing the roles of spouse and parent. The result was a transition from the companionate marriage to what we might call the *individualized marriage*.

The transition to the individualized marriage began in the 1960s and accelerated in the 1970s, as shown by an American study of the changing themes in popular magazine articles offering marital advice in every decade between 1900 and 1979 (Cancian 1987). The author identified three themes that characterized beliefs about the post-1960-style marriage. The first was self-development: Each person should develop a fulfilling, independent self instead of merely sacrificing oneself to one's partner. The second was that roles within marriage should be flexible and negotiable. The third was that communication and openness in confronting problems are essential. She then tallied the percentage of articles in each decade that contained one or more of these three themes. About one third of the articles in the first decade of the century, and again at midcentury, displayed these themes, whereas about two thirds displayed these themes in the 1970s. The author characterized this transition as a shift in emphasis "from role to self" (Cancian 1987).

During this second change in the meaning of marriage, the role of the law changed significantly as well. This transformation was most apparent in divorce law. In the United States and most other developed countries, legal restrictions on divorce were replaced by statutes that recognized consensual and even unilateral divorce. The transition to "private ordering" (Mnookin and Kornhauser 1979) allowed couples to negotiate the details of their divorce agreements within broad limits. Most European nations experienced similar legal developments (Glendon 1989; Théry 1993). Indeed, French social demographer Louis Roussel (1989) wrote of a "double deinstitutionalization" in behavior and in law: a greater hesitation of young adults to enter into marriage, combined with a loosening of the legal regulation of marriage.

Sociological theorists of late modernity (or postmodernity) such as Anthony Giddens (1991, 1992) in Britain and Ulrich Beck and Elisabeth Beck-Gernsheim in Germany (1995, 2002) also have written about the growing individualization of personal life. Consistent with the idea of deinstitutionalization, they note the declining power of social norms and laws as regulating mechanisms for family life, and they stress the expanding role of personal choice. They argue that as traditional sources of identity such as class, religion, and community lose influence, one's intimate relationships become central to self-identity. Giddens (1991, 1992) writes of the emergence of the "pure relationship": an intimate partnership entered into for its own sake, which lasts only as long as both partners are satisfied with the rewards (mostly intimacy and love) that they get from it. It is in some ways the logical extension of the increasing individualism and the deinstitutionalization of marriage that occurred in the 20th century. The pure relationship is not tied to an institution such as marriage or to the desire to raise children. Rather, it is "free-floating," independent of social institutions or economic life. Unlike marriage, it is not regulated by law, and its members do not enjoy special legal rights. It exists primarily in the realms of emotion and self-identity.

Although the theorists of late modernity believe that the quest for intimacy is becoming the central focus of personal life, they do not predict that *marriage* will remain distinctive and important. Marriage, they claim, has become a choice rather than a necessity for adults who want intimacy, companionship, and children. According to Beck and Beck-Gernsheim (1995), we will see "a huge variety of ways of living together or apart which will continue to exist side by side" (pp. 141–42). Giddens (1992) even argues that marriage has already become "just one life-style among others" (p. 154), although people may not yet realize it because of institutional lag.

The Current Context of Marriage

Overall, research and writing on the changing meaning of marriage suggest that it is now situated in a very different context than in the past. This is true in at least two senses. First, individuals now experience a vast latitude for choice in their personal lives. More forms of marriage and more alternatives to marriage are socially acceptable. Moreover, one may fit marriage into one's life in many ways: One may first live with a partner, or sequentially with several partners, without an explicit consideration of whether a marriage will occur. One may have children with one's eventual spouse or with someone else before marrying. One may, in some jurisdictions, marry someone of the same gender and build a shared marital world with few guidelines to rely on. Within marriage, roles are more flexible and negotiable, although women still do more than their share of the household work and childrearing.

The second difference is in the nature of the rewards that people seek through marriage and other close relationships. Individuals aim for personal growth and deeper intimacy through more open communication and mutually shared disclosures about feelings with their partners. They may feel justified in insisting on changes in a relationship that no longer provides them with individualized rewards. In contrast, they are less likely than in the past to focus on the rewards to be found in fulfilling socially valued roles such as the good parent or the loyal and supportive spouse. The result of these changing contexts has been a deinstitutionalization of marriage, in which social norms about family and personal life count for less than they did during the heyday of the companionate marriage, and far less than during the period of the institutional marriage. Instead, personal choice and self-development loom large in people's construction of their marital careers.

Why Do People Still Marry?

There is a puzzle within the story of deinstitutionalization that needs solving. Although fewer Americans are marrying than during the peak years of marriage in the mid-20th century, most—nearly 90%, according to a recent estimate (Goldstein and Kenney 2001)—will eventually marry. A survey of high school seniors conducted annually since 1976 shows no decline in the importance they attach to marriage. The percentage of young women who respond that they expect to marry has stayed constant at roughly 80% (and has increased from 71% to 78% for young men). The percentage who respond that "having a good marriage and family life" is extremely important has also remained constant, at about 80% for young women and 70% for young men (Thornton and Young-DeMarco 2001). What is more, in the 1990s and early 2000s, a strong promarriage movement emerged among gay men and lesbians in the United States, who sought the right to marry with increasing success. Clearly, marriage remains important to many people in the United States. Consequently, I think the interesting question is not why so few people are marrying, but rather, why so *many* people are marrying, or planning to marry, or hoping to marry, when cohabitation and single parenthood are widely acceptable options. (This question may be less relevant in Canada and the many European nations where the estimated proportions of who will ever marry are lower.)

The Gains to Marriage

The dominant theoretical perspectives on marriage in the 20th century do not provide much guidance on the question of why marriage remains so popular. The structural functionalists in social anthropology and sociology in the early- to mid-20th century emphasized the role of marriage in ensuring that a child would have a link to the status of a man, a right to his protection, and a claim to inherit his property (Mair 1971). But as the law began to recognize the rights of children born outside marriage, and as mothers acquired resources by working in the paid workforce, these reasons for marriage become less important.

Nor is evolutionary theory very helpful. Although there may be important evolutionary influences on family behavior, it is unlikely that humans have developed an innate preference for marriage as we know it. The classical account of our evolutionary heritage is that women, whose reproductive capacity is limited by pregnancy and lactation (which delays the return of ovulation), seek stable pair bonds with men, whereas men seek to maximize their fertility by impregnating many women. Rather than being "natural," marriage-centered kinship was described in much early- and mid-20th century anthropological writing as the social invention that solved the problem of the sexually wandering male (Tiger and Fox 1971). Moreover, when dependable male providers are not available, women may prefer a reproductive strategy of relying on a network of female kin and more than one man (Hrdy 1999). In addition, marriages are increasingly being formed well after a child is born, yet evolutionary theory suggests that the impetus to marry should be greatest when newborn children need support and protection. In the 1950s, half of all unmarried pregnant women in the United States married before the birth of their child, whereas in the 1990s, only one fourth married (U.S. Census Bureau 1999). Finally, evolutionary theory cannot explain the persistence of the formal wedding style in which people are still marrying (see below). Studies of preindustrial societies have found that although many have elaborate ceremonies, others have little or no ceremony (Ember, Ember, and Peregrine 2002; Stephens 1963).

The mid-20th century specialization model of economist Gary Becker (1965, 1981) also seems less relevant than when it was introduced. Becker assumed that women were relatively more productive at home than men, and that men were relatively more productive (i.e., they could earn higher wages) in the labor market. He argued that women and men could increase their utility by exchanging, through marriage, women's home work for men's labor market work. The specialization model would predict that in the present era, women with less labor market potential would be more likely to marry because they would gain the most economically from finding a husband. But several studies show that in recent decades, women in the United States and Canada with less education (and therefore less labor market potential) are *less* likely to marry (Lichter et al. 1992; Oppenheimer, Blossfeld, and Wackerow 1995; Qian and Preston 1993; Sweeney 2002; Turcotte and Goldscheider 1998). This finding suggests that the specialization model may no longer hold. Moreover, the specialization model was developed before cohabitation was widespread, and offers no explanation for why couples would marry rather than cohabit.

From a rational choice perspective, then, what benefits might contemporary marriage offer that would lead cohabiting couples to marry rather than cohabit? I suggest that the major benefit is what we might call *enforceable trust* (Cherlin 2000; Portes and Sensenbrenner 1993). Marriage still requires a public commitment to a long-term, possibly lifelong relationship. This commitment is usually expressed in front of relatives, friends, and religious congregants. Cohabitation, in contrast, requires only a private commitment, which is easier to break. Therefore, marriage, more so than cohabitation, lowers the risk that one's partner will renege on agreements that have been made. In the language of economic theory, marriage lowers the transaction costs of enforcing agreements between the partners (Pollak 1985). It allows individuals to invest in the partnership with less fear of abandonment. For instance, it allows the partners to invest financially in joint long-term purchases such as homes and automobiles. It allows caregivers to make relationship-specific investments (England and Farkas 1986) in the couple's children—investments of time and effort that, unlike strengthening one's job skills, would not be easily portable to another intimate relationship.

Nevertheless, the difference in the amount of enforceable trust that marriage brings, compared with cohabitation, is eroding. Although relatives and friends will view a divorce with disappointment, they will accept it more readily than their counterparts would have two generations ago. As I noted, cohabiting couples are increasingly gaining the rights previously reserved to married couples. It seems likely that over time, the legal differences between cohabitation and marriage will become minimal in the United States, Canada, and many European countries. The advantage of marriage in enhancing trust will then depend on the force of public commitments, both secular and religious, by the partners.

In general, the prevailing theoretical perspectives are of greater value in explaining why marriage has declined than why it persists. With more women working outside the home, the predictions of the specialization model are less relevant. Although the rational choice theorists remind us that marriage still provides enforceable trust, it seems clear that its enforcement power is declining. Recently, evolutionary theorists have argued that women who have difficulty finding men who are reliable providers might choose a reproductive strategy that involves single parenthood and kin networks, a strategy that is consistent with changes that have occurred in low-income families. And although the insights of the theorists of late modernity help us understand the changing meaning of marriage, they predict that marriage will lose its distinctive status, and indeed may already have become just one lifestyle among others. Why, then, are so many people still marrying?

The Symbolic Significance of Marriage

What has happened is that although the practical importance of being married has declined, its symbolic importance has remained high, and may even have increased. Marriage is at once less dominant and more distinctive than it was. It has evolved from a marker of conformity to a marker of prestige. Marriage is a status one builds up to, often by living with a partner beforehand, by attaining steady employment or starting a career, by putting away some savings, and even by having children. Marriage's place in the life course used to come before those investments were made, but now it often comes afterward. It used to be the foundation of adult personal life; now it is sometimes the capstone. It is something to be achieved through one's own efforts rather than something to which one routinely accedes.

How Low-Income Individuals See Marriage

Paradoxically, it is among the lower social strata in the United States, where marriage rates are lowest, that both the persistent preference for marriage and its changing meaning seem clearest. Although marriage is optional and often foregone, it has by no means faded away among the poor and near poor. Instead, it is a much sought-after but elusive goal. They tell observers that they wish to marry, but will do so only when they are sure they can do it successfully: when their partner has demonstrated the ability to hold a decent job and treat them fairly and without abuse, when they have a security deposit or a down payment for a decent apartment or home, and when they have enough in the bank to pay for a nice wedding party for family and friends. Edin and Kefalas (forthcoming), who studied childbearing and intimate relationships among 165 mothers in 8 low- and moderate-income Philadelphia neighborhoods, wrote, "In some sense, marriage is a form of social bragging about the quality of the couple relationship, a powerfully symbolic way of elevating one's relationship above others in the community, particularly in a community where marriage is rare."

Along with several collaborators, I am conducting a study of low-income families in three United States cities. The ethnographic component of that study is directed by Linda Burton of Pennsylvania State University. A 27-year-old mother told one of our ethnographers:

> *I was poor all my life and so was Reginald. When I got pregnant, we agreed we would marry some day in the future because we loved each other and wanted to raise our child together. But we would not get married until we could afford to get a house and pay all the utility bills on time. I have this thing about utility bills. Our gas and electric got turned off all the time when we were growing up and we wanted to make sure that would not happen when we got married. That was our biggest worry. . . . We worked together and built up savings and then we got married. It's forever for us.*

Another woman in our study, already living with the man she was engaged to and had children with, told an ethnographer she was not yet ready to marry him:

> *But I'm not ready to do that yet. I told him, we're not financially ready yet. He knows that. I told him by the end of this year, maybe. I told him that last year. Plus, we both need to learn to control our tempers, you could say. He doesn't understand that bills and kids and [our relationship] come first, not [his] going out and getting new clothes or [his] doing this and that. It's the kids, then us. He gets paid good, about five hundred dollars a week. How hard is it to give me money and help with the bills?*

Note that for this woman, more is required of a man than a steady job before he is marriageable. He has to learn to turn over most of his paycheck to his family rather than spending it on his friends and himself. He must put his relationship with his partner ahead of running with his single male friends, a way of saying that a husband must place a priority on providing companionship and intimacy to his wife and on being sexually faithful. And he and his partner have to learn to control their tempers, a vague referent to the possibility that physical abuse exists in the relationship. In sum, the demands low-income women place on men include not just a reliable income, as important as that is, but also a commitment to put family first, provide companionship, be faithful, and avoid abusive behavior.

How Young Adults in General See It

The changing meaning of marriage is not limited to the low-income population. Consider a nationally representative survey of 1,003 adults, ages 20–29, conducted in 2001 on attitudes toward marriage (Whitehead and Popenoe 2001). A majority responded in ways suggestive of the view that marriage is a status that one builds up to. Sixty-two percent agreed with the statement, "Living together with someone before marriage is a good way to avoid an eventual divorce," and 82% agreed that "it is extremely important to you to be economically set before you get married." Moreover, most indicated a view of marriage as centered on intimacy and love more than on practical matters such as finances and children. Ninety-four percent of those who had never married agreed that "when you marry, you want your spouse to be your soul mate, first and foremost." In contrast, only 16% agreed that "the main purpose of marriage these days is to have children." And over 80% of the women agreed that it is more important "to have a husband who can communicate about his deepest feelings than to have a husband who makes a good living." The authors of the report conclude, "While marriage is losing much of its broad public and institutional character, it is gaining popularity as a Super-Relationship, an intensely private spiritualized union, combining sexual fidelity, romantic love, emotional intimacy, and togetherness" (p. 13).

The Wedding as a Status Symbol

Even the wedding has become an individual achievement. In the distant past, a wedding was an event at which two kinship groups formed an alliance. More recently, it has been an event organized and paid for by parents, at which they display their approval and support for their child's marriage. In both cases, it has been the ritual that provides legal and social approval for having children. But in keeping with the deinstitutionalization of marriage, it is now becoming an event centered on and often controlled by the couple themselves, having less to do with family approval or having children than in the past. One might assume, then, that weddings would become smaller and that many couples would forgo a public wedding altogether. But that does not appear to have happened for most couples. The wedding, it seems, has become an important symbol of the partners' personal achievements and a stage in their self-development (Bulcroft et al. 2000).

A 1984 survey of 459 ever-married women in the Detroit metropolitan area provided information on trends in wedding practices in the United States during much of the 20th century. Whyte (1990) divided the women into a prewar group who married between 1925 and 1944, a baby boom group who married between 1945 and 1964, and a more recent group who married between 1965 and 1984. Across the more than a half century of life history that this survey elicited, several indicators of wedding rituals and activities increased over time. The percentage of women who reported a wedding in a religious institution (e.g., church or synagogue) increased from 68% to 74% across the three groups; the percentage who had a wedding reception increased from 64% to 88%; the percentage who had bridal showers or whose spouses had bachelor parties increased sharply; and the percentage who took a honeymoon rose from 47% to 60%. Some of these trends could be caused by increasing affluence, but not all. It is not obvious why affluence should lead to more religious weddings. In fact, one might have expected affluence to lead to a secularization of the marriage process and an increase in civil weddings.

In recent decades, then, when partners decide that their relationship has finally reached the stage where they can marry, they generally want a ritual-filled wedding to celebrate it. A small literature on contemporary weddings and honeymoons is developing in North America and Europe, and it treats them as occasions of consumption and celebrations of romance (Boden 2003; Bulcroft et al. 2000; Bulcroft et al. 1997; Ingraham 1999). Even low- and moderate-income couples who have limited funds and who may already have children and may be living together seem to view a substantial wedding as a requirement for marriage. Many of the women in our study said that they would not get married without a church wedding. Just going to city hall and having a civil ceremony was not acceptable to them. Similarly, some of the working-class and lower middle-class couples in the Manning and Smock (2003) study said that merely going "downtown" for a civil ceremony did not constitute an acceptable wedding (Smock 2004; Smock, Manning, and Porter 2004). Edin and Kefalas (forthcoming) write of the attitudes among the mothers they studied, "Having the wherewithal to throw a 'big' wedding is a vivid display that the couple has achieved enough financial security to do more than live from paycheck to paycheck."

The couples in our study wanted to make a statement through their weddings, a statement both to themselves and to their friends and family that they had passed a milestone in the development of their self-identities. Through wedding ceremonies, the purchase of a home, and the acquisition of other accoutrements of married life, individuals hoped to display their attainment of a prestigious, comfortable, stable style of life. They also expected marriage to provide some enforceable trust. But as I have argued, the enforcement value of marriage is less than it used to be. People marry now less for the social benefits that marriage provides than for the personal achievement it represents.

Alternative Futures

What do these developments suggest about the future of marriage? Social demographers usually predict a continuation of whatever is happening at the moment, and they are usually correct, but sometimes spectacularly wrong. For example, in the 1930s, every demographic expert in the United States confidently predicted a continuation of the low birth rates of the Depression. Not one forecast the baby boom that overtook them after World War II. No less a scholar than Kingsley Davis (1937) wrote that the future of the family as a social institution was in danger because people were not having enough children to replace themselves. Not a single 1950s or 1960s sociologist predicted the rise of cohabitation. Chastened by this unimpressive record, I will tentatively sketch some future directions.

The first alternative is the reinstitutionalization of marriage, a return to a status akin to its dominant position through the mid-20th century. This would entail a rise in the proportion who ever marry, a rise in the proportion of births born to married couples, and a decline in divorce. It would require a reversal of the individualistic orientation toward family and personal life that has been the major cultural force driving family change over the past several decades. It would probably also require a decrease in women's labor force participation and a return to more gender-typed family roles. I think this alternative is very unlikely—but then again, so was the baby boom.

The second alternative is a continuation of the current situation, in which marriage remains deinstitutionalized but is common and distinctive. It is not just one type of family relationship among many; rather, it is the most prestigious form. People generally desire to be married. But it is an individual choice, and individuals construct marriages through an increasingly long process that often includes cohabitation and childbearing beforehand. It still confers some of its traditional benefits, such as enforceable trust, but it is increasingly a mark of prestige, a display of distinction, an individualistic achievement, a part of what Beck and Beck-Gernsheim (2002) call the "do-it-yourself biography." In this scenario, the proportion of people who ever marry could fall further; in particular, we could see probabilities of marriage among Whites in the United States that are similar to the probabilities shown today by African Americans. Moreover, because of high levels of nonmarital childbearing, cohabitation, and divorce, people will spend a smaller proportion of their adult lives in intact marriages than in the past. Still, marriage would retain its special and highly valued place in the family system.

But I admit to some doubts about whether this alternative will prevail for long in the United States. The privileges and material advantages of marriage, relative to cohabitation, have been declining. The commitment of partners to be trustworthy has been undermined by frequent divorce. If marriage was once a form of cultural capital—one needed to be married to advance one's career, say—that capital has decreased too. What is left, I have argued, is a display of prestige and achievement. But it could be that marriage retains its symbolic aura largely because of its dominant position in social norms until just a half century ago. It could be that this aura is diminishing, like an echo in a canyon. It could be that, despite the efforts of the wedding industry, the need for a highly ritualized ceremony and legalized status will fade. And there is not much else supporting marriage in the early 21st century.

That leads to a third alternative, the fading away of marriage. Here, the argument is that people are still marrying in large numbers because of institutional lag; they have yet to realize that marriage is no longer important. A nonmarital pure relationship, to use Giddens' ideal type, can provide much intimacy and love, can place both partners on an equal footing, and can allow them to develop their independent senses of self. These characteristics are highly valued in late modern societies. However, this alternative also suggests the predominance of fragile relationships that are continually at risk of breaking up because they are held together entirely by the voluntary commitment of each partner. People may still commit morally to a relationship, but they increasingly prefer to commit voluntarily rather than to be obligated to commit by law or social norms. And partners feel free to revoke their commitments at any time.

Therefore, the pure relationship seems most characteristic of a world where commitment does not matter. Consequently, it seems to best fit middle-class, well-educated, childless adults. They have the resources to be independent actors by themselves or in a democratic partnership, and without childbearing responsibilities, they can be free-floating. The pure relationship seems less applicable to couples who face material constraints (Jamieson 1999). In particular, when children are present—or when they are anticipated anytime soon—issues of commitment and support come into consideration. Giddens (1992) says very little about children in his book on intimacy, and his brief attempts to incorporate children into the pure relationship are unconvincing. Individuals who are, or think they will be, the primary caregivers of children will prefer commitment and will seek material support from their partners. They may be willing to have children and begin cohabiting without commitment, but the relationship probably will not last without it. They will be wary of purely voluntary commitment if they think they can do better. So only if the advantage of marriage in providing trust and commitment disappears relative to cohabitation—and I must admit that this could happen—might we see cohabitation and marriage on an equal footing.

In sum, I see the current state of marriage and its likely future in these terms: At present, marriage is no longer as dominant as it once was, but it remains important on a symbolic level. It has been transformed from a familial and community institution to an individualized, choice-based achievement. It is a marker of prestige and is still somewhat useful in creating enforceable trust. As for the future, I have sketched three alternatives. The first, a return to a more dominant, institutionalized form of marriage, seems unlikely. In the second, the current situation continues; marriage remains important, but not as dominant, and retains its high symbolic status. In the third, marriage fades into just one of many kinds of interpersonal romantic relationships. I think that Giddens' (1992) statement that marriage has already become merely one of many relationships is not true in the United States so far, but it could become true in the future. It is possible that we are living in a transitional phase in which marriage is gradually losing its uniqueness. If Giddens and other modernity theorists are correct, the third alternative will triumph, and marriage will lose its special place in the family system of the United States. If they are not, the second alternative will continue to hold, and marriage—transformed and deinstitutionalized, but recognizable nevertheless—will remain distinctive.

ENDNOTE

Author's Note: I thank Frank Furstenberg, Joshua Goldstein, Kathleen Kieman, and Céline Le Bourdais for comments on a previous version, and Linda Burton for her collaborative work on the Three-City Study ethnography.

REFERENCES

Baehr v. Lewin. 1993. 74 Haw. 530, 74 Haw. 645, 852 P.2d 44.

Beck, U. and E. Beck-Gernsheim. 1995. *The Normal Chaos of Love.* Cambridge, England: Polity Press.

———. 2002. *Individualization: Institutionalized Individualism and Its Social and Political Consequences.* London: Sage.

Becker, G. S. 1965. "A Theory of the Allocation of Time." *Economic Journal* 75: 493–517.

———. 1981. *A Treatise on the Family.* Cambridge, MA: Harvard University Press.

Bellah, R., R. Marsden, W. M. Sullivan, A. Swidler, and S. M. Tipton 1985. *Habits of the Heart: Individualism and Commitment in America.* Berkeley: University of California Press.

Boden, S. 2003. *Consumerism, Romance and the Wedding Experience.* Hampshire, England: Palgrave Macmillan.

Bulcroft, R., K. Bulcroft, K. Bradley, and C. Simpson. 2000. "The Management and Production of Risk in Romantic Relationships: A Postmodern Paradox." *Journal of Family History* 25:63–92.

Bulcroft, K., R. Bulcroft, L. Smeins, and H. Cranage. 1997. "The Social Construction of the North American Honeymoon, 1880–1995." *Journal of Family History* 22: 462–90.

Bumpass, L. L. and H.-H. Lu. 2000. "Trends in Cohabitation and Implications for Children's Family Contexts in the United States." *Population Studies* 54:19–41.

Bumpass, L. L., K. Raley, and J. A. Sweet. 1995. "The Changing Character of Stepfamilies: Implications of Cohabitation and Nonmarital Childbearing." *Demography* 32:1–12.

Bumpass, L. L., J. A. Sweet, and A. J. Cherlin. 1991. "The Role of Cohabitation in Declining Rates of Marriage." *Journal of Marriage and the Family* 53:338–55.

Burgess, E. W. and H. J. Locke. 1945. *The Family: From Institution to Companionship.* New York: American Book.

Cancian, F. M. 1987. *Love in America: Gender and Self-Development.* Cambridge, England: Cambridge University Press.

Carrington, C. 1999. *No Place Like Home: Relationships and Family Life among Lesbians and Gay Men.* Chicago: University of Chicago Press.

Cherlin, A. 1978. Remarriage as an Incomplete Institution. *American Journal of Sociology,* 84:634–50.

———. 1992. *Marriage, Divorce, Remarriage.* Rev. ed. Cambridge, MA: Harvard University Press.

———. 2000. "Toward a New Home Socioeconomics of Union Formation." Pp. 126–44 in *Ties That Bind: Perspectives on Marriage and Cohabitation,* edited by L. Waite, C. Bachrach, M. Hindin, E. Thomson, and A. Thornton. Hawthorne, NY: Aldine de Gruyter.

Daley, S. 2000. "French Couples Take Plunge That Falls Short of Marriage." *New York Times,* April 18, pp. A1, A4.

Davis, J. A., T. W. Smith, and P. Marsden. 2003. *General Social Surveys, 1972–2002 Cumulative Codebook.* Chicago: National Opinion Research Center, University of Chicago.

Davis, K. 1937. "Reproductive Institutions and the Pressure for Population." *Sociological Review* 29:289–306.

Edin, K. J. and M. J. Kefalas. Forthcoming. *Promises I Can Keep: Why Poor Women Put Motherhood Before Marriage.* Berkeley: University of California Press.

Ember, C. R., M. Ember, and P. N. Peregrine. 2002. *Anthropology.* 10th ed. Upper Saddle River, NJ: Prentice-Hall.

England, P. and G. Farkas. 1986. *Households, Employment, and Gender: A Social, Economic, and Demographic View.* New York: Aldine.

Ermisch, J. 2001. "Cohabitation and Childbearing Outside Marriage in Britain." Pp. 109–39 in *Out of Wedlock: Causes and Consequences of Nonmarital Fertility*, edited by L. L. Wu and B. Wolfe. New York: Russell Sage Foundation.

Giddens, A. 1991. *Modernity and Self-Identity*. Stanford, CA: Stanford University Press.

———. 1992. *The Transformation of Intimacy*. Stanford, CA: Stanford University Press.

Gillis, J. R. 1985. *For Better or Worse: British Marriages, 1600 to the Present*. Oxford, England: Oxford University Press.

Glendon, M. A. 1989. *Abortion and Divorce in Western Law*. Cambridge, MA: Harvard University Press.

Goldstein, J. R. and C. T. Kenney. 2001. "Marriage Delayed or Marriage Forgone? New Cohort Forecasts of First Marriage for U.S. Women." *American Sociological Review* 66:506–19.

Hochschild, A. 1989. *The Second Shift: Working Parents and the Revolution at Home*. New York: Viking.

Hrdy, S. B. 1999. *Mother Nature: Maternal Instincts and How They Shape the Human Species*. New York: Ballantine Books.

Ingraham, C. 1999. *White Weddings: Romancing Heterosexuality in Popular Culture*. New York: Routledge.

Jamieson, L. 1999. "Intimacy Transformed? A Critical Look at the "Pure Relationship." *Sociology* 33:477–94.

Juby, H., N. Marcil-Gratton, and C. Le Bourdais. Forthcoming. *When Parents Separate: Further Findings from the National Longitudinal Survey of Children and Youth*. Phase 2 research report of the project "The Impact of Parents' Family Transitions on Children's Family Environment and Economic Well-Being: A Longitudinal Assessment." Ottawa, Ontario: Department of Justice Canada, Child Support Team.

Kiernan, K. 2002. "Cohabitation in Western Europe: Trends, Issues, and Implications." Pp. 3–31 in *Just Living Together: Implication of Cohabitation on Families, Children, and Social Policy*, edited by A. Booth and A. C. Crouter. Mahwah, NJ: Erlbaum.

Le Bourdais, C. and H. Juby. 2002. "The Impact of Cohabitation on the Family Life Course in Contemporary North America: Insights from across the Border." Pp. 107–18 in *Just Living Together: Implications of Cohabitation on Families, Children, and Social Policy*, edited by A. Booth and A. C. Crouter. Mahwah, NJ: Erlbaum.

Le Bourdais, C. and N. Marcil-Gratton. 1996. "Family Transformations across the Canadian/American Border: When the Laggard Becomes the Leader." *Journal of Comparative Family Studies* 27:415–36.

Lichter, D. T., D. K. McLaughlin G. Kephart, and D. J. Landry. 1992. "Race and the Retreat from Marriage: A Shortage of Marriageable Men?" *American Sociological Review,* 57:781–99.

Lyall, S. 2004. "In Europe, Lovers Now Propose: Marry Me a Little." *New York Times,* February 15, p. A3.

Mair, L. 1971. *Marriage*. Middlesex, England: Penguin Books.

Manning, W. and P. J. Smock. 2003, May. *"Measuring and Modeling Cohabitation: New Perspectives from Qualitative Data."* Paper presented at the annual meeting of the Population Association of America, Minneapolis, MN.

Mnookin, R. H. and L. Kornhauser. 1979. "Bargaining in the Shadow of the Law: The Case of Divorce." *Yale Law Journal* 88:950–97.

Nova Scotia (Attorney General) v. Walsh. 2002. SCC 83.

Oppenheimer V. K., H.-P. Blossfeld, and A. Wackerow. 1995. "United States of America." Pp. 150–73 in *The New Role of Women: Family Formation in Modern Societies*, edited by H. P. Blossfeld. Boulder, CO: Westview Press.

Pollak, R. A. 1985. "A Transaction Costs Approach to Families and Households." *Journal of Economic Literature* 23:581–608.

Portes, A. and J. Sensenbrenner 1993. "Embeddedness and Immigration: Notes on the Social Determinants of Economic Action. *American Journal of Sociology* 98: 1320–50.

Qian, Z. and S. H. Preston. 1993. "Changes in American Marriage, 1972 to 1987: Availability and Forces of Attraction by Age and Education." *American Sociological Review* 58:482–95.

Roussel, L. 1989. *La Famille Incertaine.* Paris: Editions Odile Jacob.

Smock, P. J. 2004. "The Wax and Wane of Marriage: Prospects for Marriage in the 21st Century." *Journal of Marriage and the Family* 66:966–79.

Smock, P. J. and S. Gupta. 2002. "Cohabitation in Contemporary North America." Pp. 53–84 in *Just Living Together: Implications of Cohabitation on Families, Children, and Social Policy,* edited by A. Booth and A. C. Crouter. Mahwah, NJ: Erlbaum.

Smock, P. J., W. D. Manning, and M. Porter. 2004, April. "'Everything's There Except Money': How Money Shapes Orientations towards Marriage among Cohabitors." Paper presented at the annual meeting of the Population Association of America, Boston.

Statistics Canada. 1997. *Report on the Demographic Situation in Canada 1996.* No. 91-209-XPE. Ottawa, Ontario: Statistical Reference Centre.

——. 2002. *Changing Conjugal Life in Canada.* No. 89-576-XIE. Ottawa, Ontario: Statistical Reference Centre.

——. 2003. *Annual Demographic Statistics, 2002.* No. 91-213-XIB. Ottawa, Ontario: Statistical Reference Centre.

Stephens, William N. 1963. *The Family in Cross-Cultural Perspective.* New York: Holt, Rinehart and Winston.

Sweeney, M. M. 2002. "Two Decades of Family Change: The Shift in Economic Foundations of Marriage." *American Sociological Review* 67:132–47.

Théry, I. 1993. *Le Démariage.* Paris: Editions Odile Jacob.

Thornton, A., and L. Young-DeMarco 2001. "Four Decades of Trends in Attitudes toward Family Issues in the United States: The 1960s through the 1990s." *Journal of Marriage and Family* 63:1009–37.

Tiger, L., and R. Fox. 1971. *The Imperial Animal.* New York: Holt, Rinehart and Winston.

Turcotte, P., and F. Goldscheider. 1998. "Evolution of Factors Influencing First Union Formation in Canada." *Canadian Studies in Population* 25:145–73.

U.S. Census Bureau. 1999. "Trends in Premarital Childbearing: 1930–1994." *Current Population Reports,* No. P23-97. Washington, DC: U.S. Government Printing Office.

——. 2003a. "Estimated Median Age at First Marriage, by Sex: 1890 to Present." Retrieved January 11, 2003 (http://www.census.gov/population/www/socdemo/hh-fam.html).

——. 2003b. "Married-Couple and Unmarried-Partner Households: 2000." *Census 2000 Special Reports,* CENSR-5. Washington, DC: U.S. Government Printing Office.

U.S. National Center for Health Statistics.1982. *Vital Statistics of the United States, 1978.* Vol. I *Natality.* Washington, DC: U.S. Government Printing Office.

——. 2003. "Births: Preliminary Data for 2002." Retrieved December 15, 2003 (http://www.cdc.gov/nchs/data/nvsr/nvsr51/nvsr51_11.pdf).

Weeks, J., B., Heaphy, and C. Donovan. 2001. *Same-Sex Intimacies: Families of Choice and Other Life Experiments.* London: Routledge.

Weston, K. 1991. *Families We Choose: Lesbians, Gays, Kinship.* New York: Columbia University Press.

Whitehead, B. D. and D. Popenoe. 2001. "Who Wants to Marry a Soul Mate? Pp. 6–16 in *The State of Our Unions, 2001.* National Marriage Project. Retrieved February 12, 2004 (http://marriage.rutgers.edu/Publications/SOOU/NMPAR2001.pdf).

Whyte, M. K. 1990. *Dating, Mating and Marriage.* New York: Aldine de Gruyter.

13

CLASHING DREAMS
Highly Educated Overseas Brides
and Low–Wage U.S. Husbands

HUNG CAM THAI

Hours before her husband's plane was due, on a rainy day in July 2000, Thanh Nguyen[1] and about thirty members of her family anxiously waited outside of Tan Son Nhut, Saigon's international airport.[2] Thanh's family was understandably excited. For many families expecting a relative or a close friend from the Vietnamese diaspora, the waiting is an event in itself: they come to the airport long before the plane is due, creating such a commotion outside that it is difficult to follow any one conversation.

I watched and listened, like a waiter at a busy restaurant—intently but discreetly. I could make out only fragments of conversations among people of a culture known for making sure: "Make sure you greet him properly," adults told young children. "Make sure the restaurant knows we are coming," men reminded women. And of course, "Make sure you always show him love and respect," Thanh's parents reminded their thirty-two-year-old daughter.

The Nguyens were prudent people. Although they knew Thanh's husband, Minh, well—he had made the long journey across the Pacific from his home in Quincy, Washington, three times in the last year—they wanted him to feel welcome and important each time he visited. Their instinct was a good one: when I visited him in Quincy, ninety miles from Seattle, the thirty-seven-year-old Minh revealed to me that he often did not feel important or respected in the small suburban town where he lived.

Seattle is one of the most heavily Vietnamese cities outside of Vietnam, and Thanh's husband is one of more than two million *Viet Kieu*, or Vietnamese people living overseas, who make up an aging diaspora that largely began emigrating in the mid-1970s.[3] Thanh will soon join Minh in Quincy as one of more than 200,000 legal marriage migrants who come to the United States each year.[4]

About a quarter of all men and more than 40 percent of all women who currently enter the United States are marriage migrants.[5] Of these marriage migrants, more than 65 percent are women. It is no news that women have

Hung Cam Thai, "Clashing Dreams: Highly Educated Overseas Brides and Low-Wage U.S. Husbands" from *Global Woman: Nannies, Maids, and Sex Workers in the New Economy,* edited by Barbara Ehrenreich and Arlie Russell Hochschild (New York: Metropolitan Books, 2002). Reprinted with the permission of the author.

dominated U.S.-bound migration since the 1930s[6] and that, historically, more women than men have migrated as spouses.[7] However, despite the fact that marriage remains the number one reason people migrate to the United States,[8] we know very little about the specific contemporary marriage migration streams or about why women overwhelmingly dominate them.[9] More familiar is the often sensationalized phenomenon of mail-order brides.[10] Though an important part of the female marriage migration puzzle, such women constitute at most 4 percent of all marriage migrants.[11]

The marriage of Minh and Thanh follows a global trend that has been gathering momentum over the last forty years: immigrant and immigrant-origin men are more and more frequently seeking wives in their countries of origin.[12] An estimated two-thirds of all marriage migrants are of the same ethnicity, and among migrants who come to the United States married to noncitizen permanent residents (presumably immigrants), almost 90 percent are women.[13] Like many international marriages between same-ethnic individuals, especially in Asia, the marriage of Minh and Thanh was arranged. Marriage arrangements come in many forms, and I have addressed these elsewhere.[14] What Minh and Tranh represent is a specific and fairly typical pattern: the marriage of the two "unmarriageables," namely of highly educated women in Vietnam to Vietnamese men who do low-wage work overseas.[15]

The Double Marriage Squeeze

Vietnamese people worldwide are pressed by what demographer Daniel Goodkind calls the "double marriage squeeze."[16] A high male mortality rate during the Vietnam War, combined with the migration of a larger number of men than women during the last quarter of the twentieth century, has produced a low ratio of men to women in Vietnam, as well as an unusually high ratio of men to women in the Vietnamese diaspora, especially in Australia and the United States. Of the fifteen most populous nations in 1989, Vietnam had the lowest ratio of men to women at the peak marrying ages. By 1999, there were approximately 92 men for every 100 women between the ages of 30 and 34 in Vietnam. The reverse situation prevails in the diaspora: in 2000, there were 129 Vietnamese-American men for every 100 women between the ages of 24 and 29. Among Vietnamese-Americans aged 30 to 34, there were about 135 men for every 100 women.[17]

Those who study marriage markets have long documented a nearly universal pattern, called the marriage gradient, whereby women tend to marry men who are older, better educated, and higher earning than they are, while men tend to marry younger women who earn less money and have less education.[18] Men "marry down" economically and socially; women "marry up." Transnational couples like Minh and Thanh, however, seem to reverse the marriage gradient. But depending on the measure one uses, it is often difficult to tell who is really marrying up, and who down.

Thanh belongs to an emerging group of highly educated women in Vietnam who have delayed or avoided marriage with local men. These women have found that too few men in Vietnam are employed and successful relative to them. More important, in the eyes of many men influenced by traditional Asian and Confucian hierarchies of gender, age, and class, a highly educated woman like Thanh is unmarriageable. As with highly educated African American women in the United States, there is a surfeit of women like Thanh in Vietnam relative to their educated male counterparts. Minh, on the other hand, belongs to a surfeit group of Viet Kieu men, many of whom are unable to find marriage partners partly because they are low-wage workers. Some of these men, though certainly not all, experienced tremendous downward mobility when they migrated overseas after the Vietnam War.

In my study of sixty-nine Vietnamese transpacific marriages, 80 percent of the men were low-wage earners like Minh. These men generally work for hourly wages, though some work in ethnic enterprises where salaries are negotiated under the table. For the most part, they work long hours for low pay. Almost 70 percent of their brides are women like Thanh, who are college-educated; about 40 percent of these women have advanced degrees, which permit them to work as doctors, lawyers, computer programmers, and the like. Of my entire sample about 55 percent were marriages between these two "unmarriageables."[19]

The double marriage squeeze is one force propelling these transpacific marriages of the two unmarriageables, but the cultural belief in the marriage gradient is at least as powerful and probably more so. The marriage gradient is a strict norm in Vietnamese culture. Many Vietnamese, including the unmarriageables themselves, believe that by making these unorthodox matches transnational ones, they somehow get around the discomfort of breaking the marriage gradient norm. It is as though despite their relative incomes and education, if the man is from a First World country, he has the "up," while a woman from Third World Vietnam has the "down." And though it is no surprise that the economic divide between the First and Third Worlds deeply penetrates the private lives of Vietnamese transpacific couples, it is not always clear who has the Third World life in marriages of the two unmarriageables.

While reaching out overseas seems a perfect solution to the double marriage squeeze, it gives rise to an unanticipated collision of gender ideologies in 90 percent of these couples. The reason is that the dreams that led both partners into the arrangement often had as much to do with gender as with economic mobility. Educated women like Thanh hope that a man living overseas in a modern country will respect women more than men at home, who may still be in the sway of ancient Vietnamese traditions. Low-wage working men like Minh, meanwhile, often look to women in Vietnam precisely because they wish to uphold those ancient traditions, which they believe have been eroded in modern American life, but which they expect a woman in Vietnam will maintain.

In their search for spouses, both parties have relied to some extent on tradition, which leads them to agree to a marriage arranged by family members.

But it is the modern, globalizing culture of Vietnam that makes the transnational match possible. In 1986, after having had no contact with the outside world for over a decade, the Vietnamese government adopted a new economic policy known as *doi moi*. It did not end state ownership, but it encouraged private enterprise, free markets, and global engagement. In the 1990s, Saigon reemerged as a major international city, first within Asia and then in the world more generally. Vietnam was projected to be one of Asia's next "tigers."[20] Enticed by an emerging labor and consumer market of eighty million people, foreign companies were eager to move their factories there and to make their products known.

Globalization rapidly opened the Vietnamese market for capital, goods, and labor. At the same time, it also opened a more personal exchange of emotions and marriage partners. But while goods and capital tend to flow in two directions, the divide between the First World economy of the West and the Third World economy of Vietnam makes it impossible for women in Vietnam to go abroad to look for grooms but very easy for Viet Kieu men to go to Vietnam for brides. Just as global corporations and factories moved to Vietnam to partake of its large supply of labor, Viet Kieu men go there to choose among its large selection of potential brides. But unlike locals who eagerly take jobs at foreign factories for the pay, Vietnamese transpacific brides have a wide range of reasons for choosing to marry Viet Kieu men.

The Highly Educated Bride

Twenty years ago, Thanh's father was a math teacher at Le Buon Phong, a prestigious high school in Saigon. After the war, Thanh's uncle, her mother's younger brother, and his family were among the several thousand Vietnamese who were airlifted out of Vietnam on April 30, 1975, when Saigon surrendered to the North Vietnamese. They eventually settled in Houston, one of the larger Vietnamese enclaves in the United States, and started a successful restaurant business specializing in *pho*, the popular Vietnamese beef noodle soup. Remittances from Thanh's uncle helped her parents open a small candy factory in the late 1980s; that factory now has more than forty employees. Thanh's parents belong to a small but very visible class of Vietnamese families who enjoy access to overseas resources. They are part of a Viet Kieu economy that has grown from roughly $35 million in 1993 to an estimated $2 billion in 2000.[21]

Thanh was only seven years old when Saigon fell. She is not as old as Minh, whose memory of the war is very strong and formative; nor is she able to put that era completely behind her, like her peers born after the war, who are eager to move forward and to join the global economy. She embraces foreign influences and appreciates the access she has to them. Many of her friends work in foreign companies as translators, or in marketing or sales; some have become local branch supervisors for international corporations such as Citibank and IBM. Nevertheless, Thanh is conscious that her parents have sustained hidden injuries from accepting remittances from her uncle in Houston, and this saddens her. She observes:

My father is a very strong man; nobody ever tells him what to do with his life, like how to raise his children. But I think it is very hard for him when he has to deal with my uncle. My uncle is a very nice man, and he cares a lot for our family. But even though he's younger than my mother, his older sister, he doesn't respect my father. He thinks my father has to listen to him about everything, like how to run his business. When he comes back to Vietnam, he always tries to change the ways my dad runs things. And my father always defers to him. He feels that because my uncle helped him financially to open up the candy factory, he has to do everything my uncle says. I know he feels very embarrassed and humiliated inside, but would never tell anyone about it.

Thanh's family is not alone in its discomfort with receiving money from abroad. Remittances create social inequality and stress between givers and receivers, and even greater inequalities between receivers and nonreceivers in the same community. Nonetheless, Thanh knows that she owes the lifestyle she enjoys at least partly to her uncle's remittances. After all, the average salary for Saigonese lawyers, according to Thanh, is a little over 2 million Vietnamese *dong* (VND), or US $150 per month, whereas the net profit of her father's candy factory averages close to VND 900 million a year. Thanh earns about VND 2.5 million a month as a part-time lawyer in a small firm that handles legal contracts of all sorts. Although her salary is six times the standard income of the average worker in Saigon, it is still low on a global scale.[22] But the remittances that gave her parents' business a leg up have also allowed Thanh, an only child, to have a greater than average degree of educational and social mobility. She has been able to obtain a good high school education, to study law, and to take lessons at international English schools in Saigon.

Most of Thanh's peers married soon after high school, but Thanh and a small group of her female friends from Le Buon Phong High School decided to continue their schooling instead. Of her seven close female friends from high school, only one did not go to college, choosing instead to marry early. The rest, including Thanh, quietly built professional careers. Most went into fields traditionally reserved for women, including education and nursing. Two pursued advanced degrees. Thanh obtained a law degree, while her friend became a prestigious physician at Vinh Bien, a private hospital catering to Saigon's middle class. Four of the seven, now in their early thirties, remain single. At the time of this writing, there is no available data on the extent of delayed marriages across class and educational levels in Vietnam. But if the paths of Thanh and her four friends who chose singlehood are any indication, a quiet gender revolution is taking place among highly educated Vietnamese women. These women have opted for singlehood in a culture where marriage is not only presumed but often coerced. Women and men who have not yet married at the appropriate age are often dismissively referred to as "*e*," or unmarketable. By contrast, women (often young and beautiful) and men (often educated and financially secure) who fare well on the marriage market are considered *dat*, or scarce goods. As Thanh explained to me,

> I am already e in Vietnam. You know, at thirty-two here, it's hard to find a decent husband. I knew that when I decided to get a good education here that many men would be intimidated by me. But it was important to me to get an education, and I know that for women, marriage is more important. In Asian cultures, but may be in Vietnam especially, the men do not want their wives to be better than them. I think for me it's harder, too, because my parents are successful here, so to the outsider, we seem very successful.

In truth, Thanh is not completely *e:* several men, sometimes with their families, have come to propose marriage to her. Arranged marriages remain common in Vietnam, although they are more common in villages than in urban areas. Young couples who marry by arrangement are susceptible to significant difficulties if class differences divide their families.[23] Individual and family success can make a Vietnamese woman, particularly if she has passed the socially accepted marriageability age, unmarriageable. Thanh had several proposals for marriage arrangements when she was in her mid-twenties, before she got her law degree, from men who wanted to marry down. Now she is thirty-two and educated; she believes that marrying up is no longer an option, since there are few available men in that category. Although she has many suitors of lesser means and education than herself, Thanh explains that she does not find marrying down to be an appealing prospect. . . .

Thanh's marriage procrastination was partly anchored in her confused class and gender status. Her upward mobility put her at the top locally, but globally, she is at the bottom, since Vietnam has low status among nations. In a traditional marriage, her husband must be the household's provider; but given that she is marrying a low-wage worker, she may end up being the one to seek economic security through her own means. Yet marrying a low-wage worker overseas looks attractive to Thanh because she knows that in Vietnam, her high educational status will not help her escape the gender subordination of marital life. She can think of few men she knows in Vietnam who show respect to their wives.

On our third and final interview, Thanh and I walked along the Saigon River. It was early evening, and the city skyline loomed in the near distance, separated from us by a cacophony of motorcycles, bicycles, and taxis. Disconsolately, Thanh explained:

> In Vietnam, it is hard being single, female, and old. People will criticize and laugh at you. People always ask me, "Where are your husband and children?" And when I think about that, I realize that I have two choices. I can marry a man in Vietnam who is much less educated and less successful than I whom I will have to support and who will likely abuse me emotionally or physically or dominate me in every possible way. Or I can marry a Viet Kieu man. At least Viet Kieu men live in modern countries where they respect women.

Ultimately, what Thanh wants in a marriage partner is someone who will respect her, and who will not seek to control her the way she sees so many Vietnamese men control their wives. . . .

The Low–Wage Working Groom

If Thanh's desire for respect stems from her upward mobility, her husband's parallel desire has everything to do with his downward mobility. Minh, whose hands, facial expressions, and graying hair make him seem older than his thirty-seven years, was the only member of his family to leave Vietnam during "Wave II" of the boat exodus that took place after the war.[24] As the eldest son, he was vested with a special status and with a good deal of responsibility for his six siblings. Both of his parents were teachers of philosophy at Le Buon Phong, where they have known Thanh's parents for many years. Today, three of Minh's sisters are teachers and his two brothers are successful merchants in Saigon.

In 1985, at the age of twenty-one, Minh was a man of intellectual ambition and curiosity. He had just completed his third year of engineering school when his parents asked him if he wanted to go to America. They didn't know anyone overseas at the time, but they knew of several people, among the many hundreds of thousands of refugees, who had safely reached a Western country. More than 90 percent of these refugees settled in France, Australia, Canada, or the United States.[25] Minh's parents also knew that as many as half of the refugees on any given boat did not reach their destinations. They died along the way due to starvation, pirate attacks, and often, in the case of women and children, in the combination of rape and murder en route to a refugee camp. Many were also caught by the Vietnamese government and severely punished with long prison sentences.

Nevertheless, Minh's parents were confident that he would survive and find a better life abroad. They spent their entire lives' savings to put him on one of the safest and most reputable boats to leave the Mekong Delta for Western lands of opportunity. These boats and their routes via refugee camps in Southeast Asia were a carefully guarded secret in Vietnam, and they were accessible only to wealthy or well-connected families. Being caught by government officials could lead to severe punishment. Many who were not wealthy, like Minh's family, managed to pool their resources so that one person, usually a son, could go. They saw this as an investment, which they made with the hope it would yield high returns.

Today, Minh considers himself one of the lucky ones who left. After surviving two years in a refugee camp in Malaysia, he was selected in 1987 for entry to the United States. Many people he met at the camp ended up in less desirable places, like Finland, Belgium, or Hungary. Back then, as now, the United States was the top-choice destination, followed by Canada, France, and Australia. Minh arrived in rural Wyoming under the sponsorship of a local Catholic church. Like many of the American churches that sponsored

Indochinese refugees from the late 1970s to the mid-1990s, Minh's church sponsored only one person.[26] He spent the first five years of his new life as the only person of color in a rural town in Wyoming, the name of which he doesn't even want to remember.

Like many Vietnamese refugees in the past three decades, Minh decided to migrate a second time. He wanted to go to Little Saigon, the most highly concentrated Vietnamese enclave outside of Vietnam, located in a seemingly quiet Los Angeles suburb that is today plagued by urban problems.[27] But he had little money and no connections in or around Los Angeles. Then one day, in one of the Vietnamese-produced newspapers that flourished in the United States following the influx of refugees, Minh read about a Chinese restaurant called the Panda Garden that needed dishwashers. Unfortunately, it was not in Los Angeles but in a small town called Quincy, ninety miles from Seattle. Minh heard that Seattle also had many Vietnamese people, and he hoped that moving there would bring him closer to other refugees.

Eleven years later, Minh still lives in Quincy and works at the Panda Garden. He is now a deep fryer and an assistant cook, which is several steps up from the dishwashing position he was first given. Although to him, an assistant cook carries less stigma than a dishwasher, it is far from the engineering career he envisaged in his pre-migration years. His responsibilities include helping the main cook with various kitchen tasks and making sure that the restaurant has a constant supply of egg rolls and wontons. Though known as one of the best and most authentic ethnic restaurants in town, the Panda serves a mainly white American clientele that, according to the restaurant's owners, probably wouldn't know the difference between authentic Chinese food and a Sara Lee frozen dinner.

Quincy is similar to many suburban towns in Middle America: it is not quite rural, but far from urban. People who live here drive to Seattle to shop and eat if they have money, but they stay in town if they want to see a movie. The town has two Chinese restaurants, a dozen other ethnic restaurants, and numerous chain-store franchises. Minh knows five other Vietnamese people in Quincy. They are all men, and three of them work with him at the restaurant. He shares a modest three-bedroom apartment with the barest of furnishings with these coworkers.

Like many Viet Kieu people, Minh sends remittances to Vietnam. But though remittances allow their receivers to enjoy First World consumption, givers often only partake of these fruits when they return to their Third World homes. In the First World settings where they live and work, some givers, like Minh, are able to sustain only a Third World consumption pattern. Minh earns approximately $1,400 a month in Quincy and sends $500 of that back to his family. That amount is much higher than the average of $160 the grooms in my study remit to their wives or families on a monthly basis. At $900, his remaining budget would be considered way below the poverty level anywhere in the United States. But the stream of cash he sends his family permits them to stay connected in the small, though conspicuous, circles of families who have overseas kin networks.

In the meantime, however, Minh finds himself lacking not only in material comforts but in the kind of respect he had come to expect before he migrated. Minh remembers vividly that in his early twenties, his peers considered him a good catch. He came from a well-respected family, and he was headed for a career in engineering. Young men he knew had not one but several girlfriends at a time, and this was accepted and celebrated during those difficult postwar years. Minh was relatively fortunate: his parents were respected teachers with small but steady incomes. They could afford to spend small amounts of money on leisure activities, and on materials that bought them some status in their pre-remittance circles. When we talked over beer and cigarettes in the hot kitchen where he worked, Minh told me:

> *Life here now is not like life in Vietnam back then. My younger brothers and sisters used to respect me a lot because I was going to college and I was about to get my degree. Many young women I met at the time liked me, too, because I came from a good family and I had status [dia di]. But now, because I don't have a good job here, people don't pay attention to me. That's the way my life has been since I came to the United States. And I don't know if I'm lucky or unlucky, but I think it's hard for a [Vietnamese] man to find a wife here if he doesn't make good money. If you have money, everyone will pay attention [to you], but if you don't, you have to live by yourself.*

For the most part, that's what Minh has done in the sixteen years since he arrived in the United States. Minh believes that money can, and often does, buy love, and that if you don't have much of it, you live by yourself. Although his yearly income puts him just above the poverty level for a single man, I discovered in a budget analysis of his expenditures that after remittances he falls well below the poverty level. The long hours that often accompany low-wage work have made it particularly difficult for him to meet and court marriage partners. If Minh worked long hours for a law firm or a corporation, he would not only get financial rewards but also the status and prestige that men often use as a trade-off in marriage markets. If he were a blue-collar white man in Quincy, he could go to church functions, bowling alleys, or bars to meet and court local women. For Minh, a single, immigrant man who does low-wage work in a low-status job with long hours in Middle America, the prospect of marriage has been, and remains, low. Even under slightly more favorable circumstances, Viet Kieu men complain of a lack of marriage partners. Men I interviewed in ethnic enclaves such as Little Saigon faced difficulties because, as one man told me, "Viet Kieu women know that there are many of us and few of them!"

Low-wage workers like Minh find it especially difficult to compete in intimate markets. Unlike women like Thanh, men like Minh are at the bottom locally, while globally they are at the top, since the United States enjoys high status among nations. That is one reason they turn to Vietnam. After all, men like Minh are in the market for more than just intimacy. They are in it for respect and for a kind of marital life that they believe they cannot obtain locally. For men in general, but especially for working-class men, as sociologist Lillian Rubin has argued in a compelling study, a worthy sense of self is deeply connected to the ability to provide economically for one's family.[28] As Minh movingly explained to me,

> *I don't know if other men told you this, but I think the main reason why a lot of Viet Kieu men go back to Vietnam for a wife is because the women here [Viet Kieu] do not respect their husbands if the husbands cannot make a lot of money. I think that's why there are a lot of Viet Kieu women who marry white men, because the white men have better jobs than us.[29] Many Viet Kieu women, even though they are not attractive and would not be worth much if there were a lot of them, would not even look at men like me because we can't buy them the fancy house or the nice cars. I need my wife to respect me as her husband. If your wife doesn't respect you, who will?*

How They Meet

Although Minh was upwardly mobile in 1985 and would have become an engineer had he remained in Vietnam, he is now an assistant cook who has spent the bulk of his adult working life confined to a small Chinese restaurant in Middle America. He hasn't read a book in recent memory. In fact, he says little about what he does, except work, or what he owns, except for a used Toyota Tercel he recently bought. Meanwhile, Thanh is a relatively successful lawyer in urban Saigon, where Chanel perfume and Ann Taylor shirts are essential components of her daily life. Thanh speaks very good English, the language we used when she and I met in Vietnam; Minh and I spoke Vietnamese when I interviewed him in Quincy. Thanh is currently working toward an English proficiency degree at an international adult English school, and her reading list includes F. Scott Fitzgerald's *The Great Gatsby*. She often prides herself that she is not as thin as the average woman in Vietnam, nor does she have the stereotypically Vietnamese long, straight black hair. Instead, Thanh has a perm with red highlights, and she spends a large part of her leisure time taking aerobics classes at the Saigonese Women's Union. She likes to joke, "Some people in Vietnam think that I'm a Viet Kieu woman."

Today Minh and Thanh live in seemingly separate worlds. The network of kin and acquaintanceship that unites them was driven by the war, but it still shares the history, memories, and connections of the prewar years. In 1997, when he was nearing his mid-thirties, Minh's family pressed him to find a suitable wife. In Vietnam, there is a strong cultural belief that one should marry in early adulthood, and most certainly before one turns thirty. In 1997, Minh, at thirty-four, was getting old in the eyes of married Vietnamese people. At twenty-eight, Thanh was considered even older as a woman, and both were very old according to Vietnamese notions of fertility. Most people are expected to have a first child, preferably a son, early to ensure patrilineal lineage. Although the average age of marriage has increased in Vietnam in the past few years, as it has worldwide, Vietnamese women are often stigmatized and considered unmarriageable at as young as twenty-five.[30] In the villages, some women are considered unmarriageable at twenty.

Transpacific marriage arrangements are not always the idea of the grooms or brides involved. More than 55 percent of the grooms I interviewed said the idea of a transpacific marriage did not occur to them until a close friend or family member suggested it. The same was true of only 27 percent of the brides. In other words, more brides than grooms expressed an initial desire for an overseas spouse, while grooms were somewhat hesitant until encouraged. The arrangement for Minh and Thanh started when Minh's siblings expressed concern that their eldest brother appeared lonely and needed a wife (though they never asked him if this was the case). After all, he was the eldest sibling but the only one who remained unmarried and childless. The average age of marriage for his three younger sisters was twenty-one and for his two brothers, twenty-four. While these ages seem lower than the current Vietnamese average of twenty-four years for women and twenty-five years for men, they were not unusual at the time, since all five siblings married in the late 1980s and early 1990.[31] Minh's next brother's eldest child is now in her first year at Le Buon Phong High School. Minh feels old when he thinks of this. He is often embarrassed when his family asks him, "Why didn't you bring your lady friend back to visit us, too?" Minh's long work hours, along with the scarcity of Vietnamese women (relative to men) in the United States in general and Quincy in particular, were among the real reasons why the lady friend was generally "too busy to come home *this time*."

Both Minh and Thanh faced structural and demographic limitations in their local marriage markets, but in different and reversed ways. Minh knew very few Vietnamese-American women, and those he knew usually earned the same amount or more than he did, which made him a less attractive marriage candidate in the United States. Among Asian-Americans, especially in California, women tend to get low-wage jobs more easily, to work longer hours, and to earn more money than men.[32] By contrast, Thanh knew many single men in Saigon, but they were far below her in educational status and made much less money than she did. Her economic and educational status made her a less attractive marriage candidate in Vietnam, but the same qualities served her well on the transpacific marriage market. As Thanh explained to me:

> *Any Viet Kieu man can come here to find a wife. And he can surely find a beautiful woman if he wants because there are many beautiful young women willing to marry anyone to go overseas. I think there is something different when you talk about Viet Kieu men coming back here to marry. The women here who marry for money, many of them will marry other foreign men, like Taiwanese and Korean men, but they have sacrificed their lives for their families because they think they can go off to another country and later send money back home. Those [non–Viet Kieu] men seldom check the family backgrounds of the women they marry, because they don't care. They, the women and the men, know it's something like prostitution, like selling oneself, even though they have weddings and everything. But it's not really a marriage. If the brides are lucky, their foreign husbands will love them and take care of them. But when it has to do*

with Vietnamese men, they are more selective. They look for a real marriage. And a marriage that will last forever. So it's important to them to check every-thing about the woman they will marry and her background. These [Viet Kieu] men want a woman who is educated and who comes from an educated family, because that means she comes from a good family. And if her family has money, he knows she just doesn't want to marry him to go overseas because she already has a comfortable life in Vietnam.

News of a split marriage market, one for foreign non–Viet Kieu men and the other for Viet Kieu men who usually have family connections, has circu-lated extensively throughout the Vietnamese diaspora. Men who want "real" marriages are careful not to meet women on their own, because they fear they will be used as passes for migration. When I visited Saigon night-clubs, cafés, and bars where overseas Vietnamese men and local women converge, I found that both men and women approached public courtship with a lack of trust. Like women in Taiwan, Thailand, Singapore, Malaysia, Hong Kong, and other Asian countries I've visited or studied, Vietnamese women who seek transpacific spouses are so afraid of being seen as prostitutes that they rarely allow themselves to be courted by foreign men in public. Some Viet Kieu men come back and visit local bars and dance clubs in search of "one-night stands" either with prostitutes or non-prostitutes, but they rarely marry women they meet in these public spaces. My sample of marriages yielded only one couple who met by any means other than kinship introduction or arrangement. That couple had met through an international Vietnamese newspaper based in Sydney. Ninety percent of the couples had their marriages arranged, and of the remaining 9 percent, the men had returned to Vietnam to court old school friends or neighbors.

If women are afraid that they will be sexually exploited, Viet Kieu men are wary of being used as a "bridge" to cross the Pacific.[33] These concerns, combined with the availability of transnational networks, have propelled women in Vietnam and Vietnamese men who live overseas to rely on mar-riage arrangements rather than engaging in individual courtship. As in the case of arranged marriages among other ethnic groups, marriage candidates in the Vietnamese diaspora believe that family members make the best judg-ments in their interests when looking for a spouse.[34] . . .

Minh's parents have known Thanh's family for more than two decades. Even though Thanh's father taught at Le Buon Phong two decades ago, and was a friend and colleague of Minh's parents, the current consumption gap between the two families has created a social distance over the years. When Minh's siblings convinced him to search for a wife in Vietnam, he was hesitant at first, but later followed their advice when his parents promised that they would invest time and care in finding the most suitable spouse. According to Minh, however, they were surprised to discover that arranging a marriage for a Viet Kieu was more complicated than they had anticipated:

I thought that it would be easy for them to find someone. I thought all they had to do was mention a few things to their friends, and within days they could describe a few possible people to me. But my parents told me that they were afraid that women just wanted to use our family to go abroad. We had many people get involved, many people wanted to be matchmakers for the family, and they added so much anxiety and fear about people's intentions. But the first goal for them was to find a woman from a wealthy family so that they were sure she wasn't just interested in money, because if she has money she would already be comfortable in Vietnam. And it would have been best if she had family in the United States already, because we would then know that they already have overseas people who help them out and they would not expect to become dependent on us. In Vietnamese, you know, there is this saying, "When you choose a spouse, you are choosing his or her whole family."

Minh's parents finally contacted Thanh's parents, after the traditional fashion in which the groom's parents represent him to propose, often with rituals and a centuries-old ceremonial language. Like most brides in my study, Thanh relied on an overseas relative—in this case her uncle, Tuan— for advice on Minh's situation in the United States. The family discovered that Minh was a low-wage worker, but a full-time worker nonetheless. During a walk Thanh and I took through the busy Ben Thanh market in the center of Saigon, she revealed that she and her family were already prepared to support a reversed remittance situation:

My father and mother didn't care about how much money Minh has. They figured that they could help us out if Minh doesn't do so well; it sounds strange and hard to believe, but my parents said that they could help us open up a business in the United States later on if Minh wants us to do that. They liked the idea that he is a hardworking man and that he comes from a good family. . . . They know he comes from a good family because he sends money back to his parents. He knows how to take care of them.

Virtually all of the locals I met in Vietnam viewed overseas men as a two-tiered group: the "successful," who were educated or who succeeded in owning ethnic enterprises, and the "indolent," who lacked full-time jobs and were perceived as being welfare-dependent or as participating in underground economies, such as gambling. Some felt that the latter group had taken up valuable spots that others from Vietnam could have filled. "If I had gotten a chance to go, I would be so rich by now," I heard many local men say. Most people, however, could not explain a man like Minh, who is neither lazy nor extremely successful. Thanh's uncle Tuan seemed to know more men in Houston who were not only unemployed but alcoholics and gamblers. Her parents were worried that their daughter was unmarriageable, because there was certainly no shortage of younger women in Vietnam for local men her age to marry. Thanh, too, was already convinced that she was "*e*." Both her parents and her uncle worried that Thanh was facing a life of permanent singlehood. Finally, they all believed that marrying Thanh to Minh, a Viet Kieu man, would be more desirable than arranging her marriage to a local man in Vietnam. Thanh's parents were confident that Minh's status as a full-time worker who sent remittances back home to his family spoke well for him as a suitable husband. Most Viet Kieu single men her uncle knew belonged to an underclass of which Minh was not a part. For Thanh, Minh's geographical advantage translated into something socially priceless: a man living in a modern country, she was sure, would respect women.

A Clash of Dreams

Highly educated women like Thanh resist patriarchal arrangements by avoiding marriages with local men. They do not want to "marry down" economically and socially—though this seems to be their only choice—because they believe that marrying local men will only constrain them to domestic roles in a male-dominated culture. As Thanh told me, some women will endure the often painful stigma of singlehood and childlessness over the oppression they could face from dominating husbands. For some of these women, the transpacific marriage market holds out hope for a different kind of marriage—one in which Vietnamese women imagine that their husbands will believe in, and practice, gender equity. Many such women will instead find themselves back in the pre-modern family life they hoped to avoid. As Minh told me, "A woman's place is in the home to take care of her husband and his family."

All but three of the twenty-eight grooms I interviewed shared Minh's view. But this conflict in gender ideology between the two unmarriageables never seemed to come to the fore until it was too late. During the migration period, each expensive phone call and visit is an occasion for love, not for discussing the details of what life will be like when the woman joins the man abroad. Most couples shared only words of joy about being together in the future.

And yet, as I interviewed the couples in their separate countries during this period, I found that the two parties usually held conflicting views of the life they would soon lead together. I did not interview all of the grooms, but I did ask all of the brides about their husbands' ideas about gender relations, and about how they envisioned the organization of their households after they joined their husbands abroad. Among other things, I asked about household division of labor, about whether the couple would live with or without kin, and about whether or not the women expected to work outside the home. Although these concerns address only a fraction of a marriage's potential promise or pitfalls, they can certainly help us understand the interplay between a husband's gender ideology and his wife's.[35]

Nearly 95 percent of the brides in Vietnam wanted to work for a wage when they joined their husbands abroad. Though wanting to work outside the home is not the ultimate measure of a modernized woman in Vietnam, it does indicate these women's unwillingness to be confined to domestic work. Some women who wanted paid jobs were not averse to the idea of doing second shift work as well.[36] However, most of the women, and virtually all of the educated ones—the unmarriageables—wanted and expected to have egalitarian relationships with their husbands. In general, they objected to traditionally female tasks, although they did not fully embrace what we might call a peer marriage.[37] For the men and women I interviewed, as for mainstream dual-career American couples, marital life consists of much more than just household tasks. But these tasks are important symbols in the economy of gratitude among married people, "for how a person wants to identify himself or herself influences what, in the back and forth of a marriage, will seem like a gift and what will not."[38]. . .

Women like Thanh want a respectful marriage based on principles of gender equality. According to these principles, women expect to work for a wage, to share in making social and economic decisions for their future households, and to have their husbands share in the household division of labor. Above all, they do *not* want to live in multigenerational households, serving as the dutiful daughter-in-law and housewife, the two often inseparable roles historically delegated to women in Vietnam. Many express that reluctance, because they know numerous Viet Kieu men who live with their parents or who plan to do so when their parents are old. In Vietnam, and more generally in Asia, elderly parents often live with their eldest sons. The daily caring work then falls to their sons' wives. Forty percent of the U.S.-based grooms and a third of all Vietnamese grooms live with their parents, most of whom are elderly and require care. Of all low-wage working men married to highly educated women, about 35 percent currently reside with their parents. Virtually all of the men in my study who resided with their parents wanted to continue to do so when their wives joined them abroad.

For Minh, the possibility that a wife will insist on an equal marriage is one of the anxieties of modern life:

> *Vietnamese women, they care for their husbands and they are more traditional. I think non-Vietnamese women and Viet Kieu women are too modern. They just want to be equal with their husbands, and I don't think that is the way husband and wife should be. . . . I mean that husband and wife should not be equal. The wife should listen to husband most of the time. That is how they will have a happy life together. If the woman tries to be equal they will have problems. . . . I know many Vietnamese men here who abandon their parents because their wives refuse to live with their parents. If my parents were in America, I would definitely plan for them to live with me when they are old. But because they are in Vietnam, they are living with one of my brothers.*

Instead of seeking peasant village women or uneducated ones, after the fashion of white men who pursue mail-order brides because they believe such women consent to subordination in marriage, men like Minh seek marriage arrangements with educated women. As Minh explains:

> *For me, I want to marry an educated woman, because she comes from a good, educated family. It's very hard to find a poor woman or an uneducated woman who comes from an uneducated family to teach their daughters about morals and values, because if they are uneducated they don't know how. I know many men, Viet Kieu and foreign men, who go to Vietnam to marry beautiful young women,*

but they don't ask why do those women marry them? Those women only want to use their beauty to go overseas, and they will leave their husbands when they get the chance. They can use their beauty to find other men. I would never marry a beautiful girl from a poor, uneducated family. You see, the educated women, they know it's important to marry and stay married forever. As they say in Vietnam, "Tram nam han phuc [a hundred years of happiness]." Educated women must protect their family's reputation in Vietnam by having a happy marriage, not have it end in divorce.

The Inflated Market of Respect

At first glance, Minh and Thanh seem to come from two vastly different social worlds, assembled only by the complexity of Vietnamese history. But at a closer look, we learn that these two lonely faces of globalization are very much alike. Both of their parents were educated and middle class. Both lack the emotional fulfillment and intimate partnership that adults of their social worlds enjoy. Both long for a kind of marital respect they perceive as scarce in their local marriage markets. Minh has experienced immense, swift downward mobility as a result of migration, and he is eager to regain the respect he has lost. Thanh has practically priced herself out of the local marriage market by acquiring an advanced degree, which she could not have obtained without her uncle's remittances. She wants a husband who respects her as an equal and who accepts that she is a modern woman. He wants to regain something he thinks men like him have lost; she wants to challenge the local marriage norm, including the very preindustrial Vietnamese family life Minh yearns for. Many men in Vietnam do live that life. As Minh told me:

My younger brothers have control over their homes. Their wives help them with their shops selling fabrics in Saigon, but their wives don't make any decisions. I think that if they lived in America, and their wives were working, they would not let my brother make all the decisions in the house. . . . And I think that Vietnamese women, when they come to the United States, they are influenced by a lot of different things. That is why there are a lot of divorces in America.

Minh believes that when he migrated to the United States, he left the respect he now craves behind him in Vietnam. Thanh imagines that the marital respect *she* craves is unobtainable in Vietnam, but awaits her in the United States. Each has inflated the true extent of the respect the other is willing to give. For though there is a quiet feminist revolution of sorts going on among highly educated women in Vietnam, that revolution has not entered the experience or expectations of the less educated, low-wage husbands living overseas. And while many of these Viet Kieu men seek reprieve from modern Western life, the women they marry have washed away those traditions during the long years that the men have been gone.

The Future of Transpacific Marriages

Surely, this clash of dreams and expectations will result in marital conflict when the couple is united overseas. Such conflicts have several potential outcomes. The happiest would have Minh joining the feminist revolution and abandoning his desire for the preindustrial, traditional family life he never had. Some men will go this route, but only a few. In other cases, such marriages may end in divorce—or worse, domestic battery. I believe the latter scenario is an unlikely one for the couples I studied. Many women like Thanh have considered the possibility and are careful to maintain contact with transnational networks that will look out for them. Seventy-five percent of the women in my study have at least one overseas relative. Virtually all the middle-class and college-educated women do.

Most likely, these marriages will resolve themselves with the men getting the respect they want and the women consenting to subordination in the name of family and kinship. Thanh will be going from the patriarchal frying pan to the patriarchal fire, but with one big difference. In the United States, her desire for gender equity will find more support, in a culture where women dare to leave their husbands if they aren't treated equally. But Thanh will still bear the burden of Vietnamese tradition, which will prevent her from leaving her husband. In Vietnam, divorce is stigmatized, and saving face is especially important to educated, middle-class families. If Thanh daringly divorces her husband, she will damage her family's reputation in Vietnam and overseas. She told me she would not be likely to take this risk. If she stays in the marriage, she will probably wind up serving as the traditional wife Minh desires.

Although globalization appears to offer some Vietnamese women an escape from local patriarchal marriages, it may in fact play more to the interests of certain Vietnamese men, offering them the opportunity to create the traditional life they've always wanted within the modern setting where they now live. Strong traditions back in Vietnam protect them against instability in their marriages. But the women they have married don't share their husbands' traditional vision of marital life. The only thing educated women like Thanh have to look forward to is more waiting—waiting for men like their husbands, who live in a modern country, simply to respect women.

ENDNOTES

1. All names have been changed to protect the privacy of informants. . . .

2. Although Saigon's name changed to Ho Chi Minh City when the South surrendered to Northern Vietnam in 1975, most people I met in contemporary Vietnam still refer to the city as Saigon, or simply Thanh Pho (the City). I use the name Saigon and Saigonese in deference to local usage.

3. More than two million people have emigrated from Vietnam since April 1975, which comes to about 3 percent of the country's current population of eighty million. Approximately 60 percent left as boat refugees; the remaining 40 percent went directly to resettlement countries. Ninety-four percent of those who left Vietnam eventually resettled in Western countries. Between 1975 and 1995, the

United States accepted 64 percent of that group; 12 percent went to Australia and 12 percent to Canada. . . .

4. I would like to thank Pierrette Hondagneu-Sotelo for pointing out the complexity and danger of lumping all migrants—legal and illegal—into one category.

5. These figures refer to individuals aged twenty and over, since aggregate data from the Immigration and Naturalization Service includes in one bracket the ages fifteen through nineteen, thus making it impossible to calculate the legal marriage age of eighteen into the marriage migration figure. Therefore, we can assume that these percentages are slightly lower than the actual numbers of marriage migrants. See United States Immigration and Naturalization Service, "Statistical Yearbook of the Immigration and Naturalization Service, 1997," *Statistics Branch* (1999); United States Immigration and Naturalization Service, "International Matchmaking Organizations: A Report to Congress By the Immigration and Naturalization Service," *A Report to Congress* (1999); and United States Immigration and Naturalization Service, "Annual Report: Legal Immigration, Fiscal Year 1997," *Statistics Branch* (1999), pp. 1–13.

6. Marion F. Houstoun, Roger G. Kramer, and Joan Mackin Barrett, "Female Predominance in Immigration to the United States since the 1930s: A First Look," *International Migration Review*, vol. 18, no. 4 (1984), pp. 908–63.

7. Guillermina Jasso, *The New Chosen People: Immigrants in the United States* (New York: Russell Sage Foundation, 1990). In recent years, there has been a lively discussion among feminist scholars about family migration, but no one has specifically looked at processes of marriage migration. See, for example, Alan Booth, Ann C. Crouter, and Nancy Landale, *Immigration and the Family: Research and Policy on U.S. Immigrants* (Mahwah, N.J.: Lawrence Erlbaum Associates Press, 1997); Nancy Foner, "The Immigrant Family: Cultural Legacies and Cultural Changes," *International Migration Review*, vol. 31, no. 4 (1997), pp. 961–74; Yen Le Espiritu, *Asian American Women and Men* (Thousand Oaks, Calif.: Sage Publications, 1997); Pierrette Hondagneu-Sotelo, *Gendered Transitions: Mexican Experiences of Immigration* (Berkeley: University of California Press, 1994); Silvia Pedraza, "Women and Migration: The Social Consequences of Gender," *Annual Review of Sociology*, vol. 17 (1991), pp. 303–25; and Patricia R. Pessar, "Engendering Migration Studies: The Case of Immigrants in the United States," *American Behavioral Scientist*, vol. 42, no. 4 (1999), pp. 577–600.

8. Ruben G. Rumbaut, "Ties That Bind: Immigration and Immigrant Families in the United States," in *Immigration and the Family: Research and Policy on U.S. Immigrants*, ed. Alan Booth, Ann C. Crouter, and Nancy Landale (Mahwah, N.J.: Lawrence Erlbaum Associates Press, 1997).

9. Migrants in at least three different streams of marriage migration can obtain, with relative ease, the papers to go abroad. The first is the *commercialized* mail-order bride stream. In their communities of origin, these brides are seen as occupying a continuum that runs from prostitutes (most commonly) to women seeking their dream husbands. Men on the receiving end are usually Caucasians from the United States, Australia, Canada, and Europe who go to "exotic lands" in search of submissive wives. See Mila Glodava and Richard Onizuka, *Mail-Order Brides: Women for Sale* (Colorado: Alaken, 1994). The second stream includes the *noncommercialized* transracial spousal migrant. This has historically included war brides of U.S. servicemen. In contemporary Vietnam and elsewhere, these couples tend to meet by working together in multinational firms, embassies, or universities. The third stream is composed of same-ethnic individuals who live in different countries and have married each other. This third stream is the topic of my research.

10. See, for example, Eve Tahmincioglu, "For Richer or Poorer: Mail-Order Brides Make for Big Business Online," *Ziff Davis Smart Business for the New Economy*, (Jan. 1, 2001), p. 40.

11. Although it is difficult to calculate whether or not marriage migrants are in transracial relationships, or how many are part of systems of commercialized mail-order brides, the best estimate we have is that about one-third of all marriage migrant couples are transracial, and that 2.7 to 4.1 percent are mail-order brides. See *Report to Congress,* 1999; Michael C. Thornton, "The Quiet Immigration: Foreign Spouses of U.S. Citizens, 1945–1985," in *Racially Mixed People in America,* ed. Maria P. Root (Newbury Park, Calif.: Sage Publications, 1992), pp. 64–76.

12. Guillermina Jasso and Mark R. Rosenzweig, "Sponsors, Sponsorship Rates and the Immigration Multiplier," *International Migration Review,* vol. 23, no.4 (1989), pp. 856–88; Jasso, 1990.

13. In the United States from 1960 to 1997, the number of marriage migrants multiplied by approximately three times. In the 1960s, only 9 percent of all immigrants were marriage migrants; by 1997, this number jumped to 25 percent. See *Report to Congress,* 1999; Jasso, 1990. Most of those who migrate to marry permanent residents are women. In 1997, for example, a total of 201,802 individuals came to the United States through legal marriage migration. Of these, 84 percent were marrying U.S. citizens and 16 percent were marrying permanent residents. Of those marrying U.S. citizens, 61 percent were women, whereas 87 percent of those marrying permanent residents were women.

14. This paper is based on extensive interviews with ninety-eight people (mainly brides and their families) in Vietnam and thirty-one people (mainly grooms) in the United States. I interviewed the brides in their homes in Saigon and in six villages dotted along a main road in the Mekong Delta. I interviewed the grooms in their homes in San Francisco, Los Angeles, Seattle, and Boston. For further details, see Hung Cam Thai, "Marriage Across the Pacific: Family, Gender and Migration in Vietnam and in the Vietnamese Diaspora" (Ph.D. dissertation, University of California, Berkeley).

15. Except in a few cases, the men who do low-wage work are also less educated than their wives; most of these grooms have barely a grade school education. Education and income are often, but not always, linked. Plumbers, for example, may earn more money than teachers. In this chapter, I refer to the men as both "low-wage workers" and "undereducated" men. The brides I describe in this chapter are "highly educated" women compared to most women in Vietnam, meaning that they all have at least a college degree and many have advanced degrees. Most of them, though not all, come from solidly middle-class Vietnamese backgrounds.

16. Daniel Goodkind, "The Vietnamese Double Marriage Squeeze," *The Center for Migration Studies of New York,* vol. 31, no. 1 (1997), pp. 108–28.

17. These calculations are based on Goodkind's 1990 data. See Goodkind, 1997. I simply added ten years to each cohort, though mortality for either sex as a whole may have caused a shift in sex ratio since 1990.

18. Tina Katherine Fitzgerald, "Who Marries Whom? Attitudes in Marital Partner Selection" (Ph.D. dissertation, Department of Sociology, University of Colorado, 1999).

19. When low-wage men travel to search for spouses abroad, they are unlikely to advertise that they work in low-wage jobs. In my study, however, most men did inform their wives, vis-à-vis matchmakers and go-betweens. Thus, I base my 55 percent figure of low-wage men married to highly educated women on information provided by the brides and their families, as well as interviews with some of the grooms. I did not find that any grooms had misrepresented themselves when I matched their stories to those of their brides. Nonetheless, although I estimate that 80 percent of the grooms in my study are low-wage workers, that number may, in fact, be higher if they misinformed their wives.

20. Andrew J. Pierre, "Vietnam's Contradictions," *Foreign Affairs,* vol. 79, no. 6 (2000).

21. Pierre, 2000.

22. Henry Dietz, "The Rich Get Richer: The Rise of Income Inequality in the United States and the World," *Social Science Quarterly* (Sept. 1991), p. 639; *Saigon: 20 Years After Liberation* (Hanoi, Vietnam: The Gioi Publishers, 1995); Vu Thi Hong, Le Van Thanh, and Troung Si Anh, *Migration, Human Resources, Employment and Urbanization in Ho Chi Minh City* (Hanoi: National Political Publishing House, 1996).

23. Daniele Belanger and Khuat Thu Hong, "Marriage and Family in Urban North Vietnam, 1965–1993," *Journal of Population*, vol. 2, no. 1 (1996), pp. 83–112; Charles Hirschman and Vu Manh Loi, "Family and Household Structures in Vietnam: Some Glimpses from a Recent Survey," *Pacific Affairs*, vol. 69 (1996), pp. 229–49; Nazli Kibria, *Family Tightrope: The Changing Lives of Vietnamese Americans* (Princeton, N.J.: Princeton University Press, 1993); Dinh Huou Tran, "Traditional Families in Vietnam and the Influence of Confucianism," in *Sociological Studies on the Vietnamese Family*, ed. Rita Lijestrom and Tuong Lai (Hanoi, Vietnam: Social Sciences Publishing House, 1991), pp. 27–53; and Steven K. Wisensale, "Marriage and Family Law in a Changing Vietnam," *Journal of Family Issues*, vol. 20 (1999), pp. 602–16.

24. Min Zhou and Carl L. Bankston, *Growing Up American: How Vietnamese Children Adapt to Life in the United States* (New York: Russell Sage Foundation, 1998).

25. Giovanna M. Merli, "Estimation of International Migration for Vietnam 1979–1989" (unpublished paper, Department of Sociology and Center for Studies in Demography and Ecology, University of Washington, Seattle, 1997).

26. Zhou and Bankston, 1998.

27. Jack Leonard and Mai Tran, "Probes Take Aim at Organized Crime in Little Saigon; Crackdown: Numerous Agencies Target Gambling, Drug Sales, Counterfeit Labels and Credit Card Scams," *Los Angeles Times*, Oct. 7, 2000, p. B-7; Richard C. Paddock and Lily Dizon, "3 Vietnamese Brothers in Shoot-out Led Troubled Lives," *Los Angeles Times*, April 15, 1991, p. A3; Richard Marosi and Mai Tran, "Little Saigon Raids Dismantle Crime Ring, Authorities Say," *Los Angeles Times*, Sept. 29, 2000, p. B-3.

28. Lillian Rubin, *Families on the Fault Line: America's Working Class Speaks About the Family, the Economy, Race and Ethnicity* (New York: HarperCollins, 1994).

29. Racial and ethnic disparities, including in interethnic and interracial intimate markets, loom large in some of the marriages I studied. For these low-wage working men, categories of class and gender are more internalized, and more to the fore in their reflections on their lived experiences.

30. Huu Minh Nguyen, "Age at First Marriage in Vietnam: Patterns and Determinants" (unpublished M.A. thesis, Department of Sociology, University of Washington, 1995); *The World's Women, 2000: Trends and Statistics*, 3rd ed., Social Statistics and Indicators, series K, no. 16 (New York: United Nations, 2000).

31. *World's Women, 2000*.

32. Yen Le Espiritu, "Gender and Labor in Asian Immigrant Families," *American Behavioral Scientist* (1999), pp. 628–47.

33. Aihwa Ong, *Flexible Citizenship* (London: Duke University Press, 1999). In one highly publicized case that spread throughout the Vietnamese diaspora, a transpacific groom "arrived to meet his bride at Los Angeles International Airport with a dozen red roses only to watch her blithely wave good-bye before she left with friends for San Jose" (Lily Dizon, "Journey Home for a Bride," *Los Angeles Times*, Sept. 19, 1994, p. A1).

34. Reena Jana, "Arranged Marriages, Minus the Parents; for Some South Asians, Matrimonial Sites Both Honor and Subvert Tradition," *New York Times*, August 17, 2000, p. D1; Molly Moore, "Changing India, Wedded to Tradition; Arranged Marriages Persist with '90's Twists," *Washington Post*, Oct. 8, 1994; Shanthy Nambiar, "Love with the Proper Stranger," *Washington Post*, 1993; Shoba Narayan, "When Life's Partner Comes Pre-Chosen," *New York Times*, 1995;

Najma Rizvi, "Do You Take This Man? Pakistani Arranged Marriages," *American Anthropologist* (Sept. 1993), p. 787.

35. According to sociologist Arlie Russell Hochschild, there are differences between what people say they believe about their marital roles and how they seem to feel about those roles. Furthermore, what they believe and how they feel may also differ from what they actually do. She distinguishes between gender ideologies and gender strategies to point out that ideology has to do with how men and women draw on "beliefs about manhood and womanhood, beliefs that are forged in early childhood and thus anchored to deep emotions." Gender strategies refer to people's plans of action and their emotional preparations for pursuing them. See Arlie Russell Hochschild and Anne Machung, *The Second Shift: Working Parents and the Revolution at Home* (New York: Viking, 1989), p. 15.

36. Hochschild with Machung, *The Second Shift: Working Parents and the Revolution at Home* (New York: Avon, 1997).

37. Pepper Schwartz, *Love Between Equals: How Peer Marriage Really Works* (New York: Free Press, 1995).

38. Hochschild with Machung, 1997.

14

PEER MARRIAGE

PEPPER SCHWARTZ

When I told people that I was beginning a research study of couples who evenly divided parenting and housework responsibilities, the usual reaction was mock curiosity—how was I going to find the three existing egalitarian couples in the universe? Despite several decades of dissecting the sexism and inequities inherent in traditional marriage, as a society, we have yet to develop a clear picture of how more balanced marital partnerships actually work. Some critics even argue that the practice of true equality in marriage is not much more common today than it was 30 years ago. In fact, authors like Arlie Hochschild have suggested that women's liberation has made prospects for equity worse. The basic theme of her provocative book, *The Second Shift*, is that women now have two jobs — their old, traditional marital roles and their new responsibilities in the work force. A look at the spectacular divorce rates and lower marriage rate for successful women provides further fuel for the argument that equality has just brought wives more, not less, burdens.

All of this figured heavily in my own commitment to exploring the alternative possibilities for marital partnership. [In 1983,] this began with *American Couples: Money, Work and Sex*, a study I did with Philip Blumstein that compared more than 6,000 couples — married, cohabiting, gay males and lesbians — looking for, among other things, what aspects of gendered behavior contributed to relationship satisfaction and durability. This study contained within it a small number of egalitarian couples, who fascinated and inspired me. We discussed them rather briefly in the book, but our editor encouraged us to make them the subject of a second study that would examine how couples manage to sustain an egalitarian partnership over time. Unfortunately, my co-author was not able to continue the project and it was not until three years ago that I began the research on what I came to call Peer Marriage. I began looking for couples who had worked out no worse than a 60-40 split on childrearing, housework and control of discretionary funds and who considered themselves to have "equal status or standing in the relationship."

I started out interviewing some of the couples originally studied for *American Couples* and then, using what sociologists call a "snowball sample," I asked those couples if they knew anyone else like themselves that I could interview. After talking to a few couples in a given network, I then would look for a different kind of couple (different class, race, educational background, etc.) in order to extend the range of my sample. I interviewed 57 egalitarian couples, but even after the formal study was over, I kept running into couples that fit my specifications and did 10 more partial interviews.

While initially my design included only Peer Marriages, I also began to interview a lot of couples who others thought to be egalitarian, but who did not meet my criteria. Instead of throwing them out of the sample, I used them as a base of comparison, dividing them into two additional categories: "Traditionals" and "Near Peers." Traditionals were couples in which the man usually had veto power over decision-making (except with the children) and in which the wife felt that she did not have — nor did she want — equal status. The Near Peers were couples who, while they believed in equality, felt derailed from their initial goal of an egalitarian marriage because of the realities of raising children and/or the need or desire to maximize male income. As a result, the husband could not be anywhere near as participatory a father as the couple had initially envisioned. These two groups proved to be a fortuitous addition to the design. It is sometimes hard to understand what peer couples are doing that allows them to fulfill an egalitarian agenda without understanding what keeps other couples from doing the same.

Even though I consider myself to be in a Peer Marriage, I found many surprises among the Peer Couples I studied. Of course, as a researcher, one is never supposed to extrapolate from one's own experience, but it is almost impossible not to unconsciously put one's presuppositions into the hypothesis phase of the research. Clearly, people make their marital bargains for many different reasons, and face different challenges in sustaining them. Here are some of the discoveries I made that I thought might be of use to therapists [and to other family scholars].

I assumed most couples would, like myself, come to egalitarianism out of the women's movement or feminist ideology. Nevertheless, while approximately 40 percent of the women and about 20 percent of the men cited feminism and a desire to be in a nonhierarchical relationship, the majority of couples mentioned other reasons. These included a desire to avoid parental models that they found oppressive in their own upbringing, the *other* partner's strong preference for an egalitarian marriage, some emotional turmoil that had led to their rethinking their relationship, or an intense desire for co-parenting. Women in particular often mentioned their own parents as a negative model. One woman said, "*I want a husband who knows how to pack his own suitcase, who puts away his own clothes, who can't tell me to shut up at will. . . . My mother may have been happy with this kind of marriage, but I'm still angry at my father for treating my mother like that — and angry at her for letting him.*" A 25-year-old husband told me, on a different theme, "*My main objective in having an equal relationship was not to be the kind of father I had. I want my kids to know me before they are adults. I want them to be able to talk to me. I want them to run to me if they hurt themselves. I want our conversations to be more than me telling them they could do better on a test or that I was disappointed they didn't make the team. I want to be all the things to my kids that my dad was not. I want us to have hugged many, many times and not just on birthdays or their wedding day.*"

Quite a few men in Peer Marriages said they really had no strong feelings about being in either traditional or egalitarian marriages, but had merely followed their wives' lead. Typical of this group was a high school basketball coach who said he had had a very traditional first marriage because that was the only arrangement that he and his wife could envision even when it wasn't working. But when he met his current wife, a policewoman who had been single quite a while, her demands for equality seemed perfectly reasonable to him. He just, more or less, fell into line with his future wife's ideas about the relationship. Many of these men told me they had always expected a woman to be the emotional architect of a relationship and were predisposed to let her set the rules.

Most of the couples, however, did have strong ideas about marriage and placed particular emphasis on equity and equality. Even if they didn't start out with a common agenda, most ended up sharing a high degree of conscious purpose. People's particular personal philosophies about marriage mattered less than the fact that their philosophies differentiated their family from a culture that reinforced the general belief that equality is neither possible nor even in the long-term interests of couples. Many people talked about how easy it is to slide into old and familiar roles or follow economic opportunities that started to whittle away at male participation in childrearing. It takes an intense desire to keep a couple on the nontraditional track and a clear sense of purpose to justify the economic sacrifices and daily complications it takes to co-parent. As one wife of 10 years said, *"We always try to make sure that we don't start getting traditional. It's so easy to do. But we really want this extraordinary empathy and respect we have. I just know it wouldn't be there if we did this marriage any other way."*

Important as relationship ideology is, Peer Marriages depend at least as much on coordinating work with home and childraising responsibilities and not letting a high earner be exempt from daily participation. Previous research had shown me the connection between a husband's and wife's relative income and their likelihood of being egalitarian. So I assumed that most of the couples I interviewed would be working couples and have relatively similar incomes. This was mostly true, although I was struck by the couples who were exceptions. Four husbands in the study had non-working wives. The men didn't want to dominate those relationships because they felt very strongly that money did not legitimately confer power. For example, one husband had inherited a great deal of money but didn't feel it was any more his than his wife's. She stayed at home with the children, but he took over in the late afternoon and on weekends. He also was the primary cook and cleaner. In another case, a husband who earned a good deal more than his wife put all the money in a joint account and put investments in her name as well as his. Over time, she had assets equal to his. While these triumphs over income differentials were exceptions, it did make me respect the fact that truly determined couples could overcome being seduced by the power of economic advantage.

However, many Peer Marriages had a significant income differential and husbands and wives had to negotiate a lot just to make sure they didn't fall into the trap of letting the higher earner be the senior decision-maker. Even more tricky, according to many, was not letting work set the emotional and task agenda of the household. The couples needed to keep their eyes on what was the tail and what was the dog so that their relationship was not sidetracked by career opportunities or job pressures. Many Peer Couples had gone through periods in which they realized that they were beginning to have no time for each other, or that one of them was more consistently taking care of the children while the other was consumed with job demands. But what distinguished those couples from more traditional marriages was that they had a competing ideology of economic or career success that guided them when their egalitarianism began to get out of kilter.

One husband, who had an architectural practice designing and building airports, had begun to travel for longer and longer periods of time until it was clear that he was no longer a true co-parent or a full partner in the marriage. After long and painful discussions, he quit his job and opened up a home office so he could spend more time with his wife and children. Both partners realized this would cause some economic privations and, in fact, it took the husband five years to get a modestly successful practice going while the wife struggled to support the family. Without minimizing how tough this period had been, the couple felt they had done the right thing. "After all," the husband said, "we saved our marriage."

This attitude helped explain another surprise in this study. I had presumed that most of the Peer Marriages I would find would be yuppie or post-yuppie couples, mostly young or baby boom professionals who were "having it all." In fact, most of them were solidly middle class: small-business owners, social workers, schoolteachers, health professionals (but not doctors). Apparently, people on career fast tracks were less willing to endanger their potential income and opportunities for promotion. There may be childrearing Peer Marriages out there comprised of litigators, investment bankers and brain surgeons — but I didn't find them. The closest I came to finding fast trackers in a Peer Marriage and family were high-earning women who had husbands who were extremely pleased with their partner's success and were willing to be the more primary parent in order to support her career.

When these women negotiated issues with their husbands in front of me, they seemed more sensitive about their husbands' feelings than men of comparable accomplishment with lower earning wives. For example, they did not interrupt as much as high-earning men in traditional marriages, and they seemed to quite consciously not pull rank when I asked them jointly to solve a financial problem. They told me, however, that they consciously had to work at being less controlling than they sometimes thought they deserved to be. A very successful woman attorney, married to another, significantly-less-prominent attorney, told me that they had some problems because he wasn't used to picking up the slack when she was called away suddenly to represent a Fortune 500 company. She found herself battling her own ambitions in order to be sensitive to his desire for her to let up a bit. As she noted, "*We [women] are not prepared to be the major providers and it's easy to want all the privileges and leeway that men have always gotten for the role. But our bargain to raise the kids together and be respectful of one another holds me back from being like every other lawyer who would have this powerful a job. Still, it's hard.*"

The other fast-track exception was very successful men in their second marriages who had sacrificed their first in their climb to the top. Mostly these were men who talked about dependent ex-wives, their unhappiness at paying substantial support and their determination not to repeat the mistakes of their first marriages. One 50-year-old man, who had traveled constantly in his first marriage raising money for pension funds, told me he was through being the high earner for the company and wanted more family time in the second part of his life. As he put it, "*I consciously went looking for someone who I could spend time with, who I had a lot in common with, who would want me to stop having to be the big earner all the time. I don't want to die before I've been a real partner to somebody who can stand on her own two feet . . . and I've been a real father.*"

When I first realized how often the desire to co-parent led couples into an egalitarian ideology, I thought this might also lead couples to prioritize their parenting responsibilities over their husband-and-wife relationship. But these were not marriages in which husbands and wives called each other "Mom" and "Dad." For the most part, these couples avoided the rigidly territorial approach I saw in Traditional and Near Peer marriages. In both of these types of couples, I observed mothers who were much more absorbed in their children, which both partners regarded as a primarily female responsibility. As a result, women had sole control over decisions about their children's daily life and used the children as a main source of intimacy, affection and unshared secrets. They related stories about things the children told them that "they would never dare tell their father." While quite a few of the mothers talked about how "close" their husbands were with their children, they would also, usually in the same story, tell me how much closer their children were with them. What surprised me was that while these traditional moms complained about father absence, very few really wanted to change the situation. Most often, it was explained that, while it would be great to have their husband home, they "couldn't afford it." But of course "afford" is a relative term and I sensed that the women really did not want the men interfering with their control over parenting. Or they would have liked more fatherly engagement but definitely not at the cost of loss of income. One young, working Near Peer Couple with four kids was discussing the husband's lesser parenting responsibilities with me when he said, "*You know, I could come home early and get the kids by 3:30. I'd like to do that.*" The wife's response was to straightforwardly insist that with four kids going to private school, his energies were best used paying for their tuitions. She preferred a double shift to a shared one because her financial priorities and her vision of what most profited her children were clear.

But there was an unexpected downside for the couples who did manage to co-parent. I was unprepared for how often Peer Couples mentioned serious conflict over childrearing. Because each partner felt very strongly about the children's upbringing, differences of opinion were not easily resolved. As one peer wife said, "*We are both capable of stepping up to the line and staying there screaming at each other.*" Another husband said, "*If you only talked to us about how we deal with disagreements about the kids, you might think we were a deeply conflicted marriage. We're not. But unfortunately, we have very different ideas about discipline and we can get pretty intense with one another and it might look bad. We went to counseling about the kids and this therapist wanted to look at our whole relationship and we had to say, 'You don't get it. This really is the only thing we argue about like this.'*"

Peers may, in fact, have more conflict about children than more Traditional partners because unlike Traditional Marriage, there is no territory that is automatically ceded to the other person and conflict cannot be resolved by one person claiming the greater right to have the final word. Still, while a majority of Peer Couples mentioned fights over child-related decisions, there were only a few Peer Marriages where I wondered if these arguments threatened the relationship. In the majority of them, the couples talked about how they ultimately, if not in the heat of battle, followed their usual pattern of talking until agreement was reached. What usually forced them to continue to communicate and reach a joint answer was their pledge to give the other partner equal standing in the relationship. Occasionally, a few people told me, they just couldn't reach a mutually satisfying answer and let their partner "win one" out of trust in his or her good judgment, not because they agreed on a given issue.

The couples that I felt might be in more trouble had recurring disagreements that they were never able to resolve over punishments, educational or religious choices or how much freedom to give kids. Furthermore, in each instance at least one partner said that the other partner's approach was beginning to erode the respect that made their relationship possible. Moreover, this particular kind of conflict was deeply troubling since many of them had organized their marriage around the expectation of being great co-parents. It may be that co-parenting requires that parenting philosophies be similar or grow together. Co-parents may have a particular need for good negotiating and communication skills so that they can resolve their differences without threatening the basis of their relationship.

In contrast with traditional or Near Peer Couples, the partners in Peer Marriages never complained about lack of affection or intimacy in their relationships. What they did mention, that other couples did not, was the problem of becoming so familiar with each other that they felt more like siblings than lovers. Some researchers have theorized that sexual arousal is often caused or intensified by anxiety, fear and tension. Many others have written about how sexual desire depends on "Yin" and "Yang" — mystery and difference. And quite a few women and men I talked to rather guiltily confessed that while they wanted equal partners, all their sexual socialization had been to having sex in a hierarchical relationship: Women had fantasies of being "taken" or mildly dominated; men had learned very early on that they were expected to be the orchestrators of any given sexual encounter and that masculinity required sexual directiveness. For men, sexual arousal was often connected with a strong desire to protect or control.

Peer Couples complained that they often forgot to include sex in their daily lives. Unlike Traditional or Near Peers, their sexual frequency did not slow down because of unresolved issues or continuing anger, at least not in any systematic ways. These couples may start to lose interest in sex even more than the other kinds of marriages because sex is not their main way of getting close. Many Traditional and some Near Peer Couples mentioned that the only time they felt that they got through to each other was in bed. Perhaps the more emotional distance couples feel with one another, the larger the role sexuality plays in helping them feel they still have the capacity for intimacy. Being less dependent on this pathway to intimacy, partners in Peer Marriage may be more willing to tolerate a less satisfactory sexual relationship.

One husband, who worked with his wife in their own advertising firm, even talked about having developed "an incest taboo," which had led to the couple entering therapy. They were such buddies during the daytime, he had trouble treating her as anything else in the evening. The therapist this couple consulted encouraged them to assume new personas in the bedroom. For example, he told them to take turns being the dominant partner, to create scenarios where they created new characters and then behaved as they thought the person they were impersonating would behave. He gave them "homework," such as putting themselves in romantic or sexy environments and allowing themselves to imagine meeting there the first time. The wife was encouraged to dress outrageously for bed every now and then; the husband occasionally to be stereotypically directive. The therapist reminded both partners that their emotional bargain was safe: they loved and respected each other. That meant they could use sex as recreation, release and exploration. They were good pupils and felt they had really learned something for a lifetime.

In another couple, it was the wife who mentioned the problem. Her husband had been the dominant partner in his previous marriage and had enjoyed that role in bed. However, she liked more reciprocity and role-sharing in sex, so he tried to be accommodating. However, early on in the relationship he began treating her, as she put it, "*too darn respectfully . . . it was almost as if we were having politically correct sex. . . . I had to remember that he wasn't my brother and it was okay to be sexually far out with him.*"

On the other hand, Peer Couples with satisfying sexual relationships often mentioned their equality as a source of sexual strength. These couples felt their emotional security with one another allowed them to be more uninhibited and made sex more likely since both people were responsible for making it happen. Women with unhappy sexual experiences with sexist men mentioned that for the first time in their lives they could use any sexual position without worrying about any larger meaning in the act. Being on the bottom just meant being on the bottom; it was not about surrendering in more cosmic ways. Being a sex kitten was a role for the evening—and not part of a larger submissive persona.

Many of the Peer Couples I interviewed had terrific sexual lives. The women, especially, felt they had finally met men with whom they could be vulnerable and uninhibited. As one woman said, "*I used to be a real market for women's books. I wanted men who fit the stereotype of Clark Gable or Kevin Costner—few words, and when they are delivered, they are real ringers, and there is a lot of eye contact and passion, and that's about as much talking as you get. Maybe it was dating all these guys who were really like that, but even as fantasy objects, I got tired of men who didn't want to explore a feeling or who were only loving when they had a hard-on. I fell in love the first time sharing Prince of Tides with the guy I was dating, and fell in love with Eric [her husband] over a discussion of Eyes on the Prize. The sexy thing was the conversation and the quality of our minds. . . . I can't imagine anything more boring or ultimately unsexy than a man—and I don't care if he looked like Robert Redford and earned like Donald Trump—who had nothing to say or if he did, didn't get turned on by what I was saying.*"

Equality brings with it the tools to have a great erotic relationship and also, at the same time, the pitfalls that can lead to sexual boredom. If couples learn that their sexual lives need not be constrained by any preconceived idea of what is "egalitarian sex" or appropriate sexual roles, there is no reason that their equality can't work for them. But couples who cannot separate their nights and days, who cannot transcend their identities in everyday life, may need guidance from a knowledgeable counselor.

What enables couples to sustain a style of egalitarian relationship in a world that encourages families to link their economic destiny with the male's career and casts women in an auxiliary worker role so that they can take responsibility for everyday childcare and household chores? In Peer Couples, a sense of shared purpose helps guide the couple back to why they are putting up with all the problems that come from putting together a new model of relationship without societal or familial supports.

Otherwise, it is all too easy for mothers to fall in love with their children and assume primary responsibility for their upbringing or for men to allow their careers to sweep them out of the home, away from their children and back into the more familiar territory they have been trained to inhabit. When this begins to happen, a couple's ideology, almost like an organization's mission statement, helps remind them what their central goal is: the marital intimacy that comes from being part of a well-matched, equally empowered, equally participatory team.

But avoiding traditional hierarchy involves a constant struggle to resist the power of money to define each partner's family roles. Peer Couples continually have to evaluate the role of work in their lives and how much it can infringe on parenting and household responsibilities. If one partner earns or starts to earn a lot more money, and the job starts to take up more time, the couple has to face what this means for their relationship—how much it might distort what they have set out to create.

Peer Couples check in with each other an extraordinary amount to keep their relationship on track. They each have to take responsibility for making sure that they are not drifting too far away from reciprocity. Peer Couples manage to maintain equity in small ways that make sure the balance in their marriage is more than an ideology. If one person has been picking up the kids, the other is planning their summer activities and getting their clothes. Or if one partner has been responsible lately for making sure extended family members are contacted, the other person takes it over for a while. If one partner really decides he or she likes to cook, then the other partner takes on some other equally functional and time-consuming job. There's no reason that each partner can't specialize, but both are careful that one of them doesn't take over all the high-prestige, undemanding jobs while the other ends up with the classically stigmatized assignments (like cleaning bathrooms, or whatever is personally loathed by that person).

Besides monitoring jobs and sharing, couples have to monitor their attitude. Is the wife being treated as a subordinate? Does one person carry around the anger so often seen in someone who feels discounted and unappreciated? Is one person's voice considered more important than the other person's? Is the relationship getting distant, and is the couple starting to lead parallel lives? Do they put in the time required to be best friends and family collaborators? Are they treating each other in the ways that would support a non-romantic relationship of freely associating friends?

There is nothing "natural" or automatic about keeping Peer Marriages going. There will be role discomfort when newly inhabiting the other gender's world. That is why some research shows that men who start being involved with a child from prenatal classes on show more easy attachment and participation in childrearing activities later. While men become comfortable with mothering over time, some need a lot of help. Children will sense who is the primary parent and that will be the person to whom they run, make demands, and from whom they seek daily counsel. One direct way of helping fathers evaluate how they are doing is to help the partners measure how much the children treat them as equally viable sources of comfort and help.

Likewise, being a serious provider is a responsibility some women find absolutely crushing. Most middle-class women were raised to feel that working would be voluntary. After they have made a bargain to do their share of keeping the family economically afloat, they may regret the pressures it puts on them. The old deal of staying at home and being supported can look pretty good after a bad day at the office. But only the exceptional relationship seems to be able to make that traditional provider/mother deal for very long and still sustain a marriage where partners have equal standing in each other's eyes. Couples have to keep reminding themselves how much intimacy, respect and mutual interest they earn in exchange for learning new roles and sustaining the less enjoyable elements of new responsibilities.

Couples who live as peers often attract others like themselves, and the building of a supportive community can modify the impact of the lack of support in the larger world. Like-minded others who have made similar decisions help a lot, especially when critical turning points are reached: such as re-evaluating a career track when it becomes painfully clear that it will not accommodate Peer Family life.

This study yielded no single blueprint for successful Peer Marriage. As in all couples, partners in Peer Marriages require a good measure of honesty, a dedication to fair play, flexibility, generosity and maturity. But most of all, they need to remember what they set out to do and why it was important, at least for them. If they can keep their eyes and hearts on the purpose of it all—if we help them do that—more Peer Marriages will endure and provide a model for others exploring the still-uncharted territory of egalitarian relationships.

15

FAMILIES FORMED OUTSIDE OF MARRIAGE

JUDITH A. SELTZER

It is a sociological truism that the meaning of cohabitation outside of marriage and other family relationships depends on the social context in which they occur. For example, many Latin American countries have long histories of socially accepted consensual unions, which may substitute for formal unions in some groups (De Vos 1999; Parrado and Tienda 1997). Laws about taxes and housing and child allowances treat unmarried and married couples the same in Sweden, where premarital cohabitation is nearly universal (Hoem 1995). In contrast, in the United States, where cohabitation was uncommon until recently, family law gives cohabitors few of the rights of married couples (Gordon 1998/1999). Similarly, U.S. children born outside of marriage lack some advantages that accrue to children born in marriage, unless the former have legally identified fathers.

As cohabitation and nonmarital childbearing become more common, individuals are less likely to think of them as deviant behaviors. Individuals also have fewer incentives to marry before having a child when children born outside of marriage are eligible for the same benefits and accorded the same social recognition as children born in marriage. In the United States, individuals are marrying and forming nonmarital families in a changing social context. Marriage, as an institution, is increasingly defined as a short-term relationship. Divorce is more acceptable now than in the past (Thornton 1989). Laws no longer assume that marriage is forever (Weitzman 1985), and celebrations of marriage are less likely to emphasize its permanence (Furstenberg 1997). The meaning of cohabitation is shifting, in part because the meaning of marriage has shifted. Marriage offers fewer benefits relative to cohabitation now than in the past. Most young people expect to marry and believe that it is important to have a good marriage and family life, but most do not believe that they must marry to live a good life (Thornton 1995).

The meaning of cohabitation and nonmarital relationships also depends on the expectations of those who form the union and on individuals' own experiences within the relationship. Individuals' attitudes on the appropriate conditions for marriage and childbearing, on whether relationships involve lifetime commitments, and on the different rights and responsibilities of women and men in cohabiting and marital relationships affect how they understand their personal relationships. Marriage is an economic arrangement, notwithstanding the expressions of love that accompany the formalization of such unions. Economic uncertainty and scarcity of economic resources increase the likelihood of cohabitation compared with marriage, but rates of cohabitation have risen among those with both low and high levels of education, an indicator of likely economic success. Individuals who decide to live together instead of marrying may do so as a way to evaluate whether their partner will end up as a good economic match (Oppenheimer 1988) or an egalitarian partner (Cherlin 2000). Once couples begin living together, they also develop new ties that bring them closer together (Berger and Kellner 1974). Having children together connects cohabiting partners in addition to the symbolic connections adults create. For some couples, these symbolic and child-based sources of solidarity may reinforce their plans to marry. For other couples, these bonds may make the idea of formalizing their union through marriage less important than when they began living together. The secular rise in the public's acceptance of cohabitation and of childbearing outside of marriage contributes to a decline in cohabiting partners' expectations about whether marriage is the "next step" in their own relationship.

The Rise in Cohabitation and Group Differences in Cohabitation

It was clear by the start of this decade that cohabitation was an important aspect of couple relationships in the United States. Between the mid-1970s and 1980s, young adults became more accepting of nonmarital cohabitation, with increasing percentages agreeing that cohabitation was a "worthwhile experiment" and that it was a good idea to live together before marrying (Thornton 1989). Approval of cohabitation is likely to continue to increase in the future through the process of cohort replacement because young adults are more likely than older adults to believe that it is all right for an unmarried couple to live together even if they have no plans to marry (Bumpass and Sweet 1995; Oropesa 1996). British data also show that compared with older persons, young adults are much more likely to say that they would advise a young person to live with a partner before they marry the partner (Kiernan and Estaugh 1993; see Thornton 1995, for a review of attitudes about cohabitation and changing family patterns). Trends in behavior follow a similar pattern, with each recent birth cohort more likely to cohabit than previous cohorts (Bumpass and Sweet 1989; Chevan 1996). Rates of cohabitation have increased even among older adults, however (Waite 1995). By 1997, there were approximately 4.1 million cohabiting couples of all ages, up from 2.9 million in 1990, an increase of 46% (Casper and Cohen 2000).

The rise in cohabitation is best understood in the context of delayed marriage for recent cohorts compared with cohorts born between the post–World War II period and the mid-1960s. About two thirds of the decline between 1970 and 1985 in the proportion of young adults married by age 25 can be attributed to the rise in nonmarital cohabitation (Bumpass, Sweet, and Cherlin 1991, Table 1). Although much discussion of cohabitation among young adults considers it a stage in the transition to first marriage, Bumpass and his colleagues showed that cohabiting unions also occur after a marriage dissolves and that rising rates of postmarital cohabitation compensated for the decline in remarriage among couples separated in the early 1980s.

These trends have continued for U.S. women in the 1990s. Nearly 40% of women aged 19 to 24 years in 1995 had ever cohabited, compared with just under 30% of women that age in the late 1980s (Bumpass and Lu 2000, Table 1). More than half of first unions in the early 1990s began with cohabitation (Bumpass and Lu, Table 3). The increase in nonmarital cohabitation occurred for all education groups and for Whites, Blacks, and Hispanics, although the increases were greater for those with a high school degree or less and for non-Hispanic Whites than for other groups (Bumpass and Lu, Table 2). Cohabitation continues to offset the decline in marriage for young women (Bumpass and Lu).

Cohabitation remains more common among those with less education and for whom economic resources are more constrained (Bumpass and Lu 2000; Clarkberg 1999; Willis and Michael 1994), perhaps because cohabiting unions require less initial commitment to fulfill long-term economic responsibilities (Clarkberg, Stolzenberg, and Waite 1995; Smock and Manning 1997). Because the institution of marriage includes expectations about economic roles, couples may think that they should reach specific financial goals, such as steady employment or housing of a certain quality, before it is appropriate to marry. Those with low incomes may also think that marriage, with its legal rules about marital property and inheritance, is irrelevant for them given their few material assets (Cherlin 1992). Consistent with higher rates of cohabitation among the economically disadvantaged, cohabitors with more financial resources are more likely to expect to marry their partners (Bumpass et al. 1991). They are also more likely to realize their expectations about marriage than cohabiting couples who are economically disadvantaged (Smock and Manning).

Cohabitation rates have increased at the same time as marriage rates have declined for both Blacks and Whites. By 1998, about two thirds of White women aged 20 to 24 were never married, nearly doubling the percentage never married in 1970. Marriage is even less common for Black women age 20–24, among whom 85% were never married in 1998 (Cherlin 1992).

Rates of marriage or nonmarriage exaggerate Black–White differences in union formation. When one considers both informal unions (cohabitation) and formal unions (marriages), the race difference in the percentage of young women who have entered a union is reduced by about one half (Raley 1996). Puerto Ricans also enter informal unions at high rates. Compared with non-Hispanic Whites, Puerto Ricans are less likely to marry their cohabiting partners (Landale and Forste 1991). Explanations for race and ethnic differences in cohabitation patterns draw on both cultural and economic factors. Landale and Fennelly (1992), for example, argued that the long history of social recognition of consensual unions in many Latin American countries explains in part why Puerto Rican women, compared to non-Hispanic White women, are less likely to formalize their unions, even when children are involved.

When men's economic circumstances are precarious, young adults delay marriage (Oppenheimer, Kalmijn, and Lim 1997). Those who are economically insecure, including those still enrolled in school, may choose cohabitation over marriage (Thornton, Axinn, and Teachman 1995; Willis and Michael 1994). Among cohabiting couples, those in which the male partner is more economically secure are more likely to marry than those in which the male partner is economically insecure (Smock and Manning 1997). Economic factors alone, however, do not explain race differences in union formation (Raley 1996), pointing again to the need for explanations that take account of both cultural and economic factors. That men's declining labor market prospects explain some, but not all, of the delay in marriage between 1960 and 1980 for Black and White men reinforces the need to consider both economic and noneconomic factors to account for temporal and cross-sectional differences in union formation (Mare and Winship 1991).

Cohabitation as a Stage Before Marriage or as an End in Itself

That family scholars in the 1980s regarded cohabitation in the United States as a transitional stage between being single and marrying is evident from the organization of the 1990 *Journal of Marriage and the Family* decade reviews. Ten years ago, cohabitation was examined in the review of research on mate selection and premarital relationships (Surra 1990). Cohabitors themselves also saw their unions as a way to assess marital compatibility (Bumpass et al. 1991, Table 7). Most either had definite plans to marry their cohabiting partner or thought they would marry their partner (Bumpass et al., Table 9). Among young adults, never-married cohabitors are usually intermediate between those who are single and those who are in first marriages on attitudes and socioeconomic characteristics. On most of these dimensions, cohabitors are more similar to single, noncohabiting adults than to those who are married (Rindfuss and VandenHeuvel 1990). Because cohabitation may occur either before a first marriage or with a new partner after a divorce, it is instructive to compare the characteristics of single and cohabiting persons, taking account of whether they have ever been married. Casper and Bianchi (Forthcoming, Table 3) show that, among 25- to 34-year-old adults, never-married singles and cohabitors are more similar to each other than they are to ever-married singles and cohabitors on education, per capita income, and use of food stamps. Ever-married singles and cohabitors resemble each other on these characteristics and are generally more disadvantaged than the never-marrieds, regardless of cohabitation status. Comparisons on other characteristics show more variation in which groups bear the greatest resemblance.

Not surprisingly, cohabiting women are more similar to married women than to single women in their sexual and contraceptive behavior due to their greater exposure to risk (Bachrach 1987). Although adults in cohabiting relationships report that they have sex more frequently than those who are married, once the younger age of cohabitors is taken into account, the difference diminishes (Laumann et al. 1994). Never-married cohabiting couples are less likely to have a child together than are married couples, but they are significantly more likely to have a child compared with single women (Manning and Landale 1996; Wu, Bumpass, and Musick 1999). However, race and economic characteristics affect the degree to which cohabiting couples' fertility resembles that of married couples (Loomis and Landale 1994; Manning and Landale 1996).

Although cohabitation is often a prelude to marriage, cohabiting unions may be an end in themselves for an increasing percentage of cohabitors. These cohabitors do not necessarily reject marriage. Instead, cohabitors are less likely to see marriage as the defining characteristic of their family lives. Fewer cohabitations end in marriage now than in the past. In the 1970s, about 60% of cohabitors who formed unions at age 25 or older married their partners within 3 years of starting to live together, compared with only about 35% in the early 1990s (Bumpass 1995, figure 6; see Bumpass 1998, for replication using different data). Thus, fewer cohabitations are a stage on the way to marriage, either because the partners never intended to marry in the first place or because other changes in their circumstances altered their intentions or their ability to fulfill their intentions.

Change in the meaning of nonmarital cohabitation also comes from the growing importance of cohabitation as a setting in which couples bear and rear children. The percentage of cohabitors who had biological children together increased from 12% in the early 1980s to 15% in the early 1990s (Bumpass, personal communication, 1999). Although these percentages are still low, the change is a 25% increase over a short time. Having a child in the relationship may change how the couple thinks of their union. For example, among Puerto Rican women interviewed in a survey that allowed them to describe their unions as either informal marriages (i.e., they thought of themselves as married) or cohabitations, women who had borne children outside formal marriage were much more likely to describe their relationship as an informal marriage than women without children (Landale and Fennelly 1992).

At the same time that cohabitors have become more likely to bear children together, the percentage of all children who are born to unmarried parents in the United States increased from about 18% in 1980 to nearly a third in 1997 (Smith, Morgan, and Koropeckyj-Cox 1996; Ventura et al. 1999), a trend I discuss further below. Cohabiting couples are responsible for much of this increase in nonmarital childbearing. In the early 1980s, cohabiting couples had 29% of nonmarital births, compared with 39% a decade later (Bumpass and Lu 2000). About 20% of nonmarital births occur in cohabiting unions after a first marriage has ended in separation or divorce, among women born since 1945 (Brown 2000). Children born to cohabiting parents begin life in a household with both biological parents, but researchers and policy makers often assume that these children live in a single-mother household.

Single women who become pregnant are increasingly likely to move in with rather than marry the father of their child. In the past, many of these pregnancies were "premarital" pregnancies that resulted in marital births; a single woman who became pregnant married the father of their child. (See Parnell, Swicegood, and Stevens 1994 on declines in "legitimation" in the postwar period.) As recently as the early 1980s, about 20% of single noncohabiting women who had a pregnancy that resulted in a live birth married by the time the child was born. By the early 1990s, only 11% did so. Over this same period, the percentage of pregnant single women who began cohabiting by the time their child was born increased from 6% to 9% (Raley forthcoming). Thus, women are almost as likely to form nonmarital cohabiting unions as marry when they have a child. Cohabiting couples also care for children brought to the union by only one of the partners. Nearly half of cohabiting couples live with children (Bumpass, personal communication, 1999), and cohabiting couples make up one fourth of all stepfamilies (Bumpass Raley, and Sweet 1995).

Stability of Cohabiting Unions

Cohabiting unions end quickly because the couple either marries or breaks up. Half end in a year or less for one of these reasons (Bumpass and Lu 2000). Compared with married couples, cohabitors are much more likely to break up. About 29% of cohabitors and only 9% of married couples break up within the first 2 years (Bumpass and Sweet 1989, Table 4). Over the past decade, cohabiting unions have become even less stable, but this is mainly because of the decline in the percentage of cohabitors who eventually marry their partners (Bumpass and Lu). Within 5 years, more than half of unions begun by cohabitation have ended, regardless of whether the couple formalized the union by marrying (Bumpass and Lu). In Canada, cohabiting unions may also be less stable than in the past (Wu and Balakrishnan 1995). Informal unions dissolve more quickly than do formal marriages because of differences in the quality of the match between partners who marry and those who do not, the strength of normative consensus favoring marriage, the legal and social institutions that support formal marriage over cohabitation, and differences in the attitudes and resources of cohabitors and those who marry.

Marriages preceded by cohabitation are more likely to end in separation or divorce than marriages in which the couple did not live together previously

(Bumpass and Lu 2000; Laumann et al. 1994; Lillard, Brien, and Waite 1995; Sweet and Bumpass 1992). For instance, about 16% of marriages preceded by cohabitation broke up within the first 5 years, compared with about 10% of marriages not preceded by cohabitation among women born in the mid-1930s. For women born a decade later who were marrying during the 1960s when divorce rates were rising, the contrast is 31% compared with 16%, respectively (Schoen 1992, Table 1). However, for women born more recently, there is some evidence of convergence in the rates of marital dissolution between those who cohabited and those who did not (Schoen; but see Bumpass and Lu 2000, who reported that the higher disruption rates for marriages preceded by cohabitation persist for a more recent period).

In Britain, premarital cohabitation is also associated with higher rates of marital disruption (Berrington and Diamond 1999). In France, however, Leridon (1990) found that premarital cohabitation does not affect the stability of first marriage. Both cohort and country variation in the association between premarital cohabitation and marital disruption support my earlier claim that the social context affects who cohabits and the meaning and consequences of cohabitation.

In the United States, higher divorce rates for couples who cohabit before marriage may be due to differences in the background, attitudes, and behavior of those who choose premarital cohabitation compared with those who do not. Yet if young adults are correct in their belief that cohabitation is a worthwhile experiment for evaluating the compatibility of a potential spouse, one would expect those who cohabit first to have even more stable marriages than those who marry without cohabiting once preexisting differences between those who cohabit before marriage and those who do not are taken into account. Alternatively, the experience of premarital cohabitation may damage the couple's prospect of having a stable marriage. (See Axinn and Thornton 1992; Sweet and Bumpass 1992.)

Evidence for whether cohabitation *causes* an increase in the chance of divorce is mixed. Young men and women with liberal gender-role attitudes are more likely to cohabit than to marry (Clarkberg et al. 1995). Similarly, those who hold more negative attitudes about marriage and are more accepting of divorce have higher rates of cohabitation and generally lower rates of marriage (Axinn and Thornton 1992). Childhood family characteristics associated with marital disruption also affect whether a person cohabits or marries. Growing up in a single-parent household increases the likelihood of cohabiting in the United States and in Great Britain (Bumpass and Sweet 1989; Thornton 1991). Longitudinal surveys do not measure all of the personality traits and attitudes that distinguish cohabitors from those who marry. Higher rates of marital disruption for those who have previously cohabited disappear when these unobserved differences are taken into account with econometric techniques (Lillard et al. 1995). For German couples, premarital cohabitation actually enhances marital stability after statistical adjustments for unmeasured differences, such as attitudes and the quality of the couple's relationship, between those who cohabit and those who do not (Brüderl, Diekmann, and Engelhardt 1997). The statistical techniques used in these studies require assumptions that are difficult to meet, but the similarity in findings and their consistency with other longitudinal analyses is reassuring on this point.

Young adults also become more tolerant of divorce as a result of cohabiting, whatever their initial views are (Axinn and Thornton 1992). Cohabitation may expose partners to a wider range of attitudes about family arrangements than those who marry without first living together. In addition, how cohabitors organize their daily lives may carry over into marriage (see below). Women and men in cohabiting couples divide housework somewhat more equally and bring home more similar earnings than married couples (Brines and Joyner 1999; Nock 1995). If these patterns carry over into marriage, they may contribute to higher divorce rates for those who cohabited before marriage because marital solidarity may depend on a specialized division of labor. Couples who cohabited before marriage may find that attempts to pursue a more egalitarian division of labor in marriage, a social institution that promotes a gendered division of labor, creates strain and conflict, which in turn increase the likelihood of divorce (Brines and Joyner). Researchers have done little to address the following questions: How and why do cohabiting couples decide to marry (or not to marry)? And how, if at all, does marriage change their behavior and feelings about the relationship (see Bumpass and Sweet forthcoming)?

On balance, both the "people who cohabit are different" and "cohabitation changes people" interpretations are supported by recent studies. None of the studies cited above provides definitive evidence on which is the better interpretation of higher divorce rates for those who cohabit before marriage. Much past research focuses on individuals and their attitudes, to the exclusion of partners' attitudes and the characteristics of their union, including how those who cohabit and those who marry organize their lives. Nevertheless, studies using different data and different methods of analysis consistently show that those who live together before marriage come from more "divorce-prone" families and hold more liberal attitudes toward divorce than do those who do not cohabit before marriage. Claims that individuals who cohabit before marriage hurt their chances of a good marriage pay too little attention to this evidence.

Paradoxically, whatever the effect of cohabiting on divorce at the level of the relationship, the instability of individual cohabiting unions stabilizes the rate of divorce. Many relationships that would have been short-term marriages dissolve before couples marry. Living together shows the couple that marriage is not for them, so they break up before formalizing their union. Demographers speculate that this removes some "high-risk" marriages from the pool of marriages that contributes to the formal divorce rate (Bumpass and Lu 2000; Bumpass and Sweet 1989). Recently, however, Goldstein's (1999) simulation provides evidence against this interpretation, suggesting that the rise in cohabitation explains little, if any, of the stabilization in the divorce rate.

How Cohabitors Organize Their Lives:
Work, Couple, and Kin Ties

That couples who cohabit differ in their attitudes about gender roles and family institutions suggests that they may organize their daily lives differently from those who choose to marry. Much of what we know about the organization of cohabiting couples' lives and how their lives compare to the lives of married couples builds on the rich information provided by Blumstein and Schwartz (1983) in their study of couple relationships in the United States. Cohabiting couples have greater flexibility in the degree to which they follow the gender-based division of labor and family responsibilities that is characteristic of formal marriage. Because some couples use cohabitation as a testing ground to evaluate a partner's compatibility, women (and men) who want to marry someone who will share most household and childrearing tasks may be particularly likely to live with a partner before marriage to observe and negotiate these arrangements. Whether the greater similarity in women's and men's roles within cohabitation than in marriage is due to the different goals that cohabitors bring to their relationship or to the lack of institutional supports for a gender-based division of labor is still an open question.

Recent data from large, national probability surveys, such as the National Survey of Families and Households (Sweet and Bumpass 1996), provide similar information on the experiences of heterosexual couples in formal and informal unions. These data show that compared with wives, women in cohabiting couples do fewer hours of housework but more hours of paid work. When differences between married and cohabiting couples in education, paid work, and the presence of children are taken into account, women in cohabiting couples still do about 6 fewer hours of housework than wives do. This is consistent with the finding cited above that compared with those who marry, cohabitors have more liberal gender-role attitudes when they begin their relationship. There are small differences, if any, in housework time for men by whether they are in formal or informal unions (Shelton and John 1993; South and Spitze 1994). In both marriage and cohabitation, women do more housework than men do, but the somewhat greater similarity between women's and men's paid and unpaid work in cohabiting unions suggests that the role responsibilities of female cohabiting partners may differ from those of female marriage partners.

Because cohabiting women perceive their relationships as less secure and as more likely to dissolve than formal marriages, they may be less willing to limit their paid labor force participation or to invest extra effort in housework to the detriment of their participation in the paid labor force. Both women and men may be less committed to their relationships when they cohabit than when they marry. Compared with those who are married, women and men in pre- and post-marital cohabiting unions see fewer costs and more benefits to breaking up (Nock 1995). A recent study in Norway also showed that a majority of cohabitors, regardless of whether they had a child together, are reluctant to marry because marriages are difficult to dissolve (Kravdal 1999, Table 6). These perceptions of the barriers to breaking up are realistic assessments. Married couples are more likely to pool their financial resources and have other relationship-specific investments, including biological children born to the union, than are cohabiting couples (Blumstein and Schwartz 1983; Loomis and Landale 1994). Another indication that spouses are more committed than are cohabitors to their relationships comes from the U.S. National Health and Social Life Survey of adults, which showed that marriages are more likely to be sexually exclusive than cohabitations, even taking account of cohabitors' more permissive values (Treas and Giesen 2000). We do not know, however, whether partners who invest more in their relationship do so because it is a good relationship or whether the relationship improves and becomes stronger as a result of the partners' investments.

Cohabiting partners may evaluate the success of their union using different criteria than do spouses in formal marriage. For instance, because they hold more egalitarian attitudes, young adult cohabitors may observe how their housework is actually divided to assess whether the relationship is "working." Cohabiting couples in which partners have similar earnings are more stable than those with dissimilar earnings. In contrast, among married couples, a more specialized division of labor, in which wives are not employed but husbands are, increases marital stability, as noted above (Brines and Joyner 1999).

Cohabiting couples face more disapproval of their relationship and receive less social support than do married couples. The lack of support may contribute to higher rates of disruption for cohabiting unions. Although the general public has grown increasingly tolerant of nonmarital cohabitation, parents may prefer that their children marry rather than cohabit. When mothers think marriage is important, their daughters are less likely to cohabit than when mothers hold less favorable attitudes about marriage (Axinn and Thornton 1992). Similarly, data from young adults in the Netherlands show that young adults' intentions to cohabit depend on whether they think that their parents and friends would support their decision (Liefbroer and Gierveld 1993).

Cohabitation may strain relationships between parents and adult children. Members of married couples describe their relationships with parents more positively than do cohabiting couples (Nock 1995). Parents also report closer relationships with married children than with cohabiting children (Aquilino 1997). On the other hand, members of cohabiting couples are almost as likely as members of married couples to have been introduced to each other by a family member, which suggests that spouses and cohabiting partners may be part of similar social circles (Laumann et al. 1994, Table 6.1) Parents whose children cohabit are also more likely than those whose children are single (and not cohabiting) to share with each other leisure activities, meals, and enjoyable times and to have emotionally close relationships (Aquilino).

Cohabitation, Childbearing, and Childrearing

Do Cohabiting Couples Marry Because They Want Children?

If cohabiting unions are experiments that young couples undertake to decide if they should marry, is there an end to the experiment or some precipitating event that prompts couple members to marry? Cohabiting couples who decide that they are ready to have children may decide to marry as a first step toward having a child. Cohabiting couples in which the woman becomes pregnant (and does not have an abortion) are more likely to marry than are couples in which the woman is not pregnant (Manning 1995), although this effect is greater for White than for Black women (Manning and Smock 1995). Pregnancy also increases marriage among cohabitors in Sweden, a setting with fewer institutional barriers to childbearing outside of formal marriage than in the United States (Bracher and Santow 1998). Cohabiting couples in the United States who already have children, whether born to the couple or in previous relationships, are more likely to marry than those without children (Manning and Smock 1995). This finding is not consistent across settings, however. In Canada, which has also experienced a rise in cohabitation, couples who have a child in their cohabiting union are less likely to marry than those who have not had a child in their union (Wu and Balakrishnan 1995). Childbearing in cohabitation reduces the chance that a couple will break up, whether or not they formalize their union (Wu and Balakrishnan).

Effects of Cohabitation on Children's Family Experiences

As noted above, much of the recent rise in childbearing outside of marriage can be attributed to childbearing in cohabiting unions. Children in these unions start life in households with both of their biological parents instead of in a single-mother household. For new parents in Oakland, California, and Austin, Texas, about half of unmarried mothers who have just had a child report that they are living with their child's father (McLanahan, Garfinkel, and Padilla 1999a; McLanahan, Garfinkel, and Waller 1999b). Even if these reports overstate the extent of cohabitation at childbirth, perhaps because the interview occurred at a time of great optimism about the strength of the couple's relationship (L. Wu, personal communication, 1999), these children are born into families in which both parents are present, at least for a time.

Inferences about children's living arrangements from parents' marital status provide a misleading picture of recent demographic trends, such as the rise of "single"-father families. For instance, Garasky and Meyer (1996) showed that treating cohabitors as two-parent families reduces estimates of the growth in "single"-father families between 1960 and 1990 from about 240% to about 120%. Cohabitation also reduces the amount of time that children will spend in a single-parent household during childhood. Estimates using marital status to infer whether both parents are present have shown that children in recent cohorts will spend a median of nearly 7 years in a single-parent household from the time they first enter it. When cohabiting parents are taken into account, the median duration drops to 3.7 years (Bumpass and Raley 1995).

At first glance, taking cohabitation into account suggests that children's lives have become more stable. Yet because cohabiting unions are usually short-term relationships, taking cohabitation into account increases the number of family disruptions children experience. Just over one third of children born in either a marital or cohabiting union will experience the break-up of their parents' relationship before the end of their teenage years, and this fraction increased in the decade between the early 1980s and the 1990s (Bumpass and Lu 2000:37). Cohabitation also affects children's experience in stepfamilies, many of which are begun informally when a parent brings a new partner into the household, rather than by formal marriage. By the early 1980s, almost two thirds of children who entered a stepfamily did so by cohabitation instead of marriage (Bumpass et al. 1995, Table 2). Once children enter a stepfamily, the rates at which they face the dissolution of their stepfamily are similar whether the stepfamily began by cohabitation or by marriage (Bumpass et al. 1995, Table 4). The similarity in rates of disruption for cohabiting and remarried stepfamilies suggests that there is less selection into cohabiting unions after a first relationship ends than into premarital cohabiting unions.

Effects of Cohabitation on Children

Adults who live with children share resources with them. A parent's cohabiting partner is likely to contribute toward the economic costs of raising the child(ren). These contributions may occur because the parent and her partner pool their incomes or because the child shares the household's public goods, such as housing, even if the cohabiting partners do not pool all of their incomes. The National Academy of Sciences report on measuring poverty recognizes that cohabiting partners' resources are important for family members' economic well-being. The report recommends that poverty measures treat cohabitors as part of the same family (Citro and Michael 1995). Cohabitors are included in the definition of "family" because of their likely pooling of income, economies of scale, and potential for continued resource sharing for several years. Although we know little about the extent to which cohabiting partners pool their incomes, Bauman (1999) finds that compared with spouses, cohabitors pool less of their income. Partners may be more likely to pool their incomes when they have a child together or have lived together a long time (Winkler 1997).

Income from a parent's cohabiting partner reduces by almost 30% the number of children in cohabiting-couple families who are in poverty (Manning and Lichter 1996). The rise in cohabitation over the past several decades implies that assessments of trends in poverty may overstate poverty in the more recent period relative to poverty rates a few decades ago. In fact, once cohabiting partners are included as family members and contributors to family income, the increase between 1969 and 1989 in child poverty from

13.1% to 18.7%, as measured by official statistics, would have been about 11% less (Carlson and Danziger 1999). Children whose parents cohabit are still more likely to be poor than those in married-couple families because of the age, education, and employment differentials between those who cohabit and those who marry.

In addition to the economic implications for children's well-being, married and cohabiting parents may follow different childrearing practices. Compared with stepfathers, male cohabiting partners devote less time to organized youth activities at school, religious, or other community organizations. Otherwise, however, stepfathers and male cohabiting partners pursue similar activities with children (Thomson, McLanahan, and Curtin 1992). Cohabiting fathers may pursue fewer organized activities because they often are arranged for children's socially recognized parents, and those who are cohabiting may be reluctant to participate unless they are married to the child's mother. We know little about how parents' cohabiting partners affect children's family experience, although studies are beginning to distinguish cohabiting-couple families from married-"intact" families and stepfamilies (Hanson, McLanahan, and Thomson 1997; Thomson, Hanson and McLanahan 1994). Efforts to compare childrearing practices of cohabiting parents to those of married biological parents and married stepparents are limited by small sample sizes, even in studies that include oversamples of cohabiting families (Bumpass and Lu 2000; Thomson et al. 1998). . . .

Behavioral and Legal Definitions of Family

Cohabitation and childbearing outside of marriage are central features of growth in families formed outside of marriage. Relationships between cohabiting couples and between many parents of babies born outside of marriage are defined by coresidence and sharing a household. Nonmarital family relationships also cross household boundaries, as when parents and children live apart after divorce. Contact and financial transfers from nonresident parents to minor children help define family ties that may be important for children's welfare (Seltzer 1991, 1994). Cohabitation, childbearing outside of marriage, and relationships between parents and minor children who live apart are all families that exist largely without formal recognition by the state, although state laws about child support are an important exception to the lack of formal recognition. Individual citizens and policy makers seek to formalize relationships between cohabiting couples and fathers and children who live apart to acquire rights and, from the policy makers' side, establish responsibilities.

Two aspects of cohabiting unions may be formalized: rights and responsibilities within the union, including property and inheritance, and rights and responsibilities with respect to the state and other third parties (e.g., Blumberg 1981, 1985). Rights within the union can be formalized by individual contracts and other legal procedures the couple members can initiate. Establishing these legal contracts may be expensive, which means that they are not universally available because cohabitation is more common among the economically disadvantaged.

Rights with respect to third parties, such as social insurance claims, access to health insurance and other "family" benefits, derive from public action, including the passage of state laws, city ordinances establishing domestic partnership licenses, and policies adopted by employers. Vermont's recent civil union legislation tries to formalize both aspects of nonmarital unions for same-sex couples. The legislation provides same-sex couples who establish a civil union with the rights and obligations of marriage and requires that when a civil union dissolves, it is governed by the laws for marital dissolution. Other domestic partner laws apply to both same-sex and opposite-sex partnerships but may limit the types of heterosexual couples who are allowed to register as domestic partners. For instance, the California Assembly bill (AB 26, 1999–2000) on domestic partners allows same-sex adult partners or seniors to register as partners if they live together and agree to be jointly responsible for each other's living expenses. The bill gives partners the same rights to hospital visitation as members of married families have, as well as rights to health insurance benefits. The substantial variation across states in the availability of domestic partnership registration, the eligibility rules, and the benefits and responsibilities of registration demonstrates public disagreement about the meaning of cohabitation and its place in the U.S. kinship system. The rapidly changing opportunities to acquire domestic partnerships and the diverse record keeping systems make it difficult to study these arrangements. We know little about the prevalence of domestic partnerships, the content of the agreements, who acquires the partnerships, and the consequences of the partnerships for the nature and stability of the relationship, although researchers are beginning to address these questions (e.g., Willetts and Scanzoni 1998). . . .

Cohabitation and Nonmarital Childbearing: Individual and Social Matters

Families matter for individuals. What happens in our families affects how we live our lives, whether we are rich or poor, the languages we speak, the work that we do, how healthy we are, and how we feel. Families also matter for the larger social group. Family members take care of each other (some better than others) and bear and rear the next generation. Within a society, the work families do depends on what people believe is the right way to treat parents, siblings, children, grandparents, and other kin. A common understanding about the obligations and rights of family members contributes to the institutionalization of family relationships. General consensus in public opinion about who should be counted as a family member and consistent laws also institutionalize relationships. Cohabitation, like remarriage, is still an incomplete institution in the United States (Cherlin 1978; Nock 1995). It takes a long time for new behaviors to become institutionalized.

The rapid increase in cohabitation and nonmarital childbearing over the past few decades suggests that these relationships may become more complete institutions in the future, but it is unlikely that they will have the preferred standing of marriage and childbearing in marriage any time soon. Cohabiting couples are very diverse, in part because they are forming their relationships under a rapidly changing set of social rules about marriage, cohabitation, and childbearing outside of marriage. The instability of the environment in which individuals make family choices hampers the enforcement of kin obligations and norms about the acceptability of informal families and makes it even more likely that individuals will experiment in their family lives.

Some cohabitors would prefer formal marriage, but their economic circumstances prevent them from achieving this goal. Others seek a different type of relationship, one with greater gender equality, than they expect to find in marriage or than they found in a previous marriage. Yet another group of cohabitors uses their informal relationship as a trial period during which they negotiate and assess whether to formalize their union through marriage. We do not know the relative size of these groups in the population nor do we know how rapidly each group is growing. The heterogeneity of cohabiting couples poses a challenge to researchers who try to understand what cohabitation means.

Adults have more choices today about whether to cohabit and whether to have a child outside of marriage because the social costs, at least to adults, of forming informal families are much less today than just a few decades ago. Choosing one's family is part of a long-term trend toward greater individual autonomy in West Europe and the United States (Lesthaeghe 1995). The ability to choose at the individual level, however, does not mean that all choices will or should have the same standing in the public sphere. Nevertheless, the inclusion of a decade review on families formed outside of marriage in the *Journal of Marriage and the Family* demonstrates the greater legitimacy of individual choice in the contemporary United States and suggests even greater variation in informal families in the near future.

ENDNOTE

Author's Note: This work was supported, in part, by a grant from the Council on Research of the UCLA Academic Senate. The paper benefited from discussion with seminar participants at the University of California, Berkeley; University of Washington; University of California, Riverside; RAND; University of Virginia; University of Wisconsin–Madison; and Notre Dame University. I am grateful to Suzanne Bianchi, Larry Bumpass, Lynne Casper, Wendy Manning, Robert Mare, Kelly Musick, R. Kelly Raley, Christine Schwartz, and Pamela Smock for helpful advice, discussion, and comments on previous versions.

REFERENCES

Aquilino, W. S. 1997. "From Adolescent to Young Adult: A Prospective Study of Parent–Child Relations during the Transition to Adulthood." *Journal of Marriage and the Family* 59:670–86.

Axinn, W. G. and A. Thornton. 1992. "The Relationship between Cohabitation and Divorce: Selectivity or Causal Influence?" *Demography* 29:357–74.

Bachrach, C. A. 1987. "Cohabitation and Reproductive Behavior in the United States." *Demography* 24:623–37.

Bauman, K. J. 1999. "Shifting Family Definitions: The Effect of Cohabitation and Other Nonfamily Household Relationships on Measures of Poverty." *Demography* 36:315–25.

Berger, R. L., and H. Kellner. 1974. "Marriage and the Construction of Reality." Pp. 157–74 in *The Family: Its Structures and Functions*, 2d ed., edited by R. L. Coser. New York: St. Martin's Press.

Berrington, A. and I. Diamond. 1999. "Marital Dissolution among the 1958 British Birth Cohort: The Role of Cohabitation." *Population Studies* 53:19–38.

Blumberg, G. G. 1981. "Cohabitation without Marriage: A Different Perspective." *UCLA Law Review* 28:1125–80.

——. 1985. "New Models of Marriage and Divorce: Significant Legal Developments in the Last Decade." In *Contemporary Marriage: Comparative Perspectives on a Changing Institution*, edited by K. Davis with A. Grossbard-Shechtman. New York: Russell Sage.

Blumstein, R. and R. Schwartz. 1983. *American Couples: Money, Work and Sex*. New York: William Morrow.

Bracher, M. and G. Santow. 1998. "Economic Independence and Union Formation in Sweden." *Population Studies* 52:275–94.

Brines, J. and K. Joyner. 1999. "The Ties That Bind: Principles of Cohesion in Cohabitation and Marriage." *American Sociological Review* 64:333–55.

Brown, S. S. 2000. "Fertility Following Marital Dissolution: The Role of Cohabitation." *Journal of Family Issues* 21:501–524.

Brüderl, J., A. Diekmann, and H. Engelhardt. 1997, August. "Premarital Cohabitation and Marital Stability in West Germany." Paper presented at the annual meeting of the American Sociological Association, Toronto.

Bumpass, L. L. 1995. "The Declining Significance of Marriage: Changing Family Life in the United States." National Survey of Families and Households Working Paper No. 66. Center for Demography and Ecology, University of Wisconsin, Madison.

——. 1998. "The Changing Significance of Marriage in the United States." Pp. 63–79 in *The Changing Family in Comparative Perspective: Asia and the United States*, edited by K. O. Masou, N. O. Tsuya, and M. K. Choe. Honolulu: East-West Center.

Bumpass, L. L. and H. H. Lu. 2000. "Trends in Cohabitation and Implications for Children's Family Contexts in the United States." *Population Studies* 54:29–41.

Bumpass, L. L. and R. K. Raley. 1995. "Redefining Single-Parent Families: Cohabitation and Changing Family Realty. *Demography* 32:97–109.

Bumpass, L. L., R. K. Raley, and J. A. Sweet. 1995. "The Changing Character of Stepfamilies: Implications of Cohabitation and Nonmarital Childbearing." *Demography* 32:425–36.

Bumpass, L. L., and J. A. Sweet. 1989. "National Estimates of Cohabitation." *Demography* 26:615–25.

——. 1995. "Cohabitation, Marriage, and Nonmarital Childbearing and Union Stability: Preliminary Findings from NSFH2." National Survey of Families and Households Working Paper No. 65. Center for Demography and Ecology, University of Wisconsin, Madison.

——. Forthcoming. "Marriage, Divorce, and Intergenerational Relationships." In *The Well-Being of Children and Families*, edited by A. Thornton. Ann Arbor: University of Michigan Press.

Bumpass, L. L., J. A. Sweet, and A. J. Cherlin. 1991. "The Role of Cohabitation in Declining Rates of Marriage." *Journal of Marriage and the Family* 53:913–27.

Carlson, M. and S. Danziger. 1999. "Cohabitation and the Measurement of Child Poverty." *Review of Income and Wealth* 2:179–91.

Casper, L. M. and S. M. Bianchi. Forthcoming. "Cohabitation." In *Trends in the American Family.* Thousand Oaks, CA: Sage.

Casper, L. M. and P. N. Cohen. 2000. "How Does POSSLQ Measure Up? Historical Estimates of Cohabitation." *Demography* 37:237–45.

Cherlin, A. J. 1978. "Remarriage as an Incomplete Institution." *American Journal of Sociology* 84:634–50.

——. 1992. *Marriage, Divorce, Remarriage.* Cambridge, MA: Harvard University Press.

——. 2000. "Toward a New Home Socioeconomics of Union Formation." Pp. 126–44 in *Ties That Bind: Perspectives on Marriage and Cohabitation,* edited by L. J. Waite, C. Bachrach, M. Hindin, E. Thomson, and A. Thornton. Hawthorne, NY: Aldine de Gruyter.

Chevan, A. 1996. "As Cheaply as One: Cohabitation in the Older Population." *Journal of Marriage and the Family* 58:656–67.

Citro, C. F. and R. T. Michael, eds. 1995. *Measuring Poverty: A New Approach.* Washington, DC: National Academy Press.

Clarkberg, J. 1999. "The Price of Partnering: The Role of Economic Well-Being in Young Adults' First Union Experiences." *Social Forces* 77:945–68.

Clarkberg, M., R. M. Stolzenberg, and L. J. Waite. 1995. "Attitudes, Values, and Entrance into Cohabitational versus Marital Unions." *Social Forces* 74:609–34.

De Vos, S. 1999. "Comment of Coding Marital Status in Latin America." *Journal of Comparative Family Studies* 30:79–93.

Furstenberg, F. F., Jr. 1997, January. *Family Change and Family Diversity: Accounts of the Past and Scenarios of the Future.* Paper prepared for the Conference on Common Values, Social Diversity, and Cultural Conflict, Center for Advanced Study in the Behavioral Sciences, Stanford, CA.

Garasky, S. and D. R. Meyer. 1996. "Reconsidering the Increase in Father-Only Families." *Demography* 33:385–93.

Goldstein, J. R. 1999. "The Leveling of Divorce in the United States." *Demography* 36:409–14.

Gordon, K. C. 1998/1999. "The Necessity and Enforcement of Cohabitation Agreements: When Strings Will Attach and How to Prevent Them. A State Survey." *University of Louisville Brandeis Law* 37:245–57.

Hanson, T. L., S. McLanahan, and E. Thomson. 1997. "Economic Resources, Parental Practices, and Children's Well-Being." Pp. 190–238 in *Consequences of Growing Up Poor,* edited by G. Duncan and J. Brooks-Gunn. New York: Russell Sage.

Hoem, B. 1995. "Sweden." Pp. 35–55 in *The New Role of Women: Family Formation in Modern Societies,* edited by H. P Blossfeld. Boulder, CO: Westview Press.

Kiernan, K. E. and V. Estaugh. 1993. *Cohabitation: Extra-marital Childbearing and Social Policy.* Occasional Paper No. 17. London: Family Policy Studies Centre.

Kravdal, O. 1999. "Does Marriage Require a Stronger Economic Underpinning than Informal Cohabitation?" *Population Studies* 53:63–80.

Landale, N. S. and K. Fennelly. 1992. "Informal Unions among Mainland Puerto Ricans: Cohabitation or an Alternative to Legal Marriage?" *Journal of Marriage and the Family.* 54:269–80.

Landale, N. S. and R. Forste. 1991. "Patterns of Entry into Cohabitation and Marriage among Mainland Puerto Rican Women." *Demography* 28:587–607.

Laumann, E. O., J. H. Gagnon, R. T. Michael, and S. Michaels. 1994. *The Social Organization of Sexuality: Sexual Practices in the United States.* Chicago: University of Chicago Press.

Leridon, H. 1990. "Cohabitation, Marriage, Separation: An Analysis of Life Histories of French Cohorts from 1968 to 1985." *Population Studies* 44:127–44.

Lesthaeghe, R. 1995. "The Second Demographic Transition in Western Countries: An Interpretation." Pp. 17–82 in *Gender and Family Change in Industrialized Countries,* edited by K. O. Mason and A. M. Jensen. Oxford, UK: Clarendon Press.

Liefbroer, A. C. and J. D. J. Gierveld. 1993. "The Impact of Rational Considerations and Perceived Opinions on Young Adults' Union Formation Intentions." *Journal of Family Issues* 14:213–35.

Lillard, L. A., M. J. Brien, and L. J. Waite. 1995. "Premarital Cohabitation and Subsequent Marital Dissolution: A Matter of Self-Selection." *Demography* 32:437–57.

Loomis, L. S. and N. S. Landale. 1994. "Nonmarital Cohabitation and Childbearing among Black and White American Women." *Journal of Marriage and the Family* 56:949–62.

Manning, W. D. 1995. "Cohabitation, Marriage, and Entry into Motherhood." *Journal of Marriage and the Family* 57:191–200.

Manning, W. D. and N. S. Landale. 1996. "Racial and Ethnic Differences in the Role of Cohabitation in Premarital Childbearing." *Journal of Marriage and the Family* 58:63–77.

Manning, W. D. and D. T. Lichter. 1996. "Parental Cohabitation and Children's Economic Well-Being." *Journal of Marriage and the Family* 58:998–1010.

Manning, W. D. and R. J. Smock. 1995. "Why Marry? Race and the Transition to Marriage among Cohabitors." *Demography* 32:509–20.

Mare, R. D. and C. Winship. 1991. "Socioeconomic Change and the Decline of Marriage for Blacks and Whites." Pp. 175–202 in *The Urban Underclass*, edited by C. Jencks and P. E. Peterson. Washington, DC: Brookings Institute.

McLanahan, S., I. Garfinkel, and Y. Padilla. 1999a. "The Fragile Families and Child Wellbeing Study: Austin, Texas." Baseline report. Center for Research on Child Wellbeing, Princeton University, Princeton, NJ.

McLanahan, S., I. Garfinkel, and M. Waller. 1999b. "The Fragile Families and Child Wellbeing Study: Oakland, California." Baseline report. Center for Research on Child Wellbeing, Princeton University, Princeton, NJ.

Nock, S. L. 1995. "A Comparison of Marriages and Cohabiting Relationships." *Journal of Family Issues* 16:53–76.

Oppenheimer, V. K. 1988. "A Theory of Marriage Timing." *American Journal of Sociology* 94:563–91.

Oppenheimer, V. K., M. Kalmijn, and N. Lim. 1997. "Men's Career Development and Marriage Timing during a Period of Rising Inequality." *Demography* 34:311–30.

Oropesa, R. S. 1996. "Normative Beliefs about Marriage and Cohabitation: A Comparison of Non-Latino Whites, Mexican Americans, and Puerto Ricans." *Journal of Marriage and the Family* 58:49–62.

Parnell, A. M., G. Swicegood, and G. Stevens. 1994. "Nonmarital Pregnancies and Marriage in the United States." *Social Forces* 73:263–87.

Parrado, E. A. and M. Tienda. 1997. "Women's Roles and Family Formation in Venezuela: New Forms of Consensual Unions?" *Social Biology* 44:1–24.

Raley, R. K. 1996. "A Shortage of Marriageable Men? A Note on the Role of Coinhabitation in Black–White Differences in Marriage Rates." *American Sociological Review* 61:973–83.

——. In press. "Increasing Fertility in Coinhabiting Unions: Evidence for the Second Demographic Transition in the United States?" *Demography*.

Rindfuss, R. R. and A. VandenHeuvel. 1990. "Cohabitation: A Precursor to Marriage or an Alternative to Being Single?" *Population and Development Review* 16:703–26.

Schoen, R. 1992. "First Unions and the Stability of First Marriages." *Journal of Marriage and the Family* 54:281–84.

Seltzer, J. A. 1991. "Relationships between Fathers and Children Who Live Apart." *Journal of Marriage and the Family* 53:79–101.

——. 1994. "Consequences of Marital Dissolution for Children." *Annual Review of Sociology* 20:235–66.

Shelton, B. A. and D. John. 1993. "Does Marital Status Make a Difference?" *Journal of Family Issues* 14:401–20.

Smith, H. L., S. P. Morgan, and T. Koropeckyj-Cox. 1996. "A Decomposition of Trends in the Nonmarital Fertility Ratios of Blacks and Whites in the United States, 1960–1992." *Demography* 33:141–51.

Smock, P. J. and W. D. Manning. 1997. "Cohabiting Partners' Economic Circumstances and Marriage." *Demography* 34:331–41.

South, S. J. and G. Spitze. 1994. "Housework in Marital and Nonmarital Households." *Sociological Review* 59:327–47.

Surra, C. A. 1990. "Research and Theory on Mate Selection and Premarital Relationships in the 1980s." *Journal of Marriage and the Family* 52:844–65.

Sweet, J. A. and L. L. Bumpass. 1992. "Disruption of Marital and Cohabitation Relationships: A Social Demographic Perspective." Pp. 67–89 in *Close Relationship Loss: Theoretical Approaches*, edited by T. L. Orbuch. New York: Springer-Verlag.

——. 1996. "The National Survey of Families and Households—Waves 1 and 2: Data Description and Documentation." Center for Demography and Ecology, University of Wisconsin, Madison. Retrieved from the World Wide Web (http://www.ssc.wisc.edu/nsfh).

Thomson, E., T. L. Hanson, and S. S. McLanahan. 1994. "Family Structure and Child Well-Being: Economic Resources vs. Parental Behaviors." *Social Forces* 73:221–42.

Thomson, E., S. S. McLanahan, and R. B. Curtin. 1992. "Family Structure, Gender, and Parental Socialization." *Journal of Marriage and the Family* 54:368–78.

Thomson, E., J. Mosley, T. L. Hanson, and S. S. McLanahan 1998. "Remarriage, Cohabitation and Changes in Mothering. National Survey of Families and Households." Working Paper No. 65. Center for Demography and Ecology, University of Wisconsin, Madison.

Thornton, A. 1989. "Changing Atitudes toward Family Issues." *Journal of Marriage and the Family* 51:873–93.

——. 1991. "Influence of the Marital History of Parents on the Marital and Cohabitational Experiences of Children." *American Journal of Sociology* 96:868–94.

—— 1995. "Attitudes, Values and Norms Related to Nonmarital Fertility." Pp. 201–15 in *Report to Congress on Out-of-Wedlock Childbearing*. U.S. Department of Health and Human Services (DHHS Pub. No. [PHS] 95-1257). Hyattsville MD: U.S. Government Printing Office.

Thornton, A., W. C. Axinn, and J. D. Teachman. 1995. "The Influence of School Enrollment and Accumulation on Cohabitation and Marriage in Early Adulthood." *American Sociological Review* 60:762–74.

Treas, J. and D. Giesen. 2000. "Sexual Infidelity among Married and Cohabiting Americans." *Journal of Marriage and the Family* 62:48–60.

Ventura, S. J., J. A. Martin, S. C. Curtin, and T. J. Mathews. 1999. "Births: Final Data for 1997." *National Vital Statistics Reports* 47(18). Hyattsville, MD: National Center for Health Statistics.

Waite, L. J. 1995. "Does Marriage Matter?" *Demography* 32:483–507.

Weitzman, L. J. 1985. "The Divorce Law Revolution and the Transformation of Legal Marriage." Pp. 301–48 in *Contemporary Marriage: Comparative Perspectives on a Changing Institution*, edited by K. Davis with A. Grossbard-Shechtman. New York: Russell Sage.

Willetts, M. C. and Scanzoni, J. 1998, August. "Redefining Family: Domestic Partnership Ordinances." Paper presented at the annual meeting of the American Sociological Association, San Francisco, CA.

Willis, R. J. and R. T. Michael. 1994. "Innovation in Family Formation: Evidence on Cohabitation in the United States." Pp. 9–45 in *The Family, the Market and the State in Ageing Societies*, edited by J. Ermisch and N. Ogawa. Oxford, UK: Clarendon Press.

Winkler, A. E. 1997. "Economic Decision-Making by Cohabitors: Findings Regarding Income Pooling." *Applied Economics* 29:1079–90.

Wu, L. L., L. L. Bumpass, and K. Musick. 1999, July. "Historical and Life Course Trajectories of Nonmarital Childbearing." Revised version of paper presented at the Conference on Nonmarital Fertility, Institute for Research on Poverty, University of Wisconsin, Madison.

Wu, Z. and T. R. Balakrishnan. 1995. "Dissolution of Premarital Cohabitation in Canada." *Demography* 32:521–32.

16

FROM THIS DAY FORWARD
Commitment, Marriage, and Family in Lesbian and Gay Relationships

GRETCHEN A. STIERS

I think we wanted to make that level of commitment to each other and we wanted to do it in a way that included friends and family. We really wanted a ritual for ourselves that would provide a marker in terms of where we were in our relationship. We both thought there was no reason that the ritual of marriage had to be an exclusively heterosexual privilege. There was no reason why lesbians couldn't also have their own rituals and ceremonies.

— MARIA SIGGIA

I guess it's not for me. I don't think it makes your relationship more valid if you have a ceremony. It seems like jumping on the bandwagon in a way. Like I can do it too! I'm just as important or as good as you are and I can get a minister, etc. I am resistant to identifying in any way with that sort of lifestyle. I think that's why I rebel a little about joint checking accounts, savings, wills, and all that because it's similar to, reminds me of heterosexism in a way. I think it's their values, what the heterosexual community has said is important to do to make one's life valid and fulfilled.

— RICHARD HUDSON

Historical evidence suggests that same-sex ceremonies are not a "new" phenomenon within lesbian and gay communities in the United States. In the past, many same-sex couples said vows, and even may have exchanged rings, to commemorate their unions. In most cases, these ceremonies took place in private without public witnesses or the support of biological family members.[1] Over the past twenty-five years, however, increasing numbers of lesbians and gay men have had "public" ceremonies: rituals in which families and friends are invited to witness the event. While these rituals focus on declaring a couple's love and commitment to each other, one of their central purposes is to garner support and validation for lesbian and gay relationships. Many same-sex ceremonies are rites of passage that not only "create family" but also "build community."

As the two epigraphs to this [reading] suggest, not all lesbians and gay men choose to have ceremonies. Among the ninety people interviewed, thirty-two had or were planning to have a same-sex ceremony. Of the remaining fifty-eight individuals, twenty-eight commented that they might have a ceremony sometime in the future; thirty stated that they did not want to have a ceremony either with their current partner or in a future relationship.

In order to examine motivations for having or not having a same-sex ceremony, this [reading] focuses on three questions: What reasons do lesbians and gay men state for having a commitment or union ceremony? What motivations do other lesbians and gay men have for considering having a ceremony? What reasons do some state for not wanting to have a ceremony? . . .

Same–Sex Ceremonies as Rites of Passage

According to anthropologist Terence Turner (1977), rites of passage are in essence a series of rituals that mark the transition from one social state to another. Although no one accepted definition of "ritual" exists within the anthropological literature, the term generally refers to acts that are conventional and repetitive celebrations or social demarcations of important events (Goody 1977). Therefore, rites of passage involve sequences of customary and standardized behaviors that designate life-changing events, such as birth, marriage, and death. . . .

Even though norms have changed in the United States, marriage remains a significant rite of passage for many heterosexual women and men. It continues to be an important rite of passage for them in part because it signals adulthood, the merging of two distinct kinship networks, the intention to have children, and the formation of a new family unit (Roth 1985). Traditional marriage rites typically (although not always) take place through a series of rituals: betrothal, engagement party, wedding shower, bachelor party, rehearsal dinner, wedding ceremony, reception, and honeymoon.

For lesbians and gay men, however, no corresponding rites of passage exist to signify important changes in their adult roles or family relationships. In part, this lack of rites and rituals has stemmed from society's long-standing condemnation of homosexuality. Lesbian and gay couples do not receive the same legitimation and support as heterosexual relationships. In sharp contrast to the approval bestowed upon married couples, parents and other relatives of lesbians and gays often invalidate homosexual relationships by acting as if these relationships do not exist, which renders them invisible, or by recognizing the relationships but considering them not genuine (Roth 1985).

Many lesbians and gay men, however, are choosing to create their own rituals and ceremonies to mark their own significant life transitions. Although these ceremonies vary in their content and structure, they are rites of passage; that is, they involve rituals of separation, transition, and integration that demarcate a couple's "partnered" status. As the following section points out, however, respondents' motivations for having a ceremony are both similar to and different from the reasons heterosexuals have weddings.

Motivations for Having a Same-Sex Ceremony

As mentioned, thirty-two respondents either had a ceremony or were planning to have one within a year. Among these respondents, same-sex ceremonies fell into two distinct categories: celebrations of recent commitments and celebrations of existing commitments. Eighteen respondents had ceremonies to acknowledge "recent" commitments — relationships that had lasted less than five years. . . . Most of these respondents used either the phrase "commitment ceremony" or "holy union" to refer to their ceremonies on their invitations. All of these ceremonies took place between six months and four years after the couples had first met. Although their current ages ranged from twenty to forty-four, most respondents were in their twenties or early thirties at the time of the ceremonies.

In addition, five respondents were planning ceremonies to celebrate "recent" commitments within the next year. These respondents had been with their partners for less than two years. Four respondents stated they were planning to have a "wedding," and one woman commented she was planning a "union ceremony." All five respondents were under the age of forty and had never been married legally.

In contrast, five lesbians and two gay men had ceremonies to celebrate their established, long-term relationships. While most of the lesbians called their ceremonies "anniversary celebrations," the gay men used the phrases "holy union" and an "exchange of vows." Regardless of their names, however, all of these ceremonies took place between ten and sixteen years after the couples first met.[2] Unlike the respondents celebrating newer commitments who were in their twenties and early thirties, these lesbians and gay men were in their thirties, forties, and fifties at the time they had their ceremonies.

Although they cannot marry legally, lesbians and gay men are aware of the purposes weddings serve in the larger community. Correspondingly, respondents who had or were planning a ceremony discussed two main reasons for their decisions: to show their commitment and love to each other and to receive public validation of their commitments from friends and family. Noticeably absent from their accounts, however, were the traditional functions of separating from their families of origin or having children.

According to Patrick Flemming, he and his partner decided to have a ceremony because "we loved each other. We felt committed to each other for our lives and we wanted to let people know that in a very ritualized, public way that they could participate in too." Kathleen O'Brien also commented on the importance of social affirmation.

> *I thought that Valerie and I deserved to have some public recognition and support of our commitment. That I deserved the right to hear myself say that I believe we have what it took and that I was willing to commit to that publicly. That our relationship deserved that intangible level of support and recognition.*

Similarly, Randall Harris stated, "At the time we started planning to do it we had not yet been living together quite a year but we knew we wanted to make a commitment in a public way with some friends and family there."

In particular, respondents who had "anniversary celebrations" emphasized the need for more "public" support of gay and lesbian relationships. In their accounts, they often used the term "public" to refer to support from friends and family as well as from the larger gay and lesbian community. As Beth Epstein commented, she and her partner wanted to celebrate their twelfth anniversary because

> we really were feeling the need for public support. We had moved to this area just a few years before. We were really still establishing roots here and felt like we just needed some support. We also just really wanted to be able to express publicly to each other our commitment to the relationship, which had undergone some changes once we moved.

Indeed, many respondents stated that it was important to create support since lesbians and gay men have few avenues for gaining social recognition for their relationships. As Melanie Obermeier remarked:

> I think people should have more ritual in their lives. There's not enough. Especially in gay relationships. You get a lot more support if your partner is straight even if you're not religious. You get a lot more ceremonies that give you landmarks and things to remember back to. You don't get those when you are gay. You have to make your own.

For a small minority of respondents, religious recognition and support also were important factors in why they had a ceremony. For Kathleen O'Brien and her partner Valerie, it was extremely important to have their "commitment ceremony" in a Unitarian church because of their religious convictions. As Kathleen explained:

> We had been attending services at the Unitarian church for probably about six months when we realized that the Unitarian Society as a religious institution, not just as a church in Lesbianville,[3] recognized the union of gay and lesbian people as legitimate as straight people. Then we knew that is where we wanted to have our ceremony because we both had a very strong religious upbringing and the power of the symbol of the church was very important to us.

Similarly, Celeste Davis stated that she and her partner, Grace, had their "holy union" in a Unitarian church because of their religious beliefs. According to Celeste, "We were going to the Unitarian church and were familiar with their dogma. Their perspective reflected our beliefs about religion and having a ceremony."

All five of the respondents who referred to their ceremonies as "holy unions" commented that making a public statement included making a commitment before God. Although Luke Fontaine and his partner, Ben, did not have their "holy union" ceremony in a church, they had strong religious convictions. As Luke recalled:

I wanted to make my commitment to Ben public and I wanted him to make his to me public. I think that making a commitment to each other before God and before witnesses is a very important step in making your relationship work. It's not so easy to walk away from something when you've made a public promise that you'll be together till death do us part.

For these respondents, same-sex ceremonies included religious recognition and support from their religious communities.

Different Motivations from Heterosexual Weddings

Similar to heterosexual weddings, same-sex ceremonies can help lesbian and gay couples integrate into kinship and community networks. For many such couples, however, the functions a ceremony performs often diverge from the heterosexual model. While same-sex ceremonies serve many of the same purposes as traditional heterosexual weddings, they differ in five important respects.

First, lesbian and gay unions do not necessarily begin the process of separating individuals from their families of origin. Since most individuals experience some level of rejection when they come out and identify as gay, typically they already have gone through a process of separation from their families. For this same reason, many same-sex ceremonies are not organized by blood family members and take place outside the traditional context of kin relations. Indeed, . . . a primary purpose of many same-sex ceremonies is to create "chosen" families that include close friends.[4]

Second, although many heterosexual couples marry in order to gain public recognition of their relationships, public support has an additional significance for lesbians and gay men. For many respondents, the desire for such support from friends and family not only stemmed from wanting affirmation as a "couple" but also acceptance as a "lesbian" or "gay" couple. As Barbara Mercer remarked, "I think having a ceremony is important to show the rest of the world because it can give more validity to the fact that these are real relationships just like straight folks have." Unless heterosexual couples are of mixed races, ethnicities, or religions, they do not automatically face the same level of social rejection as lesbian and gay couples.

The support many same-sex couples who have ceremonies receive not only affirms the couple's relationship but also can be compensation for the lack of acceptance they often feel from biological family members and "the world at large." As Maria Siggia remarked:

It was important to have that support of friends and family in terms of the kind of isolation that goes along with being part of a subculture or oppressed minority group. It seemed to us that it was very important to have some way to balance out all of the negativeness about being gay or lesbian. That it's really important to affirm our relationship and to ask people to actively support us and help out since the culture doesn't allow for that.

Other respondents also elaborated on the importance of rituals as an avenue for reinforcing the dyadic ties of lesbians and gay men. According to Melanie Obermeier:

> *It's a really hard thing to do to have a relationship, and you need all the help you can get. If you're a heterosexual you get incredible support from the community to stay together even when people shouldn't. There is almost a pressure to stay together. And in the gay community there's none. There's none of the baby showers, wedding gifts, anniversaries. None of the "You buy silver on your tenth anniversary and Hallmark cards to my lovely wife" kind of thing. We get nothing, absolutely nothing. I think these types of rituals help maintain relationships.*

Third, many respondents discussed how their ceremonies made an important statement to other lesbian and gay couples. This sentiment was articulated especially by couples whose ceremonies celebrated anniversaries. As Margaret Dubek explained:

> *We just felt really good about the fact that we were still together after ten years. There aren't too many role models in the community that are able to do that. We wanted to celebrate it for ourselves and invite our friends to help us. I think it is good for our community and our friends to know that there are some successful relationships. That we can survive all the difficulties our society puts on us. We should celebrate that.*

Kristen Johnson also remarked that it was important for other couples to have long-term, lesbian relationships as role models.

> *The tenth is a milestone and I think that comes from tradition. Even within this community, I think it was important for us and for our friends that a tenth could be celebrated even in the midst of other long-term relationships breaking up. It was a moment of celebration.*

One of the most important purposes of having a same-sex ceremony is the creation of recognition for a relationship within lesbian and gay communities. In the past, couples in long-term, monogamous relationships often received little support from other lesbians and gay men. As sociologists Philip Blumstein and Pepper Schwartz (1983) commented in their study *American Couples:* "There is a general fear in both gay and lesbian circles that relationships are unlikely to last. Long-lasting relationships are seen as quite special. They are unexpected, and therefore newly formed couples are not treated as though they will remain together for fifty years. . . . When a couple is not treated as [sacred], the less likely the partners will see themselves that way" (p. 322).

Similarly, many respondents in this study thought that long-term relationships did not receive enough support from other lesbians and gay men. To quote Melanie Obermeier again: "*Sometimes the gay community doesn't take its own relationships seriously enough and that's part of the reason we have a hard time maintaining relationships. Because even as a community we don't take ourselves seriously and recognize our own relationships.*"

Even today there remains a perception among many lesbians and gay men that same-sex couples do not remain together for very long. As authors Berger (1982) and Johnson (1990) have noted, however, many lesbians and gay men do have long-term relationships that last over ten years. Berger (1982) suggests that one reason older lesbian and gay couples seem invisible is that they do not share the same social circles as younger gays and, therefore, remain hidden to them.

Fourth, lesbian and gay ceremonies often are not celebrations of "new" commitments; that is, they may take place at any time during a couple's relationship. For example, Kristen Johnson and her partner decided to have a "tenth-anniversary celebration" instead of a commitment ceremony. According to Kristen:

> *We feel very married and have felt very married right from the year one. Because of our insecurities around our sexuality for the first three or four years we were together, we never had a service. Now we don't think it is really appropriate or necessary to have a commitment ceremony since we have that commitment and have since the year one.*

Similarly, Beth Epstein remarked:

> *We called it a "recommitment celebration." We felt that we couldn't just call it a "commitment celebration." Obviously we had already made some level of commitment to be together for twelve years. Recommitment. Like on this day we publicly recommit to each other. That somehow really captured it for both of us.*

Although heterosexual couples may live together without being married, and thus face a similar decision about publicly acknowledging their commitment, nothing prevents them from marrying. Heterosexual couples have a choice whether to marry legally; lesbians and gay men do not and, in addition, often face prejudice, which can prevent them from having a commitment ceremony.

Married heterosexual couples may decide to "renew" their vows on a significant anniversary. For such couples, wedding anniversaries are occasions to celebrate the date of their marriages. Since lesbians and gay men do not have the same kind of "formal" date to mark the length of their relationships, often they observe many different relationship anniversaries, including when they first met, had sex, moved in together, or decided to make a commitment. These anniversaries have added significance because they help to validate relationships in a society that discounts them. As a further way to gauge the legitimacy of their relationships, lesbian and gay couples may decide to have some type of ceremony when they reach a significant anniversary. In these instances, the length of the relationship becomes a substitute for conventional forms of societal recognition that heterosexual couples receive (Slater and Mencher 1991).

A few respondents stated that their ceremonies were political acts with political consequences. As Patrick Flemming shouted, "We were saying that we were gay and we were proud. So there!" Similarly, Tom Douglass replied, "I have to admit part of what we were doing was a protest. To say, 'The church says no; the state says no; we say yes!'"

Lesbians' and gay men's political motivations for having a ceremony centered not only on validating gay relationships but affirming gay identity. Ever since politician and gay activist Harvey Milk's admonishments to "come out" in the mid-1970s, being publicly open about one's sexual identity has been considered a political act within lesbian and gay culture.[5] When asked to discuss her reasons for having a ceremony, Melanie Obermeier commented on the importance of taking a stand about one's sexual identity.

> *If we don't do it for ourselves, who's going to do it for us? We're not going to hear anybody in the "het" community saying "hey, you guys, you should all be having ceremonies and celebrations." They're not going to do it for us. If we aren't out for ourselves, they won't be out for us.*

Similarly, Esther Gould remarked:

> *In fact, I think same-sex ceremonies are more legitimate than "weddings." I think they are much braver thing to do. It's so easy to be heterosexual and get married. It's hard not to, in fact. I think it's a brave and really sort of profoundly creative thing for lesbians to create a ritual like that.*

Given lesbians' and gay men's inability to marry legally, it was surprising that so few respondents specifically mentioned political motivations for having a commitment or union ceremony. In contrast to the political slogan of the 1970s, "the personal is political," most of these respondents did not stress a connection between their personal motivations and larger social change within society. In fact, some specifically commented that their ceremonies were "not political events." Their reasons for having a ceremony focused more on personal aspects of commitment than on social change.

Like heterosexuals, lesbians and gay men clearly have ceremonies because they love their partners and want to acknowledge that bond publicly. Indeed, like heterosexual weddings, lesbian and gay ceremonies serve to integrate a couple into larger kinship and community networks. At their core, same-sex ceremonies are rites of integration as well as rites of passage; their two primary objectives are the creation of family and the building of community. . . . These "family" and "community" networks are very different in form from those generated for heterosexual couples. . . .

Are Same–Sex Ceremonies Acts of Accommodation or Acts of Resistance?

During the last ten years, lesbian and gay scholars have debated whether same-sex ceremonies and the subsequent movement to legalize same-sex "marriages" act to help assimilate gay couples into the mainstream or to break down conventional meanings of marriage (Ettlebrick 1989; Stoddard 1989). Although analyzing same-sex ceremonies as rites of passage implies that they are inherently assimilationist, such ceremonies include both "strategies of accommodation" as well as "strategies of resistance." According to anthropologist Louise Lamphere (1987), strategies of accommodation are activities that help individuals endure oppressive experiences and situations in their daily lives. These strategies, however, often coexist with strategies of resistance that help undermine the coercive practices and institutions the individuals must adapt to.

In her work on immigrant women, Lamphere argues that women who work in the labor force are "active strategists" who utilize accommodative coping strategies in order to survive their specific work situations. In addition, women also use resistance strategies to undermine the authority of management and the control supervisors have over their lives. Thus women do not "passively" accept their working conditions but actively manage their work situations.

In a similar vein, anthropologist Ellen Lewin (1994) described the strategies of resistance and accommodation lesbians use to "manage" motherhood and their dual identities as lesbians and mothers. Lesbians who choose to be mothers face the opposing cultural beliefs that women "naturally" are good mothers and that homosexuality is "unnatural." Lesbians are categorized by default as "unfit" mothers. Motherhood, however, permits "lesbians to be more like other women" while at the same time it empowers them to refute "the equation of homosexuality with unnaturalness . . . allowing the lesbian mother to resist gendered constructions of sexuality" (pp. 348–49).

In creating and having same-sex ceremonies, lesbians and gay men also actively participate in both reinforcing and subverting traditional ideals about gender, sexuality, and marriage. They may utilize accommodation strategies in order to gain the status and recognition accorded married, heterosexual couples. Simultaneously, they may use resistance strategies that question the "abnormality" of homosexuality and the hegemony of traditional gender relations within marriage. Although some lesbians and gay men frame their ceremonies in the context of traditional marriage norms, others view their ceremonies as contesting these same values. Indeed, many do both. Since same-sex couples cannot marry legally, their motivations for altering the traditional wedding ceremony differ from those of heterosexual couples.

Same–Sex Ceremonies as Acts of Accommodation

Although most of the lesbians and gay men in this study who had or were planning a commitment ceremony stated that they believed their ceremonies were about "creating something new," their personal expectations about being in a committed relationship often echoed more traditional norms. The act of having a commitment ceremony often reinforces traditional marriage norms in two primary ways. First, many same-sex couples uphold a number of conventional expectations about adult relationships. In particular, they endorse the assumptions that couples "should" both make a commitment to having a long-term relationship and be sexually monogamous. Like heterosexual weddings, same-sex ceremonies reinforce the ideology that marriage is the proper site for adult sexual relations. By focusing on commitment and monogamy, they invalidate other forms of sexual expression. As sociologist Emile Durkheim ([1912] 1971) noted, rites of passage convey the "core values" of a society to ritual participants and observers. Like heterosexual weddings, same-sex ceremonies reinforce monogamy as a cultural ideal, if not always the practice of particular individuals.

Second, same-sex ceremonies are one strategy for claiming that being gay or lesbian is not all that different from being heterosexual. For some lesbians and gay men, having a ceremony may help them manage their "spoiled" identities (Goffman 1963). According to sociologist Erving Goffman (1963), all stigmatized individuals struggle with integrating their self-perceptions as being "like" everyone else with society's judgment of them as "others." Same-sex ceremonies can help lesbians and gay men cope with this "other" categorization by stressing the similarities between gay and heterosexual relationships. Indeed, within gay communities, this strategy often is referred to derogatorily as "passing" or attempting to gain "heterosexual privilege." Whether a couple has a ceremony for this reason, same-sex ceremonies are one avenue for trying to become "insiders."

Same–Sex Ceremonies as Acts of Resistance

Although same-sex ceremonies can be interpreted as strategies of accommodation that situate lesbian and gay couples within mainstream heterosexual culture, paradoxically this accommodation is accomplished through strategies of resistance that challenge marriage norms. While same-sex ceremonies reinforce some values about marriage, they simultaneously subvert a number of other conventional ideologies. When two women or two men decide to celebrate their relationship, they are asserting that marriage does not necessarily entail one man and one woman. In addition, they do not assume that they "must" take on traditional male and female gender roles within their relationships or have children in order to be part of a "family."

As many feminist scholars have noted, resistance takes place on two levels (Abu-Lughod 1990; Lewin 1994). First, direct resistance can occur on the terrain of everyday life through actions that sabotage specific institutions. For example, lesbian and gay organizations, such as the Lambda Legal Defense and Education Fund, that want to legalize same-sex marriages are working to undermine the gendered basis of the institution of marriage. In the United States, state marriage laws explicitly assert or are interpreted to imply that marriage is an act that takes place between a woman and a man. By claiming the legal right to have a commitment or wedding ceremony, lesbians and gay men challenge the gender component of marriage as well as its underlying procreative function.

Second, resistance can take place on the level of consciousness. According to anthropologist Emily Martin (1987), in women's relation to the field of medicine "there are a great many ways that women express consciousness of their position and opposition to oppression" (p. 183). In her definition of resistance, Martin includes "refusing to accept a definition of oneself" and "refusing to act as requested or required" (p. 187).

In having a ceremony, lesbians and gay men participate in both of these types of conscious resistance. They refuse to accept the social construction of homosexuality as "abnormal" by claiming that the desire to marry is a "normal" aspiration for any two adults regardless of sexual identity. In addition, those who have ceremonies question the gendered basis of marriage. Two women or two men who "marry" subvert the belief that women and men take on separate but complementary roles within a marriage and overtly resist the notion that marriage functions to support specifically defined gender roles.

Recently anthropologists have begun to argue that rites of passage do not merely transmit the "core values" of a society, as Durkheim first suggested (Baumann 1994). Rituals are spheres of "contradictory and contestable perspectives — participants having their own reasons, viewpoints, and motives, and in fact, [rituals] are made up as they go along."[6] Although participants and observers expect rituals to follow certain rules, they also have the ability to "reconstruct" rituals by changing the wording or performance of certain procedures. For example, heterosexual couples often decide on the precise wording and procedures for their wedding ceremonies and do not follow a "strict" ritual format. Over time, this process of reconstruction slowly alters the format of wedding rituals, resulting in a moderate form of cultural change.

In creating their ceremonies, however, lesbians and gay men shift the conventional meanings of the wedding ritual more overtly. They consciously seek to reformulate cultural values not only about marriage but about gender and homosexuality as well. As anthropologist Gerd Baumann (1994) notes, rituals may not only "speak to values basic to the culture. . . . They can speak as clearly and centrally to aspirations towards cultural change . . ." (p. 109). Same-sex ceremonies have a political dimension that is absent from heterosexual weddings. They challenge normative ideologies of both gender and homosexuality and "reconstruct" the very meaning of the wedding ritual, contributing to a more radical form of cultural change in marriage norms.

Analyses of same-sex ceremonies need to move beyond framing them in a simple dualistic fashion: as acts of assimilation or as acts of resistance. These ceremonies alter some cultural ideals while supporting other social norms at the same time. "Mixed" strategies of accommodation and resistance are commonly part of same-sex ceremonies. One respondent, David Gascon, remarked about the lesbian and gay ceremonies he had been to:

> *To me a wedding is a sexual contract. The gay and lesbian commitment ceremonies I've seen have been sexual contracts, companionship contracts, but there also are political statements in them. They are more about, from my perspective, a commitment toward a person than an institution like marriage. Straight people are expected to be married, whereas the gay culture hasn't expected anybody to*

do anything. The commitment has more to do with taking control and creating our own world rather than fulfilling someone else's need for us to conform.

. . . Like heterosexuals, lesbians and gay men make many choices in constructing their ceremonies. Unlike heterosexuals, however, they rarely choose only conventional customs. . . .

Conclusion

Lesbians and gay men are an integral part of the changing landscape of family life in the United States. Although they always have been part of so-called nuclear families (as spouses, parents, and children), the families they create with their own partners, children, and friends have become more visible outside of lesbian and gay communities over the last thirty years. This visibility largely has resulted from the political and legal steps they have taken to ensure their unions are accorded the same legal rights as married, heterosexual couples. Over the last twenty years, many lesbians and gay men around the country have fought for increased family, parenting, and marriage rights for same-sex couples.

The accounts in this [reading] highlight four important themes about marriage and family life in the United States today. First, what socially and legally constitutes "family" is continually (albeit slowly) being transformed. Changes in the structure of family are not new to the last few decades but have been in progress for over the last 150 years (Gordon 1988). Clearly, the increasing inclusion of same-sex couples in the social and legal matrix of family life is one important aspect of this evolution.

Second, social definitions of marriage also are changing. In contrast to the breadwinner/homemaker ideal of the 1940s and 1950s, a new "companionate" model of marriage has emerged, which stresses that partners should provide each other with emotional intimacy, companionship, and sexual fulfillment (Reissman 1990). Indeed, many lesbian and gay couples (although certainly not all) have adopted this model for their own relationships. Their relationships illustrate the potential for self-growth and long-term commitment as well as conflict in this new model of marriage.

Third, although marriage and family norms are changing, marriage remains a primary vehicle through which individuals form intimate relationships. Instead of rejecting marriage as some did in the 1970s and 1980s, today many lesbians and gay men are pushing for the right to be included in this institution. Contrary to the often-stated diatribe by the New Right that same-sex marriages would undermine the institution of marriage, most respondents believed that legal recognition of lesbian and gay unions would further strengthen the social, economic, and legal rights of all married couples (heterosexual, lesbian, or gay) over those of single individuals.

Finally, many individuals hold ambivalent or even contradictory views on the changes occurring in the institutions of marriage and family. Although women have gained more equality within marriage, husbands and wives continue to struggle over money, housework, and child care issues. Not surprisingly, many heterosexuals "remain torn by their reverence for the traditional nuclear family as it was, or seemed to be, and their acceptance of the 'new' forms of family in today's society" (Skolnick 1991:198).

The attitudes of lesbians and gay men toward family and marriage issues highlight the changes taking place in these institutions and the conflicting sentiments individuals have about them. While many respondents were critical of the institutions of marriage and family, the majority valued the ideals of love, commitment, monogamy, and family life. At the same time they were supportive of these so-called traditional values, they also argued that marriage and the family need to be redefined to reflect the families people actually create. Their attitudes both mirrored contemporary beliefs and critiqued these same expectations.

As part of the changing fabric of family life in the United States, lesbians and gay men clearly have a stake in how the institutions of marriage and family will be redefined in the future. Although the views of the people studied cannot be generalized to all lesbians and gay men, they do provide an important critique of modern ideals about intimate relationships. Clearly, the battle over who should and will be included in modern social, religious, and legal definitions of family and marriage will continue into the twenty-first century. Despite some legal setbacks, such as the passage of the Defense of Marriage Act by Congress in 1996, lesbians and gay men will continue to fight for and eventually win the battle for full equality.

ENDNOTES

1. This does not mean that no lesbians and gay men had "public" ceremonies. In fact, some Black lesbians and gay men in Harlem had highly visible same-sex ceremonies during the 1920s (Ayers and Brown 1994). Same-sex ceremonies that included public witnesses, however, were uncommon until the 1970s and 1980s.
2. Among the respondents, no ceremonies took place between five and nine years after a couple had gotten together.
3. The term "Lesbianville" was coined by the *National Enquirer* to refer to the town of Northampton, Massachusetts (1992:8; Kelliher 1992:1).
4. The phrase "chosen families" was adopted from Kath Weston, who used it to refer to the families lesbians and gay men create. Members of chosen families can include friends, blood relatives, and children (Weston 1991).
5. Harvey Milk was the first openly gay city supervisor to be elected to office in San Francisco. He was a city supervisor from June 1977 until his assassination in November 1978 (Adam 1987).
6. Gerholm quoted in Parkin 1994:13.

REFERENCES

Abu-Lughod, Lila. 1990. "The Romance of Resistance: Tracing Transformations of Power Through Bedouin Women." *American Ethnologist* 17 (1): 41–55.
Adam, Barry. 1987. *The Rise of a Gay and Lesbian Movement.* Boston: G. K. Hall.
Ayers, Tess and Paul Brown. 1994. *The Essential Guide to Lesbian and Gay Weddings.* New York: HarperCollins.

Baumann, Gerd. 1994. "Ritual Implicates 'Other': Rereading Durkheim in a Plural Society." Pp. 97–116 in *Understanding Rituals,* edited by Daniel de Copper. New York: Routledge.

Berger, Raymond. 1982. *Gay and Gray: The Older Homosexual Man.* Boston: Alyson.

Blumstein, Philip and Pepper Schwartz. 1983. *American Couples: Money, Work, Sex.* New York: William Morrow.

Durkheim, Émile. [1912] 1971. *The Elementary Forms of Religious Life.* London: George Allen and Unwin.

Ettlebrick, Paula. 1989. "Since When Is Marriage a Path to Liberation?" *OUT/LOOK* 2(2) (Fall): 14–17.

Goffman, Erving. 1963. *Stigma.* Englewood Cliffs, NJ: Prentice-Hall.

Goody, Jack. 1977. "Against Ritual: Loosely Structured Thoughts on a Loosely Defined Topic." Pp. 25–35 in *Secular Ritual,* edited by Sally Moore and Barbara Myerhoff. Amsterdam: Van Gorcum.

Gordon, Linda, ed. 1988. *Heroes of Their Own Lives.* New York: Penguin.

Johnson, Susan. 1990. *Staying Power: Long-Term Lesbian Couples.* Tallahassee, FL: Naiad Press.

Kelliher, Judith. 1992. "Enquiring Minds Wanted to Know." *Daily Hampshire Gazette,* April 14, p. 1.

Lamphere, Louise. 1987. *From Working Daughters to Working Mothers: Factory Women in Massachusetts.* Albany: State University of New York Press.

Lewin, Ellen. 1994. "Negotiating Lesbian Motherhood: The Dialectics of Resistance and Accommodation." Pp. 333–53 in *Mothering: Ideology, Experience, and Agency,* edited by Evelyn Glenn, Grace Chang, and Linda Forcey. New York: Routledge.

Martin, Emily. 1987. *The Woman in the Body: A Cultural Analysis of Reproduction.* Boston: Beacon Press.

Reissman, Catherine. 1990. *Divorce Talk: Women and Men Make Sense of Personal Relationships.* New Brunswick, NJ: Rutgers University Press.

Roth, Sally. 1985. "Psychotherapy with Lesbian Couples: Individual Issues, Female Socialization, and the Social Context." *Journal of Marriage and Family Therapy* 11 (3) :273–86.

Skolnick, Arlene. 1991. *Embattled Paradise.* New York: HarperCollins.

Slater, Suzanne and Julie Mencher. 1991. "The Lesbian Family Life Cycle: A Contextual Approach." *American Journal of Orthopsychiatry* 61 (3): 372–82.

Stoddard, Thomas. 1989. "Why Gay People Should Seek the Right to Marry." *OUT/LOOK* 2(2) (Fall): 9–13.

Turner, Terence. 1977. "Transformation, Hierarchy, and Transcendence: A Reformulation of Van Gennep's Model of the Structure of Rites de Passage." Pp. 53–70 in *Secular Ritual,* edited by Sally Moore and Barbara Myerhoff. Amsterdam: Van Gorcum.

Weston, Kath. 1991. *Families We Choose: Lesbians, Gays, Kinship.* New York: Columbia University Press.

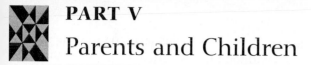

PART V
Parents and Children

In this section, we examine parent–child relationships from a variety of perspectives. Parenting remains the central focus of the sociological study of the family. Ideally, research on parenting should include both the perspectives of parents and the perspectives of children. However, until recently, more research has been done on parenthood and the perspectives of parents than on childhood and the perspectives of children. Granted, it is much easier to gain research access with adults than it is with children. Still, more research on children and childhood is needed. Family scholars are working to rectify this limitation, and we are beginning to see separate courses and books on children and childhood. One example is William A. Corsaro's book, *The Sociology of Childhood* (1997), in which he examines childhood based on his cross-cultural experiences in Italy. Two exciting new studies on children are excerpted in this section, see Readings 20 and 21.

To date, research on parenting covers a range of topics from studies on who becomes parents, to the transition to parenthood, to how people parent (types of discipline, values, etc.), to what are the consequences of parenting (e.g., how do children change people's lives, and what effects does parenting have on the marital relationship?). Research on children tends to focus on socialization, day care, the effects of parental employment on children, and the effects of divorce and remarriage on children. We begin our investigation with the historical conceptions of parent–child relationships before examining issues specifically related to parenting (i.e., single-parent families and gay and lesbian parenting) and issues specifically related to children (i.e., the effects of race and social class on children and the commercialization of contemporary childhood). In this section, I also include a study on how family influences on children have changed over three decades (Reading 20) and suggest that the reader also look at Paul R. Amato's research, "Life-Span Adjustment of Children to Their Parents' Divorce" (Reading 34), which reviews research related to the effects of divorce on children. The last section of this anthology on families and poverty also has several readings that address issues related to children, especially Demie Kurz's article "Poor Mothers and the Care of Teenage Children" (Reading 47) and Lee Rainwater and Timothy M. Smeeding's article on needed social policy changes, "Is There Hope for America's Low-Income Children?" (Reading 48).

Historical Perspectives

To understand contemporary parenting, we need to have a historical perspective. Sociologists Robert LeVine and Merry White (1987), for example, in their research on the social transformation of parenthood and childhood, argue that childhood has changed more in the past 200 years than it has in 9 millennia. This transformation of childhood has occurred on many levels, including ideological changes, socioeconomic changes, demographic changes, and educational changes. On an ideological level, LeVine and White argue that the meanings of children have changed. In Western urban areas, the economic utility of children has declined, and children have become more valued sentimentally. In addition, there is more public interest in children today, especially evident in discussions concerning children's rights and policies affecting children. On a socioeconomic level, childhood was affected by the shift from agrarian economies to urban-industrial economies. Families experienced socioeconomic improvement, and parents could now invest unilaterally in their children's lives. Levine and White point out that this socioeconomic improvement led to improved diets, sanitation, water, and housing, which resulted in decreased mortality and fertility. Arlene Skolnick (1994), a research psychologist at the Institute of Human Development at UC–Berkeley, argues that this increased longevity has encouraged stronger emotional bonds between parents and children and has lengthened the duration of parent–child relationships. Moreover, as we shall see in Readings 29 and 30, increased longevity also has made grandparent-hood a more common life experience. According to LeVine and White (1987), the final transformative change of childhood occurred with the rise of mass schooling and the Public School Movement in the United States. By 1890 most children were attending schools, which limited the amount of control parents had over their children. Children were kept out of full-time produc-tive work, and they required more resources to attend school.

These historical changes provide a background for the first reading on parenting, Maris A Vinovskis' "Historical Perspectives on Parent–Child Interactions." In this reading, Vinovskis, a historian at the University of Michigan, summarizes the major changes in parent–child relationships during the past 400 years. This summary is important because it shows that parent-hood is socially constructed; that is, what is considered important and relevant to parenting changes across cultures and over time. Moreover, the various fac-tors that influence the relationship between parents and children also change over time. Vinovskis focuses his analysis on the changes in perceptions and treatment of children and on the changes in parent–child relationships since the Middle Ages. In particular, Vinovskis examines changes in the parental love of children, the intellectual capabilities of young children, and the recognition of adolescence. His discussion of parent–child relations assesses historical changes in parental responsibility for early child care and in parental control of children.

Fertility

Over the past 200 years, birthrates have declined dramatically in the United States. In 1800 an adult woman had an average of 7 births during her life-time. By 1995 this average had dropped to 1.7 births per adult woman.

Many factors contributed to this decline in fertility, including women's increased education and workforce participation, people marrying later and divorcing more, the increased cost of raising children, the increased availability of birth control and legalized abortion, and a decrease in religious and societal pressures to have children. A key factor in the declining birthrate is a change in the ideal family size. Whereas large families were considered to be ideal in earlier centuries, today the majority of Americans think the ideal family size is two children. There also has been a significant change in attitudes toward childlessness. Prior to 1960, most Americans (85 percent) agreed with the statement that "all married couples should have children." By the mid-1980s, the percentage of Americans who agreed with this statement was 43 percent, or less than half of Americans. These data indicate that more people are separating the institution of marriage from the institution of parenthood. Societal attitudes have changed: Not all married people are expected to have children. Moreover, an increasing number of people plan to be voluntarily childless, or child free. For example, the percentage of Americans who said they expect to remain childless increased from 5 percent in 1960 to 10 percent by the mid-1980s. Thus, more people are defining their social roles in adulthood as separate from parenting.

Even though we are seeing an increase in voluntary childlessness, we are still a pronatalist society, which means that our society encourages people to have children. However, while many people are influenced by pronatalism and want children, an increasing number of Americans are attempting to control the timing of childbirth in their lives. For example, prior to 1970, 80 percent of women under 25 years of age had experienced childbirth. By 1989, only 50 percent of women under 25 years of age had experienced childbirth. Today, more and more women are delaying childbirth until their thirties, and some women are delaying it into their forties (Ventura et al. 1999). This delay has numerous consequences, both positive and negative. Couples and individuals who delay childbearing tend to be more established in their careers and have more financial resources for raising children than those who have children in their twenties. However, delayed childbearing also means there is a larger age gap between parents and children, and some people are concerned that older parents may have less energy to devote to children. On the other hand, others argue that older parents tend to be more patient with children.

One important consequence of delaying childbirth is its effect on birthrates: More people will not have children at all. Moreover, while most people (90 percent) still want to have children, due to delayed childbearing, a substantial percentage (20 percent) will have some difficulty having biological children. In fact, 15 to 20 percent of all heterosexual couples are infertile, meaning they have been trying to get pregnant for over a year. Historically and medically, the primary focus of research and intervention has been on female infertility. Now, fertility treatments and reproductive technologies focus on both men and women. Many couples have such a great desire to have biological children that they are turning to expensive and intrusive reproductive technologies to achieve their goals. Lasker and Borg (1987), for example, interviewed infertile couples who have tried using alternative or artificial insemination (AI) or in vitro fertilization (IVF), and the couples talk about their personal experiences with infertility and the internal and external pressures they feel to have children. Other people who want to parent, but who are unable to conceive their own children, are turning to foster parenting or adoption.

Single–Parent Families

Using reproductive technologies is not limited to married, heterosexual couples who are experiencing infertility. An increasing number of single, heterosexual women and lesbians also are using these technologies to get pregnant. This trend is another example of how, as mentioned earlier, parenting is increasingly separate from heterosexual marriage. In addition, there are a growing number of children being raised by never-married women and by divorced, separated, or widowed parents. The rise in single parenthood is often a subject of public debate. Many conservatives see these families as problematic because they believe they are financially dependent on welfare or inferior to the two-parent family. The second article in this section on parenting, "Single-Parent Families," examines the myths and realities of single-parent families in the United States. Stephen D. Sugarman, a professor of law at the University of California at Berkeley, provides an overview of the diversity of demographic types of single-parent families. Sugarman argues that not only are there single-parent families headed by men, but single-parent families vary in terms of marital status, socioeconomic status, race-ethnicity, and employment. Sugarman also examines the changes over time in social policies pertaining to single-parent families.

Gay and Lesbian Parenthood

While the contemporary debate around same-sex marriage stirs strong emotions in the United States, many Americans feel even more strongly about the notion that gay people might be parenting children. The reality, however, is that there are approximately 6 to 20 million children being raised in gay households and many more children, now adults, who have lesbian, gay, or bisexual parents (Joos 2003). The third reading in this section turns our attention to this controversial subject: Should gays and lesbians be allowed to parent children? Judith Stacey and Timothy J. Biblarz, sociology professors at the University of Southern California, examine the research on lesbian and gay parenthood. After reviewing the research cases for and against gay parenthood, Stacey and Biblarz specifically focus on how this research is designed and whether or not researchers' bias (either in favor of gay parenting or against it) may influence the reporting of developmental outcomes.

Stacey and Biblarz argue that research on gay parenting needs to move from a strictly psychological model to an informed sociological model that would allow differences in the developmental outcomes of children raised by gay parents to be further explored.

Research on Children

Over the last decade more research on children has been published. Two recent and exciting studies on children are excerpted in this section. The first article, "How Families Still Matter: A Longitudinal Study of Youth in Two Generations," is by a team of scholars in California, Vern L. Bengtson, Timothy J. Biblarz, and Robert E. L. Roberts. Bengtson is a professor of gerontology and sociology at the University of Southern California, Biblarz is an associate professor of sociology at the University of California, and Roberts is a professor of sociology at California State University, San Marcos. Bengtson et al. use 26 years of longitudinal data to study how parenting and children have changed across three decades, specifically comparing the Baby Boomers of the 1960s with the Generation Xers of the 1990s. After reviewing some contemporary myths about the decline and dysfunction of families, Bengtson et al. offer three important propositions as to why families still matter.

The second article that focuses on children is Annette Lareau's research, "Invisible Inequality: Social Class and Childrearing in Black Families and White Families." Similar to William Marsiglio's research on "Overlooked Aspects of Stepfathering" (Reading 27), Lareau studies parenting and its effects on children beyond the obvious domains of providing food, shelter, and other basic care. What do parents convey to their children in terms of social capital? Lareau, a professor of sociology at Temple University, began studying childrearing strategies in families of diverse racial-ethnic and social class backgrounds in order to determine the social effects of parenting on children. Lareau's intensive research is based on interviews and observations of children, aged 8 to 10, and their families in a midwestern community. Lareau found distinctive parenting practices and styles between the middle-class and working-class parents that provided middle-class children a greater sense of entitlement and advantage than working-class children. The full report of this study can be found in Lareau's recent book, *Unequal Childhood: Class, Race, and Family Life* (2003).

REFERENCES

Corsaro, William A. 1997. *The Sociology of Childhood.* Thousand Oaks, CA: Pine Forge Press.

Joos, Kristin E. 2003. "LGBT Parents and Their Children." SWS Fact Sheet. Washington, DC: Sociologists for Women in Society.

Lareau, Annette. 2003. *Unequal Childhood: Class, Race, and Family Life.* Berkeley: University of California Press.

Lasker, Judith N. and Susan Borg. 1987. *In Search of Parenthood: Coping with Infertility and High-Tech Conception.* Boston: Beacon Press.

LeVine, Robert A. and Merry White. 1987. "Parenthood in Social Transformation." Pp. 271–93 in *Parenting across the Life Span: Biosocial Dimensions,* edited by Jane B. Lancaster, Jeanne Altmann, Alice S. Rossi, and Lonnie R. Sherrod. New York: Aldine de Gruyter.

Skolnick, Arlene. 1994. "The Life Course Revolution." Pp. 62–71 in *Family in Transition,* edited by Arlene S. Skolnick and Jerome H. Skolnick. New York: HarperCollins.

Ventura, Stephanie J., et al. 1999. "Highlights of Trends in Pregnancies and Pregnancy Rates by Outcome: Estimates for the United States, 1976–96." *National Vital Statistics Reports.* Vol. 47, No. 29. Washington, DC: U.S. Department of Health and Human Services.

17

HISTORICAL PERSPECTIVES
ON PARENT–CHILD INTERACTIONS

MARIS A. VINOVSKIS

Overview

The perception and treatment of children and parent–child relationships have experienced major changes during the past 300 or 400 years. While most Western families have always been small and nuclear, the sharp boundary between the modern American family and the rest of society is a recent development. Although parents have historically been responsible for their children, they were not always closely attached to them as infants. Nor have young children been perceived and treated the same throughout history. Whether or not children were once seen as miniature adults, it is clear that they were regarded as capable of considerable intellectual training at a very early age. Furthermore, while historians differ among themselves on the existence or meaning of adolescence in earlier times, most of them agree that the life course of youth has changed considerably during the past several hundred years.

Parent–child relationships have also changed over time. Parental involvement in early child care has grown considerably since the Middle Ages, but the role of the father in the catechizing and educating of young children has diminished. At the same time, parental control over children has been greatly diminished in areas such as sexual behavior or choice of a career or spouse.

The relationship between parents and children is influenced by many factors and can vary over time. Alterations in the composition and size of the household as well as its interactions with the outside can affect the experiences of children growing up within it. Similarly, changes in the roles of parents or servants, for example, may affect the socialization of the young by that household. And any changes in the perceptions of the nature of children or their appropriate role in society is likely to influence their dealings with parents and other adults.

During the past 20 years, historians have reexamined the nature of the family as it once was, as well as the changes in the perception and treatment of children (Degler 1980b; Vinovskis 1977, 1983a). Most of these efforts, how-ever, have been focused on some particular aspect of the family or of the child, with less attention paid to their interaction. This [reading] will attempt to bring together some of these diverse studies and suggest how parenting and child development may have been different in the past than it is today. Although this analysis will draw upon historical examples from all of Western Europe since the 16th century, its primary focus will be on 17th-, 18th-, and 19th-century England and America. Furthermore, while there are many different possible definitions of family, throughout this chapter, family will refer to members of the same kin living under one roof (Stone 1977).

Nature of the Family and Household in the Past

The social context of parenting and child development is very much affected by the nature of the residence in which the child is reared. The traditional assumption (Parsons 1943; Wirth 1938) is that most children in the past grew up in extended households. After marriage, they continued to live with their parents and supported them in their old age. As a result, young children fre-quently grew up in large households where their grandparents as well as their parents played an important role in their upbringing.

Accordingly, the extended Western preindustrial household was trans-formed into an isolated nuclear one as the result of the disruptive impact of urbanization and industrialization (often incorrectly combined under the term "modernization") in the 19th and 20th centuries. While this new nuclear household was supposedly better suited to the needs of the modern economy in terms of providing a more mobile and less kin-oriented labor force, the tasks of child rearing and care of the elderly were seen to have suf-fered in the process.

Recent historical research has cast considerable doubt on the idea that the Western family evolved from extended to nuclear due to the onset of urbanization and industrialization. As Laslett (1972) and his associates have argued, most households in preindustrial Western Europe were already nuclear and therefore could not have been transformed by any recent eco-nomic changes. While some variations did exist in household size, these were surprisingly small and mainly due to the presence or absence of ser-vants or boarders and lodgers rather than relatives. Furthermore, instead of the nostalgic view of children growing up in large families, Laslett (1972) contends that most households were actually quite small (mean household size was about 4.75).

Critics (Berkner 1972, 1973) of the use of a mean household size point out that studying the average size of families at any given moment is mis-leading and incorrect because individual families increase and decrease in size and complexity over time. While only a small proportion are extended at any particular instance, a much larger proportion of them may have been extended at some point. Berkner (1972) in particular notes the prevalence of the stem family in Austria, where one of the male children continues to live with the parents after he marries and then inherits the farm after the father dies.

Although the critics of the use of mean household size are correct in questioning its conceptual and analytical utility, it is not likely that many families in preindustrial England or America had married children routinely living with them (Degler 1980a; Vinovskis 1977, 1983a). While single servants or boarders and lodgers frequently resided in the same household (Demos 1970; Modell and Hareven 1973), it was expected that married couples would establish their own separate, independent households. In some parts of Western Europe, however, such as southern France (Flandrin 1979) or the Baltic provinces (Plakens 1975), multigenerational households were more common. Furthermore, while mean household size was usually quite small in Western Europe (Laslett 1972), it was considerably larger in colonial New England (Greven 1972) because of the higher fertility and lower mortality in that region.

Even if most Western European families had always been small and nuclear, it does not mean that the social context in which children were brought up in a household remained the same. As Aries (1962) has pointed out, the medieval family was very different from its modern counterpart in that the boundary between the household and the larger society was not as rigidly drawn and the role of parents, servants, or neighbors in the socialization of children was not as differentiated and clear-cut. Stone's (1977) analysis of the late medieval and early 16th century English family confirms and expands upon many of Aries's findings. While Stone acknowledges that his categorization and periodization of the changes in English families is limited by the sources and the overlapping of these ideal family types to some degree in practice, his framework provides a useful point of departure for this analysis.

The English in the late medieval period maintained only weak boundaries between their families and the rest of society, and family members were oriented more toward kin relationships among the upper classes and toward neighbors among their poorer counterparts (Stone 1977). Marriage among property-owning classes in 16th-century England was a collective decision involving not only the family but also other kin. Individual considerations of happiness and romantic love were subservient to the need to protect the long-term interests of the lineage. Relationships within the nuclear family were not much closer than those with neighbors, relatives, or other friends.

According to Stone (1977), this open lineage family gave way to a restricted patriarchal nuclear family that predominated from 1580 to 1640, during which time loyalties to lineage, kin, and local community declined as allegiances to the state and church and kin within the household increased. As a result, the boundary between the nuclear family and the other members of society increased, while the authority of the father as head of the household within that family was enhanced. Both the state and the church provided new theoretical and practical support for patriarchy within the family, which was coupled with a new interest in children. Fathers now had added incentive to ensure that their offspring internalized the values of submissiveness to them even if it meant breaking their will at an early age. This drive toward parental dominance was particularly characteristic of the Puritans, who tended to be especially anxious about their children's upbringing. Concern about children continued as they developed, and upper-class parents sought to control their choices of both a career and a spouse.

Finally, Stone (1977) sees the growth of the closed domesticated nuclear family after the mid-17th century among the upper bourgeoisie and squirarchy caused by the rise of affective individualism. The family was now increasingly organized around the principle of personal autonomy and bound together by strong affective ties. The separation between the members of the nuclear family and their servants or boarders and lodgers widened, along with the distance between the household and the rest of society. Physical privacy became more important, and the idea of the individual's right to pursue his own happiness became more acceptable.

While the causes of the changes or the exact timing among the different social classes of the move from the open lineage family to the closed domesticated nuclear family are not always clear or agreed upon (Trumbach 1978), the occurrence of that shift is generally accepted. Children growing up in 15th-century England, for example, encountered a very different social environment in their homes and neighborhoods from those in the 18th and 19th centuries. Thus, the close-knit affective nuclear family that is most prevalent today is really only the latest stage in the longer evolution of households and family life in Western Europe in the past 500 years.

Throughout most of the preindustrial period the household also functioned as the central productive unit of society. Children received training in their own homes regarding their future occupations or were employed in someone else's household (Mitterauer and Sieder 1982). But as the economic functions of the household were transferred in the late 18th- and 19th centuries to the shop or the factory, the home environment in which the children were raised changed. Rather than being closely integrated into neighborhood activities and serving as an economic focal point, the household increasingly became a haven or escape from the outside world (Cott 1977; Lasch 1977). Furthermore, as members of the nuclear family increasingly distanced themselves from others, they came to expect and cherish more from each other emotionally (Mitterauer and Sieder 1982). As a result, whereas children growing up in the 15th century were expected and encouraged to interact closely with many other adults besides their own parents, those in the 18th and 19th centuries came to rely more upon each other and their own parents for their emotional needs.

While major changes in the nature of the family occurred in Western Europe, such changes were less dramatic in America due to the fact that when the New World was settled the closed domesticated nuclear family was already prevalent in England (Stone 1977). The families that migrated to the New World, especially the Puritans, brought with them the ideal of a close and loving family (Demos 1970; Morgan [1944] 1966). While the economic functions of the American household were altered in the 19th century, the overall change was less than the shift from an open lineage family to the closed domesticated nuclear family in Western Europe. Thus, although the relationship between parents and their children, for example, has not remained constant in America during the past 300 years, the extent of that change is probably less than in Western Europe.

Changing Perceptions and Treatment of Children

Having surveyed some of the changes in the nature of the household and the way they might affect the environment in which children were raised, the way those children were perceived and treated will now be considered. Because it is impossible, of course, to survey child development in its entirety, the focus will be confined to only three aspects: (1) parental love of children, (2) intellectual capabilities of young children, and (3) youth.

Parental Love of Children

It is commonly assumed that one of the basic characteristics of human beings is the close and immediate attachment between the newborn child and the parents — especially the mother. Consequently, child abandonment or abuse today is puzzling to many Americans, since these practices seem to contradict what is perceived to be a deeply ingrained feeling toward one's own children.

Maternal indifference to infants, however, may have been common during the Middle Ages (Aries 1962; Stone 1977). Parents did not pay much attention to newborn infants and did not display much grief if they died. According to Aries, the lack of affection toward and attention to infants continued until the 16th and 17th centuries, and Shorter (1975) argues that it persisted into the 18th and 19th centuries among the ordinary people of Western Europe. A few studies (Pollock 1983), however, question the extent of maternal indifference and inattention in the past and thereby tend to minimize any of the more recent changes perceived by other historians.

As evidence of parental indifference to infants, scholars point to the casualness with which deaths of young children were accepted and sometimes seemingly encouraged or at least tolerated. Although overt infanticide was frowned upon and increasingly prosecuted in the 16th century, it still may have been quite common in parts of Western Europe (Langer 1975). There also seems to be agreement that the practice of leaving infants at foundling hospitals or with rural wet nurses during the 17th, 18th, and 19th centuries resulted in very high mortality rates (Badinter 1981). The prevalence of wet-nursing is indicated by the fact that in the first two decades of the 19th century approximately half of the infants born in Paris were nursed commercially, even though this often resulted in more than one quarter of those infants dying (Sussman 1977). In addition, the natural children of the wet nurses also suffered and were more apt to die because they did not receive sufficient nourishment (Lehning 1982). Whether the decision to abandon an infant to a charitable institution or to a wet nurse was mainly the result of the mother's economic desperation, the difficulty of raising an out-of-wedlock child, or a lack of attachment for the young infant is not clear. But the fact that many well-to-do, married women casually chose to give their infants to wet nurses, despite the apparent higher risks of mortality, suggests that not everyone using this form of child care was driven to it by dire circumstances (Shorter 1975).

While the practice of overt infanticide and child abandonment may have been relatively widespread in parts of Western Europe (such as France), it does not seem to have been as prevalent in either England or America (Hoffer and Hull 1981; Stone 1977). Indeed, authorities in both those countries prosecuted cases of infanticide in the 16th and 17th centuries more vigorously than most other forms of murder and emphasized the importance of maternal care of the young child. Furthermore, the use of wet nurses (employed by upper-class English women) became unfashionable by the end of the 18th century (Trumbach 1978).

Although there is considerable disagreement on the extent and timing of parental indifference to infants in Western Europe, almost everyone is agreed on its presence as well as its subsequent demise. Though few individuals (Pollock 1983) have begun to challenge this interpretation—at least in its more extreme forms—most observers still concur that by the 17th and 18th centuries (or perhaps even later among French peasants and workers) parents expressed more interest in and affection for their children (Demos 1970; Morgan [1944] 1966; Stone 1977; Trumbach 1978). Indeed, the deep affection and attachment to one's own children became one of the major characteristics of the closed domesticated nuclear family. By the 19th century, many observers began to even criticize parents for being too child-centered (Wishy 1968).

While the gradual change in the reactions of parents to their newborn undoubtedly improved the situation of children generally, parents still could, if they chose, abuse their own children as long as such abuse did not result in death. Gradually, however, the state began to intervene to protect the child from harm inflicted at the workplace or at home. Yet it was not until the late 19th century that reformers in England were able to persuade lawmakers to pass legislation to protect children from abusive parents, since the parent–child relationship was regarded as sacred and beyond state intervention (Behlmer 1982). Ironically, efforts to prevent cruelty against animals preceded those to accomplish the same ends for children by nearly half a century (Turner 1980).

Intellectual Capabilities of Young Children

Child developmentalists sometimes portray the nature and capabilities of the young as invariant across cultures and over time, without taking into consideration how much of the behavior of those children can be explained by parental and societal expectations. Yet historically the perceptions and treatment of the child have been quite varied.

Some of the earliest studies (Earle 1899) of children in colonial America yielded the observation that a distinct phase of childhood did not exist. Children were expected to think and behave as adults from a very early age. As Fleming (1933) noted, "Children were regarded simply as miniature adults" (p. 60). This perception of children received strong reinforcement from Aries (1962), who argued that medieval society in general did not distinguish between children and adults and that the idea of childhood as a separate and distinct stage did not emerge until the 16th and 17th centuries.

Some recent scholars (Demos 1970, 1974; Zuckerman 1970) of the colonial American family have continued the idea that children were perceived and treated as miniature adults. But others (Axtell 1974; Kaestle and Vinovskis 1978, 1980; Stannard 1975, 1977) have questioned this interpretation by pointing out that the New England Puritans were aware that children had different abilities and temperaments from adults and that child rearing should be molded to those individual differences (Moran and Vinovskis 1983).

Young children in colonial America, however, were perceived as being more capable intellectually at an early age than their counterparts today. The Puritans believed that children should be taught to read the Bible as soon as possible because it was essential for everyone's salvation. The importance of early reading was reinforced for them by their expectation that children were likely to die at any moment and therefore had to be spiritually prepared for this eventuality (Slater 1977; Stannard 1975, 1977; Vinovskis 1972, 1976, 1981b). Indeed, the notion that children could and should learn to read as soon as they could talk was so commonly accepted by educators (Locke 1964) that they did not feel the need to elaborate upon it in their writings (Kaestle and Vinovskis 1978, 1980).

The idea of early childhood learning received a powerful boost in the first third of the 19th century, when the infant school movement swept the United States (Kaestle and Vinovskis 1978, 1980; May and Vinovskis 1976). The focus on special classes for very young children was imported from England, where infant schools had been created to help disadvantaged poor children. While most infant schools in America were initially intended to help poor children, they were quickly adopted by middle-class parents once it became evident that they were useful in helping children to develop. By the 1830s and 1840s in Massachusetts, for example, nearly 40–50 percent of 3-year-old children were attending schools and learning to read. Although some infant-school teachers were reluctant to focus on intellectual activities such as reading, pressures from parents forced most of them to provide such instruction.

During the first two centuries of settlement in the New World, the idea that 3- and 4-year-old children were intellectually capable of learning to read had gone virtually unchallenged in theory as well as practice and was reinforced by the infant-school movement of the late 1820s. Yet in the 1830s this viewpoint became strongly and successfully contested. Amariah Brigham, a prominent physician, published a popular book (1833) in which he argued that the early intellectual training of children seriously and permanently physically weakened their growing young minds and often led to insanity in later life. His dire warnings were accepted and repeated by educators as well as writers of child-rearing manuals. As a result, crucial financial support for the infant schools from the middle-class reformers dropped precipitously, and many such institutions were forced to close. Although parents were much slower than physicians and educators in abandoning early childhood education, by the 1850s and 1860s virtually no very young children (3- or 4-year-olds) could be found in Massachusetts schools. Interestingly, when the kindergarten movement was popularized in the United States in the 1860s and 1870s by Mary Peabody, a former Massachusetts infant-school teacher, it was restricted to children at least 5 or 6 years old and deliberately avoided intellectual activities such as reading.

This example of the changing attitudes on when a child could and should learn to read illustrates how alterations in the perception of children can greatly affect the type of socialization provided for them in early life. It also demonstrates how sudden and dramatic shifts in the perceptions of the child can alter the basic pattern of child care that had been accepted unquestioningly for several centuries. One might even speculate that as society becomes increasingly willing to incorporate the latest scientific and medical findings in the care of the young, and as social institutions such as the schools become more willing and able to determine how and when parents educate their children, the likelihood of frequent swings in child-rearing practices may increase.

Youth

Although the historical study of youth is now attracting more research (Gillis 1974; Kett 1977), there is still little agreement among scholars on the changes that occur in this phase of the life course. The recognition of adolescence as a particular stage of development in the past, for example, has not been conclusively demonstrated. Some historians (Demos and Demos 1969) see its emergence only in the late 19th or early 20th century, as a result of the introduction of more career choices and the sharper discontinuities in young people's lives due to urban-industrial development. Others (Hiner 1975) have challenged that interpretation by arguing for the presence of adolescence in the early 18th century. Some individuals (Kett 1977) have moved away from the issue of adolescence as a particular stage and focused instead on the changes in the lives of youth as they move from a state of dependence to one of independence, signaled by the establishment of their own household.

Rather than trying to analyze the individual emotional turmoil and tension that is often associated with adolescence today, many historians are studying other aspects of teenage development, such as patterns of school attendance and labor force participation. Here the debate, usually among economic and educational historians, revolves not around the life course experiences of the individual, but on those differences in the experiences among various ethnic groups or classes (Vinovskis 1983b). Scholars like Thernstrom (1964) argue that early school leaving in 19th-century America was mainly the result of ethnic rather than class differences, as Irish parents were more willing to have their children leave school in order to help the family earn enough money to purchase their own home. Other historians (Bowles and Gintis 1976; Katz and Davey 1978) reject this ethnic interpretation and contend that the real cause of variations in school attendance was class differences. Finally, some analysts (Kaestle and Vinovskis 1980) offer a more pluralistic interpretation that recognizes the importance of both the ethnicity and class of the parents as well as the type of community in which the children are raised.

While historians may be moving toward more agreement on the patterns of school attendance and labor force participation among youth, they are simultaneously beginning to disagree on the importance of that education. Whereas Thernstrom (1964) and most other social historians simply assumed that education was an important factor in the social functioning and mobility of 19th-century teenagers, Graff (1979) questions the benefits and necessity of literacy and education altogether. Thus, historians who have been content to analyze the patterns and causes of teenage school attendance are now being forced to reexamine its actual meaning and impact on the lives of those children.

Although American historians have tried to analyze the patterns of school attendance and labor force participation of teenagers in the past as well as the existence of adolescence as a stage of the life course, surprisingly little has been done to explore the changes in teenage sexuality, pregnancy, or childbearing (Vinovskis 1982). This is somewhat surprising, since the issue of the so-called "epidemic" of adolescent pregnancy has become so visible and symbolically important to policymakers in Washington today (Vinovskis 1981a).

In early America, adolescent sexuality, pregnancy, and childbearing were not perceived to be particular problems (Vinovskis 1982). Although the age of menarche in colonial New England biologically was low enough for teenage parenting to occur, few became pregnant because of the stringent 17th-century prohibitions against premarital sexual relations and the fact that few women married in their early teens. Even if teenage girls were sexually active and did become pregnant, their age was less of a factor in how society reacted than their general behavior. In other words, early Americans were more concerned about premarital sexual relations in general than the age of the women involved. Only in the late 19th and early 20th centuries is there differentiation between teenage and adult sexual behavior, with a more negative connotation attached to the former.

Throughout most of the 17th, 18th, and 19th centuries, there was little onus attached to teenage marriages as long as the couple was self-supporting. Because opportunities for careers for single or married women outside the home were limited, the handicaps currently associated with early childbearing did not seem as severe. Furthermore, the relatively small number of teenage marriages during these years compared to the situation today also minimized the attention that was paid to teenage childbearing in the past.

Indeed, only in the post–World War II period has the issue of teenage pregnancy and childbearing become such a major public concern. Ironically, the greatest attention to it has come during the late 1970s and early 1980s, even though the rates of teenage pregnancy and childbearing peaked in the United States in the late 1950s (Vinovskis 1981a).

Parent–Child Relations

Thus far this chapter has dealt with changes in the . . . perception and treatment of children over time. Two issues in the relationship between parents and children — (1) parental responsibility for early child care and (2) parental control of children — should also be considered.

Parental Responsibility for Early Child Care

In modern American society, it is assumed that the parents have the primary responsibility for child care until the children are enrolled in schools where they will receive most of their educational instruction. When the behavior of parents seriously threatens the well-being of the young child, the state can intervene to protect it, but this does not occur frequently. Furthermore, the physical care and early socialization of the child is almost always the responsibility of the mother — even if both parents are employed.

Historically, the primary responsibility for the upbringing of young children belonged almost exclusively to the parents, especially the father. Although in some periods and societies, such as 17th- and 18th-century New England (Moran and Vinovskis 1983), the state or church intervened in order to ensure that the children were properly catechized and instructed, it was not until the late 19th and early 20th centuries that the state was willing to remove the young child from the direct supervision of negligent or abusive parents (Behlmer 1982). It should also be noted, however, that although the state valued the family in the past, it was not irrevocably committed to it when that family was incapable of supporting its own members. Thus, in early America destitute families were sometimes disbanded and the children placed in other households in order to reduce the welfare costs to the rest of the community (Rosenkrantz and Vinovskis 1977).

If the responsibility for early child care usually resided with the parents, they did not always provide that care themselves. In the medieval household, for example, servants as well as neighbors complemented the care given the young child by the parents or their older siblings (Aries 1962; Stone 1977). In addition, as was discussed previously, many women in the past willingly or out of economic necessity relinquished the nurturing of their infants to a wet nurse (Shorter 1975; Sussman 1977).

By the 17th and 18th centuries, particularly in England and America, parents increasingly cared for their own young children and began to limit assistance from nonfamily members (Morgan [1944] 1966; Stone 1977). This trend was caused in large part by the growing affection and self-centeredness among the immediate family members in the closed domesticated nuclear family. Furthermore, parental involvement in the upbringing of their own children was especially evident among the Puritans, who insisted on the importance of the family in providing for the spiritual as well as the physical needs of the young child (Moran and Vinovskis 1982, 1983).

As the family began to play a more active role in the care of its young children, there was often a division of labor between the parents. The mother provided for the physical needs of the child while the father, as head of the household, attended to its spiritual and educational development. Indeed, the Puritans saw the father as the primary catechizer of children and household servants (Moran and Vinovskis 1983).

The importance in these areas of the Puritan father was reversed in the 18th and 19th centuries, as men stopped joining churches and therefore were deemed less suitable for overseeing the religious upbringing of their children (Moran 1979, 1980). New England Puritans came to rely more upon the mothers who, although they were less literate than the husbands, continued to join the churches. By the end of the 18th and early 19th centuries, the mother's role in early childhood care and socialization was clearly established (Kuhn 1947; Moran and Vinovskis 1983). The only major change thereafter was the growing role of the schools in the provision of formal education for the young child, as parents usually willingly relinquished that task to reluctant schoolteachers who had tried to limit the entry of young children into their classrooms (Kaestle and Vinovskis 1980).

Thus, although parents have usually been assigned the primary responsibility for the care and socialization of the young child in Western society, they have not always provided those services themselves. During the past 300 or 400 years, however, parents have increasingly nurtured and socialized, at least to some degree and frequently with the assistance of specialized institutions such as schools or churches, their own children. While the direct involvement of parents in early child care and education has grown, that of other non-related members of the household or of the neighbors has diminished; the family today is more private and self-centered than its medieval counterpart. Finally, although the father played a more important role in the catechizing and educating of young children in certain time periods and cultures, the primary provider of care and affection for the young child was usually the mother or her female substitute. The mother's role in the upbringing of the young child increased during the 18th and 19th centuries as fathers became too busy or uninterested in sharing more fully in the raising of their young offspring. While child-rearing manuals continued to acknowledge the importance of the father for the care of the young, they also recognized that the mother had become the major figure in the performance of that task (Demos 1982).

Parental Control of Children

Throughout most of Western development, parents exercised considerable control over children as long as they remained in the home. Children were expected to be obedient to their parents and to contribute to the well-being of the family. During much of this time, parents arranged the marriages of their children and greatly influenced their choice of careers.

In the medieval period, the interests of the lineage and kin were more important than those of the individual (Aries 1962; Stone 1977). Children were expected to acquiesce not only to the requests of parents, but also to the interests of the larger kinship network. Marriages were arranged in order to further the goals of the family and its kindred.

The emergence of the restricted patriarchal nuclear family weakened the claims of the lineage and kin on the allegiances of the children as the nuclear family grew closer together. The emphasis on the authority of the father as the head of the household, however, reinforced parental control over the children.

It was not until the arrival of the closed domesticated nuclear family that the rights of children as individuals were clearly recognized and acknowledged. Increasingly, children were allowed not only to veto an unsatisfactory marriage partner, but even to choose someone they loved (Stone 1977; Trumbach 1978). While dating this erosion of parental power in the selection of a child's mate may vary from one society to another, it probably occurred in America between the late 18th and 19th centuries (Smith 1973).

Parents tried to determine not only whom children should marry, but also when. According to Greven (1970), the second generation in 17th-century Andover, Massachusetts were prevented from early marriages by the unwillingness of their fathers to relinquish legal control over the land they had set aside for their sons. While this argument is plausible, Greven has been unable to establish it statistically (Vinovskis 1971). Indeed, while there is little doubt that parents often tried to influence the timing as well as the partner of their child's marriage, very few of the existing historical studies are able to ascertain the relative importance of the role of the parents—especially since many of the children may have willingly acquiesced in this process anyway. Yet the idea that a child has rights independent of and superior to those of the parents is a relatively recent development in Western society.

In Western Europe, children were also expected to turn over almost all their earnings directly to the parents—sometimes even after they had left home (Shorter 1975). Under these circumstances, the economic value of children to the family was considerably enhanced, since the additional labor or revenue from a grown child could be substantial. Although children frequently contributed some of their outside earnings to their parents in the United States, it does not seem to have been as common as in Western Europe—especially among the native-born population (Dublin 1979). This difference in parental control over the earnings of children probably reflects both the greater individuality and freedom of the child in the 19th-century American family and the fact that these families were not as economically destitute as their European counterparts. Certainly among some immigrant groups in the United States there seems to have been a stronger tradition of children, particularly girls, turning over their pay envelopes to the parents (Hareven 1982).

Over time parental control of children has been significantly diminished. Whereas in the medieval and early modern periods parents had almost unlimited control over the behavior of their children in their own households, such is no longer the case. Although parents may still influence the choice of a child's mate or career, they cannot determine them. In addition, the idea of a child giving most of his/her outside wages to the parents seems anachronistic and inappropriate today. Indeed, the development of children's rights has proceeded so far and rapidly that society is in the midst of a backlash as efforts are being made to reassert parental rights in areas such as the reproductive behavior of minor children.

Conclusion

This brief historical survey of the nature of the family and household, the perception and treatment of children, and parent–child relationships suggests that major changes have occurred in these areas during the past 300 to 400 years. While most Western families have always been small and nuclear, the sharp boundary between the modern American family and the rest of society is a recent development.

Although parents have been responsible for their children, they were not always closely attached to them as infants. Nor were young children perceived and treated the same throughout history. Whether or not children were once seen as miniature adults, it is clear that they were regarded as capable of considerable intellectual training at a very early age. Furthermore, while historians differ among themselves on the existence or meaning of adolescence in the past, most of them agree that the life course of youth has drastically changed during the past several hundred years.

Finally, parent–child relationships have changed over time as well. Parental involvement in early child care has grown greatly since the Middle Ages, but the role of the father in the catechizing and educating of young children has diminished. At the same time, parental control over the behavior of children has been greatly diminished in areas such as sexual behavior or choice of a career or spouse.

Although there have been major changes in the way society treats children, it would be very difficult to agree on the costs and benefits of those trends from the viewpoint of the child, the parents, or society. While many applaud the increasing individualism and freedom for children within the family, others lament the loss of family responsibility and individual discipline. While an historical analysis of parents and children cannot resolve such issues, it can provide us with a better appreciation of the flexibility and resilience of the family as an institution for raising the young.

ENDNOTE

Author's Note: Research was supported by the Program in American Institutions at the University of Michigan.

REFERENCES

Aries, P. 1962. *Centuries of Childhood: A Social History of Family Life.* Translated by R. Baldick. New York: Vintage Books.

Axtell, J. 1974. *The School upon a Hill: Education and Society in Colonial New England.* New Haven, CT: Yale University Press.

Badinter, E. 1981. *Mother Love: Myth & Reality.* New York: Macmillan.

Behlmer, G. K. 1982. *Child Abuse and Moral Reform in England, 1870–1908.* Stanford, CA: Stanford University Press.

Berkner, L. K. 1972. "The Stem Family and the Developmental Cycle of the Peasant Household: An Eighteenth-Century Austrian Example." *American Historical Review* 77:398–418.

——. 1973. "Recent Research on the History of the Family in Western Europe." *Journal of Marriage and the Family* 35:395–405.

Bowles, S. and H. Gintis. 1976. *Schooling in Capitalist America: Educational Reform and the Contradictions of Economic Life.* New York: Basic Books.

Brigham, A. 1833. *Remarks on the Influence of Mental Cultivation and Mental Excitement upon Health.* 2d ed. Boston, MA: Marsh, Capen and Lyon.

Cott, N. F. 1977. *The Bonds of Womanhood: "Woman's Sphere" in New England, 1780–1835.* New Haven, CT: Yale University Press.

Degler, C. 1980a. *At Odds: Women and the Family in America from the Revolution to the Present.* New York: Oxford University Press.

——. 1980b. "Women and the Family." Pp. 308–26 in *The Past Before Us: Contemporary Historical Writings in the United States,* edited by M. Kammen. Ithaca, NY: Cornell University Press.

Demos, J. 1970. *A Little Commonwealth: Family Life in Plymouth Colony.* New York: Oxford University Press.

——. 1974. "The American Family in Past Time." *American Scholar* 43:422–46.

——. 1982. "The Changing Faces of Fatherhood: A New Exploration in American Family History." Pp. 425–50 in *Father and Child: Developmental and Clinical Perspectives,* edited by S. H. Cath, A. R. Gurwitt, and J. M. Ross. Boston, MA: Little, Brown.

Demos, J. and V. Demos. 1969. "Adolescence in Historical Perspective." *Journal of Marriage and the Family* 31:632–38.

Dublin, T. 1979. *Women at Work: The Transformation of Work and Community in Lowell, Massachusetts, 1826–1860.* New York: Columbia University Press.

Earle, A. M. 1899. *Child Life in Colonial Days.* New York: Macmillan.

Flandrin, J. L. 1979. *Families in Former Times: Kinship, Household, and Sexuality in Early Modern France.* Translated by R. Southern. Cambridge: Cambridge University Press.

Fleming, S. 1933. *Children and Puritanism: The Place of Children in the Life and Thought of the New England Churches, 1620–1847.* New Haven, CT: Yale University Press.

Gillis, J. R. 1974. *Youth and History.* New York: Academic Press.

Graff, H. J. 1979. *The Literacy Myth: Literacy and Social Structure in the Nineteenth-Century City.* New York: Academic Press.

Greven, P. J. 1970. *Four Generations: Population, Land, and Family in Colonial Andover, Massachusetts.* Ithaca, NY: Cornell University Press.

——. 1972. "The Average Size of Families and Households in the Province of Massachusetts in 1764 and in the United States in 1790: An Overview." Pp. 545–60 in *Household and Family in Past Time,* edited by P. Laslett. Cambridge: Cambridge University Press.

Hareven, T. K. 1982. *Family Time & Industrial Time: The Relationship between the Family and Work in a New England Industrial Community.* Cambridge: Cambridge University Press.

Hiner, N. R. 1975. "Adolescence in Eighteenth-Century America." *History of Childhood Quarterly* 3:253–80.

Hoffer, P. C. and N. E. H. Hull. 1981. *Murdering Mothers: Infanticide in England and New England, 1558–1803.* New York: New York University Press.

Kaestle, C. F. and M. A. Vinovskis. 1978. "From Apron Strings to ABCs: Parents, Children, and Schooling in Nineteenth-Century Massachusetts." Pp. 539–580 in *Turning Points: Historical and Sociological Essays on the Family,* edited by J. Demos and S. S. Boocock. Chicago: University of Chicago Press.

———. 1980. *Education and Social Change in Nineteenth-Century Massachusetts.* Cambridge: Cambridge University Press.

Katz, M. B. and I. E. Davey. 1978. "School Attendance and Early Industrialization in a Canadian City: A Multivariate Analysis." *History of Education Quarterly* 18:271–94.

Kett, J. F. 1977. *Rites of Passage: Adolescence in America, 1790 to the Present.* New York: Basic Books.

Kuhn, A. L. 1947. *The Mother's Role in Childhood Education.* New Haven, CT: Yale University Press.

Langer, W. 1975. "Infanticide: A Historical Survey." Pp. 55–68 in *The New Psychohistory,* edited by L. DeMause. New York: The Psychohistory Press.

Lasch, C. 1977. *Haven in a Heartless World: The Family Besieged.* New York: Basic Books.

Laslett, P., ed. 1972. *Household and Family in Past Time.* Cambridge: Cambridge University Press.

Lehning, J. R. 1982. "Family Life and Wetnursing in a French Village." *Journal of Interdisciplinary History* 12:645–56.

Locke, J. 1964. *Some Thoughts Concerning Education.* Abridged and edited by F. W. Garforth. Woodbury, NY: Barron.

May, D. and M. A. Vinovskis. 1976. "A Ray of Millennial Light: Early Education and Social Reform in the Infant School Movement in Massachusetts, 1826–1840." Pp. 62–99 in *Family and Kin in American Urban Communities, 1800–1940,* edited by T. K. Hareven. New York: Watts.

Mitterauer, M. and M. Sieder. 1982. *The European Family: From Patriarchy to Partnership.* Translated by K. Oosterveen and M. Horzinger. Chicago: University of Chicago Press.

Modell, J. and T. K. Hareven. 1973. "Urbanization and the Malleable Household: An Examination of Boarding and Lodging in American Families." *Journal of Marriage and the Family* 35:467–79.

Moran, E. S. 1966. *The Puritan Family: Religion and Domestic Relations in Seventeenth-Century New England.* New York: Harper and Row.

Moran, G. F. 1979. "Religious Renewal, Puritan Tribalism, and the Family in Seventeenth-Century Milford Connecticut." *William and Mary Quarterly,* 3rd Series, 36:236–54.

———. 1980. "Sisters in Christ: Women and the Church in Seventeenth-Century New England." Pp. 47–64 in *Women in American Religion,* edited by J. W. James. Philadelphia: University of Pennsylvania Press.

Moran, G. F. and M. A. Vinovskis. 1982. "The Puritan Family and Religion: A Critical Reappraisal." *William and Mary Quarterly,* 3d Series, 39:29–63.

———. 1983. "The Great Care of Godly Parents: Early Childhood in Puritan New England." Paper presented at Biennial Meeting of the Society for Research in Child Development, Detroit, April.

Morgan, Edmund S. [1944] 1966. *The Puritan Family: Religion and Domestic Relations in 17th Century New England.* New York: Vanguard Press.

Parsons, T. 1943. "The Kinship System of the Contemporary United States." *American Anthropologist* 45:22–38.

Plakens, A. 1975. "Seigneurial Authority and Peasant Family Life: The Baltic Area in the Eighteenth Century. *Journal of Interdisciplinary History* 4:629–54.

Pollock, L. 1983. *Forgotten Children: Parent–Child Relations from 1500 to 1900.* Cambridge: Cambridge University Press.

Rosenkrantz, B. G. and M. A. Vinovskis.1977. "Caring for the Insane in Antebellum Massachusetts: Family, Community, and State Participation." Pp. 187–218 in *Kin and Communities: Families in America,* edited by A. J. Lichtman and J. R. Challinor. Washington, DC: Smithsonian Institution Press.

Shorter, E. 1975. *The Making of the Modern Family.* New York: Basic Books.

Slater, P. G. 1977. *Children in the New England Mind: In Death and in Life.* Hamden, CT: Archon Books.

Smith, D. S. 1973. "Parental Power and Marriage Patterns: An Analysis of Historical Trends in Hingham, Massachusetts." *Journal of Marriage and the Family* 35:406–18.

Stannard, D. E. 1975. "Death and the Puritan Child." Pp. 9–29 in *Death in America,* edited by D. E. Stannard. Philadelphia: University of Pennsylvania Press.

——. 1977. *The Puritan Way of Death: A Study in Religion, Culture, and Social Change.* New Haven, CT: Yale University Press.

Stone, L. 1977. *The Family, Sex and Marriage in England, 1500–1800.* New York: Oxford University Press.

Sussman, G. D. 1977. "Parisian Infants and Norman Wet Nurses in the Early Nineteenth Century: A Statistical Study." *Journal of Interdisciplinary History* 7:637–54.

Thernstrom, S. 1964. *Poverty and Progress: Social Mobility in a Nineteenth-Century City.* Cambridge, MA: Harvard University Press.

Trumbach, R. 1978. *The Rise of the Egalitarian Family: Aristocratic Kinship and Domestic Relations in Eighteenth-Century England.* New York: Academic Press.

Turner, J. 1980. *Reckoning with the Beast: Animals, Pain, and Humanity in the Victorian Mind.* Baltimore: Johns Hopkins Press.

Vinovskis, M. A. 1971. "American Historical Demography: A Review Essay." *Historical Methods Newsletter* 4:141–48.

——. 1972. "Mortality Rates and Trends in Massachusetts before 1860." *Journal of Economic History* 32:184–213.

——. 1976. "Angels, Heads and Weeping Willows: Death in Early America." *Proceedings of the American Antiquarian Society:* 86:273–302.

——. 1977. "From Household Size to the Life Course: Some Observations on Recent Trends in Family History." *American Behavioral Scientist* 21:263–87.

——. 1981a. "An Epidemic of Adolescent Pregnancy? Some Historical Considerations. *Journal of Family History* 6:205–30.

——. 1981b. *Fertility in Massachusetts from the Revolution to the Civil War.* New York: Academic Press.

——. 1982. "Adolescent Sexuality, Pregnancy, and Childbearing in Early America: Some Preliminary Speculations." Paper presented at the SSRC Conference on School-Age Pregnancies and Parenthood, Belmont Conference Center, Maryland, May.

——. 1983a. "American Families in the Past." Pp. 115–37 in *Ordinary People and Everyday Life: Perspectives on the New Social History.* Nashville, TN: American Association for State and Local History.

——. 1983b. "Quantification and the Analysis of Antebellum Education." *Journal of Interdisciplinary History* 13:761–86.

Wirth, L. 1938. "Urbanism as a Way of Life." *American Journal of Sociology* 44:1–24.

Wishy, B. 1968. *The Child and the Republic.* Philadelphia: University of Pennsylvania Press.

Zuckerman, M. 1970. *Peaceable Kingdoms: New England Towns in the Eighteenth Century.* New York: Alfred A. Knopf.

18

SINGLE–PARENT FAMILIES

STEPHEN D. SUGARMAN

What do the former First Lady Jackie Kennedy, the chief prosecutor in the O. J. Simpson case, Marcia Clark, the pop star Madonna, and the TV character Murphy Brown have in common? They all are, or at one time were, single mothers — unmarried women caring for their minor children. This [reading] concerns public policy and the single-parent family, a family type dominated by single mothers.

Because these four women are fitting subjects for *Lifestyles of the Rich and Famous*, they are a far cry from what most people have in mind when the phrase "single mother" is used. Many picture, say, a nineteen-year-old high school dropout living on welfare in public housing. Hence, just mentioning these four prominent women vividly demonstrates the diversity of single mothers. These four also illustrate the major categories of single mothers — the widowed mother, the divorced or separated mother, and the single woman who bears her child outside of marriage. (Women in this last category are often misleadingly called "never married" even though approximately one-fourth of the women who are unmarried at the birth of their child had been married at an earlier time.[1])

One further distinction should also be made here. The usual picture of the single mother is of a woman living *alone* with her children — Jackie Kennedy, Marcia Clark, and Murphy Brown. But those we call "cohabitants" are also single mothers as a legal matter, even though their children are living in two-adult households. Indeed, where the woman is cohabiting with the father of her child — Madonna — while the mother is single, from the child's perspective it is an intact family.

As with single mothers generally, these four prominent women arouse a wide range of feelings, from support to dismay, in the public at large. Jackie Kennedy surely gained the maximum empathy of our foursome when her husband was murdered in her presence. Even those women who are widowed in less horrifying ways have long been viewed as victims of cruel fate and strongly deserving of community compassion.

Not too long ago, having been divorced was by itself thought to disqualify those seeking public office or other positions of prominence. That no longer holds, as Ronald Reagan's presidency made clear. As a result, when the spotlight of fame first shined on Marcia Clark, she probably appeared to most Americans as one of many of today's divorced professional women who had the challenging task of having to balance the pursuit of her career with raising a child on her own. The grueling pressures of prosecuting her most notorious case and her subsequent publicly revealed squabbles with her former husband did, however, bring to the fore our society's general uneasiness about how well children fare in these settings, as well as our uncertainty about the appropriate roles of divorced fathers as providers of both cash and care.

In Sweden today, Madonna's family structure is commonplace. There, a very large number of men and women live together and have children together, but do not go through the formalities of marriage. Lately, in America as well, the cohabitation category, long ignored by the census, is rapidly growing. This is not to say that most Americans, unlike the Swedes, accept cohabitation as though it were marriage. Indeed, American public policy, as we will see, treats cohabitation very differently from marriage.

Perhaps because Murphy Brown is a fictional character, this has allowed those who are on the rampage against unmarried women who bear children to be candid about their feelings without having to be so openly nasty to a "real" person. Yet Murphy Brown is an awkward icon. To be sure, she flouted the conventional morality of an earlier era. She had sex outside of marriage and then decided to keep and raise her child once she discovered she had unintentionally become pregnant. Although many people in our society still rail against sex other than between married couples, sex outside of marriage has become such a widespread phenomenon that it is generally no longer a stigma. And while it would be easy to chastise Murphy Brown for carelessly getting pregnant, this also is so commonplace that it is barely remarkable any more. Indeed, Murphy Brown might have come in for more censure had she, as a single woman, deliberately become pregnant.

As for deciding to raise her child on her own, this *by itself* no longer arouses great public outcry. After all, it is not as though widowed mothers who make that decision are castigated for choosing not to remarry. As for the unmarried birth mother, shotgun weddings are seen to be less promising than they once were; abortion, while still a right, is hardly thought to be a duty; and while giving a child up for adoption is often commendable, today this is seen primarily as the route for women who do not want to, or cannot afford to, take care of their children themselves.

In short, the strongest objection by those who have assailed Murphy Brown is that she is a bad role model—in particular, that she is a bad role model for *poor* women who, unlike her, cannot provide for their children on their own, but go ahead and have them anyway, planning to turn to the state for financial and other assistance. In many quarters those single mothers are doubly condemned. First, they are seen to be prying money out of the rest of us by trading on our natural sympathy for their innocent children; yet this is said to leave taxpayers both unhappy because they have less money to spend on their own children and with the distasteful feeling that society is condoning, even promoting, the initial irresponsible and self-indulgent behavior by these poor single mothers. Then, these low-income women are rebuked as high-frequency failures as parents — for example, when their children disproportionately drop out of, or are disruptive at, school or turn to criminal behavior. Of course, not everyone disapproves of Murphy Brown or even those poor women who choose to have children on their own knowing that they will have to turn to the state for financial assistance. Many people believe that every American woman (at least if she is emotionally fit) ought to be able to be a mother if she wants to be.

These various types of single mothers are significant because they raise different issues, and, in turn, they have yielded very different policy solutions and proposals for reform. But before we turn to policy questions, some general demographic information is presented that, among other things, shows single-parent families to differ significantly from some common myths about them. The policy discussion that follows begins with a historical overview that demonstrates how American policies have changed sharply through the century. . . . The [reading] concludes with a call to refocus public attention on the needs of the children in single-parent families.

Single–Parent Family Demographics: Myths and Realities

Father-Headed Single-Parent Families

In the first place, not all single-parent families are headed by women. In 1970, three-quarters of a million children living in single-parent families lived with their father (10 percent of such families); by 1992, more than two million children lived in father-headed single-parent families (an increase to 14 percent).[2]

These families are not the subject of much policy attention, however. First, most of them are headed by divorced (or separated) men; a few are widowers. It is rare, however, that the father of a child born outside of marriage will gain physical control of that child, and this takes custodial fathers largely outside the most controversial category of single parents. Furthermore, single fathers caring for their children tend to be financially self-supporting and therefore generally beyond the purview of welfare reformers. Finally, they tend to remarry fairly quickly and hence remain heads of single-parent families for only a short time. In fact, the main public policy controversy involving these men today concerns divorce custody law — in what circumstances should fathers be able to become heads of single-parent families in the first place?

Noncustodial fathers are quite another matter — whether divorced from or never married to the mothers of their children. As we will see, they are the subject of a great deal of public attention and concern.

Unmarried as Compared to Divorced and Widowed

Turning back to families headed by single mothers, one myth is that they are predominantly women who have never been married to the father of their child. Yet there are actually more divorced (and separated) single mothers. For example, in 1992, 60 percent of single mothers were divorced or separated, and another 5 percent were widowed.[3] Moreover, because of the predominance of widowed and divorced mothers, large numbers of women become single mothers, not at their child's birth, but later on in their child's life, often not until the child is a teenager. Hence, among the children in single-parent families, living one's entire childhood apart from one's father is by no means the norm.

Cohabitants

Cohabitants with children in their household are a complicated category, and, in turn, they complicate the data.[4] As noted earlier, although the women in these families are decidedly single mothers in a legal sense, in many respects these couples resemble married couples. So, many of these households are better described as two-parent, not single-parent, families. Some demographers have recently suggested that "cohabitation operates primarily as a precursor or a transitional stage to marriage among whites, but more as an alternative form of marriage among blacks."[5]

In any case, these cohabiting households come in several varieties. One first thinks of two biological parents not married to each other but living with their child — as exemplified by Madonna and the father of her child and the Swedish model. Cohabiting mothers in this situation still often show up in U.S. surveys as though they were never-married mothers living on their own, because survey instruments tend to categorize respondents only as married or single.

A second variety of cohabiting households includes a single mother with her child who is now living with, but not married to, a man who is *not* the child's father. These women are drawn out of the ranks of the never married, the divorced, and the widowed; they, too, are frequently counted in surveys as living on their own. Moreover, in this second category especially, it is often unclear to outsiders whether the man is a de facto spouse and stepparent, a casual boyfriend, or something in between.

Yet a third category of cohabiting households contains a homosexual couple (more often two women) in which one of the partners is the legal (usually biological) parent and the other is formally a stranger (although some lesbian couples of late have successfully become dual mothers through adoption).

Working and Not

Although the myth is that single mothers (especially never-married welfare moms) spend their time lounging around the house, watching TV, doing drugs, and/or entertaining men, this is a wild exaggeration. A large proportion is in the paid labor force. Official data from 1993 show that about two-thirds of *all* women with children are in the labor force. Married women's rates are about 60 percent where the youngest child is under six and about 75 percent where the youngest child is six or older. Within the ranks of single mothers, divorced women work *more* than married women, whereas never-married women are less likely to *report* working.[6]

Single mothers often feel compelled to work full time even when their children are very young, although the official data again show a difference between divorced and never-married women. According to 1993 figures, of those women with a child under age six, 51 percent of divorced women and 26 percent of never-married women worked *full time;* on average this was slightly higher than the rate for married women, 38 percent of whom were working full time.[7]

Although fewer than 10 percent of single mothers who are receiving welfare officially acknowledge earning wages,[8] recent research by Kathryn Edin suggests that, in fact, a high proportion of them is actually employed at least part time.[9] They tend to work for cash in the underground (and sometimes illegal) economy. According to Edin's findings, they do not typically do so to be able to buy drugs or booze but, rather, in order to keep their households from utter destitution or to avoid having to live in intolerably dangerous public housing projects. They keep this work a secret from the welfare authorities because if the authorities knew, they would so cut back those women's welfare benefits to make their wages from work nearly meaningless. Although these women would be viewed by the welfare system as "cheaters," they tend to remain living in fairly impoverished circumstances. As Edin puts it, they feel compelled to break the law by the skimpiness of the welfare benefits they receive.

Poor and Nonpoor

Even with the receipt of government assistance, more than a third of family households headed by single mothers officially live below the poverty level (as compared with only 6.5 percent of families headed by a married couple).[10] Although this is a distressingly high number, to the extent that the myth is that single mothers are poor and on welfare, the myth is false. A substantial share of single mothers provides a reasonable level of material goods for their children, and more than half of all single mothers are not on welfare. In 1992, for example, about 44 percent of female-headed households with related children under age eighteen received means-tested cash assistance.[11]

Those who escape poverty for their families tend to do so primarily through earnings and secondarily through child support and government benefits (or through a combination of these sources)—although typically not by receiving welfare. In 1992, *nonpoor* single mothers received about 80 percent of their income from earnings, 8 percent from child support and alimony, 7 percent from Social Security, pensions, unemployment compensation and the like, and only just over 3 percent from welfare, food stamps, and housing assistance.[12] This is because nowhere in America today does welfare alone bring a family even close to the poverty level, and, as noted already, the rules governing welfare tend to reduce the amount of the welfare payment by nearly all the money the mother obtains from other sources. It is not surprising, then, that, in 1992, the poverty rate for single-parent families with children under age eighteen was 48.2 percent before the receipt of means-tested cash transfers and 45.2 percent after their receipt, a relatively modest reduction indeed. (Noncash benefits have a greater impact, reducing the rate to less than 40 percent.)[13] A different, and often more promising, route out of poverty for single mothers and their children is through marriage and thereby into a new family structure.

White and Nonwhite

The myth is that single mothers primarily come from racial and ethnic minorities. While it is true that these groups are disproportionately represented given their share of the population, in fact, these days more single mothers are white than any other group. For example, in 1993, 60 percent of nonmarital births were to whites and 36 percent to blacks.[14] On a cumulative basis, as of 1992 there were 5.8 million white, mother-headed family groups (including white Hispanics) as compared with three million black, mother-headed family groups (including black Hispanics)—even though 58 percent of all black family groups were headed by mothers and only 26 percent of all white family groups were headed by mothers.[15]

Change over Time

The demography of single parenting has changed a lot over the course of this century. There are many more single parents today than there were several generations ago, both in absolute numbers and, more importantly, in terms of the percentage of all children (or all parents) affected.

In 1900, the typical single parent was a widow. Male deaths through industrial and railway accidents were very visible. By contrast, divorce was then scarce (although desertion was a problem). And becoming a single mother by becoming pregnant outside of marriage was not very common, especially because so many who got pregnant promptly married the father.[16] Now, especially since the 1960s, all that is changed. Divorce is more frequent. "Illegitimacy" and cohabitation are also more prevalent than in earlier periods. For example, of women born between 1940 and 1944, only 3 percent had lived with a partner of the opposite sex by age twenty-five; of those born between 1960 and 1964, 37 percent had done so.[17] Moreover, the stigma of bearing a child outside of marriage and/or what some still call "living in sin" is much reduced.

Nonetheless, along with these changing characteristics of the single-parent family has come a change in public empathy. Earlier there was very widespread compassion for single parents and their children when single parents were mainly widows and divorcees, especially in the pre-no-fault era, when divorce usually was triggered (formally at least) by the misbehavior of the husband. Today, at least in some quarters, single mothers are loathed — those receiving welfare who have borne their children outside of marriage or who are suspected of bringing about the end of their marriages through their own selfishness. Currently, slightly more than half of those receiving welfare have had children outside of marriage as compared with but a trivial share in the 1930s and less than 30 percent as late as 1969.[18]

Changing Policies toward Single Parents

Widows

In 1909, President Theodore Roosevelt convened a historic first White House Conference on Children, which identified the poverty of widowed mothers and their children as a central policy problem. Then, if states and localities provided any assistance at all, it was too often through the squalid conditions of the "poor house" into which single-parent families might move — something of a counterpart to today's shelters for homeless families. The poor house itself was the successor to an earlier system in which desperate mothers farmed their children out to others, in effect providing young servants to those people who took these semiorphaned children into their homes, farms, and businesses. Reflecting the outlook of the social work profession that was then just getting under way, the White House Conference pushed instead for the adoption of Mothers' Pensions plans. Soon enacted, at least on paper, in most of the states, this new approach envisaged cash payments to single (primarily widowed) mothers who were certified by social workers as capable of providing decent parenting in their own homes if they only had a little more money in their pockets.[19]

Mothers' Pensions, the precursor to Aid to Families with Dependent Children (AFDC), reflected both the psychological perspective that it was best for the children to be raised in their own homes and the sociological outlook that it was appropriate for the mothers to stay at home and raise them (perhaps taking in other families' laundry or sewing, but not leaving their children to join the regular paid labor force).[20] As we will see, this benign attitude toward the payment of public assistance to single parents, which was reinforced by the adoption of AFDC in 1935 at the urging of President Franklin D. Roosevelt and maintained at least through the 1960s, is now rapidly disappearing.

Divorcees

Much earlier in the century, while widows were pitied, marital breakup was broadly frowned upon. Nonetheless, it was increasingly acknowledged that some spouses acted in intolerable ways and should be censured by allowing their spouses to divorce them. Adultery, spousal abuse, and desertion were the main categories of unacceptable marital conduct, and most of it seemed to be engaged in by husbands. As the decades rolled by, however, the divorce law requirement of severe wrongdoing by one spouse and innocence on the part of the complaining spouse soon ill-fit the attitudes of many couples themselves. Especially starting after World War II, and accelerating in the 1960s, many more couples came to realize that their marriages had simply broken down and they both wanted out. Until divorce law changed to reflect this new outlook, couples were prompted to engage in fraudulent charades (often involving the husband pretending to engage in adultery) so as to satisfy domestic relations law judges.

No-fault divorce law first emerged in California in 1970 and was rapidly followed by other states.[21] As a practical matter, not only did this reform allow couples amicably to obtain a divorce without having either one of them adjudicated as the wrongdoer but also, in most states, it permitted any dissatisfied spouse to terminate the marriage unilaterally. Whether no-fault divorce actually caused an increase in the divorce rate or merely coincided with (indeed, grew out of) the spiraling demand for divorce is unclear.[22] What is clear, however, is that divorce rates today are enormously greater than they were before 1970, thereby contributing to the great increase in single parenting.[23] As we will see, that state of affairs, in turn, has recently generated something of a backlash movement, one that seeks to reintroduce legal barriers to divorce in families with minor children.

Illegitimacy

Public policies toward illegitimacy (and, in turn, toward both abortion and teen pregnancy) have also changed significantly during this century. At an earlier time, children born outside of marriage were pejoratively labeled "bastards" and denied inheritance and other rights connected to their fathers, although their biological fathers did generally have the legal duty to support them.[24] If a single woman became pregnant, a standard solution was to promptly marry the child's father, perhaps pretending that the pregnancy arose during marriage after all. Adoption was available to some, who would be encouraged to go away before their pregnancies began to "show," only to return childless afterward as though nothing had happened. Pursuing an abortion instead then risked criminal punishment and subjected the woman to grave risks to her life and health.

Rather suddenly, a little more than two-thirds of the way through this century, policies in these areas turned around dramatically. For those who wanted it, abortion became legal. More important for our purposes, remaining unmarried and then keeping a child born out-of-wedlock became much more acceptable. For example, instead of expelling pregnant teens, schools adopted special programs for them. Fewer women gave up their newborns for adoption—for example, 19 percent of white, unmarried birth mothers did so in the 1960s, but only 3 percent did so in the 1980s.[25] The courts forced states to give many legal rights to illegitimates that had previously been enjoyed only by legitimates;[26] and many legislatures voluntarily expanded the inheritance rights and other entitlements of out-of-wedlock children.

Soon, unmarried pregnant women far less often married the biological father during the course of the pregnancy—a drop of from 52 percent to 27 percent between 1960 and 1980.[27]

Women who had children outside of marriage were no longer casually labeled unsuitable mothers and, as noted previously, soon became the largest category of single mothers receiving welfare. In terms of public acceptability, something of a high-water mark may have been reached in the early 1970s with the conversion of welfare into a "right" by the federal courts, the elimination of welfare's "suitable home" requirement, and the end to one-year waiting periods for newcomers seeking welfare.[28] This ignited an explosion of the welfare rolls,[29] and for the first time in many states, African American women gained reasonably secure access to benefits. At that time, Republican President Richard Nixon proposed turning AFDC from a complex state-federal program into a uniform national scheme.

[Near the end of the century, however, a policy backlash emerged.] Between 1967 and 1997, the proportion of African American children born outside of marriage skyrocketed from around 25 percent to nearly 70 percent; and the rate for white children is conceivably poised for a similar trajectory—and in any case has grown from 8 percent thirty years ago to around 25 percent today.[30] Now, curbing illegitimacy, or at least unmarried teen pregnancy, seems to be near the top of many politicians' lists. An indicator of how fast things have changed was Democratic President Bill Clinton's call to "end welfare as we know it" during his 1992 election campaign.

Child Support

It has been long understood that fathers have a moral obligation to provide for the financial support of their minor children. In the absent-parent context, this means paying "child support." For most of the century, however, a substantial proportion of men failed to pay the support they might have paid.[31] The default rate by divorced fathers has long been very high, and in out-of-wedlock births the father's paternity often was not even legally determined. (Stepfathers with no legal duties were frequently a more reliable source of support.) Moreover, in many states, even if noncustodial fathers paid all they owed, this was judged to be a pittance when compared with the child's reasonable needs. Deceased fathers were no more reliable, frequently dying with estates of trivial value and without life insurance.

Through the 1930s, AFDC and its predecessors were the main public response to these failures—providing means-tested cash benefits to poor children (and their mothers) deprived of the support of a breadwinner. In 1939, however, special privileged treatment was afforded widows and their children. The Social Security system was expanded so that, upon the death of the working father, "survivor" benefits would be paid to the children and their caretaker mother based upon the father's past wages.[32] This, in effect, created publicly funded life insurance for most widows and their children, with the result that today hardly any widowed mothers find it necessary to apply for welfare.

No comparable "child support insurance" was provided, however, so that divorced and never-married poor mothers have had to continue to turn to the socially less favored means-tested welfare programs instead of Social Security. On behalf of these families, the effort, much enlarged since the mid-1970s, has been to increase the amount of child support an absent father owes and to beef up child support enforcement efforts.[33] Notwithstanding those reforms, it is still estimated that more than five billion dollars of child support annually goes uncollected, and many custodial mothers are unable to collect any support for their children.[34]

Cohabitation

It appears that American society generally is becoming more accepting of cohabitation, even if it remains frowned upon in many circles. (Clearly, same-sex cohabitation continues to be highly controversial.) So far as public policy is concerned, however, marriage still makes a significant difference. For example, when children are involved and the cohabitants split up, the woman who keeps the children (as is typically the case) continues to be disadvantaged as compared with the woman who had married. Although she is entitled to support for her child, only in very special circumstances can she gain financial support for herself from her former partner. So, too, upon the death of her partner who was the father of her children, while her children can claim Social Security benefits, she does not qualify for the caretaker Social Security benefits that a legal widow would have obtained.[35] On the other hand, if she cohabits with a man who is not the father of her children, a mother and her children have been able to qualify for welfare; by contrast, were she married (or cohabiting with the father of her children), it has been extremely unlikely for them to obtain welfare. . . .

Refocusing the Policy Perspective

When it comes to single-parent families, much of our current policy focus is on parents: whether they divorce, whether they pay child support, whether they have children outside of marriage, whether they work, and so on. Suppose instead that policy attention was aimed at the *children* in single-parent families. For example, as we have seen, if a child's breadwinner parent dies, the government ordinarily assures that child far better financial security than it does if that child's breadwinner parent is simply absent from the home: Social Security steps in to satisfy the deceased parent's obligation to have provided life insurance but not the absent parent's duty to provide child support.

Comparable treatment for the latter group implies some sort of publicly funded "child support insurance" scheme. Plans of this sort (including those that would expand Social Security in exactly this way) have in fact been proposed in recent years, most notably by Irwin Garfinkel, although so far at least they have not won widespread endorsement.[36] This sort of scheme could assure all children living in single-parent families with equal financial support—say, up to the poverty level. Or, like Social Security and private child support obligations, the benefits could be related to the absent parent's past wages. In either case, unlike the rules that have governed AFDC, earnings by the custodial parent could supplement rather than replace the child support benefit.

Such a plan could be financed by general revenues or Social Security payroll taxes. But it might also be funded, at least in substantial part, by absent parents, thereby making the plan one that guarantees that a suitable level of child support will actually be provided and makes up the shortfall when the collection effort fails. Were this second approach adopted, not only should it dramatically reduce our sense of the cost of the plan, but also it should offset any tendency that the plan might otherwise have to increase divorce.

It is important to emphasize that a plan like this would much improve the lot of both many children who in the past have been dependent on AFDC and large numbers of children with working-class and even middle-class mothers whose absent fathers now default on their child support obligations. It must be conceded, however, that in view of the direction of recent welfare reform, the prospects at the moment are not favorable for any new initiative to provide cash for children in single-parent families.

A different child-centered approach, therefore, is to try to assure all children with essential goods by means other than providing cash. Ought not all American youths live in decent housing, obtain a quality education, receive adequate food, have access to decent health care, and so on? This is not the place to detail the many alternative mechanisms by which these critical items might be delivered. What needs emphasizing, however, is that any program guaranteeing these sorts of things to all children would vastly disproportionately benefit children now living in single-parent families. Moreover, if we can keep the focus on the needy and innocent members of the next generation, perhaps we can escape ideological battles over the worthiness of these children's parents. This is possibly a naive hope, but one that may be enhanced when the thing delivered to the child's family is other than money: witness the greater public and legislative popularity of the federal food stamps program and federal aid to elementary and secondary education as compared with the now-decimated federal welfare program.

The many policy reforms discussed here are unlikely to have large impacts on people like Jackie Kennedy, Marcia Clark, Madonna, and Murphy Brown. But ordinary single mothers (and their children) who are in analogous situations have a great deal at stake.

ENDNOTES

1. Dore Hollander, "Nonmarital Childbearing in the United States: A Government Report," *Family Planning Perspectives* 28(1):30, 1996.
2. *Current Population Reports* P20, No. 468, "Marital Status and Living Arrangements," 1992:xii, Table G.

3. *Current Population Reports* P-20, No. 467, "Household and Family Characteristics," 1992(March):xiv.

4. Larry L. Bumpass and R. Kelly Raley, "Redefining Single-Parent Families: Cohabitation and Changing Family Reality," *Demography* 32(1):97, 1995.

5. Wendy D. Manning and Pamela J. Smock, "Why Marry? Race and the Transition to Marriage among Cohabitors," *Demography* 32(4):509, 1995. See also Ronald R. Rindfuss and Audrey Vandenheuvel, "Cohabitation: A Precursor to Marriage or an Alternative to Being Single?" *Population and Development Review* 16:703, 1990.

6. Committee on Ways and Means, U.S. House of Representatives, Overview of Entitlement Programs, 1994 Green Book (hereafter 1994 Green Book), Table 12-2, 534.

7. 1994 Green Book, Table 12-4, 536.

8. In 1992, for example, just over 2 percent of single mothers on AFDC reported working full time and another 4 percent reported working part time. Another 12 percent were said to be seeking work. 1994 Green Book, Table 10-28, 404.

9. More specifically, Edin found that about 15 percent were working full time (typically under another name) and many others were working part time. Kathryn Edin and Christopher Jencks, "Reforming Welfare," in Christopher Jencks, *Rethinking Social Policy: Race, Poverty and the Underclass*. Cambridge: Harvard University Press, 1992, 204–35.

10. *Current Population Reports* P-60, No. 188, "Income, Poverty and Valuation of Non-Cash Benefits," 1993:xvi, Table C.

11. *Current Population Reports* P-60, No. 185, "Poverty in the U.S.," 1992:xviii, Table F.

12. 1994 Green Book, Table G-32, 1144–45.

13. 1994 Green Book, Table H-12, 1174.

14. Hollander, "Nonmarital Childbearing," 29.

15. *Current Population Reports* P-20, No. 467, "Household and Family Characteristics," 1992(March): xiv, Table F.

16. Mary Ann Mason, *Father's Property to Children's Rights*, New York: Columbia University Press, 1994, 11–16.

17. Hollander, "Nonmarital Childbearing," 30.

18. 1994 Green Book, Table 10–29, 401.

19. Winifred Bell, *Aid to Dependent Children*, New York: Columbia University Press, 1965.

20. Committee on Economic Security. Social Security in America, The Factual Background of the Social Security Act as Summarized from Staff Reports to the Committee on Economic Security, 1937.

21. Herma Hill Kay, "Beyond No-fault: New Directions in Divorce Reform," in Stephen Sugarman and Herma Hill Kay (eds), *Divorce Reform at the Crossroads*, New Haven: Yale University Press, 1990, 6–36.

22. H. Elizabeth Peters, "Marriage and Divorce: Information Constraints and Private Contracting," *American Economic Review* 76:437, 1986; Gary S. Becker, *A Treatise on the Family*, Cambridge: Harvard University Press, 1981, 228–29.

23. Centers for Disease Control and Prevention, National Center for Health Statistics, "Monthly Vital Statistics Report," 44(4), 1995.

24. Ira Mark Ellman, Paul M. Kurtz, and Katharine T. Bartlett, *Family Law: Cases, Text, Problems*, 2d ed., Charlottesville: Michie Law Publishers, 1991, 881–912.

25. Hollander, "Nonmarital Childbearing," 31.

26. *Levy v. Louisiana*, 391 U.S. 68 (1968); *Weber v. Aetna Cas. & Sur. Co.*, 406 U.S. 164 (1972).

27. Hollander, "Nonmarital Childbearing," 31.

28. *Goldberg v. Kelly*, 397 U.S. 254 (1970); *King v. Smith*, 392 U.S. 309 (1968); and *Shapiro v. Thompson*, 394 U.S. 618 (1969).

29. 1994 Green Book, Table 10-1, 325.

30. Charles Murray, "The Coming White Underclass," *Wall Street Journal*, Oct. 29, 1993, A14.

31. David L. Chambers, *Making Fathers Pay: The Enforcement of Child Support*, Chicago: University of Chicago Press, 1979.

32. Stephen D. Sugarman, "Children's Benefits in Social Security," *Cornell Law Review* 65:836–908, 1980.

33. 1994 Green Book, 455–530.

34. 1994 Green Book, Table 11-4, 463.

35. This rule was unsuccessfully challenged in *Boles v. Califano*, 443 U.S. 282 (1979).

36. Irwin Garfinkel, *Assuring Child Support*, New York: Russell Sage Foundation, 1992; Stephen D. Sugarman, "Reforming Welfare Through Social Security," *University of Michigan Journal of Law Reform* 26:817–51, 1993; Stephen D. Sugarman, "Financial Support of Children and the End of Welfare as We Know It," *Virginia Law Review* 81:2523–73, 1995.

19

(HOW) DOES THE SEXUAL ORIENTATION OF PARENTS MATTER?

JUDITH STACEY • TIMOTHY J. BIBLARZ

Today, gay marriage is taking on an air of inevitability" (*Detroit News*, "Middle Ground Emerges for Gay Couples," October 4, 1999, p. A9). So observed a U.S. newspaper from the heartland in September 1999, reporting that one-third of those surveyed in an *NBC News/Wall Street Journal* poll endorsed the legalization of same-sex marriage, while 65 percent predicted such legislation would take place in the new century (Price 1999). During the waning months of the last millennium, France enacted national registered partnerships, Denmark extended child custody rights to same-sex couples, and the state supreme courts in Vermont and in Ontario, Canada, ruled that same-sex couples were entitled to full and equal family rights. Most dramatically, in September 2000 the Netherlands became the first nation to realize the inevitable when the Dutch parliament voted over-whelmingly to grant same-sex couples full and equal rights to marriage. As the new millennium begins, struggles by nonheterosexuals to secure equal recognition and rights for the new family relationships they are now cre-ating represent some of the most dramatic and fiercely contested develop-ments in Western family patterns.

It is not surprising, therefore, that social science research on lesbigay family issues has become a rapid growth industry that incites passionate divisions. For the consequences of such research are by no means "aca-demic," but bear on marriage and family policies that encode Western cul-ture's most profoundly held convictions about gender, sexuality, and parenthood. As advocates and opponents square off in state and federal courts and legislatures, in the electoral arena, and in culture wars over efforts to extend to nonheterosexuals equal rights to marriage, child custody, adoption, foster care, and fertility services, they heatedly debate the impli-cations of a youthful body of research, conducted primarily by psycholo-gists, that investigates if and how the sexual orientation of parents affects children.

This body of research, almost uniformly, reports findings of no notable differences between children reared by heterosexual parents and those reared by lesbian and gay parents, and that it finds lesbigay parents to be as competent and effective as heterosexual parents. Lawyers and activists struggling to defend child custody and adoption petitions by lesbians and gay men, or to attain same-gender marriage rights and to defeat preemptive referenda against such rights (e.g., the victorious Knight Initiative on the 2000 ballot in California), have drawn on this research with considerable success (cf. Wald 1999). Although progress is uneven, this strategy has pro-moted a gradual liberalizing trend in judicial and policy decisions. However, backlash campaigns against gay family rights have begun to challenge the validity of the research.

In 1997, the *University of Illinois Law Review Journal* published an article by Wardle (1997), a Brigham Young University law professor, that impugned the motives, methods, and merits of social science research on lesbian and gay parenting. Wardle charged the legal profession and social scientists with an ideological bias favoring gay rights that has compromised most research in this field and the liberal judicial and policy decisions it has informed. He presented a harshly critical assessment of the research and argued for a pre-sumptive judicial standard in favor of awarding child custody to heterosex-ual married couples. The following year, Wardle drafted new state regulations in Utah that restrict adoption and foster care placements to households in which all adults are related by blood or marriage. Florida, Arkansas, and Mississippi also have imposed restrictions on adoption and/or foster care, and such bills have been introduced in the legislatures of 10 additional states (Leslie Cooper, ACLU gay family rights staff attorney, personal communication, September 27, 2000). In March 2000, a paper presented at a "Revitalizing Marriage" conference at Brigham Young University assailed the quality of studies that had been cited to support the efficacy of lesbigay parenting (Lerner and Nagai 2000). Characterizing the research methods as "dismal," Lerner and Nagai claimed that "the methods used in these studies were sufficiently flawed so that these studies could not and should not be used in legislative forums or legal cases to buttress any arguments on the nature of homosexual vs. heterosexual parenting" (p. 3). Shortly afterward, Gallagher (2000), of the Institute for American Values, broadcast Lerner and Nagai's argument in her nationally syndicated *New York Post* column in order to undermine the use of "the science card" by advocates of gay marriage and gay "normalization."

We depart sharply from the views of Wardle and Gallagher on the merits and morals of lesbigay parenthood as well as on their analysis of the child development research. We agree, however, that ideological pressures constrain intellectual development in this field. In our view, it is the pervasiveness of social prejudice and institutionalized discrimination against lesbians and gay men that exerts a powerful policing effect on the basic terms of psychological research and public discourse on the significance of parental sexual orientation. The field suffers less from the overt ideological convictions of scholars than from the unfortunate intellectual consequences that follow from the implicit hetero normative presumption governing the terms of the discourse—that healthy child development depends upon parenting by a married heterosexual couple. While few contributors to this literature personally subscribe to this view, most of the research asks whether lesbigay parents subject their children to greater risks or harm than are confronted by children reared by heterosexual parents. Because anti-gay scholars seek evidence of harm, sympathetic researchers defensively stress its absence.

We take stock of this body of psychological research from a sociological perspective. We analyze the impact that this hetero-normative presumption exacts on predominant research strategies, analyses, and representations of findings. After assessing the basic premises and arguments in the debate, we discuss how the social fact of heterosexism has operated to constrain the research populations, concepts, and designs employed in the studies to date.

We wish to acknowledge that the political stakes of this body of research are so high that the ideological "family values" of scholars play a greater part than usual in how they design, conduct, and interpret their studies. Of course, we recognize that this is equally true for those who criticize such studies (including Wardle [1997], Lerner and Nagai [2000], and ourselves). The inescapably ideological and emotional nature of this subject makes it incumbent on scholars to acknowledge the personal convictions they bring to the discussion. Because we personally oppose discrimination on the basis of sexual orientation or gender, we subject research claims by those sympathetic to our stance to a heightened degree of critical scrutiny and afford the fullest possible consideration to work by scholars opposed to parenting by lesbians and gay men.

The Case against Lesbian and Gay Parenthood

Wardle (1997) is correct that contemporary scholarship on the effects of parental sexual orientation on children's development is rarely critical of lesbigay parenthood. Few respectable scholars today oppose such parenting. However, a few psychologists subscribe to the view that homosexuality represents either a sin or a mental illness and continue to publish alarmist works on the putative ill effects of gay parenting (e.g., Cameron and Cameron 1996; Cameron, Cameron, and Landess 1996). Even though the American Psychological Association expelled Paul Cameron, and the American Sociological Association denounced him for willfully misrepresenting research (Cantor 1994; Herek 1998, 2000), his publications continue to be cited in amicus briefs, court decisions, and policy hearings. For example, the chair of the Arkansas Child Welfare Agency Review Board repeatedly cited publications by Cameron's group in her testimony at policy hearings, which, incidentally, led to restricting foster child placements to heterosexual parents (Woodruff 1998).[1]

Likewise, Wardle (1997) draws explicitly on Cameron's work to build his case against gay parent rights. Research demonstrates, Wardle maintains, that gay parents subject children to disproportionate risks; that children of gay parents are more apt to suffer confusion over their gender and sexual identities and are more likely to become homosexuals themselves; that homosexual parents are more sexually promiscuous than are heterosexual parents and are more likely to molest their own children; that children are at greater risk of losing a homosexual parent to AIDS, substance abuse, or suicide, and to suffer greater risks of depression and other emotional difficulties; that homosexual couples are more unstable and likely to separate; and that the social stigma and embarrassment of having a homosexual parent unfairly ostracizes children and hinders their relationships with peers. Judges have cited Wardle's article to justify transferring child custody from lesbian to heterosexual parents.[1]

Wardle (1997), like other opponents of homosexual parenthood, also relies on a controversial literature that decries the putative risks of "fatherlessness" in general. Thus, Wardle cites books by Popenoe (1993, 1996), Blankenhorn (1995), and Whitehead (1993) when he argues:

> [C]hildren generally develop best, and develop most completely, when raised by both a mother and a father and experience regular family interaction with both genders' parenting skills during their years of childhood. It is now undeniable that, just as a mother's influence is crucial to the secure, healthy, and full development of a child, [a] paternal presence in the life of a child is essential to the child emotionally and physically. (P. 860)

Wardle, like Blankenhorn, extrapolates (inappropriately) from research on single-mother families to portray children of lesbians as more vulnerable to everything from delinquency, substance abuse, violence, and crime, to teen pregnancy, school dropout, suicide, and even poverty.[2] In short, the few scholars who are opposed to parenting by lesbians and gay men provide academic support for the convictions of many judges, journalists, politicians, and citizens that the sexual orientation of parents matters greatly to children, and that lesbigay parents represent a danger to their children and to society. Generally, these scholars offer only limited, and often implicit, theoretical explanations for the disadvantages of same-sex parenting—typically combining elements of bio-evolutionary theory with social and cognitive learning theories (e.g., Blankenhorn 1995). Cameron et al. (1996) crudely propose that homosexuality is a "learned pathology" that parents pass on to children through processes of modeling, seduction, and "contagion." The deeply rooted hetero-normative convictions about what constitutes healthy and moral gender identity, sexual orientation, and family composition held by contributors to this literature hinders their ability to conduct or interpret research with reason, nuance, or care.

The Case for Lesbian and Gay Parenthood

Perhaps the most consequential impact that heterosexism exerts on the research on lesbigay parenting lies where it is least apparent—in the far more responsible literature that is largely sympathetic to its subject. It is easy to expose the ways in which the prejudicial views of those directly hostile to lesbigay parenting distort their research (Herek 1998). Moreover, because anti-gay scholars regard homosexuality itself as a form of pathology, they tautologically interpret any evidence that children may be more likely to engage in homoerotic behavior as evidence of harm. Less obvious, however, are the ways in which heterosexism also hampers research and analysis among those who explicitly support lesbigay parenthood. With rare exceptions, even the most sympathetic proceed from a highly defensive posture that accepts heterosexual parenting as the gold standard and investigates whether lesbigay parents and their children are inferior.

This sort of hierarchical model implies that *differences* indicate *deficits* (Baumrind 1995). Instead of investigating whether (and how) differences in adult sexual orientation might lead to meaningful differences in how individuals parent and how their children develop, the predominant research designs place the burden of proof on lesbigay parents to demonstrate that they are not less successful or less worthy than heterosexual parents. Too often scholars seem to presume that this approach precludes acknowledging almost any differences in parenting or in child outcomes. A characteristic review of research on lesbian-mother families concludes:

> [A] rapidly growing and highly consistent body of empirical work has failed to identify significant differences between lesbian mothers and their heterosexual counterparts or the children raised by these groups. Researchers have been unable to establish empirically that detriment results to children from being raised by lesbian mothers. (Falk 1994:151)

Given the weighty political implications of this body of research, it is easy to understand the social sources of such a defensive stance. As long as sexual orientation can deprive a gay parent of child custody, fertility services, and adoption rights, sensitive scholars are apt to tread gingerly around the terrain of differences. Unfortunately, however, this reticence compromises the development of knowledge not only in child development and psychology, but also within the sociology of sexuality, gender, and family more broadly. For if homophobic theories seem crude, too many psychologists who are sympathetic to lesbigay parenting seem hesitant to theorize at all. When researchers downplay the significance of any findings of differences, they forfeit a unique opportunity to take full advantage of the "natural laboratory" that the advent of lesbigay-parent families provides for exploring the effects and acquisition of gender and sexual identity, ideology, and behavior.

This reticence is most evident in analyses of sexual behavior and identity — the most politically sensitive issue in the debate. Virtually all of the published research claims to find no differences in the sexuality of children reared by lesbigay parents and those raised by nongay parents — but none of the studies that report this finding attempts to theorize about such an implausible outcome. Yet it is difficult to conceive of a credible theory of sexual development that would not expect the adult children of lesbigay parents to display a somewhat higher incidence of homoerotic desire, behavior, and identity than children of heterosexual parents. For example, biological determinist theory should predict at least some difference in an inherited predisposition to same-sex desire; a social constructionist theory would expect lesbigay parents to provide an environment in which children would feel freer to explore and affirm such desires; psychoanalytic theory might hypothesize that the absence of a male parent would weaken a daughter's need to relinquish her pre-oedipal desire for her mother or that the absence of a female parent would foster a son's pre-oedipal love for his father that no fear of castration or oedipal crisis would interrupt. Moreover, because parents determine where their children reside, even one who subscribed to J. Harris' (1998) maverick theory — that parents are virtually powerless when compared with peers to influence their children's development — should anticipate that lesbigay parents would probably rear their children among less homophobic peers.

Bem's (1996) "exotic becomes erotic" theory of sexual orientation argues that in a gender-polarized society, children eroticize the gender of peers whose interests and temperaments differ most from their own. Most children thereby become heterosexual, but boys attracted to "feminine" activities and girls who are "tomboys" are apt to develop homoerotic desires. The impact of parental genes and child-rearing practices remains implicit because parents contribute genetically to the temperamental factors Bem identifies as precursors to a child's native activity preferences, and parental attitudes toward gender polarization should affect the way those innate preferences translate into children's cognition and play. In fact, the only "theory" of child development we can imagine in which a child's sexual development would bear no relationship to parental genes, practices, environment, or beliefs would be an arbitrary one.[3] Yet this is precisely the outcome that most scholars report, although the limited empirical record does not justify it.

Over the past decade, prominent psychologists in the field began to call for less defensive research on lesbian and gay family issues (G. Green and Bozett 1991; Kitzinger and Coyle 1995; Patterson 1992). Rethinking the "no differences" doctrine, some scholars urge social scientists to look for potentially beneficial effects children might derive from such distinctive aspects of lesbigay parenting as the more egalitarian relationships these parents appear to practice (Patterson 1995; also see Dunne 2000). More radically, a few scholars (Kitzinger 1987, 1989; Kitzinger and Coyle 1995) propose abandoning comparative research on lesbian and heterosexual parenting altogether and supplanting it with research that asks "why and how are lesbian parents oppressed and how can we change that?" (Clarke 2000:28, paraphrasing Kitzinger 1994:501). While we perceive potential advantages from these agendas, we advocate an alternative strategy that moves beyond heteronormativity without forfeiting the fruitful potential of comparative research. Although we agree with Kitzinger and Coyle (1995) and Clarke (2000) that the social obstacles to lesbian (and gay) parenthood deserve rigorous attention, we believe that this should supplement, not supplant, the rich opportunity planned lesbigay parenthood provides for the exploration of the interactions of gender, sexual orientation, and biosocial family structures on parenting and child development. Moreover, while we welcome research attuned to potential strengths as well as vulnerabilities of lesbigay parenting, we believe that knowledge and policy will be best served when scholars feel free to replace a hierarchical model, which assigns "grades" to parents and children according to their sexual identities, with a more genuinely pluralist approach to family diversity. Sometimes, to bowdlerize Freud's famous dictum, a difference *really is* just a difference!

Problems with Concepts, Categories, and Samples

The social effects of heterosexism constrain the character of research conducted on lesbigay parenting in ways more profound than those deriving from the ideological stakes of researchers. First, as most researchers recognize, because so many individuals legitimately fear the social consequences of adopting a gay identity, and because few national surveys have included questions about sexual orientation, it is impossible to gather reliable data on such basic demographic questions as how many lesbians and gay men there are in the general population, how many have children, or how many children reside (or have substantial contact) with lesbian or gay parents. Curiously, those who are hostile to gay parenting tend to minimize the incidence of same-sex orientation, while sympathetic scholars typically report improbably high numerical estimates. Both camps thus implicitly presume that the rarer the incidence, the less legitimate would be lesbigay claims to rights. One could imagine an alternative political logic, however, in which a low figure might undermine grounds for viewing lesbigay parenting as a meaningful social threat. Nonetheless, political anxieties have complicated the difficulty of answering basic demographic questions.

Since 1984, most researchers have statically reproduced numbers, of uncertain origin, depicting a range of from 1 to 5 million lesbian mothers, from 1 to 3 million gay fathers, and from 6 to 14 million children of gay or lesbian parents in the United States (e.g., Patterson 1992, 1996).[4] More recent estimates by Patterson and Freil (2000) extrapolate from distributions observed in the National Health and Social Life Survey (Laumann et al. 1995). Depending upon the definition of parental sexual orientation employed, Patterson and Freil suggest a current lower limit of 800,000 lesbigay parents ages 18 to 59 with 1.6 million children and an upper limit of 7 million lesbigay parents with 14 million children. However, these estimates include many "children" who are actually adults. To estimate the number who are dependent children (age 18 or younger), we multiplied the child-counts by .66, which is the proportion of dependent children among all offspring of 18- to 59-year-old parents in the representative National Survey of Families and Households (Sweet and Bumpass 1996).[5] This adjustment reduces the estimates of current dependent children with lesbigay parents to a range of 1 to 9 million, which implies that somewhere between 1 percent and 12 percent of all (78 million) children ages 19 and under in the United States (U.S. Census Bureau 1999) have a lesbigay parent. The 12 percent figure depends upon classifying as a lesbigay parent anyone who reports that even the idea of homoerotic sex is appealing, while the low (1 percent) figure derives from the narrower and, in our view, more politically salient, definition of a lesbigay parent as one who self-identifies as such (also see Badgett 1998; Black, Maker, et al. 1998).

Across the ideological spectrum, scholars, journalists, and activists appear to presume that the normalization of lesbigay sexuality should steadily increase the ranks of children with lesbian and gay parents. In contrast, we believe that normalization is more likely to reduce the proportion of such children. Most contemporary lesbian and gay parents procreated within heterosexual marriages that many had entered hoping to escape the social and emotional consequences of homophobia. As homosexuality becomes more legitimate, far fewer people with homoerotic desires should feel compelled to enter heterosexual marriages, and thus fewer should become parents in this manner.

On the other hand, with normalization, intentional parenting by self-identified lesbians and gay men should continue to increase, but it is unlikely to do so sufficiently to compensate for the decline in the current ranks of formerly married lesbian and gay parents. Thus, the proportion of lesbian parents may not change much. Many women with homoerotic desires who once might have married men and succumbed to social pressures to parent will no longer do so; others who remained single and childless because of their homoerotic desires will feel freer to choose lesbian maternity. It is difficult to predict the net effect of these contradictory trends. However, as fewer closeted gay men participate in heterosexual marriages, the ranks of gay fathers should thin. Even if gay men were as eager as lesbians are to become parents, biology alone sharply constrains their ability to do so. Moreover, there is evidence that fewer men of any sexual orientation actually desire children as strongly as do comparable women (cf. Groze 1991; Shireman 1996), and most demographic studies of sexual orientation find a higher incidence of homosexuality among men than women (Kinsey et al. 1948; Kinsey et al. 1953; Laumann et al. 1994; Michael et al. 1994). Thus, although the ranks of intentional paternity among gay men should increase, we do not believe this will compensate for the declining numbers of closeted gay men who will become fathers through heterosexual marriages. Hence the estimate of 1 to 12 percent of children with a lesbigay parent may represent a peak interval that may decline somewhat with normalization.

A second fundamental problem in sampling involves the ambiguity, fluidity, and complexity of definitions of sexual orientation. "The traditional type of surveys on the prevalence of 'homosexuality,'" remarks a prominent Danish sociologist, "are already in danger of becoming antiquated even before they are carried out; the questions asked are partially irrelevant; sexuality is not what it used to be" (Bech 1997:211). What defines a parent (or adult child) as lesbian, gay, bisexual, or heterosexual? Are these behavioral, social, emotional, or political categories? Historical scholarship has established that sexual identities are modern categories whose definitions vary greatly not only across cultures, spaces, and time, but even among and within individuals (Katz 1995; Seidman 1997). Some gay men, for example, practice celibacy; some heterosexual men engage in "situational" homosexual activity. Some lesbians relinquish lesbian identities to marry; some relinquish marriage for a lesbian identity. What about bisexual, transsexual, or transgendered parents, not to mention those who re-partner with individuals of the same or different genders? Sexual desires, acts, meanings, and identities are not expressed in fixed or predictable packages.

Third, visible lesbigay parenthood is such a recent phenomenon that most studies are necessarily of the children of a transitional generation of self-identified lesbians and gay men who became parents in the context of heterosexual marriages or relationships that dissolved before or after they assumed a gay identity. These unique historical conditions make it impossible to fully distinguish the impact of a parent's sexual orientation on a child from the impact of such factors as divorce, re-mating, the secrecy of the closet, the process of coming out, or the social consequences of stigma. Only a few studies have attempted to control for the number and gender of a child's parents before and after a parent decided to identify as lesbian or gay. Because many more formerly married lesbian mothers than gay fathers retain custody of their children, most research is actually on post-divorce lesbian motherhood. A few studies compare heterosexual and gay fathers

after divorce (Bigner and Jacobsen 1989, 1992). If fewer self-identified lesbians and gay men will become parents through heterosexual marriages, the
published research on this form of gay parenthood will become less relevant
to issues in scholarly and public debates.

Fourth, because researchers lack reliable data on the number and location of lesbigay parents with children in the general population, there are no
studies of child development based on random, representative samples of
such families. Most studies rely on small-scale, snowball and convenience
samples drawn primarily from personal and community networks or agencies. Most research to date has been conducted on white lesbian mothers
who are comparatively educated, mature, and reside in relatively progressive urban centers, most often in California or the Northeastern states.[6]

Although scholars often acknowledge some of these difficulties (Bozett
1989; Patterson and Friel 2000; Rothblum 1994), few studies explicitly grapple with these definitional questions. Most studies simply rely on a parent's
sexual self-identity at the time of the study, which contributes unwittingly
to the racial, ethnic, and class imbalance of the populations studied.
Ethnographic studies suggest that "lesbian," "gay," and "bisexual" identity
among socially subordinate and nonurban populations is generally less visible or less affirmed than it is among more privileged white, educated, and
urban populations (Boykin 1996; Cantu 2000; Carrier 1992; Greene and
Boyd-Franklin 1996; Hawkeswood 1997; Lynch 1992; Peterson 1992).

Increasingly, uncloseted lesbians and gay men actively choose to become
parents through diverse and innovative means (Benkov 1994). In addition to
adoption and foster care, lesbians are choosing motherhood using known
and unknown sperm donors (as single mothers, in intentional co-mother
couples, and in complex variations of biosocial parenting). Both members of
a lesbian couple may choose to become pregnant sequentially or simultaneously. Pioneering lesbian couples have exchanged ova to enable both
women to claim biological, and thereby legal, maternal status to the same
infant (Bourne 1999). It is much more difficult (and costly) for gay men to
choose to become fathers, particularly fathers of infants. Some (who reside
in states that permit this) become adoptive or foster parents; others serve as
sperm donors in joint parenting arrangements with lesbian or other mothers.
An affluent minority hire women as "surrogates" to bear children for them.

The means and contexts for planned parenthood are so diverse and complex that they compound the difficulties of isolating the significance of
parental sexual orientation. To even approximate this goal, researchers
would need to control not only for the gender, number, and sexual orientation of parents, but for their diverse biosocial and legal statuses. The handful of studies that have attempted to do this focus on lesbian motherhood.
The most rigorous research designs compare donor-insemination (DI) parenthood among lesbian and heterosexual couples or single mothers (e.g.,
Chan, Brooks, et al. 1998; Flaks et al. 1995). To our knowledge, no studies
have been conducted exclusively on lesbian or gay adoptive parents or

compare the children of intentional gay fathers with children in other family forms. Researchers do not know the extent to which the comparatively high socioeconomic status of the DI parents studied accurately reflects the demographics of lesbian and gay parenthood generally, but given the degree of effort, cultural and legal support, and, frequently, the expense involved, members of relatively privileged social groups would be the ones most able to make use of reproductive technology and/or independent adoption.

In short, the indirect effects of heterosexism have placed inordinate constraints on most research on the effects of gay parenthood. We believe, however, that the time may now be propitious to begin to reformulate the basic terms of the enterprise.

Reconsidering the Psychological Findings

Toward this end, we examined the findings of 21 psychological studies (listed at the bottom of Table 1) published between 1981 and 1998 that we considered best equipped to address sociological questions about how parental sexual orientation matters to children. One meta-analysis of 18 such studies (11 of which are included among our 21) characteristically concludes that "the results demonstrate no differences on any measures between the heterosexual and homosexual parents regarding parenting styles, emotional adjustment, and sexual orientation of the child(ren)" (Allen and Burrell 1996:19). To evaluate this claim, we selected for examination only studies that: (1) include a sample of gay or lesbian parents and children and a comparison group of heterosexual parents and children; (2) assess differences between groups in terms of statistical significance; and (3) include findings directly relevant to children's development. The studies we discuss compare relatively advantaged lesbian parents (18 studies) and gay male parents (3 studies) with a roughly matched sample of heterosexual parents. Echoing the conclusion of meta-analysts Allen and Burrell (1996), the authors of all 21 studies almost uniformly claim to find no differences in measures of parenting or child outcomes. In contrast, our careful scrutiny of the findings they report suggests that on some dimensions—particularly those related to gender and sexuality—the sexual orientations of these parents matter somewhat more for their children than the researchers claimed.[7]

The empirical findings from these studies are presented in Tables 1 and 2. Table 1 summarizes findings on the relationship between parental sexual orientation and three sets of child "outcome" variables: (1) gender behavior/gender preferences, (2) sexual behavior/sexual preferences, and (3) psychological well-being. Table 2 summarizes findings on the relationship between parental sexual orientation and other attributes of parents, including: (1) behavior toward children's gender and sexual development, (2) parenting skills, (3) relationships with children, and (4) psychological well-being. Positive signs (+) indicate a statistically significant higher level of the variable

TABLE 1   Findings on the Associations between Parents' Sexual Orientations and Selected Child Outcomes: 21 Studies, 1981 to 1998

Variable Measured	Direction of Effect
Gender Behavior/Preferences	
Girls' departure from traditional gender role expectations and behaviors—in dress, play, physicality, school activities, occupational aspirations (Hoeffer 1981; Golombok, Spencer, and Rutter 1983; R. Green et al. 1986; Steckel 1987; Hotvedt and Mandel 1982).	0/+
Boys' departure from traditional gender role expectations and behaviors—in dress, play, physicality, school activities, occupational aspirations (Hoeffer 1981; Golombok et al. 1983; R. Green et al. 1986; Steckel 1987; Hotvedt and Mandel 1982).	0/+
Boys' level of aggressiveness and domineering disposition (Steckel 1987).	−
Child wishes she/he were the other sex (Green et al. 1986).	0
Sexual Behavior/Sexual Preferences	
Young adult child has considered same-sex sexual relationship(s); has had same-sex sexual relationship(s) (Tasker and Golombok 1997).	+
Young adult child firmly self-identifies as bisexual, gay, or lesbian (Tasker and Golombok 1997).	0
Boys' likelihood of having a gay sexual orientation in adulthood, by sexual orientation of father (Bailey et al. 1995).	(+)
Girls' number of sexual partners from puberty to young adulthood (Tasker and Golombok 1997).	+
Boys' number of sexual partners from puberty to young adulthood (Tasker and Golombok 1997).	(−)
Quality of intimate relationships in young adulthood (Tasker and Golombok 1997).	0
Have friend(s) who are gay or lesbian (Tasker and Golombok 1997).	+
Self-Esteem and Psychological Well-Being	
Children's self-esteem, anxiety, depression, internalizing behavioral problems, externalizing behavioral problems, total behavioral problems, performance in social arenas (sports, friendships, school), use of psychological counseling, mothers' and teachers' reports of children's hyperactivity, unsociability, emotional difficulty, conduct difficulty, other behavioral problems (Golombok, Spencer, and Rutter 1983; Huggins 1989; Patterson 1994; Flaks et al. 1995; Tasker and Golombok 1997; Chan, Raboy, and Patterson 1998; Chan, Brooks, et al. 1998).	0
Daughters' self-reported level of popularity at school and in the neighborhood (Hotvedt and Mandel 1982).	+
Mothers' and teachers' reports of child's level of affection, responsiveness, and concern for younger children (Steckel 1987).	+
Experience of peer stigma concerning own sexuality (Tasker and Golombok 1997).	+

(Continued)

(Table 1 continued)

Cognitive functioning (IQ, verbal, performance, and so on) (Flaks et al. 1995; R. Green et al. 1986).	0
Experienced problems gaining employment in young adulthood (Tasker and Golombok 1997).	0

Sources: The 21 studies considered in Tables 1 and 2 are, in date order: Hoeffer (1981); Kweskin and Cook (1982); Miller, Jacobsen, and Bigner (1982); Rand, Graham, and Rawlings (1982); Golombok, Spencer, and Rutter (1983); R. Green et al. (1986); M. Harris and Turner (1986); Bigner and Jacobsen (1989); Hotvedt and Mandel (1982); Huggins (1989); Steckel (1987); Bigner and Jacobsen (1992); Jenny, Roesler, and Poyer (1994); Patterson (1994); Bailey et al. (1995); Flaks et al. (1995); Brewaeys et al. (1997); Tasker and Golombok (1997); Chan, Raboy, and Patterson (1998); Chan, Brooks, et al. (1998); and McNeill, Rienzi, and Kposowa (1998).

 \+ = significantly higher in lesbigay than in heterosexual parent context.

 0 = no significant difference between lesbigay and heterosexual parent context.

 − = significantly lower in lesbigay than heterosexual parent context.

 ( ) = borders on statistical significance.

0/+ = evidence is mixed.

for lesbigay parents or their children, while negative signs (−) indicate a higher level for heterosexual parents or their children. Zero (0) indicates no significant difference.

While Table 1 reports the results of all 21 studies, our discussion here emphasizes findings from six studies we consider to be best designed to isolate whatever unique effects parents' sexual orientations might have on children. Four of these—Flaks et al. (1995); Brewaeys et al. (1997); Chan, Raboy, and Patterson (1998); and Chan, Brooks, et al. (1998)—focus on planned parenting and compare children of lesbian mothers and heterosexual mothers who conceived through DI. This focus reduces the potential for variables like parental divorce, re-partnering, coming out, and so on to confound whatever effects of maternal sexual orientation may be observed. The other two studies—R. Green et al. (1986) and Tasker and Golombok (1997)—focus on children born within heterosexual marriages who experienced the divorce of their biological parents before being raised by a lesbian mother with or without a new partner or spouse. Although this research design heightens the risk that in statistical analyses the effect of maternal sexual orientation may include the effects of other factors, distinctive strengths of each study counterbalance this limitation. R. Green et al. (1986) rigorously attempt to match lesbian mothers and heterosexual mothers on a variety of characteristics, and they compare the two groups of mothers as well as both groups of children on a wide variety of dimensions.[8] Tasker and Golombok (1997) offer a unique long-term, longitudinal design. Their data collection began in 1976 on 27 heterosexual single mothers and 39 of their children (average age 10) and 27 lesbian mothers and 39 of their children (also average age 10) in England. Follow-up interviews with 46 of the original children were conducted 14 years later, allowing for a rare glimpse at how children with lesbian mothers and those with heterosexual mothers fared over their early life courses into young adulthood. . . .

TABLE 2   **Findings on the Associations between Parents' Sexual Orientations, Other Attributes of Parents, and Parent–Child Relationships: 21 Studies, 1981 to 1998**

Variable Measured	Direction of Effect
Parental Behavior toward Children's Gender and Sexual Development	
Mother prefers child engages in gender-appropriate play activities (Hoeffer 1981; R. Green et al. 1986; M. Harris and Turner 1986).	0/−
Mother classifies the ideal child as masculine (if boy) and feminine (if girl) (Kweskin and Cook 1982).	0
Mother prefers that child be gay or lesbian when grown up (Golombok et al. 1983; Tasker and Golombok 1997).	0
Child believes that mother would prefer that she/he has lesbigay sexual orientation (Tasker and Golombok 1997).	+
Parenting Practices: Developmental Orientations and Parenting Skills	
Mother's developmental orientation in child rearing and parenting skill (Miller et al. 1982; McNeill et al. 1998; Flaks et al. 1995).	0/+
Spouse/partner's developmental orientation in child rearing and parenting skill (Flaks et al. 1995; Brewaeys et al. 1997).	+
Spouse/partner's desire for equal/shared distribution of childcare (Chan, Brooks, et al. 1998).	+
Degree to which mother and spouse/partner share child-care work (Brewaeys et al. 1997; Chan, Brooks, et al. 1998).	+
Similarity between mother's and spouse/partner's parenting skills (Flaks et al. 1995).	+
Similarity between mother's and spouse/partner's assessment of child's behavior and well-being (Chan, Raboy, and Patterson 1998; Chan, Brooks, et al. 1998).	+
Mother allowed adolescent child's boyfriend/girlfriend to spend the night (Tasker and Golombok 1997).	0
Residential Parent–Child Relationships	
Mother's rating of quality of relationship with child (Golombok et al. 1983; M. Harris and Turner 1986; Brewaeys et al. 1997; McNeill et al. 1998).	0
Mother's likelihood of having a live-in partner post-divorce (Kweskin and Cook 1982; R. Green et al. 1986).	+
Spouse/partner's rating of quality of relationship with child (Brewaeys et al. 1997).	+
Child's report of closeness with biological mother growing up (Tasker and Golombok 1997; Brewaeys et al. 1997).	0
Child's report of closeness with biological mother's partner/spouse growing up (Tasker and Golombok 1997; Brewaeys et al. 1997).	0/+
Child felt able to discuss own sexual development with parent(s) while growing up (Tasker and Golombok 1997).	+

(Continued)

(Table 2 continued)

Nonresidential Parent–Child Relationships

(Noncustodial) father's level of involvement with children, limit setting, and developmental orientation in child rearing (Bigner and Jacobsen 1989, 1992).	0/+
Mother's encouragement of child's contact with nonresidential father (Hotvedt and Mandel 1982).	0
Divorced mother's contact with children's father in the past year (Golombok et al. 1983).	+
Child's frequency of contact with nonresidential father (Golombok et al. 1983).	+
Child's positive feelings toward nonresidential father (Hotvedt and Mandel 1982; Tasker and Golombok 1997).	0/(+)

Parent's Self-Esteem and Psychological Well-Being

Mother's level of depression, self-esteem (Rand, Graham, and Rawlings 1982; R. Green et al. 1986; Chan, Raboy and Patterson 1998; Golombok et al. 1983).	0/+
Mother's level of leadership, independence, achievement orientation (R. Green et al. 1986; Rand et al. 1982).	0/+
Mother's use of sedatives, stimulants, in- or out-patient psychiatric care in past year (Golombok et al. 1983).	0
Mother ever received psychiatric care in adult life? (Golombok et al. 1983).	+
Mother's level of self-reported stress associated with single-parenthood (R. Green et al. 1986).	0

Sources: See Table 1.

+ = significantly higher in lesbigay than in heterosexual parent context.
0 = no significant difference between lesbigay and heterosexual parent context.
− = significantly lower in lesbigay than heterosexual parent context.
( ) = borders on statistical significance.
0/+ = evidence is mixed.

No Differences of Social Concern

The findings summarized in Tables 1 and 2 show that the "no differences" claim does receive strong empirical support in crucial domains. Lesbigay parents and their children in these studies display no differences from heterosexual counterparts in psychological well-being or cognitive functioning. Scores for lesbigay parenting styles and levels of investment in children are at least as "high" as those for heterosexual parents. Levels of closeness and quality of parent–child relationships do not seem to differentiate directly by parental sexual orientation, but indirectly, by way of parental gender. Because every relevant study to date shows that parental sexual orientation per se has no measurable effect on the quality of parent–child relationships or on children's mental health or social adjustment, there is no evidentiary basis for considering parental sexual orientation in decisions about children's "best interest." In fact, given that children with lesbigay parents probably contend with a degree of social stigma, these similarities in child outcomes suggest the presence of compensatory processes in lesbigay-parent families. Exploring how these families help children cope with stigma might prove helpful to all kinds of families.

Most of the research to date focuses on social-psychological dimensions of well-being and adjustment and on the quality of parent–child relationships. Perhaps these variables reflect the disciplinary preferences of psychologists who have conducted most of the studies, as well as a desire to produce evidence directly relevant to the questions of "harm" that dominate judicial and legislative deliberations over child custody. Less research has explored questions for which there are stronger theoretical grounds for expecting differences—children's gender and sexual behavior and preferences. In fact, only two studies (R. Green et al. 1986; Tasker and Golombok 1997) generate much of the baseline evidence on potential connections between parents' and child's sexual and gender identities. Evidence in these and the few other studies that focus on these variables does not support the "no differences" claim. Children with lesbigay parents appear less traditionally gender-typed and more likely to be open to homoerotic relationships. In addition, evidence suggests that parental gender and sexual identities interact to create distinctive family processes whose consequences for children have yet to be studied.

How the Sexual Orientation of Parents Matters

We have identified conceptual, methodological, and theoretical limitations in the psychological research on the effects of parental sexual orientation and have challenged the predominant claim that the sexual orientation of parents does not matter at all. We argued instead that despite the limitations, there is suggestive evidence and good reason to believe that contemporary children and young adults with lesbian or gay parents do differ in modest and interesting ways from children with heterosexual parents. Most of these differences, however, are not causal, but are indirect effects of parental gender or selection effects associated with heterosexist social conditions under which lesbigay-parent families currently live.

First, our analysis of the psychological research indicates that the effects of parental gender trump those of sexual orientation (Brewaeys et al. 1997; Chan, Brooks, et al. 1998; Chan, Raboy, and Patterson 1998; Flaks et al. 1995). A diverse array of gender theories (social learning theory, psychoanalytic theory, materialist, symbolic interactionist) would predict that children with two same-gender parents, and particularly with co-mother parents, should develop in less gender-stereotypical ways than would children with two heterosexual parents. There is reason to credit the perception of lesbian co-mothers in a qualitative study (Dunne 2000) that they "were redefining the meaning and content of motherhood, extending its boundaries to incorporate the activities that are usually dichotomized as mother and father" (p. 25). Children who derive their principal source of love, discipline, protection,

and identification from women living independent of male domestic authority or influence should develop less stereotypical symbolic, emotional, practical, and behavioral gender repertoires. Indeed, it is the claim that the
gender mix of parents has no effect on their children's gender behavior,
interests, or development that cries out for sociological explanation. Only a
crude theory of cultural indoctrination that posited the absolute impotence
of parents might predict such an outcome, and the remarkable variability of
gender configurations documented in the anthropological record readily
undermines such a theory (Bonvillain 1998; Brettell and Sargent 1997; Ortner
and Whitehead 1981). The burden of proof in the domain of gender and sexuality should rest with those who embrace the null hypothesis.

Second, because homosexuality is stigmatized, selection effects may
yield correlations between parental sexual orientation and child development that do not derive from sexual orientation itself. For example, social
constraints on access to marriage and parenting make lesbian parents likely
to be older, urban, educated, and self-aware — factors that foster several positive developmental consequences for their children. On the other hand,
denied access to marriage, lesbian co-parent relationships are likely to experience dissolution rates somewhat higher than those among heterosexual
co-parents (Bell and Weinberg 1978; Weeks, Heaphy, and Donovan forthcoming, chap. 5). Not only do same-sex couples lack the institutional pressures and support for commitment that marriage provides, but qualitative
studies suggest that they tend to embrace comparatively high standards of
emotional intimacy and satisfaction (Dunne 2000; Sullivan 1996; Weeks et al.
forthcoming). The decision to pursue a socially ostracized domain of intimacy implies an investment in the emotional regime that Giddens (1992)
terms "the pure relationship" and "confluent love." Such relationships confront the inherent instabilities of modern or postmodern intimacy, what Beck
and Beck-Gersheim (1995) term "the normal chaos of love." Thus, a higher
dissolution rate would be correlated with but not causally related to sexual
orientation, a difference that should erode were homophobia to disappear
and legal marriage be made available to lesbians and gay men.

Most of the differences in the findings discussed above cannot be considered deficits from any legitimate public policy perspective. They either
favor the children with lesbigay parents, are secondary effects of social prejudice, or represent "just a difference" of the sort democratic societies should
respect and protect. Apart from differences associated with parental gender,
most of the presently observable differences in child "outcomes" should
wither away under conditions of full equality and respect for sexual diver
sity. Indeed, it is time to recognize that the categories "lesbian mother" and
"gay father" are historically transitional and conceptually flawed, because
they erroneously imply that a parent's sexual orientation is the decisive characteristic of her or his parenting. On the contrary, we propose that homophobia and discrimination are the chief reasons why parental sexual
orientation matters at all. Because lesbigay parents do not enjoy the same
rights, respect, and recognition as heterosexual parents, their children

contend with the burdens of vicarious social stigma. Likewise, some of the particular strengths and sensitivities such children appear to display, such as a greater capacity to express feelings or more empathy for social diversity (Mitchell 1998; O'Connell 1994), are probably artifacts of marginality and may be destined for the historical dustbin of a democratic, sexually pluralist society.

Even in a utopian society, however, one difference seems less likely to disappear: The sexual orientation of parents appears to have a unique (although not large) effect on children in the politically sensitive domain of sexuality. The evidence, while scanty and underanalyzed, hints that parental sexual orientation is positively associated with the possibility that children will be more likely to attain a similar orientation—and theory and common sense also support such a view. Children raised by lesbian co-parents should and do seem to grow up more open to homoerotic relationships. This may be partly due to genetic and family socialization processes, but what sociologists refer to as "contextual effects" not yet investigated by psychologists may also be important. Because lesbigay parents are disproportionately more likely to inhabit diverse, cosmopolitan cities—Los Angeles, New York and San Francisco—and progressive university communities—such as Santa Cruz, Santa Rosa, Madison, and Ann Arbor (Black, Gates, et al. 2000)—their children grow up in comparatively tolerant school, neighborhood, and social contexts, which foster less hostility to homoeroticism. Sociology could make a valuable contribution to this field by researching processes that interact at the individual, family, and community level to undergird parent–child links between gender and sexuality.

Under homophobic conditions, lesbigay parents are apt to be more sensitive to issues surrounding their children's sexual development and to injuries that children with nonconforming desires may experience, more open to discussing sexuality with their children, and more affirming of their questions about sexuality (Mitchell 1998; Tasker and Golombok 1997). It therefore seems likely, although this has yet to be studied, that their children will grow up better informed about and more comfortable with sexual desires and practices. However, the tantalizing gender contrast in the level of sexual activity reported for sons versus daughters of lesbians raises more complicated questions about the relationship between gender and sexuality.

Even were heterosexism to disappear, however, parental sexual orientation would probably continue to have some impact on the eventual sexuality of children. Research and theory on sexual development remain so rudimentary that it is impossible to predict how much difference might remain were homosexuality not subject to social stigma. Indeed, we believe that if one suspends the hetero-normative presumption, one fascinating riddle to explain in this field is why, even though children of lesbigay parents appear to express a significant increase in homoeroticism, the majority of all children nonetheless identify as heterosexual, as most theories across the "essentialist" to "social constructionist" spectrum seem (perhaps too hastily) to expect. A nondefensive look at the anomalous data on this question could pose fruitful challenges to social constructionist, genetic, and bio-evolutionary theories.

We recognize the political dangers of pointing out that recent studies indicate that a higher proportion of children with lesbigay parents are themselves apt to engage in homosexual activity. In a homophobic world, anti-gay forces deploy such results to deny parents custody of their own children and to fuel backlash movements opposed to gay rights. Nonetheless, we believe that denying this probability capitulates to heterosexist ideology and is apt to prove counterproductive in the long run. It is neither intellectually honest nor politically wise to base a claim for justice on grounds that may prove falsifiable empirically. Moreover, the case for granting equal rights to nonheterosexual parents should not require finding their children to be identical to those reared by heterosexuals. Nor should it require finding that such children do not encounter distinctive challenges or risks, especially when these derive from social prejudice. The U.S. Supreme Court rejected this rationale for denying custody when it repudiated discrimination against interracially married parents in *Palmore v. Sidoti* in 1984: "[P]rivate biases may be outside the reach of the law, but the law cannot, directly or indirectly, give them effect" (quoted in Polikoff 1990:569–70). Inevitably, children share most of the social privileges and injuries associated with their parents' social status. If social prejudice were grounds for restricting rights to parent, a limited pool of adults would qualify.

One can readily turn the tables on a logic that seeks to protect children from the harmful effects of heterosexist stigma directed against their parents. Granting legal rights and respect to gay parents and their children should lessen the stigma that they now suffer and might reduce the high rates of depression and suicide reported among closeted gay youth living with heterosexual parents. Thus, while we disagree with those who claim that there are no differences between the children of heterosexual parents and children of lesbigay parents, we unequivocally endorse their conclusion that social science research provides no grounds for taking sexual orientation into account in the political distribution of family rights and responsibilities.

It is quite a different thing, however, to consider this issue a legitimate matter for social science research. Planned lesbigay parenthood offers a veritable "social laboratory" of family diversity in which scholars could fruitfully examine not only the acquisition of sexual and gender identity, but the relative effects on children of the gender and number of their parents as well as of the implications of diverse biosocial routes to parenthood. Such studies could give us purchase on some of the most vexing and intriguing topics in our field, including divorce, adoption, step-parenthood, and domestic violence, to name a few. To exploit this opportunity, however, researchers must overcome the hetero-normative presumption that interprets sexual differences as deficits, thereby inflicting some of the very disadvantages it claims to discover. Paradoxically, if the sexual orientation of parents were to matter less for political rights, it could matter more for social theory.

ENDNOTES

Author's Note: We are grateful for the constructive criticisms on early versions of this article from: Celeste Atkins, Amy Binder, Phil Cowan, Gary Gates, Adam Green, David Greenberg, Oystein Holter, Celia Kitzinger, Joan Laird, Jane Mauldon, Dan McPherson, Shannon Minter, Valory Mitchell, Charlotte Patterson, Anne Peplau, Vernon Rosario, Seth Sanders, Alisa Steckel, Michael Wald, and the reviewers and editors of *ASR*. We presented portions of this work at: UCLA Neuropsychiatric Institute Symposium on Sexuality; the Feminist Interdisciplinary Seminar of the University of California, Davis; and the Taft Lecture Program at the University of Cincinnati.

1. In *J.B.F. v. J.M.F.* (Ex parte J.M.F. 1970224, So. 2d 1190, 1988 Ala. LEXIS 161 [1998]), for example, Alabama's Supreme Court quoted Wardle's (1997) essay to justify transferring custody of a child from her lesbian mother to her heterosexual father.

2. The extrapolation is "inappropriate" because lesbigay-parent families have never been a comparison group in the family structure literature on which these authors rely (cf. Downey and Powell 1993; McLanahan 1985).

3. In March 2000, Norwegian sociologist Oystein Holter (personal communication) described Helmut Stierlin's "delegation" theory (published in German) — that children take over their parents' unconscious wishes. Holter suggests this theory could predict that a child who grows up with gay parents under homophobic conditions might develop "contrary responses." We are unfamiliar with this theory but find it likely that under such conditions unconscious wishes of heterosexual and non-heterosexual parents could foster some different "contrary responses."

4. These estimates derive from an extrapolation of Kinsey data claiming a roughly 10 percent prevalence of homosexuality in the adult male population. Interestingly, Michael et al.'s (1994) revisiting of Kinsey (Kinsey, Pomeroy, and Martin 1948; Kinsey, Pomeroy, Martin, and Gebhard 1953) suggests that Kinsey himself emphasized that different measures of sexual orientation yield different estimates of individuals with same-sex sexual orientations in the population. Had scholars read Kinsey differently, they might have selected his figure of 4 percent of the men in his sample who practiced exclusive homosexual behavior from adolescence onward, rather than the widely embraced 10 percent figure. In fact, the 10 percent number is fundamentally flawed: Kinsey found that of the 37 percent of the white men in his sample who had at least one sexual experience with another man in their lifetime, only 10 percent of them (i.e., 3.7 percent of the entire white male sample) had exclusively same-sex sexual experiences for any three-year period between ages 16 and 55.

5. This assumes that the ratio of number of dependent children to total offspring among current lesbigay parents will be roughly the same as that for all parents and children.

6. The field is now in a position to take advantage of new data sources. For example, the 1990 U.S. census allows (albeit imperfectly) for the first time the identification of gay and lesbian couples, as will the 2000 census (Black, Gates, et al. 2000). From 1989 to the present, the U.S. General Social Surveys (http://www.icpsr.umich.edu/GSS/index.html) have also allowed for the identification of the sexual orientation of respondents, as does the National Health and Social Life Survey (Laumann et al. 1995).

7. We chose to display the specific findings in each of the quantitative studies, rather than to conduct a meta-analysis, because at this stage of knowledge not enough studies are targeted to the same general "outcome" to enable a meta-analysis to reveal systematic patterns. The single meta-analysis that has been done (Allen and Burrell 1996) reached the typical "no difference" conclusion but its conclusions were hampered by this very problem. The small number of studies

available led Allen and Burrell to pool studies focused on quite different parent and child "outcomes," heightening the risk that findings in one direction effectively offset findings in another.

8. Belcastro et al. (1993) point out that R. Green et al. (1986) did not successfully match heterosexual and lesbian single-mother families on the dimension of household composition. While 39 of R. Green et al.'s 50 lesbian single-mother households had a second adult residing in them by one-plus years post-divorce, only 4 of the 40 heterosexual single mothers did so. R. Green et al. (1986) note this difference, but do not discuss its implications for findings; nor do Belcastro et al. (1993).

REFERENCES

Allen, Mike and Nancy Burrell. 1996. "Comparing the Impact of Homosexual and Heterosexual Parents on Children: Meta-Analysis of Existing Research." *Journal of Homosexuality* 32:19–35.

Badgett, M. V. Lee. 1998. "The Economic Well-Being of Lesbian, Gay, and Bisexual Adults' Families." Pp. 231–48 in *Lesbian, Gay and Bisexual Identities in Families: Psychological Perspectives*, edited by C. J. Patterson and A. R. D'Augelli. New York: Oxford University Press.

Bailey, J. Michael, David Bobrow, Marilyn Wolfe, and Sarah Mikach. 1995. "Sexual Orientation of Adult Sons of Gay Fathers." *Developmental Psychology* 31.124–29.

Baumrind, Diana. 1980. "New Directions in Socialization Research." *American Psychologist* 35:639–52.

———. 1995. "Commentary on Sexual Orientation: Research and Social Policy Implications." *Developmental Psychology* 31:130–36.

Bech, Henning. 1997. *When Men Meet: Homosexuality and Modernity*. Chicago: University of Chicago Press.

Beck, Ulrich and Elisabeth Beck-Gersheim. 1995. *The Normal Chaos of Love*. London: Polity.

Belcastro, Philip A., Theresa Gramlich, Thomas Nicholson, Jimmie Price, and Richard Wilson. 1993. "A Review of Data Based Studies Addressing the Affects [*sic*] of Homosexual Parenting on Children's Sexual and Social Functioning." *Journal of Divorce and Remarriage* 20:105–22.

Bell, Alan P. and Martin S. Weinberg. 1978. *Homosexualities: A Study of Diversity among Men and Women*. New York: Simon and Schuster.

Benkov, Laura. 1994. *Reinventing the Family: Lesbian and Gay Parents*. New York: Crown.

Bem, Daryl J. 1996. "Exotic Becomes Erotic: A Developmental Theory of Sexual Orientation." *Psychological Review* 103:320–35.

Bigner, Jerry J. and R. Brooke Jacobsen. 1989. "Parenting Behaviors of Homosexual and Heterosexual Fathers." *Journal of Homosexuality* 18:73–86.

———. 1992. "Adult Responses to Child Behavior and Attitudes toward Fathering: Gay and Nongay Fathers." *Journal of Homosexuality* 23:99–112.

Black, Dan A., Gary Gates, Seth Sanders, and Lowell Taylor. 2000. "Demographics of the Gay and Lesbian Population in the United States: Evidence from Available Systematic Data Sources." *Demography* 37:139–54.

Black, Dan A., Hoda R. Maker, Seth G. Sanders, and Lowell Taylor. 1998. "The Effects of Sexual Orientation on Earnings." Working paper, Department of Economics, Gatton College of Business and Economics, University of Kentucky, Lexington, KY.

Blankenhorn, David. 1995. *Fatherless America: Confronting Our Most Urgent Social Problem*. New York: Basic.

Bonvillain, Nancy. 1998. *Women and Men: Cultural Constructs of Gender*. 2d ed. Upper Saddle River, NJ: Prentice Hall.

Bourne, Amy E. 1999. "Mothers of Invention." *San Francisco Daily Journal*, May 21, pp. 1, 9.

Boykin, Keith. 1996. *One More River to Cross: Black and Gay in America*. New York: Anchor.

Bozett, Frederick W. 1989. "Gay Fathers: A Review of the Literature." Pp. 137–62 in *Homosexuality and the Family*, edited by F. W. Bozett. New York: Haworth Press.

Brettell, Caroline B. and Carolyn F. Sargent, eds. 1997. *Gender in Cross-Cultural Perspective*. 2d ed. Upper Saddle River, NJ: Prentice Hall.

Brewaeys, A., I. Ponjaert, E. V. Van Hall, and S. Golombok. 1997. "Donor Insemination: Child Development and Family Functioning in Lesbian Mother Families." *Human Reproduction* 12:1349–59.

Cameron, Paul and Kirk Cameron. 1996. "Homosexual Parents." *Adolescence* 31:757–76.

Cameron, Paul, Kirk Cameron, and Thomas Landess. 1996. "Errors by the American Psychiatric Association, the American Psychological Association, and the National Educational Association in Representing Homosexuality in Amicus Briefs about Amendment 2 to the U.S. Supreme Court." *Psychological Reports* 79:383–404.

Cantor, David. 1994. *The Religious Right: The Assault on Tolerance and Pluralism in America*. New York: Anti-Defamation League.

Cantu, Lionel. 2000. "Entre Hombres/Between Men: Latino Masculinities and Homosexualities." Pp. 224–46 in *Gay Masculinities*, edited by P. Nardi. Thousand Oaks, CA: Sage.

Carrier, Joseph. 1992. "Miguel: Sexual Life History of a Gay Mexican American." Pp. 202–24 in *Gay Culture in America: Essays from the Field*, edited by G. Herdt. Boston: Beacon.

Chan, Raymond W., Risa C. Brooks, Barbara Raboy, and Charlotte J. Patterson. 1998. "Division of Labor among Lesbian and Heterosexual Parents: Associations with Children's Adjustment." *Journal of Family Psychology* 12:402–19.

Chan, Raymond W., Barbara Raboy, and Charlotte J. Patterson. 1998. "Psychosocial Adjustment among Children Conceived Via Donor Insemination by Lesbian and Heterosexual Mothers." *Child Development* 69:443–57.

Clarke, Victoria. 2000. "Sameness and Difference in Research on Lesbian Parenting." Working paper, Women's Studies Research Group, Department of Social Sciences, Loughborough University, Leicestershire, UK.

Downey, Douglas B. and Brian Powell. 1993. "Do Children in Single-Parent Households Fare Better Living with Same-Sex Parents?" *Journal of Marriage and the Family* 55:55–72.

Dunne, Gillian A. 2000. "Opting into Motherhood: Lesbians Blurring the Boundaries and Transforming the Meaning of Parenthood and Kinship." *Gender and Society* 14:11–35.

Falk, Patrick J. 1994. "The Gap between Psychosocial Assumptions and Empirical Research in Lesbian-Mother Child Custody Cases." Pp. 131–56 in *Redefining Families: Implications for Children's Development*, edited by A. E. Gottfried and A. W. Gottfried. New York: Plenum.

Flaks, David K., Ilda Ficher, Frank Masterpasqua, and Gregory Joseph. 1995. "Lesbians Choosing Motherhood: A Comparative Study of Lesbian and Heterosexual Parents and Their Children." *Developmental Psychology* 31:105–14.

Gallagher, Maggie. 2000. "The Gay-Parenting Science." *New York Post*, March 30, p. 3.

Giddens, Anthony. 1992. *The Transformation of Intimacy: Sexuality, Love and Eroticism in Modern Societies*. Stanford, CA: Stanford University Press.

Golombok, Susan, Ann Spencer, and Michael Rutter. 1983. "Children in Lesbian and Single-Parent Households: Psychosexual and Psychiatric Appraisal." *Journal of Child Psychology and Psychiatry* 24:551–72.

Green, G. Dorsey and Frederick W. Bozett. 1991. "Lesbian Mothers and Gay Fathers." Pp. 197–214 in *Homosexuality: Research Implications for Public Policy*, edited by J. C. Gonsiorek and J. D. Weinrich. Newbury Park, CA: Sage.

Green, Richard, Jane Barclay Mandel, Mary E. Hotvedt, James Gray, and Laurel Smith. 1986. "Lesbian Mothers and Their Children: A Comparison with Solo Parent Heterosexual Mothers and Their Children." *Archives of Sexual Behavior* 15:167–84.

Greene, Beverly and Nancy Boyd-Franklin. 1996. "African-American Lesbians: Issues in Couple Therapy." Pp. 251–71 in *Lesbians and Gays in Couples and Families: A Handbook for Therapists*, edited by J. Laird and R. J. Green. San Francisco, CA: Jossey-Bass.

Groze, Vic. 1991. "Adoption and Single Parents: A Review." *Child Welfare* 70:321–32.

Harris, Judith Rich. 1998. *The Nurture Assumption: Why Children Turn Out the Way They Do*. New York: Free Press.

Harris, Mary B. and Pauline H. Turner. 1986. "Gay and Lesbian Parents." *Journal of Homosexuality* 12:101–13.

Hawkeswood, William. 1997. *One of the Children: Gay Black Men in Harlem*. Berkeley: University of California Press.

Herek, Gregory M. 1998. "Bad Science in the Service of Stigma: A Critique of the Cameron Group's Survey Studies," Pp. 223–55 in *Stigma and Sexual Orientation: Understanding Prejudice against Lesbians, Gay Men, and Bisexuals*, edited by G. M. Herek. Thousand Oaks, CA: Sage.

——. 2000. "Paul Cameron Fact Sheet" (Copyright 1997–2000 by G. M. Herek). Retrieved (http://psychology.ucdavis.edu/rainbow/html/facts_cameron_sheet.html).

Hoeffer, Beverly. 1981. "Children's Acquisition of Sex-Role Behavior in Lesbian-Mother Families." *American Journal of Orthopsychiatry* 51:536–44.

Hotvedt, Mary E. and Jane Barclay Mandel. 1982. "Children of Lesbian Mothers." Pp. 275–91 in *Homosexuality, Social, Psychological, and Biological Issues*, edited by W. Paul. Beverly Hills, CA: Sage.

Huggins, Sharon L. 1989. "A Comparative Study of Self-Esteem of Adolescent Children of Divorced Lesbian Mothers and Divorced Heterosexual Mothers." Pp. 123–35 in *Homosexuality and the Family*, edited by F. W. Bozett. New York: Haworth.

Jenny, Carole, Thomas A. Roesler, and Kimberly L. Poyer. 1994. "Are Children at Risk for Sexual Abuse by Homosexuals?" *Pediatrics* 94:41–44.

Katz, Jonathan Ned. 1995. *The Invention of Heterosexuality*. New York: Dutton.

Kinsey, Alfred C., Wardell B. Pomeroy, and Clyde E. Martin. 1948. *Sexual Behavior in the Human Male*. Philadelphia: W. B. Saunders.

Kinsey, Alfred C., Wardell B. Pomeroy, Clyde E. Martin, and Paul H. Gebhard. 1953. *Sexual Behavior in the Human Female*. Philadelphia: W. B. Saunders.

Kitzinger, Celia. 1987. *The Social Construction of Lesbianism*. London, England: Sage.

——. 1989. "Liberal Humanism as an Ideology of Social Control: The Regulation of Lesbian Identities." Pp. 82–98 in *Texts of Identity*, edited by J. Shotter and K. Gergen. London: Sage.

——. 1994. "Should Psychologists Study Sex Differences? Editor's Introduction: Sex Differences Research: Feminist Perspectives." *Feminism and Psychology* 4:501–506.

Kitzinger, Celia and Adrian Coyle. 1995. "Lesbian and Gay Couples: Speaking of Difference." *The Psychologist* 8:64–69.

Kweskin, Sally L. and Alicia S. Cook. 1982. "Heterosexual and Homosexual Mothers' Self-Described Sex-Role Behavior and Ideal Sex-Role Behavior in Children." *Sex Roles* 8:967–75.

Laumann, Edward O., John H. Gagnon, Robert T. Michael, and Stuart Michaels. 1994. *The Social Organization of Sexuality: Sexual Practices in the United States*. Chicago: University of Chicago Press.

——. 1995. *National Health and Social Life Survey, 1992* [MRDF]. Chicago: University of Chicago and National Opinion Research Center [producer]. Ann Arbor, MI: Inter-university Consortium for Political and Social Research [distributor].

Lerner, Robert and Althea K. Nagai. 2000. "Out of Nothing Comes Nothing: Homosexual and Heterosexual Marriage Not Shown to Be Equivalent for Raising Children." Paper presented at the Revitalizing the Institution of Marriage for the 21st Century conference, Brigham Young University, March, Provo, UT.

Lynch, F. R. 1992. "Nonghetto Gays: An Ethnography of Suburban Homosexuals." Pp. 165–201 in *Gay Culture in America: Essays from the Field*, edited by G. Herdt. Boston, MA: Beacon.

McLanahan, Sara S. 1985. "Family Structure and the Reproduction of Poverty." *American Journal of Sociology* 90:873–901.

McNeill, Kevin F., Beth M. Rienzi, and Augustine Kposowa. 1998. "Families and Parenting: A Comparison of Lesbian and Heterosexual Mothers." *Psychological Reports* 82:59–62.

Michael, Robert T., John H. Gagnon, Edward O. Laumann, and Gina Bari Kolata. 1994. *Sex in America: A Definitive Survey*. Boston, MA: Little, Brown.

Miller, Judith Ann, R. Brooke Jacobsen, and Jerry J. Bigner. 1982. "The Child's Home Environment for Lesbian vs. Heterosexual Mothers: A Neglected Area of Research." *Journal of Homosexuality* 7:49–56.

Mitchell, Valory. 1998. "The Birds, the Bees . . . and the Sperm Banks: How Lesbian Mothers Talk with Their Children about Sex and Reproduction." *American Journal of Orthopsychiatry* 68:400–409.

O'Connell, Ann. 1994. "Voices from the Heart: The Developmental Impact of a Mother's Lesbianism on Her Adolescent Children." *Smith College Studies in Social Work* 63:281–99.

Ortner, Sherry and Harriet Whitehead. 1981. *Sexual Meanings: The Cultural Construction of Gender and Sexuality*. Cambridge, England: Cambridge University Press.

Patterson, Charlotte J. 1992. "Children of Lesbian and Gay Parents." *Child Development* 63:1025–42.

———. 1994. "Children of the Lesbian Baby Boom: Behavioral Adjustment, Self-Concepts and Sex Role Identity." Pp. 156–75 in *Lesbian and Gay Psychology: Theory, Research, and Clinical Applications*, edited by B. Green and G. M. Herek. Thousand Oaks, CA: Sage.

———. 1995. "Families of the Lesbian Baby Boom: Parents' Division of Labor and Children's Adjustment." *Developmental Psychology* 31:115–23.

——— 1996. "Lesbian and Gay Parents and Their Children." Pp. 274–304 in *The Lives of Lesbians, Gays, and Bisexuals: Children to Adults*, edited by R. C. Savin-Williams and K. M. Cohen. Fort Worth, TX: Harcourt Brace College Publishers.

Patterson, Charlotte J. and Lisa V. Freil. 2000. "Sexual Orientation and Fertility." In *Infertility in the Modern World: Biosocial Perspectives*, edited by G. Bentley and N. Mascie-Taylor. Cambridge, England: Cambridge University Press.

Peterson, John. 1992. "Black Men and Their Same-Sex Desires and Behaviors." Pp. 147–64 in *Gay Culture in America: Essays from the Field*, edited by G. Herdt. Boston: Beacon.

Polikoff, Nancy D. 1990. "This Child Does Have Two Mothers: Redefining Parenthood to Meet the Needs of Children in Lesbian-Mother and Other Nontraditional Families." *Georgetown Law Journal* 78:459–575.

Popenoe, David. 1993. "American Family Decline, 1960–1990: A Review and Appraisal." *Journal of Marriage and the Family* 55:527–41.

———. 1996. *Life without Father*. New York: Free Press.

Price, Deb. 1999. "Middle Ground Emerges for Gay Couples." *Detroit News*, October 4.

Rand, Catherine, Dee L. R. Graham and Edna I. Rawlings. 1982. "Psychological Health and Factors the Court Seeks to Control in Lesbian Mother Custody Trials." *Journal of Homosexuality* 8:27–39.

Rothblum, Ester D. 1994. "'I Only Read About Myself on Bathroom Walls': The Need for Research on the Mental Health of Lesbians and Gay Men.'" *Journal of Consulting and Clinical Psychology* 62:213–20.

Seidman, Steven. 1997. *Difference Troubles: Queering Social Theory and Sexual Politics*. New York: Cambridge University Press.

Shireman, Joan F. 1996. "Single-Parent Adoptive Homes." *Children and Youth Services Review* 18:23–36.

Steckel, Alisa. 1987. "Psychosocial Development of Children of Lesbian Mothers." Pp. 75–85 in *Gay and Lesbian Parents*, edited by F. W. Bozett. New York: Praeger.

Sullivan, Maureen. 1996. "Rozzie and Harriet?: Gender and Family Patterns of Lesbian Coparents." *Gender and Society* 10:747–67.

Sweet, James and Larry Bumpass. 1996. *The National Survey of Families and Households—Waves 1 and 2: Data Description and Documentation.* Center for Demography and Ecology, University of Wisconsin–Madison, Madison, WI (http://www/ssc.wisc.edu/nsfh/home.htm).

Tasker, Fiona L. and Susan Golombok. 1997. *Growing Up in a Lesbian Family.* New York: Guilford.

U.S. Census Bureau. 1999. "Population Estimates Program." Population Division, Washington, DC. Retrieved January 5, 2000 (http://www.census.gov/population/estimates/nation/intfile2–1.txt, and natdoc.txt).

Wald, Michael S. 1999. "Same-Sex Couples: Marriage, Families, and Children, An Analysis of Proposition 22, The Knight Initiative." Stanford Institute for Research on Women and Gender, Stanford University, Stanford, CA.

Wardle, Lynn D. 1997. "The Potential Impact of Homosexual Parenting on Children." *University of Illinois Law Review* 1997:833–919.

Weeks, Jeffrey, Brian Heaphy, and Catherine Donovan. Forthcoming. *Families of Choice and Other Life Experiments: The Intimate Lives of Non-Heterosexuals.* Cambridge, England: Cambridge University Press.

Whitehead, Barbara Dafoe. 1993. "Dan Quayle Was Right." *Atlantic Monthly*, April, vol. 271, pp. 47–50.

Woodruff, Robin. 1998. Testimony re: "Subcommittee Meeting to Accept Empirical Data and Expert Testimony Concerning Homosexual Foster Parents." Hearing at the Office of the Attorney General, September 9, 1998. Little Rock, AK. Available from the authors on request.

20

HOW FAMILIES STILL MATTER
A Longitudinal Study of Youth in Two Generations

VERN. L. BENGTSON • TIMOTHY J. BIBLARZ • ROBERT E. L. ROBERTS

G3 father: I tell my sons there's going to be people you can depend upon for your whole life, and they're called your brother and your mother and your father. You can have friends now that won't be friends later, but your family will be with you the rest of your life.

In this study we have examined data concerning intergenerational continuity and change over the last three decades, comparing the Baby Boomers of the 1960s with the Generation Xers of the 1990s. We asked four questions:

(1) How different are today's youth from previous generations? Are they a "generation at risk"? (2) How have changes in family structure and roles—particularly divorce and maternal employment—affected successive generations of youth? (3) Has there been a decline over generations in parents' influence on youth? (4) What are the gender differences in achievement orientations and family influence across generations?

Underlying our inquiry have been other, more general questions: How important are families in America at the beginning of the twenty-first century? How well are contemporary families doing in terms of fulfilling their responsibilities to prepare youth for the future? How do family influences on today's youth (Generation Xers) compare with those of earlier generations?

We began examining these issues in the context of public and academic clamor about the American family: its demise, dysfunctions, or irrelevance at the start of the twenty-first century. Using twenty-six years of data from the Longitudinal Study of Generations, we tested two general hypotheses in the research literature about family influences today. The first is the "family decline" perspective, which sees American families as having lost many of their functions and much of their structure (through divorce) over recent decades. The second is the "family solidarity" hypothesis, which posits the continued importance and function of families across generations even in the context of changes such as divorce.

We approached these issues by asking whether families are still functional in their primary role of socializing their children, that is, whether family influences are still important in shaping the educational and occupational aspirations, self-esteem, and values of children in the context of high divorce rates, increased maternal employment, changing opportunity structures, and sociohistorical conditions. In analyzing our data we uncovered a number of patterns that suggest (in contrast to the family decline perspective) that families still matter greatly, and that families can and do tend to perform well those functions that are particularly relevant to the lives of children, even in different social and historical contexts, household arrangements, and living conditions.

In this [reading] we review our central findings, and place them in the context of current mass-media discussions about *how* families still matter, using those findings to untangle some myths from realities about Generation Xers and their families. We then discuss *why* families still matter, and in so doing raise questions—in the form of three propositions or hypotheses—that we hope will stimulate further research on the linkages among social change, family intergenerational relations, and children's attainments over the life course.

Myths and Realities about Generation Xers and Their Families

One contemporary myth is that Generation Xers are quite different from their parents and grandparents, that they are "slackers" because of their low-achievement orientations or a "generation at risk" because of having grown up in families of divorce or with mothers who "abandoned" them for paid employment. Our research findings challenge this image. We draw a different conclusion when we examine the evidence concerning Generation Xers' aspirations, values, and self-esteem as compared with their parents' at the same life stage. "The kids *are* all right." In fact, they're doing "quite a bit better" than their elders did when they were youth, despite the dramatic social and family structure changes of the last few decades.

A second myth is the claim that the American family is declining in importance. People who hold this myth suggest that enhancing family values should be a major public policy priority in solving America's domestic problems. Our research suggests a somewhat different conclusion. Our data indicate that families remain important as the sites for guidance and support and the socialization of children and that fathers continue to influence their children positively, many with greater involvement than their own fathers had (although as previously mentioned, their effectiveness in some areas has been diminished as a result of parental divorce). Our research also shows that the promulgation of family values policies may be misguided or ill-fated, as well as insensitive to the pluralism of American family forms and beliefs.

A third myth is that divorce is a disaster. This is the message of *The Unexpected Legacy of Divorce: A 25-year Landmark Study* (Wallerstein, Lewis, and Blakeslee 2000). This volume is based on a twenty-five-year follow-up of children in a small, clinical sample of parents in the process of divorcing, a study that began the same year as the LSOG (1971) but with a sample of troubled children. Wallerstein and her colleagues argue that the damage from divorce is serious and lasting. Our study finds less serious consequences of divorce — in fact, that divorce has relatively little impact on children's achievement orientations, self-esteem, and values (when compared directly with youth from nondivorced families). Our findings are similar to those of Hetherington and Kelly (2002), whose data suggest that 75 percent of children of divorce were functioning well after three decades, with little long-term damage.

In sum, our findings challenge the myths that Generation Xers are slackers or a lost generation, that families are declining in function and influence, and that nontraditional or "alternative" family structures spell the downfall of American youth. While rapid social change has presented families with many challenges, we find that most families are resilient and adaptive, and that American families continue to perform their socialization functions in the face of rapid social change and varied family structures. In most respects, the family decline hypothesis cannot be supported by the data in this longitudinal study.

How Families Still Matter

Based on our data, Generation X youth are neither the underachieving slackers nor the overachieving cyberspace entrepreneurs as some commentators and researchers have described them. The Generation Xers in our sample have higher educational and occupational aspirations, as well as higher levels of self-esteem, than their Baby Boomer parents had at the same age twenty-six years earlier. Particularly noteworthy are the educational and career expectations of Generation X young women, who aspire to even higher levels of achievement than do Generation X young men.

Because we have data from two successive generations of youth—as well as from their parents—we can offer some suggestions about *how* families still matter across generations, despite the obvious changes in nuclear family structures and roles over recent decades.

First, children's *feelings of solidarity and closeness* with their parents—particularly their mothers—were high in both generations, even though Generation Xers in childhood experienced rates of family disruption and maternal employment that were never experienced by their Baby Boomer parents. Solidarity with parents, in turn, was among the strongest positive predictors of youths' self-esteem and aspirations both today (Generation Xers) and in the previous generation (Baby Boomers).

Second, the effects of *parental divorce* on younger generations were not as significant as we had expected. Our evidence shows that three core dimensions of children's identity—aspirations, self-esteem, and values—are not strongly affected by the rise in divorce rate over the past thirty years. Most important, the experience of parental divorce did not erode the self-confidence of Generation X youth. Both Generation X youth who experienced parental divorce and those from traditional families had high and roughly equivalent levels of self-esteem. The late-adolescent Generation Xers who experienced their parents' divorce did have slightly lower aspirations than their Generation X counterparts whose parents did not divorce. While Generation X youth who experienced parental divorce were more materialistic than those who did not, they also held more collectivistic and less individualistic value orientations.

Third, the impact of *maternal employment* on child well-being was also not as significant as we had expected; in fact, it was negligible. One of our most important findings is that across two generations and twenty-six years, mothers' labor force participation did not harm children's status aspirations, self-esteem, or prosocial value orientations, and in some cases maternal employment proved beneficial to children (e.g., in the case of sons, maternal employment was associated with heightened self-esteem). Overall, it made little difference whether mothers worked or stayed home.

Fourth, when we examined parental influences on youths' aspirations, self-esteem, and values—the measure of the family's success in the socialization of its children—we found that *parents' ability to influence their children has not declined over recent generations.* Contrary to the hypothesis of family decline, our data indicate that the importance of parental influences for the self-esteem, aspirations, and values of their children has not diminished across generations.

Fifth, we found that *intergenerational transmission processes* are still working effectively to shape achievement orientations of youth. For one thing, these data indicate that *children learn from and model themselves after their parents* in occupational and educational aspirations and values. Children hold for themselves the values they learned from parents, such as high individualism or low materialism. For another, these data indicate the crucial role of *parental affirmation and intergenerational solidarity* in the transmission process. Children who are close to their parents have higher self-esteem and educational and occupational aspirations than those who are not close. Finally, *status inheritance* processes are important in achievement orientations. The social standing and resources of families continue to be crucial predictors of what youth come to aspire for themselves. Parental education and occupational status have a strong resemblance to the aspirations of youth in both generations—the Gen Xers as well as the Baby Boomers. Moreover, parental status and resources had the same effect on children from divorced families as they did in two-parent, long-married families.

In this study we compared the magnitude and direction of intergenerational influences on child outcomes, and the average child outcomes themselves, among families who were raising children in very different social milieus (the 1950s and 1960s in the case of our G2/G3 parent/child dyads, and the 1980s and 1990s in the case of our G3/G4 dyads), and in very different kinds of family structures and family divisions of labor over time. Our data indicate more continuity than contrast in the processes of intergenerational transmission and in the course of generational progress. With some exceptions, our families seem to be able to do well by their children, even under a variety of more or less taxing and challenging conditions. The contemporary families in our analysis, changed in many ways from their predecessors by high divorce rates and the shifting market and nonmarket responsibilities of parents, have been relatively successful in raising a generation of youth that appears well equipped to face the challenges of adulthood.

To sum up, our results demonstrate the continuing influence and enduring importance of families across recent generations, despite the effects of divorce, alternative family forms, and changing gender roles on family commitments and functions. The family is still fulfilling its basic task, the socialization of children, but in a world very different from that of the late 1950s. Its forms are more fluid; its relationship ties are both ascribed and chosen. Traditional "nuclear" family forms are no longer the norm in American society. Marriages, having evolved from "institutional" to "companionate" relationships based largely on bonds of affection, are more fragile. But despite this, family influences across generations are strong, and families still matter—much more than advocates of the family decline hypothesis would admit.

Why Families Still Matter

These findings about *how* families are important raise the question of *why.* This is particularly relevant in light of other research and family decline theory predicting that recent social trends and changes in the family have

significantly diminished intergenerational transmission processes and negatively affected child outcomes. Parental divorce, for example, has been shown
to create emotional distress, behavioral or school difficulties, and related
problems for children in the short term (Dawson 1991; Kline, Johnson, and
Tschann 1991) and over several decades (according to Wallerstein et al.
2000). The modal pattern is that children suffer substantial economic loss
following divorce (since children most often reside with their mothers), and
that children's relationships with nonresidential fathers decline over time
following divorce. The effects of maternal employment on children should
also be negative following the "family decline" hypothesis, because employment involves mothers' reallocation of time away from childrearing, and
mothers' time investments in children have been shown to be central for
many aspects of children's development.

Below we offer three propositions about why families still matter, why
Generation X children have done well, and why divorce and maternal
employment have not had (at least in our sample) the severe detrimental
effects on children predicted by some commentators and researchers. We set
forth these propositions as important issues to be tested in future research.

> *Proposition 1:* Families are adapting by expanding support across gen-
> erations. There is increasing interdependence and exchange across sev-
> eral generations of family members; this expansion has protected and
> enhanced the well-being of new generations of children.

> *Proposition 2:* Nondivorced, two-parent families are more successful
> than their counterparts a generation ago. Relational processes within
> two-parent families are changing over time in ways that have enhanced
> the well-being of new generations of children.

> *Proposition 3:* Maternal investment in children has not declined over
> generations. Despite growth in the rate of labor force participation
> among mothers, maternal investment in children has remained high and
> constant over time, and this has assured a generally positive level of
> well-being among new generations of children.

In a sense, these propositions summarize our major findings. But our
data are limited and the story they tell is incomplete. We present the propositions as issues to be tested in further research, using larger and nationally
representative samples.

Proposition 1: Families Are Adapting by Expanding Support across Generations

The apparent resiliency of Generation X children who have experienced
recent changes in family structure and roles may be accounted for by the
adaptive and compensatory processes that their families have drawn on,
particularly in times of need. These processes may often involve expanding
the family to bring additional parent-like figures and family members
into the lives of children. African American families, for example, have had a

long history of adaptation to family disruption induced (in fact, often forced) by slavery, segregation, employment discrimination, and other manifestations of racism. Research like Hill's (1999) *The Strengths of African American Families* (also Johnson 1999; Oates 1999) has emphasized the resilient capacities of African American families to care and provide for children under difficult conditions (such as fatherlessness) by forming extended and fictive kin relations. In father-absent African American families historically, the "fatherly" role was often played by someone other than a biological father, and aunts, uncles, and grandparents (biologically or socially related) have been instrumental in the rearing of children.

An important direction for further family research and theory involves the application of this "families adapt by extending kin" concept to other kinds of families, particularly those who have experienced disruptive events such as divorce. The relationships that children and parents have with their grandparents following divorce, in particular, should be carefully explored (Bengtson 2001). Emotional closeness and support from grandparents have been shown to compensate for or mitigate divorce-related family processes and custodial-parent role overload that can have a negative impact on the well-being of both adult children and grandchildren (Johnson and Barer 1987; Silverstein, Giarrusso, and Bengtson 1998). For example, greater grandparental involvement with children could compensate for the temporary declines in mothers' attention and time with her children immediately following divorce. In this situation, children would continue to receive the adult-family-member time investment that is so essential to their development. This type of compensation may ameliorate the risk of negative outcomes for today's children in divorced families.

Grandparental involvement in postdivorce families is an especially important potential source of social support (Johnson 2000; Johnson and Barer 1987) because—unlike day-care centers, after-school programs, babysitters, or nannies—grandparents typically have a high level of concern for the interests of their children and grandchildren. Grandparents today bring other strengths to their family roles. Grandparents are considerably more financially secure than they were just twenty-five years ago; they have a higher standard of living (Treas 1995). At the same time, grandparents today are healthier and much more active, with many more years ahead of them after retirement. Grandparents today, as they age, can expect fewer years with chronic illnesses and limiting disabilities than previous generations (Hayward and Heron 1999). These positive trends may make grandparent/grandchildren relationships far more important and rewarding than ever before.

In the context of the diversity of family conditions that exist today, there are pressures and opportunities to shift more familial responsibility to members of the extended family (Bengtson 2001). Contemporary families may be moving beyond the confines of the shrinking nuclear family to encompass the broader support and emotional resources of multigenerational families, relationships that are both ascribed and created, where (as Robert Frost noted), ". . . when you have to go there . . . they have to take you in."

And increasingly they do. This can be seen in the growing incidence of grandparents raising grandchildren, where the middle generations' marriages dissolve, or where there are other difficulties (such as drug addiction) that interfere with the younger adults' ability to parent. To the extent that traditional nuclear families weaken or transform themselves, the strengths and resources of the multigenerational family may take on new importance.

At the same time that exchange, dependence, and support among multiple generations of family members are becoming increasingly important, so, too, are patterns of intergenerational exchange, dependence, and support over the life course. In the new economic reality of postindustrialism, for example, many midlife parents still have their young adult children at home or at school. Generation X young adults will be in college far longer on average than their Baby Boomer parents were, extending the period of economic dependence on the resources of their parents. This extended period of intergenerational exchange and support tends to strengthen the bonds of solidarity between parents and children as well (Bengtson, Rosenthal, and Burton, 1995; Elder 1994). In an unexpected way, these examples of "prolonged parenting" by those now at midlife (that is, Baby Boomers) may reflect, in practice, the shift that we found in this study toward more collectivistic values. Especially in light of the ways in which families are diversifying, we believe that multi- and intergenerational exchange and support among family members over the life course of children must become an important object of study in examining consequences for children of recent changes in the family.

Proposition 2: Today's Nondivorced, Two-Parent Families Are More Successful than Their Counterparts a Generation Ago

A major finding in our study was the discovery of strengths in a family type that is typically used as a reference category but not as often explored in its own right: the two-biological parent family of the 1990s and beyond. The aspirations, self-esteem, and values of the Generation Xers from these families were significantly more positive than those of comparable two-parent families in the previous generation (Baby Boomer youth). In several respects, today's two-parent families seem to be more effective in the socialization of their children than yesterday's two-parent families.

It is likely these two-parent families are to some extent a select group, as less happily married or dysfunctional parents of Generation Xers would have already divorced (unlike similarly predisposed marital partners of earlier generations, who would have found divorce much more difficult to accomplish). Nevertheless, uncovering how today's two-parent families have been successful in navigating the postmodern social structure — balancing work and home, negotiating divisions of labor, and finding individual self-fulfillment while at the same time maintaining a high level of investment in children — may reveal family processes of adaptation that can be of use to all kinds of families. Once uncovered and described, these processes can also be compared — for similarity and difference—with those occurring in the new extended families that have accompanied family diversification.

There are several important questions that research on today's two-parent, long-married families should pursue. For example, are these families characterized by fairly traditional gender-based divisions of labor, or do these parents share a more equitable division of housework, childcare, paid employment, and decision-making? The uniquely high levels of humanistic and collectivistic values among Generation Xers from two-parent families in our study may be related to a greater egalitarianism between still-married mothers and fathers in the Baby Boom generation. Traditionally, women in the United States have married men who were better educated than themselves. Improvement in women's educational attainment over the past thirty years has, for the first time, reversed this trend. In fact, since 1980 marriages in which women were better educated than their husbands have become more likely than marriages in which men were better educated than their wives (Qian 1998). Women's greater education and economic power within marriage may mean that they participate in household decision-making about childrearing, consumption, and other life choices not only in their role as wives and mothers but as educational equals and breadwinners. This change within marriages may have served children well. We found, for example, that among two-biological-parent families, mother/child bonds enhanced the values and self-esteem of Generation X youth more than they did those of the previous generation.

The role of "absentee" fathers in a context of high divorce has been much investigated. We have found, consistent with other research (Amato 1994; Amato and Keith 1991), that divorced fathers have become increasingly disadvantaged in terms of their emotional bonds with their young adult children when compared with mothers. Parental divorce has reduced the ability of Baby Boomer fathers to influence their Generation X children's aspirations, self-esteem, and prosocial values, while mother/child affective bonds and maternal influence have tended to remain high. Perhaps this is a reflection of a broader cultural shift toward the "feminization of kinship" relations that has been observed by other family researchers (Fry 1995; Hagestad 1986; Rossi and Rossi 1990).

While evidence has accumulated showing decline in paternal investment in children among divorced dads, some striking evidence—particularly that assembled and analyzed by Bianchi (2000)—has also shown that today's married fathers are exhibiting an unprecedented, high level of involvement with their children. According to time diary studies between 1965 and 1998, fathers' time spent with children grew from about 25 percent to fully two-thirds the amount of time that mothers spent with children. The greater involvement of today's fathers within two-parent family contexts may be contributing to the high levels of self-esteem and ambition that we observed in the aggregate among Generation X youth. More generally, good parenting on the part of fathers—custodial or noncustodial—has been shown to enhance many dimensions of children's well-being (Lamb 1997).

We have suggested that recent demographic trends (e.g., increased longevity and active life expectancy) may have intersected with other demographic trends (growth in nonmarital fertility, divorce, remarriage, and the labor force participation of mothers) to facilitate the growth of new kinds of extended families in the United States. The numbers and kinds of multigenerational family members available to families and children have certainly increased (Bengtson 2001). The support functions served by multigenerational family members may also have increased, accordingly. This kind of family expansion appears adaptive; that is, under diverse and potentially disruptive conditions, it may be a way that families care for their children. It may also lie behind many of the findings of this study: that families of all kinds still matter for children.

We have also proposed that, over time, processes within two-biological-parent families have shifted in ways that benefit children. We believe that an intriguing and important next step is to explore potential similarities and differences in processes that occur in these new-form two-parent families, on the one hand, and these new-form extended families, on the other. For many families (probably an increasing number), close multigenerational ties are adaptive and very much needed in a fast-changing world. The adaptive strengths evolving from these family arrangements—including, perhaps, shared parenting, authoritative parenting practices (not just necessarily by parents, but also by additional parent-like figures), egalitarian household arrangements, more collectivistic and humanistic value orientations—may parallel to some extent what is occurring in today's two-parent families, including the Baby Boom parents with Generation X children in our study. It may be that through their intergenerational socialization processes and practices, both two-parent families and extended multigenerational families—though distinct in their relationship intensity or the immediacy of their responsibilities for children—engender similar patterns and strengths.

Proposition 3: Maternal Investment in Children Has Not Declined over Time

Social critics became alarmed at the huge growth in the labor force participation of mothers over the past thirty years, for fear that the well-being of new generations of children would be compromised by a lack of attention given to them by their mothers. However, our study shows nonexistent, small, or ambiguous effects of mothers' labor force participation on children. This is similar to findings of other researchers (Parcel and Menaghan 1994).

The prognostications of negative consequences were not supported empirically, in part because they rested on a shaky foundation: that the stay-at-home moms of yesteryear surely spent more time with their children than working moms do today. Bianchi (2000) has questioned this assumption. She argues that the amount of nonmarket time that mothers invested in children in the past has been overestimated. While employment rates for mothers earlier in this century were much lower than today, mothers in the past also faced more time-consuming family work and domestic chores, relied on

older children to spend time with the younger children, and had less education. Education is positively correlated with the amount of direct time mothers spend caring for children. Bianchi also suggests that the extent to which
paid work takes mothers' time away from children today has been overestimated. The net result of these often offsetting trends, according to many of
the studies Bianchi draws from, is a relatively constant level of maternal
investment in children over time, and a conclusion, consistent with the
findings of our study, that employment has generally not meant a decline in
mothers' time with and care for children.

This constancy in maternal investment may help explain why the consequences of family change for Generation X youth were not more evident. In
terms of their actual time allocation to children, the mothers of our Baby
Boomer and Generation X youth, respectively, may not have been that different. Generation X children who experienced divorce felt as close to their mothers as those who did not, suggesting again a kind of safety net provided by a
generally high and stable average level of maternal investment. Other research
has shown that in the context of divorce, mothers tend to sustain a high level
of emotional investment in children amidst spousal conflict and marital disruption, whereas fathers' relations with children diminishs as their relationship
with spouses diminish (Belsky et al. 1991). This maternal investment (the
parameters and variations of which need to be carefully explored) may be
linked to the patterns borne out by our data showing how families—divorced
or not, dual-employed or not—are bringing up children with high self-esteem
on average and aspirations that exceed those of each generation before them.

High levels of paternal investment and involvement (among both residential and nonresidential fathers) also positively affect many aspects of
children's lives, but evidence shows that, on average, levels of paternal
involvement are relatively low (Simons et al. 1996). However, if upward
trends have been occurring in the proportion of highly involved, "good
dads" as described by Furstenberg (1988), this too may be linked to some of
the findings reported here.

The Paradox of Continuity and Change across Generations

In concluding this examination of family functioning and change at the start
of the twenty-first century, we return to a question raised by philosophers
and playwrights (and more recently by social historians and social scientists)
over six millennia of human experience: *How much is changing, and how much
remains the same, across generations today?*

Karl Mannheim ([1922] 1952) called this "the sociological problem of
generations": the ongoing tension between continuity and change, affirmation
and innovation, as each new generation comes into contact with the existing
social order represented by their parents' generation, and how they attempt
to adapt to or radically change this heritage.

Mannheim used this generational tension as a means to explain the development of social and political movements in Europe throughout the eighteenth and nineteenth centuries, from cultural changes in style and art to political revolution and warfare. While Mannheim's sweeping sociopolitical theory has not been supported by subsequent analyses, his central argument has become a central premise of life-course theory today.

The paradox of change and continuity is reflected in our data on family influences on younger generations during the past three decades. We have approached this issue from three analytic levels, each central to the life-course theoretical perspective in family sociology and family psychology.

At the *macrosocial* level of analysis, it is important to recognize the changing configurations of human demography reflected in the age structures of society, the social metabolism of changes in birth and death rates, immigration and emigration, longevity and morbidity. These trends are crucial for twenty-first-century societies, and particularly for cross-generational relationships (Bengtson and Putney 2000).

At the *mesosocial* level, the life-course perspective calls us to inquire about the interactive effects of maturation, historical placement, and emerging sociohistorical events on generational differences and continuities. And at the *microsocial* level, our focus is on the processes by which generations within a family pass on the knowledge and values, and the material and psychological resources that its members need to live successfully in society.

It is within the family — the *microsocial* level — that the paradox of continuity and change, the problem of balancing individuality and allegiance, is most immediate. It is a fluid, unending process and at times contentious. At times we think that surely a break from the past has occurred: Families aren't what they used to be; families are in trouble. Yet if we look closely, we can see threads of continuity and patterns of influence across generations. These patterns within families across historical time have been the focus of our study. How do they emerge? How are they sustained? What do they tell us about the structure and function of families and intergenerational relations in our now postindustrial world?

The family is the fulcrum balancing change and continuity over time in human society. It has been so in the past; we believe it will be so in the twenty-first century. We look to the family as the context for negotiating the problems of continuity and change, of individuality and integration, between and within the generations in ways that allow the continuous re-creation of society. Families still matter.

REFERENCES

Amato, P. R. 1994. "Father–Child Relations, Mother–Child Relations and Psychological Well-Being in Early Adulthood." *Journal of Marriage and the Family* 56:1031–42.

Amato, P. R. and B. Keith. 1991. "Parental Divorce and Adult Well-Being: A Meta-Analysis." *Journal of Marriage and the Family* 53 (1): 43–58.

Belsky, J., L. Youngblade, M. Rovine, and B. Volling. 1991. "Patterns of Marital Change and Parent–Child Interaction." *Journal of Marriage and the Family* 53:487–98.

Bengtson, V. L. 2001. "Beyond the Nuclear Family: The Increasing Importance of Multigenerational Relationships in American Society. The 1998 Burgess Award Lecture." *Journal of Marriage and the Family* 63 (1): 1–16.

Bengtson, V. L. and N. Putney. 2000. "Who Will Care for Tomorrow's Elderly? Consequences of Population Aging East and West." In *Aging in the East and West: Families, States and the Elderly,* edited by V. L. Bengtson, K. D. Kim, G. C. Myers, and K. S. Eun. New York: Springer.

Bengtson, V. L., C. J. Rosenthal, and L. M. Burton. 1995. "Paradoxes of Families and Aging." Pp. 253–82 in *Handbook of Aging and the Social Sciences,* 4th ed., edited by R. H. Binstock and L. K. George. San Diego: Academic Press.

Bianchi, S. M. 2000. "Maternal Employment and Time with Children: Dramatic Change or Surprising Continuity?" Paper presented at the 2000 Presidential Address to the Population Association of American, Los Angeles, March.

Dawson, D. A. 1991. "Family Structure and Children's Health and Well Being: Data from the 1988 National Health Interview Survey on Child Health." *Journal of Marriage and the Family* 53:573–84.

Elder, G. H., Jr. 1994. "Time, Human Agency, and Social Change: Perspectives on the Life Course." *Social Psychology Quarterly* 57:4–15.

Fry, C. L. 1995. "Kinship and Individuation: Cross-Cultural Perspectives on Intergenerational Relations." Pp. 126–56 in *Adult Intergenerational Relations,* edited by V. L. Bengtson, K. W. Schaie, and L. M. Burton. New York: Springer.

Furstenberg, F. F., Jr. 1988. "Good Dads—Bad Dads: Two Faces of Fatherhood." Pp. 193–218 in *The Changing American Family and Public Policy,* edited by A. J. Cherlin. Washington, DC: Urban Institute Press.

Hagestad, G. O. 1986. "The Family: Women and Grandparents as Kin Keepers." Pp. 141–160 in *Our Aging Society,* edited by A. Pifer and L. Bronte. New York: Norton.

Hayward, M. D. and M. Heron. 1999. "Racial Inequality in Active Life among Adult Americans." *Demography* 36 (1): 77–91.

Hetherington, E. Mavis and J. Kelly. 2002. *For Better or For Worse: Divorce Reconsidered.* New York: W. W. Norton.

Hill, R. B. 1999. *The Strengths of African American Families: Twenty-five Years Later.* Lanham, MD: University Press of America.

Johnson, C. L. 1999. "Fictive Kin among Oldest Old African Americans in the San Francisco Bay Area." *Journal of Gerontology* 54:S368–S375.

———. 2000. "Perspectives of American Kinship in the Later 1990s." *Journal of Marriage and the Family,* 62 (3): 623–39.

Johnson, C. L. and B. M. Barer. 1987. "Marital Instability and the Changing Kinship Networks of Grandparents." *The Gerontologist* 27:330–35.

Kline, M., J. R. Johnson, and J. J. Tschann. 1991. "The Long Shadow of Marital Conflict: A Model of Children's Postdivorce Adjustment." *Journal of Marriage and the Family* 53:297–310.

Lamb, M. E. 1997. *The Role of the Father in Child Development.* New York: Wiley.

Mannheim, K. [1922] 1952. "The Problem of Generations." Pp. 276–322 in *Essays in the Sociology of Knowledge,* edited by K. Mannheim. London: Routledge and Kegan Paul.

Oates, L. F. 1999. "Standing in the Gap: How Male Relatives or Fictive Kin Help Single African American Mothers and Their Adolescent Children Cope with Father Absences." Thesis, Smith College School for Social Work.

Parcel, T. L. and E. G. Menaghan. 1994. *Parents' Jobs and Children's Lives.* New York: Aldine de Gruyter.

Qian, Z. C. 1998. "Changes in Assortive Mating: The Impact of Age and Education, 1970–1990." *Demography* 35:279–92.

Rossi, A. S. and P. H. Rossi. 1990. *Of Human Bonding: Parent–Child Relations across the Life Course.* New York: Aldine de Gruyter.

Silverstein, M., R. Giarrusso, and V. L. Bengtson. 1998. "Intergenerational Solidarity and the Grandparent Role." Pp. 144–158 in *Handbook on Grandparenthood,* edited by M. Szinovacz. Westport, CT: Greenwood Press.

Simons, R. L., et al. 1996. *Understanding Differences between Divorced and Intact Families: Stress, Interactions, and Child Outcome.* Thousand Oaks, CA: Sage Publications.

Treas, J. 1995. "Older Americans in the 1990s and Beyond." *Population Bulletin* 50(2):2–46.

Wallerstein, J. S., J. Lewis, and S. Blakeslee. 2000. *The Unexpected Legacy of Divorce: A 25-year Landmark Study.* New York: Hyperion Press.

21

INVISIBLE INEQUALITY
Social Class and Childrearing in Black Families and White Families

ANNETTE LAREAU

In recent decades, sociological knowledge about inequality in family life has increased dramatically. Yet, debate persists, especially about the transmission of class advantages to children. Kingston (2000) and others question whether disparate aspects of family life cohere in meaningful patterns. Pointing to a "thin evidentiary base" for claims of social class differences in the interior of family life, Kingston also asserts that "class distinguishes neither distinctive parenting styles or distinctive involvement of kids" in specific behaviors (p. 134).

One problem with many studies is that they are narrowly focused. Researchers look at the influence of parents' education on parent involvement in schooling *or* at children's time spent watching television *or* at time spent visiting relatives. Only a few studies examine more than one dynamic inside the home. Second, much of the empirical work is descriptive. For example, extensive research has been done on time use, including patterns of women's labor force participation, hours parents spend at work, and mothers' and fathers' contributions to childcare. . . .

Third, researchers have not satisfactorily explained how these observed patterns are produced. Put differently, *conceptualizations* of the *social processes* through which families differ are underdeveloped and little is known about how family life transmits advantages to children. Few researchers have attempted to integrate what is known about behaviors and attitudes taught inside the home with the ways in which these practices may provide unequal resources for family members outside the home. . . .

Fourth, little is known about the degree to which children adopt and enact their parents' beliefs. Sociologists of the family have long stressed the importance of a more dynamic model of parent–child interaction, but empirical research has been slow to emerge. . . .

I draw on findings from a small, intensive data set collected using ethnographic methods. I map the connections between parents' resources and their children's daily lives. My first goal, then, is to challenge Kingston's (2000) argument that social class does not distinguish parents' behavior or children's daily lives. I seek to show empirically that social class does indeed create distinctive parenting styles. I demonstrate that parents differ by class in the ways they define their own roles in their children's lives as well as in how they perceive the nature of childhood. The middle-class parents, both white *and* black, tend to conform to a cultural logic of childrearing I call "concerted cultivation." They enroll their children in numerous age-specific organized activities that dominate family life and create enormous labor, particularly for mothers. The parents view these activities as transmitting important life skills to children. Middle-class parents also stress language use and the development of reasoning and employ talking as their preferred form of discipline. This "cultivation" approach results in a wider range of experiences for children but also creates a frenetic pace for parents, a cult of individualism within the family, and an emphasis on children's performance.

The childrearing strategies of white and black working-class and poor parents emphasize the "accomplishment of natural growth." These parents believe that as long as they provide love, food, and safety, their children will grow and thrive. They do not focus on developing their children's special talents. Compared to the middle-class children, working-class and poor children participate in few organized activities and have more free time and deeper, richer ties within their extended families. Working-class and poor parents issue many more directives to their children and, in some households, place more emphasis on physical discipline than do the middle-class parents. These findings extend Kohn and Schooler's (1983) observation of class differences in parents' values, showing that differences also exist in the *behavior* of parents *and* children.

Quantitative studies of children's activities offer valuable empirical evidence but only limited ideas about how to conceptualize the mechanisms through which social advantage is transmitted. Thus, my second goal is to offer "conceptual umbrellas" useful for making comparisons across race and class and for assessing the role of social structural location in shaping daily life.

Last, I trace the connections between the class position of family members — including children — and the uneven outcomes of their experiences outside the home as they interact with professionals in dominant institutions. The pattern of concerted cultivation encourages an *emerging sense of entitlement* in children. All parents and children are not equally assertive, but the pattern of questioning and intervening among the white and black middle-class parents contrasts sharply with the definitions of how to be helpful and effective observed among the white and black working-class and poor adults. The pattern of the accomplishment of natural growth encourages an *emerging sense of constraint*. Adults as well as children in these social classes tend to be deferential and outwardly accepting in their interactions with professionals such as doctors and educators. At the same time, however, compared to their middle-class counterparts, white and black working-class and poor family members are more distrustful of professionals. These are differences with potential long-term consequences. In an historical moment when the dominant society privileges active, informed, assertive clients of health and educational services, the strategies employed by children and parents are not equally effective across classes. In sum, differences in family life lie not only in the advantages parents obtain for their children, but also in the skills they transmit to children for negotiating their own life paths.

Methodology

Study Participants

This study is based on interviews and observations of children, aged 8 to 10, and their families. The data were collected over time in three research phases. Phase one involved observations in two third-grade classrooms in a public school in the midwestern community of "Lawrenceville."[1] After conducting observations for two months, I grouped the families into social class (and race) categories based on information provided by educators. I then chose every third name, and sent a letter to the child's home asking the mother and father to participate in separate interviews. Over 90 percent of parents agreed, for a total of 32 children (16 white and 16 African American). A black graduate student and I interviewed all mothers and most fathers (or guardians) of the children. Each interview lasted 90 to 120 minutes, and all took place in 1989–1990.

Phase two took place at two sites in a northeastern metropolitan area. One school, "Lower Richmond," although located in a predominantly white, working-class urban neighborhood, drew about half of its students from a nearby all-black housing project. I observed one third-grade class at Lower Richmond about twice a week for almost six months. The second site, "Swan," was located in a suburban neighborhood about 45 minutes from the city center. It was 90 percent white; most of the remaining 10 percent were middle-class black children.[2] There, I observed twice a week for two months at the end of the third grade; a research assistant then observed weekly for

TABLE 1   **Frequency Distribution of Children in the Study by Social Class and Race**

Social Class	White	Black	Total
Middle class[a]	18 (Garrett Tallinger) (Melanie Handlon)	18 (Alexander Williams) (Stacey Marshall)	36
Working class[b]	14 (Billy Yanelli) (Wendy Driver)	12 (Tyrec Taylor) (Jessica Irwin)[c]	26
Poor[d]	12 (Karl Greeley) (Katie Brindle)	14 (Harold McAllister) (Tara Carroll)	26
Total sample	44	44	88

Note: The names in each cell of the table indicate the children selected to take place in the family-observation phase of the study.

[a]Middle-class children are those who live in households in which at least one parent is employed in a position that either entails substantial managerial authority or draws upon highly complex, educationally certified skills (i.e., college-level).

[b]Working-class children are those who live in households in which neither parent is employed in a middle-class position and at least one parent is employed in a position with little or no managerial authority and that does not draw on highly complex, educationally certified skills. This category includes lower-level white-collar workers.

[c]An inter-racial girl who has a black father and a white mother.

[d]Poor children are those who live in households in which parents receive public assistance and do not participate in the labor force on a regular, continuous basis.

four more months in the fourth grade.[3] At each site, teachers and parents described their school in positive terms.[4] The observations took place between September 1992 and January 1994. In the fall of 1993, I drew an interview sample from Lower Richmond and Swan, following the same method of selection used for Lawrenceville. A team of research assistants and I interviewed the parents and guardians of 39 children. Again, the response rate was over 90 percent but because the classrooms did not generate enough black middle-class children and white poor children to fill the analytical categories, interviews were also conducted with 17 families with children aged 8 to 10. . . . Thus, the total number of children who participated in the study was 88 (32 from the Midwest and 56 from the Northeast).

Family Observations

Phase three, the most intensive research phase of the study, involved home observations of 12 children and their families in the Northeast who had been previously interviewed (see Table 1). Some themes, such as language use and families' social connections, surfaced mainly during this phase. . . .

The research assistants and I took turns visiting the participating families daily, for a total of about 20 visits to each home, often in the space of one month. The observations went beyond the home: Fieldworkers followed children and parents as they participated in school activities, church services and events, organized play, visits to relatives, and medical appointments. . . .

We worked in teams of three. One fieldworker visited three to four times per week; another visited one to two times per week; and I visited once or twice per week, except for the two families for which I was lead fieldworker. The research teams' composition varied with the race of the family. Two white graduate students and I (a middle-aged white woman) visited the white families; for the black families, the teams included one white graduate student, one black graduate student, and me. All black families with male children were visited by teams that included a black male fieldworker. A white male fieldworker observed the poor family with the white boy; the remaining white fieldworkers were female. Team members met regularly to discuss the families and to review the emerging analytic themes.

Our presence altered family dynamics, especially at first. Over time, however, we saw signs of adjustment (e.g., yelling and cursing increased on the third day and again on the tenth). . . . Overall, however, family members reported in exit interviews that they had not changed their behavior significantly, or they mentioned very specific alterations (e.g., "the house got cleaner").

A Note on Class

I undertook field observations to develop an intensive, realistic portrait of family life. Although I deliberately focused on only 12 families, I wanted to compare children across gender and race. Adopting the fine-grained differentiations characteristic of current neo-Marxist and neo-Weberian empirical studies was not tenable. Further limitations were imposed by the school populations at the sites I selected. Very few students were children of employers or of self-employed workers. I decided to focus exclusively on those whose parents were employees. Authority in the workplace and "credential barriers" are the criteria most commonly used to differentiate within this heterogeneous group. I assigned the families to a working-class or middle-class category based on detailed information that each of the employed adults provided about the work they did, the nature of the organization that employed them, and their educational credentials. I also included a category traditionally excluded from class groupings: families not involved in the labor market. In the first school I studied, many children were from households supported by public assistance. Omitting them would have restricted the scope of the study arbitrarily.[5]

The three class categories conceal important internal variations. The Williams family (black) and the Tallinger family (white) have very high incomes, both in excess of $175,000; the median income among the middle-class parents was much lower.[6] Income differences among the middle-class families were not associated with differences in childrearing methods. Moreover, no other data in the study showed compelling intraclass divisions. I consider the use of one term — middle class — to be reasonable.

TABLE 2   **Summary of Differences in Childrearing Approaches**

Dimension Observed	Childrearing Approach	
	Concerted Cultivation	Accomplishment of Natural Growth
Key elements of each approach	Parent actively fosters and assesses child's talents, opinions, and skills	Parent cares for child and allows child to grow
Organization of daily life	Multiple child leisure activities are orchestrated by adults	Child "hangs out" particularly with kin
Language use	Reasoning/directives	Directives
	Child contestation of adult statements	Rare for child to question or challenge adults
	Extended negotiations between parents and child	General acceptance by child of directives
Social connections	Weak extended family ties	Strong extended family ties
	Child often in homogeneous age groupings	Child often in heterogeneous age groupings
Interventions in institutions	Criticisms and interventions on behalf of child	Dependence on institutions
	Training of child to intervene on his or her own behalf	Sense of powerlessness and frustration
		Conflict between childrearing practices at home and at school
Consequences	Emerging sense of entitlement on the part of the child	Emerging sense of constraint on the part of the child

Concerted Cultivation and Natural Growth

The interviews and observations suggested that crucial aspects of family life *cohered*. Within the concerted cultivation and accomplishment of natural growth approaches, three key dimensions may be distinguished: the organization of daily life, the use of language, and social connections. ("Interventions in institutions" and "consequences" are addressed later in the paper.) These dimensions do not capture all important parts of family life, but they do incorporate core aspects of childrearing (Table 2). Moreover, our field observations revealed that behaviors and activities related to these dimensions dominated the rhythms of family life. Conceptually, the organization of daily life and the use of language are crucial dimensions. Both must be present for the family to be described as engaging in one childrearing approach rather than the other. Social connections are significant but less conceptually essential.

All three aspects of childrearing were intricately woven into the families' daily routines, but rarely remarked upon. As part of everyday practice, they were invisible to parents and children. Analytically, however, they are useful means for comparing and contrasting ways in which social class differences shape the character of family life. I now examine two families in terms of these three key dimensions. I "control" for race and gender and contrast the lives of two black boys—one from an (upper) middle-class family and one from a family on public assistance. I could have focused on almost any of the other 12 children, but this pair seemed optimal, given the limited number of studies reporting on black middle-class families, as well as the aspect of my argument that suggests that race is less important than class in shaping childrearing patterns.

Developing Alexander Williams

Alexander Williams and his parents live in a predominantly black middle-class neighborhood. Their six-bedroom house is worth about $150,000. Alexander is an only child. Both parents grew up in small towns in the South, and both are from large families. His father, a tall, handsome man, is a very successful trial lawyer who earns about $125,000 annually in a small firm specializing in medical malpractice cases. Two weeks each month, he works very long hours (from about 5:30 A.M. until midnight) preparing for trials. The other two weeks, his workday ends around 6:00 P.M. He rarely travels out of town. Alexander's mother, Christina, is a positive, bubbly woman with freckles and long, black, wavy hair. A high-level manager in a major corporation, she has a corner office, a personal secretary, and responsibilities for other offices across the nation. She tries to limit her travel, but at least once a month she takes an overnight trip.

Alexander is a charming, inquisitive boy with a winsome smile. Ms. Williams is pleased that Alexander seems interested in so many things:

> *Alexander is a joy. He's a gift to me. He's very energetic, very curious, loving, caring person, that, um . . . is outgoing and who, uh, really loves to be with people. And who loves to explore, and loves to read and . . . just do a lot of fun things.*

The private school Alexander attends has an on-site after-school program. There, he participates in several activities and receives guitar lessons and photography instruction.

Organization of Daily Life   Alexander is busy with activities during the week and on weekends (Table 3). His mother describes their Saturday morning routine. The day starts early with a private piano lesson for Alexander downtown, a 20-minute drive from the house:

> *It's an 8:15 class. But for me, it was a tradeoff. I am very adamant about Saturday morning TV. I don't know what it contributes. So . . . it was . . . um . . . either stay at home and fight on a Saturday morning [laughs] or go do something constructive. . . . Now Saturday mornings are pretty booked up. You know, the piano lesson, and then straight to choir for a couple of hours. So, he has a very full schedule.*

TABLE 3 Participation in Activities Outside of School: Boys

Boy's Name /Race/Class	Activities Organized by Adults	Informal Activities
Middle Class		
Garrett Tallinger (white)	Soccer team Traveling soccer team Baseball team Basketball team (summer) Swim team Piano Saxophone (through school)	Plays with siblings in yard Watches television Plays computer games Overnights with friends
Alexander Williams (black)	Soccer team Baseball team Community choir Church choir Sunday school Piano (Suzuki) School plays Guitar (through school)	Restricted television Plays outside occasionally with two other boys Visits friends from school
Working Class		
Billy Yanelli (white)	Baseball team	Watches television Visits relatives Rides bike Plays outside in the street Hangs out with neighborhood kids
Tyrec Taylor (black)	Football team Vacation Bible School Sunday school (off/on)	Watches television Plays outside in the street Rides bikes with neighborhood boys Visits relatives Goes to swimming pool
Poor		
Karl Greeley (white)	Goes to swimming pool Walks dogs with neighbor	Watches television Plays Nintendo Plays with siblings
Harold McAllister (black)	Bible study in neighbor's house (occasionally) Bible camp (1 week)	Visits relatives Plays ball with neighborhood kids Watches television Watches videos

Ms. Williams' vehement opposition to television is based on her view of what Alexander needs to grow and thrive. She objects to TV's passivity and feels it is her obligation to help her son cultivate his talents.

Sometimes Alexander complains that "my mother signs me up for everything!" Generally, however, he likes his activities. He says they make him feel "special," and without them life would be "boring." His sense of time is thoroughly entwined with his activities: He feels disoriented when his schedule is not full. This unease is clear in the following field-note excerpt. The family is driving home from a Back-to-School night. The next morning, Ms. Williams will leave for a work-related day trip and will not return until late at night. Alexander is grumpy because he has nothing planned for the next day. He wants to have a friend over, but his mother rebuffs him. Whining, he wonders what he will do. His mother, speaking tersely, says:

You have piano and guitar. You'll have some free time. [Pause] I think you'll survive for one night. [Alexander does not respond but seems mad. It is quiet for the rest of the trip home.]

Alexander's parents believe his activities provide a wide range of benefits important for his development. In discussing Alexander's piano lessons, Mr. Williams notes that as a Suzuki student,[7] Alexander is already able to read music. Speculating about more diffuse benefits of Alexander's involvement with piano, he says:

I don't see how any kid's adolescence and adulthood could not but be enhanced by an awareness of who Beethoven was. And is that Bach or Mozart? I don't know the difference between the two! I don't know Baroque from Classical — but he does. How can that not be a benefit in later life? I'm convinced that this rich experience will make him a better person, a better citizen, a better husband, a better father — certainly a better student.

Ms. Williams sees music as building her son's "confidence" and his "poise." In interviews and casual conversation, she stresses "exposure." She believes it is her responsibility to broaden Alexander's worldview. Childhood activities provide a learning ground for important life skills:

Sports provide great opportunities to learn how to be competitive. Learn how to accept defeat, you know. Learn how to accept winning, you know, in a gracious way. Also it gives him the opportunity to learn leadership skills and how to be a team player. . . . Sports really provides a lot of really great opportunities.

Alexander's schedule is constantly shifting; some activities wind down and others start up. Because the schedules of sports practices and games are issued no sooner than the start of the new season, advance planning is rarely possible. Given the sheer number of Alexander's activities, events inevitably overlap. Some activities, though short-lived, are extremely time consuming. Alexander's school play, for example, requires rehearsals three nights the week before the opening. In addition, in choosing activities, the Williamses have an added concern — the group's racial balance. Ms. Williams prefers that Alexander not be the only black child at events. Typically, one or two other black boys are involved, but the groups are predominantly white and the activities take place in predominantly white residential neighborhoods. Alexander is, however, part of his church's youth choir and Sunday School, activities in which all participants are black.

Many activities involve competition. Alex must audition for his solo performance in the school play, for example. Similarly, parents and children alike understand that participation on "A," "B," or "All-Star" sports teams signal different skill levels. Like other middle-class children in the study, Alexander seems to enjoy public performance. According to a field note, after his solo at a musical production in front of over 200 people, he appeared "contained, pleased, aware of the attention he's receiving."

Alexander's commitments do not consume *all* his free time. Still, his life is defined by a series of deadlines and schedules interwoven with a series of activities that are organized and controlled by adults rather than children. Neither he nor his parents see this as troublesome.

Language Use   Like other middle-class families, the Williamses often engage in conversation that promotes reasoning and negotiation. An excerpt from a field note (describing an exchange between Alexander and his mother during a car ride home after summer camp) shows the kind of pointed questions middle-class parents ask children. Ms. Williams is not just eliciting information. She is also giving Alexander the opportunity to develop and practice verbal skills, including how to summarize, clarify, and amplify information:

As she drives, [Ms. Williams] asks Alex, "So, how was your day?"

Alex: "Okay. I had hot dogs today, but they were burned! They were all black!"

Mom: "Oh, great. You shouldn't have eaten any."

Alex: "They weren't all black, only half were. The rest were regular."

Mom: "Oh, okay. What was that game you were playing this morning? . . ."

Alex: "It was [called] 'Whatcha doin?'"

Mom: "How do you play?"

Alexander explains the game elaborately—fieldworker doesn't quite follow. Mom asks Alex questions throughout his explanation, saying, "Oh, I see," when he answers. She asks him about another game she saw them play; he again explains. . . . She continues to prompt and encourage him with small giggles in the back of her throat as he elaborates.

Expressions of interest in children's activities often lead to negotiations over small, home-based matters. During the same car ride, Ms. Williams tries to adjust the dinner menu to suit Alexander:

Alexander says, "I don't want hot dogs tonight."

Mom: "Oh? Because you had them for lunch."

Alexander nods.

Mom: "Well, I can fix something else and save the hot dogs for tomorrow night."

Alex: *"But I don't want any pork chops either."*

Mom: *"Well, Alexander, we need to eat something. Why didn't you have hamburgers today?"*

Alex: *"They don't have them any more at the snack bar."*

Mom asks Alexander if he's ok, if he wants a snack. Alexander says he's ok. Mom asks if he's sure he doesn't want a bag of chips?

Not all middle-class parents are as attentive to their children's needs as this mother, and none are *always* interested in negotiating. But a general pattern of reasoning and accommodating is common.

Social Connections   Mr. and Ms. Williams consider themselves very close to their extended families. Because the Williamses' aging parents live in the South, visiting requires a plane trip. Ms. Williams takes Alexander with her to see his grandparents twice a year. She speaks on the phone with her parents at least once a week and also calls her siblings several times a week. Mr. Williams talks with his mother regularly by phone (he has less contact with his stepfather). With pride, he also mentions his niece, whose Ivy League education he is helping to finance.

Interactions with cousins are not normally a part of Alexander's leisure time. . . . Nor does he often play with neighborhood children. The huge homes on the Williamses' street are occupied mainly by couples without children. Most of Alexander's playmates come from his classroom or his organized activities. Because most of his school events, church life, and assorted activities are organized by the age (and sometimes gender) of the participants, Alexander interacts almost exclusively with children his own age, usually boys. Adult-organized activities thus define the context of his social life.

Mr. and Ms. Williams are aware that they allocate a sizable portion of time to Alexander's activities. What they stress, however, is the time they *hold back*. They mention activities the family has chosen *not* to take on (such as traveling soccer).

Summary   Overall, Alexander's parents engaged in concerted cultivation. They fostered their son's growth through involvement in music, church, athletics, and academics. They talked with him at length, seeking his opinions and encouraging his ideas. Their approach involved considerable direct expenses (e.g., the cost of lessons and equipment) and large indirect expenses (e.g., the cost of taking time off from work, driving to practices, and forgoing adult leisure activities). Although Mr. and Ms. Williams acknowledged the importance of extended family, Alexander spent relatively little time with relatives. His social interactions occurred almost exclusively with children his own age and with adults. Alexander's many activities significantly shaped the organization of daily life in the family. Both parents' leisure time was tailored to their son's commitments. Mr. and Ms. Williams felt that the strategies they cultivated with Alexander would result in his having the best possible chance at a happy and productive life. They couldn't imagine themselves not investing large amounts of time and energy in their son's life. But, as I explain in the next section, which focuses on a black boy from a poor family, other parents held a different view.

Supporting the Natural Growth of Harold McAllister

Harold McAllister, a large, stocky boy with a big smile, is from a poor black family. He lives with his mother and his 8-year-old sister, Alexis, in a large apartment. Two cousins often stay overnight. Harold's 16-year-old sister and 18-year-old brother usually live with their grandmother, but sometimes they stay at the McAllister's home. Ms. McAllister, a high school graduate, relies on public assistance (AFDC). Hank, Harold and Alexis' father, is a mechanic. He and Ms. McAllister have never married. He visits regularly, sometimes weekly, stopping by after work to watch television or nap. Harold (but not Alexis) sometimes travels across town by bus to spend the weekend with Hank.

The McAllisters' apartment is in a public housing project near a busy street. The complex consists of rows of two- and three-story brick units. The buildings, blocky and brown, have small yards enclosed by concrete and wood fences. Large floodlights are mounted on the corners of the buildings, and wide concrete sidewalks cut through the spaces between units. The ground is bare in many places; paper wrappers and glass litter the area.

Inside the apartment, life is humorous and lively, with family members and kin sharing in the daily routines. Ms. McAllister discussed, disdainfully, mothers who are on drugs or who abuse alcohol and do not "look after" their children. Indeed, the previous year Ms. McAllister called Child Protective Services to report her twin sister, a cocaine addict, because she was neglecting her children. Ms. McAllister is actively involved in her twin's daughters' lives. Her two nephews also frequently stay with her. Overall, she sees herself as a capable mother who takes care of her children and her extended family.

Organization of Daily Life   Much of Harold's life and the lives of his family members revolve around home. Project residents often sit outside in lawn chairs or on front stoops, drinking beer, talking, and watching children play. During summer, windows are frequently left open, allowing breezes to waft through the units and providing vantage points from which residents can survey the neighborhood. A large deciduous tree in front of the McAllisters' apartment unit provides welcome shade in the summer's heat.

Harold loves sports. He is particularly fond of basketball, but he also enjoys football, and he follows televised professional sports closely. Most afternoons, he is either inside watching television or outside playing ball. He tosses a football with cousins and boys from the neighboring units and organizes pick-up basketball games. Sometimes he and his friends use a rusty, bare hoop hanging from a telephone pole in the housing project; other times, they string up an old, blue plastic crate as a makeshift hoop.

One obstacle to playing sports, however, is a shortage of equipment. Balls are costly to replace, especially given the rate at which they disappear — theft of children's play equipment, including balls and bicycles, is an ongoing problem. During a field observation, Harold asks his mother if she knows where the ball is. She replies with some vehemence, "They stole the blue and yellow ball, and they stole the green ball, and they stole the other ball."

Hunting for balls is a routine part of Harold's leisure time. One June day, with the temperature and humidity in the high 80's, Harold and his cousin Tyrice (and a fieldworker) wander around the housing project for about an hour, trying to find a basketball:

> We head to the other side of the complex. On the way . . . we passed four guys sitting on the step. Their ages were 9 to 13 years. They had a radio blaring. Two were working intently on fixing a flat bike tire. The other two were dribbling a basketball.

Harold: *"Yo! What's up, ya'll."*

Group: *"What's up, Har." "What's up? "Yo."*

> They continued to work on the tire and dribble the ball. As we walked down the hill, Harold asked, "Yo, could I use your ball?"

> The guy responded, looking up from the tire, "Naw, man. Ya'll might lose it."

Harold, Tyrice, and the fieldworker walk to another part of the complex, heading for a makeshift basketball court where they hope to find a game in progress:

> No such luck. Harold enters an apartment directly in front of the makeshift court. The door was open. . . . Harold came back. "No ball. I guess I gotta go back."

The pace of life for Harold and his friends ebbs and flows with the children's interests and family obligations. The day of the basketball search, for example, after spending time listening to music and looking at baseball cards, the children join a water fight Tyrice instigates. It is a lively game, filled with laughter and with efforts to get the adults next door wet (against their wishes). When the game winds down, the kids ask their mother for money, receive it, and then walk to a store to buy chips and soda. They chat with another young boy and then amble back to the apartment, eating as they walk. Another afternoon, almost two weeks later, the children — Harold, two of his cousins, and two children from the neighborhood — and the fieldworker play basketball on a makeshift court in the street (using the fieldworker's ball). As Harold bounces the ball, neighborhood children of all ages wander through the space.

Thus, Harold's life is more free-flowing and more child-directed than is Alexander Williams'. The pace of any given day is not so much planned as emergent, reflecting child-based interests and activities. Parents intervene in specific areas, such as personal grooming, meals, and occasional chores, but they do not continuously direct and monitor their children's leisure activities. Moreover, the leisure activities Harold and other working-class and poor children pursue require them to develop a repertoire of skills for dealing with much older and much younger children as well as with neighbors and relatives.

Language Use   Life in the working-class and poor families in the study flows smoothly without extended verbal discussions. The amount of talking varies, but overall, it is considerably less than occurs in the middle-class homes.[8] Ms. McAllister jokes with the children and discusses what is on television. But she does not appear to cultivate conversation by asking the children questions or by drawing them out. Often she is brief and direct in her remarks. For instance, she coordinates the use of the apartment's only bathroom by using one-word directives. She sends the children (there are almost always at least four children home at once) to wash up by pointing to a child, saying one word, "bathroom," and handing him or her a washcloth. Wordlessly, the designated child gets up and goes to the bathroom to take a shower.

Similarly, although Ms. McAllister will listen to the children's complaints about school, she does not draw them out on these issues or seek to determine details, as Ms. Williams would. For instance, at the start of the new school year, when I ask Harold about his teacher, he tells me she is "mean" and that "she lies." Ms. McAllister, washing dishes, listens to her son, but she does not encourage Harold to support his opinion about his new teacher with more examples, nor does she mention any concerns of her own. Instead, she asks about last year's teacher, "What was the name of that man teacher?" Harold says, "Mr. Lindsey?" She says, "No, the other one." He says, "Mr. Terrene." Ms. McAllister smiles and says, "Yeah. I liked him." Unlike Alexander's mother, she seems content with a brief exchange of information.

Social Connections   Children, especially boys, frequently play outside. The number of potential playmates in Harold's world is vastly higher than the number in Alexander's neighborhood. When a fieldworker stops to count heads, she finds 40 children of elementary school age residing in the nearby rows of apartments. With so many children nearby, Harold could choose to play only with others his own age. In fact, though, he often hangs out with older and younger children and with his cousins (who are close to his age).

The McAllister family, like other poor and working-class families, is involved in a web of extended kin. As noted earlier, Harold's older siblings and his two male cousins often spend the night at the McAllister home. Celebrations such as birthdays involve relatives almost exclusively. Party guests are not, as in middle-class families, friends from school or from extracurricular activities. Birthdays are celebrated enthusiastically, with cake and special food to mark the occasion; presents, however, are not offered. Similarly, Christmas at Harold's house featured a tree and special food but no presents. At these and other family events, the older children voluntarily look after the younger ones: Harold plays with his 16-month-old niece, and his cousins carry around the younger babies.

The importance of family ties—and the contingent nature of life in the McAllisters' world—is clear in the response Alexis offers when asked what she would do if she were given a million dollars:

> *Oh, boy! I'd buy my brother, my sister, my uncle, my aunt, my nieces and my nephews, and my grandpop, and my grandmom, and my mom, and my dad, and my friends, not my friends, but mostly my best friend—I'd buy them all clothes. . .and sneakers. And I'd buy some food, and I'd buy my mom some food, and I'd get my brothers and my sisters gifts for their birthdays.*

Summary   In a setting where everyone, including the children, was acutely aware of the lack of money, the McAllister family made do. Ms. McAllister rightfully saw herself as a very capable mother. She was a strong, positive influence in the lives of the children she looked after. Still, the contrast with Ms. Williams is striking. Ms. McAllister did not seem to think that Harold's opinions needed to be cultivated and developed. She, like most parents in the working-class and poor families, drew strong and clear boundaries between adults and children. Adults gave directions to children. Children were given freedom to play informally unless they were needed for chores. Extended family networks were deemed important and trustworthy.

The Intersection of Race and Class in Family Life

I expected race to powerfully shape children's daily schedules, but this was not evident (also see Conley 1999; Pattillo-McCoy 1999). This is not to say that race is unimportant. Black parents were particularly concerned with monitoring their children's lives outside the home for signs of racial problems.[9] Black middle-class fathers, especially, were likely to stress the importance of their sons understanding "what it means to be a black man in this society" (J. Hochschild 1995). Mr. Williams, in summarizing how he and his wife orient Alexander, said:

> *[We try to] teach him that race unfortunately is the most important aspect of our national life. I mean people look at other people and they see a color first. But that isn't going to define who he is. He will do his best. He will succeed, despite racism. And I think he lives his life that way.*

Alexander's parents were acutely aware of the potential significance of race in his life. Both were adamant, however, that race should not be used as "an excuse" for not striving to succeed. Mr. Williams put it this way:

> *I discuss how race impacts on my life as an attorney, and I discuss how race will impact on his life. The one teaching that he takes away from this is that he is never to use discrimination as an excuse for not doing his best.*

Thus far, few incidents of overt racism had occurred in Alexander's life, as his mother noted:

> *Those situations have been far and few between. . . . I mean, I can count them on my fingers.*

Still, Ms. Williams recounted with obvious pain an incident at a birthday party Alexander had attended as a preschooler. The grandparents of the birthday child repeatedly asked, "Who is that boy?" and exclaimed, "He's so dark!" Such experiences fueled the Williams's resolve always to be "cautious":

> *We've never been, uh, parents who drop off their kid anywhere. We've always gone with him. And even now, I go in and — to school in the morning — and check [in]. . . . The school environment, we've watched very closely.*

Alexander's parents were not equally optimistic about the chances for racial equality in this country. Ms. Williams felt strongly that, especially while Alexander was young, his father should not voice his pessimism. Mr. Williams complained that this meant he had to "watch" what he said to Alexander about race relations. Still, both parents agreed about the need to be vigilant regarding potential racial problems in Alexander's life. Other black parents reported experiencing racial prejudice and expressed a similar commitment to vigilance.

Issues surrounding the prospect of growing up black and male in this society were threaded through Alexander's life in ways that had no equivalent among his middle-class, white male peers. Still, in fourth grade there were no signs of racial experiences having "taken hold" the way that they might as Alexander ages. In terms of the number and kind of activities he participated in, his life was very similar to that of Garrett Tallinger, his white counterpart (see Table 3). That both sets of parents were fully committed to a strategy of concentrated cultivation was apparent in the number of adult-organized activities the boys were enrolled in, the hectic pace of family life, and the stress on reasoning in parent–child negotiations. Likewise, the research assistants and I saw no striking differences in the ways in which white parents and black parents in the working-class and poor homes socialized their children.

Others (Fordham and Ogbu 1986) have found that in middle school and high school, adolescent peer groups often draw sharp racial boundaries, a pattern not evident among this study's third- and fourth-grade participants (but sometimes present among their older siblings). Following Tatum (1997:52), I attribute this to the children's relatively young ages (also see "Race in America," *The New York Times*, June 25, 2000, p. 1). In sum, in the broader society, key aspects of daily life were shaped by racial segregation and discrimination. But in terms of enrollment in organized activities, language use, and social connections, the largest differences between the families we observed were across social class, not racial groups. . . .

Impact of Chidrearing Strategies on Interactions with Institutions

Social scientists sometimes emphasize the importance of reshaping parenting practices to improve children's chances of success. Explicitly and implicitly, the literature exhorts parents to comply with the views of professionals (Bronfenbrenner 1966; Epstein 2001; Heimer and Staffen 1998). Such calls for compliance do not, however, reconcile professionals' judgments regarding the intrinsic value of current childrearing standards with the evidence of the historical record, which shows regular shifts in such standards over time (Aries 1962; Wrigley 1989; Zelizer 1985). Nor are the stratified, and limited, possibilities for success in the broader society examined.

I now follow the families out of their homes and into encounters with representatives of dominant institutions—institutions that are directed by middle-class professionals. Again, I focus on Alexander Williams and Harold McAllister. (Institutional experiences are summarized in Table 2.) Across all social classes, parents and children interacted with teachers and school officials, healthcare professionals, and assorted government officials. Although they often addressed similar problems (e.g., learning disabilities, asthma, traffic violations), they typically did not achieve similar resolutions. The pattern of concerted cultivation fostered an *emerging sense of entitlement* in the life of Alexander Williams and other middle-class children. By contrast, the commitment to nurturing children's natural growth fostered an *emerging sense of constraint* in the life of Harold McAllister and other working-class or poor children. (These consequences of childrearing practices are summarized in Table 2.)

Both parents and children drew on the resources associated with these two childrearing approaches during their interactions with officials. Middle-class parents and children often customized these interactions; working-class and poor parents were more likely to have a "generic" relationship. When faced with problems, middle-class parents also appeared better equipped to exert influence over other adults compared with working-class and poor parents. Nor did middle-class parents or children display the intimidation or confusion we witnessed among many working-class and poor families when they faced a problem in their children's school experience.

Emerging Signs of Entitlement

Alexander Williams' mother, like many middle-class mothers, explicitly teaches her son to be an informed, assertive client in interactions with professionals. For example, as she drives Alexander to a routine doctor's appointment, she coaches him in the art of communicating effectively in healthcare settings:

> *Alexander asks if he needs to get any shots today at the doctor's. Ms. Williams says he'll need to ask the doctor. . . . As we enter Park Lane, Mom says quietly to Alex: "Alexander, you should be thinking of questions you might want to ask the doctor. You can ask him anything you want. Don't be shy. You can ask anything."*

> *Alex thinks for a minute, then: "I have some bumps under my arms from my deodorant."*

> Mom: *"Really? You mean from your new deodorant?"*

> Alex: *"Yes."*

> Mom: *"Well, you should ask the doctor."*

Alexander learns that he has the right to speak up (e.g., "don't be shy") and that he should prepare for an encounter with a person in a position of authority by gathering his thoughts in advance.

These class resources are subsequently *activated* in the encounter with the doctor (a jovial white man in his late thirties or early forties). The examination begins this way:

Doctor: *"Okay, as usual, I'd like to go through the routine questions with you. And if you have any questions for me, just fire away."* Doctor examines Alex's chart: *"Height-wise, as usual, Alexander's in the ninety-fifth percentile."*

Although the physician is talking to Ms. Williams, Alexander interrupts him:

Alex: *"I'm in the what?"*

Doctor: *"It means that you're taller than more than ninety-five out of a hundred young men when they're, uh, ten years old."*

Alex: *"I'm not ten."*

Doctor: *"Well, they graphed you at ten . . . they usually take the closest year to get that graph."*

Alex: *"Alright."*

Alexander's "Alright" reveals that he feels entitled to weigh-in with his own judgment.

A few minutes later, the exam is interrupted when the doctor is asked to provide an emergency consultation by telephone. Alexander listens to the doctor's conversation and then uses what he has overheard as the basis for a clear directive:

Doctor: *"The stitches are on the eyelids themselves, the laceration? . . . Um . . . I don't suture eyelids . . . um . . . Absolutely not! . . . Don't even touch them. That was very bad judgment on the camp's part. . . .* [Hangs up.] *I'm sorry about the interruption."*

Alex: *"Stay away from my eyelids!"*

Alexander's comment, which draws laughter from the adults, reflects this fourth grader's tremendous ease interacting with a physician.

Later, Ms. Williams and the doctor discuss Alexander's diet. Ms. Williams freely admits that they do not always follow nutritional guidelines. Her honesty is a form of capital because it gives the doctor accurate information on which to base a diagnosis. Feeling no need for deception positions mother and son to receive better care:

Doctor: *Let's start with appetite. Do you get three meals a day?"*

Alex: *"Yeah."*

Doctor: *"And here's the important question:*

Do you get your fruits and vegetables too?"

Alex: *"Yeah."*

Mom, high-pitched: *"Ooooo. . . ."*

Doctor: *"I see I have a second opinion."* [laughter]

Alex, voice rising: *"You give me bananas and all in my lunch every day. And I had cabbage for dinner last night."*

Class resources are again activated when Alexander's mother reveals she "gave up" on a medication. The doctor pleasantly but clearly instructs her to continue the medication. Again, though, he receives accurate information rather than facing silent resistance or defiance, as occurred in encounters between healthcare professionals and other (primarily working-class and poor) families. The doctor acknowledges Ms. Williams's relative power: He "argues for" continuation rather than directing her to execute a medically necessary action:

Mom: *"His allergies have just been, just acted up again. One time this summer and I had to bring him in."*

Doctor: *"I see a note here from Dr. Svennson that she put him on Vancinace and Benadryl. Did it seem to help him?"*

Mom: *"Just, not really. So, I used it for about a week and I just gave up."* Doctor, sitting forward in his chair: *"OK, I'm actually going to argue for not giving up. If he needs it, Vancinace is a very effective drug. But it takes at least a week to start. . . ."*

Mom: *"Oh. OK. . . ."*

Doctor: *"I'd rather have him use that than heavy oral medications. You have to give it a few weeks. . . ."*

A similar pattern of give and take and questioning characterizes Alexander's interaction with the doctor, as the following excerpt illustrates:

Doctor: *"The only thing that you really need besides my checking you, um, is to have, um, your eyes checked downstairs."*

Alex: *"Yes! I love that, I love that!"*

Doctor laughs: *"Well, now the most important question. Do you have any questions you want to ask me before I do your physical?"*

Alex: *"Um. . . . only one. I've been getting some bumps on my arms, right around here [indicates underarm]."*

Doctor: *"Underneath?"*

Alex: *"Yeah."*

Doctor: *"Ok. . . .Do they hurt or itch?"*

Alex: *"No, they're just there."*

Doctor: *"OK, well, I'll take a peek. . . . Any questions or worries on your part?* [looking at the mother]

Mom: *"No. . . . He seems to be coming along very nicely."*[10]

Alexander's mother's last comment reflects her view of him as a project, one that is progressing "very nicely." Throughout the visit, she signals her ease and her perception of the exam as an exchange between peers (with Alexander a legitimate participant), rather than a communication from a person in authority to his subordinates. Other middle-class parents seemed similarly comfortable. During Garrett Tallinger's exam, for example, his mother took off her sandals and tucked her legs up under her as she sat in the examination room. She also joked casually with the doctor.

Middle-class parents and children were also very assertive in situations at the public elementary school most of the middle-class children in the study attended. There were numerous conflicts during the year over matters small and large. For example, parents complained to one another and to the teachers about the amount of homework the children were assigned. A black middle-class mother whose daughters had not tested into the school's gifted program negotiated with officials to have the girls' (higher) results from a private testing company accepted instead. The parents of a fourth-grade boy drew the school superintendent into a battle over religious lyrics in a song scheduled to be sung as part of the holiday program. The superintendent consulted the district lawyer and ultimately "counseled" the principal to be more sensitive, and the song was dropped.

Children, too, asserted themselves at school. Examples include requesting that the classroom's blinds be lowered so the sun wasn't in their eyes, badgering the teacher for permission to retake a math test for a higher grade, and demanding to know why no cupcake had been saved when an absence prevented attendance at a classroom party. In these encounters, children were not simply complying with adults' requests or asking for a repeat of an earlier experience. They were displaying an emerging sense of entitlement by urging adults to permit a customized accommodation of institutional processes to suit their preferences.

Of course, some children (and parents) were more forceful than others in their dealings with teachers, and some were more successful than others. Melanie Handlon's mother, for example, took a very "hands-on" approach to her daughter's learning problems, coaching Melanie through her homework day after day. Instead of improved grades, however, the only result was a deteriorating home environment marked by tension and tears.

Emerging Signs of Constraint

The interactions the research assistants and I observed between professionals and working-class and poor parents frequently seemed cautious and constrained. This unease is evident, for example, during a physical Harold McAllister has before going to Bible camp. Harold's mother, normally boisterous and talkative at home, is quiet. Unlike Ms. Williams, she seems wary of supplying the doctor with accurate information:

Doctor: *"Does he eat something each day — either fish, meat, or egg?"*

Mom, response is low and muffled: *"Yes."*

Doctor, attempting to make eye contact but mom stares intently at paper: *"A yellow vegetable?"*

Mom, still no eye contact, looking at the floor: *"Yeah."*

Doctor: *"A green vegetable?"* Mom, looking at the doctor: *"Not all the time."* [Fieldworker has not seen any of the children eat a green or yellow vegetable since visits began.]

Doctor: *"No. Fruit or juice?"*

Mom, low voice, little or no eye contact, looks at the doctor's scribbles on the paper he is filling out: *"Ummh humn."*

Doctor: *"Does he drink milk every day?"*

Mom, abruptly, in considerably louder voice: *"Yeah."*

Doctor: *"Cereal, bread, rice, potato, anything like that?"*

Mom, shakes her head: *"Yes, definitely."* [Looks at doctor.]

Ms. McAllister's knowledge of developmental events in Harold's life is uneven. She is not sure when he learned to walk and cannot recall the name of his previous doctor. And when the doctor asks, "When was the last time he had a tetanus shot?" she counters, gruffly, "What's a tetanus shot?"

Unlike Ms. Williams, who urged Alexander to share information with the doctor, Ms. McAllister squelches eight-year-old Alexis's overtures:

Doctor: *"Any birth mark?"*

Mom looks at doctor, shakes her head no.

Alexis, raising her left arm, says excitedly: *"I have a birth mark under my arm!"*

Mom, raising her voice and looking stern: *"Will you cool out a minute?"* Mom, again answering the doctor's question: *"No."*

Despite Ms. McAllister's tension and the marked change in her everyday demeanor, Harold's whole exam is not uncomfortable. There are moments of laughter. Moreover, Harold's mother is not consistently shy or passive. Before the visit begins, the doctor comes into the waiting room and calls Harold's and Alexis' names. In response, the McAllisters (and the fieldworker) stand. Ms. McAllister then beckons for her nephew Tyrice (who is about Harold's age) to come along *before* she clears this with the doctor. Later, she sends Tyrice down the hall to observe Harold being weighed; she relies on her nephew's report rather than asking for this information from the healthcare professionals.

Still, neither Harold nor his mother seemed as comfortable as Alexander had been. Alexander was used to extensive conversation at home; with the doctor, he was at ease initiating questions. Harold, who was used to responding to directives at home, primarily answered questions from the doctor, rather than posing his own. Alexander, encouraged by his mother, was assertive and confident with the doctor. Harold was reserved. Absorbing his mother's apparent need to conceal the truth about the range of foods he ate, he appeared cautious, displaying an emerging sense of constraint.

We observed a similar pattern in school interactions. Overall, the working-class and poor adults had much more distance or separation from the school than their middle-class counterparts. Ms. McAllister, for example, could be quite assertive in some settings (e.g., at the start of family observations, she visited the local drug dealer, warning him not to "mess with" the black male fieldworker). But throughout the fourth-grade parent-teacher conference, she kept her winter jacket zipped up, sat hunched over in her chair, and spoke in barely audible tones. She was stunned when the teacher said that Harold did not do homework. Sounding dumbfounded, she said, "He does it at home." The teacher denied it and continued talking. Ms. McAllister made no further comments and did not probe for more information, except about a letter the teacher said he had mailed home and that she had not received. The conference ended, having yielded Ms. McAllister few insights into Harold's educational experience.[11]

Other working-class and poor parents also appeared baffled, intimidated, and subdued in parent-teacher conferences. Ms. Driver, who was extremely worried about her fourth-grader's inability to read, kept these concerns to herself. She explained to us, "I don't want to jump into anything and find it is the wrong thing." When working-class and poor parents did try to intervene in their children's educational experiences, they often felt ineffectual. Billy Yanelli's mother appeared relaxed and chatty in many of her interactions with other adults. With "the school," however, she was very apprehensive. She distrusted school personnel. She felt bullied and powerless. Hoping to resolve a problem involving her son, she tried to prepare her ideas in advance. Still, as she recounted during an interview, she failed to make school officials see Billy as vulnerable:

Ms. Yanelli: *I found a note in his school bag one morning and it said, "I'm going to kill you . . . you're a dead mother-f-er. . . ." So, I started shaking. I was all ready to go over there. [I was] prepared for the counselor. . . . They said the reason they [the other kids] do what they do is because Billy makes them do it. So they had an answer for everything.*

Interviewer: *How did you feel about that answer?*

Ms. Yanelli: *I hate the school. I hate it.*

Working-class and poor children seemed aware of their parents' frustration and witnessed their powerlessness. Billy Yanelli, for example, asserted in an interview that his mother "hate[d]" school officials.

At times, these parents encouraged their children to resist school officials' authority. The Yanellis told Billy to "beat up" a boy who was bothering him. Wendy Driver's mother advised her to punch a male classmate who pestered her and pulled her ponytail. Ms. Driver's boyfriend added, "Hit him when the teacher isn't looking."

In classroom observations, working-class and poor children could be quite lively and energetic, but we did not observe them try to customize their environments. They tended to react to adults' offers or, at times, to plead with educators to repeat previous experiences, such as reading a particular story, watching a movie, or going to the computer room. Compared to middle-class classroom interactions, the boundaries between adults and children seemed firmer and clearer. Although the children often resisted and tested school rules, they did not seem to be seeking to get educators to accommodate their own *individual* preferences.

Overall, then, the behavior of working-class and poor parents cannot be explained as a manifestation of their temperaments or of overall passivity; parents were quite energetic in intervening in their children's lives in other spheres. Rather, working-class and poor parents generally appeared to depend on the school (Lareau 2000), even as they were dubious of the trustworthiness of the professionals. This suspicion of professionals in dominant institutions is, at least in some instances, a reasonable response.[12] The unequal level of trust, as well as differences in the amount and quality of information divulged, can yield unequal *profits* during an historical moment when professionals applaud assertiveness and reject passivity as an inappropriate parenting strategy (Epstein 2001). Middle-class children and parents often (but not always) accrued advantages or profits from their efforts. Alexander Williams succeeded in having the doctor take his medical concerns seriously. Ms. Marshall's children ended up in the gifted program, even though they did not technically qualify. Middle-class children expect institutions to be responsive to *them* and to accommodate their individual needs. By contrast, when Wendy Driver is told to hit the boy who is pestering her (when the teacher isn't looking) or Billy Yanelli is told to physically defend himself, despite school rules, they are not learning how to make bureaucratic institutions work to their advantage. Instead, they are being given lessons in frustration and powerlessness.

Why Does Social Class Matter?

Parents' economic resources helped create the observed class differences in childrearing practices. Enrollment fees that middle-class parents dismissed as "negligible" were formidable expenses for less affluent families. Parents also paid for clothing, equipment, hotel stays, fast-food meals, summer camps, and fundraisers. In 1994, the Tallingers estimated the cost of Garrett's activities at $4,000 annually, and that figure was not unusually high.[13] Moreover, families needed reliable private transportation and flexible work schedules to get children to and from events. These resources were dispro-portionately concentrated in middle-class families.

Differences in educational resources also are important. Middle-class parents' superior levels of education gave them larger vocabularies that facilitated concerted cultivation, particularly in institutional interventions. Poor and working-class parents were not familiar with key terms profes-sionals used, such as "tetanus shot." Furthermore, middle-class parents' educational backgrounds gave them confidence when criticizing educa-tional professionals and intervening in school matters. Working-class and poor parents viewed educators as their social superiors.

Kohn and Schooler (1983) showed that parents' occupations, especially the complexity of their work, influence their childrearing beliefs. We found that parents' work mattered, but also saw signs that the experience of adult-hood itself influenced conceptions of childhood. Middle-class parents often were preoccupied with the pleasures and challenges of their work lives.[14] They tended to view childhood as a dual opportunity: a chance for play and for developing talents and skills of value later in life. Mr. Tallinger noted that playing soccer taught Garrett to be "hard nosed" and "competitive," valu-able workplace skills. Ms. Williams mentioned the value of Alexander learn-ing to work with others by playing on a sports team. Middle-class parents, aware of the "declining fortunes" of the middle class, worried about their own economic futures and those of their children (Newman 1993). This uncertainty increased their commitment to helping their children develop broad skills to enhance their future possibilities.

Working-class and poor parents' conceptions of adulthood and child-hood also appeared to be closely connected to their lived experiences. For the working class, it was the deadening quality of work and the press of eco-nomic shortages that defined their experience of adulthood and influenced their vision of childhood. It was dependence on public assistance and severe economic shortages that most shaped poor parents' views. Families in both classes had many worries about basic issues: food shortages, limited access to healthcare, physical safety, unreliable transportation, insufficient clothing. Thinking back over their childhoods, these parents remembered hardship but also recalled times without the anxieties they now faced. Many appeared to want their own youngsters to concentrate on being happy and relaxed, keeping the burdens of life at bay until they were older.

Thus, childrearing strategies are influenced by more than parents' edu-cation. It is the interweaving of life experiences and resources, including parents' economic resources, occupational conditions, and educational back-grounds, that appears to be most important in leading middle-class parents to engage in concerted cultivation and working-class and poor parents to engage in the accomplishment of natural growth. Still, the structural location of families did not fully determine their childrearing practices. The agency of actors and the indeterminacy of social life are inevitable.

In addition to economic and social resources, are there other significant factors? If the poor and working-class families' resources were transformed overnight so that they equaled those of the middle-class families, would their cultural logic of childrearing shift as well? Or are there cultural attitudes and beliefs that are substantially independent of economic and social resources that are influencing parents' practices here? The size and scope of this study preclude a definitive answer. Some poor and working-class parents embraced principles of concerted cultivation: They wished (but could not afford) to enroll their children in organized activities (e.g., piano lessons, voice lessons), they believed listening to their children was important, and they were committed to being involved in their children's schooling. Still, even when parents across all of the classes seemed committed to similar principles, their motivations differed. For example, many working-class and poor parents who wanted more activities for their children were seeking a safe haven for them. Their goal was to provide protection from harm rather than to cultivate the child's talents per se.

Some parents explicitly criticized children's schedules that involved many activities. During the parent interviews, we described the real-life activities of two children (using data from the 12 families we were observing). One schedule resembled Alexander Williams's: restricted television, required reading, and many organized activities, including piano lessons (for analytical purposes, we said that, unlike Alexander, this child disliked his piano lessons but was not allowed to quit). Summing up the attitude of the working-class and poor parents who rejected this kind of schedule,[15] one white, poor mother complained:

> I think he wants more. I think he doesn't enjoy doing what he's doing half of the time (light laughter). I think his parents are too strict. And he's not a child.

Even parents who believed this more regimented approach would pay off "job-wise" when the child was an adult still expressed serious reservations: "I think he is a sad kid," or, "He must be dead-dog tired."

Thus, working-class and poor parents varied in their beliefs. Some longed for a schedule of organized activities for their children and others did not; some believed in reasoning with children and playing an active role in schooling and others did not. Fully untangling the effects of material and cultural resources on parent's and children's choices is a challenge for future research.

Discussion

The evidence shows that class position influences critical aspects of family life: time use, language use, and kin ties. Not all aspects of family life are affected by social class, and there is variability within class. Still, parents do transmit advantages to their children in patterns that are sufficiently consistent and identifiable to be described as a "cultural logic" of childrearing. The white and black middle-class parents engaged in practices I have termed "concerted cultivation" — they made a deliberate and sustained effort to stimulate children's development and to cultivate their cognitive and social skills. The working-class and poor parents viewed children's development as spontaneously unfolding, as long as they were provided with comfort, food, shelter, and other basic support. This commitment, too, required ongoing effort; sustaining children's natural growth despite formidable life challenges is properly viewed as an accomplishment.

In daily life, the patterns associated with each of these approaches were interwoven and mutually reinforcing. Nine-year-old middle-class children already had developed a clear sense of their own talents and skills, and they differentiated themselves from siblings and friends. They were also learning to think of themselves as special and worthy of having adults devote time and energy to promoting them and their leisure activities. In the process, the boundaries between adults and children sometimes blurred; adults' leisure preferences became subordinate to their children's. The strong emphasis on reasoning in middle-class families had similar, diffused effects. Children used their formidable reasoning skills to persuade adults to acquiesce to their wishes. The idea that children's desires should be taken seriously was routinely realized in the middle-class families we interviewed and observed. In many subtle ways, children were taught that they were entitled. Finally, the commitment to cultivating children resulted in family schedules so crowded with activities there was little time left for visiting relatives. Quantitative studies of time use have shed light on important issues, but they do not capture the interactive nature of routine, everyday activities and the varying ways they affect the texture of family life.[16]

In working-class and poor families, parents established limits; within those limits, children were free to fashion their own pastimes. Children's wishes did not guide adults' actions as frequently or as decisively as they did in middle-class homes. Children were viewed as subordinate to adults. Parents tended to issue directives rather than to negotiate. Frequent interactions with relatives rather than acquaintances or strangers created a thicker divide between families and the outside world. Implicitly and explicitly, parents taught their children to keep their distance from people in positions of authority, to be distrustful of institutions, and, at times, to resist officials' authority. Children seemed to absorb the adults' feelings of powerlessness in their institutional relationships. As with the middle class, there were important variations among working-class and poor families, and some critical aspects of family life, such as the use of humor, were immune to social class.

The role of race in children's daily lives was less powerful than I had expected. The middle-class black children's parents were alert to the potential effects of institutional discrimination on their children. Middle-class black parents also took steps to help their children develop a positive racial identity. Still, in terms of how children spend their time, the way parents use language and discipline in the home, the nature of the families' social connections, and the strategies used for intervening in institutions, white and black middle-class parents engaged in very similar, often identical, practices with their children. A similar pattern was observed in white and black working-class homes as well as in white and black poor families. Thus my data indicate that on the childrearing dynamics studied here, compared with social class, race was less important in children's daily lives.[17] As they enter the racially segregated words of dating, marriage, and housing markets, and as they encounter more racism in their interpersonal contact with whites (Waters 1999), the relative importance of race in the children's daily lives is likely to increase.

Differences in family dynamics and the logic of childrearing across social classes have long-term consequences. As family members moved out of the home and interacted with representatives of formal institutions, middle-class parents and children were able to negotiate more valuable outcomes than their working-class and poor counterparts. In interactions with agents of dominant institutions, working-class and poor children were learning lessons in constraint while middle-class children were developing a sense of entitlement.

It is a mistake to see either concerted cultivation or the accomplishment of natural growth as an intrinsically desirable approach. As has been amply documented, conceptions of childhood have changed dramatically over time (Wrigley 1989). Drawbacks to middle-class childrearing, including the exhaustion associated with intensive mothering and frenetic family schedules and a sapping of children's naivete that leaves them feeling too sophisticated for simple games and toys (Hays 1996), remain insufficiently highlighted.

Another drawback is that middle-class children are less likely to learn how to fill "empty time" with their own creative play, leading to a dependence on their parents to solve experiences of boredom. Sociologists need to more clearly differentiate between standards that are intrinsically desirable and standards that facilitate success in dominant institutions. A more critical, and historically sensitive, vision is needed (Donzelot 1979). Here Bourdieu's work (1976, 1984, 1986, 1989) is valuable.

Finally, there are methodological issues to consider. Quantitative research has delineated population-wide patterns; ethnographies offer rich descriptive detail but typically focus on a single, small group. Neither approach can provide holistic, but empirically grounded, assessments of daily life. Multi-sited, multi-person research using ethnographic methods also pose formidable methodological challenges (Lareau 2002). Still, families have proven themselves open to being studied in an intimate fashion. Creating penetrating portraits of daily life that will enrich our theoretical models is an important challenge for the future.

ENDNOTES

1. All names of people and places are pseudonyms. The Lawrenceville school was in a white suburban neighborhood in a university community a few hours from a metropolitan area. The student population was about half white and half black; the (disproportionately poor) black children were bused from other neighborhoods.

2. Over three-quarters of the students at Lower Richmond qualified for free lunch; by contrast, Swan did not have a free lunch program.

3. At both sites, we attended school events and observed many parent–teacher conferences. Also, I interviewed the classroom teachers and adults involved in the children's organized activities. These interview data are not presented here.

4. Both schools had computer labs, art programs, and music programs, but Swan had many more resources and much higher average achievement scores. Graffiti and physical confrontations between students were common only at Lower Richmond. At these two sites and in Lawrenceville, white faculty predominated.

5. Here "poor" refers to the source of income (i.e., government assistance versus labor market) rather than the amount of income. Although lower class is more accurate than poor, it is widely perceived as pejorative. I might have used "underclass," but the literature has defined this term in racialized ways.

6. Dollar figures are from 1994–1995, unless otherwise noted. Income was not used to define class membership, but these data are available from the author.

7. The Suzuki method is labor intensive. Students are required to listen to music about one hour per day. Also, both child and parent(s) are expected to practice daily and to attend every lesson together.

8. Hart and Risley (1995) reported a similar difference in speech patterns. In their sample, by about age three, children of professionals had larger vocabularies and spoke more utterances per hour than the *parents* of similarly aged children on welfare.

9. This section focuses primarily on the concerns of black parents. Whites, of course, also benefited from race relations, notably in the scattering of poor white families in working-class neighborhoods rather than being concentrated in dense settings with other poor families (Massey and Denton 1993).

10. Not all professionals accommodated children's participation. Regardless of these adults' overt attitudes, though, we routinely observed that middle-class mothers monitor and intervene in their children's interactions with professionals.

11. Middle-class parents sometimes appeared slightly anxious during parent–teacher conferences, but overall, they spoke more and asked educators more questions than did working-class and poor parents.

12. The higher levels of institutional reports of child neglect, child abuse, and other family difficulties among poor families may reflect this group's greater vulnerability to institutional intervention (e.g., see L. Gordon 1989).

13. In 2002, a single sport could cost as much as $5,000 annually. Yearly league fees for ice hockey run to $2,700; equipment costs are high as well (Halbfinger 2002).

14. Middle-class adults do not live problem-free lives, but compared with the working class and poor, they have more varied occupational experiences and greater access to jobs with higher economic returns.

15. Many middle-class parents remarked that forcing a child to take piano lessons was wrong. Nevertheless, they continued to stress the importance of "exposure."

16. The time-use differences we observed were part of the taken-for-granted aspects of daily life; they were generally unnoticed by family members. For example, the working-class Yanellis considered themselves "really busy" if they had one baseball game on Saturday and an extended family gathering on Sunday. The Tallingers and other middle-class families would have considered this a slow weekend.

17. These findings are compatible with others showing children as aware of race at relatively early ages (Van Ausdale and Feagin 1996). At the two sites, girls often played in racially segregated groups during recess; boys tended to play in racially integrated groups.

REFERENCES

Aries, Philippe. 1962. *Centuries of Childhood: A Social History of the Family*. Translated by R. Baldick. London: Cape.

Bourdieu, Pierre. 1976. "Marriage Strategies as Strategies of Social Reproduction." Pp. 117–44 in *Family and Society*, edited by R. Forster and O. Ranum. Baltimore, MD: Johns Hopkins University Press.

———. 1984. *Distinction: A Social Critique of the Judgment of Taste*. Cambridge, MA: Harvard University Press.

———. 1986. "The Forms of Capital." Pp. 241–58 in *Handbook of Theory and Research for the Sociology of Education*, edited by J. C. Richardson. New York: Greenwood.

———. 1989. *The State Nobility: Elite Schools in the Field of Power*. Stanford, CA: Stanford University Press.

Bronfenbrenner, Urie. 1966. "Socialization and Social Class through Time and Space." Pp. 362–77 in *Class, Status and Power*, edited by R. Bendix and S. M. Lipset. New York: Free Press.

Conley, Dalton. 1999. *Being Black, Living in the Red: Race, Wealth, and Social Policy in America*. Berkeley: University of California Press.

Donzelot, Jacques. 1979. *The Policing of Families*. Translated by R. Hurley. New York: Pantheon.

Epstein, Joyce. 2001. *Schools, Family, and Community Partnerships*. Boulder, CO: Westview.

Fordham, Signithia and John U. Ogbu. 1986. "Black Students' School Success: Coping with the 'Burden of Acting White.'" *The Urban Review* 18:176–206.

Gordon, Linda. 1989. *Heroes of Their Own Lives: The Politics and History of Family Violence*. New York: Penguin.

Halbfinger, David M. 2002. "A Hockey Parent's Life: Time, Money, and Yes, Frustration." *New York Times*, January 12, p. 29.

Hart, Betty and Todd Risley. 1995. *Meaningful Differences in the Everyday Experience of Young American Children*. Baltimore, MD: Paul Brooks.

Hays, Sharon. 1996. *The Cultural Contradictions of Motherhood*. New Haven, CT: Yale University Press.

Heimer, Carol A. and Lisa Staffen. 1998. *For the Sake of the Children: The Social Organization of Responsibility in the Hospital and at Home*. Chicago: University of Chicago Press.

Hochschild, Jennifer L. 1995. *Facing Up to the American Dream*. Princeton, NJ: Princeton University Press.

Kingston, Paul. 2000. *The Classless Society*. Stanford, CA: Stanford University Press.

Kohn, Melvin and Carmi Schooler, eds. 1983. *Work and Personality: An Inquiry into the Impact of Social Stratification*. Norwood, NJ: Ablex.

Lareau, Annette. 2000. *Home Advantage: Social Class and Parental Intervention in Elementary Education*. 2d ed. Lanham, MD: Rowman and Littlefield.

———. 2002. "Doing Multi-Person, Multi-Site 'Ethnographic' Work: A Reflective, Critical Essay." Department of Sociology, Temple University, Philadelphia, PA. Unpublished manuscript.

Massey, Douglas and Nancy Denton. 1993. *American Apartheid*. Cambridge, MA: Harvard University Press.

Newman, Kathleen. 1993. *Declining Fortunes: The Withering of the American Dream*. New York: Basic Books.

Pattillo-McCoy, Mary 1999. *Black Picket Fences: Privilege and Peril among the Black Middle-Class*. Chicago: University of Chicago Press.

Tatum, Beverly Daniel. 1997. *Why Are All the Black Kids Sitting Together in the Cafeteria? And Other Conversations about Race*. New York: Basic Books.

Van Ausdale, Debra and Joe R. Feagin. 1996. "Using Racial and Ethnic Concepts: The Critical Case of Very Young Children." *American Sociological Review* 61:779–93.

Waters, Mary. 1999. *Black Identities: West Indian Immigrant Dreams and American Realities*. New York: Russell Sage Foundation.

Wrigley, Julia. 1989. "Do Young Children Need Intellectual Stimulation? Experts' Advice to Parents, 1900–1985." *History of Education* 29:41–75.

Zelizer, Viviana. 1985. *Pricing the Priceless Child: The Changing Social Value of Children*. New York: Basic Books.

PART VI

Motherhood and Fatherhood

In the previous section, we examined parenting and childhood; in this section, we examine more closely how parenting is gendered; that is, how parenting is similar and different between mothers and fathers. In fact, when people talk about parenthood, they are usually talking about motherhood, or they assume that mothers are the primary parent. By including separate articles on motherhood and fatherhood, I hope to correct this gender bias. Both motherhood and fatherhood need to be examined to fully understand the complexity of parenting. Moreover, as both parenthood and childhood are socially constructed, so are motherhood and fatherhood each socially constructed. That is, the expectations for and meanings of motherhood and fatherhood vary across cultures and over time. For example, as seen in the Adrienne Rich quote below, in Western culture, motherhood has been idealized to such an extent that mothers are often placed on a pedestal, but also blamed for everything that is wrong with children. Sociologist Scott Coltrane (1998) argues that "our idealized view of motherhood assumes that a dominant maternal instinct will naturally emerge and guide women's parenting because mothering is their destiny" (p. 96). Thus, many people believe that mothers have a maternal instinct, a biological desire to have children, and the innate knowledge of how to be a good mother. Instead, nothing could be further from the truth. Women's desires (as well as men's desires) to become a parent and their knowledge about parenting are learned via gender socialization and other societal messages. The section that follows is divided into two subsections, "Motherhood" and "Fatherhood."

Motherhood

A "natural" mother is a person without further identity, one who can find her chief gratification in being alone all day with small children, living at a pace tuned to theirs; that the isolation of mothers and children living in the home must be taken for granted; that maternal love is and should be, quite literally selfless; that children and mothers are the "causes" of each others' suffering.

— ADRIENNE RICH [1976] 1986

The first article in this section, "Shifting the Center: Race, Class, and Feminist Theorizing about Motherhood," by Patricia Hill Collins, challenges contemporary social constructions of motherhood. Collins, a professor of sociology and head of the Department of African American Studies at Brandeis University, has extensively researched the diverse meanings of motherhood in various racial-ethnic and social class groups. In this selection, Collins argues that scholars need to place the voices and experiences of

367

women of color at the center of feminist theorizing about motherhood. She states that until scholars "shift the center" of family scholarship away from white, middle-class, heterosexual families, they cannot understand how families are constructed differently for people of color. For example, work and family have not always been separate and conflicting spheres for women of color as they have been for white, middle-class women. Collins argues that scholars also need to understand that "motherwork" and the provision for physical survival of children vary by the racial-ethnic and social class backgrounds of mothers. For instance, the motherwork done by women of color often includes teaching children their racial-ethnic identity and helping them to understand their own culture and learn ways to survive in the dominant culture.

Following Collins' argument, Dalla and Gamble's research, "Teenage Mothering on the Navajo Reservation: An Examination of Intergenerational Perceptions and Beliefs," shifts our attention from white, middle-class families to Navajo women who become teen parents. Rochelle L. Dalla, an associate professor of family science at the University of Nebraska, Lincoln, and Wendy C. Gamble, an associate professor of human development and family at the University of Arizona, conducted this research at a Navajo reservation in Northern Arizona. Their study enables us to explore the meanings of motherhood from the perspective of one Native American tribe and challenges us to think about the cultural and structural constraints that shape motherhood. Dalla and Gamble interviewed teen mothers, teen fathers, the mothers of the teen mothers, and community informants in order to determine the various meanings of the terms "mother" and "teen parenting" among two generations of Navajo and between Navajo women and men. Dalla and Gamble reveal the complex intersection that race-ethnicity, gender, age, culture, and community can have on perceptions of teen parenting and mothering.

The third article in this section, "Mothering from a Distance: Emotions, Gender, and Intergenerational Relations in Filipino Transnational Families," by Rhacel Salazar Parreñas, also builds on many of Patricia Hill Collins' arguments (Reading 22) about shifting the center of our analysis of motherhood. Salazar Parreñas, an assistant professor of women's studies and Asian American studies at the University of Wisconsin, Madison, interviewed 72 Filipina domestic workers in Rome, Italy, and in the United States to find out how transnational work has shaped these women's perceptions and experiences of mothering their own children, left behind in the Philippines. Salazar Parreñas reveals the high emotional costs paid by Filipina women who, in order to provide their families with income, are forced to live physically apart from them. These women are caught in numerous cultural contradictions about motherhood within their own cultures of the Philippines and within the dominant cultures of Italy or the United States where they work. Moreover, the domestic labor of these transnational Filipinas enables privileged women and men in the West to have more time with their children, while depriving Filipina domestics of intensive contact with their own children.

Fatherhood

> *Biological fathers are more likely to be committed to the upbringing of their own children than are nonbiological fathers. Human beings have evolved to invest more readily in genetically related persons than in nonrelated persons. Being a father is much more than merely playing a social role. Engaged biological fathers care profoundly and selflessly about their own children, and such fatherly love is not something that can be transferred easily or learned from a script.*
>
> — DAVID POPENOE 1996:198

The first three readings on motherhood show how the construct of motherhood is ideologically laden. As motherhood is socially constructed, so is fatherhood. The quote above reflects one such construction of fatherhood that biological fathers are more committed to their children than nonbiological fathers, such as stepfathers, adoptive fathers, or foster fathers, because of their genetic ties. The author of this quote, David Popenoe, argues that the father role is innate or biologically determined and is not a role that can be learned. Many other sociologists disagree with Popenoe and believe that fatherhood is primarily a social role that is determined and shaped by the larger society. Thus, our understanding of fatherhood is influenced by a number of cultural shifts, including changes in the larger economy, changes in marriage patterns, and changes in gender roles. The social construction of fatherhood is currently in flux. Even the very definition of fatherhood has had to adapt due to the high divorce rate, a rise in the number of non coresidential fathers, and the growing use of reproductive technologies. No longer is the biological definition of fatherhood sufficient, if it ever was. This increasing complexity of fatherhood demands more research.

The current flux in the construction of fatherhood has led to a greater emphasis on father blaming in the larger society. Fathers are called many derogatory terms, including deadbeat dads, absent fathers, and uninvolved fathers. The first reading in the section on fatherhood, "Fathering: Paradoxes, Contradictions, and Dilemmas" by Scott Coltrane, addresses these views that men are not involved enough in their children's lives. Coltrane, a professor of sociology at the University of California, Riverside, has studied gender and families for over 20 years. The selection excerpted here is an overview of the social construction of fatherhood in the United States. In this reading, Coltrane examines how fathering practices have varied across cultures and through history; how different social, economic, and political contexts have produced different types of father involvement; and what the causes and consequences are of father involvement. Coltrane concludes his examination of fathering in the 21st century with some arguments about how fathering might change further in the future.

The second article on fatherhood, "What It Means to Be Daddy: Fatherhood for Black Men Living Away from Their Children" by Jennifer Hamer, also challenges traditional definitions of fatherhood. Hamer, an associate professor of Afro-American Studies and Research Program at the University of Illinois, Urbana–Champaign, decided to research what fatherhood has meant for low-income black fathers who do not reside with their children. What is fatherhood like for men who live on the margins of society in terms of their race and social class? Noncustodial black fathers are one of the more maligned and stereotyped groups among parents in the United States. Hamer's interview study challenges these stereotypes and reveals that we cannot evaluate fatherhood strictly in terms of the dominant U.S. ideal based on white, middle- and upper-class fathers. Black men face a number of economic and social barriers that prevent many of them from becoming that idealized family breadwinner. Instead, Hamer argues that we need to address these barriers with better social policies aimed toward the unique circumstances of black families. Hamer also shows how black family structure is shaped by history, the current economy, and governmental policies toward black families.

The third article on fatherhood in this section also examines an underresearched and often taken-for-granted type of father: stepfathers. William Marsiglio, a professor of sociology at the University of Florida, Gainesville, has studied men, masculinity, and fatherhood for almost 30 years. This selection is taken from Marsiglio's interview study of stepfathers reported in his recent book, *Stepdads: Stories of Love, Hope, and Repair* (2004). Like nonresidential, low-income black fathers, stepfathers also are a heavily stereotyped and disparaged group of fathers in the United States. Yet, the reality is that many children will spend a good part of their childhood growing up with stepfathers. After describing the obvious ways that a stepfather can positively influence his stepchildren's lives (that is, via discipline, supervision, financial support, and play), Marsiglio turns his attention to discovering what are the less obvious ways that stepfathers influence their stepchildren's lives. Marsiglio finds that stepfathers positively contribute to their stepchildren's lives in a number of ways, but two often unobserved ways are how stepfathers contribute to the building of a child's social capital and how stepfathers make an effort to be an ally for the biological father with his children.

REFERENCES

Coltrane, Scott. 1998. *Gender and Families.* Thousand Oaks, CA: Pine Forge Press.

Hamer, Jennifer F. 2001. *What It Means to Be Daddy: Fatherhood for Black Men Living Away from Their Children.* New York: Columbia University Press.

Marsiglio, William. 2004. *Stepdads: Stories of Love, Hope, and Repair.* Boston: Rowman and Littlefield.

Popenoe, David. 1996. *Life without Father: Compelling New Evidence that Fatherhood and Marriage Are Indispensable for the Good of Children and Society.* New York: Martin Kessler Books/The Free Press.

Rich, Adrienne. [1976] 1986. "Anger and Tenderness." Excerpt from *Of Woman Born: Motherhood Experience and Institution.* New York: W. W. Norton.

22

SHIFTING THE CENTER
Race, Class, and Feminist Theorizing about Motherhood

PATRICIA HILL COLLINS

I dread to see my children grow, I know not their fate. Where the white boy has every opportunity and protection, mine will have few opportunities and no protection. It does not matter how good or wise my children may be, they are colored.

— An anonymous African American mother in 1904
(reported in LERNER 1972:158)

For Native American, African American, Hispanic, and Asian American women, motherhood cannot be analyzed in isolation from its context. Motherhood occurs in specific historical contexts framed by interlocking structures of race, class, and gender, contexts where the sons of white mothers have "every opportunity and protection," and the "colored" daughters and sons of racial ethnic mothers "know not their fate." Racial domination and economic exploitation profoundly shape the mothering context not only for racial ethnic women in the United States but for all women.[1]

Despite the significance of race and class, feminist theorizing routinely minimizes their importance. In this sense, feminist theorizing about motherhood has not been immune to the decontextualization in Western social thought overall.[2] Although many dimensions of motherhood's context are ignored, the exclusion of race and/or class from feminist theorizing generally and from feminist theorizing about motherhood specifically merits special attention (Spelman 1988).[3]

Much feminist theorizing about motherhood assumes that male domination in the political economy and the household is the driving force in family life and that understanding the struggle for individual autonomy in the face of such domination is central to understanding motherhood (Eisenstein 1983).[4] Several guiding principles frame such analyses. First, such theories posit a dichotomous split between the public sphere of economic and political discourse and the private sphere of family and household responsibilities. This juxtaposition of a public, political economy to a private, noneconomic, and apolitical domestic household allows work and family to be seen as separate institutions. Second, reserving the public sphere for men as a "male" domain leaves the private, domestic sphere as a "female" domain. Gender roles become tied to the dichotomous constructions of these two basic societal institutions—men work and women take care of families. Third, the public/private dichotomy separating the family/household from the paid labor market shapes sex-segregated gender roles within the private sphere of the family. The archetypal white, middle-class, nuclear family divides family life into two oppositional spheres—the "male" sphere of economic providing and the "female" sphere of affective nurturing, mainly mothering. This normative family household ideally consists of a working father who earns enough to allow his spouse and dependent children to forgo participation in the paid labor force. Owing in large part to their superior earning power, men as workers and fathers exert power over women in the labor market and in families. Finally, the struggle for individual autonomy in the face of a controlling, oppressive "public" society or the father as patriarch constitutes the main human enterprise.[5] Successful adult males achieve this autonomy. Women, children, and less successful males—namely, those who are working class or from racial ethnic groups—are seen as dependent persons, as less autonomous, and therefore as fitting objects for elite male domination. Within the nuclear family, this struggle for autonomy takes the form of increasing opposition to the mother, the individual responsible for socializing children by these guiding principles (Chodorow 1978; Flax 1978).

Placing the experiences of women of color in the center of feminist theorizing about motherhood demonstrates how emphasizing the issue of father as patriarch in a decontextualized nuclear family distorts the experiences of women in alternative family structures with quite different political economies. While male domination certainly has been an important theme for racial ethnic women in the United States, gender inequality has long worked in tandem with racial domination and economic exploitation. Since work and family have rarely functioned as dichotomous spheres for women of color, examining racial ethnic women's experiences reveals how these two spheres actually are interwoven (Collins 1990; Dill 1988; Glenn 1985).

For women of color, the subjective experience of mothering/motherhood is inextricably linked to the sociocultural concerns of racial ethnic communities—one does not exist without the other. Whether under conditions of the labor exploitation of African American women during slavery and the ensuing tenant farm system, the political conquest of Native American women during European acquisition of land, or exclusionary immigration policies applied to Asian Americans and Latinos, women of color have performed motherwork that challenges social constructions of work and family as separate spheres, of male and female gender roles as similarly dichotomized, and of the search for autonomy as the guiding human quest. "Women's reproductive labor—that is, feeding, clothing, and psychologically supporting the male wage earner and nurturing and socializing the next generation—is seen as work on behalf of the family as a whole rather than as work benefiting men in particular," observes Asian American sociologist Evelyn Nakano Glenn (1986:192). The locus of conflict lies outside the household, as women and their families engage in collective effort to create and maintain family life in the face of forces that undermine family integrity. But this "reproductive labor" or "motherwork" goes beyond ensuring the survival of members of one's family. This type of motherwork recognizes that individual survival, empowerment, and identity require group survival, empowerment, and identity. . . .

. . . I use the term *motherwork* to soften the dichotomies in feminist theorizing about motherhood that posit rigid distinctions between private and public, family and work, the individual and the collective, identity as individual autonomy and identity growing from the collective self-determination of one's group. Racial ethnic women's mothering and work experiences occur at the boundaries demarking these dualities. "Work for the day to come" is motherwork, whether it is on behalf of one's own biological children, children of one's racial ethnic community, or children who are yet unborn. Moreover, the space that this motherwork occupies promises to shift our thinking about motherhood itself.

Shifting the Center: Women of Color and Motherwork

What themes might emerge if issues of race and class generally, and understanding racial ethnic women's motherwork specifically, became central to feminist theorizing about motherhood? Centering feminist theorizing on the concerns of white middle-class women leads to two problematic assumptions. The first is that a relative degree of economic security exists for mothers and their children. A second is that all women enjoy the racial privilege that allows them to see themselves primarily as individuals in search of personal autonomy instead of members of racial ethnic groups struggling for power. These assumptions allow feminist theorists to concentrate on themes such as the connections among mothering, aggression, and death, the effects of maternal isolation on mother–child relationships within nuclear family households, maternal sexuality, relations among family members, all-powerful mothers as conduits for gender oppression, and the possibilities of an idealized motherhood freed from patriarchy (Chodorow and Contratto 1982; Eisenstein 1983).

Although these issues merit investigation, centering feminist theorizing about motherhood in the ideas and experiences of African American, Native American, Hispanic, and Asian American women might yield markedly different themes (Andersen 1988; Brown 1989). This stance is to be distinguished from adding racial ethnic women's experiences to preexisting feminist theories without considering how these experiences challenge those theories (Spelman 1988). Involving much more than consulting existing social science sources, placing the ideas and experiences of women of color in the center of analysis requires invoking a different epistemology concerning what type of knowledge is valid. We must distinguish between what has been said about subordinated groups in the dominant discourse, and what such groups might say about themselves if given the opportunity. Personal narratives, autobiographical statements, poetry, fiction, and other personalized statements have all been used by women of color to express self-defined standpoints on mothering and motherhood. Such knowledge reflects the authentic standpoint of subordinated groups. Placing these sources in the center and supplementing them with statistics, historical material, and other knowledge produced to justify the interests of ruling elites should create new themes and angles of vision (Smith 1990).[6]

Specifying the contours of racial ethnic women's motherwork promises to point the way toward richer feminist theorizing about motherhood. Issues of survival, power, and identity—these three themes form the bedrock of women of color's motherwork. The importance of working for the physical survival of children and community, the dialectical nature of power and powerlessness in structuring mothering patterns, and the significance of self-definition in constructing individual and collective racial identity comprise three core themes characterizing the experiences of Native American, African American, Hispanic, and Asian American women. Examining survival, power, and identity reveals how racial ethnic women in the United States encounter and fashion motherwork. But it also suggests how feminist theorizing about motherhood might be shifted if different voices became central in feminist discourse.

Motherwork and Physical Survival

> *When we are not physically starving we have the luxury to realize psychic and emotional starvation.*
>
> —MORAGA 1979:29

Physical survival is assumed for children who are white and middle class. Thus, examining their psychic and emotional well-being and that of their mothers appears rational. The children of women of color, many of whom are "physically starving," have no such assurances. Racial ethnic children's lives have long been held in low regard. African American children face an infant mortality rate twice that for white infants. Approximately one-third of Hispanic children and one-half of African American children who survive infancy live in poverty. Racial ethnic children often live in harsh urban environments where drugs, crime, industrial pollutants, and violence threaten their survival. Children in rural environments often fare no better.

Winona LaDuke reports that Native Americans on reservations frequently must use contaminated water. On the Pine Ridge Sioux Reservation in 1979, for example, 38 percent of all pregnancies resulted in miscarriages before the fifth month or in excessive hemorrhaging. Approximately 65 percent of the children who were born suffered breathing problems caused by underdeveloped lungs and jaundice (LaDuke 1988:63).

Struggles to foster the survival of Native American, Latino, Asian American, and African American families and communities by ensuring the survival of children are a fundamental dimension of racial ethnic women's motherwork. African American women's fiction contains numerous stories of mothers fighting for the physical survival both of their own biological children and of those of the larger African American community.[7] "Don't care how much death it is in the land, I got to make preparations for my baby to live!" proclaims Mariah Upshur, the African American heroine of Sara Wright's 1986 novel *This Child's Gonna Live* (p. 143). The harsh climates that confront racial ethnic children require that their mothers, like Mariah Upshur, "make preparations for their babies to live" as a central feature of their motherwork.

Yet, like all deep cultural themes, the theme of motherwork for physical survival contains contradictory elements. On the one hand, racial ethnic women's motherwork for individuals and the community has been essential for their survival. On the other hand, this work often extracts a high cost for large numbers of women, such as loss of individual autonomy or the submersion of individual growth for the benefit of the group. Although this dimension of motherwork is essential, the question of whether women are doing more than their fair share of such work for community development merits consideration.

Histories of family-based labor have shaped racial ethnic women's motherwork for survival and the types of mothering relationships that ensue. African American, Asian American, Native American, and Hispanic women have all worked and contributed to family economic well-being (Dill 1988; Glenn 1985). Much of these women's experiences with motherwork stems from the work they performed as children. The commodification of children of color—from the enslavement of African children who were legally owned as property to the subsequent treatment of children as units of labor in agricultural work, family businesses, and industry—has been a major theme shaping motherhood for women of color. Beginning in slavery and continuing into the post–World War II period, African American children were put to work at young ages in the fields of southern agriculture. Sara Brooks began full-time work in the fields at age eleven and remembers, "We never was lazy 'cause we used to really work. We used to work like mens. Oh, fight sometime, fuss sometime, but worked on" (Collins 1990:54). Black and Latino children in contemporary migrant farm families make similar contributions to their family's economy. "I musta been almost eight when I started following the crops," remembers Jessie de la Cruz, a Mexican American mother with six grown children. "Every winter, up north. I was on the end of the row of prunes, taking care of my younger brother and sister. They would help me fill up the cans and put 'em in a box while the rest of the family was picking the whole row" (de la Cruz 1980:168). Asian American children spent long hours working in family businesses, child labor practices that have earned Asian Americans the dubious distinction of being "model minorities." More recently, the family-based labor of undocumented racial ethnic immigrants, often mother–child units doing piecework for the garment industry, recalls the sweatshop conditions confronting turn-of-the-century European immigrants.

A certain degree of maternal isolation from members of the dominant group characterizes the preceding mother–child units. For women of color working along with their children, such isolation is more appropriately seen as reflecting the placement of women of color and their children in racially and class-stratified labor systems than as resulting from patriarchal domination. The unit may be isolated, but the work performed by the mother–child unit closely ties the mothering experiences of women of color to wider political and economic issues. Children learn to see their work and that of their mother not as isolated from the wider society but as essential to their family's survival. Moreover, in the case of family agricultural labor or family businesses, women and children worked alongside men, often performing the same work. If isolation occurred, the family, not the mother–child unit, was the focus.

Children working in close proximity to their mothers received distinctive types of mothering. Asian American children working in urban family businesses report long days filled almost exclusively with work and school. In contrast, the sons and daughters of African American sharecroppers and migrant farm children of all backgrounds did not fare as well. Their placement in rural work settings meant that they had less access to educational opportunities. "I think the longest time I went to school was two months in one place," remembers Jessie de la Cruz. "I attended, I think, about forty-five schools. When my parents or my brothers didn't find any work, we wouldn't attend school because we weren't sure of staying there. So I missed a lot of school" (de la Cruz 1980:167–68). It was only in the 1950s that southern school districts stopped the practice of closing segregated African American schools during certain times of the year so that the children could work.

Work that separated women of color from their children also framed the mothering relationship. Until the 1960s, large numbers of African American, Hispanic, and Asian American women worked in domestic service. Even though women worked long hours to ensure their children's physical survival, that same work ironically denied the mothers access to their children. Different institutional arrangements emerged in African American, Latino, and Asian American communities to resolve the tension between maternal separation due to employment and the needs of dependent children. The extended family structure in African American communities endured as a flexible institution that mitigated some of the effects of maternal separation. Grandmothers are highly revered in African American communities, often because they function as primary caretakers of their daughters' and daughters-in-law's children (Collins 1990). In contrast, exclusionary immigration policies that mitigated against intergenerational family units in the United States led Chinese American and Japanese American families to make other arrangements (Dill 1988).

Some mothers are clearly defeated by this situation of incessant labor performed to ensure their children's survival. The magnitude of their motherwork overwhelms them. But others, even while appearing to be defeated, manage to pass on the meaning of motherwork for survival to their children. African American feminist thinker June Jordan (1985) remembers her perceptions of her mother's work:

> As a child I noticed the sadness of my mother as she sat alone in the kitchen at night. . . . Her woman's work never won permanent victories of any kind. It never enlarged the universe of her imagination or her power to influence what happened beyond the front door of our house. Her woman's work never tickled her to laugh or shout or dance. (P. 105)

But Jordan also sees her mother's work as being motherwork that is essential to individual and community survival.

> But she did raise me to respect her way of offering love and to believe that hard work is often the irreducible factor for survival, not something to avoid. Her woman's work produced a reliable home base where I could pursue the privileges of books and music. Her woman's work invented the potential for a completely new kind of work for us, the next generation of Black women: huge, rewarding hard work demanded by the huge, different ambitions that her perfect confidence in us engendered.

Motherwork and Power

How can I write down how I felt when I was a little child and my grandmother used to cry with us 'cause she didn't have enough food to give us? Because my brother was going barefooted and he was cryin' because he wasn't used to going without shoes? How can I describe that? I can't describe when my little girl died because I didn't have money for a doctor. And never had any teaching on caring for sick babies. Living out in labor camps. How can I describe that?

—DE LA CRUZ 1980:177

Jessie de la Cruz, a Mexican American woman who grew up as a migrant farm worker, experienced firsthand the struggle for empowerment facing racial ethnic women whose daily motherwork centers on issues of survival. A dialectical relation exists between efforts of racial orders to mold the institution of motherhood to serve the interests of elites, in this case, racial elites, and efforts on the part of subordinated groups to retain power over motherhood so that it serves the legitimate needs of their communities (Collins 1990). African American, Asian American, Hispanic, and Native American women have long been preoccupied with patterns of maternal power and powerlessness because their mothering experiences have been profoundly affected by this dialectical process. But instead of emphasizing maternal power in dealing either with father as patriarch (Chodorow 1978; Rich 1986) or with male dominance (Ferguson 1989), women of color are concerned with their power and powerlessness within an array of social institutions that frame their lives.

Racial ethnic women's struggles for maternal empowerment have revolved around three main themes. The struggle for control over their own bodies in order to preserve choice over whether to become mothers at all is one fundamental theme. The ambiguous politics of caring for unplanned children has long shaped African American women's motherwork. For example, the widespread institutionalized rape of African American women by white men both during slavery and in the segregated South created countless biracial children who had to be absorbed into African American families and communities (Davis 1981). The range of skin colors and hair textures in contemporary African American communities bears mute testament to the powerlessness of African American women in controlling this dimension of motherhood.

For many women of color, choosing to become a mother challenges institutional policies that encourage white middle-class women to reproduce and discourage low-income racial ethnic women from doing so, even penalizing them (Davis 1981). Rita Silk-Nauni, an incarcerated Native American woman, writes of the difficulties she encountered in trying to have additional children. She loved her son so much that she left him only when she went to work. "I tried having more after him and couldn't," she observes. "I went to a specialist and he thought I had been fixed when I had my Son. He said I would have to have surgery in order to give birth again. The surgery was so expensive but I thought I could make a way even if I had to work 24 hours a day. Now that I'm here, I know I'll never have that chance" (Brant 1988:94). Like Silk-Nauni, Puerto Rican and African American women have long had to struggle with issues of sterilization abuse (Davis 1981). More recently, efforts to manipulate the fertility of poor women dependent on public assistance speaks to the continued salience of this issue in the lives of racial ethnic women.

A second dimension of racial women's struggles for maternal empowerment concerns getting to keep the children that are wanted, whether they were planned for or not. For racial ethnic mothers like Jessie de la Cruz whose "little girl died" because she "didn't have money for a doctor," maternal separation from one's children becomes a much more salient issue than maternal isolation with one's children within an allegedly private nuclear family. Physical or psychological separation of mothers and children designed to disempower racial ethnic individuals forms the basis of a systematic effort to disempower their communities.

For both Native American and African American mothers, situations of conquest introduced this dimension of the struggle for maternal empowerment.

In her fictional account of a Native American mother's loss of her children in 1890, Brant explores the pain of maternal separation. "It has been two days since they came and took the children away. My body is greatly chilled. All our blankets have been used to bring me warmth. The women keep the fire blazing. The men sit. They talk among themselves. We are frightened by this sudden child-stealing. We signed papers, the agent said. This gave them rights to take our babies. It is good for them, the agent said. It will make them civilized" (1988:101). A legacy of conquest has meant that Native American mothers on so-called reservations confront intrusive government institutions such as the Bureau of Indian Affairs in deciding the fate of their children. For example, the long-standing policy of removing Native American children from their homes and housing them in reservation boarding schools can be seen as an effort to disempower their mothers. In the case of African American women under slavery, owners controlled virtually all dimensions of their children's lives — they could be sold at will, whipped, even killed, all with no recourse by their mothers. In such a situation, simply keeping and rearing one's children becomes empowerment.

A third dimension of racial ethnic women's struggles for empowerment concerns the pervasive efforts by the dominant group to control their children's minds. In her short story "A Long Memory," Beth Brant juxtaposes the loss felt in 1890 by a Native American mother whose son and daughter were forcibly removed by white officials to the loss that Brant felt in 1978 when a hearing took away her custody of her daughter. "Why do they want our babies?" queries the turn-of-the-century mother. "They want our power. They take our children to remove the inside of them. Our power" (Brant 1988:105). This mother recognizes that the future of the Native American way of life lies in retaining the power to define that worldview through educating the children. By forbidding children to speak their native languages and in other ways encouraging them to assimilate into Anglo culture, external agencies challenge the power of mothers to raise their children as they see fit.

Schools controlled by the dominant group comprise one important location where this dimension of the struggle for maternal empowerment occurs. In contrast to white middle-class children, whose educational experiences affirm their mothers' middle-class values, culture, and authority, African American, Latino, Asian American and Native American children typically receive an education that derogates their mothers' perspective. For example, the struggles over bilingual education in Latino communities are about much more than retaining Spanish as a second language. Speaking the language of one's childhood is a way of retaining the entire culture and honoring the mother teaching that culture (Anzaldúa 1987; Moraga 1979).

Jenny Yamoto (1988) describes the stress of ongoing negotiations with schools regarding her part African American and part Japanese sons. "I've noticed that depending on which parent, Black mom or Asian dad, goes to school open house, my oldest son's behavior is interpreted as disruptive and irreverent, or assertive and clever. . . . I resent their behavior being defined and even expected on the basis of racial biases their teachers may struggle with or hold. . . . I don't have the time or energy to constantly change and challenge their teachers' and friends' misperceptions. I only go after them when the children really seem to be seriously threatened" (p. 24).

In confronting each of these three dimensions of their struggles for empowerment, racial ethnic women are not powerless in the face of racial and class oppression. Being grounded in a strong, dynamic, indigenous culture can be central in racial ethnic women's social constructions of motherhood. Depending on their access to traditional culture, women of color invoke alternative sources of power.[8] "Equality per se may have a different meaning for Indian women and Indian people," suggests Kate Shanley (1988). "That difference begins with personal and tribal sovereignty — the right to be legally recognized as people empowered to determine our own destinies" (p. 214). Personal sovereignty involves the struggle to promote the survival of a social structure whose organizational principles represent notions of family and motherhood different from those of the mainstream. "The nuclear family has little relevance to Indian women," observes Shanley. "In fact, in many ways, mainstream feminists now are striving to redefine family and community in a way that Indian women have long known."

African American mothers can draw upon an Afrocentric tradition where motherhood of varying types, whether bloodmother, othermother, or community othermother, can be invoked as a symbol of power. Many African American women receive respect and recognition within their local communities for innovative and practical approaches to mothering not only their own biological children but also the children in their extended family networks and in the community overall. Black women's involvement in fostering African American community development forms the basis of this community-based power. In local African American communities, community othermothers can become identified as powerful figures through furthering the community's well-being (Collins 1990).

Despite policies of dominant institutions that place racial ethnic mothers in positions where they appear less powerful to their children, mothers and children empower themselves by understanding each other's position and relying on each other's strengths. In many cases, children, especially daughters, bond with their mothers instead of railing against them as symbols of patriarchal power. Cherríe Moraga describes the impact that her mother had on her. Because she was repeatedly removed from school in order to work, Moraga's mother would be considered largely illiterate by prevailing standards. But her mother was also a fine storyteller and found ways to empower herself within dominant institutions. "I would go with my mother to fill out job applications for her, or write checks for her at the supermarket," Moraga (1979) recounts. "We would have the scenario all worked out ahead of time. My mother would sign the check before we'd get to the store. Then, as we'd approach the checkstand, she would say — within earshot of the cashier — 'oh honey, you go 'head and make out the check,' as if she couldn't be bothered with such an insignificant detail" (p. 28). Like Cherríe Moraga and her mother, racial ethnic women's motherwork involves collaborating to empower mothers and children within oppressive structures.

Motherwork and Identity

Please help me find out who I am. My mother was Indian, but we were taken from her and put in foster homes. They were white and didn't want to tell us about our mother. I have a name and maybe a place of birth. Do you think you can help me?

— BRANT 1988:9

Like this excerpt from a letter to an editor, the theme of loss of racial ethnic identity and the struggle to maintain a sense of self and community pervade the remaining stories, poetry, and narratives in Beth Brant's volume, *A Gathering of Spirit.* Carol Lee Sanchez offers another view of the impact of the loss of self. "Radicals look at reservation Indians and get very upset about their poverty conditions," observes Sanchez. "But poverty to us is not the same thing as poverty is to you. Our poverty is that we can't be who we are. We can't hunt or fish or grow our food because our basic resources and the right to use them in traditional ways are denied us" (Brant 1988:165). Racial ethnic women's motherwork reflects the tensions inherent in trying to foster a meaningful racial identity in children within a society that denigrates people of color. The racial privilege enjoyed by white middle-class women makes unnecessary this complicated dimension of the mothering tradition of women of color. Although white children can be prepared to fight racial oppression, their survival does not depend on gaining these skills. Their racial identity is validated by their schools, the media, and other social institutions. White children are socialized into their rightful place in systems of racial privilege. Racial ethnic women have no such guarantees for their children. Their children must first be taught to survive in systems that would oppress them. Moreover, this survival must not come at the expense of self-esteem. Thus, a dialectical relation exists between systems of racial oppression designed to strip subordinated groups of a sense of personal identity and a sense of collective peoplehood, and the cultures of resistance to that oppression extant in various racial ethnic groups. For women of color, motherwork for identity occurs at this critical juncture (Collins 1990).

"Through our mothers, the culture gave us mixed messages," observes Mexican American poet Gloria Anzaldúa (1987). "Which was it to be—strong or submissive, rebellious or conforming?" (p. 18). Thus women of color's motherwork requires reconciling two contradictory needs concerning identity. First, preparing children to cope with and survive within systems of racial oppression is essential. The pressures for these children to assimilate are pervasive. In order to compel women of color to participate in their children's assimilation, dominant institutions promulgate ideologies that belittle people of color. Negative controlling images infuse the worlds of their male and female children (Collins 1990; Green 1990; Tajima 1989). Native American girls are encouraged to see themselves as "Pocahontases" and "squaws"; Asian American girls as "geisha girls" and "Suzy Wongs"; Hispanic girls as "Madonnas" and "hot-blooded whores"; and African American girls as "mammies," "matriarchs," and "prostitutes." Girls of all groups are told that their lives cannot be complete without a male partner and that their educational and career aspirations must always be subordinated to their family obligations.

This push toward assimilation is part of a larger effort to socialize racial ethnic children into their proper subordinate places in systems of racial and class oppression. But despite pressures to assimilate, since children of color can never be white, assimilation by becoming white is impossible. Thus, a second dimension of this mothering tradition involves equipping children with skills to challenge the systems of racial oppression. Girls who become women believing that they are capable only of being maids and prostitutes cannot contribute to racial ethnic women's motherwork. Mothers make varying choices in preparing their children to fit into, yet resist, systems of racial domination. Some mothers remain powerless in the face of external forces that foster their children's assimilation and subsequent alienation from their families and communities. Through fiction, Native American author Beth Brant (1988:102–103) explores the grief felt by a mother whose children had been taken away to live among whites. A letter arrives giving news of her missing son and daughter:

> *This letter is from two strangers with the names Martha and Daniel. They say they are learning civilized ways. Daniel works in the fields, growing food for the school. Martha is being taught to sew aprons. She will be going to live with the schoolmaster's wife. She will be a live-in girl. What is live-in girl? I shake my head. The words sound the same to me. I am afraid of Martha and Daniel. These strangers who know my name.*

Other mothers become unwitting conduits of the dominant ideology. "How many times have I heard mothers and mothers-in-law tell their sons to beat their wives for not obeying them, for being *hociconas* (big mouths), for being *callajeras* (going to visit and gossip with neighbors), for expecting their husbands to help with the rearing of children and the housework, for wanting to be something other than housewives," asks Gloria Anzaldúa (1987:16).

Some mothers encourage their children to fit in for reasons of survival. "My mother, nursed in the folds of a town that once christened its black babies Lee, after Robert E., and Jackson, after Stonewall, raised me on a dangerous generation's old belief," remembers African American author Marita Golden (1983). "Because of my dark brown complexion, she warned me against wearing browns or yellow and reds. . . . And every summer I was admonished not to play in the sun 'cause you gonna have to get a light husband anyway, for the sake of your children'" (p. 24). To Cherríe Moraga's mother, "on a basic economic level, being Chicana meant being 'less.' It was through my mother's desire to protect her children from poverty and illiteracy that we became 'anglocized'; the more effectively we could pass in the white world, the better guaranteed our future" (Moraga 1979:28). Despite their mothers' good intentions, the costs to children taught to submit to racist and sexist ideologies can be high. Raven, a Native American woman, looks back on her childhood: "I've been raised in white man's world and was forbade more or less to converse with Indian people. As my mother wanted me to be educated and live a good life, free from poverty. I lived a life of loneliness. Today I am desperate to know my people" (Brant 1988:221). Raven's mother did what she thought best to help her daughter avoid poverty. But ultimately, Raven experienced the poverty of not being able to be who she was.

Still other mothers transmit sophisticated skills to their children of how one can appear to submit to yet simultaneously challenge oppression. Willi Coleman's mother used a Saturday-night hair-combing ritual to impart an African American women's standpoint to her daughters:

> Except for special occasions mama came home from work early on Saturdays. She spent six days a week mopping, waxing and dusting other women's houses and keeping out of reach of other women's husbands. Saturday nights were reserved for "taking care of them girls" hair and the telling of stories. Some of which included a recitation of what she had endured and how she had triumphed over "folks that were lower than dirt" and "no-good snakes in the grass." She combed, patted, twisted and talked, saying things which would have embarrassed or shamed her at other times. (Coleman 1987:34)

Historian Elsa Barkley Brown captures the delicate balance that racial ethnic mothers must achieve. Brown (1989) points out that her mother's behavior demonstrated the "need to teach me to live my life one way and, at the same time, to provide all the tools I would need to live it quite differently" (p. 929).

For women of color, the struggle to maintain an independent racial identity has taken many forms, all revealing varying solutions to the dialectical relation between institutions that would deny their children their humanity and their children's right to exist as self-defined people. Like Willi Coleman's mother, African American women draw upon a long-standing Afrocentric feminist worldview emphasizing the importance of self-definition and self-reliance, and the necessity of demanding respect from others (Collins 1990; Terborg-Penn 1986).

Poet and essayist Gloria Anzaldúa (1987) challenges many of the ideas in Latino cultures concerning women: "Though I'll defend my race and culture when they are attacked by non-mexicanos, . . . I abhor some of my culture's ways, how it cripples its women, *como burras*, our strengths used against us" (p. 21). Anzaldúa offers a trenchant analysis of the ways in which the Spanish conquest of Native Americans fragmented women's identity and produced three symbolic "mothers." *La Virgen de Guadalupe*, perhaps the single most potent religious, political, and cultural image of the Chicano people, represents the virgin mother who cares for and nurtures an oppressed people. *La Chingada (Malinche)* represents the raped mother, all but abandoned. A combination of the first two, *la Llorona*, symbolizes the mother who seeks her lost children. "Ambiguity surrounds the symbols of these three 'Our Mothers,'" claims Anzaldúa (1987). "In part, the true identity of all three has been subverted — *Guadalupe* to make us docile and enduring, *la Chingada* to make us ashamed of our Indian side, and *la Llorona* to make us a long-suffering people" (p. 31). For Anzaldúa (1987), the Spanish conquest that brought racism and economic subordination to Indian people and created a new mixed-race Latino people simultaneously devalued women:

> No, I do not buy all the myths of the tribe into which I was born. I can understand why the more tinged with Anglo blood, the more adamantly my colored and colorless sisters glorify their colored culture's values — to offset the extreme devaluation of it by the white culture. It's a legitimate reaction. But I will not glorify those aspects of my culture which have injured me and which have injured me in the name of protecting me. (P. 22)

Latino mothers face the complicated task of shepherding their children through the racism of the dominant society and the reactions to that racism framing cultural beliefs internal to Hispanic communities. Many Asian American mothers stress conformity and fitting in as a way to challenge the system. "Our parents are painted as hard workers who were socially uncomfortable and had difficulty expressing even the smallest opinion," observes Japanese American Kesaya Noda in her autobiographical essay "Growing Up Asian in America" (1989:246). Noda questioned this seeming capitulation on the part of her parents: "'Why did you go into those camps,' I raged at my parents, frightened by my own inner silence and timidity. 'Why didn't you do anything to resist?'" But Noda (1989) later discovers a compelling explanation as to why Asian Americans are so often portrayed as conforming: "I had not been able to imagine before what it must have felt like to be an American — to know absolutely that one is an American — and yet to have almost everyone else deny it. Not only deny it, but challenge that identity with machine guns and troops of white American soldiers. In those circumstances it was difficult to say, 'I'm a Japanese American.' 'American' had to do" (p. 247).

Native American women can draw upon a tradition of motherhood and woman's power inherent in Native American cultures (Allen 1986; Awiakta 1988). In such philosophies, "water, land, and life are basic to the natural order," says Winona LaDuke (1988). "All else has been created by the use and misuse of technology. It is only natural that in our respective struggles for survival, the native peoples are waging a war to protect the land, the water, and life, while the consumer culture strives to protect its technological lifeblood" (p. 65). Marilou Awiakta (1988) offers a powerful summary of the symbolic meaning of motherhood in Native American cultures: "I feel the Grandmother's power. She sings of harmony, not dominance. And her song rises from a culture that repeats the wise balance of nature: The gender capable of bearing life is not separated from the power to sustain it" (p. 126). A culture that sees the connectedness between the earth and human survival, and that sees motherhood as symbolic of the earth itself holds motherhood as an institution in high regard.

Concluding Remarks

Survival, power, and identity shape motherhood for all women. But these themes remain muted when the mothering experiences of women of color are marginalized in feminist theorizing about motherhood. The theories reflect a lack of attention to the connection between ideas and the contexts in which they emerge. Although such decontextualization aims to generate universal theories of human behavior, in actuality the theories routinely distort or omit huge categories of human experience.

Placing racial ethnic women's motherwork in the center of analysis recontextualizes motherhood. Whereas the significance of race and class in shaping the context in which motherhood occurs is virtually invisible when white, middle-class women's experiences are the theoretical norm, the effects of race and class stand out in stark relief when women of color are accorded theoretical primacy. Highlighting racial ethnic mothers' struggles concerning their children's right to exist focuses attention on the importance of survival. Exploring the dialectical nature of racial ethnic women's empowerment in structures of racial domination and economic exploitation demonstrates the need to broaden the definition of maternal power. Emphasizing how the quest for self-definition is mediated by membership in different racial and social class groups reveals how the issue of identity is crucial to all motherwork.

Existing feminist theories of motherhood have emerged in specific intellectual and political contexts. By assuming that social theory will be applicable regardless of social context, feminist scholars fail to realize that they themselves are rooted in specific locations, and that the contexts in which they are located provide the thought-models of how they interpret the world. Their theories may appear to be universal and objective, but they actually are only partial perspectives reflecting the white middle-class context in which their creators live. Large segments of experience, those of women who are not white and middle class, have been excluded (Spelman 1988). Feminist theories of motherhood thus cannot be seen as *theories* of motherhood generalizable to all women. The resulting patterns of partiality inherent in existing theories—for example, the emphasis placed on all-powerful mothers as conduits for gender oppression—reflect feminist theorists' positions in structures of power. Such theorists are themselves participants in a system of privilege that rewards them for not seeing race and class privilege as important. Their theories can ignore the workings of class and race as systems of privilege because their creators often benefit from that privilege, taking it as a given and not as something to be contested.

Theorizing about motherhood will not be helped, however, by supplanting one group's theory with that of another—for example, by claiming that women of color's experiences are more valid than those of white middle-class women. Just as varying placement in systems of privilege, whether race, class, sexuality, or age, generates divergent experiences with motherhood, examining motherhood and mother-as-subject from multiple perspectives should uncover rich textures of difference. Shifting the center to accommodate this diversity promises to recontextualize motherhood and point us toward feminist theorizing that embraces difference as an essential part of commonality.

ENDNOTES

1. In this chapter, I use the terms *racial ethnic women* and *women of color* interchangeably. Grounded in the experiences of groups who have been the targets of racism, the term *racial ethnic* implies more solidarity with men involved in struggles against racism. In contrast, the term *women of color* emerges from a feminist background where racial ethnic women committed to feminist struggle aimed to distinguish their history and issues from those of middle-class white women. Neither term captures the complexity of African American, Native American, Asian American, and Hispanic women's experiences.

2. Positivist social science exemplifies this type of decontextualization. In order to create scientific descriptions of reality, positivist researchers aim to produce ostensibly objective generalizations. But because researchers have widely differing values, experiences, and emotions, genuine science is thought to be unattainable unless all human characteristics except rationality are eliminated from the research process. By following strict methodological rules, scientists aimed to distance themselves from the values, vested interests, and emotions generated by their class, race, sex, or unique situation. By decontextualizing themselves, they allegedly become detached observers and manipulators of nature. Moreover, this researcher decontextualization is paralleled by comparable efforts to remove the objects of study from their contexts (Jaggar 1983).

3. Dominant theories are characterized by this decontextualization. Boyd's (1989) helpful survey of literature on the mother–daughter relationship reveals that though much work has been done on motherhood generally, and on the mother–daughter relationship, very little of it tests feminist theories of motherhood. Boyd identifies two prevailing theories—psychoanalytic theory and social learning theory—that she claims form the bulk of feminist theorizing. Both of these approaches minimize the importance of race and class in the context of motherhood. Boyd ignores Marxist-feminist theorizing about motherhood, mainly because very little of this work is concerned with the mother–daughter relationship. But Marxist-feminist analyses of motherhood provide another example of how decontextualization frames feminist theories of motherhood. See, e.g., Ann Ferguson's *Blood at the Root: Motherhood, Sexuality, and Male Dominance* (1989), an ambitious attempt to develop a universal theory of motherhood that is linked to the social construction of sexuality and male dominance. Ferguson's work stems from a feminist tradition that explores the relation between motherhood and sexuality by either bemoaning their putative incompatibility or romanticizing maternal sexuality.

4. Psychoanalytic feminist theorizing about motherhood, such as Nancy Chodorow's groundbreaking work *The Reproduction of Mothering* (1978), exemplifies how decontextualization of race and/or class can weaken what is otherwise

strong feminist theorizing. Although I realize that other feminist approaches to motherhood exist—see, e.g., Eisenstein's (1983) summary—I have chosen to stress psychoanalytic feminist theory because the work of Chodorow and others has been highly influential in framing the predominant themes in feminist discourse.

5. The thesis of the atomized individual that underlies Western psychology is rooted in a much larger Western construction concerning the relation of the individual to the community (Hartsock 1983). Theories of motherhood based on the assumption of the atomized human proceed to use this definition of the individual as the unit of analysis and then construct theory from this base. From this grow assumptions that the major process to examine is that between freely choosing rational individuals engaging in bargains (Hartsock 1983).

6. The narrative tradition in the writings of women of color addresses this effort to recover the history of mothers. Works from African American women's autobiographical tradition such as Ann Moody's *Coming of Age in Mississippi*, Maya Angelou's *I Know Why the Caged Bird Sings*, Linda Brent's *Incidents in the Life of a Slave Girl*, and Marita Golden's *The Heart of a Woman* contain the authentic voices of African American women centered on experiences of motherhood. Works from African American women's fiction include *This Child's Gonna Live*, Alice Walker's *Meridian*, and Toni Morrison's *Sula* and *Beloved*. Asian American women's fiction, such as Amy Tan's *The Joy Luck Club* and Maxine Kingston's *Woman Warrior*, and autobiographies, such as Jean Wakatsuki Houston's *Farewell to Manzanar*, offer a parallel source of authentic voice. Connie Young Yu (1989) entitles her article on the history of Asian American women "The World of Our Grandmothers" and recreates Asian American history with her grandmother as a central figure. Cherríe Moraga (1979) writes a letter to her mother as a way of coming to terms with the contradictions in her racial identity as a Chicana. In *Borderlands/La Frontera*, Gloria Anzaldúa (1987) weaves autobiography, poetry, and philosophy together in her exploration of women and mothering.

7. Notable examples include Lutie Johnson's unsuccessful attempt to rescue her son from the harmful effects of an urban environment in Ann Petry's *The Street;* and Meridian's work on behalf of the children of a small southern town after she chooses to relinquish her own child, in Alice Walker's *Meridian*.

8. Noticeably absent from feminist theories of motherhood is a comprehensive theory of power and an account of how power relations shape any theories actually developed. Firmly rooted in an exchange-based marketplace with its accompanying assumptions of rational economic decision making and white male control of the marketplace, this model of community stresses the rights of individuals, including feminist theorists, to make decisions in their own interest, regardless of the impact on larger society. Composed of a collection of unequal individuals who compete for greater shares of money as the medium of exchange, this model of community legitimates relations of domination either by denying they exist or by treating them as inevitable but unimportant (Hartsock 1983).

REFERENCES

Allen, P. G. 1986. *The Sacred Hoop: Recovering the Feminine in American Indian Traditions.* Boston: Beacon Press.

Andersen, M. 1988. "Moving Our Minds: Studying Women of Color and Reconstructing Sociology." *Teaching Sociology* 16 (2): 123–32.

Anzaldúa, G. 1987. *Borderlands/La Frontera: The New Mestiza.* San Francisco: Spinsters.

Awiakta, M. 1988. "Amazons in Appalachia." Pp. 125–30 in *A Gathering of Spirit*, edited by B. Brant. Ithaca, NY: Firebrand Books.

Boyd, C. J. 1989. "Mothers and Daughters: A Discussion of Theory and Research." *Journal of Marriage and the Family* 51:291–301.

Brant, B., ed. 1988. *A Gathering of Spirit: A Collection by North American Indian Women.* Ithaca, NY: Firebrand Books.

Brown, E. B. 1989. "African-American Women's Quilting: A Framework for Conceptualizing and Teaching African-American Women's History. *Signs* 14 (4): 921–29.

Chodorow, N. 1978. *The Reproduction of Mothering.* Berkeley: University of California Press.

Chodorow, N. and S. Contratto. 1982. "The Fantasy of the Perfect Mother." Pp. 54–74 in *Rethinking the Family: Some Feminist Questions,* edited by B. Thorne and M. Yalom. New York: Longman.

Coleman, W. 1987. "Closets and Keepsakes." *Sage: A Scholarly Journal on Black Women* 4 (2): 34–35.

Collins, P. H. 1990. *Black Feminist Thought: Knowledge, Consciousness and the Politics of Empowerment.* New York: Routledge.

Davis, A. Y. 1981. *Women, Race, and Class.* New York: Random House.

de la Cruz, J. 1980. Interview. In *American Dreams: Lost and Found,* edited by S. Terkel. New York: Ballantine Books.

Dill, B. T. 1988. "Our Mothers' Grief: Racial Ethnic Women and the Maintenance of Families." *Journal of Family History* 13 (4): 415–31.

Eisenstein, H. 1983. *Contemporary Feminist Thought.* Boston: Hall.

Ferguson, A. 1989. *Blood at the Root: Motherhood, Sexuality, and Male Dominance.* New York: Unwin Hyman/Routledge.

Flax, J. 1978. "The Conflict between Nurturance and Autonomy in Mother–Daughter Relationships and within Feminism." *Feminist Studies* 4 (2): 171–89.

Glenn, E. N. 1985. "Racial Ethnic Women's Labor: The Intersection of Race, Gender and Class Oppression." *Review of Radical Political Economics* 17 (3): 86–108.

——. 1986. *Issei, Nisei, War Bride: Three Generations of Japanese American Women in Domestic Service.* Philadelphia: Temple University Press.

Golden, M. 1983. *Migrations of the Heart.* New York: Ballantine Books.

Green, R. 1990. "The Pocohontas Perplex: The Image of Indian Women in American Culture." Pp. 15–21 in *Unequal Sisters,* edited by E. C. DuBois and V. Ruiz. New York: Routledge.

Hartsock, N. 1983. *Money, Sex and Power.* Boston: Northeastern University Press.

Jaggar, A. 1983. *Feminist Politics and Human Nature.* Totowa, NJ: Rowman & Allanheld.

Jordan, J. 1985. *On Call.* Boston: South End Press.

LaDuke, W. 1988. "They Always Come Back." Pp. 62–67 in *A Gathering of Spirit,* edited by B. Brant. Ithaca, NY: Firebrand Books.

Lerner, G., ed. 1972. *Black Women in White America: A Documentary History.* New York: Vintage Books.

Moraga, C. 1979. "La Guera." Pp. 27–34 in *This Bridge Called My Back: Writings by Radical Women of Color,* edited by C. Moraga and G. Anzaldúa. Watertown, MA: Persephone Press.

Noda, K. E. 1989. "Growing Up Asian in America." Pp. 243–50 in *Making Waves: An Anthology of Writings by and about Asian American Women,* edited by Asian Women United of California. Boston: Beacon Press.

Rich, A. 1986. *Of Woman Born: Motherhood as Institution and Experience.* New York: Norton.

Shanley, K. 1988. "Thoughts on Indian Feminism." Pp. 213–15 in *A Gathering of Spirit,* edited by B. Brant. Ithaca, NY: Firebrand Books.

Smith, D. E. 1990. *The Conceptual Practices of Power: A Feminist Sociology of Knowledge.* Boston: Northeastern University Press.

Spelman, E. V. 1988. *Inessential Woman: Problems of Exclusion in Feminist Thought.* Boston: Beacon Press.

Tajima, R. E. 1989. "Lotus Blossoms Don't Bleed: Images of Asian Women." Pp. 308–17 in *Making Waves: An Anthology of Writings by and about Asian American Women,* edited by Asian Women United of California. Boston: Beacon Press.

Terborg-Penn, R. 1986. "Black Women in Resistance: A Cross-Cultural Perspective."
Pp. 188–209 in *In Resistance: Studies in African, Caribbean and Afro-American History,*
edited by G. Y. Okhiro. Amherst: University of Massachusetts Press.

Wright, S. 1986. *This Child's Gonna Live.* Old Westbury, NY: Feminist Press.

Yamoto, J. 1988. "Mixed Bloods, Half Breeds, Mongrels, Hybrids." Pp. 22–24 in
Changing Our Power: An Introduction to Women's Studies, edited by J. W. Cochran,
D. Langston, and C. Woodward. Dubuque, IA: Kendall/Hunt.

Yu, C. Y. 1989. "The World of Our Grandmothers." Pp. 33–41 in *Making Waves: An
Anthology of Writings by and about Asian American Women,* edited by Asian Women
United of California. Boston: Beacon Press.

23

TEENAGE MOTHERING ON THE NAVAJO RESERVATION

An Examination of Intergenerational Perceptions and Beliefs

ROCHELLE L. DALLA • WENDY C. GAMBLE

Teenage parenting, characterized as a "crisis" by some[1] and an "alternative life course strategy" by others,[2] comprises an issue of debate and concern among policy makers, academicians, educators, and social-service providers alike. Not surprisingly, teenage parenting has received considerable attention from behavioral scientists over the past three decades. Still, significant gaps exist in the current literature.

The majority of investigations have included Euro-American populations as the reference group, with secondary attention focused on Blacks and non-White Hispanics. Little attention has been afforded Navajo (and other Native American) teenage mothers. The individuals participating in the present study reside on the Navajo Reservation in Arizona. The Navajo Nation is the largest tribe in North America,[3] occupies the most expansive reservation,[4] and experiences higher rates of teenage childbirth among youth aged fifteen to nineteen than among similarly aged women across the

Rochelle L. Dalla and Wendy C. Gamble, "Teenage Mothering on the Navajo Reservation: An Examination of Intergenerational Perceptions and Beliefs" from *American Indian Culture and Research Journal* 25:1 (2001): 1–19. Reprinted with the permission of the authors and the UCLA American Indian Studies Center.

United States as a whole (15.8 percent versus 12 percent).[5] Beyond the public health data, little information exists regarding Navajo perceptions or attitudes toward parenting in general, or teenage parenting specifically. By focusing attention on majority groups and generalizing findings to non-majority populations, unique cultural and contextual influences are overlooked. Teenage parents, in general, do not comprise a homogenous group.[6] Knowledge of unique influences that shape attitudes and behaviors is paramount for successfully assisting youthful adaptation to the parenting role.

Accurately representing what those attitudes and behaviors are and the forces that shape them depends largely on the methodology employed by the investigator. Despite the scientific strength of obtaining multiple perspectives, most investigations of attitudes and behaviors relevant for understanding adolescent pregnancy and parenting have included teenage mothers only. Occasionally, perspectives of the teenagers' partners or from teenage fathers have been included.[7] Numerous investigations have also examined teenage parenting from a multigenerational perspective.[8] Yet investigations including the perspectives of the teenage mothers, their own mothers, and adolescent fathers simultaneously are noticeably absent in contemporary teenage parenting literature. The voices of other community members, who may provide a unique perspective on teenage parenting, have often been overlooked as well.

The teenage parenting literature also lacks a comprehensive base of information regarding the relationships between teenage mothers and their male partners, the fathers of their children. Social support literature provides cursory data regarding male partners of teenage mothers. Adolescent mothers seek more support from family members, and particularly their own mothers,[9] than from partners or husbands.[10] Racial differences are evident with regard to marital status among teenage mothers, in that White and Black women tend to remain single and live with their families of origin for extensive periods following the birth of their first child,[11] while Hispanic youth are more likely to be married or living with a partner.[12] Regardless of ethnicity, male partners often provide a relatively large portion of financial and economic support to young mothers,[13] although this tends to diminish with time.[14] Still, a paucity of information exists regarding the development and maintenance of those relationships before and after discovery of an unexpected pregnancy, or the dissolution of the relationship. This investigation seeks to explore these unanswered questions.

The primary objective of this investigation is to compare attitudes of the meaning of the term *mother*, the maternal role generally, and teenage parenting specifically among (a) two generations of Navajo and (b) individuals representing diverse roles within the community. Second, this investigation seeks to examine the relationships between adult Navajo men and women, and between teenage Navajo mothers and their partners.

This investigation attempts to address gaps identified in the teenage parenting literature by (a) examining teenage parenting among a unique population; (b) incorporating multiple points of view from individuals from

different generations who occupy various roles; (c) examining the development and dissolution of male/female teenage parenting relationships; and
(d) adopting qualitative assessment techniques to allow for the full expression of participants' attitudes and perceptions. Given the scarcity of current,
theoretically driven research-based literature on the Navajo and the lack of
empirically standardized instruments available for use with Native American populations, qualitative methods were deemed essential for the success
of this investigation.

Guiding Framework

In her seminal work, Kristin Luker explores historical-political influences
on adolescent reproductive choices and the social construction of adolescent childbearing as a "problem" or "epidemic."[15] She provides an analysis of adolescent pregnancy and parenting in the United States, with a
particular focus on Whites and Blacks. Luker argues that the social context
in which teenagers make life decisions is a product of three decades of
changes in public attitudes toward sexual and reproductive behavior,
family structure, and gender roles.[16] She contends that existing data sets
are inadequate for identifying and understanding the forces that shape the
way American teens, and particularly teens of color, make reproductive,
marital, and life decisions. She further argues that critical information,
namely how women view their own lives and circumstances, is rarely
described in the literature. The challenge for researchers of adolescent parenting is to develop frameworks that account for personal decisions about
sexuality and parenting within unique social and cultural contexts. The
present study explores the context in which Navajo adolescents make
reproductive and life choices against the backdrop of their own, their
mother's, and adult community members' perceptions of traditional and
contemporary attitudes.

Within the developmental field, Urie Bronfenbrenner's most recent formulation of Ecological Systems Theory describes the necessity of examining
the interplay between person and environment through time.[17] Other theoretical perspectives similarly argue for examining the social context. Lev
Vygotsky presents a compelling conceptualization of the processes by which
cultural factors contribute to individual development.[18] The tenets of Vygotsky's developmental theory illustrate the critical connection between culture,
history, and environment, and the resulting influence on human development.
He asserts that (a) the human species continually creates and elaborates its
environment in the form of culture; (b) the evolution of culture is seen as a
historical process that has taken different forms across space and time; and
(c) human beings are not only a culture-producing species, but are also
culture produced.[19]

An ethnogenetic model examining constancy and change in relation to
both person and environment guides this investigation. *Ethnogenetic* refers

to the process whereby people come into and modify the terms of their existence and assumes that characteristics of the social context—a product of cultural, historical, and current environmental processes—influence every transaction. A brief history of the Navajo is thus necessary to interpret current perceptions of Navajo teen pregnancy and parenting in the social context in which it emerges.

Brief Historical Background

The Navajo trace their descent matrilineally (through the mother's line) and historically reside with the wife's family after marriage.[20] Children traditionally served as a source of security for their aging parents. Extended families and the maternal role were highly valued, as evidenced in Navajo cosmological beliefs, ceremonies, and prayers.[21]

According to the Navajo, First Man and First Woman were created by the Diyin Diné (Holy People), although they had no definite form or shape.[22] First Man and First Woman built a sweathouse at the place of emergence and "sang into existence the world as the Navajo now know it."[23] As described by Maureen Trudelle Schwartz,[24] the perfect order of that world was disrupted; women began giving birth to monsters whose presence in the world resulted in the loss of reproductive capacity among plants, animals, and humans. The Diyin Diné intervened and arranged for First Man to find Changing Woman (Asdzáá Nádleehé). She matured miraculously and began menstruating after twelve days. Her menstruation symbolized the restoration of power and fertility on the earth; the Kinaaldá was celebrated in honor of the event. Changing Woman gave birth to twin sons, Monster Slayer and Born for Water, who destroyed all monsters except Hunger, Poverty, Old Age, and Lice. Changing Woman was lonely, so she created the first four Navajo clans by rubbing skin from her own body.[25] From these people, the present-day Navajo clans and all their descendants were created.[26] The life, death, and rebirth of Changing Woman is mirrored in the changing seasons; she is considered the mother of all life on earth.[27]

The significance of fertility and the role of Navajo women in providing and maintaining the life of their children is further depicted in cultural symbols and ceremonial practices. For instance, yellow-corn pollen is considered "the single most sacred item in the Navajo universe," and was fed to Changing Woman by First Man and First Woman, providing her with generative powers.[28] Moreover, contemporary Navajo females are initiated into adulthood through the traditional sacred Kinaaldá ceremony, during which young women symbolically become Changing Woman, reinforcing their own procreative powers.

Yet tremendous economic, political, and social changes have transformed the Navajo Reservation.[29] Land comprising the Navajo Reservation is rich with natural resources, including petroleum, uranium, vanadium, helium, coal, and other renewable resources.[30] The Navajo have little control over these resources, however, as profits largely go to outsiders. Wolfgang Lindig further notes that although jewelry and craft sales contribute to family income, wages earned off the reservation are becoming increasingly important.[31]

Reservation social and economic changes have resulted in dramatic transformations in the status of Navajo women. According to Mary Shepardson, stock reduction (beginning in 1933) marginalized Navajo women's status.[32] Traditionally, sheep herding was integral to Navajo subsistence and economy. Being a matrilineal society, women owned and cared for their own herds.[33] Stock reduction, a federally enforced act, devastated Navajo woman because they possessed few alternatives for wage work. Men occupied the most available and lucrative positions in forestry, irrigation, road building, and construction.[34] Between 1950 and 1980, the status of Navajo women again began to reverse with expanding educational and employment opportunities. Due to the implementation of electricity and indoor plumbing, the standard of living also began to rise, as did the health status and life expectancy of Navajo people. The inception of the Indian Health Service (IHS) in 1955 dramatically reduced maternal and perinatal mortality and morbidity.[35] Despite improved health service delivery and technological advancements, the Navajo Reservation is still characterized by persistent poverty, substandard housing, limited educational opportunities, and high rates of academic failure, unemployment and underemployment.[36]

Given the historical, social, and economic changes experienced by the Navajo, how are contemporary Navajo women, and mothers specifically, perceived in reservation communities? How do they view their own lives and circumstances, and do these views vary by generation or in light of the role the individual occupies? Does evidence exist to suggest that adolescent teenage parenting is encouraged, however subtly, through family and community attitudes, thus accounting for the higher-than-average rates of adolescent parenting on the Navajo Reservation? Finally, how are contemporary relationships between Navajo men and women, and between teenage mothers and their male partners, described? . . .

Sample

Twenty-five individuals comprised the final sample, which included teenage mothers, their mothers, community informants, and teenage fathers. Eight Navajo teenage mothers were included. Interviewees ranged in age from sixteen to nineteen (mean age = 16.8 years). When the subjects first gave birth they ranged in age from fourteen to sixteen (mean age = 15.6 years). Most (*n* = 7) had one child only, two were pregnant with their second children, and one teenager was the mother of two children. The majority (*n* = 7) of the pregnancies were unexpected. Fathers of the children ranged in age from seventeen to thirty-six (mean = 21.4). Six of the teenage women participated in an alternative education program; two attended high school. One young woman was employed part-time, and several participated in extracurricular activities such as karate and basketball. Most teen mothers ($n = 6$) lived with their families of origin, although one lived with extended family and another with her partner. On average, seven individuals resided in each household; annual household incomes averaged less than $20,000 a year.

Flexibility is a necessary component of field investigations. Thus, although the mother of each teenage participant was sought for inclusion, two compromises were made. First, one of the teenage-mother participants asked that her mother not be included in the study; her wishes were respected and her mother was not contacted. In the second case, the mother of another teen was asked to participate, but refused. The young woman's grandmother (the great-grandmother of her child) was included instead. Subsequently, seven women comprised the "grandmother" group. They ranged in age from forty-one to fifty-seven years (mean age = 44.9), with the great-grandmother being the oldest. Most of these women ($n = 6$) were divorced or separated; one was a widower. All reported being married for the first time between the ages of nineteen and twenty-three and as having their first child between the ages of twenty and twenty-four. They reported having from one to six children (mean number of children = 4.6).

Four teenage fathers also participated. They ranged in age from eighteen to twenty-one years (mean age = 19.2). Two of these men, one nineteen-year-old and the twenty-one-year-old, were the partners of two of the teenage mother participants. One of the participating fathers attended high school, two had dropped out and were employed, and one was neither employed nor a high school graduate. All were born and raised in the target community.

The final participant group ($n = 6$) was represented by individuals holding diverse roles and occupations throughout the community, including two teachers from the alternative high school; a nurse; a drug/alcohol abuse counselor; a delegate to the Navajo Nation (a position equivalent to that of a city mayor); and a traditional Navajo healer. Three, including the two alternative school teachers and the high school nurse, were Caucasian and had lived in the community for an average of 3.4 years. They were included because they had direct, extensive, and daily contact with the teenage mothers, their families, and their male partners. . . . (All participants were given pseudonyms.)

Results

The Meaning of **Mother,** *the Maternal Role, and Teenage Parenting across Different Generations and Individuals*

"Women," according to one community informant, "have always been respected among the Navajo." This statement was reiterated by many, and the reasons provided for women's high status was reportedly related to their procreative ability and familial role. One community member explained, "the role of the woman is exalted because she has babies." And according to another, "In our tradition . . . it's the women that really hold the families together."

Most of the grandmothers agreed, noting that although they were mothers and grandmothers, they continued to view their own mothers as sources of comfort and support. When asked where she found strength to raise her six children alone, one grandmother explained, "My mother — my mother is the one." Another grandmother explained,

> *Women are the head of the household. They're the ones that are the backbone of the family because they're the ones that are at home all the time. Even a long time ago, that's what my mom tells me . . . and I think it's true, even today, that women [are] still the head of the household.*

Most participants reported believing that the roles of Navajo women and the status afforded them has changed little from more traditional times. When asked to compare women's roles of the past with demands of the present, one participant explained that, "In many ways it's the same as it's always been — to be mature, responsible, to take care of the needs of the family."

Teenage parenting was described by research participants as normative in the past. But this view no longer prevails among the teenage parents, the grandmothers, or the community informants. Even the traditional Navajo healer agreed that "today, teenage parenting is too early." In contrast to traditional Navajo custom, he believes that marriage and parenthood should be postponed and educational goals pursued prior to taking on the roles and responsibilities associated with contemporary adulthood. In comparing traditional and contemporary attitudes toward teenage parenting, one grandmother explained,

> *[The girls] were married before and in that sense it was more stable, the girls knew that they were gonna be with this man and have children together and make a life. Now, the stability is not there.*

Similarly, of teenage parenting, Merlinda noted, "It's not okay. They are too young, they don't know what's happening." Unexpectedly, many of the attitudes conveyed by the grandmothers were reiterated by their teenage daughters. Because they were adolescent mothers, it was assumed that they would report greater acceptance of teenage parenting. Contrary reports emerged. Most described feelings of disapproval regarding adolescent parenthood. Palissa remarked, for instance,

> *This is not one of my everyday childhood dreams, like, "Oh, I want to have a baby." I didn't say that. When I was really young it was like, "No, I don't want to have a baby." And here it is . . . Why did I do this, why did I just turn around and go in the wrong direction?*

The shame Palissa feels is evident in her association of teenage mothering with "going in the wrong direction." Nonetheless, she believes that adolescent parenting on the Navajo Reservation is a reflection of broader, nonreservation norms, stating:

> *Traditionally, we're not supposed to have kids until we're married, but the world is changing. Now, it's just like anywhere else. We're put in a society*

where your people [non-Native, white] are like role models to us. . . . Teenagers
in cities get pregnant and here they get pregnant. This is just like anywhere else.

Although many of the young women reported deep commitment to their children and the maternal role, they also expressed guilt and shame for their unexpected pregnancies and feelings of being rejected by peers. Yana remarked, "I used to have friends but they just drifted off, they looked down on me because I got pregnant. Before they used to think I was real cool, now they just ignore me." Yana reported rejection from peers due to her unexpected pregnancy. In contrast, Rhonda A. Richardson, Nancy E. Barbour, and Donald L. Bubenzer report peers as a primary source of emotional support, interfering less than family.[37] Context, however, is significant. Yana's remark implies that the general attitude among youth was that teenage parenting was not condoned within the community, and perhaps was criticized.

Community informants reiterated that teenage parenting is not a community norm, although they did note that it is more acceptable on the Navajo Reservation than in non-reservation communities. One community informant summed up the prevailing attitude with the following remark:

. . . there's more acceptance of teenage parenting in this culture. . . . [B]ut there's
a lot of people around who say "you need to have an education, you need to go
to college, it's not good to have a baby when you're a teenager," but it will take
a long time for that to change, really radically change, because they've been
doing this for twenty thousand years.

In sum, participants described Navajo women, and mothers specifically, as powerful, strong, and family-oriented. She is perceived as the sustainer and maintainer of the Navajo family. Despite the value placed on children and life among the Navajo, teenagers were encouraged to finish school before having children. Moreover, all participants agreed that, although teenage parenting was not condoned, if an unplanned pregnancy occurred, family support typically remained strong.

The Development, Maintenance, and Dissolution of Relationships between Navajo Men and Women and Teenage Mothers and Their Male Partners

When questioned about the Navajo men and women, participants described an interesting comparison between traditional and contemporary roles. Whereas the role of the Navajo female was described as relatively consistent through time, with family as their primary responsibility, the traditional role of the Navajo male as primary economic provider no longer applied, given economic and social changes on the reservation, and particularly women's increasing economic viability.[38] Many reported feeling that loss of the traditional male economic role imparted serious consequences to the Navajo family and community, including the persistent abuse of alcohol and drugs by male youth and adult men. Navajo men were consistently described as existing on the periphery of the family unit, and as maintaining little contact with their families.

Questions relating to the male's role in the family and relationships between Navajo men and women revealed that divorce was frequently instigated by alcoholism, adultery, and abuse. Upon further probing, many grandmothers described making a choice between the health and welfare of themselves and their children and remaining with a man who threatened that security. Anita and her former husband, for instance, experienced a series of separations and reconciliations until she found her husband in a drunken stupor while in charge of their youngest child. She explained, "I thought, 'this is it, this is it. I can't go through this, the kids can't go through this—we can't live with this. It's not good for me, especially for the kids.'" Similarly, Merlinda left her husband after months of alcohol-related incidents nearly resulted in the removal of their children. Her husband had called from a bar asking her for a ride. After entering the bar to retrieve her husband, the police picked up the kids who were waiting outside, believing both parents were inside and drunk. She stated, "I thought, 'this is it, my kids aren't worth losing. I'm not going to lose my kids running around to look for a drunk person—so I divorced him.'"

Many of these women described themselves as independent and self-sufficient, with the ability to parent competently as single parents. Though single parenting is not desirable, divorce was reported as an acceptable solution to marital problems. When asked to describe her feelings about being a single parent and the sole breadwinner for a family of six, Anita replied, "[It] makes me feel stronger!" This view was shared by many of the adult women. Interestingly, despite considering themselves divorced, several of the grandmothers reported that they remained close with their former husbands and maintained frequent contact. Often, ex-husbands kept clothes and other belongings in the women's homes and they ate meals together. One of the grandmothers stated that her former husband built a home for himself directly behind hers following their divorce.

Attitudes toward divorce and separation, it was noted, had changed little across the generations. Indeed, most of the grandmothers were raised in single-parent homes. Karanna said, "My mom is in the same situation I'm in. She raised all nine of us by herself. . . . My dad was never home, he was the type that was always out there, drinking." And of her own mother's relationship with her father, Merlinda explained, "I guess finally she just decided that nothing was going to work and he'll never be home and he'll never help support her with the kids, so that's why she just let him go."

Most ($n = 7$) of the teen mothers reported being in long-term relationships (from two to six years) with the fathers of their children prior to becoming pregnant. Two of those relationships began while the women were in junior high. Only one young woman reported being single and as never developing a relationship with her daughter's father. Three of the young women described being in a long-term committed relationship with the fathers of their children. One explained,

> *[T]hey say marriage is just like you're going together. We are living together, but we're not legally married . . . papers are nothing to us . . . when we do get married the only thing that's changed throughout the whole big day [will be] my last name.*

Another described the relationship between herself and her partner in the following manner:

> *We're not married legally, but the things we've been through — the financial things, the responsibility of children, we even went to counseling. . . . [T]hose are things that a married couple goes through, so yeah, I do see us as being married 'cause we went through a lot.*

Still, it appeared that the teenage mothers were, or had been, involved in relationships very much like those their own mothers had described leaving. Although the majority of young women reported the desire for a strong, committed, and supportive relationship with the fathers of their children, most also described the unlikely probability that their wishes would materialize. When interviewed, only three of the seven young females were still involved with their children's fathers; only two of the three believed those relationships would continue. Descriptions from the teenage mothers regarding relationships with their male partners parallel those described by other investigators. Patricia L. East and Marianne E. Felice report, for instance, that contrary to the misconception of short-lived relationships between teenage mothers and their male partners, most young couples report having close relationships for some time prior to pregnancy.[39] Following delivery, however, the couple's relationship often changed with substantially decreased contact.

Four of the young mothers had recently (in the last three months) separated from their partners, primarily due to alcohol abuse and lack of emotional and financial support. When asked why she and her boyfriend had separated, for instance, Yana stated, "Because he takes drinking over his daughter and me." Several also reported being subjected to physical violence by their partners. Palissa explained:

> *[D]uring my last trimester, I'd say it was the hardest because my boyfriend wasn't there for me, he didn't see the baby being born . . . and he was very, very abusive. And, I was too young to be abused already.*

Of concern is that the words of this young woman imply that abuse was an expected part of adult male/female relationships. That she was too young to be abused was apparently more disturbing than the fact that she had been assaulted at all.

The male participants confirmed the reports of the young women. Two of the four admitted to heavy drinking and abusive behavior toward their partners. They also described providing their partners with support. Emmit, for instance, stated that he provided support by starting the vehicle in the morning and driving Monica to school and their son to daycare. He also picked them up in the evening. He reported hanging out with friends and playing basketball in the afternoon, as he had dropped out of school and was unemployed.

When asked to describe the hardest part of being a father, he replied, "just staying home; I want to go play basketball or go cruise or go do anything." Likewise, Tony was not ready to compromise his friendships and youth lifestyle for family responsibility. He and his partner were no longer together because

> *she didn't like me going out. Sometimes I used to take off with my friends and play basketball . . . and she didn't like it one bit. And I knew if I married her she'd be a lot worse and make me stay home, which I don't like doing.*

Despite traditional acceptability of teenage pregnancy in the context of marriage, grandmothers preferred that their own adolescent parenting daughters remain single, fearing that teenage marriage might prove detrimental to their daughters and grandchildren. As a case in point, Char explained not wanting her sixteen-year-old daughter to marry, even after learning of her daughter's pregnancy. She explained,

> *No, I didn't want that [marriage]. Even then I didn't want her to get married. He can still come to see her but I don't want no marriage. . . . To this day I still feel the same way. I'm not gonna change my mind just because there's a baby.*

Grandmothers reported wanting their daughters to remain single because of (a) the instability of teenage marriages and (b) their concern over the ability of the fathers to provide for their daughters and grandchildren. Marriage trends among economically disadvantaged Black families have been examined by William J. Wilson. He argues that economic viability, or the ability of a father (or soon-to-be father) to provide stable income is paramount in determining whether a couple will marry. Lacking financial support from their children's fathers, women are likely better off as single parents.[40] Perhaps changes on the Navajo Reservation, such as the expansion of economic opportunities for Navajo women, instigated changes in attitudes as well, such that generational norms, particularly in reference to marriage and teenage parenting, were also transformed. Char and others reported feeling that marriage was not expected of women, even adolescents with children. Rather, they emphasized the desire for their daughters to become self-sufficient with the ability to economically support their own families.

In sum, despite the status associated with Navajo women, incidents of physical and emotional abuse appeared frequently in participants' reports. Also, unlike the family role assigned Navajo woman, the role of the Navajo male is characterized as tenuous, as are relationships between Navajo men and women. The physical absence of men within the family sphere was often noted. Separation and divorce were reportedly common in the grandmothers' generation and among their children. Teenage mothers reported that relationships with their children's fathers began to deteriorate after the children were born. Most hoped to raise their children in environments free of drugs and alcohol, which for some meant raising their children alone. Single, teenage maternity is believed more desirable than early, unstable marriage. Grandmothers in particular encouraged their young parenting daughters to remain single.

Discussion

This investigation sought to examine perceptions of teenage mothering and relationships between Navajo men and women across generations and among individuals occupying diverse roles. The contemporary image of the Navajo mother has reportedly changed little from more traditional images emphasizing her role as giver and sustainer of life. Regardless of who was interviewed, the Navajo mother was described as the head of the family, the "kin keeper," so to speak.[41] Contrary to expectations, little evidence emerged suggesting that the high value placed on mothers, children, and life within Navajo culture accounts for the higher-than-average rates of Navajo Reservation teenage parenting. Indeed, most reported that teenage parenting was "not acceptable"; youth were expected to complete high school and gain employment prior to beginning families.

Relationships between Navajo men and women were also explored. The frequent absence of the Navajo male emerged as a central theme. Separation, divorce, and the subsequent production of female-headed households was the reported norm within the grandmother generation—a pattern being rapidly repeated by their teenage parenting daughters.

Single teenage mothering is of particular concern due to subsequently limited educational and economic opportunities. The academic careers of single teenage mothers may be severely attenuated if they are forced to drop out of high school.[42] Lacking educational and occupational skills, their ability to achieve financial independence will also be restricted. Lily Hechtman reports teenage pregnancy as the major cause of young girls leaving school.[43] Jeanne Brooks-Gunn and Lindsay Chase-Lansdale agree that a large number of teenage mothers do not complete high school, although they continue to note that Black teenagers are more likely to finish high school than their White counterparts after becoming mothers, suggesting familial support, particularly co-residence.[44]

All but one of the teenage mother participants were enrolled in an alternative school designed for youth at risk. The Navajo Reservation experiences high school dropout rates of approximately 50 percent.[45] Compared to urban dwellers, reservation-residing Native Americans experience higher rates of alcoholism, academic failure, illiteracy, illness, and poverty.[46] Subsequently, optimal well-being among children born to reservation-residing Navajo youth may be severely challenged. Although great variability exists in the developmental outcomes of teenage parents and their children.[47] The presence of multiple risk factors, with a corresponding lack of "protective factors," may result in psychosocial delays.[48] Common risk factors among teenage parenting families include father absence, multiple children in the home, maternal education less than twelve years, alcohol or drug addiction by parent, and poverty.[49] Despite the beneficial impacts of familial closeness and Navajo cohesiveness, reports from the teenage mothers, fathers, grandmothers, and other community members indicate that many of the teenagers' children are exposed to multiple risk factors identified above.

Environmental risk may prove exceptionally challenging for even the most supportive family unit.

Community contexts discouraging teenage parenting likely result in strong motivation among youth to pursue other roles reinforced within the community, such as academic success. Yet some communities, like that examined here, discourage teenage parenting but have little to offer their youth in terms of alternative roles. The tools and instruments that facilitate the building and strengthening of community assets lay, as noted by many, in providing accessible educational opportunities and youth programs. Community assets and unique programs aimed at assisting youth in obtaining their high school and college degrees would buffer many challenges associated with teenage parenting. One frequently mentioned problem was that day care services were not available for young parents attending school. The need for child care far surpassed the supply. Lacking child care, teens often missed school. The need to provide day care to parenting students was recognized, yet funding shortages limited services the school could provide. It was further reported that financial limitations severely restricted the educational opportunities of many students, not only teenage parents. To challenge and motivate youth to pursue educational goals, two needs were described: (1) role models and mentors working in career fields of interest; and (2) corporate funding to offset costs associated with secondary education.

Importantly, the Navajo culture was described as being in a state of transition, with traditional beliefs and practices becoming increasingly integrated with Western lifestyles and norms. The situation has created confusion among youth and their families, many of whom hope to maintain a distinct Navajo identity while simultaneously developing skills necessary for success in non-reservation communities. For families, teaching children about the traditional ways while finding a balance between customary behavior and contemporary expectations involves complex negotiation and sensitivity. Most of the young women reported wanting to integrate traditional Navajo practices with their own parenting, yet stated that they have little knowledge of such customs. Programmatic assistance that incorporates a holistic familial approach, traditional education, and contemporary parenting knowledge and information would likely be well-received among parenting Navajo youth.

ENDNOTES

1. Susan Codega, Kay Pasley, and Jill Kreutzer, "Coping Behaviors of Adolescent Mothers: An Exploratory Study and Comparison of Mexican-Americans and Anglos," *Journal of Adolescent Research* 5 (1990): 34–53.

2. Linda Burton, "Teenage Childbearing as an Alternative Life-Course Strategy in Multigeneration Black Families," *Human Nature* 1 (1990): 124.

3. D. Wilkins, *Diné Bibeehaáz Aanii: A Handbook of Navajo Government* (Tsaile, AZ: The Navajo Community College Press, 1987).

4. Wolfgang Lindig, *Navajo* (New York: Facts on File, Inc., 1993).

5. U.S. Department of Health and Human Services, Maternal and Child Health Branch, *Trends in Indian Health* (Washington, DC: Government Printing Office, 1991).

6. Elena Flores, Stephen Eyre, and Susan Millstein, "Sociocultural Beliefs Related to Sex among Mexican American Adolescents," *Hispanic Journal of Behavioral Sciences* 20 (1998): 60–82; Lorraine Klerman, "Adolescent Pregnancy and Parenting: Controversies of the Past and Lessons for the Future," *Journal of Adolescent Health* 14 (1993): 553–61.

7. Mark S. Kiselica and Paul Sturmer, "Is Society Giving Teenage Fathers a Mixed Message?" *Youth & Society* 24 (1993): 487–501; Patricia L. East and Marianne E. Felice, "The Partners of Adolescent Mothers," in *Adolescent Pregnancy and Parenting: Findings from a Racially Diverse Sample,* eds. East and Felice (Mahwah, NJ: Lawrence Erlbaum, 1996); Maureen A. Pirog-Good, "The Family Background and Attitudes of Teen Fathers," *Youth & Society* 26 (1995): 351–76. Research with teenage fathers has increased dramatically during the past five years.

8. Burton, "Teenage Childbearing," 123–43; see also Daphna Oyserman, Norma Radin, and Rita Benn, "Dynamics in a Three-Generation Family: Teens, Grandparents, and Babies," *Developmental Psychology* 29 (1993): 564–72; P. Lindsay Chase-Lansdale, Jeanne Brooks-Gunn, and E. S. Zamsky, "Young African-American Multigenerational Families in Poverty: Quality of Mothering and Grandmothering," *Child Development* 65 (1994): 373–93.

9. Jean Rhodes, Lori Ebert, and Adena Meyers, "Social Support, Relationship Problems and the Psychological Functioning of Young African-American Mothers," *Journal of Social and Personal Relationships* 11 (1994): 587–99; Gail Wasserman, Virginia Rauh, Susan A. Brunelli, Maritza Garcia-Castro, and Belkis Necos, "Psychosocial Attributes and Life Experiences of Disadvantaged Minority Mothers: Age and Ethnic Variations," *Child Development* 61 (1990): 566–80; Ann G. Bergman, "Informal Support Systems for Pregnant Teenagers," *Social Casework: The Journal of Contemporary Social Work* 70 (1989): 525–33; Donald G. Unger and Lois Pall Wandersman, "The Relation of Family and Partner Support to the Adjustment of Adolescent Mothers," *Child Development* 59 (1988): 1056–60.

10. Kris Kissman and Janet Shapiro, "The Composites of Social Support and Well-Being among Adolescent Mothers," *International Journal of Adolescence and Youth* 1 (1990): 247–55.

11. Patricia Voydanoff and Brenda Donnelly, *Adolescent Sexuality and Pregnancy* (Newbury Park, CA: Sage Publications, 1990); Frank Furstenberg, Jeanne Brooks-Gunn, and Lindsay Chase-Lansdale, "Teenage Pregnancy and Childbearing," *American Psychologist* 44 (1989): 313–20.

12. Diane de Anda, "Informal Support Networks of Hispanic Mothers: A Comparison across Age Groups," *Journal of Social Service Research* 7 (1984): 89–105.

13. Unger and Wandersman, "The Relation of Family and Partner Support," 1056–60.

14. Frank Furstenberg, Jeanne Brooks-Gunn, and Susan Morgan, *Adolescent Mothers in Later Life* (New York: Cambridge University Press, 1987).

15. Kristin Luker, *Dubious Conceptions: The Politics of Teenage Pregnancy* (Cambridge, MA: Harvard University Press, 1996).

16. Ibid.

17. Urie Bronfenbrenner, "Ecological Systems Theory," in *Six Theories of Child Development: Revised Formulations and Current Issues,* ed. R. Vasta (Philadelphia: Jessica Kingsley Publications, 1989), 187–249.

18. Lev Vygotsky, *Mind in Society* (Gambridge, MA: Harvard University Press, 1978).

19. Ibid.

20. Ruth Underhill, *The Navajos* (Norman: The University of Oklahoma Press, 1956); Gary Witherspoon, *Navajo Kinship and Marriage* (Chicago: University of Chicago Press, 1975).

21. Mary Shepardson, "The Status of Navajo Women," *American Indian Quarterly* 6 (1982): 149–31.

22. Maureen Trudelle Schwarz, *Molded in the Image of Changing Woman: Navajo Views on the Human Body and Personhood* (Tucson: University of Arizona Press, 1997).

23. Gary Witherspoon, *Language and Art in the Navajo Universe* (Ann Arbor: University of Michigan Press, 1977).

24. Schwarz, *Molded in the Image of Changing Woman*, 18–33.

25. Peggy Beck, Anna Lee Walters, and Nia Francisco, *The Sacred: Ways of Knowledge, Sources of Life* (Tsaile, AZ: Navajo Community College Press, 1992).

26. Underhill, *The Navajos*, 276.

27. Witherspoon, *Navajo Kinship and Marriage*, 65; Rose Smallcanyon, "Traditional Child-Rearing Practices of the Navajo Indians," *Family Perspective* 14 (1980): 125–31.

28. Witherspoon, *Navajo Kinship and Marriage*, 17.

29. Peter Iverson, *The Navajos* (New York: Chelsea House, 1990).

30. Vic Christopherson, "Rural Navajo Youth: A Challenge for Resource Development" (paper presented at the annual meeting of the Rural Sociological Society, Burlington, VA, November 1979); Stephen Kunitz and Jerrold Levy, "Ethnicity and Medical Care," in *Navajos*, ed. A. Harwood (Cambridge, MA: Harvard University Press, 1981); and Lindig, *Navajo*, 25–38.

31. Ibid.

32. Shepardson, "The Status of Navajo Women," 150–53.

33. Christine Conte, "Ladies, Livestock, Land and Lucre: Women's Networks and Social Status on the Western Navajo Reservation," *American Indian Quarterly* 6 (1982): 105–24.

34. Shepardson, "The Status of Navajo Women," 154–56.

35. B. Carol Milligan, "Nursing Care and Beliefs of Expectant Navajo Women," *American Indian Quarterly* 8 (1984): 83–101.

36. Indian Health Services, "Regional Differences in Indian Health" (U.S. Department of Health and Human Services: Office of Planning, Evaluation, and Legislation, 1992).

37. Rhonda A. Richardson, Nancy E. Barbour, and Donald L. Bubenzer, "Peer Relationships as a Source of Support for Adolescent Mothers," *Journal of Adolescent Research* 10 (1995): 278–90.

38. This idea emerged largely after federally imposed stock reduction and the increase in non-reservation employment opportunities available to Navajo men (see Shepardson, "The Status of Navajo Women," 150–54).

39. East and Felice, "The Partners of Adolescent Mothers," 103.

40. William J. Wilson, *The Truly Disadvantaged: The Inner City, the Underclass, and Public Policy* (Chicago: University of Chicago Press, 1987).

41. D. Wilkins, *Dine' Bibeehaz' Aanii*.

42. Jeanne Brooks-Gunn and Lindsay Chase-Lansdale, "Adolescent Parenthood," in *Handbook of Parenting: Status and Social Conditions of Parenting*, ed. M. H. Bornstein (Mahwah, NJ: Lawrence Erlbaum, 1995), 113–49.

43. Lily Hechtman, "Teenage Mothers and Their Children: Risks and Problems: A Review," *Canadian Journal of Psychiatry* 34 (1989): 569–75.

44. Brooks-Gunn and Chase-Lansdale, "Adolescent Parenthood," 114.

45. Flores, Eyre, and Millstein, "Sociocultural Beliefs Related to Sex among Mexican American Adolescents"; Klerman, "Adolescent Pregnancy and Parenting."

46. Teresa D. Laframboise and Kathryn Graff Low, "American Indian Children and Adolescents," in *Children of Color: Psychological Interventions with Minority Youth*, eds. J. T. Gibbs and L. H. Huang (San Francisco: Jossey-Bass, 1991) 114–47.

47. Frank Furstenberg, "As the Pendulum Swings: Teenage Childbearing and Social Concern," *Family Relations* 40 (1991): 127–38; Arlene Fulton, Kay Murphy, and Sarah Anderson, "Increasing Adolescent Mothers' Knowledge of Child Development," *Adolescence* 26 (1991): 73–81.

48. Luker, *Dubious Conceptions*.

49. Eric Dubow and Tom Luster, "Adjustment of Children Born to Teenage Mothers: The Contribution of Risk and Protective Factors," *Journal of Marriage and the Family* 52 (1990): 393–404.

24

MOTHERING FROM A DISTANCE

Emotions, Gender, and Intergenerational Relations in Filipino Transnational Families

RHACEL SALAZAR PARREÑAS

An increasing number of Filipina migrants are mothering their children from a distance. In order to provide for their families, they must leave them behind in the Philippines and take advantage of the greater labor market opportunities in other countries of Asia, Europe, and the Americas. One of the largest sources of independent female labor migrants in the world, the Philippines has seen the formation of a growing number of female-headed transnational families.[1] These families are households with core members living in at least two nation-states and in which the mother works in another country while some or all of her dependents reside in the Philippines. This article analyzes the emotional consequences of geographical distance in female-headed transnational families and examines the mechanisms by which mothers and children cope with them.

Without a doubt, mothering from a distance has emotional ramifications both for mothers who leave and children who are sent back or left behind.

The pain of family separation creates various feelings, including helplessness, regret, and guilt for mothers and loneliness, vulnerability, and insecurity for children. How are these feelings negotiated in the social reproduction of the transnational family?[2] Moreover, how are these feelings influenced by gender ideologies of mothering? The practice of mothering from a distance or "transnational mothering," as Pierrette Hondagneu-Sotelo and Ernestine Avila have called it, ruptures the ideological foundation of the Filipino family.[3] Unlike the "split households" of earlier Chinese, Mexican, and Filipino male migrants in the United States, the traditional division of labor with the father in charge of production and the mother of reproduction is contested in contemporary female-headed transnational households.[4]

This [reading] examines gender and intergenerational relations through the lens of emotion. I show that socialized gender norms in the family aggravate the emotional strains of mothers and children in transnational families and argue that the reconstitution of mothering led by female migrants from the Philippines is stalled by traditional ideologies of family life. I chose emotion as the central analytical principle of this article because emotional strains are prominent characteristics of the family life of migrant Filipina domestic workers. Moreover, these emotional strains beg to be understood systematically. As Arlie Hochschild has shown, emotions do not exist in a vacuum. Instead, they exist in the context of social structures in society. As she states, "Emotion is a sense that tells about the self relevance of reality. We infer from it what we must have wanted or expected or how we must have been perceiving the world. Emotion is one way to discover a buried perspective on matters." Regulated by "feeling rules," emotions are determined by ideologies,[5] and in the Filipino family, as in many other families, the ideology of woman as nurturer is a central determinant of the emotional needs and expectations of its members.[6] . . .

Methodology

This article is based primarily on open-ended interviews that I collected with female domestic workers in Rome and Los Angeles: forty-six in Rome and twenty-six in Los Angeles. I tape-recorded and transcribed fully each of my interviews, which were mostly conducted in Tagalog or Taglish (a hybrid of Tagalog and English), and then translated into English. I based my study on these two cities because they are two main destinations of Filipina migrants.

A little less than five months in Rome in 1995 and 1996 gave me ample time to collect forty-six in-depth interviews with Filipina domestic workers. The interviews ranged from one and one-half to three hours in length. I collected an unsystematic sample of research participants by using chain and snowball referrals. To diversify my sample, I solicited research participants from various sites in the community (e.g., church, parks, and plazas).

In Los Angeles, I collected a smaller sample of twenty-six indepth interviews with Filipina domestic workers. These interviews range from one and one-half to three hours in length. I collected these interviews between April and September 1996. . . .

Characteristics of Sample

Although there are distinguishing characteristics between my interviewees in Rome and Los Angeles, they also share many social characteristics. Differences between them include regional origin and median age. Interestingly, there arc more similarities between them. First, most of them are legal residents of their respective host societies. In Italy, thirty of forty-six interviewees have a *permesso di soggiorno* (permit to stay), which grants them temporary residency for seven years. . . . With the legislation of the Martelli Law in 1990, migrant Filipina domestic workers became eligible to sponsor the migration of their families. Nonetheless, most of my interviewees have chosen not to sponsor the migration of their children.

In Los Angeles, fifteen of twenty-six interviewees have legal documents. Most of the women acquired permanent legal status by marriage or the sponsorship of a wealthy employer. Yet many have not been able to sponsor the migration of dependents, because they have been caught in the legal bind of obtaining legal status only after their children had reached adult age, when they are no longer eligible for immediate family reunification.

Another similarity between my interviewees in Rome and Los Angeles is their high level of educational attainment. Most of them have acquired some years of postsecondary training in the Philippines. . . .

Finally, more than one-half of my interviewees are married women with children. I was surprised to stumble upon this fact, because studies have indicated that Filipina migrants are usually young and single women.[7] . . .

The median age of interviewees suggests that the children of women in Rome are fairly young, and in Los Angeles, the children are older. The median age of my interviewees in Los Angeles is high at fifty-two. . . . In Rome, the median age of interviewees is thirty-one years old, significantly lower than my sample in Los Angeles. . . .

In contrast to the trend for shorter periods of separation among Mexican migrant families, the duration of separation among Filipina migrant domestic workers extends to more than two years for most families, usually encompassing the entire duration of settlement.[8] Significantly, parents with legal documents return to the Philippines sporadically. On average, they visit their children every four years for a period of two months. They attribute the infrequency of their return to the high cost of airfare and to the fact they cannot afford to take time off work. In addition, the fear of losing their jobs prevents them from visiting their families for an extended period of time. As they are limited to short visits to the Philippines, traveling is seen as an excessive expense of funds that could otherwise be used on meeting the costs of reproducing the family.

The Structural Context of Mothering from a Distance

The globalization of the market economy has triggered a high demand for female workers from developing nations, such as the Philippines, to supply low-wage service labor in more developed nations. In postindustrial nations such as the United States and Italy, their low-wage service labor (e.g., hotel housekeeping and domestic work) is needed by the growing professional population in global cities, meaning new economic centers where specialized professional services (e.g., legal, financial, accounting, and consulting services) are concentrated.[9] In newly industrialized countries, such as Taiwan and Malaysia, globalization and the rise of manufacturing production has also generated a demand for low-wage service migrant workers. Production activities in these economies have subsumed the traditional proletariat female work force who would otherwise perform low-wage service jobs such as domestic work. This shift in labor market concentration has generated a need for the lower wage labor of women from neighboring countries in Asia to fill the demand for service employment.[10]

In globalization, even though the "denationalized" economy demands the low-wage service labor of female migrants, the "renationalized" society neither wants the responsibility for the reproductive costs of these workers nor grants them the membership accorded by the contributions of their labor to the economic growth of receiving nations.[11] The entrance of migrant Filipina domestic workers into the global economy is wrought by structural constraints that restrict their incorporation into receiving nations. For example, various countries limit the term of their settlement to temporary labor contracts and deny entry to their spouses and children.[12] As a result, migrant Filipina domestic workers with children are forced to mother from a distance.

Receiving nations curb the integration of migrant Filipina domestic workers so as to guarantee to their economies a secure source of low-wage labor. By containing the costs of reproduction in sending countries, wages of migrant workers can be kept to a minimum. Moreover, by restricting the incorporation of migrants, receiving nations can secure for their economies a supply of low-wage workers who could easily be repatriated if the economy is slow.

Sending the message that only the production and not the reproduction of their labor is desired, nations such as Singapore and Malaysia prohibit the marriage or cohabitation of migrant Filipina domestic workers with native citizens.[13] Pregnancy is furthermore prohibited for Filipina migrants in the Middle East and Asia.[14] The liberal states of the United States and Italy are not exempt from the trend of "renationalization." In the United States, for example, lawmakers are entertaining the promotion of temporary labor migration and the elimination of certain preference categories for family reunification, including the preference categories for adult children and parents of U.S. citizens and permanent residents — the trend being to continue the labor provided by migrants but to discontinue support for their reproduction. In Italy, the "guest worker" status of migrant Filipinos coupled with their restricted options in the labor market encourages the maintenance of transnational households.

Only in a few countries are migrant Filipina domestic workers eligible for family reunification. They include Canada, the United States, and Italy. However, many structural factors deter migrant Filipina domestic workers in these countries from sponsoring the migration of their children. For instance, the occupational demands of domestic work make it difficult for them to raise their children in these host societies. In Italy, low wages force most day workers to work long hours. In the United States, most of my research informants are live-in domestic workers. As such, their work arrangement limits the time that they can devote to the care of their own families.

Consequently, as I have argued elsewhere, the increasing demand for migrant women to alleviate the reproductive labor of the growing number of working women in postindustrial nations has sparked the formation of an international division of reproductive labor.[15] Under this system, migrant Filipina domestic workers perform the reproductive labor of class-privileged women in industrialized countries and are forced to leave their children behind in the Philippines. Many in turn have had to hire other women in the Philippines to perform their own household work. In fact, many of the women in my study employ paid domestic workers to care for their families in the Philippines. In this sense, we can see the formation of a three-tier chain of the commodification of mothering between middle-class women in the United States and Italy; migrant Filipina domestic workers; and Filipina domestic workers in the Philippines who are too poor to afford the costs of emigration.

Filipina migrants leave or send children back to the Philippines in order to mediate other structural forces of globalization, including the unequal level of economic development between sending and receiving nations and the rise of anti-immigrant sentiments. Negotiating the unequal development of regions in the global economy, migrant Filipina domestic workers mother from a distance to take advantage of the lower costs of reproducing—feeding, housing, clothing, and educating—the family in the Third World. In doing so, they are able to provide their families with a secure middle-class lifestyle. The lesser costs of reproduction in sending countries, such as the Philippines, enable them to provide greater material benefits for their children, including the luxury of paid domestic help and more comfortable housing as opposed to cramped living quarters forced by high rents in global cities. In this way, the family can expedite its goals of accumulating savings and property.

Migrants also form transnational households in response to the pressure of nativism in receiving societies. Nativist grassroots organizations (e.g., Americans for Immigration Control and *Lega* in Northern Italy) aimed at the further restriction and exclusion of immigration have sprouted throughout the United States and Italy.[16] With anti-immigrant sentiments brewing, migrant parents may not want to expose their children to the racial tensions and anti-immigrant sentiments fostered by the social and cultural construction of low-wage migrants as undesirable citizens. These structural constraints prolong the length of family separation in migration as it may even extend to a span of a life cycle. Among my interviewees, for example, the length of separation between mothers and their now-adult children extends to sixteen years.

The Pain of Mothering from a Distance

When the girl that I take care of calls her mother "Mama," my heart jumps all the time because my children also call me "Mama."... I begin thinking that at this hour I should be taking care of my very own children and not someone else's, someone who is not related to me in any way, shape, or form.... The work that I do here is done for my family, but the problem is they are not close to me but are far away in the Philippines. Sometimes, you feel the separation and you start to cry. Some days, I just start crying while I am sweeping the floor because I am thinking about my children in the Philippines. Sometimes, when I receive a letter from my children telling me that they are sick, I look up out the window and ask the Lord to look after them and make sure they get better even without me around to care after them. (Starts crying.) If I had wings, I would fly home to my children. Just for a moment, to see my children and take care of their needs, help them, then fly back over here to continue my work. (Author's emphasis.) (Rosemarie Samaniego, widowed, Rome, migrated in 1991, children are ten, twelve, fifteen, eighteen, and nineteen years old.)[17]

Every day Filipina domestic workers such as Rosemarie Samaniego are overwhelmed by feelings of helplessness: they are trapped in the painful contradiction of feeling the distance from their families and having to depend on the material benefits of their separation. They may long to reunite with their children but cannot, because they need their earnings to sustain their families.

Emotional strains of transnational mothering include feelings of anxiety, helplessness, loss, guilt, and the burden of loneliness. Mothers negotiate these emotional strains in three central ways: the commodification of love; the repression of emotional strains; and the rationalization of distance, that is, they use regulation communication to ease distance. In general, individual women use all three coping mechanisms, although not always consciously. For the most part, they justify their decision to leave their children behind in the Philippines by highlighting the material gains of the family. And they struggle to maintain a semblance of family life by rationalizing distance. Although a few women explicitly deny the emotional strains imposed by separation on their children, most women admit to the emotional difficulties that they themselves feel.

Knowing that they have missed the growing years of children, mothers admit experiencing loss of intimacy in transnational families. In general, a surreal timelessness is felt during separation that is suddenly catapulted back to reality the moment the family reunites.

When I came home, my daughters were teenagers already. (Starts crying.)
*When I saw my family, I dropped my bag and asked who were my daughters.
I did not know who they were but they just kept on* screaming, *"Inay,
Inay!" [Mom, Mom!] I asked them who was who and they* said, *"I'm Sally
and I'm Sandra." We were crying. I did not know who was who. Imagine!
But they were so small when I left and there they were as teenagers. . . .*
(Ermie Contado, widowed, Rome, migrated in 1981, daughters followed
her in early 1990s.)

Confronted with the absence of familiarity, transnational mothers often feel an
unsurmountable loss over their prolonged separation from their children.

For the women in my study, this pain is usually aggravated by caretaking tasks of domestic work. Taking care of children is not just taking care of
children when, in the process of doing so, one cannot take care of one's own
children. This contradiction accentuates the pain of domestic work and
results in their simultaneous aversion and desire for this job. Ruby Mercado,
a domestic worker, states: "Domestic work is depressing . . . you especially
miss your children. I do not like taking care of other children when I could
not take care of my own. It hurts too much." Although a few domestic workers
resolve this tension by avoiding childcare, many also resolve it by "pouring
love," including Trinidad Borromeo, who states, "When I take care of an elderly,
I treat her like she is my own mother."

As I have noted, transnational mothers cope with the emotional tensions
of mothering from a distance by commodifying love. In the field, I often
heard women say: "I buy everything that my children need" or "I give them
everything they want." Transnational parents knowingly or unknowingly
have the urge to overcompensate for their absence with material goods.
Ruby Mercado states:

*All the things that my children needed I gave to them and even more because
I know that I have not fulfilled my motherly duties completely. Because we were
apart (since 1983), there have been needs that I have not met. I try to hide that
gap by giving them all the material things that they desire and want. I feel
guilty because as a mother I have not been able to care for their daily needs. So,
because I am lacking in giving them maternal love, I fill that gap with
many material goods. . . .* (Author's emphasis.)

Unable to provide her four children (now between the ages of eighteen and
twenty-six) with daily acts of caregiving, Ruby, not unlike other transnational mothers, feels insecure about the emotional bonds in her family. As a
result, she has come to rely on commodities to establish concrete ties of
familial dependency.

Transnational parents struggle with and do have regrets over separation,
but they are able to withstand these hardships because of the financial gains
that they have achieved in migration.

*I have been lonely here. I have thought about the Philippines while I am
scrubbing and mopping that floor. You cannot help but ask yourself what are*

you doing here scrubbing and being apart from your family. Then, you think about the money and know that you have no choice but to be here. (Incarnacion Molina, separated, Rome, migrated in 1991, two daughters in late adolescence.)

By working outside of the Philippines, parents obtain the financial resources that they need to ensure that their children eat daily meals of meat and rice, attend college, and have secure housing.

Although many migrant laborers outside of the Philippines have attained some years of postsecondary education, they have not been able to achieve a "secure" middle-class lifestyle in the Philippines. So, why do they bother to invest in their children's college education? The education of children is a marker of material security for migrant parents. It is a central motivating factor for migration. As a domestic worker states, *"The intelligence of my children would be wasted if they don't attain a college degree, that's why I made up my mind and I prayed a lot that I have a chance to go abroad for the sake of my children's education."*[18] Parents believe that the more educated children there are in their families, the greater the resources of the family and the lesser the dependence of family members on each other, which means there would be less need for a family member to work outside of the Philippines in order to support other members of the family.

Migrant mothers also cope with separation by repressing the emotional tensions in transnational families. Considering that larger structural forces of globalization deny migrant Filipina domestic workers the right to family reunification, they sometimes cannot afford to confront their feelings. As Dorothy Espiritu — a widowed domestic worker in Los Angeles who left her four (now adult) children between the ages of nine and eighteen — explains, lingering over the painful sacrifice of separation only intensifies the emotional hardships of providing the family with material security.

In answer to my question of whether it has been difficult not seeing her children for twelve years, she answered:

> *If you say it is hard, it is hard. You could easily be overwhelmed by the loneliness you feel as a mother, but then you have to have the foresight to overcome that. Without the foresight for the future of your children, then you have a harder time. If I had not had the foresight, my children would not be as secure as they are now. They would not have had a chance. (Pauses.) What I did was I put the loneliness aside. I put everything aside. I put the sacrifice aside. Everything. Now, I am happy that all of them have completed college.*

Although mothers usually admit that emotional strains are engendered by geographical distance, they also tend to repress them. In fact, some of my interviewees strategically cope with physical distance by completely denying its emotional costs. It had primarily been mothers who had two sets of children, one in the Philippines and the other abroad, who preferred not to discuss intergenerational relationships at all.

Despite their tendency to downplay the emotional tensions wrought by the formation of transnational households, migrant mothers struggle to amend this loss by regularly keeping in contact with their children in the Philippines. To fulfill their mothering role from afar, they compress time and space and attempt to counter the physical distance in the family via the telephone and letter writing. Most of my interviewees phone and write their children at least once every two weeks. In doing so, they keep abreast of their children's activities and at the same time achieve a certain level of familiarity and intimacy. As Patricia Baclayon of Los Angeles states: "There is nothing wrong with our relationship. I pay a lot for the phone bill. Last month, I paid $170 and that's two days of wages. They write too. Last week, I received four letters."

Ironically, the rationalization of transnational distance in the family, while reassuring for parents, could be stifling for children in the Philippines. At the very least, parents are more likely to consider prolonging separation, as they are reassured that separation is manageable and does not mean the loss of intimacy. The "power geometry" in the process of time-space compression is elucidated by feminist geographer Doreen Massey as having created distinct experiences:

> This point concerns not merely the issue of who moves and who doesn't although that is an important element of it; it is also about power in relation to the flows and the movement. Different social groups [in this case, mothers and children] have distinct relationships to this anyway differentiated mobility: some people are more in charge of it than others; some initiate flows and movement, others don't; some are more on the receiving end of it than others; some are effectively imprisoned by it.[19]

In transnational families, power clearly lies with the parent, in particular the migrant parent. The process of time-space compression is unidirectional with children at the receiving end. Migrant parents initiate calls as children receive them. Migrant parents remit money to children physically immobilized in the Philippines. Children are trapped as time-space compression convinces parents that they have maintained close-knit ties and allows them to keep their children waiting even longer.

From the commodification of love to the "technological" management of distance, my interviewees have found many ways to cope with family separation. Although they ease the barriers that spatial distance has imposed on their families, many still feel that intimacy can only be fully achieved with great investment in time and daily interactions in the family.

The Pain of Growing Up in Transnational Families

Regardless of household structure, whether it is nuclear, single parent, or transnational, intergenerational conflicts frequently arise in the family. As many feminist scholars have argued, the family is not a collective unit. Instead, the family represents an institution with conflicting interests, priorities, and concerns for its members. In transnational households, intergenerational conflicts are engendered by the emotional strains of family life.

Children also suffer from the emotional costs of geographical distance with feelings of loneliness, insecurity, and vulnerability. They also crave greater intimacy with their migrant parents. For example, the children in Victoria Paz Cruz's survey offer several reasons for their desire to reunite with their migrant parents: "I want them to share with us in our daily life and I want our family to be complete"; "So that they will be there when we need them"; and "We can share our laughters and tears."[20] Denied the intimacy of daily interactions, children struggle to understand the motives behind their mothers' decision to raise them from a distance. Unfortunately, they do not necessarily do so successfully.

Three central conflicts plague intergenerational relationships between migrant mothers and the children whom they have left behind in the Philippines. First, children disagree with their mothers that commodities are sufficient markers of love. Second, they do not believe that their mothers recognize the sacrifices that children have made toward the successful maintenance of the family. Finally, although they appreciate the efforts of migrant mothers to show affection and care, they still question the extent of their efforts. They particularly question mothers for their sporadic visits to the Philippines. As I have noted, most of the mothers whom I interviewed return to the Philippines infrequently, once every four years. . . .

Conclusion

Although enabling the family to maximize its earnings, the formation of female-headed transnational households also involves an emotional upheaval in the lives of transnational mothers and the children whom they have left behind in the Philippines. A central paradox in the maintenance of such households is the achievement of financial security going hand in hand with an increase in emotional insecurity, an impact that could however be softened by an alteration of the traditional gender ideologies in the family.

In mapping out the emotional wounds imposed by geographical distance on mothers and children in transnational households, I do not mean to imply that these wounds can only be healed by the return of migrating mothers. Nor do I mean to suggest that mothers are somehow at fault for deciding to maximize their earning potential by working abroad and leaving children behind in the Philippines. The root causes of these wounds extend beyond the individual female migrant to larger structural inequalities that constrain the options that they have to provide their children with material, emotional, and moral care to the fullest. Various structural inequalities of globalization force them to sacrifice their emotional needs and those of their children for the material needs of the family. These inequalities include legal barriers preventing the migration of dependents;

social stratification and the segregation of Filipino migrant workers to informal service employment in most host societies; economic globalization and the unequal level of development among nations; postindustrialization and the demand for female migrant workers; and the rise of anti-immigrant sentiments in receiving nations.

These emotional wounds are telling of the "stalled revolution" faced by women at the beginning of this millennium as they have yet to achieve full gender parity at home and at work.[21] The ideological foundation of the Filipino family has yet to experience a major rupture even with the high rate of women's labor force participation. The responsibility for emotional care remains with women even in families with fathers who provide a tremendous amount of emotional care to their children and mothers who give a great deal of material care. It is true that feelings of pain in transnational families are fostered by separation; however, they are undoubtedly intensified by the failure in a great number of families to meet the gender-based expectations of children for mothers (and not fathers) to nurture them and also the self-imposed expectations of mothers to follow culturally and ideologically inscribed duties in the family. As shown by the emotional tensions wrought by separation and the greater resentment of children about transnational mothers, rather than fathers, traditional notions of mothering haunt migrant women transnationally. Traditional views still have a deep hold on the most basic values of the youth in the Philippines. However, we can only hope that the "reconstitution of mothering" led by numerous female migrants from the Philippines will eventually seep into and shift the consciousness, values, and ideologies of the general public toward the acceptance of multiple variances of family life.

ENDNOTES

Authors' Note: This article benefited from comments and suggestions shared by Arlie Hochschild, Charlotte Chiu, Angela Gallegos, Mimi Motoyoshi, Jennifer Lee, and three anonymous readers. The University of California President's Office, Babilonia Wilner Foundation, and the Graduate School of University of Wisconsin, Madison, provided support during the writing of this article.

1. See Victoria Paz Cruz, *Seasonal Orphans and Solo Parents: The Impacts of Overseas Migration* (Quezon City, Philippines: Scalabrini Migration Center, 1987); and Maruja Asis, "The Overseas Employment Program," in *Philippine Labor Migration: Impact and Policy,* ed. Graziano Battistella and Anthony Paganoni (Quezon City, Philippines: Scalabrini Migration Center, 1992), 68–112.

2. By social reproduction, I refer, as defined by Barbara Laslett and Johanna Brenner, to "the activities and attitudes, behaviors and emotions, responsibilities and relationships directly involved in the maintenance of life on a daily basis, and intergenerationally." See Barrie Thorne, "Feminism and the Family: Two Decades of Thought," in *Rethinking the Family: Some Feminist Questions,* ed. Barrie Thorne and Marilyn Yalom, rev. ed. (Boston: Northwestern University Press, 1992), 3–30.

3. For an excellent article on the reconstitution of mothering in transnational households, see Pierrette Hondagneu-Sotelo and Ernestine Avila, "'I'm Here, but I'm There': The Meanings of Latina Transnational Motherhood," *Gender and Society*

11 (October 1997): 548–71. For a discussion of gender ideologies in the Philippines, see Delia Aguilar, *The Feminist Challenge: Initial Working Principles toward Reconceptualizing the Feminist Movement in the Philippines* (Metro Manila, Philippines: Asian Social Institute, 1988).

4. Evelyn Nakano Glenn, "Split Household, Small Producer, and Dual Wage Earner: An Analysis of Chinese-American Family Strategies," *Journal of Marriage and the Family* 19 (February 1983): 35–46.

5. Arlie Hochschild, *The Managed Heart: Commercialization of Human Feeling* (Berkeley: University of California Press, 1983), 85.

6. See Belinda Medina, *The Filipino Family: A Text with Selected Readings* (Quezon City, Philippines: University of the Philippines Press, 1991).

7. Examples of such studies include Christine Chin, *In Service and Servitude; Foreign Female Domestic Workers and the Malaysian "Modernity" Project* (New York: Columbia University Press, 1998); and Catholic Institute for International Relations, *The Labour Trade: Filipino Migrant Workers around the Globe* (London: Catholic Institute for International Relations, 1987).

8. Pierrette Hondagneu-Sotelo, *Gendered Transitions: Mexican Experiences of Migration* (Berkeley: University of California Press, 1994).

9. For excellent discussions on the labor market incorporation of migrants in urban centers of globalization, see Saskia Sassen, *The Mobility and Flow of Labor and Capital* (New York: Cambridge University Press, 1988), and *Cities in a World Economy* (Thousand Oaks, Calif.: Pine Forge Press, 1994).

10. See Chin.

11. For a discussion of the "denationalization" and "renationalization" of societies in globalization, see Saskia Sassen, *Losing Control? Sovereignty in an Age of Globalization* (New York: Columbia University Press, 1996).

12. For instance, see Chin.

13. See Abigail Bakan and Daiva Stasiulis, introduction to *Not One of the Family: Foreign Domestic Workers in Canada*, ed. Abigail Bakan and Daiva Stasiulis (Toronto: University of Toronto Press, 1997), 3–27.

14. See Mary Lou Alcid, "Legal and Organizational Support Mechanisms for Foreign Domestic Workers," in *The Trade in Domestic Workers*, ed. Noeleen Heyzer et al. (London: Zed Books, 1994), 161–77; and Pei-Chia Lan, "Bounded Commodity in a Global Market: Migrant Workers in Taiwan" (paper presented at the Annual Meeting of the Society for the Study of Social Problems, Chicago, 6–8 Aug. 1999).

15. Rhacel Salazar Parreñas, "Migrant Filipina Domestic Workers and the International Division of Reproductive Labor," *Gender and Society* 14 (August 2000): 560–80.

16. See the anthology edited by Juan Perea, *Immigrants Out! The New Nativism and the Anti-immigrant Impulse in the United States* (New York: New York University Press, 1997).

17. I use pseudonyms to protect the anonymity of my informants.

18. Gloria Acgaoili, "Mother, Behold Your Child," *Tinig Filipino*, May 1995, 14. Italicized sections are translated from Tagalog to English.

19. Doreen Massey, *Space, Place, and Gender* (Minneapolis: University of Minnesota Press, 1994), 149.

20. Paz Cruz, 43.

21. Arlie Hochschild with Anne Machung, *The Second Shift* (New York: Avon Books, 1989).

25

FATHERING
Paradoxes, Contradictions, and Dilemmas

SCOTT COLTRANE

The beginning of the 21st century offers a paradox for American fathers: Media images, political rhetoric, and psychological studies affirm the importance of fathers to children at the same time that men are becoming less likely to live with their offspring. Although the average married father spends more time interacting with his children than in past decades, marriage rates have fallen, and half of all marriages are predicted to end in divorce. Additionally, the proportion of births to unmarried mothers has increased dramatically for all race and ethnic groups, and single-mother households have become commonplace. These contradictory tendencies — more father–child interaction in two-parent families but fewer two-parent families in the population — have encouraged new research on fathers and spawned debates about how essential fathers are to families and normal child development (Blankenhorn 1995; Silverstein and Auerbach 1999).

Scholars attribute the current paradox in fathering to various economic and social trends. Whereas most men in the 20th century were sole breadwinners, contemporary fathers' wages can rarely support a middle-class standard of living for an entire family. The weakening of the good-provider model, coupled with trends in fertility, marriage, divorce, and custody, has resulted in the average man spending fewer years living with children (Eggebeen 2002). Simultaneously, however, men rank marriage and children among their most precious goals, single-father households have increased, and fathers in two-parent households are spending more time with co-resident children than at any time since data on fathers were collected (Pleck and Masciadrelli 2003). Although married fathers report that they value their families over their jobs, they spend significantly more time in paid work and less time in family work than married mothers, with most men continuing to serve as helpers to their wives, especially for housework and child maintenance activities (Coltrane 2000). Personal, political, religious, and popular discourses about fathers reveal similar ambivalence about men's family involvements, with ideals ranging from stern patriarchs to nurturing daddies, and public portrayals frequently at odds with the actual behavior of average American fathers (LaRossa 1997). We can understand these contradictions by recognizing that fatherhood has gained symbolic importance just as men's family participation has become more voluntary, tenuous, and conflicted (Griswold 1993; Kimmel 1996).

In this [reading], I summarize how fathering practices have varied across cultures and through history; highlight how different social, economic, and political contexts have produced different types of father involvement; . . . and examine findings about causes and consequences of father involvement. I end with a short analysis of debates over family policy and offer tentative predictions about the future of fathering in America.

Cross–Cultural Variation

Fatherhood defines a biological and social relationship between a male parent and his offspring. *To father* means to impregnate a woman and beget a child, thus describing a kinship connection that facilitates the intergenerational transfer of wealth and authority (at least in patrilineal descent systems such as ours). Fatherhood also reflects ideals about the rights, duties, and activities of men in families and in society and generalizes to other social and symbolic relationships, as when Christians refer to "God the Father," Catholics call priests "Father," and Americans label George Washington "the Father" of the country. Fatherhood thus reflects a normative set of social practices and expectations that are institutionalized within religion, politics, law, and culture. Social theories have employed the concept of *social fatherhood* to explain how the institution of fatherhood links a particular child to a particular man (whether father or uncle) in order to secure a place for that child in the social structure (Coltrane and Collins 2001).

Fathering (in contrast to *fatherhood*) refers more directly to what men do with and for children. Although folk beliefs suggest that fathering entails behaviors fixed by reproductive biology, humans must learn how to parent. In every culture and historical period, men's parenting has been shaped by social and economic forces. Although women have been the primary caretakers of young children in all cultures, fathers' participation in child rearing has varied from virtually no direct involvement to active participation in all aspects of children's routine care. Except for breastfeeding and the earliest care of infants, there are no cross-cultural universals in the tasks that mothers and fathers perform (Johnson 1988). In some societies, the social worlds of fathers and mothers were so separate that they rarely had contact and seldom performed the same tasks; in other societies, men participated in tasks like infant care, and women participated in tasks like hunting (Coltrane 1988; Sanday 1981).

Drawing on worldwide cross-cultural comparisons, scholars have identified two general patterns of fathers' family involvement, one intimate and the other aloof. In the intimate pattern, men eat and sleep with their wives and children, talk with them during evening meals, attend births, and participate actively in infant care. In the aloof pattern, men often eat and sleep apart from women, spend their leisure time in the company of other men, stay away during births, and seldom help with child care (Whiting and Whiting 1975). Societies with involved fathers are more likely than societies with aloof fathers to be peaceful, to afford women a role in community decision making, to have intimate husband–wife relationships, to feature more gender equality in the society, and to include nurturing deities of both sexes in their religions. Aloof-father societies are more likely to have religious systems with stern male gods, social institutions that exclude women from community decision making, marriage systems in which husbands demand deference from wives, and public rituals that focus on men's competitive displays of masculinity (Coltrane 1988, 1996; Sanday 1981).

Research on fathering among indigenous peoples such as the African Aka suggests why involved fathering and gender egalitarianism are associated (Hewlett 1991). Anthropologists such as Hewlett have drawn on Chodorow's (1974) work to suggest that when fathers are active in infant care, boys develop an intimate knowledge of masculinity, which makes them less likely to devalue the feminine, whereas when fathers are rarely around, boys lack a clear sense of masculinity and construct their identities in opposition to things feminine by devaluing and criticizing women (Hewlett 2000). In reviews of data on father involvement over the past 120,000 years, Hewlett concluded that fathers contribute to their children in many ways, with the relative importance of different contributions varying dramatically; that different ecologies and modes of production have a substantial impact on the contributions of fathers to their children; and that fathers' roles today are relatively unique in human history (Hewlett 1991, 2000).

Historical Variation

Historical studies have focused on practices in Europe, chronicling and emphasizing men's public lives: work, political exploits, literary accomplishments, scientific discoveries, and heroic battles. This emphasis shows how various economic, political, and legal practices have structured privileges and obligations within and beyond families. For example, the historical concept of family in the West is derived from the Latin *famulus*, meaning servant, and the Roman *familia*, meaning the man's domestic property. Linking institutional arrangements with linguistic forms tells us something important about men's relationships to families. Recent historical studies have focused more directly on men's ideal and actual behaviors in families, thereby documenting complexity and diversity in past fathering practices (e.g., Griswold 1993; Kimmel 1996; LaRossa 1997; Mintz 1998; Pleck and Pleck 1997).

Before these studies, many scholars erroneously assumed that changes in fatherhood were linear and progressive (Coltrane and Parke 1998). For example, early family history emphasized that peasant families were extended and governed by stern patriarchs, whereas market societies produced nuclear families, companionate marriages, and involved fathers. In fact, historical patterns of fathering have responded to a complex array of social and economic forces, varying considerably across regions, time periods, and ethnic or cultural groups. Although it is useful to identify how men's work and production have shaped their public and private statuses, actual family relations have been diverse, and fatherhood ideals have followed different trajectories in different regions of the same country (Griswold 1993; Mintz 1998; Pleck and Pleck 1997).

The economy of the 17th and 18th centuries in Europe and America was based on agriculture and productive family households. For families that owned farms or small artisan shops, their place of work was also their home. Slaves, indentured servants, and others were expected to work on family estates in return for food, a place to live, and sometimes other rewards. In this pattern of household or family-based production, men, women, and children worked together. Regional variations could be large, and fathers and mothers often did different types of work, but many tasks required for subsistence and family survival were interchangeable, and both mothers and fathers took responsibility for child care and training (Coltrane and Galt 2000).

Because most men's work as farmers, artisans, and tradesmen occurred in the family household, fathers were a visible presence in their children's lives. Child rearing was a more collective enterprise than it is today, with family behaviors and attitudes ruled primarily by duty and obligation. Men introduced sons to farming or craft work within the household economy, oversaw the work of others, and were responsible for maintaining harmonious household relations. The preindustrial home was a system of control as well as a center of production, and both functions reinforced the father's authority (Griswold 1993). Though mothers provided most direct care for infants and young children, men tended to be active in the training and tutoring of children. Because they were moral teachers and family heads, fathers were thought to have greater responsibility for and influence on children than mothers and were also generally held responsible for how the children acted outside the home (Pleck and Pleck 1997).

Because the sentimental individualism of the modern era had not yet blossomed, emotional involvement with children in the Western world during the 17th and early 18th centuries was more limited than today. Prevailing images of children also were different from modern ideas about their innocence and purity. Religious teachings stressed the corrupt nature and evil dispositions of children, and fathers were admonished to demand strict obedience and use swift physical punishment to cleanse children of their sinful ways. Puritan fathers justified their extensive involvement in children's lives because women were seen as unfit to be disciplinarians, moral guides, or intellectual teachers. Griswold (1997) pointed out, however, that stern unaffectionate fathering, though not confined to Puritans, was not representative of all of the population. In fact, most American fathers attempted to shape and guide their children's characters, not break them or beat the devil out of them. As more privileged 18th-century fathers gained enough affluence to have some leisure time, many were affectionate with their children and delighted in playing with them (Griswold 1997).

As market economies replaced home-based production in the 19th and 20th centuries, the middle-class father's position as household head and master and moral instructor of his children was slowly transformed. Men increasingly sought employment outside the home, and their direct contact with family members declined. As the wage labor economy developed, men's occupational achievement outside the household took on stronger moral overtones. Men came to be seen as fulfilling their family and civic duty, not by teaching and interacting with their children as before, but by supporting the family financially. The middle-class home, previously the site of production, consumption, and virtually everything else in life, became a nurturing, child-centered haven set apart from the impersonal world of work, politics, and other public pursuits. The separate-spheres ideal became a defining feature of the late 19th and early 20th centuries (Bernard 1981; Coltrane and Galt 2000; Kimmel 1996).

The ideal that paid work was only for men and that only women were suited to care for family members remained an unattainable myth rather than an everyday reality for most families. Many working-class fathers were not able to earn the family wage assumed by the separate-spheres ideal, and a majority of African American, Latino, Asian American, and other immigrant men could not fulfill the good-provider role that the cultural ideal implied. Women in these families had to either work for wages, participate in production at home, or find other ways to make ends meet. Although the emerging romantic ideal held that women should be sensitive and pure keepers of the home on a full-time basis, the reality was that women in less advantaged households had no choice but to simultaneously be workers and mothers. In fact, many working-class and ethnic minority women had to leave their homes and children to take care of other people's children and houses (Dill 1988). Even during the heyday of separate spheres (in the early 20th century), minority women, young single women, widows, and married women whose husbands could not support them worked for wages.

As noted above, attempts to understand the history of fatherhood have often painted a simple before-and-after picture: *Before* the Industrial Revolution, families were rural and extended, and patriarchal fathers were stern moralists; *after* the Industrial Revolution, families were urban and nuclear, and wage-earning fathers became companionate husbands, distant breadwinners, and occasional playmates to their children. This before-and-after picture captures something important about general shifts in work and family life, but its simple assumption of unidirectional linear change and its binary conceptualization contrasting men's patriarchal roles in the past with egalitarian roles in the present is misleading (Coontz 1992). Stage models of family history have ignored the substantial regional and race/ethnic differences that encouraged different family patterns (Pleck and Pleck 1997). For example, as most of the United States was undergoing industrialization, large pockets remained relatively untouched by it. The experience of white planters in the antebellum South was both like and unlike that of men in the commercial and industrial North (Griswold 1993). Another major drawback of early historical studies is the tendency to overgeneralize for the entire society on the basis of the experience of the white middle class. Even during the heyday of separate spheres at the turn of the 20th century, minority and immigrant men were unlikely to be able to support a family. Race and class differences also intersect with regional differences: Not only did southern fathering practices differ from northern ones, but slave fathers and freedmen in the South had much different experiences than either group of white men (Griswold 1993; McDaniel 1994).

The Emergence of Modern Fathering

Throughout the 20th century, calls for greater paternal involvement coexisted with the physical presence, but relative emotional and functional absence, of fathers (LaRossa 1997). Nevertheless, some fathers have always reported high levels of involvement with their children. By the 1930s, even though mothers bore most of the responsibility for care of homes and families, three out of four American fathers said they regularly read magazine articles about child care, and nearly as many men as women were members of the PTA (Kimmel 1996). Increases in women's labor force participation during the 1940s briefly challenged the ideal of separate family and work roles, but in the postwar era, high rates of marriage and low rates of employment reinforced the ideology of separate spheres for men and women. The ideal father at midcentury was seen as a good provider who "set a good table, provided a decent home, paid the mortgage, bought the shoes, and kept his children warmly clothed" (Bernard 1981:3–4). As they had during the earlier Victorian era, middle-class women were expected to be consumed and fulfilled by wifely and motherly duties. With Ozzie and Harriet–style families as the 1950s model, women married earlier and had more children than any group of American women before them. Rapid expansion of the U.S. economy fueled a phenomenal growth of suburbs, and the consumer culture from that era idolized domestic life on radio and television. Isolated in suburban houses, many mothers now had almost sole responsibility for raising children, aided by occasional reference to expert guides from pediatricians and child psychologists (Hays 1996). Fathers of the 1950s were also told to get involved with child care—but not *too* involved (Kimmel 1996). The separate spheres of white middle-class men and women were thus maintained, though experts deemed them permeable enough for men to participate regularly as a helper to the mother (Coltrane and Galt 2000; Hays 1996).

During the mid-20th century, separate-spheres ideology and the popularity of Freud's ideas about mother–infant bonding led to widespread acceptance of concepts like *maternal deprivation,* and few researchers asked who besides mothers took care of children, although some researchers began to focus on *father absence* during the baby boom era (roughly 1946–64). Empirical studies and social theories valued the symbolic significance of fathers' breadwinning, discipline, and masculine role modeling, even though few studies controlled for social class or measured what fathers actually did with children. Studies including fathers found that they were more likely than mothers to engage in rough and tumble play and to give more attention to sons than daughters (Parke 1996; Pleck 1997). In general, research showed that child care was an ongoing and taken-for-granted task for mothers but a novel and fun distraction for fathers (Thompson and Walker 1989).

Compared to the wholesome but distant good-provider fathers pictured on television programs like *Ozzie and Harriet* and *Father Knows Best* in the 1950s, a new father ideal gained prominence in the 1980s (Griswold 1993). According to Furstenberg (1988) "[T]elevision, magazines, and movies herald the coming of the modern father – the nurturant, caring, and emotionally attuned parent. . . . Today's father is at least as adept at changing diapers as changing tires" (p. 193). No longer limited to being protectors and providers, fathers were pictured on television and in magazines as intimately involved in family life. Fatherhood proponents focused on the potential of the new ideals and practices (Biller 1976), but researchers in the 1980s reported that many fathers resisted assuming responsibility for daily housework or child care (Thompson and Walker 1989). Some researchers claimed that popular images far exceeded men's actual behaviors (LaRossa 1988), and others suggested that men, on the whole, were less committed to families than they had been in the past (Ehrenreich 1984). In the 1990s, researchers also began to examine how the modern ideal of the new father carried hidden messages about class and race, with some suggesting that the image of the sensitive and involved father was a new class/ethnic icon because it set middle-class fathers apart from working-class and ethnic minority fathers, who presented a more masculine image (Messner 1993). Others suggested that the sensitive or androgynous parenting styles of new fathers might lead to gender identity confusion in sons (Blankenhorn 1995). . . .

The Potential Influence of Fathers

As scholars pay more attention to fathers, they are beginning to understand what influence their involvement might have on child development. Most researchers find that father–child relationships are influential for children's future life chances; (Parke 1996; Pleck and Masciadrelli 2003). The focus of this research tends to be on the positive aspects of fathers' involvement, though it should be noted that because men are more likely than women to abuse children or to use inappropriate parenting techniques, increased male involvement can lead to increased risk and negative outcomes for children, particularly if the father figure does not have a long-term relationship with the mother.

Many researchers continue to focus on fathers' economic contributions to children and report that fathers' resources improve children's life chances. Longitudinal research shows that children from one-parent households (usually mother headed) are at greater risk for negative adult outcomes (e.g., lower educational and occupational achievement, earlier childbirth, school dropout, health problems, behavioral difficulties) than those from two-parent families (Marsiglio et al. 2000; McLanahan and Sandefur 1994). Although comparisons between children of divorced parents and those from first-marriage families show more problems in the former group, differences between the two are generally small across various outcome measures and do not necessarily isolate the influence of divorce or of father involvement (Crockett Eggebeen, and Hawkins 1993; Furstenberg and Harris 1993; Seltzer 1994). For children with nonresident fathers, the amount of fathers' earnings (especially the amount that is actually transferred to children) is a significant predictor of children's well-being, including school grades and behavior problems (Amato and Gilbreth 1999; McLanahan et al. 1994; Marsiglio et al. 2000). Because the great majority of children from single-parent homes turn out to be happy, healthy, and productive adults, debates continue about how such large-group comparisons should be made and how we should interpret their results in terms of fathers' economic or social contributions (Amato 2000; Coltrane and Adams 2003).

Earlier reviews suggested that the level of father involvement has a smaller direct effect on infant attachment than the quality or style of father interaction, though time spent parenting is also related to competence (Lamb et al. 1987; Marsiglio et al. 2000). Preschool children with fathers who perform 40% or more of the within-family child care show more cognitive competence, more internal locus of control, more empathy, and less gender stereotyping than preschool children with less involved fathers (Lamb et al. 1987; Pleck 1997). Adolescents with involved fathers are more likely to have positive developmental outcomes such as self-control, self-esteem, life skills, and social competence, provided that the father is not authoritarian or overly controlling (Mosley and Thomson 1995; Pleck and Masciadrelli 2003). Studies examining differences between the presence of biological fathers versus other father figures suggest that it is the quality of the father–child relationship rather than biological relationship that enhances the cognitive and emotional development of children (Dubowitz et al. 2001; Hofferth and Anderson 2003; Silverstein and Auerbach 1999). Reports of greater father involvement when children were growing up have also been associated with positive aspects of adult children's educational attainment, relationship quality, and career success (Amato and Booth 1997; Harris, Furstenberg, and Marmer 1998; Nock 1998; Snarey 1993). Because of methodological inadequacies in previous studies such as not controlling for maternal involvement, most scholars recommend more carefully controlled studies using random samples and multirater longitudinal designs, as well as advocating caution in interpreting associations between fathering and positive child outcomes (Amato and Rivera 1999; Parke 1996; Pleck and Masciadrelli 2003). It will take some time to isolate the specific influence of fathers as against the influence of mothers and other social-contextual factors such as income, education, schools, neighborhoods, communities, kin networks, and cultural ideals.

We do know that when fathers share child care and housework with their wives, employed mothers escape total responsibility for family work, evaluate the division of labor as more fair, are less depressed, and enjoy higher levels of marital satisfaction (Brennan, Barnett and Gareis 2001; Coltrane 2000; Deutsch 1999). When men care for young children on a regular basis, they emphasize verbal interaction, notice and use more subtle cues, and treat sons and daughters similarly, rather than focusing on play, giving orders, and sex-typing children (Coltrane 1996, 1998; Parke 1996). These styles of father involvement have been found to encourage less gender stereotyping among young adults and to encourage independence in daughters and emotional sensitivity in sons. Most researchers agree that these are worthy goals that could contribute to reducing sexism, promoting gender equity, and curbing violence against women (but see Blankenhorn 1995).

Demographic Contexts for Father Involvement

As Furstenberg (1988) first noted, conflicting images of fathers are common in popular culture, with nurturing, involved "good dads" contrasted with "bad dads" who do not marry the mother of their children or who move out and fail to pay child support. Recent research suggests that both types of fathers are on the rise and that the demographic contexts for fatherhood have changed significantly over the past few decades. In many industrialized countries, at the same time that some fathers are taking a more active role in their children's lives, growing numbers of men rarely see their children and do not support them financially. In the United States, for example, single-parent households are increasing, with only about half of U.S. children eligible for child support from nonresident parents via court order and only about half of those receiving the full amount (Scoon-Rogers 1999). Both trends in fatherhood—toward more direct involvement and toward less contact and financial support—are responses to the same underlying social developments, including women's rising labor force participation and the increasingly optional nature of marriage.

Marriage rates have fallen in the past few decades, with people waiting longer to get married and increasingly living together without marrying. Women are having fewer children than they did just a few decades ago, waiting longer to have them, and not necessarily marrying before they give birth (Eggebeen 2002; Seltzer 2000). One of three births in the United States is to an unmarried woman, a rate that is three times higher than it was in the 1960s, with rates for African American women highest, followed by Latinas, and then non-Hispanic whites (National Center for Health Statistics 2000). It is often assumed that nonmarital births produce fatherless children, but recent studies show that most of the increase in nonmarital childbearing from the 1980s to the 1990s is accounted for by the increase in the number of cohabiting women getting pregnant and carrying the baby to term without getting married. Historically, if an unmarried woman became pregnant, she would marry to legitimate the birth. Today, only a minority of women do so.

In addition, an increasingly large number of American fathers live apart from their children because of separation or divorce. Because most divorcing men do not seek (or are not awarded) child custody following divorce, the number of divorced men who are uninvolved fathers has risen (Eggebeen 2002; Furstenberg and Cherlin 1991), although recent research shows that the actual involvement of fathers with children after divorce varies enormously, sometimes without regard to official postdivorce court orders (McLanahan and Sandefur 1994; Seltzer 1998). The number of men with joint physical (residential) custody has grown, though joint legal (decision-making) custody is still a more common postdivorce parenting arrangement (Maccoby and Mnookin 1992; Seltzer 1998). And although single father-households have increased in recent years, single-mother households continue to outpace them five to one. Demographers suggest that because of all these trends, younger cohorts will be less likely to experience sustained involved fathering than the generations that immediately preceded them (Eggebeen 2002).

Marriage and the traditional assumption of fatherhood have become more fragile, in part because an increasing number of men face financial difficulties. Although men continue to earn about 30% higher wages than women, their real wages (adjusted for inflation) have declined since the early 1970s, whereas women's have increased (Bernstein and Mishel 1997). As the U.S. economy has shifted from heavy reliance on domestic manufacturing to global interdependence within an information and service economy, working-class men's prospects of earning a family wage have declined. At the same time, women's labor force participation has risen steadily, with future growth in the economy predicted in the areas where women are traditionally concentrated (e.g., service, information health care, part-time work). The historical significance of this shift cannot be overestimated. For most of the 19th and 20th centuries, American women's life chances were determined by their marriage decisions. Unable to own property, vote, or be legally independent in most states, daughters were dependent on fathers and wives were dependent on their husbands for economic survival. Such dependencies shaped family relations and produced fatherhood ideals and practices predicated on male family headship. As women and mothers have gained independence by entering the labor force in record numbers, it is not surprising that older ideals about marriage to a man legitimating childbearing have been challenged.

Gender and the Politics of Fatherhood

In the 1990s, popular books and articles revived a research and policy focus that had been popular in the 1960s: father absence. For example, Popenoe (1996) suggested that drug and alcohol abuse, juvenile delinquency, teenage pregnancy, violent crime, and child poverty were the result of fatherlessness and that American society was in decline because it had abandoned traditional marriage and child-rearing patterns. Such claims about father absence often rely on evolutionary psychology and sociobiology and define fathers as categorically different from mothers (Blankenhorn 1995; Popenoe 1996). Even some proponents of nurturing fathers warn men against trying to act too much like mothers (Pruett 1993). Following this reasoning, some argue for gender-differentiated parenting measurement strategies: "[T]he roles of father and mother are different and complementary rather than interchangeable and thus the standards for evaluating the role performance of fathers and mothers should be different" (Day and Mackey 1989: 402). Some label the use of measures developed on mothers to study fathers and the practice of comparing fathers' and mothers' parenting as the *deficit model* (Doherty 1991) or the *role inadequacy perspective* (Hawkins and Dollahite 1997).

Because parenting is a learned behavior for both men and women, most social scientists focus on the societal conditions that create gender differences in parenting or find proximate social causes of paternal investment that outweigh assumed biological causes (e.g., Hofferth and Anderson 2003). Nevertheless, questioning taken-for-granted cultural ideals about families can cause controversy. When Silverstein and Auerbach (1999) challenged assertions about essential differences between fathers and mothers in an *American Psychologist* article entitled "Deconstructing the Essential Father," they received widespread public and academic criticism. Their scholarly article (based on a review of research findings) was ridiculed as "silliness" and "junk science" by Wade Horn (1999; formerly of the National Fatherhood Initiative and now Assistant Secretary in the U.S. Department of Health and Human Services), and the U.S. House of Representatives debated whether to pass a resolution condemning the article (Silverstein 2002). Clearly, debates about fathers, marriage, and family values carry symbolic meanings that transcend scientific findings. The contentious political and scholarly debates about fathers that emerged in the 1990s appear to be framed by an older political dichotomy: Conservatives tend to focus on biological parenting differences and stress the importance of male headship and breadwinning, respect for authority, and moral leadership (Blankenhorn 1995; Popenoe 1996), whereas liberals tend to focus on similarities between mothers and fathers and stress the importance of employment, social services, and possibilities for more equal marital relations (Coontz 1992; Silverstein and Auerbach 1999; Stacey 1996).

A full analysis of contemporary family values debates is beyond the scope of this [reading], but elsewhere I analyze marriage and fatherhood movements using data and theories about political opportunities, resource mobilization, and the moral framing of social issues (Coltrane 2001; Coltrane and Adams 2003; see also Gavanas 2002). In general, cultural tensions in the larger society are mirrored in policy proposals and academic debates about the appropriate roles of fathers and the importance of marriage. One cannot adjudicate among various scholarly approaches to fathering without acknowledging gendered interests and understanding the political economy of expert knowledge production. Recent policies and programs promoting marriage and fatherhood using faith-based organizations are designed to advance a particular vision of fatherhood. Whether they will benefit the majority of American mothers and children is a question that cannot be resolved without more sophisticated research with controls for mothers' parenting and various other economic and social-contextual issues (Marsiglio et al. 2000; Marsiglio and Pleck forthcoming).

Prospects for the Future

The forces that are driving changes in fathers' involvement in families are likely to continue. In two-parent households (both married and cohabiting), men share more family work if their female partners are employed more hours, earn more money, and have more education. All three of these trends in women's attainment are likely to continue for the foreseeable future. Similarly, fathers share more family work when they are employed fewer hours and their wives earn a greater portion of the family income. Labor market and economic trends for these variables are also expected to continue for several decades. Couples also share more when they believe that family work should be shared and that men and women should have equal rights. According to national opinion polls, although the country has become slightly more conservative about marriage and divorce than it was in the 1970s and 1980s, the belief in gender equality continues to gain acceptance among both men and women. In addition, American women are waiting longer, on average, to marry and give birth, and they are having fewer children — additional factors sometimes associated with more sharing of housework and child care. Thus, I predict that increasing economic parity and more equal gender relations will allow women to buy out of some domestic obligations and/or recruit their partners to do more. Middle- and upper-class wives and mothers will rely on working-class and immigrant women to provide domestic services (nannies, housekeepers, child care workers, fast food employees, etc.), thereby reducing their own hours of family labor but simultaneously perpetuating race, class, and gender hierarchies in the labor market and in the society. Some fathers in dual-earner households will increase their contributions to family work, whereas others will perform a greater proportion of housework and child care by virtue of their wives' doing less. Other men will remain marginal to family life because they do not stay connected to the mothers of their children, do not hold jobs allowing them to support their children, or do not seek custody or make regular child support payments. These two ideal types—of involved and marginalized fathers—are likely to continue to coexist in the popular culture and in actual practice.

The context in which American couples negotiate fathering has definitely changed. The future is likely to bring more demands on fathers to be active parents if they want to stay involved with the mothers of their children. For fathers to assume more responsibility for active parenting, it may be necessary to change cultural assumptions that men are entitled to domestic services and that women are inherently predisposed to provide them. Further changes in fathering arc likely to be driven by women's increasing independence and earning power. Ironically, women's enhanced economic position also makes them able to form families and raise children without the father's being present. In the future, men will be even less able to rely on their superior earning power and the institution of fatherhood to maintain their connection to families and children. Increasingly, they will need to adopt different fathering styles to meet specific family circumstances and to commit to doing things men have not been accustomed to doing. Some men will be able to maintain their economic and emotional commitments to their children, whereas others will not. Some men will participate in all aspects of child rearing, whereas others will hardly see their children. Unless living wages and adequate social supports are developed for all fathers (as well as for mothers and children), we can expect that the paradoxes, contradictions, and dilemmas associated with fathering described in this chapter will continue for the foreseeable future.

Author's Note: This chapter incorporates some material from a November 21, 2002, National Council on Family Relations (NCFR) Annual Conference Special Session, "Future Prospects for Increasing Father Involvement in Child Rearing and House-hold Activities," reprinted as "The Paradox of Fatherhood: Predicting the Future of Men's Family Involvement" in *Vision 2003* (Minneapolis, MN: National Council on Family Relations/Allen). I thank Marilyn Coleman, Lawrence Ganong, Joseph Pleck, Carl Auerbach, and two anonymous reviewers for valuable feedback on an earlier draft of this chapter.

REFERENCES

Amato, P. 2000. "Diversity within Single-Parent Families." Pp. 149–72 in *Handbook of Family Diversity,* edited by D. H. Demo, K. R. Allen, and M. A. Fine. New York: Oxford University Press.

Amato, P. and A. Booth. 1997. *A Generation at Risk: Growing Up in an Era of Family Upheaval.* Cambridge, MA: Harvard University Press.

Amato, P. and J. Gilbreth 1999. "Nonresident Fathers and Children's Well-Being: A Meta-Analysis." *Journal of Marriage and the Family* 61:557–73.

Bernard, J. 1981. "The Good Provider Role: Its Rise and Fall." *American Psychologist* 36:1–12.

Bernstein, J. and L. Mishel. 1997. "Has Wage Inequality Stopped Growing?" *Monthly Labor Review* 120:3–17.

Biller, H. B. 1976. "The Father and Personality Development." In *The Role of the Father in Child Development,* edited by M. E. Lamb. New York: John Wiley.

Blankenhorn, D. 1995. *Fatherless America*. New York: Basic Books.

Brennan, R. T., R. C. Barnett, and K. C. Gareis. 2001. "When She Earns More than He Does: A Longitudinal Study of Dual-Earner Couples." *Journal of Marriage and the Family* 63:168–82.

Chodorow, N. 1974. "Family Structure and Feminine Personality." Pp. 43–66 in *Woman, Culture and Society*, edited by M. Z. Rosaldo and L. Lampher. Palo Alto, CA: Stanford University Press.

Coltrane, S. 1988. Father–Child Relationships and the Status of Women." *American Journal of Sociology* 93:1060–95.

——. 1996. *Family Man*. New York: Oxford University Press.

——. 2000. "Research on Household Labor." *Journal of Marriage and the Family* 62:1209–33.

Coltrane, S. and M. Adams. 2003. "The Social Construction of the Divorce "Problem": Morality, Child Victims, and the Politics of Gender." *Family Relations* 52:21–30.

Coltrane, S. and R. Collins. 2001. *Sociology of Marriage and the Family*. 5th ed. Belmont, CA: Wadsworth/Thomson Learning.

Coltrane, S. and J. Galt. 2000. "The History of Men's Caring." Pp. 15–36 in *Care Work: Gender, Labor, and Welfare States*, edited by M. H. Meyer. New York: Routledge.

Coltrane, S. and R. D. Parke. 1998. "Reinventing Fatherhood: Toward an Historical Understanding of Continuity and Change in Men's Family Lives." Working Paper No. 98–12A. Philadelphia: National Center on Fathers and Families.

Coontz, S. 1992. *The Way We Never Were*. New York: Basic Books.

Crockett, L. J., D. J. Eggebeen, and A. J. Hawkins. 1993. "Fathers' Presence and Young Children's Behavioral and Cognitive Adjustment." *Journal of Family Issues* 14: 355–77.

Day, R. D. and W. C. Mackey. 1989. "An Alternate Standard for Evaluating American Fathers." *Journal of Family Issues* 10:401–08.

Deutsch, F. 1999. *Halving It All*. Cambridge, MA: Harvard University Press.

Dill, B. T. 1988. "Our Mother's Grief: Racial Ethnic Women and the Maintenance of Families." *Journal of Family History* 13:415–31.

Doherty, W. J. 1991. "Beyond Reactivity and the Deficit Model of Manhood." *Journal of Marital and Family Therapy* 17:29–32.

Dubowitz, H., M. M. Black, C. E. Cox, M. A. Kerr, A. J. Litrownik, A. Radhakrishna, D. J. English, M. W. Schneider, and D. K. Runyan. 2001. "Father Involvement and Children's Functioning at Age 6 Years: A Multisite Study." *Child Maltreatment* 6:300–09.

Eggebeen, D. 2002. "The Changing Course of Fatherhood." *Journal of Family Issues* 23:486–506.

Ehrenreich, B. 1984. *The Hearts of Men*. Garden City, NY: Anchor Press/Doubleday.

Furstenberg, F. F. 1988. "Good Dads—Bad Dads." Pp. 193–218 in *The Changing American Family and Public Policy*, edited by A. Cherlin. Washington, DC: Urban Institute Press.

Furstenberg, F. F. and A. Cherlin. 1991. *Divided Families*. Cambridge, MA: Harvard University Press.

Furstenberg, F. F. and K. Harris. 1993. "When and Why Fathers Matter." Pp. 150–76 in *Young Unwed Fathers*, edited by R. Lerman and T. Ooms. Philadelphia: Temple University Press.

Gavanas, A. 2002. "The Fatherhood Responsibility Movement." Pp. 213–42 in *Making Men into Fathers*, edited by B. Hobson. New York: Cambridge University Press.

Griswold, R. L. 1993. *Fatherhood in America: A History*. New York: Basic Books.

Harris, K. H., F. F. Furstenberg, and J. K. Marmer. 1998. "Paternal Involvement with Adolescents in Intact Families." *Demography* 35:201–16.

Hawkins, A. J. and D. C. Dollahite. 1997. "Beyond the Role-Inadequacy Perspective of Fathering." Pp. 3–16. in *Generative Fathering: Beyond Deficit Perspectives*, edited by A. J. Hawkins and D. C. Dollahite. Thousand Oaks, CA: Sage.

Hays, S. 1996. *The Cultural Contradictions of Motherhood*. New Haven, CT: Yale University Press.

Hewlett, B. S. 1991. *The Nature and Context of Aka Pygmy Paternal Infant Care*. Ann Arbor: University of Michigan Press.

———. 2000. "Culture, History, and Sex: Anthropological Contributions to Conceptualizing Father Involvement." *Marriage and Family Review* 29:59–73.

Hofferth, S. L. and K. G. Anderson. 2003. "Are All Dads Equal? Biology versus Marriage as a Basis for Paternal Investment." *Journal of Marriage and Family* 65:213–32.

Horn, W. 1999. "Lunacy 101: Questioning the Need for Fathers." Retrieved April 29, 2003, from the Smart Marriages Web site (http://listarchives.his.com/smartmarriages/smartmarriages.9907/msg00011.html).

Johnson, M. 1988. *Strong Mothers, Weak Wives*. Berkeley: University of California Press.

Kimmel, M. 1996. *Manhood in America: A Cultural History*. New York: Free Press.

Lamb, M. E., J. Pleck, E. Charnov, and J. Levine. 1987. "A Biosocial Perspective on Parental Behavior and Involvement." Pp. 11–42 in *Parenting across the Lifespan*, edited by J. B. Lancaster, J. Altman, and A. Rossi. New York: Academic Press.

LaRossa, R. 1988. "Fatherhood and Social Change." *Family Relations* 37:451–57.

———. 1997. *The Modernization of Fatherhood: A Social and Political History*. Chicago: University of Chicago Press.

Maccoby, E. and R. Mnookin. 1992. *Dividing the Child*. Cambridge, MA: Harvard University Press.

Marsiglio, W., P. Amato, R. D. Day, and M. E. Lamb. 2000. "Scholarship on Fatherhood in the 1990s and Beyond." *Journal of Marriage and the Family* 62:1173–91.

Marsiglio, W. and J. H. Pleck. Forthcoming. "Fatherhood and Masculinities." In *The Handbook of Studies on Men and Masculinities*, edited by R. W. Connell, J. Hearn, and M. Kimmell. Thousand Oaks, CA: Sage.

McDaniel, A. 1994. "Historical Racial Differences in Living Arrangements of Children." *Journal of Family History* 19:57–77.

McLanahan, S. and G. Sandefur. 1994. *Growing Up with a Single Parent: What Hurts, What Helps*. Cambridge, MA: Harvard University Press.

McLanahan, S., J. Seltzer, T. Hanson, and E. Thomson. 1994. "Child Support Enforcement and Child Well-Being." Pp. 285–316 in *Child Support and Child Well-Being*, edited by I. Garfinkel, S. S. McLanahan, and P. K. Robins. Washington, DC: Urban Institute.

Messner, M. 1993. "'Changing Men' and Feminist Politics in the U.S." *Theory and Society* 22:723–37.

Mintz, S. 1998. "From Patriarchy to Androgyny and Other Myths." Pp. 3–30 in *Men in Families*, edited by A. Booth and A. C. Crouter. Mahwah, NJ: Lawrence Erlbaum.

Mosley, J. and E. Thomson. 1995. "Fathering Behavior and Child Outcomes." Pp. 148–65 in *Fatherhood*, edited by W. Marsiglio. Thousand Oaks, CA: Sage.

National Center for Health Statistics. (2000, January). "Nonmarital Birth Rates, 1940–1999." Retrieved on April 29, 2003, from the Centers for Disease Control and Prevention Web site (www.cdc.gov/nchs/data/nvsr/nvsr48).

Nock, S. 1998. *Marriage in Men's Lives*. New York: Oxford University Press.

Parke, R. D. 1996. in *Fatherhood*. Cambridge, MA: Harvard University Press.

Pleck, E. H. and J. H. Pleck. 1997. "Fatherhood Ideals in the United States: Historical Dimensions." Pp. 33–48 in *The Role of the Father in Child Development*, 3d ed., edited by M. E. Lamb. New York: John Wiley.

Pleck, J. H. 1997. "Paternal Involvement: Levels, Sources, and Consequences." Pp. 66–103 in *The Role of the Father in Child Development*, 3d ed., edited by M. E. Lamb. New York: John Wiley.

Pleck, J. H. and B. P. Masciadrelli. 2003. "Paternal Involvement: Levels, Sources, and Consequences." *The Role of the Father in Child Development*, 4th ed., edited by M. E. Lamb. New York: John Wiley.

Popenoe, D. 1996. *Life without Father: Compelling New Evidence That Fatherhood and Marriage Are Indispensable for the Good of Children and Society*. New York: Free Press.

Pruett, K. D. 1993. "The Paternal Presence." *Families in Society* 74:16 50.

Sanday, P. R. 1981. *Female Power and Male Dominance*. New York: Cambridge University Press.

Scoon-Rogers, L. 1999. *Child Support for Custodial Mothers and Fathers*. Current Population Reports, P60–196. Washington, DC: U.S. Bureau of the Census.

Seltzer, J. A. 1994. "Consequences of Marital Dissolution for Children." *Annual Review of Sociology* 20:235–66.

——. 1998. "Father by Law: Effects of Joint Legal Custody on Nonresident Fathers' Involvement with Children." *Demography* 35:135–46.

——. 2000. "Families Formed Outside of Marriage." *Journal of Marriage and the Family* 62:1247–68.

Silverstein, L. B. 2002. "Fathers and Families." Pp. 35–64 in *Retrospect and Prospect in the Psychological Study of Fathers,* edited by J. McHale and W. Grolnick. Mahwah, NJ: Lawrence Erlbaum.

Silverstein, L. B. and C. F. Auerbach. 1999. "Deconstructing the Essential Father." *American Psychologist* 54:397–407.

Snarey, J. 1993. *How Fathers Care for the Next Generation*. Cambridge, MA: Harvard University Press.

Stacey, J. 1996. *In the Name of the Family*. Boston: Beacon.

Thompson, L. and A. J. Walker. 1989. "Gender in Families: Women and Men in Marriage, Work, and Parenthood." *Journal of Marriage and the Family* 51:845–71.

Whiting, J. and B. Whiting. 1975. "Aloofness and Intimacy of Husbands and Wives." *Ethos* 3:183–207.

26

WHAT IT MEANS TO BE DADDY
Fatherhood for Black Men Living Away from Their Children

JENNIFER HAMER

Our story about fatherhood for low-income black American fathers is drawing to a close. It began by asking the reader to look at fatherhood through the eyes of this category of men. Specifically, the audience was asked to place paternal attitudes and activities of these fathers in the context of their surrounding environments and then, given the circumstances of these environments, understand parenting from their perspectives. These tasks are complicated by the barrage of public reports about high school drop-out rates, teenage pregnancy, gang violence, and stark poverty among African American children. Headlines blame fathers for their children's poor life circumstances. They are considered deadbeats, absent, and common villains.

The findings from this study of black live-away fathers move us forward in the public debate about black men and their families. They broaden our analyses and lead us to better understand that low-income black live-away fathers, like all other fathers, continuously negotiate their parenting within particular social, political, cultural, and economic circumstances. These circumstances consist of historical and contemporary social and economic injustices, cultural misrepresentations, unrealistic public expectations, and vague parental agreements with the mothers of their children. In this [reading], the reader is again asked to consider the context of black live-away fatherhood and its meaning in the fathers' world. What follows is a brief explanation of why low-income black fatherhood for them appears to contrast with the dominant paradigm. Finally, this [reading] discusses the implications of these findings for social policy.

Fatherhood on the Margins

"The world is a beautiful place," said one father of two, "if you can ignore the trash on the streets, if you can afford to pay the rent every month and eat . . . and then after all that, if you can still see your kids smile at the end of the day, the world is a beautiful place." Many black, low-income, live-away fathers experience life on the boundaries. Socially, economically, and culturally they hold a marginal position. The men interviewed worked for low wages and acquired low levels of education. They worked in jobs that required erratic schedules, demanded stringent emotional and physical labor, offered little opportunity for advancement, and afforded them little respect.

Most fathers expressed a desire to one day acquire a single job that would enable them to spend greater leisure time with their families and earn enough money to provide sufficiently for them. Said one father, "I just need to make enough so life is not a struggle . . . so I don't have so many worries." Their occupational aspirations did not seem unreasonable. A few shared their desire to become airplane pilots, corporate CEO's, and self-employed owners of profitable upscale businesses. However, references to these types of positions were generally made in jest and described as "dream" jobs.

Given their backgrounds, these fathers genuinely and realistically aspired for working-class employment. They verbally listed companies such as Coca-Cola, the U.S. Postal Service, United Parcel Service, city sanitation work, and other service or blue-collar occupations. They perceived that these employers would provide them with financial stability, family wages and retirement, paid vacation, health insurance, and other benefits. These were accouterments their low-wage labor, underground employment, and/or unemployment did not render. Fathers told of a few men that they knew who held or once held these types of occupations. "My uncle, he used to work for the telephone company before they laid him off . . . it was a good job, too," one father reported. "He bought himself a nice house . . . he bought his wife a nice car . . . beautiful." A thirty-six-year-old live-away father recalled his childhood neighbors building a new house "with a finished basement and a pool table" when the father was promoted to a supervisory position in a local glass manufacturing plant. Most surmised that these better-paying positions were today difficult to come by and were virtually nonexistent in the areas surrounding their communities.

They were correct in their assessment. Such manufacturing plants and employers continue to move away from cities and communities that house a disproportionate number of poor African American residents. Many of these fathers lived in East St. Louis, Illinois; Houston, Texas; Chicago, Illinois; St. Louis, Missouri; Detroit, Michigan; and other cities that at one time held economic promise for low-skill workers. Not having access to employment with higher wages and better benefits pained fathers. Said one father, "It's like it makes you feel bad when the snowcone van comes around and you don't have money to give to your child for snowcones . . . and yet and still, he sees all his little friends get to buy a snowcone." Another father recalled the anguish and guilt he felt when he did not visit his daughter on her birthday because he had been fired from his job and could not afford to purchase a birthday gift. "I figured her mother would go off on me for showing up without the present that I had promised," he said sadly. He found out weeks later that the mother of his child was angry not because he did not provide a gift but because he had chosen to simply not attend the celebration at all. In addition to the poor pay and low benefits of employment, these fathers, like black people in general, were faced with racial prejudices and individual acts of discrimination in their everyday encounters at work, on the bus, in stores, and on the streets.

What Fathers Do

For many black men, their situation has demanded that they develop an "ideal" of fatherhood at variance with dominant cultural and institutional norms. Ironically, their status has provided them with some freedom to set their own code of conduct for proper paternal behavior. This freedom has also enabled low-income, black live-away fathers to develop their own identity outside of mainstream expectations and norms. They are, as Le Roi Jones (1963) explains "natural nonconformists" because "being Black in a society where such a state is an extreme liability is the most extreme form of nonconformity available."[1]

Regardless of black men's uncertain status, social policies, cultural media, and social institutions direct black people to assimilate and adopt European American mainstream conceptualizations of proper attitudes and behavior. Yet, many researchers have argued that social conditions continuously deny them the means by which to live such a lifestyle. Consequently, black men are expected to assimilate into the dominant society and accept mainstream values and conceptualizations of fatherhood as if these ideals correctly reflect their own reality.[2]

Social researchers and social policy creators tend to view fatherhood in a manner significantly different from that held by the men in my study. Family policies generally reflect a patriarchal perspective that is much in keeping with the historical "ideal" of a father as family head. In this study, black live-away fathers have chosen an alternative to this tradition.

Caregiving and Formation Function

According to the fathers in this study, "ideal" live-away fathers are those who spend as much time as possible with their children. This, they perceived, was their primary paternal function. A review of parenting literature indicates that the amount of time fathers spend with their children is less important than the quality of their interaction. Even without this formal knowledge, most of these fathers attempted to involve themselves as much as possible in the daily aspects of their children's care. Fathers reported managing various responsibilities for their children's care. They picked their children up after school, counseled them, and listened to their concerns. They prepared their meals and helped with homework. When they felt mothers were weak in terms of disciplining their children, they stepped in to fill the void.

Similar to married fathers who reside full-time with their children, these men interacted with children in recreational activities as well. While they took them to various public events, they were more likely to entertain their children with low-cost activities. Such activities would include visiting with relatives, playing cards, eating lunch occasionally at McDonald's, going to the park, or simply taking a leisurely stroll. These findings strengthen research indicating that many live-away fathers may involve themselves extensively in children's caretaking. Moreover, these findings indicate that fathers may continue their involvement throughout their children's development—from infancy through adolescence.

This contrasts with studies indicating that among those experiencing divorce, noncustodial fathers decrease involvement with children over time, particularly those who were "very" involved with children prior to divorce. What this may also suggest is that if the two groups were empirically compared, never-married black live-away fathers may be more "consistently" involved with their children than those experiencing divorce. Research also suggests that married fathers who reside with their children spend about one-third of the time mothers do in direct interaction with their offspring. Additionally, they are less likely than mothers to take on responsibilities for child care, such as changing diapers, giving meals, and making medical appointments. Rather, play time takes up much more of their time with children. Many fathers in this study reported spending time with children. Their involvement was at varying levels. Some never visited their children while others cared for them on an almost daily basis. Moreover, for those who visited or cared for their children one or more times a week, what they provided may not differ markedly from the social and emotional care provided by married fathers who reside full-time with their children.[3]

The implications of this call into question the purpose of marriage as it concerns the care and well-being of children, and the impact of divorce on relationships between fathers and offspring. It may be that having never-married parents and a "very involved father' is better for the emotional stability and well-being of children than having lived with married parents who subsequently divorce. Certainly, the question warrants investigation, given the rate of divorce and rising numbers of single-parenting homes in most demographic groups across the United States.

Ideally, mothers explained, fathers should be sufficient economic providers. However, mothers readily modified this ideal to better fit the financial situations of low-skill, low-income fathers. In so doing, mothers agreed with fathers that the paternal time spent with children was more significant than the receipt of child support, but this did not mean they were completely satisfied with the extent of fathers' activities in this arena. Many expressed disappointment at what was, from their perspective, flaccid male parenting. Some mothers felt men could provide more time for their children than they actually did, particularly since they did not often provide substantial child support. Fathers did not disagree with this, but felt that pressures from work, multiple sets of children, and physical distance from children's homes strained their ability to be accessible and involved at an optimum level. Mothers acknowledged that black men in general were in a difficult position in today's contemporary social and economic spheres. However, they were often reluctant to accept men's excuses for not spending more time with their children. As one mother stated: "Women always have to make time for their kids, and we always do. . . . Fathers shouldn't be able to get off from that." Mothers too, were stressed economically and would have liked more financial support from fathers. Again, there was general acknowledgment that men also were economically "strapped." Women generally felt that to castigate men and/or pursue them for more money may have a countereffect. From their experiences, it would discourage men from visiting their children, and from contributing what little economic assistance they did provide.

Legal Bonds

Family policies and social institutions expect all fathers to provide their children with a legal bond to their ancestry and formal ties to paternal kin. In this study, none of the men indicated this was a primary element of their roles and functions as fathers. Fathers generally felt it was important for their children to know them as their "daddy." However, knowing paternity was not equated with a legal bond. Whether or not children carried their father's surname seemed of little significance to live-away fathers or custodial mothers. The majority of these men's children did not have their fathers' respective surnames. As in times of slavery, children had access to both maternal and paternal kinship networks despite the absence of sanctioned bonds between father and child.

Traditionally, European American fathers have provided their offspring with paternal surnames so that children are legally recognized as their father's child. In this way, children were able to reap the benefits of significant financial support and inheritance that formal ties to their ancestry might bring. But this particular intent has little meaning for low-income black live-away fathers. In terms of material inheritance, property, wealth, and accompanying accouterments, these men have virtually nothing to pass on to their offspring. "All I can give him," said one father in reference to his three-year-old son, "is my bills."

Provider

In U.S. society, how fathers function in their provider/breadwinner role is the basis for measuring their success or failure. Interviewed black live-away fathers consciously rejected this element as a defining feature of their success or failure as fathers. Furthermore, they considered it to be one of the least important functions of their fatherhood. Those that paid child support on a consistent basis expressed various reasons for doing so. For a few fathers, child support was a legal matter in which their nonpayment could result in legal action against them. One never-married father lived with his children and their mother for twelve years before separating from them. Without a court order, this father willingly provided consistent monthly economic support to his children. He explained:

> I have always given them everything . . . my constant love and attention . . . as much of my time as possible . . . and I make a good living so I give that, too. . . . I don't need no judge coming between me and my kids. . . . I told her [the children's mother] as long as it stays between me and you then I'll take care of my own.

Still other fathers stated that they used child support as a means to make up for the lack of time they spent with their children. Yet, no father viewed the provider role as the most important aspect of his fathering. Nor did they use this as a criterion with which to rate their performance as fathers.

For these fathers, children were primarily cared for by their mothers or another maternal family member. In addition, various maternal and paternal kinfolk provided an array of new and "hand-me-down" goods—clothing, toys, shoes, linens, and furniture that in most cases neither parent could altogether afford to purchase. For most of these fathers at least one set of their children qualified for and received government welfare benefits at some point during their lives, regardless of fathers' economic situation. Welfare benefits addressed children's essential needs—health care, nutrition requirements, and housing; however, no welfare allowances alone were sufficient.

Kin networks, social service organizations (food pantries, etc.) contributed to the survival of women and their children. Although such benefits and familial assistance did not guarantee a child the best quality of life, they nonetheless provided fathers and mothers with some sense of comfort.

Although fathers generally looked to others to assume the primary provider role for their children, they looked to themselves to "improve" their children's quality of life. They worked and sought higher education so that in the future they could help their children. In this respect, they expressed attitudes similar to those of custodial black fathers. Like their custodial counterparts, these fathers had great dreams for their offspring, and expected them to attain both academic and professional success (Robinson et al. 1985).

What Mothers Want from Their Children's Daddies

Despite their circumstances, fathers in this study well understood what policy makers and politicians expected of them as fathers. Recent welfare policies demand that states assign paternity to children and secure formal child support from fathers regardless of their economic circumstances. What was unclear to fathers in this study was that the mothers of their children tended to harbor ideals and standards of fatherhood that were similar to those espoused through social policy. They reluctantly relinquish their right to demand child support for fear of what their children may lose in the long run.

For example, custodial mothers of children are compelled to reveal paternity information or face the potential penalties that include the loss of much-needed welfare benefits. However, many of the mothers in this study were reluctant about pursuing fathers for formal payments. Many receive some informal, though inconsistent, support from children's fathers. Consequently, they were concerned that formal pursuit of consistent financial support would not only discourage men from visiting their children but might possibly land fathers in jail if they are unable to meet payment terms. Mothers were also reluctant to pursue child support for another reason: When fathers provide child support through state agencies, the state benefits received for their children are reduced. Moreover, what low-income fathers are able to provide through state agencies does not significantly improve their living conditions.

Nevertheless, mothers often reported feelings of anger toward fathers for not doing more to provide for their children. Fathers, on the other hand, tended to feel they were doing the best they could economically, given the dire straits they often experienced. They felt that relative to their fathers, they were "pretty good" dads. They also felt that mothers had, at least, some support from state and other public and private agencies, which presumably made up for many of the things they could not give. Still, fathers recognized that even these sources did not provide enough, and maintained informal arrangements with the mothers of their children. Upon request, fathers attempted to help mothers and children with purchases of food, clothing, shoes, school supplies, and other needs. They also used various sources to get toys and other extra items for their children. At the time of their interviews, few of these fathers were paying child support through official means. They did, however, feel that there was often more they could do in terms of the social and emotional role they played in their children's lives.

"Bumps in the Road"

Live-away parenting was not always easy. Fathers negotiated their paternal activities in the context of unfriendly attitudes and behaviors from some of the mothers of their children, the lack of support and guidance they received from their own parents, and employment and formal education schedules. Findings from past research on divorced live-away fathers suggest that such circumstances often serve as barriers, inhibiting men's ability to parent their children. Interviewed fathers perceived these elements as making it more difficult to perform fatherhood functions but not necessarily as "barriers" preventing them from doing what they desired to do for their children. One father referred to these "barriers" as "bumps in the road." They were considered small hurdles easily overcome by a determination to be a good father. In fact, these fathers perceived few if any permanent obstacles to their parenting. A "lack of time" and "physical proximity away from children" were the primary hurdles fathers felt that they were constantly leaping. Each was due primarily to fathers having multiple jobs, multiple families, and multiple sets of children. Mostly, these elements were considered quite simply as negative aspects of live-away fatherhood, of which fathers had little control.

Although fathers' relationships sometimes posed problems for their parenting, they were also a source of strength, providing support to their ability to perform the tasks of fatherhood. Assessing the gate-keeping activities of the mothers of their children was complex. Women generally felt their words and actions encouraged fathers' participation. From their perspective, it was often their encouragement that moved fathers to maintain involvement. From men's view, mothers were simultaneously encouraging and controlling. Women seemed to control when fathers could and could not visit with children, and enlisted the assistance of significant others (boyfriends, mothers, sisters, aunts, brothers, etc.) when fathers did not abide by their rules. Consequently, fathers expressed feelings of powerlessness. They sometimes felt like outsiders in their children's lives.

Nevertheless, most women encouraged fathers to spend time with their children, and fathers perceived that this was the most important expectation of them. Similar to the findings of Stack (1974, 1986), fathers tended to participate in their children's household as a close "friend" to the family. They ran errands, provided child care and transportation, performed yard work, and rendered various other services. In exchange, they sometimes were treated as one of the family. Mothers often provided fathers with meals, allowed them to relax around the house and watch television, and allowed them to spend time with the children in their home.

The mothers of fathers in this study also provided fathers a source of support and encouragement. Fathers' mothers encouraged their sons to spend time with their children, provided sons with comfort, and provided them with advice on childrearing and life in general. In times of disagreements, they also served as mediators between their sons and the mothers of their son's children. One woman recalled that out of anger and disappointment, she prevented her children's father from visiting with them for three months. She also refused to accept any gifts or money he offered the children. When his prodding to reconsider proved unsuccessful, the father simply took the items to his mother and the woman's mother. These women made certain the items reached their destination. "My children still needed to know I cared about them even though I did their mother wrong," the father explained. The mother agreed and relented. After some time, the two began communicating again.

The Difference between Fathers and Daddies

Fathers distinguished between two types of fathers—those who were "just" fathers and those who acted as "daddies." The former they described as "baby-makers," or those who demonstrated no care for their children. This type was presumed to have multiple children with different women; however, these relationships were rarely sustained for long periods of time. "Daddies" on the other hand, were those who expressed love, provided social support and companionship, and made their children a central part of their lives. No father in this study fit the "baby-maker" profile. It is important to note that at a glance some may have appeared to, particularly those who had no apparent contact with their children. Upon further exploration of their individual circumstances and decision making, even these relatively few men appeared to fall somewhere in between the definitions of "baby-maker" and "daddy." They expressed great love for their children, but felt overwhelmed and/or constricted by their circumstances. They also seemed to foresee few if any potential opportunities to change their situations. "Daddies" explained that they learned their father role through trial and error and from their own parents.

Mothers of fathers, in particular, provided incentive and inspiration for sons "to do right" by their children—that is, spend time and be a "daddy" to them. Yet, the lack of interaction between men and their own fathers also inspired them to be good daddies. Similar to married fathers mentioned in Blankenhorn's *Fatherless America* (1995), these men were attempting to be better fathers to their children than they felt their fathers had been to them.

Not all fathers were able to negotiate the demands of parenting into their daily lives. Some fathers were quite literally absent from their children's lives.

However, none fit the stereotype of the uncaring, selfish, absentee parent circulating in popular media. On the contrary, these fathers expressed deep concern for their children's well-being and shared emotional accounts of how their disengagement from parenting occurred. Many reported their absence was in the best interests of their children. Their ability to parent was overwhelmingly impaired by what seemed to be overlapping experiences in two or more of the following life circumstances: substance abuse, illegal employment, incarceration, and contention between themselves and the mothers of their children. Additionally, some of these fathers appeared to have experienced acute poverty as children themselves and lacked significant sources of social support that may have strengthened their ability to co-parent. While involved fathers tussled with similar obstacles, they seemed to describe having access to various forms of social and economic support throughout their childhood, during pregnancy, and following the birth of their children. Several absent fathers generally felt confounded by their situations and/or felt that their ability to change their situation for their children would be a difficult and complicated task.

Never–Married Co–Parenting Families: An Incomplete Institution

Noncustodial fatherhood was a formal aspect of American slavery. Furthermore, from this period on, the nonresident father–custodial mother family form was sustained through social, economic, and political institutions. Never-married childbearing and co-parenting is historically established and persists in significant proportions in black communities. However, as an institution in U.S. society, it is quite incomplete. Despite its increasing prevalence among most demographic groups in the United States, it has yet to be accepted and instituted as a legitimate alternative to the nuclear family.[4]

Relative to laws and norms that protect and inform bonds within marital relationships, those that protect relationships and define appropriate behavior for never-married co-parents and partners are still evolving. The never-married live-away father, custodial mother, family has yet to embody a well-established structured pattern of paternal behavior that is a fundamental part of our American culture. What is more, the state's primary emphasis on paternal financial "responsibility" is complicated by the low and inconsistent earnings of many black fathers.

Low-income black fathers and the mothers of their children seem to be developing a definition of fatherhood and a pattern of behavior that best fits these economic circumstances. The mothers of their children, who are also economically deprived, often do their best to maintain paternal ties, even if it means relinquishing their right to child support. Thus, even the development of "child support payments" as a paternal norm for low-income men remains problematic. Custodial mothers and live-away fathers find themselves negotiating and defining their social roles, functions, and interactions with little institutional guidance or support. Consequently, fathers are often unclear about what mothers expect of them as parents. Mothers are constantly assessing and reassessing means to improve fathers' paternal sensibilities and behaviors. This is particularly difficult because there seems to exist so little general public understanding or verbal agreement on what fathers are supposed to do as live-away dads.

Redefining Fatherhood and Adapting Policies to Families

Fathers in this study seemed to discuss fatherhood in a way that best preserved their sense of accomplishment. Their definition of primary paternal roles and functions placed meaning in what they were best able to do for their children. To do otherwise would serve to inhibit their potential as parents and to set themselves up for possible failure as men and as fathers. Their definition of the most important aspects of fatherhood comes from their own interactions with significant others and from their understanding of life's options. It is also within these micro- and meso-systems that live-away fathers look for and find approval for their father functions. Theirs is a "bottom-up" perspective of live-away fatherhood that draws from the daily lives of those most affected by social policy decisions. It is unlike the "top-down" view of the world that characterizes the practices of many social scientists and social policy creators.

These groups tend to view the world and define the functions of black live-away fathers in terms of the values and norms of the dominant culture. Their definition of the most "desirable" father behavior—providing child support and a paternal surname—negates the values and behaviors of those who hold dissimilar views. At a minimum it places a lesser value on opposing perspectives. Thus, while black live-away fathers express a view of fatherhood that is based on their reality, theirs is a fatherhood that is provided little to no formal support or legitimacy. Social policies addressing child support and support for black fatherless families in general do not factor in the worldview of black live-away fathers. Overall, social policy efforts are far removed from the daily experiences of black men and women. For this reason, Christopher Jencks (1993) argues that many black men and women feel justified in carrying out alternative and adaptive means of survival to provide for themselves and the well-being of their children.

Critics might point out, perhaps correctly, that the evidence presented by fathers in this study is influenced by the tendency people have to present themselves in a favorable light. In fact, measuring the effects of mothers' and fathers' attitudes and behaviors on children's well-being were beyond the scope of this study. Consequently, conclusions drawn are suggestive rather than definitive. Nevertheless, it seems black live-away fathers are developing their own form of fatherhood despite a steady barrage of negative social messages, myths, and negative stereotypes. This attests to the importance black men place on their father/child bonds. Evaluating their fatherhood strictly in terms of the dominant Western paradigm undermines and disregards the subtle strength of what they do provide and can potentially provide for the well-being of their children.

Moving Forward: Improving Circumstances for Parents and Children in Black Noncustodial Father Families

Social policy attempting to address the emotional, social, and economic well-being of black children has—to date—been largely ineffective. Relative to other groups, black children continue to have higher rates of poverty, juvenile delinquency, teenage pregnancies, death from homicide, drug use, school dropouts, and poor health. Social policies have attempted to combat such statistics by attempting to establish children's paternity, subsequently pursuing live-away fathers for formal payment of child support and by implementing various changes in welfare policy. . . .

Supporting Never-Married Co-Parents through Social Policy and Community

American families are increasingly resembling the predominant African American noncustodial father–custodial mother family form. Furthermore, regardless of race and ethnicity, noncustodial fathers frequently do not provide for the financial security of their children, even when they can afford to do so. Addressing the experiences of low-income black fathers and their children may inevitably enable social policy makers and social work practitioners to better understand and assist other groups in similar circumstances.

Low-income live-away fathers must be guaranteed full employment at livable wages if they are expected to fulfill their parental financial obligations. At the macrolevel, local, state, and federal governments must legislate both for all working people if they hope for these parents to have the means to provide enough money to boost themselves and their children out of poverty. Under current conditions and policy emphases, women with children generally gain access to breadwinner's income solely through marriage. Black women are less likely than other demographic groups to marry and/or find mates that earn breadwinner wages. Unless livable wages are instituted, the problem of childhood poverty will remain unbounded in the United States, whether or not parents reside in the same household as their shared offspring (Orloff 1993).

But men's legitimate employment and higher wages alone will not sufficiently improve the well-being of black children. The nurturing and caring aspects of live-away parenting must be further defined and strengthened through institutional and community support. Government attempts to improve the well-being of poor black children and all children will continue to be ill-effective unless researchers and policy creators adapt their perspective of low-income black never-married parents to their reality. Social policy creators must recognize the primary elements of black live-away fatherhood as a "legitimate alternative" to the traditional patriarchal notions of fatherhood, particularly under current economic conditions. Additionally, the definition of fatherhood or the "good father" must be broadened to include the varying characteristics and experiences of low-income black families. Once a more inclusive definition is developed, policy creators can identify and more adequately support family members through legislation and public discourse.

To accomplish this task is complex. Researchers and policy creators must continue to seek to find a balance between the economic provider and nurturing roles. Current policies concerning child support continue to place primary emphasis on the economic support fathers are expected to provide for their children. The everyday nurturance and care for children continues to be gendered labor, and tends to fall most heavily on the shoulders of women. Relatively little importance is placed on the social or emotional relationship between fathers and their children. Yet, the well-being of poor children requires an investment in both time and money, and each element should be a calculated factor in the determination of child support (Klawitter 1994). Some live-away fathers can provide money and time; still others can provide more of one element than the other. Feminists have been arguing for decades that an economic formula should be applied to the caregiving and nurturant roles and functions of childrearing. So too should such a formula be calculated and applied to live-away father/child and mother/child relationships to ensure that children are receiving at least a minimum of what they need for emotional, social, and economic well-being.

Presently, there is no adequate systematic means of accounting for the amount and type of care fathers provide to their children. Nor is there an adequate means of accounting for the informal economic support black live-away fathers seem to provide. Yet, while popular media, and politicians, and researchers continue to associate the presence of a father with positive well-being and quality of life outcomes for children, they have failed to adequately articulate what it is about fathers that directly links to this phenomenon. Is it, for example, the financial support they provide to the household? Is it their physical presence in the household? Is it the amount and/or type of quality and interactive time they spend with children? Or, is it some or all of the above?

Is it possible to be a good father and not provide significant financial support to one's child? For some directors of father centers in black communities the answer is yes, especially if fathers are doing the most they can for their children. According to one director: "Men want to be fathers to their children and must learn how to do so despite their inconsistent and difficult financial state." He and other program facilitators also argue that men have increased self-esteem and self-confidence, and are more patient and willing to communicate with the mothers of their children, when they are working at legally well-paying jobs. This, they contend, enables them to feel a sense of power in daily parental decision making that affects their children's behavior and well-being. Thus, these programs find themselves attempting to strike a balance between nurturing and economic parenting activities that best fit the lives of their clients.

The goals of father-centered programs would be much easier if they were expressly aided by support from other community entities. In his foreword to Andrew Billingsley's recent work on the black church and social reform, *Mighty like a River* (1999), C. Eric Lincoln argues that the church is a "vitalizing resource" for all Americans and a "defining reference" in the black community. Faith-based organizations in black communities have historically taken the lead toward social reform. Today they remain the most well-organized and entrenched networks within black America. Moreover, their leadership is often sought by politicians and policy makers for commentary and assessment of conditions for black families.

Yet, under current social and economic conditions, churches must become more ardent and vigilant social activists if they intend to continue as leaders for social change. Their leadership and membership must work as agents to address secular issues confronting black families. Moreover, dwindling resources among the poorest churches and black communities demands that faith-based organizations collaborate with other institutions and activist organizations to identify and address the needs of black mothers, fathers, and children.

Many churches have responded to the sustained secular crises among black families. Over two-thirds of 635 churches surveyed in Billingsley's study operated community outreach programs, a majority of which consisted of adult family support. However, effective support to custodial mothers and noncustodial fathers requires that church leadership and program coordinators think holistically and beyond traditional notions of family. Custodial mothers, live-away fathers, grandparents, aunts, uncles, and fictive kin all play a significant role in raising black children within the noncustodial father family form. Programs should seek to help family members to define the roles of family members and enhance positive communication and interaction, particularly between mothers and fathers.[5]

Although it exists separately from a church, the Lutheran Child and Family Services Fathers Center of East St. Louis, Illinois, attempts to do just that. Here, the Reverend Phoenix Barnes brings divorced, separated, and never-married fathers and mothers together to discuss their familial circumstances, their parental options and choices, and identify and define their appropriate roles as co-parents. The program also provides opportunities for fathers to seek employment and continued education. It also enables them to spend quality time with their children and arranges familial outings that neither parent could otherwise afford.

Faith-based programs must also be prepared to address many of the problems that may further inhibit familial well-being, such as adult unemployment, substance abuse, incarceration, and low levels of education. Most importantly, as "vitalizing" agents, churches must take the lead in supporting and institutionalizing noncustodial father family forms by articulating their circumstances and needs to social service agencies, educational systems, and cultural media, institutions that can help legitimize this family form. But churches, social service agencies, and the educational system are only part of the solution. They cannot be wholly effective without further attention paid to living wages for poor and working-class people and women's economic ability to develop and maintain autonomous households.

Inevitably, what poor and working-class black live-away fathers actually do for their children rests with society's ability to provide them access to sufficient economic means. It is equally contingent on the legitimacy and support granted to their paternal status. It is also based on their ability to interact and communicate with those who assist in the co-parenting of their children. It is further influenced by black men's ability to define and voice their own vision of fatherhood in the context of their collective economic and social circumstances. For those men who have little else to offer, the provision of nurturance, love, and affection are priceless aspects of fatherhood. Said one father, "No matter what anybody else say, we black men have got to make fatherhood work for *us*. . . . All our babies want is their daddies, and we have got to decide what that means."

ENDNOTES

1. The quote from Jones is used with caution here. Jones, or Amiri Baraka, is well known for his male chauvinism, and this study's findings and conclusions offer little support for the patriarchal ideals about male and female relationships that he espouses.
2. See Williams et al. 1995. Also see Jewell 1988; Majors and Billson 1992; Taylor 1994.
3. See Rivera, Sweeney, and Henderson 1986; Stack 1986; McClanahan 1999. Michael E. Lamb (1995) provides an excellent summary of the literature on what fathers do for their children. He also examines the influence of paternal involvement on child development. It appears that married fathers tend to provide about one-third of what mothers do regardless of whether both parents work 30 hours or more a week. One should note that the studies reviewed consist of primarily white samples. However, there are some indications that black fathers tend to do more in the household than their white counterparts. Yet, there is research that contradicts this as well. It is important to note that at least one study suggests that relative to middle-class and professional resident fathers, working-class fathers have increased their parental interaction with children more in recent decades. See Ferree (1988), whose work suggests that part of the reason for this is that women in working class families are more likely to perceive themselves and be perceived by others as sharing the breadwinning role. Thus, she is in a better position than middle-class and professional women to demand and initiate greater participation in household activities and childcare. In middle-class families the need for women's wages is less apparent and more apt to be perceived as a privilege.
4. The term "noncustodial" is used to describe a live-away father status in slavery only for lack of a better term. There are definite qualitative differences between live-away status during slavery and present-day circumstances. During the former, black men (and women) were bonded labor and had no control over where they lived and sometimes no say in the decision to partner with a particular woman. In contemporary times, blacks have a different relationship to the

market. They are no longer bonded. However, their noncustodial status is influenced by (among other factors) their relationship to the free market, their inability to find meaningful employment, and their relationship to the mother of their children.

5. Billingsley 1999. In the past decade, faith-based initiatives have increased across the nation. Federal grant availability and a general decline in the well-being of poor black communities have spurred the sharp increase in the development of nonprofit programs housed within churches. Grant monies also encourage faith-based organizations to collaborate to provide services to their communities and minimize duplication.

REFERENCES

Billingsley, Andrew. 1999. *Mighty like a River: The Black Church and Social Reform.* New York: Oxford University Press.

Blankenhorn, David. 1995. *Fatherless America: Confronting Our Most Urgent Social Problem.* New York: Basic Books.

Ferree, Myra Marx. 1988. "Negotiating Household Roles and Responsibilities: Resistance, Conflict, and Change." Paper presented at annual conference of the National Council on Family Relations, Philadelphia, November.

Jencks, Christopher. 1993. *Rethinking Social Policy: Race, Poverty, and the Underclass.* New York: Harper Perennial.

Jewell, K. Sue. 1988. *Survival of the Black Family: The Institutional Impact of U.S. Social Policy.* Wesport, CT: Praeger.

Klawitter, Marieka M. 1994. "Who Gains, Who Loses from Changing U.S. Child Support Policies?" *Policy Sciences* 27 (2–3): 197–219.

Lamb, Michael E. 1995. "The Changing Roles of Fathers." Pp. 18–35 in *Becoming a Father,* edited by Jerrold Shapiro, Michael Diamond, and Martin Greenberg. New York: Springer.

Majors, Richard and Janet Mancini Billson. 1992. *Cool Pose: The Dilemma of Black Manhood in American.* New York: Lexington.

McLanahan, Sara. 1999. "Dispelling Myths about Unwed Parents." National Summit on Supporting Urban Fathers, National Fatherhood Initiative, June 14, Washington, DC.

Orloff, Ann Shola. 1993. "Gender and Social Rights of Citizenship: The Comparative Analysis of Gender Relations and Welfare States." *American Sociological Review* 58(June):303–28.

Rivera, F., P. Sweeney, and B. Henderson. 1986. "Black Teenage Fathers: What Happens When the Child Is Born?" *Pediatrics* 78(1):151–58.

Robinson, Ira E., Wilfred Bailey, John Smith, and Bernice Bzrnett. 1985. "Self-Perception of the Husband/Father in the Intact Lower-Class Black Family." *Phylon* 46(2):136–47.

Stack, Carol. 1974. *All Our Kin: Strategies for Survival in a Black Community.* New York: Harper and Row.

———. 1986. "Sex Roles and Survival Strategies in an Urban Black Community." In *The Black Family: Essays and Studies,* 3d ed., edited by R. Staples. New York: Harper and Row.

Taylor, Ronald. 1994. "Black Males and Social Policy: Breaking the Cycle of Disadvantage." Pp. 147–66 in *The Black Male: His Present and Future Status,* edited by R. G. Majors and J. U. Gordon. Chicago: Nelson-Hall.

Williams, Norma, Kelly Himmel, Andrea Sjoberg, and D. Torrez. 1995. "The Assimilation Model, Family Life, and Race and Ethnicity in the United States:" The Case of Minority Welfare Mothers." *Journal of Family Issues* 16:380–405.

27

OVERLOOKED ASPECTS OF STEPFATHERING

WILLIAM MARSIGLIO

When we think about the everyday issues and implications associated with stepfathering, our attention likely drifts to obvious activities like discipline, supervision, financial support, and playing.[1] How assertive is the stepfather in defining the house rules or looking after his partner's child? Does he help pay for the child's food, clothes, and activities? If the mother works, does the stepdad take on the role of babysitter when she's away from home? Does he spend time doing fun things with the child?

We seldom reflect on the indirect ways a stepfather can influence a stepchild's life. Without this broader view, though, much goes unnoticed about how the complex and often ambiguous nature of stepfamily dynamics provides the stepfather with unique opportunities to make a difference in a child's life. A stepfather, just like a biological father, can influence a child's well-being in many ways, some direct, others indirect. The stepfathers' stories in my study shed light on two key indirect avenues for making a difference: contributions to building social capital and efforts to support the biological father, or, as I put it, to be the father's ally.

Another dimension of stepfathering that often flies beneath the radar is that the experience of stepfathering, like fathering, is not a one-way street. A man's willingness to get involved with his partner's child in a fatherly way means that he too may be changed by the experience. The stepfather who is mindful of how he makes a difference in a stepchild's life, as well as how he develops because of his involvement, is likely to have a much deeper understanding of what stepfamily life means to him.

Social Capital

Under the right circumstances, a father, either biological or step, can contribute to his child's well-being indirectly by providing the child with what sociologists call social capital.[2] This type of contribution goes beyond the typical cognitive and financial resources a parent can provide a child. In this study, it refers to the stepfather's contributions to either family-based or community-based relations that can affect a child's cognitive, emotional, and physical well-being. In terms of family relations, it captures a stepfather's relations with his child, the extent of his positive involvement and support. It also focuses on the extent to which a stepfather maintains a relationship with the mother based on trust, mutual respect, and a sense of loyalty. Does the stepfather share similar parenting values and conflict resolution strategies with the child's birth mother? To what extent and in what ways is the stepfather supportive of the birth mother, especially in ways that the child can notice? Is the stepfather an integral part of a coparenting team with the birth mother in which they routinely share with each other information about the child, a practice that allows each to know what is taking place in the child's life from day to day?

The other domain in which social capital comes into play involves the stepfather's set of relations with individuals and organizations directly involved with the stepchild. The individuals either interact with the child or are in a position to provide resources and opportunities if needed. Included among them are teachers, coaches, ministers, camp counselors, medical personnel, neighbors, and the child's friends, as well as the friends' parents. Individuals who presently are not involved with the child can also be viewed as part of this potential network if the stepfather has the option of bringing them into the picture to benefit the child (an acquaintance of the stepfather who hires the child for a summer job).

Taken together, these two general forms of social capital are meaningful because they enable a stepfather to expose a child to a healthy model of adult interaction, bring about closure in the child's social networks so that people important to the child can share vital information about him or her, and act as a liaison to valuable community resources for the child. If persons in the community share the stepfather's interests in helping the child, they can provide an important source of supervision while reinforcing or sanctioning the child's behavior. Similarly, if the stepfather is integrated into a larger network or community where mutual obligations, expectations, and trustworthiness prevail, the child will be exposed to social capital. Focusing on these types of connections and fatherly contributions reminds us that the stepfamily (or family) is a social system embedded in a larger social ecology replete with neighborhood, school, and peer contexts.[3] How then can a stepfather, given the ambiguous norms often associated with stepfamily life, contribute to a child's social capital and thereby affect the child's quality of life? Because the norms and arrangements associated with stepfamily life are sometimes unclear to family members[4] and are often muddled in the public eye,[5] a stepfather may be forced to work harder than a biological father if he wishes to develop social capital on behalf of a child.

When stepfathers describe their parenting circumstances, they often emphasize their desire to be part of a team. As already noted, some are more successful in achieving this arrangement than others. The "team" mentality that some of the stepfathers experience can be thought of as part of the family-based social capital they contribute to their stepchildren. This is one form of social capital that requires the birth mother's cooperation. The men's efforts to promote a team approach can sometimes be viewed as part of their general attempt to provide social support for the birth mother. When men take an active role in the hands-on parenting of stepchildren with the mother's blessing, her life becomes easier.

By definition, for a stepfather to produce community-based social capital, persons and organizations outside the family must be involved. The public face of stepfathering is relevant because a stepfather's ability to build social capital depends in part on how others foster his ability to act in a fatherly way. Yes, the stepfather must be motivated if he is to secure knowledge and connections necessary to make use of the larger social network within which his stepchild operates. Ultimately, though, motivation is not sufficient; a stepfather's ability to develop social capital depends on the cooperation of others. Put simply, if others do not respect a stepfather's desire to have a fatherly presence in the stepchild's life, he is likely to be handicapped in the type and amount of social capital he can provide. If the stepfather is not included in the network of people and organizations that are integrated into a system where obligations, expectations, and a sense of trustworthiness are shared regarding the care of children, he will be less effective in transmitting social capital to his stepchild.[6]

From a practical standpoint, opportunities to create community-based social capital are more readily available for men with school-age children who are involved in school and other activities outside the home. Because a number of the men I interviewed were involved with stepchildren who were still quite young and had little exposure to the world beyond their home, my sample is a bit limited in the breadth and depth of insights it can generate on this topic. Nevertheless, a third of the stepfathers in my sample met the target stepchild when he or she was at least seven years old, and two-thirds were currently involved with a stepchild who had reached school age. The stepfather's experiences with school-age children highlight several points germane to the development of social capital.

Several of the stepfathers spoke about how they took it upon themselves to have discussions with teachers and other child care professionals in order to understand their stepchild better and to intervene on his or her behalf. Some of these kids had been diagnosed with a learning disability or behavioral problem (for example, ADHD—attention deficit hyperactive disorder) and/or were having problems at school. Although they varied in how they went about getting involved, a number of the stepdads took their roles quite seriously. Randy, for example, describes his experience with his wife, Molly, and her son Jamie. Talking about how he and his wife responded to a teacher's suggestion that Jamie probably had ADHD, Randy says, "We were able to get him tested early and have a firm handle on all the problems, before he got into public schools. So we have in some ways been really tight with all his teachers." Continuing, "We interact with the teachers. And basically we have to because if anything happens to Jamie, Molly's going to be in somebody's face about it. So I've got to be right there to make sure she doesn't overdo the 'in the face' stuff, . . . we're kind of a good cop, bad cop team, when it comes to Jamie." By using "we" and "team" to characterize his involvement, Randy apparently sees his role in Jamie's life from a coparenting perspective. His consistent use of these words illustrates that he perceives himself as playing a critical role alongside his wife in looking out for Jamie and developing social capital to serve the child's best interests.

Brad similarly describes his initial contribution to a coparenting approach to developing social capital and being involved with his stepson Bobby, diagnosed with ADHD. He entered the picture at a time when Bobby was struggling at school and his mother was distraught over what she could do to help him improve. She had been particularly upset over one teacher's treatment of her son, while being generally dissatisfied with the response she was receiving from school personnel. Given this awkward context, Brad's initial involvement in confronting school representatives meant that he was jumping into an already volatile situation. Referring to this first meeting, Brad says, "I went basically to try and help her keep her temper, help keep the discussion at a level that was rational and not just angry at the school, expressing anger to the teachers. I failed miserably." Although Brad does not view his initial experience as a success, he recognizes that he has made a difference since then.

Like Randy, Brad felt that he was part of a parental team, with his specific role being to bring a calm and sober perspective to the meetings with school personnel. Presumably, both these men, as well as their partners, assumed that they could provide this perspective because, compared to the birth mother, they did not have the same history with and investments in the child. However, these men still saw themselves as having a vested interest in looking out for their respective stepchildren, but they implicitly recognized that their best shot at building social capital and helping the child was to monitor the birth mother. They wanted to help her make her case while building social capital, instead of antagonizing school officials to the point that it might be detrimental for the child. Each situation shows how a "crisis" in a child's life can offer a stepfather the opportunity to prove his commitment to the child and the birth mother. Although these heated situations may create tension and push partners away from each other, they can also solidify their mutual commitment as they jointly struggle to find a solution to a child's problem.

The same sort of paternal commitment is expressed by Doug as he talks about how he became very active in his nonbiological son Sammy's academic life a few years ago, when the boy was in his senior year of high school. Doug differs from Randy and Brad in that he assumes a more proactive and independent role. He describes at length a situation in which Sammy (who had on his own stopped taking the drug Ritalin earlier in the year) announced near the end of the academic year that he was probably not going to graduate with his class. On hearing the news, Doug immediately called the school principal and arranged a joint meeting the next day with a few of Sammy's teachers, the principal, Sammy, and himself. As Doug describes it, it was an intense meeting where he confronted both the teachers and Sammy about Sammy's predicament. He recalls telling the school officials: "I am here on behalf of my son. . . . He's what matters to me. . . . He's going to graduate." During that meeting, Doug negotiated an arrangement whereby the teachers agreed to tutor Sammy and Sammy agreed to resume taking Ritalin. Doug proudly finishes the story by noting that Sammy graduated on time that spring, adding "had it been let go the way it was, Sammy would not have graduated." Although Doug's wife supported his intervention on Sammy's behalf, she did so from a distance. . . .

Although situations like those described above are noteworthy in their own right, a stepfather can experience plenty of less dramatic, more pleasant opportunities to build social capital for a child. Under the right circumstances, a stepfather, like a biological father, can volunteer to participate in various school activities, affording him a chance to build relations with persons who may have contact with or be in a position to monitor his stepchild. This rings true for Calvin. While talking about his experiences at the charter school his stepdaughter Rebecca attends, he mentions that parents are required to volunteer for a certain amount of time. For his part, Calvin has stuffed packets, participated in an area cleanup, taken charge of selling candy for the safety patrol, and managed a listserv—a newsgroup for the parents. He also describes himself as having "positive interactions with the teachers." Many of these interactions occur spontaneously while he's waiting to pick Rebecca up from school. "I'll see them and talk to them at that time. There are three or four of them that were there last year and I've kind of gotten to know. . . . I'll talk to them about whatever's going on and if there's a problem. And Rebecca is usually good in school, but if there's a problem, I'll talk to them about that." Calvin's last comment highlights the opportunities parents have to develop social capital stemming from their children's needs and experiences. Both minor and more serious kinds of needs can provide an impetus for parental action. When children struggle in some way, parents are often compelled to contact members of the child's network outside the family. Building social capital for a child who has not experienced significant problems may help some parents prevent specific problems from ever occurring.

Let's stay with Calvin's story to illustrate another example of how social capital can be developed, while interpreting social capital broadly. Calvin stresses how he and his wife, Kristin, need to talk more about helping Rebecca in school because in his opinion, he and Kristin "haven't really gotten on the same page" yet. Prompted by his concerns for Rebecca's behavior, he went to a community-sponsored "parenting fair" a few days prior to the interview with Rebecca in tow. The listserv he manages came in handy because he learned about the program from one of the parents who posted information on the listserv about it. One of the workshops he attended dealt with children's problem behaviors and how to help children build self-esteem. Calvin plans to talk to Kristin about what he learned when they have some free time. This example is useful because it depicts how a stepfather, under the right set of circumstances, can serve as a liaison between the community and his family. In Calvin's case, he brought his own commitment to education with him when he got involved in Kristin's and Rebecca's lives. Consequently, he became active in promoting Rebecca's school performance, which entailed his getting involved in school-related activities, including developing a listserv for the parents. From this resource he then learned about the parent fair that he attended, prompting him to think about strengthening his family-based social capital by improving his communication with Kristin about Rebecca. Calvin's desire to participate in Rebecca's life in a fatherly way extends to his wanting to share with Kristin his knowledge about parenting, some of which he learned while at the fair. Thus his efforts to build social capital are tied to both his stepfather–child and coparenting trajectories. . . .

Father Ally

One of the indirect ways stepdads can leave their mark on their stepchildren that goes largely unnoticed in the literature about stepfamilies is how step-dads relate to biological fathers.[7] Do stepfathers make it easier or more diffi-cult for biological fathers to maintain contact and a close relationship with children with whom they do not live?

Some stepdads have little or nothing to do with biological fathers because these fathers have either walked away or been pushed away from their children, sometimes completely. A significant minority of the men who participated in my study describes the biological fathers as being out of the picture. In a small number of cases, the biological fathers may not even be aware that they have fathered a child. But most of the stepdads are directly or indirectly aware of the biological father's presence in the children's lives as well as his interaction with the children's mother. Not surprisingly, a number of the stepdads are accustomed to dealing with the biological father's continued involvement with his children. In some cases, the biolog-ical fathers are even involved on a limited basis with the children and mother together. Some of the stepdads find it eye opening, being nonresi-dent fathers themselves, because they sometimes develop a more well-rounded view of stepfamily arrangements when they have contact with men serving as stepfathers to their own children. This allows certain stepdads to relate more easily to issues involving the intersection between their roles and those of the biological father.

As my participants clearly illustrate, stepdads face a range of possible stepfamily scenarios. These scenarios differ in the frequency, type, and quality of the biological father's involvement with the children.[8] Though many of the patterns are stable over an extended period of time, they are not etched in stone. A scenario familiar today may be gone tomorrow as biological fathers get more involved or distance themselves from their children. Biological fathers may also change how they're involved. A sudden job loss may result in a father not being able to pay child support, but he may have more free time to spend with his child. Or a father may get involved, perhaps marry a woman who has her own child and begin to invest time, energy, and money in this new family. Given this type of uncertainty within stepfamilies, step-dads may, over time, face differing stepfamily scenarios where the biological father's role varies considerably.

When dealing with a biological father who is at least moderately involved in a hands-on way, a stepdad is likely to be concerned with how his own involvement will be supported or challenged. Will a biological father try to undermine the stepdad's household authority or will he encourage his child to respect the stepfather? By paying child support, being consistent with scheduled visits, speaking respectfully to the child and mother about the stepdad, and treating the stepfather cordially, a father has plenty of opportunities to ease the stepfather's transition into his various familial roles. The father can also help the stepfather thrive in the new roles. Additionally, the biological father who interacts with a stepdad in supportive ways can often improve his chances of having the stepdad act on his behalf in return. Along these lines, William, a twenty-seven-year-old man who was acting as a stepfather for his fiancée's two young boys, knew the boys' father before he became involved with the kids. William recalls having a conversation with the father during the early phases of becoming involved with the boys. He said the father "was just telling me that he was sorry that he wasn't there, but since I was there and he knows what kind of person I am, he said he felt that his kids were in competent hands. He told me that to my face." Hearing the father's sentiments made William "feel pretty good" about himself. It also helped reinforce his willingness not to say anything negative about the father in front of the kids.

The biological father who wants to remain involved in his child's life, even though he is no longer romantically involved with the child's mother, is likely to be concerned with how the stepdad affects his ability to retain his fatherly roles. A father may feel this way irrespective of the custody or residency arrangement. In many situations, the father's and stepfather's perceptions and actions can influence each other, even though they may not be conscious of their effect or acknowledge it directly. The old adage "scratch my back and I'll scratch yours" captures the experiences of many men with children as they try to settle on new ways of organizing their family roles, rights, and responsibilities in a wide range of different family settings. Although this agreement is often left unspoken, it exists nonetheless. This kind of arrangement eventually unfolded between Barry and his stepchildren's father, Sam, who had known and disliked Barry for some time before Barry got involved with his ex-wife (Lucy) and children. In Barry's words:

> *I would hear back from the kids and from other people that he overcame his dislike of me, so to speak, because he felt I was being so nice to the kids and I wasn't trying to replace him, that I was in fact saying positive things about him and trying to encourage Lucy not to be bitter. He really encouraged that. In fact,*

I was getting Christmas presents from them [biological father and his current wife] and a birthday present, things like that. He'd call me up. But we never sat down and said oh, you're a great guy, I love what you're doing.

One distinct pattern that emerged from my interviews with the stepdads was that many acted in ways that had the effect of helping the father remain active in a positive way in his child's life. From the stepfather's perspective, this activity sometimes enabled the biological father to strengthen his emotional ties with his child. Some stepfathers' efforts were intended and obvious, while others were much more subtle. If the term "ally" is used loosely, some stepdads acted like an ally to the father because they helped prevent problems or smooth over ones that probably would have tainted the father's relationship with his child had they gone unattended. For instance, a number of the stepfathers said they encouraged mothers not to say anything negative about the father in front of the children. Those who took this position thought it was counterproductive to "bad-mouth" a father in a child's presence, even though some mothers might have found this to be an effective short-term strategy to release stress. A few stepfathers, like Barry, even took it a step further. "I encouraged Lucy to try and get over her bitterness toward Sam's new wife [woman who had adulterous relationship with Sam during Lucy's marriage to him]. . . . And I never ever said anything about Sam in front of them [the kids]. In fact, I would say good things, even though I didn't always think it sometimes."

Stepdads who had kids of their own living elsewhere appeared to be the most sensitive to giving the biological father a fair shake in the stepfamily household. From their own experience, they knew how they would like to be represented to their children when they were absent. However, even stepdads who don't have their own children living elsewhere can develop empathy for a nonresident father. . . .

Some stepdads made a point of taking their own advice by going out of their way not to say anything negative about the biological father around the kids. A variation on this theme involved those who had something less than favorable to say. If they did have something to say, they did so diplomatically. Brad, a thirty-eight-year-old informal stepfather to two teenage kids, one a thirteen-year-old boy named Bobby, has endured a rather unique situation with Bobby's father, Len, who lives out of state. As mentioned previously, after experiencing severe brain damage from a car accident, Len was unable to fly his kids to see him because he lives in a group home. Brad's partner, Len's former wife, graciously makes arrangements for Len to stay at her house three times a year for a week at a time. During these visits, Brad goes over to the house and witnesses Len interacting with Bobby. Recently Brad has even taken to spending the nights. He describes how he delicately navigates the difficult situations when he feels that Len is filling Bobby's mind with unhealthy ideas.

If I see Len demonstrating one of his more egregious behaviors, I will tell Bobby, "That's not the way all men think. That's not — I don't believe that's correct.

I know he's your dad and you love him but you need to understand that there are other ways to think about that." So—I don't want to countermand him [biological father], but at the same time, sometimes it's just so out there that you feel like it needs to be—Bobby needs to understand—he's at that very impressionable age and he needs to understand that yes, your dad feels that way but not all men feel that way. That's not necessarily the way you need to think about that situation or whatever. And unfortunately it's mostly how he [biological father] feels about women.

In situations like Brad's, it may be a stretch to refer to stepdads as being an ally to the father. However, even though Brad is tempted to be critical of Len, he refrains from doing so partly out of respect for the father–son bond Len shares with Bobby. Because he cuts the father some slack, Brad can be viewed as an ally—loosely defined—who is willing to encourage Bobby to sustain his relationship with his father.

A stepdad has various opportunities to be an ally to a father by how he speaks to or interacts with the child directly. He might, for instance, make a point of saying nice things about the father, jump in to defend the father if circumstances call for it, or give advice on how to communicate with the father. Without being in the home himself, the nonresident father has a more difficult time speaking on his own behalf and explaining his behavior in a convenient and timely manner. One stepfather, Eddie, recalls several times when he consoled his stepdaughter Melissa on being disappointed by her father's irresponsible behavior. Asked if his efforts minimized Melissa's pain, and in the process helped the father's relationship with her, Eddie replies:

Well, the damage is when he does it—the damage is already done. I'm just trying to make her feel a little bit better. I guess you can say, because if he does something—if he don't call or he don't pick her up when he says he's going to pick her up, then I guess I kind of smooth things over for him. I guess you can say that. I mean—I try to make him—he's not bad. I try to make him, when he do bad things, whether he do it intentionally or not—I try to make him look like he—it's a mistake, nobody's perfect. Dad is going to make mistakes. It's okay for dad to make mistakes. He's human. It's going to be all right. He'll call you the next time. I think that—she loves her dad. When I think—if I really didn't soften the blow for her . . . I think she'd be a little ticked off at him at the time. She'd be a little mad at him. And trust me, when she gets mad she can make it hard on you.

As his comments indicate, Eddie acknowledges that he probably helps minimize his stepdaughter's disappointment and anger with her father. But when I asked Eddie specifically if he feels comfortable with the language of being called the father's "ally," he said he felt a bit uneasy with the label. Apparently Eddie has difficulty thinking of himself as the father's ally because "he [father] doesn't know half the times I cleaned up his mess." For Eddie, thinking of himself as an ally seems to necessitate an explicit agreement between the two men. It seems reasonable to conclude that Eddie acts like an ally in a functional sense, even if he does not clearly see himself as doing so and if the father is unaware of his efforts. The bottom line is that he does things as a stepdad that help the father maintain the quality of his relationship with his daughter.

Eddie's experience highlights two distinctions relevant to situations in which a stepdad acts like an ally to the father. First, does the stepfather do his work behind the scenes away from the father's view or does he actively work with the father, telling him what he is trying to accomplish? Eddie is essentially a "secret" ally because the father remains in the dark about much of what he does. A selective few, however, are more direct in making their approach and intentions known. The second distinction involves the stepfather's motivation for doing the things that are intended to enhance the father's relationship with his child. Is the stepfather making this effort because of his concern for the child, the father, or both? The driving force behind Eddie's efforts is his desire to look out for his stepdaughter's feelings. He is not particularly concerned about the father's dilemmas or feelings. In some instances, though, the stepdad empathizes with a father and goes out of his way to help him. Sometimes the stepfather may choose to play this role because he wants to be treated similarly.

Herman, a gregarious forty-two-year-old man, provides a detailed account of what it means to be an active and open father ally. In addition, he expresses his interest in helping both his stepdaughter and her father. He goes to considerable lengths to describe how he tries to keep the biological father of his three stepchildren involved in their lives. A self-described "initiator" when it comes to conversations, Herman explains that he once talked to the father on the phone and candidly told him that "you need to spend time with your kids." Compared to many stepfathers, Herman has gone the extra mile to reach out to the father and develop his own line of communication with him. Seeing the father in the stands at a high school football game, for example, Herman made a point of introducing himself to him and his current wife. Herman clarifies his assertiveness by explaining his line of thinking. "We don't have a reason not to be civil because—it's four different lives now [Herman and his wife, the father and his wife]. . . . There's no reason for us not to be civil together. Plus, we need to be civil for the kids anyhow." According to Herman, the father eventually embraced this view and they had subsequent conversations.

In addition to talking to the father directly, Herman talks frankly and forcefully to his stepchildren. He is particularly eager to have his fourteen-year-old stepdaughter, Annette, maintain contact with her father. In one instance, after Herman convinced Annette to rejoin the band, he asked her if she had told her father that she was involved in a jamfest at one of the universities in the region. As he explains,

> See, what I'm doing is, I'm pushing her up to do it, because I don't want it to seem — granted, like I told him on the phone — look man, I don't have a problem with you calling my house. I don't have a problem with you coming to my house. She's my wife now. I'm not insecure about that. I'm not insecure about

anything. I want you to spend time with your children, because they're your children.

Herman also makes a point of asking Annette if her father knows about her other school and recreational functions as they approach. In his words, "I make sure that she initiates with her father, let him know what's happening. . . . One day he's going to need you [Annette]."

Herman offers other astute comments that reveal how he believes Annette is growing closer to him over time because they live together. He worries about this and reflects on how his own fathering experiences with his son, who lives elsewhere with his mother, enable him to empathize with Annette's father.

> *She's coming more to my side because I'm with her all the time. . . . he's going to be distanced but — and that's the thing that concerns me, that after awhile I'll take on the persona of being her father and her father will be just a memory. I don't want that to be. I want him to actually be in her life. Because I'm going to be there. . . . But he'll be missing the growing-up stages in her life. She'll end up getting married and he'll miss that. Like with my son, I miss stuff. He's eleven years old now. Out of his entire life I think I've — if you put all the time that we've spent together, I've had two years, maybe three years of his life. . . . My son's got his own life now. It hurts because I've missed . . . ten years of his life that I don't even know what happened to him. I don't even know when he was sick. Did he cry? I taught him how to ride a bike. I bought him stuff. But then I miss days in the wintertime coming home, sitting out in the yard and he coming out there and sitting in the yard or helping me mow the yard. Well, I got a few days of that. So, I don't want this guy to miss that. He's got a girl. She's going to give him grandchildren. . . . She's going to go to the prom. I'm going to be there. Okay, I'm going to enjoy that because she's in the house with me, but that's one of his privileges. . . . Who's going to be there on her first date? I'm going to be the one scrutinizing this rookie coming up. Where you from, son? Okay. Tell me about yourself. He's going to miss that. You see? It's just not a good thing. I mean, it's a good thing for me, but I'm sure he should be in on that. She's his daughter. But now she's my daughter. I'm going to take responsibility for her. I have taken responsibility . . . everything I would do with my child, she gets the same.*

Listening to Herman's thought-provoking, emotional description of his efforts, it is clear that he takes pride as a proactive, nurturing, and protective father in overseeing Annette's life. In a separate interview, Herman's wife attests to his commitment to Annette. Unlike some stepfathers, Herman has a sense of security in his relationships with both his wife and Annette that provide him with the confidence necessary to incorporate the father more fully into the network of adults who have an interest in supporting Annette's transition through her teen years. In addition, the intense frustration and pain he has experienced as a nonresident father provide him a reservoir of feelings enabling him to relate to and empathize with Annette's father. As suggested previously, Herman's compassionate approach seems motivated by a genuine concern for both Annette's and her father's emotional and psychological well-being. . . .

Kids Making a Difference

Sometimes a stepfather's active involvement with a child leads him to make fundamental changes in the way he lives and sets his priorities. He may gain insights about himself, others, and life in general. When a stepfather seizes these opportunities, he often feels differently about himself.[9]

The stories the men tell about how they have been affected by being involved with stepchildren are similar in many ways to those typically shared by biological fathers. Unlike many biological fathers who make a conscious decision to have a child with their partner, most stepfathers become active with children because they get romantically involved with a woman who happens to be a mother. Concerns about how being involved with stepchildren may affect their lives may not fully register with stepfathers. They may not plan for or anticipate these consequences prior to getting seriously involved with the mother. But whether the consequences of their involvement with the kids are expected or not, some men are aware after the fact that their experiences as stepfathers have affected them.

Not surprisingly, some of the men comment on how involvement with stepchildren helped them develop a sense of purpose, become more responsible, and feel grounded. Among these men, Keith, Carl, Eddie, and Ray provide excellent examples of how being an active stepfather can affect men's lives. Keith, a stepfather of two young adolescent girls, says with conviction, "I have purpose now. That's something to do besides work and take care of Keith. That seems to be very important to me. I don't know why though. I need to have something to turn around and look back on, that's more than me, I guess." Keith's reference to being able to "look back on" his stepdaughters captures his feelings about helping others grow. These feelings are not new to Keith because he spent a number of years in a previous marriage helping raise a stepson who is now thirty years old. His long-standing and strong relationship with his stepson enabled him to feel comfortable about the prospects of devoting himself to raising children who are not biologically related to him. He anticipates that they will remain a part of his life forever.

Carl, the married stepfather of eight-year-old Vicky, shares Keith's sentiment about feeling connected to and responsible for others. Speaking of Vicky, Carl remarks,

> *She's made me more responsible. I always was fairly responsible, at least I see myself as that, but she's made me more responsible, in terms of knowing that I have people to take care of and knowing that the things that I'm doing with my life are making a difference in not just my life, but in two other people's lives. Things that I do as far as education and stuff are only going to make the opportunities for Vicky that much more, and the opportunities for us to be a family that much more.*

Carl's comments, here and elsewhere during the interview, reflect his strong commitment to care for his stepdaughter as if she were his own. This kind of sentiment apparently motivates Carl to take his work and education more seriously than if he did not have a child in his life.

Eddie identifies only one way in which being a stepfather for eight-year-old Rhendy has changed him, but he feels it is significant.

> *My sense is I know I have to work harder. . . . it's the extra stuff that she wants, so I figure I'll go out, I'll sacrifice my time for a little extra. Why not? You only live once. If I didn't get it when I was little, and my kids want it, by golly I'm going to go out and work and make sure they have it. . . . I've had to work harder just to make her happy, her life comfortable.*

Eddie's willingness to work longer hours relates partly to his interest in providing financially for his three biological children, but he focuses his remarks primarily on his current responsibilities for Rhendy. Consistent with his traditional view of men's fatherly responsibilities, Eddie takes his financial provider role quite seriously. Thus Eddie's desire to make Rhendy happy has led him to deepen his commitment to being a family man who expresses himself through his financial contribution to the family.

For Ray, being a stepfather and biological father helps him feel "grounded." Being involved in a fatherly way with his two stepchildren and one biological child gives him a "good feeling" about the "responsibility angle" of raising kids. "I like responsibility. To see that well, hey, I'm not a scared little child. I'm actually doing this. I'm actually taking care of this. This feels good. I feel strong. I feel powerful. I feel confident. That's a good deal." Ray conveys the idea that the kids in his life provide him with opportunities to perform certain adult, fatherly roles that in turn give him a sense of empowerment. Although most might find it a little odd that Ray, at age forty-two, refers to his contentment with being able to avoid the "scared little child" role, Ray's comments apparently reflect his sincere feelings about his contribution to his kids.

In some respects, Keith, Carl, and Eddie represent men who have become more future oriented because of their involvement with stepchildren. The men have a heightened sense that they need to provide for their stepkids now, as well as plan for the future. But for some of the stepfathers, their experiences with children actually encourage them to slow down and pay more attention to the present. This is what happened with Jackson, an introspective thirty-nine-year-old man who decided that he wanted to have a child with his former wife several years ago and was disappointed when he realized that she was unwilling to do so. His desire for a child was so strong that he divorced his first wife and pursued a new relationship with a longtime friend who has a small son. Jackson, who is now living his dream of being involved with a child, has found new inspiration by being around his five-year-old stepson, Mason.

> *He really got me to slow down from the — I guess I lived for quite a long time in future-oriented goals and trying to achieve something that's tomorrow,*

tomorrow, tomorrow. It's really pulled me into the present more, because just answering the questions of someone who's trying to define the world and is working very hard to define the world is — it takes a lot of energy so I can't be as future-oriented or worry about tomorrow and the next day, so that's one way, I've slowed down. And he's given me remarkable opportunities to be introspective, to think about what's important to me. . . . He says something like well, light reflects — we've got colors because light reflects off of the surface and — as he's learning these things and repeating different, very basic concepts that I have just taken for granted for most of my life, it's kind of wondrous. It makes me realize that, well, as corny as it sounds, this is really a precious thing we have. And it's very easy to get lost chasing the goals that we think are important when we're twenty or twenty-five that don't really mean that much later in life.

Here, and in other portions of his interview, Jackson emphasizes that Mason has affected his outlook on life. Jackson thinks less about promoting his business and acquiring the material symbols of success. He is more inspired by the beauty of life, nature, and being a family man. Mason has brought Jackson back to the present and into a world where he values his personal connections to others much more. . . .

Just as Jackson spoke about the ways Mason gets him to think about things that he hasn't thought about since he was a kid, other men comment on how being with their stepchildren helped them remain young. Carl, for instance, mentions that Vicky "just done wonders for me as far as making sure that I stay with my kid-self, staying with being able to read children's books and seeing it from a kid's point of view and seeing all the wonderful things that I remember as a kid, that you forget when you get into the workplace and you, the day-in-day out drudgery of paperwork." Similarly, Rodney offers that his two teenage stepchildren are responsible for making "me stay on my toes and I think they're helping me think younger than I would if I didn't have kids their age." A stepfather may not initially seek experiences such as these when he gets involved with a woman who is a mother, but they can nonetheless become powerful experiences over time.

For stepfathers who assume their place in a stepfamily without ever having kids of their own, being involved with stepchildren can offer them a unique opportunity to become less ego-centered. Gerald, even though he lived with a woman who had kids for several years, had for the most part lived the bachelor life, growing accustomed to having his living space to himself. Becoming a stepfather and living with his thirteen-year-old stepdaughter Sabrina has given Gerald a chance to expand his perspective. In his words, Sabrina

caused me, forced me, allowed me to just open my heart a little bit more than maybe I normally would. Just learning to live with somebody makes changes in an individual. I'm probably less spoiled than I was. You live with a kid you can't be — even if you want to be, you've gotta set a good example. . . . when you have kids, you have to give and take. . . . You can't necessarily show your true self.

Throughout the interview Gerald describes himself as "pissy," so his involvement with Sabrina has allowed him to change his personality while learning how to "chill a bit." Presumably, when Gerald talks about not showing his "true self" he means that he wants to shelter Sabrina from the less congenial aspects of his personality. Although he still enjoys his alone time, I got the sense that Sabrina has been drawing him out a bit from his self-centered ways, encouraging him to think of others more. Sabrina is basically helping Gerald mature.

Along similar lines, Randy, a stepfather who is unemployed because of serious physical disabilities that confine him to a wheelchair, feels that his nine-year-old stepson has made him a "better person" and forced him to think of others more. Since becoming a stepfather, Randy has become more concerned with presenting his genuine self. "He's made me realize that I got to be more truthful with myself and I can't like tell him to do something and then not really do it myself." By pretending to talk to his stepson, Randy makes the point that his stepson is likely to model his behavior: "'Take your bath and don't back talk your mama.' Well, I better take my bath and don't back talk his mama too." He adds, "I take pride in what he does. I mean more so than I do with what I would do. . . . He's made me have to live my life for somebody else, more so than I think than just if Molly [mother] and I were married." This became apparent when Randy faced serious surgery and was asked to sign a bank form in case he died. "I wasn't just worried about me. I was worried about other people and what happened to me. Now if I get sick it affects two other people, so I damn well better take care of myself. I better listen to the doctor." Randy's appreciation for his stepson is perhaps best captured in a simple statement he made: "He has given me tons more than I think I've given him."

For men who were fathers prior to getting involved with their current partner who was a single mother, becoming a stepfather meant that they were in most cases spending more time with children than they had in the recent past or, in some cases, ever. Because some of the men miss living with their children and seeing them as much as they once did, getting involved in their stepchildren's lives gives some a chance to fulfill their desires to be around children. . . .

The stories I use to capture the nature and significance of the impact stepfathers and children have on each other come from the minds, hearts, and mouths of stepfathers, and to a lesser extent the birth mothers. A more complete portrait of this impact awaits future research incorporating children's voices directly. For now, we glimpse the power a child's perspective can bring to the story of stepfatherhood by turning to Danny, one of the two fourteen-year-olds I interviewed and discussed earlier in connection with his stepfather, Thomas. After I asked him what letter grade he would assign to his stepfather, Danny was quick to reply, "I would give him an A plus. Because he's just the best thing that has happened to me. So, it's like I really appreciate what he's done and how he's affected my life and helped me get through my father leaving me and stuff." Later, while discussing different aspects of his relationship with his stepfather, Danny talks about the pride his stepfather takes in him. At one point he says, "He's like very quick to tell people how smart I am and how good grades I get and stuff. It's like, he really likes to tell people how good I am and stuff." [I: "And what does that do for you or how does that make you . . . ?"] "It just makes me feel proud, it's like . . . makes me feel proud of what I'm doing and it kind of encourages me to do more." Danny's heartfelt, thoughtful analysis pinpoints the value of parental support, whether it's from a biological father or stepfather. In this case, it is Danny's stepfather who lets him know that he is appreciated for who he is and what he does. In a number of cases, this sense of pride can be heard in the stepfathers' voices as they glowingly talk about their stepchildren. A sampling of these comments:

> *He's intrinsically a really good boy. He has a good heart. He's very sensitive. . . . I someday see him being a really good father himself because he's just got a good soul, he's got a kind heart. . . . He's nine years old and he's already, I mean he plays with kids that are two, three years old and genuinely play with 'em and keeps 'em company and has a good time with them.* [Terry, 41]

> *They're both great kids. They're fabulous kids.* [Barry, 52]

> *She has an incredible voice, a beautiful singing voice. She's really very naturally talented.* [Brad, 38]

> *She's a great kid. She's smart and she's added a whole new dimension to my life.* [Calvin, 38]

> *When you see her contemporaries acting certain ways. It made me appreciate even more what a good kid she is. I mean, she's not a typical thirteen-year-old. I think she's more sensitive. . . . She does not get into any trouble. . . . She really does occupy her time quite productively.* [Gerald, 44]

Not all the stepfathers, of course, praise their stepchildren. However, most feel at least reasonably content with their stepchildren's character. Most of the stepfathers also tend to think that they have lent a helping hand in shaping these kids. Once again, we must keep in mind that the sample of stepfathers who volunteered to be in my study probably does not fully tap the men who are struggling in their stepfathering roles or those who walked away from them. That said, the overriding impression I formed from my interviews is that most of the stepfathers are proud to be around their stepchildren and delighted to have others see them together.

ENDNOTES

1. For national survey studies of what stepfathers do with children, see Hofferth and Anderson 2003; Hofferth et al. 2002.
2. Amato 1998; Coleman 1988, 1990; Furstenberg 1998; Furstenberg and Hughes 1995; Marsiglio and Cohan 2000; Seltzer 1998a; Teachman, Paasch, and Carver 1996.

3. Recent conceptual discussions about fathering using a systems or ecological approach (Doherty, Kouneski, and Erickson 1998) or a scripting perspective (Marsiglio 1995, 1998) are also relevant to stepfathers.

4. Although there is some disagreement between the way parents and stepparents perceive the stepparent's role in a stepfamily, the greatest discrepancy is found when comparing stepchildren's perceptions. (Fine, Coleman, and Ganong 1998, 1999).

5. Cherlin 1978; Ganong and Coleman 1997.

6. Stepfathers' opportunities for providing social capital, as well as their involvement with their stepchildren in other ways, are likely to be affected by the same four factors outlined by Pleck, Lamb, and Levine (1986) dealing with fathers: motivation, skills, social supports, and institutional barriers.

7. Ahrons and Wallisch (1987) provide one of the few empirically based discussions of the relations between biological father and stepfathers, biological mothers and stepmothers, and stepfathers and stepmothers. They use longitudinal data from a sample of 98 pairs of former spouses and their current partners, identified initially in 1977 from divorce court records in Wisconsin. About 75 percent of the biological parents described the same gender stepparents as being "acquaintances rather than friends or relatives" (p. 241). But the authors add, "few reported arguments, anger, or hostility in their contract." About half of the biological parents described the stepparent to be "supportive of the biological parent's special needs as a parent" (pp. 241–42). Among biological fathers specifically, 65 percent reported that the stepparent was "usually" or "always" a "caring person" toward the children and 40 percent thought the stepfather was a good influence on the kids. Finally, 78 percent of the fathers were "mostly satisfied" with the stepfather with only 6 percent saying they were "mostly dissatisfied."

8. A considerable amount of research in recent years has focused on different aspects of nonresident fathers' involvement with their children, especially visitation and child support (Arendell 1995; Braver and O'Connell 1998; Cooksey and Craig 1998; Leite and McKenry 2002; Manning and Smock 1999; Seltzer 1991, 1998b; Seltzer and Brandeth 1995). A number of studies have also focused on how nonresident fathers' actions are related to child outcomes (for a review, see Amato and Gilbreth 1999). The main conclusion from these latter studies is that it is not how much time nonresident fathers spend with their kids that matters, but how they interact with them. In an important related study, White, and Gilbreth (2001) look at how children's outcomes are influenced by the kinds of relationships they have with their resident stepfather and nonresident father. Using national data, they conclude that "many children have good relationships with both fathers and that, even controlling for quality of relationship with the mother, good relationships with both fathers are associated with better child outcomes" (p. 155). The outcomes they address include internalizing (unhappy, sad, depressed, feels worthless or inferior) and externalizing (impulsive or acts without thinking, restless or overly active, cannot sit still) problems.

9. Although researchers have done little to explore systematically how becoming a stepfather influences men's personal lives—beyond marital adjustment, several researchers have explored the implications of biological fathers getting involved actively with their children, especially in a marital context. Hawkins and Belsky (1989) argue that by being involved in their young children's lives, fathers develop more nurturing traits. However, some research indicates that positive father involvement may lead men to experience conflict, stress, and a lower self-esteem (especially with sons), although these patterns do not appear to be related to fathers' level of satisfaction with fathering (Pleck 1997). Finally, Snarey (1993:98) suggests that fathers are more likely to express their capacity for "establishing, guiding, or caring for the next generation" (in the community at large

separate from their own children). In the latter study, being a father is interpreted as encouraging men to play a more significant role in their communities. I suspect that these types of patterns may influence stepfathers as well, though to a lesser degree.

REFERENCES

Ahrons, C. A. and Wallish, L. 1987. "Parenting in the Binuclear Family: Relationships between Biological and Stepparents," Pp. 225–56 in *Remarriage and Stepparenting: Current Research and Theory*, edited by K. Pasley and M. Ihinger-Tallman. New York: Guilford.

Amato, P. 1998. "More than Money? Men's Contributions to Their Children's Lives." Pp. 241–78, in *Men in Families: When Do They Get Involved? What Difference Does It Make?*, edited by A. Booth and N. Crouter. Mahwah, NJ: Erlbaum.

Amato, P. R. and J. G. Gilbreth. 1999. "Nonresident Fathers and Children's Well-Being: A Meta-Analysis." *Journal of Marriage and the Family* 61:557–73.

Arendell, T. 1995. *Fathers and Divorce*. Thousand Oaks, CA: Sage.

Braver, S. L. and D. O'Connell. 1998. *Divorced Dads: Shattering the Myths*. New York: Tarcher/Putnam.

Cherlin, A. J. 1978. "Remarriage as an Incomplete Institution." *American Journal of Sociology* 84:634–50.

Coleman, J. 1988. "Social Capital in the Creation of Human Capital." *American Journal of Sociology* 94:S95–S120.

——. 1990. *Foundations of Social Theory*. Cambridge, MA: Harvard University Press.

Cooksey, E. C. and P. H. Craig. 1998. "Parenting from a Distance: The Effects of Paternal Characteristics on Contact between Nonresidential Fathers and Their Children." *Demography* 35:187–200.

Doherty, W. J., E. F. Kouneski, and M. F. Erickson. 1998. "Responsible Fathering: An Overview and Conceptual Framework." *Journal of Marriage and the Family* 60:277–92.

Fine, M. A., M. Coleman, and L. H. Ganong. 1998. "Consistency in Perceptions of the Stepparent Role among Stepparents, Parents and Stepchildren." *Journal of Social and Personal Relationships* 15:810–28.

——. 1999. "A Social Constructionist Multi-Method Approach to Understanding the Stepparent Role." In *Coping with Divorce, Single Parenting, and Remarriage: A Risk and Resiliency Perspective*, edited by E. M. Hetherington. Mahwah, NJ: Erlbaum.

Furstenberg, F. F., Jr. 1998. "Social Capital and the Role of Fathers in the Family." Pp. 295–301 in *Men in Families: When Do They Get Involved? What Difference Does It Make?*, edited by A. Booth and N. Crouter. Mahwah, NJ: Erlbaum.

Furstenberg, F. F., Jr. and Hughes, M. E. 1995. "Social Capital and Successful Development among At-Risk Youth." *Journal of Marriage and the Family* 57:580–93.

Ganong, L. H. and M. M. Coleman. 1997. "How Society Views Stepfamilies." *Marriage and Family Review* 26:85–106.

Hawkins, A. J. and J. Belsky. 1989. "The Role of Father Involvement in Personality Change in Men across the Transition to Parenthood." *Family Relations* 38:378–84.

Hofferth, S. L. and K. G. Anderson. 2003. "Are All Dads Equal? Biology versus Marriage as a Basis for Parental Investment." *Journal of Marriage and the Family* 65:213–32.

Hofferth, S. L., J. Pleck, J. L. Stueve, S. Bianchi, and L. Sayer. 2002. "The Demography of Fathers: What Fathers Do." Pp 63–90 in *Handbook of Father Involvement: Multidisciplinary Perspective*, edited by C. S. Tamis-LeMonda and N. Cabrera. Mahwah, NJ: Erlbaum.

Leite, R. W. and P. C. McKenry. 2002. "Aspects of Father Status and Postdivorce Father Involvement with Children." *Journal of Family Issues* 23:601–23.

Manning, W. D. and P. J. Smock. 1999. "New Families and Nonresident Father–Child Visitation." *Social Forces* 78:87–116.

Marsiglio, W. 1995. "Fathers' Diverse Life Course Patterns and Roles: Theory and Social Interventions." Pp. 78–101 in *Fatherhood: Contemporary Theories, Research, and Social Policy*, edited by W. Marsiglio. Thousand Oaks, CA: Sage.

——. 1998. *Procreative Man.* New York: New York University Press.

Marsiglio, W. and M. Cohan. 2000. "Contextualizing Father Involvement and Paternal Influence: Sociological and Qualitative Themes." *Marriage and Family Review* 29:75–95.

Pleck, J. H. 1997. "Paternal Involvement: Levels, Sources, and Consequences." Pp. 123–67 in *The Role of the Father in Child Development*, 3d ed., edited by M. E. Lamb. New York: Wiley.

Pleck, J. H., M. E. Lamb, and J. A. Levine. 1986. "Epilogue: Facilitating Future Changes in Men's Family Roles." *Marriage and Family Review* 93:11–16.

Seltzer, J. 1991. "Relationships between Fathers and Children Living Apart: The Father's Role after Separation." *Journal of Marriage and the Family* 53:79–101.

——. 1998a. "Men's Contributions to Children and Social Policy." Pp. 303–14 in *Men in Families: When Do They Get Involved? What Difference Does It Make?* Edited by A. Booth and N. Crouter. Mahwah, NJ: Erlbaum.

——. 1998b. "Father by Law: Effects of Joint Legal Custody on Nonresident Fathers' Involvement with Children." *Demography* 35:135–46.

Seltzer, J., and Y. Brandeth. 1995. "What Fathers Say about Involvement with Children after Separation." Pp. 166–92 in *Fatherhood: Contemporary Theory, Research, and Social Policy*, edited by W. Marsiglio. Thousand Oaks, CA: Sage.

Snarey, J. 1993. *How Fathers Care for the Next Generation: A Four-Decade Study.* Cambridge, MA: Harvard University Press.

Teachman, J. D., K. Paasch, and K. Carver. 1996. "Social Capital and Dropping Out of School Early." *Journal of Marriage and the Family* 58:773–83.

White, L. and J. G. Gilbreth. 2001. "When Children Have Two Fathers: Effects of Relationships with Stepfathers and Noncustodial Fathers on Adolescent Outcomes." *Journal of Marriage and the Family* 63:155–67.

PART VII

Aging and Multigenerational Relationships

I n this section, we explore how family relationships change over time, especially as family members get older. Issues related to the elderly and their families include prolonged intergenerational family relationships, grandparenthood, care of elderly family members, housing issues, health issues, widowhood, elder abuse, and worries about socioeconomic status and poverty. Of particular interest in the United States is the number of elderly who are and will be retiring in the next couple of decades. Part of this concern is driven by changing demographics: As the baby-boom generation (individuals born between 1946 and 1964) ages and prepares to retire, there are fewer workers in the younger generations. Thus, an ongoing public concern is whether there will be enough funds in Social Security to cover the growing number of retired persons in the twenty-first century. Of course, many factors affect how well an individual will do in retirement, including two important family variables — marital status and access to dual incomes — in addition to their education, whether or not they own a home, and the amount of income and savings accrued over their lifetime. People who are single, especially women, have a greater likelihood of being impoverished in their old age than married people with dual incomes. Other issues pertaining to the elderly are the costs of long-term care, mandatory retirement, and ageism in the larger society.

Who Are the Elderly?

We tend to define the elderly by using a somewhat arbitrary age of 65. Supposedly, before 65 you are not old and after 65 you are old. Age 65 was first used in 1889 to define the elderly in Germany when Chancellor Otto Bismarck chose this age to set up a social service program because, at that time, living to age 65 was rare and, therefore, a 65-year-old was definitely considered old. In the 1930s, the U.S. Social Security Administration adopted age 65 to determine when retired persons could get benefits. Because life expectancy for both men and women has greatly increased since the 1930s, the Social Security Administration has decided to raise the age of retirement to 67.

The reality is that "old" and "aged" are really social definitions that vary from society to society and over time. Thus, what it means to be elderly in Japan is not what it means to be elderly in the United States. The elderly are more respected within certain cultures, such as that of Japan and among Native Americans. Historically, many cultures were gerontocracies, which means that the elderly were the highest group in the social stratification system:

They controlled the social resources and political power. What it means to be elderly also varies within societies: It varies between women and men, between different racial-ethnic groups, between people of different social classes, and also between people of different occupations. For example, what is "old" for a professional athlete? Or what is too "old" to become a mother? What is "old" for an academic scholar? Physical aging also varies from individual to individual based on genetic differences and life experiences, such as work, parenting, diet, supportive relationships, and socioeconomic factors.

Family scholars are less interested in the physical aspects of aging than they are in the social consequences related to aging, such as how the elderly affect intergenerational family relationships. Sociologist Matilda White Riley (1983) has researched families in the aging society of the United States and has found that increasing longevity has numerous effects on individuals and on family structure. In particular, Riley argues that family relationships are never fixed but are, instead, constantly changing, a situation that is encouraged by longer life spans. Moreover, individuals have some degree of control over their close relationships. Longevity amplifies this control: People who live longer are more likely to be able to define and choose what types of relationships they would like to have and maintain. Riley's third argument is that the lives of family members are interdependent; thus, the increasing age of one member affects all the other members. Riley's research shows that the increasing life spans provide opportunities and issues for the family that have not been experienced at any other time in history. Two family issues directly affected by longevity—grandparenthood and caring for elderly parents—are the focus of the readings in this section.

Grandparenting

The first article in this section, "Grandparenting," is by Lynne M. Casper and Suzanne M. Bianchi. Casper is a professor and social demographer at the University of Southern California, and Bianchi is a professor of sociology and director of the Maryland Population Research Center at the University of Maryland. This excerpt is taken from their award-winning book, *Continuity and Change in the American Family: Anchoring the Future* (2002). Casper and Bianchi build on Cherlin and Furstenberg's classic study of American grandparenthood (1987), which finds that while grandparenting is a relatively recent phenomenon, developing primarily after World War II, styles of grandparenting vary by social class, race-ethnicity, and age. Casper and Bianchi argue that grandparenthood has changed greatly over the past 100 years due to changes in mortality, fertility, and immigration in the United States. Casper and Bianchi also examine the current situation of increased parental involvement in both their children's and grandchildren's lives due to the rise in single parenthood and the rise of multigenerational households. More grandchildren also are living with their grandparents as their primary parents. All of these changes in grandparenting and multigenerational households create new stresses and new opportunities for families as they adapt to demographic changes. Casper and Bianchi's research reveals the extent to which grandparenthood, and families in general, are sometimes "idealized"—that is, the reality of the situation is not necessarily reflected in the wider society's beliefs about family structure.

This idealized notion of grandparenthood can be examined by studying the normative models of grandparenting in different cultures and different racial-ethnic groups. The second reading in this section, "The Strengths of Apache Grandmothers: Observations on Commitment, Culture, and Caretaking," by Kathleen S. Bahr, provides this cross-cultural analysis. Bahr, an associate professor in the Department of Home and Family Living at Brigham Young University, compares the models of grandparenting common in Anglo American culture and in Apache culture. Bahr begins by introducing these contrasting models, then she provides a detailed description of contemporary Apache grandmothering and its social context among the White Mountain Apache grandmothers living on the Fort Apache Indian Reservation. Next, Bahr makes a systematic comparison between selected themes and issues in both the Anglo American and Apache ethnic contexts, including the meanings and consequences of grandparenting for community and family life. Bahr concludes her article with a summary of ways the Apache family is experiencing strain and undergoing change. Fortunately, Apache grandmothers help to buffer most of these changes in the Apache family, but not without costs. Bahr argues that Apache grandmothers face incredible physical and emotional demands taking care of children and adults in their families.

In the larger society, other families are feeling these strains and undergoing change as well. In response, as discussed by Casper and Bianchi in Reading 28, grandparenting continues to change with more and more grandparents living in multigenerational households or actually raising their grandchildren (estimated to be approximately 4 million families in 2000), and with more families going through divorce or moving long distances away from the grandparents. Journalist Louise Kiernan (1995), for example, argues that "[t]he reality is that all issues affecting parents and their children—divorce, dual-career couples, social mobility and rapid cultural and technological shifts—are also altering the relationships grandparents have with their families" (p. 1T). In recent years, a grandparents' rights movement has arisen to help grandparents maintain or reestablish contact with grandchildren who have been separated from them due to divorce or family discord. Whatever the future of grandparenting, it remains a vital and important social role in American families.

Caring for Elderly Parents

The third reading in this section, "My Mother's Hip: Lessons from the World of Eldercare," is by Luisa Margolies. Margolies, an anthropologist, became interested in the topic of elder care after her mother broke her hip and then suffered a series of health complications that required more intervention and care by her daughter. Like many adult children, she learned her lessons about elder care in the midst of crises. In this selection, Margolies examines the elderly parent carework done by children, primarily daughters. In doing so, she builds on social worker Elaine M. Brody's classic work (1981, 1985) on "women in the middle"; that is, middle-aged women who are involved in parenting children and in caring for elderly parents at the same time. Because many of these women often work outside the home as well, they suffer severe role strain from the competing demands of work and family. Similar to Casper and Bianchi's article (Reading 28), Margolies argues that increasing numbers of elderly will need long-term care to manage chronic illnesses and complications related to aging. The reality is that dealing with aging parents eventually affects most adults, but it is women who undertake the disproportionate amount of physical care for aging and chronically ill parents. This labor, like other caretaking labor in the family, is gendered, and this uneven distribution of responsibility for care of an aging parent is an area of conflict, both within couples and between siblings. Moreover, an illness of an elderly parent can affect the entire family, both emotionally and financially, especially if expensive long-term care is needed. This selection by Margolies (Reading 30) on elder care supplements the readings on family and carework found in Part X of this anthology.

One consequence of prolonged intergenerational family relationships, and the increasing need for parent care, is the rise in reported and unreported cases of elder abuse. Family scholars are particularly concerned because the number of elder abuse cases in the United States is growing rapidly. Unfortunately, this type of abuse is severely underreported because the elderly are often ashamed of being abused. Elder abuse takes a variety of forms, from physical and sexual abuse, to emotional abuse, to neglect, to financial abuse. Moreover, the elderly, especially elderly women, are more likely to be victims of crime, including muggings, homicide, and domestic violence, than are younger people. Elder abuse is committed by family members in the home and by some nursing aide staff in nursing homes. However, because only a small percentage of the elderly (5 to 7 percent) live in nursing homes, most of this abuse occurs in private homes where a son or a daughter is caring for an elderly parent. For a more detailed discussion of elder abuse, see Reading 39 by Ola Barnett, Cindy L. Miller-Perrin, and Robin D. Perrin.

REFERENCES

Brody, Elaine M. 1981. "Women in the Middle" and Family Help to Older People." *The Gerontologist* 21:471–80.

——. 1985. "Parent Care as a Normative Family Stress." *The Gerontologist* 25 (1): 19–29.

Casper, Lynne M. and Suzanne M. Bianchi. 2002. *Continuity and Change in the American Family: Anchoring the Future*. Thousand Oaks, CA: Sage Publications.

Cherlin, Andrew J. and Frank F. Furstenberg, Jr. 1987. *The New American Grandparent: A Place in the Family, A Life Apart*. New York: Basic Books.

Kiernan, Louise. 1995. "Why It's Not Easy Being a Grandparent in the 1990s." *Des Moines Register*, November 11, pp. 1T–2T.

Riley, Matilda White. 1983. "The Family in an Aging Society: A Matrix of Latent Relationships." *Journal of Family Issues* 4 (3): 439–54.

GRANDPARENTING

LYNNE M. CASPER • SUZANNE M. BIANCHI

The most recent estimates indicate that there are 53 million grandparents in the United States and that about 70 percent of adults over age 50 are grandparents (Watson and Koblinsky 1997). Although the majority of Americans will experience the role of grandparent as they age, just how they carry out this role is likely to vary greatly. Grandparent–grandchild relations are embedded in societal, environmental, cultural, familial, and individual contexts that are interdependent and change over time (King, Russell, and Elder 1998). Because of differences in these contexts, grandparenting styles are diverse; they can range from extremely involved, as in the case of a grandparent raising a grandchild without the help of the child's parents, to very remote, as in the case of grandparents who live on the opposite coast from their grandchildren.

Since the 1940s, grandparents have often been portrayed as "rescuers" in family crises, stepping in to help out after wartime marriages dissolved due to death or divorce, or in times of economic crisis (Szinovacz 1998). More recently, increases in drug abuse, child abuse, teen and nonmarital births, divorce, the incidence of AIDS, and changes in welfare laws have presented families with new crises. The increased severity and prevalence of these crises has meant that more and more grandparents are raising their grandchildren on their own (Bryson and Casper 1999; Casper and Bryson 1998). At the same time, increased longevity and continued preferences for noninstitutional living have meant that other grandparents are in need of care and assistance and may reside with their children and grandchildren for the help they can provide (Bryson and Casper 1999). These grandparents may be in need of assistance, but they may also be able to help out with child care, light household chores, and financial contributions, although they have much less responsibility in the rearing of their grandchildren than do grandparents who are raising their grandchildren alone.

A recent front-page feature in *USA Today* highlighted three families that included grandparents and described the circumstances through which each family came to be formed. Grandparents Tom and Pat Torkelson went to live with Tom's daughter and her husband after Pat was hospitalized for cardiac problems (Kasindorf 1999). The family is doing well financially and

Mr. Torkelson works almost full-time to contribute. He enjoys a close relationship with his grandchildren, talking to them frequently and giving them advice. He also drives the youngest children to piano, dance, singing, and soccer practices. Mrs. Torkelson is home when the children get home from school and keeps an eye on them.

In contrast, Cora Stewart, a 63-year-old single grandmother in ill health, is raising her four grandchildren whose mothers could not raise them because of drug problems (Sharp 1999). The Stewart family survives on $250 a month in food stamps and $364 a month in welfare payments. For all intents and purposes, Mrs. Stewart acts as both mother and father to her grandchildren and is fully responsible for their upbringing.

The third family highlighted in the *USA Today* feature includes Mr. and Mrs. Gibson, their daughter, Amy, and their granddaughter, Nicole (El Nasser 1999). Amy Gibson got pregnant when she was 13 years old. Rather than give the baby up for adoption, the Gibsons raised their daughter and granddaughter together and say the two girls grew up more like sisters. The Gibsons are fairly well-off, and Mrs. Gibson quit her job to be home full-time with Nicole.

These stories not only illustrate the diversity of grandparent–grandchildren families and the different types of interactions grandparents and grandchildren can have, they highlight the unique processes through which each family was formed. These families were joined together by circumstances brought about by illness, drug abuse, and nonmarital childbearing, and they bear testimony to the resilience of the American family and its ability to cope with even the most severe crises. The diversity of these families also illustrates the blurring of the definition of family and of the traditional roles each member performs. In some of these families the parents are fulfilling their legal, moral, and social obligations to their children; in others, parents are sharing these responsibilities with the grandparents; and in still others, the grandparents have full responsibility.

Other demographic shifts, including improvements in life expectancy and declines in fertility and immigration, have altered opportunities for interaction between grandparents and grandchildren (Uhlenberg and Kirby 1998). Because more people are surviving to older ages, more children today will have the opportunity to establish relationships with several grandparents than was true in the past. And more grandparents will live long enough to have adult grandchildren. . . .

How Has Grandparenthood Changed over the Years?

Social and demographic shifts have altered the face of grandparenthood over the past century. Changes in mortality, fertility, and immigration can greatly affect how people experience the roles of grandparent and grandchild. In the past, when mortality was higher among adults, children and young adults were less likely than they are today to have living grandparents.

Uhlenberg (1996) used life table techniques to estimate the proportion of people who, at various ages, would have had a living grandparent at the beginning and end of the twentieth century. Less than one-fourth of infants born in 1900 would have had four living grandparents. By 2000, life expectancy among adults had improved to such an extent that more than two-thirds of newborns had all four grandparents alive. Only one-fifth of adults age 30 would have had any living grandparents in 1900, compared with more than three-fourths of those turning 30 in 2000. Many scholars have maintained that at the beginning of the twentieth century very few grandparents were alive. Although it is true that children today are more likely to have living grandparents than were children in the past, even a century ago more than 90 percent of 10-year-old children had at least one living grandparent.

Throughout most of the century, the gender gap in mortality grew and the likelihood of having a living grandmother increased more rapidly than the probability of having a surviving grandfather, especially for young adults (Uhlenberg and Kirby 1998). These differences in mortality also mean that a larger proportion of living grandparents are grandmothers and that the vast majority of great-grandparents are female.

The number of grandchildren a grandparent can expect to have is affected by the level of fertility—higher fertility rates imply more grandchildren and lower fertility rates imply fewer grandchildren. The likelihood of being a grandparent is also affected by changes in childlessness and the timing of births within the population. Changing fertility patterns over the twentieth century affected grandparenthood in three major ways (Uhlenberg and Kirby 1998). First, because of declining fertility, grandparents have fewer grandchildren today than they did in 1900. For example, it is estimated that a woman aged 60 to 64 in 1900 would have had 12.1 grandchildren; a woman in the same age group in the 1990s would have had fewer than 6 grandchildren. Second, due to a decline in childlessness, a higher proportion of older Americans are grandparents than was true a century ago. Third, because of changes in the age at which women complete their childbearing, people today are less likely than they were in 1900 still to be raising their own children when they become grandparents. This is not to say that early childbearing today does not produce overlap in these roles for some people. For example, because childbearing occurs at younger ages for blacks and Hispanics, they are more likely than whites (or Asian Americans) to become grandparents while still raising their own children (Morgan 1996). Yet overall, as fertility declines for all groups, fewer people are likely to experience this overlap than in the past.

Record numbers of immigrants poured into the United States at the beginning of the twentieth century before restrictive laws that limited immigration were passed in the 1920s. This meant that the children of immigrants typically lived in a different country than did their grandparents, and interaction between grandparents and grandchildren was infrequent. One-third of children under age 15 in 1900 had a parent who was born in another country, compared with one-fourth of children in that age group in the late 1990s (Uhlenberg and Kirby 1998).

Other social changes occurring throughout the twentieth century were also important in transforming grandparenthood. The changing economic fortunes of the older population and improvements in health have meant that grandparents today have greater opportunities for more meaningful interaction with their grandchildren. Today's grandparents are also likely to have more free time to spend with their grandchildren; they have more postretirement years and more years after they raise their own children to pursue relationships with their grandchildren. Prior to the 1960s, many documents portrayed grandparents' interactions with grandchildren in a negative light (Szinovacz 1998). Judging from the articles in *USA Today* described above, these views have diminished substantially.

Grandparenting

Styles of grandparenting are defined in part by the extent of the connectedness between grandparents and their grandchildren. The degree of this connectedness is influenced by norms, roles, interactions, sentiments, and exchanges of support (Silverstein, Giarrusso, and Bengtson 1998). Bengtson and his colleagues suggest that intergenerational connectedness between grandparents and grandchildren must be measured along a number of dimensions (Bengtson 2001; Bengtson and Schrader 1982; Mangen, Bengtson, and Landry 1988; Silverstein and Bengtson 1997). The degree of emotional closeness felt between grandparents and grandchildren and the degree to which they share beliefs and values affect connectedness. Closeness between the generations depends on structural factors that facilitate interaction between the grandparents and grandchildren, such as geographic distance and family structure. Grandparenting styles are affected by the number of activities grandparents and grandchildren share and how often they see each other. The extent to which grandparents and grandchildren receive assistance from each other is another important factor. And finally, the degree to which grandparents and grandchildren have a sense of familial duty to each other and share family values affects grandparenting styles.

In general, very few normatively explicit expectations are placed on the role behavior of grandparents. However, American grandparents generally adhere to the norm of noninterference; that is, they believe that parents should be free to raise their children as they see fit (Cherlin and Furstenberg 1985, 1986). Yet most Americans also feel obligated to provide assistance when close relatives are in need (Rossi and Rossi 1990). These two contrasting norms, along with variations in the six dimensions of grandparent–grandchild connectedness, help to explain why there is such broad diversity in grandparenting styles.

In one of the earliest studies on grandparenting, Neugarten and Weinstein (1964) used factors such as biologic continuity, emotional self-fulfillment, teaching, vicarious accomplishment, degree of formality, authority, contact, the transmission of family wisdom, and having fun to categorize the meaning of grandparenthood and the style of grandparenting. They identified the following types of grandparents: "formal," "funseeker," "surrogate parent," "reservoir of family wisdom," and "distant."

Cherlin and Furstenberg (1985, 1986), in one of the benchmark studies on grandparenthood, used nationally representative data to develop a typology of grandparenting styles based on the extent of exchange of services, the degree of parentlike behavior (authority), and frequency of contact. They labeled those who scored low on exchange of services, demonstrated little parentlike behavior, and had little contact with their grandchildren "detached" grandparents. "Passive" grandparents reported minimal exchange of services and little parentlike behavior, but had more frequent contact with their grandchildren. "Active" grandparents were those who exchanged services and/or had some parentlike influence in their grand-children's lives. Cherlin and Furstenberg (1985) further categorized active grandparents as "supportive" (those scoring high only on exchange), "authoritative" (those scoring high only on authority), or "influential" (those scoring high in both areas). Using this typology, they found that 26 percent of the grandparents in their sample were detached, 29 percent were passive, 17 percent were supportive, 9 percent were authoritative, and 19 percent were influential. According to this typology, more than 70 percent of grand-parents do not assume parentlike roles with their grandchildren. Thus, even though most grandparents have involvement with their grandchildren, the majority seem to adhere to the norm of noninterference.

In their study, Cherlin and Furstenberg (1985) also examined other differences across grandparenting styles. They found that detached and pas-sive grandparents were much older than supportive and authoritative grandparents and that influential grandparents tended to be the youngest. They interpret this finding as evidence that grandparental activity levels are determined in part by the aging process. They also found that detached grandparents had less contact with and lived farther away from their grand-children than other grandparents. They suggest that because 63 percent of detached grandparents lived more than 100 miles from their grandchildren, geographic limitations may impede such grandparents from adopting more active roles. Cherlin and Furstenberg also found that about half of the passive, supportive, and authoritative grandparents saw their grandchildren at least once a week. Therefore, the degree of contact between grandparents and grandchildren was not necessarily indicative of whether grandparents had a passive or moderately active style of grandparenting. In contrast, influential grandparents lived very close to their grandchildren and had a very high degree of contact. In regard to this finding, Cherlin and Furstenberg note that near daily contact seems to be essential to a grandparent's maintaining an influential grandparenting style.

Although family rituals, such as special family recipes and dishes, jokes, common expressions, songs, and sharing special events, were common among all grandparents, detached grandparents were the least likely to acknowledge such rituals (Bengtson 2001; Cherlin and Furstenberg 1985). They were also the least likely to report that they had close or extremely close relationships with their grandchildren.

Styles of grandparenting are related to other factors as well, including gender, lineage (paternal or maternal relation), ages of grandparents and grandchildren and their relative ages, family structure, and race. (For a recent review of this literature, see Aldous 1995.) Studies have shown that grandmothers generally have closer relationships with their grandchildren than do grandfathers (Cherlin and Furstenberg 1986). Grandmothers also interact differently with grandchildren than do grandfathers; they are more likely to interact as caregivers, whereas grandfathers are more likely to interact as mentors (Eisenberg 1988).

Divorce and premarital fertility in the parental generation also affect grandparenting styles. Grandparents are more likely to assist the middle generation when daughters are single mothers (Aldous 1985; Eggebeen and Hogan 1990). In addition, when parents divorce, the mother usually retains custody and her parents tend to have greater access to the grandchild. Aldous (1995) suggests that one of the consequences of these customary custody arrangements is that grandparents are generally less important in the lives of their descendants in the male line. This may be particularly salient for black families, because single-mother families are more prevalent among blacks.

Yet even apart from single parenting, the intergenerational linkages between mothers and adult daughters tend to be somewhat stronger than those between mothers and sons (Silverstein and Bengtson 1997). This predisposes grandchildren to have more contact with maternal grandparents. Feelings of closeness are also stronger between adult children and mothers (Bengtson 2001; Silverstein and Bengtson 1997), further increasing the likelihood that grandmothers more than grandfathers will be influential in the lives of their grandchildren.

The ages of the grandparents and grandchildren also affect grandparenting styles. Younger grandparents are more likely to be involved with their grandchildren (Troll 1983), yet grandparents who are too young may not be prepared for the role of grandparent and may feel overburdened by the prospect of having to raise both their own children and their children's children (Burton and Bengtson 1985; Troll 1985). Older grandparents are more often detached or passive in their grandparenting styles. Research suggests that older grandparents often lack the energy to interact with their grandchildren (Burton and Dilworth-Anderson 1991). Grandchildren's ages also matter; grandparents tend to be more highly involved with young grandchildren and less involved with adolescent grandchildren (Troll 1983). In addition, whereas grandparents feel responsible for disciplining and advising younger grandchildren, they feel responsible for sharing wisdom with older grandchildren (Thomas 1989).

Research in the area of grandparent roles and grandparent–grandchild relationships has also focused on how historical and experimental events shape the way the grandparent role is enacted (Cherlin and Furstenberg 1986; Hagestad 1985). Children who grew up in cohesive families with affectionate parents exhibit stronger feelings of obligation as mature adults when they are enacting the grandparent role (Rossi and Rossi 1990). Childhood experiences with grandparents also influence how grandparents interact with their own grandchildren (King and Elder 1997). Also, relations between grandchildren and grandparents depend on current relations between grandchildren and their parents and, more important, on relations between their parents and grandparents (King and Elder 1995).

A few researchers have also investigated cultural differences in grandparenting styles. Young black adults tend to believe that grandparents should have a parental role in rearing grandchildren and that the boundary between parent and grandparent roles is malleable. In contrast, young white adults hold attitudes consistent with the norm of noninterference — grandparents should maintain contact, but leave the role of parenting to the parent (Kennedy 1990). Cherlin and Furstenberg (1985) report similar black–white differences with regard to the norm of noninterference. Sotomayor (1989) found that Mexican American grandparents believe they have an important function in helping to rear their grandchildren. Asian American families are more likely to reject the norm of noninterference; Kamo (1998) suggests that this may be explained in part by Confucian ethics, under which children belong to the entire extended family.

Grandparents and Single Parenting

The involvement of grandparents in the lives of their daughters (and sons) who become single parents is receiving increased attention with court cases over grandparents' visitation rights and welfare reform measures that highlight the responsibilities of (grand)parents whose teenage daughters become mothers. The 2000 Census even included a new set of questions, mandated as part of welfare reform, on grandparents' support of grandchildren to address this important issue.

Research suggests that grandparents increase the assistance they provide to their adult children after their children experience divorce (Hirshorn 1998). As in the case of the Gibsons in the *USA Today* article cited earlier, grandparents also frequently coparent or raise their grandchildren who are born into single-parent families. In these cases grandparents may provide child care, act as coparents or as surrogate parents, and help out with expenses.

Table 1 illustrates the importance of grandparents in mother–child families. In 1998, about 17 percent of unmarried mothers with children lived in the homes of their parents. These single mothers are likely to benefit from sharing residences with their parents; grandparents can help out by providing food and shelter, caring for their grandchildren, and providing parenting advice. The table also shows that the proportion of single mothers living with their parents is the highest for Hispanics (22 percent), followed by blacks (18 percent)

TABLE 1   **Coresidence with Parents and Receipt of Child Care in Single-Mother Families by Race (in percentages)**

	Total	White	Black	Hispanic
Single mothers living with their parents	16.7	14.5	17.5	21.7
Preschoolers with grandparents as primary child-care providers[a]				
All preschoolers of employed mothers	16.3	14.1	22.1	22.4
With married mothers	13.5	12.1	18.0	19.5
With unmarried mothers	25.4	24.8	25.1	29.2

Source: Data on single mothers living with parents are from the Current Population Survey, March supplement, 1998; data on preschoolers are from the Survey of Income and Program Participation, 1994.
Note: Race-ethnicity categories are white, non-Hispanic; black, non-Hispanic, and Hispanic.
[a]Care provided while the mother was at work.

and whites (15 percent). These findings provide further evidence that "distant grandparenting" and the norm of noninterference may be more prevalent among whites, perhaps in part because the higher economic status of white single-parent families, on average, means they less often require direct (grand)parental assistance. Grandparents also coreside with and provide support to sons who are single fathers. Data . . . indicate that about 1 out of 10 single fathers lived with his children's grandparent(s) in 1998. Hagestad (1996) has used the expression "Family National Guard" to describe the ways in which elders, especially grandparents, provide assistance when necessary, and the living arrangement data are consistent with this notion of grandparents as a reserve to be called upon during times of need.

Living arrangements data such as those shown in Table 1 provide only a snapshot of grandparental assistance to single mothers and underestimate the proportion of single mothers who ever receive assistance from their parents during their years of single parenting. A much higher 36 percent of single mothers live at some point in their parents' homes (Bumpass and Raley 1995, Table 3). Coresidence with a parent is especially prevalent among black single mothers, 57 percent of whom have lived in their mothers' (and/or fathers') homes while raising children without their children's father present. Grandparent coresidence is especially likely in cases where there is a birth before marriage: 60 percent of white and 72 percent of black single mothers who had a child before marrying resided at some point with their parent(s).

Data from the Survey of Income and Program Participation give us an idea of another type of help grandparents provide to single parents: child care. In 1994, one-fourth of preschoolers with unmarried mothers had grandparents as primary child-care providers while their mothers worked, compared with only 14 percent of children with married mothers (see Table 1). Slightly more Hispanic preschoolers with unmarried mothers had grandparents as their primary care providers than did their black and white counterparts (29 percent, 25 percent, and 25 percent, respectively). Data also suggest that grandparents are more likely to provide primary care for their grandchildren when their children are never married than when they are divorced or separated (Casper 1997, Table 2). Thus, as single parenthood shifts toward women who have never married, grandparents may be providing financial and child-care assistance for increasing numbers of single mothers and their children (Ghosh, Easterlin, and Macunovich 1993).

Grandparent interaction with grandchildren in single-parent families blurs the boundaries of the traditional roles of parenthood and grandparenthood. To the extent that grandparent involvement substitutes for the nonresident parent's involvement or compensates for time and resources the single parent cannot give to children, single parents may experience different "degrees" of raising children alone and grandparents may experience different degrees of parenting and grandparenting.

Multigenerational Families with Grandparents

In the 1990s, amid the passage of the new welfare legislation and continued discussion of the decline of the family, grandparenting research shifted toward the examination of different kinds of households containing grandparents and grandchildren (Szinovacz 1998). The three types of grandparent–grandchild families depicted in the *USA Today* articles noted earlier provide a real-life example of the diversity of these families. The main structural difference among these families is that Mrs. Stewart and the Gibsons took their grandchildren into their homes and had primary responsibility for parenting them, whereas the Torkelsons moved in with their adult children and were supplemental caregivers for their grandchildren. These two household structures, with homes maintained by either the grandparents or the parents, imply different caregiving scenarios in which the roles of the grandparents vary enormously.

Researchers, public policy makers, and the media first began to notice the increases in grandparent-maintained households around 1990, prompting them to question why this was happening. An explosion of analytic research occurred in the early to mid-1990s that sought to answer this question and to examine further the area of grandparent caregiving in general. These studies identified several explanations for the increase in the numbers of grandparents raising and helping to raise their grandchildren. Increasing drug abuse among parents, teen pregnancy, divorce, the rapid rise of single-parent households, mental and physical illnesses of parents, AIDS, crime, child abuse and neglect, and incarceration are a few of the most common explanations offered (for a review of these causes, see Minkler 1998).

CPS data for the 1990s confirm the researchers' impressions, showing that more grandparents were taking their children and grandchildren into their homes. In 1990, there were 2.1 million grandparent-maintained households

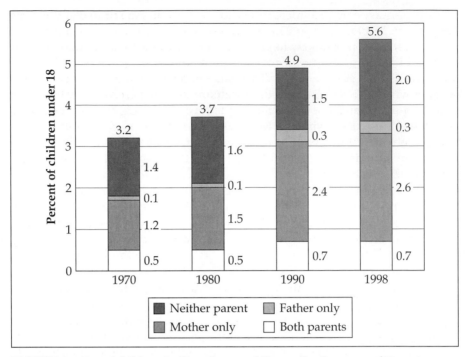

FIGURE 1   Grandchildren in Grandparents' Homes by Presence of Parents
Source: U.S. Census, 1970, 1980; Current Population Survey, March Supplements, 1990, 1998.

in the United States, constituting 6.3 percent of all family households. By 1998, this number had increased to 2.6 million, representing 7.4 percent of all family households. The number of children residing with grandparents increased as well. Figure 1 shows that in 1970, 2.2 million or 3.2 percent of American children lived in households maintained by grandparents. By 1998, this number had risen to 4 million, or 5.6 percent. Thus the number of children living in their grandparents' homes increased by more than 80 percent over the 28-year period. Substantial increases occurred among all types of households maintained by grandparents, regardless of the presence or absence of the grandchildren's parents, but increases were greatest among children with only one parent in the household. The majority of change for most household types occurred in the decade of the 1980s. Although the proportion of children living *only* with their grandparents (i.e., no parent present) did not increase in the 1970s and 1980s, the greatest growth in the 1990s was registered in these skipped-generation living arrangements. This means that the 1990s was a decade marked by increasing numbers of grandparents with sole responsibility for raising their grandchildren.

Given the increase in this type of family, it is not surprising that the popular media began to focus attention on the growing number of children being raised by their grandparents (e.g., Culter 1991; Norris 1991). It wasn't long before federal lawmakers followed suit—both the Senate and the

House of Representatives recognized that this trend constituted a pressing issue for public policy and held congressional hearings on the matter in 1992. The Senate hearings of the Special Committee on Aging focused on the causes of the trend (U.S. Senate 1992), whereas the House hearings, held by the Select Committee on Aging, examined the new roles and responsibilities of grandparents (U.S. House of Representatives 1992). Both sets of hearings also highlighted policy deficiencies in the areas of grandparents' rights and grandparents' access to public assistance. In January 1995, then-President Clinton signed a formal proclamation declaring 1995 the "Year of the Grandparent," recognizing the "extraordinary place that grandparents hold in our families and communities."

The recent increase in numbers of grandparents raising their grandchildren is particularly troubling because both these grandparents and their grandchildren often suffer significant health problems. Researchers have documented high rates of asthma, weakened immune systems, poor eating and sleeping patterns, physical disabilities, and hyperactivity among grandchildren being raised by their grandparents (Dowdell 1995; Minkler and Roe 1996; Shore and Hayslip 1994). Grandparents raising grandchildren also appear to be in poorer health than their counterparts; studies have noted high rates of depression, poor self-rated health, and multiple chronic health problems among grandparents raising their grandchildren (Dowdell 1995; Minkler and Roe 1993). For example, Minkler et al. (1997) found that grandparents raising grandchildren were twice as likely to be clinically depressed as were grandparents who play more traditional roles.

These families are also more likely than other kinds of families to experience economic hardship. A number of studies have focused on the economic well-being of grandparents and their grandchildren, documenting their disproportionately high poverty rates (Bryson and Casper 1999; Casper and Bryson 1998; Chalfie 1994; Fuller-Thomson, Minkler, and Driver 1997; Rutrough and Ofstedal 1997).

At the other end of the spectrum are growing concerns for the well-being of adults who are taking their aging mothers and fathers into their homes and providing care for them, often at the same time they are raising children of their own. Demographic shifts—the extension of the life span, aging of the population, fewer children per family, increasing divorce and remarriage, and the delay in childbearing—have contributed to the sense of urgency in this matter. In this type of household, the flow of resources is usually from the parent to the grandparent. Grandparents in this situation may be more limited in the roles they can play in their grandchildren's lives. They are likely to be older and to have older grandchildren than grandparents who provide homes for their grandchildren. They are also more likely to have health problems (Bryson and Casper 1999).

Despite the trend toward independent living among older Americans, research has shown that many families who have older kin in frail health provide extraordinary care (Horowitz 1985; Stone, Cafferata, and Sangl 1987).

Providing intensive care can have many negative consequences for caregivers, including increased stress and strained relationships (Semple 1992; Stommel et al. 1995). The level of stress in these households is also likely to affect how grandparents and grandchildren experience their relationships.

REFERENCES

Aldous, Joan. 1985. "Parent–Adult Child Relations as Affected by the Grandparents' Status." Pp. 117–32 in *Grandparenthood,* edited by Vern L. Bengtson and Joan F. Robertson. Beverly Hills, CA: Sage.

——. 1995. "New Views of Grandparents in Intergenerational Context." *Journal of Family Issues* 16:104–22.

Bengtson, Vern L. 2001. "Beyond the Nuclear Family: The Increasing Importance of Multigenerational Bonds." *Journal of Marriage and the Family* 63:1–16.

Bengtson, Vern L. and Sandi S. Schrader. 1982. "Parent-Child Relations." Pp. 115–86 in *Research Instruments in Social Gerontology,* vol. 2, *Social Roles and Social Participation,* edited by David J. Mangen and Warren A. Peterson. Minneapolis: University of Minnesota Press.

Bryson, Ken and Lynne M. Casper. 1999. *Co-resident Grandparents and Their Grandchildren.* Current Population Reports, Series P-23, No. 198. Washington, DC: Government Printing Office.

Bumpass, Larry L. and R. Kelly Raley. 1995. "Redefining Single-Parent Families: Cohabitation and Changing Family Reality." *Demography* 32:97–109.

Burton, Linda M. and Vern L. Bengtson. 1985. "Black Grandmothers: Issues of Timing and Continuity of Roles." Pp. 61–77 in *Grandparenthood,* edited by Vern L. Bengtson and Joan F. Robertson. Beverly Hills, CA: Sage.

Burton, Linda M. and Peggy Dilworth-Anderson. 1991. "The Intergenerational Family Roles of Aged Black Americans." *Marriage and Family Review* 16:311–30.

——. 1997. *Who's Minding Our Preschoolers? Fall 1994 (Update).* Current Population Reports, Series P-70, No. 62. Washington, DC: Government Printing Office.

Casper, Lynne M. and Ken Bryson. 1998. "Co-resident Grandparents and Their Grandchildren: Grandparent-Maintained Families." Working Paper No. 26, Population Division, U.S. Bureau of the Census, Washington, DC.

Chalfie, Deborah. 1994. *Going It Alone: A Closer Look at Grandparents Rearing Grandchildren.* Washington, DC: American Association of Retired Persons.

Cherlin, Andrew J. and Frank F. Furstenberg, Jr. 1985. "Styles and Strategies of Grandparenting." Pp. 97–116 in *Grandparenthood,* edited by Vern L. Bengtson and Joan F. Robertson. Beverly Hills, CA: Sage.

——. 1986. *The New American Grandparent: A Place in the Family, a Life Apart.* New York: Basic Books.

Culter, Lawrence. 1991. "More and More, Grandparents Raise Grandchildren." *New York Times,* April 7, p. C12.

Dowdell, Elizabeth B. 1995. "Caregiver Burden: Grandparents Raising Their High-Risk Children." *Journal of Psychosocial Nursing* 33 (3): 27–30.

Eggebeen, David J. and Dennis P. Hogan. 1990. "Giving between Generations in American Families." *Human Nature* 1:211–32.

Eisenberg, Anne R. 1988. "Grandchildren's Perspectives on Relationships with Grandparents: The Influence of Gender across Generations." *Sex Roles* 19:205–17.

El Nasser, Haya. 1999. "Raising Grandkids: No Day at the Beach." *USA Today,* July 1, p. A1.

Fuller-Thomson, Esme, Meredith Minkler, and Diane Driver. 1997. "A Profile of Grandparents Raising Grandchildren in the United States." *Gerontologist* 37:406–11.

Ghosh, Susmita, Richard A. Easterlin, and Diane J. Macunovich. 1993. "How Badly Have Single Parents Done? Trends in the Economic Status of Single Parents since

1964." Presented at the annual meeting of the Population Association of America, March, Cincinnati.

Hagestad, Gunhild O. 1985. "Continuity and Connectedness." Pp. 31–48 in *Grandparenthood,* edited by Vern L. Bengtson and Joan F. Robertson. Beverly Hills, CA: Sage.

———. 1996. "On-Time, Off-Time, Out of Time? Reflections of Continuity and Discontinuity from an Illness Process." Pp. 204–22 in *Adulthood and Aging: Research on Continuities and Discontinuities,* edited by Vern L. Bengtson. New York: Springer.

Hirshorn, Barbara A. 1998. "Grandparents as Caregivers." Pp. 200–14 in *Handbook on Grandparenthood,* edited by Maximiliane E. Szinovacz. Westport, CT: Greenwood.

Horowitz, Amy. 1985. "Family Caregiving to the Frail Elderly." Pp. 194–246 in *Annual Review of Gerontology and Geriatrics,* vol. 5, edited by Carl Eisdorfer. New York: Springer.

Kamo, Yoshinori. 1998. "Asian Grandparents." Pp. 97–112 in *Handbook on Grandparenthood,* edited by Maximiliane E. Szinovacz. Westport, CT: Greenwood.

Kasindorf, Martin. 1999. "Three Generations, One Happy Family." *USA Today,* July 1, p. D8.

Kennedy, Gregory E. 1990. "College Students' Expectations of Grandparent and Grandchild Role Behaviors." *Gerontologist* 30:43–48.

King, Valerie and Glen H. Elder, Jr. 1995. "American Children View Their Grandparents: Linked Lives across Three Rural Generations." *Journal of Marriage and the Family* 57:165–78.

———. 1997. "The Legacy of Grandparenting: Childhood Experiences with Grandparents and Current Involvement with Grandchildren." *Journal of Marriage and the Family* 59:848–59.

King, Valerie, Steven T. Russell, and Glen H. Elder, Jr. 1998. "Grandparenting in Family Systems: An Ecological Perspective." Pp. 53–69 in *Handbook on Grandparenthood,* edited by Maximiliane E. Szinovacz. Westport, CT: Greenwood.

Mangen, David J., Vern L. Bengtson, and Pierre H. Landry. 1988. *Measurement of Intergenerational Relations.* Newbury Park, CA: Sage.

Minkler, Meredith. 1998. "Intergenerational Households Headed by Grandparents: Demographic and Sociological Contexts." Pp. 3–18 in *Grandparents and Other Relatives Raising Children: Background Papers from Generations United's Expert Symposium,* edited by Generations United. Washington, DC: Generations United.

Minkler, Meredith, and Esme Fuller-Thomson, Doriane Miller, and Diane Driver. 1997. "Depression in Grandparents Raising Grandchildren: Results of a National Longitudinal Study." *Archives of Family Medicine* 6:445–52.

Minkler, Meredith and Kathleen M. Roe. 1993. *Grandmothers as Caregivers: Raising Children of the Crack Cocaine Epidemic.* Newbury Park, CA: Sage.

———. 1996. "Grandparents as Surrogate Parents." *Generations* 20:34–38.

Morgan, S. Philip. 1996. "Characteristic Features of Modern American Fertility." Pp. 19–66 in *Fertility in the United States: New Patterns, New Theories,* edited by J. B. Casterline, Ronald D. Lee, and Karen A. Foote. New York: Population Council.

Neugarten, Bernice L. and Karol K. Weinstein. 1964. "The Changing American Grandparent." *Journal of Marriage and the Family* 26:199–204.

Norris, Michele. 1991. "Grandmothers Who Fill Void Carved by Drugs." *Washington Post,* August 30, p. C12.

Rossi, Alice S. and Peter H. Rossi. 1990. *Of Human Bonding: Parent–Child Relations across the Life Course.* New York: Aldine de Gruyter.

Rutrough, Thyne S. and Mary Beth Ofstedal. 1997. "Grandparents Living with Grandchildren: A Metropolitan–Nonmetropolitan Comparison." Presented at the annual meeting of the Population Associate of America, March.

Sharp, Deborah. 1999. "After a Lifetime of Work, a Second Family to Raise." *USA Today,* July 1, p. D8.

Shore, Ron J. and Bert Hayslip, Jr. 1994. "Custodial Grandparenting: Implications for Children's Development." Pp. 171–218 in *Redefining Families: Implications for*

Children's Development, edited by Adele Eskeles Gottfried and Allen W. Gottfried. New York: Plenum.

Silverstein, Merril and Vern L. Bengtson. 1997. "Intergenerational Solidarity and the Structure of Adult Child–Parent Relationships in American Families." *American Journal of Sociology* 103:429–60.

Silverstein, Merril, Roseann Giarrusso, and Vern L. Bengston. 1998. "Intergenerational Solidarity and the Grandparent Role." Pp. 144–58 in *Handbook on Grandparenthood,* edited by Maximiliane E. Szinovacz. Westport, CT: Greenwood.

Sotomayor, M. 1989. "The Hispanic Elderly and the Intergenerational Family." *Journal of Children in Contemporary Society* 20:55–65.

Stommel, Manfred, Barbara A. Given, Charles W. Given, and Clare Collins. 1995. "The Impact of the Frequency of Care Activities on the Division of Labor between Primary Caregivers and Other Care Providers." *Research on Aging* 17:412–33.

Stone, Robyn, Gail Lee Cafferata, and Judith Sangl. 1987. "Caregivers of the Frail Elderly: A National Profile." *Gerontologist* 27:616–26.

Szinovacz, Maximiliane E. 1998. "Grandparent Research: Past, Present, and Future." Pp. 1–22 in *Handbook on Grandparenthood,* edited by Maximiliane E. Szinovacz. Westport, CT: Greenwood.

Thomas, Jeanne L. 1989. "Gender and Perceptions of Grandparenthood." *International Journal of Aging and Human Development* 29:269–82.

Troll, Lillian E. 1983. "Grandparents: The Family Watchdogs." Pp. 63–74 in *Family Relationships in Later Life,* edited by Timothy H. Brubaker. New York: Free Press.

———. 1985. "The Contingencies of Grandparenting." Pp. 135–49 in *Grandparenthood,* edited by Vern L. Bengtson and Joan F. Robertson. Beverly Hills, CA: Sage.

Uhlenberg, Peter. 1996. "Mortality Decline in the Twentieth Century and Supply of Kin over the Lifecourse." *Gerontologist* 36:681–85.

Uhlenberg, Peter and James B. Kirby. 1998. "Grandparenthood over Time: Historical and Demographic Trends." Pp. 23–39 in *Handbook on Grandparenthood,* edited by Maximiliane E. Szinovacz. Westport, CT: Greenwood.

U.S. House of Representatives. 1992. *Grandparents: New Roles and Responsibilities.* Select Committee on Aging Publication No. 102-876. Washington, DC: Government Printing Office.

U.S. Senate. 1992. *Grandparents as Parents: Raising a Second Generation.* Special Committee on Aging Serial No. 102-24. Washington, DC: Government Printing Office.

Watson, Jeffrey A. and Sally A. Koblinsky. 1997. "Strengths and Needs of Working-Class African-American and Anglo-American Grandparents." *International Journal of Aging and Human Development* 44:149–65.

29

THE STRENGTHS OF APACHE GRANDMOTHERS
Observations on Commitment, Culture, and Caretaking

KATHLEEN S. BAHR

"**M**y great grandmother is a special person to me because she did a good job of raising my mother. I am happy for what she has done and for what she is still doing for us." So begins a tribute written by Garrett Dazen, a fifth grader, published in the *Fort Apache Scout*, June 1, 1990. To persons unacquainted with Apachean families (including several Apache populations as well as the Navajo), this tribute may hint of possible failure in the family system: What happened that made it necessary for the great grandmother to raise the mother? In fact, rather than signaling family failure, the statement is testimony to one of the great strengths of Apache families, a traditional pattern of responsibility and care that continues to serve families and protect children.

This [reading] compares two normative models of grandparenting, one common in Anglo American culture and the other an Apache pattern. The introduction of these contrasting models is followed by a description of contemporary Apache grandmothering and its social context, as enacted by White Mountain Apache grandmothers living on the Fort Apache Indian Reservation. Finally, there is a systematic comparison of selected themes and issues in both ethnic contexts, and of the meanings and consequences of grandparenting for community and family life.

Ethnicity and "Normal" Family Development

Wilson (1984a), commenting on social scientific studies of black families, observed that there had been much more attention paid to their pathologies and disorganization than to their remarkable strength and resilience. So it also is with studies of Indian families. People who know very little else about Indian Americans share stereotypes about the poverty, violence, and alcoholism that characterize their families. Yet Anglo Americans are generally unaware of the tenacity of Indian family values and the maintenance of strong kinship ties and family identity among them in the face of almost insurmountable odds.

In family matters, as in other patterns of behavior, it has been assumed by white Americans that their own cultural norms for acceptable behavior are the "right" ones, normal and morally superior to other patterns. Thus, in scholarship as well as popular stereotypes, Anglo American family patterns have been held up as optimal standards. To the degree that the families of ethnic minorities have differed, they have been defined as deficient, disorganized, or immoral (Wilson 1984b:1333). "Help" in better adjusting and conforming to majority standards, often unsought, has been offered or imposed on Indian peoples by teachers, counselors, missionaries, social workers, politicians, and other professionals.

One of the purposes of this [reading] is to call into question the superiority of the standard "white" family pattern as it applies to grandparenting. Another is to document the continuing commitment of many Apachean grandmothers as bearers of the cultural heritage and of ultimate responsibility for the physical well-being of their families. Defined by her culture and often by circumstance as "caretaker of last resort," she devotes extraordinary effort and personal sacrifice to performing the grandmother role.

Models of Grandparenting: Anglos and Apacheans

Family scientists sometimes talk of "the" family life cycle, or "developmental stages," as if such cycles and stages were part of humanity's genetic heritage rather than social constructions. In practice, there are many ethnic and individual variations in such stages and cycles. With respect to grandparenting, many of the standard models of family life in American assume a configuration where grandparents are acknowledged as kin, but play a peripheral role in the lives of the families of their children and grandchildren. In the usual "family life cycle" model, with "stages" often presented as universals without significant ethnic qualification, American older couples "launch" their children and move into an "empty nest" stage. This is described as a stage when parents should be able to consider their parenting tasks "done," and now are free to pursue their own interests in ways heretofore impossible because of child-rearing responsibilities.

In reality many parents do not "launch" their adult children and many are directly involved in the care of grandchildren (according to the U.S. Census Bureau, 24 percent of unmarried adults aged 25 to 39 were living in the parental household, and about 5 percent of American grandchildren live in a grandparent-headed household, 1991b:9, 11). However, these variations do little to weaken the strength of the norm. In fact, to vary from this norm is sometimes labeled as being "out of phase," that is, not finished with parenting at ages when most people are said to be enjoying the "freedom" associated with an "empty nest."

Being thus out of phase is reported to be associated with perceptions of high personal stress and unhappiness. The stresses are assumed to be severe if adult children and grandchildren return to live in the grandparental home. Such grandparents are said to be "developmentally disadvantaged":

> In the home with adult children, the parents' development may also suffer. As individuals, these parents are often prevented from experiencing the freedom necessary to develop further interests without the burdens of children at home. (Clemens and Axelson 1985:262)

The family structure of this three-generation household is described as "inappropriate or off-balance." It is said that "most parents do not welcome the return of these children and view their stay as a short-term arrangement," and that "older adult children and those whose sojourn [in the parental household] becomes long-term appear to both cause and experience more stress" (p. 263). In the same vein, Hagestad and Burton (1986) argue that

> the entry into grandparenthood has become a normal, expectable part of middle age, *a time when daily involvement in the demands of parenthood have ceased*. When the transition does not come in the expected life context, it may disrupt resolution of developmental tasks and hamper involvement in other roles. [Emphasis added] (P. 471)

Beyond the expectation that they will be "freed from the commitments of the child-rearing years," "the normal expectable life" of the modern Anglo grandparent also includes the assumption that they "have attained a certain level of economic security, and at a time when they are still healthy and vigorous" (Hagestad and Burton 1986:473). The combination of health and a degree of economic security means that many continue to maintain a social and economic life independent of children and grandchildren. Consider Cowgill's (1986) depiction of "Western" grandparenting:

> In Western society, despite the fact that grandparents have generally been relieved of any authoritative responsibility for the discipline and upbringing of grandchildren, the relationship is usually rather formal and distant. Grandparents are interested in and take pride in the accomplishments of grandchildren, but they are not usually intimate with them, and there is relatively little affect in the relationship. But in this case, the distance results not from any interference based on authority but from physical separation and conflicting social involvement. . . . Thus both grandparents and grandchildren tend to be preoccupied with interests and activities with their age peers, and all of this tends to minimize contacts, reduce interaction, and attenuate the relationship. (P. 92)

In contrast to this normative Anglo American pattern[1] is an American Indian standard that defines the grandparent as very important in the socialization and care of children. Rather than being without responsibility or right to intervene in the rearing of the new generation, grandparents are both authorized and expected to play a major role. Among the Sioux, a new child is called "little grandmother" or "little grandfather" to help impress on her the important role of the grandparent. This custom also encourages respect for the very young and is a reminder that the grandparent generation is the model, "that you are going to grow up to be a grandparent some day and, as such, you must remember to keep these things in mind. And mutual respect and affection develop because this is a known role for the future as well as the kind one can play at when one is a child. It is a very important thing" (Attneave 1981:47).

The expectation that grandparents will play a major role in the physical care and training of their grandchildren is common among most Indian peoples. In fact, it is one of the notable similarities among the wide diversity of tribes (Ryan 1981).

Many ethnographic reports emphasize the key role Apachean grandparents have played in the rearing of their grandchildren. Shomaker (1989) notes that among the Navajo the grandparent often adopted the grandchild, and the alliance between the grandparent and grandchild was considered

> the strongest bond in Navajo culture; this was a warm association in which perpetuation of traditional teaching could be effected. The fostered child became known to others as *child of the grandparent,* changing in status from that of the biological grandchild. The biological mother withdrew from her role as parent to a more distant relationship, similar to that of an older sister. The grandchild lived with the grandparents until adulthood. [Emphasis added] (P. 3)

Historically, the Apaches were hunters, gatherers, and farmers, and Apache women played a major role in providing for their families (Stockel 1991). Their involvement as providers began when they were young girls and continued into old age for as long as they were physically able. Young Apache mothers, perhaps accompanied by an older daughter, roamed long distances to gather food and fuel. Grandmothers, less physically able, stayed close to home and cared for the children. "Older women supervised, answered questions, trained the girls, and taught them to identify various plants and how to shell, husk, and strip wild foods to obtain the edible parts" (Stockel 1991:14).

Goodwin (1942), a close observer of the Western Apache in the 1930s, described the relationship between grandmothers and grandchildren this way:

> Grandparents love to watch their grandchildren at play. It is common for a grandmother to give a small child the run of her wickiup, the child passing and repassing in front of her with a most annoying frequency, stepping over her, lolling against her, pulling at her dress, all of which she accepts with a calm inattention truly remarkable. If the child is too much in the way, the grandparent may turn about in feigned anger and dismiss it with a sharp word. The child usually obeys. Occasionally, a child will defy a grandparent. *The parents do not interfere but leave the matter to the grandparent entirely.* If the encounter ends in the child's

crying, it cannot run to the parents for sympathy. *The child's attitude toward its grandparents is not duplicated with* any other relative. The grandparent's good-naturedness and willingness to do things are taken for granted, and I have never heard a maternal grandparent mentioned with any dislike or fear. They are usually spoken of with a feeling of affection, intimacy, and respect. [Emphasis added] (P. 218)

Goodwin (1942) also writes of "a decided lack of restraint" among grown grandchildren in asking for help from grandparents. "Where a young man hesitates to use another relative's dwelling, he makes himself entirely at home with his maternal grandparents, using their belongings, lying on their beds, asking for food and money" (p. 219). To some degree, the generosity of grandparents was reciprocated by the grandchildren. At the very least, they were expected to respect the grandparents. Among the Navajo at the turn of the century, "Grandchildren served as eyes, ears, hands, and feet for their frail elderly grandparents" (Shomaker 1989:2). Adult daughters assumed the primary responsibility for the care of their elderly parents, but they were often assisted in this effort by young grandsons and granddaughters.

In a 1989 interview, an Apache medicine man told me about his relationship with his grandmother in these words:

Grandmother and I took care of each other, in her wickiup. When I was little, grandmother and I went on a donkey to get wood. My mother was with my dad, but I was with grandmother. My mother sent my sister and I to sleep with my grandmother. They [your parents] always want you to respect the older people. You never walk over them and you never talk back to them. You always listen and then they cook for you and you learn a lot of things from them.

When the Apaches lived off the land, this system of cross-generational reciprocity ensured that family members shared the necessities of life and also knowledge about life. A changing tribal economy in a changing regional and national economic system, including the modern trend toward a cash economy, has complicated but not eliminated the traditional system of reciprocal amity and responsibility.

Apache Grandmothering Today: Patterns and Contexts

As part of an exploratory study of grandparenting and family change among Navajo and Apache grandmothers, beginning in 1989 and continuing through 1991, I conducted loosely structured, in-depth interviews with 13 grandmothers, four adult daughters, a medicine man, and an Anglo elementary school teacher, all residents of the Fort Apache reservation in Arizona.[2] Potential respondents were chosen by a "snowball sampling" technique. They were members of a network that included a long-term friend and former student of mine who had been raised on the reservation.

Early in each interview, I questioned the grandmother about her children and grandchildren and sketched a genogram (Bahr 1990) of her extended family. The genogram then served as a systematic guide or "map" to her family, helping me to keep relationships straight and ask appropriate questions as the interview proceeded.

The interview data have been supplemented by published research on Apachean peoples and occasional references in the tribal newspaper to problems of parenting and grandparenting in the White Mountain Apache community. The following descriptions of contemporary Apache summarize and illustrate behaviors that I observed or that were reported by my informants or other cited sources. It is not maintained that they are statistically representative of all Apache grandmothers.

The project's initial focus was on the place of grandmothers in transmitting traditional values and teaching family work skills, that is, on grandmothers as the custodians of culture. However, I was quickly impressed by the creativity and strength shown by these grandmothers in provisioning their households. They are custodians of the culture, but many of them are also responsible for the sheer physical support of their children and grandchildren. The present discussion emphasizes their responsibilities as providers and nurturers more than their role as custodians of culture.

Role Expectations and Performance

Apache culture values the extended family and exemplifies it in many forms. In these multigenerational settings family members feel, as one respondent put it, that "there is always someone to care for the children." In many instances, the household member who seems to feel the greatest obligation to the children is the grandmother. Therefore, she tends to be the "someone" of last resort.

I was particularly interested by the acceptance of heavy obligations of child care and support by women whose counterparts in Anglo society tend to celebrate their freedom from such responsibilities. Although it is not clear precisely what percentage of Apache grandmothers assume such obligations, the pattern is well-known and quite visible in the community. Rough estimates of its frequency may be made from results of the 1990 U.S. Census. Because the Census reports list heads of household by age but not grandparent status, we cannot tell how many grandparents are caring for grandchildren. However, there are published figures for total numbers of grandchildren living in grandparent-headed households. In 1990 an Apache child was at least 3.5 times more likely to be living in the home of a grandparent than was her Anglo American counterpart.[3] Judging from what I saw and was told, the number of grandchildren living with grandparents varies considerably from day to day and week to week. Nevertheless, it is clear this is a fairly common arrangement, affecting at least one-fifth of the children on a continuing basis.[4]

The recognition of the grandmothers' ultimate responsibility is a well-established part of the Apachean culture. There is general recognition and respect in the community for these women who carry on the nurturing and caretaking functions of the "grandmother role" with energy and deep commitment until incapacitated by illness or taken by death. There are many reasons for this pattern. As indicated earlier, it is "traditional" in the sense that historically the grandmother's role was a well-defined, essential part of normal family life. For many Apache families, the need for traditional grandmothering continues and is perhaps heightened by the modern pattern of women's employment outside the home, which means that many children need supplemental care. High rates of single parenthood and of alcohol abuse put additional children at risk. There are also many grown children, marginally employed or unemployed, who continue to be supported, at least in part, by their parents or grandparents.

Many of the more economically stable members of Apache families live off the reservation, often in another state, insulated from much of the day-to-day pressure to make ends meet. When things get hard for the unemployed on the reservation, it is culturally appropriate to call upon grandparents for aid. Under such circumstances it is fairly common for adult children, with or without partners, to live with their parents, and in many cases the task of caring for and teaching their children falls almost entirely to the grandmothers.

There is also the powerful force of cultural tradition and family example. For some of these women, the memory of having been raised by a grandmother translates into the expectation that they themselves need not be a truly responsible "parent" until they reach the grandmother stage. At that point, however, they recognize that the responsibility to be "parent of last resort" is now theirs.

A related explanation for the willingness to continue nurturing behavior at an age when many women in the wider society have "graduated" to leisure and, at most, sporadic child care is that the grandmothers feel fulfilled by doing it. Caring for children and grandchildren is a source of deep satisfaction for them. In fact, the chief regret expressed by the grandmothers I interviewed was that they couldn't do more for their children and grandchildren. That sense of needing to do more was cited as the most difficult thing about being a grandmother:

> *It's finding the time . . . having the chance to really talk with my teenage grandson and granddaughter. She needs to be advised about different ways of dressing and caring for herself and all these things. It seems that the time is too limited, that you can't sit down and talk without having [all of my grandchildren] pulling at me. . . . There are ways that we can deal with it, like go by yourself and get [that one] individual, but then I always feel guilty [when] the other one says, "Can I go? I want to go with you." Before I know it, I have two or three with me, without getting the chance with that one. . . . You know you are swamped by them, and then my daughter, too, still needs advice, and I need the time to spend with [her], and it is getting so that she is pushed out by these [grand]kids.*

In the past few years of economic recession, Apache grandmothers enacting their traditional roles, serving as caretakers of last resort for adult children and grandchildren, have been especially hard hit. What is remarkable is that their definitions of their problems do not question the role definition that assigns them ultimate responsibility but, rather, focus on changes and other obstacles that make it harder for them to live up to the cultural expectations. A mother of five with 11 grandchildren acknowledged that the challenge of trying to feed her household kept her in a state of continual stress. Like many Apache grandmothers, the size of her household varies. At the time of the interview, two preschool-aged grandchildren, two adult daughters, and an ex-son-in-law were living with her. Other adult children and grandchildren lived nearby and were frequent visitors. She was proud to have "a real close family." Her only problem was

> the feeding part of it. It is hard to feed a big family, and it is hard when just one family is not up to feeding the children, and they have to come over here and we feed them. But my grandmother, she only had a bag of beans, flour, salt and baking soda, and a bag of potatoes. But we ate good; it didn't hardly cost her anything. She fed us three times a day. But with these children [who belonged to a daughter who had recently quit work following the birth of another baby] . . . seems like we don't have anything to eat half the time. But in those days, I don't know how my grandmother managed, [but we seemed] to have plenty all of the time.

Many community members continue to recognize the grandmothers as the last line of responsibility for families in trouble. An elementary school teacher and long-term observer of the community commented,

> When you hear of a death in the family . . . you pray it's not the grandmother, because they are the only ones there for the children in many families. I would say, in at least 15, maybe 20, percent of the students I have had, they live with their grandmother. Their mother may be around part of the time, but it is the grandmother they go home to, who comes to school to see how they are doing. . . . And they really are the only ones many times that aren't drinking. . . . And they many times are the ones who worry about getting kids their clothes and getting them into school and trying to make sure that the kids are there [attending school].

Children who do not have an able grandmother to supplement and back up the efforts of their other caretakers are disadvantaged.

What happens if the grandmother has passed away? One of the grandmothers I talked to said that sometimes other relatives don't want to take the responsibility for the children the deceased grandmother was caring for, and then they are taken to a group home sponsored by the tribe. Usually, however, some close relative will assume responsibility. In her own case, this informant recalled, she was fortunate because she had a third "grandmother," a caring older relative in addition to her two grandmothers. "I guess [she] was my mom's aunt," she said:

my grandmother's sister, and after my grandmother passed away she kind of took over. . . . She taught us a lot of things. By this time my other sisters were too small to remember my real grandmother. . . . They more or less thought of her as our real grandmother.

The grandmothers I interviewed were committed to their families and devoted their lives to them. They were models of energy and industry. Such characteristics are expected of Apache grandmothers, and it was apparent that there was an accepted standard of grandmother behavior. Everyone seemed to know a grandmother or two who didn't fare too well, and some of the grandmothers I interviewed had things to say about other grandmothers—and grandchildren—who didn't measure up. For example, grandmothers whose caring behavior consisted merely of "baby-sitting" were seen as deficient, and so were some whose drinking habits made them incapable of caring for their households. Others manifested less commitment than my informants thought appropriate. I did not interview any of these "below-par" grandmothers—they were not identified to me by name—but plainly they were defined as a small and deviant minority.

Many grandmothers that outsiders might define as exploited or domi-nated by children and grandchildren do not see themselves as "giving in" but, rather, define their actions as the most loving, altruistic responses they know how to give, under the circumstances. They may not define being "used" by their children as exploitation. The caring grandmother is unlikely to assert herself. Rather, she gives in because "she loves her children and grandchildren," and she feels "like they are part of her." Take the grand-mother who, when asked what was the most difficult thing about being a grandmother, was interrupted by her grown daughter who insisted, "Let me answer for her: Saying 'No.'" The daughter elaborated,

Like if one of my sisters comes and says, "I want to go here and I want you to take care of my children," when my Mom would want to do something else, she doesn't know how to say no. So she ends up with the kids. That's the problem.

The grandmother's reply revealed a different ethic: "I don't mind them being there. I raised a lot of my own, so having my grandkids there doesn't make too much difference." She further showed her priorities in answering a question about what was most difficult about being a grandmother: "the worry." She said she worried especially about the grandchildren who did *not* live with her and who, she felt, were not well supervised at home.

Most of these grandmothers impressed me as pragmatic and world-wise. They knew that generosity required wisdom, that gifts should not be given indiscriminately. Also, they recognized that they were personally vulnerable and were sometimes exploited. Some were openly critical of the grown children—generally not their own—who they thought took unfair advantage of parental generosity. One told of seeing a grandmother in a grocery store spending her meager Social Security checks on disposable diapers, and offered her opinion that "Grandmother shouldn't be buying those. Grandmother should buy herself good food that she likes to eat."

It was also suggested that some grandmothers might appear to be overly tolerant or generous because they were trying to make up for past mistakes. In the words of one Apache mother,

> *This one grandmother, she's trying to win their love. Try to win their love back. Somewhere she made a mistake, maybe through her drinking in her younger days, maybe the days when she was having a good time.*

There was some evidence to support her judgment. While I did not specifically ask, two grandmothers volunteered that they had been fairly heavy drinkers when their children were young, and often had left their children either to care for themselves or in the care of a grandmother. Their recollections were often poignant: "And the kids would be wondering, 'what happened to my mom?'"

Coping Strategies

Apache grandmothers, despite their limited resources, rarely turn away their own. Grandmothers too old or unskilled to participate in the conventional labor market somehow manage, as "caretakers of last resort," to support themselves and their households. Often they survive by the creative application of traditional skills.

Many are still "gatherers," combing nearby lands for anything that can be sold for cash. "Anything" includes digging for worms to sell to fishermen, retrieving quills from roadkill porcupines to use in making earrings, scavenging the countryside for aluminum cans to sell to recycling centers, and harvesting native plants to sell and to supplement the family diet. They make lunches to sell in town, sew traditional dresses, or do craftwork, making dolls, cradle boards, beadwork, and jewelry. The usual market for these products is local residents more than tourists. Often such products are sold at places of employment on paydays.

A key to the grandmother's very survival is the operation of the informal economy, whereby goods, services, and money are exchanged and transferred. The system does not always work smoothly and predictably, particularly where alcohol is involved. There also seems to be a pattern where men—sons, brothers, husbands—are more willing than daughters or sisters to take advantage of the generosity of the grandmothers. On the other hand, a daughter with an alcohol or drug problem can be as exploitive as any man.

Creative coping strategies and the workings of the informal economy are illustrated in the following brief profiles of two of the grandmothers. Grandmother A has 10 children and 17 grandchildren. When I interviewed her, two grown daughters and a preschool grandson were living with her. Three teenaged grandsons and their mother live nearby and spend a lot of time with her. When I first arrived at her home, she was mixing dough to make tortillas for another of her daughters who lives in the area.

Grandmother A receives a small income from the Veterans Administration and from Social Security, "not much, but it helps out a little." The daughter who lives nearby receives AFDC and food stamps and contributes about $10 a month to the family income, "to buy meat sometimes, or whatever." One of her sons also helps out, "off and on, not that much."

How does Grandmother A supplement this meager income? I asked if she made crafts or helped the resident grandson's other grandmother "pick worms" for sale to fishermen. "No," she said, "I have a bad heart and I have rheumatoid arthritis. What I usually do is chop wood and wash and that is about it." She is resourceful and lives simply, cooking with wood, making her own tortillas. Because of her health problems, she has not grown a garden for several years. She does, however, gather the yellow pollen from cattails and sells that to get a little extra cash.

She takes her grandchildren with her to gather the cattails, because she can't get into the water where they grow but the children can. Then she lays the cattails in the sun to dry. As they dry, she shakes out the pollen. It is a time-consuming process. It takes many cattails to get enough pollen to fill one baby-food jar. This year, she said, a jar of pollen sells for about $20, or about $5 for one tablespoon. The pollen is used in Sunrise Dance ceremonies throughout the year.

I had difficulty discovering just how much money the pollen harvest yields. When I expressed surprise that all that work would net her only about a hundred dollars, she explained, in the essential spirit of the nurturing grandmother, that

> sometimes I just give it out free, 'cause a lot of our people are on welfare and food stamps, and it is really hard for them. . . . If they have money, they can go ahead and buy yellow powder but they can't do that with their food stamps.

Her grandsons contribute to the welfare of the household by gathering and chopping wood and cleaning house. They sweep and mop the floors and wash the dishes. She told me with satisfaction that her 3½-year-old grandson

> picks up the broom and says, "Grandma, let me sweep." He brings the wood in. And sometimes he wants to help me with the dishes, and he pulls up a chair and is standing there.

How does she see her role as grandmother? She insisted that what she does is assuredly "not baby-sitting." Instead, "They need me, and I need to be there with them to talk with them or do something with them."

Grandmother B bore 11 children, four of whom grew to adulthood. Three are still living. At present her brother lives with her. Much of the time, so do three grandsons, children of her oldest son. Her aged mother lived with her until her death a few months ago. Her mother's passing has taken away the Social Security checks that for several years were the household's only regular income. A sister who provided moral support and occasional transportation also died recently. Now the challenges of paying the rent, buying food, and making the lengthy trip to the tribal offices to apply for her monthly allotment of food stamps are much harder than before.

After her mother's death, Grandmother B went to a daughter's home in another state. On her return she discovered that her alcoholic son, father of the three grandsons who often live in her home, had claimed her food stamps. There was nothing left to enable her to buy food for the month. I asked what she thought she would do about this crisis. She looked around her home and said, "I've been thinking I could have a yard sale. I could sell a lot of this stuff."

She has only limited reading skills, and in the wake of her mother's recent death her life has been further complicated by the arrival of various official forms that must somehow be interpreted and dealt with. Even taking advantage of the transfer payments available to her ends up being a hardship. To obtain food stamps, she must apply in person each month at an office many miles away, and then, two weeks later, she must again make the trip to personally pick up the stamps. If she is unable to get a ride, she hitchhikes, and the round trip plus the waiting in line and application process may take an entire day. It can be even worse for mothers with small children in tow who have to wait in the food-stamp line in wet or freezing weather.

After the food stamps, her main source of income is "picking worms" for fishermen. Her grandsons help in this enterprise, and sometimes so do other kinfolk or temporary household members. One morning when I picked Grandmother B up to accompany me to some interviews, she told how the night before her grandsons had come to report that they had watered the grass "real good" at their maternal grandmother's house and now there were lots of worms coming up. So they had all gone over there and within about 30 minutes had picked up enough worms to make a two-inch layer in the bottom of a large can. As we drove away, we saw the boys out on the road selling worms. On a good day in summer—a weekend or holiday— Grandmother B may gross as much as $50 selling worms. Weekdays are slower: A good day's receipts may total only $10 to $15. Winters are hard. When the ground freezes worm-picking is over, and along with that loss of income comes the additional expense of having to buy wood to heat her modest home. Sometimes members of her church help out and give her wood.

As summer wanes, Grandmother B becomes a crafts worker. When she can get the materials, she makes dolls and beautiful doll clothes. When she can get silver, she makes jewelry. Her out-of-state daughter often sends fabrics and trims for the dolls. Finding an effective way to market her products is always a challenge. Grandmother B has no car and must depend on others for transportation. The small community where she lives has no stores, and the nearest commercial center is about 15 miles away. Relatives and friends passing through sometimes deliver items to distant customers or even market them for her.

There is also some direct sustenance from the land. The grandsons fish at a nearby lake. When they are successful, their catch is a significant addition to family meals. When someone kills an elk, it is butchered, cut up, and distributed to friends and relatives. Of course, Grandmother B and many others like her, grandmothers whose lives exemplify the tribal ethic of sharing and who are known to be primary economic supports for children and grandchildren, are included in the community distribution network.

And so the stories go. One grandmother makes and sells cradle boards, real ones for the Apache mothers who use them and miniature decorative models for the tourist trade. Another makes and sells the traditional Apache "camp dresses." Another walks along the riverbanks gathering aluminum cans to sell and occasionally is paid to teach special classes at local schools. Yet another works two jobs, as support staff in the local public schools during the school year and in a forestry camp during the summer.

Finally, as indicated above, some grandmothers also receive financial support from children and other relatives who live off-reservation. The Apache values of sharing, family commitment, and community support extend beyond the reservation boundary lines.

Summary and Discussion

In the modern Anglo milieu of "expressive individualism" (Bellah et al. 1985), older adults, and especially retired adults, are often portrayed as having reached an age of entitlement, when they deserve to be rewarded for years of work and can expect to "enjoy the good life." To those so entitled, high levels of family demand, conflict, and stress signal pathology, not maturity.

In contrast, the Apache grandmothers I talked to seemed reconciled to a "conflict" orientation to life: They accepted the reality that conflict and stress were embedded in the processes of family living. Whether they saw such experiences as growth-producing, at least they seemed to recognize that now, in the full strength of their maturity, such experiences and the responsibility to make the best of them were their lot as *grandmothers*. Resourceful, patient, even resigned, most were willing to lose themselves in the service of their families. At a life stage when many in Anglo society defined themselves as "retired" and perhaps redundant, the Apache grandmothers had arrived at the pinnacle of maturity and responsibility.

The other side of the coin is that many young Apache mothers seem to feel that now is their time to serve individualistic interests, to seek personal goals, or simply to "have a good time." Their attitudes and activities, while not always approved by the grandmothers, are defined as a normal stage of life. But if the mothers can sometimes avoid the challenging responsibilities of child care and child rearing, the grandmothers cannot. The developmental sequence has run its course, and their time has come.

It is instructive to compare some specific aspects of Apache (A) and Anglo American grandparenting (AA). In making these comparisons, I have cited some relevant descriptions of grandparenting in other tribes where they parallel my own observations of Apache grandparenting. Also, I generalize about Anglo American grandparenting according to what I perceive are central tendencies or dominant patterns reported in the literature. It is recognized that there are many other Anglo American patterns, including some that involve high commitment, frequent interaction, active economic support of grown children and grandchildren, and even formal educational efforts to improve grandparenting performance.[5]

1. Obligation and Responsibility

AA: A grandparent is a "spoiler" of grandchildren, one who may interact or give gifts but who "can have meaningful relationships with their grandchildren with minimal obligation and responsibility" (Link 1987:29).

A: For grandmothers in particular, grandparenting means heavy obligation and responsibility: "The older woman's role was that of a parent substitute within the family system" (Ryan 1981:35).

2. Gender Differences in Grandparental Role Behavior

AA: Grandmothers are more important than grandfathers in both role definition and role enactment. "Grandmothers tend to have warmer and closer relationships and serve more often as surrogate parents than grandfathers. Their close involvement in the mother role in relationships with their own children is a determining factor" (Link 1987:31).

A: Grandmothers are much more important than grandfathers. In this characteristic the Apache and Anglo patterns are similar in direction, but the role of the grandmother as provider is much enhanced among the Apache, and so is her position in the memory of Apache children (and among Indian children of other tribes as revealed in their writings as adults). In both Anglo and Apache society, the grandmothers' priority over grandfathers is partly a function of their greater longevity and partly a culturally prescribed greater affinity and responsibility for children generally.

3. Grandparents as Part of a Viable, Functioning Family Network

AA: Kinship ties are valued and maintained between parents, adult children, and grandchildren, but economic and residential units families tend to be nuclear and two-generational (parents and children). Family households have well-defined, fairly stable boundaries. Individual households tend to be independent.

A: Kinship ties are valued and maintained, and individual households are likely to involve cross-generational and multinuclear (e.g., cousins, aunts, and uncles) members. Family households have loosely defined, rather permeable, boundaries. Individual households tend to be interdependent. Ryan (1981:28) identifies the traditional interdependent family as the key to overcoming the problems faced by many American Indians today. "The individuals I knew who were not successful were not successful because their family was not complete," he says, and the missing elements he points to are grandmothers, grandfathers, aunts and uncles.

4. Economic Security and Economic Responsibilities

AA: Elder status, retirement, and grandparenthood are typically times of fairly secure economic status. Grandparents are more likely than others to own their homes and have accumulated savings. Financial costs of rearing and educating their grandchildren are expected to be borne by the children's parents.

A: Elder status and grandparenthood are times of heavy economic demand. Adult children and grandchildren may become the economic responsibility of the grandparents, adding to the financial burdens of the older years because in the low-income reservation milieu it has been difficult to accumulate savings. Pensions, Social Security, food stamps, and other transfer payment programs do not begin to cover the Apache grandmother's expenses, and, as a consequence, she often works as hard as ever in her life, for as long as she is able.

Apache grandmothers are busy in good causes. Some of them are elderly, many have health problems, but they exhibit a rich variety of economic activities, in both the informal and the formal economy. Generally they not only make enough to support themselves, but also provide much and sometimes all of the support for their large, often-multigenerational households. Whether married or single, they take financial responsibility for themselves and many others.

These are strong, industrious women. Only one of more than a score of Apache and Navajo grandmothers I got to know in the course of this research was not actively working at cottage enterprises or formal employment, or both, in an effort to improve the economic status of her family. That lone exception was also the oldest grandmother I encountered. Many of these women were suffering considerable physical hardship, from handicaps, accidents, aging, and illness; several showed signs of sheer physical exhaustion; some were psychologically stretched by the responsibilities of child care along with serving as economic providers and cultural models. Most had relatively low-level job skills, in the accepted sense of formal education, human capital, and preparation for successful competition in the labor force.

Despite multiple disadvantages, these Apache grandmothers were among the most influential and active participants in community life. Occupying the respected role of grandmother, enacting a tribal role definition that includes wisdom, energy, and resourcefulness, they stand out as the effective "managers" of much of the local economy and models of independence, courage, and strength in contexts where dependence, frustration, and resignation might be seen as more realistic adjustments.

It is not merely that they are individually strong and committed. To the degree that anyone is truly responsible for the future of the Apache society and culture, I believe it is the grandmothers. More than the tribal politicians, the medicine men, the teachers, the local celebrities, or the upwardly mobile migrants to urban America, it is the local grandmothers who anchor the heritage and, very often, the physical well-being of the Apache people.

Like families in the rest of America, the Apache family is experiencing strain and undergoing change. Like families elsewhere, many Apache mothers and fathers have occupations and lifestyles that take them away from home and severely limit their time with their children. It might even be argued that the poverty and accompanying social problems that afflict the Apache people make their families particularly vulnerable to a host of problems that would have destroyed a lesser people. In the face of the problems they confront, it is fortunate that, unlike much of the rest of America, they do not set aside their older women as "retired" or irrelevant. Rather, they place them in demanding, high-status, high-intensity roles that direct their insights and energies to the benefit of the community's youngest and most helpless members. The combination of high role expectations and the sheer scale of physical and emotional need they confront seem to inspire almost superhuman efforts from them. Looking at their lives and challenges, one may conclude that Apache grandmothering is very hard on the grandmothers. On the other hand, it plainly is very good for the Apache community as a whole and for Apache posterity.

ENDNOTES

1. In highlighting this general or "normative" pattern, I do not mean to downplay the diversity of grandparenting behavior among both Anglo and Indian populations. There is exceptional and deficient grandparenting in all societies, and millions of American grandparents are currently raising their grandchildren. Even so, I believe the literature in general, and the illustrative works cited, support a clear Anglo–Apache difference in cultural expectations about what constitutes good grandparenting and the social status accorded grandparents.

2. The Fort Apache Reservation occupies portions of Navajo, Gila, and Apache counties in east central Arizona. In 1990 the population of the Fort Apache Reservation was 10,394, of whom 9,825 were Indian Americans. There were 2,232 households (1,974 family households), with an average household size of 4.35. The Apache population is young: 45 percent are under age 18, and the median age is 20.9. Of the family households, 31 percent were headed by women ("female householder, no husband present") (U.S. Bureau of the Census 1991a:58, 1992:285).

3. According to the 1990 U.S. Census, of the 4,453 children under age 18 on the Fort Apache Reservation, 759 (17.0 percent) lived in households headed by one or both grandparents. In the entire United States, the corresponding rate was 4.9 percent (U.S. Bureau of the Census 1991b:9; 1992:285).

4. Of course this pattern is not the only pattern among the White Mountain Apache, nor the typical one. In addition to the 17 percent of all children living in households headed by a grandparent, 55 percent lived in married-couple families including at least one of their parents, 17 percent in single-parent families headed by their mothers, 4 percent in single-parent families headed by their fathers, and the remainder with other relatives or nonrelatives or in institutions (U.S. Bureau of the Census 1992:285). Plainly, the parent or parents are still the primary caretakers for the majority of children. However, even where parents are in place and functioning, Apache culture strongly encourages grandparents to participate in the socialization and nurturing of their grandchildren. Both patterns—grandparent dominant and grandparent supportive and supplemental—seem to be within the "norm."

5. As with Cowgills' statement, quoted earlier, that in the "Western" model of grand-parenting, grandchild–grandparent relationships usually are "rather formal and distant," so also the following generalizations on "minimal obligation and responsibility" need to be qualified. Not only are millions of American grandparents standing in for parents and raising their grandchildren, but substantial numbers are making a conscious effort to improve their grandparenting skills, as indicated in the emergence of formal curricula and a published literature on grandparent education (cf. Strom and Strom 1991a, 1991b, 1992).

REFERENCES

Attneave, Carolyn. 1981. "Discussion." Pp. 46–51 in *The American Indian Family: Strength and Stresses*, edited by John Red Horse, August Shattuck, and Fred Hoffman. Isleta, NM: American Indian Social Research and Development Associates.

Bahr, Kathleen. 1990. "Student Responses to Genogram and Family Chronology." *Family Relations* 39:243–49.

Bellah, Robert N., Richard Madsen, William M. Sullivan, Ann Swidler, and Steven M. Tipton. 1985. *Habits of the Heart: Individualism and Commitment in American Life.* Berkeley: University of California Press.

Clemens, Audra W. and Leland J. Axelson. 1985. "The Not-So-Empty-Nest: The Return of the Fledgling Adult." *Family Relations* 34:259–64.

Cowgill, Donald O. 1986. *Aging Around the World.* Belmont, CA: Wadsworth.

Goodwin, Grenville. 1942. *The Social Organization of the Western Apache.* Chicago: University of Chicago Press.

Hagestad, Gunhild O. and Linda M. Burton. 1986. "Grandparenthood, Life Context, and Family Development." *American Behavioral Scientist* 29 (4, March/April): 471–84.

Link, Mary S. 1987. "The Grandparenting Role." *Lifestyles: A Journal of Changing Patterns* 8 (3&4, Spring/Summer): 27–45.

Ryan, Robert A. 1981. "Strengths of the American Indian Family: State of the Art." Pp. 25–43 in *The American Indian Family: Strength and Stresses*, edited by John Red Horse, August Shattuck, and Fred Hoffman. Isleta, NM: American Indian Social Research and Development Associates.

Shomaker, Dianna J. 1989. "Transfer of Children and the Importance of Grandmothers among the Navajo Indians." *Journal of Cross-Cultural Gerontology* 4:1–18.

Stockel, H. Henrietta. 1991. *Women of the Apache Nation.* Reno: University of Nevada Press.

Strom, Robert D. and Shirley K. Strom. 1991a. *Becoming a Better Grandparent: Viewpoints on Strengthening the Family.* Newbury Park, CA: Sage.

——. 1991b. *Grandparent Education: A Guide for Leaders.* Newbury Park, CA: Sage.

——. 1992. *Achieving Grandparent Potential: Viewpoints on Building Intergenerational Relationships.* Newbury Park, CA: Sage.

U.S. Bureau of the Census. 1991a. *1990 Census of Population and Housing, Summary Population and Housing Characteristics: Arizona.* Washington, DC: U.S. Government Printing Office.

——. 1991b. *Marital Status and Living Arrangements, March 1990.* Current Population Reports, Series P-20, No. 450. Washington, DC: U.S. Government Printing Office.

——. 1992. *1990 Census of Population, General Population Characteristics: Arizona.* Washington, DC: U.S. Government Printing Office.

Wilson, Melvin N. 1984a. "The Black Extended Family: An Analytical Consideration." *Developmental Psychology* 22:246–58.

——. 1984b. "Mothers' and Grandmothers' Perceptions of Parental Behavior in Three-Generational Black Families." *Child Development* 55:1333–39.

30

MY MOTHER'S HIP
Lessons from the World of Eldercare

LUISA MARGOLIES

The question of who will care for the elderly is not as simple as it used to be. Fifty years ago, few middle-aged people had frail, elderly parents. Now, nearly 90 percent of baby boomers have parents who survive to advanced ages. Families composed of several generations are not unusual; nor is it uncommon for an elderly child to care for an aged parent. Parents may require different types and degrees of care, depending on their age and health status. Many people older than eighty-five can manage on their own, particularly if they have a spouse to share the tasks, but nearly half need limited to substantial assistance in carrying out their daily activities and can remain at home only with the help of family caregivers or hired aides.

Transformations in family structure have wrought fundamental changes in the nature of caregiving. Thanks to geographical mobility and the decline in fertility, the extended family is almost extinct, and fewer children are around to care for aging parents. Divorce, remarriage, and multiple career paths for men and women have made rendering consistent care increasingly difficult.

The issue of who should care for the elderly has become muddled with moralistic arguments. Some historians contend that economic imperatives were the moral underpinning of the large extended families of the past. In the countryside, adult children toed the line because their parents controlled the means of production and allocated the family's economic resources. One honored one's parents and took care of them in their old age. Ireland's system of impartible inheritance, for instance, obligated children to seek their fortunes elsewhere. The youngest son, however, continued to live with his parents and was committed to caring for them throughout their lives. This child was amply compensated on his parents' death by being made the sole recipient of the family estate.

Even among urban families, where no such economic imperative reigned, adult children felt a heavy obligation to care for their surviving parents. Numerous children worked out the logistics of caregiving without the aid of Social Security and national medical entitlements. Surviving parents normally lived with a primary caregiver but also rotated among their other children. The children had an unquestioned duty to their parents, and the lines of caregiving were clearly delineated.

When I think about my grandparents and great-grandparents, the idea of removing them from home was inconceivable. Both sets of paternal great-grandparents lived to advanced ages and were cared for by my paternal grandparents. My father had fond memories of talking to his grandparents daily: All he had to do was walk down the long hallway of the large apartment to their separate quarters. Both sets of his grandparents died naturally at home of "old age." My paternal grandfather "dropped dead" at the relatively young age of fifty-seven, but my paternal grandmother lived into her eighties in her only daughter's home. When she grew senile and frail, her three sons contributed a monthly stipend for her medical care. My maternal grandmother also died young, but my maternal grandfather was lucky to have had four adoring daughters who spoiled him after he was widowed. He continued to live with his youngest daughter after she married, but he liked to circulate among his other daughters for weeks at a time. He helped raise his youngest daughter's children, and he was an integral member of her household until his sudden death at age seventy-four from a ruptured hernia.

It was not until the Medicare and Medicaid Acts of 1965 were passed that the idea of living with and being cared for by one's family changed. In one swift moment, the extended family was rendered superfluous as commercial nursing homes, financed by government contributions, took over the role of caring for the frail elderly. The cultural ties that bound multiple generations together in a single household rapidly attenuated, and the first Medicare generation to reach old age gained the dubious distinction of caring for itself.

Today, filial piety is nearly an anachronism, and ethicists argue about the moral obligations children should have toward their aging parents. The argument goes something like this: Children did not ask to be born and therefore do not have the same degree of commitment toward their parents that parents have toward them. Parents must raise their children and see them safely into young adulthood, but this does not necessarily obligate children to bear the burden of caring for a failing parent later. Because parents are simply discharging their normal responsibilities, the "parental sacrifice account" of filial obligation in which grown children "owe" their old parents care is nonsense (even though many grown children still subscribe to it). In *Am I My Parents' Keeper?* (1988), Norman Daniels argues that we cannot view children's obligations as equivalent to parental duties. We should not fall into the trap of appealing to the "traditionalist" view of a golden age of moral and emotional bonds as a signal for returning to outmoded values. Caregiving obligations were different in the "good old days," when parents died relatively young after brief illnesses. Long-term care duties can now be so burdensome, he adds, that it would be imprudent to depend exclusively on individuals to care for their elderly.

What ethicists are trying to tell us is that we should not rely indiscriminately on implicit contracts to ensure that growing numbers of frail elders are properly cared for. Daniel Callahan, founding director of the bioethics research institute The Hastings Center, observes that some moral obligations *do* exist for family members to care for one another. But he also warns that "unlimited self-sacrifice on the part of the caregiver, in a time of rapidly increasing life expectancy and chronic illness, encounters heavy, and perhaps mounting resistance" (1987:101). . . .

Today, seven in ten care recipients suffer from medical conditions that are long term or chronic in nature (AARP 1997:14). Chronic conditions can turn caregiving into an endless nightmare, because the elderly are older, sicker, and frailer than ever before. Living with a chronic condition is like living with an uninvited guest who refuses to leave, no matter how many hints are given. Chronic diseases are incurable and relentlessly progressive. They sap one's strength even as one tries to manage them. These are just the physical effects. The illness is also the main element that segregates the sufferer from normal interactions with the outer world, taking on a dynamic of its own and tightening its tedious grip over every aspect of his or her daily life.

The chronically ill exist in a state of limbo. My colleague Robert Murphy, who suffered from the disabling effects of an inoperable tumor on the spine, described his feelings of alienation and sense of stigmatization in *The Body Silent:*

> *My identity has lost its stable moorings and has become contingent on a physical flaw. . . . The long-term physically impaired are neither sick nor well, neither dead nor fully alive, neither out of society nor wholly in it. They are human beings but their bodies are warped or malfunctioning, leaving their full humanity in doubt. . . . The sick person lives in a state of social suspension until he or she gets better. The disabled spend a lifetime in a similar state. They are neither fish nor fowl; they exist in partial isolation from society as undefined, ambiguous people (1987:104, 131).*

Chronic diseases have to be nurtured because they form a permanent part of one's life. One has to both monitor the illness and learn how to cope. All this takes up a lot of time and energy. In *Good Days, Bad Days,* Kathy Charmaz notes that chronic illness is "intrusive" because it forces its sufferer to make constant adjustments. The illness is like being on a roller-coaster—there are good days and bad days, depending on the "intrusiveness" of the symptoms (1991:42–49). When chronically ill people feel "well," they push themselves in the foolish attempt to persuade themselves that they are not actually ill. Then they become overtaxed and relapse quickly, only to be bitterly reminded of their illness by experiencing renewed episodes of pain and fatigue. . . .

How many times have chronically ill people been asked by well-meaning observers, "What do you do with yourself all day?" Just going to the supermarket may constitute the day's major outing and consume all of one's meager resources. How many adult children wonder why a parent takes "all day" to accomplish a "minor" task because they are insensitive to the illness's dominant role in limiting a person's capacity to perform routine chores? The interrogators cannot understand how pervasive the consequences of chronic disease are.

Each modification of one's surroundings to eliminate physical obstacles, and each limitation of activities, is a reminder of one's condition. One is forced to simplify as the illness progresses. People give up cherished activities like driving and entertaining and differentiate themselves from the people around them by parking in special handicapped spots or sitting down in the supermarket. They may have to purchase adaptive devices to compensate for physical limitations. They may stop picking up relatives at the airport, stop going to the mall, and "forget" to walk or exercise. Sick people often cannot be bothered with such niceties as setting a pretty table or filling the house with plants, and they may dispense with common courtesies because they feel "entitled." Chronic sufferers may end up reducing their living space to a well-traveled path between one room and another or confining themselves to a favorite chair. Nothing is more painful than the day the chronically ill person realizes he or she cannot manage alone. Caregiving then becomes a question of not only helping the elderly run their households, but also of providing them with hands-on continuing care. The caregiver must come to accept that she or he may not be able to alleviate the suffering of an ailing parent who is on a downhill course. "Sometimes, it means sharing their suffering, helping them to shoulder the burden," notes Richard Gunderman (2002:42).

Paradoxically, technological advances, which seemed to offer so much promise for the elderly, have scarcely affected our ability to care equitably for those who have most benefited from them. We have yet to come up with morally comfortable solutions that will ensure the continuing well-being of our aging society and keep pace with the remarkable achievements of modern medicine. Although the biomedical approach to medicine has dealt admirably with acute diseases, it has shortchanged the care of our senior population. According to a recent report on eldercare, "The gap is plugged by programs of long-term institutional care and informal home care that are at worst inhumane and niggardly, and at best starved for adequate funds and well-trained health care workers and social workers" (JIRGIB 1994:S11). Callahan posed the right question when he asked what the appropriate balance should be between the provision of acute health care and the provision of long-term care for the chronically ill elderly. He calls for a different type of medicine today — one that knows its limitations and focuses on the care of the chronically ill (1993:209).

Family members currently provide the bulk of long-term care services to the elderly and underwrite some $38 billion of the $70 billion expended on long-term care. Recent projections suggest that these expenditures will more than double in the next twenty-five years to keep pace with the galloping growth of the senior population. Meanwhile, Medicare entitlements continue to rest on theories about aging that prevailed more than forty years ago. Families who care for ailing relatives at home rarely receive the benefit of community-based programs or services because of Medicare's skewed emphasis on acute-care reimbursements for inpatients. Compare our glaringly deficient programs with those in many European countries, where both home-nursing and institutional care are incorporated into comprehensive social-security systems that are financed by a percentage of the wage base assessed exclusively for eldercare. Germany, for example, has a universal, compulsory long-term care program that is administered by a sickness fund whose contributions come from monthly deductions shared equally between employees and employers. The elderly are provided with nursing-home and home-health care benefits, and family caregivers receive formal training and earn pension credits (Wiener and Cuellar 1999). Those who choose to stay at home (the majority) receive a monthly stipend; their caregivers are covered by social-security insurance and receive various supports, such as respite care. In contrast, the American system puts the onus of caregiving squarely on the patient's family. It fails both the recipient and the giver of care.

Who are the care recipients, and how are they cared for? A national survey of family caregiving shows that the mean age of care recipients is seventy-seven years and seven months, but nearly 25 percent are older than eighty-five. Sixty percent are female, and a little more than 40 percent are widowed. Some 22.4 million families provide assistance to an aging relative. Adult children constitute 37 percent of all caregivers, and nearly one-fifth of care recipients live with their caregivers. The majority of family caregivers devote an average of three hours each day to rendering care, despite such competing demands as paid employment. Forty percent of caregivers perform the equivalent of a full-time job and have borne the responsibility for an average of four-and-a-half years. Twenty percent of caregivers have been fulfilling this role for more than five years (AARP 1997).

Family caregivers provide an eclectic variety of services for the elderly, including assistance with marketing, shopping, banking, car repairs, housekeeping, cooking, assorted chores, doctors' appointments, and financial management. The next level of attention involves hands-on personal care, such as bathing, dressing, toileting, and administering medication. Another type of assistance falls within the rubric of nursing and may involve the performance of complicated medical procedures.

One usually takes on the role of caregiver spontaneously, without anticipating the enormous complications to come. Caregiving functions tend to expand almost insidiously as the care recipients grow increasingly infirm or have unexpected crises. Caregivers will go to considerable lengths to provide the necessary care at home, even if they have to hire full-time aides or appeal to the services of a case manager to coordinate the different types of care. Nursing homes, for the most part, are still considered places of last resort. Brakman concludes that, "when elder parents do take up residence in a nursing home, this is often experienced by the child and the elder as a moral, emotional, and physical failure" (1994:27).

Caregiving is overwhelmingly women's work. Women make up 77 percent of the adult children providing hands-on care and are likely to rearrange their professional and personal lives to manage the unpredictable needs of their parents. Caregiving takes an important place alongside women's other roles as workers, wives, mothers, and homemakers. The typical caregiving daughter is middle-aged and squarely "in the middle" in terms of the demands competing for her time and energy. Some 41 percent of caregivers are still raising children younger than eighteen when they first undertake the caregiving role. Women generally serve as primary caregivers to an older female relative; today, that relative is likely to be one's mother. In the past forty years, the proportion of fifty-year-old women with living mothers has risen from 37 percent to nearly 70 percent. It is common for a fifty-year-old woman to have a mother who is living but perhaps not well—that is, with a chronic illness or some frailty. This daughter may have put off childbearing in favor of career development during her thirties; now she finds herself the mother of children approaching adulthood while confronting menopause and her own eventual mortality. She may end up spending more years caring for an elderly parent than raising her children. For these women, the issues surrounding caregiving pose an enormous challenge.

Various researchers have commented that daughters look on caregiving not as a set of discrete tasks but as a diffuse responsibility that never ends (Brody 1981; Rutman 1996). Daughters feel intimately responsible for their parents' well-being and will go to great lengths to preserve the recipient's sense of dignity. They try to uphold an image of the parent as he or she was by presenting that fictional vision, as far as possible, to the public sphere. In *Who Cares for the Elderly? Public Policy and the Experiences of Adult Daughters* (1991), Emily Abel views this act of protecting a parent's sense of personhood as a kind of moral guardianship. Daughters seem to have an intuitive, nonverbal engagement with their parents that allows them to translate their parents' feelings.

Why do middle-aged women have such a difficult time setting limits on their role as caregivers to their parents? First, these women traditionally have been raised to be nurturers and expect to make sacrifices. They learned this from their stay-at-home mothers, and even though women are now in the working world, shrugging off old values is hard. Daughters are still the ones who hold families together and embody the moral underpinnings of the family unit, even though the nature of family dynamics has clearly changed.

Caregiving is not something most daughters have to think about very hard. They just do it because they have to. Caregiving is often a natural, spontaneous act for one's parents. Daughters have an overwhelming desire to provide care when a parent needs it and do not expect anything in return. I have yet to come across a daughter who can proceed comfortably with her own life while ignoring the obvious needs of a parent. Take the case of

Elaine Simmons, the visiting nurse who came to my parents' home for eighteen months to give Mother her Calcimar injections. Elaine held a full-time job while caring for a daughter with developmental difficulties and a husband brain-disabled in a freak accident. She also found time to be a caring daughter to an ailing father who traveled between his home up North and hers in South Florida. She coordinated every detail of her father's care for several years while respecting his wishes to retain a separate and distant household. Elaine was so good-natured and concerned about her patients that one would never know she carried such weighty responsibilities at home. She juggled her affairs so that each family member received attention without feeling slighted. Such intense caregiving seems to emanate from a sense of connectedness, according to Abel (1991:91), rather than from any notion of repaying a parent or canceling a moral debt.

Two of my closest friends cared for their fathers with such abnegation that they had to rework their professional lives. George Ann worked for a global nonprofit organization, a job that kept her traveling much of the year. When her widowed father broke his hip, she bought a house in Vermont, moved him in with her, and took a more sedentary job. Her father had emphysema and had been seriously depressed since his wife's death. George Ann saw him through congestive heart failure, several minor strokes, and many bouts of pneumonia, but she never considered putting him in a nursing home, even though her absent brother kept urging her to take the step. During the nearly four years George Ann lived in Vermont, her brother visited their father once. Two years after her father's death, George Ann still could not forgive her brother for his failure to participate in their father's care. By contrast, Carmen Nieves, a colleague in the Canary Islands, was fortunate to have both a brother and a husband to share in caregiving tasks. Nevertheless, she refused to leave her father for more than a few days at a time, despite numerous professional invitations abroad. Her father suffered from advanced Parkinson's disease and was eventually confined to a wheelchair. Not only did Carmen Nieves cater to his bodily needs; she also made sure he took part in the family's activities by seating him in the front parlor, where he could greet and chat with everyone who entered the house. He was a retired schoolmaster and enjoyed the comings and goings of his granddaughter and her friends. Carmen Nieves' brother occasionally covered for her when she went out in the evening; it was understood that they would share the responsibility for their ailing father. The care was accomplished in a low-key, unobtrusive manner, and her father's death was a blow to the entire family.

Aspects of caregiving can be gratifying, but as the parent's needs increase, caregiving takes over more and more of a daughter's life. Women may assume the tasks willingly when a parent is relatively independent or step in for an emergency without knowing what to expect in the future (Guberman, Maheu, and Maille 1992). Daughters are likely to take unpaid leaves of absence, reduce their working hours, relinquish their jobs, eliminate their vacations, and abandon their social activities to keep pace with the pressing demands of caregiving. But the progressive deterioration of the parent cannot be stemmed, and in the end daughters often feel frustrated and angry about their own powerlessness.

Caregiving is hard work. It is not something to undertake lightly or to walk away from in the middle. It is not only physically taxing; it is emotionally wearing. Eldercare is also more complicated than it was in the past and can involve multiple tasks over many years. "It is hypocritical to envision it as anything but a hard, bankrupting job," says Theodore Roszak. "The extensive care that the frail and infirm require is uniquely the result of modern medicine. Nobody in any previous culture was expected to handle demands of this magnitude and live a life of their own" (2001:121). The caregiver must give unconditional support and function as the parent's advocate without being patronizing. Many daughters have likened the experience of caring for a frail parent to that of caring for a growing child, because the daughter assumes the role of parent. Yet the experience is inherently different because the daughter is a witness to her parent's decline, and the result is not hard to envision. What the daughter does to make an ailing parent more comfortable may ensure the status quo for a while, but it is never enough in the long run. Women tend to see the deterioration of a parent under their care as a personal affront and are burdened with guilt. It is hard for a daughter to act objectively amid such intense involvement.

Daughters who care for their mothers are particularly stressed because they identify so closely with their mothers' decline. Although their roles are now reversed, daughters continue to look upon mothers as the original nurturers. Daughters are not only constantly reminded of how their mothers used to be; they are also terrified of their mothers' infirmities, which "foreshadow" their coming old age. The anthropologist Robert Rubinstein, who studied the social context of caregiving by collecting daughters' narratives, concludes that, no matter how dependent mothers are on daughters, the relationship continues to remain one between a mother who has raised a child and her middle-aged daughter. This is the last chance for mothers and daughters to examine and work out crucial aspects of their relationship (1995:258).

When elderly people have both sons and daughters, the daughters inevitably end up as the primary caregivers. Sometimes, adult daughters share equally in the tasks of caregiving, but that is the exception rather than the rule. "Contingencies such as geographical proximity, gender roles, or interpersonal relationships conspire to make the burdens unequal, and often unfair, in practice," notes Harry Moody (1992:92). Sons who share in caregiving tasks usually expect their sisters to provide the personal care while they carry out the more "masculine" tasks related to managing the household.

Considering the broad range of caregiving duties performed by family members, the need to share the responsibility becomes obvious. Barbara Tarlow (1996) believes that the caregiving role should be negotiated among adult children because not everyone is cut out to be a good caregiver or is willing to make the necessary sacrifices. Good caregiving encompasses a number of indispensable qualities without which the experience can be transformed into a traumatic burden for all concerned. Some children may feel that a paid surrogate is an adequate substitute for personal caregiving. The neglected parent's emotional hurt is not easily forgotten. It is not uncommon for the elderly care recipient to feel abandoned when adult children are distant and uninvolved.

Men rise admirably to the occasion when daughters are lacking. Some of the finest stories in the caregiving literature are about men caring tenderly for their parents and feeling as much of a moral responsibility as women do. In *The Time of Their Dying*, Stephen Rosenfeld talks about the importance of investing time, unstintingly, in the care of a parent: "One must be there. Time and again I realized how futile it was to extract information or convey emotion at a distance" (1977:180). The journalist and writer Nick Taylor, who was sucked into the caregiving vortex as an only child, also experienced such sentiments. His memoir, *A Necessary End*, should be read by every potential caregiver because it depicts so nakedly his intense involvement with both parents as they declined. His caretaking career encompassed the period from 1983 to 1991. At first he felt he had to decide how much of his life he should sacrifice to care for his ailing parents. But then he plunged fully into the caregiving fray as he tried to deal with one crisis after another. . . . No matter what he did, he never felt he had a handle on the situation, and he had no siblings to share his pain. . . .

Tom Koch, the author of *Mirrored Lives: Aging Children and Elderly Parents*, cared for his father with total dedication. He became a frequent flyer between Vancouver and Buffalo, New York.

> *unable to stay in Buffalo and unwilling to stay away. Each new medical crisis returned me to Norm's house, and as he grew weaker, each new responsibility tied me closer to the world that Norm progressively relinquished. . . . I could not leave; it was impossible for me to fly that far knowing how tenuous was the balance in our Buffalo world. . . . This was the pattern, a gradual diminishment and a series of small incidents, as we waited for calamity to strike (1990:173, 175).*

Koch's book illustrates how the strands of connectedness bind failing parents and caring children even closer together as their private world crumbles. . . .

In *Looking After*, John Daniel depicts the nitty-gritty of caregiving in frank, unapologetic terms. He was a reluctant caregiver for a mother who had moved into his home after she became increasingly forgetful. Daniel had conflicting feelings because she had never been a "mothering" type. He was annoyed and acted churlishly at times: "My mother had been a strong and vibrant woman. It grieved me to see her reduced to a stooped crone who dithered over vegetables at the store, who couldn't remember what she'd read half an hour before, who forgot to take the pills I placed directly in front of her at breakfast. It more than grieved me — it enraged me . . . because I was stuck with caring for a feeble old mother and didn't want to be" (1996:92). Yet he mourned his mother after she died and chastised himself. "In the time since her death, I've found myself saying, 'I'm sorry, Mama, I'm so sorry.' . . . I berated myself for not being strong enough to bear the modest office of caregiving. I blamed myself for my mother's irrevocable absence from the world" (1996:204, 214).

Researchers have consistently shown that family caregiving engenders family conflicts. Rare is the family that manages to stay together and act harmoniously under the multiple stresses of caring for failing parents. The national survey on family caregiving found that some 25 percent of care-givers report family conflict (AARP 1997:22). The conflict generally arises between the primary caregiver and the other siblings (Brody et al. 1989). Because most primary caregivers are women, sisters frequently find them-selves on the outs with their brothers. "When caregivers are asked directly about relations with siblings," writes Amy Horowitz, "significant numbers do report deteriorated relations" (1985:210). Many siblings care deeply about their parents but do not engage in the actual care. Brothers may feel that hands-on care can be provided adequately by hiring outsiders, but daugh-ters often believe that no outsider can care for their parents the way they do and are more sensitive to the fact that vulnerable parents may prefer their children's help. Brothers may act as though their sisters' careers are expend-able or less relevant because they cling to the outmoded, sexist notion that men are the principal wage earners. Caregiving itself is devalued because it is an unremunerated personal activity—women's work—that receives little recognition beyond the family sphere.

Many wonder how much longer women can bear the emotional burden of caregiving. The responsibility is often imposed on the daughter with little discussion or planning, because girls have been socialized to "care" while boys are directed to "act." Despite the revolution in gender roles, people still assume that women will continue to provide the bulk of the hands-on care. Richard Martin and Stephen Post note that some women may have the inner resources to "shoulder this monumental responsibility" and may "live lives of significant self-abnegation," yet they question the ability of women to hold up under the increasing pressure (1992:62).

Explosions are likely to occur when the primary caregiver feels the effects of burnout and verbalizes her resentment to less involved siblings. A little more than half of all caregivers feel that other relatives are not doing their share. Caregivers are distressed not only by their siblings' lesser par-ticipation but also by their siblings' lack of emotional and instrumental sup-port for their role as principal caregiver. The other siblings often take the caregiving sister for granted. Caregivers rightly feel that absent siblings are the least fit to criticize their efforts or offer unsolicited advice, especially when they are not there to witness the daily happenings. Absent children, however, may feel slighted by the primary caregiver because they are not consulted or kept abreast of changes. . . .

Numerous factors affect the quality of sibling relationships. First and foremost, siblings cannot afford to be angry with their parents, so they must take out their fear and frustration on one another. A failing parent is too often caught up in his or her own problems to focus on the undercurrents of care. Some siblings revive childhood rivalries and other old conflicts in the context of caregiving. Yet caregiving is sufficiently stressful to produce conflicts among siblings who previously enjoyed harmonious relationships. Adult children bicker about the type of care that is appropriate — should it be a nursing home or some sort of home arrangement? They squabble over the disbursement of the parents' funds — one sibling may feel that the parents' savings should be used to fund their care, another that those life savings are sacred and should be held for eventual inheritance. Parents who lived through the Depression may be loath to deplete the savings that took a lifetime to amass and worry that their medical expenses will leave nothing for the children. Siblings may have questions about inheritance and wills but feel that discussing such matters in the context of caregiving is tasteless. So they remain silent, and their silence breeds tension and taints their relationship. The possibilities for friction among siblings are endless. Primary caregivers may be so depressed and exhausted from sleeplessness, poor diet, lack of respite, and the endless routine that they cannot cope graciously with a difficult sibling. "Coming together to face a parent's illness requires an altogether different degree of cooperation and communication among siblings than organizing holiday dinners and family reunions," warn Nancy Hooyman and Wendy Lustbader in *Taking Care of Your Aging Family Members* (1986:45).

If filial obligations were shared more evenly and not simply left to dutiful daughters, families would be able to function as more effective caregivers to their parents. The burdens of contemporary caregiving can be extremely unfair, creating a new class of human casualties who will be unable to age successfully because of the disproportionate demands on their time and resources. "Increasing pressures on adult children to personally take care of their frail relative's every need is socially irresponsible," says Laura Olson in a detailed study of the political economy of long-term care (1993:179). The solution, she says, is to implement social policies that will address not only the needs of the care recipients but also those of the caregivers.

In a cogent summing up of the problem, Carol Levine notes that she eventually realized she had done nothing wrong in her caregiving. It was the system that was out of whack. "I feel abandoned by a health care system that commits resources and rewards to rescuing the injured and ill, but then consigns such patients and their families to the black hole of chronic 'custodial' care" (2000:74). Only in the United States are family members inducted into a volunteer labor force because the health-care system, predicated on outmoded social policies, has not yet grappled with the issue of caring for our nation's oldest citizens. The void in long-term care programs will only expand unless Medicare abandons its antiquated premises and comes to terms with the pressing needs of our rapidly aging society.

An equitable health-care system would empower potential caregivers by allowing them to choose to take on the caregiving role rather than forcing the role on them. In a timely essay on the institutional care of the elderly,

Bela Blasszauer puts it aptly: "A society can, indeed, very well be judged on the basis of how it takes care of its elderly" (1994:14). Good care must be an ethical concern for everyone, and caring for the frail elderly must be the social responsibility of an entire nation.

REFERENCES

AARP. 1997. "Family Caregiving in the U.S.: Findings from a National Survey." Final Report. Washington, DC: National Alliance for Caregiving and American Association of Retired Persons (AARP).

Abel, Emily K. 1991. *Who Cares for the Elderly? Public Policy and the Experiences of Adult Daughters.* Philadelphia: Temple University Press.

Blasszauer, Bela. 1994. "Institutional Care of the Elderly." *Hastings Center Report* 24 (5): 14–17.

Brakman, Sarah-Vaughan. 1994. "Adult Daughter Caregivers." Symposium. Caring for an Aging World: Allocating Scarce Resources. *Hastings Center Report* 24 (5): 26–28.

Brody, Elaine M. 1981. "Women in the Middle and Family Help to Older People." *Gerontologist* 21 (5): 471–80.

Brody, Elaine M., Christine Hoffman, Morton H. Kleban, and Claire B. Schoonover. 1989. "Caregiving Daughters and Their Local Siblings: Perceptions, Strains, and Interactions." *Gerontologist* 29 (4): 529–38.

Callahan, Daniel. 1987. *Setting Limits: Medical Goals in an Aging Society.* Washington, DC: Georgetown University Press.

———. 1993. *The Troubled Dream of Life: Living with Mortality.* New York: Simon and Schuster.

Charmaz, Kathy. 1991. *Good Days, Bad Days: The Self in Chronic Illness and Time.* New Brunswick, NJ: Rutgers University Press.

Daniel, John. 1996. *Looking After: A Son's Memoir.* Washington, DC: Counterpoint.

Daniels, Norman. 1988. *Am I My Parents' Keeper? An Essay on Justice between the Young and the Old.* New York: Oxford University Press.

Guberman, N., P. Maheu, and C. Maille. 1992. "Women as Family Caregivers: Why Do They Care?" *Gerontologist* 32 (5): 607–17.

Gunderman, Richard B. 2002. "Is Suffering the Enemy?" *Hastings Center Report* 32 (2): 40–44.

Hooyman, Nancy R. and Wendy Lustbader. 1986. *Taking Care of Your Aging Family Members: A Practical Guide.* New York: Free Press.

Horowitz, Amy. 1985. "Family Caregiving to the Frail Elderly." Pp. 194–246 in *Annual Review of Gerontology and Geriatrics.* New York: Springer.

JIRGIB (Joint International Research Group of the Institute of Bioethics). 1994. "What Do We Owe the Elderly? Allocating Social and Health Care Resources." *Hastings Center Report, Special Supplement* 24 (2).

Koch, Tom. 1990. *Mirrored Lives: Aging Children and Elderly Parents.* Westport, CT: Praeger.

Levine, Carol. 2000. "The Loneliness of the Long-Term Care Giver." Pp. 71–80 in *Always on Call: When Illness Turns Families into Caregivers,* edited by Carol Levine. New York: United Hospital Fund of New York.

Martin, Richard J. and Stephen G. Post. 1992. "Human Dignity, Dementia and the Moral Basis of Caregiving." Pp. 55–68 in *Dementia and Aging: Ethics, Values and Policy Choices,* edited by Robert H. Binstock, Stephen G. Post, and Peter J. Whitehouse. Baltimore: Johns Hopkins University Press.

Moody, Harry R. 1992. "A Critical View of Ethical Dilemmas in Dementia." Pp. 86–106 in *Dementia and Aging: Ethics, Values and Policy Choices,* edited by Robert H. Binstock, Stephen G. Post, and Peter J. Whitehouse. Baltimore: Johns Hopkins University Press.

Murphy, Robert F. 1987. *The Body Silent*. New York: Henry Holt.

Olson, Laura Katz. 1993. "The Political Economy of Productive Aging: Long-Term Care."Pp. 167–85 in *Achieving a Productive Aging Society*, edited by Scott A. Bass, Francis G. Caro, and Yung Ping Chen. Westport, CT: Auburn House.

Rosenfeld, Stephen S. 1977. *The Time of Their Dying*. New York: W. W. Norton.

Roszak, Theodore. 2001. *Longevity Revolution: As Boomers Become Elders*. Berkeley, CA: Berkeley Hills Books.

Rubinstein, Robert L. 1995. "Narratives of Elder Parental Death: A Structural and Cultural Analysis." *Medical Anthropological Quarterly* 9 (2): 257–76.

Rutman, Deborah. 1996. "Caregiving as Women's Work: Women's Experiences of Powerfulness and Powerlessness as Caregivers." *Qualitative Health Research* 6 (1): 90–111.

Tarlow, Barbara. 1996. "Caring: A Negotiated Process That Varies." Pp. 56–82 in *Caregiving: Readings in Knowledge, Practice, Ethics and Politics*, edited by Suzanne Gordon, Gordon, Patricia Benner, and Nel Noddings. Philadelphia: University of Pennsylvania Press.

Taylor, Nick. 1994. *A Necessary End*. New York: Doubleday/Nan A. Talese.

Wiener, Joshua M. and Alison Evans Cuellar. 1999. "Public and Private Responsibilities: Home- and Community-Based Services in the United Kingdom and Germany." *Journal of Aging and Health* 11 (2): 417–44.

PART VIII

Divorce, Remarriage, and Blended Families

I n this section, we examine divorce, remarriage, and blended families. Until recently, much more research has been done on divorce than on remarriage and blended families. Hopefully, in the future, this research imbalance will be corrected further because we need more information on the diverse types of families formed after a divorce. Remember that in Part IV, we discovered that many couples are choosing to cohabit instead of remarrying after a divorce, because of their unhappiness with the institution of marriage. Other individuals are remarrying after a divorce and forming blended families. The term *blended families* is used to describe these postdivorce families reuniting via cohabitation or marriage, and it is more inclusive than the term *stepfamilies*, which usually refers only to postdivorce families that have remarried.

A marriage can be terminated in one of three ways: annulment, divorce, or widowhood. Historically, most marriages in the United States ended via widowhood. Divorce has existed in the United States since colonial times, but it was rare, and divorce policies were inconsistent due to different colonies being settled by groups of people with differing values and beliefs. The Puritans in the northeastern colonies, for example, did allow divorce under certain conditions, whereas the southern colonies did not allow it (Riley 1991). In the northern colonies, spouses wanting to end a marriage via divorce had to prove the marriage had not fulfilled its contractual obligation; that is, the wife was barren and could not produce children or the husband had deserted the family and was not providing for them. Other traditional grounds for divorce included adultery, fraud, drunkenness, and later, physical cruelty. However, cruelty alone usually was not sufficient enough grounds for a divorce because of its vagueness.

In the 1970s, many states introduced no-fault divorce laws, which were designed to eliminate fault-based grounds for divorce (Weitzman 1985). Moreover, it was hoped that no-fault divorce would eliminate the adversarial process and lead to financial settlements that were more equitable and based on economic need. Family responsibilities postdivorce also were to be redefined as more gender neutral. No-fault divorce accomplished some of these goals, especially making it much easier to obtain a divorce because neither spouse had to be proven at fault. By eliminating blame common in fault divorces, no-fault divorces can reduce the trauma of divorce proceedings. However, divorce is still adversarial for many couples. Moreover, financial settlements are not necessarily equitable nor based on financial need as is evidenced by the numerous parents who are behind in child-support payments. Alimony or spousal support is awarded less often today, so it is more important for women to be financially independent regardless of their marital status.

Some states are working to change divorce laws because they believe the no-fault divorce laws are too lenient and make it too easy for a family to break up (Yepsen 1995). Instead of having no-fault divorces, these states want to move back to a system whereby a spouse would have to show specific grounds for divorce and one of the spouses would be blamed for the failure of the marriage. Louisiana, for example, is pushing for covenant marriages, which would make divorce very difficult to obtain. Other scholars argue that in order to reduce the postdivorce conflicts between ex-spouses and children, we should remove divorce from our adversarial legal system and, instead, use mediation. Joyce Hauser in her book *Good Divorces, Bad Divorces: A Case for Divorce Mediation* (1995) argues that mediation is the best method for advancing harmony and justice during and after a divorce. Unfortunately, few people know that divorce mediation exists as an option. Another innovative program, in Atlanta and Indianapolis, is a court-ordered class for divorcing parents called "Children Cope with Divorce." All divorcing parents are required to attend the four-hour course on how to lessen the impact of divorce on their children (Walker 1992).

Why is the divorce rate so high? There are many reasons, including infidelity, money and employment conflicts, differences in spousal age and education, substance abuse, and family violence. In fact, not only is family violence a precursor of divorce, it also is often a consequence of divorce. Many battered wives report an escalation in family violence both during divorce proceedings and after. Another reason why divorce rates are so high is that the United States is a society which overemphasizes romantic love, so our relationship expectations are too high for most couples to achieve. People enter into marriages with unrealistic expectations about romance and the relationship. Moreover, the public attitude toward divorce is more favorable. There is less social stigma today for divorced persons than there was 50 years ago or even 30 years ago. It is important to note that divorce rates vary by age, race-ethnicity, and religion. Moreover, divorce rates tend to be higher in western and southern states than in northeastern and midwestern states.

Myths about Divorce

There are many myths about divorce, including the belief that Americans are anti-marriage and that divorce is an easy and casual process. Moreover, people tend to have nostalgic views about the family such as the idealized notion that marriage *used to be* a wonderful and stable relationship. In reality, married life has not always been blissful, and many marriages have been full of violence, substance abuse, and other problems. The difference is that, today, a person does not have to stay in an abusive situation or in an unhappy marriage. Constance Ahrons addresses these and other misconceptions about divorce in her article "No Easy Answers: Why the Popular View of Divorce Is Wrong." Ahrons is a professor emerita of sociology at the University of Southern California. Ahrons began her research on divorce in 1976 when she was on the faculty at the University of Wisconsin, Madison. A single parent herself, Ahrons decided that instead of following the traditional route of looking for deviance or pathology, she would study how families reorganized themselves after divorce and that she would look for the "good divorces," divorces in which children and adults were leading healthy lives in spite of divorce. Her numerous publications, based on several major research studies and 30 years of clinical experience, have introduced new concepts in and new ways of looking at divorce. The research reported in this selection is taken from Ahrons' recent book *We're Still Family: What Grown Children Have to Say about Their Parents' Divorce* (2004). The impetus behind this excerpt came from Ahrons' public lectures on divorce. In her audiences, she often found people who had several misconceptions about divorce, including the myth that all of the consequences of divorce are negative. In this reading, Ahrons reviews seven popular misconceptions about divorce that make good divorces invisible in our society.

Divorce Is a Gendered Experience

One reality of divorce is that the experience of divorce is very gendered. What women and men think about and experience in going through a divorce is often different. Sociologist Catherine Riessman, for example, in her 1990 book on the gendered experience of divorce, has found that many women express that divorce had many positive consequences for their lives, including feeling independent and learning to survive on their own, feeling free from subordination, and learning the competencies involved in managing a daily life, such as learning to do household repairs and controlling their own money. Moreover, many women express being challenged by needing to reenter the job market or by going back to school to finish their education. Other women express positive changes in their social relationships, where they are learning to nurture new friendships and relationships. Of course, not all the consequences of divorce are positive for women, but Riessman's research shows some of the personal growth that can occur due to this transition in marital status.

The second article in this section, "The Social Self as Gendered: A Masculinist Discourse of Divorce," by Terry Arendell, examines the gendered experience of divorce for men. Arendell, a professor of sociology at Colby College, has done extensive research on gender, the sociology of the family, and divorce. She recently investigated the extent of father absence after divorce in an interview study of 75 divorced New York fathers. She found that men's perspectives on divorce and their interactions with their families postdivorce reveal similar patterns of coping and maintenance of their gender identities. Arendell concludes that these divorced men share a "masculinist discourse of divorce." This discourse involves unique understandings and definitions of the family, including a devaluation of the former wife and diverse strategies for interacting with ex-wives and children. For example, she found that many divorced fathers use father absence as a strategy to control situations of conflict and emotional tension. Other divorced fathers use fathers' rights rhetoric to argue that they have been the primary victims of divorce.

One example of concern about fathers' involvement after divorce is the increasing intervention of the state in child custody and support issues. Even though there is great scholarly debate concerning the effects of divorce on children (see Reading 34, by Paul Amato, for a complete overview), some recent research has shown that absent fathers have a negative impact on children's well-being because of the lack of parental and economic support (McLanahan and Sandefur 1994). Many states have implemented stronger sanctions against fathers who are not paying child support. These men have been labeled "Deadbeat Dads," because of the billions of dollars in child support that is owed to children. States are concerned that this lack of child support may be contributing to increasing numbers of women and children on welfare, and they are going after fathers (and some mothers) to get it. In Massachusetts, for example, where over $18 billion is owed in child support, parents who are found to owe child support could lose their driver's license, their lottery winnings, their business license, and even their freedom. In Iowa, once a year, the *Des Moines Register* publishes a list of names of all parents (fathers and mothers) who are delinquent in child support. After this list comes out, the public shaming effectively enables the state to collect a substantial amount of unpaid support. Some states will even legally garnish a delinquent parent's wages, which means the state will take out of the paycheck the amount owed for child support, before the individual receives his or her paycheck.

The Effects of Divorce on Children and on the Community

The effects of divorce on children also are addressed in the third reading in this section. In particular, another concern regarding divorce is how supportive the community will be to single parents and children after a divorce occurs. Nathalie Friedman examines this issue in her article, "Divorced Parents and the Jewish Community." Little research has been done on how divorce among Jews is affecting ties to the Jewish community. In addition to providing an overview concerning factors and problems related to divorce in Jewish families, Friedman investigates whether divorce erodes Jewish commitment and involvement. She specifically focuses on whether the family still attends synagogue, whether the children's Jewish education continues, and whether the divorced family maintains any other ties with the Jewish community. Friedman concludes that there are many obstacles to community participation after a divorce and that the Jewish community needs to recognize that these divorced families need support.

The fourth reading in this section on divorce, remarriage, and blended families also focuses on the effects divorce has on children. Paul R. Amato, a professor of sociology, demography, and family studies at Pennsylvania State University, has been researching divorce for several years. In this selection, "Life-Span Adjustment of Children to Their Parents' Divorce," Amato reviews all of the research related to the effects of divorce on children. This research is important because there is a great deal of debate in the family literature concerning the effects divorce has on children. A large part of this debate depends on what variables the researcher is studying because the experience of divorce varies so widely in families. Clearly, parents and children experience divorce in multiple ways, and how parents manage the divorce transition greatly affects their parenting and their children. Key variables that need to be examined are short-term versus long-term effects, and how the effects vary between girls and boys and between older and younger children. Amato discusses the differences between these effects and how parental divorce affects children's well-being. He concludes by suggesting policy changes that would improve the lives of children after divorce.

Remarriage and Stepfamilies

As argued earlier, not everything about divorce is necessarily negative. Many individuals go on to marry again and often form stepfamilies or blended families. The last article in this section, "The Modern American Stepfamily: Problems and Possibilities," by Mary Ann Mason, a professor of social welfare at the University of California at Berkeley, examines remarriage and stepfamilies. Mason's work builds on the earlier work of Cherlin (1978) and of Cherlin and Furstenberg (1994), who found that parents, stepparents, and their children and stepchildren have numerous problems in forming successful new families. Due to the lack of social and institutional support for stepfamilies and blended families, Cherlin and Furstenberg argue that remarriage is an incomplete institution. Mason demonstrates their argument in her research by examining current state and federal policies and laws pertaining to stepfamilies. Mason first reviews social and economic functioning of stepfamilies before she turns her attention to the problematic legal conceptions of stepparenting and stepfamilies. Mason argues that we need a new conceptualization of stepparent rights and responsibilities. Mason's arguments should be compared to those of William Marsiglio (Reading 27), in his article "Overlooked Aspects of Stepfathering," which examines divorce, stepchildren, and stepfathers in particular.

REFERENCES

Ahrons, Constance. 2004. *We're Still Family: What Grown Children Have to Say about Their Parents' Divorce*. New York: HarperCollins.

Cherlin, Andrew J. 1978. "Remarriage as an Incomplete Institution." *American Journal of Sociology* 84:634–50.

Cherlin, Andrew J. and Frank F. Furstenberg, Jr. 1994. "Stepfamilies in the United States: A Reconsideration." *Annual Review of Sociology* 20:359–81.

Hauser, Joyce. 1995. *Good Divorces, Bad Divorces: A Case for Divorce Mediation*. Lanham, MD: University Press of America.

McLanahan, Sara and Gary Sandefur. 1994. *Growing Up with a Single Parent: What Hurts, What Helps*. Cambridge, MA: Harvard University Press.

Riessman, Catherine. 1990. *Divorce Talk: Women and Men Make Sense of Personal Relationships*. New Brunswick, NJ: Rutgers University Press.

Riley, Glenda. 1991. *Divorce: An American Tradition*. New York: Oxford University Press.

Walker, Lou Ann. 1992. "To Ease Broken Hearts." *Parade Magazine*, December 6, p. 12.

Weitzman, Lenore J. 1985. *The Divorce Revolution: The Unexpected Social and Economic Consequences for Women and Children in America*. New York: Free Press.

Yepsen, David. 1995. "Branstad Seeks Change in Iowa's Divorce Laws." *Des Moines Register*, November 12, p. 7B.

31

NO EASY ANSWERS
Why the Popular View of Divorce Is Wrong

CONSTANCE AHRONS

Everyday meat and potato truth is beyond our ability to capture in a few words.
— ANNE LAMOTT, *BIRD BY BIRD*

It was a sunny, unseasonably warm Sunday morning in October. In a quaint country inn in New Jersey, surrounded by a glorious autumn garden, my young grandchildren and I waited patiently for their Aunt Jennifer's wedding to begin. The white carpet was unrolled, the guests were assembled, and the harpist was playing Pachelbel's Canon.

A hush came over the guests. The first member of the bridal party appeared. Poised at the entry, she took a deep breath as she began her slow-paced walk down the white wedding path. Pauline, my grandchildren's stepgreat-grandmother, made her way down the aisle, pausing occasionally to greet family and friends. A round of applause spontaneously erupted. She had traveled fifteen hundred miles to be at her granddaughter's wedding, when only days before, a threatening illness made her presence doubtful.

Next in the grand parade came the best man, one of the groom's three brothers. Proudly, he made his way down the aisle and took his position, ready to be at his brother's side. Then the two maids of honor, looking lovely in their flowing black chiffon gowns, made their appearance. My grandchildren started to wiggle and whisper: "It's Aunt Amy [my younger daughter]! And Christine [the longtime girlfriend who cohabits with Uncle Craig, my daughters' halfbrother]!" As they walked down the aisle and moved slowly past us, special smiles were exchanged with my grandchildren—their nieces and nephew.

Seconds later, my youngest granddaughter pointed excitedly, exclaiming, "Here comes Mommy!" They waved excitedly as the next member of the bridal party, the matron of honor—*their mother, my daughter*—made her way down the path. She paused briefly at our row to exchange a fleeting greeting with her children.

Next, the groom, soon officially to be their "Uncle Andrew," with his mother's arm linked on his left, and his father on his right. The happy

Constance Ahrons, "No Easy Answers: Why the Popular View of Divorce is Wrong" from *Wr're Still Family: What Grown Children Have to Say About Their Parents' Divorce* (New York: HarperCollins, 2004). Copyright © 2004 by Constance Ahrons. Reprinted with the permission of the author and the Sandra Dijkstra Literary Agency.

threesome joined the processional. Divorced from each other when Andrew was a child, his parents beamed in anticipation of the marriage of their eldest son.

Silence. All heads now turned to catch their first glimpse of the bride. Greeted with oohs and aahs, Aunt Jennifer was radiant as she walked arm in arm with her proud and elegant mother, their stepgrandmother, Grandma Susan. Sadly missed at that moment was the father of the bride, my former husband, who had passed away a few years earlier.

When I told friends in California I was flying to the East Coast for a family wedding, I stumbled over how to explain my relationship to the bride. To some I explained: "She's my exhusband's daughter by his second wife." To others, perhaps to be provocative and draw attention to the lack of kinship terms, I said, "She's my daughters' sister." Of course, technically she's my daughters' halfsister, but many years ago my daughters told me firmly that that term "halfsister" was utterly ridiculous. Jennifer wasn't a half anything, she was their *real* sister. Some of my friends thought it strange that I would be invited; others thought it even stranger that I would travel cross-country to attend.

The wedding reception brought an awkward moment or two, when some of the groom's guests asked a common question, "How was I related to the bride?" With some guilt at violating my daughters' dictum, but not knowing how else to identify our kinship, I answered, "She is my daughters' halfsister." A puzzled look. It was not that they didn't understand the relationship, but it seemed strange to them that I was a wedding guest. As we talked, a few guests noted how nice it was that I was there, and then with great elaboration told me stories about their own complex families. Some told me sad stories of families torn apart by divorce and remarriage, and others related happy stories of how their complex families of divorce had come together at family celebrations.

At several points during this celebratory day, I happened to be standing next to the bride's mother when someone from the groom's side asked us how we were related. She or I pleasantly answered, "We used to be married to the same man." This response turned out to be a showstopper. The question asker was at a loss to respond. First and second wives aren't supposed to be amicable or even respectful toward one another. And certainly, first wives are not supposed to be included in their exhusband's new families. And last of all, first and second wives shouldn't be willing to comfortably share the information of having a husband in common.

Although it may appear strange, my exhusband's untimely death brought his second and first families closer together. I had mourned at his funeral and spent time with his family and friends for several days afterward. A different level of kinship formed, as we—his first and second families— shared our loss and sadness. Since then, we have chosen to join together at several family celebrations, which has added a deeper dimension to our feelings of family.

You may be thinking, "This is all so rational. There's no way my family could pull this off." Or perhaps, like the many people who have shared their stories with me over the years, you are nodding your head knowingly, remembering similar occasions in your own family. The truth is we are like many extended families rearranged by divorce. My ties to my exhusband's family are not close, but we care about one another. We seldom have contact outside of family occasions, but we know we're family. We hear stories of each other's comings and goings, transmitted to us through our mutual ties to my daughters, and now, through grandchildren. But if many families, like my own, continue to have relationships years after divorce, why don't we hear more about them?

Quite simply, it's because this is not the way it's supposed to be. My family, and the many others like mine, don't fit the ideal images we have about families. They appear strange because they're not tidy. There are "extra" people and relationships that don't exist in nuclear families and are awkward to describe because we don't have familiar and socially defined kinship terms to do so. Although families rearranged and expanded by divorce are rapidly growing and increasingly common, our resistance to accepting them as normal makes them appear deviant.

Societal change is painfully slow, which results in the situation wherein the current realities of family life come into conflict with our valued images. Sociologists call this difference "cultural lag," the difference between what is real and what we hold as ideal. This lag occurs because of our powerful resistance to acknowledging changes that challenge our basic beliefs about what's good and what's bad in our society.

Why Good Divorces Are Invisible

Good divorces are those in which the divorce does not destroy meaningful family relationships. Parents maintain a sufficiently cooperative and supportive relationship that allows them to focus on the needs of their children. In good divorces children continue to have ties to both their mothers and their fathers, and each of their extended families, including those acquired when either parent remarries.

Good divorces have been well-kept secrets because to acknowledge them in mainstream life threatens our nostalgic images of family. If the secret got out that indeed many families that don't fit our "mom and pop" household ideal are healthy, we would have to question the basic societal premise that marriage and family are synonymous. And that reality upsets a lot of people, who then respond with familiar outcries that divorce is eroding our basic values and destroying society.

Although we view ourselves as a society in which nuclear families and lifelong monogamous marriages predominate, the reality is that 43 percent of first marriages will end in divorce. Over half of new marriages are actually remarriages for at least one of the partners. Not only have either the bride or groom (or both) been divorced but increasingly one of them also has parents who are divorced.

Families are the way we organize to raise children. Although we hold the ideal image that marriage is a precursor to establishing a family, modern parents are increasingly challenging this traditional ideal. Families today arrange— and rearrange—themselves in many responsible ways that meet the needs of children for nurturance, guidance and economic support. Family historian Stephanie Coontz, in her book *The Way We Never Were*, shows how the "tremendous variety of workable childrearing patterns in history suggests that, with little effort, we should be able to forge new institutions and values."[1]

One way we resist these needed societal changes is by denying that divorce is no longer deviant. We demean divorced families by clinging to the belief that families can't exist outside of marriage. It follows then that stories of healthy families that don't fit the tidy nuclear family package are rare and stories that show how divorce destroys families and harms children are common. In this way, bad divorces appear to represent the American way of divorce and good divorces become invisible.

Messages That Hinder Good Divorces

When the evils of divorce are all that families hear about, it makes coping with the normal transitions and changes that inevitably accompany divorce all the more difficult. Negative messages make children feel different and lesser, leading to feelings of shame and guilt. Parents who feel marginalized in this way are less likely to think about creative solutions to their problems. That all of this unnecessary anxiety is fueled by sensationalized reports of weak findings, half-truths and myths of devastation is deplorable. Only by sorting out the truths about divorce from the fiction can we be empowered to make better decisions, find healthy ways to maintain family relationships, and develop important family rituals after divorce. Let's take a close look at the most common misconceptions about divorce.

Misconception 1: Parents Should Stay Married for the Sake of the Kids

This is a message that pervades our culture, and it rests on a false duality: Marriage is good for kids, divorce is bad. Underlying this premise is the belief that parents who divorce are immature and selfish because they put their personal needs ahead of the needs of their children, that because divorce is too easy to get, spouses give up on their marriages too easily and that if you're thinking about divorcing your spouse, you should "stick it out till the kids are grown." A popular joke takes this message to its extreme. A couple in their nineties, married for seventy years, appears before a judge in their petition for a divorce. The judge looks at them quizzically and asks, "Why now, why after all these years?" The couple responds: "We waited until the children were dead."

The research findings are now very clear that reality is nowhere near as simple and tidy. Unresolved, open interparental conflict between married spouses that pervades day-to-day family life has been shown again and again to have negative effects on children. Most experts agree that when this is the case it is better for the children if parents divorce rather than stay married. Ironically, prior to the initiation of no-fault legislation over twenty years ago, in most states this kind of open conflict in the home was considered "cruel and inhumane" treatment and it was one of the few grounds on which a divorce would be granted — if it could be proved.

But the majority of unsatisfying marriages are not such clear-cut cases. When most parents ask themselves if they should stay married for the sake of their children, they have clearly reached the point where they are miserable in their marriages but wouldn't necessarily categorize them as "high-conflict." And here is where, in spite of the societal message, there is no agreement in the research findings or among clinical experts. That's because it's extremely complex and each individual situation is too different to allow for a "one-size-fits-all" answer.

A huge list of factors comes into play when assessing whether staying married would be better for your kids. For example,

- Is the unhappiness in your marriage making you so depressed or angry that your children's needs go unmet because you can't parent effectively?
- Do you and your spouse have a cold and distant relationship that makes the atmosphere at home unhealthy for your children?
- Do you and your spouse lack mutual respect, caring or interests, setting a poor model for your children?
- Would the financial hardships be so dire that your children will experience a severely reduced standard of living?

Add to this your child's temperament, resources and degree of resilience, and then the personal and family changes that take place in the years after the divorce, and you can see how the complexities mount.

It is a rare parent who divorces *too easily*. Most parents are responsible adults who spend years struggling with the extremely difficult and complex decision of whether to divorce or stay married "for the sake of the children." The bottom line is that divorce is an adult decision, usually made by one spouse, entering into in the face of many unknowns. Without a crystal ball, no one knows whether their decision will be better for their children. . . .

Misconception 2: "Adult Children of Divorce" Are Doomed to Have Lifelong Problems

If your parents divorced when you were a child, you are often categorized as an ACOD, an "adult child of divorce," and we all know there's nothing good to be said about that. I dislike this label because it is stigmatizing. It casts dark shadows over divorcing parents and their children, results in feelings of shame and guilt, and is another way of pathologizing divorce.

Years ago I coined a term, "divorcism," to call attention to the stereotypes and stigma attached to divorce. To put children with divorced parents in a special category is divorcism in action. It stereotypes them as a group with problems, and like all stereotypes it ignores individual differences.

If your parents didn't divorce, are you then called an "adult child of marriage"? No, you're just "normal." Normal kids must have two parents of different genders who live in the same household; anything else is abnormal, and if you're abnormal then you must be dysfunctional. That's the way the American family story goes.

Perhaps the worst outcome of this labeling is that it makes parents and children feel that this one event has doomed them and they don't have the power to change anything. This pinpointing of divorce as the source of personal problems is pervasive. Parents worry that whatever problems their kids have, even when they are normal developmental issues, were caused by the divorce. Children are encouraged to blame the divorce for whatever unhappiness they may feel, which makes them feel helpless about improving their lives. Teachers are often too quick to identify divorce as the reason for a child's school behavior problem. The greater society points a finger at divorce as the reason for a wide range of greater social problems.

The truth is that, for the great majority of children who experience a parental divorce, the divorce becomes part of their history but it is not a defining factor. Like the rest of us, most of them reach adulthood to lead reasonably happy, successful lives. Although children who grew up with divorced parents certainly share an important common experience, their ability to form healthy relationships, be good parents, build careers, and so on, are far more determined by their individual temperaments, their sibling relationships, the dynamics within their parents' *marriages* and the climate of their *postdivorce* family lives.

Misconception 3: Divorce Means You Are No Longer a Family

There's this myth that as long as you stay married your family is good but as soon as you announce you're separating, your family is thrown into the bad zone. Your family goes from being "intact" to being "dissolved," from two-parent to single parent, from functional to dysfunctional. Even though we all know that people don't jump from happy marriages right into divorce, there is an assumption that the decision to separate is the critical marker. It doesn't seem to matter whether your marital relationship was terrible, whether you were miserable and your children troubled. Just as long as you are married and living together in one household, the sign over the front door clearly states to the world, "We're a normal family."

The inaccurate and misleading message that divorce destroys families is harmful to both parents and children because it hides and denies all the positive ways that families can be rearranged after divorce. It sends the destructive message to children that divorce means they only get to keep one parent and they will no longer be part of a family. Although two-parent first-married households now represent less than 25 percent of all households,[2] and an increasing number of children each year are raised by unmarried adults, many people cling to the belief that healthy families can only be two-parent married families and social change is always bad and threatening to our very foundations.

When Julie, one of the participants in my study, married recently, she walked down the aisle with a father on either side. On her left was her biological father, on her right was her stepfather of eighteen years. Her mother was her matron of honor, who joined her former and present husbands, all standing together to witness the marriage. Two best men, the groom's eleven-year-old twin sons from his first marriage, stood next to him. Helen, the groom's former wife, sat close by, accompanied by Tony, her live-in partner.

While this wedding ceremony doesn't fit the traditional pattern, Don and Julie have joined the three-quarters of American households who have living arrangements other than that of the "traditional" family.

My older daughter thanked me for coming to Jennifer's wedding. She told me that my being there made it possible for her to share this happy occasion with *all* her family, instead of feeling the disconnections that some children feel in divorced families. This bonding spreads to the third generation so that my grandchildren know us all as family.

The truth is that although some divorces result in family breakdown, the vast majority do not. While divorce changes the form of the family from one household to two, from a nuclear family to a binuclear one, it does not need to change the way children think and feel about the significant relationships within their families. This does not mean that divorce is not painful or difficult, but over the years, as postdivorce families change and even expand, most remain capable of meeting children's needs for family.

Misconception 4: Divorce Leaves Children without Fathers

This message is linked closely with the preceding one because when we say that divorce destroys families we really mean that fathers disappear from the family. The myths that accompany this message are that fathers are "deadbeat dads" who abandon their kids and leave their families impoverished. The message strongly implies that fathers don't care and are unwilling or unable to make continuing commitments to their children. While this reflects the reality for a minority of divorced fathers, the majority of fathers continue to have loving relationships with their children and contribute financially to their upbringing.

The truth is that many fathers do spend less time with their children after divorce, but to stereotype them as parents who abandon their children only creates more difficulty for both fathers and their children. It establishes a myth that men are irresponsible parents who don't care about their children, when in reality most feel great pain that they are not able to see their children more frequently. In the vast majority of divorces, over 85 percent, mothers are awarded sole custody, or in the case of joint custody, primary residence. This means that most fathers become nonresidential parents after divorce. Being a nonresidential father is a difficult role with no preparation or guidelines.

Most of the research on dads after divorce focuses on absentee fathers, while involved fathers are frequently overlooked. Many fathers continue to be excellent parents after divorce and in fact some fathers and children report that their relationships actually improve after the divorce. In much the same way that good divorces are invisible in the public debate, so are involved fathers.

Misconception 5: Exspouses Are Incapable of Getting Along

When I first started to study divorce in the early 1970s, it was assumed in the literature that any continuing relationship between exspouses was a sign of serious pathology, an inability to adjust to the divorce, to let go and to move on with their lives.

In the late 1970s, when joint custody was first introduced, it was met with loud cries of skepticism from the opposition. How could two parents who couldn't get along well enough to stay married possibly get along well enough to continue to share parenting? Two decades ago I confronted the skeptics by writing several articles arguing that we needed to accept the reality of our divorce rates and needed to transform our values about parenting after divorce. The issue was no longer *whether* divorced parents should share parenting to meet their children's needs but *how*.[3]

Although there have been many legal changes over the years, and some form of joint custody legislation exists now in all states, questions about its viability still prevail. These accusations, citing joint custody as a failed "social experiment," are not based on research findings, which are still very limited and inconclusive, but instead on the ill-founded stereotype that all divorcing spouses are bitter enemies, too lost in waging their own wars to consider their children. Certainly this is true for some divorcing spouses, the ones that make headlines in bitter custody disputes, but it is not true for the majority.

Although we have come to realize that parents who divorce still need to have some relationship with one another, the belief that it's not really possible still lingers. In fact, when exspouses remain friends, they are viewed as a little strange and their relationship is suspect. Yet, the truth is that many divorced parents *are* cooperative and effective coparents. Like good divorces and involved fathers, they are mostly invisible in the media.

Despite much resistance, joint custody has become increasingly common, and new words, such as "coparents," have emerged in response to this reality. The newest edition of *Webster's College Dictionary* (2000) recognizes the term, defining it as separated or divorced parents who share custody and child rearing equally. While I don't agree that coparenting is limited only to those parents who share child rearing equally, or even that those who coparent need to share equally in time or responsibility, the inclusion of the word in the dictionary sanctions important new kinship language for divorced families, thereby advancing our ability to acknowledge complex family arrangements.

Misconception 6: Divorce Turns Everyone into Exfamily; In-laws Become Outlaws

When it comes to the semantics of divorce-speak, all of the kinship ties that got established by marriage dissolve abruptly. On the day of the legal divorce, my husband and all of his relatives suddenly became exes. But even though the kinship is *legally* terminated, meaningful relationships often continue. My friend Jan, during her fifteen-year marriage, formed a very close relationship with her mother-in-law. Now, twenty years later, she still calls her eighty-two-year-old exmother-in-law "Mom," talks with her several times a week, and has dinner with her weekly. Exmother-in-law is certainly not an adequate description of this ongoing relationship.

As a culture we continue to resist accepting divorce as a normal endpoint to marriage even though it is an option chosen by almost half of those who marry. It is this cultural lag, this denial of current realities that causes the inaccurate language, not only for the family ties that continue but also for the family we inherit when we, our former spouses, our parents, or our children remarry. Kinship language is important because it provides a shorthand way for us to identify relationships without wading through tedious explanations.

We have terms like "cousin," "great-aunt" or uncle, and "sister-in-law" that help us quickly identify lineage in families. Even these kinship terms are sometimes inadequate and confusing. For example, "sister-in-law" can mean my brother's wife, or my husband's sister, or my husband's brother's wife. And even though you don't know exactly *how* she is related to me, you do at least know that she belongs in the family picture. The in-law suffix quickly tells you that we are not blood relatives but we are related through marriage lines.

Our failure to provide kinship language that recognizes some kind of viable relationship between parents who are no longer married to each other, as well as language that incorporates old and new family as kin, makes children feel that their identity is shattered by divorce. It is no wonder that we remain in the dark ages when it comes to normalizing complex families after divorce and remarriage.

Our language and models for divorce and remarriage are inadequate at best and pejorative at worst. Relegating the relationship between divorced spouses who are parents to the term "exspouse" hurls children and their parents into the dark territory of "exfamily." The common terms of "broken home," "dissolved family," and "single-parent family" all imply that children are left with either no family or only one parent.

This lack of positive language is one more way that the invisibility of good divorces impacts postdivorce families.

Misconception 7: Stepparents Aren't Real Parents

One of the implications of the high divorce rate is that the shape and composition of families have changed dramatically in the last twenty years. All over the world, weddings no longer fit the traditional model: there are stepparents, half siblings, stepsiblings, stepchildren, intimate partners of parents, stepgrandparents and even, on rare occasions, exspouses of the bride or groom.

To complicate the wedding picture even more, one or both of the bride's and groom's parents may have been divorced. And given that well over half of those who divorce eventually remarry, we are likely to find that the majority of those who have divorced parents also have stepparents. Add the dramatic increase in cohabitation to that equation and it is not unusual for an "unmarried intimate partner" of one of the parents to be present as well. These complex families require photographers to quickly switch to their wide-angle lens and totally revamp their traditional formats for wedding photos.

Over half the children today have adults in their lives for whom they can't attach socially accepted kinship terms. They lack social rules that would help them know how they are supposed to relate and how to present these adults to the social world around them. I am reminded here of a *Herman* cartoon, showing a boy holding his report card and asking his teacher: "Which parent do you want to sign it: my natural father, my stepfather, my mother's third husband, my real mother, or my natural father's fourth wife who lives with us?"

As the cartoon clearly suggests, there are real and natural parents, and then there are stepparents. Stepmothers are stereotyped in children's literature as mean, nasty, and even abusive. The only time we hear about stepfathers is when the media highlights the sensationalized case of sexual abuse. Added to these negative images is the reality that stepparents have no legal rights to their stepchildren. The research on stepparents is still very limited and positive role models are lacking.

Children and their new stepparents start off their relationships with two strikes against them. They have to fight an uphill battle to overcome negative expectations, and they have to do so without much help from society. Since almost 85 percent of the children with divorced parents will have a stepparent at some time in their lives, it is shocking that we know so little about how these relationships work. Clearly, societal resistance to recognizing the broad spectrum of postdivorce families has hindered the development of good role models for stepchildren and their stepparents.

Painting a False Picture

Taken together, these negative messages paint a false picture of divorce, one that assumes family ties are irretrievably broken so that postdivorce family relationships appear to be nonexistent. Despite these destructive messages, many divorced parents meet the needs of their children by creating strong families after divorce. Without a doubt, divorce is painful and creates stress for families, but it is important to remember that most recover, maintaining some of their kinship relationships and adding new ones over time.

By making good divorces invisible we have accepted bad divorces as the norm. In so doing, children and their divorced parents are being given inaccurate messages that conflict with the realities they live and make them feel deviant and stigmatized. It is time we challenge these outdated, ill-founded messages and replace them with new ones that acknowledge and accurately reflect current realities.

The Distortions of Oversimplifying

Just a little over a decade ago, in January 1989, the *New York Times* Magazine ran a cover story called "Children after Divorce," which created a wave of panic in divorced parents and their children. Judith Wallerstein and her coauthor, Sandra Blakeslee, a staff writer for the *New York Times,* noted their newest unexpected finding. Calling it the "sleeper effect," they concluded that only ten years after divorce did it become apparent that girls experience "serious effects of divorce at the time they are entering young adulthood."[4]

When one of the most prestigious newspapers in the world highlights the findings of a study, most readers take it seriously. "That 66 percent of young women in our study between the ages of nineteen and twenty-three will suffer debilitating effects of their parents' divorce years later" immediately became generalized to the millions of female children with divorced parents. The message—just when you think everything may be okay, the doom of divorce will rear its ugly head—is based on a *mere eighteen out of the grand total of twenty-seven women* interviewed in this age group.[5] This detail wasn't mentioned in the fine print of the article but is buried in the appendix of the book that was scheduled for publication a month after the *New York Times* story appeared. And it is on this slim data that the seeds of a myth are planted. We are still living with the fallout.

In sharp contrast to Wallerstein's view that parental divorce has a powerful devastating impact on children well into adulthood, another psychologist made headlines with a completely opposite thesis. In her book, *The Nurture Assumption: Why Children Turn Out the Way They Do,* Judith Rich Harris proposes that what parents do makes little difference in how their children's lives turn out. Half of the variation in children's behavior and personality is due to genes, claims Harris, and the other half to environmental factors, mainly their peer relationships. For this reason, Harris asserts parental divorce is not responsible for all the ills it is blamed for.

These extreme positions—of divorce as disaster and divorce as inconsequential—oversimplify the realities of our complex lives. Genes and contemporary relationships notwithstanding, we have strong evidence that parents still make a significant difference in their children's development. Genetic inheritance and peer relationships are part of the story but certainly not the whole story. . . .

It should come, then, as no surprise that reports of the findings about divorce are often contradictory and confusing. It is impossible for any study to take account of all the complexities of real life, or of the individual differences that allow one family to thrive in a situation that would create enormous stress, and frayed relationships, in another. But it is in these variations that we can begin to make sense of how divorce impacts the lives of individuals and families.

ENDNOTES

1. Stephanie Coontz, *The Way We Never Were* (New York: Basic Books, 1992), p. 230.
2. Jason Fields and Lynne Casper, *America's Families and Living Arrangements: March 2000,* Current Population Reports, Pp. 20–53. (Washington, DC: U.S. Census Bureau, 2001).
3. See the following articles for more information: Constance Ahrons, "Redefining the Divorced Family: A Conceptual Framework for Postdivorce Family System Reorganization," *Social Work* 25 (1980): 437–41; "Divorce: A Crisis of Family Transition and Change," *Family Relations* 29 (1980): 533–40; "Joint Custody Arrangements in the Postdivorce Family," *Journal of Divorce* 3 (1980): 189–205; and "The Binuclear Family: Two Households, One Family," *Alternative Lifestyles* (1979): 499–515.
4. Judith Wallerstein and Sandra Blakeslee, "Children After Divorce," *New York Times* (January 22, 1989), p. 19.
5. Judith Wallerstein and Sandra Blakeslee, *Second Chances* (New York: Ticknor & Fields, 1989), Table 2 appendix, p. 315.

32

THE SOCIAL SELF AS GENDERED
A Masculinist Discourse of Divorce

TERRY ARENDELL

Divorce functions as a prism, making available for examination an array of issues. Pulled into question are the shape and dictates of extrafamilial institutions and practices, such as the juridical and economic; and the character of family life, parenting, and domestic arrangements. Also brought into view are matters of interpersonal relations and gender identity: It is "unfamiliar situations" which call forth "taken as given

Terry Arendell, "The Social Self as Gendered: A Masculinist Discourse of Divorce" from *Symbolic Interaction* 15, no. 2 (Summer 1992). Copyright © 1992 by JAI Press. Reprinted with permission of the author and the University of California Press.

identities" and present opportunities to observe the effects of identity upon behavior (Foote 1981:338). . . . Thus investigation of participants' perspectives on and responses to divorce and the postdivorce situation can illumine processes not only of interactional adjustment in the context of change but also of identity maintenance and alteration.

Family and identity transitions are located within a broader sociocultural context: The gender hierarchy and belief system and gender roles are being questioned and altered, although at broadly discrepant rates (Hochschild 1989; Pleck 1985). Specifically, the conventions of masculinity — "those sets of signs indicating that a person is a 'man,' or 'not a woman' or 'not a child'" (Hearn 1987:137) and which are "the social reality for men in modern society" (Clatterbaugh 1990:3) — are being challenged. Indeed, Kimmel (1987) has concluded that contemporary men, like men in other periods characterized by dramatic social and economic change, "confront a crisis in masculinity" (p. 153). Divorce both exemplifies and prompts a crisis in gender identity (Riessman 1990; Vaughan 1986).

Men's perspectives on, actions in, and adjustments to divorce have been relatively neglected in divorce research. Yet they are significant for understanding contemporary social arrangements and processes as well as for broadening understanding of men's lives: How men define their situations and act in divorce points to their positions in a gender-structured society and to their understandings of the nature of social practices, relationships, and selves. To paraphrase an argument made with regard to the study of a gendered division of labor in families, the ways in which divorced fathers "use motive talk to account for, disclaim, and/or neutralize their behavior or changes in their behavior need to be more fully explored and developed" (Pestello and Voyandoff 1991:117).

Methodology

Based on data obtained through intensive interviews examining postdivorce situations, experiences, and feelings with a sample of 75 divorced fathers (Arendell 1995), this article explores the problem of the social self as gendered and specifically, the nature of the masculinist self. All participants were volunteers who responded to notices and advertisements placed in newsletters, magazines, and newspapers or to referrals from other participants. The men ranged in age from 23 to 59 years with a median age of 38.5 years. Sixty-four interviewees were white, three were black, four Hispanic, two Asian American, and two Native American. All respondents were residents of New York State, had one or more minor children, and had been divorced or legally separated for at least 18 months. The median time divorced or separated was 4.8 years. At the time they were interviewed, 18 men were remarried, 5 were living with a woman in a marital-like relationship, and the others were unmarried. Nearly half of the sample had some college education with over one-third having completed college and approximately one-sixth having earned a graduate or professional degree. Occupationally, one-third of the employed respondents worked in blue-collar and two-thirds worked in white-collar positions. Six men were unemployed at the time of the interview, three by choice.

The respondents were fathers to a total of 195 children ranging in age from 2 to 25 with a median age of 9.5 years. The number of children per father ranged from one to six; the mean number of children was 2.6 and the median was 2. Child custody arrangements varied among the men: six fathers had primary physical custody, five had co- or shared physical custody with their former wives, and 64 were noncustodial fathers. Two of those categorized as noncustodial fathers actually had split custody arrangements; each had one child living with him and another two children living with their mothers. A total of eleven fathers were "absent" fathers, meaning that they had no contact with any of their children for at least the past twelve months; another four fathers were "absent" from one or more but not all of their children.

The sample overrepresents "involved" fathers; for example, only 15 percent were "absent" compared to the national figure of about 50 percent (Furstenberg, Morgan, and Allison 1987) and 85 percent were noncustodial parents compared to a national figure of 90 percent (U.S. Bureau of the Census 1989). Additionally, with only a few exceptions, the nonresidential fathers repeatedly maintained that they desired increased access to and involvement with their children; many wished for more satisfying relations with their children.

Interviews were open-ended, tended to be long, lasting between two and five hours, and were conducted primarily in 1990 with some occurring in late 1989 and early 1991. Seven respondents participated in follow-up interviews. An interview instrument, initially developed and revised on the basis of 15 earlier interviews in another state, was used as a reference to ensure that certain areas were covered during the discussions. All interviews were tape recorded and transcribed. Data were analyzed using the constant comparative method and coding paradigm developed in works on grounded theory (Glaser and Strauss 1967; Strauss 1989).

A Masculinist Discourse of Divorce

What the data in this study of divorce provide is a richly descriptive testimony of the men's perspectives on and actions in family and divorce. These divorced fathers, largely irrespective of variations in custody, visitation, marital, or socioeconomic class status, shared a set of dispositions, practices, and explanations with which they managed their identities, situations, and emotional lives. They held in common a body of *gender strategies:* plans of action "through which a person tries to solve problems at hand given the cultural notions of gender at play" and through which an individual reconciles beliefs and feelings with behaviors and circumstances (Hochschild 1989:15).

In similar ways, they accounted for past and present actions and described and implied intended future lines of activity, including, significantly, the probable meanings of such movement. The participants shared a *discourse* — a particular "matrix of perceptions, appreciations, and actions" (Bourdieu 1987:83). More specifically, they shared a *masculinist discourse of divorce.* . . .

Considered specifically in this article are the interviewees' understandings and definitions of family, encompassing issues of gender differences and a *broken* family and the processes of devaluation of the former wife. Then examined is the related use of a rhetoric of *rights*. Following this is a brief discussion and analysis of the contrasting perspectives and actions of the divergent group, the postdivorce "androgynous" fathers. Lastly, several of the implications of the findings are specified.

Definition of Family

Gender Differences

The family was shown to be a threshold of masculinity in these men's accounts; it was the primary social group (Cooley 1981) that conveyed and reinforced the constructs of gender. The family of origin served as the nursery and early classroom of gender acquisition, and the family of procreation (that formed through marriage) served as a workshop where gender identity was continuously retooled. Then, as the marriage ended and the postdivorce situation entered, the family and its changes evoked a questioning of masculine identity. Made particularly evident in the divorcing process was that beneath the jointly created and shared reality of married life (Berger and Kellner 1964) were distinctive experiences and understandings, organized according to and understood in terms of gender — the "his" and "hers" of married life (Bernard 1981; Riessman 1990). Nearly all of the respondents expressed a belief that gender differences had been at play in their marriages and divorces; while some regretted the consequences of the differences and attributed marital problems to them, most nonetheless expressed confidence that, compared to their former wife's, their own experiences and perceptions had been, to use their terms, the more valid, reasonable, logical, reliable, or objective ones.

Communication patterns and conversational styles in their marriages varied along gender lines, reflecting and reinforcing gender differences. The men usually expected and reported themselves to be less expressive and self-disclosing in marriage than their former wives; they also claimed to have felt pressured during marriage to be otherwise (see also Cancian 1987; Riessman 1990; Tannen 1990). One participant, in a remark about the differences between men and women which was similar in substance to most others' comments about gender differences, noted:

> Men compartmentalize. It's just a different pattern of doing things, it has to do with the differences between men and women. I think men are always a few

months, a few steps, behind women in a relationship. And men don't talk to each other the way women do to each other so men don't know what's going on outside of the things they are already most familiar with. They are at a disadvantage, they usually don't know what's going on.

Despite its gendered and therefore problematic character, marriage, for a large majority of these men, was essential to family; indeed, family was predicated upon the enduring "successful marriage." The "successful" and desired marriage, however, was defined in a paradoxical way as being both the traditional marriage and the companionate marriage. That is, on the one hand, most of these men wanted a marital arrangement in which they were ultimately, even if largely benignly, the dominant spouse, befitting men in relationships with women according to the conventions of masculinity. On the other hand, these men wanted a relationship in which they were equal co-partners, forging mutually a high degree of intimacy and seeking reciprocally to meet the other's needs and desires. This next person, a co-custodial parent who had opted to leave his marriage two years earlier but was now hoping for a marital reconciliation, explained his position:

> *I'm not talking about a marriage and family with a patriarchal model, but the priority of the relationship between a man and a woman as a husband and wife. I want an equal relationship, a partnership. But let me word it this way, I would like her to be able to trust me to be the leader of the family. When there are times we can't sit down at the table and make decisions cooperatively, then I will make the decisions and she will trust me. I want to be able to do that in a marriage. What I need and want is the trust from her to be able to be the leader of the family. I want her to be the first one to say: "We've talked about it and I'll let you decide." I guess I expect her to relinquish the control of the situation first.*

The improbability, even impossibility, of having simultaneously both types of marriage was largely obscured by the gender assumptions held. By conceiving of themselves as more rational, logical, and dependable than their wives, for example, assertions repeated in various ways throughout their accounts of marriage and divorce, these men were able to make claims to both types of marriage without acknowledging the contradictions or tensions between them.

The explanation for the failure to have the desired and lasting companionate marriage was the existence of fundamental differences between themselves as *men* and their former wives as *women*. In specifying these differences, the men rehearsed and reinforced the cultural stereotypes of gender and their expectations that they be the dominant partner. . . . Perceiving themselves to be fundamentally dissimilar from women had enabled these men to objectify their wives during marriage, at least as their retrospective accounts indicated, and to thereby discount or reconstruct the meanings of their communications in particular ways. . . . Accepting the conventional beliefs in gender differences and asserting the preeminence of their levels of rationality and insight served to strengthen the respondents' identities as masculine selves. For example:

> *I just mostly stayed rational and reasonable during the months we considered separation, but she just got crazier and crazier through the whole thing. I should have been prepared for that; I always knew during the marriage not to take her too seriously because she could be so illogical. I mean, you know, it's men's rationality that keeps a marriage together to begin with.*

Likewise, having dismissed or redefined a wife's expression of marital discontent was justified through claims to basic superiority. One man noted:

> *She kept saying she was unhappy, that I worked too much and was never home, and that I neither listened to or appreciated her, that I didn't help out with the kids, maybe even didn't care about them. But I insisted she was just depressed because her father had died. It just made sense but I couldn't get her to see it.*

By redefining a wife's expressed feelings of discontent with the marriage or him as a partner, an individual could rationalize and discount his own participation in the demise of the marriage. Through such disclaimers, the estranged husband reinforced his definitions of the situation and of self. . . .

A wife's sentiments about and assessments of their marriage could be discounted; entering into the wife's point of view, or attempting to "take the role of the other" — defined by Mead (1934:254) as "a uniquely human capacity which assumes the attitude of the other individual as well as calling it out in the other" — was not a constitutive element of a husband's range of activities in the conventional marital relationship. Women spoke a "different language," as one man summed up the differences between men and women which lead to divorce, a language not to be taken too seriously, or at least not as seriously as one's own *as a man*.[1] This posture toward a wife's perspectives and feelings carried over into the postdivorce situation where differences and conflicts of interest were typically highlighted and multiplied.

A "Broken Family"

Family, within the masculinist discourse of divorce, was understood to be a *broken family*, consisting essentially of two parts: the male-self and the wife-and-children or, as referred to, "'me' and 'them.'" Even men who had sought the divorce, about one-third of the group, and several of those who had primary or shared custody of children, understood and discussed the post-divorce family as being a *broken* one. Most of the noncustodial fathers perceived themselves to have been marginalized from the family, and nearly all felt stigmatized as divorced fathers. For instance:

> *You're not part of the family, part of the society anymore. You really don't have a proper place, a place where you have input into what goes on in your life. You're treated as if you're just scum, that's what you are really.*

One father, using the language of *broken* family explicitly, summed up the dilemma he faced, suggesting that with the fracturing of the family went a loss of power and authority:

> *I guess I'm sort of at a loss in all of this; I just don't know what to do to fix a broken family. I can't say I didn't want the divorce, it was a mutual decision. But I just hadn't understood before how it would break the family into pieces. It's really become them and me and I don't know what to do. I keep thinking of the rhyme: "Humpty Dumpty sat on a wall, Humpty Dumpty had a great fall. All the king's horses and all the king's men, couldn't put Humpty together again." I ran it by my ex last week and asked her if she had any Super-Glue, but she didn't think it was funny.*

The definition of the postdivorce family as a *broken* one had several sources, including the belief that family is predicated on the marriage. Other sources of the view were acceptance of the conventional definition that masculinity is the measure of mature adulthood in comparison to both femininity and childhood (Broverman et al. 1970; Phillips and Gilroy 1985),[2] meaning, therefore, that men are different in distinctive ways from women and children, and of the ideology, if not the actual practice, of a traditional gender-based family division of labor: child-rearing and caretaking are the responsibilities primarily of women, whether or not they are employed, and economic providing is the responsibility primarily of men (Cohen 1989; Hochschild 1989).[3]

Another and related factor in the view that the postdivorce family consisted of "me" and "them" was the understanding that the respective parent–child relationship differed, a perception shared by divorced mothers as well, according to other studies (Arendell 1986; Hetherington, Cox, and Cox 1976). . . . In contrast to the unique and independent mother–child unit, the father–child relationship was mediated in varying ways by the wife, consistent with her marital role as emotional worker (Hochschild 1983, 1989), and so was dependent on her actions. One father, who had read extensively about the psychological effects of divorce on children, compared the outcomes of his two divorces:

> *I would have to say that my children's primary attachment really was with their mother. I think that's typical in families, mothers are just better trained, maybe it's an instinct for parenting. Maybe fathers just don't make the effort. Anyway, even after my first divorce, I found that my ex-wife was vital to my relationship with the child of our marriage: She thought it was important that he maintain contact with me and that I be a part of his life. So she really encouraged him to do this and so it continued to be a relationship. She ran a kind of interference between us. He's 21 now and we have a good, solid relationship, but my children of this last marriage are essentially withdrawn from me. Their mother, my second wife, never really facilitated our relationship.*

The retreat by former wives from the activity of facilitating the relationship between children and their fathers after divorce was interpreted as a misuse of power, and often as an overt act of hostility or revenge. In addition to the use and misuse of their psychological power in interpersonal relations (see also Pleck 1989), former wives exercised power by interfering with visitation, denigrating them as fathers and men to their children, provoking interpersonal conflicts, being uncooperative in legal matters, and demanding additional money. . . . Nearly all of the men had an acute sense that their own power and authority in the family had been seriously eroded through divorce (Arendell 1992; Riessman 1990). This perception was central to the crisis in gender identity and was not limited to noncustodial fathers: More than half of the primary or co-custodial fathers argued that their former wives had usurped power illegitimately and at their expense. Moreover, former spouses had attained or appropriated dominance only partly through their own actions: The judiciary and legal system and the institutional and informal gender biases of both were accomplices and even instigators.

> *The legal system is such a crock, I can't believe it. The legal system is so for the woman and so against the man, it's just incredible. And the result is that all of these women get to go around screwing their ex-husbands.*

Another person explained:

> *When we went to court after the divorce was over because of disagreements over support and visitation, the court did nothing. The situation is as it is today [with the mother interfering with his visitation] because the judge did nothing except hold meeting after meeting, delay after delay. The judge even said she was an unfit mother. She violated every aspect of the agreement, she obstructed. But they let her do it.*

In support of their assertions about the unjustness of the system, numerous men cited the lack of a legal presumption in favor of joint child custody in New York State. Over half of the fathers argued (erroneously) that joint custody is not allowed in New York State (*Family Law* 1990) and nearly all of the noncustodial fathers, most of whom were granted what they called the "standard visitation arrangement"—every other weekend and one evening a week—complained bitterly about their limited access to their children.

Consistent with the categorization of "me" and "them," the perceived centrality of the former wife, and their own limited parental involvement, children most often were talked about as if they were extensions of their mothers rather than separate, unique persons. Thus, identity as a divorced father was intermixed with identity as a former spouse, adding further ambiguity and uncertainty to their place and activities in the changed family. Further, nearly all of the noncustodial and a third of the custodial fathers viewed their children as being instruments of their mothers in the postdivorce exchanges between the parents. . . . Fathers tended to merge their children with their former wives in other ways as well. In explaining their motives for or the consequences of actions, the majority of men frequently shifted from their children as the subject to their former wife. For instance,

> *I wanted the kids to have a house. So it remains as it is, with them [the kids] living in it, until the youngest is 18. But that was my biggest mistake. I should have had the house sold. Then I could have really gotten away from her [the former wife] and had no ties to her at all.*

The approach of not disaggregating the children from the former wife served varying functions. On the one hand, this approach bolstered the primacy of the former spouse in the postdivorce situation, granting her a position of centrality and augmenting the charges against her, and, on the other hand, it reduced her status by categorizing her with the children. Children's experiences and feelings could be discounted more easily than if they were respected as independent persons, thus creating more emotional distance between them. . . . Not surprisingly, then, fathers satisfied with their parent–child relations were the exception: They included the postdivorce "androgynous" fathers and eight others. The majority were discontented with and disconcerted by the nature of their interactions with, emotional connections to, and levels of involvement with their children. Most characterized their relations with their children as being strained or superficial, distrustful, and unfulfilling.

Devaluing a Wife's Family Activities

Most of the respondents specifically devalued the family activities done both during and after marriage by the former wife (Riessman 1990). Through deprecating the former partner's activities, the men were able to buttress various assertions, including that they had been the dominant spouse and had been mistreated badly by the divorce settlement. Over a third of the fathers contended that they had been exceptional men in their marriages—a "superman," as several fathers quipped, in contrast to the popularized notion of "superwoman"—carrying the major share of income-earning and participating equally or near equally in caretaking activities. These particular fathers especially generalized their critique of their former wife's activities to a broad indictment of women's family roles, thus further reinforcing their beliefs in male superiority. As one noncustodial father, whose career development had demanded exceptionally long work weeks and whose former wife had stayed home during the marriage with the children, said:

> *After all, I was able to do it [work and family] all, while she did next to nothing, so I don't see what these women are complaining about.*

The devaluing of a former wife's activities also helped sustain the perception that, at least in retrospect, her economic dependence during marriage had been unfair, as was any continued exchange of resources after divorce. The implicit marriage contract operative during marriage, involved a culturally defined and socially structured gender-based division of labor and exchange (Weitzman 1985), was to be terminated upon divorce. Child support was viewed as a continuation of support for the undeserving former spouse. Of the 57 fathers (three-quarters of the sample) who were paying child support consistently or fairly regularly, almost two-thirds were adamant in their assertions that men's rights are infringed upon by the child support systems.[4] One man, in a representative statement, said:

> *I, a hard-working family man, got screwed, plain and simple. The court, under the direction of a totally biased judge, dictated that she and her children, our children, can relate to me simply as a money machine: "Just push the buttons and out comes the money, no strings attached." And leave me without enough money even to afford a decent place to live.*

"Adding insult to injury," as one irate father put it, was the demonstrated and undeniable reality that each time money defined as child support was passed to her, the former wife gained discretionary authority over its use, being accountable to neither the former husband or any institutional authority. Resentment over the child support system and the former wife's unwarranted power over his earnings was the explanation for various actions of resistance. Such common behaviors included refusing to pay support, providing a check without funds in the bank to cover it, and neglecting to pay on time so that the former spouse was pushed into having to request the support check. Other actions were more idiosyncratic; for example, one father of three described his strategy for protesting the payment of child support:

> *I put the check in the kids' dirty clothes bag and send it home with them after they visit. I used to put it in the clean clothes, but now I put it in the dirty clothes bag. One woman told me her husband sent back the kids' clothes with a woman's sock, then the next time a woman's bra. I won't go that far, it's too low. But I suspect even this keeps her angry and off-balance, and she can't say a word to me about it. She knows I can simply withhold it, refuse to pay it.*

The respondents defined their postdivorce situations and actions primarily in terms of the former wife, and a preoccupation with her was sustained whether or not there was continued direct interaction. Contributing were overlapping factors: lingering feelings about her, characterized generally by ambivalence, frustration and anger and remaining intense for over a third of the men (see also Wallerstein and Blakeslee 1989); the perception that she held a position of dominance in the postdivorce milieu together with the processes of devaluing her significance; and the continuing relevance of issues pertaining to their children and finances.

A Rhetoric of Rights

A rhetoric of *rights* was interspersed throughout the men's accounts: It was basic to their understanding of family and their place in it and to their postdivorce actions, perspectives, and relationships. Attitudes held toward *rights* and its use were largely independent of particular experiences. Men satisfied with their divorce and postdivorce experiences spoke of *rights* in ways analogous to those men who were intensely dissatisfied with nearly every aspect of their divorce, the general exception being the small group characterized as "androgynous" fathers. . . .

That *rights* were to be secured in relation to another, and primarily the former wife, demystified the assertions and implications that what was at issue were matters of abstract principles of justice. Central among the various issues framed within the rhetoric of *rights* were the privileges of position of husband and father as held, or expected to be held, in the family prior to separation and divorce. As one father referring to the dominant pattern in which mothers receive custody and fathers pay child support pointedly said,

> *Divorce touches men in the two most vulnerable spots possible: rights to their money and rights to their children.*

The rhetoric of *rights* had a distinctive and complex connotation: that which was expected, desired, and believed to be deserved *as a man*. This person, for example, insisted repeatedly and explicitly throughout much of his account that his *rights* had been continuously violated. He had obtained primary custody of their children after "forcing my wife out of our home" and claiming that "she deserted us" in response to her request for a divorce:

> *The legal system abuses you as a man. You know: you have no rights. That is, you're treated as a nonperson or as a second, third, fourth or fifth class citizen. They look at us: you know, "Who is that guy with the mother?" Suddenly we're just sperm donators or something. We're a paycheck and sperm donators and that's our total function in society. The legal bias for the mother is incredible. You pull your hair and spend thousands of dollars and say, "Aren't I a human being?" I mean I saw on TV: gay rights, pink rights, blue rights, everybody has rights and they're all demonstrating. I said, "Don't men have rights too? Aren't these my children? Isn't this my house? Don't they bear my name?" I mean I was the first one to hold each of them when they were first born. I was there for it all. . . . None of my rights were protected, but had I been a woman, you can bet that if I were a female, I'd have had these things automatically, without any fight at all. . . .*

This father remained locked in a power struggle with his former wife, especially as he actively resisted her involvement with the children. Like many of the men in the study and even though he was a custodial parent, his relations with his children were continuously filtered through his relations and feelings about their mother. . . .

The rhetoric of *rights* then was multifaceted, consisting of complex and overlapping themes pertaining to self-identity and involving issues of personal efficacy, dominance, and control. It served to define, reaffirm, and reassert a masculine self. *Rights* was a euphemism for male privilege within the family and the stratified gender system generally, and provided a means for characterizing one's place and experiences in the social order and in divorce. *Rights* then provided a framework for defining the self in relation to others, a particularly important function in a context characterized by rapid changes and ambiguity, and for explaining the changing locus of power and various actual or threatened losses. . . .

"Androgynous" Fathers

The "androgynous" fathers, 9 out of the 75 fathers in the study, differed from the majority in broadly consistent ways. Variations in postdivorce custody status alone did not account for the differences between this small group of fathers and the others. Three of these fathers had primary custody of their children and two shared custody with their former spouses (which in their cases involved dividing equally the time spent with and caring for their children). The other four men were noncustodial fathers who were extensively involved with their children. Only one had remarried, a noncustodial father.

Eight of these men, and two of the others, marveled at how they had "learned to become a father only after divorcing." Six had found it necessary to make major alterations in their behaviors and priorities in order to become involved, nurturing fathers. For example, this postdivorce "androgynous" father assumed his role as a custodial parent of three young children suddenly when his wife left:

> It was terrifying at first, just terrifying. I remember the night she walked out the door. And I cried at the thought of it: I said to myself, "How in the hell am I going to do this?" I was raised in a stereotypical way, stereotypically male. I did not cook. I did not particularly clean. I was working a lot so it was "come home and play with the baby." The youngest was just a year and a half, one was going towards three, and the oldest one was just about four. So it was like playtime. I didn't have any responsibility for their daily care. I'd hardly changed a diaper before. I didn't know what parenting was about, really. I mean, who teaches us how to parent? I really didn't know how to ask for help. I don't truly remember the first year. It was day by day by day. After about a year, I managed to figure out that I had my act together. But it goes deeper than all of that. I had to learn to relate to them.

After describing in some detail his strategies for coping in the new and stressful situation, he assessed the personal changes:

> I actually think I'm a better person, to be honest with you, and certainly a far better parent than I ever would have been had she not left. Not that it would be by choice [single parenting], but however you'd like it to be, I would rather have done what I've done. What happened by becoming single is that I was forced into all of this. Now I admit I lost the playtime when they were little, and that's my greatest regret, and all of that. And it's been very hard financially because I'm always limited in how much I can work and I felt I couldn't change jobs. But I've shared so much more with them than any other father I know, they just don't even know what I'm talking about. Now I can't imagine what life will be like when they're grown and leave home. I feel like I'll be starting all over. I thought I had this ball game all figured out.

The postdivorce family was not characterized as a *broken* one by these fathers. Comparatively little use was made of the language of *rights* to frame experiences, relations, or feelings, although fundamental legal issues were sometimes intrinsic to their experiences also. The postdivorce family context was not characterized as a battleground on which the struggle for *rights* was actively fought and there was no talk of divorce or gender wars. Instead, family was represented in various ways as a network of relationships which, as a result of the divorce, necessitated changes in assumptions and interactions.

The areas in which these men were particularly unique were their positive assessments of their relations with their children, overall level of sustained postdivorce parental involvement, and perceptions that the postdivorce father–child relationship depended centrally on their own actions. Interactions with the former wife were aimed primarily at fostering and maintaining cooperation and open communication; the objective was to view and relate to her primarily as the other parent, the mother of the children, and not as the former wife. Thus, issues of the relationship and interpersonal tensions between them were generally subordinated to those regarding their children's well-being and their own parenting. Unlike the majority, for example, the "androgynous" fathers had little if anything to say about postdivorce father absence other than that they neither understood it nor perceived it to be an optional line of action, regardless of the extent of tensions or differences with the former wife (Arendell 1992). [Thus,] . . . with only one exception, the postdivorce "androgynous" fathers viewed their postdivorce parenting activities as being part of a team effort, done collaboratively with the former spouse. They were part of a *parenting partnership*.[5] . . .

Issues of gender identity were present, in significant ways, however, for this subset of men also. Although they raised questions about and challenged the conventions of masculinity, its constraints and consequences, they too were agents of and participants in the masculinist discourse of divorce by virtue of their gender identity, status, and experiences in a gendered-structured society. Because the postdivorce adaptive strategies and attitudes they adopted were often inconsistent with the major themes of the gendered divorce discourse, extensive intra-gender conflict was experienced (Rosenblum 1990). Reflective about and deliberately rejecting of what they perceived to be the typical behaviors and explanations of fathers after divorce, these men "paid a price" for their divergence (see also Coltrane 1989). They were beset with doubts about their actions and motives. Seeking alternative lines of action, they too, nonetheless, used as their measure of self, the norms of masculinity. One custodial father who was struggling with questions of motive and objective said,

> I just have to keep asking myself: "Why are you doing this?" I need to constantly ask myself if I'm doing this for my child or for some other reason. Am I trying to prove something?

Self-doubt was reinforced by inexperience and a sense of isolation: They were largely unprepared for parenting in the postdivorce context and had found few, if any, adequate male role models for their situations as divorced parents. In lamenting the lack of a male role model, four of these fathers observed that their exemplar for parenting was their mother, two noted that theirs was their former wife, and another credited his sister. . . . In not conforming more fully to the conventions of masculinity, the men found themselves subject to question and even ridicule, especially from male co-workers and relatives: Certain performances of gender carry more status and power than others, and theirs were defined as deviant. As one man noted, in describing his lingering uncertainty about his decisions "to find another way,"

> *Even my father and brother told me to get on with my life, to start acting "like a man" and to let this child go, that my involvement with him would just inter-fere with my work and future relationships with women. They told me that other people were going to think I was a wimp, you know, unmanly, for not standing up to my former wife.*

Interpersonal and cultural pressures to conform to gender conventions were reinforced by structural practices and arrangements. The traditional gender-based division of labor, persisting not only in the domestic but also in the employment arena, hindered these fathers' attempts to act in ways generally deemed to be unconventional for men. Impediments included work schedules and demands, the gender wage gap, cultural definitions of male career success, and perceived, if not real, gender biases in the legal system as well as the culture. Individually confronting the conventions of masculinity and challenging the relevance in their situations of gender pre-scriptions did not alter dominant ideologies or institutionalized arrange-ments or constraints (see also Cohen 1989; Risman 1989).

Conclusion and Implications

The masculinist discourse of divorce, constructed and anchored in interac-tion and reinforced by the stratified social order, made available a set of prac-tices and dispositions that prescribed and reaffirmed these men's gendered identities. But the template of familial relations and interpersonal interac-tions offered was a restricted one, often unsuited for the ambiguous and emergent character of the postdivorce circumstance. Even as the altered, and often stressful, situation called for continued interactional adjustments, negotiations, and alignment, lines of action were aimed instead primarily at repair and reassertion of self as autonomous, independent, and controlling. Those few men who sought out and engaged in some alternative behaviors also were both agents in and constrained by the gendered divorce discourse.

. . . The perspectives on and actions in family and divorce provided by the participants in this exploratory study invite further investigation into various postdivorce paternal behaviors, including, for example, noncompli-ance with child support orders and limited other forms of parental support, father absence after divorce, repeat child custody challenges, and the phenomenon of "serial fathering." While often counterproductive to the development and sustaining of mutually satisfying father–child relationships, these behaviors, nonetheless, may be understood by the actors as meaningful and appropriate responses given their perspectives and circumstances. The points of view, explanations, and motives underlying such behaviors warrant further investigation and analysis. So too do the findings that men typically are less satisfied with divorce than are women (Riessman 1990; Wallerstein 1989).

Clearly much more study of divorce is called for since divorce as a common event appears to be here to stay. Careful attention must be given to the voices and viewpoints of all participants in divorce—children, women, and men. A fundamental part of the research agenda needs to be consideration of the effects of gender on divorce outcomes because divorce, like marriage, is not gender neutral. But a focus on individuals' definitions of and adjustments to divorce must be coupled with investigation of the effects of institutional practices and arrangements and cultural biases. . . . Called for then, in brief, are continual assessments of what is transpiring in the lives of families; a conscious revisiting of our assumptions about family and the relations between married and former spouses, and parents and children; and a recasting of society aimed at empowering individuals to move beyond the constraints of gender roles and, most significantly, the constraints of gender identity.

ENDNOTES

Author's Note: This paper is a revision of one presented at the 1991 Gregory Stone Symposium held at the University of California, San Francisco, and the research was funded in part by a PSC-CUNY grant. Appreciation is extended to Joseph P. Marino, Jr., for the many useful and provocative discussions regarding this work; Arlie R. Hochschild for her thoughtful commentary on an earlier draft; and to the anonymous reviewers for their constructive remarks on earlier drafts of the paper.

1. That most of the participants readily asserted that the superiority of their perceptions and definitions gave them the prerogative to dismiss the wife's point of view is consistent with various theoretical arguments regarding the effects of stratification and differential socialization on interactions (Chodorow 1978; Gilligan 1982; Harding 1983). Glenn (1987), for example, noted: "It can be readily observed in a variety of situations that subordinates (women, servants, racial minorities) must be more sensitive to and responsive to the point of view of superordinates (men, masters, dominant racial groups) than the other way around" (p. 356).
2. Goffman (1975), for example, early on observed that "ritually speaking, females are equivalent to subordinate males and both are equivalent to children" (p. 5) in depictions of gender in advertisements. He suggested that relations between men and women are based on the parent–child complex.
3. For a relevant analysis of gender division of labor in families which uses the meso domain or mesostructural approach, see Pestello and Voyandoff (1991). Although not utilized, the meso domain or mesostructural approach could be applied to the data obtained in this study; see, for example, Maines (1979, 1982) and Hall (1987, 1991).

4. The New York State Child Support Standards Act of 1989 (referred to usually by the fathers in the study as the new Child Support Guidelines) was held almost unanimously by these fathers to be grossly unjust and biased against noncustodial parents, primarily fathers; the extensive media coverage given to the Support Guidelines had reinforced many men's sense of being victimized by divorce. Moreover, according to the men in the study, the New York State Child Support Standards Act leads fathers to conclude that they should seek sole custody in order to avoid paying the mandated levels of child support.

5. I am using the term *parenting partnership* rather than shared parenting or co-parents because it suggests a greater flexibility than do the other two terms. . . . The term is also more appropriate for the postdivorce situation than shared parenting or co-parents because the latter are commonly used in reference to parenting activities done in the context of marriage.

REFERENCES

Arendell, Terry. 1986. *Mothers and Divorce: Legal, Economic and Social Dilemmas.* Berkeley: University of California Press.

——. 1992. "After Divorce: Investigations into Father Absence." *Gender & Society* (December).

——. 1995. *Fathers and Divorce.* Newbury Park, CA: Sage.

Berger, Peter and H. Kellner. 1964. "Marriage and the Social Construction of Reality." *Diogenes* 46:1–25.

Bernard, Jessie. 1981. "The Good-Provider Role: Its Rise and Fall." *American Psychologist* 36:1–12.

Bourdieu, Pierre. 1987. *Outline of a Theory of Practice.* Cambridge: Cambridge University Press.

Broverman, I., M. Broverman, F. Clarkson, P. Rosenkrantz, and S. Vogel. 1970. "Sex-Role Stereotypes and Clinical Judgments of Mental Health." *Journal of Consulting and Clinical Psychology* 34:1–7.

Cancian, Francesca. 1987. *Love in America: Gender and Self Development.* New York: Cambridge University Press.

Chodorow, Nancy. 1978. *The Reproduction of Mothering.* Berkeley: University of California.

Clatterbaugh, Kenneth. 1990. *Contemporary Perspectives on Masculinity: Men, Women and Politics in Modern Society.* Boulder, CO: Westview Press.

Cohen, Theodore. 1989. "Becoming and Being Husbands and Fathers: Work and Family Conflict for Men." Pp. 220–34 in *Gender in Intimate Relationships: A Microstructural Approach,* edited by Barbara J. Risman and Pepper Schwartz. Belmont, CA: Wadsworth.

Coltrane, Scott. 1989. "Household Labor and the Routine Production of Gender." *Social Problems* 36:473–90.

Cooley, Charles. 1981. "Self as Sentiment and Reflection." Pp. 169–74 in *Social Psychology through Symbolic Interaction,* 2d ed., edited by Gregory Stone and Harvey Farberman. New York: Wiley.

Family Law of the State of New York. 1990. Flushing, NY: Looseleaf Law.

Foote, Nelson. 1981. "Identification as the Basis for a Theory of Motivation." Pp. 333–42 in *Social Psychology through Symbolic Interaction,* 2d ed., edited by Gregory Stone and Harvey Farberman. New York: Wiley.

Furstenberg, Frank, S. Philip Morgan, and Paul Allison. 1987. "Parental Participation and Children's Well-Being after Marital Dissolution." *American Sociological Review* 52:695–701.

Gilligan, Carol. 1982. *In a Different Voice: Psychological Theory and Women's Development.* Cambridge, MA: Harvard University Press.

Glaser, Barney and Anselm Strauss. 1967. *The Discovery of Grounded Theory.* New York: Aldine.

Glenn, Evelyn Nakano. 1987. "Gender and the Family." Pp. 348–80 in *Analyzing Gender*, edited by Beth Hess and Myra Marx Ferree. Beverly Hills, CA: Sage.

Goffman, Erving. 1975. *Gender Advertisements*. New York: Harper & Row.

Hall, Peter. 1987. "Interactionism and the Study of Social Organization." *The Sociological Quarterly* 28:1–22.

——. 1991. "In Search of the Meso Domain: Commentary on the Contributions of Pestello and Voyandoff." *Symbolic Interaction* 14 (2): 129–34.

Harding, Sandra. 1983. "Why Has the Sex/Gender System Become Visible Only Now?" Pp. 311–24 in *Discovering Reality: Feminist Perspectives on Epistemology, Metaphysics, Methodology, and Philosophy of Science*, edited by Sandra Harding and Merrill Hintikka. Dordrecht, Holland: D. Reidel.

Hearn, Jeff. 1987. *The Gender of Oppression: Men, Masculinity and the Critique of Marxism*. New York: St. Martin's Press.

Hetherington, Elizabeth, Mavis Cox, and Richard Cox. 1976. "Divorced Fathers." *The Family Coordinator* 25:417–28.

Hochschild, Arlie R. 1983. *The Managed Heart: Commercialization of Human Feeling*. Berkeley: University of California Press.

Hochschild, Arlie R., with Anne Machung. 1989. *The Second Shift*. New York: Viking Press.

Kimmel, Michael. 1987. "The Contemporary Crisis of Masculinity in Historical Perspective." Pp. 121–54 in *The Making of Masculinities: The New Men's Studies*, edited by Harry Brod. Boston: Allen & Unwin.

Maines, David. 1979. "Mesostructure and Social Process." *Contemporary Sociology* 8:524–27.

——. 1982. "In Search of Mesostructure: Studies in the Negotiated Order." *Urban Life* 11:267–79.

Mead, George H. 1934. *Mind, Self, and Society*. Chicago: University of Chicago Press.

Pestello, Frances and Patricia Voyandoff. 1991. "In Search of Mesostructure in the Family: An Interactionist Approach to Division of Labor." *Symbolic Interaction* 14 (2): 105–28.

Phillips, Roger and Faith Gilroy. 1985. "Sex-Role Stereotypes and Clinical Judgments of Mental Health: The Brovermans' Findings Reexamined." *Sex Roles* 12 (1/2): 179–93.

Pleck, Joseph. 1985. *Working Wives/Working Husbands*. Beverly Hills, CA: Sage.

——. 1989. "Men's Power with Women, Other Men, and Society: A Men's Movement Analysis." Pp. 21–29 in *Men's Lives*, edited by Michael Kimmel and Michael Messner. New York: Macmillan.

Riessman, Catherine. 1990. *Divorce Talk: Women and Men Make Sense of Personal Relationships*. New Brunswick, NJ: Rutgers University Press.

Risman, Barbara. 1989. "Can Men 'Mother'? Life as a Single Father." Pp. 155–64 in *Gender in Intimate Relationships: A Microstructural Approach*, edited by Barbara J. Risman and Pepper Schwartz. Belmont, CA: Wadsworth.

Rosenblum, Karen. 1990. "The Conflict between and within Genders: An Appraisal of Contemporary Femininity and Masculinity." Pp. 193–202 in *Families in Transition*, edited by Arlene Skolnick and Jerome Skolnick. Glenview, IL: Scott, Foresman.

Strauss, Anselm. 1989. *Qualitative Analysis in the Social Sciences*. Cambridge: Cambridge University Press.

Tannen, Deborah. 1990. *You Just Don't Understand: Men and Women in Conversation*. New York: Ballantine Books.

U.S. Bureau of the Census. 1989. *Statistical Abstracts of the United States, 1988. National Data Book and Guide to Sources*. Washington, DC: U.S. Government Printing Office.

Vaughan, Diane. 1986. *Uncoupling: Turning Points in Relationships*. New York: Oxford University Press.

Wallerstein, Judith and Sandra Blakeslee. 1989. *Second Chances: Men, Women, and Children a Decade after Divorce*. New York: Ticknor & Fields.
Weitzman, Lenore. 1985. *The Divorce Revolution: The Unexpected Social and Economic Consequences for Women and Children in America*. New York: Free Press.

33

DIVORCED PARENTS AND THE JEWISH COMMUNITY

NATHALIE FRIEDMAN

According to conservative estimates, almost one of every two marriages that took place in the United States in the past 15 years will end in divorce; by 1990 half of all children under 18 will have lived for some time with a single (divorced) parent.

Some sociologists view these projections with relative equanimity as reflections of and necessary adaptations to social change. Others hear the death knell of the family as we have known it and predict increased alienation of youth, more women and children living in poverty, and the loss of the grandparent–grandchild relationship.

Most observers of the Jewish scene agree that the divorce rate among Jews is somewhat below that of the general population.[1] Projections of current rates suggest that at least one in every three or four Jewish couples married over the past 15 years will divorce, leaving an increasing number of Jewish children to grow up in the care of a single parent. The high divorce rate among Jews has triggered a good deal of unease within the Jewish community. The reasons for concern are many. A high Jewish divorce rate threatens the basic family structure, traditionally so essential to Jewish identity. It is likely to mean fewer children being born to Jewish families. And it is seen as raising a number of social, psychological, and economic problems that erode Jewish commitment, participation, and involvement.

Little, however, is actually known about the impact of divorce on ties to the Jewish community. Do the social, economic, and psychological problems that often accompany divorce erode Jewish commitment and involvement? Are synagogue affiliation and attendance affected? Does the child's Jewish education continue? Do families turn to the Jewish community, and does that community serve in any way as a support system before, during, or after divorce? What about those with only minimal or no Jewish communal involvement prior to divorce — to whom do they turn, and how do they cope in the aftermath of divorce?

This study examines these questions from the perspective of the divorced parents.

Through interviews with 40 women and 25 of their former husbands, it explores the nature of the couples' communal ties both before and after their divorces, and inquiries particularly into the impact of divorce on their religious affiliations. The study also focuses on the degree of support that Jewish communal institutions provided these couples and suggests how the institutions can become more responsive to the needs of Jewish single-parent families.

The sample selected for study spanned the religious spectrum from ultra-Orthodox to unaffiliated. The research design called for extensive interviews with 40 sets of parents: 10 Orthodox (including two ultra-Orthodox), 10 Conservative, 10 Reform, and 10 unaffiliated — all divorced or separated from one to five years and with at least one child aged 3 to 16 at the time the marriage was dissolved.

The research design presented several problems when it came to classifying the family's religious orientation. How, for example, would one classify a family where the mother said she was unaffiliated and her ex-spouse called himself Conservative? What about the family in which the mother was affiliated with a Reform temple but identified herself as Conservative? Should a family be classified by its affiliation during the marriage or after the divorce? Since one purpose of the research was to look at Jewish identity and affiliation *after* a divorce, it was decided to classify families on the basis of the temple or synagogue with which the custodial parent was affiliated, unless that parent clearly designated herself or himself otherwise. And, because the religious affiliation of a husband might differ from that of his wife, data were also collected on the current religious status of each parent, on the family during the marriage, and on each parent at the time he or she was growing up. Thus the religious odysseys of the 40 families could be traced, and Jewish affiliation after the divorce could be compared with that in the immediate and more distant past. . . .

The final sample consisted of 40 mothers and 25 fathers ranging in age between 31 and 62. All had lived in the New York City metropolitan area during their marriages. Fifteen of the fathers could not be interviewed — four were not living in the United States or their whereabouts were unknown; four were not contacted at the wife's request; and seven refused. Interviews with the mothers were conducted between the fall of 1983 and the summer of 1984, and averaged about two hours in length. Interviews with fathers were somewhat less lengthy, both because the mother had already provided the basic family information and because fathers were less likely to offer details about activities and feelings. . . .

One note of caution. This research was not designed to permit generalization to the entire population of Jewish divorced persons. Its purpose, rather, was to uncover patterns, relationships, causal links, and critical variables that might provide clues to how communal institutions can better serve that rapidly increasing phenomenon, the Jewish single-parent family. . . .

Ties to the Jewish Community during the Marriage

During the years they were married, the patterns of affiliation and observance of these 40 couples varied widely. About half were completely unaffiliated with a synagogue or temple, had minimal or no home observance, and gave their children no Jewish education. For example, only 20 of the 40 couples had actually been members of synagogues or temples in the various communities in which they had lived while married. Among the other 20 couples, four said that they had never joined but had occasionally attended services at neighborhood synagogues or temples; six said they occasionally went to their parents' or in-laws' synagogues for the High Holy Days; 10 couples stated that they had neither belonged to nor attended any house of worship.

It is difficult to attach denominational labels to the 20 couples who were affiliated while married, for some had joined synagogues of different denominations as they moved from one community to another or as their children grew ready for Sunday or Hebrew school. As one mother explained:

> First we lived in Queens, and we belonged to a Conservative synagogue there. Then we moved farther out on the Island, and when our son was ready for Sunday school we joined the Reform temple because that was where most of the Jewish families on our block belonged. . . .

Just prior to separation, however, eight couples were affiliated with Orthodox and five with Conservative synagogues; seven belonged to Reform temples; and 20 were unaffiliated.

Absence of synagogue affiliation or attendance generally, but not necessarily, precluded some form of Jewish education for the children. In eight instances, the divorce had occurred before the child was old enough for Sunday or Hebrew school, and in eight others, although the children were of age, they had not received any Jewish education. In 16 families children had attended a Sunday or Hebrew school, and in eight families an Orthodox day school or yeshiva. Observance in the home during the marriage ranged from "zero," as one respondent put it, to strictly Orthodox. For 12 families, observance of the Sabbath and holidays was simply not a part of their lives. As one commented:

> Home observance? None. I guess you could say we were borderline Christians because we observed Christmas, but also a little Hanukkah.

Several noted that, although they did not observe at home, they would occasionally go to their parents' or in-laws' for a Seder or a holiday meal. Ten families characterized their home observance as "minimal." As one explained:

> *We'd observe the Sabbath and holidays off and on — no regularity. Mostly in an "eating" sense, I guess. You know — a special meal. . . .*

If there was any one holiday observed by these families, it tended to be Hanukkah:

> *We used to light the menorah and give the children gifts.*

> *We thought it was important to celebrate Hanukkah because the children saw so much Christmas around them.*

Several of the families said that, although they never attended services and their home observance was at best "limited," they kept their children home from school on Rosh Hashanah and Yom Kippur because "we wanted them to know they were Jewish."

In nine families home observance was fairly regular, including candles on Friday night and the celebration of such holidays as Passover, Hanukkah, Purim, and Simchat Torah with family meals, a Seder, and special foods. Respondents in this group, however, were quick to add that they did not keep kosher homes. Typical was this woman's response:

> *We didn't have a kosher home, but we did celebrate all the holidays — Hanukkah, Seders, Purim (I'd get hamantaschen). Friday night was always special — not in a religious sense — but we had chicken and challah, and we tried not to make other plans on Friday nights.*

Finally, nine families characterized themselves as "observant," "strictly observant," or "Orthodox." Their homes ranged from "kosher" to "strictly kosher," and all the holidays as well as the Sabbath were observed, with their positive and negative commandments. . . .

In sum, the ties of these 40 couples to the Jewish community during the marriage varied widely. At the one extreme were about half the families with no synagogue or other Jewish organizational affiliation and minimal or no home observance. About one in four families described strong Jewish institutional ties, regular synagogue attendance, and strict home observance of the Sabbath, holidays, dietary laws, and other religious rituals. In between were some 10 families who were affiliated with a temple or synagogue, attended services frequently, and marked the Sabbath and/or religious holidays with some degree of regularity. Even among those with only the most tenuous institutional connections, however, Jewish education for the children was not necessarily precluded; four of these families sent their children to Sunday or Hebrew schools and one (as long as the grandparents paid for it) to a day school.

The Divorce Experience

Factors Leading to the Divorce

The couples' reasons for ending their marriages probably reflect the experiences of most divorced couples in America. Some attributed the breakup to such unacceptable behavior on the part of their partners as violence or wife abuse (three cases), alcoholism or gambling (two cases), homosexuality (one case), and infidelity (five cases). These reasons were particularly frequent among the Orthodox couples. Although infidelity was cited as a factor in five instances, in only three was it regarded as the determining factor.

The word most frequently used by respondents as they spoke about the factors leading to the divorce was "incompatibility." This word proved to mean different things to different respondents. Some, for example, explained that they had married quite young and had grown apart over the years. In other instances, "incompatibility" referred to temperamental or personality differences. One man, for example, complained about his ex-wife's inability to communicate:

> *We weren't on the same wave length. Her tuner is way down while mine tends to be all the way up.*

A woman said of her ex-husband:

> *He's a very selfish person — totally involved with himself, egocentric. I just needed more love and affection — it was lonely living with him.*

A third kind of incompatibility was the couple's disagreement over the woman's role as wife, mother, and employed person. Often, this disagreement arose in the course of the woman's pursuit of personal growth, self-development, and career. One woman said:

> *Once I went back to work it became clear that our interests were different. He was opposed to my going back to work. His idea of my role was to bring up the children, entertain, be at home for him. But I felt that I had to develop as a person, find my own identity that was not just a part of him and the children. . . .*

Finally, several respondents suggested that the prevailing social climate, in which divorce carried no stigma, was a factor in the breakup of their marriages. As one said:

> *We are probably products of our age — an age of divorce. I think that a lot of divorces that have taken place would not have taken place thirty years ago. People's expectations are higher when it comes to happiness in marriage.*

The decision to divorce was generally initiated by the woman and accepted, often reluctantly, by the man. In those few instances where the divorce was initiated by the man, the cause was quite specific: He had met another woman; his wife was an "adulteress"; he couldn't make it financially and felt overwhelmed by marital and parental responsibilities. Only one of the 25 men interviewed attributed the divorce to *his* need for self-fulfillment or personal space.

The Jewish Factor

Was there a Jewish factor in the divorce decision? The answer is "yes and no." On one hand, with only a few exceptions, respondents said that religious or Jewish issues were not precipitating factors. On the other hand, as the marriage bonds weakened, dissension over these issues surfaced in 14 of the 40 couples.

In three of the five interfaith marriages, religious issues were cited by at least one of the partners. In nine other instances, while both partners were Jewish, they came from different religious backgrounds and Jewish issues surfaced. For example:

> First of all, there was another woman, but that was just the straw that broke the camel's back. Basically, we were just not compatible—we had different values about almost everything. And eventually, even our differences over Judaism got to me—he ate nonkosher outside while I was strictly kosher; and he worked on Shabbos while I wanted him to go to shul with me and the boys. . . .

In three cases where dissension over religious issues surfaced, both partners came from fairly similar backgrounds. In one instance, where both were from Conservative homes, the wife complained that her husband was too passive about Jewish observance and participation and that she was tired of having to take the lead. In another instance, although both partners had come from Orthodox homes and had attended religious day schools, the wife said:

> He was always less religious than I, and we bickered a lot about it. I wanted to cover my head, and he thought that was silly. I didn't want to eat in a nonkosher restaurant, and he thought it was okay as long as we ate dairy. He opened up the mail and rode up in the elevator on Shabbos, and I wouldn't.

These findings suggest that when husband and wife come from similar religious backgrounds religious issues rarely surface. When the marriage is mixed (and that term is used to denote marriages in which the Jewish backgrounds are different as well as interfaith marriages), however, religious issues often contribute to the incompatibility of the partners. . . .

The Importance of the Get

Orthodox and Conservative rabbis will not marry a divorced person who has not obtained the religious divorce decree, the *get*. If a woman without a *get* marries again, any child of the remarriage will be illegitimate in Jewish law. The law imposes no such penalty on a man. Should he remarry without a *get*, a child of that marriage would be legitimate. If a wife refuses to accept the *get* from her husband, Jewish law provides alternative ways for the man to be declared free to remarry. The woman whose husband refuses to provide a *get* has no similar recourse. Thus the law places the obligation to obtain a *get* upon the woman and gives the man a unique advantage in negotiating a divorce settlement.

Ten of the 40 women in the sample had obtained a *get* at the time of, or subsequent to, their divorces. Most were either Orthodox or Conservative. One of two Reform women who had obtained a *get* said:

> *The rabbi insisted that I must have it to remarry — if ever I should. My ex paid for it.*

The other Reform woman had herself insisted on the *get*:

> *I insisted on an Orthodox* get. *I had been married religiously in a Conservative synagogue, and it was important to me to have the most religious divorce I could get. He [the ex] would not pay for it, but at least he went through it. His mother can't understand why I wanted it.*

One young woman from the Hasidic community in Flatbush was still trying, after almost five years, to obtain a *get*.

> *I've asked, I've tried, but he just won't do it. I've gone to some local rabbis for help but haven't gotten anywhere. Unfortunately, you need money to get them [the rabbis] to help you, and I don't have it. . . .*

Eight women said that they would obtain a *get* should they decide to remarry. None of them anticipated any difficulty. Fully half of the women in the sample, however, neither requested a *get* nor had any intention of doing so. Many had never heard of a *get*; it was simply "not an issue," "irrelevant," "nonsense," or "something that would never have occurred to us." From the perspective of the traditional Jewish community, should these women remarry and bear children, the absence of a *get* could have serious ramifications when their children, in turn, are ready to marry.[2]

Single-Parent Families in the Jewish Community

The Affiliated

Between the time of the divorce and the time of the interview — an average of four years — changes had occurred in the pattern of Jewish affiliation of the people in the sample. Of the 20 families that had been unaffiliated during the marriage, three became affiliated with a Reform temple or school, three with a Conservative synagogue or school, and four with an Orthodox synagogue and day school.[3] In addition, two families that had been affiliated with an orthodox synagogue during the marriage identified themselves as Conservative at the time of the interview; another moved from Conservative to Reform and still another from Reform to Conservative. Two of these latter changes stemmed from geographic moves and two from dissatisfaction with a particular Sunday or Hebrew school.

More significant is the finding that, after the divorce, 10 previously unaffiliated families had joined the ranks of the affiliated, while none had moved from affiliated to unaffiliated status. This finding appears to run counter to the belief that divorce necessarily erodes Jewish affiliation and identification. Although the data offered here are too few to refute this belief, these 10 cases suggest factors that may explain the "return" of the unaffiliated. The word "return" is used advisedly because, among the 10 families that had been unaffiliated during the marriage but developed some tie afterward, there were five custodial parents who had grown up in affiliated homes. One woman, for example, who had married a non-Jew against the wishes of her parents, said:

> When the girls got to be old enough, I decided they should have some kind of Jewish education. I guess it's a little strange, because during the marriage we really did nothing Jewish. But I find myself getting more and more conservative with age. Maybe it's that being the child of Holocaust parents, I feel a particular responsibility to pass on a Jewish tradition. So now the girls are in a Reform Hebrew school, and we go to services on Friday night. They love it.

Another woman, also divorced from a non-Jew, had similar sentiments:

> The minute my son was old enough, I enrolled him at the nursery school of the Conservative synagogue here. It was highly recommended as a place where there's real Jewish involvement. I wanted him to have this, especially after the absence of all of this with his father. We go to shul all the time, and I'm enrolled in the women's Bat Mitzvah class. When I was young, I never went to Hebrew school — only my brothers did. My son is very close to my parents [Conservative]. We're with them on all the holidays. . . .

[Another] "returnee" commented:

> We never belonged to anything during the marriage, although occasionally we went to my parents' Conservative synagogue. I put the children in a Conservative Hebrew school just as soon as they were old enough, and we go every Sabbath together. I was brought up in a Conservative synagogue but never went to Hebrew school — although my brother did. I wanted the children to know what it was all about. In fact, at first I had put them in a religious day school, but they had to leave it as part of the divorce settlement. It was important to my ex that they not go, and it didn't matter that much to me. . . .

These women had three things in common: a traditional Jewish home background; a husband who wished to have little to do with Jewish communal life; and a child old enough for some form of religious education. It is possible, of course, that had their marriages remained intact, these women would still have seen to it that their children received some form of Jewish education. It appears, however, that the dissolution of their marriages actually removed a barrier to their return to a more traditional Jewish life.

Four women came from completely unaffiliated homes and had been — as one put it — "borderline Christians" while married. Three who lived in the Bronx came under the influence of a rabbi well known for his community activism, his personal warmth and understanding, and his readiness to embrace anyone who expressed a desire to lead a traditional Jewish life. The fourth was referred by a friend to a similarly outgoing rabbi on Manhattan's West Side. All four engaged in religious study, became Sabbath observers, koshered their homes, attended synagogue regularly, and sent their children to religious day schools.

What moved these four women to take on what has been called "the yoke of Orthodoxy"? In each case the key factor was a charismatic rabbi willing to devote considerable time to the family. As one woman remarked: . . .

> *Someone had told me about this day school, and I liked the way it looked so I decided my son should go. That's how I met the rabbi. He was the one who arranged for the* get. *I didn't even know such a thing existed. He invited me to come to the shul, and I liked it. He explained to me about being kosher, and I did the house, little by little. . . .*

In all 10 families that moved from unaffiliated to affiliated status, it was the mother who, after the divorce, established the synagogue affiliation, enrolled the children in a religious school, and initiated observance in the home. These women did not have to deal with their ex-husbands about matters of Jewish observance and affiliation. But those fathers who still saw their children regularly did not object to the new patterns of observance and affiliation. One father commented:

> *It's true that my ex has become quite involved Jewishly because of the children. But no, it hasn't been a problem for me. I try to encourage the girls. I pick them up from Hebrew school when it's my day. I took them to shul on Purim — I even made their costumes. . . .*

A father who had himself grown up in an Orthodox home noted:

> *When we got married, I had had my fill of religion, and I moved completely away from it — no synagogue affiliation. But since the divorce, my wife has gotten very involved, and our son is at a yeshiva. The rabbi there is very special — he believes in bringing people back in any way that he can. As a result, I find that I've slowly been moving back to religion over the past few years.*

Every family that had been affiliated during the marriage retained an affiliation after the divorce. Children who had been attending Sunday or Hebrew school, day school or yeshiva, continued their Jewish educations at least until their Bar Mitzvahs or Bat Mitzvahs. Since generally it was the mother who had custody, she was the one who met with teachers and attended parent meetings, Hebrew school plays, and special Sabbath programs. In several instances, however, the father, rather than the mother, took the lead in ensuring the continued affiliation and participation of the children. For example, one father said:

> *During the marriage, I guess you might say we sank to the lower common denominator — hers. Whatever minimal observance there was, was because of the children. Now I go to synagogue more than ever, and I'm the one that*

supervises the children's Jewish education. I spend a lot more time with my parents, and when I have the children on a weekend I take them to my parents' synagogue.

One mother was quite explicit about the fact that she felt that the children's Jewish education was their father's responsibility:

I occasionally go to the temple on a Sabbath with the children, but I decided that I did not want control over that whole area. As part of the divorce, I gave that responsibility — the kids' Jewish education — to him. I didn't want to have anything to do with it. I felt I had enough responsibility in other areas. I wouldn't say "don't go," but I wanted him to take control. I make my ex drive the car pools for all the kids' Jewish activities.

Her ex-husband confirmed this:

I live in the city, but I drive out to Long Island four times a week to see the children. Twice a week I pick up my son from Hebrew school at the temple and then take both kids for supper. On Saturdays I participate with them in a special parent–child religious and education program at the temple. Then on Sunday I come out again and pick up my daughter from Sunday school and take the kids for the day.

This father was clearly exerting every possible effort to keep his children identified and affiliated Jewishly. . . .

Contrary to the belief that divorce is a major factor in the erosion of Jewish affiliation and identity, the sample in this study presented no case of a family *dis*affiliating after the breakup of the marriage. It is true that a number of men and women became synagogue or temple dropouts, particularly after their children passed the age of Bar Mitzvah or Bat Mitzvah. But children who had attended Hebrew or Sunday school before their parents' divorce continued to do so after. And among the previously unaffiliated, fully half moved to affiliated status and provided some form of religious education for their children.

The Unaffiliated

At the time of the interviews, 10 custodial parents classified themselves as unaffiliated. None attended religious services except for an occasional visit to a temple during the High Holy Days, and even that was rare. Nevertheless, several of these parents maintained some institutional ties to the Jewish community. A West Side mother explained:

The children go to the community Hebrew school. It's good because no one pounds you. Once in a while, they go to services there. I say, "Go if you want to." My ex stuck them in this school and then wouldn't pay the tuition. I was ready to take them out, but then they told me they'd take both boys for free. It didn't matter to me — they'll do anything to keep those kids there. . . .

Several unaffiliated parents noted that they were considering Jewish education for their children. One mother commented:

Now that she's 10, I think I would like her to have some Jewish education. No Hebrew, and nothing religious – just cultural. The problem is that it would have to be during the week only – no weekends, because we rotate weekends, and I don't think my ex would go for that. . . .

With a few exceptions, parents who identified themselves as unaffiliated spoke positively about Judaism. A woman put it this way:

I have a keen emotional sense of being Jewish. It's important for me to be identified as a Jew. So many thousands of years that a people has survived! I have a sympathy and empathy for my people that I want to pass on to my children.

A man who had been married to a non-Jewish woman said:

Since the divorce, I feel that I've become closer to things Jewish. I've become more cognizant of the Jewish tradition, and, as a single parent, I feel a responsibility to provide some of this for the kids. For example, I have them every other weekend, and I light candles with them, saying the prayer. Sometimes we do it at my parents; sometimes they each have a friend over; but often it's just the three of us – the kids and me. I also think that as I've gotten a bit older, I've been able to reflect on the traditions, and they have become more valuable to me. . . .

Thus even among those who were unaffiliated and disinterested in organized religion, there existed a sense of identification as Jews, sympathy for Jewish causes, and attachment to Jewish traditions.

Obstacles to Community Participation

Most families in the sample maintained, and some increased, existing ties to the Jewish community after the divorce. A number reported excellent experiences that illustrate how the Jewish community can reach out to single parents and their children. A majority of the respondents, however, mentioned obstacles to participation in Jewish communal life as a result of their changed marital status. Finances posed one kind of barrier. But equally, if not more, serious were lack of social support and a sense of stigmatization.

Financial Obstacles Most of the rabbis and school personnel interviewed for *The Jewish Community and Children of Divorce* had insisted that no one was forced to drop out of synagogue or Hebrew or day school for financial reasons. While interviews with parents in this study confirmed that none had *left* because of inability to pay, several respondents – particularly mothers – explained that the synagogue's financial policy had prevented them from joining in the first place. One said:

I've seen Judaism lose children for financial reasons. At the temple that I first thought I would join after my divorce, I found that they charged the same amount for me as for a couple with several children, so I never joined. Frankly, I could have afforded it, but it was the principle. And there are a lot of people who are embarrassed to ask for special consideration or to say, "I can't afford that much.". . .

Several were grateful that after the divorce their children were able to continue in the day school on scholarships, but one noted:

> *I have a scholarship which gives me one-third off, but every chance that they get, they throw the scholarship in your face. They have bingo, and if you're on scholarship you're supposed to help out, but it's during the day, and I can't go. They said, "It's your obligation; you're on scholarship, you know." I find that very degrading. Do they think I want to be on scholarship? . . .*

These perceptions of second-class status may or may not have been rooted in reality, but they were widely felt and frequently voiced.

Lack of Outreach   More common than financial complaints among respondents were feelings that the synagogue or temple could do far more "reaching out" to the single parent and child, both at the time of the divorce and after. All denominations were criticized in this respect. Said one woman bitterly about the neighborhood Reform temple:

> *Support from the temple at the time of the divorce? No — it never occurred to the rabbi to call me. He spoke with my husband — but, of course, my husband had been a member of the board of directors for 10 years. It certainly would have been nice, considering the fact that I had also been involved in that temple for 10 years, if they had encouraged me to stay on as a member.*

Said one woman about the suburban Reform temple that she still attended:

> *I must say that the temple did not reach out to us at all. When we "fell out," no one followed up. They never tried. I was right there kind of waving for their attention, but they never touched me. It's too bad — they put all their efforts into the strong supporters, the regulars. They should try to reach the hesitants, like us.*

Her ex-husband confirmed this:

> *I used to go regularly to classes at the temple. But after the divorce, they did not reach out in any way, shape, or form — except to ask me to pay the bills. Then when I couldn't pay — no response. Nothing! The rabbi never said a word. He made no overtures, never said, "Would you like to come in and talk?" or "How are you doing?" or "My door is open."*

Complaints about lack of outreach on the part of Orthodox institutions were expressed less frequently, but they did occur. . . . Generally, after a divorce, it is the man who leaves the household and finds housing elsewhere. Several fathers said that they would have appreciated some attempt on the part of the rabbi in the new neighborhood to draw them into the synagogue or temple. One said:

> *When I first joined the new temple — largely so that my daughter could go to Hebrew school there — I told them my situation and made arrangements about dues, mail, tuition bills, and everything. I go to services regularly, but the rabbi has never approached me. . . .*

Stigmatization   Lack of outreach efforts was usually blamed on the rabbi. Many respondents, however, spoke about their general sense of discomfort as single parents in the synagogue or school, of "feeling different," of not being welcomed by the congregation or other parents. As one woman put it:

> I'm thinking of dropping my membership. As I see it, the temple [Reform] is regarded as the exclusive province of the family. The widowed or divorced are seen as obstacles — maybe even as threats. At times, I feel almost ostracized. Let me give you just one subtle example. I used to be a frequent reader of the Haftorah [weekly reading from the Prophets]; since my divorce almost four years ago, I have not been asked once.

The problem is particularly critical for the Orthodox divorced woman, according to one such respondent:

> Divorced fathers get very different treatment than divorced mothers. The whole attitude is different. You should see how respectfully the teachers at the children's yeshiva treat the fathers when they come into the school. Part of it is probably money, but that shouldn't mean that the mother should get less respect. Some of the teachers give you a look as if to say, "What more can we expect from these children since their mother is divorced?" That attitude is all wrong. . . .

The fathers, too, expressed discomfort as single parents in the synagogue. As one observed:

> There seems to be something inherent in Judaism that means a mass denial about divorce. When it happens, it's something shameful, a disgrace. People try to pretend that there's nothing wrong, and as a result they ignore you and the pain you're going through.

As these men and women spoke of the discomfort and aloneness they felt in the synagogue, several acknowledged that the problem was not present only there. One man said:

> Sure it's hard. They're all couples at the temple, and it's a lonely feeling. But it's lonely being single in the temple, in the Jewish community, or anywhere I go. It's just lonely being single!

Positive Experiences

Although most respondents had negative feelings about the failure of the synagogue or the community to reach out to them, several had only praise and appreciation for the ways they and their children had been drawn in and made to feel comfortable. Said one about the Reform suburban temple to which she belonged:

> The rabbi was extremely supportive of me and the children after the divorce. He tried to pay special attention to the children. He made a point of talking to them about things that interested them — like baseball. I was on the PTA board at the time, and he insisted that I continue. He encouraged me to remain active, to

come to services Friday night, [to] work in the PTA. He made me feel that I was as good as everyone else!

Two Orthodox institutions, one in Manhattan and one in the Bronx, were warmly praised. One woman described the atmosphere:

The shul [in Manhattan] made a real effort to pull me in, as well as to pull in the boys, who were going to Hebrew school there. They have separate fees for single parents that are adjusted according to your ability to pay. They are warm, congenial. They never make you feel pitiable or like a sore thumb. . . .

About the synagogue in the Bronx, a mother said:

I love the shul. It's such a warm place. The men are wonderful to my son. For example, they make sure to put him on their shoulders and carry him around on Simchat Torah. It's little things like that, but they're important. They make him feel so welcome that he really loves going there.

Occasionally, one respondent praised and another criticized the same temple or synagogue. Perceptions vary, of course, and experiences as well. But one factor may be, as some respondents pointed out, the receptivity and behavior of the individual. The suggestion was made, for example, that the single parent has a responsibility to take some initiative. One said:

There's just so much a synagogue can do for a single parent. As difficult as it is, it's important that we make ourselves get out there and push ourselves a little so we'll get accepted, invited, and involved. I did it, and it worked.

Another suggested:

I think it has less to do with the synagogue than with the woman herself. You can't sit around and wait for the synagogue to come to you. If you want to be involved, you have to stop kvetching and go out and do it!

These comments underscore the fact that the individual as well as the synagogue has an outreach responsibility. Nevertheless, the extent to which the synagogue or temple reaches out and welcomes the single-parent family probably determines whether that family will remain involved in the Jewish community.

The Bar Mitzvah and Bat Mitzvah

In *The Jewish Community and Children of Divorce*, rabbis identified a range of problems—financial, ceremonial, social, psychological—that may confront the postdivorce couple at the time of their child's Bar Mitzvah or Bat Mitzvah. In this study, the parents themselves were asked how they had coped with this even if it had occurred after their divorce. Parents with youngsters between 9 and 12 were asked if they had given any thought to the event and, if so, what their expectations and plans were.

A total of 15 families had celebrated a Bar Mitzvah or Bat Mitzvah after the parents' divorces. Five felt that things had gone very well. Recalled one mother:

Our son's Bar Mitzvah went beautifully, largely because of the rabbi's sensitivity. For example, normally the father and the mother sit next to each other on the pulpit, but he arranged for us to sit on opposite sides. It also helped that his father's woman friend did not come. We each invited our own friends, and our son invited the entire religious school class. So there was a head table of fourteen boys, and that made our son feel good. . . .

In six cases, the parent(s) reported a few problems. One father related:

The Bat Mitzvah took place shortly after the divorce, and I just say that although it went all right, I felt that it was a great source of acrimony in that postdivorce period. Still, we tried not to take our own problems out on our daughter. . . .

In four cases, the Bar Mitzvah or Bat Mitzvah provoked many problems. One mother explained:

The Bar Mitzvah itself didn't go too badly. We divided the aliyahs *[blessings over the Torah], and for our son's sake we tried very hard to behave civilly. But up until the day itself, it was a difficult time. My ex absolutely didn't want a Bar Mitzvah, while my son wanted one like crazy. We had terrible fights over money since my ex thought the whole thing was unnecessary. In the end, he paid for half, but he really gave me a hard time.*

The father's side of the story was somewhat different:

It's not that I didn't want a Bar Mitzvah — I just didn't want one of those big, fancy affairs. I wanted to take my son to Israel instead and just have a small affair here. But his mother wouldn't let him go. So in the end, it was the big, fancy affair, and I got stuck paying for half of it.

Eight families with children between 9 and 12 contemplated the approaching Bar Mitzvah or Bat Mitzvah with anxiety and concern. The mother of a 9-year-old said:

I worry about everything already. A Bar Mitzvah is usually a big function — 100 to 150 people, and I don't know many people. Whom will I invite? I don't have a wide circle of friends anymore. Also, I guess my ex should be there, but I don't think I'd want that. And then, there's the cost — who is going to pay? . . .

Five families anticipated the Bar Mitzvah or Bat Mitzvah with pleasure. One father said:

We'll make the Bat Mitzvah a very simple affair, just as our older daughter's was, before the divorce. I'm sure it will go fine.

A mother who looked forward to the Bar Mitzvah of her son in two years said:

My ex and I get along very well. We're very friendly, so I know it won't be a problem.

Several couples reported that at the time of an older child's Bar Mitzvah or Bat Mitzvah they had already decided to separate. These parents postponed their divorces until after the ceremony so as not to mar the occasion for the child or for their respective families, underscoring the fact that many Jews—Orthodox, Conservative, Reform, and even unaffiliated—view the Bar Mitzvah or Bat Mitzvah as a significant event. . . .

Summary and Conclusions

Although the sample of 40 divorced couples was too small to permit any generalizations, the study suggests that divorce does not necessarily result in erosion of Jewish identity and community involvement but may, especially for families with young children, open the way for a restoration or strengthening of Jewish affiliation. The determining factor may well be the warmth and sensitivity with which the synagogue, temple, or other Jewish institution welcomes and involves such single-parent families.

In the conference that followed publication of *The Jewish Community and Children of Divorce*, we suggested that some rabbis, particularly among the Orthodox, are concerned that efforts to deal with the single-parent family may be seen as condoning, even encouraging, divorce. Said one rabbi at the conference:

> *A problem that emerges from giving special treatment to single parents in relation to institutional activities and fees is the loss of the couple advantage. The subtle indication of approval which emerges from such a response may shift the pro-family balance, which is part of the Jewish value system.*

While this concern is understandable, it is self-defeating. The divorce rate among Jews has risen, and even among the Orthodox divorced families have become increasingly visible. These families face all the problems associated with the breakup of marriage and, in addition, find, all too often, that the Jewish community is indifferent and unresponsive to their plight. Programs of premarital and marital counseling may help to reduce the incidence of divorce among Jews, but it will not make the problem go away. Single-parent families are a growing segment of the community. Their needs must be recognized, acknowledged, and addressed.

ENDNOTES

1. Chaim I. Waxman, *America's Jews in Transition* (Philadelphia: Temple University Press, 1983).
2. The Jewish community has taken steps to address the problem of the recalcitrant husband. A number of Orthodox rabbis are now asking couples to sign a simple prenuptial agreement stating that, in the event the marriage is dissolved civilly, both parties will agree to give or receive a *get*. The Conservative movement has incorporated a prenuptial agreement in its *ketubah* (marriage contract), and a recent case suggests that the civil courts will enforce such an agreement.

   To combat ignorance about the fact that a *get* is necessary for children of subsequent marriages to be legitimate under Jewish law, as well as to address the problem of the recalcitrant husband, an organization called GET (Getting Equitable Treatment) was formed several years ago in New York City. The organization seeks to assist men and women who are involved in battles over the *get*, as well as to forestall such problems through community education.

3. The postdivorce "family" is defined as the custodial parent and child(ren).

34

LIFE–SPAN ADJUSTMENT OF CHILDREN TO THEIR PARENTS' DIVORCE

PAUL R. AMATO

Children have always faced the threat of family disruption. In the past, death was more likely to disrupt families than was divorce. Around the turn of the century in the United States, about 25 percent of children experienced the death of a parent before age 15, compared with 7 percent or 8 percent who experienced parental divorce.[1] As a result of the increase in longevity, the proportion of dependent children who lost a parent through death decreased during this century; currently, only about 5 percent of children are so affected. But the divorce rate increased over this same period, and at current rates, between two-fifths and two-thirds of all recent first marriages will end in divorce or separation.[2] The high rate of marital dissolution means that about 40 percent of children will experience a parental divorce prior to the age of 16.[3] Although a substantial risk of family disruption has always been present, today it is much more likely to be caused by divorce than by death.

Americans traditionally have believed that a two-parent family is necessary for the successful socialization and development of children. Consequently, it was assumed that parental death leads to many problems for children, such as delinquency, depression, and even suicide in later life — assumptions that appeared to be confirmed by early research.[4]

More recent studies indicate that, although parental death disadvantages children, the long-term consequences are not as severe as people once believed.[5] Nevertheless, many social scientists assumed that children who "lost" a parent through divorce experienced serious problems similar to those experienced by children who lost a parent through death. Furthermore, whereas the death of a parent is usually unintended and unavoidable, marital dissolution is freely chosen by at least one parent. Consequently, the question of the impact of divorce on children took on moral overtones. These concerns, combined with the dramatic increase in the rate of divorce during the last few decades, resulted in a proliferation of studies on the effects of divorce on children.

This research literature does not always lead to firm conclusions. Many gaps exist in our knowledge, and weaknesses in study methodology mean that many findings are tentative at best. Nevertheless, a consensus is beginning to emerge among social scientists about the consequences of divorce for children. And, in spite of its limitations, this knowledge can help to inform policies designed to improve the well-being of children involved in parental marital dissolution. . . .

How Do Children of Divorce Differ from Other Children?

Those who delve into the published literature on this topic may experience some frustration, as the results vary a good deal from study to study. Many studies show that children of divorce have more problems than do children in continuously intact two-parent families.[6] But other studies show no difference,[7] and a few show that children in divorced families are better off in certain respects than children in two-parent families.[8] This inconsistency results from the fact that studies vary in their sampling strategies, choice of what outcomes to measure, methods of obtaining information, and techniques for analyzing data.

A technique known as *meta-analysis* was recently developed to deal with this situation.[9] In a meta-analysis, the results of individual studies are expressed in terms of an "effect size" which summarizes the differences between children in divorced and intact groups on each outcome. Because these effect sizes are expressed in a common unit of measure, it is possible to combine them across all studies to determine whether significant effects exist for each topic being reviewed. It is also possible to examine how design features of studies, such as the nature of the sample, might affect the conclusions.

In 1991, Amato and Keith pooled the results for 92 studies that involved more than 13,000 children ranging from preschool to college age.[10] This meta-analysis confirmed that children in divorced families, on average, experience more problems and have a lower level of well-being than do children in continuously intact two-parent families. These problems include lower academic achievement, more behavioral problems, poorer psychological adjustment, more negative self-concepts, more social difficulties, and more problematic relationships with both mothers and fathers.

To determine if there are also differences in adjustment when children of divorce grow into adulthood, Amato and Keith carried out a second meta-analysis of 37 studies in which they examined adult children of divorce.[11] These results, based on pooled data from 80,000 adults, suggest that parental divorce has a detrimental impact on the life course. Compared with those raised in intact two-parent families, adults who experienced a parental divorce had lower psychological well-being, more behavioral problems, less education, lower job status, a lower standard of living, lower marital satisfaction, a heightened risk of divorce, a heightened risk of being a single parent, and poorer physical health.

The view that children adapt readily to divorce and show no lingering negative consequences is clearly inconsistent with the cumulative research in this area. However, several qualifications temper the seriousness of this conclusion. First, the average differences between children from divorced and continuously intact families are small rather than large. This fact suggests that divorce is not as severe a stressor for children as are other things that can go wrong during childhood. For example, a recent meta-analysis of studies dealing with childhood sexual abuse revealed average effect sizes three to four times larger than those based on studies of children of divorce.[12] Second, although children of divorce differ, on average, from children in continuously intact two-parent families, there is a great deal of overlap between the two groups. . . .

This diversity helps us to understand why the *average* effects of divorce are relatively weak. Divorce may represent a severe stressor for some children, resulting in substantial impairment and decline in well-being. But for other children, divorce may be relatively inconsequential. And some children may show improvements following divorce. In other words, to inquire about the effects of divorce, as if all children were affected similarly, is to ask the wrong question. A better question would be, "Under what conditions is divorce harmful or beneficial to children?" This point is returned to below.

Variations by Gender of Child

Some researchers are interested in measuring differences in adjustment between children of divorce and children in intact families based on such variables as gender, ethnicity, age, and cohort membership in attempts to identify groups that may respond differently to divorce. Summarized below are the major findings with regard to the relationship between these variables and adjustment.

Several early influential studies found that boys in divorced families had more adjustment problems than did girls.[6] Because these studies have been widely cited, many have come to accept this finding as incontrovertible. Given that boys usually live with their mothers following family disruption, the loss of contact with the same-sex parent could account for such a difference. In addition, boys, compared with girls, may be exposed to more conflict, receive less support from parents and others (because they are believed to be tougher), and be picked on more by custodial mothers (because they resemble their fathers). Other observers have suggested that boys may be more psychologically vulnerable than girls to a range of stressors, including divorce.[13] However, a number of other studies have failed to find a gender difference in children's reactions to divorce,[8,14] and some studies have found that girls have more problems than do boys.[15]

Amato and Keith tried to clarify this issue in their meta-analytic studies by pooling the results from all studies that reported data for males and females separately.[10,11] For children, the literature reveals one major gender difference: The estimated negative effects of divorce on social adjustment are stronger for boys than for girls. Social adjustment includes measures of popularity, loneliness, and cooperativeness. In other areas, however, such as academic achievement, conduct, or psychological adjustment, no differences between boys and girls are apparent. Why a difference in social adjustment, in particular, should occur is unclear. Girls may be more socially skilled than boys, and this may make them less susceptible to any disruptive effects of divorce. Alternatively, the increased aggressiveness of boys from divorced families may make their social relationships especially problematic, at least in the short term.[16] Nevertheless, the meta-analysis suggests that boys do not always suffer more detrimental consequences of divorce than do girls.

The meta-analysis for adults also revealed minimal sex differences, with one exception: Although both men and women from divorced families obtain less education than do those from continuously intact two-parent families, this difference is larger for women than for men. The reason for the greater vulnerability of women is somewhat unclear. One possibility is that non-custodial fathers are less likely to finance the higher education of daughters than sons.

Variations by Ethnicity of Child

There is a scant amount of research on how divorce affects nonwhite children of divorce. For example, because relatively little research has focused on this population, Amato and Keith were unable to reach any conclusions about ethnic differences in children's reactions to divorce.[10] The lack of information on how divorce affects nonwhite children is a serious omission in this research literature.

With regard to African American children, some research has suggested that academic deficits associated with living with a single mother are not as pronounced for black children as for white children.[17]

In relation to adults, Amato and Keith show that African Americans are affected less by parental divorce than are whites. For example, the gap in socioeconomic attainment between adults from divorced and nondivorced families of origin is greater among whites than among African Americans. This difference may have to do with the fact that divorce is more common, and perhaps more accepted, among African Americans than among whites. Also, because extended kin relations tend to be particularly strong among African Americans, single African American mothers may receive more support from their extended families than do single white mothers.[18] Alternatively, given the large number of structural barriers that inhibit the attainment of African Americans, growing up in a divorced single-parent family may result in relatively little additional disadvantage.

We need additional research on divorce in different racial and ethnic groups, including African Americans, Asian Americans, Hispanics, and Native Americans. In addition to the adjustment of children of divorce, we need information on relationships between children and custodial and noncustodial parents, the role of extended kin in providing support, and, in general, how culture moderates the impact of marital dissolution on children.

Variations by Age of Child

Some of the best descriptions of how divorce affects children of different ages come from the work of Wallerstein and Kelly, who conducted detailed interviews with children and parents.[19] Although their sample appears to have overrepresented parents who had a difficult time adjusting to divorce, many of their conclusions about age differences have been supported by later studies. Observation of children during the first year after parental separation showed that preschool age children lack the cognitive sophistication to understand the meaning of divorce. Consequently, they react to the departure of one parent with a great deal of confusion. Because they do not understand what is happening, many become fearful. For example, a child may wonder, "Now that one parent is gone, what is to stop the other parent from leaving also?" Young children also tend to be egocentric, that is, they see themselves at the center of the world. This leads some children to blame themselves for their parents' divorce. For example, they may think, "Daddy left because I was bad." Regression to earlier stages of behavior is also common among very young children.

Children of primary school age have greater cognitive maturity and can more accurately grasp the meaning of divorce. However, their understanding of what divorce entails may lead them to grieve for the loss of the family as it was, and feelings of sadness and depression are common. Some children see the divorce as a personal rejection. However, because egocentrism decreases with age, many are able to place the blame elsewhere—usually on a parent. Consequently, older children in this age group may feel a great deal of anger toward one, or sometimes both, parents.

Adolescents are more peer-oriented and less dependent on the family than are younger children. For this reason, they may be impacted less directly by the divorce. However, adolescents may still feel a considerable degree of anger toward one or both parents. In addition, adolescents are concerned about their own intimate relationships. The divorce of their parents may lead adolescents to question their own ability to maintain a long-term relationship with a partner.

The work of Wallerstein and Kelly suggests that children at every age are affected by divorce, although the nature of their reactions differs. But are these reactions more disturbing for one group than for another? Wallerstein and Kelly found that preschool children were the most distressed in the period following parental separation. However, 10 years later, the children of preschool age appeared to have adjusted better than children who were older at the time of family disruption.[20]

Many other studies have examined age at the time of divorce to see if it is associated with children's problems. However, these studies have yielded mixed and often inconsistent results, and the meta-analyses of children and adults were unable to cast much light on these issues.[21] A common problem in many data sets is that age at divorce and time since divorce are confounded. In other words, for a group of children of the same age, the younger they were at the time of divorce, the more time that has elapsed. But if we examine children whose parents all divorced at about the same time, then the more time that has passed, the older children are at the time of the study. Similarly, if we hold constant the age of the child at the time of divorce, then length of time and current age are perfectly correlated. In other words, it is impossible to separate the effects of age at divorce, length of time since divorce, and current age. Given this problem, it is not surprising that research findings are unclear. Nevertheless, it is safe to say that divorce has the potential to impact negatively on children of all ages.

Year of Study

One additional noteworthy finding that emerged from the meta-analyses by Amato and Keith concerns the year in which the study was conducted. These researchers found that older studies tended to yield larger differences between children from divorced and intact families than studies carried out more recently. This tendency was observed in studies of children (in relation to measures of academic achievement and conduct) and in studies of adults (in relation to measures of psychological adjustment, separation and divorce, material quality of life, and occupational quality). The difference persisted when the fact that more recent studies are more methodologically sophisticated than earlier studies was taken into account.

This finding suggests that more recent cohorts of children are showing less severe effects of divorce than earlier cohorts. Two explanations are worth considering. First, as divorce has become more common, attitudes toward divorce have become more accepting, so children probably feel less stigmatized. Similarly, the increasing number of divorces makes it easier for children to obtain support from others in similar circumstances. Second, because the legal and social barriers to marital dissolution were stronger in the past, couples who obtained a divorce several decades ago probably had more serious problems and experienced more conflict prior to separation than do some divorcing couples today. Furthermore, divorces were probably more acrimonious before the introduction of no-fault divorce. Thus, children of divorce in the past may have been exposed to more dysfunctional family environments and higher levels of conflict than were more recent cohorts of children.

Why Does Divorce Lower Children's Well-Being?

Available research clearly shows an association between parental divorce and children's well-being. However, the causal mechanisms responsible for this association are just beginning to be understood. Most explanations refer to the absence of the noncustodial parent, the adjustment of the custodial parent, interparental conflict, economic hardship, and life stress. Variations in these factors may explain why divorce affects some children more adversely than others.

Parental Absence

According to this view, divorce affects children negatively to the extent that it results in a loss of time, assistance, and affection provided by the noncustodial parent. Mothers and fathers are both considered potentially important resources for children. Both can serve as sources of practical assistance, emotional support, protection, guidance, and supervision. Divorce usually brings about the departure of one parent — typically the father — from the child's household. Over time, the quantity and quality of contact between children and noncustodial parents often decreases, and this is believed to result in lower levels of adjustment for these children as compared with children from intact families.[22]

The parental-absence explanation is supported by several lines of research. For example, some studies show that children who experience the death of a parent exhibit problems similar to those of children who "lose" a parent through divorce.[23] These findings are consistent with the notion that the absence of a parent *for any reason* is problematic for children. Also consistent with a parental absence perspective are studies showing that children who have another adult (such as a grandparent or other relative) to fill some of the functions of the absent parent have fewer problems than do children who have no substitute for the absent parent.[24] In addition, although the results of studies in the area of access to the noncustodial parent and adjustment are mixed,[25] in general, studies show that a close relationship with both parents is associated with positive adjustment after divorce. One circumstance in which high levels of access may not produce positive adjustment in children is in high-conflict divorces. When conflict between parents is marked, frequent contact with the noncustodial parent may do more harm than good.[26]

Custodial Parental Adjustment and Parenting Skills

According to this view, divorce affects children negatively to the extent that it interferes with the custodial parents' psychological health and ability to parent effectively. Following divorce, custodial parents often exhibit symptoms of depression and anxiety. Lowered emotional well-being, in turn, is likely to impair single parents' child-rearing behaviors. Hetherington and colleagues found that, during the first year following separation, custodial parents were less affectionate toward their children, made fewer maturity demands, supervised them less, were more punitive, and were less consistent in dispensing discipline.[27]

Research provides clear support for this perspective. Almost all studies show that children are better adjusted when the custodial parent is in good mental health[28] and displays good child-rearing skills.[29] In particular, children are better off when custodial parents are affectionate, provide adequate supervision, exercise a moderate degree of control, provide explanations for rules, avoid harsh discipline, and are consistent in dispensing punishment. Also consistent with a parental adjustment perspective are studies showing that, when custodial parents have a good deal of social support, their children have fewer difficulties.

Interparental Conflict

A third explanation for the effects of divorce on children focuses on the role of conflict between parents. A home marked by high levels of discord represents a problematic environment for children's socialization and development. Witnessing overt conflict is a direct stressor for children. Furthermore, parents who argue heatedly or resort to physical violence indirectly teach children that fighting is an appropriate method for resolving differences. As such, children in high-conflict families may not have opportunities to learn alternative ways to manage disagreements, such as negotiating and reaching compromises. Failure to acquire these social skills may interfere with children's ability to form and maintain friendships. Not surprisingly, numerous studies show that children living in high-conflict two-parent families are at increased risk for a variety of problems.[30] It seems likely, therefore, that many of the problems observed among children of divorce are actually caused by the conflict between parents that precedes and accompanies marital dissolution.

Studies show that children in high-conflict intact families are no better off—and often are worse off—than children in divorced single-parent families.[31] Indeed, children in single-parent families may show improvements in well-being following divorce if it represents an escape from an aversive and dysfunctional family environment. Furthermore, a study by Cherlin and colleagues shows that many, but not all, of the difficulties exhibited by children of divorce, such as behavioral problems and low academic test scores, are present *prior* to parental separation, especially for boys.[32] This finding is consistent with the notion that the lowered well-being of children is partly attributable to the conflict that precedes divorce. In addition, conflict may increase around the time of the separation, and parents often continue to fight long after the divorce is final. Indeed, many studies show that children's adjustment is related to the level of conflict between parents following divorce.[33] It should be noted here that postdivorce adjustment may also be influenced by residual effects of conflict that occurred during the marriage.

Economic Hardship

Divorce typically results in a severe decline in standard of living for most custodial mothers and their children.[34] Economic hardship increases the risk of psychological and behavioral problems among children[35] and may negatively affect their nutrition and health.[36] Economic hardship also makes it difficult for custodial mothers to provide books, educational toys, home computers, and other resources that can facilitate children's academic attainment. Furthermore, economically pressed parents often move to neighborhoods where schools are poorly financed, crime rates are high, and services are inadequate.[37] Living under these circumstances may facilitate the entry of adolescents into delinquent subcultures. According to this view, divorce affects children negatively to the extent that it results in economic hardship.

Studies show that children's outcomes—especially measures of academic achievement—are related to the level of household income following divorce. For example, Guidubaldi and colleagues found that children in divorced families scored significantly lower than children in intact two-parent families on 27 out of 34 outcomes; taking income differences into account statistically reduced the number of significant differences to only 13.[38] Similarly, McLanahan found that income accounted for about half of the association between living in a single-parent family and high school completion for white students.[39] However, most studies show that, even when families are equated in terms of income, children of divorce continue to experience an increased risk of problems. This suggests that economic disadvantage, although important, is not the sole explanation for divorce effects.

Life Stress

Each of the factors noted above—loss of contact with the noncustodial parent, impaired child rearing by the custodial parent, conflict between parents, and a decline in standard of living—represents a stressor for children. In addition, divorce often sets into motion other events that may be stressful, such as moving, changing schools, and parental remarriage. And of course, parental remarriage brings about the possibility of additional divorces. Multiple instances of divorce expose children to repeated episodes of conflict, diminished parenting, and financial hardship.[40] For some children of divorce, stress accumulates throughout childhood.

Research generally supports a stress interpretation of children's adjustment following divorce. Divorces that are accompanied by a large number of other changes appear to have an especially negative impact on children.[41] Furthermore, parental remarriage sometimes exacerbates problems for children of divorce,[42] as does a second divorce.[43]

A General Perspective on How Divorce Affects Children

All five explanations for the effects of divorce on children appear to have merit, and a complete accounting for the effect of divorce on children must make reference to each. Because of variability in these five factors, the consequences of divorce differ considerably from one child to the next.

Consider a divorce in which a child loses contact with the father, the custodial mother is preoccupied and inattentive, the parents fight over child support and other issues, the household descends abruptly into poverty, and the separation is accompanied by a series of other uncontrollable changes. Under these circumstances, one would expect the divorce to have a substantial negative impact on the child. In contrast, consider a divorce in which the child continues to see the noncustodial father regularly, the custodial mother continues to be supportive and exercises appropriate discipline, the parents are able to cooperate without conflict, the child's standard of living changes little, and the transition is accompanied by no other major disruptions in the child's life. Under these circumstances, one would predict few negative consequences of divorce. Finally, consider a high-conflict marriage that ends in divorce. As the level of conflict subsides, the previously distant father grows closer to his child, and the previously distracted and stressed mother becomes warmer and more attentive. Assuming no major economic problems or additional disruptive changes, this divorce would probably have a positive impact on the child.

Overall, to understand how divorce affects children, it is necessary to assess how divorce changes the total configuration of resources and stressors in children's lives.[44] The five factors described above should also be considered when evaluating policy alternatives aimed at improving the well-being of children of divorce.

What Interventions Might Benefit Children of Divorce?

Concern for the well-being of children of divorce leads to a consideration of how various policies and interventions might reduce the risk of problems for them. The most commonly discussed interventions include lowering the incidence of divorce, joint custody, child-support reform, enhancing the self-sufficiency of single mothers, and therapeutic programs for children and parents. Interventions suggested in this article are considered in the light of available research evidence.

Lowering the Incidence of Divorce

In the United States during the twentieth century, divorce became increasingly available as the result of a series of judicial decisions that widened the grounds for divorce. In 1970, no-fault divorce was introduced in California; presently it is available in all 50 states.[45] Under most forms of no-fault divorce, a divorce can be obtained without a restrictive waiting period if one partner wants it even if the other partner has done nothing to violate the marriage contract and wishes to keep the marriage together. This fact raises an interesting question: If the law were changed to make marital dissolution more difficult to obtain, and if doing so lowered the divorce rate, would we see a corresponding improvement in the well-being of children?

Several considerations suggest that this outcome is unlikely. First, although legal divorces occurred less often in the past, informal separations and desertions were not uncommon, especially among minorities and those of low socioeconomic status.[46] From a child's perspective, separation is no better than divorce. If the legal system were changed to make divorce more difficult, it would most likely increase the proportion of children living in separated but nondivorced families. It would also increase the proportion of people who spend their childhoods in high-conflict, two-parent families. As noted above, high-conflict two-parent families present just as many problems for children as do divorced single-parent families, perhaps more so. Given that the legal system cannot stop married couples from living apart or fighting, changing the legal system to decrease the frequency of divorce is unlikely to improve the well-being of children.

Is it possible to lower the frequency of divorce by increasing marital happiness and stability? The government could enact certain changes toward this end, for example, by changing the tax code to benefit married parents. It is possible that such a policy would enhance the quality and stability of some marriages; however, providing these benefits to married-couple families would increase the relative disadvantage of single parents and their children, an undesirable outcome. Alternatively, the government could take steps to promote marriage preparation, enrichment, and counseling. Increasing the availability of such services would probably help to keep some marriages from ending in divorce. However, as Furstenberg and Cherlin suggest, the rise in divorce is the result of fundamental changes in American society, including shifts in personal values and the growing economic independence of women, factors that cannot be affected easily by government policies.[47] As such, any actions taken by government to strengthen marriage are likely to have only minor effects on the divorce rate.

Increasing the Incidence of Joint Physical Custody

The history of custody determination in the United States has changed over time primarily in response to societal influences. In the eighteenth century, fathers usually were awarded custody of their children as they were considered the dominant family figure and were most likely to have the financial means to care for them. In the nineteenth century, the preference for custody moved toward women. The reason for this shift was probably occasioned, in part, by the industrial revolution and the movement of men from the home to the workplace to earn a living. Women, in this circumstance, were needed to care for the children while men were at work and became the primary caretakers of children. At this time, child developmental theorists also focused on the importance of the mother–child relationship, and the assumption was that the children were usually better off under the custody of their mother. Recently, society has moved toward a dual-earner family, and child developmentalists have emphasized the importance of both parents to the child. These changes are currently reflected in the law which emphasizes the importance of maintaining relationships with both parents. The result has been an increased interest in joint custody, which is now available as an option in most states.[41] *Joint physical custody* provides legal rights and responsibilities to both parents and is intended to grant children substantial portions of time with each parent. *Joint legal custody,* which is more common, provides legal rights and responsibilities to both parents, but the child lives with one parent.

Joint legal custody may be beneficial to the extent that it keeps both parents involved in their children's lives. However, studies show few differences between joint legal and mother-custody families in the extent to which fathers pay child support, visit their children, and are involved in making decisions about their children, once parental income, education, and other predivorce parental characteristics are taken into account.[48] Although joint legal custody may have symbolic value in emphasizing the importance of both parents, it appears to make little difference in practice.

In contrast, joint physical custody is associated with greater father contact, involvement, and payment of child support.[49] Fathers also appear to be more satisfied with joint physical custody than with mother custody. For example, Shrier and colleagues found in 1991 that joint-custody fathers were significantly more satisfied than sole-maternal-custody fathers in two areas, including their legal rights and responsibilities as a parent and their current alimony and child support financial arrangements.[50] Joint physical custody may be beneficial if it gives children frequent access to both parents. On the other hand, residential instability may be stressful for some children. Although few studies are available, some show that children in joint physical custody are better adjusted than are children with other custody arrangements,[51] and other studies show no difference.[52]

However, these results may present a picture that is too optimistic. Courts are most likely to grant joint physical custody to couples who request it. A large-scale study by Maccoby and Mnookin in California showed that couples with joint physical custody, compared with those who receive sole custody, are better educated and have higher incomes; furthermore, couples who request joint custody may be relatively less hostile, and fathers may be particularly committed to their children prior to divorce.[53] These findings suggest that some of the apparent positive "effect" of joint custody is a natural result of the type of people who request it in the first place.

It is unlikely that joint physical custody would work well if it were imposed on parents against their will. Under these conditions, joint custody may lead to more contact between fathers and their children but may also maintain and exacerbate conflict between parents.[54] Maccoby and Mnookin found that, although conflict over custody is relatively rare, joint custody is sometimes used to resolve custody disputes. In their study, joint custody was awarded in about one-third of cases in which mothers and fathers had each initially sought sole custody; furthermore, the more legal conflict between parents, the more likely joint custody was to be awarded. Three and one-half years after separation, these couples were experiencing considerably more conflict and less cooperative parenting than couples in which both had wanted joint custody initially. This finding demonstrates that an award of joint custody does not improve the relationship between hostile parents.

As noted above, studies show that children's contact with noncustodial parents is harmful if postdivorce conflict between parents is high. To the extent that joint physical custody maintains contact between children and parents in an atmosphere of conflict, it may do as much (or more) harm than good.[55] Joint custody, therefore, would appear to be the best arrangement for children when parents are cooperative and request such an arrangement. But in cases where parents are unable to cooperate, or when one parent is violent or abusive, a more traditional custody arrangement would be preferable.

Does research suggest that children are better adjusted in mother- or father-custody households? From an economic perspective, one might expect children to be better off with fathers, given that men typically earn more money than do women. On the other hand, children may be cared for more competently by mothers than fathers, given that mothers usually have more child-care experience. Studies that have compared the adjustment of children in mother- and father-custody households have yielded mixed results, with some favoring mother custody, some favoring father custody, and others favoring the placement of the child with the same-sex parent.[21]

A recent and thorough study by Downey and Powell,[56] based on a large national sample of children, found little evidence to support the notion that children are better off with the same-sex parent. On a few outcomes, children were better off in father-custody households. However, with household income controlled, children tended to be slightly better off with mothers. This finding suggests that the higher income of single-father households confers certain advantages on children, but if mothers earned as much as fathers, children would be better off with mothers. The overall finding of the study, however, is that the sex of the custodial parent has little to do with the children's adjustment. In general, then, it does not appear that either mother or father custody is inherently better for children, regardless of the sex of the child.

Child Support Reform

It is widely recognized that noncustodial fathers often fail to pay child support. In a 1987 study by the U.S. Bureau of the Census, about one-third of formerly married women with custody had no child support award. And among those with an award, one-fourth reported receiving no payments in the previous year.[57] In the past, it has been difficult for custodial mothers to seek compliance with awards because of the complications and expense involved. New provisions in the 1988 Family Support Act allow for states to recover child support payments through the taxation system.[58] Starting in

1994, all new payments will be subject to automatic withholding from parents' paychecks.

Child support payments represent only a fraction of most single mothers' income, usually no more than one-fifth.[59] As such, stricter enforcement of child support payments cannot be expected to have a dramatic impact on children's standard of living. Nevertheless, it is usually highly needed income. As noted above, economic hardship has negative consequences for children's health, academic achievement, and psychological adjustment. Consequently, any policy that reduces the economic hardship experienced by children of divorce would be helpful. Furthermore, the extra income derived from child support may decrease custodial mothers' stress and improve parental functioning, with beneficial consequences for children. Consistent with this view, two studies show that regular payment of child support by noncustodial fathers decreases children's behavior problems and increases academic test scores.[60] Furthermore, in these studies, the apparently beneficial effect of child support occurred in spite of the fact that contact between fathers and children was not related to children's well-being.

Research indicates that the majority of fathers are capable of paying the full amount of child support awarded; in fact, most are capable of paying more. Based on these considerations, it would appear to be desirable to increase the economic support provided by noncustodial fathers to their children. This would include increasing the proportion of children with awards, increasing the level of awards, and enforcing child support awards more strictly. A guaranteed minimum child support benefit, in which the government sets a minimum benefit level and ensures full payment when fathers are unable to comply, would also improve the standard of living of many children.[61]

Requiring fathers to increase their economic commitment to children may also lead them to increase visitation, if for no other reason than to make sure that their money is being spent wisely. A number of studies have shown that fathers who pay child support tend to visit their children more often and make more decisions about them than do fathers who fail to pay.[62] If increasing the level of compliance increases father visitation, it may increase conflict between some parents. On the other hand, some children may benefit from greater father involvement. Overall, the benefits of increasing fathers' economic contribution to children would seem to outweigh any risks.

Economic Self-Sufficiency for Single Mothers

As noted above, stricter enforcement of child-support awards will help to raise the standard of living of single mothers and their children. However, even if fathers comply fully with child-support awards, the economic situation of many single mothers will remain precarious. To a large extent, the economic vulnerability of single mothers reflects the larger inequality between men and women in American society. Not only do women earn less than men, but many married women sacrifice future earning potential to care for children by dropping out of the paid labor force, cutting back on the number of hours worked, taking jobs with more-flexible hours, or taking jobs closer to home. Thus, divorcees are disadvantaged both by the lower wages paid to women and by their work histories. In the long run, single mothers and their children will achieve economic parity with single fathers only when women and men are equal in terms of earnings and time spent caring for children.

In the short term, however, certain steps can be taken to allow single mothers receiving public assistance to be economically self-sufficient. These steps would include the provision of job training and subsidized child care.[63] Although these programs operate at government expense, they are cost-effective to the extent that women and children become independent of further public assistance. Furthermore, many single mothers are "penalized" for working because they lose government benefits, such as health care and child care. Welfare reform that removes work disincentives by allowing women to earn a reasonable level of income without losing health-care and child-care benefits would be desirable. In fact, changes in these directions are being implemented as part of the Family Support Act of 1988.[64] Given that the employment of single mothers does not appear to be harmful to children and can provide a higher standard of living for children than does welfare, and given that economic self-sufficiency would probably improve the psychological well-being of single mothers, it seems likely that these changes will benefit children.

Therapeutic Interventions for Children

According to Cherlin, there are still no firm estimates on the proportion of children who experience harmful psychological effects from parental divorce.[2] Research suggests that, in many cases, children adjust well to divorce without the need for therapeutic intervention. However, our current understanding is that a minority of children do experience adjustment problems and are in need of therapeutic intervention. The type of therapeutic intervention suited for children varies according to the type and severity of the adjustment problems and the length of time they are expressed by the child. The major types of therapeutic interventions include child-oriented interventions and family-oriented interventions.[65]

Child-oriented interventions attempt to help children by alleviating the problems commonly experienced by them after divorce. Some intervention programs include private individual therapy. However, many single parents are unable to afford private therapy for their children and may enroll them in programs in which counselors work with groups of children.

Typically, in these sessions, children meet on a regular basis to share their experiences, learn about problem-solving strategies, and offer mutual support. Children may also view films, draw, or participate in role-playing exercises. Small groups are desirable for children of divorce for several reasons. Not only can they reach large numbers of children, but the group itself is therapeutic: Children may find it easier to talk with other children than with adults about their experiences and feelings. Most group programs are located in schools; such programs have been introduced in thousands of school districts across the United States.

Evaluations of these programs have been attempted, and in spite of some methodological limitations, most are favorable: Children from divorced families who participate, compared with those who do not, exhibit fewer maladaptive attitudes and beliefs about divorce, better classroom behavior, less anxiety and depression, and improved self-concept.[66] Although much of the evidence is positive, it is not entirely clear which components of these programs are most effective. For example, improvement may be brought about by a better understanding of divorce, newly acquired communication skills, or the support of other students. Although more evaluation research is needed, the evidence is positive enough to warrant further development and introduction of therapeutic programs for children.

In addition to child-focused interventions, there are *family-focused interventions* including both educational and therapeutic programs. These programs are aimed at divorcing parents, with the intention of either improving parenting skills or reducing the level of conflict over children.[67] In principle, therapeutic interventions that improve parental child-rearing skills or decrease the level of conflict between parents should benefit children, although this effect has not yet been demonstrated.

What Directions Should Future Research Take?

All things being equal, existing research suggests that a well-functioning nuclear family with two caring parents may be a better environment for children's growth and development than a divorced single-parent family. Children of divorce, as a group, are at greater risk than children from intact families, as a group, for many psychological, academic, and social problems. And adults raised in divorced single-parent families, as a group, do not achieve the same level of psychological and material well-being as those raised in continuously intact two-parent families. However, we need to keep in mind that many children are better off living in single-parent households than in two-parent families marked by conflict. Furthermore, we need to recognize that most single parents work hard to provide their children with a loving and structured family life. Many single-parent families function well, and most children raised in these settings develop into well-adjusted adults. Blaming single parents as a group for the problems experienced by children of divorce is a pointless exercise.

At this time, our knowledge about children and divorce needs to be expanded in certain directions. The long-term effect of divorce on children is the basic question that needs to be addressed. The answers to this question will inform social policy and the court system, shape models of intervention, and influence parental decision making. This type of information should be obtained from longitudinal and longitudinal-sequential designs. Needed are studies that begin prior to divorce, as well as studies that follow children of divorce through adolescence and into adulthood.[68]

Also needed are data on how a variety of factors—relations with parents, parental adjustment, economic well-being, conflict, and exposure to stressors—combine to affect children's response to divorce. This research should make it possible to determine which children lose the most through divorce, which children are relatively unaffected, and which children benefit.

Information on how divorce affects children in different racial and ethnic groups is another area of research that would be informative from the standpoint of both clinical and economic intervention.[18] And more evaluation of various interventions, both legal (joint custody, mediation, child support reform) and therapeutic, is also needed.

It is important to focus on establishing policies that will help narrow the gap in well-being between children of divorce and children from intact families. High divorce rates and single-parent families are facts of life in American society. If it is impossible to prevent children from experiencing parental divorce, steps must be taken to ease the transition.

ENDNOTES

1. Furstenberg Jr., F. F., and Cherlin, A. J. *Divided Families: What Happens to Children When Parents Part.* Cambridge, MA: Harvard University Press, 1991, pp. 1–15; Uhlenberg, P. Death and the family. *Journal of Family History* (1980) 5:313–20.

2. Cherlin, A. *Marriage, divorce, remarriage.* Rev. ed. Cambridge, MA: Harvard University Press, 1992.

3. Bumpass, L. Children and marital disruption: A replication and update. *Demography* (1984) 21:71–82.

4. For examples, see the articles in *The Child in His Family: The Impact of Disease and Death.* E. J. Anthony, ed. New York: Wiley, 1973.

5. Crook, T., and Eliot, J. Parental death during childhood and adult depression: A critical review of the literature. *Psychological Bulletin* (1980) 87:252–59.

6. See, for example, Guidubaldi, J., Cleminshaw, H. K., Perry, J. D., and McLoughlin, C. S. The impact of parental divorce on children: Report of the nationwide NASP study. *School Psychology Review* (1983) 12:300–23; Hetherington, E. M., Cox, M., and Cox, R. Effects of divorce on parents and children. In *Nontraditional Families.* M. E. Lamb, ed. Hillsdale, NJ: Lawrence Erlbaum Associates, 1982, pp. 223–88.

7. See, for example, Baydar, N. Effects of parental separation and reentry into union on the emotional well-being of children. *Journal of Marriage and the Family* (1988) 50:967–81; Enos, D. M., and Handal, P. J. Relation of parental marital status and perceived family conflict to adjustment in white adolescents. *Journal of Consulting and Clinical Psychology* (1986) 54:820–24; Mechanic, D., and Hansell, S. Divorce, family conflict, and adolescents' well-being. *Journal of Health and Social Behavior* (1989) 30:105–16.

8. Amato, P. R., and Ochiltree, G. Child and adolescent competence in intact, one-parent, and stepfamilies. *Journal of Divorce* (1987) 10:75–96.

9. See Glass, G. V., McGaw, B., and Smith, M. L. An evaluation of meta-analysis. In *Meta-analysis in Social Research.* Newbury Park, CA: Sage, 1981.

10. Amato, P. R., and Keith, B. Parental divorce and the well-being of children: A meta-analysis. *Psychological Bulletin* (1991) 100:26–46.

11. Amato, P. R., and Keith, B. Parental divorce and adult well-being: A meta-analysis. *Journal of Marriage and the Family* (1991) 53:43–58.

12. Kendall-Tackett, K. A., Williams, L. M., and Finkelhor, D. Impact of sexual abuse on children: A review and synthesis of recent empirical studies. *Psychological Bulletin* (1993) 113:164–80.

13. Rutter, M. Sex differences in children's responses to family stress. In *The Child in His Family.* Vol. 1. E. J. Anthony and C. Koupernik, eds. New York: Wiley, 1970.

14. See, for example, Booth, A., Brinkerhoff, D. B., and White, L. K. The impact of parental divorce on courtship. *Journal of Marriage and the Family* (1984) 46:85–94; Smith, T. E. Parental separation and adolescents' academic self-concepts: An effort to solve the puzzle of separation effects. *Journal of Marriage and the Family* (1990) 52:107–18.

15. Slater, E., Steward, K. J., and Linn, M. W. The effects of family disruption on adolescent males and females. *Adolescence* (1983) 18:931–42.

16. See Peterson, J. L., and Zill, N. Marital disruption, parent–child relationships, and behavior problems in children. *Journal of Marriage and the Family* (1986) 48:295–307; Hetherington, E. M., and Chase-Lansdale, P. L. The impact of divorce on life-span development: Short and long term effects. In *Life-span Development and Behavior.* P. B. Baltes, D. L. Featherman, and R. M. Lerner, eds. Hillsdale, NJ: Lawrence Erlbaum Associates, 1990.

17. Hetherington, E. M., Camara, K. A., and Featherman, D. L. Achievement and intellectual functioning of children in one-parent households. In *Achievement and Achievement Motives.* J. T. Spence, ed. San Francisco: W. H. Freeman, 1983.

18. Del Carmen, R., and Virgo, G. N. Marital disruption and nonresidential parenting: A multicultural perspective. In *Nonresidential Parenting: New Vistas in Family Living.* C. Depner and J. Bray, eds. Newbury Park, CA: Sage, 1993, pp. 13–36.

19. Wallerstein, J. S., and Kelly, J. B. *Surviving the Breakup: How Children and Parents Cope with Divorce.* New York: Basic Books, 1980.

20. Wallerstein, J. S., and Blakeslee, S. *Second chances: Men, Women, and Children a Decade after Divorce.* New York: Ticknor and Fields, 1989.

21. For a summary of these studies, see Amato, P. R. Children's adjustment to divorce: Theories, hypotheses, and empirical support. *Journal of Marriage and the Family* (1993) 55:23–38.

22. Furstenberg Jr., F. F., and Nord, C. W. Parenting apart: Patterns of child-rearing after marital disruption. *Journal of Marriage and the Family* (1985) 47:893–904; Selzer, J. A. Relationships between fathers and children who live apart: The father's role after separation. *Journal of Marriage and the Family* (1991) 53:79–101.

23. This trend was confirmed in the meta-analysis by Amato and Keith; see note 11. For examples of studies, see Amato, P. R., Parental absence during childhood and depression in later life. *Sociological Quarterly* (1991) 32:543–56; Gregory, I. Introspective data following childhood loss of a parent: Delinquency and high school dropout. *Archives of General Psychiatry* (1965) 13:99–109; Saucier, J., and Ambert, A. Parental marital status and adolescents' optimism about their future. *Journal of Youth and Adolescence* (1982) 11:345–53. Our meta-analysis also showed that, although children who experience parental death are worse off than those in intact two-parent families, they have higher levels of well-being than do children of divorce.

24. Cochran, M., Larner, M., Riley, D., et al. *Extending Families: The Social Networks of Parents and Their Children.* Cambridge, MA: Cambridge University Press, 1990; Dornbusch, S., Carlsmith, J. M., Bushwall, S. J., et al. Single parents, extended households, and the control of adolescents. *Child Development* (1985) 56:326–41.

25. Kelly, J. B. Current research on children's postdivorce adjustment: No simple answers. *Family and Conciliation Courts Review* (1993) 31:29–49.

26. Amato, P. R., and Rezac, S. J. Contact with nonresident parents, interparental conflict, and children's behavior. Paper presented at the Annual Meeting of the Midwest Sociological Society. Chicago, IL, 1993; Healy, Jr., J. Malley, J., and Stewart, A. Children and their fathers after parental separation. *American Journal of Orthopsychiatry* (1990) 60:531–43.

27. See Simons, R. L., Beaman, J., Conger, R. D., and Chao, W. Stress, support, and antisocial behavior traits as determinants of emotional well-being and parenting practices among single mothers. *Journal of Marriage and the Family* (1993) 55:385–98.

28. Kline, M., Tschann, J. M., Johnston, J. R., and Wallerstein, J. S. Children's adjustment in joint and sole physical custody families. *Developmental Psychology* (1989) 25:430–38. Guidubaldi, J., and Perry, J. D. Divorce and mental health sequelae for children: A two-year follow-up of a nationwide sample. *Journal of the American Academy of Child Psychiatry* (1985) 24:531–37; and Kalter, N., Kloner, A., Schreiser, S., and Olka, K. Predictors of children's postdivorce adjustment. *American Journal of Orthopsychiatry* (1989) 59:605–18.

29. Guidubaldi, J., Cleminshaw, H. K., Perry, J. D., et al. The role of selected family environment factors in children's postdivorce adjustment. *Family Relations* (1986) 35:141–51; see note 6, Hetherington, Cox, and Cox. See note 28, Kalter, Kloner, Schreiser, and Olka; see note 16, Peterson and Zill.

30. Emery, R. Interparental conflict and the children of discord and divorce. *Psychological Bulletin* (1982) 92:310–30; Grych, J. H., and Fincham, F. D. Marital conflict and children's adjustment: A cognitive-contextual framework. *Psychological Bulletin* (1990) 108:267–90.

31. See note 14, Booth, Brinkerhoff, and White. See note 7, Enos and Handal; and Mechanic and Hansell; Long, N., Forehand, R., Fauber, R., and Brody, G. H. Self-perceived and independently observed competence of young adolescents as a function of parental marital conflict and recent divorce. *Journal of Abnormal Child Psychology* (1987) 15:15–27; see note 16, Peterson and Zill.

32. Cherlin, A. J., Furstenberg Jr., F. F., Chase-Lansdale, P. L., et al. Longitudinal studies of effects of divorce on children in Great Britain and the United States. *Science* (1991) 252:1386–89. Similar findings were reported by Block, J. H., Block, J., and Gjerde, P. R. The personality of children prior to divorce. *Child Development* (1986) 57:827–40.

33. Johnston, J. R., Kline, M., and Tschann, J. M. Ongoing postdivorce conflict: Effects on children of joint custody and frequent access. *American Journal of Orthopsychiatry* (1999) 59:576–92; Kurdek, L. A., and Berg, B. Correlates of children's adjustment to their parents' divorces. In *Children and divorce*. L. A. Kurdek, ed. San Francisco: Jossey-Bass, 1983; Shaw, D. S., and Emery, R. E. Parental conflict and other correlates of the adjustment of school-age children whose parents have separated. *Journal of Abnormal Child Psychology* (1987) 15:269–81. It is also probable that children's problems, to a certain extent, exacerbate conflict between parents.

34. Duncan, G. J., and Hoffman, S. D. Economic consequences of marital instability. In *Horizontal Equity, Uncertainty, and Economic Well-being*. M. David and T. Smeeding, eds. Chicago: University of Chicago Press, 1985; Weitzman, L. J. *The Divorce Revolution: The Unexpected Social and Economic Consequences for Women and Children in America*. New York: Free Press, 1985.

35. McLeod, J. D., and Shanahan, M. J. Poverty, parenting, and children's mental health. *American Sociological Review* (1993) 58:351–66.

36. Williams, D. R. Socioeconomic differentials in health: A review and redirection. *Social Psychology Quarterly* (1990) 52:81–99.

37. McLanahan, S., and Booth, K. Mother-only families: Problems, prospects, and politics. *Journal of Marriage and the Family* (1989) 51:557–80.
38. See note 6, Guidubaldi, Cleminshaw, Perry, and McLoughlin.
39. McLanahan, S. Family structure and the reproduction of poverty. *American Journal of Sociology* (1985) 90:873–901.
40. For a review of the effects of serial marriages (involving three or more marriages) and divorces on child adjustment, see Brody, G. H., Neubaum, E., and Forehand, R. Serial marriage: A heuristic analysis of an emerging family form. *Psychological Bulletin* (1988) 103:211–22.
41. Hodges, W. F., Tierney, C. W., and Buchsbaum, H. K. The cumulative effects of stress on preschool children of divorced and intact families. *Journal of Marriage and the Family* (1984) 46:611–19; Stolberg, A. L., and Anker, J. M. Cognitive and behavioral changes in children resulting from parental divorce and consequent environmental changes. *Journal of Divorce* (1983) 7:23–37.
42. See note 7, Baydar. Hetherington and her colleagues found that the remarriage of the custodial mother was associated with increased problems for girls but decreased problems for boys. Hetherington, E. M., Cox, M., and Cox, R. Long-term effects of divorce and remarriage on the adjustment of children. *Journal of the American Academy of Child Psychiatry* (1985) 24:518–30.
43. Amato, P. R., and Booth, A. The consequences of parental divorce and marital unhappiness for adult well-being. *Social Forces* (1991) 69:895–914.
44. For similar perspectives, see Hetherington, E. M. Coping with family transitions: Winners, losers, and survivors. *Child Development* (1989) 60:1–14; Kurdek, L. A. An integrative perspective on children's divorce adjustment. *American Psychologist* 36:856–66.
45. Glendon, M. A. *The Transformation of Family Law: State, Law, and Family in the United States and Western Europe.* Chicago: University of Chicago Press, 1989. See note 34, Weitzman.
46. See note 45, Glendon; Sweet, J. A., and Bumpass, L. L. *American Families and Households.* New York: Russell Sage Foundation, 1990.
47. See note 1, Furstenberg and Cherlin.
48. Seltzer, J. Legal custody arrangements and children's economic welfare. *American Journal of Sociology* (1991) 96:895–929.
49. Arditti, J. A. Differences between fathers with joint custody and noncustodial fathers. *American Journal of Orthopsychiatry* (1992) 62:186–95; Bowman, M., and Ahrons, C. R. Impact of legal custody status on fathers' parenting postdivorce. *Journal of Marriage and the Family* (1985) 47:481–88; Dudley, J. R. Exploring ways to get divorced fathers to comply willingly with child support agreements. *Journal of Divorce* (1991) 14:121–33; Leupnitz, D. A comparison of maternal, paternal, and joint custody: Understanding the varieties of postdivorce family life. *Journal of Divorce* (1986) 9:1–12.
50. See note 49, Arditti; Little, M. A. The impact of the custody plan on the family: A five-year follow-up. *Family and Conciliation Courts Review* (1992) 30:243–51; Shrier, D. K., Simring, S. K., Shapiro, E. T., and Greif, J. B. Level of satisfaction of fathers and mothers with joint or sole custody arrangements. *Journal of Divorce and Remarriage* (1991) 16:163–69.
51. Buchanan, C. M., Maccoby, E. E., and Dornbusch, S. M. Adolescents and their families after divorce: Three residential arrangements compared. *Journal of Research on Adolescents* (1992) 2:261–91; Glover, R. J., and Steele, C. Comparing the effects on the child of postdivorce parenting arrangements. *Journal of Divorce* (1989) 12:185–201; Wolchik, S. A., Braver, S. L., and Sandler, I. N. Maternal versus

joint custody: Children's postseparation experiences and adjustment. *Journal of Clinical Child Psychology* (1985) 14:5–10.

52. Kline, M., Tschann, J. M., Johnston, J. R., and Wallerstein, J. S. Children's adjustment in joint and sole physical custody families. *Developmental Psychology* (1988) 25:430–38; Leupnitz, D. *Child custody.* Lexington, MA: D. C. Heath, 1982; Pearson, J., and Thoennes, N. Custody after divorce: Demographic and attitudinal patterns. *American Journal of Orthopsychiatry* (1990) 60:233–49.

53. See note 49, Arditti; note 52, Pearson and Thoennes; Steinman, S. The experience of children in a joint custody arrangement: A report of a study. *American Journal of Orthopsychiatry* (1981) 24:554–62; Macoby, E. E., and Mnookin, R. H. *Dividing the Child: Social and Legal Dilemmas of Custody.* Cambridge, MA: Harvard University Press, 1992.

54. Nelson, R. Parental hostility, conflict, and communication in joint and sole custody families. *Journal of Divorce* (1989) 13:145–57.

55. Buchanan, C. M., Maccoby, E. E., and Dornbusch, S. M. Caught between parents: Adolescents' experience in divorced homes. *Child Development* (1991) 62:1008–29; Johnston, J. R., Kline, M., and Tschann, J. M. Ongoing postdivorce conflict: Effects on children of joint custody and frequent access. *American Journal of Orthopsychiatry* (1989) 59:576–92.

56. Downey, D., and Powell, B. Do children in single-parent households fare better living with same-sex parents? *Journal of Marriage and the Family* (1993) 55:55–71.

57. U.S. Bureau of the Census. *Child Support and Alimony: 1987.* Current Population Reports, Series P-23, No. 167. Washington, DC: U.S. Government Printing Office, 1990.

58. Public Law No. 100–485, reprinted in 1988 *U.S. Code Cong. & Admin. News,* 102 Stat. 2343.

59. See note 34, Duncan and Hoffman.

60. Furstenberg Jr., F. F., Morgan, S. P., and Allison, P. D. Paternal participation and children's well-being after marital dissolution. *American Sociological Review* (1987) 52:695–701; King, V. Nonresidential father involvement and child well-being: Can dads make a difference? Paper presented at the annual meeting of the Population Association of America. Cincinnati, OH, 1993.

61. For a discussion of child-support reform, see Garfinkel, I. *Assuring Child Support: An Extension of Social Security.* New York: Russell Sage Foundation, 1992; Garfinkel, I., and McLanahan, S. S. *Single Mothers and Their Children: A New American Dilemma.* Washington, DC: Urban Institute Press, 1986.

62. Seltzer, J. A., and Bianchi, S. M. Children's contact with absent parents. *Journal of Marriage and the Family* (1988) 50:663–77; Seltzer, J., Schaeffer, N. C., and Charng, H. Family ties after divorce: The relationship between visiting and paying child support. *Journal of Marriage and the Family* (1989) 51:1013–32.

63. Britto, K. The Family Support Act of 1988 Welfare Reform (Public Law 100–485). Vol. 2, No. 3. National Conference of State Legislatures. Denver, CO, 1989.

64. Aldous, J. Family policy in the 1980s: Controversy and consensus. *Journal of Marriage and the Family* (1990) 52:1136–51.

65. Grych, J., and Fincham, F. D. Interventions for children of divorce: Toward greater integration of research and action. *Psychological Bulletin* (1992) 111:434–54.

66. Anderson, R. F., Kinney, J., and Gerler, E. R. The effects of divorce groups on children's classroom behavior and attitudes toward divorce. *Elementary School Guidance and Counseling* (1984) 19:70–76; Crosbie-Burnett, M., and Newcomer, L. L. Group counseling children of divorce: The effects of a multimodel intervention. *Journal of Divorce* (1989) 13:69–78. Pedro-Carroll, J., and Cowan, E. L. The children

of divorce intervention program: An investigation of the efficacy of a school-based intervention program. *Journal of Consulting and Clinical Psychology* (1985) 53:603–11; Stolberg, A. J., and Garrison, K. M. Evaluating a primary prevention program for children of divorce. *American Journal of Community Psychology* (1985) 13:111–24.

67. Bloom, B. L., Hodges, W. F., and Caldwell, R. A. A preventive program for the newly separated: Initial evaluation. *American Journal of Community Psychology* (1982) 10:251–64; Bloom, B. L., Hodges, W. F., Kern, M. B., and McFaddin, S. C. A preventive intervention program for the newly separated: Final evaluations. *American Journal of Orthopsychiatry* (1985) 55:9–26; Zibbell, R. A. A short-term, small-group education and counseling program for separated and divorced parents in conflict. *Journal of Divorce and Remarriage* (1992) 18:189–203.

68. Wallerstein, J. S. The long-term effects of divorce on children: A review. *Journal of the American Academy of Child Adolescent Psychiatry* (1991) 30:349–60.

35

THE MODERN AMERICAN STEPFAMILY: PROBLEMS AND POSSIBILITIES

MARY ANN MASON

Cinderella had one, so did Snow White and Hansel and Gretel. Our traditional cultural myths are filled with the presence of evil stepmothers. We learn from the stories read to us as children that stepparents, particularly stepmothers, are not to be trusted. They may pretend to love us in front of our biological parent, but the moment our real parent is out of sight they will treat us cruelly and shower their own children with kindnesses. Few modern children's tales paint stepparents so harshly, still the negative image of stepparents lingers in public policy. While the rights and obligations of biological parents, wed or unwed, have been greatly strengthened in recent times, stepparents have been virtually ignored. At best it is fair to say that as a society we have a poorly formed concept of the role of stepparents and a reluctance to clarify that role.

Indeed, the contrast between the legal status of stepparents and the presumptive rights and obligations of natural parents is remarkable. Child support obligations, custody rights, and inheritance rights exist between children and their natural parents by virtue of a biological tie alone, regardless of the quality of social or emotional bonds between parent and child, and regardless of whether the parents are married. In recent years, policy changes have extended the rights and obligations of natural parents, particularly in regard to unwed and divorced parents, but have not advanced with regard to stepparents. Stepparents in most states have no obligation during the marriage to support their stepchildren, nor do they enjoy any right of custody or control. Consistent with this pattern, if the marriage terminates through divorce or death, they usually have no rights to custody or even visitation, however long-standing their relationship with their stepchildren. Conversely, stepparents have no obligation to pay child support following divorce, even if their stepchildren have depended on their income for many years. In turn, stepchildren have no right of inheritance in the event of the stepparent's death (they are, however, eligible for Social Security benefits in most cases).[1]

Policymakers who spend a great deal of time worrying about the economic and psychological effects of divorce on children rarely consider the fact that about 70 percent of mothers are remarried within six years. Moreover, about 28 percent of children are born to unwed mothers, many of whom eventually marry someone who is not the father of their child. In a study including all children, not just children of divorce, it was estimated that one-fourth of the children born in the United States in the early 1980s will live with a stepparent before they reach adulthood.[2] These numbers are likely to increase in the future, at least as long as the number of single-parent families continues to grow. In light of these demographic trends, federal and state policies affecting families and children, as well as policies governing private-sector employee benefits, insurance, and other critical areas of everyday life, may need to be adapted to address the concerns of modern stepfamilies.

In recent years, stepfamilies have received fresh attention from the psychological and social sciences but little from legal and policy scholars. We now know a good deal about who modern stepfamilies are and how they function, but there have been few attempts to apply this knowledge to policy. This [reading] first of all reviews the recent findings on the everyday social and economic functioning of today's stepfamilies, and then examines current state and federal policies, or lack of them in this arena. Finally, the sparse set of current policy recommendations, including my own, are presented. . . .

The Modern Stepfamily

The modern stepfamily is different and more complex than Cinderella's or Snow White's in several important ways. First, the stepparent who lives with the children is far more likely to be a stepfather than a stepmother, and in most cases the children's biological father is still alive and a presence, in varying degrees, in their lives. Today it is divorce, rather than death, which usually serves as the background event for the formation of the stepfamily, and it is the custodial mother who remarries (86 percent of stepchildren live primarily with a custodial mother and stepfather),[3] initiating a new legal arrangement with a stepfather.[4] . . .

In most stepfamilies the noncustodial parent, usually the father, is still alive (only in 25 percent of cases is the noncustodial parent dead or his whereabouts unknown). This creates the phenomenon of more than two parents, a situation that conventional policymakers are not well equipped to address. However, according to the National Survey of Families and Households (NSFH), a nationally representative sample of families, contact between stepchildren and their absent natural fathers is not that frequent. Contact falls into four broad patterns: Roughly one-quarter of all stepchildren have no association at all with their fathers and receive no child support; one-quarter see their fathers only once a year or less often and receive no child support; one-quarter have intermittent contact or receive some child support; and one-quarter may or may not receive child support but have fairly regular contact, seeing their fathers once a month or more. Using these data as guides to the quality and intensity of the father–child relationship, it appears that relatively few stepchildren are close to their natural fathers or have enough contact with them to permit the fathers to play a prominent role in the children's upbringing. Still, at least half of natural fathers do figure in their children's lives to some degree.[5] The presence of the noncustodial parent usually precludes the option of stepparent adoption, a solution that would solve the legal ambiguities, at least, of the stepparent's role. . . .

Some children may spend time a good deal of time with nonresidential stepparents, and they may become significant figures in the children's lives. But for our purpose of reassessing the parental rights and obligations of stepparents, we will focus only on residental stepparents, since they are more likely to be involved in the everyday support and care of their stepchildren. Moreover, the wide variety of benefits available to dependent children, like Social Security and health insurance, are usually attached only to a residential stepparent. . . .

The classic longitudinal studies by Hetherington and colleagues,[6] spanning the past two decades, provide a rich source of information on how stepfamilies function. Hetherington emphasizes that stepchildren are children who have experienced several marital transitions. They have usually already experienced the divorce of their parents (although the number whose mothers have never before wed is increasing) and a period of life in a single–parent family before the formation of the stepfamily. In the early stages of all marital transitions, including divorce and remarriage, child–parent relations are often disrupted and parenting is less authoritative than in nondivorced families. These early periods, however, usually give way to a parenting situation more similar to nuclear families.[7]

The Heatherington studies found that stepfathers vary in how enthusiastically and effectively they parent their stepchildren, and stepchildren also vary in how willingly they permit a parental relationship to develop.

Indeed, many stepfather–stepchild relationships are not emotionally close. Overall, stepfathers in these studies are most often disengaged and less authoritative as compared with nondivorced fathers. The small class of residential stepmothers exhibits a similar style.[8] . . .

The age and gender of the child at the time of stepfamily formation are critical in his or her adjustment. Early adolescence is a difficult time in which to have remarriage occur, with more sustained difficulties in stepfather–stepchild relations than in remarriages where the children are younger. Young (preadolescent) stepsons, but not necessarily stepdaughters, develop a closer relationship to their stepfathers after a period of time; this is not as likely with older children.[9]

Other researchers have found that in their lives outside the family, stepchildren do not perform as well as children from nondivorced families, and look more like the children from single-parent families. It seems that divorce and remarriage (or some factors associated with divorce and remarriage) increase the risk of poor academic, behavioral, and psychological outcomes.[10]

The difficulties of the stepfamily relationship are evident in the high divorce rate of such families. About one-quarter of all remarrying women separate from their new spouses within five years of the second marriage, and the figure is higher for women with children from prior relationships. A conservative estimate is that between 20 percent and 30 percent of stepchildren will, before they turn eighteen, see their custodial parent and stepparent divorce.[11] This is yet another disruptive marital transition for children, most of whom have already undergone at least one divorce.

Other researchers look at the stepfamily more positively. Amato and Keith analyzed data comparing intact, two-parent families with stepfamilies and found that while children from two-parent families performed significantly better on a multifactored measure of well-being and development, there was a significant overlap. A substantial number of children in stepfamilies actually perform as well as or better than children in intact two-parent families. As Amato comments, "Some children grow up in well-functioning intact families in which they encounter abuse, neglect, poverty, parental mental illness, and parental substance abuse. Other children grow up in well-functioning stepfamilies and have caring stepparents who provide affection, effective control and economic support."[12] Still other researchers suggest that it may be the painful transitions of divorce and economically deprived single-parenthood which usually precede the formation of the stepfamily that explain the poor performance of stepchildren.[13]

Perhaps a fairer comparison of stepchildren's well-being is against single-parent families. Indeed, if there were no remarriage (or first marriage, in the case of unmarried birth mothers), these children would remain a part of a single-parent household. On most psychological measures of behavior and achievement, stepchildren look more like children from single-parent families than children from never-divorced families, but on economic measures it is a different story. The National Survey of Families and Households

(NSFH) data show that stepparents have slightly lower incomes and slightly less education than parents in nuclear families, but that incomes of all types of married families with children are three to four times greater than the incomes of single mothers. Custodial mothers in stepfamilies have similar incomes to single mothers (about $12,000 in 1987). If, as seems plausible, their personal incomes are about the same before they married as after, then marriage has increased their household incomes more than threefold. Stepfathers' incomes are, on average, more than twice as great as their wives' and account for nearly three-fourths of the family's income.[14]

In contrast to residential stepparents, absent biological parents only rarely provide much financial or other help to their children. Some do not because they are dead or cannot be found; about 26 percent of custodial, remarried mothers and 28 percent of single mothers report that their child's father is deceased or of unknown whereabouts. Yet even in the three-quarters of families where the noncustodial parent's whereabouts are known, only about one-third of all custodial mothers (single and remarried) receive child support or alimony from former spouses, and the amounts involved are small compared to the cost of raising children. According to NSFH data, remarried women with awards receive on average $1780 per year, while single mothers receive $1383. Clearly, former spouses cannot be relied on to lift custodial mothers and their children out of poverty.[15]

The picture is still more complex, as is true with all issues relating to stepfamilies. Some noncustodial fathers have remarried and have stepchildren themselves. These relationships, too, are evident in the NSFH data. Nearly one-quarter (23 percent) of residential stepfathers have minor children from former relationships living elsewhere. Two-thirds of those report paying child support for their children.[16] [There] is a growing class of fathers who frequently feel resentful about the heavy burden of supporting two households, particularly when their first wife has remarried.

In sum, although we have no data which precisely examine the distribution of resources within a stepfamily, it is fair to assume that stepfathers' substantial contributions to family income improve their stepchildren's material well-being by helping to cover basic living costs. For many formerly single-parent families, stepfathers' incomes provided by remarriage are essential in preventing or ending poverty among custodial mothers and their children. (The data are less clear for the much smaller class of residential stepmothers.)

While legal dependency usually ends at eighteen, the economic resources available to a stepchild through remarriage could continue to be an important factor past childhood. College education and young adulthood are especially demanding economic events. The life-course studies undertaken by some researchers substantiate the interpersonal trends seen in stepfamilies before the stepchildren leave home. White reports that viewed from either the parent's or the child's perspective, relationships over the life-course between stepchildren and stepparents are substantially weaker than those between biological parents and children. These relationships are not monolithic, however; the best occur when the stepparent is a male, there are no stepsiblings, the stepparent has no children of his own, and the marriage between the biological parent and the stepparent is intact.[17] On the other end, support relationships are nearly always cut off if the stepparent relationship is terminated because of divorce or the death of the natural parent. . . .

. . .One study of perceived normative obligation to stepparents and stepchildren suggests that people in stepfamilies have weaker, but still important, family ties than do biological kin.[18] In terms of economic and other forms of adult support, even weak ties cannot be discounted. They might, instead, become the focus of public policy initiatives.

Stepfamilies in Law and Public Policy

Both state and federal law set policies that affect stepfamilies. Overall, these policies do not reflect a coherent policy toward stepparents and stepchildren. Two competing models are roughly evident. One, a "stranger" model, followed by most states, treats the residential stepparent as if he or she were a legal stranger to the children, with no rights and no responsibilities. The other, a "dependency" model, most often followed by federal policymakers, assumes the residential stepfather is, in fact, supporting the stepchildren and provides benefits accordingly. But there is inconsistency in both state and federal policy. Some states lean at times toward a dependency model and require support in some instances, and the federal government sometimes treats the stepparent as if he or she were a stranger to the stepchildren, and ignores them in calculating benefits.

State law governs the traditional family matters of marriage, divorce, adoption, and inheritance, while federal law covers a wide range of programs and policies which touch on the lives of most Americans, including stepfamilies. As the provider of benefits through such programs as [TANF] and Social Security, the federal government sets eligibility standards that affect the economic well-being of many stepfamilies. In addition, as the employer of the armed forces and civil servants, the federal government establishes employee benefits guidelines for vast numbers of American families. And in its regulatory role, the federal government defines the status of stepfamilies for many purposes ranging from immigration eligibility to tax liability. . . .

State Policies

State laws generally give little recognition to the dependency needs of children who reside with their stepparent; they are most likely to treat the stepparent as a stranger to the children, with no rights or obligations. In contrast to the numerous state laws obligating parents to support natural children born out of wedlock or within a previous marriage, only a few states have enacted statutes which specifically impose an affirmative duty on stepparents. The Utah stepparent support statute, for example, provides simply that "[a] stepparent shall support a stepchild to the same extent that a natural or adoptive parent is required to support a child."[19] This duty of support ends upon the termination of the marriage. Most states are silent on the obligation to support stepchildren.[20]

A few states rely on common law, the legal tradition stemming from our English roots. The common law tradition leans more toward a dependency model. It dictates that a stepparent can acquire the rights and duties of a parent if he or she acts *in loco parentis* (in the place of a parent). Acquisition of this status is not automatic; it is determined by the stepparent's intent. A stepparent need not explicitly state the intention to act as a parent; he or she can "manifest the requisite intent to assume responsibility by actually providing financial support or by taking over the custodial duties."[21] Courts, however, have been reluctant to grant *in loco* parental rights or to attach obligations to unwilling stepparents. In the words of one Wisconsin court, "A good Samaritan should not be saddled with the legal obligations of another, and we think the law should not with alacrity conclude that a stepparent assumes parental relationships to a child."[22]

At the extreme, once the status of *in loco parentis* is achieved, the stepparent "stands in the place of the natural parent, and the reciprocal rights, duties, and obligations of parent and child subsist." These rights, duties, and obligations include the duty to provide financial support, the right to custody and control of the child, immunity from suit by the stepchild, and, in some cases, visitation rights after the dissolution of the marriage by death or divorce.

Yet stepparents who qualify as *in loco parentis* are not always required to provide support in all circumstances. A subset of states imposes obligation only if the stepchild is in danger of becoming dependent on public assistance. For example, Hawaii provides that

> [a] stepparent who acts in loco parentis is bound to provide, maintain, and support the stepparent's stepchild during the residence of the child with the stepparent if the legal parents desert the child or are unable to support the child, thereby reducing the child to destitute and necessitous circumstances.[23]

Just as states do not regularly require stepparents to support their stepchildren, they do not offer stepparents the parental authority of custody and control within the marriage. A residential stepparent generally has fewer rights than a legal guardian or a foster parent. According to one commentator, a stepparent "has no authority to make decisions about the child—no authority to approve emergency medical treatment or even to sign a permission slip for a field trip to the fire station."[24]

Both common law and state statutes almost uniformly terminate the stepparent relationship upon divorce or the death of the custodial parent. This means that the support obligations, if there were any, cease and that the stepparent has no rights to visitation or custody. State courts have sometimes found individual exceptions to this rule, but they have not created any clear precedents. Currently only a few states authorize stepparents to seek visitation rights, and custody is almost always granted to a biological parent upon divorce. In the event of the death of the stepparent's spouse, the noncustodial, biological parent is usually granted custody even when the stepparent has, in fact, raised the child. In one such recent Michigan case, *Henrickson* v. *Gable*,[25] the children, aged nine and ten when their mother died, had lived with their stepfather since infancy and had rarely seen their biological father. In the ensuing custody dispute, the trial court left the children with their stepfather, but an appellate court, relying upon a state law that created a strong preference for biological parents, reversed this decision and turned the children over to their biological father.

Following the stranger model, state inheritance laws, with a few complex exceptions, do not recognize the existence of stepchildren. Under existing state laws, even a dependent stepchild whose stepparent has supported and raised the child for many years is not eligible to inherit from the stepparent if there is no will. California provides the most liberal rule for stepchild recovery when there is no will, but only if the stepchild meets relatively onerous qualifications. Stepchildren may inherit as the children of a deceased stepparent only if "it is established by clear and convincing evidence that the stepparent would have adopted the person but for a legal barrier."[26] Very few stepchildren have been able to pass this test. Similarly a stepchild cannot bring a negligence suit for the accidental death of a stepparent. In most instances, then, only a biological child will inherit or receive legal compensation when a stepparent dies.

Federal Policies

The federal policies that concern us here are of two types: federal benefit programs given to families in need, including AFDC (until 1997) and Supplemental Security Income (SSI), and general programs not based on need, including Social Security as well as civil service and military personnel employee benefits. Most of these programs follow the dependency model. They go further than do most states in recognizing or promoting the actual family relationship of residential stepfamilies. Many of them (although not all) assume that residential stepparents support their stepchildren and accordingly make these children eligible for benefits equivalent to those afforded to other children of the family.

Despite the fact that federal law generally recognizes the dependency of residential stepchildren, it remains wanting in many respects. There is a great deal of inconsistency in how the numerous federal programs and policies treat the stepparent–stepchild relationship, and the very definitions of what constitutes a stepchild are often quite different across programs. Most of the programs strive for a dependency-based definition, such as living with or receiving 50 percent of support from a stepparent. However, some invoke the vague definition "actual family relationship," and some do not attempt any definition at all, thus potentially including nonresidential stepchildren among the beneficiaries. In some programs the category of stepchild is entirely absent or specifically excluded from the list of beneficiaries for some programs. . . .

Stepchildren are even more vulnerable in the event of divorce. Here the stranger model is turned to. As with state law, any legally recognized relationship is immediately severed upon divorce in nearly all federal programs. The children and their stepparents become as strangers. Social Security does not provide any cushion for stepchildren if the deceased stepparent is divorced from the custodial parent. Under Social Security law, the stepparent–stepchild relationship is terminated immediately upon divorce and the stepchild is no longer eligible for benefits even if the child has in fact been dependent on the insured stepparent for the duration of a very long marriage.[27] If the divorce were finalized the day before the stepparent's death, the child would receive no benefits. . . .

New Policy Proposals

. . . All of the proposals I review base their arguments to a greater or lesser degree on social science data, although not always the same data. The proposers may roughly be divided into three camps. The first, and perhaps smallest camp, I call *negativists*. These are scholars who view stepfamilies from a sociobiological perspective and find them a troublesome aberration to be actively discouraged. The second, and by far largest group of scholars, I term *voluntarists*. This group acknowledges both the complexity and the often distant nature of stepparent relationships, and largely believes that law and policy should leave stepfamilies alone, as it does now. If stepparents wish to take a greater role in their stepchildren's lives, they should be encouraged to do so, by adoption or some other means. The third camp recognizes the growing presence of stepfamilies as an alternate family form and believes they should be recognized and strengthened in some important ways. This group, I call them *reformists*, believes the law should take the lead in providing more rights or obligations to stepparents. The few policy initiatives from this group range from small specific reforms regarding such issues as inheritance and visitation to my own proposal for a full-scale redefinition of stepparents' rights and obligations.

The negativist viewpoint on stepparenting, most prominently represented by sociologist David Popenoe, relies on a sociobiological theory of reproduction. According to this theory, human beings will give unstintingly to their own biological children, in order to promote their own genes, but will be far less generous to others. The recent rise in divorce and out-of-wedlock births, according to Popenoe, has created a pattern of essentially fatherless households that cannot compete with the two-biological-parent families.

Popenoe believes the pattern of stepparent disengagement revealed by many researchers is largely based on this biological stinginess.

> If the argument . . . is correct, and the family is fundamentally rooted in biology and at least partly activated by the "genetically selfish"

activities of human beings, childbearing by non-relatives is inherently problematic. It is not that unrelated individuals are unable to do the job of parenting, it is just that they are not as likely to do the job well. Stepfamily problems, in short, may be so intractable that the best strategy for dealing with them is to do everything possible to minimize their occurrence.[28] . . .

Popenoe goes beyond the stranger model, which is neutral as to state activity, and suggests an active discouragement of stepparent families. He believes the best way to obstruct stepfamilies is to encourage married biological two-parent families. Premarital and marital counseling, a longer waiting period for divorce, and a redesign of the current welfare system so that marriage and family are empowered rather than denigrated are among his policy recommendations. . . .

The second group of scholars, whom I call voluntarists, generally believe that the stepparent relationship is essentially voluntary and private and the stranger model most clearly reflects this. The legal bond formed by remarriage is between man and wife — stepchildren are incidental; they are legal strangers. Stepparents may choose, or not choose, to become more involved with everyday economic and emotional support of their stepchildren; but the law should not mandate this relationship, it should simply reflect it. These scholars recognize the growth of stepfamilies as a factor of modern life and neither condone nor condemn this configuration. Family law scholar David Chambers probably speaks for most scholars in this large camp when he says,

> In most regards, this state of the law nicely complements the state of stepparent relationships in the United States. Recall the inescapable diversity of such relationships — residential and non-residential, beginning when the children are infants and when they are teenagers, leading to comfortable relationships in some cases and awkward relationships in others, lasting a few years and lasting many. In this context it seems sensible to permit those relationships to rest largely on the voluntary arrangements among stepparents and biological parents. The current state of the law also amply recognizes our nation's continuing absorption with the biological relationship, especially as it informs our sensibilities about enduring financial obligations.[29]

Chambers is not enthusiastic about imposing support obligations on stepparents, either during or following the termination of a marriage, but is interested in promoting voluntary adoption. He would, however, approve some middle ground where biological parents are not completely cut off in the adoption process.

Other voluntarists are attracted by the new English model of parenting, as enacted in the Children Act of 1989. Of great attraction to American voluntarists is the fact that under this model a stepparent who has been married at least two years to the biological parent may voluntarily petition for a residence order for his or her spouse's child. With a residence order the stepparent has parental responsibility toward the child until the age of sixteen. But this order does not extinguish the parental responsibility of the noncustodial parent.[30] In accordance with the Children Act of 1989, parents, biological or otherwise, no longer have parental rights; they have only parental responsibilities, and these cannot be extinguished upon the divorce of the biological parents. In England, therefore, it is possible for three adults to claim parental responsibility. Unlike biological parental responsibility, however, stepparent responsibility does not usually extend following divorce. The stepparent is not normally financially responsible following divorce, but he or she may apply for a visitation order.

The third group, whom I call reformists, believe that voluntary acts on the part of stepparents are not always adequate, and that it is necessary to reform the law in some way to more clearly define the rights and responsibilities of stepparents. The American Bar Association Family Law Section has been working for some years on a proposed Model Act to suggest legislative reforms regarding stepparents' obligations to provide child support and rights to discipline, visitation, and custody. A Model Act is not binding anywhere; it is simply a model for all states to consider. Traditionally, however, Model Acts have been very influential in guiding state legislative reform. In its current form, the ABA Model Act would require stepparents to assume a duty of support during the duration of the remarriage only if the child is not adequately supported by the custodial and noncustodial parent. The issue is ultimately left to the discretion of the family court, but the Model Act does not require that the stepparent would need to have a close relationship with a stepchild before a support duty is imposed. The Model Act, however, does not describe what the rule should be if the stepparent and the custodial parent divorce.

The proposed statute is rather more complete in its discussion of stepparent visitation or custody rights following divorce. It takes a two-tiered approach, first asking if the stepparent has standing (a legal basis) to seek visitation and then asking if the visitation would be in the best interests of the child. The standing question is to be resolved with reference to five factors, which essentially examine the role of the stepparent in the child's life (almost an *in loco parentis* question), the financial support offered by the stepparent, and the detriment to the child from denying visitation. The court, if it finds standing, then completes the analysis with the best interests standard of the jurisdiction. The Model Act's section on physical custody also requires a two-tiered test, requiring standing and increasing the burden on the stepparent to present clear and convincing proof that he or she is the better custodial parent.

The ABA Model Act is a worthwhile start, in my opinion, but it is little more than that. At most it moves away from a stranger model and provides a limited concept of mandatory stepparent support during a marriage, acknowledging that stepchildren are at least sometimes dependent. It also gives a stepparent a fighting chance for visitation or custody following a divorce. It fails to clarify stepparents' rights during the marriage, however, and does not deal with the issue of economic support at the period of maximum vulnerability, the termination of the marriage through death and divorce. Moreover, the Model Act, and, indeed, all the existing reform proposals, deal only with traditional legal concepts of parenthood defined by each state and do not consider the vast range of federal programs, or other public and private programs, that define the step parent–stepchild relationship for purposes of benefits, insurance, or other purposes.

I propose, instead, a new conceptualization of stepparent rights and responsibilities, a de facto parent model, that will cover all aspects of the stepparent–stepchild relationship and will extend to federal and private policy as well. My first concern in proposing a new framework is the welfare of the stepchildren, which is not adequately dealt with in either the stranger or the dependency model. The failure of state and, to a lesser extent, federal policy to address coherently the financial interdependencies of step relationships, described earlier, means that children dependent upon a residential stepparent may not receive adequate support or benefits from that parent during the marriage, and they may not be protected economically in the event of divorce or parental death. . . .

A second reason for proposing a new framework is to strengthen the relationship of the stepparent and stepchildren. While research generally finds that stepparents are less engaged in parenting than natural parents, research studies do not explain the causes; others must do so. In addition to the sociobiologists' claim for stingy, genetically driven behavior, sociologists have posited the explanation of "incomplete institutionalization."[31] This theory is based on the belief that, by and large, people act as they are expected to act by society. In the case of stepfamilies, there are unclear or absent societal norms and standards for how to define the remarried family, especially the role of the stepparent in relation to the stepchild.

Briefly, my new model requires, first of all, dividing stepparents into two subclasses: those who are de facto parents and those who are not. De facto parents would be defined as "those stepparents legally married to a natural parent who primarily reside with their stepchildren, or who provide at least 50 percent of the stepchild's financial support." Stepparents who do not meet the de facto parent requirements would, in all important respects, disappear from policy.

For the purposes of federal and state policy, under this scheme, a de facto parent would be treated virtually the same as a natural parent during the marriage. The same rights, obligations, and presumptions would attach vis-à-vis their stepchildren, including the obligation of support. These rights and duties would continue in some form, based on the length of the marriage, following the custodial parent's death or divorce from the stepparent, or the death of the stepparent. In the event of divorce the stepparent would have standing to seek custody or visitation, but the stepparent could also be obligated for child support of a limited duration. Upon the death of a stepparent, a minor stepchild would be treated for purposes of inheritance and benefits as would a natural child.

So far this proposal resembles the common law doctrine of *in loco parentis*, described earlier, where the stepparent is treated for most purposes (except inheritance) as a parent on the condition that he or she voluntarily agrees to support the child. In the de facto model, however, support is mandatory, not voluntary, on the grounds both that it is not fair to stepchildren to be treated by the law in an unequal or arbitrary manner and that child welfare considerations are best met by uniform support of stepchildren. Furthermore, in the traditional common law *in loco parentis* scenario, the noncustodial parent had died and was not a factor to be reckoned with. Under this scheme, creating a de facto parent category for stepparents would not invalidate the existing rights and obligations of a noncustodial biological parent. Rather, this proposal would empower a stepparent as an additional parent.

Multiple parenting and the rights and obligations of the stepparent and children following divorce or death are controversial and difficult policy matters that require more detailed attention than the brief exposition that can be offered here. Multiple parenting is the barrier upon which many family law reform schemes, especially in custody and adoption, have foundered. It is also one of the reasons that there has been no consistent effort to reformulate the role of stepparents. Working out the details is critical. For instance, mandating stepparent support raises a central issue of fairness. If the stepparent is indeed required to support the child, there is a question about the support obligations of the noncustodial parent. Traditionally, most states have not recognized the stepparent contribution as an offset to child support.[32] While this policy promotes administrative efficiency, and may benefit some children, it may not be fair to the noncustodial parent. An important advance in recognizing the existence of multiple parents in the nonlinear family is to recognize multiple support obligations. The few states that require stepparent obligation have given limited attention to apportionment of child support obligations, offering no clear guidelines. I propose that state statutory requirements for stepparent obligation as de facto parents also include clear guidelines for apportionment of child support between the noncustodial natural parent and the stepparent. . . .

Another facet of multiple parenting is legal authority. If stepparents are required to accept parental support obligations, equal protection and fairness concerns dictate that they must also be given parental rights. Currently, state laws, as noted earlier, recognize only natural or adoptive parents; a stepparent currently has no legal authority over a stepchild, even to authorize a field trip. If stepparents had full parental rights, in some cases, as when the parents have shared legal custody, the law would be recognizing the parental rights of three parents, rather than two. While this sounds unusual, it is an accurate reflection of how many families now raise their children. Most often, however, it would be only the custodial parent and his or her spouse, the de facto parent, who would have authority to make decisions for the children in their home.

Critics of this scheme may argue that adoption, not the creation of the legal status of de facto parent, is the appropriate vehicle for granting a stepparent full parental rights and responsibilities.[33] If, as discussed earlier, nearly three-quarters of stepchildren are not being supported by their non-custodial parents, policy initiatives could be directed to terminating the non-paying parents' rights and promoting stepparent adoption. Adoption is not possible, however, unless the parental rights of the absent natural parent have been terminated—a difficult procedure against a reluctant parent. Normally, the rights of a parent who maintains contact with his or her child cannot be terminated even if that parent is not contributing child support. And when parental rights are terminated, visitation rights are terminated as well in most states. It is by no means clear that it is in the best interests of children to terminate contact with a natural parent, even if the parent is not meeting his or her obligation to support.[34] As discussed earlier, a large percentage (another 25 percent or so), of noncustodial parents continue some contact with their children, even when not paying support.[35] And while stepparent adoption should be strongly encouraged when it is possible, this solution will not resolve the problem of defining the role of stepparents who have not adopted.

Extending, in some form, the rights and obligations following the termination of the marriage by divorce or death is equally problematical. Currently, only a few courts have ruled in favor of support payments following divorce, and these have been decided on an individual basis. Only one state, Missouri, statutorily continues stepparent support obligations following divorce.[36] It would clearly be in the best interests of the child to experience continued support, since a significant number of children may sink below the poverty line upon the dissolution of their stepfamily.[37]

Since the de facto model is based on dependency, not blood, a fair basis for support following divorce or the death of the custodial parent might be to require that a stepparent who qualified as a de facto parent for at least one year must contribute child support for half the number of years of dependency until the child reached maturity. If a child resided with the stepparent for four years, the stepparent would be liable for support for two years. If the biological noncustodial parent were still paying support payments, the amount could be apportioned. While it may be said that this policy would discourage people from becoming stepparents by marrying, it could also be said to discourage divorce once one has become a stepparent. Stepparents might consider working harder at maintaining a marriage if divorce had some real costs.

Conversely, stepparents should have rights as well as responsibilities following divorce or the death of the custodial parent. Divorced or widowed stepparents should be able to pursue visitation or custody if they have lived with and supported the child for at least one year. Once again, multiple parent claims might sometimes be an issue, but these could be resolved, as they are now, under a primary caretaker, or a best interest standard.

The death of a stepparent is a particular period of vulnerability for stepchildren for which they are unprotected by inheritance law. While Social Security and other federal survivor benefits are based on the premise that a stepchild relies on the support of the residential stepparent and will suffer the same hardship as natural children if the stepparent dies, state inheritance laws, notoriously archaic, decree that only biology, not dependency, counts. State laws should assume that a de facto parent would wish to have all his dependents receive a share of his estate if he died without a will. If the stepchildren are no longer dependent, that assumption would not necessarily prevail. The same assumption should prevail for insurance policies and compensation claims following an accidental death. A dependent stepchild, just as a natural child, should have the right to sue for loss of support.

On the federal front, a clear definition of stepparents as de facto parents would eliminate the inconsistencies regarding stepparents which plague current federal policies and would clarify the role of the residential stepparent. For the duration of the marriage, a stepchild would be treated as a natural child for purposes of support and the receipt of federal benefits. This treatment would persist in the event of the death of the stepparent. The stepchild would receive all the survivor and death benefits that would accrue to a natural child.[38]

In the case of divorce, the issue of federal benefits is more complicated. Stepchildren and natural children should not have identical coverage for federal benefits following divorce, again, but neither is it good policy to summarily cut off children who have been dependent, sometimes for many years, on the de facto parent. A better policy is to extend federal benefits for a period following divorce, based on a formula which matches half the number of years of dependency, as earlier suggested for child support. For instance, if the stepparent resided with the stepchild for four years, the child would be covered by Social Security survivor benefits and other federal benefits, including federal employee benefits, for a period of two years following the divorce. This solution would serve children by at least providing a transitional cushion. It would also be relatively easy to administer. In the case of the death of the biological custodial parent, benefits could be similarly extended, or continued indefinitely if the child remains in the custody of the stepparent. . . .

Ultimately, state law defines most of these stepfamily relationships, and it is difficult, if not impossible to achieve uniform reform on a state-by-state basis. In England it is possible to pass a single piece of national legislation, such as the Children Act of 1989, which completely redefines parental roles. In America, the process of reform is slower and less sure. Probably the first step in promoting a new policy would be for the federal government to insist all states pass stepparent general support obligation laws requiring stepparents acting as de facto parents (by my definition) to support their stepchildren as they do their natural children. This goal could be accomplished by making stepparent general support obligation laws a prerequisite for receiving federal welfare grants. Federal policy already assumes this support in figuring eligibility in many programs, but it has not insisted that states change their laws. Precedent for this strategy has been set by the Family Support Acts of 1988 in which the federal government mandated that states set up strict child support enforcement laws for divorced parents and unwed fathers at AFDC levels in order to secure AFDC funding.[39] The second, larger step would be to require limited stepparent support following divorce, as described previously. Once the basic obligations were asserted, an articulation of basic rights would presumably follow.

Conclusion

Stepfamilies compose a large and growing sector of American families that is largely ignored by public policy. Social scientists tell us that these families have problems. Stepparent–stepchildren relationships, poorly defined by law and social norms, are not as strong or nurturing as those in nondivorced families, and stepchildren do not do as well in school and in other outside settings. Still, stepfamily relationships are important in lifting single-parent families out of poverty. When single or divorced mothers marry, the household income increases by more than threefold, rising to roughly the same level as nuclear families. A substantial portion of these families experiences divorce, however, placing the stepchildren at risk of falling back into poverty. It makes good public policy sense then, both to strengthen these stepfamily relationships and to cushion the transition for stepchildren should the relationship end.

ENDNOTES

1. Mary Ann Mason and David Simon, "The Ambiguous Stepparent: Federal Legislation in Search of a Model," *Family Law Quarterly* 29:446–48, 1995.
2. E. Mavis Hetherington and Kathleen M. Jodl, "Stepfamilies as Settings for Child Development," in Alan Booth and Judy Dunn (eds.), *Stepfamilies: Who Benefits? Who Does Not?* New Jersey: 1994, 55; and E. Mavis Hetherington, "An Overview of the Virginia Longitudinal Study of Divorce and Remarriage: A Focus on Early Adolescence," *Journal of Family Psychology* 7:39–56, 1993.
3. U.S. Bureau of Census, 1989.
4. Divorce is not always the background event. An increasing, but still relatively small number of custodial mothers have not previously wed.
5. Mary Ann Mason and Jame Mauldon, "The New Stepfamily Needs a New Public Policy," *Journal of Social Issues* 52(3):5, Fall 1996.
6. Hetherington and Jodl, "Stepfamilies as Settings for Child Development," 55–81.
7. Ibid., 76.
8. E. Mavis Hetherington and William Clingempeel, "Coping with Marital Transitions: A Family Systems Perspective," *Monographs of the Society for Research in Child Development* 57:2–3, Serial No. 227, New York: 1992; E. Thomson, Sara McLanahan, and R. B. Curtin, "Family Structure, Gender, and Parental Socialization, *Journal of Marriage and the Family* 54:368–378, 1992.
9. Hetherington and Jodl, "Stepfamilies as Settings for Child Development," 64–65.
10. Thomson, McLanahan, and Curtin, "Family Structure, Gender, and Parental Socialization," 368–78.

11. L. Bumpass and J. Sweet, *American Families and Households*, New York: Russell Sage Foundation, 1987, 23.

12. Paul Amato, "The Implications of Research Findings on Children in Stepfamilies," in Alan Booth and Judy Dunn (eds.), *Stepfamilies: Who Benefits? Who Does Not?* New Jersey: Erlbaum, 1994, 84.

13. Nicholas Zill, "Understanding Why Children in Stepfamilies Have More Learning and Behavior Problems than Children in Nuclear Families." in Alan Booth and Judy Dunn (eds.) *Stepfamilies: Who Benefits? Who Does Not?* New Jersey: Erlbaum, 1994, 89–97.

14. Mason and Mauldon, "The New Stepfamily Needs a New Public Policy," 7.

15. Ibid., 8.

16. Ibid.

17. Lynn White, "Stepfamilies Over the Lifecourse: Social Support." in Alan Booth and Judy Dunn (eds.), *Stepfamilies: Who Benefits? Who Does Not?* New Jersey: Erlbaum, 1994, 109–139.

18. A. S. Rossi and P. H. Rossi, *Of Human Bonding: Parent–Child Relations across the Life Course*, New York: A. de Gruyter, 1990.

19. Utah Code Ann. 78-45-4.1.

20. Margaret Mahoney, *Stepfamilies and the Law*, Ann Arbor: University of Michigan Press, 1994, 13–47.

21. *Miller v. United States,* 123 F.2d 715, 717 (8th Cir, 1941).

22. *Niesen v. Niesen,* 157 N. W.2d 660 664(Wis. 1968).

23. Hawaii Revised Stat. Ann., Title 31, Sec. 577-4.

24. David Chambers, "Stepparents, Biologic Parents, and the Law's Perceptions of 'Family' after Divorce," in S. Sugarman and H. H. Kay (eds.), *Divorce Reform at the Crossroads*, New Haven: Yale University Press, 1990, 102–29.

25. *Henrickson v. Gable.*

26. Cal. Prob. Code, Sec. 6408.

27. 42 U.S.C. sec. 416(e), 1994.

28. David Popenoe, "Evolution of Marriage and Stepfamily Problems," in Alan Booth and Judy Dunn (eds.), *Stepfamilies: Who Benefits? Who Does Not?* New Jersey: 1994, 3–28.

29. Chambers, "Stepparents, Biologic Parents, and the Law's Perceptions of 'Family' after Divorce," 26.

30. Mark A. Fine, "Social Policy Pertaining to Stepfamilies: Should Stepparents and Stepchildren Have the Option of Establishing a Legal Relationship?" in Alan Booth and Judy Dunn (eds.), *Stepfamilies: Who Benefits? Who Does Not?* New Jersey: Erlbaum, 1994, 199.

31. Andrew Cherlin, "Remarriage as an Incomplete Institution," *American Journal of Sociology* 84:634–49, 1978.

32. S. Ramsey and J. Masson, "Stepparent Support of Stepchildren: A Comparative Analysis of Policies and Problems in the American and British Experience." *Syracuse Law Review* 36:649–66, 1985.

33. Joan Hollinger (ed.-in-chief), et al., *Adoption Law and Practice*, New York: Matthew Bender, 1988.

34. Katherine Bartlett, "Re-thinking Parenthood as an Exclusive Status: The Need for Alternatives When the Premise of the Nuclear Family Has Failed," *Virginia Law Review* 70:879–903, 1984.

35. Mason and Mauldon, "The New Stepfamily Needs a New Public Policy," 5.

36. Vernon's Ann. Missouri Stats. 453.400, 1994.

37. Mason and Mauldon, "The New Stepfamily Needs a New Public Policy," 5.

38. Mason and Simon, "The Ambiguous Stepparent: Federal Legislation in Search of a Model," 471.

39. 100 P.L. 485; 102 Stat. 2343 (1988).

PART IX

Families and Violence

In this section, we examine domestic violence, or the violence that occurs between family members and relational intimates within and outside the household. Domestic violence takes many forms, including dating violence, spousal and partner abuse, child abuse and incest, elder abuse, and violence between same-sex couples. The four primary types of family violence are physical abuse, verbal abuse, sexual abuse, and neglect. The legal definitions of domestic violence vary, but most tend to focus on physical and sexual abuse, not on verbal abuse and neglect. For example, a common legal definition reads that family violence is "any assault, battery, sexual assault, sexual battery, or criminal offense resulting in the physical injury or death of one family or household member by another who is or was residing in the same single dwelling unit" (Section 415.602, Florida Statutes). Another problem with legal definitions is that every state has its own definition of domestic violence, which means that judicial policy concerning family violence varies from state to state. Thus, one of the first issues in studying family or domestic violence is getting a clear working definition of the terms used to describe it and identifying behaviors that are consistent between states and policymakers.

Moreover, the terms *domestic violence* and *family violence* themselves are seen as problematic by some researchers. Sociologist Demie Kurz (1998), for example, argues that how family violence research is framed and compartmentalized obscures its prevalence and impact. One problematic way family violence research has been framed is the argument that men and women are equally violent in their families and intimate relationships. That is, some researchers have tried to make domestic violence gender neutral—an assertion that has created some debate concerning the gendered nature of family violence data (Gelles 1993). Most family sociologists find that domestic violence is gendered: Women are abused more frequently and in different contexts than men. Moreover, the majority of official data-gathering agencies have found women to be the main victims. For example, statistics show that domestic violence is the leading cause of injury to women between 15 and 44 years old in the United States—it injures more women than car accidents, muggings, and rapes combined (FBI *Uniform Crime Reports* 1991). This gendered nature of family violence has led Kurz and other scholars to conclude that family violence should be identified as violence against women. Similarly, Wardell, Gillespie, and Leffler (1983) state that "when researchers take gender into account, it becomes clear that physical violence against women should be compared, not with elder abuse, but with related types of violence against women, such as rape, marital rape, sexual harassment, and incest, all of which also result from male dominance" (p. 328).

Violence against Women

The first reading in this section, "Gender, Diversity, and Violence: Extending the Feminist Framework, is by Kersti A. Yllö. Yllö, a professor of sociology at Wheaton College, has been studying domestic violence, especially batter-ing, marital rape, and abuse during pregnancy, for over 25 years. In this selection, Yllö builds on Kurz's and others' arguments that we need to ana-lyze domestic violence using a gendered lens. She argues that to understand domestic violence, we need to understand not only how violence is gen-dered but also how violence reflects power, especially coercive control. In addition, Yllö advocates that feminist theory and analysis needs to go fur-ther in looking at the effects of intersectionality on family violence; that is, the intersection of gender with race-ethnicity, social class, sexuality, and so on. Thus, this first reading on family violence provides a theoretical basis from which to understand and analyze multiple types of family violence.

Another important aspect of family violence is examining domestic vio-lence within diverse cultural groups in the United States. Many abused immigrant and refugee women are isolated because they face access barriers to U.S. legal and social systems. These women frequently are separated from family and community networks that could help them and have difficulties with language and cultural differences between their countries of origin and the United States. For example, Jang, Lee, and Morello-Frosch (1990) have argued that immigration laws hurt women. New immigrants who marry can be denied U.S. citizenship if the marriage lasts less than two years. This law makes it difficult for women to leave violent relationships. Jang et al. conclude that the United States needs to provide immigrant women with cultural and language access to women's shelters, to increase the collaboration between immigrant community agencies and domestic violence projects, and to initiate legislative action to better protect battered immigrant women.

The second reading in this section, "Lifting the Veil of Secrecy: Domestic Violence against South Asian Women in the United States," is by Satya P. Krishnan, Malahat Baig-Amin, Louisa Gilbert, Nabila El-Bassel, and Anne Waters. Krishnan is an associate professor in the Department of Health and Social Services at New Mexico State University. She and her colleagues use focus groups to explore and discuss a variety of issues concerning domestic violence against South Asian women, some of whom are recent immigrants. The focus groups define domestic violence, and the women talk about their experiences with violence and their decisions regarding staying in or leaving an abusive relationship. Of particular importance is the number of barriers that South Asian women face in leaving a violent spouse. In addition to the legal and immigrant barriers discussed previously by Jang et al., South Asian women face cultural barriers, such as prescribed marriage and gender roles; community and structural barriers, such as a lack of knowledge about social programs and social and material support; and individual barriers, such as fear for safety of themselves and their children and the lack of job and language skills. Krishnan et al. conclude that there is much work to be done in South Asian immigrant communities to help women who are experiencing violence.

Violence in Same–Sex Relationships

Another underserved population that is experiencing high rates of domestic violence is gay and lesbian couples. Part of this invisibility is due to the myth that domestic violence occurs only between men and women in family relationships. The reality is that the abuse of power and violence can occur in any human relationship, including those of same-sex couples. The third reading in this section, "Toward a Better Understanding of Lesbian Battering," by Claire M. Renzetti, examines same-sex family violence. Renzetti is a professor of sociology at St. Joseph's University in Philadelphia, where she teaches courses on gender, families, and criminology. Renzetti began researching lesbian battering in 1985, after a student initially sparked her interest in the topic by giving her a copy of the *Philadelphia Gay News*, which contained an ad for a speak-out on lesbian battering. Renzetti called the contact person listed in the ad to get more information, and after several more phone conversations, she arranged for Renzetti to meet with members of a support group for battered lesbians. Together they developed the project that produced the selection excerpted here from Renzetti's book *Violent Betrayal: Partner Abuse in Lesbian Relationships* (1992). Renzetti also has had the privilege of speaking with many courageous lesbian survivors of same-sex partner abuse, who have spoken out about their experiences largely to help others. She continues to study, write about, and lecture on lesbian battering, and she is currently conducting additional general research on women's use of violence in intimate relationships. Renzetti concludes her article with similar arguments to those of Yllö (Reading 36) and Krishnan et al. (Reading 37) that more support services need to be provided to women who are survivors of violence.

Elder Abuse

The last reading in this section, "Abuse of Elders," by Ola Barnett, Cindy L. Miller-Perrin, and Robin D. Perrin, professors at Pepperdine University, turns our attention to another type of domestic violence occurring within the family. This wider lens is important because we tend to think of family violence as occurring only between partners and spouses, when, in fact, an abuse of power can occur in any family or intimate relationship. In this reading, excerpted from *Family Violence across the Lifespan: An Introduction* (2005), Barnett et al. provide an overview of what elder abuse is, the prevalence of abuse, and the characteristics of abused elders and of those persons who are abusing the elderly. After reviewing several decades of research, they found that elder abuse is much more common than previously thought, with five times more cases going unreported than those that are reported. Even with some increased attention in recent years, many people still do not recognize elder abuse, and unlike other types of family violence, elder abuse is more easily hidden from authorities because the elderly may not interact with the public. Clearly, much more research and public attention needs to be focused on this egregious family problem.

REFERENCES

Barnett, Ola, Cindy L. Miller-Perrin, and Robin D. Perrin. 2005. *Family Violence across the Lifespan: An Introduction.* Thousand Oaks, CA: Sage Publications.

FBI. 1991. *Uniform Crime Reports for the United States.* Washington, DC: U.S. Department of Justice.

Gelles, Richard J. 1993. "Through a Sociological Lens: Social Structure and Family Violence." Pp. 31–46 in *Current Controversies on Family Violence,* edited by Richard J. Gelles and Donileen R. Loseke. Thousand Oaks, CA: Sage Publications.

Jang, Deeana, Debbie Lee, and Rachel Morello-Frosch. 1990. "Domestic Violence in the Immigrant and Refugee Community." *Response,* Issue 77, 13(4): 2–6.

Kurz, Demie. 1998. "Old Problems and New Directions in the Study of Violence against Women." Pp. 197–208 in *Issues in Intimate Violence,* edited by Raquel Kennedy Bergen. Thousand Oaks, CA: Sage Publications.

Renzetti, Claire M. 1992. *Violent Betrayal: Partner Abuse in Lesbian Relationships.* Thousand Oaks, CA: Sage Publications.

Wardell, L., C. Gillespie, and A. Leffler. 1983. "Science and Violence against Women." Pp. 69–84 in *The Dark Side of Families: Current Family Violence Research,* edited by D. Finkelhor, Richard Gelles, H. Hotaling, and Murray Straus. Beverly Hills, CA: Sage Publications.

36

GENDER, DIVERSITY, AND VIOLENCE
Extending the Feminist Framework

KERSTI A. YLLÖ

Violence within the family is as complex as it is disturbing. Compressed into one assault are our deepest human emotions, our sense of self, our power, and our hopes and fears about love and intimacy, as well as the social construction of marriage and its place within the larger society. Despite the issue's complexity, the most fundamental feminist insight into all of this is quite simple: Domestic violence cannot be adequately understood unless gender and power are taken into account.

Looking at domestic violence through a feminist lens is not a simple matter, however. Developing a theoretical, empirical, political, and personal understanding of violence requires us to analyze its complex gendered nature. This involves the psychologies of perpetrator and victim and their interactions, gendered expectations about family relationships and dynamics, and the patriarchal ideology and structure of society within which individuals and relationships are embedded. Increasingly, feminists of color are pointing to the important impact of race-ethnicity and class in shaping all of these dimensions. Although there is a range of feminist perspectives, there is a broad consensus that family violence is profoundly shaped by gender and power.

Feminist understanding of domestic violence has its roots in social action. Feminist academic work, theoretical analyses, and methodological debates flow out of feminist practice. The feminist perspective, with its origins in social movements, is strong on practical programs and critiques of prevailing perspectives. But it is not yet a fully developed, distinctive framework for the explanation of domestic violence, and in this limitation we are in good company, for no single view is complete. Although a feminist lens may not be sufficient for seeing the full picture of domestic violence, I believe that it is a necessary lens without which any other analytic perspective is flawed. Gender and power are key elements of domestic violence, whether one takes a sociological or a psychological perspective.

After briefly reviewing the gender and power analysis so central to the feminist perspective, I turn to one of the pressing issues feminists are now addressing: a fuller, more nuanced incorporation of race-ethnicity and class into our analysis. The feminist focus on women as a victimized class has obscured the diversity among women (as well as among the men who perpetrate the violence). I point to new directions in feminist theory that, I believe, hold the potential to move us to a more inclusive and more powerful analysis.

Domestic Violence, Gender, and Control

As social constructionists point out, the phenomena we study (including physical violence) are not simply "out there" to be discovered through direct observation. Rather, definitions of problems are socially created through ongoing controversy as well as collaboration. Observation is always theory laden, and this is especially true when the phenomenon under scrutiny is as politically and emotionally fraught as violence (see Yllö, 1988).

The focus we choose for our work (including our theoretical formulations, our empirical research, our policy recommendations, and our social activism) is crucially important. . . . The family [is] the overarching rubric for defining the problem. It then falls to feminists, who tend to focus on *domestic violence* (a term that has become synonymous with battering), to explain why our analysis is largely limited to woman abuse. In the *Handbook of Marriage and the Family*, for example, Suzanne Steinmetz (1987) dismisses feminist theory as "constricted" and of "limited utility as a theory of family violence" (p. 749).

An important question that has been largely overlooked during the 30-year explosion of the family violence field is whether "family violence" is a unitary phenomenon that requires an overarching theory. I argue that feminist analysis has made an enormous contribution to our understanding of wife abuse, yet it has produced relatively less insight into child abuse or elder abuse. However, I do not regard this as evidence that feminist theory is constricted, since it has also made significant contributions to our understanding of stranger rape, acquaintance rape, sexual harassment in the workplace, and murder. Further, this analysis of violence against women (whether in the family or outside it) rests within even broader feminist analysis of all aspects of women's lives in patriarchal society. A feminist analysis of violence connects it to the pervasive sexism in our norms, values, and institutions.

When a man rapes his wife because he feels that it is her "wifely duty" to submit, this is not just a conflict of individual interests, as a sociological analysis might contend. This conflict is deeply gendered, and the husband's perceived entitlement has strong institutional support. When a man with a personality disorder batters his wife when she burns his dinner or tries to get a job, our understanding of the violence is incomplete if we deny the gendered aspects of his controlling behavior. To say simply that domestic violence is about gender and power may seem like nothing more than a sound bite. But it is far more than that—it is a concise expression of a complex body of feminist theory and research. A full discussion of this work would fill volumes; in this [reading] I can only outline the coercive control view of domestic violence.

In her review essay on feminism and family research, Myra Marx Ferree (1990) states that "feminists agree that male dominance within families is part of a wider system of male power, is neither natural nor inevitable, and occurs at women's cost" (p. 866). Feminist work in family violence explores and articulates the ways in which violence against women in the home is a critical component of the system of male power. Violence grows out of inequality within marriage (and other intimate relations that are modeled on marriage) and reinforces male dominance and female subordination within the home and outside it. In other words, violence against women (whether in the form of sexual harassment at work, rape by a date, or a beating at home) is a part of male control (Dobash and Dobash 1998; Hanmer and Maynard 1987). It is not gender neutral any more than the economic division of labor or the institution of marriage is gender neutral.

The conceptualization of violence as coercive control was not deduced from an abstract theoretical model. Rather, it grew inductively out of the day-to-day work of battered women and activists who struggled to make sense of the victimization they saw. As the shelter movement grew and survivors and activists joined together to discuss their experiences, a clearer vision of what domestic violence is and how to challenge it emerged.

A control model of domestic violence, known as the "Power and Control Wheel," developed by the Domestic Abuse Intervention Project in Duluth, Minnesota, is shown in Figure 1. This model has been used across the country in batterers' groups, support groups, and training sessions, as well as in empirical studies (see Shepard and Pence 1999). It provides a valuable, concise framework for seeing the interconnections between violence and other forms of coercive control or *control tactics*. The wheel connects physical and sexual violence to the hub of power and control with a number of "spokes": minimization and denial, intimidation, isolation, emotional abuse, economic abuse, use of children, threats, and assertion of male privilege.

When one looks at these control tactics in a bit more detail, through research based on extensive interviews with battered women and batterers (Jones and Schechter 1992; Ptacek 1988), the close-up picture of domestic violence that develops is one of domination. The following is an interview excerpt from my study of women who were physically abused during their pregnancies.

S., a 31-year-old white woman, describes the control and violence in her marriage that eventually resulted in a miscarriage:

> *I didn't even realize he was gaining control and I was too dumb to know any better. . . . He was gaining control bit by bit until he was checking my pantyhose when I'd come home from the supermarket to see if they were inside out. . . . He'd time me. He'd check the mileage on the car. . . . I was living like a prisoner. . . . One day I was at Zayers with him . . . and I was looking at a sweater. He insisted*

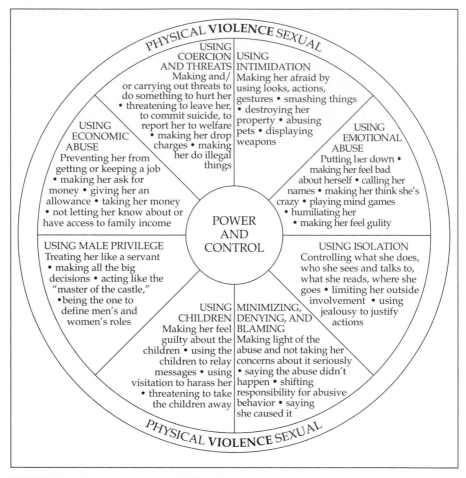

FIGURE 1   Power and Control Wheel

Source: Reprinted with permission from Minnesota Program Development, Inc., Domestic Abuse Intervention Project, 206 W. 4th Street, Duluth, MN 55806.

> *I was looking at a guy. I didn't even know there was a guy in the area, because it got to the point that I, I had to walk like I had horse-blinders on. . . . You don't look anybody in the eye. You don't look up because you are afraid.*

At one point, S. was insulted by a friend of her husband's, and she was furious. She recalls:

> *I told him, who the hell was he? And I threw a glass of root beer in his face. My husband gave me a back hand, so I just went upstairs to the bedroom and got into a nightgown. And he kept telling me to come downstairs and I said "No—just leave me alone." . . . He come up and went right through the door. Knocked the whole top panel off the door and got into the room. Ripped the nightgown right off my back, just bounced me off every wall in that bedroom. Then he threw*

me down the stairs and . . . outside in the snow and just kept kicking me and saying it was too soon for me to be pregnant. . . . His friend was almost rooting him on.

The coercive control model of domestic violence is an important theoretical alternative to psychological explanations focused only on personality disorders and the sociology of interpersonal conflict. It identifies violence as a tactic of entitlement and power that is deeply gendered, rather than as a symptom of a disorder or as a conflict tactic that is individual and gender neutral. It has deepened our understanding of family violence in substantial and significant ways. However, it is not the final analysis. Although it provides a potent description of violence and its context, it should be seen as the beginning, not the completion of our work.

Commonality and Diversity

One area where feminist theory has fallen short concerns the racial-ethnic and class diversity among women. Drawing on radical feminist analysis, we have conceptualized women as a class, oppressed in a dichotomous sex-gender system. During the last decade, important work by feminists of color have challenged this view as simplistic and limiting (Crenshaw 1994; Richie 1996). This conceptualization is constricted by what Adrienne Rich (1979) called "white solipsism" — a type of tunnel vision in which white experience is assumed to describe human experience.

We are currently undergoing a period of rich intellectual and political debate about the interconnections among gender, race, and class and their implications for understanding violence. I suggest that feminist theory stands out among the different family violence frameworks in addressing these issues. Race is far more than a variable affecting rates of violence or a factor to be controlled. Like gender, race-ethnicity infuses all aspects of family life and its social context. I next touch upon promising theoretical work, mostly by women of color, that needs more attention and integration into our analyses and practices.

An important concept for analyzing diversity and violence is the idea of intersectionality, developed by legal scholar Kimberlé Crenshaw (1993, 1994). She makes the point that

> although violence is a common issue among women, such violence usually occurs within a specific context — that often varies considerably depending on the race, class, and other social characteristics of the woman. . . . These characteristics can be better understood and addressed through a framework that links them to broader structures of subordination which intersect sometimes in fairly predictable ways. (1993:15)

Further, she suggests that we consider both structural and political intersectionality. Structurally, the intersection of race, class, and gender creates particular circumstances for different battered women. Deciding how to respond to abuse is very different for a Latina who is trying to establish legal residence through her husband than it is for an employed white woman who is a U.S. citizen. Politically, intersectionality has implications for activism and intervention. Crenshaw urges us to supersede identity politics and the notion of unitary groups in conflict (blacks versus whites, males versus females, gays versus straights, and so on) and to recognize each of these groups as multidimensional within themselves and, at their best, effective coalitions. So, women can be a coalition of gay, straight, Latina, middle class, poor, African American, white, and so on with structural and political commonalties and differences. A feminist theory that emphasizes only the commonality of gender erases the texture of women's lives and is less useful than it might be. Feminist scholars and activists who are mindful of these inter-sections can develop theory, research, and interventions to move us forward.

In *The Color of Privilege: Three Blasphemies on Race and Feminism* (1996), Aida Hurtado offers a useful and challenging framework for considering intersectionality, although she does not address domestic violence directly. She develops a theory of gender subordination as relational, explaining why subordination is experienced differently by white women and women of color. It is often tempting to see these as differences in attitude—as simple reflections of culture (for example, different values regarding family)—or social location (the greater likelihood that women of color live in poverty). Hurtado argues that the theoretically important factor is women's *relation-ship* to white male power. She points out that women of color have been exploited for their labor and sexuality, yet they have been rejected as legiti-mate reproducers of white men's offspring. White women, in contrast, have been seduced into compliance because they are needed to biologically reproduce the next generation of the power structure (p. vii). White women, especially of the upper and middle classes, live *within* circles of power and are intimately connected to those who subordinate them.

Hurtado's theory is particularly useful in an analysis of violence in the home, because she helps us see how feminist theory to date has been myopic. The political consciousness that has informed the women's move-ment grew out of an examination of the public-private distinction and the realization by white, educated women that gender oppression occurred in the intimacy of their own homes. The radical slogan "The personal is politi-cal," according to Hurtado, "identifies and rejects the public-private distinc-tion as a tool by which women are excluded from public participation while the daily tyrannies of men are protected from public scrutiny" (p. 18). From this viewpoint, battering is a prime example of this intimate oppression, and much of feminist activism has attempted to bring it to public attention, to sanction it through the criminal justice system, and to offer women refuge from their homes.

This work has undoubtedly been important and has saved lives. It has, however, assumed that the private-public split applies similarly to all women. Hurtado contends that "the political consciousness of women of color stems from an awareness that the public is personally political" (p. 18).

People of color have not had the luxury of a private realm. Through welfare programs, public housing, sterilization programs, police presence, and disproportionate arrest and incarceration rates, public systems of social control invade their private realm. Poor women of color are acutely aware of their distance from the white male power structure that may evict or deport them or imprison their sons. Their activism, then, more often focuses on these public issues rather than the subordination or abuse they may experience from their intimate partners who are, otherwise, relatively powerless. Their experiences with the racism of the criminal justice system and other service providers make them reluctant to use the same avenues of redress that white battered women turn to.

In contrast, women who are physically integrated into the centers of power have a very different experience of gender subordination. Thus white feminists have been more concerned with expectations of docility, gender socialization, housework, body image, and intimate violence. These observations have been made before; however, the implication usually has been that some essential difference exists between the submissive, white women victimized within their homes and the strong, black women heading families. A relational theory of gender subordination offers a clear structural explanation for the differences: They reflect women's connection to or distance from white male power.

As Hurtado points out, the women's movement is the only political movement in history to develop its own clinical approach—feminist therapy (p. 18). There is a real question about the extent to which therapy, which deals with oppression at the individual and interpersonal level, can address the needs of all women. So far, feminist therapy has focused heavily on issues of intimacy with white men and has been utilized largely by those women who are struggling with the seduction of men in power. Yet, feminist therapy, like feminist theory, is addressing the challenges posed by feminists of color who question its assumptions (Bograd 1999). This is not to argue that feminist therapy has not made important contributions, but rather that we should not assume that approaches of value for some women will be of value for all women. Further, a truly radical feminist therapy will help to transcend the divisions between those women privileged by their association with white male power and those distanced and oppressed by it.

The discussion in this [reading] has been largely about gender subordination and rather little about family violence. Nevertheless, I hope that the implications for our work, both scholarly and applied, are becoming clear. The feminist approach to violence will become more analytically powerful and more practically useful if we add to its depth and complexity by addressing the intersection of race-ethnicity, class, and gender. It is not enough to include these factors as variables in models that ignore the structural conditions of oppression. Nor is it enough to invoke "race-class-gender" as a political mantra in superficial analyses. There is an enormous amount of intellectual, political, and practical work to be done to reach more synthetic understandings and solutions.

Research and Intervention at the Intersection

The feminist analysis of intimate violence to date has emphasized women's commonality. The point feminists have made over and over again has been that *all* women are vulnerable to such violence, which cuts across racial, ethnic, and class lines. This position has proven to be very effective politically precisely because of the relational character of gender subordination that Hurtado identifies. Whether we're training judges, police, or medical doctors, or lobbying for stronger criminal justice sanctions or the Violence against Women Act, we have made the point that the victims can be "*your* sisters, daughters, and friends." We have seen that Social Security is sacred, while welfare is vilified. Therefore, we have emphasized the connections to the white men in power and downplayed violence in poor communities of color because we knew that funding would not be forthcoming if victims were seen as "other." Political favor flows more easily to "worthy" (read white, middle-class) victims. Using the strategy, feminists have successfully changed laws, policies, and procedures and gained funding for services that have helped large numbers of women.

However, Crenshaw (1994:105) points out that there is a thin line between debunking the stereotypical beliefs that only poor and minority women are battered and pushing them aside to focus on victims for whom mainstream politicians and media are more likely to express concern.

Unfortunately, one of the unintended consequences of this approach is that the differences among women have been "white-washed" and that those who are most victimized have been pushed aside. The reality that poor women (who are disproportionately women of color) experience more extensive and severe violence coupled with fewer options tends to become lost.

Angela Browne and her colleagues (Browne and Bassuk 1997) have done important work on the relationship between poverty and intimate violence. Their well-designed study of housed and homeless poor women revealed horrific rates of physical and sexual abuse. The researchers found that an astounding 83 percent of very low-income mothers had been victims of severe physical violence and/or sexual abuse during their lifetimes. Homelessness and substance abuse were closely connected problems. The enormity of these women's troubles can be more fully understood through such examinations of class, poverty, and the welfare system; a gender analysis alone is inadequate.

The gender-race-class intersection was an unexpected finding in a study by Eileen Abel (1999) that compared female "victims" with women who had been adjudicated as "batterers." The study was based on a sample of women drawn from three domestic violence victim service programs ($N = 51$) and three batterer intervention programs ($N = 67$) in the state of Florida. There were few statistical differences between the "victims" and "batterers" in exposure to violence *by their partners*, except that the women identified as batterers were *more* likely to have been threatened and forced to have sex than their victim counterparts. The women who had been labeled as batterers were also more likely to have previously sought medical treatment (62 percent versus 38 percent), whereas victims were more likely to have previously used domestic violence victim services (67 percent versus 33 percent). Abel discovered another important difference between the two groups: Women of color were overrepresented in the batterers group (42 percent nonwhite) compared to the victims group (26 percent). The mean income of women in the batterers group was $26,000; in the victims group it was more than $46,000. So, despite higher levels of victimization and injury, poorer and minority women are more likely to be mandated into batterer treatment through the criminal justice system, while victim services are more likely to offer support to white, financially more stable women. While the Abel study offered no details of the women's use of violence or the process by which they came to be in the two groups, her research does raise questions about the impact of class and race on battered women's experiences with state intervention and social services.

The race-gender intersection also proved critical in a study of 1,870 partner violence reports to police by Bourg and Stock (in Marin and Russo 1999). They found that, overall, men were more likely to be identified as batterers; however women who were so identified were more likely to be charged with a serious crime. In particular, "black women were more likely to be arrested on felony charges (84%) than white men were (19%) *for similar behavior*" (p. 23, emphasis mine). Given the overall high arrest rates in communities of color, it is not surprising that black women are arrested and charged disproportionately.

These studies provide support for the proposition that individuals' distance from the white male power structure shapes their chances of abuse as well as the response of social services and the criminal justice system. However, these studies offer just a glimpse of how race intersects with gender in the institutional response to violence, since race was not their main focus. One study that does take this intersection as its central concern is Beth Richie's *Compelled to Crime: The Gender Entrapment of Battered Black Women* (1995). Her research on battered women jailed on Rikers Island, New York, reveals just how complex the race-class-gender intersection is. The battered African American women she interviewed were entrapped in a series of paradoxes. For example, Richie found that the battered women in her sample were more likely to come from stable families in which their parents had high expectations of them. These women struggled to maintain relationships despite ongoing abuse because they were so committed to traditional gender norms and family values. Unfortunately for these women, these efforts led to illegal activities in response to violence and coercion by their male partners (p. 4). Women from more disadvantaged and unstable families were more likely to walk away from violent partners because they had few expectations of an enduring family.

Compounding what Richie refers to as the battered women's "gender entrapment" in their abusive relationships are their experiences with social services and the criminal justice system. Compared to the white battered women in the study, the African American women were less likely to turn to social services for help. Further, none wanted their partners arrested or jailed, whereas the white women had often turned to the police for help. Here, Hurtado's (1996) emphasis on distance from the white male power structure is illuminating. The institutions that feminists have worked hard to make responsive to battered women have certainly changed, but those changes seem to better serve white women rather than all women.

Richie's (1996) study serves as a warning to those who ignore race or who might too easily assume that the effects of race, class, and gender are simply additive. Although Richie focused on the most extreme cases, her nuanced analysis of the intersection of race, class, and gender serves as a model of feminist research that can guide us in further work on the full spectrum of family violence.

Looking Forward

Feminists have made enormous contributions to our understanding of and interventions in intimate violence. Gender and coercive control remain critical conceptual tools in this work. The challenge before us is to deepen and extend our analysis. The centrality of gender is the subject of as much controversy as ever. From researchers using the Conflict Tactics Scales comes the assertion that women are as violent as men in the home. Antifeminist activists use these data to champion an artificial "equality" of abuse that erases the terror and injury of battering and undermines programs designed to intervene with violent men and support battered women. In response, feminists must work hard to elucidate women's shared subjection. We must not relent in asserting women's commonality of experience with coercive control. The Power and Control Wheel (which has been translated into dozens of languages and dialects) speaks to battered women of every color in disparate communities around the globe.

Yet, as surely as we must assert women's commonality in response to the antifeminist backlash, we must recognize, understand, and draw on the power of the diversity among us. A feminist analysis that assumes gender oppression is a unitary phenomenon will fall far short of its transformative potential. The social location of a black battered woman or an abused illegal immigrant is profoundly different from that of a beaten middle-class white woman—despite the subjection of all three to the coercive control of their partners. These differences are not essential to racial or ethnic groups. Rather, they reflect cultural differences, structural inequalities, and our differing relationships to white male power.

Doing feminist work in this field is, in many ways, more challenging than ever. It is certainly true that we have been heard and have more funding and more influence than in the early years of the movement. We have succeeded in making what was once a private trouble into a public issue. Feminist research and activism have influenced institutional realms from the police and courts to medical, mental health, and social services. After more than

25 years of work, we are at a point where the once glaring indifference to violence against women has been confronted and, in many places, transformed. There have been dramatic changes in law, policy, protocols, and practice. In a recent address titled "The Color of Violence against Women," Angela Davis (2000) pays tribute to the anti-violence movement that has criminalized the once-private act of battering. Yet she challenges us by arguing that "given the racist and patriarchal patterns of the state, it is difficult to envision the state as the holder of solutions to the problem of violence against women of color." A critical task now is to develop more of what some have called "culturally sensitive" or "culturally competent" analysis and interventions. We must remember that this cultural sensitivity must be linked to challenges of structural inequalities and power relations. The work before us is, in many ways, more complex and difficult than what we have accomplished thus far.

The final point I make is not about feminism or violence per se, but about the nature of the debate and controversy around these issues. I am disturbed by the deep cleavages that have resulted from attacks, counterattacks, and highbrow name calling. Feminist scholars and activists with strong convictions are labeled ideologues, "feminist fundamentalists" (Erickson 1992), and "dogmatic." At the same time, feminists deepen the chasm by dismissing nonfeminist insights too quickly and hastily deciding who "gets it" and who doesn't. In the early years of family violence research and the battered women's movement, these divisions were largely focused on gender politics. More recently, challenges from scholars and activists of color (some feminists, some not) are pushing us forward toward more inclusive and transformative work. Our contentious history should give us pause. White feminists taking up the challenge to address race must recognize the potential dangers of this work. As Jim Ptacek (1999) notes, "In a fiercely divided society, public discussions of class, race, and violence entail risks. Wittingly or unwittingly, those who name these interconnections arouse powerful racist images, even when their goals are to displace them" (p. 19).

One way that white feminists can further the work on the race-class-gender intersection is to interrogate our own racial privilege (Lewis 1997). "Culturally sensitive" theories and interventions focused on people of color should not be seen as alternatives to the prevailing work, which is somehow assumed to be culturally neutral. Race is not a black issue any more than gender is a women's issue.

I believe that our future work cannot evade these difficult matters. Openness and respectful listening to different viewpoints will be essential. Careful consideration of potential unintended consequences of our work will be more important than ever. Recognition of the power of the coalitions (rather than the divisions) among us will be crucial. It will not be easy to answer Angela Davis's (2000) question, "How do we develop analyses and organizing strategies against violence against women that acknowledge the race of gender and the gender of race?" It will be difficult. But in addressing this question, I believe, lies the radical potential of feminism.

ENDNOTE

Author's Note: Thanks are given to Michelle Harris for her comments and suggestions.

REFERENCES

Abel, E. 1999. "Comparing the Social Service Utilization, Exposure to Violence, and Trauma Symptomology of Domestic Violence 'Victims' and Female 'Batterers.'" Paper presented at the Seventh International Family Violence Research Conference, University of New Hampshire.

Bograd, M. 1999. "Strengthening Domestic Violence Theories: Intersections of Race, Class, Sexual Orientation, and Gender." *Journal of Marital and Family Therapy* 25: 275–89.

Browne, A. and S. Bassuk. 1997. "Intimate Violence in the Lives of Homeless and Poor Housed Women." *American Journal of Orthopsychiatry* 67 (2): 261–78.

Crenshaw, K. 1993. "Race, Gender, and Violence against Women." Pp. 230–32 in *Family Matters: Readings on Family Lives and the Law,* edited by M. Minow. New York: New Press.

Crenshaw, K. 1994. "Mapping the Margins: Intersectionality, Identity Politics, and Violence against Women of Color." Pp. 93–118 in *The Public Nature of Private Violence,* edited by M. Fineman and R. Mykitiuk. New York: Routledge.

Davis, A. 2000. "The Color of Violence against Women." Keynote address of the Color of Violence Conference at the University of California at Santa Cruz. Retrieved April 29, 2004 (www.arc.org/C_Lines/CL Archive/story3_3_02.html).

Dobash, R. E. and R. P. Dobash. 1998. *Rethinking Violence against Women.* Thousand Oaks, CA: Sage.

Erickson, B. 1992. "Feminist Fundamentalism: Reactions to Avis, Kaufman, and Bograd." *Journal of Marital and Family Therapy* 18:263–67.

Ferree, M. M. 1990. "Beyond Separate Spheres: Feminism and Family Research." *Journal of Marriage and the Family* 52:866–84.

Hanmer, J. and M. Maynard. 1987. *Women, Violence, and Social Control.* Atlantic Highlands, NJ: Humanities.

Hurtado, A. 1996. *The Color of Privilege: Three Blasphemies on Race and Feminism.* Ann Arbor: University of Michigan Press.

Jones, A. and S. Schechter. 1992. *When Love Goes Wrong.* New York: HarperCollins.

Lewis, A. 1997. "Theorizing Whiteness: Interrogating Racial Privilege." Working Paper No. 568, Center for Research on Social Organization, University of Michigan.

Marin, A. and N. Russo. 1999. "Feminist-Perspectives on Male Violence against Women." Pp. 18–35 in *What Causes Men's Violence against Women?,* edited by M. Harway and J. O'Neil. Thousand Oaks, CA: Sage.

Ptacek, J. 1988. "Why Do Men Batter Their Wives?" Pp. 133–57 in *Feminist Perspectives on Wife Abuse,* edited by K. Yllö and M. Bograd. Newbury Park, CA: Sage.

——. 1999. *Battered Women in the Courtroom.* Boston: Northeastern University Press.

Rich, A. 1979. *On Lies, Secrets, and Silence: Selected Prose, 1966–1978.* New York: Norton.

Richie, B. E. 1995. *Compelled to Crime: The Gender Entrapment of Battered Black Women.* New York: Routledge.

——. 1996. "Battered Black Women: A Challenge for the Black Community." *Black Scholar* 16 (2): 40–44.

Shepard, M. and E. Pence. eds. 1999. *Coordinating Community Response: Lessons from Duluth and Beyond.* Thousand Oaks, CA: Sage.

Steinmetz, S. K. 1987. "Family Violence: Past, Present, and Future." Pp. 725–65 in *Handbook of Marriage and the Family,* edited by M. B. Sussman and S. K. Steinmetz. New York: Plenum.

Yllö, K. 1988. "Political and Methodological Debates in Wife Abuse Research." Pp. 28–50 in *Feminist Perspectives on Wife Abuse,* edited by K. Yllö and M. Bograd. Newbury Park, CA: Sage.

37

LIFTING THE VEIL OF SECRECY

Domestic Violence against South Asian Women in the United States

SATYA P. KRISHNAN • MALAHAT BAIG–AMIN
LOUISA GILBERT • NABILA EL–BASSEL • ANNE WATERS

I would always be in fear. Even though I worked, I had to be home at a certain time. Even if I was five minutes late or if there was a traffic jam or something, I could not tell him that. I was in fear all the time. I was in fear that I would lose my mind if I go home late. I constantly made plans to be home on time.

— AN INTERVIEWEE'S COMMENTS

The image of a woman being abused by those who claim to love and honor her is horrifying. However, such abuse is one that many of us have heard of or, perhaps, experienced in our own lives. Domestic violence has been a part of our living landscape since the beginning of time and is still a significant component of many women's lives. Despite their abusive domestic circumstances, many women strive to work quietly, raise children, care for their families, and try to establish a "normal" existence in society.

Owing to the efforts of many dedicated community activists, the prevalence of domestic violence among South Asian women in the United States is no longer a secret. The efforts of these advocates have been crucial in bringing acknowledgment, recognition, and understanding to the issues surrounding domestic violence in South Asian immigrant communities. As the number of immigrants to the United States increases, the endeavors of these activists have begun to shed light on a neglected public health issue in a singularly underserved group, the South Asian American community.[1] Our interests in the issues of domestic violence among South Asian women stem from our research interests in immigrant women's health issues in general and our commitment to [ending] violence against women. . . .

Violence in Intimate Relationships: Issues in the Larger Society

Women often experience their greatest risk of violence not from acquaintances and strangers but from their intimate male partners.[2] Domestic violence is one of the most significant causes of injury to women, affecting about two million women in the United States every year. Today, domestic violence is being referred to as a "national epidemic" by physicians, public health experts, and politicians and is slowly becoming a part of the public consciousness in the United States.[3] Domestic violence, specifically intentional physical or nonphysical harm, or both, perpetrated by an intimate partner against a woman is pervasive and often an unrecognized cause of chronic physical and mental health problems.[4] These chronic health problems include such physical traumas as multiple contusions, fractures, bruises, bites, as well as burns on the face, head, abdomen, or genitals. In addition to direct injuries, victims may also suffer from chronic stress-related disorders such as gastric distress, lower back and pelvic pain, headaches, insomnia, and hyperventilation.[5] A variety of psychological and mental health symptoms such as anxiety disorders and panic attacks, depression, sense of helplessness and declining coping skills, self-blame, as well as lowered self-esteem may further accompany these physical impairments.[6]

Domestic Violence in South Asian Communities

The recent recognition of domestic violence in the United States and around the world as an extensive and long-existing phenomenon is largely due to the global efforts of battered women themselves. It is undeniable that the activities of community-based agencies and women's organizations have brought increasing policy, media, and research attention to intimate violence.[7] As the issues of domestic violence move from the private to the public arena in the larger community, a similar trend is reflected among South Asians in the United States.[8] Two factors appear to influence this shift: (1) the emergence and investment of South Asian women's groups and community-based organizations such as Manavi, Apna Ghar, and Sakhi for South Asian women and (2) the increased willingness of South Asian battered women to tell their stories to formal support systems.

In fact, South Asian community organizations and women's groups have played a pivotal role in bringing recognition to domestic violence within their communities. While they serve as safe havens for individual battered women, these agencies simultaneously aim to bring about social change by focusing attention on domestic violence itself. Generally, individual care comes in the form of counseling and emotional support, as well as intervention during emergencies. Social change, on the other hand, is attempted through publicizing particular issues of South Asian women in abusive relationships, training social and health-care workers, and influencing as well as improving legislation regarding domestic violence. Consequently, the visibility of women's groups and community-based organizations, and the willingness of South Asian women to talk about their experiences of violence, have begun to construct a clearer and more realistic picture of women's lives in South Asian immigrant communities.

Of the immigrants living in the United States, 2.8 percent are Asian, and the 1990 census indicates that a million are South Asians—Bangladeshi, Indian, Pakistani, Nepali, and Sri Lankan.[9] One estimate suggests that the incidence of domestic violence in these communities is about 20 to 25 percent.[10] However, this may be an underestimation because domestic violence cases in these communities often are underreported owing to underutilization of existing social and health services.[11] Issues such as immigration status, language barriers, lack of knowledge about helping services and organizations, social and cultural barriers, fear and isolation, as well as concerns of safety for themselves and their children, are often responsible for this underutilization. This constellation of issues can have a profound effect on how South Asian women respond to violence in intimate relationships. These issues, real and perceived, add to the vulnerability of battered South Asian women and influence the way they address violence in their personal lives.

Despite the prevalence of domestic violence among South Asian women living in the United States, little systematic understanding and documentation of the problem exists.[12] A lack of comprehension of the cultural and social factors that define domestic violence, difficulties in reaching out to victims, and the continued reluctance of many women to seek help all contribute to perpetuating intimate violence in our communities. However, current changing conditions within South Asian communities suggest the need for research approaches that can systematically record the scope and particularities of that violence. Such research will also provide better understanding of the factors and correlates of intimate violence, so that culturally appropriate and effective prevention and intervention strategies can be designed.

In this [reading], we hope to lift the veil of secrecy shrouding domestic violence by offering realistic views of South Asian women's experiences, concerns, needs, solutions, and hopes through the words, thoughts, ideas, and courage of the women themselves.

Domestic Violence Research and Focus Groups

In our work, we have used focus groups extensively to explore, discuss, and elaborate on a variety of issues concerning domestic violence among South Asian women living in the United States. A focus group discussion, very simply, is a qualitative method of gathering information from a group of eight to fifteen people who have at least one interest in common.[13] We chose to use focus groups over other methods because of their comfortable, safe, and sharing format. We observed that while participants told their own stories in these groups, they also heard from other women in similar circumstances and developed a sense of kinship and support for one another.

We conducted several focus groups in Chicago and in New York City, where the local South Asian women's organizations assisted us in contacting and recruiting participants for groups. Between five and ten South Asian (Indian, Pakistani, and Bangladeshi) women participated in each of the discussion groups. Some of the issues explored during the group sessions included

- Personal, family, and community definitions and perceptions of domestic violence and its consequences;
- The type, context, and circumstances in which violence occurred;
- Effects and consequences of this violence on the women themselves and their children, and on other aspects of women's lives;
- Personal, family, and community norms, attitudes, perceptions, and acceptance of domestic violence;
- The issues of social support, both formal and informal, and the types of coping strategies used;
- Factors that perpetuate domestic violence in women's lives and those that alleviate the problem;
- Barriers to care- and help-seeking behaviors and the women's suggestions for change; and
- Whether migration has affected women's domestic violence experiences.

The focus group discussions were led by two facilitators who helped to moderate the discussions among participants. For South Asian women who were still in abusive situations, these discussion sessions proved to be "safe havens" where they felt comfortable about articulating their experiences of domestic violence and discussing a variety of other related issues. Furthermore, these discussions also appeared to be "therapeutic" and "empowering," as the participants themselves indicated that they welcomed the opportunity to talk about their lives and the violence and meet others in situations similar to theirs.

South Asian Women Define Domestic Violence

The recent interest in domestic violence has fueled a debate about what constitutes the phenomenon. Experts, politicians, activists, advocates, and academics have suggested varying definitions, including those rooted in feminist perspectives, those from the family preservation point of view, and others from the ecological standpoint. An important missing ingredient in this ongoing argument is the viewpoint of battered women, in this case, South Asian women in abusive relationships. Although their definitions may differ from those of the professionals, the South Asian women participating in our focus groups knew intuitively what was "not right" or what was "wrong" in their domestic lives. Meena, a young Indian woman who recently moved to the United States, had a very simple definition of violence and declared, "Beating is domestic violence."[14]

While Meena focused on the physical aspects of domestic violence, Kismat, a Pakistani mother of four, emphasized the psychological aspects of such abuse. She focused on the constant lack of respect from her spouse, which constituted domestic violence to her. This lack of respect often translated into jealousy and suspicion and led to various types of abuse and violence, including physical beatings. She said, "[Domestic violence] is when husbands do not give respect to their wives and are always suspicious. The persons who live with each other must have respect for each other."

Definitions of spousal violence offered by the women participating in the focus groups were not limited to physical or overt forms of abuse only. Their notion of ill treatment included emotional and verbal abuse, as well as subtle mistreatments such as standing around to overhear conversations with friends and family members. Munni, an Indian woman living in the Chicago area for a number of years, provided quite a comprehensive definition of domestic violence: "Emotional abuse is domestic violence. And verbal abuse, being suspicious, beating, and not supporting financially is domestic violence. Sometimes men think that they should treat women like a pair of shoes."

These interpretations of domestic violence indicate that the South Asian women in the focus groups understood intuitively that their experiences of physical, emotional, and psychological abuse were not normative. They were also able to distinguish among various types of domestic violence such as physical, psychological, emotional, verbal, and sexual. This distinction affected the consequences of abuse, as well as the demands on the women's coping skills. Clearly, these women recognized abuse in their relationships, even when it was perpetrated in subtle and quiet ways.

Although the women were quite willing to discuss their overall situations, cultural as well as community influences were obvious in the emphasis they placed on certain types of abuse and their reluctance to discuss others. For example, many of the focus group participants felt that verbal, psychological, and emotional abuse were more pervasive and therefore critical in their lives but felt that, unlike physical abuse, these were harder to document and explain. Furthermore, all women were significantly more reticent about broaching the subject of sexual abuse.

Another culture-specific aspect was that the women did not necessarily blame themselves for the violence in their domestic relationships but considered it more a consequence of "bad fate." This ability to contextualize domestic violence in terms of bad fate gave the participants the patience, tolerance, and dignity they needed to cope with it. Sheba, an Indian mother of two grown-up children, explained: "I don't think it was my fault at all. This was my fate. I just thought that this was part of my life. You know, no one's life is perfect. There's one thing or another in everyone's life. And I just look at this [domestic violence] as something that I had to tolerate."

Obedient Daughters, Faithful Wives, and Caring Mothers: Sexual Abuse in Conjugal Relationships

All of the participating women were very reluctant to acknowledge, include, and discuss sexual abuse as an integral part of domestic violence. Sexual abuse was by far the hardest topic to introduce in the discussions, and the women even refused to elaborate on the reasons for this discomfort. One can only speculate about their rationale in terms of the women's lack of ease with issues of sex, sexuality, and self-disclosure. Although they perceived the focus groups to be "safe" and "nonjudgmental," the majority of women were conscious of the constraints of their social norms. They were socialized to be "obedient daughters," "faithful wives," and "caring mothers," and these social norms required conformity to certain behavioral standards: subservience, propriety, and putting others' needs ahead of their own. These expectations ruled out any discussion regarding sex, pleasure, and personal enjoyment. The fact that they had moved into the public arena with their stories of domestic violence was already a great departure from tradition, and to discuss sexual abuse, another taboo issue, would have further taxed their coping skills.

Decision to Stay: Insights into a Process

Recent research indicates that women's length of stay in violent relationships varies with ethnicity, assimilation to the dominant culture and acculturation levels, attitudes, and norms about family, marriage, sex roles, and domestic violence, as well as other sociodemographic characteristics. In light of these studies, we tried to examine the factors that affect South Asian women's motivations to remain in violent relationships. Thus, the women participating in the focus groups spent a substantial amount of time exploring why each stayed in their abusive situations. Their discussions indicated a decision-making process that was personal, yet complex. The following were some considerations extracted from the women's testimonies regarding the process itself:

1. Evaluation of the pros and cons of their domestic circumstances;
2. Perceived choices and options available to them;
3. Concern for their children's safety and future;
4. Immigration status and financial stability;
5. Value placed on opinions and concerns of family members and community;
6. A sense of self-blame, guilt, and personal responsibility; and
7. Perceptions of societal norms and expectations of them.

Contrary to popular belief, the decisions these women made were neither irrational nor arbitrary. Most women based their decisions on a clear rationale. For example, Hala, a young Muslim woman, assessed her situation and found no relevant and viable solutions to her problem. In addition, she believed that she was expected to "tolerate" the violence she was experiencing. Thus, she based her decision to stay with her abusive spouse on these perceptions: I guess that's the way its supposed to be. Women, they take it. They don't fight back, you know, like women here [American women in the United States] do. Asian women, however much educated they are, they don't fight back. That's the way I was—just be quiet, or walk out, or get out of the house, or go to the other room. Roja, another focus group participant, declared unceremoniously, "In my case, it was financial dependence."

The issue of economic dependency as a salient reason for continuing in a violent relationship was a theme that emerged often. Many of the participants were partially or totally dependent on their spouses for their finances, as well as other resources. Some perceived this dependency to be stronger than it may have been in actuality. Social isolation and lack of information about formal service provisions also contributed to exaggerating this problem of dependency. For some women in the focus groups, marriage had provided them with financial resources, a decent home, class privileges, respectability, and legitimacy in their community and families that they did not have before. In essence, the women had received respectability, a higher social class, and material comforts in exchange for private mistreatments. This exchange was a strategic choice that some participants indicated they made consciously, for themselves and for their children, for a limited length of time or for a lifetime.

For some participants, social norms, family traditions and marriage, and acceptance of men as authorities in the family were adequate reasons for maintaining their abusive relationships. Jila, a focus group participant, succinctly stated her reason for not leaving her violent husband: "Because we feel respect for our parents [and] we should try to keep good relations with our husbands—no matter what." Kamini, another woman in the groups, expressed similar sentiments: "For me, it's like everyone should be together, sit together, and there should be love amongst everyone. And it is a good impression for the children. This is what is in my faith and in my culture. Divorce in our family is very difficult. If you have children, you have to stay together for their sake. Children need to have both mother and father."

Barriers to Leaving: A Glimpse into South Asian Women's Worlds

For most people, it is extremely difficult to comprehend why a woman continues to endure and cope with violence in her home. In our group discussions, South Asian women provided glimpses into a process of decision making that is often poorly understood and judged harshly. Despite the fear and uncertainty that most of these women face daily they seem to find a way to examine their own lives, available options, and their own capabilities in terms of complexities engendered by living in a "foreign" country. This rather calm and rational scrutiny in the midst of an otherwise chaotic life seemingly helped the group participants find reasons for continuing in their violent relationships and coming to terms with it.

Values and Norms-Related Factors

Many of the barriers to leaving that these women experienced were not individual at all. Rather, women based their decisions to stay on factors such as family and cultural values. [The values and norms that created barriers for these women include:]

1. Societal, community, and family norms;
2. Community and family expectations; and
3. Patriarchy and prescribed gender roles.

The effects of these factors are illustrated in Munni's account of the circumstances of her marriage and conjugal life: "When I got married, my father said to my husband, 'My respect and honor is in your hands. Please take care of my daughter.' From then on he was my husband. It was my job to take care of him. For my family honor, family respect, and to maintain [this] respect, we have to just put up with it [violence]. Because of the family!" This is even more clear in Nilufer's statement "My husband forced me to have more children for citizenship purposes. I am sure that what he really wanted was to have sons. He hates daughters. I couldn't even tell you how much. Back in Pakistan, it is understood that girls are no good, and you shouldn't have them." Along with the perceived relevance of patriarchy in families, Nilufer's understanding and acceptance of gender positions is evident in this statement.

Support Factors

[The focus group discussions also centered on three support factors:]

1. Lack of social support;
2. Lack of structural support and material resources; and
3. Lack of knowledge of available formal support networks and systems.

Suman, an Indian single mother living in New York with a young daughter, discussed the lack of social support she experienced: "I have no relatives. I have nobody, just me and my daughter now. It is hard, very hard." Savitri, a mother of three children, discussed the lack of structural support and material resources in terms of the availability of affordable baby-sitting and public transportation. She felt that a scarcity of both had prevented her from developing necessary skills to become self-sufficient and independent. "I have a baby-sitting problem. The day care that is on our side is very expensive. Taking the public transport to another place itself costs five dollars," she lamented.

The lack of knowledge about available formal assistance programs can often prove to be an important reason why some South Asian women choose to continue in their violent domestic relationships. Roja, who had recently moved to Chicago from India, expressed her dilemma and her reasons for staying in her violent relationship: "And this is a new culture [the United States], language problem, no money, and with children. Where to go? And moreover, no relatives. There is nowhere to go. And there is no way to get out."

During discussions about support factors, focus group participants indicated the magnitude of their sense of isolation when they were attempting to address problems surrounding abuse in their lives. Suman declared, "It's quite difficult to make the adjustment and adapt to the new culture, and it takes quite a bit of time. There are difficulties and problems. Especially when there is no one to turn to."

Individual Factors

These individual factors emerged from the focus group discussions:

1. Fear for safety for themselves and their children;
2. Fear for their future and possible deportation;
3. Inability to handle and cope with the stress of living alone in the United States;
4. Lack of job skills, language skills, and other life skills;
5. Desire to stay in the relationship or inability to accept and address the violence in their lives; and
6. Fear for the children's future.

Leela, a woman living in Chicago, focused on some of the personal factors that formed barriers for her: "My English speaking isn't very good. So getting a job and working is not a possibility yet. So I cannot get the things I need without the English. In addition I do not have a green card." Roja, another woman in Chicago, indicated racism as a factor contributing to her abusive situation: "My life now is for my children. That's why I need to work and support them. I had to swallow my hopes. I have to put all my hopes in my children. There are many tensions from the outside. He [the husband] wants what he had back home [in terms of a job]. A woman accepts whatever she can get, because we want to survive and support the family. Although the men have the education, they cannot find a suitable job or sometimes they do not want to work. So there is frustration outside and inside the home for all of us."

Why Leave Now? Why South Asian Women Walk Out of Their Marriages

Despite the hopelessness and lack of support they experienced, some of the South Asian women took the "uncharacteristic" and "unlikely" step of leaving their abusive relationships for good. Many indicated that they were seriously considering this option. Others stated that they were trying hard to cope with their present, violence-filled circumstances and hoping to "make them [their marriages] work."

Those who walked away from their abusive relationships indicated that they did so not because of one defining moment, or a single violent episode, but because of the sum total of their experiences. They had reached the end of their tolerance and recognized that they could seek and receive support and assistance from formal systems. Those who had walked away from their violent relationships, however, also acknowledged that it had been excruciatingly difficult and painful to start living on their own. They indicated that the support they received from local South Asian women's organizations and culturally sensitive domestic violence shelters was crucial in their decision making and follow-through processes. Also significant in their decision making was the support they received from informal kin and friendship networks such as friends, family members, neighbors, and co-workers. For those who were continuing in their present abusive circumstances, having a job and interacting with their colleagues at work, talking to supportive siblings, family members, and friends, the support and understanding of their children, and their own unwavering religious faith had all helped them to continue to cope. These factors gave them hope for a better future and life.

Hopes for the Future: Living in Peace and Tranquillity

Despite difficult circumstances and lives filled with violence and fear, the participating South Asian women expressed hopes and expectations for a better future. Those who had left their violent lives encouraged others to consider this option and offered to help in any way possible. Madhu, an Indian woman who participated in one of the focus groups in Chicago, voiced this optimism: "My hopes are that I want to study [and] I am doing a job in the library now. It's a good position, but I want to move ahead. So that's why I want to study more. I don't want a restaurant or a store job." Kismat, a Pakistani woman and a mother of four, expressed her desires in terms of her children. She remarked, "My life is with my children. I want to see my children have a good life with a good education, have good jobs. This is my biggest wish and hope." Sheba, who had started a life on her own, had this advice for other participants: "You need to make yourself good and show that you don't have less of anything. You can raise your children without him. And better than him. And you can be happy. You need to begin to say this to yourself and foster these kinds of thoughts."

During these discussions, the participants indicated that it was important to address domestic violence through simple and tangible strategies that were empowering and meaningful to women. They suggested that these strategies need to focus first and foremost on providing life skills, job skills, and language skills so that women could slowly find the peace and tranquillity that had eluded them for so long. Their suggestions included providing the following services: English classes, transportation, baby-sitting services, advice about legal issues and immigration laws, job training such as computer classes, some seed money to start their lives again, and support groups where they can talk with others and help others.

Their focus was simple, narrow, and targeted toward themselves. They felt that with these kinds of tangible assistance and services, they could emerge from behind the veil of secrecy, talk about their lives in public, not feel responsible for the violence in their lives, and, like other people, live a life of dignity and peace. . . .

Learning from Women

Although there has been a long history of domestic violence in South Asian communities, only recently have attempts been made to document these issues systematically in these communities in the United States. Our experience is that focus group discussions are extremely effective in exploring a variety of issues regarding domestic violence in these communities. Our work with South Asian women revealed that violence experienced by South Asian women was defined by a variety of unique cultural, familial, and community factors and norms. Socioeconomic factors, immigration status, and a host of perceived barriers, including linguistic ones, further defined their experiences. Our focus group discussions revealed a complex picture of domestic violence among the participating South Asian women. Issues of patriarchy, gender roles and expectations, constricting family and community norms, attitudes and traditions about spousal violence, lack of decision-making power, and economic independence are still important in South Asian communities and have aggravated the problem of domestic violence further. Despite this bleak picture, the South Asian women who participated in our groups exhibited enviable resiliency and coping abilities. Their hopes for a peaceful and violence-free life for themselves and their children spoke volumes about their courage. With the help of South Asian women's organizations and other community-based organizations, and through their own willingness to speak out, South Asian women have begun to challenge their communities to confront domestic violence with sensitivity and urgency. Although the process has been initiated, there is much work to be done. Part of the task is to document the nature and incidence of this atrocity systematically and implement culturally sensitive, as well as effective, interventions that address issues in South Asian contexts.

ENDNOTES

1. K. A. Huisman, "Wife Battering in Asian American Communities," *Violence against Women* 2 (1996): 260–83.

2. M. P. Koss, L. A. Goodman, A. Browne, L. F. Fitzgerald, G. P. Keita, and N. F. Russo, *No Safe Haven: Male Violence against Women at Home, at Work, and in the Community* (Washington, DC: American Psychological Association, 1994).

3. J. Abbott, J. McLain-Koziol, and S. Lowenstein, "Domestic Violence against Women: Incidence and Prevalence in an Emergency Department Population," *Journal of the American Medical Association* 273 (1995): 1763–77.

4. D. Berrios and D. Grady, "Domestic Violence. Risk Factors and Outcomes," *Western Journal of Medicine* 155, no. 2 (1991): 133–35.

5. V. F. Parker, "Battered," *RN (TWP)* 58, no. 1 (1995): 26–29.

6. A. L. Kornblit, "Domestic Violence: An Emerging Health Issue," *Social Science and Medicine* 39 (1994): 1181–88.

7. S. D. Dasgupta and S. Warrier, "In the Footsteps of 'Arundhati': Asian Indian Women's Experience of Domestic Violence in the United States," *Violence against Women* 2, no. 3 (1996): 238–59.

8. M. Abraham, "Addressing the Problem of Marital Violence among South Asians in the United States: A Sociological Study of the Role of Organizations," paper presented at the meetings of the International Sociological Association (1994); and "Transforming Marital Violence from a 'Private Problem' to a 'Public Issue': South Asian Women's Organizations and Community Empowerment," paper presented at the meetings of the American Sociological Association (1995). These papers have since been published as "Ethnicity, Gender, and Marital Violence: South Asian Women's Organizations in the United States," *Gender and Society* 9 (1995): 450–68; and "Speaking the Unspeakable: Marital Violence against South Asian Immigrant Women in the United States," *Indian Journal of Gender Studies* 5, no. 2 (June–December 1998).

9. U.S. Bureau of the Census, *1990 Census of the Population: Social and Economic Characteristics, United States* (Washington, DC: U.S. Government Printing Office, 1993).

10. Koss et al., *No Safe Haven.*

11. C. K. Ho, "An Analysis of Domestic Violence in Asian American Communities: A Multicultural Approach to Counseling," *Woman and Therapy* 9 (1990): 129–50.

12. Abraham, "Addressing the Problem" and "Transforming Marital Violence."

13. T. L. Greenbaum, *The Practical Handbook and Guide to Focus Groups Research* (Lexington, MA: Lexington, 1988).

14. Names of all participants have been changed to protect their identity.

38

TOWARD A BETTER UNDERSTANDING
OF LESBIAN BATTERING

CLAIRE M. RENZETTI

What do we now know about violence in lesbian relationships, and where do we go from here? . . .

It appears that violence in lesbian relationships occurs at about the same frequency as violence in heterosexual relationships. The abuse may be physical and/or psychological, ranging from verbal threats and insults to stabbings and shootings. Indeed, batterers display a terrifying ingenuity in their selection of abusive tactics, frequently tailoring the abuse to the specific vulnerabilities of their partners. We have seen that there is no "typical" form of abuse, even though some types of abuse are more common than others. What emerged as significant in my research was not the forms of abuse inflicted, but, rather, the factors that appear to give rise to the abuse, and the consequences of the abuse for batterers and especially for victims.

The factor that in this study was most strongly associated with abuse was partners' relative dependency on one another. More specifically, batterers appeared to be intensely dependent on the partners whom they victimized. The abusive partner's dependency was a central element in an ongoing, dialectic struggle in these relationships. As batterers grew more dependent, their partners attempted to exercise greater independence. This, in turn, posed a threat to the batterer, who would subsequently try to tighten her hold on her partner, often by violent means. The greater the batterer's dependency, the more frequent and severe the abuse she inflicted on her partner. In most cases, the batterer eventually succeeded in cutting her partner off from friends, relatives, colleagues, and all outside interests and activities that did not include the batterer herself. Still, though she apparently had her partner all to herself in a sense, her success in controlling her partner seemed only to fuel her dependency rather than salve it.

The intense dependency of the batterer typically manifests itself as jealousy. It is not enough for the batterer to possess her partner; she must also guard her from all others who could potentially lure her away. The battering victim is subjected to lengthy interrogations about her routine activities and associations.

She is repeatedly accused of infidelity, and although the accusations are almost always groundless, her denials rarely satisfy the batterer. Violence is a frequent end product of the batterer's jealous tirades. The overdependency of the batterer may also manifest itself through substance abuse, especially alcohol abuse. When under the influence of alcohol or drugs, she may feel strong, more independent, more aggressive. She may act on these perceptions by becoming violent and abusive, especially toward her partner. This is particularly likely if, along with the belief that alcohol or drugs make her powerful, she or her partner or both of them also believe that an individual under the influence of alcohol or drugs is not responsible for her actions. Thus substance abuse appears to be a facilitator rather than a cause of lesbian battering.

Another factor that emerged as a potential facilitator of lesbian partner abuse was a personal history of family violence. Although a number of researchers have found that childhood exposure to domestic violence may increase one's likelihood of being victimized in an intimate relationship as an adult, the participants in my study did not report a high incidence of exposure to domestic violence in their families of origin. Their batterers were more likely than they were to have been victimized, but there were almost as many abusive partners who grew up in nonviolent households as there were those who grew up in violent ones.

Exposure to domestic violence as a child may put one at risk of becoming abusive toward one's own partner as an adult, but the data from my study also suggest that a personal history of abuse can become, for both batterer and victim, a means to legitimate the battering. In other words, the belief that childhood exposure to domestic violence predisposes one toward violent behavior or victimization as an adult may facilitate lesbian battering much the same way substance abuse does—that is, by forming the basis of an excuse for the batterer's behavior.

One issue that remains unclear is how an imbalance of power in the relationship may contribute to partner abuse. Like other researchers who have examined the relationship between power imbalance and battering among homosexual couples, few strong associations emerged from my study. This is probably due in large part to the complexity of the concept of power. Power is multifaceted. With respect to some dimensions of power (e.g., decision making, the division of household labor), batterers could be considered the more powerful partners. However, in terms of other indicators of power (e.g., economic resources brought to the relationship), victims tended to be more powerful. It is also unclear when an imbalance of power in these terms emerges in abusive relationships; the data from my study indicate that, at least with regard to decision making, victims often ceded power to batterers in an attempt to appease them and perhaps avoid further abuse. This evidence lends support to the hypothesis that batterers are individuals who feel powerless and use violence as a means to achieve power and dominance in their intimate relationships.

The power imbalance–domestic violence link is one that obviously deserves further attention in future research. If batterers use violence as a means to overcome feelings of powerlessness, what are the sources of these feelings? Are they a further outgrowth of dependency needs? In addition, researchers need to clarify what elements compose the power construct so that the dimensions of power relevant to the etiology of lesbian partner abuse can be distinguished and addressed.[1]

It is doubtful that we will ever be able to predict with precision which relationships, be they homosexual or heterosexual, will become violent. However, findings from my research and that of others we have reviewed point to several factors that may serve as markers for identifying lesbian relationships that are particularly at risk for violence. Figure 1 presents a decision tree designed to assist lesbian partners, counselors, battered women's advocates, and others in assessing this risk. I also urge readers who feel they are at risk, or who think they may be involved in a battering relationship, to apply Figure 1 as a checklist to their own relationships.

What if one is involved in an abusive relationship? Where may one go for help? . . . As the findings of my research make clear, battered lesbians experience tremendous difficulty obtaining the help they want and need. Help sources available to battered heterosexual women (e.g., the police and the legal system, shelters, relatives) generally are not perceived by lesbian victims as viable sources of help. Or, if help is sought from these sources, lesbian victims do not typically rate it as highly effective. Even those whom lesbian victims consider to be good sources of help (i.e., counselors and friends) frequently deny the abuse or refuse to name it battering.

Based on the data gathered in my study, it is not overstating the point to say that battered lesbians are victimized not only by their partners, but also by many of those from whom they seek help. Consequently, additional research is urgently needed on ways to improve help providers' responses to battered lesbians. We will take up this issue in the sections that follow.

Providing Help to Battered Lesbians

Research has consistently documented the difficulties battered heterosexual women encounter when they seek help to address the battering. Nevertheless, battered heterosexual women appear to have considerably more success in getting effective help—or at least in eliciting positive responses from help providers—than battered lesbians do. As Pharr (1986) has pointed out:

> There is an important difference between the battered lesbian and the battered non-lesbian: the battered non-lesbian experiences violence within the context of a misogynist world; the lesbian experiences violence within the context of a world that is not only woman-hating, but is also homophobic. And that is a great difference. Therefore, an initial step in improving responses to battered lesbians is for help providers to confront and overcome their homophobia. (P. 204)

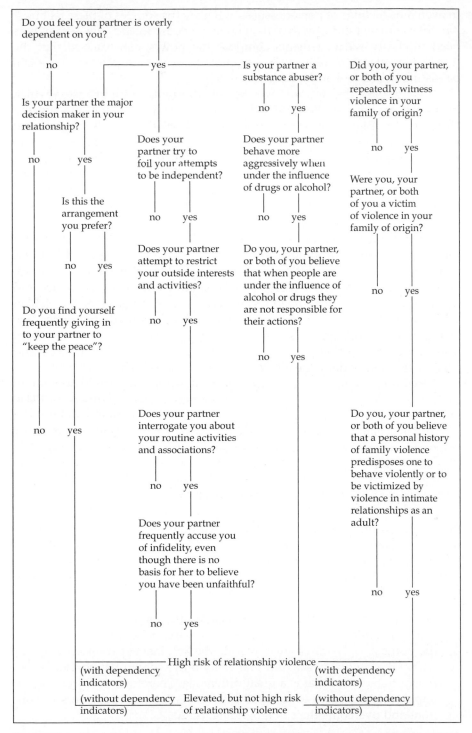

FIGURE 1   Decision Tree for Assessing Risk for Violence in Lesbian Relationships

As Elliott (1990) says, "Before you . . . can acknowledge lesbian battering, you must first acknowledge lesbian relationships" (n.p.).

While informal help providers (e.g., heterosexual friends, family members) cannot be forced to attend homophobia workshops, all official or formal help providers—that is, police personnel, shelter volunteers and paid staff, crisis hotline staffers, counselors, physicians, and emergency room personnel—should be required to participate in such workshops as part of their routine training. There are a number of excellent resources available that can be utilized for such sessions. Perhaps the best is *Confronting Homophobia,* edited by Julie Guth and Pamela Elliott of the Lesbian Advocacy Committee of the Minnesota Coalition for Battered Women. The manual includes not only training materials, but also suggestions for trainers and workshop leaders, sample training formats, and evaluation forms.

Confronting Homophobia is part of a two-volume set; the second volume, *Confronting Lesbian Battering,* is specifically designed for battered women's advocates as a resource for developing effective responses to lesbian victims. The value of *Confronting Lesbian Battering* is that it addresses the many myths that surround lesbian partner abuse and sensitively guides readers through a rethinking of our operating models of intimate violence.

In a survey of 1,505 service providers that I conducted in 1991, two thirds (66.6 percent) of the 557 service providers who responded indicated that their staff receive antihomophobia training; 56.4 percent indicated that volunteers also receive this training. However, only 47.9 percent reported that their staff received any training specifically about lesbian battering and 40.6 percent reported that volunteers receive such training. Thus, in addition to homophobia workshops, help providers also must be educated about lesbian battering, and this education must include an analysis of the many myths about partner abuse: that it is a male/female problem; that it typically involves "mutual battering"; that it is always the physically larger or "masculine" partner who batters. Education in this regard, however, should extend beyond official help providers to the communities, both lesbian and non-lesbian. This may be undertaken in the context of community speakouts in which participants are assured safe space. It may also be done through the distribution of pamphlets or flyers and through public service advertisements. In particular, battered women's agencies should determine if their ads and literature imply (or explicitly state) that all batterers are heterosexual men and all victims of battering are heterosexual women. Often, the sex-specific pronoun "he" is used in reference to batterers, and "she" is used in reference to victims. In my survey of service providers, 96.4 percent of those who responded said they welcome battered lesbians as clients, yet just 37 percent reported that they do outreach to lesbians. Similarly, 77.7 percent said that at least some of the written materials they make available use inclusive language, but only 25.9 percent indicated that their written materials explicitly address the problem of lesbian battering and just 29.8 percent reported that they have written material specifically about lesbian battering available. Just as efforts have been made to make agency materials racially-inclusive, so too should they be inclusive of lesbians and gay men.

Strategies such as these not only educate help providers, the lesbian and gay community in general, and the heterosexual public, but may also assist lesbians involved in abusive relationships in recognizing themselves as battered, which is their first step in getting free. Still, education without action is of little use. What responses from others would lesbian victims find most helpful? This question was posed to the participants in my study of lesbian battering. Their answers have been incorporated into the following discussions.[2]

The Legal System and Alternatives

A current debate among advocates for battered lesbians is whether or not the legal system should be utilized to resolve the problem of violence in lesbian relationships. Those who support the use of the legal system maintain that bringing the force of legal authority to bear on the batterer can effectively put an end to her abuse and, at the same time, hold her accountable for her actions. From this perspective, lesbians are entitled to equal protection by the law. The difficulties are that in most states, the domestic violence statutes do not explicitly apply to homosexual couples, and in those states where they do apply, the police and the courts do not consistently or fairly enforce them in cases involving homosexual couples. Those who hold this position maintain that advocates should lobby for the revision of domestic violence statutes to include homosexual couples, and serve as watchdogs to ensure that the statutes are consistently and fairly enforced when lesbians and gay men turn to the police and courts for help.[3]

Opponents of utilizing the legal system in cases of lesbian battering point first to its well-documented mistreatment of cases involving heterosexual couples. According to Irvine (1990), "The courts deal so poorly with heterosexual abuse cases that in a case involving two lesbians they would have a 'field day'" (p. 29). Second, many see the legal system as inappropriate for resolving problems between lesbian partners. As one advocate put it: "I have a personal hatred and bias against women using the legal system and the police system in their fights with each other. I find it offensive as a feminist. Resolution of disputes between lesbians should not take place in a white male judicial court" (quoted in Irvine 1990:29).

Only two of the participants in my study indicated that they would find intervention by the police and the courts helpful. One said she would like to have legal sanctions available that are tougher than restraining orders. The second participant said that the homophobia of the police needs to be addressed. She found the police to be helpful in stopping the battering in the short-run, but reported that they were blatantly homophobic in their response to her.

If the police and the legal system should not be utilized by battered lesbians, what are their alternatives? One is mediation. The role of the mediator is to facilitate communication between partners so that they themselves can develop a mutually beneficial and impartial resolution to their conflicts (e.g., separation, a signed agreement in which the abusive partner promises to end the violence) without resorting to formal legal action (Felstiner and Williams 1978; Folberg and Taylor 1984).

The informal and private nature of mediation may make it especially appealing to lesbian victims, particularly if they prefer that most people (e.g., their families, colleagues at work, etc.) not know about their sexual orientation. However, Ellis (1988) and others (e.g., Bahr, Chappell, and Marcos 1987) warn that mediation may have limited success in ending partner abuse. Their research indicates that the more hostile the relations between partners, the less likely they are to successfully complete mediation. In addition, mediators, in their effort to be impartial, may overlook inequalities of power between partners, not only with regard to economic resources, but also in terms of fear or psychological domination. Mediation also implies co-responsibility on the part of the partners and fails to hold batterers accountable for their behavior. Weighing these findings against the potential value of mediation for lesbian victims, research should be undertaken to evaluate the effectiveness of existing mediation programs in assisting both lesbian and heterosexual clients.

Apart from the police, the courts, and mediators, battered lesbians may also turn to other formal help providers, especially shelters and counselors, for assistance. How might the responses of these professionals be improved?

Shelters and Counselors

Nineteen participants in my study stated that having a safe place to which they could go for refuge from their batterers would have been most helpful to them.[4] We have already noted that shelters can only become viable sources of help to battered lesbians when shelter staff confront and overcome their homophobia, and when lesbian partner abuse is explicitly recognized as a serious problem in public service advertisements and literature for battered women. Lesbian victims of partners abuse need to know that local battered women's shelters are open to them and that they are welcome there.

Once the battered lesbian arrives at the shelter, staff there must, of course, make good on their promise of providing her with safe space, emotional support, and other assistance that they routinely provide to battered heterosexual women. Shelter staff must not minimize the abuse experienced by the battered lesbian simply because her batterer is a woman. Lesbian battering is "real" battering, and many of the needs of battered lesbians are the same as those of battered heterosexual women.

At the same time, however, battered lesbians have several unique concerns. One of the most important is deciding to whom among shelter staff and residents one will make one's sexual orientation known. As Geraci (1986) explains:

> If a lesbian does not choose to come out this right must be respected. It is important to keep in mind that in the lesbian community at large, battering between women is a non-issue—it violates the idea of a safe,

peaceful world of women. . . . A battered lesbian who seeks shelter is making a very courageous step which could cause her to lose the support of many of her lesbian sisters. (P. 78)

She also runs the risk of incurring hostility and ostracism from other shelter residents.[5] Among the service providers I surveyed, 92.3 percent said that their clients' sexual orientation was treated confidentially, although the majority also indicated their confidentiality policies regarding sexual orientation were not explicit.

Another serious concern of battered lesbians in shelters is the extent to which they are actually safe from their batterers. While shelter locations are well-guarded secrets from men, and both staff and residents are severely sanctioned if they disclose this information, we have already noted that the location of shelters is often well-known in the lesbian community, primarily because lesbians have been very active in the battered women's movement and because of the widely held belief that all batterers are men. Consequently it has been suggested that as an alternative to traditional residential shelters, a network of safe houses be established for battered lesbians (Irvine 1990). In Minneapolis–St. Paul, for example, a network of lesbians takes victims into their individual homes (Ojeda-Zapata 1990). Irvine (1990) points out that a drawback of this approach is that lesbian victims are not afforded the peer support that may be available at the shelters. However, a support group for battered lesbians may fill this gap (Porat 1986).

The Lesbian Battering Intervention Project of the Minnesota Coalition for Battered Women has compiled a checklist to assist shelter staff in determining if they are adequately prepared to serve battered lesbians. They have kindly permitted me to reprint it here (see Table 1). Many of the issues raised in this checklist also apply to counselors from whom lesbian victims seek help. Seventeen of the lesbian victims in my study identified specific responses from counselors that they would have found helpful. Three were cited repeatedly.

First, participants indicated that they needed professional help in regaining their self-esteem and building a strong sense of self-worth. They expressed the desire for counselors to focus therapy sessions on these goals. Importantly, however, respondents emphasized that counselors should not treat their low self-esteem as a cause of their battering but, rather, as a result of it. Lenore Walker's (1979:239) suggestions with respect to counseling battered heterosexual women are applicable here. Walker maintains that individual therapy with battered women should be more action-oriented than analytic. "The realities of present alternatives and future goal planning are explored in individual therapy. The battered woman needs to recognize concrete steps she can take to improve her situation. . . . Intervention and collaboration with other helpers are important corollaries of individual psychotherapy." These methods will help the battered woman rebuild her self-esteem and recognize and constructively experience her feelings of anger.

Closely related to this were the two other responses participants most would have appreciated from counselors—specifically, for counselors to

TABLE 1   Checklist for Shelter Programs

1. Do all written materials use inclusive language (no pronouns) and address the issue of lesbian battering?
   Mission
   Philosophy statement
   Brochures
   Arrival and departure forms
   Welcome letters, house rules, etc.

2. Is homophobia identified as an oppression and a form of violence?
   In the philosophy statement
   In the house rules

3. Are policies inclusive of lesbians?
   Does the definition of family in personal policies include lesbian families?
   Does the affirmative action statement include sexual/affectional orientation?
   Does the policy on confidentiality include confidentiality for lesbians and consequences for violating the policy?

4. Is the recruitment of staff, volunteers, and board members addressing homophobia?
   Are candidates questioned about homophobia and providing services to lesbians?
   Are position announcements distributed to reach lesbians?
   Do job qualifications include commitment to confront homophobia?
   Is homophobia training included for all new staff, volunteers, and board members?
   Does the program have a commitment to lesbian involvement at all levels?

5. Is the program prepared to respond to the needs of battered lesbians?
   Is information available on resources for battered lesbians?
   Does the library, video library, and/or magazine rack contain lesbian books, videos, periodicals, or articles?
   Is the Children's Program staff familiar with issues confronting lesbian mothers? (custody, coming out to children, etc.)
   Is the Women's Program familiar with issues confronting battered lesbians? (dangers of using the "system," closeting, etc.)
   Are all services prepared to include battered lesbians? (support group, intervention program, legal advocates, etc.)

6. Has the issue of lesbian battering been integrated into the program on an ongoing basis? (One or two trainings will not remove barriers or fix the problem.)

Source: Written by Lisa Vecoli for the Minnesota Coalition for Battered Women, Lesbian Battering Intervention Project; printed in Elliott 1990, pp. 73–74.

identify their experiences as battering and for them not to lay blame for the abuse on those who were victimized. Like shelter staff, counselors must not minimize the abuse because it was inflicted by a woman, nor deflect attention away from the abuse and onto the abused's "other problems." Battered lesbians, like battered heterosexual women, may also benefit from group therapy and support groups, but counselors should not assume that couples counseling is more appropriate for lesbian partners involved in abusive relationships than for heterosexual couples. As Lydia Walker (1986) has pointed out, why should counselors assume that lesbian batterers are less manipulative and more likely than men to control their violence? These are false assumptions.

This is not to say that treatment for batterers should be ignored. To the contrary, a focus of future research should be on identifying the unique treatment needs of lesbian batterers and developing treatment programs specifically for them. (The vast majority of treatment programs for batterers are male-centered, and men who batter women also tend to be overtly homophobic. Thus such programs would be inappropriate and probably ineffective for lesbian batterers.) If a lesbian victim presents herself for treatment, however, the counselor must keep in mind that she alone—not her partner, nor she and her partner as a couple—is the client. Couples counseling should only be attempted at the request of the victim. The model offered by Walker (1979:245–48) may be applicable to lesbian couples, if both therapists involved are lesbians. However, even if a battered lesbian requests couples counseling, it should be attempted only if her safety can be ensured, and she should be apprised of its low probability of success in abusive relationships.

As noted [by other researchers], the couples counseling approach is based on a family systems or codependency model that sees both partners sharing responsibility for the abusive nature of their relationship. Although it has, perhaps, intuitive appeal, the codependency model is inherently victim-blaming. It may be especially damaging when the woman who has been abused fought back or defended herself against the battering. Victims who have fought back or defended themselves, we have seen, typically experience guilt or shame over their use of violence. They often question whether they are truly victims or are batterers themselves. Counselors, like others, appear to apply the label "mutually abusive" too readily and uncritically to lesbian victims who come to them for help. Thus they reinforce rather than reverse the women's low self-esteem and perpetuate the myth that the abuse is at least partially their fault.

Counselors must learn to evaluate the dialectic nature of the abusive relationship and to distinguish between battering and self-defense (or fighting back). To do this, they, along with shelter staff and other advocates, must first ask themselves some hard questions about their own acceptance of the myth of mutual battering (Walker 1986:76):

> Why are female batterers more "believable" when they blame their partner, why do workers see self-defense as "mutual battering" if the batterer is a woman, and why is it easier to believe that somehow a battered lesbian is part of the "violence problem" than to believe that a heterosexual woman is part of the "violence problem"? I challenge workers in the movement to think about how they would respond to a battered woman who says she provokes him or that she is as much to blame as him because she hits him first sometimes.

Relatives, Friends, and Community

The major barrier to relatives becoming viable sources of help for battered lesbians, as they are for battered heterosexual women, is their homophobia. However, it is probably more difficult to convince relatives to attend homophobia workshops than it is for any other group of help providers we have discussed here. Perhaps family members will be motivated by the fact that if they do confront and overcome their homophobia, they can effectively help their loved ones free themselves from abusive relationships: Recall our finding that the more helpful lesbian victims found their relatives to be, the sooner they ended the abusive relationship.

It is friends, though, especially friends in the lesbian community, from whom battered lesbians most often seek help. And it was to friends and the community that the majority of the study participants directed their suggestions for improving responses to lesbian victims.

The primary need expressed by lesbian victims is for their friends to allow them to confide in them. Thirty-two of the study participants wrote that they wanted their friends to lend emotional support, listen to them when they tried to make them aware of the problem, and reassure them that the abuse was not their fault. Twenty women said they wished their friends had named the violence "battering" instead of excusing or denying it. Fifteen women would have liked their friends to help them leave the relationship, either by offering physical assistance in moving or by verbally affirming their decision to end the relationship.

In short, friends and the community itself must recognize that battering is a problem among lesbian couples, and that its consequences are as serious as those of heterosexual battering — perhaps more serious, in fact, given that lesbians who are victimized are doubly stigmatized and have fewer sources of help available to them. Belief is essential, and like other help providers, friends and the community must not reflexively apply the label "mutual battering" simply because the partners involved are both women or because they know that the victim sometimes fought back. The words of the study participants, of course, convey these sentiments best:

Most helpful would have been the respect shown by believing that there actually was a problem — my friends brushed it off, didn't believe [she] was abusive, said it was a two-way street. [Questionnaire 14]

To listen, believe, ask questions to gain understanding, but no "Why didn't you just do . . . ?" Offer practical help to get away. Encouragement to talk about it. No victim blaming. No judgmental crap about how my batterer is really my sister. Treat me as you would treat any woman who has been the victim of a violent crime. [Questionnaire 39]

Support, genuine understanding. My friends knew but tried to ignore it and suggested that I overlook her "moods" because "she's just that way."

Acknowledging that lesbian battering is a serious problem may indeed be unpleasant, even painful, for the lesbian community. But until such acknowledgment is made, until victims' needs are effectively and sensitively met, and until batterers are challenged and held accountable for their behavior, all lesbians are unsafe and the struggle for the creation of a peaceful, egalitarian community of women is violently betrayed.

ENDNOTES

1. Others (see, e.g., Island and Letellier 1991 and Coleman 1990) have hypothesized that internalized homophobia may be an underlying factor in homosexual partner abuse either by motivating a partner to be violent or by increasing one's risk of victimization. Although I did not examine internalized homophobia in my study, the issue was the focus of much discussion at my meetings with the Working Group on Lesbian Battering. Certainly the phenomenon of internalized homophobia deserves attention in future studies of homosexual partner abuse. However, the problem of developing a reliable and valid measure of internalized homophobia—a problem perhaps more difficult to resolve than that of measuring partners' relative power in a relationship—confronts researchers who wish to explore this issue further.

2. Eighty-nine participants responded to the questionnaire item, "Whether or not you sought help, please describe what response from others would have been most helpful to you." One woman wrote simply that she had gotten the help she needed. One felt that money/financial assistance would have been most helpful. And a third participant wrote, "Take my alcohol away." The majority of the women, however, responded with more than one answer.

3. According to Fagan (1989), research on heterosexual domestic violence indicates that legal sanctions appear to be most effective in deterring batterers with brief and relatively nonsevere histories of abusive behavior. At the same time, however, Fagan notes that, for any legal sanctions to be effective, they cannot be weak. Weak legal interventions may reinforce violence simply by not adequately penalizing it.

4. Two participants indicated that in addition to safe shelter space, they needed transportation. One suggested establishing an escort service that could be called upon at any time to transport victims to a safe space. Four women also requested hotline services, and four felt that a support group for battered lesbians would be helpful.

5. Grover (1990:43) points out that children of battered lesbians who accompany their mothers to shelters must also have their privacy rights respected. "Children may be used as closeting for their mothers and themselves. They may not know who is safe to come out to and who is not. A conversation with mom about how her family typically handles this is essential."

REFERENCES

Bahr, S., C. B. Chappell, and A. Marcos. 1987. "An Evaluation of a Trial Mediation Programme." *Mediation Quarterly* (Winter):37–52.

Coleman, V. E. 1990. "Violence between Lesbian Couples: A Between Groups Comparison." Ph.D. dissertation. University Microfilms International (9109022).

Elliott, P. 1990. "Introduction." In *Confronting Lesbian Battering*, edited by P. Elliott. St. Paul: Minnesota Coalition for Battered Women.

Ellis, D. 1988. "Marital Conflict Mediation and Post-Separation Wife-Abuse." Presented at the annual meeting of the American Society of Criminology, Chicago, November.

Fagan, J. 1989. "Cessation of Family Violence: Deterrence and Discussion." Pp. 377–425 in *Family Violence*, edited by L. Ohlin and M. Tonry. Chicago: University of Chicago Press.

Felstiner, W. and L. Williams. 1978. "Mediation as an Alternative to Criminal Prosecution: Ideology and Limitations." *Law and Human Behavior* 2:221–39.

Folberg, J. and A. Taylor. 1984. *Mediation*. San Francisco: Jossey-Bass.

Geraci, L. 1986. "Making Shelters Safe for Lesbians." Pp. 77–79 in *Naming the Violence*, edited by K. Lobel. Seattle, WA: Seal.

Grover, J. 1990. "Children from Violent Lesbian Homes." Pp. 42–43 in *Confronting Lesbian Battering*, edited by P. Elliott. St. Paul: Minnesota Coalition for Battered Women.

Guth, J. and P. Elliott, eds. 1991. *Confronting Homophobia*. St. Paul: Minnesota Coalition for Battered Women.

Irvine, J. 1990. "Lesbian Battering: The Search for Shelter." Pp. 25–30 in *Confronting Lesbian Battering*, edited by P. Elliott. St. Paul: Minnesota Coalition for Battered Women.

Island, D. and P. Letellier. 1991. *Men Who Beat the Men Who Love Them*. New York: Harrington Park.

Ojeda-Zapata, J. 1990. "Battering No. 1 Lesbian Problem." *St. Paul Pioneer Press-Dispatch*, October 21. (Located in *Newsbank* [microform], Social Relations, 1990, 72:D3-5, fiche.)

Pharr, S. 1986. "Two Workshops on Homophobia." Pp. 202–22 in *Naming the Violence*, edited by K. Lobel. Seattle, WA: Seal.

Porat, N. 1986. "Support Groups for Battered Lesbians." Pp. 80–87 in *Naming the Violence*, edited by K. Lobel. Seattle, WA: Seal.

Walker, L. 1986. "Battered Women's Shelters and Work with Battered Lesbians." Pp. 73–76 in *Naming the Violence*, edited by K. Lobel. Seattle, WA: Seal.

Walker, L. E. 1979. *The Battered Woman*. New York: Harper & Row.

39

ABUSE OF ELDERS

OLA BARNETT • CINDY L. MILLER-PERRIN

ROBIN D. PERRIN

Case History: Jenny and Jeff Jr. — Dwindling Assets, Dwindling Devotion

Several years after my husband's death, my mother-in-law, Jenny, who was 91, became unable to care for herself. She went to live with my brother-in-law, Jeff Jr., and his wife, Marianne. Although my own aging mother was dying, I took time to visit Jenny, who had always been a loving mother-in-law.

Over the next year, Jeff Jr. became Jenny's guardian, and she made out a new will giving one-third of her estate to each of us — myself, Jeff Jr., and Marianne. I didn't understand this sudden change from the previous division of half for each son, but I said nothing; after all, I was a widowed daughter-in-law.

As Jenny continued to deteriorate, I asked Jeff Jr. if he was planning to put Jenny in a retirement home where she would receive around-the-clock care. He said he couldn't afford to place her in a home and that he and Marianne would care for her at home. I was amazed. Jeff Jr. had sold Jenny's home for a probable yield of $150,000 in cash. Jeff Jr. and Marianne owned a mini-estate as well as stocks and bonds; they were probably worth $2 million.

I was puzzled by what was going on with Jenny and Jeff Jr., but then I became seriously concerned when I heard a number of rumors from Jenny's other relatives and friends. They said that Jeff Jr. and Marianne had offered financial advice to several aging relatives. Each had changed his or her will to name Jeff Jr. and Marianne the beneficiaries, and each had died shortly thereafter of neglect and malnutrition.

Over the next few months, I became alarmed when Jenny "refused to come to the phone" to speak to me. Marianne told me that "Jenny couldn't walk far enough to get to the phone." After 2 weeks, I drove several hours to visit her. I was appalled when I arrived. There was Jenny, sitting alone in a hot room that smelled like urine. She would not speak to me. She was in the maid's quarters, with no television and no phone. She was dirty and unkempt. There were no diapers in the room, the small refrigerator held only a piece of moldy bologna, and Jenny had not taken her medications. Later, when I expressed my concern to Jeff Jr., he said that he was going to hire a couple to come in and take care of her. I left feeling some sense of relief that Jenny's ordeal would soon be over.

A week later, I received a call from the caretaker couple. Frightened by Jenny's condition when they arrived to care for her, they had called the para-medics, who took Jenny to the hospital, and then they called me. Doctors diag-nosed Jenny's condition as malnutrition, dehydration, and "neglect." The caretakers said that Jeff Jr. and Marianne had gone on a vacation, leaving no money for food or diapers, no instructions, no telephone numbers or itinerary — not even any information about when they would return. Finally, I felt compelled to call the county adult protective services (APS) agency. Someone there promised to visit the premises and soon did so. I also called some other relatives, who started making unscheduled visits to see Jenny.

Jeff Jr. and Marianne continue to take unexpected vacations to visit other aging relatives who may "need financial management services in the near future." I fear that Jeff Jr. and Marianne hope to come home someday to find that Jenny has simply "passed away in her sleep." I am constantly uneasy about Jenny's situation. I frequently call APS to see if they can do something more, and I keep "popping in" to check up on Jenny when Jeff Jr. and Marianne are away from home.

Jenny, by all accounts, is doing better now. She is clean and has food in the refrigerator. The caretakers drop in every day briefly and bring in food and diapers on their own. Jenny is still alone most of the time, and she seems too frightened to say much. As Jenny's life is slowly ending, I feel that my life is "on hold." I wish I knew for sure that everything that can be done to protect Jenny is being done. It's in God's hands now.

Violence against elders has been a perpetual feature of American social history. As with other forms of family violence, however, there has been an ebb and flow in the visibility and invisibility of elder abuse. During the 1980s, violence against elders received heightened consideration, especially violence perpetrated by informal caretakers, such as relatives (Social Services Inspectorate 1992). The year 2002 brought international attention to elder abuse through the work of the World Health Organization (cited in Cook-Daniels 2003; Nelson 2002). Only recently, however, has elder abuse attracted scholarly examination at all consonant with other subfields of family violence. As a result, there is a surprising dearth of methodologically sound research on violence against elders.

Any type of problem afflicting the elderly, of course, is likely to multiply with the rapid increase of elderly in the population. According to the U.S. Bureau of the Census (2000), in 2000 there were almost 35 million elderly (65+ years of age) in the United States, 12.4% of the total population. This figure is apt to rise through at least the first few decades of the twenty-first century, as the post–World War II baby boom generation ages.

Changes in economic conditions, families and family mobility, women's roles, and traditional methods of elder care appear to have contributed to increasing rates of elder abuse (see Kosberg and Garcia 1995; Kwan 1995). One dilemma is that in American society there are no clear norms or moral rules about who is responsible for elder care (Phillipson 1993). Adult children are not legally required to help elderly parents in need. Moreover, many elders are childless, homosexual elders in particular (Cahill and Smith 2002). Because of this lack of moral and legal standards concerning responsibility for the elderly, it is difficult to know who society should hold accountable for their care or neglect. This ambiguity places the elderly in an especially vulnerable position.

Further complicating matters is the fact that even in cases of interpersonal violence involving elderly persons, it is often not clear who is the victim and who is the perpetrator. Indeed, some violence in which elders are involved can be categorized as mutual violence (e.g., Phillipson 1992). Elders may strike out at their caregivers, for instance, in reaction to the loss of personal freedom they feel when the caregivers find it necessary to curtail the elders' behavior (e.g., when the caregiver will not let the elder leave the house alone) (Meddaugh 1990). Taken together, these problems have generated a literature on elder abuse that lacks coherence and precision. In sum, the nascency of research on elder abuse leaves numerous gaps in current knowledge, thus creating a large number of uncertainties. . . .

Scope of the Problem

If an elderly father wishes to wear a food-stained jacket, are his offspring-caregivers supposed to enforce some sort of cleanliness standard to avoid being neglectful? What can a caregiver do if an elder decides to drink too much alcohol or otherwise act foolishly? What if an adult son decides to let his increasingly dependent father fend for himself? Is the son an abuser?

What Is Elder Abuse?

Arguably, the debate about what constitutes family violence is more pronounced in the area of elder abuse than in other subfields. State legislatures and various professional groups (e.g., in the fields of medicine and social work) all define elder abuse dissimilarly. In addition to definitional questions, additional challenges have arisen. To define elder abuse, one must, for example, specify the meanings of *elder* (i.e., age requirements), *dependency*, and *self-neglect*. The Joint Commission on Accreditation of Healthcare Organizations (JCAHO 2002) suggests defining an elder as someone 60 years of age or older. Congress also favors age 60 (Stiegel 2003).

Sexual Abuse   Direct forms of sexual abuse of elders encompass intercourse, molestation, sexualized kissing, oral/genital contact, and digital penetration. Indirect forms of sexual abuse include unwanted sexual discussions, exhibitionism, forced viewing of pornography, and exposed masturbation (see Ramsey-Klawsnik 1991). A surprising newer type of sex abuse has come to light in the form of pornographic Web sites that display older victims who were too mentally incapacitated to give consent. These sites offer still photographs of elderly women posed in every conceivable sexual activity. Viewers can also play short video clips of elderly women engaged in sexual activities. These media materials are classified as pornography, but laws regarding the use of older women hinge on the adults' ability to consent. Police officers who are specially trained in child and elder sexual abuse investigate these cases (Calkins 2003).

Financial Abuse   Financial abuse of elders consists of a number of behaviors: (a) misusing a durable power of attorney, bank account, or guardianship; (b) failing to compensate transfers of real estate; (c) charging excessive amounts for goods and services delivered to an elder; (d) using undue influence to gain control of an elder's money or property; and (e) predatory lending, Internet, telemarketing, or other frauds (Sweeney 2003).

Taxonomies of Elder Abuse   Boudreau (1993) distinguishes five broad categories of abuse most frequently cited in the literature: physical, psychological, financial/material, unsatisfactory living arrangement (e.g., unclean home), and violation of individual or constitutional rights. Although experts concur that physical violence constitutes abuse, they disagree over whether some behaviors, such as "violation of constitutional rights," are abuse. At what point, for example, do a caregiver's actions become a violation of an elder's constitutional rights? Does a daughter who makes her elderly mother wear a bib at dinner violate the mother's constitutional rights?

In creating a more widely acknowledged classification system, Hudson (1991) solicited opinions from 63 professionals in diverse specialties such as law, medicine, psychology, public health, and social work. Over three successive rounds of decision making, these experts attempted to reach consensus about the appropriateness of certain theoretical definitions of elder abuse.

Representative of one series of judgments, participants categorized mistreatment into two major classes (elder abuse and elder neglect) with two modes of intent (unintentional and intentional). Each round resulted in greater and greater specificity with more and more subdefinitions. The final taxonomy consists of four forms of elder abuse: physical, social, psychological, and financial. With one exception, senior adults in a follow-up study agreed with the experts' definitions. Leaders in the field believe that some forms of abuse (e.g., yelling) must occur several times to reach the level of abuse, whereas the interviewed elders believed even one such occurrence is abusive (Hudson et al. 2000). It is important to acknowledge that elders find disrespect a very painful type of abuse, although it is not included in these taxonomies (Cook-Daniels 2003). Note that the taxonomy excludes self-neglect and does not list sexual abuse separately. Insertion of sexual abuse into the physical abuse category may be unfortunate, because sexual abuse represents a distinctive form of elder abuse. Table 1 presents the taxonomy of elder abuse developed by Hudson et al. (2000).

Gay, Lesbian, Bisexual, and Transgendered Elders Although dating violence and intimate partner violence (IPV) among younger gay, lesbian, bisexual, and transgendered (GLBT) persons have gained some recognition, older GLBT individuals often go unidentified and unassisted by medical and mental health personnel. Both **heterosexism** (denigration of non-heterosexual behavior) and **homophobia** (fear or hatred of homosexual orientation) plague GLBT elders. An abusive caregiver, as one example, can threaten to "out" a gay elder if the gay elder will not comply with the caregiver's demands (see Cahill and Smith 2002).

Elder Abuse among Minorities Some racial-ethnic groups have distinctive views about elder abuse (Hudson et al., 2000). Korean Americans, for example, traditionally participate in a type of co-ownership of elder parents' financial assets, an arrangement that many African Americans and Whites consider a form of financial exploitation. Another cultural difference is that Korean Americans judge it inappropriate to tell outsiders "family business"; thus they do not report elder abuse at a rate comparable to either African Americans or Whites (Moon and Benton 2000). Korean Americans are also especially likely to blame elder victims for their own abuse (Moon and Benton 2000). Interestingly, as Asian immigrants' children become Americanized, they are beginning to change the habit of keeping aging parents at home and are putting them in assisted living centers (Kershaw 2003). A survey of 2,702 White, African American, and Hispanic female victims in Illinois found some differences among types of abuse experienced. In particular, about four times as many Hispanic women and three times as many White women reported sexual abuse as did African American women (Grossman and Lundy 2003). . . .

TABLE 1   Theoretical Definitions of Elder Mistreatment and Abuse by Delphi Panel of Elder Mistreatment Experts

Level I	
Elder mistreatment	Destructive behavior that is directed toward an older adult; occurs within the context of a relationship connoting trust; and is of sufficient intensity and/or frequency to produce harmful physical, psychological, social, and/or financial effects of unnecessary suffering, injury, pain, loss, and/or violation of human rights and poorer quality of life for the older adult
Personal/social relationship	Persons in close personal relationships with an older adult connoting trust and some socially established behavioral norms, for example, relatives by blood or marriage, friends, neighbors, any "significant other"
Professional/business relationship	Persons in a formal relationship with an older adult that denotes trust and expected services, for example, physicians, nurses, social workers, nursing aides, bankers, lawyers, nursing home staff, home health personnel, and landlords
Level II	
Elder abuse	Aggressive or invasive behavior/action(s), or threats of same, inflicted on an older adult and resulting in harmful effects for the older adult
Elder neglect	The failure of a responsible party(ies) to act so as to provide, or to provide what is prudently deemed adequate and reasonable assistance that is available and warranted to ensure that the older adult's basic physical, psychological, social, and financial needs are met, resulting in harmful effects for the older adult
Level III	
Intentional	Abusive or neglectful behavior or acts that are carried out for the purpose of harming, deceiving, coercing, or controlling the older adult so as to produce gain for the perpetrator (often labeled *active* abuse/neglect in the literature)
Unintentional	Abusive or neglectful behavior or acts that are carried out, but *not* for the purpose of harming, deceiving, coercing, or controlling the older adult, so as to produce gain for the perpetrator (often labeled *passive* abuse/neglect in the literature)
Level IV	
Physical	Behavior(s)/actions in which physical force(s) is used to inflict the abuse; or available and warranted physical assistance is not provided, resulting in neglect
Psychological	Behavior(s)/action(s) in which verbal force is used to inflict the abuse; or available and warranted psychological/emotional assistance/support is not provided, resulting in neglect

(Continued)

(Table 1 Continued)

Social	Behavior(s)/action(s) that prevents the basic social needs of an older adult from being met; or failure to provide available and warranted means by which an older adult's basic social needs can be met
Financial	Theft or misuse of an older adult's funds or property; or failure to provide available and warranted means by which an older adult's basic material needs can be met

Source: "Elder Mistreatment: A Taxonomy with Definitions by Delphi," by M. F. Hudson, 1991, *Journal of Elder Abuse and Neglect,* 3 (2): 14. Copyright 1991 by Margaret F. Hudson. Reprinted with permission.

Prevalence of Abuse

The rates of elder abuse in Australia, Canada, Great Britain, and Norway appear to be roughly similar to estimated rates in the United States (Kurrle and Sadler 1993; Ogg and Bennett 1992; Podnieks 1992). The estimated proportion of Finnish elders seeking shelter from abuse is 3% to 6% (cited in Kivela 1995). In Greece, the estimate for physical abuse is quite high, 15% (Pitsiou-Darrough and Spinellis 1995). A recent survey of 355 elderly Chinese in Hong Kong revealed a 2% rate for physical abuse and a 20.8% rate for verbal abuse (Yan and Tang 2001). In another study, 18% of 4,000 elderly Japanese reported knowing of an elder victim (Tsukada, Saito, and Tatara 2001). A survey of older women ($M = 75$ years) in Ireland, Italy, and the United Kingdom suggested the elder abuse rate was approximately 20% (Ockleford et al. 2003).

In most foreign countries, elders receive support and care through informal care systems (i.e., family) rather than through formal institutions (e.g., nursing homes). In Finland there are no government programs of any sort for elder care (cited in Kivela 1995), and in Australia there are no adult protective services (Dunn 1995). In Israel, only 15% of dependent elderly receive help from public authorities; the rest rely on informal sources (Lowenstein 1995). In Greece, elder abuse is "just one more problem," and victims must wait their turn for help from social agencies (Johns and Hydle 1995). European support services are only marginally involved in assisting elder abuse victims. Less than a third of victims report receiving any assistance, and agencies fail to collect data on elder victims who seek assistance (Ockleford et al. 2003).

Laws regarding elder abuse vary throughout the world. In contrast to the United States, many countries assign responsibility for elder care to adult children. In India, all financially able children are legally responsible for parental care (Shah, Veedon, and Vasi 1995). In Finland, however, as many as 20% of elders have no children or family of any sort to offer support (or abuse) (cited in Kivela 1995). In Ireland, refusing to provide necessities of life to any child or any aged or sick person is a misdemeanor (Horkan 1995).

Israel has no special legal provisions for elders, but they are protected under a general Protection of Helpless Persons law (Lowenstein 1995). As of 1994, South Africa had no laws dealing with elder abuse (Eckely and Vilakazi 1995). . . .

Because elder abuse is particularly underrecognized and underreported, prevalence estimates are complicated. Unlike children, who usually go out of the house at least to attend school, elders who live alone and seldom leave their homes are practically invisible. Although similar to other intimate violence victims in not reporting all of their mistreatment, elders are more likely than younger victims to report crimes (Klaus 2000). The National Elder Abuse Incidence Study (NEAIS), based on APS data, showed that reports of elder abuse rose significantly over the period from 1986 to 1996. Apparently, elder abuse is not as hidden as it once was (National Center on Elder Abuse [NCEA] 1998).

Nonetheless, the NEAIS found more than five times as many unreported cases as reported cases. Some elements of reluctance to report are mental incapability, nonrecognition of abuse, fear of others' disbelief, stigma, and fear of loss of independence (Stiegel 2001). By contrast, increased reporting rates are associated with lower SES [socioeconomic status] of elders, more community training of area professionals, and higher agency service rating scores (Wolf and Donglin 1999). . . .

Official Estimates   The U.S. Bureau of Justice Statistics recently disseminated analyses of criminal victimization of persons age 65 and older averaged over the years 1992–1997. Although the research was somewhat limited by government-specified samples and methodology, statistician Patsy A. Klaus (2000) provided a large number of core findings about elder abuse. She established that, compared with younger persons, elders suffer a much smaller proportion of violent crimes, including murders—about one-tenth as many as younger people.

Klaus used the FBI's *Supplementary Homicide Reports (SHR)* to estimate murder rates. One unexpected factor related to eldercide is that a number of "gray murders," unrecognized murders of elderly people, have occurred. An obstacle in grappling with this issue is the low autopsy rate for elder deaths, less than 1% in recent years. Attending physicians, not pathologists, determine cause of death for most seniors, and research has found a discordance rate of 44% between physicians' and pathologists' determinations of cause of death (Burton, as cited in Soos 2000).

Annual homicide rates averaged over the years 1992–1997 from *SHR* analyses revealed gender and racial differences. Elder males were perpetrators of homicide at a rate twice as great as females. Blacks were overrepresented as murder victims and perpetrators. Males also committed the majority of homicide-suicides occurring at age 55+ years (Cohen, Llorente, and Eisendorfer 1998). Dawson and Langan (1994) found in a study for the U.S. Bureau of Justice Statistics that sons and daughters commit only 11% of all homicides of victims age 60+ years. Of these patricides and matricides, sons kill fathers (53%) about as often as they kill mothers (47%), but daughters kill fathers (81%) much more often than they kill mothers (19%). . . .

In a survey conducted in 2000 under the auspices of the National Association of Adult Protective Services Administrators, Teaster (2003) amassed reports on elder/adult abuse from state APS agencies. The number of elder/adult abuse reports received by APS associations reached 472,813. In states that responded, APS investigated 396,398 reports, and APS workers confirmed 166,019 cases. Data from 40 states indicated that 41.9% of the unsubstantiated reports were for self-neglect, 20.1% were for physical abuse, and 13.2% were for caregiver neglect/abandonment. The amount of financial abuse of the elderly is unknown, but may affect 10.5% to 49.3% of abused elders (NCEA 1998; Teaster 2003).

Self-Report Estimates   Recognizing the need for more generalizable and inclusive data, Pillemer and Finkelhor (1988) conducted telephone interviews with 2,020 Boston area residents age 65 and older. They estimated prevalence rates of three different kinds of elder abuse: physical, psychological, and neglect. They did not, however, assess financial abuse. Using a modified version of the Conflict Tactics Scale (CTS1; Straus 1979), they defined physical abuse as any violent act (e.g., pushed, grabbed, shoved, beat up) committed by a caregiver (spouse, child, or other coresident) since the respondent had turned 65. They defined neglect as withholding assistance with daily living (e.g., meal preparation, housework) 10 or more times in the preceding year. Finally, they designated psychological abuse as "chronic verbal aggression" (e.g., insulted, swore at, threatened) occurring more than 10 times a year.

Of 2,020 elders interviewed, 63 (3.2%) reported being abused. Specifically, 2% reported being physically abused, 1.1% reported being psychologically abused, and 0.4% reported being neglected (in the past year) (Pillemer and Finkelhor 1988). From these figures, the researchers estimated that 701,000–1,093,560 elders were abuse victims each year in the United States. Findings of the NEAIS indicated that the number of older people abused annually was much smaller, 450,000 (NCEA 1998). The sampling procedure for the NEAIS, however, garnered extensive criticism (e.g., Cook-Daniels 1999; Otto and Quinn 1999). A group of studies pinpointed the level of any elder abuse as falling between 19.1% and 59.4% (cited in Brandl and Cook-Daniels 2002). . . .

As expected, nearly all elderly sexual assault victims are women and nearly all perpetrators are men. In a small study, Mouton, Rovi, Furniss, and Lasser (1999) found that husbands were guilty of forcing sex among 7% of older women. These older women had been battered throughout their lifetimes. A large percentage (80%) of sexual assault victims in a nursing home study were impaired. These women were in wheelchairs, were bedridden, or had dementia.

Injury Estimates   Injury estimates arise from both official and self-report data. The latest official numerical summary from the National Electronic

Injury Surveillance System–All Injury Program provides the most comprehensive and reliable data concerning injuries of elders seeking treatment at hospital emergency departments ("Public Health" 2003). This program furnishes national, annualized, weighted estimates of nonfatal, nonsexual, physical assaults categorized by intent. During 2001, roughly 33,026 elders received treatment in emergency departments (rate = 72/100,000). The majority of elders treated were men (55.4%). Primary injuries were as follows: (a) contusion/abrasion, 31.9%; (b) laceration, 21.1%; and (c) fracture, 12.7%. The primary sources of injury were assaults as follows: (a) by body part, 20.3%; (b) blunt object, 17.1%; (c) push, 14.4%; and (d) undetermined (31.8%). Perpetrators were most likely to be family members or acquaintances.

The 1992–1997 NCVS analysis of self-report data revealed that elders sustained 36,290 injuries annually. Relatives/intimates injured 41%, and others known to the victims caused 59% of injuries (Klaus 2000). A different account indicates that genital injuries are exceptionally common among older sexual assault victims (age 55+) relative to younger assault victims (ages 18–54). Of the 53 women making up the older group in this study sample, 27 sustained genital injuries compared with 7 injuries among the 53 women in the younger group (Muram, Miller, and Cutler 1992). Another outcome for abused elders is a greater likelihood of death compared with nonabused elders, even though cause of death may not be directly traceable to injuries or ill health (Lachs et al. 1998). . . .

Searching for Patterns: Who Is Abused and Who Are the Abusers?

Elder abuse researchers have tried to classify types of elders who may be especially vulnerable to abuse and types of individuals who are most apt to abuse elders. They have examined issues of family relationship, gender, age, and race, as well as mental health and alcohol abuse. Kosberg and Nahmiash (1996) have developed a conceptual framework for categorizing characteristics of victims and abusers that includes the following factors: living arrangements, gender, SES, health, age, psychological factors, problem behaviors, dependence, isolation, financial problems, family violence, and lack of social support. Given definitional, sampling, and methodological limitations of available research, social scientists accept identified patterns as preliminary in nature.

Characteristics of Abused Elders

Research on elder abuse has revealed few consistent differences, if any, between victims and nonvictims. In their review of the literature, Brandl and Cook-Daniels (2002) were unable to uncover any standard victim profile. Compared with members of all other age and ethnic groups, an elderly White female is the least likely person to sustain a violent victimization

(Klaus 2000). Chu's (2001) analysis of elder homicides revealed that risk factors for victimization are gender (male) and race (African American).

The American Bar Association's Commission on Legal Problems of the Elderly has outlined some risk factors, screening techniques, and remedies relevant to financial abuse of elders. Risk factors appear to be abuser dependency on elder or elder dependency on abuser, elder's physical frailty or impairment, social isolation, and substance abuse or psychiatric conditions of either abuser or elder victim (Stiegel 2001).

Age   Because not all researchers and organizations define the status of elder in the same way, the victim characteristic of age is difficult to pin down. Some state APS agencies typically serve all adults, without regard to age, whereas others serve only elders, defined as persons 60 or 65 years of age. The fastest-growing group of elders in the United States today is made up of individuals 80 years old and older, and these elders are targets of abuse and neglect significantly more often than others (NCEA 1998).

Gender   The data available concerning gender are somewhat contradictory. APS reports for the 2000 survey revealed that, of substantiated cases, more than half of elder abuse victims (56.0%) were female (Teaster 2003). In contrast, data from an older Boston self-report community survey indicated that more than half of the victims in that sample were male (52%). Even more important, the Boston study suggests that the victimization rate for men (5.1%) is double that for women (2.5%). One explanation for this finding is that 65% of the respondents were women. Equivalent numbers of male and female victims suggest that risk of victimization is greater for men (Pillemer and Finkelhor 1988). Chu's (2001) analysis of *SHR* data points to more intimate partner homicide victimization of males than of females. Of course, a large number of offender–victim relationships of murder victims are unknown.

Socioeconomic Status and Race   Some studies have found no racial disparities in rates of elder abuse (e.g., Pillemer and Finkelhor 1988), whereas others have (e.g., Klaus 2000). One investigation of the relationship between SES and elder abuse revealed that poor elders in the United States are no more likely to be abused than middle-class elders (Boudreau 1993). Another appraisal found that retired elders are at no greater risk than those still working (Bachman and Pillemer 1991). One team of researchers has suggested that members of various racial/ethnic groups may differ more in the behaviors they view as abusive than in actual frequency of abusive behaviors experienced (Moon and Williams 1993).

Hudson and Carlson (1999) found the following abuse rates among 924 North Carolinians age 40+ years: African Americans, 9.2%; Whites, 7.7%; and Native Americans, 4.3%. One appraisal of 597 agency cases revealed that European Americans (Whites) were more likely to suffer from self-neglect, African Americans from neglect by others, and both races equally from physical or financial abuse (Longres 1992).

Other Factors Studies suggest that there may be some relationship between living arrangements and elder abuse. Several researchers have found that significant numbers of abused elders live in the same homes as their abusers (e.g., Lachs et al. 1997; Vladescu et al. 1999). In a study of three model projects, staff rated "changes in living arrangements" as the most effective intervention strategy and "changes in the circumstances of the perpetrator" as the least effective. Of 266 cases for which data on resolutions were available, more than one-third judged the problem as "completely" resolved and another third believed that "some progress" in resolution had been made. Victim receptivity to intervention was a key variable in successful resolution, and perpetrator lack of receptivity was pivotal in unresolved cases (Wolf and Pillemer 1989).

If elders become more isolated, however, they may become easier prey to other kinds of abuses, such as financial exploitation. Living arrangements possibly affect the likelihood of victimization in regard to gender. If elderly men are more likely to be living with someone, their rate of abuse may increase while women's decreases (see Paveza et al. 1992; Pillemer and Finkelhor 1988). An apparent ecological risk factor for elder abuse is the rate of reported child abuse in a community. Presumably, factors that affect child abuse rates, such as community resources and differing characteristics of caseworkers, may account for this correlation (Jogerst et al. 2000).

Older IPV victims often do not leave their abusers. A recent study identified three major reasons why abused elder women stay with their abusers: (a) pragmatic concerns, such as economic insufficiency; (b) belief systems common to their generation and inadequate societal assistance; and (c) aging and health issues (Zink et al. 2003). Because their plight is seldom recognized by professionals, they receive little assistance toward leaving. In addition, few shelter programs nationwide are prepared to meet the needs of older battered women (see AARP 1994; Boudreau 1993; McFall 2000; Vinton 1998; Vinton, Altholz, and Lobell 1997). Shelter eligibility requirements may restrict entry to IPV victims, so that elders victimized by adult children and grandchildren are not admitted. . . .

Characteristics of Elder Abusers

There are so many noncontinuities among research results that a high degree of uncertainty exists about the typical characteristics of elder/adult abusers. Customary risk factors for elder homicide perpetrators are gender (male) and race (African American) (Chu 2001). One might think, however, that women would be the most likely abusers because they provide most informal family caregiving for elders (Arber and Ginn 1999). Several variables may be descriptive of a subset of elder abusers: (a) cognitive impairments or mental illnesses (Collins and O'Connor 2000); (b) financial dependency on the abused elder (e.g., Bendik 1992); (c) substance abuse problems, arrest records, and poor employment records (see Greenberg, McKibben, and Raymond 1990); and (d) social isolation (Bendik 1992).

Age   With only 10 states reporting on this topic, the 2000 APS survey mentioned above determined ages of elder abuse perpetrators as follows: (a) under 18 years, 5.9%; (b) 18 to 35, 18.4%; (c) 36 to 50, 24.8%; (d) 51 to 65, 10.4%; (d) 65+, 8.9%; and (e) not reported, 31.6% (Teaster 2003). Many abusive caretakers in Pillemer and Finkelhor's (1988) community survey were over age 50 (75%), and some were over 70 (20%). Abusers who are elders themselves may suffer from dementia or other problems that render them less able to care for dependent elders and more likely to abuse those elders. Although some neglect by such elders may be conscious and premeditated, some may result from ignorance or incompetence. Accounting for intentionality of abuse in such cases is another important issue (Glendenning 1993).

Gender   Even though women usually shoulder the major burden of elder care (Deitch 1993), they seem not to be the primary elder abusers. With only 17 states responding, the 2000 APS survey ascertained that with the exception of neglect, most abusers were male (52%) and a third (33%) were females, with the gender of the remainder (15%) unknown (Teaster 2003). A number of studies have found sons to be more abusive than daughters toward elderly parents (e.g., Crichton et al. 1998; Wolf and Pillemer 1997). One study, however, found opposite results when neglect was included as a category of abuse (Anetzberger 1998; Dunlop et al. 2000).

Relationship to Victim   There has been considerable discussion about which group of family members or others is most likely to abuse elders/adults. Family members consist of spouses, parents, children, grandchildren, siblings, and other relatives. Many empirical data show that adult children are the primary offenders (e.g., Brownell, Berman, and Salamone 1999; Vladescu et al. 1999). The NEAIS-2000 survey of APS agencies, for instance, indicated that adult children are the largest category of abusers, 39% to 80% (NCEA 1998).

In contrast, several other comparisons have indicated that elder abuse is primarily "spouse abuse grown old," an extension of IPV into old age (Harris 1996). Several international evaluations have also found data congruent with the spouse abuse thesis. Grossman and Lundy (2003), for example, found notable discrepancies in accounts of victim–offender relationships arising from different service agencies. Although agencies serving domestic violence victims reported that husbands or ex-husbands perpetrated the largest proportion of abuse, APS organizations reported that adult children committed most of the abuse. In reality, available data cannot settle this debate with certitude. With so much ambiguity about definitions and types of reporters, not to mention underreporting biases and large gaps in data caused by nonresponding organizations, there is much room for error.

Data from the APS 2000 survey, with 25 states reporting, indicated that the majority of confirmed elder/adult abusers (61.7%) were family members (Teaster 2003). Of family perpetrators, 30.2% were spouses or intimate partners, and 17.6% were adult children. Institutional staff committed 4.4% of abuses. A Canadian investigation of 128 elders 60+ years for whom services had been requested uncovered the following rates for abusers: spouse, 48%; adult child, 30%; and acquaintance, 22% (Lithwick et al. 1999). Although most of the abuse (87%) was psychological, spouses did perpetrate most physical abuse (31%).

In an examination of 1,855 substantiated elder abuse and neglect cases from January 1993 through June 1993, the Los Angeles County Department of Community and Senior Citizen Services (1994) determined that 66% of the suspected abusers were family members (35% offspring, 18% other relationships, and 14% spouses). Other suspects were care custodians (12%), no relationship (14%), unknown (4%), and health practitioners (3%).

Lithwick et al. (1999) ascertained that adult children carried out substantially more financial abuse (59%) and neglect (49%) than did spouses (financial abuse, 13%; neglect, 23%). Acquaintances, however, perpetrated the highest amount of financial abuse (75%), but less neglect (30%) and physical abuse (7%). In a small study of 28 cases of elder sexual assault, incestuous assaults were most frequent. These included 11 adult sons, 1 grandson, and 2 brothers. Spouses were perpetrators in 7 cases. The remainder were 1 boyfriend, 2 boarders, 1 friend, 1 distant relative, and 2 unrelated caretakers (Ramsey-Klawsnik 1991). . . .

Public Attitudes toward Abuse of Elders

Some members of society may have attitudes condoning violence against elders (Yan and Tang 2003). Emblematic of this problem is the concept of postmaturity, the idea that elders are living too long. Some believe that older people have had their "day in the sun" and now should just "fade away" (Ansello 1996). Kosberg and Garcia (1995) have formulated a list of six viewpoints that promote elder abuse: ageism, sexism, proviolence attitudes, reactions to abuse, negative attitudes toward people with disabilities, and family caregiving imperatives. When caregivers hold such attitudes, they are likely to miss signs of elder abuse (Fulmer et al. 1999).

Attitudes held by some members of the current elder cohort also have the effect of hiding abuse. Several anecdotal or qualitative reports have indicated that older women may feel humiliated to admit being abused by a family member. In fact, most abused elder women . . . do not seek help from anyone (Brandl et al. 2003; J. Mears 2003). The elderly women served by agencies tend to believe such mottos as "What goes on at home stays at home." They also have a strong ethic about "not being a burden" on their children. Such attitudes pose a challenge to agency personnel who wish to reach out to and help abused elders. In listening to older women's opinions, personnel at Project REACH in Maine learned to avoid using stigmatizing terms such as *domestic violence* and *battered woman* when placing advertisements about support groups. Using a trial-and-error procedure, they fashioned ads that used terminology suitable for attracting needy and isolated older women. They found that ads referring to the "concerns of older women," for example, were more palatable to their target audience than ads that mentioned the "abuse of older women" (see Brandl et al. 2003; London 2003; J. Mears 2003).

Various popular media tend to perpetuate stereotypes of older people, depicting them as primarily supportive of children and grandchildren or as cranky and laughable. The entertainment media include relatively few depictions of elders who lead rewarding lives (see London 2003). Although there is no adequate research on the topic, it probably is true that most Americans find it inappropriate for elders to be sexually active. Some nursing homes make it possible for elder residents to have privacy for sexual activities by providing door locks and keys, but others make such activities impossible by allowing residents no privacy.

Section Summary

Experts have advanced several theories to explain elder abuse. Learning theory accentuates the notion of the acquisition of abusive behaviors during childhood and their manifestation in adulthood, with the elder parent as victim. So little research has been conducted, however, that it is too early to evaluate this explanation.

Social exchange theory, as applied to elder abuse, posits that just as aging parents (or spouses) need more and more care, they are less and less able to offer rewards or benefits to those who care for them. This imbalance implies that caring for an elder "doesn't pay," so a caretaker might just as well neglect the elder. Social interactionism is related to social exchange theory but depends on elder abuse perpetrators' perceptions of an imbalance in the exchange.

A common theme in explanations of elder abuse is the situational stress of the caregiver. This model assumes that the dependency of an elder, brought about by impairments, raises the "costs" of elder care but not the benefits to the caregiver. Presumably, dependent elders' needs create such powerful feelings of stress in their caregivers that the caregivers may lose control and abuse the elders. For many middle-aged adult children caring for aging parents, the stress generated by this responsibility potentiates the stress from caring for their own children. Although most studies indicate little relationship between physical health indicators and abuse, a few have found that an elder's physical dependency clearly plays a role in vulnerability to abuse. Certainly, one might surmise that impairments of disabled persons make them vulnerable to abuse.

The individual differences (psychopathology of the abuser) theory presumes that elder abuse most likely results from the deviance and dependency of abusers. A large body of evidence demonstrates that perpetrators do tend to have far-ranging problems, such as alcohol abuse and emotional difficulties. The psychological status of abusers, in fact, may be a better predictor of elder abuse than characteristics of victims.

Given that all of these theories have limitations, it may be necessary to identify a configuration of related factors or to integrate theories. Situational stress, for example, in combination with particular personality types, might set the stage for elder mistreatment. Public attitudes toward elders, GLBT persons, and the disabled contribute to their abuse by intimates, acquaintances, and the entire health care system.

REFERENCES

AARP [American Association of Retired Persons]. 1994. "Survey of Services for Older Battered Women." Unpublished manuscript, Washington, DC.

Anetzberger, G. J. 1998. "Psychological Abuse and Neglect: A Cross-Cultural Concern to Older Americans." Pp. 141–51 in *Understanding and Combating Elder Abuse in Minority Communities,* edited by Archstone Foundation. Long Beach, CA: Archstone Foundation.

Ansello, E. F. 1996. "Understanding the Problem." Pp. 9–29 in *Abuse, Neglect, and Exploitation of Older Persons: Strategies for Assessment and Intervention,* edited by L. A. Baumhover and S. C. Beall. Baltimore: Health Professions Press.

Arber, S. and J. Ginn. 1999. "Gender Differences in Informal Caring." Pp. 321–39 in *The Sociology of the Family: A Reader,* edited by G. Allan. Oxford: Blackwell.

Bachman, R. and K. A. Pillemer. 1991. "Retirement: Does It Affect Marital Conflict and Violence?" *Journal of Elder Abuse and Neglect* 3 (2): 75–88.

Bendik, M. F. 1992. "Reaching the Breaking Point: Dangers of Mistreatment in Elder Caregiving Situations." *Journal of Elder Abuse and Neglect* 4 (3): 39–59.

Boudreau, F. A. 1993. "Elder Abuse." Pp. 142–58 in *Family Violence: Prevention and Treatment,* edited by R. L. Hampton, T. P. Gullotta, G. R. Adams, E. H. Potter III, and R. P. Weissberg. Newbury Park, CA: Sage.

Brandl, B. and L. Cook-Daniels. 2002. *Domestic Abuse in Later Life.* Washington, DC: National Resource Center on Domestic Violence.

Brandl, B., M. Herbert, J. Rozwadowski, and D. Spangler. 2003. "Feeling Safe, Feeling Strong: Support Groups for Older Abused Women." *Violence against Women* 9:1490–1503.

Brownell, P., J. Berman, and A. Salamone. 1999. "Mental Health and Criminal Justice Issues among Perpetrators of Elder Abuse." *Journal of Elder Abuse and Neglect* 11 (4): 81–94.

Cahill, S. and K. Smith. 2002. "Policy Issues Affecting Lesbian, Gay, Bisexual, and Transgender People in Retirement." *Generations* 26 (2): 49–54.

Calkins, P. 2003, July/August. "Cross-Discipline Gains in Indiana." *Victimization of the Elderly and Disabled* 6:17–18, 30.

Chu, L. D. 2001. "Homicide and Factors That Determine Fatality from Assault in the Elderly Population." UMI No. 3032861. *Dissertation Abstracts International* 62 (11): 5063B.

Cohen, D., M. Llorente, and C. Eisendorfer. 1998. "Homicide/Suicide in Older Persons." *American Journal of Psychiatry* 155:390–96.

Collins, P. G. and A. O'Connor. 2000. "Rape and Sexual Assault of the Elderly: An Exploratory Study of Ten Cases Referred to the Irish Forensic Psychiatry Service." *Irish Journal of Psychological Medicine* 17:128–31.

Cook-Daniels, L. 1999, May/June. "Interpreting the National Elder Abuse Incidence Study." *Victimization of the Elderly and Disabled* 2:1–2.

———. 2003, January/February. "2003 Is the Year Elder Abuse Hits the International Stage." *Victimization of the Elderly and Disabled* 5:65–66, 76.

Crichton, S. J., J. B. Bond, Jr., C. D. H. Harvey, and J. Ristok. 1998. "Elder Abuse: Feminist and Ageist Perspectives." *Journal of Elder Abuse and Neglect* 10 (3/4): 115–30.

Dawson, J. M. and P. A. Langan. 1994. *Murder in Families.* NCJ Publication No. 143498. Annapolis Junction, MD: U.S. Bureau of Justice Statistics.

Deitch, I. 1993, August. "Alone, Abandoned, Assaulted: Prevention and Intervention of Elder Abuse." Paper presented at the annual meeting of the American Psychological Association, Toronto.

Dunlop, B. D., M. B. Rothman, K. M. Condon, K. S. Hebert, and I. L. Martinez. 2000. "Elder Abuse: Risk Factors and Use of Case Data to Improve Policy and Practice." *Journal of Elder Abuse and Neglect* 12 (3/4): 95–122.

Dunn. P. F. 1995. "'Elder Abuse' as an Innovation to Australia: A Critical Overview." Pp. 13–30 in *Elder Abuse: International and Cross-Cultural Perspectives,* edited by J. I. Kosberg and J. L. Garcia. Binghamton, NY: Haworth.

Eckely, S. C. A. and P. A. C. Vilakazi. 1995. "Elder Abuse in South Africa." Pp. 171–82 in *Elder Abuse: International and Cross-Cultural Perspectives.* Binghamton, NY: Haworth.

Fulmer, T. T., M. Ramirez, S. Fairchild, D. Holmes, M. J. Koren, and J. Teresi. 1999. "Prevalence of Elder Mistreatment as Reported by Social Workers in a Probability Sample of Adult Day Health Care Clients." *Journal of Elder Abuse and Neglect* 11 (3): 25–36.

Glendenning, F. 1993. "What Is Elder Abuse and Neglect?" Pp. 1–34 in *The Mistreatment of Elderly People,* edited by P. Decalmer and F. Glendenning. London: Sage.

Greenberg, J. R., M. McKibben, and J. A. Raymond. 1990. "Dependent Adult Children and Elder Abuse." *Journal of Elder Abuse and Neglect* 2 (1/2): 73–86.

Grossman, S. E. and M. Lundy. 2003. "Use of Domestic Violence Services across Race and Ethnicity by Women Aged Fifty-Five and Older." *Violence against Women* 9:1442–52.

Harris, S. B. 1996. "For Better or for Worse: Spouse Abuse Grown Old." *Journal of Elder Abuse and Neglect* 8 (1): 1–33.

Horkan, E. M. 1995. "Elder Abuse in the Republic of Ireland." Pp. 119–37 in *Elder Abuse: International and Cross-Cultural Perspectives.* Binghamton, NY: Haworth.

Hudson, M. F. 1991. "Elder Mistreatment: A Taxonomy with Definitions by Delphi." *Journal of Elder Abuse and Neglect* 3 (2): 1–20.

Hudson, M. F., C. Beasley, R. H. Benedict, J. R. Carlson, B. F. Craig, and S. C. Mason. 2000. "Elder Abuse: Some Caucasian-American Views." *Journal of Elder Abuse and Neglect* 12 (1): 89–114.

Hudson, M. F. and J. R. Carlson. 1999. "Elder Abuse: Its Meaning to Caucasians, African Americans, and Native Americans." Pp. 187–204 in *Understanding Elder Abuse in Minority Populations,* edited by T. Tatara. Washington, DC: Taylor and Francis.

JCAHO [Joint Commission on Accreditation of Healthcare Organizations]. 2002. *How to Recognize Abuse and Neglect.* Oakbrook Terrace, IL: Author.

Johns, S. and I. Hydle. 1995. "Norway: Weakness in Welfare." Pp. 139–56 in *Elder Abuse: International and Cross-Cultural Perspectives,* edited by J. I. Kosberg and J. L. Garcia. Binghamton, NY: Haworth.

Jogerst G. J., J. D. Dawson, A. J. Hartz, J. W. Ely, and L. A. Schweitzer. 2000. "Community Characteristics Associated with Elder Abuse." *Journal of the American Geriatric Society* 48:513–18.

Kershaw, S. 2003. "Elder Care Americanized." *Los Angeles Daily News,* October 20, p. 12.

Kivela, S. L. 1995. "Elder Abuse in Finland." Pp. 31–44 in *Elder Abuse: International and Cross-Cultural Perspectives,* edited by J. I. Kosberg and J. L Garcia. Binghamton, NY: Haworth.

Klaus, P. A. 2000. *Crimes against Persons Age Sixty-Five or Older, 1992–97.* NCJ Publication No. 176352. Washington, DC: U.S. Department of Justice. Retrieved December 8, 2003 (http://www.ojp.usdoj.gov/bjs/pub/pdf/cpa6597.pdf).

Kosberg, J. I. and J. L. Garcia. 1995. "Introduction to the Book." Pp. 1–12 in *Elder Abuse: International and Cross-Cultural Perspectives,* edited by J. I. Kosberg and J. L. Garcia. Binghamton, NY: Haworth.

Kosberg, J. I. and D. Nahmiash. 1996. "Characteristics of Victims and Perpetrators and Milieus of Abuse and Neglect." Pp. 31–49 in *Abuse, Neglect, and Exploitation of Older Persons: Strategies of Assessment and Intervention,* edited by L. A. Baumhover and S. C. Beall. Baltimore: Health Professions Press.

Kurrle, S. E. and P. M. Sadler. 1993. "Australian Service Providers: Responses to Elder Abuse." *Journal of Elder Abuse and Neglect* 5 (1): 57–76.

Kwan, A. Y. 1995. "Elder Abuse in Hong Kong." Pp. 65–80 in *Elder Abuse: International and Cross-Cultural Perspectives,* edited by J. I. Kosberg and J. L. Garcia. Binghamton, NY: Haworth.

Lachs, M. S., C. Williams, S. O'Brien, L. Hurst, and R. Horwitz. 1997. "Risk Factors for Reported Elder Abuse and Neglect: A Nine-Year Observational Cohort Study." *Gerontologist* 37:469–74.

Lachs, M. S., C. Williams, S. O'Brien, K. A. Pillemer, and M. Charlson. 1998. "The Mortality of Elder Mistreatment." *Journal of the American Medical Association* 280:428–32.

Lithwick, M., M. Beaulieu, S. Gravel, and S. M. Straka. 1999. "The Mistreatment of Older Adults: Perpetrator–Victim Relationships and Interventions." *Journal of Elder Abuse and Neglect* 11 (4): 95–112.

London, M. 2003, May/June. "Crafting Support Services for Older Women." *Victimization of the Elderly and Disabled* 6:5–6.

Longres, J. F. 1992. "Race and Type of Maltreatment in an Elder Abuse System." *Journal of Elder Abuse and Neglect* 4 (3): 61–83.

Los Angeles County Department of Community and Senior Citizen Services. 1994. *Abuse by Others: 1/93 through 6/93.* Los Angeles: Author.

Lowenstein, A. 1995. "Elder Abuse in a Forming Society: Israel." Pp. 81–100 in *Elder Abuse: International and Cross-Cultural Perspectives,* edited by J. I. Kosberg and J. L. Garcia. Binghamton, NY: Haworth.

McFall, C. 2000, March/April. "Rainbow Services: A New Beginning for Older Battered Women." *Victimization of the Elderly and Disabled* 2:86.

Mears, J. 2003. "Survival Is Not Enough: Violence against Older Women in Australia." *Violence against Women* 9:1478–89.

Meddaugh, D. I. 1990. "Reactance: Understanding Aggressive Behavior in Long-Term Care." *Journal of Psychosocial Nursing and Mental Health Services* 28 (4): 28–33.

Moon, A. and D. Benton. 2000. "Tolerance of Elder Abuse and Attitudes toward Third-Party African American, Korean American, and White Elderly." *Journal of Multicultural Social Work* 8:283–303.

Moon, A. and O. J. Williams. 1993. "Perceptions of Elder Abuse and Help-Seeking Patterns among African American, Caucasian American, and Korean American Elderly Women." *Gerontologist* 33:386–95.

Mouton, C., S. Rovi, K. Furniss, and N. Lasser. 1999. "The Association between Health and Domestic Violence in Older Women: Results of a Pilot." *Journal of Women's Health and Gender-Based Medicine* 9:1173–79.

Muram, D., K. Miller, and A. Cutler. 1992. "Sexual Assault of the Elderly Victim." *Journal of Interpersonal Violence* 7:70–76.

National Center on Elder Abuse [NCEA]. 1998. *The National Elder Abuse Incidence Study: Final Report.* Madison, WI: Author.

Nelson, D. 2002. "Violence against Elderly People: A Neglected Problem." *Lancet* 360:1094.

Ockleford, E., Y. Barnes-Holmes, R. Morichelli, A. Moriaria, F. Scocchera, F. Furniss, et al. 2003. "Mistreatment of Older Women in Three European Countries." *Violence against Women* 9:1453–64.

Ogg, J. and G. C. J. Bennett. 1992. "Elder Abuse in Britain." *British Medical Journal* 305: 998–99.

Otto, J. M. and K. Quinn. 1999, January/February. "The National Elder Abuse Incidence Study: An Evaluation by the National Association of Adult Protective Services Administrators." *Victimization of the Elderly and Disabled* 2:4.

Paveza, G. J., D. Cohen, C. Eisdorfer, S. Freels, T. Semla, J. W. Ashford, et al. 1992. "Severe Family Violence and Alzheimer's Disease: Prevalence and Risk Factors." *Gerontologist* 32:493–97.

Phillipson, C. 1992. "Confronting Elder Abuse: Fact and Fiction." *Generations Review* 2:3.

———. 1993. "Abuse of Older People: Sociological Perspectives." Pp. 88–101 in *The Mistreatment of Elderly People,* edited by P. Decalmer and F. Glendenning. London: Sage.

Pillemer, K. A. and D. Finkelhor. 1988. "The Prevalence of Elder Abuse: A Random Sample Survey." *Gerontologist* 28:51–57.

Pitsiou-Darrough, E. N. and C. D. Spinellis. 1995. "Mistreatment of the Elderly in Greece." Pp. 45–64 in *Elderly Abuse: International and Cross-Cultural Perspectives,* edited by J. I. Kosberg and J. L. Garcia. Binghamton, NY: Haworth.

Podnieks, E. 1992. "National Survey on Abuse of the Elderly in Canada." *Journal of Elder Abuse and Neglect* 4 (5): 5–58.

"Public Health and Aging: Nonfatal Physical Assault Related Injuries among Persons Aged >60 Years Treated in Hospital Emergency Departments—United States, 2001." 2003. *Morbidity and Mortality Weekly Report* 52:812–16.

Ramsey-Klawsnik, H. 1991. "Elder Sexual Abuse: Preliminary Findings." *Journal of Elder Abuse and Neglect* 3 (3): 73–90.

Shah, G., R. Veedon, and S. Vasi. 1995. "Elder Abuse in India." Pp. 101–18 in *Elder Abuse: International and Cross-Cultural Perspectives.* Binghamton, NY: Haworth.

Social Services Inspectorate. 1992. *Confronting Elder Abuse: An SSI London Region Survey.* London: Her Majesty's Stationery Office.

Soos, J. N., Sr. 2000, September/October. "Gray Murders: Undetected Homicides of the Elderly Plus One Year." *Victimization of the Elderly and Disabled* 3:33–34, 42.

Stiegel, L. A. 2001. *Financial Abuse of the Elderly: Risk Factors, Screening Techniques, and Remedies.* Chicago: American Bar Association, Commission on Legal Problems of the Elderly. Retrieved December 8, 2003 (http://www.abanet.org/elderly/financial_abuse_of_the_elderly.doc).

———. 2003, July/August. "Washington Report." *Victimization of the Elderly and Disabled* 6:19–20.

Straus, M. A. 1979. "Measuring Intrafamily Conflict and Aggression: The Conflict Tactics Scale (CTS)." *Journal of Marriage and the Family* 41:75–88.

Sweeney, P. M. 2003, July/August. "Exploitation of Adults on the Internet." *Victimization of the Elderly and Disabled* 6:17, 29–30.

Teaster, P. B. 2003. *A Response to the Abuse of Vulnerable Adults: The 2000 Survey of State Adult Protective Services.* Washington, DC: National Center on Elder Abuse.

Tsukada, N., Y. Saito, and T. Tatara. 2001. "Japanese Older People's Perception of 'Elder Abuse.'" *Journal of Elder Abuse and Neglect* 13 (1): 71–89.

U.S. Bureau of the Census. 2000. *U.S. Population Estimates, by Age, Sex, Race, and Hispanic Origin.* Current Population Reports No. P25–1095. Retrieved December 8, 2003 (http://www.census.gov/population/estimates/nation/intfile2-1.txt).

Vinton, L. 1998. "A Nationwide Survey of Domestic Violence Shelters' Programming for Older Women." *Violence against Women* 4:559–71.

Vinton, L., J. A. Altholz, and T. Lobell. 1997. "A Five-Year Follow-Up Study of Domestic Violence Programming for Battered Older Women." *Journal of Women and Aging* 9:3–15.

Vladescu, D., K. Eveleigh, J. Ploeg, and C. Patterson. 1999. "An Evaluation of a Client-Centered Case Management Program for Elder Abuse." *Journal of Elder Abuse and Neglect* 11 (4): 5–22.

Wolf, R. S. and L. Donglin. 1999. "Factors Affecting the Rate of Elder Abuse Reporting to State Protective Services Programs." *Gerontologist* 39:222–28.

Wolf, R. S. and K. A. Pillemer. 1989. *Helping Elderly Victims: The Reality of Elder Abuse.* New York: Columbia University Press.

———. 1997. "The Older Battered Woman: Wives and Mothers Compared." *Journal of Mental Health and Aging* 3:325–36.

Yan, E. and Tang, C. S. 2001. "Prevalence of Pyschological Impact of Elder Abuse." *Journal of Interpersonal Violence* 16:1158–74.

———. 2003. "Proclivity to Elder Abuse: A Community Study on Hong Kong Chinese." *Journal of Interpersonal Violence* 18:999–1017.

Zink, T., S. Regan, C. J. Jacobson, Jr., and S. Pabst. 2003. "Cohort, Period, and Aging Effects: A Qualitative Study of Older Women's Reasons for Remaining in Abusive Relationships." *Violence against Women* 9:1429–41.

PART X

Families, Work, and Carework

In 1800, women whose work consisted largely in caring for families without pay were widely considered productive workers. By 1900, however, they had been formally relegated to the census category of "dependents" that included infants, young children, the sick, and the elderly.

— Economist NANCY FOLBRE

What is adequate for the "typical" employee — a male — has to be accepted without question by females who wish to participate in the male world.

— NORTON 1994:220

Early in the morning she rises,
The woman's work is never done.
And it's not because she doesn't try,
She's fighting a battle with no one on her side.

She rises up in the morning,
And she works 'til way past dusk.
The woman better slow down,
Or she's gonna come down hard.

Early in the morning she rises,
The woman's work is never done.

— *Woman's Work* by TRACY CHAPMAN

These three quotes reflect controversial feelings about families and work. The first quote shows how "work" is defined and redefined by governmental agencies. The redefinition may not value the work that some groups, namely women, do in society. The second quote refers to the work world as being structured for and around men and men's lives. The final quote, from song lyrics written by Tracy Chapman, illustrates that the vast amount of work women do both within the workplace and at home is compounded by women's roles and by the sex-based division of labor within the family. All three quotes suggest that there is conflict between the institution of the family and the institution of work. Moreover, they suggest that these worlds are separate, gendered worlds. Students tend to affirm the ideology of "separate spheres" for family and work by believing that their work lives will be unaffected by their family lives and vice versa. In this section, we challenge this ideology by showing that work and families cannot be separated and are, in fact, intimately related. Thus, we want to explore how work outside the home shapes families and how families shape work.

In addition, we examine the work done inside the home, specifically the various types of unpaid labor, such as housework, child care, kin work, food preparation, and other caretaking activities. Of particular interest to family scholars is the question "Who is doing most of this unpaid labor in the home?" Some of this labor is done by children and teenagers in the form of household chores. However, the vast majority of household labor, up to 80 percent, is done by adult women; this includes preparing meals, washing dishes, cleaning the house, shopping, laundry, and paying the bills (Demo and Acock 1993). Unfortunately, most of this labor is invisible or is seen as something women do out of love for their partners and children. Thus, as apparent in the preceding data and in the above quotes, family work is very gendered. There are different expectations concerning women and men both in the workplace and in the home. The gendered nature of work is a theme throughout the five readings in this section.

Families and Paid Employment

Until recently, most of the research on families and work focused on the interaction between paid employment and families. For example, how do dual-career couples and commuter couples organize work and family life? Do workplace structures create artificial barriers between work and families? How do employed parents, in general, balance their work lives and family lives? This question is the central theme of the first two readings in this section. The first reading, "The Work–Home Crunch," by Kathleen Gerson and Jerry A. Jacobs, examines the contemporary dilemma of why so many Americans feel overworked. Gerson, a professor of sociology at New York University, and Jacobs, a professor of sociology at the University of Pennsylvania, teamed up to study whether or not Americans were truly overworked and neglecting their family duties. The result of their research is a fascinating book titled *The Time Divide: Balancing Work and Family in Contemporary Society* (2004). In this selection, Gerson and Jacobs argue that while some Americans are working longer hours, many others are working less. What is more significant is that many people are having a difficult time finding a balance between their work and family obligations. Their research examines why Americans feel more time-squeezed, especially single parents and two-income couples.

The second reading that examines how Americans balance work and home life is by Arlie Russell Hochschild titled "The Emotional Geography of Work and Family Life." Hochschild, a professor of sociology at the University of California, Berkeley, has written extensively on gender, work, and family life. In this selection, taken from *The Time Bind: When Work Becomes*

Home and Home Becomes Work (1997), Hochschild discusses her research into a *Fortune* 500 company to see how people are balancing their work and family lives. Her goal in this study was to determine how these workers manage the work–family "speed-up" created by working mothers, inflexible jobs, and increased work hours for both men and women. She was especially interested in the difficulties of dual earner families in dealing with child care, housework, and spending time together as a family. She found that people work too many hours, which hurts the work–family balance, yet people resist family-friendly employment policies, such as flextime, shared jobs, family leaves, and working part-time. Why? Most people reported that they do not need the pay *nor* are they worried about layoffs. Instead, Hochschild found that work and family both are emotional cultures, but many people prefer being at work to being with their family because they receive more positive reinforcement at work.

A second question often found in the research literature is "How does father's or mother's employment affect children?" In their book *Parents' Jobs and Children's Lives* (1994), sociologists Toby L. Parcel and Elizabeth G. Menaghan consider the effects of parental working conditions on children's cognitive and social development. They also focus on how parental work affects the home environments that parents create for their children and how these home environments influence the children directly. Psychologist Lois Hoffman ([1985] 1987) also studied the effects of maternal and parental employment on children and found that parental employment shapes family values, influences the worker's psychological state, and imposes time schedules and domestic chores. Of particular importance is Hoffman's findings on the effects of maternal employment. Hoffman states that the belief that maternal employment has only negative effects on children is a myth and that there is over 50 years of research to disprove this myth. Instead, she argues that employed mothers have several positive effects on their children, including the fact that they are more likely to encourage independence in their children and are more likely to challenge the traditional sex-based division of labor in the home, thus influencing the sex role socialization of children. Moreover, if mothers are happily employed, their satisfaction with their employment has positive spillover effects on their parenting and family life.

But what if mothers decide to take time off from their jobs to raise their children? The third reading in this section on families and paid employment, "The Mommy Tax," by Ann Crittenden, looks at the financial penalities working women pay if they take time off from work to stay home and raise children. Crittenden, an award-winning journalist and author, became interested in the hidden and not-so-hidden economic costs of motherhood after taking time off from her job at the *New York Times* to stay home with her child. She found that the costs easily totaled over a million dollars in terms of lost salary, promotions, and retirement savings. The amount of income women are penalized for childbearing varies by age and profession, but the overall amount working mothers are losing is staggering. Moreover, it is not always easy for women to return to their former jobs after taking family leave. Crittendon's groundbreaking book, *The Price of Motherhood: Why the Most Important Job in the World Is Still the Least Valued* (2001), is excerpted here.

Housework

In addition to challenging the primary breadwinning role of men, women entering the workforce have greatly impacted the family in other ways as well. Specifically, women and their social roles have changed dramatically, but social structures and ideologies have not changed. Arlie Russell Hochschild, in her book *The Second Shift: Working Parents and the Revolution at Home* (1989), talks about a stalled revolution for women in the home. Women have made great strides by entering the workforce and competing directly with men. At home, however, men are resisting the changes in gender roles, and women are having to take on a greater share of the domestic work. The results are increased conflicts in marriages, women taking up the "second shift" of housework after they come home from work, and in some cases, an increased likelihood for divorce. Hochschild finds that a critical battleground in many dual-earner households is the division of household labor. While many couples say they want gender equity in housework, the reality is that women end up doing more of the housework, enough to create a second shift after they complete their first shift of paid employment.

Building on the work of Arlie Russell Hochschild and other scholars who have studied household labor, the fourth reading in this section, "No Place Like Home: The Division of Domestic Labor in Lesbigay Families," by Christopher Carrington, investigates how housework is actually divided in lesbian, gay, and bisexual households. Carrington, an associate professor of sociology at San Francisco State University, conducted in-depth interviews with 52 lesbigay families and did extensive observations in 8 of these households. In this selection, Carrington reports his findings related to the division of domestic labor and the resulting power dynamics in gay households. He found that, like many heterosexual couples, gay couples believe their households are much more egalitarian than they really are. Not only is much of the domestic work invisible, but couples find a variety of ways to justify the unequal burden of work in their relationship. Some couples do maintain an egalitarian division of labor with the help of hiring labor from the service economy. Most couples end up with one person specializing in domesticity and the other in paid work.

Kin Work, Elder Care, and Child Care

As described earlier, unpaid labor in the home involves much more than cleaning the house and doing the laundry. Recently, studies of families and work have begun to examine the diverse types of labor that occur inside the household. For example, for her book *Feeding the Family: The Social Organization of Caring as Gendered Work* (1991), sociologist Marjorie DeVault studied the amount of work that goes into planning and preparing family meals. This work is invisible until you begin to examine all of the steps prior to setting a cooked meal on the table. DeVault argues that food preparation in the United States is usually done by women, who spend hours planning meals, clipping food coupons, grocery shopping, preparing and cooking food. Moreover, this labor is more complex because women often are paying attention to the nutritional value of food and the personal preferences of individual family members. In addition, the meaning of food varies; in many households family meals actually help facilitate family relationships and mark special events. Thus, women are literally creating "family" by bringing family members together around the dinner table and helping to facilitate relationships. DeVault also finds that this work varies across households and income groups.

Another scholar, Micaela di Leonardo, an anthropologist, introduced the concept of kin work and shows how it shapes family relationships among Italian Americans in Northern California. Di Leonardo (1987) defines kin work as

> the conception, maintenance, and ritual celebration of cross-household kin ties, including visits, letters, telephone calls, presents, and cards to kin; the organization of family gatherings; the creation and maintenance of quasi-kin relations; decisions to neglect or intensify particular ties; the mental work of reflection about all of these activities; and the creation and communication of altering images of family and kin vis-à-vis the images of others, both folk and mass media. (Pp. 442–43)

Thus, kin work involves a variety of activities that create and maintain family ties. Similar to other types of work done within the household, kin work is often invisible and undervalued. It is also work primarily done by women, and it is not until this works stops, due to illness or divorce, that the amount of labor invested in maintaining families becomes visible. In addition, di Leonardo argues that this concept of kin work can be observed cross-culturally and across social class and racial-ethnic groups.

Two final and critically important areas related to families, work, and carework are elder care and child care. Some issues related to elder care have already been addressed in several earlier readings in this volume, including Readings 28, 30, and 39. Similar to many other types of domestic labor and carework, elder care is primarily done by women in their families. Child care also is addressed in a number of other readings, but this last reading focuses on the difficulty parents have in finding child care in the United States. Dan Clawson and Naomi Gerstel, both professors of sociology at the University of Massachusetts at Amherst, examine preschool and child care programs in this selection, "Caring for Our Young: Child Care in Europe and the United States." By comparing early childhood programs and child care in the United States to programs in Europe, Clawson and Gerstel find that U.S.

preschool and child care programs are greatly uneven. While there are some high-quality U.S. programs, most are too expensive or have so many children waiting to attend that few families can access them. Moreover, child care workers, as a group, tend to be grossly underpaid, and there is high turnover in their positions. Clawson and Gerstel conclude that we, as a society, could learn a great deal from observing different European approaches to child care, especially since the United States has no comprehensive national policies on preschool or child care and most of the existing programming and funding is fragmentary at best.

REFERENCES

Crittenden, Ann. 2001. *The Price of Motherhood: Why the Most Important Job in the World Is Still the Least Valued.* New York: Metropolitan Books.

Demo, David H. and Alan C. Acock. 1993. "Family Diversity and the Division of Domestic Labor: How Much Have Things Really Changed?" *Family Relations* 42:323–31.

DeVault, Marjorie L. 1991. *Feeding the Family: The Social Organization of Caring as Gendered Work.* Chicago: University of Chicago Press.

di Leonardo, Micaela. 1987. "The Female World of Cards and Holidays: Women, Families, and the Work of Kinship." *Signs: Journal of Women in Culture and Society* 12 (3): 440–53.

Gerson, Kathleen and Jerry A. Jacobs. 2004. *The Time Divide: Balancing Work and Family in Contemporary Society.* Cambridge, MA: Harvard University Press.

Hochschild, Arlie Russell, with Anne Machung. 1989. *The Second Shift: Working Parents and the Revolution at Home.* New York: Viking Press.

Hochschild, Arlie Russell. 1997. *The Time Bind: When Work Becomes Home and Home Becomes Work.* New York: Metropolitan Books.

Hoffman, Lois. [1985] 1987. "The Effects on Children of Maternal and Paternal Employment." Pp. 362–95 in *Families and Work,* edited by Naomi Gerstel and Harriet Engel Gross. Philadelphia: Temple University Press.

Norton, Sue M. 1994. "Pregnancy, the Family, and Work: An Historical Review and Update of Legal Regulations and Organizational Policies and Practices in the United States." *Gender, Work, and Organization* 1:217–26.

Parcel, Toby L. and Elizabeth G. Menaghan. 1994. *Parents' Jobs and Children's Lives.* New York: Aldine de Gruyter.

40

THE WORK–HOME CRUNCH

KATHLEEN GERSON • JERRY A. JACOBS

M ore than a decade has passed since the release of *The Overworked American*, a prominent 1991 book about the decline in Americans' leisure time, and the work pace in the United States only seems to have increased. From sleep-deprived parents to professionals who believe they must put in long hours to succeed at the office, the demands of work are colliding with family responsibilities and placing a tremendous time squeeze on many Americans.

Yet beyond the apparent growth in the time that many Americans spend on the job lies a more complex story. While many Americans are working more than ever, many others are working less. What is more, finding a balance between work and other obligations seems increasingly elusive to many workers — whether or not they are actually putting in more time at work than workers in earlier generations. The increase in harried workers and hurried families is a problem that demands solutions. But before we can resolve this increasingly difficult time squeeze we must first understand its root causes.

Average Working Time and Beyond

"There aren't enough hours in the day" is an increasingly resonant refrain. To most observers, including many experts, the main culprit appears to be overwork — our jobs just take up too much of our time. Yet it is not clear that the average American is spending more time on the job. Although it may come as a surprise to those who feel overstressed, the average work week — that is, hours spent working for pay by the average employee — has hardly changed over the past 30 years. Census Bureau interviews show, for example, that the average male worked 43.5 hours a week in 1970 and 43.1 hours a week in 2000, while the average female worked 37.1 hours in 1970 and 37.0 hours in 2000.

Why, then, do more and more Americans feel so pressed for time? The answer is that averages can be misleading. Looking only at the average experience of American workers misses key parts of the story. From the perspective

Kathleen Gerson and Jerry A. Jacobs, "The Work-Home Crunch" from *Contexts* 3, no. 4 (Fall 2004): 29–37. Copyright © 2004 by the American Sociological Association. Reprinted with the permission of the author and the University of California Press Journals.

of individual workers, it turns out some Americans are working more than ever, while others are finding it harder to get as much work as they need or would like. To complicate matters further, American families are now more diverse than they were in the middle of the twentieth century, when male-breadwinner households predominated. Many more Americans now live in dual-earner or single-parent families where all the adults work.

These two trends — the growing split of the labor force and the transformation of family life — lie at the heart of the new time dilemmas facing an increasing number of Americans. But they have not affected all workers and all families in the same way. Instead, these changes have divided Americans into those who feel squeezed between their work and the rest of their life, and those who have more time away from work than they need or would like. No one trend fits both groups.

So, who are the time-squeezed, and how do they differ from those with fewer time pressures but who may also have less work than they may want or need? To distinguish and describe the two sets of Americans, we need to look at the experiences of both individual workers and whole families. A focus on workers shows that they are increasingly divided between those who put in very long work weeks and who are concentrated in the better-paying jobs, and those who put in comparatively short work weeks, who are more likely to have fewer educational credentials and are more likely to be concentrated in the lower-paying jobs.

But the experiences of individuals does not tell the whole story. When we shift our focus to the family, it becomes clear that time squeezes are linked to the total working hours of family members in households. For this reason, two-job families and single parents face heightened challenges. Moreover, women continue to assume the lion's share of home and child care responsibilities and are thus especially likely to be squeezed for time. Changes in jobs and changes in families are putting overworked Americans and underemployed Americans on distinct paths, are separating the two-earner and single-parent households from the more traditional households, and are creating different futures for parents (especially mothers) than for workers without children at home.

A Growing Divide in Individual Working Time

In 1970, almost half of all employed men and women reported working 40 hours a week. By 2000, just 2 in 5 worked these "average" hours. Instead, workers are now far more likely to put in either very long or fairly short work weeks. The share of working men putting in 50 hours or more rose from 21 percent in 1970 to almost 27 percent in 2000, while the share of working women putting in these long work weeks rose from 5 to 11 percent.

At the other end of the spectrum, more workers are also putting in shorter weeks. In 1970, for example, 5 percent of men were employed for

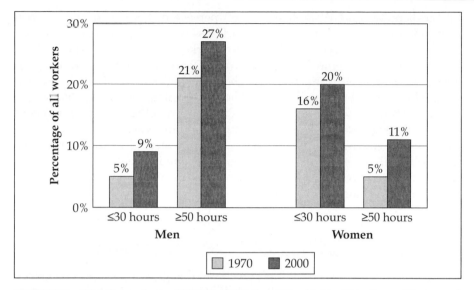

FIGURE 1 **The Percentage of Men and Women Who Put in 30 or Fewer Hours and Who Put in 50 or More Hours a Week in 1970 and 2000**

Source: March, 2000 Current Population Reports Surveys; nonfarm wage and salary workers

30 or fewer hours a week, while 9 percent worked these shortened weeks in 2000. The share of employed women spending 30 or fewer hours on the job also climbed from 16 percent to 20 percent (see Figure 1) In total, 13 million Americans in 2000 worked either shorter or longer work weeks than they would have if the 1970s pattern had continued.

These changes in working time are not evenly distributed across occupations. Instead, they are strongly related to the kinds of jobs people hold. Managers and professionals, as one might expect, tend to put in the longest work weeks. More than 1 in 3 men in this category now work 50 hours or more per week, compared to only 1 in 5 for men in other occupations. For women, 1 in 6 professionals and managers work these long weeks, compared to fewer than 1 in 14 for women in all other occupations. And because jobs are closely linked to education, the gap in working time between the college educated and those with fewer educational credentials has also grown since 1970.

Thus, time at work is growing most among those Americans who are most likely to read articles and buy books about overwork in America. They may not be typical, but they are indeed working more than their peers in earlier generations. If leisure time once signaled an elite lifestyle, that no longer appears to be the case. Working relatively few hours is now more likely to be concentrated among those with less education and less elite jobs.

Workers do not necessarily prefer these new schedules. On the contrary, when workers are asked about their ideal amount of time at work, a very different picture emerges. For example, in a 1997 survey of workers conducted by the Families and Work Institute, 60 percent of both men and women responded that they would like to work less while 19 percent of men and women said that they would like to work more. Most workers—both women and men—aspire to work between 30 and 40 hours per week. Men generally express a desire to work about 38 hours a week while women would like to work about 32 hours. The small difference in the ideal working time of men and women is less significant than the shared preferences among them. However, whether their jobs require very long or comparatively short work weeks, this shared ideal does stand in sharp contrast to their job realities. As some workers are pressured to put in more time at work and others less, finding the right balance between work and the rest of life has become increasingly elusive.

Overworked Individuals or Overworked Families?

Fundamental shifts in family life exacerbate this growing division between the over- and under-worked. While most analyses of working time focus on individual workers, time squeezes are typically experienced by families, not isolated individuals. A 60-hour work week for a father means something different depending on whether the mother stays at home or also works a 60-hour week. Even a 40-hour work week can seem too long if both members of a married couple are juggling job demands with family responsibilities. And when a family depends on a single parent, the conflicts between home and work can be even greater. Even if the length of the work week had not changed at all, the rise of families that depend on either two incomes or one parent would suffice to explain why Americans feel so pressed for time.

To understand how families experience time squeezes, we need to look at the combined working time of all family members. For example, how do married couples with two earners compare with those anchored by a sole, typically male, breadwinner? For all married couples, the work week has indeed increased from an average of about 53 hours in 1970 to 63 hours in 2000. Given that the average work week for individuals did not change, it may seem strange that the couples' family total grew so markedly. The explanation for this apparent paradox is both straightforward and crucial: married women are now far more likely to work. In 1970, half of all married-couple families had only male breadwinners. By 2000, this group had shrunk to one quarter (see Figure 2). In 1970, one-third of all married-couple families had two wage-earners, but three-fifths did in 2000. In fact, two-earner families are more common today than male-breadwinner families were 30 years ago.

Each type of family is also working a little more each week, but this change is relatively modest and certainly not large enough to account for the larger shift in total household working time. Two-earner families put in close to 82 working hours in 2000 compared with 78 hours in 1970. Male-breadwinner couples worked 44 hours on average in 1970 and 45 hours

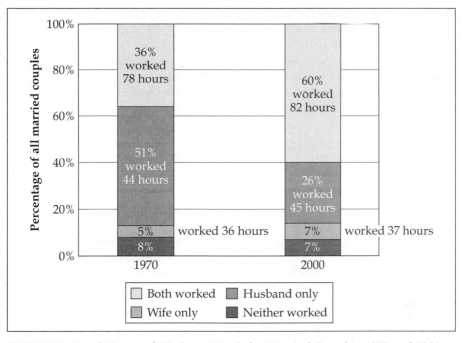

FIGURE 2   Total Hours of Work per Week for Married Couples, 1970 and 2000

Source: March, 2000 Current Population Reports Surveys; nonfarm married couples aged 18–64

in 2000. The vast majority of the change in working time over the past 30 years can thus be traced to changes in the kinds of families we live in rather than to changes in how much we work. Two-earner couples work about as much today as they did 30 years ago, but there are many more of them because more wives are working.

Single parents, who are overwhelmingly mothers, are another group who are truly caught in a time squeeze. They need to work as much as possible to support their family, and they are less likely to be able to count on a partner's help in meeting their children's daily needs. Although these households are not displayed in Figure 2, Census Bureau data show that women headed one-fifth of all families in 2000, twice the share of female-headed households in 1970. Even though their average work week remained unchanged at 39 hours, the lack of childcare and other support services leaves them facing time squeezes at least as sharp. Single fathers remain a much smaller group, but their ranks have also grown rapidly. Single dads work almost as much as single moms—37 hours per week in 2000. Even though this represents a drop of two hours since 1970, single fathers face time dilemmas as great as those facing single mothers. Being a single parent has always posed daunting challenges, and now there are more mothers and fathers than ever in this situation.

At the heart of these shifts is American families' growing reliance on a woman's earnings—whether or not they depend on a man's earnings as well.

Women's strengthened commitment to paid employment has provided more economic resources to families and given couples more options for sharing the tasks of breadwinning and caretaking. Yet this revolution in women's work has not been complemented by an equal growth in the amount of time men spend away from the job or in the availability of organized childcare. This limited change at the workplace and in men's lives has intensified the time pressures facing women.

Dual–Earner Parents and Working Time

The expansion of working time is especially important for families with children, where work and family demands are most likely to conflict. Indeed, there is a persisting concern that in their desire for paid work, families with two earners are shortchanging their children in time and attention. A closer looks reveals that even though parents face increased time pressure, they cope with these dilemmas by cutting back on their combined joint working time when they have children at home. For example, U.S. Census data show that parents in two-income families worked 3.3 fewer hours per week than spouses in two-income families without children, a slightly wider difference than the 2.6 hours separating them in 1970. Working hours also decline as the number of children increases. Couples with one child under 18 jointly averaged 81 hours per week in 2000, while couples with three or more children averaged 78 hours. Rather than forsaking their children, employed parents are taking steps to adjust their work schedules to make more time for the rest of life.

However, it is mothers, not fathers, who are cutting back. Fathers actually work more hours when they have children at home, and their working hours increase with the number of children. Thus, the drop in joint working time among couples with children reflects less working time among mothers. Figure 3 shows that in 2000, mothers worked almost 4 fewer hours per week than married women without children. This gap is not substantially different than in 1970.

This pattern of mothers reducing their hours while fathers increase them creates a larger gender gap in work participation among couples with children compared to the gender gap for childless couples. However, these differences are much smaller than the once predominant pattern in which many women stopped working for pay altogether when they bore children. While the transition to raising children continues to have different consequences for women and men, the size of this difference is diminishing.

It is also important to remember that the rise in working time among couples is not concentrated among those with children at home. Though Americans continue to worry about the consequences for children when both parents go to work, the move toward more work involvement does not reflect neglect on the part of either mothers or fathers. On the contrary, employed mothers continue to spend less time at the workplace than their

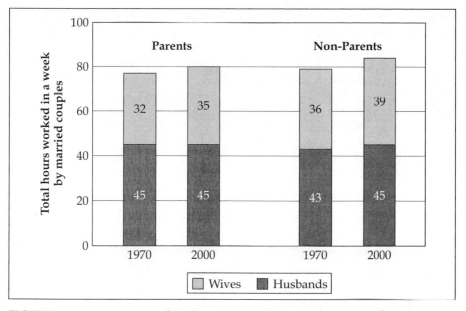

FIGURE 3   Average Hours of Work per Week of Couples (parents and non-parents)
Source: March, 2000 Current Population Reports Surveys; nonfarm married couples aged 18-64

childless peers, while employed fathers today do not spend substantially more time at work than men who are not fathers.

Solving the Time Pressure Puzzle

Even though changes in the average working time of American workers are modest, many American families have good reason to feel overworked and time-deprived. The last several decades have witnessed the emergence of a group of workers who face very long work weeks and live in families that depend on either two incomes or one parent. And while parents are putting in less time at work than their peers without children at home, they shoulder domestic responsibilities that leave them facing clashes between work demands and family needs.

The future of family well-being and gender equality will depend on developing policies to help workers resolve the time pressures created by the widespread and deeply rooted social changes discussed above. The first step toward developing effective policy responses requires accepting the social transformations that sent women into the workplace and left Americans wishing for a balance between work and family that is difficult to achieve. Unfortunately, these changes in the lives of women and men continue to evoke ambivalence.

For example, mothers continue to face strong pressures to devote intensive time and attention to child rearing. Indeed, generally they want to, despite the rising economic and social pressure to hold a paid job as well. Even though most contemporary mothers are counted on to help support their families financially, the United States has yet to develop the childcare services and flexible jobs that can help workers meet their families' needs. Whether or not mothers work outside the home, they face conflicting expectations that are difficult to meet. These social contradictions can be seen in the political push to require poor, single mothers to work at a paid job while middle-class mothers continue to be chastised for spending too much time on their jobs and away from home.

To a lesser but still important extent, fathers also face intensifying and competing pressures. Despite American families' increasing reliance on women's earnings, men face significant barriers to family involvement. Resistance from employers and co-workers continues to greet individual fathers who would like to spend less time at work to care for their children. For all the concern and attention focused on employed mothers, social policies that would help bring men more fully into the work of parenting get limited notice or support. New time squeezes can thus be better understood by comparing the large changes in women's lives with the relative lack of changes in the situation for men. The family time bind is an unbalanced one.

Even as family time has become squeezed, workers are also contending with changes in the options and expectations they face at work. Competitive workplaces appear to be creating rising pressures for some workers, especially professionals and managers, to devote an excessive amount of time to their jobs, while not offering enough work to others. In contrast to these bifurcating options, American workers increasingly express a desire to balance the important work of earning a living and caring for a new generation.

Finding solutions to these new time dilemmas will depend on developing large scale policies that recognize and address the new needs of twenty-first-century workers and their families. As we suggest in our book, *The Time Divide*, these policies need to address the basic organization of American work and community institutions. This includes revising regulations on hours of work and providing benefit protections to more workers, moving toward the norm of a shorter work week, creating more family-supportive workplaces that offer both job flexibility and protections for employed parents, and developing a wider array of high-quality, affordable childcare options.

Extending protections, such as proportional benefits and overtime pay, to workers in a wider range of jobs and occupations would reduce the built-in incentives employers have to extract as much work as possible from professionals and managers while offering less work to other employees. If professionals and managers were given overtime pay for overtime work, which wage workers are now guaranteed under the Fair Labor Standards Act, the pressures on these employees to put in endless workdays might lessen. Yet, the Bush administration recently revised these rules to move more employees into the category of those ineligible for overtime pay. Similarly, if part-time workers were offered fringe benefits proportional to the hours they work (such as partial pensions), there would be fewer reasons for employers to create jobs with work weeks so short that they do not provide the economic security all families need.

Reducing the average work week to 35 hours would also reduce the pressures on workers and help them find a better work–family balance. While this goal may seem utopian, it is important to remember that the 40-hour standard also seemed unimaginably idealistic before it was adopted in the early twentieth century. Other countries, most notably France, have adopted this standard without sacrificing economic well-being. A shorter work week still would allow for variation in work styles and commitments, but it would also create a new cultural standard that better reflects the needs and aspirations of most contemporary workers. It would also help single parents meet their dual obligations and allow couples to fashion greater equality in their work and caretaking responsibilities.

Time at work is clearly important, but it is not the whole story. The organization of the workplace and the structure of jobs also matters, especially for those whose jobs and occupations require intensive time at work. Among those putting in very long work weeks, we find that having job flexibility and autonomy helps ease the perceived strains and conflicts. The work environment, especially in the form of support from supervisors and co-workers, also makes a difference. In addition, we find that workers with access to such family-friendly options as flexible work schedules are likely to use them, while workers without such benefits would like to have them.

Flexibility and autonomy are only useful if workers feel able to use them. Women and men both express concern that making use of "family-friendly" policies, such as extended parental leaves or nonstandard working hours, may endanger their future work prospects. Social policies need to protect the rights of workers to be involved parents without incurring excessive penalties at the workplace. Most Americans spend a portion of their work lives simultaneously immersed in work for pay and in parenting. Providing greater flexibility at the workplace will help workers develop both short- and longer-term strategies for integrating work and family life. However, even basic changes in the organization of work will not suffice to meet the needs of twenty-first-century families. We also need to join the ranks of virtually all other industrialized nations by creating widely available, high-quality and affordable childcare. In a world where mothers and fathers are at the workplace to stay, we need an expanded network of support to care for the next generation of workers.

These changes will not be easy to achieve. But in one form or another, they have been effectively adopted in other societies throughout the modern world. While no one policy is a cure-all, taken together they offer a comprehensive approach for creating genuine resolutions to the time pressures that confront growing numbers of American workers and their families. Ultimately, these new time dilemmas cannot be resolved by chastising workers (and, most often, mothers) for working too much. Rather, the time has come to create more flexible, family-supportive, and gender-equal workplaces and communities that complement the twenty-first-century forms of work and family life.

RECOMMENDED RESOURCES

Bond, James T. 2003. *Highlights of the National Study of the Changing Workforce*. New York: Families and Work Institute. Bond reports findings from a major national survey of contemporary American workers, workplace conditions and work-family conflict.

Gornick, Janet and Marcia Meyers. 2003. *Families That Work: Policies for Reconciling Parenthood and Employment*. New York: Russell Sage Foundation. This important study compares family-supportive policies in Europe and the United States.

Hays, Sharon. 1997. *The Cultural Contradictions of Motherhood*. New Haven, CT: Yale University Press. Hays examines how American mothers continue to face pressure to practice intensive parenting even as they increase their commitment to paid work.

Heymann, Jody. 2000. *The Widening Gap: Why America's Working Families Are in Jeopardy and What Can Be Done about It*. New York: Basic Books. Drawing from a wide range of data, this study makes a compelling case for more flexible work structures.

Hochschild, Arlie Russell. 1997. *The Time Bind: When Home Becomes Work and Work Becomes Home*. New York: Metropolitan Books. This is a rich study of how employees in one company try to reconcile the tensions between spending time at work and caring for their families.

Jacobs, Jerry A. and Kathleen Gerson. 2004. *The Time Divide: Work, Family and Gender Inequality*. Cambridge, MA: Harvard University Press. An overview of trends in working time, our book shows why and how time pressures have emerged in America over the past three decades, how they are linked to gender inequality and family change, and what we can do to alleviate them.

Robinson, John P. and Geoffrey Godbey. 1999. *Time for Life: The Surprising Ways Americans Use Their Time*. University Park: Pennsylvania State University Press. Drawing on time diaries, Robinson and Godbey conclude that Americans' leisure time has increased.

Schor, Juliet. 1991. *The Overworked American: The Unexpected Decline of Leisure*. New York: Basic Books. This early and original analysis of how Americans are overworked sparked a national discussion on and concern for the problem.

41

THE EMOTIONAL GEOGRAPHY OF WORK AND FAMILY LIFE

ARLIE RUSSELL HOCHSCHILD

Over the last two decades, American workers have increasingly divided into a majority who work too many hours and a minority with no work at all. This split hurts families at both extremes, but I focus here on the growing scarcity of time among the long-hours majority. For many of them, a speed-up at the office and factory has marginalised life at home, so that the very term "work–family balance" seems to them a bland slogan with little bearing on real life. In this [reading], I describe the speed-up and review a range of cultural responses to it, including "family-friendly reforms" such as flextime, job sharing, part-time work and parental leave. Why, I ask, do people not resist the speed-up more than they do? When offered these reforms, why don't more take advantage of them? Drawing upon my ongoing research in an American Fortune 500 company, I argue that a company's "family-friendly" policy goes only as deep as the "emotional geography" of the work-place and home, the drawn and redrawn boundaries between the sacred and the profane. I show how ways of talking about time (for example, separating "quality" from "quantity" time) become code words to describe that emotional geography. . . .

A Work–Family Speed–Up

Three factors are creating the current speed-up in work and family life in the United States. (By the term "family," I refer to committed unmarried couples, same-sex couples, single mothers, two-job couples and wage-earner–housewife couples. My focus is on all families who raise children.) First of all, increasing numbers of mothers now work outside the home. In 1950, 22 per cent of American mothers of children eighteen and under worked for pay; in 1991, 67 per cent did. Half of the mothers of children age one year and younger work for pay.

Second, they work in jobs which generally lack flexibility. The very model of "a job" and "career" has been based, for the most part, on the model

of a traditional man whose wife cared for the children at home. Third, over
the last 20 years, both women and men have increased their hours of work.
In her book *The Overworked American*, the economist Juliet Schor argues that
over the last two decades American workers have added an extra 164 hours
to their year's work — an extra month of work a year (Schor 1992:26). Compared to 20 years ago, workers take fewer unpaid absences, and even fewer
paid ones. Over the last decade, vacations have shortened by 14 per cent
(Schor 1992:12–13). The number of families eating evening meals together
has dropped by 10 per cent (Blyton 1985; Fuchs 1991).[1] Counting overtime
and commuting time, a 1992 national sample of men averaged 48.8 hours of
work, and women, 41.7 (Galinsky, Bond, and Friedman 1993:9). Among
young parents, close to half now work more than 8 hours a day. Compared
to the 1970s, mothers take less time off for the birth of a child and are more
likely to work through the summer. They are more likely to work continuously until they retire at age 65. Thus, whether they have children or not,
women increasingly fit the profile of year-round, life-long paid workers, a
profile that has long characterised men. Meanwhile, male workers have not
reduced their hours but, instead, expanded them.

Not all working parents with more free time will spend it at home tending
children or elderly relatives. Nor, needless to say, if parents do spend time at
home, will all their children find them kind, helpful and fun. But without a
chance for more time at home, the issue of using it well does not arise at all.

Cool Modern, Traditional, Warm Modern
Stances toward the Speed–Up

Do the speed-up people think the speed-up is a problem? Does anybody
else? If so, what cultural stances toward gender equity, family life and capitalism underly the practical solutions they favour? If we explore recent writing on the hurried life of a working parent, we can discern three stances
toward it.

One is a *cool modern* stance, according to which the speed-up has become
"normal," even fashionable. Decline in time at home does not "marginalise"
family life, proponents say; it makes it different, even better. Like many other
popular self-help books addressed to the busy working mother, *The Superwoman Syndrome*, by Marjorie Schaevitz, offers busy mothers tips on how to
fend off appeals for help from neighbours, relatives, and friends, how to stop
feeling guilty about their mothering. It instructs the mother how to frugally
measure out minutes of "quality time" for her children and abandons as
hopeless the project of getting men more involved at home (Schaevitz 1984).
Such books call for no changes in the workplace, no changes in the culture
and no changes in men. *The solution to rationalisation at work is rationalisation
at home.* Tacitly such books accept the corrosive effects of global capitalism
on family life and on the very notion of what people need to be happy and
fulfilled (Hochschild 1994).

A second stance toward the work–family speed-up is *traditional* in that it calls for women's return to the home, or *quasi-traditional* in that it acquiesces to a secondary role, a lower rank "mommy track," for women at work (Schwartz 1989). Those who take this sort of stance acknowledge the speed-up as a problem but deny the fact that most women now have to work, want to work, and embrace the concept of gender equity. They essentialise different male and female "natures," and notions of time, for men and women — "industrial" time for men, and "family" time for women (Hareven 1982).[2]

A third *warm modern* stance is both humane (the speed-up is a problem) and egalitarian (equity at home and work is a goal). Those who take this approach question the terms of employment — both through a nationwide programme of worksharing (as in Germany), a shorter working week, and through company-based family-friendly reforms.[3] What are these family-friendly reforms?

- flextime; a workday with flexible starting and quitting times, but usually 40 hours of work and the opportunity to "bank" hours at one time and reclaim them later;
- flexplace; home-based work, such as telecommuting;
- regular or permanent part-time; less than full-time work with full- or pro-rated benefits and promotional opportunities in proportion to one's skill and contribution;
- job sharing; two people voluntarily sharing one job with benefits and salary pro-rated;
- compressed working week; four 10-hour days with 3 days off, or three 12-hour days with 4 days off;
- paid parental leave;
- family obligations as a consideration in the allocation of shift work and required overtime.[4]

Together, worksharing and this range of family-friendly reforms could spread work, increase worker control over hours, and create a "warm modern" world for women to be equal within.[5] As political goals in America over the last 50 years, worksharing and a shorter working week have "died and gone to heaven" where they live on as Utopian ideals. In the 1990s, family-friendly reforms are the lesser offering on the capitalist bargaining table. But are companies in fact offering these reforms? Are working parents pressing for them?

The news is good and bad. Recent nationwide studies suggest that more and more American companies offer their workers family-friendly alternative work schedules. According to one recent study, 88 per cent of 188 companies surveyed offer part-time work, 77 per cent offer flextime of some sort, 48 per cent offer job-sharing, 35 per cent offer some form of flexplace, and 20 percent offer a compressed working week (Galinsky, Friedman, and Hernandez 1991).[6] (But in most companies, the interested worker must seek and receive the approval of a supervisor or department head. Moreover, most policies do not apply to lower-level workers whose conditions of work are covered by union contracts.)

But even if offered, regardless of need, few workers actually take advantage of the reforms. One study of 384 companies noted that only nine companies reported even one father who took an official unpaid leave at the birth of his child (Friedman 1991:50). Few are on temporary or permanent part-time. Still fewer share a job. Of workers with children ages 12 and under, only 4 per cent of men and 13 per cent of women worked less than 40 hours a week (Galinsky et al. 1991:123).

Inside a Fortune 500 Company

Why, when the opportunity presents itself, do so few working parents take it? To find out, I set about interviewing managers, and clerical and factory workers in a large manufacturing company in the northeastern United States—which I shall call, simply, the Company. I chose to study this Company because of its reputation as an especially progressive company. Over the last 15 years, for example, the Company devoted millions of dollars to informing workers of its family-friendly policies, hiring staff to train managers to implement them, making showcase promotions of workers who take extended maternity leaves or who work part-time. If change is to occur anywhere, I reasoned, it was likely to be within this Company.

But the first thing I discovered was that even in this enlightened Company, few young parents or workers tending elderly relatives took advantage of the chance to work more flexible or shorter hours. Among the 26,000 employees, the average working week ranged from 45 to 55 hours. Managers and factory workers often worked 50 or 60 hours a week while clerical workers tended to work a more normal, 40-hour, week. Everyone agreed the Company was a "pretty workaholic place." Moreover, for the last 5 years, hours of work had increased.

Explanations That Don't Work

Perhaps workers shy away from applying for leaves or shortening their hours because they can't afford to earn less. This certainly explains why many young parents continue to work long hours. But it doesn't explain why the wealthiest workers, the managers and professionals, are among the *least* interested in additional time off. Even among the Company's factory workers, who in 1993 averaged between eleven and twelve dollars an hour, and who routinely competed for optional overtime, two 40-hour-a-week paychecks with no overtime work were quite enough to support the family. A substantial number said they could get by on one paycheck if they sold one of their cars, put in a vegetable garden, and cut down on "extras." Yet, the overwhelming majority did not want to.

Perhaps, then, employees shied away from using flexible or shorter hour schedules because they were afraid of having their names higher on the list of workers who might be laid off in a period of economic downturn. Through the 1980s, a third of America's largest companies experienced some layoffs, though this did not happen to managers or clerical workers at this company.

By union contract, production workers were assured that layoffs, should they occur, would be made according to seniority and not according to any other criteria—such as how many hours an employee had worked. Yet, the workaholism went on. Employees in the most profitable sectors of the Company showed no greater tendency to ask for shorter or more flexible hours for family reasons than employees in the least profitable sectors.

Is it, then, that workers who could afford shorter hours didn't *know* about the Company's family-friendly policies? No. All of the 130 working parents I spoke with had heard about alternative schedules and knew where they could find out more.

Perhaps the explanation lies not with the workers but with their managers. Managers responsible for implementing family-friendly policies may be openly or covertly undermining them. Even though Company policy allowed flexibility, the head of a division could, for reasons of production, openly refuse a worker permission to go part-time or to job-share, which some did. For example, when asked about his views on flextime, the head of the engineering division of the Company replied flatly, "My policy on flextime is that there is no flextime." Other apparently permissive division heads had supervisors who were tough on this issue "for them." Thus, there seemed to be some truth to this explanation for why so few workers stepped forward.[7]

But even managers known to be co-operative had few employees asking for alternative schedules. Perhaps, then, workers ask for time off, but do so "off the books." To some extent, this "off the books" hypothesis did hold, especially for new fathers who may take a few days to a week of sick leave for the birth of a baby instead of filing for "parental leave," which they feared would mark them as unserious workers.

Even counting informal leaves, most women managers returned to full-time 40- to 55-hour work schedules fairly soon after their 6 weeks of paid maternity leave. Across ranks, most women secretaries returned after 6 months; most women production workers returned after 6 weeks. Most new fathers took a few days off at most. Thus, even "off the books," working parents used very little of the opportunity to spend more time at home.

Far more important than all these factors seemed to be a company "speed-up" in response to global competition. In the early years of the 1990s, workers each year spoke of working longer hours than they had the year before, a trend seen nationwide. When asked why, they explained that the Company was trying to "reduce costs," in part by asking employees to do more than they were doing before.

But the sheer existence of a company speed-up doesn't explain why employees weren't trying to actively resist it, why there wasn't much backtalk.

Parents were eager to tell me how their families came first, how they were clear about that. (National polls show that next to a belief in God, Americans most strongly believe in "the family.") But, practices that might express this belief—such as sharing breakfast and dinner—were shifting in the opposite direction. In the minds of many parents of young children, warm modern intentions seemed curiously, casually, fused with cool modern ideas and practices. In some ways, those within the work–family speed-up don't seem to want to slow down. What about their experience makes this true? . . .

Work and Family as Emotional Cultures

Through its family-friendly reforms, the Company had earned a national reputation as a desirable family-friendly employer. But at the same time, it wasn't inconvenienced by having to arrange alternate schedules for very many employees. One can understand how this might benefit a company. But how about the working parents?

For the answer, we may need a better grasp of the emotional cultures, and the relative "draw" of work and family. Instead of thinking of the workplace or the family as unyielding thing-like structures, Giddens suggests that we see structures as fluid and changeable. "Structuration," Anthony Giddens tells us, is the "dynamic process whereby structures come into being" (Giddens 1976:121, 157). For structures to change, there must be changes in what people do. But in doing what they do, people unconsciously draw on resources, and depend on larger conditions to develop the skills they use to change what they do (Giddens 1976:157).

With this starting point, then, let us note that structures come with—and also "are"—emotional cultures. A change in structure requires a change in emotional culture. What we lack, so far, is a vocabulary for describing this culture, and what follows is a crude attempt to create one. An emotional culture is a set of rituals, beliefs about feelings and rules governing feeling which induce emotional focus, and even a sense of the "sacred."[8] This sense of the sacred selects and favours some social bonds over others. It selects and reselects relationships into a core or periphery of family life.

Thus, families have a more or less *sacred core* of private rituals and shared meanings. In some families what is most sacred is sexuality and marital communication (back rubs, pillow talk, sex), and in other families the "sacred" is reserved for parental bonds (bedtime cuddles with children, bathtime, meals, parental talk about children). In addition, families have secondary zones of less important daily, weekly, seasonal rituals which back up the core rituals. They also have a profane outer layer, in which members might describe themselves as "doing nothing in particular"—doing chores, watching television, sleeping. The character and boundaries of the sacred and profane aspects of family life are in the eye of the beholder. "Strong families" with "thick ties" can base their sense of the sacred on very different animating ideas and practices. Families also differ widely on how much one member's sense of the sacred matches another's and on how much it is the occasion for expressing harmony or conflict. Furthermore, families creatively adapt to new circumstances by ritualising new activities — for example, couples in commuter marriages may "ritualise" the phone call or the daily e-mail exchange. Couples with "too much time together" may de-ritualise meals, sex, or family events. Furthermore, families have different structures of sacred-ness. Some have thick actual cores and thin peripheries, others have a porous core and extensive peripheral time in which people just "hang out." But in each case, emotional culture shapes the experience of family life.

Emotional cultures stand back-to-back with ideas about time. In the con-text of the work–family speed-up, many people speak of actively "managing time, finding time, making time, guarding time, or fighting for time." Less do they speak of simply "having" or "not having" time. In their attempt to take a more active grip on their schedules, many working parents turn a tele-phone answering machine on at dinner, turn down work assignments and social engagements, and actively fight to defend "family time."

One's talk about time is itself a verbal practice that does or doesn't reaf-firm the ritual core of family life. In the core of family life, we may speak more of living in the moment. Because a sacred activity is an end in itself, and not a means to an end, the topic of time is less likely to arise. If it does, one speaks of "enjoying time," or "devoting time." With the work–family speed-up, the term "quality time" has arisen, as in "I need more quality time with my daughter," a term referring to freedom from distraction, time spent in an attitude of intense focus. In general, we try to "make" time for core family life because we feel it matters more.

In the intermediate and peripheral zones of family life, we may speak of "having time on our hands, wasting or killing time." In the new lexicon, we speak of "quantity time."[9] In general, we feel we can give up peripheral time, because it matters less. More hotly contested is the time to participate in a child's school events, help at the school auction, buy a birthday gift for a babysitter, or call an elderly neighbour.

With a decline in this periphery, the threads of reciprocity in the com-munity and neighbourhood grow weaker. By forcing families to cut out what is "least important," the speed-up thins out and weakens ties that bind it to society. Thus, under the press of the "speed-up," families are forced to give up their periphery ties with neighbours, distant relatives, bonds sus-tained by "extra time." *The speed-up privatises the family.* The "neighbourhood goes to work," where it serves the emotional interests of the workplace. Where are one's friends? At work.

Although the family in modern society is separated from the workplace, its emotional culture is ecologically linked to and drawn from it. Both the family and workplace are also linked to supportive realms. For the family, this often includes the neighbourhood, the church, the school. For the work-place, this includes the pub, the golf club, the commuter-van friendship network.

A loss of supportive structure around the family may result in a gain for the workplace, and vice versa. Insofar as the "periphery" of family life protected its ritual core, to a certain degree for working parents these ties are not so peripheral at all.

A gender pattern is clear. Because most women now must and for the most part want to work outside the home, they are performing family rituals less. At the same time, men are not doing them very much more. Together, these two facts result in a net loss in ritual life at home.

At the same time, at some workplaces, an alternative cultural magnet is drawing on the human need for a centre, a ritual core. As family life becomes de-ritualised, in certain sectors of the economy, the engineers of corporate cultures are re-ritualising the workplace. Thus, the contraction of emotional culture at home is linked to a socially engineered expansion of emotional culture at work.

Work like a Family, and Family, for Some, like Work

At a certain point, change in enough personal stories can be described as a change in culture, and I believe many families at the Company are coming to this turning-point now. Pulled toward work by one set of forces and propelled from the family by another set of forces, a growing number of workers are unwittingly altering the twin cultures of work and family (Kanter 1977; Lasch 1977). As the cultural shield surrounding work has grown stronger, the supportive cultural shield surrounding the family has weakened. Fewer neighbourhood "consultants" talk to one when trouble arises at home, and for some, they are more to help out with problems at work.

These twin processes apply unevenly; the pull toward work is stronger at the top of the occupational ladder, and marginalisation of family life, more pronounced at the bottom. Indeed, the picture I shall draw is one in a *wide array* of work and family "structurations" resulting from various combinations of social forces.

The Model of Family as a Haven in a Heartless World

When I entered the field, I assumed that working parents would *want* more time at home. I imagined that they experienced home as a place where they could relax, feel emotionally sheltered and appreciated for who they "really are." I imagined home to feel to the weary worker like the place where he or she could take off a uniform, put on a bathrobe, have a beer, exhale—a picture summed up in the image of the worker coming in the door saying, "Hi honey, I'm home!" To be sure, home life has its emergencies and strains but I imagined that home was the place people thought about when they thought about rest, safety and appreciation. Given this, they would want to maximise time at home, especially time with their children. I also assumed that these working parents would not feel particularly relaxed, safe or appreciated at work, at least not more so than at home, and especially not factory workers.

When I interviewed workers at the Company, however, a picture emerged which partly belied this model of family life. For example, one 30-year-old factory shift supervisor, a remarried mother of two, described her return home after work in this way:

> *I walk in the door and the minute I turn the key in the lock my oldest daughter is there. Granted she needs somebody to talk to about her day. The baby is still up. . . . She should have been in bed two hours ago and that upsets me. The oldest comes right up to the door and complains about anything her father said or did during the evening. She talks about her job. My husband is in the other room hollering to my daughter, "Tracy, I don't ever get no time to talk to your mother because you're always monopolizing her time first before I even get a chance!" They all come at me at once.*

The un-arbitrated quarrels, the dirty dishes, and the urgency of other people's demands she finds at home contrast with her account of going to work:

> *I usually come to work early just to get away from the house. I go to be there at a quarter after the hour and people are there waiting. We sit. We talk. We joke. I let them know what is going on, who has to be where, what changes I have made for the shift that day. We sit there and chit-chat for five or ten minutes. There is laughing. There is joking. There is fun. They aren't putting me down for any reason. Everything is done in humour and fun from beginning to end. It can get stressful, though, when a machine malfunctions and you can't get the production out.*

Another 38-year-old working mother of two, also a factory worker, had this to say:

> *My husband is a great help (with caring for their son). But as far as doing housework, or even taking the baby when I'm at home, no. When I'm home, our son becomes my job. He figures he works five days a week, he's not going to come home and clean. But he doesn't stop to think that I work seven days a week. . . . Why should I have to come home and do the housework without help from anybody else? My husband and I have been through this over and over again. Even if he would pick up the kitchen table and stack the dishes for me when I'm at work, that would make a big difference. He does nothing. On his weekends off, I have to provide a sitter for the baby so he can go fishing. When I have my day off, I have the baby all day long. He'll help out if I'm not here. . . . The minute I'm here he lets me do the work.*

To this working mother, her family was not a haven, a zone of relief and relaxation. It was a workplace. More than that, she could only get relief from this domestic workplace by going to the factory. As she continued:

I take a lot of overtime. The more I get out of the house, the better I am. It's a terrible thing to say, but that's the way I feel!

I assumed that work would feel to workers like a place in which one could be fired at the whim of a profit-hungry employer, while in the family, for all its hassles, one was safe. Based as it is on the impersonal mechanism of supply and demand, profit and loss, work would feel insecure, like being in "a jungle." In fact, many workers I interviewed had worked for the Company for 20 years or more. But they were on their second or third marriages. To these employed, *work* was their rock, their major source of security, while they were receiving their "pink slips" at home.

To be sure, most workers *wanted* to base their sense of stability at home, and many did. But I was also struck by the loyalty many felt toward the Company and a loyalty *they felt* coming from it, despite what might seem like evidence to the contrary—the speed-up, the restructuring. When problems arose at work, many workers felt they could go to their supervisors or to a human resources worker and resolve it. If one division of the Company was doing poorly, the Company might "de-hire" workers within that division and rehire in a more prosperous division. This happened to one female engineer, very much upsetting her, but her response to it was telling:

I have done very well in the Company for twelve years, and I thought my boss thought very highly of me. He'd said as much. So when our division went down and several of us were de-hired, we were told to look for another position within the Company or outside. I thought, "Oh my God, outside!" I was stunned! Later, in the new division it was like a remarriage. . . . I wondered if I could love again.

Work was not always "there for you," but increasingly "home," as they had known it, wasn't either. As one woman recounted, "One day my husband came home and told me, 'I've fallen in love with a woman at work. . . . I want a divorce.'"

Finally, the model of family-as-haven led me to assume that the individual would feel most known and appreciated at home and least so at work. Work might be where they felt unappreciated, "a cog in the machine"—an image brought to mind by the Charlie Chaplin classic film on factory life, *Modern Times*. But the factory is no longer the archetypical workplace and, sadly, many workers felt more appreciated for what they were doing at work than for what they were doing at home. For example, when I asked one 40-year-old technician whether he felt more appreciated at home or at work, he said:

I love my family. I put my family first . . . but I'm not sure I feel more appreciated by them (laughs). My 14-year-old son doesn't talk too much to anyone when he gets home from school. He's a brooder. I don't know how good I've been as a father. . . . We fix cars together on Saturday. My wife works opposite shifts to what I work, so we don't see each other except on weekends. We need more time together—need to get out to the lake more. I don't know . . .

This worker seemed to feel better about his skill repairing machines in the factory than his way of relating to his son. This is not as unusual as it might seem. In a large-scale study, Arthur Emlen found that 59 per cent of employees rated their family performance "good or unusually good" while 86 per cent gave a similar rating to their performance on the job (Friedman 1991:16).

This overall cultural shift may account for why many workers are going along with the work–family speed-up and not joining the resistance against it. A 1993 nationally representative study of 3400 workers conducted by The Families and Work Institute reflects two quite contradictory findings. On one hand, the study reports that 80 per cent of workers feel their jobs require "working very hard" and 42 per cent "often feel used up by the end of the work day." On the other hand, when workers are asked to compare how much time and energy they *actually* devoted to their family, their job or career and themselves, with how much time they would *like* to devote to each, there was little difference (Galinsky et al. 1993:1, 98). Workers estimate that they actually spend 43 per cent of their time and energy on family and friends, 37 per cent on job or career, and 20 per cent on themselves. But they *want* to spend just about what they *are* spending – 47 per cent on family and friends, 30 per cent on the job, and 23 per cent on themselves (Galinsky et al. 1993:98). Thus, the workers I spoke to who were "giving" in to the work–family speed-up may be typical of a wider trend.

Causal Mechanisms

Three sets of factors may exacerbate this reversal of family and work cultures; trends in the family, trends at work, and a cultural consumerism which reinforces trends in the family and work.

First, half of marriages in America end in divorce – the highest divorce rate in the world. Because of the greater complexity of family life, the emotional skills of parenting, woefully underestimated to begin with, are more important than ever before. Many workers spoke with feeling about strained relationships with stepchildren and ex-wives or husbands (White and Riesmann 1992). New in scope, too, are the numbers of working wives who work "two shifts," one at home and one at work, and face their husband's resistance to helping fully with the load at home – a strain that often leaves both spouses feeling unappreciated (Hochschild 1989).

Second, another set of factors apply at work. Many corporations have emotionally engineered for top and upper middle managers a world of friendly ritual and positive reinforcement. New corporate cultures call for "valuing the individual" and honouring the "internal customer" (so that requests made by employees within the Company are honoured as highly as those by customers outside the Company). Human relations employees give seminars on human problems at work. High-performance teams, based on cooperation between relative equals who "manage themselves," tend to foster intense relations at work. The Company frequently gives out awards for outstanding work at award ceremonies. Compliments run freely. The halls are hung with new plaques praising one or another worker on recent accomplishments. Recognition luncheons, department gatherings and informal birthday remembrances are common. Career planning sessions with one's supervisor, team meetings to talk over "modeling, work relations, and mentoring" with co-workers all verge on, even as they borrow from, psychotherapy. For all its aggravation and tensions, the workplace is where quite a few workers feel appreciated, honoured, and where they have real friends. By contrast, at home there are fewer "award ceremonies" and little helpful feedback about mistakes.

In addition, courtship and mate selection, earlier more or less confined to the home-based community, may be moving into the sphere of work. The later age for marriage, the higher proportion of unmarried people, and the high divorce rate all create an ever-replenishing courtship pool at work. The gender desegregation of the workplace and the lengthened working day also provide opportunity for people to meet and develop romantic or quasi-romantic ties. At the factory, romance may develop in the lunchroom, pub, or parking lot; and for upper management levels, at conferences, in "fantasy settings" in hotels and dimly lit restaurants (Kanter 1990:281).

In a previous era, an undetermined number of men escaped the house for the pub, the fishing hole, and often the office. A common pattern, to quote from the title of an article by Jean Duncombe and Dennis Marsden, was that of "workaholic men" and "whining women" (Duncombe and Marsden 1993). Now that women compose 45 per cent of the American labour force and come home to a "second shift" of work at home, some women are escaping into work too—and as they do so, altering the cultures of work and home.

Forces pulling workers out of family life and into the workplace are set into perpetual motion by consumerism. Consumerism acts as a mechanism which maintains the emotional reversal of work and family (Schor 1992). Exposed to advertisements, workers expand their material "needs." To buy what they now "need," they need money. To earn money, they work longer hours. Being away from home so many hours, they make up for their absence at home with gifts which cost money. They "materialise" love. And so the cycle continues.

Once work begins to become a more compelling arena of appreciation than home, a self-fulfilling prophecy takes hold. For, if workers flee into work from the tensions at home, tensions at home often grow worse. The worse the tensions at home, the firmer the grip of the workplace on the worker's human needs, and hence the escalation of the entire syndrome.

If more workers conceive of work as a haven, it is overwhelmingly in some sense *against their wishes*. Most workers in this and other studies say they value family life above all. Work is what they do. Family is why they live. So, I believe the logic I have described proceeds despite, not because of, the powerful intentions and deepest wishes of those in its grip.

Models of Family and Work in the Flight Plan of Capitalism

To sum up, for some people work may be becoming more like family, and family life more like work. Instead of the model of the *family* as haven from work, more of us fit the model of *work* as haven from home. In this model, the tired parent leaves a world of unresolved quarrels, unwashed laundry and dirty dishes for the atmosphere of engineered cheer, appreciation and harmony at work. It is at work that one drops the job of *working* on relating to a brooding adolescent, an obstreperous toddler, rivaling siblings or a retreating spouse. At last, beyond the emotional shield of work, one says not, "Hi honey, I'm home," but "Hi fellas, I'm here!" For those who fit this model, the ritual core of family life is not simply smaller, it is less of a ritual core.

How extensive is this trend? I suspect it is a slight tendency in the lives of many working parents, and the basic reality for a small but growing minority. This trend holds for some people more than others and in some parts of society more than in others. Certain trends — such as the growth of the contingency labour force — may increase the importance of the family, and tend toward reinstalling the model of family as haven and work as "heartless world." A growing rate of unemployment might be associated with yet a third "double-negative" model according to which neither home nor work are emotional bases, but rather the gang at the pub, or on the street.

But the sense of sacred that we presume to be reliably attached to home may be more vulnerable than we might wish.

Most working parents more deeply want, or want to want, a fourth, "double-positive" model of work–family balance. In the end, these four patterns are unevenly spread over the class structure — the "haven in a heartless world" more at the top, the "double-negative" more at the bottom, the "reverse-haven" emerging in the middle.

Each pattern of work and family life is to be seen somewhere in the flight plan of late capitalism. For capitalist competition is not simply a matter of market expansion around the globe, but of local geographies of emotion at home. The challenge, as I see it, is to understand the close links between economic trends, emotional geographies, and pockets of cultural resistance. For it is in those pockets that we can look for "warm modern" answers.

ENDNOTES

1. Less time away from work means less time for children. Nationwide, half of children wish they could see their fathers more, and a third wish they could see their mothers more (Coolsen, Seligson, and Garbino 1986; Hewlett 1991:105). A growing number of commentators draw links, often carelessly, between this decline in family time and a host of problems, including school failure and alcohol and drug abuse (Hewlett 1991).

2. In her book *When Giants Learn to Dance*, the sociologist Rosabeth Kanter suggests an alternative to mommy-tracking — company "time outs." A company requires workers to work ten weeks of 9- or 10-hour days preparing to ship a product, and then take a week-long "time out" after the product is shipped. In contrast to

"mommy-tracking," these time-outs are available to men as well as women. Those who take advantage of them aren't placed on a lower track (Kanter 1990). But by design, time-outs suit the needs of the *company* more than the worker. Time-outs presume the acceptance of an industrial notion of time for men and women, and pay the worker back for this acceptance, offering periodic rest-stops in it. It does not challenge the culture of capitalism but softens the worker up, the better to accept it (Kanter 1990:359).

3. On the political agenda for the 1950s, through the 1970s, bills proposing a shorter working week were vetoed by the United States Congress, strongly opposed by business, and have since disappeared from American public discourse (Blyton 1985; McCarthy and McGaughey 1981; Owen 1989).

4. Since factory workers are normally excluded in company consideration of these reforms, this option is normally excluded from "family-friendly reforms." In addition, seniority is the unquestioned principle applied in allocating shifts (see Engelstad 1983). Unions often oppose it adamantly since it adds a principle that competes with the principle of seniority used to determine who gets to work which shift.

5. The option of shorter or more flexible schedules should not be confused with the growth of "contingency jobs" which pair flexibility with a loss of job security and benefits. As activists in and outside companies conceive of family-friendly reforms, they make "good" jobs better and don't substitute bad jobs for good ones.

6. Many studies show that family-friendly reforms pay for themselves. Those who quit their jobs for family reasons are often the most, not the least, productive workers. In addition, each trained worker who quits costs the company money in recruiting and training a replacement.

7. The CEO's pronouncement about family-friendly reforms and the managers' nonexecution of them resemble an episode in Leo Tolstoy's *War and Peace*. In the novel, the Russian Emperor Alexander dispatches an envoy, Balashev, to deliver a critical message to Napoleon, to halt his advance toward Moscow. Balashev is detained by a series of people and, when he meets Napoleon, forgets to deliver the message.

8. Taking inspiration from Émile Durkheim, Erving Goffman brilliantly applied a notion of the sacred to the individual, though Goffman does not apply this idea to the unit intermediate between society and the individual—the family.

9. The workplace speed-up has itself exacerbated a "rationalisation" of family life. In the nineteenth century, Tamara Hareven argues, events were measured in "family time," according to a family timetable (births, marriages, deaths) and by family units (generations) and oriented to family needs (the need to tend newborns, the dying). Formerly resistant to rationalisation, in the last 30 years family life has become increasingly planned, and geared to the industrial clock. "Quality time" is demarcated from "quantity time," just as time at the office "working" is designated as separate from time "goofing off around the water cooler." One shouldn't, one feels, be chatting aimlessly in a "quantity" sort of way when one is having "quality" time with a child. Even life-cycle events such as marriages and births are now sometimes planned according to the needs of the office (Martin 1992).

REFERENCES

Blyton, Paul. 1985. *Changes in Working Time: An International Review*. New York: St. Martin's Press.

Coolsen, P., M. Seligson, and J. Garbino. 1986. *When School's Out and Nobody's Home*. Chicago: National Committee for the Prevention of Child Abuse.

Duncombe, Jean and Dennis Marsden. 1993. "Workaholics and Whining Women, Theorizing Intimacy and Emotion Work: The Last Frontier of Gender Inequality?" Unpublished paper, Department of Sociology, University of Essex, England.

Engelstad, Fredrik. 1993. "Family Structure and Institutional Interplay." Pp. 72–90 in *Family Sociology – Developing the Field*, edited by Annlang Leira. Oslo: Institut fur Samfunnsforskning.

Friedman, D. 1991. *Linking Work–Family Issues to the Bottom Line*. New York: Conference Board.

Fuchs, V. 1991. "Are Americans Under-Investing in Their Children?" *Society* (September/October): 14–22.

Galinsky, Ellen, James Bond, and Dana Friedman. 1993. *The Changing Workforce: Highlights of the National Study*. New York: Family and Work Institute.

Galinsky, Ellen, Dana E. Friedman, and Carol A. Hernandez. 1991. *The Corporate Reference Guide to Work–Family Programs*. New York: Families and Work Institute.

Giddens, Anthony. 1976. *New Rules of Sociological Method*. New York: Basic Books.

——. 1991. *Modernity and Self-Identity*. Stanford, CA: Stanford University Press.

Hewlett, Sylvia Ann. 1991. *When the Bough Breaks: The Costs of Neglecting Our Children*. New York: Basic Books.

Hochschild, Arlie. 1983. *The Managed Heart: The Commercialization of Human Feeling*. Berkeley: University of California Press.

——. 1994. "The Commercial Spirit of Intimate Life and the Abduction of Feminism: Signs from Women's Advice Books." *Theory, Culture & Society* 2 (May): 1–24.

Hochschild, Arlie, with Anne Machung. 1989. *The Second Shift: Working Parents and the Revolution at Home*. New York: Viking Press.

Kanter, Rosabeth Moss. 1977. *Work and Family in the United States: A Critical Review and Agenda for Research and Policy*. New York: Russell Sage Foundation.

——. 1990. *When Giants Learn to Dance: Mastering the Challenges of Strategy, Management, and Careers in the 1990s*. S & S Trade.

Lasch, Christopher. 1977. *Haven in a Heartless World*. New York: Basic Books.

Martin, Joanne. 1992. *Cultures in Organizations: Three Perspectives*. New York: Oxford University Press.

McCarthy, Eugene and William McGaughey. 1981. *Nonfinancial Economics: The Case for Shorter Hours of Work*. New York: Praeger.

Owen, John. 1989. *Reduced Working Hours: Cure for Unemployment or Economic Burden?* Baltimore: Johns Hopkins University Press.

Schaevitz, Marjorie Hansen. 1984. *The Superwoman Syndrome*. New York: Warner Books.

Schor, Juliet B. 1992. *The Overworked American: The Unexpected Decline of Leisure*. New York: Basic Books.

Schwartz, Felice N. 1989. "Management Women and the New Facts of Life." *Harvard Business Review* 1 (January/February): 65–76.

Tolstoy, Leo. 1966. *War and Peace*. New York: Norton.

White, Lynn K. and Agnes Riesmann. 1992. "When the Brady Bunch Grows Up: Step-, Half- and Full-Sibling Relationships in Adulthood." *Journal of Marriage and the Family* 54 (February): 197–208.

42

THE MOMMY TAX

ANN CRITTENDEN

In the U.S. we have no way to address women's economic disadvantages except through the concept of gender. We see the problem as discrimination on the basis of gender. But what's really going on is a disadvantaging of mothers *in the workforce.*

—SUSAN PEDERSON, HISTORIAN

On April 7, 1999, the Independent Women's Forum, a conservative antifeminist organization, held a news conference at the National Press Club in Washington, D.C. Displayed in the corner of the room was a large green "check," made out to feminists, for ninety-eight cents. The point being made was that American women now make ninety-eight cents to a man's dollar and have therefore achieved complete equality in the workplace.

The sheer nerve of this little exercise in misinformation was astonishing. Upon closer examination, it turned out that the women who earn almost as much as men are a rather narrow group: those who are between the ages of twenty-seven and thirty-three and who have never had children.[1] The Independent Women's Forum was comparing young childless women to men and declaring victory for all women, glossing over the real news: that mothers are the most disadvantaged people in the workplace. One could even say that motherhood is now the single greatest obstacle left in the path to economic equality for women.

For most companies, the ideal worker is "unencumbered," that is, free of all ties other than those to his job. Anyone who can't devote all his or her energies to paid work is barred from the best jobs and has a permanently lower lifetime income. Not coincidentally, almost all the people in that category happen to be mothers.

The reduced earnings of mothers are, in effect, a heavy personal tax levied on people who care for children, or for any other dependent family members. This levy, a "mommy tax," is easily greater than $1 million in the case of a college-educated woman.[2] For working-class women, there is increasing evidence both in the United States and worldwide that mothers' differential responsibility for children, rather than classic sex discrimination, is the most important factor disposing women to poverty.[3]

"This is the issue that women's and children's advocates should be raising," argues Jane Waldfogel, a professor at Columbia University School of Social Work. "Women's equality is not about equal access to education or equal job opportunities anymore — those things are done. The part that's left is the part that has to do with family responsibilities."[4]

The much-publicized earnings gap between men and women narrowed dramatically in the 1980s and early 1990s. All a girl had to do was stay young and unencumbered. The sexual egalitarianism evident in so many television sit-coms, from *Friends* to *Seinfeld* to *Ally McBeal*, is rooted in economic reality. Young women don't need a man to pay their bills or take them out, any more than men need a woman to iron their shirts or cook their dinner. Many childless women under the age of thirty-five firmly believe that all of the feminist battles have been won, and as far as they're concerned, they're largely right.

But once a woman has a baby, the egalitarian office party is over. I ought to know.

Million–Dollar Babies

After my son was born in 1982, I decided to leave the *New York Times* in order to have more time to be a mother. I recently calculated what that decision cost me financially.

I had worked full-time for approximately twenty years, eight of those at the *Times*. When I left, I had a yearly salary of roughly $50,000, augmented by speaking fees, freelance income, and journalism awards. Had I not had a child, I probably would have worked at least another fifteen years, maybe taking early retirement to pursue other interests. Under this scenario, I would have earned a pension, which I lost by leaving the paper before I had worked the requisite ten years to become vested. (The law has since changed to allow vesting after five years with one employer.)

My annual income after leaving the paper has averaged roughly $15,000, from part-time freelance writing. Very conservatively, I lost between $600,000 and $700,000, not counting the loss of a pension. Without quite realizing what I was doing, I took what I thought would be a relatively short break, assuming it would be easy to get back into journalism after a few years, or to earn a decent income from books and other projects. I was wrong. As it turned out, I sacrificed more than half of my expected lifetime earnings. And in the boom years of the stock market, that money invested in equities would have multiplied like kudzu. As a conservative estimate, it could have generated $50,000 or $60,000 a year in income for my old age.

At the time, I never sat down and made these economic calculations. I never even thought about money in connection with motherhood, or if I did, I assumed my husband would provide all we needed. And had I been asked to weigh my son's childhood against ten or fifteen more years at the *Times*, I doubt whether the monetary loss would have tipped the scales. But still, this seems a high price to pay for doing the right thing.

The mommy tax I paid is fairly typical for an educated middle-class American woman. Economist Shirley Burggraf has calculated that a husband and wife who earn a combined income of $81,500 per year and who are equally capable will lose $1.35 million if they have a child. Most of that lost income is the wages forgone by the primary parent.[5] In a middle-income family, with one parent earning $30,000 per year as a sales representative and the other averaging $15,000 as a part-time computer consultant, the mommy tax will still be more than $600,000. Again, this seems an unreasonable penalty on the decision to raise a child, a decision that contributes to the general good by adding another productive person to the nation.

In lower-income families, the mommy tax can push a couple over the brink. Martha F. Richie, a former director of the U.S. Census Bureau, told me, "There is anecdotal evidence—no real research—that for a lower-earning married couple the decision to have a child, or a second child, throws them into poverty."[6]

Those who care for elderly relatives also discover that their altruism will be heavily penalized. A small survey of individuals who provided informal, unpaid care for family members found that it cost them an average of $659,139 in lost wages, Social Security, and pension benefits over their lifetimes. The subjects reported having to pass up promotions and training opportunities, use up their sick days and vacations, reduce their workload to part-time, and in many cases even quit their paid jobs altogether. This exorbitant "caring tax" is being paid by an increasing number of people, three-quarters of them women. A 1997 study discovered that one in four families had at least one adult who had provided care for an elderly relative or friend.[7]

The mommy tax is obviously highest for well-educated, high-income individuals and lowest for poorly educated people who have less potential income to lose. All else being equal, the younger the mother, and the more children she has, the higher her tax will be, which explains why women are having fewer children, later in life, almost everywhere.

The tax is highest in the Anglo-Saxon countries, where mothers personally bear almost all the costs of caring, and lowest in France and Scandinavia, where paid maternity leaves and public preschools make it easier for mothers to provide care without sacrificing their income. . . .

Sixty Cents to a Man's Dollar

In the Bible, in Leviticus, God instructs Moses to tell the Israelites that women, for purposes of tithing, are worth thirty shekels while men are worth fifty—a ratio of 60 percent.[8] For fifty years, from about 1930 to 1980, the value of employed women eerily reflected that biblical ratio: The earnings of full-time working women were only 60 percent of men's earnings. In the 1980s, that ratio began to change. By 1993, women working full-time were earning an average of seventy-seven cents for every dollar men earned. (In 1997, the gap widened again, as the median weekly earnings of full-time working women fell to 75 percent of men's earnings.)

But lo and behold, when we look closer, we find the same old sixty cents to a man's dollar. The usual way to measure the gender wage gap is by comparing the hourly earnings of men and women who work full-time year-round. But this compares only the women who work like men with men—a method that neatly excludes most women. As we have seen, only about half of the mothers of children under eighteen have full-time, year-round paying jobs.[9]

To find the real difference between men's and women's earnings, one would have to compare the earnings of all male and female workers, both full- and part-time. And guess what one discovers? The average earnings of *all* female workers in 1999 were 59 percent of men's earnings.[10] Women who work for pay are still stuck at the age-old biblical value put on their labor.

My research turned up other intriguing reflections of the 60 percent ratio: A survey of 1982 graduates of the Stanford Business School found that ten years after graduation, the median income of the full- and part-time employed female M.B.A.s amounted to $81,300, against the men's median income of $139,100. Again, the women's share is 58 percent. Another study, of 1974 graduates of the University of Michigan Law School, revealed that in the late 1980s the women's average earnings were 61 percent of the men's— despite the fact that 96 percent of the women were working, and that the men and women were virtually identical in terms of training. The authors of this study concluded that the women's family responsibilities were "certainly the most important single cause of sex differences in earnings."[11] . . .

The Cost of Being a Mother

A small group of mostly female academic economists has added another twist to the story. Their research reveals that working mothers not only earn less than men, but also less per hour than childless women, even after such differences as education and experience are factored out. The pay gap between mothers and nonmothers under age thirty-five is now larger than the wage gap between young men and women. . . .

Why do working mothers earn so much less than childless women? Academic researchers have worried over this question like a dog over a bone but haven't turned up a single, definitive answer.[12]

Waldfogel argues that the failure of employers to provide paid maternity leaves is one factor that leads to the family wage gap in the United States. This country is one of only six nations in the world that does not require a paid leave. (The others are Australia, New Zealand, Lesotho, Swaziland, and

Papua New Guinea.[13]) With no right to a paid leave, many American mothers who want to stay at home with a new baby simply quit their jobs, and this interruption in employment costs them dearly in terms of lost income. Research in Europe reveals that when paid maternity leaves were mandated, the percentage of women remaining employed rose, and women's wages were higher, unless the leaves lasted more than a few months.[14]

In the United States as well, women who are able to take formal paid maternity leave do not suffer the same setback in their wages as comparably placed women who do not have a right to such leaves. This is a significant benefit to mothers in the five states, including California, New York, and New Jersey, that mandate temporary disability insurance coverage for pregnancy and childbirth.[15]

Paid leaves are so valuable because they don't seem to incur the same penalties that employers impose on even the briefest of unpaid career interruptions. A good example is the experience of the 1974 female graduates of the University of Michigan Law School. During their first fifteen years after law school, these women spent an average of only 3.3 months out of the workplace, compared with virtually no time out for their male classmates. More than one-quarter of the women had worked part-time, for an average of 10.1 months over the fifteen years, compared with virtually no part-time work among the men. While working full-time, the women put in only 10 percent fewer hours than full-time men, again not a dramatic difference.

But the penalties for these slight distinctions between the men's and women's work patterns were strikingly harsh. Fifteen years after graduation, the women's average earnings were not 10 percent lower, or even 20 percent lower, than the men's, but almost 40 percent lower. Fewer than one-fifth of the women in law firms who had worked part-time for more than six months had made partner in their firms, while more than four-fifths of the mothers with little or no part-time work had made partner.[16]

Another survey of almost 200 female M.B.A.s found that those who had taken an average of only 8.8 months out of the job market were less likely to reach upper-middle management and earned 17 percent less than comparable women who had never had a gap in their employment.[17]

Working-class women are also heavily penalized for job interruptions, although these are the very women who allegedly "choose" less demanding occupations that enable them to move in and out of the job market without undue wage penalties. The authors of one study concluded that the negative repercussions of taking a little time out of the labor force were still discernible after twenty years.[18] In blue-collar work, seniority decides who is eligible for better jobs, and who is "bumped" in the event of layoffs. Under current policies, many women lose their seniority forever if they interrupt their employment, as most mothers do. Training programs, required for advancement, often take place after work, excluding the many mothers who can't find child care.[19]

Mandatory overtime is another handicap placed on blue-collar mothers. Some 45 percent of American workers reported in a recent survey that they had to work overtime with little or no notice.[20] In 1994 factory workers put in the highest levels of overtime ever reported by the Bureau of Labor Statistics in its thirty-eight years of tracking the data. Where does that leave a woman who has to be home in time for dinner with the kids? Out of a promotion and maybe out of a job. Increasingly in today's driven workplace, whether she is blue- or white-collar, a woman who goes home when she is supposed to go home is going to endanger her economic well-being.

The fact that many mothers work part-time also explains some of the difference between mothers' and comparable women's hourly pay. (About 65 percent of part-time workers are women, most of whom are mothers.)[21] Employers are not required to offer part-time employees equal pay and benefits for equal work. As a result, nonstandard workers earn on average about 40 percent less an hour than full-time workers, and about half of that wage gap persists even for similar workers in similar jobs.

Many bosses privately believe that mothers who work part-time have a "recreational" attitude toward work, as one Maryland businessman assured me. Presumably, this belief makes it easier to justify their exploitation. But the working conditions they face don't sound very much like recreation. A recent survey by Catalyst, a research organization focused on women in business, found that more than half of the people who had switched to part-time jobs and lower pay reported that their workload stayed the same. Ten percent reported an increase in workload after their income had been reduced. Most of these people were mothers.[22]

Another factor in the family wage gap is the disproportionate number of mothers who operate their own small businesses, a route often taken by women who need flexibility during the child-rearing years. Female-owned small businesses have increased twofold over small businesses owned by men in recent years.[23] In 1999, women owned 38 percent of all U.S. businesses, compared with only 5 percent in 1972, a remarkable increase that is frequently cited as evidence of women's economic success. One new mother noted that conversations at play groups "center as much on software and modems as they do on teething and ear infections."[24]

Less frequently mentioned is the fact that many of these women-owned businesses are little more than Mom-minus-Pop operations: one woman trying to earn some money on the side, or keep her career alive, during the years when her children have priority. Forty-five percent of women-owned businesses are home-based. And the more than one-third of businesses owned by women in 1996 generated only 16 percent of the sales of all U.S. businesses in that year.[25]

In 1997, although women were starting new businesses at twice the rate of men, they received only 2 percent of institutional venture capital, a principal source of financing for businesses with serious prospects for growth. Almost one-quarter of female business owners financed their operations the same way that they did their shopping: with their credit cards.[26]

Some researchers have suggested that mothers earn less than childless women because they are less productive. This may be true for some mothers who work at home and are subject to frequent interruptions, or for those who are exhausted from having to do most of the domestic chores, or distracted by creaky child-care arrangements. But the claim that mothers have lower productivity than other workers is controversial and unproven. It is easier to demonstrate that working mothers face the same old problem that has bedeviled women in the workplace for decades: [discrimination]. . . .

How to Lower the Mommy Tax

Until now, narrowing the gender wage gap in the United States has depended almost entirely on what might be called the "be a man" strategy. Women are told to finish school, find a job, acquire skills, develop seniority, get tenure, make partner, and put children off until the very last minute. The longer a woman postpones family responsibilities, and the longer her "pre-parental" phase lasts, the higher her lifetime earnings will be.

Ambitious women of the baby-boom generation and younger have by and large tried to be a man in this way. A good example is Susan Pedersen, a historian who achieved tenure at Harvard in the mid-1990s. By that time, she was married and in her late thirties, but she had postponed having children until her academic career was secure. Motherhood was something she wanted very much, she commented during an interview, but it posed a serious threat to her professional dreams and had to be delayed.[27]

As Pedersen's success demonstrates, this strategy does work—for the very small number who are able to pull it off. And women who have their children later in life do have higher lifetime earnings and a wider range of opportunities than younger mothers. The advice dished out by writers like Danielle Crittenden—no relation—an antifeminist ideologue who has urged women to marry and have their babies young, ignores this, along with some other hard truths. Crittenden never tells her readers that young parents tend to separate and divorce much more frequently than older couples, leaving young mothers and children vulnerable to poverty. Large numbers of the women who end up on welfare are there because they have done exactly what she recommends: married and had children young and then been left to support them alone.[28]

But trying to be a man has its own risks. Many baby-boomer women postponed families only to discover that when they wanted to become pregnant, it was too late. . . . And millions of women don't feel that being a man is the way they want to live their lives. Increasingly, young women are saying that they don't want to put off children until they almost qualify for membership in AARP.

An alternative strategy is followed in countries like France and Sweden, where the government, private employers, and/or husbands share much more of the costs of raising children. This makes it far easier for women to be mothers and to work. In France, for example, families with two preschool-age children receive about $10,000 worth of annual subsidies, including free health care and housing subsidies and excellent free preschools.[29] As a result, child poverty is unusual, and the pay gap between mothers and others is much smaller in France than in the United States or the United Kingdom.

Whenever Europe is singled out as a model, the usual response is that Americans would never support such generous social policies. But in fact, the United States already does have an extremely generous social welfare state. But unlike the welfare states of western Europe, the American government doesn't protect mothers; it protects soldiers.

Men who postpone or interrupt civilian employment for military service pay a tax on their lifetime earnings that is quite comparable to the mommy tax. White men who were drafted during the Vietnam War, for example, were still earning approximately 15 percent less in the early 1980s than comparable nonveterans.[30] This "warrior wage gap" is strikingly similar to the family wage gap, again indicating that mothers' lower earnings are not entirely attributable to gender discrimination.

But there is unquestionable discrimination in the way the government has responded to the financial sacrifices that soldiers and parents, particularly mothers, make. All Americans are asked to "make it up" to veterans of the military: The damage to a caregiver's pocketbook is unmitigated, while the damage to a veteran's wallet has legitimized a massive relief effort. . . .

The benefits paid to military veterans are so lavish that they are now second only to Social Security in terms of government payments to individuals. And they do an excellent job of reducing the warrior tax. The educational benefits in particular help veterans overcome many of the economic disadvantages they suffer by leaving the workplace for a few years.

A congressional study in the early 1990s concluded that the veterans of World War II who took advantage of the G.I. Bill to earn a college degree enjoyed incomes of up to 10 percent more than they might otherwise have earned. Society was also the beneficiary, for the additional taxes paid by the college-educated veterans during their working lives more than paid for the program.[31]

It hardly needs to be said that there is no G.I. Bill, no health care, no subsidized housing, and no job preferences for mothers. As things now stand, millions of women sacrifice their economic independence and risk economic disaster for the sake of raising a child. This says a lot about family values, the nation's priorities, and free riding.

A third way to reduce the mommy tax would be to expand the antidiscrimination laws to cover parents. Joan Williams, a law professor at American University's Washington College of Law, argues that the design of work around masculine norms can be reconceptualized as discrimination. As an example, Williams suggests that if a woman works full-time, with good job evaluations for a significant period, then switches to part-time because of family responsibilities and is paid less per hour than full-time employees doing similar work, she could claim discrimination under the Equal Pay Act. Williams believes that disparate-action suits could also be filed against employers whose policies (including routine and mandatory overtime, promotion tracks, resistance to part-time work) have a disparate impact on women, producing disproportionate numbers of men in top-level positions.[32]

The essential point is that existing laws, and new laws preventing discrimination against people with caregiving responsibilities, could go a very long way toward improving mothers' lifetime earnings.

The Ultimate Mommy Tax: Childlessness

The cost of children has become so high that many American women are not having children at all. One of the most striking findings of Claudia Goldin's survey of white female college graduates is their high degree of childlessness (28 percent). Now that the baby-boomer generation is middle-aged, it is clear that more than one-quarter of the educated women in that age group will never have children. Indeed, the percentage of all American women who remain childless is also steadily rising, from 8 to 9 percent in the 1950s to 10 percent in 1976 to 17.5 percent in the late 1990s.

Is this rising childlessness by choice? Goldin thinks not. She found that in 1978, while in their twenties, almost half of the college-educated boomers who would remain childless had said that they did want children. Goldin calculated that almost one-fifth of this entire generation (19 percent) of white college graduates was disappointed in not having a child. This is the ultimate price of the "be a man" strategy that has been forced on working women. For women in business, the price is staggering. A recent Catalyst survey of 1,600 M.B.A.s found that only about one-fifth of the women had children, compared with 70 percent of the men.[33]

Educated black women have had, if anything, an even harder time combining children with their careers. Many of the most accomplished black women now in their forties and fifties, including Oprah Winfrey, Anita Hill, Eleanor Holmes Norton (the congressional representative for the District of Columbia), and Alexis Herman, secretary of labor in the Clinton administration, have forgone motherhood. These women apparently discovered that the price of success included the lack of parental obligations. And educated black women face an additional problem—an acute shortage of eligible black men.

Americans have a hard time realizing that such deeply personal choices as when or whether to have a child can be powerfully circumscribed by broader social or economic factors. American women, in particular, are stunningly unaware that their "choices" between a career and a family are much more limited than those of women in many European countries, where policies are much more favorable to mothers and children.

ENDNOTES

1. This calculation was made by economist June O'Neill, using data from the National Longitudinal Survey of Youth. June O'Neill and Solomon Polachek,

"Why the Gender Gap in Wages Narrowed in the 1980s," *Journal of Labor Economics* 11 (1993): 205–28. See also June O'Neill, "The Shrinking Pay Gap," *Wall Street Journal*, October 7, 1994.

2. The concept of the mommy tax was inspired by development economist Gita Sen, who has described the extra economic burden borne by women as a "reproduction tax."

3. I don't mean to suggest that old-fashioned sex discrimination, even against women who are able to perform as "ideal" workers, is not still alive and well, as numerous recent complaints, from the brokerage offices of Smith Barney to the machine shops of Mitsubishi, can attest. Simply being female still sentences women in virtually every occupation and at every level to lower earnings than men in similar positions. But overt in-your-face discrimination has thankfully declined steadily in recent decades.

4. Jane Waldfogel, personal communication, October 1996.

5. Burggraf assumes that the more flexible parent's earnings average $25,750 a year, versus $55,750 for the primary breadwinner. She then multiplies $30,000 (the difference between what the two parents earn) by 45 (the years in a working lifetime) to get the $1,350 million. *The Feminine Economy and Economic Man*, p. 61.

6. Martha Ritchie, personal communication, January 1995.

7. Sara Rimer, "Study Details Sacrifices in Caring for Elderly Kin," *New York Times*, November 27, 1999. The National Alliance for Caregivers estimates that the number of employed people who provide care for elderly family members will grow to between 11 and 15.6 million in the first decade of the twenty-first century.

8. Amity Shlaes, "What Does Woman Want?" *Women's Quarterly* (summer 1996): 10.

9. According to June O'Neill, an economist and former head of the Congressional Budget Office, "Full-time year-round workers are not likely to be representative of all workers. Women are less likely to be in this category than men." See June O'Neill and Solomon Polachek, "Why the Gender Gap in Wages Narrowed in the 1980s," *Journal of Labor Economics* 2, no. 1, pt. 1 (1993): 208–209.

10. U.S. Bureau of the Census, *Money Income in the U.S.: 1995*, Current Population Reports, P60–209, Washington, D.C., March 2000, pp. 46–49.

11. Robert G. Wood, Mary E. Corcoran, and Paul N. Courant, "Pay Differentials among the Highly-Paid: The Male–Female Earnings Gap in Lawyers' Salaries," *Journal of Labor Economics* 11, no. 3 (1993): 417–41.

12. See Paula England and Michelle Budig, "The Effects of Motherhood on Wages in Recent Cohorts: Findings from the National Longitudinal Survey of Youth," unpublished paper, 1999.

13. Elizabeth Olson, "U.N. Surveys Paid Leave for Mothers," *New York Times*, February 16, 1998.

14. Christopher J. Ruhm, "The Economic Consequences of Parental Leave Mandates: Lessons from Europe," *Quarterly Journal of Economics* CXIII, no. 1 (1998): 285–317. Ruhm found that longer leaves (of nine months or more) were associated with a slight reduction in women's relative wages, but Waldfogel discovered that mothers in Britain who exercised their right to a ten-month paid maternity leave and returned to their original employer had wages no different from those of childless women.

15. Heidi Hartmann, Institute for Women's Policy Research, personal communication, January 8, 1995. Hartmann's research has shown that fully 11 percent of women who have no paid leave have to go on public assistance during their time with a new baby.

16. Wood, Corcoran, and Courant, "Pay Differentials," pp. 417–28.

17. This 1993 study was coauthored by Joy Schneer of Rider University's College of Business Administration and Frieda Reitman, professor emeritus at Pace University's Lubin School of Business.

18. Joyce Jacobsen and Arthur Levin, "The Effects of Intermittent Labor Force Attachment on Female Earnings," *Monthly Labor Review* 118, no. 9 (September 1995): 18.

19. For a good discussion of the obstacles to mothers' employment in relatively well-paying blue-collar work, see Williams, *Unbending Gender*, pp. 76–81.

20. This survey of 1,000 workers was conducted by researchers at the University of Connecticut and Rutgers University, and was reported in the *Wall Street Journal*, May 18, 1999.

21. A survey of more than 2,000 people in four large corporations found that 75 percent of the professionals working part-time were women who were doing so because of child-care obligations. Only 11 percent of the male managers surveyed expected to work part-time at some point in their careers, compared with 36 percent of women managers. *A New Approach to Flexibility: Managing the Work/Time Equation* (New York: Catalyst, 1997), pp. 25–26.

22. There is other evidence that many so-called part-timers are increasingly working what used to be considered full-time—thirty-five to forty hours a week—for lower hourly pay than regular full-timers. See Reed Abelson, "Part-Time Work for Some Adds Up to Full-Time Job," *New York Times*, November 2, 1998.

23. In the five years from 1988 through 1992, the number of women-owned sole proprietorships, partnerships, and similar businesses soared 43 percent, compared with overall growth of 26 percent in such businesses. *Wall Street Journal*, January 29, 1996.

24. Tracy Thompson, "A War Inside Your Head," *Washington Post Magazine*, February 15, 1998, p. 29.

25. Information on women-owned businesses provided by the National Foundation for Women Business Owners in Washington, D.C., September 2000.

26. Noelle Knox, "Women Entrepreneurs Attract New Financing," *New York Times*, July 26, 1998.

27. Susan Pedersen, personal interview, June 1996.

28. Being a young mother obviously worked for Crittenden, who was affluent enough to have purchased a $1.3-million home in Washington, D.C., while still in her mid-thirties. But not many mothers enjoy such options.

29. Barbara Bergmann, personal conversation, January 4, 1999.

30. Joshua D. Angrist, "Lifetime Earnings and the Vietnam Era Draft Lottery: Evidence from Social Security Administrative Records," *American Economic Review* 80, no. 3 (June 1990): 313–31.

31. David O'Neill, "Voucher Funding of Training Programs: Evidence from the G.I. Bill," *Journal of Human Resources* 12, no. 4 (fall 1977): 425–45; and Joshua D. Angrist, "The Effects of Veterans' Benefits on Education and Earnings," *Industrial and Labor Relations Review* 46, no. 4 (July 1993): 637–57.

32. Williams, *Unbending Gender*, pp. 101–10.

33. The theory that much of the childlessness among educated American women is involuntary was supported by an informal class survey of the graduates of Harvard and Radcliffe class of 1971. Roughly one-fifth of both the men and the women were still childless in 1996, when the class was in its mid- to late forties. But many more women than men said they were childless because of "circumstances."

43

NO PLACE LIKE HOME
The Division of Domestic Labor in Lesbigay Families

CHRISTOPHER CARRINGTON

Sterling never cleaned toilets, he still doesn't clean toilets; he intends to clean the toilets, but right about the time when he gets to it, I have already cleaned the toilets.

—WAYNE OSMUNDSEN, 35-YEAR-OLD SOCIAL WORKER

The common metaphorical use of laundry, as in the phrase "to air their dirty laundry in public," connotes several things about actual laundry, most notably a common expectation that dirty laundry should remain hidden. This chapter violates that common expectation, in both a metaphorical and in a literal sense.

Stigmatized and oppressed communities often struggle with the menacing question of how to deal with "dirty laundry." Many lesbian and gay authors feel the need to present ourselves, and our communities, to the dominant culture in ideal terms, a feeling that I have often shared. These portrayals, as opposed to the empirical realities, often reflect the efforts of lesbigay people to provide a respectable image of ourselves in a society often bent on devaluing and marginalizing us. Undoubtedly, the observations made here regarding the division of domestic work in lesbigay families violate the expectation that dirty laundry remain closeted.

The public portrayals and presentations of egalitarianism among lesbigay families do not cohere with the household realities that prevail among them. Two components of the research strategy used here expose the gap between public portrayals and empirical realities. First, the use of back-to-back interviews instead of joint interviews produces discrepancies in answers to the most routine of questions about domesticity. As Aquilino (1993) reveals, interviews often produce much higher estimates of spousal contributions to domestic work when the spouse is present than when he or she is not. Second, the fieldwork component of this research offers behavioral observations that reveal significant gaps between what participants say in interviews and what participants do in everyday life. The commitment to the ideology of familial egalitarianism within the lesbian and gay community, and among the subset of lesbigay families, is palpable. Yet, the empirical reality for many of these families is something quite different, something much more akin to patterns among heterosexual families (Gerson 1985, 1993). Moreover, when a particular family achieves something close to parity in the distribution of domestic activities, this almost always occurs under unique social conditions: great affluence, relative impoverishment, or among a distinct minority of couples with significantly diminished senses of themselves as family. In this [reading] I examine each of these exceptions and what motivates lesbigay people to portray their relationships in ideal terms both to themselves and to the outside world. I will also consider what factors seem to most significantly influence the actual division of domestic labor among lesbigay families.

The Egalitarian Myth

There exists among the lesbigay families studied here a prevalent and persistent commitment to viewing both one's own relationship and those of other lesbians and gays as egalitarian. Most participants in this study, when asked to describe in general terms how they divide up household responsibilities in their relationship, relied upon the language of egalitarianism. Typical responses included: "Oh I would say it's fifty-fifty around here," or "we pretty much share all of the responsibilities," or "everyone does their fair share," or "it's pretty even." These perceptions persist even in the face of obvious empirical observations to the contrary. Many lesbigay family members fail to make much of a distinction between what they consider equal and what they consider fair. The blurring of these two quite distinct matters is necessary to maintaining the myth of egalitarianism. . . .

Consequently, one must remain aware of the distinct possibility that intense pressures exist upon a participant's answers to questions about the division of domesticity. I think these pressures go a long way in explaining why lesbigay families, when asked about domestic activities, particularly in public settings, often joke about the matter. The humor masks the awkward feelings such questions produce. And after a few humorous exchanges, and possibly a little dig or two, the families make a concerted effort to reestablish the perception of equality. The research of Hochschild (1989) indicates that heterosexual families do exactly the same; they construct myths of egalitarianism. But there is more to the story among lesbigay families than meets the eye. . . .

The Management of Gender Identity and Domesticity

Gender looms as a significant matter in the portrayal as well as the organization of domesticity in lesbigay families. Like many other scholars of gender,

I find that domestic work results not only in the creation of goods and services but also in the creation of gender (Berk 1985; Brines 1994; Coltrane 1989; DeVault 1991; Ferree 1990; Hochschild 1989; Petuchek 1992; West and Zimmerman 1987). The potential for domesticity resulting in the construction of gender identity means different things to lesbian women and gay men. For lesbians, the capacity of domesticity to construct gender carries important consequences for partners whose paid-work obligations prevent them from engaging in much domesticity. Examples abound. Many of the lesbian women employed in time- and energy-consuming occupations expressed guilt about, and made much humor of their inattentiveness to and lack of participation in, domesticity. Their partners often provide cover for them, assigning credit for domestic tasks that they really did not do, or emphasizing some femininity-producing activity that compensates. . . .

The Invisibility of Domesticity and the Egalitarian Myth

Much of domesticity is invisible. Many of the forms of domestic labor rest upon a foundation of unobserved efforts that consume an individual's time and energy. Monitoring the house for cleanliness, monitoring the calendar for birthdays, monitoring the catalog for appropriate gifts, monitoring the cupboard for low supplies, monitoring the moods of one's spouse, and monitoring the family finances all are expressions of domesticity, and all are mostly invisible. The vast stores of accumulated knowledge about domestic things go unobserved by most: the knowledge of a family member's food tastes, dietary requirements, clothing size, the last gift one bought for them, work schedule, and the last time the cat received a rabies shot are all forms of domesticity and are hidden in the heads of those who hold responsibility for doing these things.

This invisibility, even to those who do it, sometimes produces seemingly inexplicable feelings of anger and resentment. Domestic work often becomes the site of enduring conflict between partners in relationships. Joe McFarland and Richard Neibuhr have been together for just under four years. Their relationship is "on the rocks," as Richard puts it. They reluctantly agreed to an interview. The family recently bought a house together, using money from Joe's inheritance from his previous lover, who died in the late 1980s. Both Richard and Joe conceive of their domestic relationship in strongly egalitarian terms despite what to me resembles a clear pattern of specialization with Richard doing much of the domestic labor in the family—not just much of the invisible work, but the visible work as well. Richard is not happy about the situation, although he has difficulty finding the words:

> *I think things are pretty equal in the relationship, although I wish Joe would appreciate my contributions more, and maybe be a little more helpful. It's hard to describe, but I feel like I do a lot of stuff to make our life better, but he doesn't really care about that. I think he thinks I'm just nagging him. If I ask him to do certain things, like, for instance, I asked him to call someone about going out to*

a movie on Friday night. He got annoyed. He says that if I want to go out to a movie with someone, then I should call. He thinks that's my interest. It's funny, though, because if I don't do it, he will ask how come we're not doing anything, and complain that we don't really have many friends. I get sort of frustrated about it, but I don't push it too much. He feels like I am dominating his space, imposing on his free time too much, not respecting his boundaries. He's very big on boundaries, he gets that from his therapist, who thinks that he needs to keep his own space.

A similar conversation took place with Joe. Notice how the advice of the therapist actually influences the division of domesticity:

CC: *Tell me about continuing discussions/points of conflict or unre-solved feelings with your spouse over these kinds of cleaning tasks.*

Joe: *My therapist is of the opinion that Richard lacks empathy for me, and/or maybe empathy for people in general, and doesn't under-stand that for me, time down and time alone is a chance for me to think my own thoughts, feel my feelings, expand my emotional life through reading or television. Richard doesn't have any appreciation for that. Consequently, the therapist thinks he lacks empathy. He asks me to do things that are his interests, and that's not fair to me.*

CC: *What kind of things?*

Joe: *Well, like stuff for the house. I mean, I paid for the house, or at least mostly, and I don't really care that much how the house looks. I mean, I want it clean, but a little messy is not a big deal. If he wants it a certain way, he can do it. I need my space.*

Richard feels frustration because Joe won't help with domesticity. If Richard expresses those sentiments, they actually become illegitimate because they are understood as an imposition of Richard's "interests" upon Joe. Both Richard and Joe conceive of their relationship as egalitarian with the differ-ences over domesticity actually reflecting different individual "interests." The advice of the therapist, or at least the way it gets understood and deployed in the relationship, legitimates Joe's claim to private time and relaxation, and delegitimates Richard's desire for help.

Several months after these interviews I ran into Richard at the gym. He had just joined, and we talked for a while. He told me he was coming back to the gym to "get in shape, and get a man." He then reported that he and Joe had broken up, and that I was part of the reason. He said he wanted to thank me for helping him to get out of his relationship. I felt perplexed, guilty, mortified. Here is my rough approximation, scribbled on the back on my workout card, of what transpired that day at the gym:

CC: *I am very sorry; I certainly didn't intend any harm.*

Richard: *Oh, it's okay, it's not really about you, but what you helped me learn about myself.*

CC: *What do you mean?*

Richard: *Well, that interview helped me to realize just how much I actually do, and did for that jerk.*

CC: *Like what are you thinking of?*

Richard: *Well, like all those questions about going out and buying things for the house. You know, I did all of that. And I did it because I wanted us to have a nice home, to be a family. But, being a family, he thinks, is all about me and my needs. He says I am codependent. He just couldn't appreciate what I was doing for us. The interview made it so clear just how much I had taken for granted. I actually sat down and wrote a list up, thinking of the things that you asked about. Then I realized, I confronted him with it, but he basically thinks those things are my interests, and if I want to do them, that's all about me. Well, I knew I had to get out, and find someone else who appreciates me more.*

The sociologist as homewrecker was not quite what I envisioned for myself. But this situation led me to wonder about why so much of domesticity is hidden from those who do it through discourses about individual "interests" and in narrow conceptions of what domesticity actually is. Families hide much of domesticity, closet it, and drape the door with the ideological veneer of egalitarianism for quite practical reasons. First, as previously suggested, they do it to avoid the stigma associated with violating gender expectations. Second, and perhaps more significantly, they do it to avoid conflicts and to preserve relationships existing in a broader socioeconomic context that does not enable families to actually produce much equality. When thinking about Joe and Richard and the demise of that relationship I can see the dilemma that many relationships face. . . .

. . . The character of Joe's and Richard's paid employment greatly determines the organization of domesticity. Richard works in human resources, as a benefits counselor, for a suburban community. He works thirty-nine hours per week in a public-sector job with extensive family-friendly benefits, mostly negotiated by his union. He works mostly with heterosexual women, many of whom also hold responsibility for family life. Richard earned $31,000 dollars in 1993. He earns much less than Joe, who earned $52,000 the same year. Joe's work exhausts him, allowing little time, much less energy, for doing family. His work frequently seeps into family time. Concealing domesticity in the language of "interests" prevented Richard and Joe from reflecting upon paid work and family conflict. In fact, concealing the matter allowed them to avoid hard choices, including the possibility of Joe seeking alternate employment, with the potential for a reduced standard of living. They also could have acknowledged Richard's specialization in domestic matters, something they both seemed unprepared to accept. Richard understood their conflict in terms of personality, without much awareness of the impact of paid work upon what happened to them.

The Egalitarian Pattern

A minority of lesbigay families do achieve a rough equivalence in the distribution of domestic work, even using a broad and inclusive conception of domesticity. Roughly 25 percent (thirteen) of the families I studied approach this rough parity. The participants in these families appear to take responsibility for, as well as spend similar amounts of time on domestic matters. Interview data and field observations reveal patterns of specialization among many of these families, although they still approach equity. For instance, in several families, one person pursues much of the feeding work while another manages housework and kin work. Some families go to great lengths to achieve this parity. For example, three families use quite extensive "chore wheels." Chore wheels list many of the major housework items—and in one family much of the feeding work was listed as well—but none of them listed consumption, kin work, or status work-related chores. These families share a number of distinct sociological characteristics explaining much of the parity in the division of domesticity, and to those characteristics I will now turn.

Egalitarianism: Reliance on the Service Economy

Wealthier lesbigay families often purchase much domesticity in the marketplace, therein enhancing the egalitarianism within the relationship. In contrast to working/service-class and middle-class lesbigay families, these affluent families rely extensively on the service economy, or upon an army of low-paid workers without fringe benefits who provide much of the domestic labor. This pattern closely resembles one detected by Hertz (1986) in a study of upper-middle-class, dual-career heterosexual families who achieved greater equity in their relationships through reliance on service workers. Eight of the ten wealthiest families in this study hire someone to do housework for them. Four of those eight hire Latina women who work for an hourly rate without benefits. No family earning less than the study's median income hires someone to clean. Seven of the wealthiest ten families frequently either rely on laundry services or include laundry as a responsibility of the domestic workers who come to clean. Two families earning below the median income take laundry on a consistent basis to a laundry service. Six of the wealthiest twenty families hire someone to care for their lawns or gardens. Four families, all earning above the median income, hire someone to walk their dogs during the day. As mentioned in [my book] one in five lesbigay families eat at least four meals per week in a restaurant. Sixteen of those twenty-one families earn above the median income.

A very clear picture emerges here. Some lesbigay families achieve partial equity in their relationships through reliance on the labors of mostly working-poor people. One can see some of these workers behind the counters of taquerias, laundries, pasta shops, coffee shops, and delis in lesbigay neighborhoods, although many others one cannot see because their labors are more hidden (domestics, gardeners, laundry workers, daycare providers). These workers are for the most part Latino, Asian, and African American women, and young gay men and lesbians. Their labors contribute much to the achievement of egalitarianism within the families of the affluent.

Egalitarianism and Female-Identified Professional Occupations

The egalitarian pattern emerges with notable strength among those families where both individuals, regardless of gender, work in traditionally female-identified professional occupations: primary/secondary teaching, social work, healthcare assessment (nurses, dietitians, occupational therapy), librarians, school counseling, social work, and public-sector human resources jobs. A disproportionate number of lesbians and gay men in this study work in these professions. It remains an open question whether this pattern reflects the broader population of lesbigay people (Badgett and King 1997). Popular mythology holds that lesbigay people are everywhere, and perhaps they are, but lesbigay people in long-term relationships don't seem to be. It may well be the case that these forms of employment actually nourish longer-term relationships, providing at least one, and in the case of some egalitarian families, all family members the opportunity to pursue family matters more readily. When the primary partners in relationships work in these fields they establish a greater degree of equality between them in the distribution of domesticity. Why?

These forms of employment often feature *real* forty-hour work weeks, and they often offer paid vacation, paid holidays, more holidays, family leave, paid sick days, flex-time, flex place, as well as employee assistance programs offering services to families facing alcohol, drug, and domestic violence concerns. All of these family-friendly policies create a somewhat more conducive environment for doing family work. In contrast, lesbigay people working in other professional occupational categories infrequently receive such benefits, or they seem reluctant to take advantage of them, even if offered. Moreover, very few people in these professions report working more than forty hours per week for wages. This is not to say that these forms of employment are all dandy. In fact, they often feature short career ladders, glass ceilings, lower wages, and less control over the content of one's work than do male-dominated professional jobs (Glazer 1991; Preston 1995). In a sense, discrimination relegates lesbigay professionals into the female-dominated professions and enables them to do more domesticity. When looking at lesbigay professionals in the male-dominated occupations, including the engineers, physicians, attorneys, and middle-level managers, a starkly different pattern emerges, one encouraging a clear division of labor within the relationship. Moreover, most of the female-dominated professions do not require one to use one's residence in order to serve clients, or to entertain them very much. This reduces the amount of housework, feeding work, consumption work, and kin work within such households.

Egalitarianism and Downsizing the Family

There is one other form of the truly egalitarian family: the downsized family. These families, mostly composed of male couples, engage in relatively little domesticity. Similar to the affluent egalitarians, these families also rely on the service economy to provide domesticity, although they rely on it much less extensively. These families often live in urban environments, usually sharing a living space with multiple adults. These guys, mostly in their late twenties or early thirties, are often in their first relationship. They spend very little time in the places where they live, instead hanging out in cafés, bars, restaurants, gyms, and dance clubs. They don't put much effort into feeding work, eating out at cheap taquerias and hamburger joints through-out much of the week, or eating instant ramen noodles or microwaved frozen dinners. If they engage in body building, as many seem to, they eat simple meals of vegetables, bread, and pasta when they eat at home. They don't do much consumption work, although they do make joint purchases of CDs, linens and towels, and some used furniture. These joint purchases often become emblematic of their relationships. These couples do very little kin work, calling biolegal relatives mostly, but usually on major holidays or at Mother's Day, with each person responsible for his or her own biolegal relations. Even in these austere circumstances, domesticity often comes to play a crucial role in the creation of the relationship. For instance, several of these young-male couples understood the time they spent together doing laundry at laundromats as expressions of their relational identity, particularly when they mixed clothing items together for washing and drying.

The Specialization Pattern

One person specializes in domesticity in roughly three of four (thirty-eight) of the lesbigay families studied. This pattern actually parallels Blumstein and Schwartz's finding that longer-term families frequently consist of one person who places more emphasis on domesticity and one who places the emphasis on paid work (1983:172). In this study, the longer the family has been together, the more pronounced the specialization becomes. For instance, only among families together longer than nine years (twenty-one families), and mostly earning higher incomes, do I find someone working part-time by choice in order to handle domestic activities (seven families), or someone engaging in homemaking full-time (three families). Interestingly, these highly specialized, longer-term lesbigay families conceive of their circumstances as *equal,* although I suspect they really mean *fair.* They consider things fair in light of a whole series of spoken and unspoken matters ranging from the number of hours someone works for wages to the pleasures one garners from domesticity. Let me now turn to some of the central factors encouraging specialization in domesticity or in paid work within lesbigay families.

Paid employment exerts the greatest influence upon the division of domesticity in most lesbigay families. The number of hours paid work requires, where the work takes place, the length of the commute to work, the pay, the prestige, and difficulty of the work all conflate to encourage a pattern of specialization. The relative resources that each person brings to the relationship from paid work influences the division of labor. In most cases the person with less earning potential, or with less occupational prestige, picks up a disproportionate share of domestic labor. This finding parallels the "relative resource" model put forward to explain the division of domestic labor among heterosexual families (Blood and Wolfe 1960; Brines 1994). The pursuit of such resources (money, benefits, stock options, prestige, and networks) also takes time, usually leaving the pursuant with little time left to handle domesticity. In this sense, my findings parallel the "time availability" explanation (Acock and Demo 1994; Coverman 1985; Hiller 1984;) of the division of domestic labor. However, unlike some resource theory, my analysis does not conceive of domesticity as a great unpleasantness that the person with more resources (e.g., income, prestige, and education) forces onto the person with fewer. Such a view reduces domesticity to its unpleasant aspects and conceals its attractive ones, therein leaving us with no convincing explanation of why some people prefer, and orient themselves toward, domesticity (Ferree 1976, 1980). Rather, I detect a pattern of family members attempting to maximize the quality of their household lives both through providing income and through providing domesticity. Among the affluent participants, each family member pursues income, and the family purchases meals, laundry, house-cleaning, and so on in the service economy. Most lesbigay families can't afford this, even with both working full-time, and therein, they must pursue a different strategy. Longer-term families recognize the importance of domesticity to relational and family stability, and many of them pursue a strategy to attain both domesticity and financial well-being. The most obvious strategy consists of encouraging the family member with the greatest economic opportunity to pursue paid work vigorously. This has its limits, but the pattern occurs in the majority of households, and becomes stronger over time.

Gravitating toward Domesticity

Practical economic concerns and occupational characteristics play the largest role in determining who gravitates toward domestic involvement. In a few instances those who gravitate toward domesticity "choose" employment that complements their family commitments. In most instances the character of one's paid employment facilitated participation in domesticity, with very little "choice" or much reflection on the matter. Some people appear to make conscious choices about domesticity, but the choices are constrained by economic and occupational realities. For instance, only among affluent families does the choice exist to work part-time for wages, devoting the remaining time to personal and/or family life. Similarly, those in professional careers frequently find it easier to merge work and family concerns together. Recall the professionals making phone calls to friends and family from work, as well as arranging their work schedule to pursue domestic matters. Working- and service-class lesbigay families don't have these options. I want to emphasize the importance of context to the question of "choice" here. Some participants choose to ensconce themselves in domesticity, but few really possess that option. Some participants choose to take on a disproportionate share of domestic labor, but most simply find themselves doing the work without much sense of choice. That doesn't necessarily mean they feel unhappy or conceive of things as unfair—some do, and some don't. Rather, they often simply adjust in light of the expectations and opportunities associated with their own paid work and the paid work of other family members.

Family-Friendly Careers and Jobs

Many of the women and men in these specialized families are employed within traditional female-identified occupations (teaching, nursing, and so on). They take on a disproportionate share of domesticity, especially when they are in relationships with individuals in professional, managerial, or executive positions. The pattern is quite apparent among school teachers. The summer recess, holiday breaks, the capacity to do schoolwork at home, and lower salaries all conflate to encourage teachers to pick up a disproportionate share of domestic life. Few of the teachers anticipated this state of affairs at the beginning of their relationships. The experience of one teacher, Andrew Kessler, illustrates the dynamic. In the summer of 1997, at a northern California gay resort area popularly known as the Russian River, I ran into Andrew, a third-grade teacher, whom I originally interviewed back in 1994. He has taught school for eight years now, and is in a relationship with a computer software consultant. During casual conversation he commented on returning home from vacation to begin his "summer housewife stint." I asked: "How is it that you came to play that role?" Andrew responded:

> *Well, it's kind of strange. I think it happened because I have the summer off. I wasn't really that into domestic things when we first got together. I was just out of school and I was very gung-ho about my teaching. Part of it has to do with Darren's job. He works a lot and he works pretty hard, and so I think I feel a little bit of obligation to try to ease the burden on him. He earns a lot, and that makes our life pretty great. It's funny, though, I don't really feel like I was forced to do the house and stuff. More like, I came to like it over time. I felt a certain accomplishment about it, about keeping it nice. Darren couldn't really do that much, given the hours he works, and he travels some. So I think it fell to me to create more of a sense of home for us. Some of it's quite boring, of course, but I like some of it too.*

Andrew's experience is actually quite common among lesbigay families. Andrew did not really choose to become domestically oriented; rather, over time, he gravitated in that direction. Andrew's explanations of why he prepares evening meals, meets service and delivery people at the house, and does much of the consumption work all point to paid work, either the relative flexibility of his own career, or the inflexibility of his partner's career. In Andrew's case the pull toward domestic involvement began early in his work experience, and in some ways this left him less cognizant of the ways that work influences family life. For others, the pull came later, and they have a much stronger sense of how work influences family life.

Fanny Gomez, now forty-four and in her second long-term relationship as well as her second career, recently finished school and began working as a social worker. In her first relationship she did very little in terms of domesticity. She worked sixty hours per week as an accountant for a large commercial real estate firm. After her first relationship broke up she decided she wanted to make a lot of changes in her life. Mostly she wanted to pursue a career that made her happier, and one that would "make some contribution to improving other people's lives." When she and her new partner, Melinda Rodriquez, moved in together, she realized that neither of them was particularly adept at domestic tasks. They wanted to eat meals together at home, but "the meals didn't seem that satisfying." Fanny decided to spend some time learning how to cook. She bought some cookbooks and attended a cooking course on Saturdays, something she "would not have had the energy to do when she was working at the real estate firm." Her new job, doing social work with elderly Latinos as part of a city-funded program, is stressful but it has more limits. Fanny says she works thirty-eight hours a week and "not an hour more," unlike her old job, where they knew no limits, where "my whole life was about that firm." She also receives more holiday time and more vacation time. She doesn't earn as much as she used to, but she's happier. Fanny noticed that her new job, and her new relationship with Melinda, a midlevel sales manager for a computer technology firm, brought new responsibilities on the home front:

> Fanny: *We've had some fights about housecleaning over the past couple of years. She says she doesn't have time to do the stuff, and I sort of understand that, but I don't think it's fair that I have to do it. But, I think I realized that if I didn't, then nobody would. And I am here more often than she is. I get home earlier, and I leave for work later. Because I get home earlier, it's easier for me to cook, and to stop by the store and stuff.*
>
> CC: *How is this different from your first relationship?*
>
> Fanny: *I never would have done that sort of thing in my first relationship. In fact, I've sort of gone through a transition. I had no interest in cooking when I was with Janet. But in this relationship, it seems more important to me. I guess I missed the meal time that I had with Janet, and I wanted to have that again with Melinda, but Melinda wasn't into doing it, so I sort of picked it up. I think Melinda appreciates it though.*

On the one hand, Fanny contributed to her new involvement in domestic life through choices she made about work. On the other hand, Fanny's work and the work of her new lover, Melinda, changed Fanny. Fanny's search for more fulfillment in her career brought her into an occupational context that facilitated more domestic involvement.

Fanny, a social worker, and Andrew, the teacher, are not alone. Of the twenty-eight professionals that work as nurses, primary/secondary-school teachers, counselors, social workers, librarians, and community college instructors, eighteen are more domestically involved than their partners while six appear equally involved and four of those six are in relationships with partners in similar occupations.

In addition to the female-identified professional career tracks that seem to encourage domestic involvement, those individuals who work at home as artisans, writers/editors, or independent service contractors, as well as those who are students, retired, or underemployed, also bear a disproportionate share of domesticity. Twenty-four participants do much of their paid work at home—work ranging from accounting services to daycare to running a bed and breakfast to book editing to building furniture. Of these twenty-four participants, eighteen carry a greater share of the domesticity. These participants often weave their paid work with their family work. . . .

In sum, many participants gravitate toward domesticity not out of choice, or because of a strong interest in domestic pursuits, or even because they possess certain skills. Rather, they gravitate toward domesticity because the character of their paid work and that of other family members encourages their involvement. Many of these domestically involved individuals have not made a big decision to focus on family life. Rather, because of many small decisions, they gravitated toward the domestic. The decision to start the evening meal because one arrives home earlier than others facilitated increased feeding work. For those who work at home, the decision to clean the bathroom or do the laundry during the day led them into increased housework. For those with more flexible work schedules, the time to shop for consumer goods led them into increased responsibility for consumption work. Some participants do make a conscious commitment to greater involvement in domestic and family matters, and I will address them in the next section, but most do not. Their domestic careers appear to develop residually, accumulating slowly and unreflectively over the course of their relationships. They then become the experts and begin to feel the responsibility for domesticity.

Domestic by Choice

Few individuals actually choose, in a particularly conscious manner, to become more involved in family and domestic affairs. However, some do, and for a variety of reasons—reasons often reflecting growing disenchantment with paid work, or concern about maintaining an endangered relationship, or simply a love of domestic life. However, the nature of these choices varies dramatically across social class. The two men who conceive of themselves as homemakers are notable examples of choosing domestic involvement, as well as one woman, Virginia Kirbo, who works ten hours per week. All three made conscious choices to forgo paid employment in favor of concentrating on family and community life. All three are in relationships with highly successful, well-paid individuals. These families dwell in exquisite yet labor-intensive homes. I found the daily schedules of all three quite stunning, for not only do they maintain homes thick in domesticity, but also these three people expend great energy volunteering in the nonprofit sector.

John Chapman, forty-seven years old, once worked as a successful graphic artist. Over the past decade he gave up his successful graphic art practice in favor of "keeping the house" and "doing good things for the community." He consciously decided that "some of the fun went out of his work, especially serving so many corporate clients." He felt that serving corporate clients created a "factorylike feel" to what he thought of as an "artistic and creative enterprise." The factorylike character of the work distracted from his satisfaction with his work, and he decided he wanted to do more work for nonprofit organizations. The rising income and career success of his partner, Theodore Fairchild, made it possible for John to do more of this kind of work, and eventually he stopped taking on new contracts.

John now does graphic work only as a volunteer. He serves on the board of directors of two of San Francisco's largest AIDS service providers. For one, he edits the monthly newsletter and maintains the website. He spends two mornings a week volunteering at a hospice for people dying of AIDS-related diseases. He has served his local Episcopal church in almost every leadership and volunteer capacity over the last decade, most recently chairing a ministerial search committee for the parish. He volunteers as a guide every other Saturday at the Conservatory of Flowers, in Golden Gate Park, where he blends his personal interest in gardening with his sense of public service. He spends two nights of every month working for the Stop AIDS Project, where he takes to the streets of the Castro and "gets to tell the young ones how to practice safer sex." John and Theodore live in a spectacular Victorian residence in the Presidio Heights section of San Francisco. John maintains the house and an elaborate garden. They entertain often, and always have meals at home, something that John feels is very important to their relationship. John's experience is quite unique, for few lesbigay families earn enough money to make such choices.

Hindered Work Opportunities

While some of the more affluent participants became disillusioned with their careers and "chose" to emphasize domestic life instead, many other participants found themselves unable to get onto career or promotional tracks or ran into glass ceilings and consequently shifted to a domestic focus. The lack of job/career opportunities resulted in a greater emphasis on domesticity for at least eleven of the families I studied. Five of these families came to San Francisco due to an employment opportunity for one member of the family.

These families migrated with hopes of finding suitable employment for both partners, but this didn't always happen. Carey Becker, forty-three years old and working part-time as a radiology technician, shares her life with Angela DiVincenzo, a special education teacher. Five years ago they moved to San Francisco from New Jersey. A suburban Bay Area school district offered Angela a position creating a new curriculum and program for special education. Carey, who worked as a full-time radiologist back East, discovered that she lacked the proper credentials for employment in California, and that few employment opportunities existed. Carey took a part-time position with hopes of finding something full-time. She never did. Initially, Carey picked up a larger share of the domesticity:

> CC: *Describe the impact of significant job changes on your*
> *relationship.*
>
> Carey: *The move to San Francisco had a major impact, and I think it still*
> *does. I am still trying to get into the kind of work I would like to*
> *do. Although, I don't know if it's possible now. The market for*
> *radiology techs is not very hot. I have thought about what else*
> *I could do. Angela just wants me to be happy, and she hasn't put*
> *any pressure on me to find something else. The part-time position*
> *actually is thirty hours, and now that Angela's school district*
> *offers domestic partnership, I don't need to worry about going*
> *without insurance.*
>
> CC: *Did the move change what you do in the relationship?*
>
> Carey: *In some ways, it did. I do a lot more of the housework and stuff now.*
> *I don't really mind it too much. Angela works pretty hard, and I try*
> *to contribute what I can to our relationship. . . .*

In a similar fashion, some lesbians and gay men ran into the proverbial glass ceiling at work and consequently reconceived of their careers as jobs, set limits on how much work could encroach on family life, and developed a new interest in domesticity. This pattern emerged with marked strength among lesbigay professionals and managers working in predominantly heterosexual contexts. . . .

Unsuccessful efforts to enter or progress in paid work, whether due to lack of credentials, discrimination, or too short career ladders, created disenchantment with notions of meritocracy and undivided commitment to work. As a result, the affected individuals shifted focus and infused greater effort and meaning into family matters.

Preserving Relationships

Finally, another dynamic bolstering active participation in domesticity springs from efforts to preserve a cherished relationship. At some point in their life together, several lesbigay families faced hard choices of maintaining two careers or maintaining the relationship. In most cases, these longer-term lesbigay families struck a deal. Sometimes the deal included someone turning down a promotion; in other cases the deal included a diminution of work involvement for one while the other put more into paid work. Narvin Wong and Lawrence Shoong, together for just over five years, faced just such a crisis about a year before I interviewed them. Narvin, a healthcare consultant, made the decision to do independent consulting. He saw a lucrative economic opportunity and the chance to exert greater influence over his work, and he decided to take it. The decision also meant a great increase in the number of hours that he would work. Meanwhile, Lawrence had taken a promotion to a nursing position with a large, well-funded research project. The position entailed a pay increase and was much more prestigious, given that the project was associated with a major medical research center. The position required Lawrence to work many evenings with research subjects, and diminished the amount of time he could spend at home and with Narvin. About six months into their new work situations conflict began to develop at home. The conflicts initially circled around housework, but eventually expanded to questions about emotional availability, and the energy available for sexual interaction. Lawrence reflects on a question about the impact of work on his family life:

CC: *Describe the impact of significant job changes on family/ relationship.*

Lawrence: *Narvin's choice to go into independent consulting created some big changes, changes in his attitude, and changes in our life together. He has very high expectations for himself. He went to an Ivy League business school, and I think he puts lots of pressures on himself to succeed. The problem was that I felt left out, sort of abandoned. I took the position at the medical center, and suddenly I wasn't around in the evenings, and I felt like our relationship just went into a spiral. I loved working at the medical center. I got to work with really great people, and the work was interesting, and I was putting in quite a few hours, more than I used to at Marin General. But after a while I began to feel like I no longer had a life with Narvin. We talked about it, and I asked him about working less on weekends, and maybe trying to have a little more energy for us being together.*
He was pretty stubborn, though.

CC: *What was he stubborn about?*

Lawrence: *His career and his consulting work. He just felt so strong about trying to make it go.*

CC: *So, what did you guys do?*

Lawrence: *Well, I gave up the job at the lab. I mean, we talked about it, and I realized that I still wanted a relationship with him. He was in a tough place. It wasn't like he could easily go back to the hospital where he was; not at that level, you don't really go back. After a few months Narvin was making decent money, and I just decided I would rather be here at night. So I applied for a day shift position at St. Stephens, and they took me. They were a little surprised that I was leaving the medical center, but the woman who hired*

me was pretty understanding. I mean, I told her that I needed
more time for my relationship. Once I got back onto the day
shift, things really improved. I was able to come home at a decent
hour, and keep things going around here, and be with Narvin,
even if he spends most of his time in his office,
I can still go in there and talk to him, and we can have dinner
together.

CC: *What else did you mean by "keep things going around here"?*
Lawrence: *Just taking care of stuff.*
CC: *What stuff do you mean?*
Lawrence: *Everything, from laundry to shopping. I am trying to get the*
house to feel more like a home, more lived in. Of course, he thinks
I am spending too much, so I have to watch that, but yeah, just
doing a lot of stuff around here to keep things going, and to take
the pressure off of him. . . .

Lawrence and Narvin preserved their relationship, but not without Lawrence's willingness to place more emphasis on family life. Both of them view the choices made as practical, and both anticipate a financial gain from Narvin's commitment to his consulting business.

On the whole, those individuals who gravitate toward greater domestic involvement than their partners often share common socioeconomic characteristics. Frequently they share their lives with partners who earn more, have greater career opportunities, work more hours, and work outside the home. In addition, more domestically involved participants often work in occupations that offer real forty-hour work weeks, more flexible work schedules, the ability to work at home, more holiday and vacation time, and affiliation with colleagues who also share family obligations. Domestically involved participants seldom recognize the confluence of factors encouraging their domesticity. Instead, they rely on the vocabulary of individual choice, psychological disposition, and "interests," ignoring the social context in which such dispositions and interests develop. . . .

Pragmatic Choices and the Sense of Fairness

I have seen a practicality in the ways that lesbigay families sort and arrange domesticity, whether the family is egalitarian or specialized. Such practicality does not create equality, however. True equality, measured with a plumb line, eludes many of these families, but that has little to do with the families per se, and much more to do with the character and quality of employment opportunities that avail themselves to these families. If the reality is that only one member of the family can make money in a fulfilling way, then lesbigay families adjust to that reality.

Many lesbigay relationships don't survive, for a wide variety of reasons. I would add to that list the dilemmas of domesticity—not just the conflicts over who does what but the often overlooked fact that the opportunity to pursue domestic things is not available to everyone. If all of the family must toil at unpleasant and poorly compensating work in order to make ends meet, they do, and they try to fit domesticity in where they can. Of course, these are the families that often don't make it, and that should not be so surprising because without the resources, time, and energy to create family, it withers.

REFERENCES

Acock, A. and D. Demo. 1994. *Family Diversity and Well-Being*. Thousand Oaks, CA: Sage.

Aquilino, W. S. 1993. "Effects of Spouse Presence during the Interview on Survey Responses Concerning Marriage." *Public Opinion Quarterly* 55 (3): 358–76.

Badgett, L. and M. King. 1997. "Lesbian and Gay Occupational Strategies." In *Homo Economics: Capitalism, Community, and Lesbian and Gay Life*, edited by A. Gluckman and B. Reed. New York: Routledge.

Berk, S. F. (1985). *The Gender Factory: The Apportionment of Work in American Households*. New York: Plenum Press.

Blood, R. and D. Wolfe. 1960. *Husbands and Wives*. Glencoe, IL: Free Press.

Blumstein, P. and P. Schwartz. 1983. *American Couples*. New York: Morrow.

Brines, J. 1994. "Economic Dependency, Gender, and the Division of Labor at Home." *American Journal of Sociology* 100:652–88.

Coltrane, S. 1989. "Household Labor and the Routine Production of Gender." *Social Problems* 36 (5): 473–90.

Coverman, S. 1985. "Explaining Husband's Contribution in Domestic Labor." *Sociological Quarterly* 26:81–97.

DeVault, M. 1991. *Feeding the Family: The Social Organization of Caring as Gendered Work*. Chicago: University of Chicago Press.

Ferree, M. 1976. "Working-Class Jobs: Housework and Paid Work as Sources of Satisfaction." *Social Problems* 23:431–41.

———. 1980. "Satisfaction with Housework: The Social Context." In *Women and Household Labor*, edited by S. F. Berk. Beverly Hills, CA: Sage.

———. 1990. "Beyond Separate Spheres: Feminism and Family Research." *Journal of Marriage and the Family* 52:866–84.

Gerson, K. 1985. *Hard Choices*. Berkeley: University of California Press.

———. 1993. *No Man's Land: Men's Changing Commitments to Family and Work*. New York: Basic Books.

Glazer, N. 1991. "Between a Rock and a Hard Place: Women's Professional Organizations in Nursing and Class, Racial, and Ethnic Inequalities." *Gender and Society* 5 (3): 351–72.

Hertz, R. 1986. *More Equal than Others*. Berkeley: University of California Press.

Hiller, D. 1984. "Power Dependence and Division of Family Work." *Sex Roles* 10:1003–19.

Hochschild, A., with A. Machung. 1989. *The Second Shift: Working Parents and the Revolution at Home*. New York: Viking.

Petuchek, J. L. 1992. "Employed Wives' Orientation to Breadwinning: A Gender Theory Analysis." *Journal of Marriage and the Family* 54:548–58.

Preston, J. 1995. "Gender and the Formation of a Woman's Profession." In *Gender Inequality at Work*, edited by J. Jacobs. Mountain View, CA: Sage.

West C. and D. Zimmerman. 1987. "Doing Gender." *Gender and Society* 1 (2): 125–51.

44

CARING FOR OUR YOUNG
Child Care in Europe and the United States

DAN CLAWSON • NAOMI GERSTEL

When a delegation of American child care experts visited France, they were amazed by the full-day, free *écoles maternelles* that enroll almost 100 percent of French three-, four-, and five-year-olds:

> Libraries better stocked than those in many U.S. elementary schools. Three-year-olds serving one another radicchio salad, then using cloth napkins, knives, forks and real glasses of milk to wash down their bread and chicken. Young children asked whether dragons exist [as] a lesson in developing vocabulary and creative thinking.

In the United States, by contrast, working parents struggle to arrange and pay for private care. Publicly funded child care programs are restricted to the poor. Although most U.S. parents believe (or want to believe) that their children receive quality care, standardized ratings find most of the care mediocre and much of it seriously inadequate.

Looking at child care in comparative perspective offers us an opportunity—almost requires us—to think about our goals and hopes for children, parents, education, and levels of social inequality. Any child care program or funding system has social and political assumptions with far-reaching consequences. National systems vary in their emphasis on education; for three- to five-year-olds, some stress child care as preparation for school, while others take a more playful view of childhood. Systems vary in the extent to which they stress that children's early development depends on interaction with peers or some version of intensive mothering. They also vary in the extent to which they support policies promoting center-based care as opposed to time for parents to stay at home with their very young children. Each of these emphases entails different national assumptions, if only implicit, about children and parents, education, teachers, peers, and societies as a whole.

What do we want, why, and what are the implications? Rethinking these questions is timely because with changing welfare, employment, and family patterns, more U.S. parents have come to believe they want and need a place for their children in child care centers. Even parents who are not in the labor force want their children to spend time in preschool. In the United States almost half of children less than one year old now spend a good portion of their day in some form of non-parental care. Experts increasingly emphasize the potential benefits of child care. A recent National Academy of Sciences report summarizes the views of experts: "Higher quality care is associated with outcomes that all parents want to see in their children." The word in Congress these days, especially in discussions of welfare reform, is that child care is good — it saves money later on by helping kids through school (which keeps them out of jail), and it helps keep mothers on the job and families together. A generation ago, by contrast, Nixon vetoed a child care bill as a "radical piece of social legislation" designed to deliver children to "communal approaches to child rearing over and against the family-centered approach." While today's vision is clearly different, most attempts to improve U.S. child care are incremental, efforts to get a little more money here or there, with little consideration for what kind of system is being created.

The U.S. and French systems offer sharp contrasts. Although many hold up the French system as a model for children three or older, it is only one alternative. Other European countries provide thought-provoking alternatives, but the U.S.-French contrast is a good place to begin.

France and the United States: Private versus Public Care

Until their children start school, most U.S. parents struggle to find child care, endure long waiting lists, and frequently change locations. They must weave a complex, often unreliable patchwork in which their children move among relatives, informal settings, and formal center care, sometimes all in one day. Among three- to four-year-old children with employed mothers, more than one out of eight are in three or more child care arrangements, and almost half are in two or more arrangements. A very small number of the wealthy hire nannies, often immigrants; more parents place their youngest children with relatives, especially grandmothers, or work alternate shifts so fathers can share child care with mothers (these alternating shifters now include almost one-third of families with infants and toddlers). Many pay kin to provide child care — sometimes not because they prefer it, but because they cannot afford other care, and it is a way to provide jobs and income to struggling family members. For children three and older, however, the fastest-growing setting in the United States is child care centers — almost half of three-year-olds (46 percent) and almost two-thirds of four-year-olds (64 percent) now spend much of their time there.

In France, participation in the *école maternelle* system is voluntary, but a place is guaranteed to every child three to six years old. Almost 100 percent of parents enroll their three-year-olds. Even non-employed parents enroll their children, because they believe it is best for the children. Schools are open from 8:30 A.M. to 4:30 P.M. with an extended lunch break, but care is available at modest cost before and after school and during the lunch break.

Integrated with the school system, French child care is intended primarily as early education. All children, rich and poor, immigrant or not, are part of the same national system, with the same curriculum, staffed by teachers paid good wages by the same national ministry. No major political party or group opposes the system.

When extra assistance is offered, rather than targeting poor children (or families), additional resources are provided to geographic areas. Schools in some zones, mostly in urban areas, receive extra funding to reduce class size, give teachers extra training and a bonus, provide extra materials, and employ special teachers. By targeting an entire area, poor children are not singled out (as they are in U.S. free lunch programs).

Staff in the French *écoles maternelles* have master's degrees and are paid teachers' wages; in 1998, U.S. preschool teachers earned an average of $8.32 an hour, and child care workers earned $6.61, not only considerably less than (underpaid) teachers but also less than parking lot attendants. As a consequence, employee turnover averages 30 percent a year, with predictably harmful effects on children.

What are the costs of these two very different systems? In almost every community across the United States, a year of child care costs more than a year at a public university—in some cases twice as much. Subsidy systems favor the poor, but subsidies (unlike tax breaks) depend on the level of appropriations. Congress does not appropriate enough money and, therefore, most of the children who qualify for subsidies do not receive them. In 1999, under federal rules 15 million children were eligible to receive benefits, but only 1.8 million actually received them. Middle- and working-class families can receive neither kind of subsidy. An Urban Institute study suggests that some parents place their children in care they consider unsatisfactory because other arrangements are just too expensive. The quality of care thus differs drastically depending on the parents' income, geographic location, diligence in searching out alternatives, and luck.

The French system is not cheap. According to French government figures, the cost for a child in Paris was about $5,500 per year in 1999. That is only slightly more than the average U.S. parent paid for the care of a four-year-old in a center ($5,242 in 2000). But in France child care is a social responsibility, and thus free to parents, while in the United States parents pay the cost. Put another way, France spends about 1 percent of its Gross Domestic Product (GDP) on government funded early education and care programs. If the United States devoted the same share of its GDP to preschools, the government would spend about $100 billion a year. Current U.S. government spending is less than $20 billion a year ($15 billion federal, $4 billion state).

Other European Alternatives

When the American child care community thinks about European models, the French model is often what they have in mind. With its emphasis on education, the French system has an obvious appeal to U.S. politicians, educators, and child care advocates. Politicians' central concern in the United States

appears to be raising children's test scores; in popular and academic literature, this standard is often cited as the major indicator of program success.
But such an educational model is by no means the only alternative. Indeed,
the U.S. focus on the French system may itself be a telling indicator of U.S.
experts' values as well as their assessments of political realities. Many advocates insist that a substantial expansion of the U.S. system will be possible
only if the system is presented as improving children's education. These
advocates are no longer willing to use the term "child care," insisting on
"early education" instead. The French model fits these priorities: It begins
quasi-school about three years earlier than in the United States. Although the
French obviously assist employed parents and children's center activities are
said to be fun, the system is primarily touted and understood as educational —
intended to treat children as pupils, to prepare them to do better in school.

The 11 European nations included in a recent Organization for Economic
Cooperation and Development study (while quite different from one another)
all have significantly better child care and paid leave than the United States.
Each also differs significantly from France. Offering alternatives, these models
challenge us to think even more broadly about childhood, parenting, and the
kind of society we value.

Non–School Model: Denmark

From birth to age six most Danish children go to child care, but most find
that care in non-school settings. Overseen by the Ministry of Social Affairs
(rather than the Ministry of Education), the Danish system stresses "relatively unstructured curricula" that give children time to "hang out." Lead
staff are pedagogues, not teachers. Although pedagogues have college degrees
and are paid teachers' wages, their role is "equally important but different"
from that of the school-based teacher. "Listening to children" is one of the
government's five principles, and centers emphasize "looking at everything
from the child's perspective."

The Danish model differs from the French system in two additional ways
that clarify its non-school character. First, in the Danish system, pedagogues
care for very young children (from birth to age three as well as older children
ages three to six). The French preschool (*école maternelle*) model applies only to
children three and older. Before that, children of working parents can attend
crèches. *Crèche* staff, however, have only high school educations and are paid
substantially less than the (master's-degree-trained) *écoles maternelles* teachers.
Second, while the *écoles maternelles* are available to all children, the Danish
system (like the French *crèches*) is available only to children with working parents because it is intended to aid working parents, not to educate children.

The Danish system is decentralized, with each individual center required
to have a management board with a parent majority. But the system receives
most of its money from public funding, and parents contribute only about
one-fifth of total costs.

Given its non-school emphasis, age integration, and the importance it assigns to local autonomy, the Danish system might be appealing to U.S. parents, especially some people of color. To be sure, many U.S. parents — across race and class — are ambivalent about child care for their youngest children. Especially given the growing emphasis on testing, they believe that preschool might give them an edge, but they also want their children to have fun and play — to have, in short, what most Americans still consider a childhood. Some research suggests that Latina mothers are especially likely to feel that center-based care, with its emphasis on academic learning, does not provide the warmth and moral guidance they seek. They are, therefore, less likely to select center-based care than either white or African American parents, relying instead on kin or family child care providers whom they know and trust. U.S. experts' emphasis on the French model may speak not only to political realities but also to the particular class and even more clearly race preferences framing those realities.

Mothers or Peers

The United States, if only implicitly, operates on a mother-substitute model of child care. Because of a widespread assumption in the United States that all women naturally have maternal feelings and capacities, child care staff, who are almost all women (about 98 percent), are not required to have special training (and do not need to be well paid). Even for regulated providers, 41 out of 50 states require no pre-service training beyond orientation. Consequently, in the United States the child–staff ratio is one of the most prominent measures used to assess quality and is central to most state licensing systems. The assumption, based on the mother-substitute model, is that emotional support can be given and learning can take place only with such low ratios.

Considering the high quality and ample funding of many European systems, it comes as a surprise that most have much higher child-staff ratios than the United States. In the French *écoles maternelles*, for example, there is one teacher and one half-time aide for every 25 children. In Italy, in a center with one adult for every eight children (ages one to three years) the early childhood workers see no need for additional adults and think the existing ratios are appropriate. Leading researchers Sheila Kamerman and Alfred Kahn report that in Denmark, "what is particularly impressive is that children are pretty much on their own in playing with their peers. An adult is present all the time but does not lead or play with the children." In a similar vein, a cross-national study of academic literature found substantial focus on adult–child ratios in the United States, but very little literature on the topic in German-, French-, or Spanish-language publications. Why not? These systems have a different view of children and learning. Outside the United States, systems often center around the peer group. In Denmark the role of staff is to work "alongside children, rather than [to be] experts or leaders who teach children." Similarly, the first director of the early childhood services in Reggio, Italy, argues that children learn through conflict and that placing children in groups facilitates learning through "attractive," "advantageous," and "constructive" conflict "because among children there are not strong relationships of authority and dependence." In a non-European example, Joseph Tobin, David Wu, and Dana Davidson argue that in Japan the aim is ratios that "keep teachers from being too mother-like in their interactions with students. . . . Large class sizes and large ratios have become increasingly important strategies for promoting the Japanese values of groupism and selflessness." Such practices contrast with the individualistic focus in U.S. child care.

Family Leaves and Work Time

When we ask how to care for children, especially those younger than three, one answer is for parents to stay home. Policy that promotes such leaves is what one would expect from a society such as the United States, which emphasizes a mothering model of child care. It is, however, European countries that provide extensive paid family leave, usually universal, with not only job protection but also substantial income replacement. In Sweden, for example, parents receive a full year and a half of paid parental leave (with 12 months at 80 percent of prior earnings) for each child. Because so many parents (mostly mothers) use family leave, fewer than 200 children under one year old in the entire country are in public care. Generous programs are common throughout Europe (although the length, flexibility, and level of payment they provide vary).

The United States provides far less in the way of family leaves. Since its passage in 1993, the Family and Medical Leave Act (FMLA) has guaranteed a 12-week job-protected leave to workers of covered employers. Most employers (95 percent) and many workers (45 percent), however, are not covered. And all federally mandated leaves are unpaid.

The unpaid leaves provided by the FMLA, like the private system of child care, accentuate the inequality between those who can afford them and those who can't. Although the FMLA was touted as a "gender neutral" piece of legislation, men (especially white men) are unlikely to take leaves; it is overwhelmingly women (especially those who are married) who take them. As a result, such women pay a wage penalty when they interrupt their careers. To address such inequities, Sweden and Norway have introduced a "use it or lose it" policy. For each child, parents may divide up to a year of paid leave (say nine months for the mother, three for the father), *except* that the mother may not use more than eleven months total. One month is reserved for the father; if he does not use the leave, the family loses the month.

```
2002–2003 FEE SCHEDULE
(Prices effective until July 1, 2003)

Application Fee     $50.00
(nonrefundable/annual fee)
Materials Fee      $30.00 Full-time Enrollment
(nonrefundable)/   $20.00 Part-time Enrollment
Tuition Deposit* (due in two installments)
a.  Space Guarantee Fee** $150.00
    (due upon acceptance to the school)
b.  Balance due two months prior to starting date
*Amount equal to one month's tuition
**See enrollment contract for refund conditions.


    Full-time              $859.00/month


Morning Preschool (9:00 A.M.–1:00 P.M.)
    three mornings     $321.00/month
    four mornings      $397.00/month
    five mornings      $462.00/month


Afternoon Preschool (1:00 P.M.–5:00 P.M.)
    three afternoons   $285.00/month
    four afternoons    $350.00/month
    five afternoons    $404.00/month


Kindergarten Program (11:25 A.M.–5:00 P.M.)
    three days         $339.00/month
    four days          $416.00/month
    five days          $486.00/month


•  Extended Care (hour before 9:00 A.M. and
   the hour after 5:00 P.M.)        $5.25/hour
•  Unscheduled Drop-in              $6.25/hour


Participating Parents (P.P.) & Board Members
receive tuition credit. P.P. credit is $25.00 per
day of participation. Board credits vary with
position.
```

FIGURE 1   Tuition and Fees for the U.S. Preschool Illustrated Here [Kensington Nursery School], a Non-profit, Parent-Run Cooperative That Costs Almost $ 1,000 per Month

Finally, although not usually discussed as child care policy in the United States, policy makers in many European countries now emphasize that the number of hours parents work clearly shapes the ways young children are cared for and by whom. Workers in the United States, on average, put in 300 hours more per year than workers in France (and 400 more than those in Sweden).

Conclusion

The child care system in the United States is a fragmentary patchwork, both at the level of the individual child and at the level of the overall system. Recent research suggests that the quality of care for young children is poor or fair in well over half of child care settings. This low quality of care, in concert with a model of intensive mothering, means that many anxious mothers privately hunt for high-quality substitutes while trying to ensure they are not being really replaced. System administrators need to patch together a variety of funding streams, each with its own regulations and paperwork. Because the current system was fashioned primarily for the affluent at one end and those being pushed off welfare at the other, it poorly serves most of the working class and much of the middle class.

Most efforts at reform are equally piecemeal, seeking a little extra money here or there in ways that reinforce the existing fragmentation. Although increasing numbers of advocates are pushing for a better system of child care in the United States, they rarely step back to think about the characteristics of the system as a whole. If they did, what lessons could be learned from Europe?

The features that are common to our peer nations in Europe would presumably be a part of a new U.S. system. The programs would be publicly funded and universal, available to all, either at no cost or at a modest cost with subsidies for low-income participants. The staff would be paid about the same as public school teachers. The core programs would cover at least as many hours as the school day, and "wrap-around" care would be available before and after this time. Participation in the programs would be voluntary, but the programs would be of such a high quality that a majority of children would enroll. Because the quality of the programs would be high, parents would feel much less ambivalence about their children's participation, and the system would enjoy strong public support. In addition to child care centers, parents would be universally offered a significant period of paid parental leave. Of course, this system is expensive. But as the National Academy of Science Report makes clear, not caring for our children is in the long term, and probably even in the short term, even more expensive.

Centers in all nations emphasize education, peer group dynamics, and emotional support to some extent. But the balance varies. The varieties of European experience pose a set of issues to be considered if and when reform of the U.S. system is on the agenda:

- To what degree should organized care approximate school and at what age, and to what extent is the purpose of such systems primarily educational?
- To what extent should we focus on adult–child interactions that sustain or substitute for mother care as opposed to fostering child–child interactions and the development of peer groups?

- To what extent should policies promote parental time with children versus high-quality organized care, and what are the implications for gender equity of either choice?

These are fundamental questions because they address issues of social equality and force us to rethink deep-seated images of children and parents.

ENDNOTE

Author's Note: We would like to thank Amy Armenia, Michelle Budig, Mary Ann Clawson, Nancy DeProsse, Fran Deutsch, Eva Gerstel, Nancy Folbre, Joya Misra, Maureen Perry-Jenkins, Ruby Takanishi, and Robert Zussman for comments and suggestions.

RECOMMENDED RESOURCES

Cooper, Candy J. 1999. *Ready to Learn: The French System of Early Education and Care Offers Lessons for the United States.* New York: French American Foundation.

Gornick, Janet and Marcia Meyers. 2001. "Support for Working Families: What the United States Can Learn from Europe." *The American Prospect* (January 1–15): 3–7.

Helburn, Suzanne W. and Barbara R. Bergmann. 2002. *America's Childcare Problem: The Way Out.* New York: Palgrave/St. Martin's.

Kamerman, Sheila B. and Alfred J. Kahn. 1995. *Starting Right: How America Neglects Its Youngest Children and What We Can Do about It.* New York: Oxford University Press.

Moss, Peter. 2000. "Workforce Issues in Early Childhood Education and Care Staff." Paper prepared for consultative meeting on International Developments in Early Childhood Education and Care, The Institute for Child and Family Policy, Columbia University, May 11–12.

Organization for Economic Co-operation and Development. *Starting Strong – Early Education and Care: Report on an OECD Thematic Review.* Online. www.oecd.org.

Shonkoff, Jack P. and Deborah Phillips, eds. 2000. *From Neurons to Neighborhoods: The Science of Early Childhood Development.* Washington, DC: National Academy of Sciences.

PART XI

Families and Poverty

Why is poverty important to study in the sociology of the family? Poverty deeply affects many people's lives, with many people suffering from hunger and a lack of adequate housing. The problems of poverty are compounded when these people have families. Family demographer Daniel Lichter (1997) reports that in 1994 "15.3 million or 21.8 percent of all American children lived in poor families. Although children comprised only 26.7 percent of the U.S. population, they accounted for 40.1 percent of all poor persons" (p. 123). Thus, the majority of people in poverty are mothers and their children. Low socioeconomic status greatly influences family structure and relationships, and it also affects the quality of life and resources available to the family. The articles selected for this section reflect many of the issues currently facing families in poverty. Readers also may want to examine Shirley A. Hill's article (Reading 6), "Black Families: Beyond Revisionist Scholarship," and Jennifer Hamer's research on low-income African Americans and fatherhood (Reading 26).

Explanations of Poverty

There are two primary explanations of poverty used in research on families and poverty: cultural deficiency models or structural analyses. Sociologist Maxine Baca Zinn (1989) argues that cultural explanations of poverty see culture as the villain. Poor people are seen to have distinctive values, aspirations, and psychological characteristics that restrict their abilities and foster behavioral deficiencies which keep families poor from generation to generation. For example, the 1965 *Moynihan Report* on African American families in poverty blamed the poverty on African American women who were too matriarchal and strong. Another theorist, Nicholas Lemann (1986a, 1986b), argued that African Americans raised in a southern culture of poverty had "loose" attitudes toward marriage, high illegitimacy rates, and family disintegration. According to Lemann, African Americans who migrated from southern to northern cities in the United States took this culture of poverty with them. Baca Zinn argues that the problems with culture-of-poverty arguments are numerous, including the fact that these theories blame the victims and their culture for being poor and ignore larger, macrostructural forces that could be keeping them poor. The culture of poverty thesis has been disproved by researchers using the University of Michigan's Panel Study of Income Dynamics (PSID). Studies that have examined family incomes over a period of years found that most families are not in poverty for a long enough time to create a culture of poverty. Instead, income data show that there is a high turnover in the individual families who are poor in any given year. Thus, individual motivation also cannot be used as a primary explanation of poverty.

Instead of focusing on individual and cultural explanations of poverty, Baca Zinn argues that we need to look at structural explanations of poverty. Structural explanations include studying the structure of the family. Sociologist William Julius Wilson (1987) in his research on family structure and poverty found that many family variables affect poverty rates including marital status, high divorce rates, female-headed households, the number of adults earning an income in the household, and the availability of marriageable men. Other structural variables include transformations in the economy, such as deindustrialization and the switch from manufacturing to a service economy. These changes in the economy led to many jobs being deskilled or moved from urban centers, causing high rates of unemployment. Thus, the opportunity to find a decent-paying, blue-collar job is much harder today than it was 30 years ago. Baca Zinn argues that structural changes in urban areas also are affecting rates of poverty. More inner-city neighborhoods are isolated in deteriorating cities, with little public transportation and fewer cars to get people to jobs and resources in the suburbs.

The first reading, "As American as Apple Pie: Poverty and Welfare," by Mark Rank, builds on Baca Zinn's arguments concerning structural analyses of poverty. Rank, a professor of social welfare in the George Warren Brown School of Social Work at Washington University in St. Louis, was trained in sociology at the University of Wisconsin, Madison. Rank specializes in the study of poverty, social welfare, economic inequality, and social policy. In this selection, Rank dispels many myths about poverty in the United States, especially the stereotype that poor people consist only of those individuals on the fringes of society. Instead, Rank argues that most Americans will experience poverty and turn to public assistance at some point in their lives. Thus, poverty is as American as apple pie. Rank utilizes data from the Panel Study of Income Dynamics and other longitudinal data sets to show the prevalence of poverty before turning his attention to a discussion of why the poverty rate is so high in the United States.

Welfare Reform in the United States

The second article in this section, "Flat Broke with Children: The Ground-Level Results of Welfare Reform," is by Sharon Hays. Hays, a professor of sociology and gender studies at the University of California, San Diego, spent three years researching poor families in this ethnographic study of poor mothers and their children. Her research was published in the award-winning book *Flat Broke with Children: Women in the Age of Welfare Reform* (2003). The goal of Hays' research was to discover how the Personal Responsibility Act of 1996, a welfare reform act at the federal level, was actually impacting the lives of women and children. Were women successfully getting off of welfare and finding good-paying jobs? Or, at least, finding jobs that paid their bills and child care costs? In this selection, Hays discusses her experiences researching women in poverty and the successes and problems of recent welfare reform legislation.

Women and Children in Poverty

The third reading in this section, "Poor Mothers and the Care of Teenage Children," by Demie Kurz, builds on the arguments made about poverty by the previous two authors, Rank (Reading 45) and Hays (Reading 46). Kurz is a professor of women's studies and sociology at the University of Pennsylvania, where she writes and teaches about women and families in the United States. In this selection, Kurz examines why there is so much public hatred for poor women in the United States: The public sees poor women on welfare as being too dependent on welfare, too lazy to find work, and too fertile. Another erroneous belief that Kurz discusses is that many women on welfare are having more babies so that they can collect additional welfare. In fact, former Republican Congressman Newt Gingrich once said that "congressional leaders argue that governmental programs "reward dependency" and have "had the unintended consequences of making welfare more attractive than work" (cited in Lundgren-Gaveras 1996:136). Kurz questions several of these myths regarding poor women on welfare by examining the challenges these women face as they try to raise their teenage children. First, Kurz identifies the work poor mothers do and the strategies they use to manage their teenage children. Second, Kurz locates the work poor mothers do for their teenage children within larger systems of racial and social class privilege and examines the obstacles they face. Systems of privilege grant more resources to white, higher-income women; poorer women and women of color face different economic realities, including barriers to finding well-paid employment, child care, and time to parent and do the unpaid labor of housework.

The last reading in this section on families and poverty, "Is There Hope for America's Low-Income Children?," is by Lee Rainwater and Timothy M. Smeeding. Rainwater is a professor of sociology emeritus at Harvard University who, since the late 1950s, has extensively researched families and poverty. Smeeding, the Maxwell Professor of Public Policy at Syracuse University, has studied the economics of public policy and the effects of poverty programs on families. In this selection, Rainwater and Smeeding make several policy suggestions to improve the lives of children in poverty. The policies are not radical in and of themselves: parental employment, child care subsidies and child support, affordable and available child care, and parental leave policies. Moreover, many European nations already have several of these social policies in place to make sure that few families with children live in poverty. The primary question is: Why has the United States not developed a comprehensive policy program to reduce child poverty rates and improve the well-being of children?

REFERENCES

Baca Zinn, Maxine. 1989. "Family, Race, and Poverty in the Eighties." *Signs: Journal of Women in Culture and Society* 14 (4): 856–74.

Hays, Sharon. 2003. *Flat Broke with Children: Women in the Age of Welfare Reform.* New York: Oxford University Press.

Lemann, Nicholas. 1986a. "The Origins of the Underclass: Part 1." *Atlantic Monthly,* June, pp. 31–35.

———. 1986b. "The Origins of the Underclass: Part 2." *Atlantic Monthly,* July 54–68.

Lichter, Daniel T. 1997. "Poverty and Inequality among Children." *Annual Review of Sociology* 23:121–45.

Lundgren-Gaveras, Lena. 1996. "The Work–Family Needs of Single Parents: A Comparison of American and Swedish Policy Trends." *Journal of Sociology and Social Welfare* 23:131–47.

Moynihan, Daniel P. [1965] 1967. "The Negro Family: The Case for National Action." Pp. 39–132 in *The Moynihan Report and the Politics of Controversy,* edited by L. Rainwater and W. L. Yancy. Cambridge, MA: MIT Press.

Wilson, William Julius, with Kathryn Neckerman. 1987. "Poverty and Family Structure: The Widening Gap between Evidence and Public Policy Issues." Pp. 63–92 in *The Truly Disadvantaged,* by William Julius Wilson. Chicago: University of Chicago Press.

45

AS AMERICAN AS APPLE PIE
Poverty and Welfare

MARK R. RANK

For many Americans, the words poverty and welfare conjure images of people on the fringes of society: unwed mothers raising several children, inner-city black men, high school dropouts, the homeless, and so on. The media, political rhetoric, and often even the research of social scientists depict the poor as alien and often undeserving of help. In short, being poor and using welfare are perceived as outside the American mainstream.

Yet, poverty and welfare use are as American as apple pie. Most of us will experience poverty during our lives. Even more surprising, most Americans will turn to public assistance at least once during adulthood. Rather than poverty and welfare use being an issue of *them*, it is more an issue of *us*.

The Risk of Poverty and Drawing on Welfare

Our understanding about the extent of poverty comes mostly from annual surveys conducted by the Census Bureau. Over the past three decades, between 11 and 15 percent of Americans have lived below the poverty line in any given year. Some people are at greater risk than others, depending on age, race, gender, family structure, community of residence, education, work skills and physical disabilities.

Studies that follow particular families over time—in particular, the Panel Study of Income Dynamics (PSID), the National Longitudinal Survey (NLS), and the Survey of Income and Program Participation (SIPP)—have given us a further understanding of year-to-year changes in poverty. They show that most people are poor for only a short time. Typically, households are impoverished for one, two, or three years, then manage to get above the poverty line. They may stay above the line for a while, only to fall into poverty again later. Events triggering these spells of poverty frequently involve the loss of a job and its pay, family changes such as divorce, or both.

There is, however, an alternative way to estimate the scope of poverty. Specifically, how many Americans experience poverty at some point during adulthood? Counting the number of people who are ever touched by poverty,

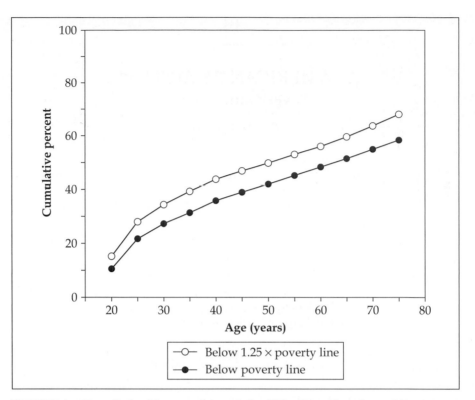

FIGURE 1   Cumulative Percent of Americans Who Have Experienced Poverty
Source: Panel Study of Income Dynamics

rather than those who are poor in any given year, gives us a better sense of the scope of the problem. Put another way, to what extent is poverty a "normal" part of the life cycle?

My colleague Tom Hirschl and I have constructed a series of "life tables" built from PSID data following families for over 25 years. The life table is a technique for counting how often specific events occur in specific periods of time, and is frequently used by demographers and medical researchers to assess risk, say, the risk of contracting breast cancer after menopause. It allows us to estimate the percentage of the American population that will experience poverty at some point during adulthood. We also calculated the percentage of the population that will use a social safety net program— programs such as food stamps or Aid to Families with Dependent Children (AFDC, now replaced by the Temporary Assistance for Needy Families [TANF] program)—sometime during adulthood. Our results suggest that a serious reconsideration of who experiences poverty is in order.

Figure 1 shows the percentage of Americans spending at least one year living below the official poverty line during adulthood. It also graphs the percentage who have lived between the poverty line and just 25 percent above it—what scholars consider "near poverty."

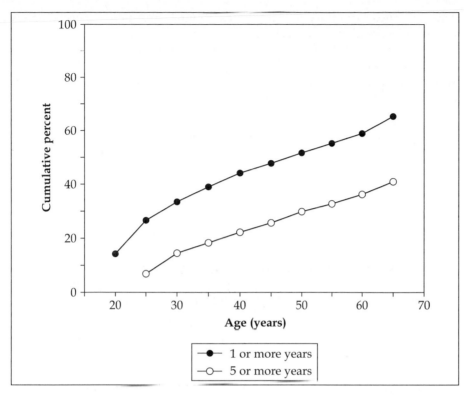

FIGURE 2   Cumulative Percent of Americans Who Have Received Welfare
Source: Panel Study of Income Dynamics

By the age of 30, 27 percent of Americans will have experienced at least one year in poverty and 34 percent will have fallen below the near-poverty line. By the age of 50, the percentages will have risen to 42 and 50 percent, respectively. And, finally, by the time Americans have reached the age of 75; 59 percent will have spent at least a year below the poverty line during their adulthood, while 68 percent will have faced at least a year in near poverty.

If we included experiences of poverty in childhood, these percentages would be even higher. Rather than an isolated event that occurs only among the so-called "underclass," poverty is a reality that a clear majority of Americans will experience during their lifetimes.

Measuring impoverishment as the use of social safety net programs produces even more startling results. Figure 2 draws on the same PSID survey to show the proportion of people between the ages of 20 and 65 who will use one of the major need-based welfare programs in the United States, including food stamps, Medicaid, AFDC, Supplemental Security Income, and other cash subsidies such as general assistance. By the time Americans reach the age of 65, approximately two-thirds will have, as adults, received assistance for at least a year, while 40 percent will have used a welfare program in at least five separate years. (Again, adding childhood experiences would only raise the rates.) Contrary to stereotypes, relying on America's social safety net is widespread and far-reaching.

Of course, people with disadvantages such as single parents or those with fewer skills will have even higher cumulative rates of poverty and welfare use than those shown in Figures 1 and 2. Yet to portray poverty as an issue affecting only marginalized groups is clearly a mistake.

Why Is the Risk of Poverty So High?

Time   First, most discussions of poverty look at single years, or five or ten years at a stretch. The life table techniques employed in Figures 1 and 2 are based upon assessing the risk of poverty across a lifetime, more than 50 years. Over so many years, individuals face many unanticipated events—households split up, workers lose their jobs, family members become sick, and so on—that become financial emergencies. The familiar saying of being "one paycheck away from poverty" is particularly apt. For example, it is estimated that families with average incomes have enough assets to maintain their standards of living for just over one month.

The Safety Net   A second reason poverty rates are so high is that there is little government help to tide households over during financial emergencies. Although most Americans will eventually rely on need-based government aid (as shown in Figure 2), that assistance often fails to save them from poverty. Contrary to the rhetoric about vast sums being spent on public assistance, the American welfare system can be more accurately described as minimal. Compared to other Western industrialized countries, the United States devotes far fewer resources to assisting the economically vulnerable.

Most European countries provide a wide range of social and insurance programs that effectively keep families from falling into poverty. These include substantial cash payments to families with children. Unemployment assistance is far more generous in these countries than in the United States, often providing support for more than a year following the loss of a job. Furthermore, universal health coverage is routinely provided along with considerable support for child care.

These social policies substantially reduce the risk of poverty in Europe and Canada, while U.S. social policies—aside from programs specifically directed to aid the elderly—have reduced poverty modestly at best. As economist Rebecca Blank notes in *It Takes a Nation*, "the national choice in the United States to provide relatively less generous transfers to low-income families has meant higher relative poverty rates in the country. While low-income families in the United States work more than in many other countries, they are not able to make up for lower governmental income support relative to their European counterparts" (pp. 141–42).

Scholars who have used the Luxembourg Income Study (LIS), an international collection of economic surveys, have documented the inability of the American safety net to reduce the risk of poverty. For example, Finnish social scientist Veli-Matti Ritakallio has examined the extent to which cash assistance reduces poverty across eight European countries, Canada, and the United States. European and Canadian programs reduce rates of poverty by an average of 79 percent from what they would have been absent the assistance. Finland, for instance, reduced the percentage of its residents who would have been poor from 33 percent down to 4 percent. In contrast, the United States was only able to reduce its percentage in poverty at any given time from 29 percent to 18 percent. As a result, the current rates of U.S. poverty are among the highest in the industrialized world.

The Labor Market   A third factor elevating the risk of American poverty across the life course is the failure of the labor market to provide enough jobs that pay well enough. During the past 30 years, the U.S. economy has produced increasing numbers of low-paying jobs, part-time jobs, and jobs without benefits. For example, the Census Bureau estimated that the median earnings of workers who were paid hourly wages in 2000 was $9.91. At the same time, approximately 3 million Americans were working part-time because of a shortage of full-time jobs. As journalist Barbara Ehrenreich and others have shown, these jobs simply do not support a family.

A higher percentage of the U.S. workforce falls into this low-wage sector than is true in comparable developed countries. For example, economist Timothy Smeeding and his colleagues have found that 25 percent of all American full-time workers could be classified as being in low-wage work (defined as earning less than 65 percent of the national median for full-time jobs). This was by far the highest percentage of the countries analyzed, with the overall average of non-U.S. countries falling at 12 percent.

In addition, there are simply not enough jobs to go around. Labor economist Timothy Bartik used several different approaches to estimate the number of jobs that would be needed to significantly reduce poverty in the United States. Even in the booming economy of the late 1990s, between 5 and 9 million more jobs were needed in order to meet the needs of the poor and disadvantaged.

To use an analogy, the demand for labor versus the supply of decent paying jobs might be thought of as an ongoing game of musical chairs. That is, the number of workers in the labor market is far greater than the number of jobs that pay a living wage. Using SIPP data for 1999, I estimated this imbalance as ranging between 9 percent and 33 percent, depending upon how poverty and labor market participation were defined. Consequently, between 9 and 33 percent of American household heads were either in non-living-wage jobs or looking for work. The very structure of the labor market ensures that some families will lose out at this musical chairs game and consequently will run a significant risk of poverty.

Some may point out that U.S. rates of unemployment are fairly low when compared to European levels. Yet Bruce Western and Katherine Beckett demonstrate that these lower rates are largely a result of extremely high rates of incarceration. By removing large numbers of American men from the labor force and placing them into the penal system (thus out of our musical chairs analogy altogether), unemployment rates are kept artificially low. When this factor is taken into account and adjusted for, U.S. unemployment rates fall more into line with those of Europe.

Changing the Poverty Paradigm

A life course perspective shows us that Americans are highly susceptible to experiencing poverty first-hand. Understanding the normality of poverty requires us to rethink several of our most enduring myths. Assuming that most Americans would rather avoid such an experience, it becomes in our enlightened self-interest to ensure that we reduce poverty and establish an effective safety net. This risk-sharing argument has been articulated most notably by the philosopher John Rawls. As well as being charitable, improving the plight of those in poverty is an issue of common concern.

We are also beginning to recognize that, as a nation, we pay a high price for our excessive rates of poverty. Research shows that poverty impairs the nation's health, the quality of its workforce, race relations, and, of course, its future generations. Understanding the commonality of poverty shifts how we choose to think about the issue—from a distant concept of *them*, to an active reality of *us*. In addition, much of the public's resistance to assisting the poor and particularly those on welfare is the perception that the poor are often undeserving of assistance, that their poverty arises from a lack of motivation, questionable morals, and so on. Yet my analysis suggests that, given its pervasiveness, poverty appears systemic to our economic structure. In short, we have met the enemy, and they are us. C. Wright Mills made a similar point about unemployment:

> When, in a city of 100,000, only one man is unemployed, that is his personal trouble, and for its relief we properly look to the character of the man, his skills, and his immediate opportunities. But when in a nation of 50 million employees, 15 million men are unemployed, that is an issue, and we may not hope to find its solution within the range of opportunities open to any one individual. The very structure of opportunities has collapsed. Both the correct statement of the problem and the range of possible solutions require us to consider the economic and political institutions of the society, and not merely the personal situation and character of a scatter of individuals.

So too with poverty. That America has the highest poverty rates in the Western industrialized world and that most Americans will experience poverty during their lifetimes has little to do with individual motivation or attitudes. Rather, it has much to do with a labor market that fails to produce enough decent paying jobs, and social policies that are unable to pull individuals and families out of poverty when unforeseen events occur. The United States has the means to alleviate poverty, and a range of models from other countries to borrow from. Allowing our policies to be mired in self-righteous moralism while millions of citizens suffer is unconscionable. It is time to shift the debate from one of blame, to one of justice and common concern.

RECOMMENDED RESOURCES

Bartik, Timothy H. 2002. "Poverty, Jobs, and Subsidized Employment." *Challenge* 45 (3): 100–11. An argument for the importance of labor demand policies that encourage job growth and improved wages for low-income workers.

Blank, Rebecca. 1997. *It Takes a Nation: A New Agenda for Fighting Poverty*. New York: Russell Sage Foundation. A review of the characteristics, nature, and current strategies for addressing American poverty.

Ehrenreich, Barbara. 2001. *Nickel and Dimed: On (Not) Getting By in America*. New York: Henry Holt and Company. A first-hand account of trying to survive on low-wage work in three different settings.

O'Connor, Alice. 2001. *Poverty Knowledge: Social Science, Social Policy, and the Poor in Twentieth-Century U.S. History*. Princeton, NJ: Princeton University Press. O'Connor critiques the dominant social science emphasis in the past 40 years on analyzing individual attributes as the primary cause of poverty.

Patterson, James T. 2000. *America's Struggle against Poverty in the Twentieth Century*. Cambridge, MA: Harvard University Press. A historical overview of American social policy directed at the alleviation of poverty.

Rank, Mark R. Forthcoming. *One Nation, Underprivileged: How American Poverty Affects Us All*. New York: Oxford University Press. A new perspective on understanding and addressing U.S. poverty.

Rank, Mark R. and Thomas A. Hirschl. 2001. "Rags or Riches? Estimating the Probabilities of Poverty and Affluence across the Adult American Life Span." *Social Science Quarterly* 82 (4): 651–69. An examination of the likelihood that Americans will experience poverty or affluence at some point during their adulthood, which suggests a new conceptualization of social stratification.

Ritakallio, Veli-Matti. 2001. "Trends of Poverty and Income Inequality in Cross-National Comparison." Luxembourg Income Study Working (Paper) No. 272. Maxwell School of Citizenship and Public Affairs, Syracuse University, Syracuse, New York. Ritakallio uses the Luxembourg Income Study to assess the effectiveness of government policy in reducing poverty among nine developed countries.

Smeeding, Timothy M., Lee Rainwater, and Gary Burtless. 2001."U.S. Poverty in a Cross-National Context." Pp. 162–89 in *Understanding Poverty*, edited by Sheldon H. Danziger and Robert H. Haveman. Cambridge, MA: Harvard University Press. The authors compare the extent of poverty in the United States and other developed countries.

Western, Bruce and Katherine Beckett. 1999. "How Unregulated Is the U.S. Market? The Penal System as a Labor Market Institution." *American Journal of Sociology* 104 (January): 1030–60. This study shows the role that incarceration plays in lowering overall U.S. unemployment rates.

46

FLAT BROKE WITH CHILDREN
The Ground–Level Results of Welfare Reform

SHARON HAYS

It's hard to date it precisely, but I think my severe case of cognitive disso-nance set in on a summer evening in 1999. As part of my research on welfare reform, I'd spent the afternoon playing on the floor with Sammy, the four-year-old son of a welfare recipient. I was struck by his intelligence and creativity and imagined that if his mom were middle-class, she'd soon be having him tested and charting the gifted and talented programs he'd attend.

But Sammy's mom, Celia, had other things on her mind. Cradling her infant daughter, she told me that she had been recently diagnosed with cancer. Her doctor wanted her to start treatments immediately. Although she'd been working at a local Fotomart for three months, the welfare office still helped her with the costs of child care — costs she couldn't otherwise manage on her $6 per hour pay. When she asked her boss about flexible hours to manage the cancer treatments, he told her she was just too easily replaced. She'd also checked with her welfare caseworkers; they told her that if she lost her job she'd have to quickly find another or risk being cut off the wel-fare rolls. I talked to her about the Social Security Disability program, even though I knew that she had only a slim chance of getting help there. Celia had an eighth-grade education, no financial assets, few job skills, and no extended family members with sufficient resources to see her through. And she needed those cancer treatments now.

Under the old welfare system, she could have simply returned to full welfare benefits. Yet, knowing what I did from my research into the worlds of low-wage work, welfare, and disability, I was sure there was now virtu-ally nowhere for her to turn, save all those local charities that were already incredibly overburdened. I didn't have the heart to tell her.

When I went home that night, the local television news was interview-ing a smiling former welfare mother recently employed at a supermarket chain. It was a story of redemption — the triumph of individual willpower and American know-how — and the newscaster cheerfully pronounced it a

Sharon Hays, "Flat Broke with Children: The Ground Level Results of Welfare Reform" from *Dissent* (Fall 2003). Reprinted with the permission of the Foundation for the Study of Independent Social Ideas.

marker of the "success" of welfare reform. That's when the dissonance set in. I've been suffering from it ever since.

From one point of view, it makes perfect sense that so many have celebrated the results of the 1996 Personal Responsibility Act. The welfare rolls have been cut by more than half—from twelve million recipients in 1996 to five million today. Among those who have left welfare, the majority (60 percent to 65 percent) are employed. Add to this the fact that public opinion polls show that almost no one liked the old system of welfare and most people (including most welfare recipients) agree that the principles behind reform—independence, self-sufficiency, strong families, a concern for the common good—are worthy ideals.

The problem is that there is a wide gap between the more worthy goals behind reform and the ground-level realities I found in the welfare office. There is also a tremendous amount of diversity hidden in those large-scale statistical accountings of the results of reform—and much of it is a great deal more disheartening than it first appears. After three years of ethnographic research inside two (distant and distinct) welfare offices, after interviewing more than 50 caseworkers and about 130 welfare mothers, and after five years of poring over policy reports on reform, it is clear to me that the majority of the nation's most desperately poor citizens are in worse shape now than they would have been had the Personal Responsibility Act never been passed.

Between Success and Failure

Political speeches, policy reports, and the popular media all cite the declining rolls and the employment of former recipients as the central evidence of the success of welfare reform. By these standards, Celia and her children would count as a success.

Of course there are genuine success stories. Take Sally. With a good job at the phone company, medical benefits, sick leave and vacation leave, a nine-to-five schedule, possibilities for advancement, and enough income to place her and her two kids above the poverty line, she was better off than she'd ever been on welfare benefits or in any of the (many) low-wage, no-benefit jobs she'd had in the past. And there was no question that the supportive services that came with reform had helped her to achieve that success. She got her job through a welfare-sponsored training program offered by the phone company. Welfare caseworkers had helped her out with clothing for work, bus vouchers, and a child care subsidy that got her through the training. "I think welfare's better now," she told me. "They've got programs there to help you. They're actually giving you an opportunity. I'm working and I feel like I can make it on my own."

Monique was also helped by reform. A messy divorce with an abusive (and stalker) husband had cost her her job as a nursing assistant. With two young sons to worry about, she sought help from the welfare office. Fortunately, she lived in one of the few states with a welfare policy that exempted domestic-violence victims from the immediate demand to find work. Using special funds made available by reform, welfare caseworkers not only provided her with a welfare check, but also helped her to manage car repairs and the down payment on an apartment. Once she and her children were settled, her boss planned to hire her again. If Monique could remain hidden from her ex-husband, things would work out just fine. Like Sally, she was grateful for the help she'd received from the welfare office.

About one-half of the welfare mothers I met experienced at least temporary successes like these. Yet under the terms of reform, the long-term outlook for the majority is not so positive. And in many cases it is difficult to distinguish the successes from the failures.

Proponents of reform would mark Andrea, for instance, as "successful." When I met her, she was earning $5.75 an hour, working thirty-five hours a week at a Sunbelt City convenience store. After paying rent, utility bills, and food costs for her family of three, she was left with $50 a month to cover the costs of child care, transportation, clothing, medical bills, laundry, school costs, furniture, appliances, and cleaning supplies. Just four months off the welfare rolls, Andrea was already in trouble. Her phone had been turned off the month before, and she was unsure how she'd pay this month's rent. Her oldest daughter was asking for new school clothes, her youngest had a birthday coming soon, and Andrea couldn't take her mind off the upcoming winter utility bills. If she were single, she told me, she would manage somehow. But with children to worry about, she knew she couldn't make it much longer.

National-level accountings of reform would also place Teresa and her three children in the plus column. When I met her, she had a temporary (three-month) job at a collection agency. Thanks to public housing and the time-limited child care subsidy offered by the welfare office, she was making ends meet. Teresa was smart and capable, but had only a high school diploma and almost no work experience. She'd spent more of her adult life outside the mainstream economy — first married to a drug dealer, then working as a street-level prostitute, and finally, drug free, on welfare. As much as Teresa thought she was doing better than ever and spoke of how happy she was to be getting dressed up every morning and going out to work, she was still concerned about the future. The child care costs for her three kids would amount to nearly three-quarters of her paycheck if she had to cover them herself. And her job, like that child care subsidy, was only temporary. Given her résumé, I wondered just what career ladder she might find to offer her sufficient income and stability to stay off the welfare rolls and successfully juggle her duties as both primary caregiver and sole breadwinner for those three kids.

The cycle of work and welfare implied by these cases is the most common pattern among the welfare-level poor. It is a cycle of moving from welfare to low-wage jobs to mounting debts and problems with child care, husbands, boyfriends, employers, landlords, overdue utility bills, broken-down cars, inadequate public transportation, unstable living arrangements, job layoffs, sick children, disabled parents, and the innumerable everyday contingencies of low-income life—any and all of which can lead a poor family back to the welfare office to repeat the cycle again. Most of the people caught up in this cycle face a number of social disadvantages from the start. Welfare recipients are overwhelmingly mothers (90 percent), they are disproportionately non-white (38 percent are black, 25 percent Latino, and 30 percent white), nearly half are without high-school diplomas (47 percent), the majority have experience in only unskilled jobs, about half suffer from physical or mental health disabilities, almost as many have a history of domestic violence, and all have children to care for. At the same time, most welfare recipients have work experience (83 percent), and most want to work. This was true long before welfare reform. Yet given their circumstances, and given the structure of low-wage work, it is not surprising that many have found it difficult to achieve long-term financial and familial stability.

Of those who have left the rolls since reform, a full 40 percent are without work or welfare at any given time. Of the 60 percent who do have jobs, their average wage is approximately $7 per hour. But most former recipients do not find full-time or year-round work, leaving their average annual wage estimated at just over $10,000 a year. Following this same pattern, about three-quarters of the families who left welfare are in jobs without medical insurance, retirement benefits, sick days, or vacation leave; and one-quarter work night or evening shifts. It is true that their average annual wages amount to more income than welfare, food stamps, and Medicaid combined. Yet, as Kathryn Edin and Laura Lein demonstrated in *Making Ends Meet*, taking into account the additional costs associated with employment (such as child care, transportation, clothing), working poor families like these actually suffer more material hardship than their counterparts on welfare.

The reality behind the declining welfare rolls is millions of former welfare families moving in and out of low-wage jobs. Some achieve success, most do not. Approximately one-third have found themselves back on welfare at least once since reform. Overall, two-thirds of those who have left welfare are either unemployed or working for wages that do not lift their families out of poverty. And there are still millions of families on welfare, coming in anew, coming back again, or as yet unable to find a way off the rolls.

The Personal Responsibility Act itself produced two primary changes in the lives of the working/welfare poor. On the one hand, welfare reform offered sufficient positive employment supports to allow poor families to leave welfare more quickly, and in some cases it offered just the boost that was needed to allow those families to achieve genuine long-term financial stability. On the other hand, welfare reform instituted a system of rules, punishments, and time limits that has effectively pressured the poor to steer clear of the welfare office.

A central result of welfare reform, in other words, is that a large proportion of desperately poor mothers and children are now too discouraged, too angry, too ashamed, or too exhausted to go to the welfare office. Nationwide, as the welfare rolls were declining by more than half, the rate of dire (welfare-level) poverty declined by only 15 percent. To put it another way: whereas the vast majority of desperately poor families received welfare support prior to reform (84 percent), today less than half of them do. Why are all these mothers and children now avoiding welfare? To make sense of this part of the story, one needs to understand the complicated changes that have taken place inside welfare offices across the nation. I can here offer only a glimpse.

Punishment and the Push to Work

Upon arrival at the Arbordale welfare office, the first thing one sees is a large red sign, two feet high, twelve feet long, inquiring, "HOW MANY MONTHS DO YOU HAVE LEFT?" This message is driven home by caseworkers' incessant reminders of the "ticking clock," in the ubiquity of employment brochures and job postings, and, above all, by a carefully sequenced set of demanding rules and regulations.

The pressure is intense. It includes the job search that all new clients must start immediately (forty verifiable job contacts in thirty days), the "job readiness" and "lifeskills" workshops they are required to attend, the (time-consuming and difficult) child support enforcement process in which they must agree to participate, and the constant monitoring of their eligibility for welfare and their progress toward employment. Welfare mothers who are not employed within a specified period (thirty days in Arbordale, forty-five in Sunbelt City) are required to enroll in full-time training programs or take full-time unpaid workfare placements until they can find a job. Throughout, these working, training, and job-searching welfare mothers are expected to find somewhere to place their children. Although welfare recipients are all technically eligible for federal child care subsidies, only about one-third receive them. With only a $350 welfare check (the average monthly benefit for a family of three), child care arrangements can be very difficult to manage.

In Sunbelt City the pressure to get off the welfare rolls is introduced even more directly and forcefully. As is true in about half the states nationwide, Sunbelt City has a "diversionary" program designed to keep poor mothers and children from applying for welfare in the first place. Before they even begin the application process, potential welfare clients are required to attend the diversion workshop. The three workshops I went to all focused on the importance of "self sufficiency," the demanding nature of welfare requirements, and the advantages of work—and left most of the poor mothers in attendance weary and confused.

For those who persisted through the application process, their compliance to the rules of reform was ensured not just by the long-term threat of time limits, but by the more immediate threat of sanctions. Any welfare mother who fails to follow through with her job search, workfare placement, training program, child support proceedings, reporting requirements, or the myriad of other regulations of the welfare office is sanctioned. To be sanctioned means that all or part of a family's welfare benefits are cut, while the "clock" keeps ticking toward that lifetime limit. National statistics suggest that about one-quarter of welfare recipients lose their benefits as a result of sanctions.

Inside the welfare offices of Arbordale and Sunbelt City many of the women I met became so disheartened that they simply gave up and left the rolls. This included women who made it through some portion of the job search, or the employment workshops, or even took a workfare placement, but just couldn't manage the pressure. Some were sanctioned, others left on their own. Connected to these, but harder to count, were all those poor mothers who gave up before they got started. Eligibility workers in Arbordale estimated that as many as one-quarter of those who started the application process did not complete it. Caseworkers in Sunbelt City guessed that about one-third of the mothers who attended their diversion workshops were ("successfully") diverted from applying for benefits. In Arbordale, about one-quarter gave up before completing the application process.

Sarah was one example of a "diverted" potential welfare client. She was the full-time caregiver for her grandchild on a lung machine, her terminally ill father, and her own two young children. She'd been managing with the help of her father's Social Security checks and her boyfriend's help. But her boyfriend had left her, and medical bills were eating up all her father's income. Sarah discovered at her initial Arbordale welfare interview that in order to receive benefits she would need to begin a job search immediately. Because no one else was available to care for her father or grandchild, she said, it just didn't make sense for her to get a job. I met her as she conveyed this story to her friends in the Arbordale waiting room, fluctuating between tones of anger and sadness. "I have to swallow my pride, and come in here, and these people just don't want to help you no more," she told us. Leaving the office, she vowed never to return. As was true of so many others, it was unclear to me what she would do.

Sonya was one example of the many sanctioned welfare clients I met, though her case was more dramatic than most. She was so quiet and shy that I wondered if anyone would notice how she'd been affected by reform. Twenty years old, with a tenth-grade education and two children, she'd been on welfare most of the time since she gave birth to her oldest son at age thirteen. She'd had only one job in her lifetime, and that lasted for just four months. In the hours I spent with her, it became clear to me that she suffered from serious mental health problems — matching clinical definitions of depression and obsessive-compulsive disorder. She rarely left her apartment and lived in fear that she would catch a cold, or pneumonia, or worse. When I commented on her spotlessly clean and carefully decorated apartment, she told me that she completely rearranged it at least once a month and sometimes once a week. I watched her feed lunch to her son: every can, jar, plate, and utensil in her kitchen was precisely ordered, and she was unable to continue our conversation until all the dishes were washed and dried and the counters disinfected, twice, for good measure. When we talked about the possibilities for employment, she explained that she found it necessary to take four showers a day, and worried that she couldn't handle this with a full-time job, especially, she said, since buses don't always run on schedule. In responding to my question about the men in her life she let me know, quietly, that her father had sexually abused her as a child. (She did not volunteer and I did not ask if her pregnancy at age twelve was the result of that abuse.) Sonya had been sanctioned for failing to carry out her job search. Without welfare income, she had no idea what she would do. I worried, a lot, about how she and her kids would get by.

Kendra might be included among those who found themselves too ashamed, discouraged, or exhausted to return to the welfare office when she needed help. One of the first welfare clients I met, Kendra was much loved by the caseworkers who knew her. She was sweet, quietly charming, and deeply earnest. Twenty-six years old, with two daughters aged six and eight, she had a history of working only part-time, on and off, in unskilled jobs. She'd finally landed a secure and meaningful job, she thought, working at a homeless shelter run by the Salvation Army. Even though it was the night shift and the pay was low, she felt good about helping out the homeless, and was grateful for the mentoring and support she'd received from the welfare office. She still didn't make enough money to get by without child care help and an income supplement from welfare, but was hoping for a raise, studying for her high school equivalency exam, and thinking about taking a second job. She was cheerful when last I saw her. Six months later her caseworkers told me how quickly Kendra's life had unraveled. In a heated argument, one of Kendra's brothers had shot and killed her other brother. One brother was dead, the other on his way to prison. Kendra fell apart emotionally, lost her job, and left the welfare rolls. Two caseworkers spent a day off trying to find her (an extremely rare undertaking), but no one knew where she had gone.

All these women and their children have contributed to the decline of the welfare rolls. They are a central basis for the celebration of reform. They are also a central basis for my case of cognitive dissonance.

The Costs

In focusing on the hardships wrought by reform, I do not mean to suggest that the successes of welfare reform are trivial or inconsequential. Those successes matter. I also don't mean to imply that all welfare mothers are saints and victims. They aren't. But there are many other issues at stake in the reform of welfare.

Reading the daily news these days, one can't help but notice that the topic of poverty has lost its prominence, especially relative to the early days of reform. One reason for this neglect, it seems to me, has been the highly effective campaign pronouncing the triumph of the Personal Responsibility Act. Like all the information that was invisible in popular accounts of the invasion of Iraq, the ground-level hardship and human costs of reform are largely hidden from view. Yet the price tag on welfare reform is real.

By 2002, the National Governors' Association found itself begging Congress not to follow through on plans to increase the pressure on welfare offices and welfare recipients across the nation—the costs, they explained, would be far too high for already stretched state budgets to bear. The U.S. Conference of Mayors found itself pleading with the Bush administration for more financial help to manage the rising populations of the hungry and homeless in American cities. Food banks were running short on food, homeless shelters were closing their doors to new customers, and local charities were raising their eligibility requirements to contend with rising numbers of people in need. The Medicaid system was in crisis, and large numbers of poor families were no longer receiving the food stamps for which they were eligible. Half of the families who left welfare had no money to buy food; one-third have had to cut the size of meals, and nearly half have had trouble paying their rent or utility bills.

In the meantime, only a fraction of welfare families have actually hit their federal lifetime limits on welfare benefits: just 120,000 welfare mothers and children had reached their limits by 2001. Given the work/welfare cycling process, and given that many families can survive at least temporarily on below-poverty wages and pieced-together alternative resources, it will take many more years for the full impact of reform to emerge. But, over the long haul, we can expect to see rising rates of hunger, homelessness, drug abuse, and crime. More children will wind up in foster care, in substandard child care, or left to fend for themselves. More disabled family members will be left without caregivers. Mental health facilities and domestic violence shelters will also feel the impact of this law, as will all the poor men who are called upon to provide additional support for their children.

Of course, this story is not apocalyptic. The poor will manage as they have always managed, magically and mysteriously, to make do on far less than poverty-level income. Many of the most desperate among them will simply disappear, off the radar screen, off to places unknown.

In any case, assessing the results of welfare reform is not just a question of its impact on the poor. It is also a question of what this law says about our collective willingness to support the nation's most disadvantaged and about the extent to which welfare reform actually lives up to the more worthy goals it purports to champion.

47

POOR MOTHERS AND THE CARE
OF TEENAGE CHILDREN

DEMIE KURZ

"Mother blaming" in public discourse and social research has created stereotypes of poor mothers that obscure many aspects of their lives (Garey and Arendell 2001; Hays 1996). In popular thinking, poor families, especially single-mother families and families of color, are typically found deficient and blamed for the failures of their children (Baca Zinn and Dill 1994; Roberts 1995). They are said to lack the proper style of discipline or to fail to monitor their children's social activities or schoolwork. In social science research, it has also been difficult to gain an understanding of the work that poor mothers do on behalf of their children and the obstacles they face. According to Garey and Arendell (2001), many researchers attribute children's problems to the failed parenting of their mothers.

In order to get beyond these stereotypes, . . . I examine the challenges poor mothers face as they raise their teenage children. I focus on two of the things mothers are most concerned about during their children's teenage years — keeping their children safe and helping them succeed in school. I describe the work they do and the strategies they use to manage their teenage children.

Mothers view raising teenage children as difficult. As their children become more independent, parents lose a lot of control over where their teenage children go and with whom, whereas peers and activities outside the home in the neighborhood exert a strong influence on teenage lives. Thus, at this stage of parenting, the quality of neighborhoods, including how safe they are and what kinds of resources they have, is critical to the lives of children and the work of parenting. The common view of the family as a self-contained private unit where parents control what goes on inside the four walls of the house and protect children from the dangers of the outside world does not hold for families with teenage children, especially poor families. As I describe, mothers are constantly trying to guide and control their teenage children, but their teenagers are very often out of the house, with friends.

My second goal . . . is to locate the work poor mothers do for their teenage children and the obstacles they face within larger systems of racial and class privilege. Until recently, mothers have typically been viewed as sharing a uniform, unchanging status (Glenn 1994). This view has obscured the fact that mothers do the work of parenting under very different conditions. Systems of racial and class privilege grant more resources to White, higher-income women; poorer women and non-White women face harsher conditions and have fewer social supports. In this chapter, in addition to describing the work poor mothers do, I identify these mechanisms of privilege.

Unfortunately, the way that privilege structures mothers' lives and the consequences this has for poor women and children have often been invisible. Until recently, researchers who study youth and families have tended to focus on the quality of parent–child relationships and on what happens inside households, rather than on the broader conditions under which parents do their work. Much of this research has been dominated by a social psychological perspective that explores the relationship between characteristics of mothers and the problems of their children (Phoenix, Woollett, and Lloyd 1991). Since crime rates and indicators of school failure are higher among children of the poor than other children, it has been assumed that bad parenting is the cause of children's problems (Garey and Arendell 2001). A major problem with this work is that it has neglected the community context within which parenting takes place (Simons et al. 1997).

Recently, some researchers have begun to turn their attention to rebuilding an older tradition of research on neighborhoods and resources that has been neglected for some time (Anderson 1999; Brooks-Gunn et al. 1993; Furstenberg et al. 1999; National Research Council 1996; Simons et al. 1997; Wilson 1991). These researchers have focused on the connection between neighborhood characteristics, parent characteristics, and outcome measures for children and youth. This research produces some interesting findings, but except in unusual cases, such as the work of Furstenberg et al. (1999), it does not focus on mothers' experiences or the actual work they do for their children under conditions of hardship.

Scholars in one group, including scholars of color, have challenged dominant, universalized conceptions of motherhood and have highlighted the role of race and class, as well as gender inequality, in shaping the work of mothers (Baca Zinn and Dill 1994; Collins 1991; Glenn 1994; Segura 1994). They argue that the experiences of minority families are different from other families. The root of this difference, they claim, is not cultural, but is due to differences in resources, with minority families being much less likely to have adequate resources to raise their families. These scholars view White women's experiences and the experiences of women of color as relational— connected in interlocking systems of inequality that provide greater access to resources for some, and less for others.

Understanding the context of power and inequality within which mothers do their parenting is critical not only for research, but also to inform social policy, which, like a lot of research, frequently ignores the environments in which parents must raise children and often blames and even punishes them when their children get into trouble. For example, laws in some jurisdictions hold parents criminally liable for the truancy or delinquency of their teenage children. Certain jurisdictions have statutes that mandate that parents be imprisoned if their children are repeatedly truant (Cahn 1996).

. . . After describing the sample on which my conclusions are based, I [will] examine the work poor mothers do and the strategies they use to try to keep their children safe and ensure that they do well in school. I then describe the time constraints poor mothers face as they do this work, which are greater than those of other mothers. In describing mothers' work, I demonstrate how systems of privilege disadvantage these poor mothers, while they advantage higher-income women. I also show how race further disadvantages the African American mothers in my sample.

Sample and Data

[My] data and conclusions are from an interview study of parents, primarily mothers, and teenage children. [Here] I focus on mothers, who do the majority of the work of parenting and of constructing and maintaining families, including families with teenagers (Larson and Richards 1994). I have interviewed mothers from four samples, three of them random samples. Two are from the city of Philadelphia, one of parents of high school students, one of parents of 22-year olds. A third random sample is from a suburban White middle-class community and includes interviews with parents of junior high and high school students. The fourth is from a snowball sample of upper-middle class mothers who are professionals, from different urban and suburban neighborhoods. Although these samples are not representative of the state they are in or of the nation as a whole, they do provide data on families with a range of income, race, and urban–suburban differences.[1]

To date, I have interviewed 81 mothers and 17 fathers, 65% White, 30% Black, and 5% other. Sixty percent are from the city of Philadelphia and 40% are from middle- and upper middle-class suburbs of Philadelphia. The sample includes single mothers, lesbian mothers, and mothers of children with disabilities. I have also interviewed 25 teenagers, analyzed data from 50 more teenagers, and done focus groups with three groups of high school students and two groups of college students.

Safety

All mothers want to protect their children from harm and keep them physically safe. In my sample, all mothers fear for their children's safety. Recent highly publicized incidents of school violence have made mothers particularly fearful. Statistics indicate the dangers adolescents face. Over half of today's youth between the ages of 10 and 17 have experienced two or more risk behaviors, including drug or alcohol abuse, school failure, delinquency, and crime, as well as unsafe sex and intercourse leading to teenage pregnancy (Lerner, Entwisle, and Hauser 1994; Zill and Nord 1994), and 10% of these youth engage in all of these behaviors (Dryfoos 1990). Tragically, the mortality rates among adolescents have been increasing, with particularly high rates of injury and death occurring in poor communities (Carnegie Corporation 1995).

Although mothers in my sample believe their children need more freedom as they get older, they worry greatly about their teens as they circulate more widely in the world among peers. They worry about the harm that could come to their children from others on the streets, in school, and when they are driving or in cars with other teenagers. They also worry that their own teenage children could engage in unsafe or illegal activities or get involved with what they believe is the wrong group of peers. Mothers worry about their teenagers' friendships with other teens if those teens look like "bad kids." They also don't want their teens spending time in empty houses where they might use alcohol or drugs or have sex. There are specific gender components to parents' concerns. Mothers have greater fear for their girls than their boys over issues of sexuality and worry that their daughters could be taken advantage of, raped, or become pregnant. Parents of boys worry more about accidents and physical violence.

Parents adopt many strategies to monitor their children's social life. For example, they try to keep their teenagers close to home. They make rules about when their children can go out and where. They try to persuade their children not to associate with certain peers and they monitor their teenagers for signs of trouble—for example, by watching carefully for signs of alcohol and drugs. Some parents buy cell phones and pagers for their children in order to communicate with them frequently. To keep their children close to home, some remodel their basements and tell their teenagers to invite their friends to come over and "hang out" there. Many mothers try to get their children involved in school and church groups to keep them out of trouble. For girls, they make special rules about when they can date, the age of the boys they can see, and where they can go on dates.

Not only do parents use many similar strategies to keep their children safe, but according to recent data, parents across different income groups are equally competent in their use of these strategies. Furstenberg et al. (1999), in their study of working-class and poor neighborhoods with a wide range of income levels, indicate that there are no significant differences across these neighborhood groups in mothers' competencies at parenting. These data run counter to stereotypes in popular and academic thinking that find poor parents, particularly poor mothers, deficient in their parenting.

Although all parents are fearful for their children's safety and work hard to protect their children, parents in unsafe neighborhoods face greater dangers, and poor mothers have to do more work to keep their children safe. Poor mothers' accounts feature many more examples of violence, crime, school truancy, and dropping out of school than do those of other mothers. They live in neighborhoods with high crime rates where the dangers mothers fear, such as gangs, are right outside their front doors on the street and in the neighborhood (Anderson 1999).

How do poor mothers cope with danger? Furstenberg et al. (1999) and Litt (1999) argue that poorer mothers become more restrictive of their children's activities. Although it is possible to restrict the movements and activities of younger children, however, it is more difficult to restrict the activities of older children. They want and need to go out. Some mothers do manage to monitor their teenage children's actions very carefully. Others try to teach their children about danger, a task that can be difficult because teenage children don't necessarily see things the same way as their parents and may not feel they are in danger. This grandmother, who is raising her 15-year-old grandson, says:

> R (Respondent):   *My grandson doesn't think there's a soul out there gonna bother him. I don't know why but I be so afraid when he's out and my phone ring my heart goes, dear Lord Jesus, don't let it be bad news. That's how afraid I am for him. Now just last year in, ah, November. My cousin, my cousin's son got killed, 17 years old, over there in (name of neighborhood) around the corner from the house.*
>
> *She always tell him, stay away from that corner, stay away from that corner. When somebody had an argument with somebody. The person said — I be back. And the person came back, both of them got shot.*
>
> *Her son, both of her sons. The youngest got shot and died. The other one got shot in the shoulder here somewhere. The guy that they were shooting at didn't even get a scratch. Now see this is what I tell my son. I say, they don't have to be at you.*
>
> I (Interviewer):   *And what does he say?*
>
> R: *"Oh, grandmom, ain't nobody gonna bother me. You, you always think something be happening to people. You shouldn't think like that." He just don't believe me. He just do not believe that he can get in harm's way out there. But I prays all the time when he's out in that street. When my son's out in that street, I, I pray.*

All mothers try to educate their children about danger but as this quotation illustrates, for poor mothers in high-crime neighborhoods there is an immediate urgency about this task.

Mothers in poor neighborhoods have to have particularly well-developed monitoring strategies for handling issues of safety, for example, reading the signs of potential danger on the street.

> I: *Is living in a neighborhood like this, does that have an impact on raising children?*
>
> R: *Um, yes, because you have to be more aware of what's going on. Um, you know, you have to know what to um, protect them against. What to tell them. You know, give them different signs to look out for. So, yeah, it does have an impact.*
>
> I: *What do you tell them? What kinds of things do they have to look out for?*
>
> R: *OK, for instance, my son takes a bus to go to school. He's in high school now. And that corner is bad, the corner on the left of us. So he can't walk down by that direction. He has to catch . . . You know, he has to go the other way, the opposite way really, a block out of his way to catch the bus to go to school and also to come home. And when they want to go outside it's*

> *just, you know, it's just seem like it's crowded or like something that's going . . . You know, sometimes you can just feel it. They just . . . Because something's going on. You know, they have to come in. They have to stay in the house.*
>
> *Or if they outside, they have to come in. Um, they wouldn't go to the store. And if you see like groups of, you know, boys out there and stuff like that, you know, my husband or myself will go. It's safer for one of us to go as opposed to my son.*
>
> I: *Okay. How big is a dangerous group?*
>
> R: *Oh, wow, it can be from three on up. But a lot times if it's a group even three if they want to start trouble, you know, three against one that's all.*

Another mother spoke of how she and her husband would instruct their children in what to do when they heard the shots of drug dealers. Two mothers who live in the inner city memorize the color of their children's clothing before they leave the house. That way, if they hear of an accident or shooting involving teenage children on the radio or television, they may be able to identify their children.

Many African American mothers do not feel they can turn to the police to help them if their children are in trouble. They don't trust the police and feel their children would be treated much more harshly by them than White children would be. This is in contrast to some of the White middle-class mothers in my sample who, if their children are engaging in risky or illegal behavior (using drugs, stealing things), are sometimes happy when their children have a police encounter. They feel this will "knock some sense" into their children.

As previously noted, part of keeping children safe, parents believe, is keeping them associated with the right kind of peers. This is harder to do for mothers in poor neighborhoods where there are more antisocial gangs. Anderson (1999), in an ethnographic study in a low-income African American neighborhood, demonstrated the pressures on many young men to join gangs and on girls to become pregnant. Mothers in my sample fear "losing" their children to groups of peers, or "bad kids." One African American mother expressed her fears about raising a Black male in our society. When I asked one woman, "What do you worry about most with your kids?" she answered:

> *I worry about school, them finishing school, and that they're ok. And with a Black male in this society . . . They want to prove themselves. They want to be a man. I'm constantly telling my son, "You are your own person. You don't have to prove yourself. You don't have to do what the group wants. Walk away."*

Another thing that mothers in more dangerous neighborhoods do is try to maintain good relations with young people in the neighborhood. One mother, who was very careful to keep a good relationship with neighborhood teenagers, held them accountable when they were doing something they shouldn't be doing, but also welcomed them into her house and treated them with a respectful attitude. This mother served as an "other mother" for neighborhood children, checking in on them and supporting them because she cared about them (Collins 1991). She was also watching out for these children so they would not give her trouble. According to her, one of her neighbors simply got angry at neighborhood youths for disorderly behavior and they then harassed her. Another family in a poor neighborhood was being harassed in their neighborhood by teenagers who were destroying property. These parents challenged the teenagers, who then threatened to firebomb their house. This family then moved to a working-class suburb.

Another strategy mothers use to keep children out of danger is to get teenagers involved in activities in the neighborhood and in their schools. Poor schools and neighborhoods have few organized activities or community centers, however. Many mothers try to keep their teenage children involved in church activities, but as they get older, many teenagers do not want to attend church. Other mothers encourage their children to get paying jobs to keep them away from what they perceive as bad influences. Some urban teenagers do find jobs at fast-food restaurants, but there is a lot of competition for these jobs from older low-skilled workers who can't find other jobs (Newman 1999).

Keeping teenage children safe involves a lot of work that our typical conceptions of mothers as nurturers do not capture. Mothers must persuade, reason with, lecture at, and negotiate with their teenage children, who have strong opinions of their own. Many parents and teenagers have arguments about where their teenage children can go, the hours they keep, and curfews. Teenage children can and do conceal information from their parents. Parenting at this stage involves careful knowledge of the neighborhood in order to be alert for signs of danger; bargaining skills; and a willingness to change as teenagers become older and gain more autonomy.

Ultimately, the most important strategy for creating safety and opportunities for children is moving to neighborhoods that provide these things. More privileged parents can use their incomes to move to neighborhoods where there are good schools, community activities, and police protection, even to "gated communities." If poorer parents move, however, it can be costly. The family mentioned earlier that did manage to move to a fairly safe working-class suburb to escape the harassment of neighborhood teenagers is now experiencing much greater financial difficulty than it did in the city. The family's mortgage in the new neighborhood is almost four times what it was in the city, and the family is having a difficult time covering basic expenses.

Poorer people, of course, usually don't have the ability to move. Housing policies in the United States create shortages of low- and moderate-income housing. Private markets provide housing for middle- and upper-income citizens, who then support zoning laws that exclude moderate- and low-income housing from their neighborhoods. The federal government fails to provide adequate financial support for moderate- and low-income housing as low-income people in poor neighborhoods struggle to keep their houses from deteriorating (Massey and Denton 1993). Further, there is a history of excluding racial and ethnic minorities from white neighborhoods.

Work in Support of Children's Schooling

The other key concern of mothers is that their children do well in school. All mothers in my sample believe that getting a high school diploma and college education, or a higher degree, is critical for their children's future success and express a strong interest in having their children succeed in school. Higher income parents send their children to high-quality public schools or pay for private school. They have the time to become involved in schools and a sense of entitlement about their right to do so. If their children need extra help, they can pay for tutoring and for coaching in test taking.

Poorer parents, however, face obstacles to helping their children do well in school, and the schools their children attend are often of low quality. Because education in the United States is financed primarily through local property taxes, poorer school districts have less money to pay their teachers than suburban districts and receive less money for equipment. Parents of children in city schools speak of poor facilities, overcrowded classrooms, and teachers who are too burdened to care.

> *They need computers. And there aren't enough computers in their school. My best friend, she's white, she told me that in the better neighborhoods they have a room with computers and the children can go to that room and everyone has one. That makes me angry. That's not fair. Our schools are overcrowded and we don't have enough computers.*

Parents also complain of not getting notified if their children skip school or have some other problem. Some mothers don't think their children are getting adequate college counseling.

> I: *So do you think_is a good school?*
> R: *It is good, but it is understaffed. The counselors have too many students. I went to talk to one of the counselors of my child who is a senior. I said to him, "Do you know who my son is?" He said, "Well, he has to come and talk to me." I couldn't believe it. My son is a senior and he doesn't know him! He doesn't have a clue. I don't think the counselor is filling out the right papers for my son for his college applications.*

McDonough's (1997) study of counseling programs in the high schools of children from a broad range of socioeconomic backgrounds demonstrates that college counseling is of much higher quality at schools in higher income neighborhoods.

Because poorer schools have inadequate resources and don't teach children as much, many poorer mothers try to make up for these deficiencies. Some work with their children at home—trying to motivate them to work harder in school, getting them to do homework, monitoring their television time, working with them to learn things, and keeping them from other distractions. One mother left her full-time job both to take care of a sick relative and to have the time to go over school lessons with her daughter, a high school student who had been getting poor marks in school. Every night, while the mother made dinner, she would have her daughter read parts of her English and social studies assignments and then have her repeat the material in her own words. This child began to do much better in school. Some mothers try to get their children into summer programs.

Due to the lower quality of schooling and the disaffection of some students, absentee rates in poorer urban schools are high (Neild 1999). Parents whose children refuse to go to school for periods of time spend a great deal of energy trying to get their children to school, sometimes being late for work and jeopardizing their jobs. One mother, who was worried about how teachers viewed her daughter, visited her daughter's school and talked to all her teachers to counter a possible perception that her daughter didn't care about school. This mother, who was African American, said that she was sure that her daughter was trying to act "cool" in school, which meant acting as if she didn't care, to please her peers. But this mother said that her daughter did care, and she wanted the teachers, who were White and who she felt might not understand her daughter's behavior, to know that. Some mothers, who said they had taught their children how to be assertive, also coached their children in how to remain respectful to authority in school. Another thing that mothers do to keep their daughters in school is try to keep them from getting pregnant. [They] expend considerable time and energy teaching their daughters to avoid pregnancy.

Besides helping their children individually, many poor mothers go to great lengths to find better schools or programs for their children. Some school districts do have school choice programs that allow families to choose a school other than their neighborhood school. According to some researchers, however, poorer parents have a more difficult time researching all the options and complying with the requirements of applying to other schools (Moore and Davenport 1990). Neild (1999), in a study of the Philadelphia School District, demonstrated that factors outside of parents' control also influence the outcome of the school choice process. For example, schools themselves play a role in school choice, with personnel in wealthier schools encouraging their students to apply for the better schools and advocating for them in the admissions process. Further, there is a limited number of high-quality schools to choose from in the district, so only half of students who opt for school choice are accepted to any one of the schools to which they apply. White students are advantaged in this process because the larger district is trying to keep them. Their acceptance rates at the higher ranked schools are higher than those of equally qualified minority students.

The alternative for some lower income people in the city is Catholic school or private Christian school, options that a number of mothers in my sample had considered. Furstenberg et al. (1999) demonstrated that the children of city parents who send their children to Catholic and other private schools do better in school. These options cost money, however. Some parents in my sample had to take their children out of Catholic school because they could not afford the cost. They believe that this had a negative impact on their children.

R: *It [Catholic school] was good and the smaller, you know, classrooms and stuff like that because I know how it is once you get out of . . . once my son got out of the Catholic school and he had all his independence, he wasn't learning. He felt he could do whatever he wanted.*

I: *He got out of the Catholic school after?*

R: *Fifth grade.*

I: *Okay. How come he left the Catholic school?*

R: *Because at the time I was unable to keep, you know, the tuition up.*

One mother, whose husband was a veteran of the Armed Forces, found a veterans' boarding school that she thought would be good for her children. She hated to send her children away to boarding school and missed them terribly, but her children could attend for free, and when they began to do much better in school, she felt she had made the right decision. A few parents try to get their children into a public school in another district. Few can afford to pay the fees for schools in other districts, however, so they have to pretend that their children live in another district. This requires considerable paperwork, as well as the cooperation of a person in that district who will allow the student to use an address illegally. Mostly only a close relative or friend would provide the false address, so this course of action is not open to many poor parents, who are less likely to have friends or relatives in more affluent neighborhoods. Many poor parents seriously consider moving, to get into a better school district, but most have to resign themselves to not being able to afford to move. This mother tries to make herself feel better about not being able to move by rationalizing that all neighborhoods are similar:

All I can do is have an imagination. Now if I was this and I was that . . . you know . . . would have gone to better schools . . . or live in a better neighborhood . . . but nowadays all the neighborhoods are about the same. You have ups and down in all of them. So you raise 'em the best way you know how . . . wherever you at. And give 'em the best education you can afford to give . . . you know . . . and hope they do the best they can with it.

Actions that parents take on behalf of their children's schooling can be critical. Although I do not have a specific numerical count of parents' actions, many poorer parents in my sample were doing the kinds of things I have discussed. In my interviews, mothers described how, when trouble occurs, they take action—talk to their children's teachers, try to get more homework for their children, coach their children, and if these things don't work, they try to get their children into a different program or school, although, as I have described, this is difficult to do. Furstenberg et al. (1999), in their study of urban families, found that poorer mothers were helping their children with homework at the same rate as other mothers.

Unfortunately, school personnel are not typically aware of all the extra, invisible work that parents do to make up for a deficient system that deprives lower income people of decent schooling for their children. Researchers have studied how teachers are much more likely to respond to the requests of middle-class parents than to those of working-class and poor parents because middle-class parents have more cultural capital, or more legitimacy and influence, based on their education and their membership in higher status social networks (Lareau 1989). School personnel also tend to be more responsive to White parents than to African American parents (Lareau and Horvat 1999). To create more fairness and equity in schooling, educational policies would have to ensure that resources were much more fairly distributed across social class and ethnic groups. Sadly, at this time, the inequality between school systems in the United States is large and growing, and children from poorer families are not getting the educational opportunities that better off families can provide.

Time to Parent

Not only do unsafe neighborhoods and poor schools create extra work and disadvantage for poor mothers, but these mothers have less time to do parenting work. In public discourse, there is much attention to work–family debates. In these debates, however, writers typically do not distinguish between workers at different income levels or focus on the diversity of experiences among women and the hardships faced by poorer women; often professional women are taken as the norm (Kurz 2000). However, poor mothers' paid labor gives them less time than other women to do the tasks of parenting. In my sample, many working mothers experience stress as they attempt to combine paid work and family life, but more higher income women work at part-time jobs or jobs with flexible hours or hours that accommodate their children's schedules (such as school teaching). Poorer women in my sample have more hours of work, less flexibility in their hours, more night jobs, more oppressive job conditions, and no money to purchase household help. This can lead to less time with children, as well as more physical exhaustion, more health problems, and little vacation time (Kurz 2000; Litt 1999).

Single mothers can have particular difficulty getting time to parent. Although being a single mother can be less stressful than living in a bad marriage, when fathers participate in childrearing, they can make a difference in helping relieve burdens of mothers. Fathers can help whether or not they are married to mothers, but fathers living with mothers undoubtedly help more. Single mothers also typically have less income than other mothers (Kurz 1995). In my sample, single mothers often had to work two jobs to make ends meet. They were unhappy about this because it meant they had less time with their children and sometimes had to leave them unsupervised. For some poor mothers, the lack of time is an even greater hardship because poorer mothers are more likely to have children who are sick or who have disabilities and therefore need extra care (Polit, London, and Martinez 2001).

One woman in my sample, after being widowed, had to work at two jobs for three years. She worked for 16 hours a day and said it was exhausting and she had to rely on family members and neighbors to check in on her children, who were alone a lot. Another woman had to work three jobs to meet her expenses when her marriage ended. She ended up having a stroke. She and her two sons live in her father's house. Her father has been ill and the house badly needs repairs, but this woman's disability payments are too low to cover expenses for house repairs. Another single mother finds that her low-status job as a nurse's aid is particularly stressful.

> *My job is very stressful. Sometimes when I come home I go to my room. I say to my kids, don't bother me for an hour. I can't talk to anyone for an hour. I have to have that. My kids have all these questions. I have to take time. It helps me keep my sanity.*
>
> *The RN's have more education. They give more of the work to you. If you don't do it their way, you get written up. We're the grunts. I agree, I'm not a brain surgeon, but we do important work.*
>
> *Nursing homes are run by corporations now. What's happening is a sin. People are locked up. I'm supposed to handle the medication for 30 people. That's scary. The medications for many of them are complicated. They don't take the proper precautions. The supplies are not well stocked, like the diapers.*
>
> *Sometimes I get low. Sometimes my family gets away with murder. Last night I just didn't feel like cooking. We got pizza. I dug in my purse. I don't have the money, but . . .*

Other nurse's aids also talk about very stressful work conditions. On the other hand, I interviewed some registered nurses whose higher status jobs enabled them to negotiate for flexible hours and in some cases part-time jobs, which those who had partners could afford to take.

Glenn (1992) argued that poor mothers are supporting the reproductive labor of White women and paying a price. As she and others have pointed out, racial-ethnic women don't have the money to hire help in their homes the way White professional women do. Indeed, they are the ones who often provide that help. Racial-ethnic women also provide more of the lower level reproductive labor in the public sphere that mothers depend on, including day care and care of the elderly (Glenn 1992). Such work, which pays poorly, enables women who can afford it to work at higher level jobs that pay more money and to buy more services in their own homes, whereas poorer mothers have to take on additional paid work to make ends meet.

The Fate of Children

Although the majority of teenagers do not get into serious trouble, as the statistics presented earlier indicate, some do. In my sample, poor mothers report more serious problems with their children than other mothers, although mothers of all class backgrounds report problems. Middle-class and professional mothers reported drug use and driving accidents, with several reporting a death of a teenager of relatives or neighbors due to drug overdoses.

Although some of these mothers reported that their children had had contact with the police, few had been arrested or prosecuted. Poor mothers whose children had problems reported children dropping out of school, getting arrested, or going to prison, as well as deaths. These mothers speak of "losing" their children to peer groups. Minority youth are at greater risk for punishment than White teenagers. In recent years, the criminal justice system has tightened its surveillance of youth and meted out harsher penalties to them, including trying some youth as adults. Minority youth are held under more suspicion by the criminal justice system and are arrested and convicted at higher rates than White youth (Dohrn 2000). The woman quoted next, who is African American, tried to understand how one of her sons managed to finish high school and successfully complete training as an auto mechanic, while the other went to prison.

R: *After my husband's death, one son kept it all in and one didn't. One strayed away and one didn't . . . so. It's just the way life is. You all keep on going, you know.*

I: *So what happened to him?*

R: *He just got with the wrong crowd and got in trouble. Got to stay in jail for it that's all. He only was two credits away from graduating high school. He was only two credits . . . He was the best . . . he was the brains. Yeah he was the brains. But he was the one that had all the knowledge and didn't use it right . . . that's all. But he had two points . . . that's all he had . . . and all he had to do was finish school . . . but he didn't do that.*

I: *So what did he get in trouble for?*

R: *Cars . . . stealing . . . sellin' . . . he was in with all the crowds. And he took the rap for 'em . . . . so. And I mean he didn't do it . . . but he took the rap on himself. So he had to pay the price then. He didn't want to give them up and he had to do it . . . so that's what he did . . . he learned the hard way . . . that's all. He had to learn the hard way.*

I: *Right. So whenever he gets out . . . you think he'll be able to . . . stay away from that crowd?*

R: *We hope so. Most of them are grown up and a lot of them are married and moved on with their life . . . so . . . . there ain't too many of them out here now. Most all of them is growed up. While he was in there serving time they was growin' up. Stuff that they did . . . but he's the one that got caught with most of the stuff. So . . . he'll come around . . . I guess.*

I: *Right. So . . . and that took a lot of your time and . . .*

R: *It took all our time. Family . . . friends . . . and all.*

One mother reported that her child is failing in school because he won't attend classes or do his homework, and that he has just had his first encounter with the police after he was involved in a fight in the neighborhood. Another woman, whose child is in prison for 5 years for theft, was feeling hopeful that her son will get on the right path when he is released because he completed a high school equivalency course in prison. A woman whose son died of AIDS, which was brought on by his drug use, reflected on the periods of homelessness the family endured while her son was growing up and their impact on her son's turning to drug use.

Unfortunately, recent data indicate that teenage children of very poor mothers who were enrolled in the welfare-to-work programs that were the precursors of welfare reform have experienced more problems than children of mothers who were on welfare but not in work programs (Lewin 2001). These data seem to indicate that the invisible work mothers do keeping their children safe and helping them in school is very important. Because welfare reform requires mothers to spend more hours in the workplace, they do not have as much time to monitor the activities of their teenage children and guide them along paths that lead to successful outcomes (Scott et al. 2002).

Conclusion

The evidence presented here demonstrates the difficulties poor mothers face at this stage of their parenting career, when teenagers are out in the world with their peers—difficulties in keeping their children safe and in getting them through school while living in environments with few resources. Poor mothers are forced to do extra work to make up for the deficits in their neighborhoods and schools, and they have less time to parent than other mothers. Poor mothers work hard, constantly and creatively strategizing the best ways to keep their children safe and productive. Undoubtedly their efforts make a great difference in the lives of their children. Although their work is difficult and they face greater uncertainty about whether their children will make their way safely in the world, their actions remain unrecognized and they continue to be stigmatized.

These data indicate that current frameworks in scholarship that focus on mothers as responsible for what happens to their children are inadequate and misleading. They envision the family as a self-contained unit where parents control what goes on inside the four walls of the house. We must expand these frameworks to include the conditions and environments within which mothers work, environments that are shaped by race and class hierarchies. These hierarchies are structured in such a way that poor women, who work at low wages, often at service jobs and jobs caring for others, are supporting the reproductive labor of wealthier women, who have more time to raise their children. Wealthier mothers benefit from policies that favor the private sector and keep taxes low, whereas poor mothers must sometimes take on extra jobs to make ends meet. As Glenn and others have stated, the positions of poor and nonpoor mothers are relationally constructed—their experiences are not just different, but connected in systematic ways (Baca Zinn and Dill 1994; Glenn 1992). Research on the parenting of poor mothers must locate the experiences of nonpoor mothers within these relations.

In addition, political leaders and policymakers must think more broadly about "family policy," which should include a consideration of neighborhoods, zoning laws, and school financing. It is essential that government policies make up for failures in the market and equalize conditions for mothers and families and provide funding for safer neighborhoods, better schools, and work—family policies that enable mothers to participate in school life. We also need policies that encourage fathers to do more of the work of raising children, including giving them flexible schedules that enable them to participate more at home.

Finally, a host of measures must be taken to raise the incomes of poorer mothers, who desperately need more money to move to better neighborhoods, get better schooling, and have more time to raise their children. The trend toward regressive tax policies must be halted in favor of progressive ones, the minimum wage must be increased, and policies ensuring a living wage must be enacted. Such a change in priorities requires transforming ideologies of individualism and privatization, as well as racial privilege.

ENDNOTES

Author's Note: The author acknowledges the support of the Philadelphia Education Longitudinal Study and the MacArthur Family Study, Department of Sociology, University of Pennsylvania, for the research on which this chapter is based. The author also thanks Francesca Cancian and Andrew London for helpful comments.

1. These samples were drawn from school records. The suburban sample was drawn from one school district. One of the urban ones was drawn from the entire school district of Philadelphia, including neighborhood schools, schools that require some admission, and highly selective magnet schools. The other was drawn from four neighborhoods selected to represent working-class and low-income neighborhoods, both White and African American. The city samples were randomly drawn from a larger survey sample, which had also been drawn randomly.

REFERENCES

Anderson, Elijah. 1999. *Code of the Street: Decency, Violence, and the Moral Life of the Inner City.* New York: W. W. Norton.

Baca Zinn, Maxine and Bonnie Thornton Dill. 1994. "Difference and Domination." Pp. 3–12 in *Women of Color in U.S. Society,* edited by Maxine Baca Zinn and Bonnie Thornton Dill. Philadelphia: Temple University Press.

Brooks-Gunn, Jeanne, Greg J. Duncan, P. K. Klebanov, and N. Sealand. 1993. "Do Neighborhoods Influence Child and Adolescent Development?" *American Journal of Sociology* 99 (2): 353–95.

Cahn, Naomi. 1996. "Pragmatic Questions about Parental Liability Statutes." *Wisconsin Law Review* 3:339–445.

Carnegie Corporation. 1995. *Great Transformations: Preparing Youth for a New Century.* New York: Carnegie Corporation.

Collins, Patricia Hill. 1991. *Black Feminist Thought: Knowledge, Consciousness, and the Politics of Empowerment.* New York: Routledge.

Dohrn, Bernadine. 2000. "'Look Out Kid It's Something You Did': The Criminalization of Children." Pp. 157–87 in *The Public Assault on America's Children: Poverty, Violence, and Juvenile Injustice,* edited by Valerie Polakow. New York: Teachers College Press.

Dryfoos, J. G. 1990. *Adolescents at Risk: Prevalence and Prevention.* Oxford: Oxford University Press.

Furstenberg, Frank F., Thomas D. Cook, Jacquelynne Eccles, Glenn H. Elder, and Arnold Sameroff. 1999. *Managing to Make It: Urban Families and Adolescent Success.* Chicago: University of Chicago Press.

Garey, Anita and Terry Arendell. 2001. "Children, Work, and Family: Some Thoughts on 'Mother-Blame.'" Pp. 293–304 in *Working Families: The Transformation of the American Home,* edited by Rosanna Hertz and Nancy Marshall. Berkeley: University of California Press.

Glenn, Evelyn Nakano. 1992. "From Servitude to Service Work. Historical Continuities in the Racial Division of Paid Reproductive Labor." *Signs* 18 (1): 1–43.

——. 1994. "Social Constructions of Mothering: A Thematic Overview." Pp. 1–29 in *Mothering: Ideology, Experience, and Agency,* edited by Evelyn Nakano Glenn, Grace Chang, and Linda Rennie Forcie. New York: Routledge.

Hays, Sharon. 1996. *The Cultural Contradictions of Motherhood.* New Haven, CT: Yale University Press.

Kurz, Demie. 1995. *For Richer, For Poorer: Mothers Confront Divorce.* New York: Routledge.

——. 2000. "Work–Family Issues of Mothers of Teenage Children." *Qualitative Sociology* 23 (4): 435–51.

Lareau, Annette. 1989. *Home Advantage: Social Class and Parental Intervention in Elementary Education.* Lanham, MD: Rowman & Littlefield.

Lareau, Annette and Erin McNamara Horvat. 1999. "Moments of Social Inclusion and Exclusion: Race, Class, and Cultural Capital in Family–School Relationships." *Sociology of Education* 72:37–53.

Larson, R. and M. H. Richards. 1994. *Divergent Realities: The Emotional Lives of Mothers, Fathers, and Adolescents.* New York: Basic Books.

Lerner, R. M., Doris R. Entwisle, and Stuart T. Hauser. 1994. "The Crisis among Contemporary American Adolescents: A Call for the Integration of Research, Policies, and Programs." *Journal of Early Adolescence* 4 (1): 14.

Lewin, Tamar. 2001. "Surprising Results in Welfare-to-Work Studies." *New York Times,* July 31, p. 16.

Litt, Jacquelyn. 1999. "Managing the Street, Isolating the Household: African American Mothers Respond to Neighborhood Deterioration." *Race, Gender & Class* 6 (3): 90–108.

Massey, Douglas S. and Nancy A. Denton. 1993. *American Apartheid: Segregation and the Making of the Underclass.* Cambridge, MA: Harvard University Press.

McDonough, Patricia M. 1997. *Choosing Colleges: How Social Class and Schools Structure Opportunity.* Albany: State University of New York Press.

Moore, D. and S. Davenport. 1990. "School Choice: The New Improved Sorting Machine." Pp. 187–223 in *Choice in Education,* edited by William Boyd and Herbert Walberg. Berkeley, CA: McCutchan.

National Research Council. 1996. *Youth Development and Neighborhood Influences: Challenges and Opportunities.* Washington, DC: National Academy Press.

Neild, Ruth. 1999. "Same Difference: School Choice and Educational Access in an Urban District." Dissertation, University of Pennsylvania.

Newman, Katherine S. 1999. *No Shame in My Game: The Working Poor in the Inner City.* New York: Knopf and the Russell Sage Foundation.

Polit, Denise F., Andrew S. London, and John M. Martinez. 2001. *The Health of Poor Urban Women: Findings from the Urban Change Project.* New York: Manpower Demonstration Research Corporation.

Roberts, Dorothy. 1995. "Racism and Patriarchy in the Meaning of Motherhood." Pp. 224–49 in *Mothers in Law: Feminist Theory and the Legal Regulation of Motherhood,* edited by Martha A. Fineman and Isabel Karpin. New York: Columbia University Press.

Scott, Ellen K., Kathryn Edin, Andrew S. London, and Joan Maya Mazelis. 2002. "My Children Come First: Welfare-Reliant Women's Post-TANF Views of Work–Family Trade-Offs and Marriage." *For Better or For Worse: Welfare Reform and the Well-Being of Children and Families*, edited by Greg J. Duncan and P. Lindsay Chase-Lansdale. New York: Russell Sage Foundation.

Segura, Denise. 1994. "Working at Motherhood: Chicana and Mexican Immigrant Mothers Employment." Pp. 211–33 in *Mothering: Ideology, Experience, and Agency*, edited by Evelyn Nakano Glenn, Grace Chang, and Linda Rennie Forcie. New York: Routledge.

Simons, Ronald L., Christine Johnson, Rand D. Conger, and Frederich O. Lorenz. 1997. "Linking Community Context to Quality of Parenting: A Study of Rural Families". *Rural Sociology* 62 (2): 207–30.

Wilson, William Julius. 1991. "Studying Inner-City Dislocations: The Challenge of Public Agenda Research." *American Sociological Review* 56 (1): 1–14.

Zill, Nicholas and Christine W. Nord. 1994. *Running in Place: How American Families are Faring in a Changing Economy and an Individualistic Society*. Washington, DC: Child Trends.

48

IS THERE HOPE FOR AMERICA'S LOW–INCOME CHILDREN?

LEE RAINWATER • TIMOTHY M. SMEEDING

Despite high rates of economic growth and improvements in the standard of living in industrialized nations throughout the twentieth century, a significant percentage of American children are still living in families so poor that normal health and growth are at risk (Duncan et al. 1998; Duncan and Brooks-Gunn 1997a, 1997b). The previous [research has] shown that it does not have to be this way: In many other countries child poverty afflicts only one-half to one-quarter as many children as in the United States.

These numbers are startling and worrisome. For more affluent nations, child poverty is not a matter of affordability—it is a matter of priority. This country made a commitment nearly sixty years ago to deal with old-age poverty, and that effort has been fairly successful (Burtless and Smeeding 2001). When we found ourselves discussing the large federal and state budget surpluses at the beginning of the twenty-first century, that was a period when we could have made a serious commitment to reduce child poverty in the United States. This opportunity was missed. Even today, with the economy in a brief recession, making a commitment to spend the modest amount of money it would take to bring about a large reduction in child poverty is well within our grasp. Of course, such a policy would need to conform to American values (market work and self-reliance), utilize American social institutions (such as the income tax system), and continue the successful antipoverty efforts of the 1990s, such as the Earned Income Tax Credit.

Consider tax policy for a moment. There are progressive substitutes for the recent 2001–2002 regressive federal income tax reductions that would shore up income support for the working poor. For instance, as part of an expanded tax reduction plan, we could make the child tax credit refundable for working families with no federal income tax obligations; these families do pay Social Security and Medicare taxes, of course. Similarly, we could expand the Earned Income Tax Credit and link it to the child tax credit (Sawicky and Cherry 2001). These modest measures would be relatively inexpensive and effective first steps in the process of further reducing child poverty for the working poor.

While such changes are meant to be suggestive, our study underlines the need for a comprehensive policy to reduce child poverty rates and improve the well-being of children. Policymakers committed to reducing child poverty must address each of the six problem areas (employment, parental leave, child care, child-related tax policy, child support, and education) identified in this [reading]. And they must also consider the much smaller number of children living in families with no parent who can work.

Employment

The most important step in reducing poverty among children is to ensure that at least one parent is employed. In particular, the labor market position of mothers needs to be improved, as their earnings are crucial for maintaining an adequate standard of living in a society where two-income families dominate. Obviously, this is doubly true for single parents, where subsidized child care is an absolute necessity for employment.

In low-wage, high-employment societies such as the United States, employment is both a virtue and a challenge. Working mothers feel better about themselves when they are employed, and children feel better about their parents when they are employed (Chase-Lansdale et al. 2003). However, low-skill employment is almost always low-paying, sometimes requires working nonstandard hours, can involve long commutes, and is vulnerable to layoffs when the economy turns down. Thus, while employment is important, it needs to be supported by flexibility in work schedules and other public support services (Haveman 2003). For two-parent families, some mixture of these policies will suffice. For single parents who must act as both provider and caretaker, employment must be coordinated with their children's needs. To be successfully employed, parents, especially mothers, need state support to facilitate that employment. The evidence is that low-income American single mothers work more hours than single mothers in any other nation (Osberg 2002).

The evidence is also clear that American single mothers receive the least income support of any nation's low-income mothers (Smeeding 2003). American policymakers therefore must find a better mix of income support and work that makes all working single parents nonpoor (see also Gornick and Meyers 2003).

Parental Leave, Child Care Subsidy, and Child Support

In many cases, parents—particularly mothers—need state support to enable them to work and to adequately take care of their children. The development of parental leave programs, guarantees for child support not paid by absent parents, and affordable child care are important conditions for keeping mothers in the full-time workforce and preventing poverty among their children. Child support enforcement measures are important and have become more successful over the past decade. But their potential for reducing child poverty is limited, since many of the parents who fail to pay child support are low earners themselves. The policy design issue is to find a public way to ensure child support, while not reducing the efforts that absent parents make to support their children.

The United States has lagged in these areas in all dimensions: our family leave is not universal and is, in fact, relatively short and unsubsidized; we have no child support insurance to protect single mothers from absent fathers who do not pay their obligated child support; and our child care support system helps the rich more than it helps the poor, despite many recent welfare reform–related efforts to expand child care subsidies for low-income parents (Gornick and Meyers 2003; Ross 1999).

According to the evidence presented [in other research], Sweden has low child poverty rates not only because of unique cultural characteristics but because as a society it has integrated women—mothers in general and single mothers in particular—into its labor force. In its configuration of welfare state policies, Sweden has traditionally stressed the importance of women's continued attachment to the labor market and supported them as wage earners by providing child care, a good parental leave program, and a comprehensive system of child care support.

Adequate parental leave programs and child care provisions are clearly important conditions for keeping mothers in full-time employment. For instance, the increased availability in the United Kingdom of child care, maternity leave, and more family-friendly corporate policies has increased the employment continuity of British women around the time of childbirth and thus reduced the indirect cost of children to their parents (Davies and Joshi 2001). It is also reported that British women can increasingly afford to make use of child care services. However, the direct cost of child care services still proves to be too high for women with smaller earnings potential. This is one of the main reasons why British women with low earnings potential, as well as those with middle earnings potential and more than one child, are more likely to stay home (see, for example, Meyers et al. 2001).

Child Care

Clearly, the introduction of comprehensive child care provisions should be complemented by measures that would make it possible for women with lower earnings potential to make use of these services. The greater the cost of child care services relative to the mother's wage potential, the less likely it is that she will seek employment. It is therefore important to expand public support for child care services that reduces the direct cost of those services, with direct subsidies and also with indirect support through refundable child care tax credits, which would (partially) compensate low-income families' remaining expenditures for this type of service.

In 1989 the European Commission published a "Communication from the Commission on Family Policies" that underlined the importance of affordable, accessible, and high-quality child care arrangements to member states' efforts to increase the labor participation of women (European Commission 1989; Kamerman and Kahn 2001). The British government's 1998 green paper "Meeting the Childcare Challenge" (United Kingdom 1998) contains several proposals for improving access to child care in Britain that are now being implemented. Clearly, the lack of affordable child care support is not a uniquely American problem, but it does cripple efforts by single parents in this country to find steady employment and make work economically viable.

Many governments seem to have understood the need for such measures. According to Sheila Kamerman and Alfred Kahn (2001), child care services continued to increase in supply during the 1990s in most nations, including the United States. Many governments have extended existing parental leave policies, and these policies were even introduced for the first time in a few other countries. In 1998 President Clinton pushed an initiative to improve child care for working families that would have made child care more affordable in various ways and doubled the number of children receiving child care subsidies to more than two million by the year 2003. Unfortunately, most elements of the proposal were not enacted into law. The expansion of affordable child care services was still on the political agenda in 2003, but the recession from 2001 to 2003 forced many state governments to cut back on child care services and subsidies in the face of rising state government deficits. While child care subsidies continued, even during the recession, for many single parents who were leaving welfare, support was more generally needed for parents in families who had already left welfare and become independent of the welfare system.

Parental Leave

Parental leave policy is another area where much could be done. In 2000, Canada instituted paid family leave as a national policy, and Australia did the same in 2003. In the United States, where unpaid family leave is very short and still unpaid, California has made a first step by instituting a paid family leave policy for some workers. Other states are likely to follow suit. The actions of these states may pave the way toward a more effective and expansive federal policy in the near future (Gornick and Meyers 2003; Ross 1999).

Parental leave programs and comprehensive and affordable child care services represent, of course, only some of the policy measures needed to integrate mothers into the workforce. Improving the skills of low-skilled workers (often women), job counseling, the removal of various structural obstacles (such as unemployment traps), and transportation assistance are also important initiatives that would make it easier for mothers to work full-time.

Child Support

The provision of steady, reliable child support is another important element of the semiprivate safety net in the United States and elsewhere. It is a widely held value that parents should support their children. The problem in doing so is often that absent fathers cannot or do not pay, owing to weak enforcement of child care laws or low earnings capacity. While significant progress has been made in upgrading child support enforcement for divorced mothers, much still remains to be accomplished for unmarried mothers (Ellwood and Blank 2001). Enforcement is uneven across states, paternity establishment by unwed mothers varies greatly across states, and often the fathers of the children of unwed mothers do not earn enough to support themselves, much less their children.

In Europe a different set of values prevails. The well-being of the child and the mother is usually the foremost value, and the absent father's willingness and ability to pay are of secondary concern. In these countries full child support is guaranteed by governments when absent fathers cannot or will not pay (Skevik 1998). While universal guaranteed child support on the European level would not fit American values, a more modest system might be achievable. When the custodial mother has established paternity and the absent father is deemed unable to pay (owing to imprisonment, unemployment, or low wages), a modest level of guaranteed child support—say, $2,000 per year for a first child and $1,500 for a second—could be a very important source of steady support for a single mother who is not otherwise receiving such aid. Similarly, states could increase the dollar amount of child support allowed to "pass through" to mothers receiving Temporary Assistance to Needy Families (TANF) without penalty, a measure that would increase the monthly amount received by the mother to $150 or $250, rather than only the first $50, which is the norm.

Child–Related Income Tax Policy

The minimum wage is insufficient to meet the income needs of working families with children. Full-time work at the current minimum wage leaves a family of three far below the poverty line, and the Earned Income Tax Credit does not fully close the gap. If we continue to pursue this policy line, additional child-related tax benefits are necessary to ensure that working families with children are not poor. Making families headed by parents with low earnings potential more dependent on market income is not sufficient to end child poverty in a period of increased earnings inequality and slack labor markets (Haveman 2003). Earnings are often not sufficient to protect households with children from poverty, and although children living in two-parent dual-earner families are far less likely to be poor, poverty rates among children living in working single-parent families remain very high in the United States.

In recent years several countries have introduced or increased minimum wages, but these often remain insufficient to keep households with children out of poverty. Governments are reluctant to further increase the minimum-wage levels in their countries because they risk aggravating the unemployment problem faced by low-skilled workers. The "living wage" laws, which pay hourly wages of seven to nine dollars per hour to governmental contractors in some parts of the United States, are rarely applied to the private sector for this same reason—many fewer employees will be hired at this level of labor cost. Since the expansion of low-wage work might improve the job prospects of less-educated workers and make it easier for single-earner households to acquire a second income, we do not advocate significantly higher minimum wages, and certainly not "living wages" for all U.S. workers. It is clear, however, that many governments should do more to support the working poor when wages are insufficient to keep a family from becoming poor. The United States EITC is one important way to supplement earnings and help working families meet their financial responsibilities. However, it does not always guarantee that a family will avoid poverty (Moffitt 2002).

There is evidence of an increasing role for refundable tax credits in the support given to low-income working-age households in other nations as well. Many OECD countries offer social tax breaks and allowances to replace cash benefits, although they tend to be less important in countries with relatively high direct tax levies, such as Denmark, Finland, the Netherlands, and Sweden. In Germany, the value of tax allowances for the cost incurred in raising children alone amounted to almost 0.6 percent of the German GDP in 1993 (Adema and Einerhand 1998). Both the Netherlands and the United Kingdom have specific tax subsidies for single-parent families, and, as we mentioned before, many countries also use tax credits to compensate these families for expenditures such as child care costs. Yet we must emphasize that such measures have less effect on the incomes of families with earnings that are too low to fully benefit from them. It is therefore important that tax credits for child care and similar measures aimed at families with low earnings be made refundable.

In addition to the EITC, the American income tax system contains a set of tax credits that are partially refundable, but not to low-income parents who do not make enough to pay federal income tax. The several plans that have been proposed to integrate these two programs would produce a single family tax credit with more benefit adequacy and lower work disincentives than in the phase-down regime of the EITC (Cherry and Sawicky 2000; Sawicky and Cherry 2001). Adoption of these programs would give a well-targeted boost to the incomes of working poor parents.

Investment in a Socially–Oriented Education Policy

Central to the promotion of employment in a knowledge-based society is quality education for all children, regardless of their financial situation or their health. Such policies could reduce the likelihood that child poverty is passed on from generation to generation (Gregg and Machin 2001; Büchel et al. 2001). A special effort needs to be made to target education resources to the areas where they can do the most good for poor children in bad schools and to prepare low-income children for elementary school more generally.

It is the responsibility of every democracy to provide an equal opportunity from birth for every child. We sorely need to give increased attention to the quality of schooling in low-income areas and develop better and more widespread preschool programs in low-income areas if we are to increase the chances of reducing adult poverty among the next generation of children. Making schools more accountable may be a partial answer to this need, but the legislation entitled "Leave No Child Behind" is insufficient by itself to reach this goal (Smeeding 2002).

An American Income Support Package for Families with Children

The previous six policy arenas can be drawn together into a benefit or "income" package that includes a role for the state, for the family, and for work, and a package that conforms to American values. Clearly, work alone is not enough to guarantee escape from poverty for low-income working families, especially single parents (Haveman 2003). The EITC is a good step, but it is not enough by itself to reach the goal. Additional refundable tax credits, subsidized child care, guaranteed child support (for those who meet specified criteria), and paid family leave must also be woven into the policy mix. This combination of work and benefits should increase the incomes and well-being of children whose mothers work. And both low-income students and their schools need to be better prepared to advance and thrive.

Policy efforts must be redoubled to meet the needs of mothers who cannot work and of households with no workers. Perhaps the answer lies in disability policy — for example, through the Supplemental Security Income (SSI) program. We will not delve into these issues here, except to say that the remaining TANF caseload (about two million households as of early 2003) is a manageable issue that could be tackled by a reauthorization of welfare reform targeted not only at removing these last welfare recipients from the rolls but at meeting their divergent and serious human needs.

Finding the Will Is Finding the Way

The findings [of our research] underline the need for a comprehensive policy to reduce child poverty rates and improve the well-being of children. Human capital concerns in industrialized countries offer an overwhelming and very practical case for adequate investment in succeeding generations. Especially in the affluent economies of the industrialized world, there are no valid economic excuses for high child poverty rates. We can all afford low child poverty rates.

But no two countries can fight poverty in exactly the same way. Each nation's policies must fit its own national culture and values. Thus, the policy suggestions made here must be hewn together into a system of child poverty reduction that will work in the United States. Moreover, these policies cannot simply be taken off the shelf and plugged in. It takes political leadership to make such policies national priorities and to make programs mesh in a supportive fashion.

In recent years Prime Minister Tony Blair of the United Kingdom has shown that when a nation makes a commitment to reduce child poverty, much can be accomplished (see, for example, Bradshaw 2001; Walker and Wiseman 2001). Since 1997 the Blair government has spent an additional 0.9 percent of GDP (about $1,900 per family) on poor families with children (Hills 2002). An equivalent degree of effort in the United States would cost $90 billion. The high poverty rates of the late 1990s in the United Kingdom are now being gradually reduced (Bradshaw 2001; Hills 2002). Unfortunately, not all countries share this priority, particularly not the United States (Danziger 2001; Smeeding 2002).

The American social assistance system has now achieved a primary goal: increasing work and reducing welfare dependence for low-income mothers. Fewer than five million persons (two million cases) remain dependent on TANF benefits. The "welfare problem" is no longer. However, as welfare rolls have been trimmed, corresponding decreases in child poverty have not been achieved because market income alone is not enough to bring about serious reductions in child poverty. The United States needs to make this goal a top priority for its political agenda. Even a commitment of $45 billion — half the effort of the Blair government — could at least partially fund most of the policy options listed in this [reading]. The integrity of our democratic values will be ensured and the cultural and economic fabric of our society enriched when we can say that many fewer children grow up poor in America.

REFERENCES

Adema, William and Marcel Einerhand. 1998. "The Growing Role of Private Social Benefits." Labor Market and Social Policy Occasional Paper No. 32. Paris; Organization for Economic Cooperation and Development, April 17.

Bradshaw, Jonathon. 2001. "Child Poverty under Labour." In *An End in Sight?: Tackling Child Poverty in the United Kingdom,* edited by Geoff Fimister. London: Child Poverty Action Group.

Büchel, Felix, Joachim R. Frick, Peter Krause, and Gerg G. Wagner. 2001. "The Impact of Poverty on Children's School Attendance: Evidence from West Germany." In *Child Well-Being, Child Poverty, and Child Policy in Modern Nations: What Do We Know?,* edited by Koen Vleminckx and Timothy M. Smeeding. Bristol, England: Policy Press.

Burtless, Gary and Timothy M. Smeeding. 2001. "The Level, Trend, and Composition of Poverty." In *Understanding Poverty,* edited by Sheldon H. Danziger and Robert G. Haveman. New York and Cambridge, MA: Russell Sage Foundation and Harvard University Press.

Chase-Lansdale, P. Lindsay, Robert A. Moffitt, Brenda J. Lohman, Andrew J. Cherlin, Rebekah Levine Coley, Laura D. Pittman, Jennifer Roff, and Elizabeth Votruba-Drzal. 2003. "Mothers' Transitions from Welfare to Work and the Well-Being of Preschoolers and Adolescents." *Science* 299 (March): 1548–52.

Cherry, Robert and Max B. Sawicky. 2000. "Giving Tax Credit Where Credit Is Due: A 'Universal Unified Child Credit' That Expands the EITC and Cuts Taxes for Working Families." Briefing Paper. Washington, DC: Economic Policy Institute (April). Available at www.cpinet.org/briefingpapers/EITC_BP.pdf.

Danziger, Sheldon H. 2001. "After Welfare Reform and an Economic Boom: Why Is Child Poverty Still So Much Higher in the United States than in Europe?" Paper presented to the Eighth Foundation for International Studies on Social Security (FISS) Conference on Support for Children and Their Parents: Why's, Ways, Effects, and Policy. Sigtuna, Sweden (June).

Davies, Hugh and Heather Joshi. 2001. "Who Has Borne the Cost of Britain's Children in the 1990s?" In *Child Well-Being, Child Poverty, and Child Policy in Modern Nations: What Do We Know?,* edited by Koen Vleminckx and Timothy M. Smeeding. Bristol, England: Policy Press.

Duncan, Greg J. and Jeanne Brooks-Gunn, eds. 1997a. *The Consequences of Growing Up Poor.* New York: Russell Sage Foundation.

———. 1997b. "Income Effects across the Life Span: Integration and Interpretation." In *The Consequences of Growing Up Poor,* edited by Greg J. Duncan and Jeanne Brooks-Gunn. New York: Russell Sage Foundation.

Duncan, Greg J., Wei-Jun J. Yeung, Jeanne Brooks-Gunn, and Judith Smith. 1998. "How Much Does Childhood Poverty Affect the Life Chances of Children?" *American Sociological Review* 63 (3, June): 406–23.

Ellwood, David and Rebecca Blank. 2001. "The Clinton Legacy for America's Poor." Research Working Paper No. RWP01-028. Cambridge, MA: Harvard University, Kennedy School of Government (July).

European Commission. 1989. "Communication from the Commission on Family Policies (COM [89] 363 final)." *Social Europe: Official Journal of the European Communities* 1 (94): 121–29.

Gornick, Janet and Marcia K. Meyers. 2003. *Families That Work: Policies for Reconciling Parenthood and Employment.* New York: Russell Sage Foundation.

Gregg, Paul and Stephen Machin. 2001. "Child Experiences, Educational Attainment, and Adult Labor Market Performance." In *Child Well-Being, Child Poverty, and Child Policy in Modern Nations: What Do We Know?,* edited by Koen Vleminckx and Timothy M. Smeeding. Bristol, England: Policy Press.

Haveman, Robert. 2003. "When Work Alone Is Not Enough." *LaFollette Policy Report* 13 (2): 1–15.

Hills, John. 2002. "The Blair Government and Child Poverty: An Extra One Percent for Children in the United Kingdom." London School of Economics. Unpublished paper.

Kamerman, Sheila B. and Alfred J. Kahn. 2001. "Child and Family Policies in an Era of Social Policy Retrenchment and Restructuring." In *Child Well-Being, Child Poverty, and Child Policy in Modern Nations: What Do We Know?*, edited by Koen Vleminckx and Timothy M. Smeeding. Bristol, England: Policy Press.

Meyers, Marcia K., Janet C. Gornick, Laura R. Peck, and Amanda J. Lockshin. 2001. "Public Policies That Support Families with Young Children: Variation across U.S. States." In *Child Well-Being, Child Poverty, and Child Policy in Modern Nations: What Do We Know?*, edited by Koen Vleminckx and Timothy M. Smeeding. Bristol, England: Policy Press.

Moffitt, Robert. 2002. "From Welfare to Work: What the Evidence Shows." Welfare Reform and Beyond 13. Washington, DC: Brookings Institution (January).

Osberg, Lars. 2002. "Time, Money, and Inequality in International Perspective." Luxembourg Income Study Working Paper No. 334. Syracuse, NY: Syracuse University, Maxwell School of Citizenship and Public Affairs, Center for Policy Research (November).

Ross, Katherin. 1999. "Labor Pains: Maternity Leave Policy and the Labor Supply and Economic Vulnerability of Recent Mothers." Ph.D. dissertation, Syracuse University.

Sawicky, Max B. and Robert Cherry. 2001. "Making Work Pay with Tax Reform." Issue Brief No. 173. Washington, DC: Economic Policy Institute (December 21). Available at www.epinet.org/Issuebriefs/ib173/ib173.pdf.

Skevik, Anne. 1998. "The State–Parent–Child Relationship after Family Break-Ups: Child Maintenance in Norway and Great Britain." In *The State of Social Welfare, 1997: International Studies on Social Insurance and Retirement, Employment, Family Policy, and Health Care,* edited by Peter Flora, Philip R. de Jong, Julian Le Grand, and Jun-Young Kim. London: Ashgate.

Smeeding, Timothy M. 2002. "No Child Left Behind?" *Indicators* 1 (3): 6–30, 67.

———. 2003. "Real Standards of Living and Public Support for Children: A Cross-National Comparison." Paper presented at the Bocconi Workshop on Income Distribution and Welfare, Milan, Italy, May 30, 2002. Revised January 2003.

United Kingdom. Department for Education and Skills. 1998. "Meeting the Child Care Challenge." National Child Care Strategy Green Paper. London: Department for Education and Skills (May). Available at www.dfes.gov.uk/childcare.

Walker, Robert and Michael Wiseman. 2001. "The House That Jack Built." *Milken Institute Review* (Fourth Quarter): 52–62.